COLLEGE AND UNIVERSITY CURRICULUM

Developing and Cultivating Programs of Study that Enhance Student Learning

Edited by
Lisa R. Lattuca
Pennsylvania State University

Jennifer Grant Haworth
Loyola University Chicago

Clifton F. Conrad
University Of Wisconsin, Madison

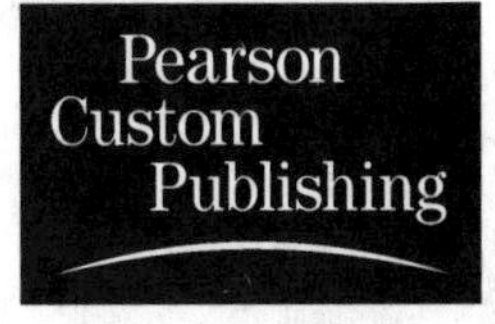

Cover Art: "Untitled," by Jan Lhormer.

Printed in the United States of America

10 9 8 7 6 5 4 3 2 1

Please visit our web site at www.pearsoncustom.com

ISBN 0–536–67146-x

BA 993951

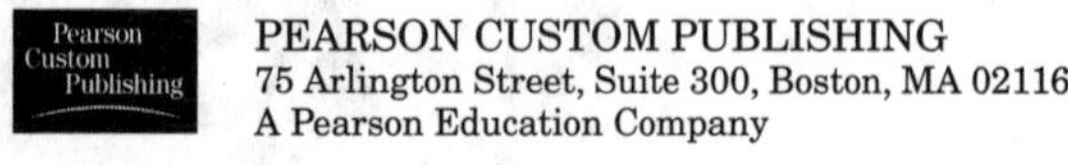

PEARSON CUSTOM PUBLISHING
75 Arlington Street, Suite 300, Boston, MA 02116
A Pearson Education Company

CONTENT

INTRODUCTION

LISA R. LATTUCA, PENNSYLVANIA STATE UNIVERSITY
JENNIFER GRANT HAWORTH, LOYOLA UNIVERSITY CHICAGO
CLIFTON F. CONRAD, UNIVERSITY OF WISCONSIN–MADISON

Since the primary audience for this reader is faculty and students in higher education graduate programs who are studying curriculum, this volume has been designed to serve both as a curriculum text and instructional text. Therefore, our animating principle in assembling this collection of readings is to engage instructors, students, and others in critical reflection and dialogue about curricular, teaching and learning, and assessment issues in higher education. The reader provides a broad and comprehensive treatment of the postsecondary curriculum. In addition, at the end of each of chapter, it offers one or two case studies that furnish opportunities to explore how the issues discussed within each chapter might find expression in practice and to apply what has been learned to the problems addressed in each case study.

This reader should also assist other stakeholders in higher education institutions, particularly administrators and staff who are charged with the responsibility of planning, designing, and evaluating general education, undergraduate major, and graduate programs in their work. The selections cover topics that few other higher education curriculum texts address collectively, such as theoretical perspectives on curricula, contextual influences on faculty and curricula in higher education, course design, pedagogy, learners and learning, assessment, innovation, and change and thus offer a primer for those engaged in the process of developing and revising programs and courses.

In our attempt to be comprehensive, we have assembled a set of readings that span a number of continua. We have included selections that describe the variety of theoretical and epistemological approaches to curricula, from modern and rationalist models to poststructuralist perspectives. We have included readings advancing traditional and pluralist viewpoints. We have included a number of primary documents that provide an historical perspective on the curriculum in higher education as well as contemporary readings that comment on current issues and concerns that are often linked to these historical concerns and events. The selected articles also represent theoretical and applied concerns and challenge readers to bridge those concerns by discovering and enacting myriad intersections of theory and practice.

Overview of the Volume

The organizing concept behind this volume is that of the *academic plan* as described in *Shaping the College Curriculum: Academic Plans in Action* (Stark and Lattuca, 1997). The concept of the academic plan is based on the notion that whether intentionally or not, every curriculum includes eight interacting elements: purpose, content, sequence or arrangement of subject matter, learners, instructional processes, instructional resources, evaluation strategies, and adjustments (or changes to the plan). In any curriculum, these elements exist in relation to one another, so that changes or decisions made regarding one element of an academic plan reverberate to varying degrees through that plan. Furthermore, all academic plans are themselves embedded in overlapping institutional and societal contexts. (For a complete discussion of the academic plan concept, see the selection in Chapter Three of this volume entitled "Creating Academic Plans.")

The four parts of this reader include selections that address both the elements of academic plans and the organizational, disciplinary, and sociocultural influences that shape decisions about these elements. In effect, we used the academic plan concept as a heuristic to suggest the dimensions of higher education curricula that should be covered in this volume. We then selected readings that illustrated these dimensions, including perspectives that extended and occasionally challenged the idea of the academic plan.

The first two parts of the reader focus primarily on the elements of purpose and content, which are typically closely related in discussions about why we educate and how we should educate. Part One, "Curriculum in Context: Definitional, Historical, and Philosophical Perspectives," is divided into two sections. The first section, "Theoretical Perspectives on Curriculum," spans an array of theoretical and epistemological beliefs that influence conceptualizations of curricula from the modern to the postmodern. The second, "Historical and Contemporary Perspectives," offers readings that describe and sometimes contrast prominent ideas about the purposes and content of higher education curricula. This section therefore includes selections on liberal, general, and professional education, as well as multiculturalism.

In Part Two, "Proposals and Critiques of the Contemporary Undergraduate Curriculum," the focus broadens as concerns about learners and their learning are raised through contemporary discussions of how purpose, content, and instructional processes can be combined to create learning environments that encourage or discourage individuals' cognitive, personal, and social development. This part of the reader includes a range of competing perspectives that have animated historic and contemporary debates over curriculum in (primarily) undergraduate education, including some highly visible proposals for curriculum reform aimed at enacting the beliefs and values of their authors. These selections invite reflection on questions such as: What political, economic, cultural, and institutional forces influence the undergraduate curriculum? What counts as knowledge and how should it be organized and taught? Whose values should be represented in the curriculum?

Attention to learners, instructional processes, and evaluation and assessment animate the third part of this volume, "Curriculum under Construction: Design and Assessment Concerns." Here we include selections that explore the influence of external and internal contexts on higher education curricula, as well as the effects of faculty members' disciplinary perspectives on curricular decisions. Several readings provide an overview of different approaches to curriculum design, highlighting various elements of the academic plan: learners, instructional processes, and instructional resources. The chapter concludes with an examination of evaluation and assessment at the classroom, program, and institutional levels.

The academic plan concept includes an adjustment loop; evaluation and assessment results provide the basis for informed changes in the plan. Attempts to revise curricula often awaken us to the realities of the political and other environments in which a plan exists. Part Four, "Curriculum in Revision: Curricular Change and Innovation," offers readings on the politics of curriculum implementation and change and invites readers to review critically the ways in which we approach and implement academic change in higher education. Selections provide examples of large- and small-scale curricular reforms and change processes, and comment on a variety of obstacles to innovation.

Curriculum in Context: Definitional, Historical, and Philosophical Perspectives

In the first part of this volume we invite readers to explore how various philosophical and epistemological commitments influence beliefs about the nature, purpose, and processes of education. We have organized the readings into two sections: "Theoretical Perspectives on the Curriculum" and "Historical and Contemporary Perspectives on the Curriculum."

Theoretical Perspectives on the Curriculum

We open this section with a chapter from Gerald Posner's book, *Analyzing the Curriculum*, in which Posner introduces five influential perspectives that have shaped curricula in the United States and elsewhere. Posner's discussion of the impact of these perspectives—traditional, experiential, structure of the disciplines, behavioral, and cognitive—on educators' thoughts about what should be taught demonstrates the range of approaches that have informed curricula in K–12 and higher education institutions. Posner analyzes each of the five perspectives by asking questions such as:

- How does learning occur and how is it facilitated?
- What kinds of content are most important and how should content be organized for instruction?
- How should educational progress be evaluated?
- What is and should be the relationship between schools and the society at large?

To be sure, answers that college and university faculty provide to the question of how learning occurs are influenced in part by their epistemological and philosophical commitments. Understanding the paradigms that lead to particular answers about how we learn is critical to reflection on both practice and theory. These paradigms are the subject of William Reid's article " 'Reconceptualist' and 'Dominant' Perspectives in Current Theory: What Do They Have to Say to Each Other?" Relying on previous discussions of dominant and reconceptualist perspectives, Reid first describes what is often an antagonistic dialogue between the two. The dominant perspective focuses on knowledge, skills, objectives, testing and evaluation. The reconceptualist position argues that learning is about people, their histories, identities, and possibilities. Reid interprets this as a schism between the philosophical and the practical: in one camp are those who are concerned with educational principles and in the other are those who are concerned with taking action. Rather than simply dwelling on these contrasts, Reid searches for areas of agreement between these perspectives (e.g., their celebration of individualism, the rejection of historically sanctioned authority, and relativistic epistemologies) and argues for greater dialogue among theorists that recognizes the complexity of the curriculum and the limitations of each viewpoint.

Bill Tierney's article, "Cultural Politics and the Curriculum in Postsecondary Education," extends this line of thinking, examining how faculty cultures and beliefs about knowledge and learners are at the heart of their educational choices. Tierney compares rational and critical perspectives on the curriculum, noting differences in epistemological assumptions, values, ideologies, and understandings of academic organizations and cultures. He asks us to consider how the answers to the following questions influence what we teach and how we teach: What is the relationship between the learner and what is to be learned? What counts as knowledge? What and how can we know? Arguing that faculty act on ideologies regardless of whether they recognize them, Tierney further contends that we must examine the values and commitments of organizational participants if we are to understand how they have shaped the curriculum in a specific context. The challenge, of course, is to confront and manage differences in these understandings and positions on knowledge and on curricula.

Echoing themes from Reid and Tierney, Francis Hunkins and Patricia Hammill analyze the assumptions of the modernist paradigm that forms the basis for rational schemes of curriculum development in their article, "Beyond Tyler and Taba: Reconceptualizing the Curriculum Process." Although Hunkins and Hammill ask educators to reflect on the assumptions of scientific-modernism and perhaps to challenge basic tenets that have guided their actions, they acknowledge that they can offer no specific plan; they neither know where we have moved or toward what we should be moving. Their suggestion is that educators learn to play a postmodern game without rules, that is, to create and conceive curricula that rely less on guidelines and more on a holistic appreciation of the complexity and dynamism of our systems of learning.

This assessment of the shortcomings of modernist views of the curriculum is shared by William Doll, who similarly critiques modernist curriculum models. Doll, however, is more willing to imagine what a postmodern curriculum might be. His vision replaces the step-by-step approach of Tyler and Taba with criteria that attend to the postmodern sensibilities of openness, nonlinearity, connection, and integration. In "Curriculum Possibilities in a 'Post'-Future," Doll suggests that four R's—richness, recursion, relations, and rigor—might become as foundational to future curricula as were the three R's of reading, 'riting, and 'rithmetic of the 19th and

20th centuries. Unlike their predecessors, however, Doll's four R's stress processes rather than products and encourage instructors and students to create and recreate curricula as they engage in a collaborative and spontaneous journey.

Historical and Contemporary Perspectives on Curriculum

Debates about the purposes of education recur throughout the history of higher education in the United States. At the center of these debates are questions of what should be the purposes and content of education. Should higher education focus on eternal questions of humanity or on the concerns of everyday life? Should it primarily benefit the individual or the community? What is the best preparation for citizenship in a democratic society? The first two articles in this section offer some historical background for understanding the continuing debates about the ends of higher education. The opening chapter from Clif Conrad and Jean Wyer's monograph, *Liberal Education in Transition,* provides an overview of the history of liberal learning from ancient Greece to the present, focusing its discussion of contemporary concerns for liberal education in the context of U.S. higher education. Similarly in "Recurring Debates about the College Curriculum," Joan Stark and Lisa Lattuca examine the history of U.S. higher education for evidence of continuing curricular debates about liberal (or general) education and specialized education, as well as competing views on student choice, access to higher education, instructional processes, and evaluation.

To assist readers in better understanding the commitments of those engaged in these debates, we have reprinted excerpts from two historical documents that address the question of whether higher education should be classical or practical, general or specialized. (Part Two of the reader includes contemporary readings on educational purposes and content.) The excerpt from the Yale Report of 1828, written by Jeremiah Day (then president of Yale) and professor James Kingsley, staunchly defends the classical curriculum against the charge that it was increasingly irrelevant to the needs of men who would serve a growing and changing United States. The appropriate goal of a college education, the authors observed, is to "lay the foundation of a superior education" that would prepare men for the study of a profession and balance the character and intellect. The Yale Report thus saw professional education as supplemental, and subsequential, to a broader classical education.

The debate regarding general and specialized education also finds expression in a chapter of the influential 1945 report of the University Committee on General Education in a Free Society. Often referred to as the Harvard Redbook, this document advocates a higher education that not only preserves and transmits the heritage of the U.S. (and thereby educates citizens about the democracy in which they live), but also honors innovation and experimentation through specialized study. According to the authors, the aim of education "should be to prepare an individual to become an expert in some particular vocation or art and in the general art of the free man and citizen" (p. 54). The Redbook contributed significantly to curricular revision efforts at many U.S. colleges and universities although the Harvard faculty never adopted it.

In "Dewey versus Hutchins: The Next Round," Tom Ehrlich explores the tension between general and specialized (and professional) education. He recounts the 1936 dialogue between two prominent educational figures, John Dewey and Robert Maynard Hutchins, who had differing ideas about the means and ends of education. Ehrlich first considers how each answered the basic questions raised in the debate: What is the purpose of education and who should be students? What should be learned? What should the learning process be? He then brings the debate to the present by examining contemporary educational practices, such as community service and problem-based learning, which might contribute to the goals of education for democracy and civic engagement, and by stressing the need for effective assessment of student learning.

Current educational practices are also the concern of Carol Geary Schneider and Robert Shoenberg. In "Contemporary Understandings of Liberal Education," Schneider and Shoenberg identify key themes in recent changes in general education and graduation requirements at institutions across the U.S. and explore their educational potential. Arguing that teaching and learning are in a period of transition, they see a significant shift away from general education that emphasizes subject matter and toward a version of liberal learning that is conceived in terms of the development of students' intellectual skills. Schneider and Shoenberg provide an accounting of the learning goals that they believe are "implicit" in contemporary campus efforts to reconceptualize undergraduate education.

Recognizing the prominence of concerns about diversity in higher education, we include Patrick's Hill's rationale for multiculturalism in higher education in this section. Hill discusses four frameworks that have been used to comprehend diversity and their ramifications for approaches to higher education: relativism, perennialism, hierarchism, and pluralism. His defense of multicultural education is built on a version of cultural pluralism that is strongly influenced by John Dewey, for whom the inclusion of diverse perspectives was not only an ethical imperative but also the key to successful democracy. He also answers six common objections to the kind of curricular and organizational restructuring that he believes a commitment to multiculturalism demands.

Finally, we end Part One of the reader with a case study of curricular reform at Franklin Pierce College. In 1992 Franklin Pierce replaced its general education distribution requirements with a common core of courses based on the theme of "The Individual and Community." In this reflective case study, "Civic Education and Academic Culture: Learning to Practice What We Teach," Craig Platt compares the challenges that students taking a "civic arts curriculum" face with the challenges faculty faced in developing this common core curriculum. He writes:

> Consider again the things we ask of students when we engage them in a civic arts education: We want them to learn to engage in dialogue with people whose points of view may differ from theirs, to integrate other perspectives with their own, and to make choices about important issues in an uncertain world. We expect them to recognize and value their connectedness to the larger world around them and to find ways to integrate and balance legitimate claims of the individual with those of the collective. (p. 25)

These are the very skills, Platt claims, that faculty must develop if they are to work toward a coherent curriculum in the service of democracy. Yet faculty beliefs, disciplines, and values strongly influence their commitments to particular educational purposes and content and may get in the way of good intentions. Platt offers some thoughts about practices that can develop the collaborative spirit needed to reform the curriculum, and his reflections demonstrate how the elements of the academic plan cannot be understood separate from the contexts in which they are embedded.

Proposals and Critiques of the Contemporary Undergraduate Curriculum

Part Two of the reader familiarizes readers with a range of competing perspectives on undergraduate education and invites reflection on the ways in which the college and university curriculum responds to political, economic, cultural, and institutional forces. The selections included here reveal strong and divisive beliefs about the kinds of knowledge and values that should be part of the undergraduate curriculum and advance differing perspectives on how that knowledge should be taught.

Many of the selections in Part Two were published during the 1980s and early 1990s, a period in which a substantial number of reports described a variety of ills affecting higher education curricula and proposed, with varying degrees of specificity, plans for reforms. These reports often stressed the need for greater prescription in postsecondary curricula. Nodding to student demand for more choice of majors and elective courses, many colleges and universities in the 1960s and 1970s relaxed requirements for the baccalaureate degree by reducing the number of required courses needed for graduation and permitting more elective courses or expanding the range of courses that would fulfill those requirements. Additional changes occurred in major concentration programs where students in many institutions could select from an array of courses to fulfill basic requirements and/or create majors based on their personal interests. The expansion of knowledge and the creation of new disciplines, fields of study, and specializations also contributed to the development of conditions conducive to the growth and diversification of postsecondary curricula.

In "Curricular Transformations: Traditional and Emerging Voices in the Academy," Jennifer Haworth and Clif Conrad summarize the curricular positions taken by those who support traditional forms of education (such as Bennett,

Cheney, and Bloom) and those who call for an education that recognizes and incorporates the diverse cultural and other perspectives represented in contemporary society (including Levine, Giroux and Nussbaum). Their introduction not only frames the debates for readers, but also places them in the social, economic, and political context of the 1980s and early 1990s, tracing the influence of external forces on curricula in U.S. colleges and universities.

In 1984, the National Endowment for the Humanities (NEH), under the leadership of William Bennett, issued one of the first reports examining higher education. In *To Reclaim a Legacy: A Report on the Humanities in Higher Education,* Bennett maintains that colleges and universities have lost a clear sense of the purpose of education. Defining the primary goal of education as learning about civilization and culture, he argues that students should study Western literature, history, and culture to obtain an understanding of the origins and development of their civilization and culture, as well as a sense of major trends in art, religion, politics, and society. Few college graduates, he asserts, receive adequate instruction in their own culture because faculty have succumbed to pressure for enrollments and to intellectual relativism rather than assume "intellectual authority" for what students should learn (p. 20). Bennett also criticizes faculty who teach the humanities in a "tendentious, ideological manner" that overtly value or reject particular social stances (p. 16). For advocates of the Western canon like Bennett, the push for student choice and relevance in the curriculum had backfired, leaving U.S. democracy and society in disarray.

Bennett believes that knowledge of Western civilization and culture should be fostered through careful reading of masterworks of English, American, and European literature. He also recommends that students become familiar with the history, literature, religion and philosophy of at least one non-Western culture or civilization. Five years later, Bennett's successor at the NEH, Lynne Cheney, issued *50 Hours: A Core Curriculum for College Students*. Arguing, like Bennett, that a common core curriculum was key to a coherent education, Cheney proposes a required curriculum that stressed the study of Western civilization, but also includes the study of additional civilizations, foreign languages, science, mathematics, and social sciences.

Allan Bloom picked up the charges against the epistemological position of relativism that Bennett leveled, but expanded these views into an indictment of multicultural education and its emphasis on openness to diversity. In "Our Virtue," one of the opening chapters of *The Closing of the American Mind*, Bloom argues that students have been taught to value openness and to reject judgments based on values. "The recent education of openness . . . does not demand fundamental agreement or the abandonment of old or new beliefs in favor of the natural ones [a reference to the doctrine of natural rights]. It is open to all kinds of men, all kinds of life-styles, all ideologies. There is no enemy other than the man who is not open to everything" (p. 27). Ultimately concerned with how in the absence of shared values Americans can live in common, Bloom argues that by recognizing and accepting man's natural rights, we find a fundamental basis of unity and sameness. "Class, race, religion, national origin or culture all disappear or become dim when bathed in the light of natural rights, which give men common interests and make them truly brothers" (p. 27).

Historian Lawrence Levine challenges the claims made by conservative and traditional critics that the university has been politicized by leftist radicals who have forced feminism and multiculturalism into the curriculum and thereby diluted students' knowledge and appreciation of Western culture and knowledge. In "Through the Looking Glass," the first chapter of his book *The Opening of the American Mind*, Levine writes: "What is happening in the contemporary university is by no means out of the ordinary; certainly it is not a radical departure from the patterns that have marked the history of the university—constant and often controversial expansion and alteration of curricula and canons and incessant struggle over the nature of that expansion and alteration" (p.15). Levine's goal is to debunk what he considers to be hyperbolic claims about the state of the university curriculum, admonishing critics to remember that the current state of the country may be reflected in college and university curricula, but it is not caused by universities, their students, or their faculties

Similarly, Henry Giroux contends that higher education curricula, pedagogy, and the disciplines themselves are the products of "messy relations of worldly values and interests"

(p. 89). In "De-centering the Canon: Prefiguring Disciplinary and Pedagogical Boundaries," he argues that the liberal arts are not simply a self-contained discourse on the good life and democracy. Rather, Giroux claims, they enact a particular vision that draws upon specific values and that relies on particular relations of power, class, gender, and ethnicity that privileges some but not all. The debate about the liberal arts therefore must be reconfigured so that it addresses how power and knowledge intersect to produce and legitimate particular values, social identities, and representations. Rather than identify sacrosanct texts to be transmitted to students, Giroux argues for a critical pedagogy that not only focuses on the production of knowledge and social identities that empowers or disempowers individuals, but that also deliberately constructs the educational conditions that support critical thinking about these issues. Giroux's goal of social transformation will be realized, he suggests, when we develop educational practices that enable individuals to become critical (rather than just good) citizens who are willing to reconstruct their communities so that the principle of social justice shapes their political, social, and economic lives.

"Citizens of the World," a chapter from Martha Nussbaum's *Cultivating Humanity: A Classical Defense of Reform in Liberal Education*, sits between the traditionalists who conceive of a curricular canon that will teach us to live in common and the pluralists who believe that an overemphasis on Western thought is dysfunctional to life in a global society. Nussbaum shares Bloom and Bennett's concerns about the place of the humanities in general education and similarly considers the study of the humanities an important tool in the development of informed and capable citizens. Nussbaum's citizens, however, study cultures other than their own not simply to learn how their own is superior, but to understand its limitations. Like Giroux, Nussbaum supports a diverse curriculum so that students develop sympathetic understandings of distant cultures and of different ethnic and religious minorities. But she parts company with advocates of multiculturalism who see differences (in gender, ethnicity, sexual orientation, class, religion, etc.) as critical to understanding individuals and their communities. Instead, she contends that it is through the study of other cultures that we can learn what is common in humanity and she disparages identity politics as "divisive and subversive of the aims of a world community" (p. 67). Nussbaum concludes with a discussion of more and less successful efforts at incorporating diverse perspectives into the college and university curriculum.

While all of the selections in Part Two call for curricular reform of some kind, most focus on critiquing current conditions and offering visions of a better future. There have been, however, a number of reports from a variety of educational associations that have proposed comprehensive and concrete plans for change in undergraduate education, which a special emphasis on curriculum, teaching, and learning issues. We have included three such reports here; these focus their attention on three common institutional types: liberal arts colleges, community colleges, and research universities.

In 1985, the Association of American Colleges (AAC) published *Integrity in the College Curriculum: A Report to the Academic Community*, which described the work of the AAC Project on Redefining the Meaning and Purpose of a Baccalaureate Degree. The authors of this report argue that contemporary students are less well prepared for collegiate study, more vocationally oriented, and more materialistic than those in previous generations. The baccalaureate credential has become more important than the course of study, and colleges and universities have surrendered to the demands of the marketplace rather than developing creative approaches to a changing environment. The report also chastises faculty for abdicating their corporate responsibility for the undergraduate curriculum, claiming they are "more confident about the length of a college education than its content and purpose" and that the major in most institutions has become little more than "a gathering of courses taken in one department" (p. 2). To correct some of these ills, the report identifies nine content-related experiences that constitute a "minimum required curriculum" expected to provide students with the general knowledge, behaviors, and attitudes needed by citizens and workers in the contemporary world. Echoing previous calls, the AAC report urges faculty to take responsibility for designing educational experiences that provide students with a "vision of the good life, a life of responsible citizenship and human decency" (p. 6).

Focusing exclusively on the research university, the Boyer Commission on Educating Undergraduates in the Research University argues that undergraduate education at these institutions is in a state of crisis. Baccalaureate students, it argues, are treated as second-class citizens: "An undergraduate at an American research university can receive an education as good or better than anything available anywhere in the world but that is not the normative experience" (p. 5). Instead of trying to implement a model of undergraduate education modeled on much smaller liberal arts colleges, *Reinventing Undergraduate Education: A Blueprint for America's Research Universities* recommends that universities use the resources of their graduate and research programs to strengthen the quality of undergraduate education by crafting an experience available *only* at research institutions. This experience would be based, in part, on interdisciplinary study; learning through inquiry; student involvement on faculty research projects; mentoring and internships to develop knowledge and skills; and through a general education curriculum built on inquiry-based learning and communication of information and ideas.

Learning is also the touchstone of Terry O'Banion's "Creating More Learning-Centered Community Colleges." Viewing the mission of community colleges as consistent with calls for higher education reform that stress learning and the need to overhaul the traditional architecture of higher education institutions, O'Banion describes an idealized "learning college" that is based on the activities of community colleges that are engaged in the process of becoming more learner-centered. He argues that the inherited architecture of colleges and universities—time-bound, place-bound, bureaucracy-bound, and role-bound—thwarts reform efforts and must be changed before institutions can put learning first. O'Banion proposes six principles that can be summarized simply as follows: "The learning college places learning first and provides educational experiences for learners anyway, anyplace, anytime" (p. 15). These six principles form the basis for a new kind of learning-centered institution.

The case study for this chapter, Alpha University, is reprinted from the American Council of Education's *Dialogues for Diversity: The Project on Campus Community and Diversity*. The case revolves around a curriculum committee discussion of the relative priorities and merits of two possible curricula—one focused on multiculturalism and the other based on more traditional liberal arts objectives. The conversation among four professors, each representing a different discipline or field of study, invites readers to consider their own beliefs about teaching, assumptions about the nature of knowledge, and ideas regarding the purposes and scope of education.

Curricula under Construction: Design and Assessment

In Part Three we include selections that focus on designing and assessing courses and academic programs as academic plans. These readings provide an overview of different approaches to curriculum design, encouraging consideration of (a) the influence of societal, institutional, and disciplinary forces on curricular design, and (b) the central concerns of learners, pedagogy, and assessment. We open with Stark and Lattuca's "Defining Curriculum: An Academic Plan," which describes the academic plan concept in detail, briefly outlining the eight elements of the plan (purpose, content, sequence, learners, instructional processes, instructional resources, evaluation, and adjustment). Stark and Lattuca also discuss the impact of organizational, internal, and external contexts and factors influence academic plans.

Marcia Mentkowski and her colleagues discuss the curricular framework they have developed in "Thinking through a Curriculum for Learning that Lasts." Drawing on more than 20 years of curriculum innovation and design at Alverno College, Mentkowski and her colleagues define curriculum as a dynamic process with interactive elements rather than a static set of structures. Based on a review of the literature, Mentkowski and her associates offer a model of the curriculum that places six key curricular elements in a set of concentric circles. The elements, which include organized learning experiences, conceptual frameworks, missions and philosophy, and evaluation/assessment, are not mutually exclusive; rather each element blends with others to form an interactive whole that is focused on learners and their learning. This conceptualization challenges educators to understand the dynamic of curriculum change and to ask how and why curricula are continually being reshaped.

A selection focusing specifically on the influence of academic disciplines on thinking about the curriculum is Lattuca and Stark's "Will Disciplinary Perspectives Impede Curriculum Reform?" The authors analyze ten reports on reforming the academic major written by faculty task forces from ten disciplinary associations. In brief, the task force reports responded to a charge by the American Association of Colleges as part of a three-year review of liberal arts and sciences majors. That charge was to decide what the content and structure of the major would be if it were to achieve the goals of coherence, connectedness with other forms of knowledge, development of critical perspectives, and greater inclusiveness. The reports revealed that different disciplines were more or less able and willing to answer the charge of redefining the major, revealing epistemological differences that had been previously suggested by theorists and researchers who studied disciplinary differences in research and teaching activities.

Theories of learning and development are the focus of several of the selections in Part Three. In "What Does It Take to Learn?" Ference Marton and Shirley Booth conjoin the question "How do we gain knowledge of about the world?" In the process of answering this question, Marton and Booth consider some of the dominant theories of learning proposed by philosophers and theorists from Plato (learning as recollection) to Pavlov, Watson and Skinner (advocates of behavioral psychology), to Chomsky (structuralism), to Piaget (individual constructivism), and through cognitivism and situated cognition (or social constructivism, the description preferred by Marton and Booth). Marton and Booth are inclined toward this last theoretical position, which to their minds dissolves the dividing line between the individual's inner and outer worlds: "There is not a real world 'out there' and a subjective world 'in here.' The world is not constructed by the learner, nor is it imposed upon her; it is constituted as an internal relation between them" (p. 13).

In a chapter from her book *Creating Contexts for Learning and Self-Authorship: Constructive-Developmental Pedagogy*, Marcia Baxter Magolda focuses on the development of students as learners and as individuals. According to Baxter Magolda, self-authorship has cognitive, intrapersonal, and interpersonal dimensions that are part of single mental activity rather than separate entities: the cognitive component involves epistemological assumptions, the intrapersonal component involves assumptions about the self, and the interpersonal component concerns assumptions about relations between the self and others. Baxter Magolda views constructive-developmental theory as one lens for examining and understanding students' experiences in particular contexts. After reviewing theories of epistemological development, Baxter Magolda uses her own model to illustrate how cognitive, interpersonal and interpersonal development are integrated in students' attempts at meaning-making and self-authorship.

Numerous researchers and theorists have proposed theories of learning that highlight the social and contextualized nature of learning (e.g., Lave, 1988; Rogoff, 1990; Lave and Wenger, 1991; Greeno, 1997). Variously described as situated cognition, situated learning, situativity, or sociocultural theories, these theories rest on the claim that learning cannot be understood apart from its historical, cultural, and institutional contexts. Moreover, they cast learning as a fundamentally social and cultural activity and their guiding framework contrasts sharply with behavioral and cognitive models in which learning is conceptualized as an individual activity and as an artifact that can be cleanly separated from the contexts in which it takes place. The chapter by Marton and Booth included in this chapter briefly explains this perspective.

In "On Two Metaphors for Learning and the Dangers of Choosing Just One," Anna Sfard examines the entailments of two basic metaphors of learning—the acquisition metaphor, which she associates with cognitive views of learning, and the participation metaphor, which encompasses situated learning theories. Sfard argues that the cognitive perspective portrays knowledge as an entity that can be acquired in one task setting and transferred to another. She compares this perspective with one in which learning is situated according to an individual's position in the world of social affairs. While the central metaphor of "position" is operative in both sets of theories, situated learning theories define position with regard to social circumstances while cognitive theories conceptualize position more narrowly. For example, the cognitive perspective defines context as the task (e.g., learning how to analyze a text) and the features of the environment (the instructional setting in which the learning task occurs). In comparison, the socio-cultural perspective extends the understanding of context so it includes both the immediate context and larger social, cultural, and historical contexts in which a particular interaction takes place. Sfard critically examines both of these metaphors and their implications, and maintains that we need both; each has something that the other cannot provide and the tension between these two seemingly conflicting metaphors is a protection against theoretical excess and a source of power.

A number of selections with a distinctly pragmatic focus complement the theoretical perspectives and models that open Part Three. These readings, all of which focus on improving practice, are supported by empirical research that provides a strong rationale for their use on college and university campuses. The first of these selections is an publication from the Joint Task Force on Student Learning sponsored by three collaborating higher education associations: the American Association for Higher Education, the American College Personnel Association, and the National Association of Student Personnel Administrators. *Powerful Partnerships: A Shared Responsibility for Learning* is anchored in the belief that collaborations between academic and student affairs personnel and organizations are needed to bring about action on the lessons gleaned from research on student learning. Such partnerships can aid institutions as they attempt to enact ten basic principles of learning and collaborative action. *Powerful Partnerships* both describes these principles and provides evidence of current practices that support these principles.

Stephen Ehrmann, in an article on technology and higher education, warns that those seeking information about whether new technologies foster better student learning may be asking useless questions. In "Asking the Right Questions: What Does Research Tell Us about Technology and Higher Learning?" Ehrmann admonishes those who seek universal answers to questions about the comparative teaching effectiveness and costs of technology. He also counsels that questions about technology that do not consider content, teaching methods, the suitability of methods and media, and usage issues are unlikely to yield widely acceptable answers. Ehrmann ultimately concludes that technology can enable important curriculum changes, but faculty and institutions must make strategic choices about how it will influence a student's total course of study.

In 1987, the *AAHE Bulletin* published the "Seven Principles of Good Practice in Undergraduate Education," a widely known distillation of research findings on the undergraduate experience. In another article in the *Bulletin,* Implementing the seven principles: Technology as lever," Arthur Chickering and Stephen Ehrmann describe cost-effective and appropriate ways to use technology—computers, video, and telecommunications technologies—to advance the Seven Principles. The authors note that the range of technologies that can be used to foster active learning among students is impressive, but that students, faculty, and institutions need to work together to use these technologies effectively and efficiently.

Tom Angelo offers yet another set of principles for enhancing learning that are based on accumulated research findings in "A Teacher's Dozen: Fourteen General, Research-Based Principles for Improving Higher Learning in Our Classrooms." Angelo briefly describes 14 principles and offers implications for or applications to teaching and classroom assessment. He notes that for each principle there will be exceptions and individual faculty must determine which principles apply, to whom, when, where and how.

Four selections in Part Three consider issues of assessment and evaluation of student learning and academic programs. We have included selections that address assessment at the program and institutional levels. A fourth selection provides specific guidelines for periodic review of the undergraduate major.

Marcia Mentkowski's article, "Creating Context Where Institutional Assessment Yields Educational Improvement," provides a comprehensive primer on designing a successful institution-wide assessment program. Based on the extensive assessment experience of Alverno college faculty and administrators, Mentkowski outlines a number of essential elements of a successful assessment effort.

In the chapter "Qualitative Program Assessment: Tests to Portfolios" from *Assessment in Higher Education: Politics, Pedagogy, and Portfolios,* Patrick Courts and Kathleen McInerney offer an account of one faculty's movement from institutional assessment based on standardized tests to more authentic forms of assessment. Candid and detailed, this article describes the process by which faculty members developed and pilot tested a series of assessments only to find that none provided the kind of information that would be most useful to them as they worked to improve their own undergraduate programs. Courts and McInerney present a case history of the move to performance assessments and also offer guidance to colleges and individuals engaged in the task of designed assessment programs.

Also included in this section are three chapters from the American Association of College's handbook, *Program Review and Educational Quality in the Major*. Based on the AAC publication, *The Challenge of Connecting Learning* (1991), which provided organizational principles for liberal learning in arts and sciences fields, this set of program review guidelines reflects the findings of the AAC's three-year review of arts and sciences majors that was conducted from 1988 to 1991. Chapter Two of the guidebook sets out a framework for program review that consists of 13 characteristics of strong programs that were articulated in the *Challenge of Connecting Learning*. Chapter Three offers suggestions for procedures to be used in organizing program reviews, and Chapter Four provides questions to be asked in a program review process focused primarily on learning in the major.

Program quality in master's programs is the subject of two chapters from *Emblems of quality: Developing and Sustaining High-Quality Programs*, by Jennifer Haworth and Clif Conrad. Haworth and Conrad note that discussions of program quality generally take one or more of five views: programs can be judged by the quality of their faculty, the quality of their students, the quality of their resources, the rigor of their academic requirements or some combination of these. After critiquing each of these views, Haworth and Conrad argue for a learning-centered view of quality that judges quality programs as those that, from the perspectives of different stakeholders, provide learning experiences that positively affect students' growth and development. Based on interviews with faculty, administrators, and students in 47 programs, the authors compile a list of 17 characteristics of an ideal, high-quality master's program that cluster into five kinds of program attributes, each of which contributes to enriching learning experiences for students: diverse and engaged participants; participatory culture; interactive teaching and learning; connected program requirements; and adequate resources. In the readings included here, the authors describe these clusters of attributes and challenge administrators, faculty and institutional researchers to use their theory as a "thinking device" for understanding and assessing quality in their graduate programs.

Part Three concludes with two case studies, one that focuses on the redesign of an introductory economics course and the other that describes a comprehensive curriculum revision. In "Beyond Chalk and Talk: Strategies for a New Introductory Economics Curriculum" Meenakshi Rishi describes a course revision intended to make economics more interesting and challenging to a diverse study body. The new course supplemented textbook readings with articles, films, and invited speakers to enable students to explore and assess economic theory and practice. Where the traditional course emphasized abstract analytical modeling, the new course employed the analytical categories of race, gender, and class. In addition, Rishi intentionally created an interactive classroom environment based on cooperative learning activities rather than competition. Examples of classroom discussions vividly illustrate the impact of these changes.

A Policy Perspectives publication from the Institute for Higher Education Research at the University of Pennsylvania profiles changes in the curriculum at Rensselaer Polytechnic Institute. Maria Ianozzi documents the institutional challenges, such as budget deficits and poor attendance in lecture classes, that led RPI to create a curriculum that was more student-centered and that included innovative use of technology and interactive courses. These interactive studio courses, which replaced large lecture classes, are the focus of this case study.

Curriculum in Revision: Curricular Change and Innovation

Given the vast number of colleges and universities in the U.S. one might surmise that there would be almost an equally large number of curricular models and approaches to teaching and learning. However, most institutions offer similar programs of general and specialized education and most faculty teach using standard lecture and discussion methods. Truly innovative higher education institutions and programs are fairly rare and change tends to be incremental and slow.

Still the history and process of change and innovation offers many lessons to those in higher education. In this chapter we include readings that explore a number of dimensions of curricular change and innovation, both historical and contemporary, and that provide insights into instructional and pedagogical innovations, program revision, and institutional transformation.

We begin Part Four with a classic reading on curricular innovation. In 1978, Gerald Grant and David Riesman published *The Perpetual Dream: Reform and Experiment in the American College*, a study of contemporary reform movements in U.S. colleges and universities. In the second chapter of their book, Grant and Riesman focus on what they termed "telic reforms," those reforms that offer a different conceptualization of the ends of undergraduate education. They distinguish telic reforms from popular reforms that simply eased curriculum requirements for students. Arguing that the few telic reform efforts in U.S. colleges and universities have an impact on campuses and individuals beyond their immediate contexts, Grant and Riesman profile a small number of institutions with distinctive visions of higher education. These include the few colleges, like St. John's, that offer a neoclassical curriculum, typically based on close readings of the Great Books; institutions that emphasize the aesthetic dimension of learning such as Oberlin and Black Mountain; colleges and universities for which the value of community, typically associated with humanistic psychology, drove curricular decision making; and activist-radical institutions that are committed to social, political, and curricular change, such as Antioch and Goddard. Grant and Riesman argue that these different types of institutions were bound together in their aversion to the university model, their belief that the disciplines are subordinate to some greater good and purpose, and their willingness to develop interdisciplinary forms and discourses.

Innovation in the community college is the subject of George Boggs and Diane Michael's discussion of curricular and institutional change. "The Palomar College Experience" chronicles the process of reshaping a typical community college into a learning college that bases its work, programs, and policies primarily on the basis of what they contribute to student learning outcomes. Boggs and Michael offer a case history that begins with the impetus for the paradigm shift from an organizational paradigm that stressed the provision of instruction to one predicated on producing learning. Boggs and Michael detail the involvement of each area of the college in realizing the vision of the learning college, demonstrating how changes in the courses, programs, and pedagogy were supplemented by changes in student services and human resources that supported the learning mission of the college.

Scholars who argue that teaching about women of color is the starting point for transforming the curriculum offer another perspective on curricular change. In "Changing the Curriculum in Higher Education," Margaret Anderson contends that creating an inclusive curriculum requires more than incorporating women into the college and university curriculum. While teaching about women of color brings to the forefront previously overlooked intersections of gender, race, ethnicity, and class, it also alters prior ways of thinking in substantial ways. Using the field of women's studies as an example, Anderson illustrates how critiques of traditional knowledge and knowledge production challenge disciplinary assumptions, facts, and theories and begin the process of transforming the curriculum.

In "Transforming the Curriculum: Teaching about Women of Color" Johnnella Butler illustrates how the inclusion of women of color in the curriculum raises awareness and understanding of all women; once students and faculty see that all women are not white, the importance of the categories of race, ethnicity, and class in the study of gender becomes apparent. Still, the goal of curricular change isn't simply to add women or men of color to the curriculum to achieve balance. Instead, the goal is transformation of Western understandings of sameness and difference, the objective and the subjective, feminine and masculine, the rational and the intuitive so they are no longer seen as oppositional but as existing in interaction. To achieve this, Butler advocates a critical pedagogy that works not merely toward tolerance of difference, but toward an egalitarian world based on communal relationships.

The process of curricular change in general education is the subject of an excerpt from *Revitalizing General Education in a Time of Scarcity: A National Chart for Administration and Faculty* (Kanter, Gamson, London, & Arnold, 1997). Drawing on a survey of 71 institutions and 15 campus visits, the authors examine the processes of organizational change, comparing more and less successful efforts. To supplement the summary numbers from the survey, which focus on the composition and size of committees, the duration of the process, and the budget expenditures required, the authors explored the campus contexts in which these change efforts occurred. Using brief case studies of individual colleges and universities, the authors demonstrate how variations in these contexts influenced the success of particular efforts. Insights from these cases illustrate the importance of involving faculty as key stakeholders in curriculum reform, the need to ensure sufficient resources for design and implementation of programs, and the hazards of different management and accountability systems.

Carol Geary Schneider and Robert Shoenberg also focus on impediments to curricular change in "Habits Hard to Break: How Persistent Features of Campus Life Frustrate Curricular Reform." Schneider and Shoenberg argue that the organizational and structural realities of academic environments often inhibit curricular reform. These include the rhetoric and curricular organization that are associated with academic disciplines and departments and that encourage students to focus their studies narrowly rather than exploring the connections among disciplines and fields. There is, Schneider and Shoenberg suggest, no need for such insularity; because they serve as learning communities for students, departments need to rethink their educational aims and provide learning experiences that prepare students for life and work in a complex world. Similarly, traditional conceptions of general education and the major, in which the former provides breadth of study and the latter, depth, have prevented educators from thinking holistically about how each curricular component should develop students' communication, analytical, critical and scientific thinking skills, as well as their societal perspectives and responsibilities. Schneider and Shoenberg also encourage educators to question their assumptions about the proper length of an undergraduate degree, current transfer credit policies that equate similar course titles with similar educational experiences, the use of credits completed as a surrogate for performance-based assessments of learning, and the negative impact of faculty reward systems on curricular and pedagogical innovation. The authors see hope for change in the emerging consensus about what really matters in undergraduate education.

The human dimension of curricular change is the subject of the selection by Patricia MacCorquodale and Judy Lensink, "Integrating Women into the Curriculum: Multiple Motives and Mixed Emotions." The authors present the results of an evaluation of a four-year curriculum revision project to integrate women into the curriculum at the University of Arizona. They analyze faculty members' motivations for participating in the project, the nature of their resistance or openness to concept of integration, and the various outcomes faculty experienced as these related to attitudes of resistance or acceptance. MacCorquodale and Lensink also examine the influence of the revised curricula on students who took the revised courses and students in comparison courses.

Part Four closes with a selection that contrasts the processes employed by two respected universities as they attempted to institute significant core curriculum reforms on their campuses. Alison Schneider's article, "When Revising a Curriculum, Strategy May Trump Pedagogy: How Duke Pulled Off an Overhaul While Rice Saw Its Plans Collapse," provides a case study of the political dimensions of curricular change. The article profiles the successful and carefully orchestrated curriculum change effort at Duke University, comparing it with an unsuccessful and contentious attempt at Rice University. Schneider suggests that although the institutions hoped to implement similar kinds of reform, Duke's effectiveness can be traced at least in part to an extensive communication effort in which key faculty players were courted to consensus.

References

Association of American Colleges. (1991). *The challenge of connected learning*. Washington, DC: Author.

Bennett, W. J. (1984). *To reclaim a legacy: A report on the humanities in higher education*. Washington, DC: National Endowment for the Humanities.

Bloom, A. (1987). *The closing of the American mind*. NY: Simon & Schuster.

Boyer Commission on Educating Undergraduates in the Research University. (1996). *Reinventing undergraduate education: A blueprint for America's research universities*.

Committee on the Objectives of a General Education in a Free Society. (1945). *General education in a free society: Report of the Harvard Committee*. Cambridge, MA: Harvard University Press.

Giroux, H. (1992). *Border crossings: Cultural workers and the politics of education*. New York: Routledge.

Greeno, J, G. (1997). On claims that answer the wrong question. *Educational Researcher, 26*(1): 5–17

Lave, J. (1988). *Cognition in practice: Mind, mathematics and culture in everyday life*. Cambridge, UK: Cambridge University Press.

Lave, J. and Wenger, E. (1991). *Situated learning: Legitimate peripheral participation*. NY: Cambridge University Press.

Levine, L. R. (1996). *The opening of the American mind: Canons, culture, and history*. San Francisco: Beacon.

Marton, F. & Booth, S. (1997). *Learning and Awareness*. Mahwah, NJ: Lawrence Erlbaum Associates.

Nussbaum, M.C. (1997). *Cultivating humanity: A classical defense of reform in liberal education*. Cambridge, MA: Harvard University Press.

O'Banion, T. (1997). Creating more learning-centered community colleges. League for Innovation in the Community College.

Platt, C. (1998). Civic education and academic culture: Learning to practice what we teach. *Liberal Education*, 84 (1), 18–25.

Rogoff, B. (1990). *Apprenticeship in thinking: Cognitive development in social context*. NY: Oxford University Press.

PART ONE

CURRICULUM IN CONTEXT: DEFINITIONAL, HISTORICAL, AND PHILOSOPHICAL PERSPECTIVES

Section A

Theoretical Perspectives on Curriculum

CHAPTER 1

THEORETICAL PERSPECTIVES ON CURRICULUM

GEORGE J. POSNER

What have been the most significant perspectives on curriculum development in the United States?

What would proponents of each perspective propose for the reform of today's curriculum?

Every curriculum represents a choice as to how to approach the education of students. The particular approach chosen by the developers of a curriculum stems in part from how they formulate the problem to which they are responding. For example, if the problem were formulated as "cultural illiteracy," then the curriculum would likely emphasize those aspects of our culture about which people are presumed to be ignorant.[1] If the problem were formulated as the school's lack of relevance to children's lives, then the curriculum would likely emphasize activities or content that students can relate to everyday living. If the problem were formulated as a lack of educational equality for students of different backgrounds and capabilities, then the curriculum would likely emphasize ways to remedy or compensate for perceived disadvantages.

The problem formulation influences but does not determine the curriculum. Cultural illiteracy can be solved by having students read the "Great Books," learn the basic concepts of each discipline of knowledge, or develop a critical awareness of the contradictions of daily life in Western culture. Education for relevance might mean learning marketable skills, studying pop culture, or becoming social activists. Educational equality might be achieved by establishing a "core curriculum" for all students but providing special classes that allow for differences in pace, e.g., accelerated and basic classes; native language, e.g., bilingual education; and disabling conditions, i.e., self-contained classes. Or it might be achieved by requiring all students not only to study the same core program, but to do so in heterogeneous and mainstreamed classes. Educational problems can be responded to with various curricula. The approach chosen depends on the beliefs and assumptions (often termed "philosophies" or "perspectives") of the people who develop the curriculum.

In this chapter we introduce five different, coherent, but not mutually exclusive perspectives on curriculum. I call them "perspectives" because I want to think about the view of education each of them permits, what features of the educational landscape each allows us to see, and what each obscures from our view. Each perspective represents a particular, coherent set of assumptions about education. These assumptions can be considered distinctive answers to questions like the following:

How does learning occur, and how is it facilitated?

What objectives are worthwhile, and how should they be expressed?

What kinds of content are most important, and how should the content be organized for instruction?

Source: "Theoretical Perspectives on Curriculum," by George J. Posner, reprinted from *Analyzing the Curriculum,* Second Edition, 1995, McGraw-Hill Companies.

How should educational progress be evaluated?

What is and should be the relationship between schools and the society at large?

Each perspective chooses which of these questions it will address. Some perspectives are more comprehensive than others and thus address a broader set of questions.

The five perspectives are named as follows: *traditional, experiential, structure of the disciplines* (or *disciplines,* for short), *behavioral,* and *cognitive.* In subsequent chapters we select from these five perspectives ones representing conflicting views about particular curriculum components. By contrasting divergent perspectives, we will be able to bring the assumptions associated with each component into sharper relief.

Although this chapter is primarily intended as an introduction to the five theoretical perspectives, it does lead to curriculum analysis questions in its own right. Some curricula have been strongly influenced by one or more theoretical perspectives. M:ACOS, for example, was dominated by both the structure-of-the-disciplines and cognitive perspectives. As you begin your curriculum analysis, you should ask yourself whether your curriculum was strongly influenced by and thus reflects, a particular theoretical perspective—and if so, which one. For now you can only form hypotheses. The perspectives are described in this chapter in only introductory fashion, emphasizing their historical and intellectual roots. Subsequent chapters will provide more detail about each perspective and will help you identify specific ways in which these perspectives influenced various components of your curriculum, even though the curriculum as a whole may not reflect a pure case.

At the end of the book's final chapter you will ask yourself whether your curriculum, as a consequence of a particular theoretical perspective, evidences any significant blind spots. In that chapter we consider the limitations of theoretical perspectives and the ways in which an eclectic approach addresses these limitations.

Before presenting the five theoretical perspectives, a few caveats are necessary.

1. These perspectives summarize many, but certainly not all, approaches that curricula take. That is, they are representative, but not exhaustive. They are not the only perspectives possible, but they are important ones. However, it is entirely possible that you may find a curriculum that has no elements of any of these five perspectives, but instead represents an entirely different one.
2. Each perspective may be regarded as a "family" of approaches to curriculum. Although there may be disputes within families, i.e., family squabbles, each family represents a coherent set of assumptions underlying a curriculum's emphasis.
3. Many actual curricula cannot be neatly categorized as belonging to only one of these perspectives. The five families represent analytic and pedagogical tools rather than actual curricula. You will need to use them in subsequent chapters to help you analyze your curriculum.
4. Presentation of the perspectives here is somewhat oversimplified in order to avoid technical jargon.

With these caveats in mind, we will now examine the five theoretical perspectives. Note that each perspective can be summarized by an overarching question directing our attention to its central focus, as depicted in Table 1-1.

Traditional

What is now called "traditional" education by many writers was, at an earlier period in history, actually a response to a contemporary problem. The problem in the United States during the late

TABLE 1-1
The Five Perspectives: Central Questions

1. *Traditional* What are the most important aspects of our *cultural heritage* that should be preserved?
2. *Experiential* What *experiences* will lead to the healthy growth of the individual?
3. *Structure of the disciplines* What is the *structure of the disciplines* of knowledge?
4. *Behavioral* At the completion of the curriculum, what should the learners be *able to do*?
5. *Cognitive* How can people learn to *make sense* of the world and to *think* more productively and creatively?

nineteenth century was "the seemingly intractable problem of universal schooling in an increasingly urban society" (Cremin, 1975, p. 20). William Torrey Harris, then superintendent of the St. Louis school system and a learned philosopher in his own right, believed that education needed to focus on transmitting the cultural heritage of Western civilization. For Harris, education was the process "by which the individual is elevated into the species" (Harris, 1897, p. 813). Therefore, the curriculum, according to Harris, should make the accumulated wisdom of "the race" available to all children. The textbook would make a common body of facts equally accessible to the children, thereby serving as an antidote for the opinion-dominated newspapers of the day. The teacher, using the lecture-recitation method, would be the driving force in the process and would be responsible for getting students to think about what they read. Examinations would monitor and classify the students as they progressed through a graded educational system. As Cremin points out, "all the pieces were present for the game of curriculum making that would be played over the next half-century; only the particular combinations and the players would change" (Cremin, 1975, p. 22). I might add that the game remains the same to this day.

One of its leading critics, John Dewey, describes traditional education as follows: "The subject matter of education consists of bodies of information and skills that have been worked out in the past; therefore the chief business of the school is to transmit them to the new generation . . ." (Dewey, 1938, pp. 17–18). One of the leading contemporary proponents of the traditional perspective, humanities professor E. D. Hirsch, Jr. says essentially the same thing in somewhat different terms:" . . . the basic goal of education in a human community is acculturation, the transmission to children of the specific information shared by the adults of the group or polis" (Hirsch, 1987, p. xvi).

Perhaps because they dominated educational practice, traditional educators after Harris did not need to make their underlying assumptions explicit. That is, until recently they did not have to explicate their theories of learning, of motivation, of knowledge, or of school and society.

Today, the traditional perspective is promoted by writers such as political scientist Allan Bloom (1987); historian Diane Ravitch (1985); Hirsch (1987); and former Secretary of Education and chairman of the National Endowment for the Humanities William Bennett, most recently head of former President George Bush's antidrug campaign (1984, 1988). Hirsch and Bennett, because they have deliberately and eloquently expressed this perspective and wish to apply it to the curriculum of both elementary and secondary public education, will serve as our modern-day traditionalists in this book.

In his widely read 1983 article "Cultural Literacy," and his 1987 book of the same title, Hirsch argues that "to be culturally literate is to possess the basic information needed to thrive in the modern world" (1987, p. xiii). That basic information is composed of the facts that "literate" Americans possess—not what they should but what they do in fact possess. Literacy requires more than learning skills; it requires "the early and continued transmission of specific information" (p. xvii). Without this information, people are unable to communicate with one another: "Only by piling up specific, communally shared information can children learn to participate in complex cooperative activities with other members of their community" (p. xv).

Although Bennett appears to agree with Hirsch's emphasis on specific information, he represents the more generally accepted traditional view, which includes not only "worthwhile knowledge" but also "important skills and sound ideals" as educational goals (Bennett, 1988, p. 6). Like Hirsch and other traditionalists, Bennett believes that there should exist a core curriculum, a curriculum with an "irreducible essence . . . of common substance" (p. 6).

Although the traditionalists lost ground to progressive educators during the first half of this century, the current wave of popularity of traditional views demonstrates the resilience of this perspective. We will see that most other curriculum perspectives can be understood, in part, as responses to traditional education. Because these other emphases represent insurgent points of view, they have been much more deliberate in explicating their underlying theories.

Experiential[2]

Beginning toward the end of the nineteenth century, the traditional perspective exemplified by the views of Harris came under attack. Its critics claimed that its authoritarian posture was in conflict with the nature of a democracy, that its view of children as passive recipients of information was inconsistent with the growing body of psychological knowledge, and that its approach to school knowledge as compartmentalized, isolated from everyday living, static, and absolute made schools increasingly irrelevant to life in a rapidly changing and complex world. A new perspective was emerging that placed at its focal point the experience of the child.

The view that curriculum can be considered in terms of the experiences of students is essentially a twentieth-century development. Simply stated, an experiential view is based on the assumption that everything that happens to students influences their lives, and that, therefore, the curriculum must be considered extremely broadly, not only in terms of what can be planned for students in schools and even outside them, but also in terms of all the unanticipated consequences of each new situation that individuals encounter. The consequences of any situation include not only what is learned in a formal sense, but also all the thoughts, feelings, and tendencies to action that the situation engenders in those individuals experiencing it. But since each individual differs in at least some small ways from all others, no two individuals can experience the same situation in precisely the same way. Thus the experiential view of education makes enormous demands on anyone who attempts to make practical curriculum decisions, for it assumes that the curriculum is more or less the same as the very process of living and that no two individuals can or should live precisely the same lives. The twentieth-century development of experiential education revolves around efforts, first, to understand how curriculum can be considered in this broadest possible way, and second, to develop clear and workable principles to guide practical decisions about such curricula.

The historical roots of experiential education can be traced to the Enlightenment in Europe during the seventeenth and eighteenth centuries. During that time, philosophers such as Hobbes (1962) and Descartes (1931) emphasized the importance of both mind and sense impressions, thus laying a basis for the development of modern psychology and an emphasis in modern education on both reasoning and empiricism. Locke (1913) argued that learning arises directly from experience, from how sense impressions of the external world "write" on the mind, which he likened to a *tabula rasa*, or blank slate. Rousseau (1962) added to such ideas his notions about the primacy of the individual, arguing that by nature individuals are pure until corrupted by the influence of society, and advocating a pedagogy that protected the experiences and spontaneous development of children. During the nineteenth century, other child-centered pedagogies that were advanced by such European educational pioneers as Pestolozzi and Froebel, and that further emphasized the needs, interests, and experiences of developing children, gained increasing prominence in Europe and gradually began to come to the attention of American educators.

The results of these new influences were soon to be felt. In the United States at the beginning of the nineteenth century almost all formal education was based on the training of the mind. Formal education was limited to a small proportion of the population, however, and training in the practical skills needed by the masses to get along in American society went on primarily through apprenticeships and the activities of daily living. During the nineteenth century, major sociological changes in the United States gradually caused the curriculum of many schools to become increasingly oriented toward practical subjects and social utility. This change occurred as the nation became increasingly urbanized and industrialized, and as compulsory school attendance laws were passed. Given these internal changes and the emergence of child-centered pedagogy in Europe, the United States at the end of the nineteenth century was poised on the brink of an immense educational revolution.

The catalyst for this revolution was the development around the turn of the century of pragmatic philosophy and the progressive educational movement. John Dewey's ideas were the principal basis for both. Dewey believed that traditional philosophies were inadequate largely because they viewed reality as external to the individual. Such philosophies emphasized either thinking or sensing as the best way of knowing reality, but not both. Education based on traditional philosophies therefore emphasized as the best criterion of curriculum choice either training of the mind (reasoning) or training of the senses (empiricism). Dewey contended that under the former criterion curricula became unduly academic and intellectual, while under the latter they became unduly vocational and social. Neither criterion alone could emphasize properly balanced individual development. In contrast, Dewey believed that reality is not external to the individual; it is found within the experience of the individual, the composite of both the individual's internal reactions, such as thoughts and feelings, and external reactions, such as actions, to the influences of the external world. Reality itself is in constant flux as both individuals and their world constantly change. For Dewey, therefore, the only way of knowing if a belief is true is to weigh the consequences of testing it in action. True beliefs are those that have good consequences for the further development of the experience of the individual. These and similar ideas advanced by other American philosophers coalesced into pragmatic philosophy, the basis for experiential education, in which the curriculum is based on the needs and interests of students and is subject to constant change and reorganization in order to foster the best possible consequences for the further development of each student's experiences.

Any form of experiential education that is consistent with Dewey's ideas therefore rejects neither reasoning nor empiricism as a criterion of curriculum choice, but it does combine them in a way that at the beginning of the twentieth century was new. To the two older criteria for curriculum choice in American schools, the development of reasoning, then associated with academic subjects believed useful in the training of mind, and the development of empiricism, then associated with practical subjects believed to lead to socially useful skills, Dewey added a new criterion: the development or healthy growth of individual experience. The addition of this third criterion brought the first two into balance. In order to lead to healthy growth, no longer could a curriculum be justified as solely academic and intellectual or as solely vocational and social. Any subject or activity chosen for or recommended to individual students should contribute to both their intellectual and social development, and to their personal development as well. Dewey believed that, as individuals thus developed in healthy ways, so, too, would American society develop and progressively change in healthy ways.

The immediate challenge for the newly formed progressive education movement was, of course, to develop principles and forms of education that would be based on personal experience and promote the development in the individual of both intelligence and socially useful skills; however, in the early decades of the century progressive education was part of the wider progressive social reform movement. It was part of a response to a whole host of ills brought on by major changes in national life. Educators and the public alike increasingly believed that American schools should contribute directly to the solution of the nation's most intractable problems. When in 1918 the National Education Association (NEA) issued the famous *Cardinal Principles of Secondary Education,* which exemplified the national mood, the organization was suggesting that curricula be nearly as broad as life itself in order to deal with seven aims: health, command of fundamental processes, worthy home membership, vocational preparation, citizenship, worthy use of leisure time, and development of ethical character (NEA, 1918).

The magnitude of these demands on the progressive educational movement brought both the opportunity on a broad scale to reconstruct the curricula of American schools and disagreement about how curricula should be organized. Despite Dewey's explanations, many progressives did not keep the three basic criteria of curriculum choice in reasonable balance. Some emphasized what they considered a scientific study of individuals and society in order to create curricula that would efficiently fit individuals into prevailing social structures. Others emphasized curricula that would protect the free and spontaneous development of children. Still others emphasized curricula intended directly to reconstruct society itself.[3] Although during the 1920s and 1930s the traditional academic curriculum that American schools had inherited as a legacy of the nineteenth century gradually incorporated different progressive emphases, there were few real experiments in genuinely experiential education, and most of these were of small scale and short duration.

The major exception was the Eight-Year Study, possibly the most important and most successful experiment ever undertaken in American schools.[4] It compared nearly 1,500 students who attended 30 progressive, experimental secondary schools with an equal number of students from traditional schools, following all students through their eight high school and college years, mostly during the middle and late

1930s. No two experimental schools were alike. Each freely developed its own curriculum; however, almost all these curricula were developed directly and cooperatively by the students and teachers of the schools in accordance with their own perceived needs and interests. Furthermore, comparisons between experimental and traditional students were made in terms of the development of individual experience, including academic, vocational, social, and personal considerations. Thus the study was clearly an experiment designed to measure the success of curricula developed in general accordance with Dewey's basic principles. Comparisons seemed to indicate that students from the experimental schools, which emphasized experiential education, did slightly better academically in college than did students from the traditional schools, but were decidedly better off in terms of their overall development in a whole host of things such as thinking, taking initiative for their own lives, and social adjustment.

Even while the Eight-Year Study was still in progress, Dewey had issued a warning and a clarification in *Experience and Education* (1938) to those progressive educators who were still confused about experiential education and how to properly balance the three basic criteria of curriculum choice: that is, how to promote the development of intelligence, the development of socially useful skills, and the healthy growth of individual experience. Dewey pointed out that all education, like all living, is a process of experiencing, but not all experiences are equally or genuinely educative. Experience must be judged by its quality. High-quality, or educative, experiences are those that contribute to the healthy growth of further experience; low-quality, or "miseducative," experiences are those that distort or arrest the healthy growth of experience. The problem for the educator is to make suggestions to individual students about subject matter, materials, and activities that will contribute to educative experiences. In general, the highest-quality experiences are those that help individuals become increasingly autonomous and intelligent in guiding their own future educative experiences. The quality of the personal experiences that the curriculum contributes to is more important than how it is organized or whether it is primarily academic, vocational, or social.

Unfortunately, both the example of the Eight-Year Study and the significance of Dewey's message were obscured by World War II, and after the war ended, the national mood turned increasingly conservative. Progressive education was increasingly viewed by the general public as something whose time had come and gone, even as something that was now largely responsible for the same ills in American schools that the progressives themselves had identified and denounced earlier in the century. The general public, of course, made no distinctions between forms of progressive education that were consistent with Dewey's views of experience and forms that were inconsistent. As we shall shortly see, the national debate about education in the late 1940s and the 1950s—very much like the national debate of the 1980s—became a call for more emphasis on traditional forms of academic education, and by the time that call was answered by the nationally sponsored, academically oriented curricula, the Progressive Educational Association itself had quietly faded out of existence. Except for a brief period during the late 1960s and early 1970s of national attention to free schools and open classrooms, some of which were genuinely devoted to experiential education and some of which were merely reactions to the academic emphases of the time, the national mood has remained unreceptive to progressive education, the fundamental experiment in modern education begun at the start of the century.

So that part of the experiment devoted to experiential education remains incomplete. Experiential education has been talked about a great deal, it has been tried out on a small scale, a few of its tenets have even seeped into typical American classrooms, but the challenge remains largely the same at the end of this century as it did at the beginning: to understand how curriculum can be considered in the broadest possible way, as whatever experience fosters the healthy growth of further experience, and to develop clear and workable principles to guide practical decisions about such curricula. Good experiential education is consistent with Dewey's views about fostering the intelligent autonomy of individual students.

Although Dewey's views were criticized during the 1950s, they were rediscovered by reformers in the late 1960s, forming the basis for the "alternative schools" movement. More recently, Eliot Wigginton (1985), through his widely publicized Foxfire program, has given Deweyan ideas a rebirth in a modern form.

Structure of the Disciplines

Abuses and distortions of Deweyan ideas provided educational critics of the 1950s, like Arthur Bestor and Admiral Hyman Rickover, a scapegoat for America's inability to gain a decisive competitive edge over the Russians in the Cold War that followed World War II. Books such as *Educational Wastelands* (Bestor, 1953), accusing American education of being intellectually "flabby," turned the questions of what schools should teach and who should decide this matter into issues of national concern. These critics laid the groundwork for a perspective that returned the focus of the curriculum to subject matter, and in particular to the disciplines of knowledge and the way scholars in those disciplines understand their structure. But as Atkin and House point out, there were significant political and educational antecedents to these issues:

> Before the mid-1950s . . . there was a lively education debate, and it was a curriculum debate. It centered on the decades-old battle between professors in liberal arts colleges and professors in schools of education. This heated internecine conflict over who trains teachers and what they should learn had been in progress at least since the late 1800s. (Atkin & House, 1981, p. 6)

The liberal arts professors representing the specific subject matters of the school curriculum regarded the education professors, particularly the progressive educators with an experiential perspective, as too general and fuzzy-headed. The education professors accused the subject-matter professors of being too narrow (Foshay, 1970). Atkin and House contend that World War II had a profound influence on this debate.

> . . . World War II and, particularly, the development of the atom bomb, greatly strengthened both the self-confidence of university-based academic scholars and their political power. The development of the practical application of atomic energy was seen as a triumph of theoretical, intellectual effort. Furthermore it was considered university-based and an achievement of professors. The fruits of research were seen by the American people, as never before, as having an impact on daily life. The United States had been increasingly enamored of technology during the preceding decades, but the developments were seen as a result of inventiveness and industry, rather than of science and theoretical inquiry. Edison and Ford had been the popular embodiments of American progress in the decades before World War II.
>
> With the Allied victory over Germany and Japan, Einstein became a cultural hero. This quintessential professor—pipe-smoking, unkempt, apparently unworldly—had developed as an act of mind the basis for defeating the Axis power. People like him had worked intensely during the war to translate theory to an awesome weapon that had saved the world from enslavement. Professors captured the respect of the American public, and academic life was seen, for the first time perhaps, as crucial to our national survival. . . . There was a boost to professors and importance of a university education which had never been seen before and, many people think, is unlikely to be seen again. (Atkin & House, 1981, p. 6)

Because of these events and because of the international political climate of the time, education at all levels was regarded as crucial to the achievement of national goals. The most direct beneficiary of these developments was the university professor. Probably for the first time, university-based scholars in mathematics and science were seen as having a legitimate influence on elementary and secondary curriculum.

> University professors had long been lamenting the quality of precollege education in the battles over teacher education policy. They had been saying for 50 years that students were arriving at the university without necessary preparation. The information high school graduates possessed was insufficient, inaccurate or unimportant—sometimes all three. What the education system needed was more involvement by university professors in the creation of curriculum for the schools; more involvement, that is, by professors in the academic disciplines that constituted the high school curriculum. (Atkin & House, 1981, pp. 6–7)

It was in this climate that Max Beberman at the University of Illinois formed a group of mathematicians and engineers at his university for the purpose of improving the high school mathematics curriculum. The group, formed in 1951 and called the University of Illinois Committee on School Mathematics (UICSM), "analyzed secondary-school mathematics courses and concluded that they seldom included concepts developed after the year 1700, and almost never focused on the mathematical ideas professors considered important" (Atkin & House, 1981, p. 7). Beberman himself demonstrated at the University High School that he could successfully teach secondary school students topics like set theory. In 1952, UICSM developed instructional materials for use by other teachers under a grant from the Carnegie Corporation. This grant allowed UICSM to expand, involving more mathematicians and more schools in which it could try out the experimental materials. The "new math" was born (Atkin & House, 1981).

By the mid-1950s, these developments were paralleled by developments in physics, this time spearheaded by a group of professors at MIT and Harvard under the leadership of Jerrold Zacharias (Zacharias & White, 1964). These scientists, after analyzing the secondary school physics curriculum, reached the same conclusions that Beberman and his colleagues had reached earlier. The physics curriculum did not include the topics that these physicists regarded as the most important. Instead, high school physics textbooks emphasized technology, in particular the physical principles underlying the operation of everyday devices like refrigerators and automobile engines.

> In the Cambridge setting, Zacharias, himself involved in defense work during World War II and emboldened by successes to be achieved by well-mobilized minds, attracted a group of outstanding physicists to work on high school curriculum. Several of these physicists also had been involved in weapons development just a few years earlier.
>
> By 1956, the 6-year-old National Science Foundation, which in its charter had been given responsibility for improving the state of American science education as well as science, began to fund Zacharias' Physical Science Study Committee (PSSC). The verve, motivation, optimism, and esprit of PSSC seemed to many observers to be reminiscent of the organization that developed the atom bomb, and by this time Americans were convinced that great minds and plenty of money could do almost anything, even change the secondary school curriculum.
>
> It probably is no coincidence that these early nationally oriented attempts to change the curriculum were in the fields of mathematics and science. It was these subjects that were associated with success in the war effort. It was these fields that represented increasingly for the American people an unqualified good. UICSM and PSSC received considerable publicity in the nation's education press, and there were feature stories in magazines such as *Time*. The tenor of the publicity, as might be imagined, was that the outstanding scholars associated with these new projects were in the process of remedying extraordinary deficiencies in the existing education system. Indeed, they were about to "reform" the curriculum. The clear inference for the public was that schools had been mismanaged, the curriculum was antiquated, and all this was, in an almost criminal fashion, depriving youngsters and society of a rightful education. The education "establishment" was seen increasingly by the public as it had been seen for decades by academics, as self-serving, unresponsive, and probably a bit dull-witted. (Atkin & House, 1981, pp. 7–8)

On October 4, 1957, these developments took on a sudden urgency with the dramatic launching of Sputnik I by the Soviet Union:

> The defense of the United States suddenly was seen as threatened. A sense of crisis permeated the nation. Professors testified in the Congress, and their testimony was believed. They said that our national well-being depended, in part, on high-quality precollege science education. (p. 8)

It was in this context that scientists like Zacharias had been attempting to update the physics curriculum. They quickly realized that the "knowledge explosion" had created too much subject matter to allow them simply to add modern physics to the existing curriculum. They found that they needed to establish priorities. Zacharias's solution was twofold: (1) teach only the most fundamental concepts in physics; (2) teach students how to derive the rest of physics knowledge from those concepts. In a sense, children could learn a lot "while keeping very little in mind" (Bruner, 1971, p. 20). Although this notion began with physics, it quickly spread to other sciences.

These efforts provided the basis for a conference in 1959 at Woods Hole, Massachusetts, sponsored by the National Science Foundation and other foundations. Jerome Bruner's (1960) report on that conference, entitled *The Process of*

Education, proposed a theoretically reasonable solution to the ongoing debate between the subject-matter specialists and education generalists based on the work of Zacharias, Beberman, and others attending the conference. This report provided the principles upon which a structure-of-the-disciplines perspective was based. First, Bruner proposed that subject matter is dynamic, something evolving, instead of a given. Second, he proposed that each discipline has its own way of conducting inquiry. There is not one scientific method, but many. Third, he proposed that the purpose of education should be to develop in children's minds several different "modes of inquiry." These proposals struck a compromise between the education professors and those in the academic disciplines. After all, both groups were, and always had been, interested in fostering understanding (Foshay, 1970). Bruner's proposal was a reasonable resolution of the dilemma and spread rapidly. In the words of Bruner (1971, pp. 19–22):

> Let me reconstruct the period in which *The Process of Education* came into being. The year 1959 was a time of great concern over the intellectual aimlessness of our schools. Great strides had been made in many fields of knowledge, and these advances were not being reflected in what was taught in our schools. A huge gap had grown between what might be called the head and the tail of the academic procession. There was great fear, particularly that we were not producing enough scientists and engineers.
>
> It was the period, you will recall, shortly after Sputnik. The great problem faced by some of my colleagues in Cambridge, Massachusetts, at the time was that modern physics and mathematics were not represented in the curriculum, yet many of the decisions that society had to make were premised on being able to understand modern science. Something had to be done to assure that the ordinary decision maker within the society would have a sound basis for decision. The task was to get started on the teaching of science and, later, other subjects. . . .
>
> The prevailing notion was that if you understood the structure of knowledge, that understanding would then permit you to go ahead on your own; you did not need to encounter everything in nature in order to know nature, but by understanding some deep principles, you could extrapolate to the particulars as needed. Knowing was a canny strategy whereby you could know a great deal about a lot of things while keeping very little in mind.
>
> This view essentially opened the possibility that those who understood a field well—the practitioners of the field—could work with teachers to produce new curricula. For the first time in the modern age, the acme of scholarship, even in our great research institutes and universities, was to convert knowledge into pedagogy, to turn it back to aid the learning of the young. It was a brave idea and a noble one, for all its pitfalls. . . .
>
> The rational structuralism of Woods Hole had its internal counterpoise in intuitionism—the espousal of good guessing, of courage to make leaps, to go a long way on a little. It was mind at its best, being active, extrapolative, innovative, going from something firmly held to areas which were not so firmly known in order to have a basis for test. . . .
>
> During the early sixties, in various projects, it was discovered again and again how difficult it was to get to the limit of children's competence when the teaching was good. It was Socrates and the slave boy constantly being replayed. No wonder then that we concluded that any subject could be taught in some honest form to any child at any stage in his development. This did not necessarily mean that it could be taught in its final form, but it did mean that basically there was a courteous translation that could reduce ideas to a form that young students could grasp. *Not* to provide such translation was discourteous to them. The pursuit of this ideal was probably the most important outcome of the great period of curriculum building in the sixties.
>
> With all of this there went a spirit and attitude toward students. The learner was not one kind of person, the scientist or historian another kind. The schoolboy learning physics did so as a physicist rather than as a consumer of some facts wrapped in what came to be called at Woods Hole a "middle language." A middle language talks *about* the subject rather than talking the subject. . . .

The metaphor of the student as neophyte scientist nicely captures the essence of this perspective. Once we understand that this metaphor provided the foundation for the perspective, the emphasis on students' active participation in scientific inquiry, the dominant role of university scientists, and the importance of providing students with the fundamental concepts of the disciplines all make perfect sense.

Behavioral

The dominance of scientists and mathematicians in curriculum development during the 1950s and early 1960s did not go unnoticed by behavioral psychologists. They were concerned that all the knowledge they had gained during the previous fifty years about how children learn was being ignored. Furthermore, with all the federal dollars being committed to curriculum development since Sputnik, they wanted a piece of the action. They argued that the strictly disciplines-based curricula were failing to teach science and mathematics effectively, that there was much more to curriculum development than providing materials that reflected the structure of the disciplines. According to these psychologists, curriculum development needed to focus not on content, but on what students should be able to do—i.e., the behaviors they learn—as a consequence of instruction. Further, educators need to take into account how students acquire these behaviors—i.e., the conditions of learning—as they plan instruction. In order to understand these criticisms and proposals, we must first consider the development of these views.

The roots of behavioral views, like most other views, can be traced back to Greek philosophers, particularly Aristotle. In an important work on memory and recollection, Aristotle argued that imagery is the basis for memory, that the associations a person makes between images are the basis for recollection, and that the principles of comparison, contrast, and contiguity are the basis for all associations. That is, the differences and similarities between images, as well as when they occur, account for the ways in which we relate our images, and those relationships in turn determine what we remember at any given time. Many of Aristotle's ideas found expression in the classical empiricism of John Locke (1913) in the seventeenth and David Hume (1957,1967) in the eighteenth century. This view of knowledge was based on the assumption that all knowledge is rooted in sense impressions, i.e., the effects that seeing, hearing, touching, tasting, and smelling things in the world have on our minds. These sense impressions form the building blocks of experience, much as atoms form the building blocks of the physical world—as Sir Isaac Newton proposed at about this same time. These "atoms" of experience are then connected by associations into complex ideas. However, as Hume (1957) so succinctly put it, no matter how complex the ideas, "there is nothing in the mind which was not first in the senses."

The founder of behavioral psychology is often considered to be Edward Thorndike. His highly influential work near the beginning of the twentieth century in the areas of mental measurement, the laws of learning, the psychology of arithmetic, and transfer of training also established him as the founder of educational psychology. In addition, his exhaustive works on behavioral objectives in arithmetic contributed to his influence on the curriculum field during its formative years in the beginning of the twentieth century.

It was Thorndike's preeminence and his promise of a behaviorally based science of education that led to the parallel emergence and common behavioral roots of educational psychology and curriculum as fields of professional study.

While Thorndike provided the necessary scientific basis, Franklin Bobbitt provided the necessary technology for a behaviorally based theory of curriculum. His two major works, *The Curriculum* (1918) and *How to Make a Curriculum* (1924), established behavioral analysis, termed "life-activity analysis," and specific objectives derived from the analysis as the principal methods of curriculum development. As long as one could assume that preparation for current life activities also prepares people to live in tomorrow's world, Bobbitt's methods seemed reasonable. Furthermore, basing curriculum on actual life activities, rather than on traditional subject matter, seemed to be consistent with the progressive movement sweeping the nation at the time. However, once educators realized that they were living in a rapidly changing world, and that life-activity analysis could lead educators to develop curricula that reinforced the existing social structure and were doomed to technological obsolescence, they began to regard Bobbitt's methods as too conservative. But Bobbitt's technology for developing curricula based on activity analysis left a legacy. After Bobbitt many educators believed that curriculum development is a process best left to experts, i.e., those with specialized knowledge. This belief transformed the field to one based on a technical production framework.

Ralph Tyler continued the technical production and objectives orientation of curriculum into the 1930s, 1940s, and 1950s. In his seminal book, *Basic Principles of Curriculum and Instruction* (1949), he presented a method for analyzing each curriculum objective into its substantive, i.e., content, dimension and its behavioral dimension.[5] Tyler's notion of the behavioral aspect of an objective served as the basis for Benjamin Bloom's (1956) highly influential work on a taxonomy (a classification) of objectives. Bloom's taxonomy systematized the behavioral dimension and, in doing so, reinforced the belief that objectives are fundamentally expressions of the behaviors that educators want learned—as opposed to the content teachers want to teach or the experiences educators want students to have.

While Bobbitt provided educators with the technology to identify important objectives, Robert Mager and Fred Keller provided the technologies necessary for expressing those objectives in clear, unambiguous terms; their work gave teachers a blueprint they could use to redesign their courses according to behavioristic principles. Mager's little book *Preparing Instructional Objectives* (1962) has done more to influence educator's beliefs about objectives—and in particular, their proper form—than any other work. Likewise, Keller's (1968) approach to teaching, termed Personalized System of Instruction (PSI), has arguably done more to change college instruction than any other single innovation. In this approach, a course is broken down into a step-by-step series of behaviors, each of which must be "mastered" before the student is allowed to move on. By uncritically transferring their extensive experience in industrial training to public education, Mager and Keller were able to stipulate the requirements for well-formed objectives and for effective course organization, respectively. The major requirement for Magerian objectives is a verb that expresses observable behaviors. Mager's insistence on observable behaviors and his stipulation of a simple procedure for writing this type of objective, and Keller's requirements for content sequence and for student progress through that sequence, have provided educators with straightforward, if not reductionistic, technologies for implementing B. F. Skinner's (1968) behavioristic psychology of learning.

Cognitive

In primary and secondary education, as in the universities, a challenge to the behavioral orientation that dominated psychology came from cognitive psychologists. Ironically, the foundations of modern cognitive views can also be traced to Greek philosophy, but in this case to Plato. Although some of Plato's theory now seems strange, his views had a strong influence on antecedents of contemporary cognitive psychology. Plato believed that a person's knowledge and ideas are innate, or inborn; all that a teacher needs to do is help the person recall them. Therefore, according to Plato learning is recollection, and recollection is the search for and discovery of innate ideas followed by the construction of new concepts from those ideas. Plato's rendition of Socratic dialogues has remained, for many educators, the prototype of great teaching. Socrates seemed capable of teaching complex, abstract ideas without appearing to tell his students anything. As implausible as Plato's view of innate ideas might seem to us now, it has been very influential and formed the basis for many modern ideas of learning as discovery.

In spite of Plato's influence, the predominant views about learning and knowledge through the nineteenth century were empiricist ones, according to which all knowledge derives from sensations and the associations made between them. Modern cognitive views, though rooted in Platonic idealism formulated more than 2,000 years earlier, may, therefore, be understood as a response to nineteenth-century empiricism. By arguing that the empiricist account of knowledge is fundamentally flawed, Immanuel Kant in the nineteenth century established the foundation for the cognitive perspective. Sensations and associations, he argued, are insufficient as an account of knowledge. Kant then asked the fundamental cognitive question: "What goes on in the mind that allows us to form knowledge?" His answer was that empiricists failed to take into account the structure of the mind. The mind, he said, has categories that structure perceptions. Experience does not consist of raw sensations, but of sensations structured by the mind.

In part because some of the methods used by some cognitive psychologists to study the mind proved to be unreliable (particularly the method known as introspection), the work of most cognitive psychologists was discredited and ignored for almost a century.

For example, the work of the Swiss psychologist Jean Piaget went largely unnoticed for thirty years until the 1950s. Piaget as he sought to understand the development of intelligence, was particularly interested in children's beliefs about space, e.g., volume; time; natural phenomena, e.g., the sun; and moral questions (Piaget, 1929). By providing detailed accounts of how these beliefs develop and how young children's thinking differs from that of adults, Piaget provided educators with an in-depth understanding of children's minds and convinced many educators that they must wait until the child is cognitively "ready," before teaching abstract concepts. Furthermore, his notion that the mind both "assimilates" new ideas into an existing structure and also "accommodates" new ideas by reorganizing this structure has formed the basis for modern constructivism and conceptual change theory, to be discussed later in this book.

While Piaget was showing educators the cognitive limitations on abstract thinking in young children, Noam Chomsky (1968) was portraying the incredible accomplishment that young children manage to complete within two to three years, namely, language acquisition. He developed a mode of analyzing the structure of language, showing that language is far more complex than previously believed, and that behaviorist accounts of language development are incapable of explaining these complexities. He argued that innate structures (a "language acquisition device") are necessary for explaining how someone learns such a complex language in so short a period of time. In his argument he made an important and highly influential distinction between competence (which he defined as the existence of mental structures, such as understanding of grammatical rules) and performance (in other words, observable behaviors, such as utterances). The study of the relationship between knowledge and performance continues to be of fundamental concern to cognitive psychologists studying such topics as problem solving, language, decision making, and even teaching.

Although the work of Piaget, Chomsky, and many others has provided the basis for modern cognitive views of education, little direct attention had been given to problems of learning per se until David Ausubel's (1968) work on "meaningful learning." Although Ausubel approached the problem from a different perspective, he joined the behavioral psychologists in criticizing the proponents of the disciplines-based curricula, particularly for their use of "discovery learning" and for their failure to distinguish between the "logical structure" of the disciplines and the "psychological structure" of the learner (Ausubel, 1964). His work and that of "schema" theorists like Richard Anderson (1977) after him established the view that "the single most important determinant of learning is what the learner already knows; ascertain that and teach him accordingly" (Ausubel, 1968).

Much of the recent work in this field has been aimed at discovering what it is that learners already know, i.e., their existing concepts and beliefs; how that knowledge affects their performance on school-related tasks such as comprehension and problem solving; and how to teach learners to perform difficult tasks and to understand abstract ideas (Bereiter & Scardamalia, 1992). This range of concerns has produced a variety of approaches to curriculum, all of which can be considered cognitively oriented, including those based on child development,[6] concept learning,[7] and the thinking process.[8] Most recently, the notion of the "thinking curriculum" attempts to resolve conflicts among these different views by . . .

> offering a perspective on learning that is thinking- and meaning-centered, yet insists on a central place for knowledge and instruction. Cognitive scientists today share with Piagetians a constructivist view of learning, asserting that people are not recorders of information (as in the traditional perspective) but builders of knowledge structures. To know something is not just to have received information but also to have interpreted it and related it to other knowledge. To be skilled is not just to know how to perform some action (as in the behavioral perspective) but also to know when to perform it and to adapt the performance to varied circumstances. . . . Thinking and learning merge in today's cognitive perspective, so that cognitive and instructional theory (and we might add, curriculum theory) is, at its heart, con-

cerned with the Thinking Curriculum. (Resnick & Klopfer, 1989, pp. 3–4)[9]

Summary

To summarize the five perspectives, we can imagine asking the proponents of each one how they would advocate reforming schooling in general and curriculum in particular. Their responses might be as follows:

1. *Traditional* Schools need to return to the basics, that is, to a mastery of basic literacy and computational skills, to a knowledge of basic facts and terminology that all educated people should know, and to a set of common values that constitute good citizenship.
2. *Experiential* Schooling is too detached from the interests and problems of the students, that is, from their ordinary life experience. Make schooling more functionally related to the students' experience, that is, less contrived and artificial, and students will grow more and become better citizens.
3. *Structure of the disciplines* There is too large a gap between school subject matter and the scholarly disciplines from which they derive. Reduce that gap by engaging students of all ages in genuine inquiry using the few truly fundamental ideas of the disciplines, and students will develop both confidence in their intellectual capabilities and understanding of a wide range of phenomena.
4. *Behavioral* There is too much vague talk about objectives, and there are too many unsystematic approaches to the development of curricula. Just decide what the successful graduates should be able to do in very specific measurable terms, analyze those behaviors to identify their prerequisite skills, provide opportunities for students to practice each skill with feedback to the point of mastery, and then evaluate the students' performance. We have the technology to ensure that all students master what they need to know. We need only the determination to implement our knowledge.
5. *Cognitive* Schools emphasize rote learning too much and do not put enough emphasis on real understanding and thinking. Curricula need to allow students to construct their own knowledge based on what they already know and to use that knowledge in purposeful activities requiring decision making, problem solving, and judgments.

Perspectives not only provide vantage points that increase our educational vision but also may influence and be influenced by our views of reality. An understanding of this point is essential before you attempt to use the perspectives for curriculum analysis.

A theoretical perspective functions as a metaphor for thinking and talking about the mind, teaching, and curriculum. Traditional curricula conjure up the metaphor of the mind as a storehouse, while cognitive curricula appear to view the mind as a garden. Behavioral curricula conceive of teaching as shaping behavior, structure-of-the-disciplines curricula view teaching as the induction of novices into a community of scholars, and experiential curricula consider teaching to be working behind the scenes to facilitate and guide student-directed projects. Behavioral perspectives conceive of curricula as the specific destinations or targets toward which education is aimed, whereas traditional perspectives imagine curricula as encyclopedic repositories of ideas, skills, people's names, events, books, and values that all students should master.

Metaphors such as these are powerful. They affect the language we use to discuss education, and they make certain proposals reasonable and others unreasonable. They even help determine what we consider to be common sense. For example, the claim by behaviorists that you cannot determine your itinerary and mode of travel until you decide specifically where you want to go is used as an appeal for highly specific educational objectives.

But we must always be cautious of metaphors. Although they help us understand the unfamiliar in terms of the familiar, they also distort. The things or experiences that a metaphor equate are never really exactly the same. That is, all metaphors have inherent limitations. They can be taken too far. More important, unless we are aware of our use of metaphors and their limitations we can become captive to them and encapsulated by them (Zais, 1976). The experienced curriculum analyst is continually monitoring the use of metaphors in educational discourse, particularly in curriculum proposals.

Curriculum Analysis Question

1. What perspective, if any, does the curriculum represent?

As you answer the question, remember that at this point you can only hypothesize about the curriculum's perspective. Don't be afraid to go out on a limb here. Subsequent chapters will enable you to test your hypothesis. If you can see no perspectives, don't hesitate to say so.

Notes

1. See, for example, writers like E. D. Hirsch, Jr. (1987), William Bennett (1988), and Allan Bloom (1987).
2. I wish to thank George Willis for his contribution to this section of the book.
3. See Cremin (1961).
4. See Aikin (1942).
5. See Bloom, Hastings, and Madaus (1971) for an elaboration of this two-dimensional analysis of objective.
6. Typically based on the work of Piaget (1929) or Kohlberg (1971).
7. Typically based on the work of Ausubel (1968) or Bruner, Goodnow, and Austin (1956).
8. For example, those derived from the work of Taba (1967) on inductive thinking, Sternberg (1985) on critical thinking, and deBono (1970) and Torrance (1965) on creative, or "lateral," thinking.
9. Interestingly, although the cognitive and the behavioral psychologists may bitterly debate the way people learn, both psychologies represent technical production perspectives on curriculum. Both consider learning to be the purpose of education, although they may come to blows about what it means to learn something and how best to facilitate the process. Furthermore, both perspectives consider curriculum development to be a technical process requiring the expertise of psychologists, although they obviously each consider their own brand of psychology to be the most useful.

CHAPTER 2

"RECONCEPTUALIST" AND "DOMINANT" PERSPECTIVES IN CURRICULUM THEORY: WHAT DO THEY HAVE TO SAY TO EACH OTHER?

WILLIAM A. REID

The field of curriculum is complex, ramified, multifaceted, full of idiosyncrasy. But this article is not about the field of curriculum as a whole: it is about two major perspectives which—in books, papers, and conferences—have tended to dominate it over the last 20 years: the "Reconceptualist Perspective" and the "Dominant Perspective." The first was, I believe, so named by William Pinar and was celebrated in his substantial edited volume, *Curriculum Theorizing: The Reconceptualists,* which appeared in 1975.[1] The second was described by Philip Jackson in the introduction to his 1992 *Handbook of Curriculum Research,* in which he explained how, successively, Bobbitt, Tyler, and Schwab had all been engaged in a common enterprise and had each propounded their own version of the perspective "at different stages of its development."[2] Both Pinar and Jackson, in their choice of title, made a somewhat extravagant claim: "Reconceptualist" implies newness in a field in which, we must suspect, there is very little that's new to be said, and "Dominant" implies a superiority that is at odds with the facts. However, in a situation in which we have claims of dominance and counterclaims of a clean sweep and a fresh beginning, we may legitimately ask the question, Do these perspectives actually have something to say to each other? Or are they pursuing incompatible agendas?

In attempting to answer these questions, I follow Pinar and Jackson in postulating a basic agreement among Reconceptualists and Dominants centering around an equally basic *disagreement:* Should we approve of or deplore proposals to design curriculums through the application of "scientific" principles? (For other purposes, of course, we might be more interested in the ways in which neither of the groups presents a unified front.[3]) But, though the rhetoric of the dialogue between Reconceptualists and Dominants has been antagonistic, the less than clear-cut nature of the controversy in this diverse field should prompt us to ask: What do they have to say to each other?

The question of what Reconceptualism has to say to the Dominant Perspective is the easier one to answer. We could say that the whole raison d'être of Reconceptualism lay in the proposition that something desperately needed to be said to adherents of the Dominant Perspective.

But first let me say what, following Jackson, I understand the Dominant Perspective to be. This is a view of curriculum that had its roots in the late 19th century and came to fruition in the United States of the 1920s. (I stress here that we are talking about an American view. It is not a European view.) The Dominant Perspective, in its own way and its own time, set out to "reconceive" curriculum. It took curriculum making, which, to that point, could be seen as a traditional craft, and attempted

Source: "Reconceptualist and Dominant Perspectives in Current Theory: What Do They Have to Say to Each Other?" by William Reid, reprinted from *Journal of Curriculum and Supervision*, Vol. 13, No. 3, 1998, Association for Supervision and Curriculum.

to turn it into a science. In Jackson's words, it construed the task of curriculum as being to "decide what goals or objectives the school should seek to attain" and then "to devise learning experiences that promise to achieve those goals and objectives."[4] To people who had to manage new or rapidly expanding school systems in the early part of the century, this was an attractive message; and it was one that was made popular by association with the century's obsession with efficient business management. If schools could be seen as commercial enterprises run on principles that enabled decisions to be made through a scientific analysis of ends and means, then the task of the curriculum specialist became both less complicated and more prestigious.

To what, then, was the Dominant Perspective a reaction? I would say it was to ideas of curriculum making that started not with objectives, but with an idea of what it means to be educated. This was the old European view, which modern America has difficulty in accommodating, though it obstinately refuses to go away (the strongest criticism that David Snedden, an early proponent of scientific curriculum making, could throw against a proposal of the 1918 *Cardinal Principles* report was that "it would please a Prussian philosopher").[5] People who thought about what education meant—and there were such people in the United States: John Dewey, for example, or Nicholas Murray Butler—were philosophers. But the supporters of the Dominant Perspective saw themselves not as philosophers but as scientists. And scientists, they thought, were empiricists.

This, as I understand it, was what the Reconceptualists wanted to complain about. Thoroughgoing empiricism in curriculum making destroys the idea of education. Education is about people: their histories, their destinies, their identities, their possibilities. But the Dominant Perspective is about items of knowledge, about specific skills, about setting objectives, about testing and evaluation. The Reconceptualists wanted to put the person back into the curriculum, and in that way to restore the conception of education that the Dominant Perspective seemed prepared to throw away. Their particular target of complaint was Ralph Tyler—though others also came in for their share of criticism. I've always thought it unfair that Tyler was the one who got picked on: a case of the wrong man in the wrong place. The worst that could be said about him was that he was not one to make a stand about anything: the consummate politician, perhaps, never anxious to stake out too clear a position. As a student of Bobbitt at Chicago, his Dominant Perspective credentials were impeccable. But I don't get the impression that he was strongly devoted to "scientific" curriculum making in the sense that Bobbitt understood it. His was a more "pragmatic" stance (using that word in its nontechnical, nonphilosophical sense): "Let's get together and see how we can fix this up." Of course, for those to whom educational ideals are important, that could be almost as bad as treating curriculum making as a science.

But if the targets were not always well chosen, there is no doubt about the clarity of the message of Reconceptualism: people matter, education matters, and if the Dominant Perspective cannot accommodate ideas like that, it deserves all the criticism we can throw at it and should make way for a perspective with a more human face.

What, then, about the possibility of messages traveling the other way? In the early days of Reconceptualism, that wasn't something to think about. Radical movements prosper on a sense of their own righteousness and on the demonization of all opposition. The idea that the other side may have something to say that is worth listening to is not to be taken seriously. But 20 years later, with the arrival of maturity, perhaps such thoughts can be entertained.

The main idea that the Dominant Perspective might press upon Reconceptualists is that having a notion of what education should achieve is not a substitute for making a curriculum. In the end, curriculum is about making choices, about devising programs for action, about getting organized and putting those programs into practice. This, of course, is the strength of the Dominant Perspective. Although we may object to its conception of the nature of action, it recognizes that, in the end, action is what curriculum is about. Reconceptualists, on the other hand, sometimes give the impression either that talking is more important than doing or that talking can be a substitute for doing.

I would say, then, that there is something that needs to be said on both sides and that some kind of dialogue should be possible. We are in a situation in which, apparently, the two essential components of curriculum have fallen apart. Those who are concerned with educational principles—the philosophical problem—have set up one camp, and those who are concerned with what it means to take action—the practical problem—have set up another. And this raises two important questions: How has this situation come about? And is it as bad as it looks?

Principles or Action?

As I have suggested, the separation of notions of education into a search for philosophical principles on the one hand and of curriculum as action on the other is largely, though not entirely, an American phenomenon, and I think it arises because the United States, compared, for example, with the countries of Europe, is a revolutionary society. In spite of recent advances, Europeans bear the imprint of thousands of years of history. This expresses itself in strong collectivist feelings associated with the legacies of religion and monarchy. A collectivist cultural tradition lingers.[6] Europeans have much less of a problem than Americans with the idea that they belong to cultures that transcend individuals. Americans, on the other hand, see their society as being centrally about the celebration of individualism. As has been frequently pointed out, this may, in some ways, be an illusion. Sociologists have described, on the one hand, the conformity to local or corporate cultures of the Americans, and, on the other, the lack of respect for authority shown, for example, by the French.[7]

But illusions are powerful in matters of how nations organize themselves. If we look at the high school curriculum, we can see that in European countries it is based on a clear idea of what cultural traditions students should be inducted into if they are to be considered "educated Germans," "educated Norwegians," and so on. Secondary school courses are largely based on disciplines, such as science, literature, or history, and are continuous over a number of years. Graduation depends on achievement across the range of these disciplinary courses. Such an idea is almost entirely absent from the American high school. Students pick and choose, within certain limitations, from among a vast array of credit courses. They then graduate on the basis of individual accumulations of credits that may have very little in common. Of course, there is a collectivist aspect to the experience of high school; but it is social, not curricular.[8]

Here we see the effects of what have been described as the "paradoxes of education in a republic."[9] These arise from the problems created by the abandonment of traditional sources of authority and the association of authority with the people at large. The paradoxes center around utility, tradition, and rationality.

First, let us consider utility. As soon as traditional sources of authority are cast aside, so that things are no longer learned because socially, culturally, historically, they are *good* to learn, the question of *why* anything should be learned becomes perplexing. Everyone is now their own authority on what should be learned, which tends to reduce the definition of common learning to what is "useful" to learn. In the early days of the Dominant Perspective in curriculum, much ingenuity was devoted to organizing surveys to discover what was useful to know. And this is a legacy that endures. In a 1991 report entitled *What Work Requires of Schools,* we read:

> Whether they go next to work, apprenticeship, the armed services, or college, all young Americans should leave high school with the know-how they need to make their way in the world . . . Parents must insist that their sons and daughters master this know-how and that their local schools teach it.[10]

Secondly, the paradox of tradition: modern republicanism was a "literary" invention; certainly, the founders of the American republic were steeped in the classics and in the "great books" generally. But in the republican curriculum, texts are replaced by textbooks. There is probably no curriculum in the world that is so dominated by textbooks as that of the American high school. Textbooks are, of course, the natural allies of useful learning. What we "need" to know is best detached from its intellectual origins. It can become part of a repertoire of knowledge without touching us deeply.

The third paradox relates to rationality. Because, in the republic, citizens must not rely on received wisdom but must think for themselves, the exercise of rationality is represented as the highest virtue. But this has the consequence that each thinker's personal views must seem to be true, whereas all other views are merely opinions. Therefore,

> . . . there can be no authoritative teaching concerning the necessity, hierarchy, or even the content of studies. No faculty must "impose

> its ideas" on students . . . truth is retained, but as a private possession, a nonuniversal, uncontrollable, inarguable, unreachable truth, a truth "true for me" alone.[11]

We can see, then, why the Dominant Perspective found fertile soil. The question for American educators became not, What knowledge is good, or true, or beautiful? but, What knowledge is useful? (Spencer's essay "What Knowledge Is of Most Worth,"[12] virtually ignored by his English contemporaries, was the bible of early American curriculum theorists like David Snedden.) And the scientific paradigm seemed to lend itself uniquely to the discovery and incorporation into curriculums of useful knowledge.

In such a situation, the philosophical pursuit of ideas about the nature of education was not merely redundant but positively obstructive. However, idealism can be held at bay only for so long. Useful knowledge, scientifically established and rationally taught, may, in its way, respect individualism and solve the problem of authority in the curriculum, but it leaves a lot of wants unsatisfied. Idealism demands respect, but how is it to be expressed when the notion of a collective cultural tradition is not available? Reconceptualism was able to provide an answer because it grew from the same stock as the Dominant Perspective.

Though Reconceptualism arrived at a different answer to the question of how curriculum should be thought about, it accepted a lot of the same premises as the Dominant Perspective. It too rejected the idea of historically sanctioned authority, celebrated individualism, and represented knowledge as relativistic—as personal and not subject to cultural validation. It too is thoroughly republican. Here is, perhaps, a fundamental reason why dialogue is difficult. Reconceptualism changes the answer but does not change the basic question: How do we respond to a situation in which the paramountcy of individualism thwarts the search for a consensus on ideals? It uses a different language to talk about curriculum, but it confronts the same problem within the same cultural parameters. Where the Dominant Perspective tries to maintain consensus by substituting utility for a collective idealism, Reconceptualism announces that the collectivist project is hopeless, and all that is left is the pursuit of individual visions. The two versions have to be in competition. One could perhaps see the later perspective as simply following the logic of the earlier one beyond the point at which its elaborators called a halt. Those whose agenda was to build school districts had reasons for limiting the acceptance of individuality and relativism and endorsing the scientific establishment of useful knowledge; those who came later and had no active agenda of curriculum making could afford to be bolder in their substitution of republican for monarchical virtues and to present the curriculum as something that should be the construction of the individual and for the individual, a means of pursuing a purely personal agenda. That would seem to be an unavoidable end point, once the idea of a collective cultural tradition has been abandoned as a source of principles for the making of curriculum.

But, having oversimplified matters in the interest of highlighting the essential nature of the two perspectives, I should now return to the point at which I said, "We are in a situation in which, *apparently*, the two essential components of curriculum (notions of education and prescriptions for action) have fallen apart." I have hinted at ways in which Reconceptualism arises from quite old-fashioned ideas. Now I shall examine the claim of the Dominant Perspective to be truly dominant, and suggest some ways in which, under its general umbrella, curriculum theorists have continued to concern themselves with collective conceptions of the nature and purposes of education.

How Dominant Is the Dominant Perspective?

I would say that the Dominant Perspective is dominant only in terms of academic and organizational acceptance. We know that it shapes the substance of many texts and guidelines on curriculum development because of certain inherent advantages. First, it lends itself to bureaucracy. Research proposals, policy statements, mandates, and evaluation reports can all be presented in formats ideally suited to the bureaucratic machine if they are couched in the language of rationally prescribed objectives. Secondly, it lends itself to a generic language of academic discourse. Journal articles, research paradigms, encyclopedias, manuals, can all emerge exuding an aura of scientific objectivity and progress.

But where practical applications are concerned, I doubt it has been so strong. First, some of the curriculum specialists claimed by Jackson as representative of the Dominant Perspective—and I have suggested that Ralph Tyler might be one—have been much more pragmatic than scientific in their approaches. While deploying a lot of "dominant" language, their use of it has been rather loose and ad hoc. This is, in fact, quite a sensible way of facing the problem of how the individualistic pursuit of "useful knowledge" can take place on grounds that have some pretense to educational merit. The answer, in this case, is to understand "educational grounds" as being "what we in the community understand to be important." Let some local homespun philosophy, which would prefer not to be spelled out by academics, stand behind the programs we put in place. But, though this is an answer to the problem, it is not one that would recommend itself to idealists, who know that local homespun philosophies can be lacking in their appreciation of nobler social aspirations.

Another answer that is found both in practice and among academic curriculum people is a purposeful, or more often instinctive, use of the kind of "deliberative" approach suggested by Joseph Schwab—another theorist claimed by Jackson for the Dominant camp. Schwab too was concerned by the separation of curriculum making from educational ideals but had the advantage of a historical appreciation of how the problem had arisen. His career at the University of Chicago in the 1940s put him in an interesting situation. First of all, he had a real curriculum problem to solve: How should Robert Hutchins's vision for the undergraduate college be realized? After several false starts following Hutchins's arrival as president in 1930, the disruption of the war years finally provided an opportunity for the introduction of an innovative program, which Schwab worked on with Richard McKeon and others. Secondly, he was able to face both ways, toward the curriculum traditions of Europe and toward the curriculum theory of the New World. The European connection stemmed largely from McKeon, who had worked with Dewey, had studied at the Sorbonne, and had developed a strong interest in classical and medieval philosophy. But Schwab also had direct access to the New World of curriculum that the Education Department at Chicago had, after Dewey's departure, nurtured through Judd, Bobbitt, and Tyler. Perhaps more than any other person at the time, Schwab was driven, intellectually and practically, to confront the question of how the separation of the components of curriculum could be reversed.

His solution, as expressed in his "Practical" papers,[13] focused on the sociocultural context within which curriculum making should take place. Through his concern with who should make curriculum and under what circumstances, it might appear that Schwab bypassed the question of what the role of educational ideals should be. But this would be a simplistic conclusion. Schwab's prescription lends to his deliberating group a character that defines how ideals should be established. He insists that each representative of a body of experience must discover the experience of others and the relevance of these radically different experiences of curriculum making for a partial coalescence of these bodies of experience to occur.[14]

In other words, the behavior of his participants in curriculum deliberations is expected to be modeled on a particular vision of liberal education. Curriculum is represented as arising from a "learning community" that promotes the discourse of exchange, of conversation, through which persons, face-to-face, come to know each other, understanding not only what each means, but why they mean it—the kind of understanding that makes possible joint decision making and action.[15]

To a great extent this reflects the old European approach to curriculum making: the curriculum results not from "scientific" reasoning, in the narrow sense, but from the exercise of *Wissenschaft*, broadly understood as the apprehension of a multiplicity of rational ways of understanding. But at the same time it recognizes the changed circumstances of the United States of the 20th century. Schwab appreciates that respect for multiple ways of understanding can no longer be taken for granted. Where a belief exists that problems can be treated as having no history and that there is no means of solution other than that demanded by a rational, "scientific" calculus, education must precede rather than follow curriculum making. Taking this first step is enabled by allowing that the nature of curriculum problems must be eclectically discovered. Where the possibility of a collective idealism has ceased to exist, the consensus that curriculum making requires must depend on a process that achieves at least a temporary and limited agreement on ideals among some relevant group. Schwab sets out to show how, through the arts of deliberation, such an ad hoc accommodation can be brought about.

Conclusion

If, then, we appreciate that attempts to maintain curriculum as an arena of action are not confined to the Dominant Perspective as the literature has narrowly defined it, and if we also appreciate that the task of Reconceptualism should be to consider advocacy of collectivist, as well as individual, sources of educational ideals (even if these have to be created, à la Schwab, rather than simply inherited), a basis can exist for dialogue between Dominants and Reconceptualists on how the disparate components of curriculum might be reunited.

The first step is for both perspectives to entertain the possibility that the questions they are addressing are too large and too subtle to be encompassed by the tools they are bringing to bear on them. The promoters of both perspectives, in the interests of taking up a clear antithetical position, have simplified reality. On the one side, the reality is that the practical concerns of curriculum making cannot be accommodated by an approach that reduces them to a rational science, and rational science has never, in fact, been up to the job. On the other side, the reality is that the lack of ideals promoted by rampant individualism cannot be remedied by discourse that celebrates individualism, and an existential philosophy is not up to that job. To the extent that both sides consider the limitations they share and work to overcome them, dialogue could become both possible and fruitful. The two sides of this particular argument—the practical and the ideal—could and should set out to recapture their natural relationship. In doing so, they would restore to curriculum some of the complexity that is its natural endowment and that is imperiled when discourse becomes centered on disagreement between hegemonic power blocks.

Notes

1. William F. Pinar, ed., *Curriculum Theorizing: The Reconceptualists* (Berkeley, CA: McCutchan, 1975).
2. Philip W. Jackson, ed., *Handbook of Curriculum Research* (New York: Macmillan, 1992), p. 21.
3. For example, William A. Reid, "Does Schwab Improve on Tyler? A Response to Jackson," *Journal of Curriculum Studies* 25 (November 1993): 499–510.
4. Philip W. Jackson, ed., *Handbook of Curriculum Research* (New York: Macmillan, 1992), p. 26.
5. E. A. Krug, *The Shaping of the American High School, 1880–1920* (Madison: University of Wisconsin Press, 1969), p. 398.
6. William A. Reid, "Systems and Structures or Myths and Fables? A Cross-Cultural Perspective on Curriculum Content," in *Didaktik and/or Curriculum? An International Dialogue*, ed. Bjorg B. Gundem and Stephan Hopmann (New York: Peter Lang, forthcoming).
7. Margaret Wolfenstein, "French Parents Take Their Children to the Park," in *Childhood in Contemporary Cultures*, ed. Margaret Mead and Margaret Wolfenstein (Chicago: University of Chicago Press, 1967).
8. Alan Peshkin, *Growing Up American* (Chicago: University of Chicago Press, 1978).
9. Eva T. H. Brann, *Paradoxes of Education in a Republic* (Chicago: University of Chicago Press, 1979).
10. Secretary's Commission on Achieving Necessary Skills, *What Work Requires of Schools: A SCANS Report for America 2000* (Washington, DC: U.S. Department of Labor, 1991), pp. vi–vii.
11. Eva T. H. Brann, *Paradoxes of Education in a Republic* (Chicago: University of Chicago Press, 1979), p. 126.
12. Herbert Spencer, "What Knowledge Is of Most Worth?" in *Essays on Education* (London, Dent: 1911), pp. 1–44. See also E. A. Krug, *The Shaping of the American High School, 1880–1920* (Madison: University of Wisconsin Press, 1969), pp. 401–402.
13. T. Westbury and N. J. Wilkof, eds., *Science, Curriculum, and Liberal Education: Selected Essays* (Chicago: University of Chicago Press, 1978), pp. 287–383; Joseph J. Schwab, "The Practical 4: Something for Curriculum Professors to Do," *Curriculum Inquiry* 13, no. 3 (1983): 239–265.
14. T. Westbury and N. J. Wilkof, eds., *Science, Curriculum, and Liberal Education: Selected Essays* (Chicago: University of Chicago Press, 1978, pp. 367–368.
15. Joseph J. Schwab, "Education and the State: Learning Community," in *The Great Ideas Today*, ed. Robert M. Hutchins and Mortimer J. Adler (Chicago: Encyclopaedia Britannica, Inc., 1976), pp. 247–248.

CHAPTER 3

CULTURAL POLITICS AND THE CURRICULUM IN POSTSECONDARY EDUCATION

WILLIAM G. TIERNEY

At Women's College (a pseudonym) a faculty member reflects about faculty life and the institution's attempts at curricular overhaul. He says, "People despair so much. No matter how much we try, there is always an air of despair that we are never successful." At a second institution, Entrepreneurial University, a longtime faculty member in the natural sciences talks about his colleagues in other departments as obstacles to curricular reform:

> They're a bunch of slimy little bastards up on the hill. The tension on this campus will never go away; nothing will get done as long as that large slug of people is here. They're just rabble-rousers. Some of these guys have coffee klatches and all they do is plot against us. It's a constant battle. They just sit around and plot.

Entrepreneurial University's apparent stalemate and the despair of Women's College faculty underscore the difficulties of curricular change. Authors have often analyzed the problems associated with academic change in postsecondary education by relying on rationalist premises of the organization and the curriculum (Bennett, 1983; Chickering, Halliburton, Berquist, & Lindquist, 1977; Tucker, 1984). In this paper, I will employ a critical framework of an educational organization and the curriculum as developed by Henry Giroux (1983, 1988a, 1988b), Roger Simon (1987), and Peter McLaren (1986, 1989), among others. My purpose will be to highlight the curriculum as a site of competing discourses about the nature and content of academic knowledge. In my view, faculty conflicts at institutions such as Women's College and Entrepreneurial University are not precipitated merely by differences of opinion about curricular decisions or by ineffective decisionmaking structures; instead, conflict often takes place because of competing cultural definitions of what counts for knowledge.

To elaborate on the idea that the curriculum is a site of ongoing negotiation and contestation I will view postsecondary organizations as cultures that are socially constructed and invested with dynamic processes. An organizational culture has an ideology that helps determine how knowledge gets defined. I will argue that how we come to terms with definitions of knowledge and the curriculum is permeated and shaped by a cultural politics of the organization. My objectives are twofold. First, I hope to extend our understanding of how culture gets expressed in academic organizations by way of the curriculum; second, I wish to touch on how the curriculum might be viewed as an empowering agent for students as they become involved in the struggle for democracy in the 21st century.

The data for the paper comes from a year-long research project in which I investigated curricular decisionmaking in seven postsecondary institutions (Tierney, 1989). I visited each institution twice for

Source: "Cultural Politics and the Curriculum in Postsecondary Education," by William G. Tierney, reprinted from *Journal of Education* (1989), with permission from the Trustees of Boston University and the author.

about a week at a time. Through ethnographic interviews and observations, I analyzed data from over 250 individuals. For the purpose of this paper, I will discuss two of the seven institutions.

The paper has four parts. In Part One, after briefly discussing a rationalist approach to the curriculum and the inherent underlying organizational premises, I will outline a critical approach to the culture of an educational organization. In doing so, I will consider the curriculum as a component of culture. I will then provide additional data from Women's College and Entrepreneurial University in Parts Two and Three. In Part Four I will conclude by discussing the implications of a critical view of the organization and the curriculum.

Approaches to the Curriculum

A Rational View

In general, previous writers about higher education's curriculum have acted as if only one epistemological position exists about knowledge. From this perspective, knowledge exists "out there," external and independent of the knower. It is as if knowledge were a jigsaw puzzle that can be shaped into multiple parts; even though different representations can be drawn, the pieces of the puzzle are the same to all of the organizational players. For students to become intellectually engaged they must learn the different pieces of the puzzle. As Diane Ravitch argues, "Students cannot learn to ask critical questions or to think conceptually about the past or about their own lives as political actors unless they have sufficient background knowledge" (1988, p. 129). According to Ravitch, "background knowledge" concerns particular facts that all students must know for "any kind" of thinking. Her assumption is that knowledge is neutral, a body of facts that wait to be learned.

Previous research on the curriculum in higher education, such as that by Paul Dressel (1971) and by Lewis Mayhew and Patrick Ford (1971), highlight the problems that occur when we assume that knowledge is neutral. Each author has struggled to develop a taxonomy of postsecondary curricular models. In general, the models relate to the explicit emphases institutions have for the curriculum. Combining the work of Dressel and Mayhew and Ford, William Berquist (1977) has arrived at the following list of curricular models in higher education:

1. *Heritage Based: A* curriculum designed to inculcate students with a knowledge of the past.
2. *Thematic Based:* A specific problem (such as the environment) is identified and studied in-depth.
3. *Competency Based:* Students learn specific skills such as proficiency in language and mathematics.
4. *Career Based:* The curriculum is designed to prepare students for a specific career.
5. *Experience Based:* Opportunities are created for the student to learn outside of the classroom.
6. *Student Based:* The curricular emphasis is on providing students with opportunities to control what they learn.
7. *Values Based:* The curriculum emphasizes specific institutional values.
8. *Future Based:* The institution devises the curriculum with a concern for what students will need in the future.

All these models as delineated by Berquist share three characteristics. In all of them, the curriculum is (1) ahistorical, (2) created by outsiders and not by participants such as teachers and students, and (3) ideologically neutral. That is, first, it is possible to discuss the curriculum in terms of its immediate context rather than historically. Second, since meaning and definition reside within each model, issues such as the class, race, and gender of teachers or students are not inherently important. Third, the models are decontextualized from the situations in which they reside so that ideological concerns are of little consequence. The overriding assumption is that issues such as history or ideology and class are germane only in models where they are made important; otherwise one can develop a curriculum that is ahistorical and ideologically neutral.

My concern with such lists is that in compiling them we blind ourselves to the way postsecondary institutions and the curriculum serve, reproduce, and challenge the social order of the society in which they reside. The implicit assumption remains: a singular reality exists to which all of the models apply. As opposed to investigating how the curriculum operates as a set of filters through which we define and choose what counts as knowledge, Berquist's work and much other previous research about higher education's curriculum functions as a unifying epistemological myth about the nature of knowledge; the institution simply arranges the elements of knowledge according to a particular curricular model. I am suggesting that we need to unmask the inherent values of a particular epistemological position and show the conflict that it conceals.

Each of the above curricular models has implicit values that need to be unearthed. A heritage-based model, for example, certainly will have different curricular offerings depending upon whose history and whose culture is included. Similarly, a value-based curriculum couched in conservative religious mores will differ from one that premises itself on a theology of liberation. Moreover, each model subscribes to particular views of history and values.

By pointing out that different institutions subscribe to different curricular formulations I am saying more than simply that one institution differs from another. Clearly, the curriculum of Oral Roberts University will differ from that of Stanford University or Evergreen State College. My point is twofold. First, we must accept that higher education's curriculum is culturally constructed and that, as a cultural construction, the curriculum is inherently partisan.

Second, if the curriculum is culturally constructed and partisan, then we must examine its relationship to knowledge and power, rather than seeking to fit it into a taxonomic model. Curricular structures imply dominant modes of discourse that deny particular groups a voice. To comprehend the curriculum in this manner we must move toward an understanding of the curriculum that delineates the inherent premises and values of the organization. We must articulate the underlying conflicts of our epistemological positions and trace the hidden geography of an organization's culture.

Such a study will unveil that different institutions have quite different conceptions of knowledge based on their historical situation, the participants who enact the curriculum, and the context where the institution resides. In short, not only the puzzles will be different, but the pieces the organizational players use to put the puzzle together will also differ. In this light, the relative importance of one curricular model or another is not significant. We can neither find one best curricular model to which all institutions must subscribe, nor build a taxonomy of models that will adequately describe the curricular universe. Instead, as McLaren expresses it, we ask

> how and why knowledge gets constructed the way it does, and how and why some constructions of reality are legitimated and celebrated by the dominant culture while others clearly are not. Critical pedagogy asks how our everyday commonsense understandings—our social constructions or "subjectivities" get produced and lived out. In other words, what are the social functions of knowledge? (1989, p. 169)

Asking how the organizational participants construct their reality implies that different realities exist. Not only will institutions arrive at different curricular models; the institutions also will begin with differing conceptions of what counts as knowledge.

A Critical View

The overarching premise of a critical view of the organization is that the organization's culture focuses the participants' understanding of their relationship to society through an organizational web of patterns and meanings that constantly undergo contestation and negotiation. Interpretation and interaction are highlighted. Rather than view reality as objective and external to the participants, the critical perspective assumes that reality is defined through a process of social interchange that cannot be readily mapped, graphed, or controlled. There is no one single, simple, unilinear rationality; there are multiple, competing rationalities.

A critical perspective on organizational culture, and hence on the curriculum, rests on four assumptions which stand in sharp distinction to rationalist premises. First, culture is not necessarily understandable either to organizational participants or to researchers. Since culture is an act of interpretation, what each person observes and interprets varies. A second, related assumption is that organizational actions are mediated by equifinal processes. That is, the construction of meaning does not imply that all individuals interpret reality similarly. Third, it is impossible to codify abstract reality. Fourth, culture is interpretive, a dialectical process of negotiation between the researcher and the researched.

Given these assumptions, a critical investigation of the curriculum differs from the more traditional studies in four ways. First, in the rational view, everyone has the same pieces of the curricular puzzle; in the critical view the curriculum is a key interpretive element that highlights how knowledge gets defined. Simon is helpful in understanding this point:

> If education is not to be viewed as a process within which knowledge is transmitted or conveyed but rather as a process of production and regulation of our social and physical world, every time we help organize narratives in our classroom we are implicated in the organization of a particular way of understanding the world and the concomitant vision of one's place in that world and in the future. (1987, p. 376)

Thus, not only will organizational actors develop different organizational puzzles, but they are also likely to draw upon different pieces to construct a puzzle, and the forms, shapes, and constructs of the puzzles themselves will differ.

Second, a critical understanding of the curriculum also struggles to understand how different constituencies come to terms with and help define their own relations within the organization and within society; the assumption is that different groups interpret curricular formations in manifold ways. Consequently, the organization's participants are at the center of understanding curricular content and meaning.

Third, rather than try to create taxonomies of curricular models, the assumption is that the curriculum is an abstraction and therefore cannot be codified. Finally, the role of the researcher as an interpreter of the curricular landscape takes on increased importance.

As opposed to the rationalist preoccupation with developing curricular taxonomies, the critical perspective highlights ideology, defined by Peter Berger "as a set of ideas which is used to legitimate vested interests of sectors of society" (1963, p. 111). Within an organization, ideology is that component of culture which speaks to the establishment and reconstitution of patterns of belief and meaning (Geertz, 1973). By viewing the curriculum through a cultural and ideological lens the critical theorist struggles to unearth the invisible curricular structures which we take for granted. The critical theorist brings into question the discourses that occur around a college's curriculum—treats the dialogues as something more than rational deliberations over the merits of various possible texts or courses. Instead, a critical study struggles to understand the dialogue in terms of the interactive relationships among individuals, as well as the relationship of the organization to society. A critical study seeks to learn how those relationships determine relations of knowledge and power.

An investigation of ideology seeks to reveal how ideology reflects the organization's culture. The multitude of cultural artifacts that exist in a college or university, such as the manner in which meetings take place, spatial and temporal arrangements, and the organization's structure, are examples of expressive cultural symbols that aid the researcher in coming to terms with institutional ideology. In so doing, a critical investigation looks for cultural artifacts and symbols that not only reinforce and sustain ideology, but also those symbols that contradict the dominant ideology.

I am suggesting that the culture of an educational organization has a dominant ideology that gets expressed by way of the curriculum. As employed here, ideology concerns both the production and the interpretation of meaning through the enactment of culture. The beliefs and values that organizational participants use to shape the curriculum derive in part from the ideology. The importance of understanding the significance of an organization's ideology concerns both the participants' ability to come to terms with how the organization produces meaning, and how the participants support, contradict, or resist those meanings. The comprehension of how ideology works, for example, enables us to investigate the assumptions of the organizational participants' definition of knowledge and what they believe should or should not go into a curriculum.

To expand on these ideas I turn now to a discussion of the two institutions mentioned at the outset of this article. At Women's College we will explore cultural conflict that occurs due to disagreements over how the institution's ideology gets defined. At Entrepreneurial University we will investigate an institution whose participants also have opposing views, yet the conflict occurs because of the lack of any overt ideological definition. At each institution, the discourse and conflict center on the curriculum.

Women's College

Burton Clark (1987) and Kuh and Whitt (1988) have tried to unearth the archaeology of faculty discourse. They have noted how faculty operate in four interdependent cultures that influence a faculty's beliefs and attitudes: (1) the culture of the institution, (2) the culture of the national system of higher education, (3) the culture of the academic profession, and (4) the culture of the discipline. I will consider the different cultures of the faculty at Women's College, and the conflicts which those differences create in regard to the curriculum.

At Women's College two of these four cultures take precedence: the culture of the discipline and the culture of the institution. Each culture is a different layer of meaning that is in constant motion and change so that a faculty member quite often has different, even contradictory stimuli requiring his or her attention and framing present possibilities. And different cultures provide different interpretations about the institution's mission and curriculum.

Women's College, a hundred-year-old liberal arts institution, has 2,500 students and a student-teacher ratio of 10 to 1. Students from throughout the nation attend Women's, and faculty positions are actively sought after; nevertheless, some individuals feel that the distinctiveness of Women's has slipped in recent years.

Women's College still remains a single-sex college, but how individuals interpret the mission and curriculum has become a source of heated debate. For example, one traditionally-minded faculty member notes, "The debate . . . is very loud. What does it mean to think of ourselves as a women's college? Some say that it means the curriculum should be different, about women. I think it means women go here. Period." An opposing viewpoint is expressed by an English professor who states, "Our mission should incorporate scholarship on and by women." An African American professor comments, "Our mission is what we are. We create brilliant Christian women in the Euro-centric tradition. If we are serious about cultural diversity—to serve women of all colors—then we need to realize the serious deficiencies." Another professor contradicts that contention: "I think students should have a common body of knowledge. I like Hirsch's book, *Cultural Literacy,* and feel we can do the same for higher education."

Each of the viewpoints has strong cultural dimensions that affect how the speakers view the overriding ideology of the institution. For example, those faculty who identify the mission of the institution as one in which a women-centered curriculum ought to be addressed are trying to create a specific allegiance to the institution. "The battle," says one professor, "is to incorporate scholarship on women, education about women. That's where we should devote our time, teaching our students about women's education." Faculty who adhere to this line of thinking are more likely to declare fidelity to other scholars across disciplines within the institution than to seek disciplinary rewards outside of the college.

On the other hand, a faculty member who believes quite strongly that the college must orient toward the disciplines comments, "I don't believe a discipline is an historic accident. The person who is productive here gives little to the college. The discipline is essential. People use commitment to the college as a substitute for being good in the discipline." A second person echoes similar sentiments when speaking about what a new dean should attempt to do. "Respect the autonomy of the departments. What a departmental structure should be is a replication of the discipline. I want departments to tell us what should be done and not some politically-minded group who advocates for a particular point of view." Both speakers reflect the faculty culture of the discipline; their orientation is toward a disciplinary culture rather than an institutional culture (Tierney, 1989a).

The disagreements over the ideology of the institution highlight the relation of power to knowledge. Those individuals who once defined knowledge through disciplinary channels now find themselves in a battle with an increasingly vocal and large segment of the faculty who reject the disciplines. That is, how the essentially younger faculty define what counts for knowledge differs radically from the previously accepted norms. Yet a shift in power has not fully occurred. As with most institutions, the older, tenured faculty at Women's College have greater authority and voice in controlling the decision-making processes that define knowledge. Consequently, debate and argument take place not only about how knowledge gets defined, but also over how decisions get made, and who participates in those decisions.

The curriculum becomes a cultural clash between the two groups of faculty oriented toward the different cultures. The curriculum takes on added significance not just as a pedagogic tool for inculcating students with particular values, but as the raison d'etre of the college. I am suggesting that institutional culture is not simply imposed on individuals; rather, the interactions of different faculty cultures play an important role in determining the culture of the organization and the form the curriculum ultimately takes. The possibilities for action, and the inability to perceive solutions, in part derive from the different orientations of the faculty that get played out by way of the curriculum.

Often the most innocuous institutional artifacts take on increased cultural importance because of the participants' interpretations. For example, at Women's College people who resist change are known as "dinosaurs." There are young "dinosaurs" and old "dinosaurs." Even the "dinosaurs" use the term about themselves. A young professor has an inflatable dinosaur sitting on his office bookshelf. He explains the term by saying, "The politics of pedagogy is very evident here. If you're not a traditionalist like I am then you think that the lecture is elitist and discussion is central. I believe there is value in lecturing, in getting across the facts to young people." "Someone started a rumor," relates another individual, "that the feminists in the administration building were taking all the lecture podiums out of the classrooms so that the faculty would not be able to lecture any more." Thus, even inert objects such as lecture podiums become highly charged cultural symbols.

Groups relate symbolic objects and discourses to particular images that are in some way tied to the ideological nature of the institution. That is, culture and ideology are interrelated. Cultural symbols such as dinosaurs or lecture podiums reflect ideology. Again, Berger's concept of ideology is that it is a set of ideas used for legitimation. Within the web of culture the participants reaffirm, reconstitute, or resist ideology. The presence or absence of a lecture podium is a cultural artifact that participants use to reaffirm or deny the dominant ideology of the institution. Conversely, with this example, the ideological "idea" concerns pedagogy: what is the legitimate manner to convey knowledge?

In general, previous investigations of the curriculum have not thought about how the curriculum change process is linked to the cultural makeup of the faculty and the institution or the overriding ideologies implicit at the cultural level. The point is not that one can do away with one cultural form or another, or necessarily that one cultural formation is wrong and another right. The first task is to understand how the participants' cultures interact with one another, and how the interactions hinder or hasten each individual's ability to comprehend the cultural web in which they are enmeshed. Once we understand how cultures interact within the organizational web, we can devise strategies that seek to embolden and empower all participants.

Entrepreneurial University

My purpose in this section is to bring into focus the confusion and conflict that takes place when no explicit ideology exists to help the participants define the culture of their institution. As opposed to Women's College, Entrepreneurial University does not have a dominant ethos that creates debate about what kind of institution it should become; instead, on the surface we find an institution whose participants believe they lack an overarching ideology.

Entrepreneurial University, almost 150 years old, has a wealthy, articulate student body, a faculty with a strong reputation, and a beautiful campus facility. Full-time faculty are about 250, and student FTE enrollment is close to 3,500. Tuition is more than $10,000. Over 80% of the freshman class will graduate within four years.

Entrepreneurial University is an institution that operates in what one individual terms "the entrepreneurial model." She explains, "No, we really don't know what we're about other than what everyone else is about—teaching, research, and service. What we are, what's great, is that people can go out and start something if they want to. It's like starting a small business." Another individual concurs: "There's lots of flexibility here. There are lots of spaces to do things so we can scoot through the cracks. It's like the ad they use for the Army. 'Be all you can be!'"

Entrepreneurial has a potpourri of innovative programs that faculty have devised. Departmental initiatives have blossomed and individuals have devised a number of courses or programs that do not need university sanction. Yet, while the atmosphere of the university encourages individual ideas, it stymies any effort to define an overarching premise of the institution by means of general education requirements and the like. No important curricular changes on an institutional level have occurred in over two decades.

Consequently, some students spend their freshman year together studying the same set of courses with a core faculty. Other students choose courses from a more traditional freshman general education sequence that consists of choices from many different curricular areas. Still other students spend an intensive amount of time in one course, and some students become immediately involved in their majors to meet the rigorous demands of premedical or engineering degrees.

Although Entrepreneurial's faculty do not agree that one body of knowledge must be taught, the faculty are similar to the more traditional, disciplinary oriented faculty of Women's College in the sense that in general they assume that what they teach is value-neutral. One individual, for example, comments:

> I'm involved in the freshman seminar, and it really shakes students up, they really end up questioning what they're all about. But I honestly don't care what they believe. We don't teach one ideological stance here. Students can pick and choose, and we're quite open about it.

I ask four students who turn out to be "political conservatives" if they feel particular political views are being taught. They laugh and nod their heads affirmatively as one student explains:

> In some classes it doesn't matter, like science or engineering. In some classes it does matter, like Latin American studies or Political Science. That's where the really liberal faculty are, but they're very open about what they believe and we're free to disagree and debate them. I like having them tell their side of the story so I can be prepared when I get out in the real world to defeat the kind of crazy ideas they have. So I'd say they have an ideology, but it's not doctrinaire or anything. It's just a typical liberal professor. But they are open to debate.

If we return to the assumptions of the critical approach, we need to locate what both individuals say in terms of their underlying assumptions about knowledge. The professor comments that he is value-neutral because he does not "care what they believe." The student feels that some classes are ideological—political science, for example—and others such as science and engineering are not. Further, the student implies that because faculty are "open to debate," ideology is relatively unimportant. From a critical perspective, by their comments both individuals are interpreting their experiences only on a surface level. They do not see how the structures of knowledge, the way courses are defined and structured, what is taught and what is absent, have strong ideological parameters. A critical perspective denies knowledge can ever be neutral.

Entrepreneurial's approach to learning is in line with its mission—one that gives faculty members wide latitude in defining their relationship to the institution. The shared conviction of the participants about the mission, in fact, is the belief that faculty have the freedom to teach whatever they want. Unlike Women's College, Entrepreneurial's faculty do not debate what they should teach; instead they have more of a smorgasbord approach to learning. In some courses students are taught to think about their relationship to concepts such as sexism or racism, but in general the curriculum does not have an overarching concern with how knowledge is produced or why particular subjects are studied and others not.

What does not take place, then, is any sense of an institutional debate over how knowledge gets defined. Absent is an institutional struggle to come to terms with whose interests are advanced and whose interests are ignored by particular definitions of knowledge. Paradoxically, in this respect knowledge is seen as both ahistorical and eternal. By not questioning how they define knowledge the participants lack any sense of the social and historical context in which they operate. Yet the lack of questioning on the part of some of the participants also leads them to assume that their definitions of knowledge are eternal and never-changing.

In part, Entrepreneurial's lack of success at curricular overhaul exemplifies the multiple interpretations the faculty bring to the institution, and the lack of specificity the mission provides. "I won't try anymore;" states a music professor. "I put in my time trying to come up with a general education component, and nothing happened." Another individual comments, "We make attempts at change, some of them are very serious attempts, too. But we always fail."

A dean concludes, "We have a very good curriculum. Students learn here. But I think most people have given up the expectation that we will reach consensus around a common core of knowledge." One other faculty member agrees with the dean, but sighs and says, "Yet deep down, I think many of us wish we could agree, wish we could find a common core."

"We have very strong disagreements about the nature of knowledge," concludes a longtime professor. "At the least, we have reached a peaceful impasse where we agree to disagree." Curricular innovations rarely occur—not because the decisionmaking process is too cumbersome, and not because the institution lacks the necessary funds to carry out any changes, but because cadres of people operate from adumbrated institutional ideologies.

The lack of an overarching definition leads to confusion for many faculty members, especially newer ones, about their role. Between my visits to the campus three faculty members are denied tenure; the rumor is that they spent too much time on their teaching, and not enough effort on research. A young faculty member comments, "I think we're two-faced. We talk about teaching. The search committee tells you how important teaching is, and as soon as you get here, the terms change. It's not fair." Another new professor comments, "It seems like we're spinning our wheels, wasting our time, when we should be talking about the curriculum. Isn't that what a teaching institution is about?"

The issue goes beyond accounting for whether teaching is more important than research. The tenure denials and the junior faculty's interpretation of them stand as a vivid illustration of how people learn about and redefine institutional ideology. As noted, at Entrepreneurial there is not a narrow definition of what someone can or cannot do. Instead, broad definitions exist; individuals operate within the context of the definitions and provide their own interpretations. When clear examples arrive such as the denial of tenure to someone, the individual reformulates an understanding of the institution. Curiously, the redefinition in this example does not so much promote what Entrepreneurial is, but what it is not. It is not that the institution is for research, but that it does not reward teaching.

In part, the conflict at Entrepreneurial University is not that disagreements arise over what a curriculum should look like, but that no one has a sense of a guiding vision of the institution other than in the broadest of terms. In general, the individualist logic of Entrepreneurial University allows faculty the freedom to construct their own interpretations of the curriculum. Examples such as a tenure denial provide singular interpretations for individuals; nevertheless, an overriding sense of institutional purpose is absent. With its "realist" epistemology, Entrepreneurial does carry out what it says it will do; the shared conviction of the institution is a dictum that one is free to do as he or she chooses. But it appears that individuals want more from the institution. The confusion and conflict arise when new faculty are unsure how to interpret the mission, or when older faculty feel disenfranchised.

Discussion

Given these two case studies, how might we think about the competing voices of the faculty and their disagreements about the curriculum? As Clark asks, "Beyond weakening attachment to attenuating broad principles, is there anything left, any linkage that somehow connects the many parts to the whole?" (1987, p. 141). And given the "weakening attachment," is there any reason to believe that we should expect curricular coherence in an institution?

I offer two tentative answers. First I will address how we might act in an organizational world that appears beset by loose connections. I will then offer one idea about how we might work toward curricular coherence from a critical view.

1. ***Action in a cultural web.*** From the critical perspective taken here, "anchoring ideologies become a crucial element" (Clark, 1987, p. 144) in orchestrating the diverse interests of the various constituencies toward a common goal. I maintain that individuals in postsecondary organizations need to explicate institutional ideologies and, as Giroux states, "address the reconstruction of social imagination in the service of human freedom" (1988a, p. 120). That is, critical educators first need to accept that all organizations exist in a cultural network where ideologies operate; they then will struggle to construct their organizations based on a concern for social justice and empowerment.

By calling for the explication of "anchoring ideologies" I run the risk of painting organizations as if they are composed of Durkheimian collectivities. Clearly, I am not interested in how a critical or cultural approach to organizations can hold fragmented constituencies together merely "for the good of the order" (Rhoades, 1989, p. 29). However, as with others (Giroux, 1988a; McLaren, 1989), I am concerned with coming to terms with how those of us who work in educational organizations can promote democracy and empowerment among our constituencies. I maintain that concentrating on the cultures and ideologies in which colleges and universities operate and delineating the ways in which they pose negative and positive moments for various constituencies will provide understandings that allow for the creation of democratic organizations.

As we have seen at Entrepreneurial, academe is a cultural network composed of contradictory groupings of faculty. The faculty often have only tenuous bonds to one another, either within the institution or across institutions. Clearly, the professor who calls his colleagues "slimy little bastards" has found little in common with faculty in other disciplines at Entrepreneurial. In part, his disappointment and anger stem from the rigor he feels as a scientist, and what he perceives is the academic shallowness of his colleagues in the social sciences and humanities. He continues, "The humanities used to think kids should take whatever they want; now they want to redo the curriculum to meet their agenda. They've never listened to the scientists." The professor's sentiments are also found at Women's College among those who want to sustain the traditional liberal arts curriculum. We heard, for example, one professor speak disparagingly of those who had a "political agenda" as opposed to individuals like himself who were more disciplinary oriented.

However, the analysis of institutional differences should extend beyond merely summarizing the conflicts by political groupings—liberal vs. conservative, young vs. old, disciplinary vs. interdisciplinary, scientists vs. social scientists, and the like. We need to try to understand the conflicts. As I have argued elsewhere (Tierney, 1987) culture arises in relation to a number of internal institutional characteristics as well as factors external to the institution. The struggle is to be able to understand the characteristics and comprehend the cultural differences. Rather than try to ameliorate or ignore the differences, we must confront them and figure out ways to deal with them.

I am suggesting that organizational leaders need to create conditions that allow for an overt ideological commitment on the part of the organization's participants. What I hope I have shown in this paper is that whether or not participants actively commit themselves to a specific ideology, within all cultures ideology is at work. The participants may be conscious of ideology, as are some of the faculty at Women's College, or they may be unaware of their ideological stance as at Entrepreneurial. Nevertheless, to speak of organizational culture, and human action within it, is to speak of the ideologies to which the participants commit themselves. Necessarily, then, organizational participants need to unearth the inherent assumptions that operate in their missions and cultures and create an ongoing reflexive discourse that works toward achieving collective understandings. Such understandings, however, do not imply a Durkheimian unity. Instead, we need to work toward unearthing the positive and negative ideological moments at work in an organization and come to terms with how the various cultural forms give voice to some, and silence others.

My assumption is that when institutional discourse is about common and communal goals, rather than capturing markets or assuming a neutral view of knowledge, then the participants will move closer toward achieving collective understandings that are rooted in the cultures of the organization. I am proposing that, as Michael Katz states, "bonds of reciprocal obligation [which make] the preservation of the community an object of desire and not merely a matter of prudence or a command of duty" (1987, p. 179) are of central importance as we approach the 21st century.

I do not believe, however, that organizational participants will be able to provide a definitive answer to the question of institutional ideology. The ideology of an institution is a map that undergoes constant reinterpretation due to the cultural web's reconfiguration. Yet simply because we cannot provide an absolute answer to what institutional ideology is, does not mean we should avoid the question. As Denneny states, if the question of ideology "cannot be solved, [it] can be thought about; one can strive to reach not an answer but perhaps greater clarity about the issue, and in the process better locate oneself in the contemporary world" (1989, p. 16).

2. ***A critical view of curriculum in a cultural web.*** As opposed to rationalist conceptions of the curriculum, I have offered a critical view. A critical perspective disavows a pedagogy that imparts disembodied knowledge. Instead, a curriculum of difference engages students so that they comprehend how what they are learning relates to their own lives, their own experiences. In doing so, I am suggesting that institutional participants need to link their discussions about the curriculum with the ideology of not only what they are, but also what they want to become. This view maintains that vast possibilities exist for administrators, faculty, and students to redefine the nature of the learning experience beyond what "background knowledge" one must have to be considered well-educated. As Daniel McLaughlin states:

> Curriculum becomes more than a sequence of decontextualized, apolitical skills. It is designed to help the learner connect academic concepts to a problemized world. As the classroom focus shifts from curriculum that is arbitrary to curriculum that scrutinizes problems immediate to the lives of the students, the teacher's role changes. The teacher becomes coach, an expert who can help solve problems. In the process, pedagogy becomes problem-solving, and curriculum becomes cultural politics. (1988, p. 20)

By attempting such an approach we ought to be aware of the inherent premises about the curriculum that I am arguing for in this paper. In working from the assumption that a curriculum is a powerful process that helps structure how organizational participants think about and organize knowledge, I reject the idea that the primary purpose of a curriculum is to inculcate youth with the accumulated wisdom of society. Institutional curricula need to be investigated from the perspective of whose knowledge, history, language, and culture is under examination. Conversely, the organization's participants need to uncover those whose voices are not present in a curricular discourse and give life to them.

From this perspective, we cannot consider curricular models divorced from the contexts in which they are situated. Not only must we understand the organizations in which curricula operate, but we must also investigate the cultures that surround the curriculum. By way of excavating cultural artifacts such as the pedagogical practices used to convey knowledge or the decisional processes called upon to decide what counts for knowledge, we gain a fuller understanding of the curriculum's relationship to knowledge and power than if we tried to create decontextualized taxonomies of higher education's curriculum.

In conclusion, I offer some questions we might raise when we study or participate in curricular change in higher education. An investigation of the kind I am suggesting might revolve around questions such as:

- How do we define knowledge?
- What accounts for a knowledgeable individual?
- How has what we defined as knowledge changed over time?
- Whose interests have been advanced by these forms of knowledge?
- Whose interests have been superseded or ignored by such forms?
- How do we transmit knowledge?
- What is the method used to determine what counts for knowledge?
- Who controls the decisionmaking?
- Who participates and who does not in curricular decisions?

Clearly, these kinds of questions will unearth different answers than many of the current questions in vogue in the higher education community concerning assessment, quality, and excellence. I am suggesting, then, an alternative approach to the study of the curriculum in higher education—one that utilizes critical theory in the interest of creating educational communities based on notions of democracy and social justice.

References

Bennett, J. B. (1983). *Managing the Academic Department, Cases and Notes.* New York: Ace/Macmillan.

Berger, P (1963). *Invitation to Sociology.* Garden City, NY: Longman.

Berquist, W (1977). Eight Curricular Models. In A. Chickering et al. (Eds.), *Developing the College Curriculum* (pp. 87–108). Washington, DC: Council for the Advancement of Small Colleges.

Chickering, A., Halliburton, D., Berquist, W, & Lindquist, J. (1977). *Developing the College Curriculum: A Handbook for Faculty and Administrators.*

Washington, DC: Council for the Advancement of Small Colleges.

Clark, B. (1987). *The Academic Life.* Princeton, NJ: Carnegie Foundation for the Advancement of Teaching.

Denneny, M. (1989). Chasing the Crossover Audience. *Out/look,* 1(4), 16–21.

Dressel, P (1971). *College and University Curriculum.* Berkeley, CA: McCutchan. Geertz, C. (1973). *The Interpretation of Cultures.* New York: Basic Books.

Giroux, H. (1983). *Theory and Resistance in Education: A Pedagogy for the Opposition.* South Hadley, MA: Bergin & Garvey.

Giroux, H. (1988a). *Schooling and the Struggle for Public Life.* Minneapolis: University of Minnesota Press.

Giroux, H. (1988b). *Teachers as Intellectuals.* Granby, MA: Bergin & Garvey.

Grumet, M. (1978). Curriculum as theater. *Curriculum Inquiry,* 8(1), 37–64.

Katz, M. B. (1987). *Reconstructing American Education.* Cambridge: Harvard University Press.

Kuh G., & Whitt, E. (1988). *Using the Cultural Lens to Understand Faculty Behavior,* Paper presented at the annual meeting of the American Educational Research Association, New Orleans.

Mayhew, L., & Ford P. (1971). *Changing the Curriculum.* San Francisco: Jossey-Bass.

McLaren, P. (1986). *Schooling as a Ritual Performance.* London: Routledge & Kegan Paul.

McLaren, P. (1989). *Life in Schools.* White Plains, NY: Longman.

McLaughlin, D. (1988). Critical Theory and Literacy Program Development. *Journal of Navajo Education,* 6(1), 10–21.

Ravitch, D. (1988). A Response to Michael Apple. *Teachers College Record,* 90(1), 128–130.

Rhoades, G. (1989). *Academic Culture and Professional Mandate.* Submitted for publication.

Simon, R. (1987). Empowerment as a Pedagogy of Possibility. *Language Arts,* 64(4), 370–382.

Tierney, W G. (1989). *Academic Work and Institutional Culture: Constructing Knowledge.* Submitted for publication.

Tierney, W G. (1989). *Curricular Landscapes, Democratic Vistas: Transformative Leadership in Higher Education.* New York: Praeger.

Tucker, A. (1984). *Chairing the Academic Department: Leadership Among Peers.* New York: Ace/Macmillan.

CHAPTER 4

BEYOND TYLER AND TABA: RECONCEPTUALIZING THE CURRICULUM PROCESS

FRANCIS P. HUNKINS AND PATRICIA A. HAMMILL

Introduction

These are dynamic times in the realm of curriculum. As we near the next century, we are asking ourselves if we finally should rid ourselves of our technological rationality and assume a new posture. A rising cacophony of voices is demanding that we detach ourselves from our technological-modern past and form a new paradigm—a post-modern perspective. We are being urged to purge ourselves of our adherence to the Tyler rationale, to get beyond Tyler and Taba.

Many critics of Tyler and scientist-modernism appear to be urging us to wipe clear our slate of the past. However, as Toulmin (1990) states, the idea of starting again with a clean slate is a myth. And it is folly to assume that we must destroy all that was before in order to nurture a new start. To accept a new paradigm, to move beyond Tyler and Taba, does not require destroying our very past and discrediting these two curriculum thinkers. There is no new starting line where we can assemble and then advance into our futures with certainty. Indeed, such thinking is part of the very modernity that many of us wish to leave. All that we can do is to begin where we discover ourselves, and at the time in which we find ourselves. These are times of excitement and uncertainty, not times in which we can advance a "self-sustaining, tradition-free intellectual system" (Toulmin, 1990, p. 1979).

All realms of scholarship are immersed in these times in forming not just a new paradigm, but paradigms. To assume that there is only one paradigm is to assume that we can attain a new certainty, which really is anathema to being postmodern in perspective. Postmodernism is essentially a *metaparadigm* encompassing all realms of thinking and action (Kung cited in Doll, 1993). While postmodernism has spawned new avenues of investigation and ways of conceptualizing physics, chemistry, biology, and mathematics, as well as the arts, it has not—and indeed cannot by its very posture—furnish us with a consensus on what it really is or whether it will be the dominant mode of our thinking in the 21st century.

As Doll (1993) asserts, the implications of a postmodern perspective for the reality of education and curriculum in particular are staggering, while remaining for many frustratingly fuzzy. We currently do not know how this urging of a shift to postmodernism will play out within the curriculum realm. We should take pleasure, however, in the fact that we will be involved in the shaping of our own immediate and distant futures. We can recognize that we are in an evolving system, moving toward the edge of chaos, and that this place is the zone where new ideas are generated, new

Source: "Beyond Tyler & Taba: Reconceptualizing the Curriculum Process," by Francis P. Hunkins and Patricia A. Hammill, reprinted from *Peabody Journal of Education*, Vol. 69, No. 3, Spring 1994.

paradigms are formulated, and new questions are posed (Lewin, 1992).

To recognize an edge we must have some vision of the total area from whence we have come. We cannot fully grasp a paradigm shift to postmodernism if we fail to understand our history of modernism. We cannot accept modernism as a thing of the past unless we have a sense of our past.

The Legacy

Modernism or modernity is not synonymous with contemporaneousness (Selznick, 1992). If that were the case, all societies would be modem in their time period. Rather, modernism refers to those attributes of technology that advanced societies have developed since the 18th century. Some would place the beginning date with Newton. The hallmark of modernism is a society in which emphasis is placed on the rational, the impersonal or objective, and the fragmentation of thought and action. It is a society of prizing and accepting certainty, a society privileging a mechanical view of the world. It is a society that employs the rational, the scientific, in addressing the problems of human life and society (Toulmin, 1990).

Bobbitt and Modernism

Modernism achieved its pinnacle in this century. In the early decades, increasing numbers of educators eagerly accepted the tenets of modernism and the approach called *scientism*. Many believed that by employing the rational, the precise, and the mechanistic, they would be able to address the problems of human life and society. Education, looked at as a mechanical system, could be quantified and managed. In being modern, one could bring efficiency and effectiveness to the schools and their curricula.

Bobbitt is credited with bringing the scientism or modernism message to education and to the field of curriculum in particular. His book, *The Curriculum*, published in 1918, is often considered the first book devoted specifically to the curriculum and to consider curriculum as a science. Bobbitt believed that it was possible to be precise in determining just what the curriculum should contain. It was the responsibility of the curriculum decision maker to outline what knowledge was important for each subject, and to identify the objectives that would be appropriate for those subjects. Once done, one then had to develop those activities that would enable the learner to master the content.

While in looking back we may think Bobbitt was "wrong-headed," we must recognize that he was essentially engaged in embracing an existing paradigm that had not been employed within educational thinking. Bobbitt's view about the use of scientism in curriculum activity greatly affected the field of curriculum. He was most influential in developing principles of curriculum-making that involved determining aims, objectives, the needs of students, and learning experiences. He noted that the objectives of the curriculum could be derived from the study of needs, something still being advocated today. Perhaps his greatest contribution is his argument that the process of curriculum-making is not specific to any particular content, but rather cuts across subject matter. As Cornbleth (1990) points out, although not relating her comments to Bobbitt, the process of curriculum development was decontextualized both conceptually and operationally. It set the stage for conceptualizing curriculum development as precise and predictable, resulting in a tangible product. The entire process and its resultant product were seen as separate from curriculum policymaking, design, practice, and even evaluation (Cornbleth, 1990).

Bobbitt, and later Tyler, did their work well—so well that the approach to curriculum development and thinking about curriculum is still very much in evidence, even with all of the dialogue about paradigm shifts to postmodern ways of thinking about the field. Indeed, the foundation that Bobbitt laid down is still the mainstream view regarding curriculum development in today's schools. This view is most difficult to budge, for the very nature of what we are being urged to employ in the place of modernism commands no consensus. There is no precise new system by which we can finally overturn the work of Bobbitt and later Tyler and Taba. This is not surprising since we do not want to deal with "mists"; we want to know specifics. We measure the worth of suggestions by their specificity rather than their heuristic value of making us challenge the details and assumptions of our thinking, of our ways.

Ralph Tyler, Prime Technocrat

Tyler was greatly influenced by Bobbitt and others similarly oriented. His book *Basic Principles of Curriculum and Instruction*, published in 1949, epitomized modernism. It has come to have an enormous influence on the field of curriculum. Despite all the criticism of Tyler, his thinking is still dominant in schools across the nation.

If we are to move beyond Tyler we must first recognize that we could not be at this juncture, debating the merits of a new paradigm for curriculum development, if Tyler had not written his 128-page book and presented four basic questions to the field: (a) What educational purposes should the school seek to attain? (b) What educational experiences can be provided that are likely to attain these purposes? (c) How can these educational experiences be effectively organized? (d) How can we determine whether these purposes are being attained?

These four questions have become known as the Tyler rationale for creating curriculum. These questions and the method implicit in dealing with them have such appeal because they appear to be so reasonable. Even Doll (1993) acknowledges that they *are* reasonable, but only if we accept a modernist, linear, cause-effect framework. We would argue that the continuing popularity of Tyler at the level of schools and school districts, and perhaps even on a few university campuses (despite all the rhetoric at national curriculum conferences), is due to the very reasonableness and workability of the rationale, regardless of one's context. Educators in classrooms and on local curriculum committees feel a sense of comfort knowing that curriculum is essentially a plan composed of identifiable components (objectives, subject matter, methods, and materials). Likewise, they feel a sense of calm knowing that the procedures for creating such a curriculum are knowable and predetermined in a manner that will assure an efficient and orderly creating and control of the curriculum. The procedures for creating curriculum, taking this viewpoint, are essentially value neutral (Cornbleth, 1990). Certainly, we exhibit values as to what content we wish to include, and perhaps even the experiences we wish students to have, but many assert that we at least can relax a bit in knowing that the procedures by which we bring curricula into existence are essentially beyond argument. We know what to do!

To even suggest that educators reflect on the assumptions behind their actions is to be somewhat confrontational. Even many not disturbed by such confrontation feel that we are asking them to forsake a professionalism that has been won only after much effort. The entire push for being scientific was an attempt to bring not only precision to curricular action, but a professionalism to the field itself. We borrowed management by objectives from the field of business. We looked to the various scientific management movements throughout this century to furnish us with ideas as to how to go about our business.

Tyler gave us a techno-speak that enabled us to be part of the modernism of this century. In a very real sense, the Tyler Rationale gave us slogans and shared ideals and views of curriculum and its creation. We could share common visions; we could communicate with a shared language. As Cornbleth (1990) notes, this technological orientation enabled us to have a sense of community gaining comfort in knowing that we were following the right path. We were exhibiting an aura of curriculum expertise that was exportable to any and all who wished to be involved in creating programs. We could identify the problems that needed to be addressed, we could determine the objectives, we could select the necessary experiences, and we could assure people that we had, indeed, obtained what we had set out to do. And administrators could take pride that their staffs had indeed been efficient in carrying out their curricular responsibilities. In those instances where this was not the case, administrators knew that there were outside experts who could be brought in to do the job of determining goals and objectives, and outlining the means to attain them. It could all be mapped out in linear fashion. In a sense, all we had to do was connect the dots and the outline of the program would become evident. Then our task was just to color within the lines and the curriculum would be covered.

Tyler's message, perhaps, would not now be so dominant if he had been a voice crying in the wilderness. But Tyler had company, and he still has. Hilda Taba was a colleague of Tyler's who gave an added boost to his rationale for the curriculum world.

Hilda Taba

Taba's thinking regarding curriculum and curriculum development also reflected the modernism-scientistic tradition. In her seminal book on curriculum development, *Curriculum Development: Theory and Practice* (1962), she argued that there was a definite order to curriculum development, and that pursuing such order would result in a more thoughtful and dynamically conceived curriculum. Like Tyler, she noted that all curricula are composed of certain elements. She accepted the assumption of componentiality. Not only could we define things in terms of their components, we could actually take these components apart and put them back together again. These units were essential to all the curricula, and in identifying them we could manage them in ways that would make them predictable (Berger, Berger, & Kellner, cited in Cornbleth, 1990).

In the procedure that Taba advanced for creating curricula, Tyler's modernism influence is evident. The model has definite steps, each to be engaged in one at a time such that a curriculum plan for teaching would result, addressing the objectives created at the outset of the process. Taba did differ from Tyler and others of the scientific bent in that she believed that teachers should have an active role in the procedure for creating curricula.

Her seven-step model of curriculum development gives even more detail to the process than do Tyler's questions.

1. Diagnosis of needs. The teacher or curriculum designer begins the process by identifying the needs of students for whom the curriculum is to be planned.
2. Formulation of objectives. Here the teacher or curriculum designer selects those specific objectives that require attention in light of the needs identified. These objectives, perceived actually as ends, allow a precision to the process and enable curriculum makers to view learning as an observable outcome that could be measured.
3. Selection of content. From the objectives selected, one can determine the subject matter of the curriculum.
4. Organization of content. While Tyler dealt rather broadly with the organization of educational experiences, Taba was more specific, actually separating the organization of content from the selection and organization of experiences. Again, this step made it clear to teachers or curriculum designers the components of the content and how they were to be organized to attain expected results.
5. Selection of learning experiences. Taba was explicit in noting that selecting learning experiences was a different component in the curriculum development process. Experiences could only be selected after the content or subject matter had been determined.
6. Organization of learning experiences. Once the experiences were selected, they needed to be placed into a sequence to optimize students' learning. Again, the assumption is that this sequence could be determined prior to the students actually becoming engaged in their learning.
7. Evaluation and means of evaluation. Like Tyler, Taba's final step engaged the curriculum planner in determining just what objectives had been accomplished. Actually, in the approach, the means of evaluation are determined prior to the actual implementation of the curriculum.

There have been variations of Tyler's and Taba's approaches to curriculum development, but most of the models extant today draw heavily on this technocratic mentality. Most are presented as if there is total agreement as to approach; most appear to be decontextualized from their social context; and most give the illusion that there is a timeless precision to the process.

In arguing that we should go beyond Tyler and Taba, we are asking educators to reflect on the assumption of scientism-modernism, and perhaps to challenge basic tenets that have guided educators' actions for most of this century. It is not to suggest that we generate a specific plan to replace Tyler and Taba. It is not to purport that we know where we have moved or even to suggest toward what we should be moving. At this juncture, perhaps we only should realize that some of us are in the process of moving. As to our destination, we cannot say.

Challenges, Transitions, Transformations

Arguing getting beyond Tyler and Taba is not so much to criticize their work and their times as it is to recognize that we are in different times—times that challenge us to think in novel ways about our realities and how to generate curricula within them. Tyler and Taba reflected a view of modernism: that life could be viewed as mechanical, that there existed a stable-state universe, that the process of curriculum development could be compartmentalized and decontextualized, that goals could be separated from the experiences designed to address those goals.

Currently, we are realizing with increasing sophistication that life is organic, not mechanical; the universe is dynamic, not stable; the process of curriculum development is not passive acceptance of steps, but evolves from action within the system in particular contexts; and that goals emerge oftentimes from the very experiences in which people engage. Curriculum gains life as it is enacted (Cornbleth, 1990). We are in a time that is encouraging the projection of new meanings, and suggesting ways to organize these myriad interpretations. The times, being identified as postmodern, are encouraging the achievement and employment of multiple awarenesses (Giroux, 1991).

Post-modernism is not just a one-world movement. It involves the thinking and actions of myriad scholars from diverse disciplines. The very crossing of these disciplinary lines has generated new ideas and practices—has triggered hybrid subject matter and invited a most heterogeneous audience to dialogue. The focus of the dialogue is to contest knowledge and to critique a total view, the primacy of reason, and the universality of general knowledge (Jencks, 1992).

The prime challenge is to query meta-narratives and accepted "stories" of the way things are in the world, and to reject the notion that we can bracket our reality. In many ways, the post-modernist is behaving in ways similar to those persons delving into the science of complexity. These individuals are convinced that through creative questioning and inventing of paradigms, they can come to understand more fully the spontaneous self-organizing dynamics of the world in ways never before imagined (Waldrop, 1992).

In rejecting grand narratives about ways to create curriculum and to generate paradigms, curricularists can address—even celebrate—the complexity of curricular deliberations and educational programs. Accepting post-modern views as well as those of complexity, curricularists can realize that what are called for at this juncture in time are plural codings of reality and actions, and multiple communications of the phenomena we are attempting to engage (Jencks, 1992). There is an attempt to assert differences in thinking, to distance ourselves from homogeneous thinking about curriculum and its development. Post-modernism asserts that there is indeed no structure or master narrative in which we can wrap ourselves for comfort (Hutcheon, 1992). There is no master curriculum plan that we can generate for all times. Master plans are illusions.

A stretch to the edges actually pushes us to the limits of possibility. It challenges us to engage in experiencing the limits—the limits of our language, our subjectivity, our identities, our views, and our systematization of approaches to curricular action. Such challenge demands a rethinking of the bases upon which we function (Hutcheon, 1992). It invites us to play with forms emerging in dynamic shadows.

Emerging Forms of Dynamic Shadows

Suggesting we go beyond Tyler and Taba is more than recommending that we follow new rules. As Lyotard (1992) submits, we are invited to play the game *without* rules, and from the very playing, to invent new rules. We are enticed to play with emerging forms in dynamic shadows of thinking, trying to put shape to what has previously been unimaginable and unpresentable.

In urging that curricularists play in these shadows, we are saying that we need to create, to conceive, curricula without the direction of pre-established rules. We need to gain excitement from engaging in the curricular game without what Lyotard calls the solace of good forms, the consensus of a taste that would enable us to share collectively a common vision. In a real sense, going beyond Tyler and Taba is engaging in action that is seeking the formulation of new rules, the shaping of forms emerging in the mist of the edge of our thinking. We are asked to create new metaphors to guide our dealings with the world. Our challenge is not that of supplying a clear reality, but inventing allusions to the conceivable and engaging ourselves in the dynamics of the system (Lyotard, 1992).

To play with forms emerging from dynamic shadows places our focus on forms and wholes, in contrast to segments, parts, and their arrangements. To get beyond Tyler and Taba is to suggest that we engage in a holistic approach to conceptualizing the curriculum and its creation. If we consider the whole, we will be immersed in considering the dynamics of the system. We will come to realize that order will emerge from such dynamics (Lewin, 1992).

This new thinking within the realm of post-modern and complexity denies the validity and usefulness of the mechanical notion of the universe. We are urged to reject the clock metaphor to explain our worlds and come to apply biology as a more useful paradigm. It is more productive for curricularists to think of curricula as comprising ecological systems. In employing the language of biology within a post-modern framework, we recognize that diversity and differentiation are the commonplace, not the exceptional (Toulmin, 1990). Getting away from traditional thinking, in our case Tyler's and Taba's, we manifest more discriminating and discerning means of processing curriculum questions. No master narrative or rationale directs our curriculum actions.

The biology metaphor enables us to consider the curriculum and its creation as comprising a living system. Instead of looking at an external manipulation of distinct parts, we accept that we are viewing worlds, immersed within the ongoing behavior of an ecological entity. We celebrate curricula as living systems that never really settle down. There is a perpetual novelty (Waldrop, 1992). The systems contain internal dynamics that make them both complex and adaptive, allowing for an immense realm of possibilities.

In a dynamic world, we need approaches to curriculum development and to curriculum itself that are adaptive under conditions of constant change and unpredictability. We need for these and anticipated times curricular systems that enable us to process perpetual novelty, that privilege the notion of emergence (Waldrop, 1992). We want emergence of forms, emergence of actions, emergence of systems, and emergence of results (Lewin, 1992).

Further, we need to realize that we are not outsiders who create and manage these systems. We are integral parts of the very systems and views we generate. The ways in which we engage in curriculum development and the conceptions we formulate of curriculum emerge from our engagement with these procedures and notions. Our involvement within the social contexts, both large and small, will influence and shape our curriculum formulations. Our actions over time cause us to realize, even celebrate, the increase in complexity within the total realm of the curriculum field. Our willingness to immerse ourselves and others in curriculum deliberations and dialogue is testimony to our faith that we will be able from our actions to add memory and information from times past, times present, and anticipated times in ways that will increase our collective curricular wisdom (Waldrop, 1992).

Post-Modern Curriculum Development

It is much easier to indicate where we have been than to indicate where we are going. As humans, we want purposefulness; the desire is part of being human (Doll, 1993). We want specifics; we judge the quality of dialogue by the number of specifics we can glean. We possess a need for action that leads to closure, to resolving our problems, to defining our actions. In taking this stance, we derive understanding and management of our worlds. If we are to go beyond Tyler and Taba, what will we specifically put in their place?

The procedures that Tyler and Taba advocated were predicated on a positivistic certainty (Doll, 1993). There were distinct points in the process that had definite purpose. In post-modern curriculum development, we are suggesting that the stress is not on the specific steps of action, but on the relations that result when people get together for the purpose of creating curricula. Rather than bring certainty to the process, there is a pragmatic doubt that results from realizing that decisions are not based on some privileged meta-narrative, but rather on the dynamics of human experiences within the local milieu.

One of the surprises of post-modernism is its acceptance of the chaotic, the emergent currents of change. Harvey (1992) quotes from Foucalt that we should "develop action, thought, and desires by proliferation, juxtaposition, and disjunction. We should prefer what is positive and multiple, difference over uniformity, flows over unities, mobile arrangements over systems. Believe that what is productive is not sedentary but nomadic."

Curriculum development in the post-modern vein would stress play rather than certain purpose; chance over certain design; process and performance over a static, finished work; participation of players over distance of players from the process; a dispersal of ideas over a centering of ideas; a combination of ideas over a narrow selection, action driven by desire rather than symptom; and a system characterized by indeterminacy rather than determinacy (Hassan, cited in Harvey, 1992).

Accepting the post-modern stance, we recognize that there can be no one way of creating curricula. There is no one meta-narrative or meta-theory through which we can generate curricula. There are no rules for creating programs that can be considered universal or having the posture of truths. Going beyond Tyler and Taba is going into the realm of thought and action in which we have a plurality of procedures or language games for discourse about curriculum development. There is no permanence—all is fluid, but from fluid motions come patterns. In curriculum development, we need to utilize the motion, the ferment, to develop the curriculum. How we actually engage in such creative curriculum development is unclear: "It is a problem we will need to live with for generations" (Doll, 1993, p. 148).

As we live with this idea of dynamic patterns emerging from being engaged, from considering curriculum development as an ongoing social activity molded by myriad contextual influences, we will begin to see patterns of necessary curricular actions. The modern paradigm of Tyler and Taba will take time to be replaced by a post-modern paradigm (Doll, 1993). We now know, however, that curriculum development is not the algorism that has been central to much of modernist thinking. Rather, curriculum development is more of a playful dance—a process in which the dancers (both teachers and students) engage in a dialogue of motions (goal setting, content selection, experience design), and are thus transformed in ways influenced by the dynamics of the local "dance" situation (Doll, 1993).

Initial attempts to get beyond modernism in curriculum development are sure to appear rather slight. Perhaps it is more the attempt to move on than the actual results of such moving that should be our focus. For instance, Cornbleth (1990) cites Goodman's work on critical curriculum design, noting that his five phases of curriculum development (developing curriculum themes, exploring resources, developing learning activities, pupil evaluation, and unit evaluation) do sound conventional. But it is in discussing these stages that we see that he is attempting to get us beyond Tyler and Taba. Rather than ask what content students can learn for specific purposes, Goodman raises questions as to what topics would enrich children's lives and expand their learning horizons. Also, he raises questions that address not the pieces of knowledge, but the holistic nature of knowledge. There is an emphasis on the uncertainty, ambiguity, and dynamism of knowledge, rather than a false sense of precision (Cornbleth, 1990). Central to the process of curriculum development is a perpetual, deep questioning of the "dance," the dancers themselves, and their locales.

An Example

There is danger in setting to paper a curriculum development model that will get us beyond Tyler and Taba. That danger is that the model suggested may be interpreted with the modernism mentality. Doll (1993) has suggested an alternative to the Tyler rationale. While his suggestions are not dealing exactly with how one actually creates a curriculum, we do get an idea as to how one might "dance" through the implied process. Doll presents four criteria for a curriculum designed to foster a postmodern view: Richness, Recursion, Relations, and Rigor. We consider these four criteria to be fluid points of reference in the creation of the curriculum. These criteria seem to imply different questions for teachers and students to pose when developing curricula.

In dealing with *richness,* curriculum designers—and we think it important to note that these players are teachers, students, and interested parties from the wider community—query themselves as to the depth of the curriculum that can be experienced so that students' lives are enriched. What layers of meaning can be arranged for students; what variety of interpretations can be selected or encouraged? At this juncture, involved parties ask themselves what is the "'right amount' of indeterminacy, anomaly, inefficiency, chaos, disequilibrium, dissipation, lived experienced" (Doll, 1993, p. 176). It is this right amount that cannot be predetermined, as would have been the case in determining scope within a modern framework of thinking. The right amount is an issue to be continually negotiated among students, teachers, and text. But, Doll asserts, one thing that cannot be negotiated is the fact that the curriculum must have some disturbing qualities. It is this very nature of the post-modern curriculum, celebrating an unstable order, that allows this means of curriculum planning to foster the creation of a rich and, it is hoped, transforming curriculum.

The second criterion for a post-modern curriculum, *recursion,* suggests to curriculum developers that they are to participate in a development process that has both stability and change. The general categories of knowledge may be the same, but the particulars addressed will vary. As people think about aspects of the curriculum, their thoughts will continually cycle back to previous thoughts and be changed and enriched in the process. Having the curriculum development process be recursive encourages the participants to engage in reflective interaction with all the players. The very act of curriculum development not only enables a listing of curricular possibilities for students to experience, but also creates a culture for all the players.

Doll (1993) notes that in creating a curriculum that is recursive, there is no fixed beginning or ending. All seeming endings are new beginnings. The components of the curriculum being designed are not perceived as disconnected units or even connected units. Rather, what is suggested for the curriculum is perceived as differing series of opportunities for students and teachers to engage in reflection, in constructing meaning. Everything suggested to be done leads to other things to be done, considered. The curriculum is designed to allow for continually going back to and then incorporating previous points and insights into a growing sense of understanding.

The third criterion, *relations,* suggests that in designing a post-modern curriculum, we need to think more about the relations between the parts of the curriculum than centering our attention on the parts. It is important that content selected encourage individuals to relate to it and to other students also experiencing said content. The emphasis on relations brings students and teachers into dialogue. It suggests that the resulting curriculum essentially cannot arise outside the school and classroom. It cannot be generated by persons who create educational materials. Certainly, it cannot be created by textbook authors. The criteria of relations makes evident that curriculum construction is a social activity being played out within particular frameworks; it is a human activity full of surprises, and we must allow for the surprises in our actions (Cornbleth, 1990). This differs from the technical modern approach of listing steps with the cannon of no surprises.

The frameworks within which the relations exist make clear that what people bring to the dialogue, to the conversations, to the teaching and teaming, is influenced by the contexts they are experiencing. The process of creating curricula is interactive. We have people participating in a type of ecological system, able to be adaptive and self-regulatory.

Rigor is the fourth criterion that Doll presents for a post-modern curriculum. While rigor is not a step in the process, it is a criterion to consider as one engages in curriculum development. Rigor demands that curriculum creators constantly question their actions and the results of their actions. It is being aware of (a) the assumptions one brings to the curriculum "dance" and (b) the fact that these assumptions contain values that influence the very process. It means getting beneath the surface appearances—challenging claims (Cornbleth, 1990).

Another aspect of rigorously creating a curriculum is realizing the impossibility of being certain that one has attained the correct answer. The search must go on with individuals striving for new combinations, interpretations, and patterns (Doll, 1993). Indeed, contrary to the scientific heritage in creating curricula, one seeks to enrich the imagination. In many ways, the scientific heritage, in stressing the one correct answer, has served to impoverish the imagination. Approaching curriculum development from a post-modern stance means addressing the paradox of imagination (Postman, 1993). Being scientific or modern in curriculum development has led to the weeding-out of the proliferation of new ideas. In contrast, being post-modern is to cultivate new ideas and novel ways of dealing with them.

It appears that the model of curriculum development implied by Doll has the features of being self-organizing as opposed to mechanistic, of being non-linear in action compared to linear, of being conducive to creativeness and openness as opposed to being deterministic, and drawing its essence from chaos theory as opposed to Newtonian mechanics (Jencks, 1992). Curriculum development in a post-modern posture beyond Tyler and Taba is ecological in view, holistic and interconnected, interrelated and semi-autonomous, and heterarchical rather than hierarchical.

However, despite much heated debate, this new "model" is not the antithesis of the modern. As Jencks argues, post-modern is a complexification and hybridization of the modern. In going beyond Tyler and Taba, it appears that this is exactly what we are doing. Rather than denying our Tylerian past, we are adding needed complexity and creativity— imagination, if you will—to our heritage. We are transforming, rather than overturning, what Tyler and Taba urged us to consider.

Our adherence to the modern has served as a safe harbor. It is time to take the educational ship and ourselves with it out of safe harbor, into the challenges, uncertainties, and dynamics of a chaotic ocean. We are invited to sail uncharted waters, discover and create new worlds, and to share stories of adventure so as to establish new educational communities.

References

Bobbitt, F. (1918). *The curriculum.* New York: Arno Press.

Cornbleth, C. (1990). *Curriculum in context.* London: The Falmer Press.

Doll, W., Jr. (1993). *A post-modern perspective on curriculum.* New York: Teachers College Press.

Giroux, H. A. (Ed.). (1991). *Postmodernism, feminism, and cultural politics.* Albany: State University of New York Press.

Harvey, D. (1992). The condition of postmodernity. In C. Jencks (Ed.), *The post-modern reader* (pp. 299–316). New York: St. Martin's Press.

Hutcheon, L. (1992). Theorizing the postmodern. In C. Jencks (Ed.), *The post-modern reader* (pp. 76–93). New York: St. Martin's Press.

Jencks, C. (Ed.). (1992). *The post-modern reader.* New York: St. Martin's Press.

Lewin, R. (1992). *Complexity.* New York: Macmillan.

Lyotard, J. E. (1992). What is postmodernism. In C. Jencks (Ed.), *The post-modern reader* (pp. 138–150). New York: St. Martin's Press.

Postman, N. (1993). *Technopoly.* New York: Alfred A. Knopf.

Selznick, P. (1992). *The moral commonwealth.* Berkeley: The University of California Press.

Taba, H. (1962). *Curriculum development: Theory and practice.* New York: Harcourt, Brace, & World.

Toulmin, S. (1990). *Cosmopolis.* Chicago: The University of Chicago Press.

Tyler, R. W. (1949). *Basic principles of curriculum and instruction.* Chicago: University of Chicago Press.

Waldrop, M. M. (1992). *Complexity.* New York: Simon & Schuster.

CHAPTER 5

CURRICULUM POSSIBILITIES IN A "POST"-FUTURE

WILLIAM E. DOLL, JR.

The art born as the echo of God's laughter [has] created the fascinating imaginative realm where no one owns the truth and everyone has the right to be understood.[1]

It is necessary to rethink the world not in terms of its laws and its regularities, but rather in terms of perturbations and turbulences, in order to bring out its multiple forms, uneven structures, and fluctuating organizations.[2]

The great end of education is to discipline rather than to furnish the mind; to train it to the use of its own powers, rather than to fill it with the accumulations of others.[3]

The third statement above has been known in the curriculum field for so many decades it has turned into a cliché. In fact, it has become a shibboleth for progressive educators. Paradoxically, I suspect it may have its origins in Yale president Jeremiah Day's spirited defense of his university's classical curriculum in the late 1820s.[4] But whatever its origins, the statement assumes the "mind" to be a *thing* (a vessel to be filled) or an *organ* (a muscle to be trained) or a *living being* (a creature with powers to be disciplined). All three of these metaphors have played a role in American thought on curriculum. The Progressive movement, particularly from the 1930s through the 1960s, encompassed each of these trends, as well as the *laissez-faire* approach for which it may be best known—leave the child alone and ability, like a sunflower, will burst forth. The view of mind expressed in these metaphors—oddly both anthropocentric and mechanical—had neither strong intellectual foundations nor a record of practical achievements.[5] I believe it is a view we need to replace, possibly with Dewey's or Whitehead's or Bruner's versions of mind as an active, self-organizing, self-abstracting process, a process to which we give the label "mind."[6]

But dealing with mind as anything other than a machine (brain) or an anthropocentric metaphor (vital force) has been almost impossible. The "thingness" of mind, a residue from Descartes' mind-body split, stubbornly persists. As a result, we have considered curriculum only in its "thingness" sense, only in its noun form (a racecourse to be traversed), and not in its infinitive verb form (*currere*—to run, especially the course). In the latter, the emphasis is on the activity of running or, metaphorically, on the activity of our making meaning from the course—our interpreting, or dialoguing with the course. This *currere* view makes mind "a verb" (to use Dewey's phrase: an active, meaning-seeking and meaning-making verb).[7] The implications of considering mind as a verb are

Source: "Curriculum Possibilities in a "Post"-Future," by W. E. Doll, Jr., reprinted from *Journal of Curriculum and Supervision*, Vol. 8, No. 4, 1993, Association for Supervision and Curriculum.

just beginning to receive critical acceptance.[8] At issue is whether or not such acceptance will result in fundamental curricular change.

In the late 1960s, Joseph Schwab pronounced the curriculum field "moribund."[9] Two decades later, Donald Schön said the same thing but in different words, discussing the deadening effect of the "technico-rational" model.[10] The curriculum reform movements of the time, whether structural-Piagetian or behavioral-competence, did little to encourage educators to disagree with Schwab or to disown Shön. Curriculum remained bereft, without theoretical or practical guidance. Students, teachers, administrators, parents—all evidenced a malaise that is still apparent.

We are now in the midst of a budding new movement, characterized by Schön's "reflective practitioner."[11] Will this be but another passing fad, another in the list of 20th-century educational "reforms"—which themselves inevitably end up being reformed? Or will it, combined with such movements as site-based management, school choice, the decentralization of school control, and a rising entrepreneurial spirit, lead to meaningful curriculum and school change, indeed, to school and curriculum redefinition? It is far too early to answer this question with any confidence; and certainly issues of student achievement, teacher "burn-out," and increasing societal demands on the school do not provide encouraging early indicators. Yet, as we prepare to move into a new century, a new millennium, I see encouraging signs.

The level of curriculum discourse has definitely improved over the past decades. As William Pinar says, curriculum has moved from "an exclusively practice-oriented field to a more theoretical, historical, and research-oriented" one.[12] The increase in quantity and quality of journals, articles, discussions, conversations, research studies, and doctorates of a theoretical nature has given the field an awareness of itself. However, this theoretical and historical awareness has not yet influenced school classrooms; there, curriculum is still very much practice-oriented, with little reflection on these practices. However, a rising groundswell of dissatisfaction—from corporations, parents, community groups, even teachers and administrators—questions how well these practices are working. In short, the time may be right for more fundamental change. Yale president Benno Schmidt's leaving his university post for the Edison Project can be seen in this light. In fact, as one reporter has said: "Mr. Schmidt's career choice reflects a clear judgment: Edison is the future, Yale is history."[13]

Fundamental changes certainly are prominent in a number of other fields as diverse as architecture and theology. In fact, we are currently immersed in a "post" era: post-Communist, post-national, post-industrial, post-patriarchal, post-structural. To cover all these "posts," I choose the overarching term "post-modern" and use the hyphen to indicate that the new era, while breaking with the past, does not negate that past. In fact, as Charles Jencks says, at the heart of post-modernism lies a "paradoxical dualism or double coding which its hybrid name entails: the continuation of Modernism and its transcendence."[14] Thus, the movement is Janus-faced, looking both backward and forward, to the past and to the future. This double or dual coding gives post-modernism its paradoxical and startling power—to honor the past and yet to laugh at it (to ensure that we do not get caught in the hyperbole and hypocrisy such honoring brings); to build for the future and yet to doubt whether such a future will emerge. This is a worldview wherein traditional categories, such as order and disorder, are not diametrically opposed or separated but are entwined, each within the other, each reinforcing and sustaining the other.

Our present curriculum frames—those of the Tyler/Taylor rationale, of competency-based instruction, of Madeline Hunter's "seven steps"—are not constructed to use and welcome paradox and eclectism, indeterminacy, self-organization, or satire and play. Yet these qualities inhere in a "post" worldview and define a post-modern perspective—to the degree such a perspective can be defined. To study post-modernism (or any of the other "posts") for curricular implications means to question much of what we have heretofore considered natural or normal. Such *fundamental* questioning, of course, is frightening; we worry about the collapse of stability, of the order we have known, of the values we hold dear. But as post-modern complexity theory shows, the collapse of simple, linear, preset order does not necessarily lead to *disruptive* chaos. Rather, a new kind of order—that labeled "chaotic order"—often emerges.[15] Although the phrase seems oxymoronic, it is not; it refers to the subtle, complex, nonlinear order we now see permeating the universe—an order the Hubble telescope is helping us "see"[16] By modernist standards this order does seem quirky and chaotic, really no order at all; but in a post-modern frame the complexity of chaotic order is both natural and beautiful—as shown in those magnificent computer designs of recursive spirals, or in the more natural designs of clouds forming, surf breaking, and smoke curling.[17]

Obviously, this is not the simple, symmetrical, Euclidean order we consider "natural". Instead we find complexity, chaos, and contingency built into this new order. Its complexity appears far more pervasive in nature than do the simple and symmetrical Euclidean shapes modernists favored. The study of this nonlinear, or fractal, order began only in the mid-1970s. Understanding its paradoxical qualities is one of the challenges for post-modernism.

Post-modernism is still too young to define itself, and indeed, it may never, or never want to, do so.[18] For to define the word in our usual, modernist sense of definition is to go against the very spirit of post-modernism; that is, definitions limit and close rather than generate and open. Those working on such a definition or nondefinition range from nihilistic deconstructivists to process theologians.[19] But the issues of paradox, indeterminacy, self-organization, and play seem appropriate concepts on which to base a working frame for post-modernism. We might begin by looking at each of these four qualities in terms of their curricular implications. Then we might attempt to find criteria for judging a "good" post-modern curriculum. These criteria could possibly serve a post-modern curriculum as Ralph Tyler's criteria served the modernist curricula.

Let us begin with indeterminacy, that bugaboo of all modernists theories. As Dewey pointed out in *The Quest for Certainty,* Western philosophy has sought certainty—through philosophy and mathematics—since the time of Plato.[20] The Forms were permanent and determinative—worldly objects being but imperfect copies of the Forms. Descartes in the 17th century thought he had found *the method* "for rightly conducting reason for seeking truth."[21] Newton, three-quarters of a century later, was believed to have discovered *the principle* (gravity) that held the universe together. Laplace, writing after Newton, called him "the most fortunate" of men who ever lived "inasmuch as there is but one universe, and it can therefore happen to put one man in the world's history to be the interpreter of its laws."[22] Further, Laplace argued, it is possible to determine the course of all future planetary movements by knowing *with precision* the present planetary positions. All one needs to do after the data are collected is "the sums."[23] This procedure has been analogized into a linear, cause-effect relationship, so that we now define the "scientific" approach (that most favored by education and the social sciences) as the collection of data and the placing of that data into a set formula. This mathematical modeling method underlies much of economic forecasting, psychometrics, and numerous doctoral dissertations. It is pervasive enough to be considered a semiparadigm for our "rightly conducting reason for seeking truth."

In the early 1900s, Werner Heisenberg became bothered by the indeterminacy he found in his study of the subatomic world. Movement in this world did not fit the patterns of linear order science had been following since Newton and Laplace. He and Bohr spent long hours arguing with Einstein over the nature and role of indeterminacy in the universe—Einstein always holding that "God does not throw dice." Indeed probability theory was developed to help tame the randomness Heisenberg and others found in nature. Still, doubts lingered, and today with the advent of complexity/chaos theory we not only question God's gender but also have doubts as to whether the dice may not be loaded. Indeterminacy, nonlinearity, and a skewed (or "ordered") randomness seem to be woven into the fabric of the universe. The complexity of this fabric is stunningly beautiful, as the computer-generated recursions show; but understanding this fabric requires us to deal with such post-modern paradoxes as "ordered randomness" and "chaotic order."[24]

In curriculum matters, the metaphysical commitment to certainty has encouraged us to structure the curriculum *only* in sequential linear terms (a step-by-step, explanation-first process) and to consider learning *only* as a direct result of teaching.[25] Such sequential ordering and cause-effect epistemology (based on a metaphysical commitment to determinism and certainty) underlie Tyler's modernist rationale for a well-designed curriculum. As Dewey pointed out well before Tyler wrote his rationale, such a view assumes the learner to be a receiver, not a creator, of knowledge, a spectator who in the most creative of moments can only discover that which already is. A curriculum based on these assumptions emphasizes transmission, linearity, and measurement rather than transformation, nonlinearity, and creation.

As might be expected, post-modernism sees indeterminacy in a positive, not a negative, manner. Once one moves beyond seeking certainty, it is possible to see indeterminacy as that which encourages, indeed entices, us to participate in the generation of meaning. The openness of indeterminacy invites us to dialogue with the situation at hand, to communicate with it and with each other. In Wolfgang Iser's phrasing, indeterminacy (especially in a text) "allows a spectrum of actualizations," actualizations that arise from our dialogue, our creative participation.[26] In this manner we, as makers, initiate *"performances" of meaning.* Such performance, of course, is always influenced by text and teacher (their role is to influence in a dialogical way), but the meaning making is ours. Thus, meaning is made, not received. The making of meaning requires, but is not guaranteed by, an open, indeterminate system.

Indeterminacy becomes a meaningful concept only to the degree self-organization is operable. Without self-organization, indeterminacy does not take on the character of "primal soup" from which order arises; rather, indeterminacy remains nebulous or loosely and poorly formed. For indeterminacy to have its own sense of power and being, to be a rich and generative *dissipative structure,* in Prigogine's use of this term, self-organization must be real and operable.[27] Self-organization, with its spontaneous creation of new forms, has been around for as long as life has existed. As Jean Piaget says, auto- or self-regulation is the *essence of life itself.*[28] It is the primary hypothesis of his theory of cognitive development.

Biological evolution, of course raises the issue of self-organization—new species emerging from the competition for survival. But the Darwinian view has paid no attention to purposiveness; the emergent species arise randomly, not willfully. It is in Piaget's and Prigogine's writings that we find this sense of *looser teleology* (one in which intentionality is entwined with chance).

Piaget saw humans developing cognitive structures through interaction with the environment. However, with his set stages and fixed sequences there is little if any role for chance. A strong sense of structuralism overlaps Piaget's constructivism. On the other hand, Prigogine's "dialogue with nature" is a good deal more open-ended. The future is unpredictable, dependent on the eventful interactions that have preceded any moment in time. But both Prigogine and Piaget agree that time does have "an arrow"; the past cannot be rerun. In this arrow of time, new ideas, forms, species arise from the interaction between and among events. In this way chance and purpose become codeterminers.

In terms of curriculum, this means there needs to be *just enough* perturbation, disturbance, disequilibrium (Piaget), or dissipation (Prigogine) built in so that self-organization will be stimulated. The teacher's role is to present the curriculum in just enough of a challenging, controversial, "chaotic" manner so that self-organization will be encouraged. Such a role for curriculum, for the teacher—one wherein the teacher becomes "readily confrontable" by the students—is quite different from what we have developed using the Tyler rationale.[29] The Tyler rationale has led us to emphasize precisely defined, well-articulated, preset goals and a delivery system that matches the clarity of the goal statements. Dissipation and disequilibrium are neither desirable nor necessary. In fact, in the operable curriculum model developed between the 1950s and 1990s—evidenced in the behavioral objectives movements, competency-based assessment, and Madeline Hunter's set steps—the student has been looked upon more as a receiver of information than as a constructor or generator of meaning. The issues John Dewey wrestled with, challenged, and fought for in the early decades of this century—centering around the difference between the student as a spectator to others' knowledge or as a personal creator of meaning—remain in this last decade of the century. Educationally, we are mired in modernism.

Playfulness and paradox—indeed, playing with paradox—may present ways of getting out of this bog, of breathing new life into our moribund curriculum. Paradox is very much part of our "post" world; it lies at the heart of quantum reality—a reality that accepts that electrons may be considered either as oscillating waves or particle pellets. The choice is ours. Hence we may legitimately say that electrons are both waves and particles. To explain reality in such contrary and contradictory terms is a paradox that modernist thought cannot fathom.

Some post-structuralists, such as Gilles Deleuze, take paradox beyond the microworld of science into the existentialness of being, to the concept of self.[30] Descartes, one of modernism's fathers, held that self was inherently contained within, and yet existed apart from, the body. He thought self to be the "I" of consciousness, the "I" that defines our being—physical and intellectual. His famous phrase "cogito ergo sum" means "thinking accounts for being." Separated from the body yet paradoxically located in the body, "mind" for Descartes was the essence of conscious being, the "I-ness" or subjectivity that defines human being.[31] This consciousness manifests itself in the human's ability to plan, create purpose, have thoughts. Yet, paradoxically again, these purposes, plans, thoughts, were themselves believed to "mirror" an outer (and static) reality. Thus, human consciousness was basically to form itself into a receptive mode in which its "mirroring" of the outer reality would be clear, precise, accurate.[32] This is why Descartes worked so hard on founding *the method* "for rightly conducting reason for seeking truth." The method is basically copying, and its pedagogical power has been felt from his day to ours.

Foucault and other post-structuralists argue there is no fixed self, that we need to "erase" such a concept from our discourse.[33] An "I" isolated from "others" and subjects separated from objects render both the I and the subjects meaningless. *Self* is understood only in relation to *other*. Both are needed, each becomes the *sine qua non* of the other. Self without an other is not a self. The same can be said about subject and object; neither exists without the other, neither exists independently and in isolation.

A pedagogy based on Cartesian-modernist separation is either a copy-model pedagogy or, at best, a discovery pedagogy. In the former, curriculum is the fixed truths and procedures to be passed on generation to generation, person to person. It is a transmitted curriculum. The teacher-student separation is simple: the teacher teaches, the learner learns. A discovery pedagogy provides more flexibility and openness; the object is not "to furnish the mind" but "to train it to the use of its own powers." However, the separation between subject and object is still presumed: the discovered is that which is already there. One has gone beyond transmission to a limited form of transformation; the subject undergoes limited, controlled, and predictable change, but the external reality remains dominant, unchanged, and controlling.

A pedagogy based on paradox, a paradoxical pedagogy as it were, shifts the focus from this subject-object split to their integration, conjunction, union. The paradox of subject-object, or teacher-learner, or text-reader is that neither is the other, yet neither is without the other. Each needs the other for its own sense of being. This shifts the focus of curriculum from receiving or developing to *dialoguing, negotiating, interacting*. These are not words or concepts found in either the Tyler rationale or in modernist curriculum thought. They imply (and use) indeterminacy, openness, self-organization. They are the words of a transformative curriculum, a *currere*-oriented curriculum, one focusing not on the external attributes of the racecourse but on the process of traversing the course, of negotiating with self, others, and the course.

Play, is a good medium for developing skills in dialoguing, negotiating, interacting. A transformative curriculum looks to and uses play for the development of these skills. Pre-modern, tribal, and medieval cultures honored play through the roles of the shaman, the fool, the jester. Shakespeare used word play extensively in his comedies, even in his tragedies and histories. However, except in kindergarten—with its origins in German romanticism—play has not been an integral or accepted part of the academic curriculum. As David Hamilton points out, our current, modernist curriculum is well-grounded in Calvinist theology.[34] A strong separation divides work and play. Work is the route to eternal salvation; play (the "devil's work") leads to idleness and damnation.[35]

Play, however, especially intellectual play, has a great deal to offer a post-modern curriculum. Play deals not with the present and foundational, but with the absent and the possible. Its very nature invites dialogue, interpretation, interaction. Its free-following form encourages participation. All of these activities are essential to meaning making; they are key elements in what Bruner calls the "narrative mode" of learning.[36] Whereas the analytic mode (which we use in lectures, textbooks, recitations) is transmittive and preset, the narrative mode is transformative and open-ended. Needless to say, the former mode has a set methodology—as evidenced in most curriculum methods courses. The latter mode asks the teacher and students to be playful—with the material and with each other. This mode (metaphorical rather than logical) also places a great burden on the teacher: to help students develop their play with and metaphoric use of ideas, forms, procedures, and patterns to create productive happenings. This is not an easy task.

Another advantage of play, once one is attuned to its nature, is that its freedom allows challenge and exploration in a nonhostile and nonthreatening way. Rap music at its best does this. At its worst, rap crosses the thin, invisible, imaginary line between productive and destructive happenings. Play, like its counterpart chaos, if it is to develop into creativity, needs a sense of boundary or attraction to an "event" (to use a Whitehead term).[37] Such, of course, will not always happen, and the teacher's role in helping such creativity occur is tenuous and delicate. Nondirection leaves all to chance—a point that bothered Piaget immensely; over-direction robs the event of its spontaneity and uniqueness, resulting in mediocrity—a point that bothered Piaget just as much. Creative development occurs in the tension between chance and direction. This tension, which Kuhn calls "essential," must always be maintained.[38]

The Four R's

The Tyler rationale, with its emphasis on closure—choosing "purposes," "experiences," "methods of organization," and then evaluating to "determine whether these purposes [experiences, methods] are being attained"—is so much a product of modernist thinking that it is hardly appropriate to use it as a set of criteria for a post-modern curriculum.[39] A new educational mind-set and curriculum frame require a new set of criteria to determine what constitutes a good or quality post-modern curriculum. Toward this end, I propose using the R's of *richness, recursion, relations,* and *rigor* as criteria. As the three R's of "reading, 'riting, and 'rithmetic" were foundational to late 19th- and early 20th-century curricula, I propose the four R's as potentially foundational for the last years of this century and the early ones of the next.

Richness

The paramount feature of a post-modern curriculum is openness—defined here as generativity, multiple layers of interpretation, and varied realms of meaning. To achieve openness, the curriculum needs to be *rich;* that is, it needs to be filled with enough ambiguity, challenge, perturbation to invite the learner to enter into dialogue with the curriculum and with those working in the curriculum. Meaning making occurs through dialogue and interaction. Thus, the curriculum needs to be *rich* enough in depth and breadth to encourage meaning making. Both the curriculum and the teacher must be challenging and open enough to invite and encourage participation.

Here is a pedagogic creed I try to follow in dialoguing with students:

> In a reflective relationship between teacher and student, the teacher does not ask the student to accept the teacher's authority; rather, the teacher asks the student *to suspend disbelief in that authority,* to join with the teacher in inquiry, into that which the student is experiencing. The teacher agrees to help the student understand the meaning of the advice given, to be readily confrontable by the student, and to work with the student in reflecting on the tacit understanding each has.[40]

The sort of dialogue advocated here can occur best when the curriculum is rich with problems, perturbations, possibilities.

While richness in the sense of having multiple layers of interpretation, meaning, and problematics does produce an exciting curriculum, it also produces one akin to the current view of the nature of the world in which we live. Descartes' set method for "rightly conducting reason for seeking truth"—a foundation of positivist philosophy—was based on the assumption that the universe we live in (indeed, reality itself) is stable, consonant, and simply ordered. As Newton was fond of saying: "Nature is comformable to Herself and simple."[41] It is this metaphysical assumption, of course, that encouraged Newton to look for the same order in the movement of the planets (the spheres) that existed in apples falling to the ground. Hence was born the concept of gravity. Today order is also posited, but not Newton's simple uniform order. Now order is seen as complex, self-generative, "lumpy," and inherently unstable. Quantum physics shows us a universe (and reality) born quirky and "quarky." Instead of simple order, we posit complex, chaotic order. From the richness of this milieu comes an order which, as we engage it, transforms both ourselves and itself. This is the nature of our creative universe as we now see it.[42]

A creative curriculum, like a creative universe, emerges through dialogue. The product is not preset but emerges through the process—a favorite point of Dewey's. This is why Rorty advocates we "keep the conversation going."[43] To challenge, then, is to develop a curriculum *rich* enough to keep conversation "going and going and going and going."

Recursion

Recursion means to *return*. It is from the Latin *recurrere* (to run back). The connection with curriculum as *currere* is obvious. A recursive curriculum emphasizes the notion of returning—to look at itself, yet again, in a new light, for the first time. This metaphorical playing happens more easily in the humanities than in the sciences. In mathematics, recursion is synonymous with mathematical iteration—working an equation in a nonlinear way so that the solution y (in an x-y formula) is fed back into the equation as a new x. This is done over and over, each new solution (y) becoming input (x) for the next repetition of the equation. It is these recursions/iterations that make up the marvelous fractal computer graphics one sees in chaos mathematics, the Mandelbrot and Julia sets.

In the humanities, however, recursion has a broader meaning. Here, it refers to the act of a mind or self "looping back," "turning around," or reflecting on itself, and in this way actually creating itself as a conscious self—the highest expression of human awareness. In education, recursion means displaying, to self and others, "what one has thought and then turning around on it and reconsidering it."[44] Through this "turning around" or "reconsidering"—which is akin to Dewey's concept of reflection, a second looking—transformation, growth, development occur. A recursive curriculum, then, leaves room for students (or a class) to loop back on previous ideas, to run back or revisit what has gone before. Such a *nonlinear* approach to curriculum represents a definite departure from the *linear* lesson plans, course syllabi, and textbook constructions educators have worked with and accepted for so long. A recursive curriculum is dialogical; its development is open, dependent on the ongoing interaction among teachers, students, texts, cultures. The art of curriculum construction—no mean feat when these four elements are diverse—consists of coordinating and directing these forces. As with Dewey's concept of growth, this coordination and direction must be neither overemphasized nor underemphasized.

Relations

A linear curriculum has a definite beginning, middle, end. A nonlinear curriculum is more akin to a matrix, maybe even to the computer graphics of a Mandelbrot set. A matrix, sphere, or Mandelbrot blob has no beginning or ending, just an ever increasing middle, a middle filled with connections and interconnections. The heart of the curriculum process calls for adding continuously to these connections, making the overall system deeper, richer, darker. Characterizing curriculum in terms of "dark" systems may be an unfamiliar concept; but as more interconnections are made, the points where they meet become darker, richer, more ambiguous. Shakespeare's poetry has lived for centuries not because of its simplicity but because of the richness of its multiple interpretations. The Newtonian metaphysical idea of simplicity—nature comformable and simple—is passé.

The Mandelbrot set appears mostly black, with luminescent colors at the fringes. The dark blob—itself almost symmetically ordered—represents an area where the equation generating the set is strong, powerful, "alive" with relations. On the fringes, filled with dynamic luminescence and all sorts of weird and fascinating shapes, the equations border on extinction, wandering off into nothingness. Paradoxically, the borders and fringes display the most visual, mathematical, and aesthetic excitement. Here is where the spirals and swirls for which the set is known occur. Here lie Prigogine's "far-from-equilibrium" situations, the most fragile, the most generative, the most transformative.

At the center of the set, the relations are rich with interpretations, but stable. The fringes reveal relations that are also among the most exciting, but that border on extinction. Transposing this metaphor into classroom teaching and curriculum suggests the teacher needs to help the students deal with the richness of multiple but stable interpretations as well as the excitement of tenuous and "far out" ones. Both types of interpretations exist. Without its fringes, the Mandelbrot set is nothing but a blob; but the fringes could not exist without the stability of the blob, the center and core of the set.

Just as richness applies to more than curriculum, to reality in a cosmological sense, so also do relations. In a cosmology such as that described by Whitehead, Prigogine, or process theology—all of which move away from considering Newton's "hard, massy, impenetrable particles" (atoms) as the ultimate essence of reality—*relations* become foundational or essential. Relations form the heart of these cosmologies. The same can be said of post-modernism or post-structuralism in general—*relations,* not things, become the prime focus. Relations, of course, are far more flexible than "impenetrable particles." Relations require interpretation and dialogue for the assessment of meaning; particles require precise measurement and definition. Such precise measurement and definition are not possible in a quantum world, as both Heisenberg and Gödel have shown. Therefore, a post-modern frame substitutes relations for particles as its chief characteristic. The curriculum field, however, has yet to make such a shift. Our current concept envisions curriculum as a prearranged set of linear particles, not as a gathering or matrix of interrelated "occasions." Shifting from particles to relations helps us understand with greater depth Whitehead's statements: "Do not teach too many subjects," but "what you teach, teach thoroughly." "Let the main ideas which are introduced . . . be few and important, and let them be thrown into every combination possible."[45]

Rigor

In some ways *rigor* is the most important of the four R's. If richness most distinguishes a post-modern curriculum, then rigor is what makes richness rich. The problems, perturbations, and possibilities that constitute richness need to be ordered (albeit loosely) if they are to shed new and interesting light on a subject. Without such loose ordering, they become merely a jumbled collection of disconnected perturbations, useful to no one. Rigor molds these into a coherent and dynamic unity; rigor is the struggle to work through the problems, perturbations, and possibilities to achieve a sense of coherence and integration not evident (maybe not present) when the struggle began. Rigor enables coherence to emerge from disequilibrium, chaos, and confusing complexity.

The word *rigor* (from the Latin of the same spelling and *rigere* in the infinitive verb form) means stiffness, severity, strictness. *Rigor mortis* is the obvious and direct carryover from Latin to contemporary usage. In a methodological sense, to be rigorous is to be severe and strict in applying a procedure, with no loose, humanist, personal, subjective infringements. In the deductive sciences, this rigor leads to the closure that logic provides for our "rightly conducting reason"; in the empirical sciences, rigor reduces possible causes to the one influential cause. In the Tyler rationale, rigor produces the close (or high) correlation between the purposes intended and the results achieved; this is what educational evaluation is all about.

Moving into a hermeneutic frame or into the narrative or post-modern mode softens rigor's harshness and severity. In those modes rigor means not so much strict conformity to a preset procedure as the careful exploration of multiple possibilities and unstated assumptions. Here one looks deeply, critically, generatively, and even contrarily into the "matter at hand." (It is hard to leave the language of modernism, even to express post-modern thoughts.) One explores thoroughly that which interpretation and metaphor present. Rather than deny the role personalness and subjectivity play in interpretation, one uses personalness and subjectivity to help achieve better, deeper, more comprehensive understanding. If, as humans, we are makers of meaning and not merely discoverers or followers of others' meanings, then rigor in this hermeneutic and heuristic sense needs to be included as a criterion of good curriculum.

It should go without saying that the criteria presented here in the four R's are as far removed from the open and progressive movements as they are from the behavioral movements associated with the Tyler rationale.

Notes

1. Milan Kundera, *The Art of the Novel,* trans. Linda Asher (New York: Grove Press, 1988), p. 164.

2. Josué Harai and David Bell, "Introduction: Journal à Plusieurs Voies," in *Michel Serres' Hermes*, ed. Josué Harai and David Bell (Baltimore, MD: Johns Hopkins University Press, 1983), p. xxvii.
3. Anonymous.
4. Herbert M. Kliebard, *Forging the American Curriculum: Essays in Curriculum History and Theory* (New York: Routledge, 1992), pp. 6–11.
5. Richard Rorty, *Philosophy and the Mirror of Nature* (Princeton, NJ: Princeton University Press, 1980).
6. David Olson, "The Mind According to Bruner," *Educational Researcher* 21 (May 1992): 29–31.
7. John Dewey, *Art as Experience* (New York: Perigee Books, G. P. Putnam's Sons, 1980). Original work published in 1934.
8. Jerome Bruner, *Acts of Meaning* (Cambridge: Harvard University Press, 1990); William E. Doll, Jr., *A Postmodern Perspective on Curriculum* (New York: Teachers College Press, 1992).
9. Joseph Schwab, *Science, Curriculum, and Liberal Education: Selected Essays*, ed. Ian Westbury and Neil Wilkof (Chicago: University of Chicago Press, 1978), pp. 287–321.
10. Donald A. Schön, *The Reflective Practitioner: How Professionals Think in Action* (New York: Basic Books, 1983); Donald A. Schön, *Educating the Reflective Practitioner* (San Francisco; Jossey-Bass, Inc., 1987).
11. Donald A. Schön, *The Reflective Practitioner: How Professionals Think in Action* (New York: Basic Books, 1983); Donald A. Schön, *Educating the Reflective Practitioner* (San Francisco: Jossey-Bass, Inc.. 1987); Donald A. Schön, *The Reflective Turn: Case Studies in and on Educational Practice* (New York: Teachers College Press, 1991); James G. Henderson, *Reflective Teaching: Becoming an Inquiring Educator* (New York: Macmillan, 1991); Tom Russell and Hugh Munby, eds., *Teachers and Teaching: From Classroom to Reflection* (London: Falmer Press, 1992).
12. William Pinar, ed., *Contemporary Curriculum Discourses* (Scottsdale, AZ: Gorsuch Scarisbrick, Publishers, 1988), p. 2.
13. "Bye, Bye, Eli," *Wall Street Journal*, May 27, 1992, p. A 14.
14. Charles Jencks, *What Is Postmodernism?* (New York: St. Martin's Press, 1987), p. 10.
15. Katherine Hayles, *Chaos and Order* (Chicago: University of Chicago Press, 1991).
16. Eric J. Chaisson, "Early Results from the Hubble Space Telescope," *Scientific American* 266 (June 1992): 44–51; Richard T. Fienberg, "COBE Confronts the Big Bang," *Sky and Telescope* 84 (July 1992): 34–36; Stephen P. Maran, "Hubble Illuminates the Universe," *Sky and Telescope* 83 (June 1992): 619–625. Obviously, there is nothing new in this "new order." The newness lies in our perceptions, both conceptual and visual.
17. Peter Garrison, "Glued to the Set," *Harvard Magazine* 91 (January–February 1989): 31.
18. Stephen E. Toulmin, *Return to Cosmology: Postmodern Science and the Theology of Nature* (Berkeley: University of California Press, 1982).
19. José G. Merquior, *From Prague to Paris: A Critique of Structuralist and Post-Structuralist Thought* (London: Verso, 1986); David R. Griffin, *The Reenchantment of Science: Postmodern Proposals* (Albany: State University of New York Press, 1988).
20. John Dewey, *The Quest for Certainty: A Study of the Relation of Knowledge and Action* (New York: G. P. Putnam, 1960). Original work published in 1929.
21. René Descartes, *Discourse on the Method*, trans. L. J. Lafleur (New York: The Liberal Arts Press, 1950). Original work published in 1637.
22. Edwin A. Burtt, *The Metaphysical Foundations of Modern Physical Science: A Historical and Critical Essay* (New York: Doubleday Anchor Books, 1955), p. 31. Original work published in 1932.
23. Ibid., p. 96.
24. John P. Briggs and David F. Peat, *Looking Glass Universe: The Emerging Science of Wholeness* (New York: Simon and Schuster, 1984); John P. Briggs and David F. Peat, *Turbulent Mirror* (New York: Harper and Row, 1989).
25. John Dewey, *The Quest for Certainty: A Study of the Relations of Knowledge and Action* (New York: G. P. Putnam, 1960), original work published in 1929; Edwin A. Burtt, *The Metaphysical Foundations of Modern Physical Science: A Historical and Critical Essay* (New York: Doubleday Anchor Books, 1955), original work published in 1932; Richard Rorty, *Philosophy and the Mirror of Nature* (Princeton, NJ: Princeton University Press, 1980).
26. Wolfgang Iser, *The Act of Reading* (Baltimore, MD: The Johns Hopkins University Press, 1978), p. 61.
27. Ilya Prigogine, *From Being to Becoming: Time and Complexity in the Physical Sciences* (San Francisco: W. H. Freeman and Company, 1980); Ilya Prigogine and Isabelle Stengers, *Order Out of Chaos: Man's New Dialogue with Nature* (New York: Bantam Books, 1984).
28. Jean Piaget, *Biology and Knowledge: An Essay on the Relations Between Organic Regulation and Cognitive Processes*, trans. Beatrix Walsh (Chicago: University of Chicago Press, 1971), ch. 1.

29. Donald Schön, *The Reflective Practitioner: How Professionals Think in Action* (New York: Basic Books, 1983), p. 296.
30. Gilles Deleuze, *The Logic of Sense*, trans. Mark Lester and Charles Stivale (New York: Columbia University Press, 1990).
31. René Descartes, "Description of the Human Body," trans. John Cottingham, in *The Philosophical Writings of Descartes*, vol. 1 (London: Cambridge University Press, 1985), pp. 314–324. Original work published in 1664.
32. Richard Rorty, *Philosophy and the Mirror of Nature* (Princeton, NJ: Princeton University Press, 1980).
33. Michel Foucault, *The History of Sexuality, Vol. 1: An Introduction*, trans. Robert Hurley (New York: Vintage Books, 1978); Michel Foucault, *The History of Sexuality, Vol. 2: The Use of Pleasure*, trans. Robert Hurley (New York: Vintage Books, 1985); Michel Foucault, *The History of Sexuality, Vol. 3: The Care of Self*, trans. Robert Hurley (New York: Vintage Books, 1986).
34. David Hamilton, *Toward a Theory of Schooling* (Philadelphia: Falmer Press, 1989).
35. William E. Doll, Jr., *Play and Mastery: A Structuralist View* (paper presented at the Terman Memorial Conference, Stanford, 1978).
36. Jerome Bruner, *Actual Minds, Possible Worlds* (Cambridge: Harvard University Press, 1986), ch. 2.
37. Alfred N. Whitehead, *Science and the Modern World* (New York: Free Press, 1967), original work published in 1925; Alfred N. Whitehead, *The Aims of Education* (New York: Free Press, 1967), original work published in 1929.
38. Thomas S. Kuhn, *The Essential Tension: Selected Studies in Scientific Traditions and Change* (Chicago: The University of Chicago Press, 1977).
39. Ralph W. Tyler, *Basic Principles of Curriculum and Instruction* (Chicago: The University of Chicago Press, 1949), pp. 1–2.
40. Assimilated from Donald Schön, *The Reflective Practitioner: How Professionals Think in Action* (New York: Basic Books, 1983), pp. 296–297.
41. Isaac Newton, *Opticks*, 4th ed. (New York: Dover Publications, Inc., 1952), p. 397. Original work published in 1730.
42. Ilya Prigogine and Isabelle Stengers, *Order Out of Chaos: Man's New Dialogue with Nature* (New York: Bantam Books, 1984); Paul Davies, *The Cosmic Blueprint: New Discoveries in Nature's Creative Ability to Order the Universe* (New York: Simon and Schuster, 1988); Paul Davies, *The Mind of God: The Scientific Basis for a Rational World* (New York: Simon and Schuster, 1992).
43. Richard Rorty, *Philosophy and the Mirror of Nature* (Princeton, NJ: Princeton University Press, 1980), p. 377.
44. Jerome Bruner, *Actual Minds, Possible Worlds* (Cambridge: Harvard University Press, 1986), p. 129.
45. Alfred N. Whitehead, *The Aims of Education* (New York: Free Press, 1957), p. 2. Original work published in 1929.

Section B

Historical and Contemporary Perspectives on Curriculum

CHAPTER 6

LIBERAL EDUCATION: A DYNAMIC TRADITION

CLIFTON F. CONRAD AND JEAN C. WYER

Liberal education is a difficult concept to define. It is ambiguous in both theory and practice. Its numerous synonyms and related terms have given it a normative status in our educational lexicon. Thus, more often than not, historical accounts of liberal education, as well as the myriad of prescriptive treatises and value-laden apologias about it, are frequently more of a revelation of their authors' personal philosophy than an exposition on the nature of liberal education itself. This study differs only in our acknowledgment of such preliminary biases and our recognition that if there is to be important and lively debate, a clear concept of liberal education is necessary.

This overview points to a potent, rich, "liberal" tradition that encompasses more than the acquisition of skills and knowledge per se. It defines a tradition of liberal education that speaks to the ultimate questions of society and the individual. The first section looks at the European roots of liberal education while the second examines the development of the liberal arts in American colleges and universities.

The Classical and Medieval Background

The various expressions "liberal disciplines," "liberal arts," "liberal studies" and their contemporary counterpart, "liberal education," have historical referents more numerous than even their names imply. The liberal disciplines among the Romans were a form of the Greek *enkuklios paideia,* which consisted of instruction in the basic literacy skills—both verbal and quantitative (Levine 1978, p. 492). The liberal arts of the Middle Ages consisted of the split between the *trivium* (grammar, rhetoric, and logic) and the *quadrivium* (arithmetic, geometry, astronomy, and music). However, it was the *trivium*, particularly logic, that dominated scholarly inquiry throughout the Middle Ages (Schachner 1962, p. 14). Liberal studies as they emerged during the Renaissance were the secular component of an education that seriously attempted to link learning with conduct in the effort to create a virtuous and noble man. Throughout the history of education, there also have been those who regarded the liberal arts as a fixed, immutable body of knowledge, subject neither to question nor criticism.

In twentieth-century America, liberal education often is used synonymously with general education, referring to that part of one's studies that lies outside the chosen area of vocational or academic specialization. More affirmatively, it sometimes refers to the curricular component that introduces students to a common cultural heritage and the seminal creations of civilization. Still others regard liberal education as an antiquated remnant from an elitist society that provides cultural refinement and little else. Most recently it has been identified as a *process* through which the

Source: "Liberal Education in Transition," by Clifton F. Conrad and Jean C. Wyer, reprinted from *AAHE-ERIC Higher Education Research Report,* No. 3, 1980, American Association for Higher Education.

"whole person" is developed, and also as a type of cognitive immersion in fundamental ways of knowing and in advanced intellectual reasoning skills (Levine 1978, pp. 3–4). Our contemporary confusion over the idea of liberal education makes a historical analysis a necessary as well as difficult task.

Liberal education—its formal ideals and its practice—has changed dramatically over the 2,500-year history of Western civilization. Still, to a degree unknown to other forms of education and training, liberal education has been solidly rooted in a cultural ideal that first emerged among the Greeks in the fifth century B.C. This account will trace the historical development of that ideal before returning to examine its Greek origins in more detail.

In the first century B.C., the erudite Roman scholar, Varro (116–27 B.C.), wrote what is regarded as the first encyclopedic work on the liberal arts; his *Disciplinarum libri novum* is one of the earliest known usages of "liberal" in conjunction with education and knowledge (Boyd 1966, p. 69). Four hundred years later Martianus Capella (c. 424), a lawyer and rhetorician, wrote *De Nuptiis Philogiae et Mercurii et de Septem Artius Liberalibus Novem,* an immensely popular work which practically became dogma during the Middle Ages (Schachner 1962, pp. 13–14; Boyd 1966, p. 94). Within a century and a half, Cassiodorus (c. 490–585) gave all-important scriptural sanction to seven liberal arts. As Abelson notes, it was during this time that church leaders admitted the necessity of "incorporating secular studies into the Christian curriculum, and since the secular studies had been definitely seven in number for over a century and a half, reasons were found from a Christian standpoint explaining scripturally that their number seven was divinely sanctioned" (1906, p. 9). Thus, with Cassiodorus, the subjects of the medieval curriculum were limited in scope and number, and the idea of learning and knowledge outside the domain of theology and Scripture was kept alive.

However, a comfortable balance did not emerge between Christian precepts and the liberal arts until 800 years later. Pietro Paolo Vegerio's (1349–1420) treatise, "On the Manners of a Gentleman and on Liberal Studies," was an influential` early Renaissance work that helped bring about several changes. Vergerio insisted on the value of an all-round education, the primacy of morality over learning, and the need to stretch the liberal arts to include literature, history, and "knowledge of nature" (Boyd 1966, pp. 163–164).

By the end of the thirteenth century, the major medieval universities had been formed—Paris, Bologna, Oxford, and Cambridge—along with at least 80 others (Haskins 1957, p. 20). During this period the three original professions of law, medicine, and theology were incorporated into the university curriculum—although their study could not be undertaken until the student was well grounded in the liberal arts. This general education for the man of affairs was an integral part of a university education. The liberal arts were transformed from a narrow epistemic construct, allowing merely for the survival of knowledge and scholarly inquiry, into a dynamic cultural ideal thriving in a new setting, the university, and, more generally, flourishing in an age of discovery and rebirth. Indeed, as our historical label for this era implies, this was a period of rebirth—a renaissance of classical knowledge and values.

The "new" knowledge incorporated into the liberal arts was actually regained knowledge, regained *through* the Spice Routes and Islamic culture but *from,* the ancient Greeks, particularly Aristotle. To a large extent, it was this injection of Greek thought into medieval Europe that set human civilization on a course out of the Dark Ages. Even in our own time, such prominent educational leaders and theorists as Mortimer Alder, Mark Van Doren, and Robert Hutchins have espoused a perennial philosophy of education that embraces the ideals of classical culture. Indeed, it was the Greek emphasis on our common humanity—as a means to create both personal and public excellence—that has made the liberal arts ideal so tenacious and potent a force.

In his classic study of Greek education, Werner Jaeger maintains that "the structure of every society is based on the written or unwritten laws which bind its members. Therefore, education in any human community . . . is the direct expression of its active awareness of a standard" (1939, p. xiv). Fortunately for us, the Greeks were supremely aware of their ideals, and they worked hard to achieve them. The ideal of a liberal education, if not its etymological root, was captured by the Greeks in two concepts: *paideia* and *areté. Paideia* meant education, or more broadly, culture, and in practice it was inextricably linked to *areté,* the ability to live one's life well, and the knowledge of what it is to be human (Drew 1978, p 304).

The Greeks earnestly sought an answer to the question, "What type of *paideia* leads to *areté*?" Their answer took the form of what we now refer to as liberal education.

Within the relatively short history of ancient classical Greece, the ultimate aim of education developed from an ideal of man as the mentally courageous and physically fit warrior, to the responsible citizen immersed in the civic affairs and artistic creations of society, to the reflective individual engaged in *eudaimonia*, the rational contemplation of the highest ideas and ideals (Jaeger 1939, p. 6). *Areté*, the strived-for ideal in Greek society, was far from impractical, since it involved all three aims of this historically developed ideal. *Eudaimonia*, the highest form of *areté* as conceived by Aristotle, was never meant to supplant the other forms of *areté* but rather to illuminate their role and significance within a broader context. It was considered the highest and most uniquely human art of thinking, the most noble use of leisure. Perhaps Lewis Mumford expresses the point most effectively as he addresses our own time and situation:

> In fact, without leisure our expansion in industry would be almost meaningless; for we need a plentitude of time if we are to select and assimilate all the genuine goods that modern man now commands. *Schola* means leisure; and leisure makes possible the school. The promise of a life economy is to provide schooling for the fullest kind of human growth—not for the further expansion of the machine (1979, p. 456).

In the very act of seeking *areté* the Greeks created a culture that became an educative force.

In an article dealing with the Greek ideals of liberal education, Murchland writes, "The endless quest for definitions and intellectual clarity was not empty verbalizing or mere intellectual gamesmanship. It was based on their belief that practice and theory were interdependent, two aspects of a unified moral activity" (1976, p. 23). Liberal education, then, was metaphysically grounded in this unique conception of an education that *is* culture and not simply *about* culture or the transmission of culture and knowledge. Furthermore, education for *areté* was a moral activity; it was not moral in a narrow religious context but rather in the sense that there was something vital at stake, an idea or situation that demanded free choice and commitment along with a concomitant willingness to bear grave risks. And ultimately for the ancient Greeks, the very life and health of each individual and society as a whole was at stake. Within such an intense context, then, the Socratic maxim "know thyself" was, fundamentally, a personal and moral inquiry . . . but not a private one (the opposite of personal is impersonal). This blend of personal excellence with the public good was dramatically embodied in *areté*. To know one's self was to know what it is to be a human being.

This brief sketch, of course, offers an understanding of liberal education at odds with those who have characterized such education as highly theoretical and esoteric, elitist, or even frivolous. Certainly, it is true that if there has been any form of education that has treasured the pursuit of knowledge for its own sake, it has been liberal education; but rarely, if ever, have its great advocates claimed knowledge as an end in itself, as the ultimate aim of education. Murchland (1979, p. 47) identifies this ivory-tower interpretation as a fairly recent phenomenon and in reference to liberal education writes, "Pure reason has no place in this tradition for there is no use of reason that does not have some emotive base and some moral payoff. This conviction was the cornerstone of Greek and medieval philosophers of education" (1976, p. 23).

Almost all contemporary proponents of liberal or general education have sought to nullify the vision of liberal education as impractical, usually through emphasizing the sustaining link between a democratic society and its educational structures (Drew 1978; Harvard Committee 1945; Hutchins 1936; Van Doren 1959) and through advocating the role of liberal education in developing a fully human individual (Chickering 1969; McGrath 1976; Murchland 1976, 1979). At some point, many proponents refer to the Greek example and attempt to show its relevance for contemporary American society and the individual.

In summary, Greek education was primarily a moral enterprise that attempted to bind together theory with practice, the ideal with reality, and the freedom of the individual with the Good of the State. It provided an ideal for education flexible enough to adjust to changing times and societies but also concrete enough to remain potent for almost 2,500 years. With this conception of liberal education solidly rooted in the thought and practice of classical Greece, we turn now to the United States to trace its historical development on a new continent.

The Liberal Arts in America

Most historians of higher education in this country identify three broad historical periods and align their accounts accordingly (Brubacher and Rudy 1976; Rudolph 1962; Schmidt 1957). The first period (from roughly 1636 to 1828) saw the transplantation of the seventeenth-century English and Scottish universities, with their classical curriculum packaged in a theological framework. The early colleges were adapted first to the needs of the fledgling colonies and later to the requirements of an emerging nation. The second period (1828–1862) was characterized by the birth of the modern university and marked by its clashes with the sectarian entrenchment of the traditional liberal arts schools. The third period began with the Morrill Act of 1862 and was quickly followed by the widespread implementation of the German university model emphasizing research and specialization. During these years the liberal arts as a distinct tradition declined in educational significance. Our close historical proximity and contemporary confusion over the goals and mission of higher education have worked to halt the definitive identification of a fourth period emerging in the late twentieth century.

As an institutional type and as a curricular component, liberal education flourished in the two earlier periods but declined dramatically in educational significance and impact with the rise of the comprehensive university. Indeed, the failure of the liberal arts schools to adjust effectively to the changing pressures and needs of an expanding society is, at least in part, the explanation for their own decline and the immense success of more versatile and open forms of higher education. It is also one fundamental cause of our contemporary divisions between vocational and theoretical, research university and liberal arts college, and even between the sciences and the humanities. By the mid-twentieth century, the status quo lay firmly within the multi-purpose, multi-mission universities; and the majority of liberal arts colleges and university undergraduate programs derived their actual curricular offerings, if not their educational rhetoric, from the academic specialists, the professional schools, the immediate needs of society, or some combination of the three.

Throughout most of this century there have been attempts to revitalize liberal education and purposively illustrate its relationship to society and to the other forms of higher education—be they professional, vocational, or disciplinary specialization. However, as Mumford pointed out almost 50 years ago, "We have still to build up a satisfactory equivalent for the old classic curriculum" (1979, p. 96). This has remained true through the 1970's. Moreover, one can no longer assume, on philosophical grounds, that any sort of consensus on liberal education can actually be achieved.

During the colonial period and into the nineteenth century the liberal arts institutions did adjust to their new environment. The transplantation of the classical curriculum occurred initially in 1636 with the founding of Harvard, followed by William and Mary in 1693 and Yale in 1701. All three were governed by lay boards and, although their fundamental mission included the training of clergymen, none required specific doctrinal examinations of either their entering or graduating students (Brubacher and Rudy 1976, p. 8).

Furthermore, and again unlike their European counterparts, the colonial colleges were organized and supported through three disparate sources: religious groups, private philanthropy and, especially, state and local government (Schmidt 1957, p. 33). The scarcity of students, monies, and scholars; the lack of "New World" traditions and cultural precedents; and the nurtured Enlightenment ideals of religious toleration and democratic governance worked together to create all of these changes in the noncurricular aspects of higher education. In comparison, the curricular innovations were, at first, relatively minor. The *trivium* and *quadrivium* and the emphasis on Greek and Latin rarely were tampered with until after the Revolutionary War.

The Protestant denominations had pervasive influence and, to a degree based upon denominational type and geographical area, their doctrines and rules blended with the Greek-rooted classical studies. Even in these early colonial colleges with rigidly prescribed courses of study, constant recitation, scholastic disputations, and stern moral exhortations there was change. The liberal arts were expanded to include at least an introduction to moral and natural philosophy (essentially, these were the progenitors of the social and natural sciences, respectively) as well as separate courses in mathematics and ancient history. A moral philosophy course, usually taught by the college president, often served as a capstone to the college experience. This was a particularly intriguing element in the early colonial liberal arts curriculum, which has experienced something of a contemporary rebirth in the form of senior seminars. The moral philosophy course of the eighteenth century was unique, however, not for its elaborate attempts to unify knowledge but rather in its view of reason as free from theological domination and the medieval scholastic mode of inquiry (Earnest 1953, pp. 28–29).

By the end of the eighteenth century, innovation in higher education was establishing some momentum. The curriculum was continuously being stretched beyond the original seven liberal arts. This was partly an attempt to meet the needs of a growing frontier nation; but perhaps more significantly, curricular expansion was in accordance with the growing role of intellectual inquiry and the rapid expansion of knowledge that marked the Enlightenment of Western Europe in general.

One of the first serious attempts to enlarge the classical curriculum occurred in the booming commercial center of Philadelphia, where Benjamin Franklin and the Reverend William Smith worked together to create the College of Philadelphia (later the University of Pennsylvania). Latin and Greek were discontinued after the first year of study; under the rubric of moral and natural philosophy, many modern-day subjects such as history, politics, trade and commerce, physics, and zoology were taught; and rhetoric and literary criticism were emphasized at the expense of grammar and syntax. In the following century, the newly created state universities (Georgia, 1785; North Carolina, 1789; Vermont, 1789; South Carolina, 1801; and Ohio University, 1804) followed Philadelphia's example, avoiding the limitations of the unitary, four-year classical plan of study under sectarian sponsorship. The progressive forces were determined to make American education less sectarian (if not less religious) and more scientific, practical, and general (Hofstadter and Smith 1961, p. 148).

In 1779 Thomas Jefferson had attempted similar reforms at The College of William and Mary with partial success. But it was over a quarter of a century later with the opening of the University of Virginia that a truly nonsectarian, publicly-controlled, Enlightenment-inspired institution was born. The University of Virginia had eight academic departments with rotating chairmanships, elective freedom, a diminished emphasis on the dominant in *loco parentis* outlook, imported European scholars, and equal respect for the sciences as well as the traditional liberal arts. Indeed, Jefferson's University of Virginia marks a peak in education reform, in sharp contrast to the well-known Yale Report of 1828.

The Yale Report was more than a local proclamation issued by President Jeremiah Day and Professor James Kingsley; it was the first unified American statement of educational philosophy that was concerned specifically with the nature of liberal education. Until its pronouncement, the numerous educational innovations—from the gradual introduction of the natural sciences to the deemphasis of Latin and Greek—were regarded as changes occurring among institutions of liberal learning. The Reverend Smith's proposal for the College of Philadelphia was entitled, "A Scheme of Liberal Education." Thomas Jefferson spoke of providing a liberal education at the University of Virginia (Hofstadter and Smith 1961, p. 175). And Benjamin Rush, a noted proponent for academic change in his day, still referred to higher education as a "liberal or learned education" in 1798 (Hofstadter and Smith 1961, p. 172). By the 1820's, however, this conception of liberal education began to change. Liberal education began to be associated with the antiquated classical curriculum, sectarianism, and in *loco parentis*—rather than regarded as an educational ideal or even simply as a synonym for higher education, as had often been the case.

Almost a decade before the Yale Report, Daniel Webster had argued the Dartmouth College Case before the United States Supreme Court. The outcome of this landmark case delineated the distinguishing legal features between public and, private institutions and, like the Yale Report, it was a victory for conservative forces. It meant that private colleges could be initially granted charters from the government and then remain free of governmental control. These two events became effective barriers against the advancing democratic forces pressing for control of higher education and more radical curricular reform. Neither their private status nor their conservative philosophy endeared the private liberal arts college to the larger public. The Yale Report was at odds with the general temper and mood of Jacksonian democracy and to many, then and now, it was a shockingly reactionary statement.

Essentially, the Yale Report was a reaffirmation of the medieval course of studies. The Report spoke of mental "discipline" and supplying the mind with "furniture" or knowledge; and it soundly rejected the appropriateness of any form of professional or vocational education within the undergraduate college experience. Rather, students were expected to develop "mental power which would be transferred at will from one study to another and from studies in general to the occupations of life" (Brubacher and Rudy 1976, p. 289). This mental rigor was equated with self-denial and strength of character and with moral righteousness itself. Yet ironically, an attitude of paternalism and authoritarianism dominated Yale and the hundreds of small, denominational liberal arts colleges that adhered to the principles and guidelines outlined in the Report. One had to search outside the domain of mental discipline and moral piety to discover educational institutions that respected their students as mature, individual young adults.

Jeremiah Day and James Kingsley had stressed that the rationale underlying the Report was the development of mental discipline. Later in the century, President Porter of Yale claimed (much as Cardinal Newman had in his essays on university education in 1853) that liberal education was an end in itself, intrinsically superior to practical studies. However, embedded in the Yale Report itself lay yet another, more abiding rationale that went, essentially, unconsidered until the twentieth century; that was the idea of the development of the whole man:

> The great object of a collegiate education . . . is to give that expansion and balance of the mental powers, those liberal and comprehensive views, and those fine proportions of character, which are not found in him whose ideas are always confined to one particular channel (Hofstadter and Smith 1961, p. 282).

But whatever the rationale, liberal education as defined and defended by President Jeremiah Day and his faculty was considered by many as aristocratic, unnecessarily rigid, irrelevant and, moreover, based on an erroneous faculty psychology of "mental discipline." Yale, however, along with some of the other older, denominational schools, had felt threatened by the new programs of instruction and so the boundaries were laid between college and universities, liberal studies and sciences. The numerous sectarian private colleges—with their odd juxtaposition of classical learning and fervent Protestantism in a rugged frontier setting—prospered and, in the meantime, Yale became known as the "Mother of Colleges."

Several years before the Yale Report, Edward Everett and George Ticknor left Harvard for advanced study in Germany. Over the next one hundred years, more than nine thousand American students followed their example (Blackman 1969, p. 523). Many of these students returned with new Ph.D.'s; more significantly, however, they returned with the German idea of a university education and a determination to implant those methods and ideals in American higher education. The concepts of *lernfreiheit* (the German equivalent to elective freedom, based on the assumption of "student as mature adult") and *lehrfreiheit* (the Old World predecessor to academic freedom and, implicitly, the beginnings of a truly professional status for the professor) were introduced, along with the research orientation, the advocacy of theoretical science, and the emphasis on advanced disciplinary specialization. By 1825 several changes in these directions had been taken by the Board of Trustees at Harvard; and although many of these reforms were temporarily forestalled by a negative faculty reaction, the foundation for change had been laid.

In many established schools the new methods and subjects of study, falling outside the purview of the traditional liberal arts, were either incorporated into the academic curriculum as a "parallel course of study" or slowly merged into the traditional curriculum (Rudolph 1962, pp. 114–115). The newly-established institutions, on the other hand, were far less hesitant to grant technical studies full status as Rensselaer did in 1824, the Union College of Engineering in 1845, and later Cornell in 1868. In the spirit of Jacksonian democracy the American public was demanding vocationally-oriented programs, and most employers felt that colleges should offer more practical training to match the nation's growing industrial needs (Conrad 1978b, p. 49).

The Yale Report only briefly slowed this trend, acting as an ideological barrier by segregating the smaller, denominational colleges with their static vision of liberal education from the larger, newer universities. The universities offered more practical training in the spirit of

American pragmatism as well as advanced study adopted from the example of German scientific research.

One commentator claims that, "The most important single event in the gradual unfolding of the curriculum from the general-liberal to the utilitarian-vocational was the Morrill Act (Land Grant Act) of 1862" (Conrad 1978b, p. 56). Whether or not it was the most important event, there can be no doubt that the Act greatly fortified the trend already under way. Yale had by 1854 instituted a parallel course of study with the creation of what would later be named the Sheffield Scientific School. The Morrill Act established state institutions of higher education supported by endowments of land from the federal government. It specified that agriculture and engineering and other technical areas of study form the major part of the curriculum. However, it was almost as an afterthought that the following clause was added to the Act: "without excluding other scientific and classical studies." Indeed, if anything, the early land-grant university still tended to imitate its classical predecessors, much to the chagrin of the pragmatic American farmer (Brubacher and Rudy 1976, p. 63). Eventually, however, the Morrill Act, along with the birth of the graduate school (John Hopkins University in 1876) and the growth of the elective system (by the end of the nineteenth century Harvard students had almost complete elective freedom), worked to create the modern university.

These were important historical developments for liberal education. The inclusion of graduate research and study and undergraduate education within the same institution dealt a severe blow to liberal studies. Because a separate graduate faculty was rarely established at the universities, the same instructor often taught students ranging from freshmen to doctoral candidates. Moreover, the institutional framework often rewarded research and disciplinary specialization, not freshmen advising or undergraduate instruction, and particularly not general studies and interdisciplinary instruction. The dramatic increase in elective freedom was, undoubtedly, a healthy reaction against the antiquated, lockstep classical curriculum; but in its excesses it, too, served to weaken the ideal of liberal education as a total, integrated experience. Indeed, many of the undergraduate schools within the comprehensive universities became preparatory schools for the professions and the graduate departments. Liberal education, regarded as the ideal of higher education in the eighteenth century and as a major institutional form of higher education in the nineteenth century, had become regarded, by the turn of the century, in an even more limited sense as one component, sometimes a minor component, of the undergraduate curriculum. The broader classical nuances seemed either abandoned or forgotten.

The election of A. Lawrence Lowell as President of Harvard in 1909 marked the beginning of a reaction against elective freedom, overspecialization, and the lack of educational unity within the undergraduate curriculum. As Lowell saw it, the ideal college

> . . . ought to produce, not defective specialists but men intellectually well-rounded, of wide sympathies and unfettered judgments. At the same time they ought to be trained for hard and accurate thought, and this will not come merely by surveying the elementary principles of many subjects. It requires mastery of something, acquired by continuous application" (in Schmidt 1957, p. 209).

Lowell's rebellion against the disintegration of the intellectual core to the undergraduate experience found support in various, and sometimes unexpected, quarters throughout the twentieth century.

Of course, the ideal of liberal education as the creation of mentally and morally disciplined gentlemen via the lockstep classical curriculum was in force among the small, denominational liberal arts colleges well into the twentieth century. Many of this century's reformers, however, have sought new foundations and new curricular structures in their attempt to reintegrate the ideals of liberal education with the realities of contemporary society. Irving Babbit and Norman Foerster were leading humanists of the early 1900's who, along with their counterparts within higher education, rebelled against the banality of pragmatism and the methodological stranglehold of the sciences. Their cause for "liberal culture" and against specialization supported the ideal of the well-rounded man who was well-acquainted with the standards of past civilizations (Veysey 1965, pp. 180–251). John Dewey and his "progressive" followers offered a philosophy of education based on the nature and needs of a modern, democratic industrial society. The curriculum was to be based upon the principle of problem-solving, and experience would precede the trappings of departmentalism and the vacuity of pure theory. Flexibility and diversity, the concepts of fluidity and change, were predominant (Dewey 1967). Following in the tradition of Cardinal Newman, Robert Hutchins placed emphasis on the Great Books and tradition, as well as the prevailing uniformity and power of human reason. His ideal curriculum would reveal underlying values and transmit the enduring truths of our Western intellectual heritage (Hutchins 1936).

The visions of these three philosophies of higher education shaped the nature of curricular reform and, although the Great Books program at St. John's College is an almost exact construct of Hutchins' ideals, most attempts at reform in liberal education drew from some mixture of these philosophical positions. They found expression in such schemes of general education as the contemporary civilization courses at Columbia University beginning in 1919, collegiate education at Meiklejohn's Experimental College at the University of Wisconsin, Morgan's experiential education at Antioch in Ohio, and Aydelotte's honors and independent study at Swarthmore in 1921.

The years immediately following World War II and the publication of Harvard's report, *General Education in a Free Society* (Harvard Committee 1945), saw yet another surge of interest in liberal education. Although the Harvard report used the expression "general education," attempting to avoid the lingering elitist connotations of the liberal arts (and undoubtedly in reaction to the continuing push toward "special" or "specialized" education), the report was a vital reaffirmation of faith in the utility and educational force of liberal education. According to the Harvard report, "The task of modern democracy is to preserve the ancient ideal of liberal education and to extend it as far as possible to all the members of the community" (Harvard Committee 1945, p. 53). The report concludes that what is necessary is a "general education capable at once of taking on many different forms and yet of representing in all its forms the common knowledge and the common values on which a free society depends" (p. 53). As Frederick Rudolph points out in his history of the American undergraduate curriculum, however, the report failed in its attempt to reinvigorate the curriculum. It was regarded by many as too conformist or too authoritarian; by most, it was regarded as unrealistic in its high expectations of faculty cooperation and interdisciplinary instruction (Rudolph 1977, pp. 262–264).

By the 1960's any revitalization of liberal or general studies inspired by the twentieth-century Harvard descendant of the Yale Report seemed entirely dissipated within the virtual free-for-all of the distribution approach. In turn, liberal education was in disarray. The philosophy of objective, value-free knowledge had lost its purgative quality and iconoclastic stance of the nineteenth century, and by the mid-twentieth century had become as dogmatic and as unmindful of its own presumptions and values as had its theological and idealist predecessors. This narrow concept of the scientific method, often coupled with a broad application, seriously undermined the Greek tradition of liberal education. In addition, two distinguishing characteristics of American higher education—the uncoordinated diversity of curricula and institutional missions and the corporate structure of administration and governance—seemed antithetical or, at best, indifferent to liberal studies.

However, two other features, clearly demarcating American higher education from its global counterparts, have supported liberal education. The extracurricular emphasis and its modern institutional embodiment, student personnel services, have served since the colonial period to expand the mission and influence of college beyond the purely academic or vocational. In addition, the very persistence of the belief in, and attempted practice of, general and liberal studies in a higher education setting is almost uniquely American. Other nations have focused on professional education and academic specialization, claiming either that they have provided general education in the secondary schools or that they do not have the necessary economic resources to support programs and institutions of liberal studies. However, in the United States liberal education continues to be a more widely discussed, problematic concept.

Yet another feature of American colleges and universities, the radical expansion of opportunity and the resulting plurality of students, raises a challenge for the future of liberal education. The ongoing vitality of the liberal education ideal may well rely most heavily on its ability to adjust to a society seeking higher education for all its citizens. Liberal education as an institutional type still maintains an uneasy balance between its expectation of "quality" incoming students and its desire for an enriching, diverse student body. What areas of liberal or general studies can or should be stressed for a pluralistic student body is open for debate. During the 1970's these tensions remained unresolved as the final vestiges of the classic liberal arts curriculum disappeared. We have yet to witness the emergence of some definitive model of liberal education that embodies the Greek ideals, bringing into closer association those ideals and the practice of liberal education.

Bibliography

Abelson, Paul. *The Seven Liberal Arts: A Study in Medieval Culture.* New York: Teachers College, Columbia University, 1906.

Blackman, Edward B. "General Education." In *Encyclopedia of Education Research,* edited by Robert L. Ebel. 4th edition. New York: Macmillan, 1969: 522–537.

Boyd, William. *The History of Western Education.* New York: Barnes and Noble, 1966.

Brubacher, John S., and Rudy, Willis. *Higher Education in Transition: A History of American Colleges and Universities,* 1636–1976. 3rd rev. ed. New York: Harper and Row, 1976.

Chickering, Arthur. *Education and Identity.* San Francisco: Jossey-Bass, 1969.

Conrad, Clifton R. *The Undergraduate Curriculum: A Guide to Innovation and Reform.* Boulder, Colorado: Westview, 1978b.

Dewey, John. *Democracy and Education.* New York: The Free Press, 1967. Originally published in 1929.

Drew, Lewis H. "The Greek Concept of Education and Its Implications for Today." *Liberal Education* 64 (October 1978): 302–319.

Earnest, Ernest. *Academic Procession: An Informal History of the American College 1636 to 1953.* Indianapolis: Bobbs-Merrill, 1953.

Harvard Committee. *General Education in a Free Society.* Cambridge, Massachusetts: Harvard University Press, 1945.

Haskins, Charles Homer. *The Rise of Universities.* Ithaca, New York: Cornell University Press, 1957.

Hofstadter, Richard, and Smith, Wilson. *American Higher Education: A Documentary History.* Vols. 1 and 2. Chicago: The University of Chicago Press, 1071.

Hutchins, Robert Maynard. *The Higher Learning in America.* New Haven, Connecticut: Yale University Press, 1936.

Jaeger, Werner. *Paideia: The Ideals of Greek Culture.* New York: Oxford University Press, 1939.

Levine, Arthur. *Handbook on Undergraduate Curriculum.* A Report for the Carnegie Council on Policy Studies in Higher Education. San Francisco: Jossey-Bass, 1978.

McGrath, Earl J. *General Education and the Plight of Modern Man.* Indianapolis: Lilly Endowment, 1976.

Mumford, Lewis. *Interpretations and Forecasts: 1922–1972.* New York: Harcourt, Brace, and Jovanovich, 1979.

Murchland, Bernard. "The Eclipse of the Liberal Arts." *Change* 8 (November 1976): 22–26, 62.

_____. "Reviving the Connected View." *Commonweal* 106 (February 2, 1979): 42–48.

Rudolph, Frederick. *The American College and University.* New York: Vintage, 1962.

_____. *Curriculum: A History of the American Undergraduate Course of Study Since 1636.* San Francisco: Jossey-Bass, 1977.

Schachner, Nathan. *The Medieval Universities.* New York: A. S. Barnes and Company, 1962.

Schmidt, George P. *The Liberal Arts College: A Chapter in American Cultural History.* New Brunswick, New Jersey: Rutgers University Press, 1957.

Van Doren, Mark. *Liberal Education.* Boston: Beacon Press, 1959.

Veysey, Laurence R. *The Emergence of the American University.* Chicago: The University of Chicago, 1965.

CHAPTER 7

RECURRING DEBATES ABOUT THE COLLEGE CURRICULUM

JOAN S. STARK AND LISA R. LATTUCA

Influences Create a Complex Educational Environment

Curricular planning in American higher education has been characterized by periodically recurring debates about key issues, superimposed on a long-term trend toward diversification of institutions, educational missions, students, and programs. The debates have been created by influences acting on the educational environment from outside colleges as well as within them. These influences have modified the educational environment substantially during the relatively short history of American higher education; consequently, the perspectives of educators and the academic plans they create have also evolved. Educators have responded to external influences somewhat more frequently than they have initiated change.

Current and historical influences that shape the educational environment can be categorized into external, organizational, and internal influences. To illustrate, external influence may be felt from changes in the nation's economy and from state governing board mandates. Organizational influences may come from missions assigned to an academic program by a higher level of authority in a college or from a change in the program's resource allocation. Internal influences stem from changes in faculty expertise or faculty decisions about teaching newly emerging knowledge. These are just a few examples of the many influences that affect the educational environment today. Because academic plans are constructed within an educational environment, it is important to acknowledge the complex set of influences that causes the environment to change (see Figure 7-1).

To place today's influences in historical perspective, we have identified recurring debates about persistent issues, and have interpreted the debates in terms of the elements of an academic plan. We have also provided timelines showing our estimates of periods of intense debate for each issue discussed. The key debates since the Civil War period that have shaped today's courses of study inform our understanding of the current college curriculum and of recent reform efforts. Some of today's proposals seem aimed, in the short run at least, at increasing the homogeneity of higher education rather than sustaining the long-term trend toward diversification. Historical perspective helps us to recognize that this may be but a short-term event within the greater trend toward diversity. Our discussion of the historical background of each periodic debate is necessarily brief.

The trend toward diversification—of institutional missions, of students, of academic programs, and of financial support and accountability—is reflected in changes that have occurred over time to

Source: "Recurring Debates About the College Curriculum," by Joan S. Stark and Lisa R. Lattuca, reprinted from *Shaping the College Curriculum: Academic Plans in Action*, 1997, Allyn and Bacon.

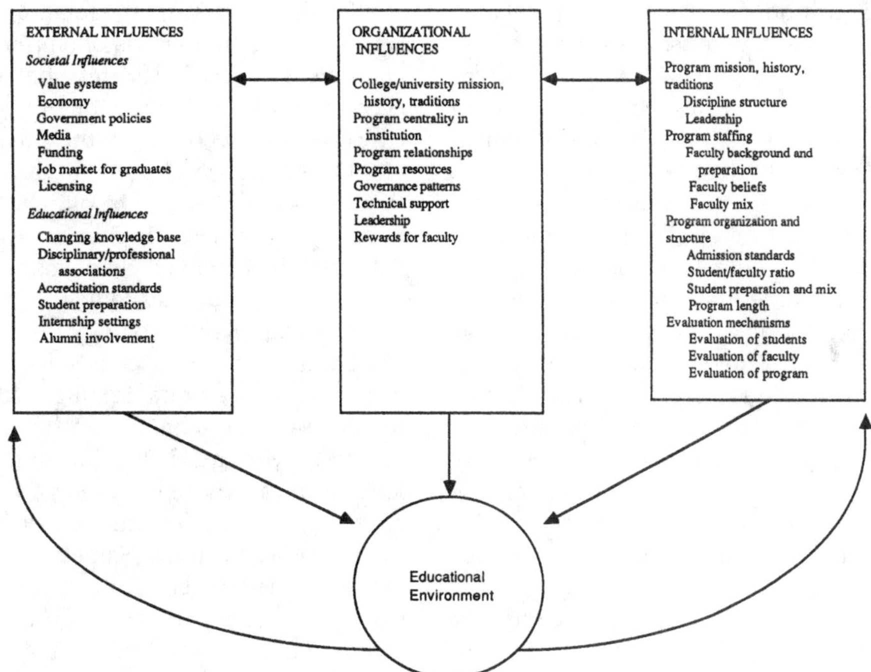

Figure 7-1 Influences on Educational Environments.

specific elements of the academic plan (purpose, content, sequence, learners, instructional resources, instructional process, and evaluation). Thus, while most issues related to developing academic plans have surfaced at several periods, the discussions are not the same each time. Some have likened curriculum at all levels of American education to a swinging pendulum because of apparently recurring patterns (see, for example, Cuban, 1990; Hansen & Stampen, 1993; SREB, 1979). Like a pendulum, history may repeat itself, but never exactly.

The three types of influences on the curriculum—internal, organizational, and external—are not, of course, independent of each other. For example, we have classified accrediting agencies as an influence external to a given academic program and faculty influences as internal. Yet both regional and specialized accrediting agencies comprise groups of colleges and programs that voluntarily conform to particular standards, and most examiners are faculty. Thus, accrediting is strongly influenced by faculty expertise; and while the accrediting process is usually viewed as external, it is not entirely so. When we speak of accreditation we are speaking of the interaction of external and internal influences. We also focus on a single direction of influence—from society (external) to higher education (internal and organizational), rather than the reverse. Yet colleges do help to shape society just as society shapes the academic plans developed by colleges. Such a discussion would exceed our scope here since our primary interest is the development and improvement of academic plans, not societal change.

Although our attempt to categorize influences simplifies discussion and helps to keep us aware of the varied influences acting on curriculum and their importance, it also highlights the complexity, interrelatedness, and countercurrents of the influences as they ebb and flow. Such complexity constantly reminds us that developing or analyzing academic plans in the American educational environment is not a simple task.

Patterns of Curriculum Debate

In the foreword to Rudolph's *Curriculum: A History of the American Course of Study since 1636*, Clark Kerr (1977, p. x) observed that curriculum is the battleground on which society debates education. Because we focused our attention on topics closely allied with elements of the academic plan, the five debates we have identified for discussion are similar to, but not identical with, Kerr's list of key battles.

Our first discussion focuses on educational *purpose* and includes debates about whether education should be general or vocationally-oriented, whether undergraduates should pursue only broad education or should specialize, and whether education should transmit a common view of culture or one adapted to include students' varied cultural backgrounds and interests. Kerr subsumed most of these discussions under the rubric of "general education versus specialized study." These debates have coincided with a trend toward increasing diversity in institutions and educational missions.

Our second discussion focuses on a series of external influences that have fostered increasing diversity of *learners*. This discussion encompasses the debates Kerr labeled "elitism versus egalitarianism" and "mass versus individualized education." Although it is difficult to document and attribute deliberate periods of elitism, we have identified alternating periods of relatively stronger and weaker emphasis on access and, perhaps, periodic neglect of the expanding pool of students. Debates about access, however, must be viewed in the context of a long-term trend toward broadened access.

Third, we discuss *content* by examining the debate Kerr called "prescription versus choice." With the rapid proliferation of knowledge, academic programs and courses have also changed, but not without considerable debate about the necessity and desirability of those changes. This debate, of course, also involves questions of institutional mission as well as the balance between general and specialized education.

Our fourth topic, *instructional process*, describes relatively few periods of modest educational experimentation at the course, program, and college level. We address experiments with instructional processes and structural arrangements, of which the one Kerr singled out ("subject-based versus competency-based education") is but one example. However, after only modest change thus far, the pace of change in instructional process is escalating as the information revolution continues.

Finally, we discuss the relation of these four sets of debates to periods of emphasis on *evaluation and adjustment*. Society has emphasized accountability—whether for funds or "quality control"—many times in the past. Often this emphasis has been intended to change the direction or pace of change. Despite these occasional periods of emphasis, higher education evaluation and adjustment mechanisms have remained idiosyncratic and unsystematic.

Although Kerr's analogy of the curriculum as a battleground for society's debates is appealing, the analogy of navigating a ship may better portray how changes in curriculum have occurred over time. Diversification has been the long-term direction, but along the way society and educators have suggested periodic adjustments and corrections. Sometimes the demand for adjustment has been intense and urgent, possibly resulting in overcorrections. At other times change has been a gradual veering. The most significant undulations in the intensity of debate about change have been produced by external influences; intensity has increased with societal turbulence related to financial developments (such as economic depression), technological developments (the industrial and information revolutions), international economic competition, and international or domestic conflicts (wars or police actions). Relatively speaking, the debates produced by internal influences within colleges have been mere flutters and the changes less dramatic, sometimes intensifying and sometimes retarding corrections sought by society. Meanwhile, overall, the course toward greater diversity in curriculum has continued.

The Educational Purpose Issue: Debating the Balance of General and Specialized Studies

Periodic debate has accompanied the gradual change from education designed with a common purpose—to prepare young men for gentlemanly status—to education to prepare today's students of all ages for useful life and work. The debate was initially inspired by changing societal needs, but it also reflected the tension between students' backgrounds, interests, and precollege preparation, on the one hand, and professors' judgments about the preservation, transmission, and creation of knowledge on the other. Figure 7-2 shows some of the periods

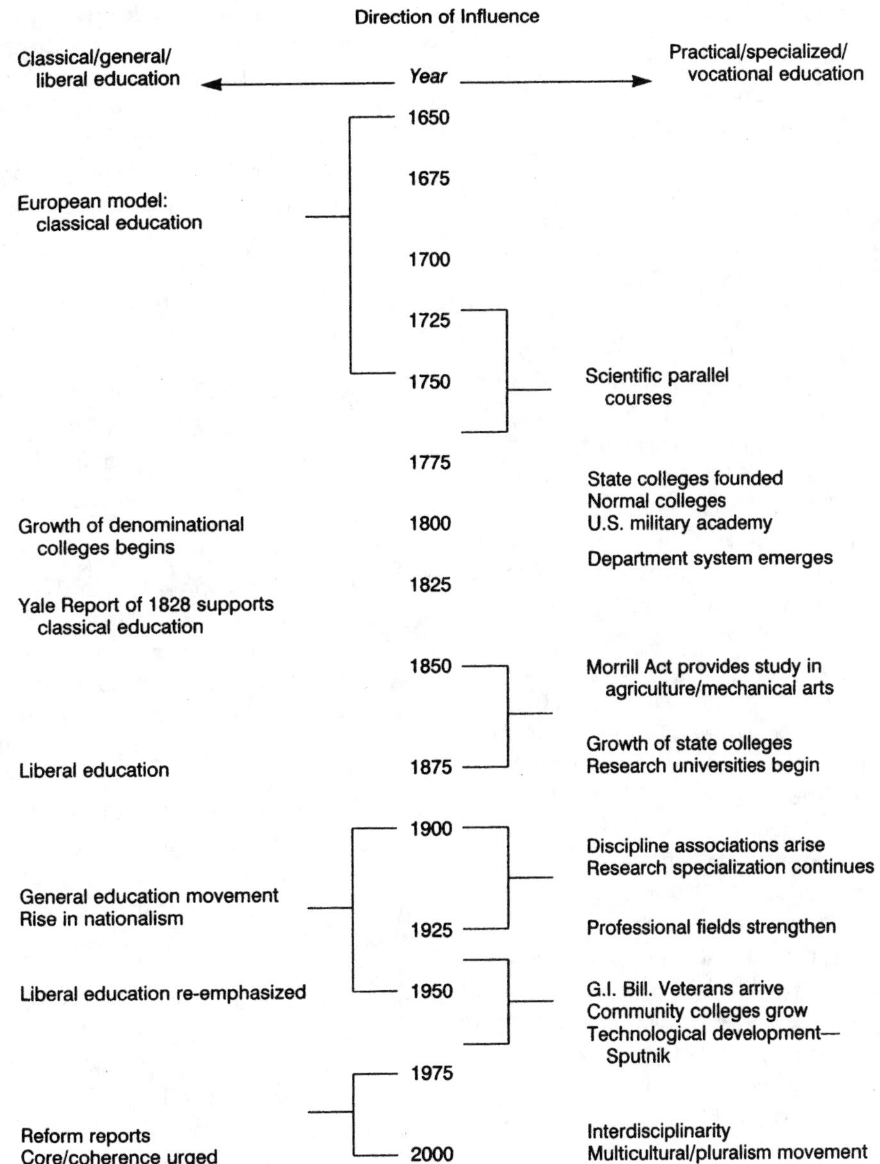

Figure 7-2 Periods of Emphasis on General and Specialized Education.

when general and specialized education have been emphasized during American higher education history.

The debate over educational purposes has been accompanied (and perhaps encouraged) by the evolution of distinctly different types of higher education institutions, including technical schools, liberal arts colleges, state universities, private two-year colleges, community colleges, and research universities. In fall 1993, 3,632 four-year and two-year collegiate institutions existed in the fifty United States, each slightly different from the others in its educational purpose or mission (*Chronicle of Higher Education Almanac,* 1995, p. 17). Postsecondary education also includes from 5,000 to 7,000 career or specialized schools, enrolling over 5.5 million students, which we will not include in our discussion. ("Characteristics of the Nation's," 1993, p. 11, Table 2).

Three Missions Solidify

Discussion of general versus specialized educational purposes became polarized at the end of the nineteenth century, when three types of college missions could be clearly distinguished. The first was a utilitarian mission, based on the belief that colleges should train citizens to participate in the nation's economic and commercial life. Institutions espousing this type of mission offered programs characterized by career-oriented programs, particularly studies like business and science, buttressed by general education electives. The Morrill Land-Grant Act of 1862 provided the framework for large numbers of state institutions, particularly those stressing agriculture, to follow this model. By the 1920s, teacher education and other occupationally useful fields, like business and engineering (of interest primarily to male students) and social work and nursing (demanded primarily by women), began to move into four-year colleges and universities, particularly in state-sponsored institutions. Today, many state colleges still emphasize a mission of practical education and social improvement through economic growth and upward mobility. These colleges attempt to meet the practical educational needs of their regional constituencies, providing relatively open access to training in the skilled professions and service in matters of civic concern, including the education of teachers. State colleges have now been joined in this mission by some "comprehensive" private colleges with varied programs. While the state colleges accepted liberal arts education to buttress career programs, many private comprehensives added preprofessional and occupational majors to supplement liberal arts programs. In search of varied funding sources and clienteles, some of these new comprehensives, both public and private, have developed large "extension" programs serving students far from their home campuses.

The research university, patterned after the German model and dedicated to the production of new knowledge, espoused another type of mission. In its purest form, the research mission had little place or need for undergraduates. However, financial concerns and faculty sentiment convinced most universities to retain their undergraduate programs rather than become exclusively research institutes serving only graduate students. This group of institutions now includes not only the universities that have historically pursued new knowledge, but also an increasing number of doctorate-granting universities, including some that evolved from state colleges. The research universities, both public and private, continue to devote large segments of their resources to the discovery of new knowledge, both in the arts and sciences and in the many professional fields that now make up separate colleges within the universities. Although undergraduate students typically constitute less than half of their enrollment, the prestige of research activities and advanced degrees often draws students interested in specialized study with research-oriented professors. The tension between general and specialized study is exacerbated when some faculty groups try to stem early undergraduate specialization, while other groups advocate it.

A third mission, especially prominent just before the turn of the century, grew from the previous classical model of education and evolved into today's liberal arts model. This mission, and the resulting curriculum, stressed understanding and improving society more than the "classic" education offered earlier. Above all else, however, the liberal arts movement sustained the faculty belief in classical education. Today, the belief remains strong that studying the liberal arts, including classic authors, improves students' ability to think, to appreciate knowledge, and to serve. These abilities, in turn, are believed to transfer to other tasks and settings, allowing graduates to serve society. Thus, many of these colleges specifically prepare students for entrance into professional schools, such as law and medicine. Prototypic liberal arts colleges maintain their mission of educating students to think critically about many subjects and ideas thereby producing broadly educated citizens, some of whom will seek more advanced specialized study. Most of these colleges discourage early specialization, particularly in vocational fields.

As knowledge expanded rapidly, faculty members in all three types of institutions became more interested in advancing new specializations and less concerned with defending the existing classical course with its emphasis on rhetoric, ancient languages and moral philosophy. Departments emerged to organize the curriculum, and close associations of scholars in similar fields motivated faculty members to stay on the forefront of knowledge. (Harvard and the University of Virginia are both said to have created the first academic departments around 1825.) Thereafter, it became possible for students, too, to specialize, expanding their broad education to include concentration in a single field. The last half of the nineteenth century saw an increase in the number of subjects being taught, the emergence of new fields like science and psychology, and increasingly more social and technological needs to be filled. The development of majors in these new subjects helped focus students' academic programs. The major field is said to have been created partly to stem the rising tide of student free choice of courses in the late 1800s and has become an important component of education in nearly all four-year colleges.

Despite the early introduction of Harvard Law School in 1817, most colleges did not include professional schools as we know them today until early in the twentieth century when the prestigious professions of medicine, dentistry, and law joined the university. These fields and their foundation disciplines in the sciences and social sciences gained stronger footholds in the college curriculum as the knowledge base for such professions expanded.

The Twentieth Century

After 1900, the pendulum swung back, again emphasizing general education. Faculty groups reacted to the threat of overspecialization by launching a period of general education reform in the first thirty years of the 1900s (Bell, 1966). Between 1915 and 1935 the number of courses in social ethics increased, reminiscent of the eighteenth century's emphasis on moral philosophy. The rise of international communism and World War I increased awareness of political ferment abroad. Ideological discussions again joined technical discussions in college classrooms. During the Great Depression of 1929–1932, students, faced with a dismal job market, wanted career flexibility, and also began to reduce specialization by majoring in more general fields.

In 1945, Harvard University produced *General Education in a Free Society,* popularly called the Harvard "Redbook," which focused on citizens' need for general education. It came just when World War II had pressed the curriculum again toward specialization. The President's Commission on Higher Education in 1947 called for balance: "Colleges must find the right relationship between specialized training on the one hand, aiming at a thousand different careers, and the transmission of a common cultural heritage toward a common citizenship on the other" (Zook, 1948, p. 49).

From the 1950s to the 1970s, specialization was again in vogue, fueled by the enormous needs during World War II for technological development, the practical outlook of the career-oriented returning veterans, and the fear of obsolescence generated by the Russian launching of Sputnik in October 1957. Even private colleges formerly devoted to the liberal arts introduced new career-oriented majors in an attempt to keep up with technology and to maintain their share of the student market.

A new type of institution, the two-year community college, began before 1910 but developed most rapidly after 1940, offering occupational studies and diversifying college missions even further. The community colleges, originally designed to provide academic foundations for students planning to transfer to four-year institutions, began to provide short-term and long-term vocational training of types previously provided by employers. These colleges meet the needs of local communities and employers for vocational programs as distinctive as horticulture, welding, refrigeration technology, or animal training. Local influences, which once encouraged denominational colleges to focus on the classics, now encourage specialized occupational programs for community colleges.

Finally, like comprehensive colleges, community colleges also defined service to their communities as part of their mission, offering leisure-time pursuits for senior citizens. Increasingly, they have contracted with local businesses to offer professional development courses tailored to employees specific needs. Some offer programs for adult members of the community with special needs who are beyond the age of eligibility for secondary school services. The missions of community colleges overlaps somewhat with those of other undergraduate institutions. Two-year and four-year colleges compete in many areas, particularly for students who wish to specialize in occupational programs.

Current Diversity

The Carnegie classification, developed in the mid-1970s and revised in 1987 and again in 1994, provides a snapshot of existing colleges and universities that is relevant to discussing curriculum because it is based on the major missions we have described: the types of academic degrees granted, the numbers of professional programs offered, and the amounts of external research funds obtained and spent. Within the subpopulation of liberal arts colleges, the college's selectivity in choosing its student body is also a criterion for classification. After these variables have formed the basic categories, the Carnegie classification further subdivides colleges by private and public sponsorship as shown in Table 7-1.

The types of available specializations, like the types of colleges, have diversified and proliferated. In 1991–1992, 1,136,553 bachelor's degrees were granted (*Chronicle of Higher Education Almanac*, 1994, p. 31) (In addition to the commonly known Bachelor of Arts and Bachelor of Science degrees, there are many additional types of bachelor's degrees, ranging from the B.Mus. (music) to the B.B.A. (business administration) and the B.S.W. (social work). Table 7-2 describes the percentage of all undergraduate degrees conferred in various specializations in 1989–1990.

The wide scope of content subjects taught in two-year and four-year institutions can be grasped by reviewing the U.S. Office of Education coding system that colleges use to report their majors, courses taught and degrees granted. This comprehensive system, the Integrated Postsecondary Education Data System (IPEDS), classifies and describes courses and programs currently offered in postsecondary schools of all types. The main categories of this system are shown in Table 7-3.

In four-year college programs, academic specializations within the arts and sciences are of four types: an academic discipline major (typically intended to prepare students for graduate

TABLE 7-1
Carnegie Classification of Colleges: Numbers of Institutions and Students, 1994

	Enrollment (Thousands)					*Number of Institutions*				
					Percentage					*Percentage*
Type of Institution	*Total*	*Public*	*Private*	*Public*	*of Total*	*Total*	*Public*	*Private*	*Public*	*of Total*
Total	15,263	12,072	3,191	79.1	100.0	3,595	1,576	2,019	43.8	100.0
Doctorate-granting institutions:	3,981	3,111	869	78.2	26.1	151	85	85	64.0	6.6
Research universities I	2,030	1,652	379	81.3	13.3	88	59	29	67.0	2.5
Research universities II	641	488	153	76.2	4.2	37	26	11	70.3	1.0
Doctoral universities I	658	467	191	70.9	4.3	51	28	23	54.9	1.4
Doctoral universities II	651	505	147	77.5	4.3	60	38	22	63.3	1.7
Master's colleges and universities**:	3,139	2,291	848	73.0	20.6	529	275	254	52.0	14.7
Master's colleges and universities I	2,896	2,177	719	75.2	19.0	435	249	186	57.2	12.1
Master's colleges and universities II	243	114	129	46.9	1.6	94	26	68	27.7	2.6
Baccalaureate colleges***:	1,053	275	777	26.2	6.9	637	86	551	13.5	17.7
Baccalaureate colleges I	268	20	248	7.5	1.8	166	7	159	4.2	4.6
Baccalaureate colleges II	784	255	529	32.5	5.1	471	79	392	16.8	13.1
Associate of arts colleges	6,527	6,234	292	95.5	42.8	1,471	963	508	65.5	40.9
Specialized institutions	548	145	404	26.4	3.6	693	72	621	10.4	19.3
Tribal colleges and universities*	15	15	0	100.0	0.1	29	29	0	100.0	0.8

Source: From *A Classification of Institutions of Higher Education.* Princeton, NJ: The Carnegie Foundation for the Advancement of Teaching, 1994, p. xiv. Enrollment figures are adapted from U.S. National Center for Education Statistics data. Copyright 1994, The Carnegie Foundation for the Advancement of Teaching. Reprinted with permission.

Note: Enrollments are rounded to the nearest 1,000.
*Figure excludes institutions with unavailable enrollment figures.
**Formerly called "comprehensive colleges" and universities.
***Formerly called "liberal arts colleges."

TABLE 7–2
Undergraduate Degrees Conferred in 1989–1990, by Major Specialization

	Associate Degrees N=429,946	*(percent)*	*Bachelors Degrees N=1,015,239*
Agriculture and natural resources	1.1		1.3
Architecture and environmental design	0.4		0.9
Area and ethnic studies	—*		0.4
Business and management	24.8		24.3
Communications	0.9		4.8
Computer and information science	1.8		3.0
Education	1.7		9.6
Engineering	13.0		0.4
Fine and applied arts	3.0		3.7
Foreign languages	—		1.1
Health professions	13.8		5.8
Home economics	2.4		1.4
Law	0.9		0.1
Letters	.01		4.9
Library science	—		—
Life sciences	0.2		3.6
Mathematics	0.2		1.5
Military science	—		—
Physical sciences	0.5		1.7
Psychology	0.3		4.8
Public affairs and services	3.9		3.4
Social sciences	0.6		10.6
Theology	0.1		0.5
Interdisciplinary studies	30.2		4.1
Total	99.8		99.9

Source: From *Race/Ethnicity Trends in Degrees Conferred by Institutions of Higher Education: 1978–79 through 1988–89,* National Center for Education Statistics, Table 8.

Notes:
*<.01
Types of degrees under a category may differ at the two degree levels. *Example:* An associate degree in education may connote preparation to be a teacher's aide or a plan to major in teacher education upon transfer; a bachelor's degree recipient may become a certified teacher. Some categories, such as letters, include several disciplines or subdisciplines such as general English, literature, speech, creative writing and so on. Public affairs includes social work.

school in academic or prestigious professional fields), a general education or liberal studies major, an interdisciplinary major, and a planned preprofessional major. Four-year public and private comprehensive colleges (and, increasingly, nonselective liberal arts colleges) also offer undergraduate career studies (professional) majors that prepare students for entry-level positions in diverse occupations, and two-year colleges offer more technical occupational concentrations.

The proliferation of career-oriented undergraduate majors in nonselective four-year colleges, both public and private, has provided programs attractive to students. The most common career majors in recent years have been business and management, education, engineering, and combined health professions. These choices are influenced by many factors, of which the job market is the most prominent. For example, the choice of education as a major by young women students declined drastically as opportunities for new entrants to teaching jobs decreased in the 1970s and, simultaneously, opportunities for women in formerly male-dominated fields like business and engineering increased. Some specialized programs that require more than four years of undergraduate study, such as architecture and pharmacy, are found in larger universities.

About 34% of students who attend a two-year college study arts and sciences; 20% study technological fields; 20% study business; and the remaining 25% study health, trades, and other services (*Condition of Education,* 1994, p. 84). Like

TABLE 7-3
Major Categories of Academic Programs, According to the Integrated Postsecondary Education Data System

01	Agricultural Business and Production	29	Military Technologies
02	Agricultural Sciences	30	Multi/Interdisciplinary Studies
03	Conservation and Renewable Natural Resources	31	Parks, Recreation, Leisure and Fitness Studies
04	Architecture and Related Programs	32	Personal Improvement and Leisure Programs
05	Area, Ethnic and Cultural Studies	33	Citizenship Activities
08	Marketing Operations, Marketing and Distribution	34	Health-related Knowledges and Skills
09	Communications	36	Leisure and Recreational Activities
10	Communications Technologies	37	Personal Awareness and Self-Improvement
11	Computer and Information Sciences	38	Philosophy and Religion
12	Personal and Miscellaneous Services	39	Theological Studies and Religious Vocations
13	Education	40	Physical Sciences
14	Engineering	41	Science Technologies
15	Engineering-Related Technologies	42	Psychology
16	Foreign Languages and Literatures	43	Protective Services
19	Home Economics	44	Public Administration and Services
20	Vocational Home Economics	45	Social Sciences and History
21	Technical Education/Industrial Arts Programs	46	Construction Trades
22	Law and Legal Studies	47	Mechanics and Repairers
23	English Language and Literature/Letters	48	Precision Production Trades
24	Liberal Arts and Sciences, General Studies, and Humanities	49	Transportation and Materials-Moving Workers
25	Library Science	50	Visual and Performing Arts
26	Biological Sciences/Life Sciences	51	Health Professions and Related Sciences
27	Mathematics	52	Business, Management and Administrative Services
28	Reserve Officers Training Corps	53	High School, Secondary Diplomas/Certificates

the four-year program, the two-year college curriculum may also include a general education segment, a major specialization, and some electives. But this distribution takes place in a total of 60 credits or fewer (two years if pursued full time), rather than in 120 credits or four years of work.

The proportions of various types of content students include in academic programs has been well documented over the years (Blackburn et al., 1976; Dressel & DeLisle, 1970; Toombs, Amey, & Fairweather, 1989). Studies of college requirements for students' coursework showed a trend between 1970 and the mid-1980s toward an increase in the portion of students' programs devoted to specialization or supporting coursework.

Approaching the Twenty-first Century

Many students at research, doctoral, or comprehensive universities begin their studies in the arts and sciences colleges in their universities. Even those who least often follow this pattern (engineering and fine arts students), usually must take some arts and science courses. Thus, the typical four-year college degree consists of about 120 credits divided into three parts: 33%–40% general education in arts and sciences, and the remaining 60%–66% divided between the major or specialization and other courses—usually electives or specific collegewide requirements. Because of the persistence of the debate about the balance of general and specialized study, considerable effort is being undertaken to document actual student course patterns (see, e.g., the studies by Adelman, 1990, 1992b; Ratcliff, 1992b; Zemsky, 1989).

General Study. According to the American Council on Education (El-Khawas, 1990), 86% of colleges and universities currently require all students to complete a certain amount of general education coursework. Many colleges use distribution requirements, requiring students to take a specified number of courses in varied areas to achieve breadth of knowledge and a course in English to demonstrate competence in writing and/or other communication skills. Forty-five percent of all colleges and universities require students to take courses focused on Western civilization and/or world civilization (El-Khawas, 1990). According to an analysis of the high school graduating class of 1972, students who attended college typically took more of these types of courses than the minimum their college required (Adelman, 1990). In 1967, 43% of the average student's course work was reported to be in general education (Dressel & DeLisle, 1970), decreasing to 33.4% in 1974 (Blackburn et al., 1976), but increasing again to 38% in 1988 (Toombs, Amey, & Fairweather, 1989; Locke 1989). In addition to increasing the proportion of credits allocated to general education in total, colleges were beginning to require at least one course in mathematics by the late 1980s. According to Lawrence Locke (1989), only 33% of colleges required mathematics as part of general education in 1967, decreasing to 20% in 1974 but rising to 65% in 1988. In 1992, half of the nation's four-year colleges were engaged in general education reform (El-Khawas, 1993).

Specialization. The important concepts of a major field and the methods of inquiry to be taught are determined by the society of scholars in that field. This group interprets the discipline; adapts it to society's needs; and typically is responsible for including new material, new questions, and new ways of thinking in the curriculum. The disciplinary major may be defined specifically and tightly as an academic plan if there is consensus of scholars in a field; it is usually more loosely structured if the discipline is in transition or lacks consensus on the questions of interest or the ways of studying them. Especially in colleges and universities where faculty participate externally in the scholarship of their field, the major plan also may reflect ferment due to recent advances.

Typically, the broad academic plan for the undergraduate disciplinary major follows a sequence in which the student gains increasingly more depth of knowledge in the field. It has an introductory course (which may double as a general education requirement), a set of intermediate courses, and some advanced courses. It may require a thesis, a senior paper, or some other "synthesizing" experience such as a seminar or comprehensive examination. Some students who major in an academic discipline plan to continue study in the field at the graduate level, but a much greater number finish college and seek work in varied occupations, some related to the major, some not.

An interdisciplinary major (or a double major) may combine two or even three fields of the student's choice; or, if there is sufficient student interest, a college may formalize an interdisciplinary major by drawing courses from several academic departments. Often an interdisciplinary major brings the methods and questions of several disciplines to bear on a particular problem or genre of problems. Examples are urban studies, Near Eastern cultures, or international relations.

Some colleges offer general education or liberal studies majors, which may involve greater flexibility and wider choice of courses than do majors in specific disciplines. The liberal studies major generally lacks the structure of the formal discipline or interdisciplinary major and is intended for students who wish to learn in many fields but resist specialization. In some colleges, it is viewed as a catch-all category for students who are undecided about which specific field to pursue in depth, or as an "escape hatch" for unmotivated students. Such negative reaction to the liberal studies major in some colleges provides evidence of how far higher education has moved from a general core curriculum toward one centered around a specialized major program of study.

A preprofessional major is usually a recommended set of courses qualifying a student to apply to a graduate-level professional school such as law, medicine, veterinary medicine, or dentistry. Frequently, a special advisor is assigned to preprofessional aspirants to help them choose the necessary courses and apply to the graduate school. But advanced professional schools typically do not require a specific major, so students who take a collection of relevant subjects often can present themselves as appropriately prepared. In many colleges, students are advised to study an appropriate disciplinary major in depth, rather than pursue a preprofessional major.

Students who pursue professional majors often practice their future occupation in fieldwork settings as undergraduates. In these fields, the major conveys a knowledge base of skills, attitudes, and behaviors needed for entry to a specific occupation on receipt of the bachelor's degree. Educators have long debated what to call these undergraduate majors. Some theorists have referred to them as preparation for the "semiprofessions" to distinguish them from the study of the "learned" or "prestigious" professions such as law, medicine, and dentistry. In comparison to occupational training for the laboring or blue-collar occupations, these fields seem to be professional because they require four to six years of college training. Some of the fields we include among the undergraduate professions are architecture, business, education, engineering, journalism, library science, nursing, occupational therapy, physical therapy, pharmacy, public administration, and social work. Today, more than 50% of U.S. college students enroll in these types of programs that, we suggest, appropriately may be called collegiate career studies.

Collegiate career studies often are viewed more favorably by students and groups external to the university than by some faculty members in the collegiate organization who accuse them of deflecting students from academic discipline majors they traditionally see as more appropriate higher learning. In fact, professional education concentrates on preparing students for ambiguous situations calling for informed, complex judgment. Students in such professional programs also consider questions of how the knowledge was gained, what usefulness it has to society, and how it can continue to be advanced, as well as what specific career uses it has for the aspiring professional. Collegiate career education that asks these questions differs from education that teaches students to perform specific well-defined tasks in an occupation.

Occupational majors, as typically offered in two-year colleges and some four-year colleges, help students to apply knowledge in specific and usually predictable situations. Although they may enjoy their work and be committed to it, graduates in these fields are not expected to be concerned about advancing knowledge in their occupation or about continuing to be independent learners. Occupational educators tend to be clear about the specific skills they are teaching and how to measure when they have been mastered. Performance-oriented subjects lend themselves to instructional processes based on diagnosis, grading, and prescription of additional practice to achieve competence. Cohen (1979, pp. 57–58) suggests that community college occupational programs may be conveniently grouped into three sets: (1) production—manufacturing, construction, mining, skilled trades, design, processing, and engineering fields; (2) commerce and general business—banking and finance, sales, advertising, marketing, communications, hospitality and tourism, retail and wholesale distribution; (3) services—allied health, education, law, criminal justice, public safety, and civil service.

Preparation for occupational positions may require less than two years and may take place on a year-round basis rather than in the traditional academic semesters. This preparation often addresses specific community manpower needs, and the college accepts additional job placement obligations as well as other support and guidance obligations for students. Still, colleges expect occupational majors to develop basic literacy and mathematical skills. These general education components may be an unpopular part of the program if students lack intellectual motivation.

Despite favorable federal and state funding of occupational programs to meet hiring needs, these programs suffer from some disrespect when placed in colleges. Students who pursue occupational majors in community colleges and later attempt to continue their education in four-year colleges without similar offerings, may have difficulty in obtaining transferable college credit, partly because occupational programs often are not offered in parallel form at four-year colleges. Indeed, some occupational programs require that faculty members with practical experience in trade fields but nonstandard credentials (by college standards) be hired. Yet a large portion of the student population in the mid-1990s attends college to obtain occupational training in many fields, from health services to industrial trades and office systems. These enrollments are continuing to grow. In some areas of the country, community colleges have replaced vocational high schools in serving area hiring needs.

The Debate Continues

Today, increased specialized knowledge promotes continued segmentation of occupational fields into subspecialties like nuclear engineering or pediatric social work. Sometimes such disciplinary splintering is encouraged by federal and state government to address social needs. Over 350 years, the move toward program diversification has included several cycles of diminished and renewed emphasis on specialization. In the 1990s, once again, increased rhetoric supports general studies, especially concern for preserving the cultural heritage and helping students broaden their outlooks. However, faculty cite expanding knowledge bases and increasingly demanding disciplinary accrediting agencies as unrelenting pressures toward specialized study. The specialization and diversification of academic programs surely are closely related, and both are opposed by advocates of breadth rather than depth.

The three missions, utilitarian, research, and liberal arts, still form the primary basis for the diversity among colleges, but now the debate over general and specialized study sometimes occurs within a single complex institution. For example, the concept of liberal arts as a foundation for life or further study for all college students dominates the undergraduate programs in many large universities or, as Clark Kerr called them "multiversities." Here the colleges of arts and sciences typically provide a core liberal arts curriculum before students branch out into more specialized studies. Clearly, they endorse a general form of education for all, in preference to specialization in either an academic discipline or a professional field. Yet professional schools within the same universities offer career-oriented education, and some prefer to enroll their students as freshmen. In large universities, organizational influences enter the debate, and competition for resources may be strong. As program is pitted against program and college against college in the budget process, the historical debate on the relative merits of general versus specialized study is often revisited in very pragmatic terms.

Learners: Periods of Emphasis on Access

The issue of access focuses on learners and grows from the debate Kerr called "elitism versus egalitarianism." A steady long-term trend toward increased access for learners has been marked by periods when strong advocacy faltered or attention turned to other issues. Calls for "quality control" sometimes camouflage stereotypes and prejudices about the capabilities or efforts of nontraditional learners. Pockets of restricted access are hardly ancient history; Princeton University first admitted Blacks after World War II, and Harvard did not abolish its admissions quota for undergraduate women until 1975.

The increased diversity of college students is strikingly illustrated by examining statistics over the last 120 years of American higher education. In 1850 it is estimated that only 1% of the population actually finished college. The rapid rise in bachelor's degrees granted after records were begun in 1870 is shown in Figure 7-3.

Opportunity Increases

The Industrial Revolution and the spread of settlement across the continent inspired change. The needs of the country—and thus its potential students—now included expertise in areas such as surveying and agriculture. An education encompassing these more practical subjects appealed to a broader spectrum of the population, and public pressure led to passage of the 1862 Morrill Land-Grant Act so that "every American citizen is entitled to receive some form of higher education" (Brubacher & Rudy, 1976, p. 66). America was producing a growing number of families willing to finance a son's education if it fitted him for entry into a world of greater opportunity. During the Civil War, some colleges also filled classes by admitting women, a trend that continued as a result of reformist ideals. The post-Civil War period and the passage of a second Morrill Act in 1890 made college education available for Black Americans, primarily by creating segregated colleges.

During the rest of the nineteenth century, access increased but assumptions of educational elitism remained, especially for women and Blacks. While more White men from outside the upper classes sought the education provided by the new and more practical institutions, Black Americans did not have full access to the types of education provided to White students until well after World War II. Figure 7-4 shows the periods of emphasis on access.

Improved Preparation Fuels Rapid Growth

In 1870 less than 2% of the 18- to 24-year-old population was enrolled in college (Snyder, 1993). In the same year, most of the nation's existing colleges offered preparatory programs because many students were not ready for college-level study (Rudolph, 1977, p. 160). Thus, the next

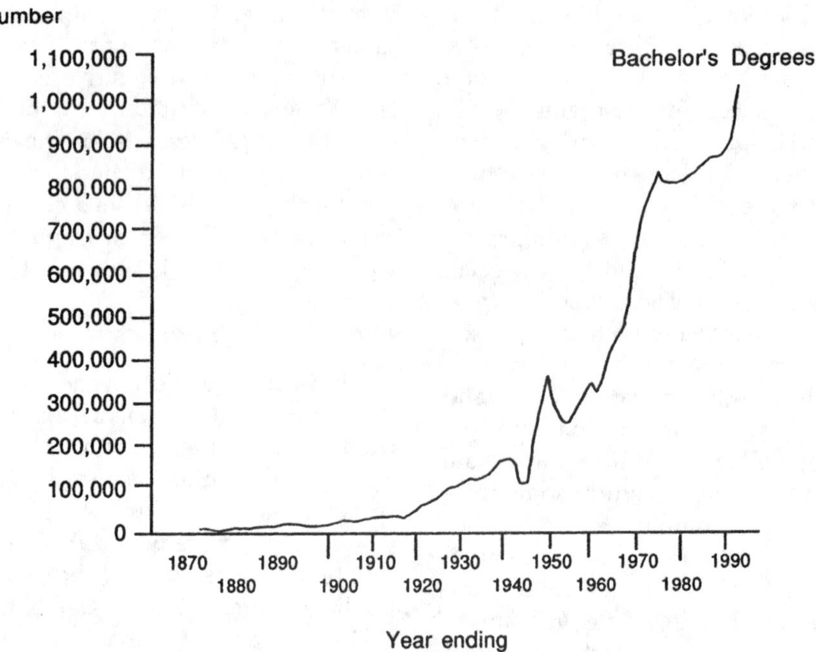

Figure 7-3 Bachelor's Degrees Conferred by U.S. Institutions of Higher Education: 1869–1870 to 1989–1990. *Source:* Adapted from Thomas Snyder (Ed.), *120 Years of American Education: A Statistical Portrait.* Washington, DC: Department of Education, National Center for Education Statistics.

period of increased access awaited expansion and improvements in public high school education. After 1870, high school attendance grew rapidly (Rudolph, 1977, p. 158). The University of Michigan developed the first articulation agreements with secondary schools during the 1870s, and thereafter the increasing standardization of the high school curriculum meant that college preparation did not require private schooling or expensive tutoring.

The influx of Jewish immigrants from Europe around the turn of the century brought a new immigrant group greatly interested in the intellectual life (Wechsler, 1977). This group swelled enrollments at colleges and universities in eastern cities and challenged them to help prepare a new professional class of doctors, lawyers, businessmen, professors, and scientists. However, in the period immediately following World War I, many eastern colleges began to limit entering class size in a possible return to elitism. They selected the best and the brightest students by using newly developed standardized admissions tests intended to assure adequate preparation. While in many ways raising admission standards was a positive step, at some universities the action represented scarcely veiled anti-Semitism. Some eastern urban institutions, eager to reduce what they considered detrimentally large concentrations of Jewish students on campus, claimed a strong concern for students' "character" and thus freed themselves to make decisions based on criteria other than academic preparation and potential.

The "Typical" Student Disappears

Although most smaller liberal arts colleges encouraged primarily full-time residential students until well after World War II, many urban institutions in the areas heavily populated by immigrants became commuter schools and established large evening divisions in the early twentieth century. World War II was, however, the most significant catalyst in diversifying college student attendance nationwide. The Servicemen's Readjustment Act of 1944, popularly known as the G.I. Bill, was stimulated by worries about the possible effects of mass unemployment when large numbers of service personnel were demobilized. Although the government assumed that only a small number would take advantage of the offer to finance their education, about 2.2 million veterans returned

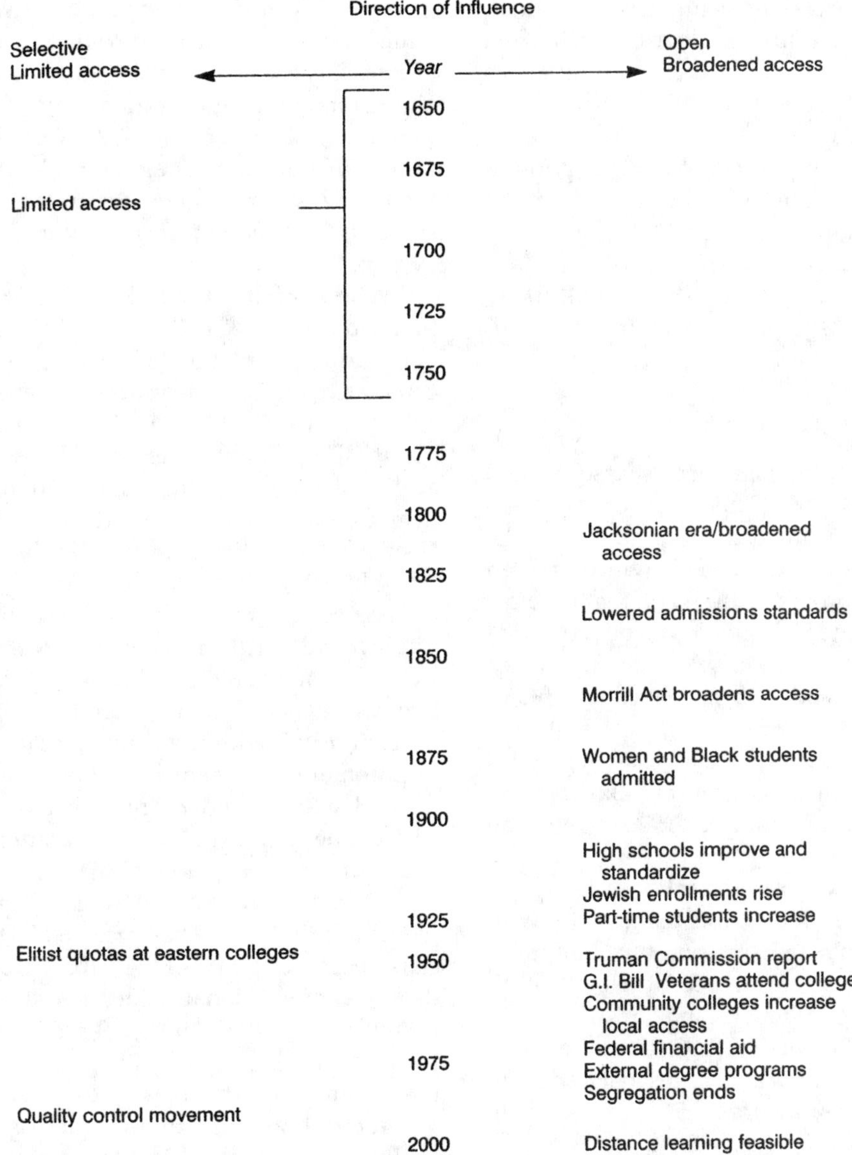

Figure 7-4 Periods of Emphasis on Access.

to college. Their attendance challenged existing visions of the typical student, required massive expansion of higher education, and paved the way for further enrollment growth and increasing student diversity in following decades.

When the President's Commission on Higher Education published its 1947 report entitled *Higher Education for Democracy,* it affirmed the usefulness of a college or university education and asserted that citizens were "entitled" to higher education whether or not they could personally afford it. Further, the report declared that the nation would benefit when postsecondary education, appropriate to student needs and talents, had been made available to all who had the requisite ability (then estimated at 50% of the population).

After the Supreme Court declared segregation illegal in the 1960s, Black Americans gained entry to colleges previously closed to them. During the 1960s, women also began to enter college in larger numbers. In the late 1960s, "external degree" colleges, or "universities without walls," sprang up to serve adult learners unable to attend formal classes on campuses. This small but distinctive group of colleges, which often award some degree credit for life experiences outside of formal education, often station faculty in locations convenient to clusters of students. An ever-increasing portion of the U.S. population has attended college. A recent study of the high school graduating class of 1980 found that 66% had entered some form of postsecondary education by 1986 (Ottinger, 1989, p. 46). Today the "typical" college student may be a U.S. citizen of any age or background.

Entitlement for Learners

Notions of entitlement and access strengthened throughout the 1950s. The report of the President's Commission laid the foundation for the Higher Education Act of 1972, which created grant and loan programs based on the principle that college attendance should not be precluded for capable students because of inability to pay. In 1972, this legislation to supply college financial aid to all needy and deserving students bolstered college attendance once more and increased student choice among existing colleges. It also led to strong federal influence on higher education.

The public two-year sector began to expand in the mid-1900s. Today, most states join with local governmental units to sponsor community-oriented colleges that account for 37% of all undergraduate enrollments and 46% of all public college enrollments. In 1992–1993, these colleges (and a few four-year colleges that also grant two-year degrees) awarded 514,756 associate degrees (*Chronicle of Higher Education Almanac,* 1995, p. 20). Citizens feel entitled to attend a community college near their home regardless of their financial resources or previous record of academic success.

Maintaining Access in the Twenty-first Century

With entitlement and antidiscrimination laws firmly in place, the final thirty years of the twentieth century are characterized by most observers as a period of strong continuing emphasis on access. This period witnessed a continued increase in numbers and diversity of students pursuing postsecondary study. In fall 1993, 14.3 million students, of whom 86% were undergraduates, were enrolled in American collegiate education, the highest enrollment in history (*Chronicle of Higher Education Almanac,* 1995, p. 8). Of the total number of students, 11,190,000 were in public colleges and 3,117,000 were in private colleges. Four-year colleges enrolled 8,740,000, while two-year colleges enrolled 5,566,000 students (*Chronicle of Higher Education Almanac,* 1995, p. 8).

Whereas only about 5% of the U.S. population had completed college in 1940; in 1989, 21% of the adult population (25 years and older) had completed four or more years of college. By 1993, 53% of individuals in the 35–39-year-old age group (born right after World War II) had attended some college, 25% had bachelor's degrees, and 8% had advanced degrees (National Center for Education Statistics, 1994b, pp. 68–69).

A higher percentage of our adult population attends college than in any other nation in the world, and adult enrollment is still rising. Approximately 56% of all college enrollees are over 24 years old; many attend on a part-time basis and live with their own nuclear families or parental families instead of same-age roommates. Part-time students recently have made up 43% of the undergraduate population in two- and four-year colleges combined.

Women made up 54.8% of college enrollments in 1991–1992. They received 58% of associate degrees and 54% of the 1,105,000 bachelor's degrees. International students also contribute to diversity. In 1991–1992, 419,585 international students enrolled in U.S. colleges; nearly half of them were undergraduates.

Yet, not all agree that full access has been achieved. Educational levels remain considerably higher for White adults than for Blacks or Hispanics. In the 35- to 39-year-old age group, only 43% of Blacks and 31% of Hispanics have attended some college, 15% of Black and 11% of Hispanic citizens have bachelor's degrees, and less than 4% of each of these minority groups has advanced degrees (*Condition of Education,* 1994, pp. 68–69). Table 7-4 gives the percentage of various ethnic groups that received undergraduate degrees in 1991–92. Although the number enrolled has reached record highs since 1990, Black and Hispanic students, who are disproportionately enrolled in two-year colleges, have also received a relatively lower proportion of bachelor's degrees than white students.

TABLE 7-4
Percentage of Earned Undergraduate Degrees Conferred on Students by Ethnic Group (1991–1992)

	Associate's Degrees (N = 504,231)	*Bachelor's Degrees (N = 1,136,553) (percent)*
American Indian/Alaskan Native	0.8	0.5
Asian/Pacific Islander	3.1	4.1
Black non-Hispanic	7.8	6.4
Hispanic	5.3	3.6
White	79.4	82.4
Nonresident alien	1.6	2.5
Race unknown	1.9	0.6

Source: From *The Chronicle of Higher Education Almanac,* 1994, p. 31.

Furthermore, composite figures obscure very different student bodies at different colleges. Table 7-5 gives a summary view from 1989–1990 for students with selected characteristics by type and control of the college in which they are enrolled (*Condition of Education,* 1994, p. 140). Clearly, older part-time students who live off campus and are financially independent more commonly attend public two-year colleges.

The community colleges are the largest and fastest growing single segment of higher education (*Community and Junior Colleges: A Recent Profile,* 1990). They will continue to experience substantial enrollment gains (El-Khawas, 1992) since technical support and related jobs—those often prepared for at community colleges—are expected to grow over 30% between 1988 and 2000, more rapidly than any other occupational group. ("College Graduates in the Labor Market," 1990).

A common target for continued attack by advocates of greater access is student "tracking." Although it is alleged to take place at all levels of education, some argue that community colleges—which were supposed to equalize access to higher education—are particularly guilty of legitimizing inequality by keeping minority students in the least prestigious types of institutions

TABLE 7-5
Percentage of Undergraduate Students with Selected Characteristics, by Type and Control of Postsecondary Institution, 1989–1990

	Public			*Private, Nonprofit*		
		Four-year			*Four-year*	
Characteristic	*Non-Ph.D.- Two-year*	*Non-Ph.D.- Granting*	*Ph.D.- Granting*	*Two-year*	*Non-Ph.D- Granting*	*Ph.D. Granting*
Attended part-time	70.1	30.8	24.1	28.5	26.9	17.2
Lived off campus	98.7	78.4	73.9	72.4	57.6	57.2
24 years of age or older	56.2	32.6	25.0	34.2	31.7	21.2
Married	34.8	19.6	14.5	19.9	20.0	11.4
Financially independent	65.6	41.0	32.5	45.1	38.1	27.7
Family income (dependent students)						
Low	19.8	19.3	14.6	21.7	20.9	15.3
Lower middle	23.8	20.3	17.8	21.7	17.6	14.3
Middle	19.3	21.5	20.6	22.5	18.5	14.8
Upper middle	21.3	21.5	23.0	14.2	19.3	19.1
Upper	15.7	17.4	24.0	19.9	23.6	36.6
Parents' highest education level						
High school graduate or less	47.9	38.4	29.0	44.3	36.0	22.7
Bachelor's degree or higher	28.4	37.4	48.7	33.2	43.1	62.2

Source: From *The Condition of Education by the National Center for Education Statistics,* 1994, p. 140.

(Brint & Karabel, 1989). One writer notes, "The democratic American system is still dogged by the ghost of Plato and the ancient superstition of fundamental inequality" (Featherstone, 1989, p. 343).

Many educators proudly labeled the U. S. system "mass higher education" and saw open access as an attained goal. Others, however, believe a period of reduced emphasis on access occurred under Republican federal and state administrations in the 1980s and 1990s, when officials questioned affirmative action policies and sought to reduce funding to support students. The critics of these actions, typically of Democratic leanings, urge renewed emphasis to ensure that all deserving students have access not only to postsecondary education but to postsecondary education of equal quality.

The sheer numbers of students have caused many to characterize the U.S. system of higher education as "universal." This term is exaggerated in that many Americans still do not attend college, but the nation has moved far from the elitist concepts of education. External influences, including several important wars, waves of immigration, desegregation, and the shift from an agrarian to a postindustrial society, have caused colleges to accept a dramatically diverse population. The nation has moved steadily from a view of education as the privilege for a few to an entitlement for citizens of all ages, races, and interests. Though more slowly, the colleges have followed.

Today, with the information society in full swing, many states are attempting to reach the last bastion of learners who cannot easily commute to campuses by developing advanced technological systems for "distance education." We may expect to see continued discussion of lifelong entitlements to support such learners, particularly for job retraining. In this sense, concerns for access and for vocational preparation are not separable.

Content Debates: Prescription versus Choice in Courses and Programs

New college missions and broader access for students have been accompanied by an increase in the variety of courses and programs colleges and universities offer. This variety has led to periodic debates about whether students should choose their own courses of study or whether institutions should prescribe requirements for all. The variations in intensity of the debate provide a very clear illustration of another recurring pattern in American curriculum history. Despite this debate's obvious periodicity, however, it is difficult to separate it from discussions of the relative virtues of general versus specialized education.

The debate between advocates of choice and prescription dates from at least 1820 (see Figure 7-5). Each recurrence of the debate includes a temporary victory for one side or the other but never a lasting truce. Each sector of higher education has sometimes settled the issue of content requirements temporarily, while another sector is just beginning its discussion. Even during periods when the debate about elective studies has been overshadowed by other topics, individual proponents and opponents of student choice have been vocal. Yet it is possible to identify broad patterns in this debate for higher education as a whole.

Pressure for Choice Increases

Several mid-nineteenth-century events fostered efforts for increased student choice in their studies. The Morrill Act encouraged elective choice as the land-grant institutions "fostered the emancipation of American higher education from the purely classical and formalistic tradition" (Brubacher & Rudy, 1976, p. 66). The Civil War era initiated new choices of studies geared to the needs of women and Black Americans.

The forty-year campaign for the elective system waged between 1869 and 1909 by Charles William Eliot, president of Harvard University, is legendary. Through Eliot's efforts, Harvard had abolished all requirements by 1898. Yet detractors claimed that the new elective system failed to guide students toward clear and coherent educational programs. With insufficient guidance, some students studied an array of subjects at an introductory level while avoiding pursuit of any subject in depth. Between 1885 and 1905, educators responded by shaping the system of general education and major/minor concentrations that is still common today. The major system, first introduced in 1885 at Indiana University and put in place at Harvard by 1910, coincided with the rise of specializations, retreated from the ideology of total choice, and, as some saw it, remedied the lack of structure and coher-

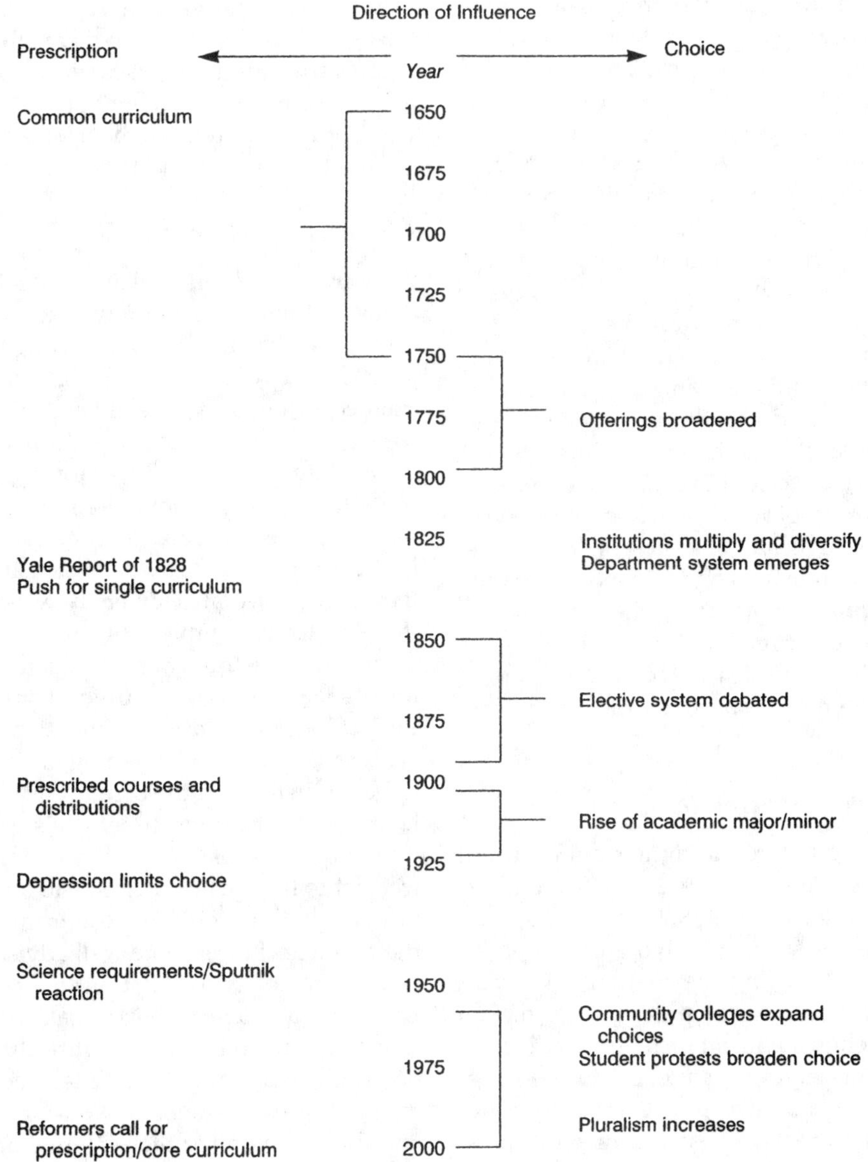

Figure 7-5 Debates about Content: Choice and Prescription.

ence that resulted when colleges abandoned all or most requirements (Rudolph, 1977, p. 227). The system of the major and general education distribution requirements was widely established by 1920.

Under this system, colleges allowed students to choose an area of specialization but required a general education program covering "distribution requirements" in subjects the faculty believed supplied important common knowledge. Departments specified basic foundation courses and other specific requirements for the majors, and then allowed students latitude to fill other credit hour requirements. The majors, therefore, could be nearly as structured as the total college requirements that had preceded them prior to the elective system. Minors were more freely chosen.

As the twentieth century continued, however, the new majors in academic fields such as language, history, and chemistry were supplemented by newer choices in career studies, such as business and education. Additional new majors like sociology and psychology grew out of disciplines like philosophy. The number of choices among fields in which to specialize continued to grow. As options increased, more educators became concerned that students share a common knowledge of Western culture and values. This view, fostered by World War I's nationalism, led to reintroduction of humanities and social science core courses and renewed emphasis on general education requirements.

Then, in 1957, when the Russian launching of the satellite Sputnik challenged notions of U.S. competitiveness and scientific preparedness, the scientific specialists had their day. Educators created more serious scientific requirements for students in high school and college, a different type of victory for advocates of a prescribed curriculum. They strengthened and expanded the distribution requirements that required students to sample each of several fields of knowledge, including laboratory science. This method of preventing students' escape from the laboratory became the norm in most colleges.

Students Advocate Greater Choice

It was not long before the tighter distribution requirements were eliminated, modified, or evaded by students. In the 1960s and 1970s, students became the strongest advocates of greater choice. Students facing the Vietnam War but denied adult choices on campuses protested curricular restrictions. With an increasingly diverse set of students entering college and a strong social-reform agenda sweeping the country, they labeled requirements as "establishment"—poisonous to individual development and freedom. Conrad and Wyer (1980) described this period as a "virtual free-for-all of the distribution approach" (p. 17). The height of student choice may have been in 1971; in this year Amherst College eliminated all general education requirements. At about the same time, experimental institutions like Hampshire College were allowing students to design completely individualized programs.

Despite many concessions to student demands during this turbulent period, most colleges retained, even if they did not fully enforce, programs in general education (required or distributed in groups of courses), a major field of study or combined related studies, and limited electives. As the job market tightened in the 1970s and 1980s, students themselves selected more structured and practical programs to enhance their employment options. In some colleges, academic credit is given for life experience, for remedial study, and for career exploration.

Choice as the Century Turns

Although checks and balances exist in most colleges, student choice today is unquestionably broad—among institutions, among majors, and among elective courses. Many students complete their education in a different college than where they began, a trend that is still increasing. But some states have acted to coordinate and systematize student movement. California, for example, has evolved a three-tier system of higher education (University of California system, California State University system, and California Community College system) and arranged these three tiers in a hierarchical master plan. Students who are best prepared academically may attend the University of California system as beginning undergraduates. Others must attend the community or state colleges and transfer for upper-division work.

About 20% of community college students transfer to four-year colleges. The transferability of courses they took may determine whether their course choices were well advised. What is called a major specialization in a transfer curriculum at a two-year college may be the approximate equivalent of the introductory and beginning specialization (intermediate level) courses for the same field at a four-year college and directly credited there. But what is called a major specialization in an occupational program at a two-year college is not often offered at a four-year college and, thus, may not be transferable.

A related constraint on flexibility of course choice is the amount of articulation between two- and four-year colleges. Faculty and administrators increasingly work out agreements about the linkages. But faculty in upper-division fields, such as accounting, and advisors in some pre-professional fields such as medicine and other health-related professions (31% of all organic chemistry courses are taken at community colleges), sometimes express concern about the rigor of community college courses and refuse to accept them. In some states this concern may be valid. Increasingly, however, syllabi are coordinated between the two levels of colleges to reduce variation in course content and level. This promotion of student access also has the effect of limiting student choice of colleges and courses.

Major fields of study also have control over courses students choose. Different demands result in different ratios of general education courses to major courses for students and also may determine the number of courses students are free to chose as electives. According to the Office of Educational Research and Improvement ("Curricular Content of Bachelor's Degrees," 1986) students majoring in both quantitative fields and the humanities traditionally have tended to take 60% of their work in their majors, social science majors about 50%, and business and education majors less than 35%. However, students often use their electives to support and enhance the major. Some majors, such as teacher education and engineering, may require a more extensive number of course credits for a degree than some others. Thus, in reality, up to three-quarters of a student's coursework may be taken in the major and closely related fields, with only a third or less in general education. Many educators lament the fact that students manage to avoid studying some fields, especially sciences and mathematics. Some are particularly concerned about the foreclosure of opportunities for some ethnic groups because, while choices may theoretically exist, students are poorly prepared to choose and succeed in courses in these fields. Some ethnic and gender-related patterns are illustrated in Table 7-6.

More often than educators would like, students' choices are limited by their previous preparation and academic success. Because most community colleges have open-door admissions policies, they are somewhat more likely than four-year colleges to offer compensatory programs for students who need to develop basic skills before or concurrent with college work. Ninety percent of two-year colleges offer at least one remedial course ("College-Level Remedial Education," 1989). In most colleges, enrollment in these developmental or remedial programs is voluntary, but a few well-known colleges like Miami-Dade Community College require students to acquire basic skills before taking courses that require their use.

TABLE 7-6
Percent of Bachelor's Degree Recipients Who Took One or More Courses in Selected Subjects, by Sex and Race/Ethnicity, 1985–1986

		Sex		*Race/Ethnicity*				
Subject	*Total*	*Men*	*Women*	*White*	*Black*	*Hispanic*	*Asian*	*American Indian*
Arts	63.1	59.0	67.4	63.6	63.3	59.0	59.1	64.1
English literature/letters	86.8	87.2	86.7	87.1	85.5	89.4	83.9	78.5
Foreign language	36.1	31.9	40.2	35.6	34.3	49.8	39.2	32.4
Philosophy and religion	52.6	53.0	52.5	53.1	53.6	46.6	50.4	57.6
Area and ethnic studies	9.0	6.7	10.2	8.0	13.5	8.2	19.3	6.1
Psychology	65.3	60.3	71.5	66.3	72.3	60.6	55.9	63.6
Economics	52.8	59.9	45.7	52.9	54.1	49.7	48.1	47.6
Geography	14.2	14.6	14.3	14.8	9.7	10.9	17.7	19.3
Political science	40.6	43.1	37.4	40.3	41.8	42.8	30.5	45.0
Sociology/anthropology	61.0	55.6	65.9	61.4	61.8	57.4	47.5	53.5
History	63.2	64.7	62.8	64.2	64.6	63.3	49.2	55.5
Life sciences	52.9	46.6	59.9	53.9	55.7	49.1	43.8	45.5
Physical sciences	66.9	72.4	62.4	68.2	55.3	56.5	76.8	62.8
Mathematics	78.1	82.8	74.0	78.4	78.1	77.3	78.5	76.2
Computer and information sciences	42.1	48.1	37.6	42.9	40.2	40.3	46.3	35.5
Engineering	17.7	27.0	8.6	17.4	14.7	16.5	32.2	18.7
Education	36.3	29.5	43.6	36.8	44.2	36.5	24.1	30.2
Business/management	53.7	58.1	49.6	53.8	60.8	51.4	43.7	56.0

Source: From *The Condition of Education by the National Center for Education Statistics,* 1994, p. 82.

Although only 2% of U.S. colleges have a totally prescribed academic program (Dey, Astin, & Hurtado, 1989), "core curricula" based on the belief that all students should have a common experience or be exposed to particular knowledge are on the increase. According to the American Council on Education, eight of ten American colleges expect all students to complete a "core amount" of course work in general education (El-Khawas, 1988). Most of these requirements allow students choice among sets of courses in several disciplinary domains but the "core" may also be:

- A set of courses (perhaps six to eight) required for all students
- A single common course required of all students, perhaps one that spans disciplines
- Two or three required and linked courses in each of several disciplinary domains

Required core courses at the upper-division level are increasing as well. About 52% of baccalaureate and comprehensive colleges now have such requirements at the upper-division level as well as in the lower division (El-Khawas, 1992, p. 38).

In earlier days educators' prescription of content often stemmed from internal and organizational influences within the college or university, including strong beliefs about student needs. Traditionally, the periodic debate about the relative merits of student choice was limited to higher education leaders and faculty advocates of the various positions. Recently, with increases of public funding, however, government officials have frequently entered the debate on the grounds of both quality maintenance and cost containment. What was once an internal debate continues to develop external dimensions.

Figure 7-6 provides a graphic representation of the relation (and overlap) of academic programs in the various types of U.S. postsecondary study as well as how it may build on the foundation of precollege preparation. The diagram shows that there are many choices and options within the universe of postsecondary education. One cost-related concern is that the abundance of choices and options is costly and duplicative. Belief is strong in some quarters that flexibility for students to stop out, repeat previous education, and move among colleges freely is sapping public resources. Still, an alternative view persists that citizens are entitled to make their own educational choices and to learn throughout their lifetime.

Instructional Process: Occasional Innovation

Changes in instructional process have frequently accompanied temporary victories in the debate about content choice and prescription. Prior to Civil War times, faculty typically thought that students' minds would be disciplined and improved by memorizing and reciting moral prescriptions and by logical disputation. These instructional processes were based on beliefs that ways of thinking transfer from topic to topic and that educators and clergymen knew best what students should learn.

Instructional processes began to change in the mid-1800s as land-grant colleges focused instruction on improving agricultural and business production. Learning by demonstration and by laboratory practice were necessary in these more practical fields. The extension movement, intended to bring new techniques to farmers, also reinforced changes in instructional methods by serving adult farmers with distinctly individual and pragmatic goals. Possibly because few records were kept, there is little evidence that this gradually changing emphasis on instructional process (outlined in Figure 7–7) actually involved much debate among educators.

Early Educational Experiments

Debated or not, distinct periods of educational experimentation occurred in the history of higher education, notably in the 1920s, 1930s, 1960s, and 1990s. Experimentation with teaching methods was first stimulated by scientific studies in the psychology of learning, which Thorndike began at Columbia University in the early 1900s. By 1914 his idea of disciplining the mind had lost credibility (Bigge & Shermis, 1992, p. 28). Also in the early 1900s, John Dewey and his followers urged that learning be based on learner experiences, and successfully promoted course instruction based on discussions, projects, and fieldwork rather than memorization and recitation. At the same time, particularly from 1925 to 1935, experimental colleges such as "The College" founded by Robert Maynard Hutchins at Chicago and The Experimental College by

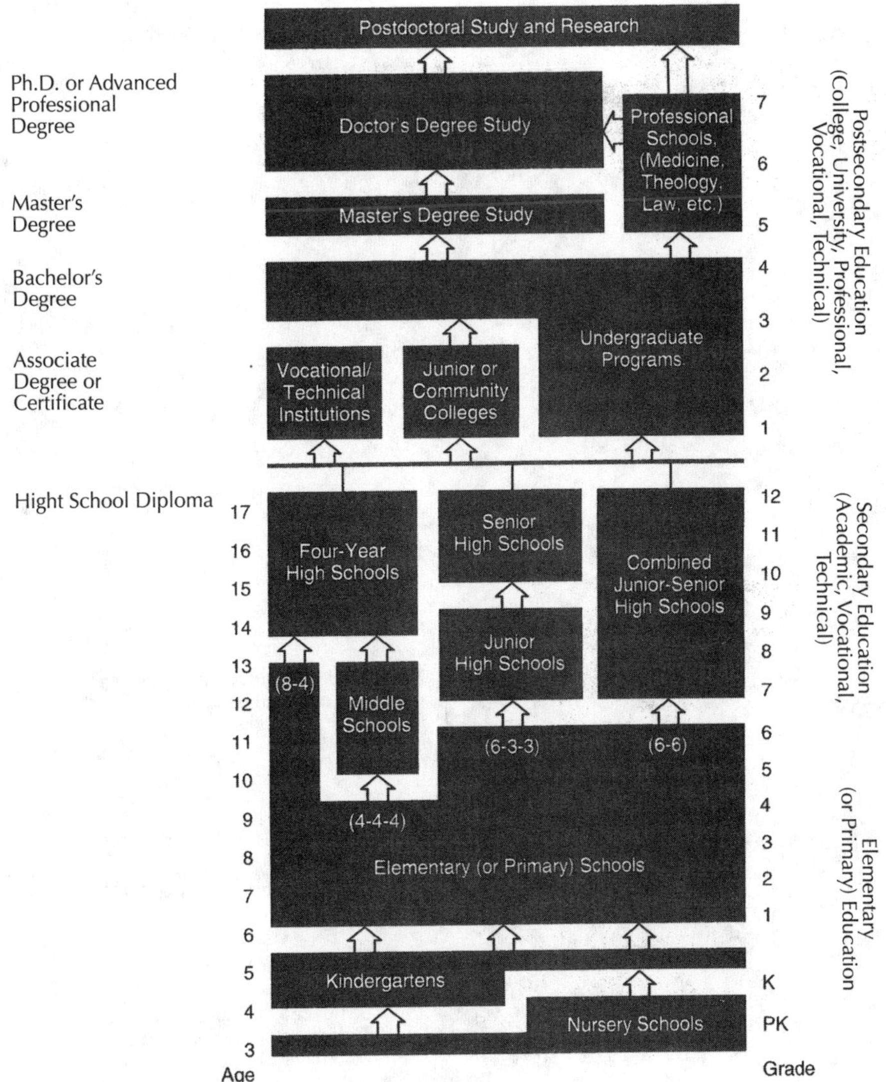

Figure 7-6 The Structure of Education in the United States.
Source: From *Mini-Digest of Education Statistics* by National Center for Educational Statistics, November 1994, pp. 5–6.

Alexander Meiklejohn at Wisconsin emphasized coherence and connection within the classical tradition of general education.

The emphasis on social values during the 1920s led to further emphasis on classroom discussion. This movement toward learner involvement was readily accepted in the lower schools; but lecturing and demonstration remained primary among college teachers. The discussion method's influence was again checked by rapid enrollment increases following World War II and, in some universities, by professors' interest in better research rather than better teaching. Individualized education became the victim of mass education as the need to process large numbers of students encouraged lecturing as the dominant instructional mode and the use of graduate assistants to teach undergraduate courses.

Student Activists Encourage Relevance and Freedom

Several alternatives to large lecture classes were tried again in the 1960s as students protested the impersonality of many college procedures. Many small colleges experimented with competency-

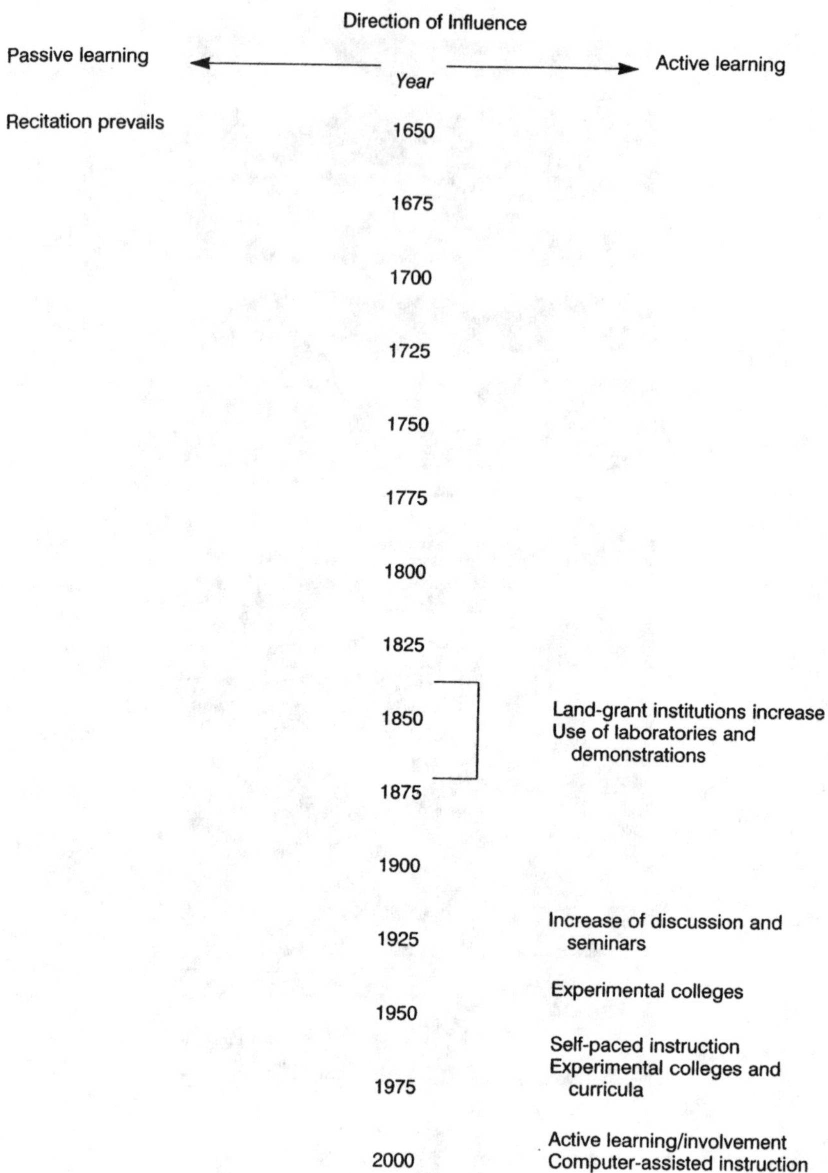

Figure 7-7 Periods of Change in Instructional Processes.

based learning and mastery learning programs like the Keller plan of self-paced instruction (Keller, 1968). Competency-based education adapted the "behavioral objective" movement in elementary and secondary schools that encouraged teachers to specify precisely each behavior students were expected to demonstrate. In colleges, proponents of self-paced instructional systems were seldom so specific; instead they believed that students should understand the learning objectives, engage a subject intensively at their own pace, and take examinations when they felt prepared to demonstrate competence. During this same period, demands for "relevance" prompted some colleges to create study arrangements that required immersion in one subject at a time (such as the one-month intensive term, typically scheduled in January in the 4–1–4 calendar system), living and learning experiences in dormitories, and more flexible grading systems that allowed students to experiment with new topics without threat of failure. While educationally exciting, many of these experiments were short lived because they consumed large amounts of faculty time and often limited students' chances for transfer or graduate school admission. Many changes in term structures or grading practices were never fully accepted, even among faculty in the colleges that experimented with them; thus, reversion to more traditional instructional processes was rapid during the 1980s. This era of emphasis on student needs did, however, succeed in making discussion of instructional processes acceptable, if not fashionable, among some college professors.

Some of the innovations, notably pass/fail grading, independent study, and student-created majors, have endured. Some instructional reforms from this era, originally tried in nonselective colleges of tenuous financial circumstances, are now found in the most stable and selective institutions. Most of the changes are structural, however, rather than broad-scale changes in philosophy of teaching. Faculty attitudes toward some of the procedural changes reluctantly adopted in the 1960s and 1970s resembled attitudes their predecessors had held in resisting earlier changes. For example, introduction of pass/ fail grading involved lengthy debates on many campuses; the final result was that students were allowed only a limited number of such grading options per term. This was a compromise that pacified students while retaining the traditional grading structure, just as earlier faculties had allowed the granting of a second-class scientific degree while retaining the classical curriculum.

Levine (1978) traced some of the sources and results of specific curricular reforms. His reports indicate periodic change in the predominant view of educational purpose and related instructional processes. We have summarized his ideas about curricular reform in 1960s and 1970s and added our own summary of the decade of the 1980s.

1960s Dominant educational philosophies were education for life (relevance) and education for personal development. Characteristic experiments included new interdisciplinary studies (ethnic studies, environmental studies) and reduced requirements including independent study, student-created majors, pass/fail grading, and experimental colleges.

1970s The U.S. college became committed to social justice and universal access. New groups of nontraditional students were admitted and, to accommodate them, variable scheduling, alternatives to courses, off-campus study, credit for experience, and compensatory education were introduced. Eventually, a strong concern for education and work emerged.

1980s This decade saw a revival of the 1940s reforms—a trend away from electives and toward greater structure. More prescribed distribution requirements emerged except in two-year colleges, where requirements continued to be reduced. Observers began expressing concern for quality and its measurement and about general rather than specialized education. Experimental colleges and free universities had almost disappeared.

Instructional Change: A Muted Debate Gains in Volume

Among educational debates, debate about instructional processes has been muted, a lifted eyebrow compared to the raised voices generated by purpose, access, and choice. Most discussions about instructional process have remained internal until recently. In the 1980s and 1990s, however, several developments have focused increased attention on instruction. One influence, largely from internal sources, was increasing support from psychologists for more active student involvement in learning activities. This view, stemming from credible faculty colleagues but encouraged by external groups such as higher education associations, is encouraging professors to reduce their dependence on lectures in favor of group processes, discovery activities, simulations, and fieldwork. Critical thinking skills, endorsed as educationally important by most faculty members, are now believed to develop less as a result of the specific course content than as a result of appropriate instructional processes for engaging the content.

The most dramatic advances in instruction, however, are likely to come from external sources, especially technology. As computers become more and more common, colleges have had little choice but to embrace them. Instructional processes will continue to change, perhaps substantially, within a few years as new skills and ways of thinking emerge in response to electronic media. Unlike earlier media, computers have initiated new forms of instruction centered on the learner as an independent agent, often pursuing learning alone except for the help of a computer program. These new instructional media seem especially likely to increase both access and student choice as well. Unparalleled changes and educational expansions, due to both development of computers and new advances in cognitive psychology, are likely to affect all of the other debates we have discussed.

Evaluation Debates: Emphasis on Quality Control

The recurring emphasis on evaluation may be viewed as a pattern of continuing discussion in its own right. Alternatively, since the appeal for curriculum corrections in each of the other debates is often made in the name of quality control or its financial counterpart, accountability, evaluation may be seen as part of each other debates we have described. When repeated debates focus on purpose, access, and choice, calls for evaluation to assure quality may be the mechanism for refocusing the curriculum. To cite the frequently used pendulum analogy, calls for quality control or accountability are often effective in slowing the pendulum or act to change its direction.

The sources of demand for quality-control mechanisms are varied. They emanate from society at some times, from educators or students at other times, but most frequently from funders of higher education. At various times during U.S. history, these funders have been churches, philanthropic foundations, business and industry, and state and federal governments. Examples of demands for accountability to these varied sponsors have always been abundant. Today, more frequently than in the past, the demands focus on the curriculum.

Calls for evaluation and adjustment can be linked to the debate about general and specialized education. For example, when educators and government officials believe that educational purpose has veered too far toward specialized vocationalism, they may initiate discussions about the neglect of general education, using quality-control rhetoric to "correct" the course of colleges. Conversely, if educational purpose seems too general to serve the country's civic and commercial needs, educators and statespersons raise issues of economic accountability and technological competitiveness in an effort to increase the specialized capability of students and colleges.

Evaluation debates have obvious connections to debates on increased access that have caused higher education to adjust academic standards. When educators and the public perceive access as too open, they blame it for decline in standards and tighten admissions or financial aid mechanisms. Implicitly, if not explicitly, the question becomes: In what ways is quality sacrificed when almost everyone can enter college? Each of these events—lowering entrance standards in early colleges seeking to extend access or increase enrollments, the development of agricultural and mechanic arts in the land-grant movement, the development of open-access community colleges, and finally financial programs to help new groups of students—has produced a backlash of concern about quality. Fear of decreased quality has followed most periods of increased diversity. In some cases, institutions developed remedial programs to improve student quality; in others, they chose to restrict access and enrollments.

The debate about choice is also related to evaluation. When educators or the public perceive that student freedom to make content choices within the academic program has become too great and that students are choosing unwisely, they see a greater number of required courses as the way to restore quality and academic rigor. Cycles of relaxed curricular requirements to provide more choice for students give way to cycles of tightened requirements to increase "rigor." The 1920s and the 1980s illustrate the content/prescription versus quality debate. In the 1920s elitism under the guise of quality control countered what some perceived as excessively open access. Subsequently, in the 1980s, calls for quality control in the form of increased prescription indirectly countered both access and specialization. It is perhaps most appropriate, then, to define our present stage in curriculum history as one in which colleges and universities are pressed toward greater prescription in deference to strong and continuing external demands for both accountability and quality control.

Government Funding and Quality Control

Throughout U.S. history the funding of all types of colleges has become more heterogeneous. As states began to provide some funds for independent colleges and financial assistance to their students, and as public colleges have successfully competed for private donations, institutions that had been private have become quasi-public, while some that had been public have become quasi-private. Indeed, interested parties in states with large state-supported universities as far flung as Michigan and Oregon, sometimes talk about becoming privatized by necessity when states support lags. In contrast, within the last fifty years, formerly private universities like the University of Pennsylvania have become "state-related" or "state-assisted." For all colleges, however, governmental control has strengthened with increases in student support and subsidies for academic research. Today, colleges face demands for evaluation and quality control from many sources, although accountability to the federal and state governments is key.

Federal support for higher education originally was very small, and, despite a few proposals, no "national" university or ministry of education was ever founded. But federal funds were channeled to higher education through special-purpose legislation such as the Morrill Land-Grant Act (1862), the Hatch Act, and the second Morrill Act (1890). With each new federal initiative, recordkeeping and evaluation processes developed to ensure that funds were properly spent. These factors created the first period of emphasis on quality control in the final decade of the nineteenth century.

The second period of increasing accountability ensued when World War II helped forge ties between universities and the federal government. Because the nation needed defense research and because it was efficient to use talent and resources already in place, the federal government directly funded research at major universities, an arrangement that continued after the war. The Servicemen's Readjustment Act of 1944 (G.I. Bill) enlisted accrediting agencies (voluntary associations of colleges) to assure the government that colleges were of appropriate quality to teach returning G.I.s with federal entitlements. While the accreditors did not exactly welcome this responsibility, they accepted it because it firmly entrenched their role by leaving quality control in the hands of educators. (For a more thorough discussion, see Stark and Associates, 1977.) Recently, the ability of accreditors to monitor quality has been seriously questioned. They remain the official evaluators, but many additional government mechanisms now coexist.

The National Defense Education Act (1958), and the Higher Education Act (1965) and its subsequent amendments (1968 and 1972) spurred the development of bookkeeping and accountability requirements. Especially after 1972, when new types of students began using tuition funds from public coffers, the federal government felt an increased responsibility to monitor many aspects of college activity and responsiveness. Research universities and colleges that accept students with federal grants and loans are regularly subject to new quality-control initiatives. Community colleges are subject to local (usually county or school district) control as well. In many states, articulation agreements between the community colleges and the four-year state colleges increase uniformity in the curriculum.

In this complex system of higher education, who can call for evaluation and adjustment in college missions, programs, and access policies? Nearly everyone, it seems—all government levels as well as private agencies—takes part in the shaping and reshaping of college missions and thus of their academic programs. As a consequence, some institutions shift their missions, their funding sources, their academic plans, and even their names in response to societal influences and financial pressures.

Current Pressure for Evaluation

The nation periodically reacts to exposure of student deficiencies with reform movements intended to tighten requirements, access, or both. An emphasis on quality often has alternated with an emphasis on equity. The 1980s witnessed a search for both quality and equity of access. Figure 7-8 shows the historical periods of emphasis on evaluation, accountability, and quality control.

Academic aptitude and achievement test data show that students attending college now have a broad range of preparation. College admissions test scores declined substantially beginning about 1968, and the decline continued through the 1970s, raising concern about preparation. Scholastic Aptitude Test scores reached their lowest point in the early 1980s. Since 1983,

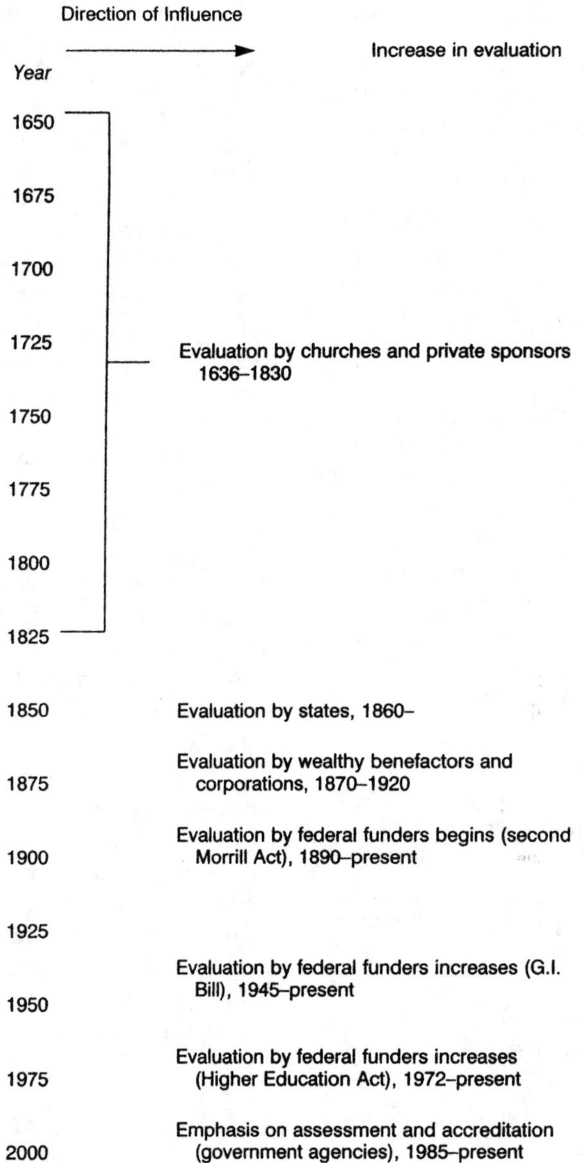

Figure 7-8 Periods of Emphasis on Evaluation, Accountability, and Quality Control.

scores have been fairly stable (verbal ability) or rising (mathematical ability), despite 8%o more students taking the tests (*Condition of Education,* 1994, pp. 64–65). There are varying interpretations of how well prepared students really are for college in the 1990s, partly depending on the data source and the period used for comparison. (For example, student self-report data from the UCLA/ACE Cooperative Institutional Research Program often conflict with test scores from Advanced Placement Tests and data from high school records.)

In response to questionable preparation, one of the 1980s reform initiatives has been to strengthen high school requirements and extend the school year; some states have reported improved student learning as a result. Nevertheless, many college students still require compensatory education, even in basic skill areas, to proceed with college work. Today's "compensatory" or "developmental" programs provide remediation that is similar to the college preparatory divisions in the mid-1800s prior to the full development of secondary schools.

The distinction between compensatory education and college-level general education is not clear even to those sponsoring such programs. In Table 7-7 we illustrate on the left the skills and knowledge that the College Board identified in 1983 as essential preparation for college. On the right are the "experiences" that the Association of American Colleges identified in 1985 as necessary for a liberal education. Because the types of experiences, understandings or skills are so similar, the difference between secondary school and college must be one of depth or focus. But the level of proficiency is ambiguous and subject to interpretation, possibly deliberately so, to accommodate the wide diversity of American students and colleges.

Although the public is currently concerned about the value of a college degree, both educators and the public feel obliged to meet the special needs of students whose pre-college opportunities have been limited. Since at least 1960, increasing numbers of students are arriving on campus with nontraditional preparation. One in seven high school diplomas recently awarded (1991) was earned through the General Equivalent Diploma (GED), and increasing numbers of these students—an all-time high of 60% in 1993—indicated plans to continue their education ("Participation in GED Program," 1994). But of the high school seniors who took the 1992 American College Testing Program entrance tests (ACT), almost half reported that they had not completed a core program in high school. This is true even though the ACT assessment is generally taken by those who consider themselves college-bound. ("1992 ACT Scores Remain Stable," 1993, p. 2). Like those mentioned earlier, these figures about student preparation conflict. Possibly, secondary school course enrollment is not a good indicator of subject mastery.

Whatever the correct interpretation of these conflicting data, in 1989, 90% of two-year public colleges and 64% of four-year public colleges offered remedial courses, and most offered college credits for taking them. ("College-level Remedial Education," 1989). Thirty percent of all college freshmen in the United States took at least one remedial course (in mathematics, writing, or reading). Roueche (1977) has mentioned a number of important characteristics of compensatory education programs and has urged that students who need them should be identified and more actively recruited for them.

Some representatives of the public argue that compensatory education at the college level should not be funded because the same education is paid for twice. Others indicate that the increased diversity and access of college education to the population is sufficient justification for serving these special student needs. According to

TABLE 7-7
Expected Understandings for High School and College

Academic Preparation for College (College Board, 1983)	*Experiences Appropriate for a Liberal Education (Association of American Colleges, 1985)*
Basic competencies	
Reading	Literacy (reading, writing, speaking, listening)
Writing	
Speaking and listening	
Mathematics	Understanding numerical data
Reasoning	Inquiry/critical analysis/logical thinking
Studying	
Computer competence	
Basic academic subjects	
English	Literacy
Arts	The arts
Mathematics	Understanding numerical data
Science	Scientific understanding
Social studies	Historical consciousness
Foreign languages	International/multicultural experience
	Values
	Study in depth

its strongest advocates, students should be offered the opportunity but should not be compelled to take compensatory education courses.

Although the public has increasingly sought quality control, colleges have only begun to develop procedures for evaluating whether the academic plans they devise fully support excellence, Public agencies are asking such questions as: How will the government know if "developing institutions," particularly historically Black colleges and universities (HBCUs), are maintaining their mission and thus their eligibility for funding? How will states know if the special missions they have assigned to specific institutions are being fulfilled? How will federal officials know that students receiving financial aid funds are getting high-quality education in the colleges they attend? Increasingly, as planners and policymakers at high levels of government bureaucracies continue to ask these questions, colleges must respond with appropriate systems for evaluation and adjustment. The debate about quality control and accountability shows no sign of abating. Indeed, this debate sparked a widespread discussion about the quality of higher education in the 1980s and 1990s.

As the extensive curricular diversity that we have described has led to public uncertainty about who is studying (and learning) what in various types of colleges, government agencies have sponsored researchers in developing new techniques to evaluate the outcomes of education. Studies of academic plans and their results, sadly neglected by colleges in the past, now are receiving considerable attention. To illustrate the range of activity in examining academic plans, we mention five types of increasingly complex and sophisticated studies.

1. Student self-reports about their academic behavior and learning progress
2. Surveys of institutional curricula
3. Studies that count what courses colleges offer (catalog studies) and what courses students select from these offerings (transcript studies)
4. Studies that not only count what courses students take but examine patterns and sequences of course taking
5. Studies that count courses, examine patterns and sequences, and relate the patterns to measures of academic achievement

Influences and Potential Reforms

Historian Frederick Rudolph characterized the curriculum as a battleground for society, a locus and transmitter of values, a social artifact, a reproduction of the national ideology, a reflection of faculty research interests and student desires, a mixture of the cultural and the utilitarian, and sometimes a creature of convenience. Surely, it has been all of these things. The main thesis of Rudolph's history, and ours, is that curriculum history is American history because of the continual interaction between curriculum and society. Social change, Rudolph held, often has been more rapid than the colleges' capacity to respond. College response has, by and large, been developed according to a pragmatic model, responding to various external and internal influences.

All in all, we believe that the relationship between academic plans and influences on the educational environment reflects a heavy societal influence toward access and toward a balance between general and specialized education. Debates about student choices among academic programs and the design of instructional processes more clearly reflect influences internal to colleges and universities. We have suggested, however, that this balance of internal and external forces may be changing as a result of new calls for quality control through external evaluation. As more perspectives are taken into account, even the design of academic plans may move farther from educators' models and more toward the pragmatic models of curriculum change.

The theoretical model we introduced is potentially very helpful in describing influences on the educational environment and enhancing understanding of how they relate to academic plan elements. The model places the development of the academic plan in the context of an educational environment responsive to society, as well as to educators. We will suggest that certain types of influences act more directly on certain elements of academic plans than on others. In other words, some parts of the academic plan are open to direct societal influences, while others are sheltered by internal influences.

Our examination of these trends and recurring debates in curriculum history will help us to keep in mind the current set of influences as we discuss demands for reform in today's college curriculum and responses of educators. Now that societal influences have increased access and choice, academic decisions are more subject to public debate and potentially more volatile. Colleges are increasingly aware of the ideas of interested factions that debate matters once left to university presidents and faculties. Over time, curriculum planning in colleges has become more political and less "rational." Yet, it is also more responsive to U.S. society and, consequently, more vulnerable to demands for accountability and quality control from many sources. For these reasons, our theoretical framework recognizes both a rational component in developing and evaluating academic plans within colleges and universities, and the more political set of influences from both inside and outside institutions that affect the planning process directly and indirectly. The rational component and the political component meet in the reform initiatives of the final decades of the twentieth century, which we will consider next.

Bibliography

1992 ACT scores remain stable. (1993). *ACTIVITY,* Newsletter of the American College Testing Program, *30*(3), 2.

Adelman, C. (1990). A college course map: *Taxonomy and transcript data.* Washington, DC: U.S. Department of Education, Office of Educational Research and Improvement.

Adelman, C. (1992b, October). *Tourists in our own land: Cultural literacies and the college curriculum.* U.S. Department of Education, Office of Educational Research and Improvement.

Association of American Colleges (AAC). (1985). *Integrity in the college curriculum: A report to the academic community.* Washington, DC: Author.

Bell, D. (1966). *The reforming of general education: The Columbia College experience in its national setting.* Garden City, NJ: Anchor, Doubleday.

Bigge, M. L., & Shermis, S. S. (1992). *Learning theories for teachers* (5th ed.), New York: HarperCollins.

Blackburn, R. T., Armstrong, E., Conrad, C., Didham, J., & McKune, T. (1976). *Changing practices in undergraduate education: A report prepared for the Carnegie Council on Policy Studies.* Berkeley, CA: Carnegie Foundation for the Advancement of Teaching.

Brint, S., & Karabel, J. (1989). American education, meritocratic ideology, and the legitimization of inequity: The community college and the problem of American exceptionalism *Higher Education, 18*(6), 725–735.

Brubacher, J. S., & Rudy, W. (1976). *Higher education in transition: A history of the American colleges and universities, 1636–1976* (3rd ed., rev. and enl.). New York: Harper & Row.

Characteristics of the nation's postsecondary institutions: Academic year: 1992–93. (December 1993). Washington, DC: U.S. Department of Education, Office of Educational Research and Improvement (NCES 93–476).

Chronicle of Higher education. (1994, September 1). *1994 Almanac, 41*(1), Whole issue.

Chronicle of Higher Education. (1995, September 1). *1995 Almanac, 42*(1), Whole issue.

Cohen, A. M. (Ed.). (1979). *Shaping the curriculum* (New Directions for Community Colleges No. 25). San Francisco: Jossey-Bass.

College Board. (1983). *Academic preparation for college: What students need to know and be able to do.* New York: Author.

College graduates in the labor market: Today and the future. (1990). *ACE Research Briefs 1*(5).

College-level remedial education in the fall of 1989 (NCES 91–191). Washington, DC: National Center for Education statistics.

Community and junior colleges: A recent profile. (1990). *ACE Research Briefs, 1*(4).

Conrad, C. F., & Wyer, J. C. (1980). *Liberal education in transition* (AAHE-ERIC Higher Education research Report No. 3). Washington, DC: American Association for Higher Education.

Cuban, L. (1990, January). Reforming again, again, and again. *Educational researcher, 19*(1), 3–13.

Curriculum content of bachelor's degrees (1986, November). *OERI Bulletin.* CS 86–317b. Washington, DC: U.S. Department of Education, Office of educational Research and Improvement.

Dressel, P. L., & DeLisle, F. H. (1970). *Undergraduate curriculum trends.* Washington, DC: American Council on Education.

El-Khawas, E. (1988). *Campus trends, 1988.* Washington, DC: American council on education.

El-Khawas, E. (1990). *Campus trends, 1990.* Washington, DC: American council on education.

El-Khawas, E. (1992). *Campus trends, 1992.* Washington, DC: American council on education.

El-Khawas, E. (1993). *Campus trends, 1993.* Washington, DC: American council on education.

Featherstone, J. (1989). Playing Marco Polo: A response to Harry Judge. *Comparative Education, 25*(3), 339–344.

Hansen, W. L., & Stampen, J. O. (1993). Higher education: No better access without better quality. *Higher Education Extension Service Review, 4*(2).

Harvard Committee. (1945). *General education in a free society.* Cambridge, MA: Harvard University Press.

Keller, F. S. (1968). Goodbye teacher . . . *Journal of Applied Behavior Analysis, 1,* 76–89.

Kerr, C. (1977). Foreword. In F. Rudolph. *Curriculum: A history of the American undergraduate course of study since 1936.* San Francisco: Jossey-Bass.

Levine, A. (1978). *Handbook on undergraduate curriculum.* San Francisco: Jossey-Bass.

Locke, L. (1989, July/August). General education: In search of facts. *Change: The Magazine of Higher Learning, 21*(4), 20–23.

National Center for Education statistics. (1994a, November). The structure of education in the United States. In *Mini-digest of education statistics* (NCES 94–131). Washington, DC: U.S. Department of Education, Office of Educational Research and Improvement.

National Center for Education Statistics. (1994b). *The condition of education, 1994* (NCES 94–149). Washington, DC: U.S. Department of Education, Office of Educational Research and Improvement.

Ottinger, C. (Ed.). (1989). *Higher education today: Facts in brief.* Washington, DC: American Council on Education.

Participation in GED programs remains high, (1994, June 27). *Higher Education and National Affairs, 43*(12), 3.

Ratcliff, J. L. (1992b). What we can learn from coursework patterns about improving the undergraduate curriculum. In J. L. Ratcliff (Ed.). *Assessment and curriculum reform* (New Directions for Higher Education No. 80, pp. 5–22). San Francisco: Jossey-Bass.

Roueche, J. E. (Ed.). (1977). *Increasing basic skills by developmental studies* (New Directions for Higher education No. 20). San Francisco: Jossey-Bass.

Rudolph, F. (1977). *Curriculum: A history of the American undergraduate course of study since 1636.* San Francisco: Jossey-Bass.

Snyder, T. (Ed.). (1993). *120 years of American education: A statistical portrait.* Washington, DC: Department of Education. National Center for Education Statistics.

Southern Regional Education Board. (1979). The search for general education: The pendulum swings back. *Issues in Higher Education* No. 15. Newsletter of the Southern Regional Education Board, Atlanta, GA.

Stark, J. S., & Associates. (1977). *The many faces of educational consumerism.* Lexington, MA: D. C. Heath.

Stark, J. S., Zaruba, K., Lattuca, L. R., & Francis, M. C. (1994). *Recurring debates in the college curriculum.* Ann Arbor: University of Michigan. Unpublished paper.

Toombs, W., Amey, M., & Fairweather, J. (1989, January 7). *Open to view: A catalog analysis of general education.* Paper given at the Association of American Colleges, Washington, DC.

Wechsler, H. S. (1977). *The qualifying student: A history of selective college admissions in America.* New York: Wiley.

Zemsky, R. (1989). *Structure and coherence: Measuring the undergraduate curriculum.* Washington, DC: Association of American Colleges.

Zook, G. (Chairman). (1948). *Higher education for democracy: A report of the President's Commission on Higher Education.* New York: Harper & Row.

CHAPTER 8

THE YALE REPORT OF 1828

Yale's leadership in furnishing the largest number of college presidents and, with Princeton, faculty members to the new colleges of the South and West made this the most influential document in American higher education in the first half of the nineteenth century. It was written as the reply of the Yale Corporation and faculty to Connecticut critics of the classical college curriculum who, like exponents of vocations, or "practical" studies elsewhere in the 1820s, were specifically opposing the retention of the "dead" languages. The two authors of the Report, which was somewhat shortened for publication in Benjamin Silliman's famous magazine and to which was added a seven-page endorsement by a committee of the Yale Corporation, were President Jeremiah Day (1773–1867) and Professor James L. Kingsley (1778–1852). Day, who wrote the first part, was officially connected with Yale for sixty-nine years as tutor, professor, president, and member of the Corporation; his successful presidency was marked by its stability, conservatism, and caution. Kingsley, author of the second part, taught at Yale from 1801 to 1851; his outstanding scholarship made him eminent in the fields of classics, mathematical science, and New England history. Their work quieted the critics of the college and intrenched the classics at Yale for the rest of the century. Not until the 1850s did men such as Francis Wayland attempt to soften the impact of the Report in some other institutions by their efforts toward curricular change and expansion.

Modern discussions of the Report can be found in R. Freeman Butts, *The College Charts Its Course: Historical Conceptions and Current Proposals* (New York, 1939), pp. 18–25; George P. Schmidt, *The Liberal Arts College: A Chapter in American Cultural History* (New Brunswick, N.J., 1957), pp. 55–58; and Richard Hofstadter and C. DeWitt Hardy, *The Development and Scope of Higher Education in the United States* (New York, 1952), pp. 15–17.

Remarks by the Editor [Benjamin Silliman]

The following papers relate to an important subject, respecting which there is at present some diversity of opinion. As the interests of sound learning, in relation both to literature and science, and to professional and active life, are intimately connected with the views developed in the subjoined reports, they are therefore inserted in this Journal, in the belief that they will be deemed both important and interesting by its readers.

At a Meeting of the President and Fellows of Yale College, Sept 11th, 1827, the Following Resolution Was Passed

That His Excellency Governor Tomlinson, Rev. President Day, Rev. Dr. Chapin, Hon. Noyes Darling, and Rev. Abel McEwen, be a committee to inquire into the expediency of so altering the regular course of instruction in this college, as to leave out of said course the study of the *dead languages*,

---

Source: "Appendix A: A Documentary History of Undergraduate Curriculum: 12 Salient Events," by A. Levine, reprinted from *Excerpts From Primary Documents: The Yale Report, Morrill Act*, 1978, Harvard Redbook, Truman Commission, Carnegie Foundation for the Advancement of Teaching.

substituting other studies therefor; and either requiring a competent knowledge of said languages, as a condition of admittance into the college, or providing instruction in the same, for such as shall choose to study them after admittance; and that the said committee be requested to report at the next annual meeting of this corporation.

This committee, at their first meeting in April, 1828, after taking into consideration the case referred to them, requested the faculty of the college to express their views on the subject of the resolution.

The expediency of retaining the ancient languages, as an essential part of our course of instruction, is so obviously connected with the object and plan of education in the college, that justice could not be done to the particular subject of inquiry in the resolution, without a brief statement of the nature and arrangement of the various branches of the whole system. The report of the faculty was accordingly made out in *two parts;* one containing a summary view of the plan of education in the college; the other, an inquiry into the expediency of insisting on the study of the ancient languages. . . .

Report of the Faculty, Part I

. . . We are decidedly of the opinion, that our present plan of education admits of improvement. We are aware that the system is imperfect: and we cherish the hope, that some of its defects may ere long be remedied. We believe that changes may, from time to time be made with advantage, to meet the varying demands of the community, to accommodate the course of instruction to the rapid advance of the country, in population, refinement, and opulence. We have no doubt that important improvements may be suggested, by attentive observation of the literary institutions in Europe; and by the earnest spirit of inquiry which is now so prevalent, on the subject of education.

The guardians of the college appear to have ever acted upon the principle, that it ought not to be stationary, but continually advancing. Some alteration has accordingly been proposed, almost every year, from its first establishment. . . .

Not only the course of studies, and the modes of instruction, have been greatly varied; but whole sciences have, for the first time, been introduced; chemistry, mineralogy, geology, political economy, etc. By raising the qualifications for admission, the standard of attainment has been elevated. Alterations so extensive and frequent, satisfactorily prove, that if those who are entrusted with the superintendence of the institution, still firmly adhere to some of its original features, it is from a higher principle, than a blind opposition to salutary reform. Improvements, we trust, will continue to be made, as rapidly as they can be, without hazarding the loss of what has been already attained.

But perhaps the time has come, when we ought to pause, and inquire, whether it will be sufficient to make *gradual* changes, as heretofore; and whether the whole system is not rather to be broken up, and a better one substituted in its stead. From different quarters, we have heard the suggestion, that our colleges must be *new-modelled;* that they are not adapted to the spirit and wants of the age; that they will soon be deserted, unless they are better accommodated to the business character of the nation. As this point may have an important bearing upon the question immediately before the committee, we would ask their indulgence, while we attempt to explain, at some length, the nature and object of the present plan of education at the college. . . .

What then is the appropriate object of a college? It is not necessary here to determine what it is which, in every case, entitles an institution to the *name* of a college. But if we have not greatly misapprehended the design of the patrons and guardians of this college, its object is to *lay the foundation of a superior education:* and this is to be done, at a period of life when a substitute must be provided for *parental superintendence.* The ground work of a thorough education, must be broad, and deep, and solid. For a partial or superficial education, the support may be of looser materials, and more hastily laid.

The two great points to be gained in intellectual culture, are the *discipline* and the *furniture* of the mind; expanding its powers, and storing it with knowledge. The former of these is, perhaps, the more important of the two. A commanding object, therefore, in a collegiate course, should be, to call into daily and vigorous exercise the faculties of the student. Those branches of study should be prescribed, and those modes of instruction adopted, which are best calculated to teach the art of fixing the attention, directing the train of thought, analyzing a subject proposed for investigation; following, with accurate discrimination, the course of argument; balancing nicely the evidence presented to the judgment; awakening, elevating, and controlling the imagination; arranging, with skill, the treasures which memory gathers; rousing and guiding the powers of genius. All this is not to be effected by a light and hasty course of study; by reading a few books, hearing a few lectures, and spending some months at a literary institution. The habits of thinking are to be formed, by long continued and close application. The mines of science must be penetrated far below the surface, before they will disclose their treasures. If a dexterous performance of the manual operations, in many of the mechanical arts, requires an apprenticeship, with diligent attention for years; much more does the training of the powers of the mind demand vigorous, and steady, and systematic effort.

In laying the foundation of a thorough education, it is necessary that all the important mental faculties be brought into exercise. . . . In the course of instruction in this college, it has been an object to maintain such a proportion between the different branches of literature and science, as to form in the student a proper *balance* of character. From the pure mathematics, he learns the art of demonstrative reasoning. In attending to the physical sciences, he becomes familiar with facts, with the process of induction, and the varieties of probable evidence. In ancient literature, he finds some of the most finished models of taste. By English reading, he learns the powers of the language in which he is to speak and write. By logic and mental philosophy, he is taught the art of thinking; by rhetoric and oratory, the art of speaking. By frequent exercise on written composition, he acquires copiousness and accuracy of expression. By extemporaneous discussion, he becomes prompt, and fluent, and animated. It is a point of high importance, that eloquence and solid learning should go together; that he who has accumulated the richest treasures of thought, should possess the highest powers of oratory. To what purpose has a man become deeply learned, if he has no faculty of communicating his knowledge? And of what use is a display of rhetorical elegance, from one who knows little or nothing which is worth communicating? . . .

No one feature in a system of intellectual education, is of greater moment than such an arrangement of duties and motives, as will most effectually throw the student upon the *resources of his own mind.* Without this, the whole apparatus of libraries, and instruments, and specimens, and lectures, and teachers, will be insufficient to secure distinguished excellence. The scholar must form himself, by his own exertions. The advantages furnished by a residence at a college, can do little more than stimulate and aid his personal efforts. The *inventive* powers are especially to be called into vigorous exercise. . . .

In our arrangements for the communication of knowledge, as well as in intellectual discipline, such branches are to be taught as will produce a proper symmetry and balance of character. We doubt whether the powers of the mind can be developed, in their fairest proportions, by studying languages alone, or mathematics alone, or natural or political science alone. As the bodily frame is brought to its highest perfection, not by one simple and uniform motion, but by a variety of exercises; so the mental faculties are expanded, and invigorated, and adapted to each other, by familiarity with different departments of science.

A most important feature in the colleges of this country is, that the students are generally of an age which requires, that a substitute be provided for *parental superintendence.* When removed from under the roof of their parents, and exposed to the untried scenes of temptation, it is necessary that some faithful and affectionate guardian take them by the hand, and guide their steps. This consideration determines the kind of government which ought to be maintained in our colleges. As it is a substitute for the regulations of a family, it should approach as near to the character of parental control as the circumstances of the case will admit. It should be founded on mutual affection and confidence. It should aim to effect its purpose, principally by kind and persuasive influence; not wholly or chiefly by restraint and terror. Still, punishment may sometimes be necessary. There may be perverse members of a college, as well as of a family. There may be those whom nothing but the arm of law can reach. . . .

Having now stated what we understand to be the proper *object* of an education at this college, viz. to lay a solid *foundation* in literature and science; we would ask permission to add a few observations on the *means* which are employed to effect this object.

In giving the course of instruction, it is intended that a due proportion be observed between lectures, and the exercises which are familiarly termed *recitations;* that is, examinations in a text book. The great advantage of lectures is, that while they call forth the highest efforts of the lecturer, and accelerate his advance to professional eminence, they give that light and spirit to the subject, which awaken the interest and ardor of the student. . . . Still it is important, that the student should have opportunities of retiring by himself, and giving a more commanding direction to his thoughts, than when listening to oral instruction. To secure his steady and earnest efforts, is the great object of the daily examinations or recitations. In these exercises, a text-book is commonly the guide. . . . When he comes to be engaged in the study of his *profession,* he may find his way through the maze, and firmly establish his own opinions, by taking days or weeks for the examination of each separate point. Text-books are, therefore, not as necessary in this advanced stage of education, as in the course at college, where the time allotted to each branch is rarely more than sufficient for the learner to become familiar with its elementary principles. . . .

We deem it to be indispensable to a proper adjustment of our collegiate system, that there should be in it both professors and tutors. There is wanted, on the one hand, the experience of those who have been long resident at the institution, and on the other, the fresh and minute information of those who, having more recently mingled with the students, have a distinct recollection of their peculiar feelings, prejudices, and habits of thinking. At the head of each great division of science, it is necessary that there should be a professor, to superintend the department, to arrange the plan of instruction, to regulate the mode of conducting it, and to teach the more important and difficult parts of the subject. But students in a college, who have just entered on the first elements of science, are not principally occupied with the more abstruse and disputable points. Their attention ought not to be solely or mainly directed to the latest discoveries. They have first to learn the principles which have been in a course of investigation, through the successive ages; and have now become simplified and settled. Before arriving at regions hitherto unexplored, they must pass over the intervening cultivated ground. The professor at the head of a department may, therefore, be greatly aided, in some parts of the course of instruction, by those who are not as deeply versed as himself in all the intricacies of the science. Indeed we doubt, whether elementary principles are always taught to the best advantage, by those whose researches have carried them so far beyond these simpler truths, that they come back to them with reluctance and distaste . . .

In the internal police of the institution, as the students are gathered into one family, it is deemed an essential provision, that some of the officers should constitute a portion of this family; being always present with them, not only at their meals, and during the business of the day; but in the hours allotted to rest. The arrangement is such, that in our college buildings, there is no room occupied by students, which is not near to the chamber of one of the officers.

But the feature in our system which renders a considerable number of tutors indispensable, is the subdivision of our classes, and the assignment of each portion to the particular charge of one man. . . .

The course of instruction which is given to the undergraduates in the college, is not designed to include *professional* studies. Our object is not to teach that which is peculiar to any one of the professions; but to lay the foundation which is common to them all. There are separate schools for medicine, law, and theology, connected with the college, as well as in various parts of the country; which are open for the reception of all who are prepared to enter upon the appropriate studies of their several professions. With these, the academical course is not intended to interfere.

But why, it may be asked, should a student waste his time upon studies which have no immediate connection with his future profession? . . . In answer to this, it may be observed, that there is no science which does not contribute its aid to professional skill. "Every thing throws light upon every thing." The great object of a collegiate education, preparatory to the study of a profession, is to give that expansion and balance of the mental powers, those liberal and comprehensive views, and those fine proportions of character, which are not to be found in him whose ideas are always confined to one particular channel. When a man has entered upon the practice of his profession, the energies of his mind must be given, principally, to its appropriate duties. But if his thoughts never range on other subjects, if he never looks abroad on the ample domains of literature and science, there will be a narrowness in his habits of thinking, a peculiarity of character, which will be sure to mark him as a man of limited views and attainments. Should he be distinguished in his profession, his ignorance on other subjects, and the defects of his education, will be the more exposed to public observation. On the other hand, he who is not only eminent in professional life, but has also a mind richly stored with general knowledge, has an elevation and dignity of character, which gives him a commanding influence in society, and a widely extended sphere of usefulness. His situation enables him to diffuse the light of science among all classes of the community. Is a man to have no other object, than to obtain a *living* by professional pursuits? Has he not duties to perform to his family, to his fellow citizens, to his country; duties which require various and extensive intellectual furniture? . . .

As our course of instruction is not intended to complete an education, in theological, medical, or legal science; neither does it include all the minute details of *mercantile, mechanical,* or *agricultural* concerns. These can never be effectually learned except in the very circumstances in which they are to be practiced. The young merchant must be trained in the counting room, the mechanic, in the workshop, the farmer, in the field. But we have, on our premises, no experimental farm or retail shop; no cotton or iron manufactory; no batter's, or silversmith's, or coachmaker's establishment. For what purpose, then, it will be asked, are young men who are destined to these occupations, ever sent to a college? They should not be sent, as we think, with an expectation of *finishing* their education at the college; but with a view of laying a thorough foundation in the principles of science, preparatory to the study of the practical arts. . . .

We are far from believing that theory *alone,* should be taught in a college. It cannot be effectually taught, except in connection with practical illustrations. . . . To bring down the principles of science to their practical application by the laboring classes, is the office of men of superior education. It is the separation of theory and practice, which has brought reproach upon both. Their union alone can elevate them to their true dignity and value. The man of science is often disposed to assume an air of superiority, when he looks upon the narrow and partial views of the mere artisan. The latter in return laughs at the practical blunders of the former. The defects in the education of both classes would be remedied, by giving them a knowledge of scientific principles, preparatory to practice.

We are aware that a thorough education is not within the reach of all. Many, for want of time and pecuniary resources, must be content with a partial course. A defective education is better than none. If a youth can afford to devote only two or three years, to a scientific and professional education, it will be proper for him to make a selection of a few of the most important branches, and give his attention exclusively to these. But this is an imperfection, arising from the necessity of the case. A partial course of study, must inevitably give a partial education. . . .

A partial education is often expedient; a superficial one, never. . . .

But why, it is asked, should *all* the students in a college be required to tread in the *same steps?* Why should not each one be allowed to select those branches of study which are most to his taste, which are best adapted to his peculiar talents, and which are most nearly connected with his intended profession? To this we answer, that our prescribed course contains those subjects only which ought to be understood, as we think, by every one who aims at a thorough education. They are not the peculiarities of any profession or art. These are to be learned in the professional and practical schools. But the principles of sciences, are the common foundation of all high intellectual attainments. As in our primary schools, reading, writing, and arithmetic are taught to all, however different their prospects; so in a college, all should be instructed in those branches of knowledge, of which no one destined to the higher walks of life ought to be ignorant. What subject which is now studied here, could be set aside, without evidently marring the system[?] Not to speak particularly, in this place, of the ancient languages; who that aims at a well proportioned and superior education will remain ignorant of the elements of the various branches of the mathematics, or of history and antiquities, or of rhetoric and oratory, or natural philosophy, or astronomy, or chemistry, or mineralogy, or geology, or political economy, or mental and moral philosophy?

It is sometimes thought that a student ought not to be urged to the study of that for which he has *no taste or capacity.* But how is he to know, whether he has a taste or capacity for a science, before be has even entered upon its elementary truths? If he is really destitute of talent sufficient for these common departments of education, he is destined for some narrow sphere of action. But we are well persuaded, that our students are not so deficient in intellectual powers, as they sometimes profess to be; though they are easily made to believe, that they have no capacity for the study of that which they are told is almost wholly useless.

When a class have become familiar with the common elements of the several sciences, then is the proper time for them to *divide off* to their favorite studies. They can then make their choice from actual trial. This is now done here, to some extent, in our Junior year. The division might be commenced at an earlier period, and extended farther, provided the qualifications for admission into the college, were brought to a higher standard.

If the view which we have thus far taken of the subject is correct, it will be seen, that the object of the system of instruction at this college, is not to give a *partial* education, consisting of a few branches only; nor, on the other hand, to give a *superficial* education, containing a smattering of almost everything; nor to *finish* the details of either a professional or practical education; but to *commence* a *thorough* course, and to carry it as far as the time of residence here will allow. It is intended to occupy, to the best advantage, the four years immediately preceding the study of a profession, or of the operations which are peculiar to the higher mercantile, manufacturing, or agricultural establishments. . . .

Our institution is not modeled exactly after the pattern of *European* universities. Difference of circumstances has rendered a different arrangement expedient. It has been the policy of most monarchical governments, to concentrate the advantages of a superior education in a few privileged places. In England, for instance, each of the ancient universities of Oxford and Cambridge, is not so much a single institution, as a large number of distinct, though contiguous colleges. But in this country, our republican habits and feelings will never allow a monopoly of literature in any one place. There must be, in the union, as many colleges, at least, as states. Nor would we complain of this arrangement as inexpedient, provided that starvation is not the consequence of a patronage so minutely divided. We anticipate no disastrous results from the multiplication of colleges, if they can only be adequately endowed. We are not without apprehensions, however, that a feeble and stinted growth of our national literature, will be the consequence of the very scanty supply of means to most of our public seminaries. . . .

Although we do not consider the literary institutions of Europe as faultless models, to be exactly copied by our American colleges; yet we would be far from condemning every feature, in systems of instruction which have had an origin more ancient than our republican seminaries. We do not suppose that the world has learned absolutely nothing, by the experience of ages; that a branch of science, or a mode of teaching, is to be abandoned, precisely because it has stood its ground, after a trial by various nations, and through successive centuries. We believe that our colleges may derive important improvements from the universities and schools in Europe; not by blindly adopting all their measures without discrimination; but by cautiously introducing, with proper modifications, such parts of their plans as are suited to our peculiar situation and character. The first and great improvement which we wish to see made, is an elevation in the standard of attainment for admission. Until this is effected, we shall only expose ourselves to inevitable failure and ridicule, by attempting a general imitation of foreign universities. . . .

It is said that the public now demand, that the doors should be thrown open to all; that education ought to be so modified, and varied, as to adapt it to the exigencies of the country, and the prospects of different individuals; that the instruction given to those who are destined to be merchants, or manufacturers, or agriculturalists, should have a special reference to their respective professional pursuits.

The public are undoubtedly right, in demanding that there should be appropriate courses of education, accessible to all classes of youth. And we rejoice at the prospect of ample provision for this purpose, in the improvement of our academics, and the establishment of commercial high schools, gymnasia, lycea, agricultural seminaries, etc. But do the public insist, that every college shall become a high school, gymnasium, lyceum, and academy? Why should we interfere with these valuable institutions? Why wish to take their business out of their hands? The college has its appropriate object, and they have theirs. . . . What is the characteristic difference between a college and an academy? Not that the former teaches more branches than the latter. There are many academies in the country, whose scheme of studies, at least upon paper, is more various than that of the colleges. But while an academy teaches a little of every thing, the college, by directing its efforts to one uniform course, aims at doing its work with greater precision, and economy of time; just as the merchant who deals in a single class of commodities, or a manufacturer who produces but one kind of fabrics, executes his business more perfectly, than be whose attention and skill are divided among a multitude of objects. . . .

But might we not, by making the college more accessible to different descriptions of persons, enlarge our *numbers,* and in that way, increase our income? This might be the operation of the measure, for a very short time, while a degree from the college should retain its present value in public estimation; a value depending entirely upon the character of the education which we give. But the moment it is understood that the institution has descended to an inferior standard of attainment, its reputation will sink to a corresponding level. After we shall have become a college in *name only,* and in reality nothing more than an academy; or half college, and half academy; what will induce parents in various and distant parts of the country, to send us their sons, when they have academies enough in their own neighborhood? There is no magical influence in an act of incorporation, to give celebrity to a literary institution, which does not command respect for itself, by the elevated rank of its education. When the college has lost its hold on the public confidence, by depressing its standard of merit, by substituting a partial, for a thorough education, we may expect that it will be deserted by that class of persons who have hitherto been drawn here by high expectations and purposes. Even if we should not immediately suffer in point of *numbers,* yet we shall exchange the best portion of our students, for others of inferior aims and attainments.

As long as we can maintain an elevated character, we need be under no apprehension with respect to numbers. Without character, it will be in vain to think of retaining them. It is a hazardous experiment, to act upon the plan of gaining numbers first, and character afterwards. . . .

The difficulties with which we are now struggling, we fear would be increased, rather than diminished, by attempting to unite different plans of education. It is far from being our intention to dictate to other colleges a system to be adopted by them. There may be good and sufficient reasons why some of them should introduce a partial course of instruction. We are not sure, that the demand for thorough education is, at present, sufficient to fill all the colleges in the United States, with students who will be satisfied with nothing short of high and solid attainments. But it is to be hoped that, at no very distant period, they will be able to come up to this elevated ground, and leave the business of second-rate education to the inferior seminaries.

The competition of colleges may advance the interests of literature: if it is a competition for *excellence,* rather than for numbers; if each aims to surpass the others, not in an imposing display, but in the substantial value of its education. . . .

Our republican form of government renders it highly important, that great numbers should enjoy the advantage of a thorough education. On the Eastern continent, the few who are destined to particular departments in political life, may be educated for the purpose; while the mass of the people are left in comparative ignorance. But in this country, where offices are accessible to all who are qualified for them, superior intellectual attainments ought not to be confined to any description of persons. *Merchants, manufacturers,* and *farmers,* as well as professional gentlemen, take their places in our public councils. A thorough education ought therefore to be extended to all these classes. It is not sufficient that they be men of sound judgment, who can decide correctly, and give a silent vote, on great national questions. Their influence upon the minds of others is needed; an influence to be produced by extent of knowledge, and the force of eloquence. Ought the speaking in our deliberative assemblies to be confined to a single profession? If it is knowledge, which gives us the command of physical agents and instruments, much more is it that which enables us to control the combinations of moral and political machinery. . . .

Can merchants, manufacturers, and agriculturists, derive no benefit from high intellectual culture? They are the very classes which, from their situation and business, have the best opportunities for reducing the principles of science to their practical applications. The large estates which the tide of prosperity in our country is so rapidly accumulating, will fall mostly into their hands. Is it not desirable that they should be men of superior education, of large and liberal views, of those solid and elegant attainments, which will raise them to a higher distinction, than the mere possession of property; which will not allow them to hoard their treasures, or waste them in senseless extravagance; which will enable them to adorn society by their learning, to move in the more intelligent circles with dignity, and to make such an application of their wealth, as will be most honorable to themselves, and most beneficial to their country?

The active, enterprising character of our population, renders it highly important, that this bustle and energy should be directed by sound intelligence, the result of deep thought and early discipline. The greater the impulse to action, the greater is the need of wise and skillful guidance. When nearly all the ship's crew are aloft, setting the topsails, and catching the breezes, it is necessary there should be a steady hand at helm. Light and moderate learning is but poorly fitted to direct the energies of a nation, so widely extended, so intelligent, so powerful in resources, so rapidly advancing in population, strength, and opulence. Where a free government gives full liberty to the human intellect to expand and operate, education should be proportionably liberal and ample. When even our mountains, and rivers, and lakes, are upon a scale which seems to denote, that we are destined to be a great and mighty nation, shall our literature be feeble, and scanty, and superficial?

CHAPTER 9

THEORY OF GENERAL EDUCATION

HARVARD COMMITTEE

1 Heritage and Change

We have tried so far to sketch in broad outline the growth of American education and to indicate the factors which have determined this growth. The very momentum of its development, like that which has marked American life generally, left a legacy of disturbance and maladjustment undreamed of in simpler times. A passage from Machiavelli's *Discourses* comes to mind in which, after asking why the Roman Republic showed signs of confusion in the period of its fastest growth, he observes that such confusion was inevitable in so vigorous a state. "Had the Roman Commonwealth," he concludes, "grown to be more tranquil, this inconvenience would have resulted that it must at the same time have grown weaker, since the road would have been closed to that greatness to which it came. For in removing the causes of her tumults, Rome must have interfered with the causes of her growth." Just so in the United States, the most ideally planned educational system would have found itself in conflict with the unforeseen forces set loose by the growth and development of the country. But this very growth, the source of the gravest problems to education, is at the same time the index of its strength and promise.

In order to pass judgment on the actualities of education and to make reasonable proposals for revising the present system, it is necessary to have an insight, however tentative, into the ideal aims of education in our society. The present chapter will accordingly consider what can, perhaps overformally, be called a philosophy of American education, and especially that part of it which is general education.

It was remarked at the end of the previous chapter that a supreme need of American education is for a unifying purpose and idea. As recently as a century ago, no doubt existed about such a purpose: it was to train the Christian citizen. Nor was there doubt how this training was to be accomplished. The student's logical powers were to be formed by mathematics, his taste by the Greek and Latin classics, his speech by rhetoric, and his ideals by Christian ethics. College catalogues commonly began with a specific statement about the influence of such a training on the mind and character. The reasons why this enviable certainty both of goal and of means has largely disappeared have already been set forth. For some decades the mere excitement of enlarging the curriculum and making place for new subjects, new methods, and masses of new students seems quite pardonably to have absorbed the energies of schools and colleges. It is fashionable now to criticize the leading figures of that expansive time for failing to replace, or even to see the need of replacing, the unity which they destroyed. But such criticisms, if just in themselves, are hardly just historically. A great and necessary task of

Source: "Theory of General Education," by Harvard Committee, reprinted from *General Education in a Free Society*, 1945, Harvard Educational Review.

modernizing and broadening education waited to be done, and there is credit enough in its accomplishment. In recent times, however, the question of unity has become insistent. We are faced with a diversity of education which, if it has many virtues, nevertheless works against the good of society by helping to destroy the common ground of training and outlook on which any society depends.

It seems that a common ground between some, though not all, of the ideas underlying our educational practice is the sense of heritage. The word heritage is not here taken to mean mere retrospection. The purpose of all education is to help students live their own lives. The appeal to heritage is partly to the authority, partly to the clarification of the past about what is important in the present. All Catholic and many Protestant institutions thus appeal to the Christian view of man and history as providing both final meaning and immediate standards for life. As observed at the outset, it is less than a century since such was the common practice of American education generally, and certainly this impulse to mold students to a pattern sanctioned by the past can, in one form or another, never be absent from education. If it were, society would become discontinuous.

In this concern for heritage lies a close similarity between religious education and education in the great classic books. Exponents of the latter have, to be sure, described it as primarily a process of intellectual discipline in the joint arts of word and number, the so-called *trivium* (grammar, logic, rhetoric) and *quadrivium* (arithmetic, geometry, astronomy, music). But, since the very idea of this discipline goes back to antiquity and since the actual books by which it is carried out are in fact the great books of the Western tradition, it seems fairer, without denying the disciplinary value of such a curriculum, to think of it as primarily a process of opening before students the intellectual forces that have shaped the Western mind. There is a sense in which education in the great books can be looked at as a secular continuation of the spirit of Protestantism. As early Protestantism, rejecting the authority and philosophy of the medieval church, placed reliance on each man's personal reading of the Scriptures, so this present movement, rejecting the unique authority of the Scriptures, places reliance on the reading of those books which are taken to represent the fullest revelation of the Western mind. But be this as it may, it is certain that, like religious education, education in the great books is essentially an introduction of students to their heritage.

Nor is the sense of heritage less important, though it may be less obvious, a part of education for modern democratic life. To the degree that the implications of democracy are drawn forth and expounded, to that degree the long-standing impulse of education toward shaping students to a received ideal is still pursued. Consider the teaching of American history and of modern democratic life. However ostensibly factual such teaching may be, it commonly carries with it a presupposition which is not subject to scientific proof: namely, the presupposition that democracy is meaningful and right. Moreover, since contemporary life is itself a product of history, to study it is to tread unconsciously, in the words of the hymn, where the saints have trod. To know modern democracy is to know something at least of Jefferson, though you have not read him; to learn to respect freedom of speech or the rights of the private conscience is not to be wholly ignorant of the *Areopagitica* or the *Antigone*, though you know nothing about them. Whether, as philosophers of history argue, being conditioned by the present we inevitably judge the past by what we know in the present (since otherwise the past would be unintelligible) or whether human motives and choices do not in reality greatly change with time, the fact remains that the past and the present are parts of the same unrolling scene and, whether you enter early or late, you see for the most part the still-unfinished progress of the same issues.

Here, then, in so far as our culture is adequately reflected in current ideas on education, one point about it is clear: it depends in part on an inherited view of man and society which it is the function, though not the only function, of education to pass on. It is not and cannot be true that all possible choices are open to us individually or collectively. We are part of an organic process, which is the American and, more broadly, the Western evolution. Our standards of judgment, ways of life, and form of government all bear the marks of this evolution, which would accordingly influence us, though confusedly, even if it were not understood. Ideally it should be understood at several degrees of depth which complement rather than exclude each other. To study the American present is to discern at best the aims and purposes of a free society animating its imperfections. To study the past is immensely to enrich the meaning of the present and at the same time to clarify it by the simplification of the writings and the issues which have been winnowed from history. To study either past or present is to confront, in some form or another, the philosophic and religious fact of man in history and to recognize the huge continuing influence alike on past and present of the stream of Jewish and Greek thought in Christianity. There is doubtless a sense in which religious education, education in the great books, and education in modern democracy may be mutually exclusive. But there is a far more important sense in which they work together to the same end, which is belief in the idea of man and society that we inherit, adapt, and pass on.

This idea is described in many ways, perhaps most commonly in recent times, as that of the dignity of man. To the belief in man's dignity must be added the recognition of his duty to his fellow men. Dignity does not rest on any man as a being separate from all other beings, which he in any case cannot be, but springs from his common humanity and exists positively as he makes the common good his own. This concept is essentially that of the Western tradition: the view of man as free and not as slave, an end in himself and not a means. It may have what many believe to be the limitations of humanism, which are those of pride and arise from making man the measure of all things. But it need not have these limitations, since it is equally compatible with a religious view of life. Thus it is similar to the position described as cooperation without uniformity, agreement on the good of man at the level of performance without the necessity of agreement on ultimates. But two points have now been added. First, thus stated, the goal of education is not in conflict with but largely includes the goals of religious education, education in the Western tradition, and education in modern democracy. For these in turn have been seen to involve necessary elements in our common tradition, each to a great extent implied in the others as levels at which it can be understood. Certainly no fruitful way of stating the belief in the dignity and mutual obligation of man can present it as other than, at one and the same time, effective in the present, emerging from the past, and partaking of the nature not of fact but of faith. Second, it has become clear that the common ground between these various views—namely, the impulse to rear students to a received idea of the good—is in fact necessary to education. It is impossible to escape the realization that our society, like any society, rests on common beliefs and that a major task of education is to perpetuate them.

This conclusion raises one of the most fundamental problems of education, indeed of society itself: how to reconcile this necessity for common belief with the equally obvious necessity for new and independent insights leading to change. We approach here the one previously mentioned concept of education which was not included under the idea of heritage: namely, the views associated with the names of James and Dewey and having to do with science, the scientific attitude, and pragmatism. This is hardly the place to try to summarize this body of thought or even to set forth in detail its application by Mr. Dewey to education. To do so would be virtually to retrace the educational controversies of the last forty years. But, at the risk of some injustice to Mr. Dewey's thought as a whole, a few points can be made about it. It puts trust in the scientific method of thought, the method which demands that you reach conclusions from tested data only, but that, since the data may be enlarged or the conclusions themselves combined with still other conclusions, you must hold them only tentatively. It emphasizes that full truth is not known and that we must be forever led by facts to revise our approximations of it. As a feeling of commitment and of allegiance marks the sense of heritage, so a tone of tough-mindedness and curiosity and a readiness for change mark this pragmatic attitude.

Here, then, is a concept of education, founded on obedience to fact and well disposed, even hospitable, to change, which appears at first sight the antithesis of any view based on the importance of heritage. Such hostility to tradition well reflects one side of the modern mind. It is impossible to contemplate the changes even of the last decades, much less the major groundswell of change since the Renaissance, without feeling that we face largely new conditions which call for new qualities of mind and outlook. Moreover, it is obviously no accident that this pragmatic philosophy has been worked out most fully in the United States. Yet, in spite of its seeming conflict with views of education based on heritage, strong doubt exists whether the questioning, innovating, experimental attitude of pragmatism is in fact something alien to the Western heritage or whether it is not, in the broadest sense of the word, a part of it.

The rest of the present volume would hardly suffice for this sweeping subject. But it can be observed even here that we look back on antiquity not simply out of curiosity but because ancient thought is sympathetic to us. The Greek idea of an orderly universe, of political freedom under rationally constructed laws, and of the inner life itself as subject to the sway of reason, was certainly not achieved without skepticism, observation, or the test of experience. The ancient atomists and medical writers and, to a large extent, Socrates himself relied precisely on induction from observed facts. Socrates, the teacher and the gadfly of the Athenian city, impressed on his pupils and the public at large the duty of man to reflect on his beliefs and to criticize his presuppositions. Socrates was an individualist proclaiming that man should form his opinions by his own reasoning and not receive them by social indoctrination. And yet, it was this same Socrates who died in obedience to the judgment of the state, even though he believed this judgment to be wrong. Again, historical Christianity has been expressly and consistently concerned with the importance of this life on earth. The doctrine of the Incarnation, that God took the form of man and inhabited the earth, declares this concern. While perhaps for Greek thought, only the timeless realm had importance, in Christian thought the process of history is vested with absolute significance. If the ideal of democracy was rightly described above in the interwoven ideas of the dignity of man (that is, his existence as an independent moral agent) and his duty to his fellow men (that is, his testing by outward performance), the debt of these two ideas to the similarly interwoven commandments of the love of God and the love of neighbor is obvious.

These evidences of a consistent and characteristic appeal throughout Western history to the test of reason and experience are not adduced for the purpose of minimizing the huge creativeness of the modern scientific age or of glozing over its actual break from the past. In the well-known opening chapters of his *Science and the Modern World* in which he inquires into the origin of modern science, Mr. Whitehead pictures it as inspired by a revolt against abstract reasoning and a respect for unique fact. So considered, the first impulse of modern science was antirational or, better, antitheoretical, in the sense that it was a reaction against the most towering intellectual system which the West has known, namely, scholasticism. But be this question of origin as it may, there is no doubt that the modern mind received one of its characteristic bents in the empiricism, the passion for observation, and the distrust of abstract reasoning which have attended the origin and growth of science.

But there also seems no doubt that what happened was a shift, perhaps to some degree a restoration, of emphasis within the Western tradition itself rather than a complete change in its nature. It is a mistake to identify the older Western culture with traditionalism. Classical antiquity handed on a working system of truth which relied on both reason and experience and was designed to provide a norm for civilized life. Its import was heightened and vastly intensified by its confluence with Christianity. But when, in its rigid systematization in the late Middle Ages, it lost touch with experience and individual inquiry, it violated its own nature and provoked the modernist revolt. The seeming opposition that resulted between traditionalism and modernism has been a tragedy for Western thought. Modernism rightly affirms the importance of inquiry and of relevance to experience. But as scholasticism ran the danger of becoming a system without vitality, so modernism runs the danger of achieving vitality without pattern.

While, then, there are discontinuities between the classical and the modern components of our Western culture, there are also continuities. For instance, it would be wrong to construe the scientific outlook as inimical to human values. Even if it were true that science is concerned with means only, it would not follow that science ignores the intrinsic worth of man. For the values of human life cannot be achieved within a physical vacuum; they require for their fulfillment the existence of material conditions. To the extent that classical civilization failed to mitigate the evils of poverty, disease, squalor, and a generally low level of living among the masses, to that extent it failed to liberate man. Conversely, to the extent that science, especially in its medical and technological applications, has succeeded in dealing with these evils, it has contributed to the realization of human values. Thus science has implemented the humanism which classicism and Christianity have proclaimed.

Science has done more than provide the material basis of the good life; it has directly fostered the spiritual values of humanism. To explain, science is both the outcome and the source of the habit of forming objective, disinterested judgments based upon exact evidence. Such a habit is of particular value in the formation of citizens for a free society. It opposes to the arbitrariness of authority and "first principles" the direct and continuing appeal to things as they are. Thus it develops the qualities of the free man. It is no accident that John Locke, who set forth the political doctrine of the natural rights of man against established authority, should have been also the man who rejected the authority of innate ideas.

Students of antiquity and of the Middle Ages can therefore rightly affirm that decisive truths about the human mind and its relation to the world were laid hold of then, and yet agree that, when new application of these truths was made through a more scrupulous attention to fact, their whole implication and meaning were immensely enlarged. Modern civilization has seen this enlargement of meaning and possibility; yet it is not a new civilization but the organic development of an earlier civilization. The true task of education is therefore so to reconcile the sense of pattern and direction deriving from heritage with the sense of experiment and innovation deriving from science that they may exist fruitfully together, as in varying degrees they have never ceased to do throughout Western history.

Belief in the dignity and mutual obligation of man is the common ground between these contrasting but mutually necessary forces in our culture. As was pointed out earlier, this belief is the fruit at once of religion, of the Western tradition, and of the American tradition. It equally inspires the faith in human reason which is the basis for trust in the future of democracy. And if it is not, strictly speaking, implied in all statements of the scientific method, there is no doubt that science has become its powerful instrument. In this tension between the opposite forces of heritage and change poised only in the faith in man, lies something like the old philosophic problem of the knowledge of the good. If you know the good, why do you seek it? If you are ignorant of the good, how do you recognize it when you find it? You must evidently at one and the same time both know it and be ignorant of it. Just so, the tradition which has come down to us regarding the nature of man and the good society must inevitably provide our standard of good. Yet an axiom of that tradition itself is the belief that no current form of the received ideal is final but that every generation, indeed every individual, must discover it in a fresh form. Education can therefore be wholly devoted neither to tradition nor to experiment, neither to the belief that the ideal in itself is enough nor to the view that means are valuable apart from the ideal. It must uphold at the same time tradition and experiment, the ideal and the means, subserving, like our culture itself, change within commitment.

2 General and Special Education

In the previous section we have attempted to outline the unifying elements of our culture and therefore of American education as well. In the present section we shall take the next step of indicating in what ways these cultural strands may be woven into the fabric of education. Education is broadly divided into general and special education; our topic now is the difference and the relationship between the two. The term, general education, is somewhat vague and colorless; it does not mean some airy education in knowledge in general (if there be such knowledge), nor does it mean education for all in the sense of universal education. It is used to indicate that part of a student's whole education which looks first of all to his life as a responsible human being and citizen; while the term, special education, indicates that part which looks to the student's competence in some occupation. These two sides of life are not entirely separable, and it would be false to imagine education for the one as quite distinct from education for the other—more will be said on this point presently. Clearly, general education has somewhat the meaning of liberal education, except that, by applying to high school as well as to college, it envisages immensely greater numbers of students and thus escapes the invidium which, rightly or wrongly, attaches to liberal education in the minds of some people. But if one clings to the root meaning of liberal as that which befits or helps to make free men, then general and liberal education have identical goals. The one may be thought of as an earlier stage of the other, similar in nature but less advanced in degree.

The opposition to liberal education—both to the phrase and to the fact—stems largely from historical causes. The concept of liberal education first appeared in a slave-owning society, like that of Athens, in which the community was divided into freemen and slaves, rulers and subjects. While the slaves carried on the specialized occupations of menial work, the freemen were primarily concerned with the rights and duties of citizenship. The training of the former was purely vocational; but as the freemen were not only a ruling but also a leisure class, their education was exclusively in the liberal arts, without any utilitarian tinge. The freemen were trained in the reflective pursuit of the good life; their education was unspecialized as well as unvocational; its aim was to produce a rounded person with a full understanding of himself and of his place in society and in the cosmos.

Modern democratic society clearly does not regard labor as odious or disgraceful; on the contrary, in this country at least, it regards leisure with suspicion and expects its "gentlemen" to engage in work. Thus we attach no odium to vocational instruction. Moreover, in so far as we surely reject the idea of freemen who are free in so far as they have slaves or subjects, we are apt strongly to deprecate the liberal education which went with the structure of the aristocratic ideal. Herein our society runs the risk of committing a serious fallacy. Democracy is the view that not only the few but that all are free, in that everyone governs his own life and shares in the responsibility for the management of the community. This being the case, it follows that all human beings stand in need of an ampler and rounded education. The task of modern democracy is to preserve the ancient ideal of liberal education and to extend it as far as possible to all the members of the community. In short, we have been apt to confuse accidental with fundamental factors, in our suspicion of the classical ideal. To believe in the equality of human beings is to believe that the good life, and the education which trains the citizen for the good life, are equally the privilege of all. And these are the touchstones of the liberated man: first, is he free; that is to say, is he able to judge and plan for himself, so that he can truly govern himself? In order to do this, his must be a mind capable of self-criticism; he must lead that self-examined life which according to Socrates is alone worthy of a free man. Thus he will possess inner freedom, as well as social freedom. Second, is he universal in his motives and sympathies? For the civilized man is a citizen of the entire universe; he has overcome provincialism, he is objective, and is a "spectator of all time and all existence." Surely these two are the very aims of democracy itself.

But the opposition to general education does not stem from causes located in the past alone. We are living in an age of specialism, in which the avenue to success for the student often lies in his choice of a specialized career, whether as a chemist, or an engineer, or a doctor, or a specialist in some form of business or of manual or technical work. Each of these specialties makes an increasing demand on the time and on the interest of the student. Specialism is the means for advancement in our mobile social structure; yet we must envisage the fact that a society controlled wholly by specialists is not a wisely ordered society. We cannot, however, turn away from specialism. The problem is how to save general education and its values within a system where specialism is necessary.

The very prevalence and power of the demand for special training makes doubly clear the need for a concurrent, balancing force in general education. Specialism enhances the centrifugal forces in society. The business of providing for the needs of society breeds a great diversity of special occupations; and a given specialist does not speak the language of the other specialists. In order to discharge his duties as a citizen adequately, a person must somehow be able to grasp the complexities of life as a whole. Even from the point of view of economic success, specialism has its peculiar limitations. Specializing in a vocation makes for inflexibility in a world of fluid possibilities. Business demands minds capable of adjusting themselves to varying situations and of managing complex human institutions. Given the pace of economic progress, techniques alter speedily; and even the work in which the student has been trained may no longer be useful when he is ready to earn a living or soon after. Our conclusion, then, is that the aim of education should be to prepare an individual to become an expert both in some particular vocation or art and in the general art of the free man and the citizen. Thus the two kinds of education once given separately to different social classes must be given together to all alike.

In this epoch in which almost all of us must be experts in some field in order to make a living, general education therefore assumes a peculiar importance. Since no one can become an expert in all fields, everyone is compelled to trust the judgment of other people pretty thoroughly in most areas of activity. I must trust the advice of my doctor, my plumber, my lawyer, my radio repairman, and so on. Therefore I am in peculiar need of a kind of sagacity by which to distinguish the expert from the quack, and the better from the worse expert. From this point of view, the aim of general education may be defined as that of providing the broad critical sense by which to recognize competence in any field. William James said that an educated person knows a good man when he sees one. There are standards and a style for every type of activity—manual, athletic, intellectual, or artistic; and the educated man should be one who can tell sound from shoddy work in a field outside his own. General education is especially required in a democracy where the public elects its leaders and officials; the ordinary citizen must be discerning enough so that he will not be deceived by appearances and will elect the candidate who is wise in his field.

Both kinds of education—special as well as general—contribute to the task of implementing the pervasive forces of our culture. Here we revert to what was said at the start of this chapter on the aims of education in our society. It was argued there that two complementary forces are at the root of our culture: on the one hand, an ideal of man and society distilled from the past but at the same time transcending the past as a standard of judgment valid in itself, and, on the other hand, the belief that no existent expressions of this ideal are final but that all alike call for perpetual scrutiny and change in the light of new knowledge. Specialism is usually the vehicle of this second force. It fosters the open-mindedness and love of investigation which are the wellspring of change, and it devotes itself to the means by which change is brought about. The fact may not always be obvious. There is a sterile specialism which hugs accepted knowledge and ends in the bleakest conservatism. Modern life also calls for many skills which, though specialized, are repetitive and certainly do not conduce to inquiry. These minister to change but unconsciously. Nevertheless, the previous statement is true in the sense that specialism is concerned primarily with knowledge in action, as it advances into new fields and into further applications.

Special education comprises a wider field than vocationalism; and correspondingly, general education extends beyond the limits of merely literary preoccupation. An example will make our point clearer. A scholar—let us say a scientist (whether student or teacher)—will, in the laudable aim of saving himself from narrowness, take a course in English literature, or perhaps read poetry and novels, or perhaps listen to good music and generally occupy himself with the fine arts. All this, while eminently fine and good, reveals a misapprehension. In his altogether unjustified humility, the scientist wrongly interprets the distinction between liberal and illiberal in terms of the distinction between the humanities and the sciences. Plato and Cicero would have been very much surprised to hear that geometry, astronomy, and the sciences of nature in general, are excluded from the humanities. There is also implied a more serious contempt for the liberal arts, harking back to the fallacy which identifies liberal education with the aristocratic ideal. The implication is that liberal education is something only genteel. A similar error is evident in the student's attitude toward his required courses outside his major field as something to "get over with," so that he may engage in the business of serious education, identified in his mind with the field of concentration.

Now, a general education is distinguished from special education, not by subject matter, but in terms of method and outlook, no matter what the field. Literature, when studied in a technical fashion, gives rise to the special science of philology; there is also the highly specialized historical approach to painting. Specialism is interchangeable, not with natural science, but with the method of science, the method which abstracts material from its context and handles it in complete isolation. The reward of scientific method is the utmost degree of precision and exactness. But, as we have seen, specialism as an educational force has its own limitations; it does not usually provide an insight into general relationships.

A further point is worth noting. The impact of specialism has been felt not only in those phases of education which are necessarily and rightly specialistic; it has affected also the whole structure of higher and even of secondary education. Teachers, themselves products of highly technical disciplines, tend to reproduce their knowledge in class. The result is that each subject, being taught by an expert, tends to be so presented as to attract potential experts. This complaint is perhaps more keenly felt in colleges and universities, which naturally look to scholarship. The undergraduate in a college receives his teaching from professors who, in their turn, have been trained in graduate schools. And the latter are dominated by the ideal of specialization. Learning now is diversified and parceled into a myriad of specialties. Correspondingly, colleges and universities are divided into large numbers of departments, with further specialization within the departments. As a result, a student in search of a general course is commonly frustrated. Even an elementary course is devised as an introduction to a specialism within a department; it is significant only as the beginning of a series of courses of advancing complexity. In short, such introductory courses are planned for the specialist, not for the student seeking a general education. The young chemist in the course in literature and the young writer in the course in chemistry find themselves in thoroughly uncomfortable positions so long as the purpose of these courses is primarily to train experts who will go on to higher courses rather than to give some basic understanding of science as it is revealed in chemistry or of the arts as they are revealed in literature.

It is most unfortunate if we envisage general education as something formless—that is to say, the taking of one course after another; and as something negative, namely, the study of what is not in a field of concentration. Just as we regard the courses in concentration as having definite relations to one another, so should we envisage general education as an organic whole whose parts join in expounding a ruling idea and in serving a common aim. And to do so means to abandon the view that all fields and all departments are equally valuable vehicles of general education. It also implies some prescription. At the least it means abandoning the usual attitude of regarding "distribution" as a sphere in which the student exercises a virtually untrammeled freedom of choice. It may be objected that we are proposing to limit the liberty of the student in the very name of liberal education. Such an objection would only indicate an ambiguity in the conception of liberal education. We must distinguish between liberalism in education and education in liberalism. The former, based as it is on the doctrine of individualism, expresses the view that the student should be free in his choice of courses. But education in liberalism is an altogether different matter; it is education which has a pattern of its own, namely, the pattern associated with the liberal outlook. In this view, there are truths which none can be free to ignore, if one is to have that wisdom through which life can become useful. These are the truths concerning the structure of the good life and concerning the factual conditions by which it may be achieved, truths comprising the goals of the free society.

Finally, the problem of general education is one of combining fixity of aim with diversity in application. It is not a question of providing a general education which will be uniform through the same classes of all schools and colleges all over the country, even were such a thing possible in our decentralized system. It is rather to adapt general education to the needs and intentions of different groups and, so far as possible, to carry its spirit into special education. The effectiveness of teaching has always largely depended on this willingness to adapt a central unvarying purpose to varying outlooks. Such adaptation is as much in the interest of the quick as of the slow, of the bookish as of the unbookish, and is the necessary protection of each. What is wanted, then, is a general education capable at once of taking on many different forms and yet of representing in all its forms the common knowledge and the common values on which a free society depends.

3 Areas of Knowledge

We have gradually moved from the less to the more specific, until now we have reached the topic of actual outcomes of education. In this section we shall deal with general education only; and our question will take two forms: what characteristics (traits of mind and character) are necessary for anything like a full and responsible life in our society; and, by what elements of knowledge are such traits nourished? These two questions, these two aspects, are images of each other. We have repeatedly found ourselves until now describing general education, at one time, as looking to the good of man in society and, at another time, as dictated by the nature of knowledge itself. There is no escape from thus shifting from one face of the same truth to the other. But temporarily and for the sake of clarity it may be useful to separate the two questions and consider first the elements of knowledge, and later the characteristics.

Tradition points to a separation of learning into the three areas of natural science, social studies, and the humanities. The study of the natural sciences looks to an understanding of our physical environment, so that we may have a suitable relation to it. The study of the social sciences is intended to produce an understanding of our social environment and of human institutions in general, so that the student may achieve a proper relation to society—not only the local but also the great society, and, by the aid of history, the society of the past and even of the future. Finally, the purpose of the humanities is to enable man to understand man in relation to himself, that is to say, in his inner aspirations and ideals.

While all this is obvious and even trite, it is hardly adequate. Subject matters do not lend themselves to such neat distinctions. To consider only one example, psychology, which has been classified as a natural science in the above list, surely has, or ought to have, something to say about human nature. A more serious flaw of this classification is that it conceives of education as the act of getting acquainted with something, and so as the acquiring of information. But information is inert knowledge. Yet, given this limitation, such an approach has its merits because it directs the student's attention to the useful truth that man must familiarize himself with the environment in which nature has placed him if he is to proceed realistically with the task of achieving the good life.

A much better justification of the way in which the areas of learning are divided is in terms of methods of knowledge. Let us start with the difference between the natural sciences and the humanities. The former describe, analyze, and explain; the latter appraise, judge, and criticize. In the first, a statement is judged as true or false; in the second, a result is judged as good or bad. The natural sciences do not take it on themselves to evaluate the worth of what they describe. The chemist is content to state the actual structure of his compound without either praising or deploring the fact. Natural science measures what can be measured, and it operates upon its materials with the instruments of formal logic and mathematics. Yet these latter are not themselves science or even the final arbiters of science. Science serves a harsher master—the brute facts of physical reality. Logic and mathematics are triumphs of abstraction. These are the media by which a scientific argument is pursued. But when the argument has by these means yielded a solution, this in turn must meet the question, "is it real?" "is it true?" By this final appeal to things as they are, or as they appear to be, the argument stands or falls.

In contrast to mathematics and the natural sciences, the humanities explore and exhibit the realm of value. For example, in literature the student is presented with various ways of life, with the tragic and the heroic outlook, or with the merely pathetic and ridiculous. His imagination is stirred with vivid evocations of ideals of action, passion, and thought, among which he may learn to discriminate. The intelligent teacher will explore the great arts and literatures in order to bring out the ideals toward which man has been groping, confusedly yet stubbornly. And of course the arts have done as much through form as through content; they disclose varying standards of taste.

Although techniques have been developed for the study of natural phenomena, no comparable progress has been made in our insight into values. We can measure a physical body, but we cannot measure an ideal, nor can we put critical standards under a microscope so as to note all their elements with precision. Science aims at precision and gets it. This is true, partly because science will not bother itself with facts when these do not lend themselves to the methods of exact observation. It limits itself to events that recur and to things which permit measurement. To the extent that an object is truly unique and occurs only once it is not the stuff of science. For example, every society is to a degree unique; hence the student of social phenomena is still baffled in his search for strict uniformities.

To admit that a difference exists between the methods of science and our insight into values is one thing; to go on from there and assert that values are wholly arbitrary is a different and wholly unjustified conclusion. It has been thought that, since the words right and wrong as applied to ethical situations do not have the same meaning as right and wrong when applied to mathematical propositions, no rational criteria are involved; and that one is at liberty to choose any set of standards more or less from the air and apply them to the problems which come to hand. Or by way of reaction some persons have gone to the opposite extreme of setting up fixed dogmas and imposing them by sheer authority. But standards are the reflection neither of personal whims nor of dogmatic attitudes. In the realm of values, critical analysis of complex situations is possible by rational methods and in the light of what other men have thought upon such matters. Here we return to what was said earlier in this chapter about the twin contribution of heritage and innovation to human beliefs. Starting with a few premises, for instance with those involved in our commitment to a free society, the mind can proceed to analyze the implications of these premises and also to modify their initial meaning by the aid of experience. While there can be no experimenting with ideals, there is experience of values in application, and there is heaping up of such experience. While there can be no precise measurement, there is intelligent analysis of codes and standards. While there are no simple uniformities, there are moral principles which command the assent of civilized men. Of all this more presently; our conclusion is that value-judgments are, or at least can be, rational in so far as they are informed and disciplined; they are communicable and can become matters of intelligent discussion and persuasion.

Finally, on this basis the social studies may be said to combine the methods of the natural sciences and of the humanities, and to use both explanation and evaluation. For instance, the historian is obviously concerned with facts and events and with the causal relations between happenings; yet he is no less concerned with values. A historical fact is not merely a fact: it is a victory or a defeat, an indication of progress or of retrogression, it is a misfortune or good fortune. We do not mean by this that a historian passes moral judgments on events and nations. We do mean that a historian is selective; that out of the infinity of events he chooses those that have a bearing on man's destiny. A similar situation is disclosed in economics, which is a judicious mixture, not always acknowledged or even realized, of factual objective study and normative judgment. The classical, if not the contemporary, economist is engaged on the one hand in a description and analysis of this or that economic institution, and on the other hand with a criticism of what he describes and analyzes in the light of the norm of a sound economy. From this point of view the object of philosophy would appear to be the bringing together of both facts and values. Philosophy asks the question: what is the place of human aspirations and ideals in the total scheme of things?

The method of science can be set off against the method of social studies and humanities taken together in the following way. In science, new findings are constantly being made in such a way that the sum of these findings constitutes the current view of truth. Science is knowledge for which an exact standard of truth exists; as a result, within any particular present there is common agreement about what is scientific truth; or if the agreement is lacking there are determinate criteria commonly agreed upon, by the application of which the issue can be settled. But in the other two fields there is often no common agreement as to what is valid within any given present; there is diversity of schools and doctrines, the reason being that a standard of exact truth or exact rightness is lacking. In the sciences, thought is progressive; the later stage corrects the earlier and includes the truth of the earlier. Were Galileo able to return to the land of the living, who doubts that he would regard later changes in physical theory as an improvement on his own? In consequence, the history of its thought is strictly irrelevant to science. But it is impossible to say with the same assurance that our philosophy or art, though presumably better than the cave man's, is better than that of the Greeks or of the men of the Renaissance. The work of any genius in art or philosophy or literature represents in some sense a complete and absolute vision. Goethe does not render Sophocles obsolete, nor does Descartes supersede Plato. The geniuses that follow do not so much correct preceding insights as they supply alternative but similarly simple and total insights from new perspectives. For this reason historical knowledge has a special importance in philosophy, and the achievements of the past have a significance for the arts and literature which is certainly not true of science.

At this point the impatient reader will interject that the distinctions which we have made do not really distinguish. We have said that literature exhibits life as it might be; yet is it not a fact that literature also depicts life as it is? We have said that economics is concerned with norms as well as actualities; yet surely mathematical economics is an analytical study and nothing else.

And conversely, the reader may add, it is false that science is wholly restricted to the techniques of measurement. The very method of science, the way in which it defines a fact and its essential presuppositions, is not subject to scientific proof. All this we admit without reservation. The distinctions we have made are rough and inexact; the total area of learning is more like a spectrum along which the diverse modes of thought are combined in varying degrees, approximating to purity only at the extreme ends.

Nevertheless, these distinctions retain their importance at least for pragmatic, that is, educational reasons. If it is true that in questions of government the words right and wrong, true and false, lack the exactitude which they have in questions of mathematics, the fact must be of the essence of teaching government and history. Clearly, education will not look solely to the giving of information. Information is of course the basis of any knowledge, but if both the nature of truth and the methods of asserting it differ as between the areas, the fact must be made fully apparent. As Mr. Whitehead has said, a student should not be taught more than he can think about. Selection is the essence of teaching. Even the most compendious survey is only the rudest culling from reality. Since the problem of choice can under no circumstances be avoided, the problem becomes what, rather than how much, to teach; or better, what principles and methods to illustrate by the use of information. The same conflict between the factual aspects of a subject and the need of insight into the kind of truth with which it deals arises in an acute form in that most factual of disciplines, natural science itself. While a heaping up of information is peculiarly necessary in the teaching of science, information is not enough. Facts must be so chosen as to convey not only something of the substance of science but, also and above all, of its methods, its characteristic achievements, and its limitations. To the extent that a student becomes aware of the methods he is using, and critically conscious of his presuppositions, he learns to transcend his specialty and generates a liberal outlook in himself.

4 Traits of Mind

At the time of his examination the average student hardly remembers more than 75 per cent of what he was taught. If he were a sophomore when he took the course, how much does he recall by the time of his graduation, how much five years later, how much, or how little, when he returns on his twenty-fifth reunion? Pondering on all this, the pessimist might well conclude that education is a wholly wasteful process. He would of course be wrong, for the simple reason that education is not a process of stuffing the mind with facts. Yet he would be partly right because the student soon forgets not only many facts but even some general ideas and principles. No doubt we are exaggerating. Those students particularly who have been able to unite what they learned in school or college with later studies or with their jobs do retain a surprising amount of information. Nevertheless, the real answer to the pessimist is that education is not merely the imparting of knowledge but the cultivation of certain aptitudes and attitudes in the mind of the young. As we have said earlier, education looks both to the nature of knowledge and to the good of man in society. It is to the latter aspect that we shall now turn our attention—more particularly to the traits and characteristics of mind fostered by education.

By characteristics we mean aims so important as to prescribe how general education should be carried out and which abilities should be sought above all others in every part of it. These abilities, in our opinion, are: *to think effectively, to communicate thought, to make relevant judgments, to discriminate among values.* They are not in practice separable and are not to be developed in isolation. Nor can they be even analyzed in separation. Each is an indispensable coexistent function of a sanely growing mind. Nonetheless, since exposition requires that one thing be discussed at one time, our description of these abilities must take them up in turn.

By *effective thinking* we mean, in the first place, logical thinking: the ability to draw sound conclusions from premises. Yet by logical thinking we do not mean the equipment of the specialist or what a student would learn by taking a course in formal logic. We are concerned with the student who is going to be a worker, or a businessman, or a professional man, and who does not necessarily look forward to a career in scholarship or in pure science. As a plain citizen he will practice his logical skills in practical situations—in choosing a career, in deciding whom to vote for, or what house to buy, or even in choosing a wife. But perhaps the last case is just the point where logical skills fail, although European parents might disagree.

Logical thinking is the capacity to extract universal truths from particular cases and, in turn, to infer particulars from general laws. More strictly, it is the ability to discern a pattern of relationships—on the one hand to analyze a problem into its component elements, and on the other to recombine these, often by the use of imaginative insight, so as to reach a solution. Its prototype is mathematics which, starting with a few selected postulates, makes exact deductions with certainty. Logical thinking is involved to a degree in the analysis of the structure of a painting as well as in that of a geometrical system. In moving toward a solution, the trained mind will have a sharp eye for the relevant factors while zealously excluding all that is irrelevant; and it will arrange the relevant factors according to weight. For instance, in voting during a presidential election our citizen should consider whether the candidate has sound policies, whether he has the ability to get on with Congress, whether he has a good grasp of international relations, and, in these troubled times, whether he has an understanding of military strategy. These are some of the factors which are relevant to the problem in hand. But the looks of the candidate most probably, and his religious denomination surely, are irrelevant. Prejudice brings in irrelevancies and logic should keep them out.

Effective thinking, while starting with logic, goes further so as to include certain broad mental skills. Thus an effective thinker is a man who can handle terms and concepts with skill and yet does not confuse words with things; he is empirical in the widest sense of the word, looking outward to nature. He is not satisfied merely with noting the facts, but his mind ever soars to implications. He knows when he knows and when he does not; he does not mistake opinion for knowledge. Furthermore, effective thinking includes the understanding of complex and fluid situations, in dealing with which logical methods are inadequate as mental tools. Of course thinking must never violate the laws of logic, but it may use techniques beyond those of exact mathematical reasoning. In the fields of the social studies and history, and in the problems of daily life, there are large areas where evidence is incomplete and may never be completed. Sometimes the evidence may be also untrustworthy; but, if the situation is practical, a decision must be made. The scientist has been habituated to deal with properties which can be abstracted from their total background and with variables which are few and well defined. Consequently, where the facts are unique and unpredictable, where the variables are numerous and their interactions too complicated for precise calculation, the scientist is apt to throw up his hands in despair and perhaps turn the situation over to the sentimentalist or the mystic. But surely he would be wrong in so doing; for the methods of logical thinking do not exhaust the resources of reason. In coping with complex and fluid situations we need thinking which is relational and which searches for cross bearings between areas; this is thinking in a context. By its use it is possible to reach an understanding of historical and social materials and of human relations, although not with the same degree of precision as in the case of simpler materials and of recurring events. As Aristotle says, "It is the mark of an educated man to expect no more exactness than the subject permits."

A further element in effective thinking is the imagination, by which we mean whatever is distinctive in the thinking of the poet. Logical thinking is straight, as opposed to crooked, thinking; and that of the poet may be described as curved thinking. Where the scientist operates with abstract conceptions the poet employs sensuous images; imagination is the faculty of thinking in terms of concrete ideas and symbols. Instead of reading a prosaic analysis of exuberant vitality, we may get a direct vision of it in Manet's portrait of the boy with the flute. We may study human nature in the psychologist's abstract accounts of it, or we may see it in the vivid presentations of imagined individuals like Othello, Becky Sharp, Ulysses, and Anna Karenina. The reader might demur that imagination has little to do with effective thinking. Yet the imagination is most valuable in the field of human relations. Statistics are useful, but statistics alone will not carry us very far in the understanding of human beings. We need an imagination delicately sensitive to the hopes and the fears, the qualities and the flaws of our fellow man, and which can evoke a total personality in its concrete fullness. In practical matters, imagination supplies the ability to break with habit and routine, to see beyond the obvious and to envisage new alternatives; it is the spur of the inventor and the revolutionary, no less than of the artist.

It may be noted that the three phases of effective thinking, logical, relational, and imaginative, correspond roughly to the three divisions of learning, the natural sciences, the social studies, and the humanities, respectively.

Communication—the ability to express oneself so as to be understood by others—is obviously inseparable from effective thinking. In most thinking, one is talking to oneself; and good speech and writing are the visible test and sign of good thinking. Conversely, to speak clearly one must have clear ideas. You cannot say something unless you have something to say; but in order to express your ideas properly you also need some skill in communication. There is something else too: the honest intent to make your ideas known, as against the desire to deceive or merely to conceal. Communication is not speaking only but listening as well; you cannot succeed in communicating your ideas unless the other person wishes to hear and knows how to listen. As there are two kinds of language, oral and written, communication breaks up into the four related skills of speaking and listening, writing and reading.

Communication is that unrestricted exchange of ideas within the body politic by which a prosperous intellectual economy is secured. In its character as the sharing of meanings it is the instrument by which human beings are welded into a society, both the living with the living and the living with the dead. In a free and democratic society the art of communication has a special importance. A totalitarian state can obtain consent by force; but a democracy must persuade, and persuasion is through speech, oral or other. In a democracy issues are aired; talked out of existence or talked into solution. Failure of communication between the citizens, or between the government and the public, means a breakdown in the democratic process. Nevertheless, whereas people have been brought together nearer than ever before, in a physical sense, by the improvement of mechanisms of transportation, it cannot be said that mutual understanding among individuals and among peoples has made a corresponding advance. Skills, crafts, professions, and scholarly disciplines are apt to surround themselves by high walls of esoteric jargon. Other barriers are erected through the tendency to convert communication into propaganda, whether it be political propaganda, or economic propaganda, as for instance in some types of advertising. Thus, effective communication depends on the possession not only of skills such as clear thinking and cogent expression but of moral qualities as well, such as candor.

In older days, a course on rhetoric was a normal part of the curriculum. Rhetoric to us suggests oratory, and today we are suspicious of or at least indifferent to oratory. Yet the art of rhetoric meant the simple skill of making one's ideas clear and cogent; it did not necessarily mean high-flown speeches. The simplest example of communication is conversation. It is a truism to say that conversation is a lost art. The question is, where was it lost? If we carry on less, or less good, conversation than our ancestors did, is it because we have lost the art, or because, having become technicians, we have little to say that is suitable for general conversation, or because we are much more interested in doing things—driving, for example, or playing bridge? Learned persons are apt to disparage conversation as trivial or frivolous, but unjustly so. If you are looking for the uncovering of important truths during a dinner party, of course you may be disappointed; but that is because you will be looking for the wrong thing. The contribution of general conversation is the revelation and impact of personality. While nothings are being bandied about and trivial words, like the lightest balloons, are launched into the air, contact with personalities is being achieved through characteristic inflections and emphases, through readiness or shyness of response. In conversation the idea is inseparable from the man; conversation is useful because it is the most unforced and natural means of bringing persons together into a society. Beyond its social function, conversation is a delight in itself. It is an art, yet it loses its value if it becomes artificial. Its essence is spontaneity, impetus, movement; the words of a conversation are evanescent, things of the moment, while written words are formalized, rigid, and fixed. Starting with simple things like the weather and minor personal happenings, it proceeds to weave a pattern of sentiments and ideas, and through these of persons, which is fugitive just because it is alive.

Perhaps we have wandered too far from the serious—or should we say the ponderous—aspects of our problem. Yet we had a point to make: that language needs to be neither high learning nor high literature in order to be communication. What we have in mind is the language of a businessman writing a plain and crisp letter, of a scientist making a report, of a citizen asking straight questions, of human beings arguing together on some matter of common interest.

The *making of relevant judgments* involves the ability of the student to bring to bear the whole range of ideas upon the area of experience. It is not now a question of apprehending more relationships within ideas but of applying these to actual facts. The most competent instructor of military science is not necessarily the best officer in the field. An adequate theory of ball playing is conceivable, but an abstract knowledge of it would not make a good ballplayer any more than a course on poetics, however good, would make a good poet. It is not the power to distinguish or state the universal formula, for separated contemplation, which heightens our skill. It is the power to use the formula in the new concrete situations as they fleet past us which education aims to advance. In Plato's myth the philosopher who has obtained the vision of the good must return to the cave and use his vision in order to guide himself among the shadows. Initially and inevitably he is confused; only after long habituation is he able to find his way around and properly to apply his concepts to his concrete experience. There is no rule to be learned which could tell the student how to apply rules to cases; the translation from theory to practice involves an art all its own and requires the skill which we call sagacity or judgment.

To some degree every school or college is separated from life by high walls, visible or invisible; it holds reality at arm's length. And up to a point this is necessary and proper. While it is true that the present is our only fact, nevertheless we cannot see the present so long as we are immersed in it; we need the perspective afforded by distance in time and in space. One of the aims of education is to break the stranglehold of the present upon the mind. On the other side is the fact that youth is instinctive and ardent; to subject youth to a steady diet of abstractions alone would be cruel and unnatural. Moreover, abstractions in themselves are meaningless unless connected with experience; and for this reason all education is in some sense premature. The adult who rereads his great authors realizes how much he had missed of their meaning when he read them in school or college. Now his reading is more rewarding because his range of experience is greater. One might conceive fancifully of another scheme of life in which work comes first and education begins later, say at forty-five. The advantages of this scheme are obvious. Not only would the mature student be amply equipped with the depth of experience necessary for the understanding of the great authors, but the financial problem would be solved. The student would have saved enough money from his work, or perhaps his children would support him.

But such utopias are not for us; we have to deal with harsh realities. Education must be so contrived that the young, during the very process of their schooling, will realize the difference between abstractions and facts and will learn to make the transition from thought to action. A young man who has been nourished with ideas exclusively will be tempted by the sin of intellectual pride, thinking himself capable of dealing with any problem, independently of experience. When he later comes into contact with things, he will stumble or perhaps in self-defense withdraw into sterile cleverness. As we have seen, the aptitude of making relevant judgments cannot be developed by theoretical teaching; being an art, it comes from example, practice, and habituation. The teacher can do a great deal nonetheless; he can relate theoretical content to the student's life at every feasible point, and he can deliberately simulate in the classroom situations from life. Finally, he can bring concrete reports of actual cases for discussion with the students. The essential thing is that the teacher should be constantly aware of the ultimate objectives, never letting means obscure ends, and be persistent in directing the attention of the student from the symbols to the things they symbolize.

Discrimination among values involves choice. The ability to discriminate in choosing covers not only awareness of different kinds of value but of their relations, including a sense of relative importance and of the mutual dependence of means and ends. It covers also much that is analogous to method in thinking; for example, the power to distinguish values truly known from values received only from opinion and therefore not in the same way part of the fabric of experience. Values are of many kinds. There are the obvious values of character, like fair play, courage, self-control, the impulse of beneficence and humanity; there are the intellectual values, like the love of truth and the respect for the intellectual enterprise in all its forms; there are the aesthetic values, like good taste and the appreciation of beauty. As for the last, people are apt to locate beauty in picture galleries and in museums and to leave it there; it is equally, if not more, important to seek beauty in ordinary things, so that it may surround one's life like an atmosphere.

Add to all this that the objective of education is not just knowledge of values but commitment to them, the embodiment of the ideal in one's actions, feelings, and thoughts, no less than an intellectual grasp of the ideal. The reader may object that we are proposing a confusion, that we are suggesting the turning of school or college into a moral reformatory or a church. For is not the purpose of educational institutions to train the mind and the mind only? Yet it is not easy, indeed it is impossible, to separate effective thinking from character. An essential factor in the advancement of knowledge is intellectual integrity, the suppression of all wishful thinking and the strictest regard for the claims of evidence. The universal community of educated men is a fellowship of ideals as well as of beliefs. To isolate the activity of thinking from the morals of thinking is to make sophists of the young and to encourage them to argue for the sake of personal victory rather than of the truth. We are not so naive as to suggest that theoretical instruction in the virtues will automatically make a student virtuous. Rather, we assert that the best way to infect the student with the zest for intellectual integrity is to put him near a teacher who is himself selflessly devoted to the truth; so that a spark from the teacher will, so to speak, leap across the desk into the classroom, kindling within the student the flame of intellectual integrity, which will thereafter sustain itself.

The problem of moral values and character is more complex. Here the college does not play quite the same role as the school. Clearly we have a right to expect the school to be engaged directly in moral education. But although the college shares in this responsibility, it cannot be expected to use the same direct approach. The college will have to confine itself to providing a proper discrimination of values and will trust to the Socratic dictum that the knowledge of the good will lead to a commitment to the good. Nevertheless, we must recognize a difference between the responsibility of both school and college to train the intellect and their responsibility to form character. In some sense, the former responsibility is a unique one for the educational institution. But in the sphere of moral instruction the school shares its responsibilities with numerous other institutions, of which the family is the most important. Moreover, the school's responsibility is less than that of the family in this field. To use an earlier figure there is danger in regarding the school as a modern Atlas to whom is entrusted the bearing of the whole task of the formation of man. To change the metaphor, a wise society does not put all its eggs in one basket. By the same token, the school cannot remain uninterested in the task of moral education. Just as liberal education, while strictly liberal, must somehow be oriented toward vocationalism, so in this general way will school and college be oriented toward moral character.

Discrimination in values is developed by the study of all the three areas of learning. We have seen that the humanities point both to moral and to aesthetic values. It may be true, as we have said earlier, that ethical neutrality is a guiding rule for the historian as scholar. Nevertheless, the historian or social scientist, as *teacher,* should probably go further and present to the student the human past and human institutions not merely as facts but as attempted embodiments of the good life in its various phases. In the natural sciences facts are studied in abstraction from values. But this separation, while pragmatically valid, leads to disaster if treated as final. Values are rooted in facts; and human ideals are somehow a part of nature.

5 The Good Man and the Citizen

General education, we repeat, must consciously aim at these abilities: at effective thinking, communication, the making of relevant judgments, and the discrimination of values. As was noted earlier, one of the subtlest and most prevalent effects of specialism has been that, through its influence, subjects have tended to be conceived and taught with an eye, so to speak, to their own internal logic rather than to their larger usefulness to students. In a course in history, for example, little concern will be felt for a student's ability to express himself, which will be left to English, or for his ability to think logically, which will fall to mathematics. Good teachers will, to be sure, always say of their subject that it subserves these higher aims, and to their great credit many do seek these aims. But the organization of knowledge into rigid, almost autonomous units, works against them. One of the few clear facts about the unclear and much disputed question of the transfer of powers from one subject to another is that it will tend not to take place unless it is deliberately planned for and worked for. Again, every course, whether general or special, may be expected to contribute something to all these abilities. Doubtless some courses will contribute more to some traits and others to others, but these abilities are after all of quite universal importance. Communication is basic to science as well as to literature; the power to think effectively is as essential to all forms of speech as it is to mathematics. Indeed, it will not be fostered as it should even by mathematics, unless the logical movements which find their purest form in theorems and equations are expressly given wider use. The power to discriminate between values is involved in this very act of wider application. Finally, the mastery of any one of the three large areas of learning will be of little use to the student unless he can relate his learning to the realities of experience and practice.

Human personality cannot, however, be broken up into distinct parts or traits. Education must look to the whole man. It has been wisely said that education aims at the good man, the good citizen, and the useful man. By, a good man is meant one who possesses an inner integration, poise, and firmness, which in the long run come from an adequate philosophy of life. Personal integration is not a fifth characteristic in addition to the other four and coordinate with them; it is their proper fruition. The aim of liberal education is the development of the whole man; and human nature involves instincts and sentiments as well as the intellect. Two dangers must be mentioned. First, there is the danger of identifying intelligence with the qualities of the so-called intellectual type—with bookishness and skill in the manipulation of concepts. We have tried to guard against this mistake by stressing the traits of relevant judgment and discrimination of values in effective thinking. Second, we must remember that intelligence, even when taken in its widest sense, does not exhaust the total potentialities of human nature. Man is not a contemplative being alone. Why is it, then, that education is conceived as primarily an intellectual enterprise when, in fact, human nature is so complex? For instance, man has his emotions and his drives and his will; why should education center on the training of the intellect? The answer is found in the truth that intelligence is not a special function (or not that only) but a way in which all human powers may function. Intelligence is that leaven of awareness and reflection which, operating upon the native powers of men, raises them from the animal level and makes them truly human. By reason we mean, not an activity apart, but rational guidance of all human activity. Thus the fruit of education is intelligence in action. The aim is mastery of life; and since living is an art, wisdom is the indispensable means to this end.

We are here disputing the doctrine, sometimes described as the classical view, that in education, reason is a self-sufficient end. Yet it was Plato himself who urged that the guardians of the state should be courageous as well as wise, in other words, that they should be full-blooded human beings as well as trained minds. We equally oppose the view at the other extreme that vitality and initiative, unregulated by the intellect, are adequate criteria of the good man. Whenever the two parts of the single aim are separated, when either thought or action is stressed as an exclusive end, when the teachers look only to scholarly ability and the students (and perhaps the public too) only to proficiency in activities and to "personality" (whatever that may mean), then indeed wholeness is lost. And what is worse, these qualities themselves, in proportion as they are divorced from each other, tend to wither or at least to fall short of fulfilling their promise.

We are not at all unmindful of the importance of religious belief in the completely good life. But, given the American scene with its varieties of faith and even of unfaith, we did not feel justified in proposing religious instruction as a part of the curriculum. The love of God is tested by the love of neighbor; nevertheless the love of God transcends merely human obligations. We must perforce speak in purely humanistic terms, confining ourselves to the obligations of man to himself and to society. But we have been careful so to delimit humanism as not to exclude the religious ideal. Yet we are not arguing for an education which is student-centered. As man is the measure of the abstract values, so in their turn do these values measure man. Like an ellipse, an educational institution has two centers, not one. And although the geometrical metaphor forbids it, truth compels us to add a third, namely, society.

Just as it is wrong to split the human person into separate parts, so would it be wrong to split the individual from society. We must resist the prevalent tendency, or at any rate temptation, to interpret the good life purely in terms of atomic individuals engaged in fulfilling their potentialities. Individualism is often confused with the life of private and selfish interest. The mandate of this committee is to concern itself with "the objectives of education in a free society." It is important to realize that the ideal of a free society involves a twofold value, the value of freedom and that of society. Democracy is a *community* of free men. We are apt sometimes to stress freedom—the power of individual choice and the right to think for oneself—without taking sufficient account of the obligation to cooperate with our fellow men; democracy must represent an adjustment between the values of freedom and social living.

Eighteenth-century liberalism tended to conceive the good life in terms of freedom alone and thought of humanity in pluralistic terms (like matter in Newtonian physics) as an aggregate of independent particles. But a life in which everyone owns his home as his castle and refrains from interfering with others is a community in a negative sense only. Rugged individualism is not sufficient to constitute a democracy; democracy also is fraternity and cooperation for the common good. Josiah Royce defined the good life in terms of loyalty to a shared value. Of course when union is stressed to the exclusion of freedom we fall into totalitarianism; but when freedom is stressed exclusively we fall into chaos. Democracy is the attempt to combine liberty with loyalty, each limiting the other, and also each reinforcing the other.

It is important, however, to limit the idea of the good citizen expressly by the ideal of the good man. By citizenship we do not mean the kind of loyalty which never questions the accepted purposes of society. A society which leaves no place for criticism of its own aims and methods by its component members has no chance to correct its errors and ailments, no chance to advance to new and better forms, and will eventually stagnate, if not die. The quality of alert and aggressive individualism is essential to good citizenship; and the good society consists of individuals who are independent in outlook and think for themselves while also willing to subordinate their individual good to the common good.

But the problem of combining these two aims is one of the hardest tasks facing our society. The ideal of free inquiry is a precious heritage of Western culture; yet a measure of firm belief is surely part of the good life. A free society means toleration, which in turn comes from openness of mind. But freedom also presupposes conviction; a free choice—unless it be wholly arbitrary (and then it would not be free)—comes from belief and ultimately from principle. A free society, then, cherishes both toleration and conviction. Yet the two seem incompatible, If I am convinced of the truth of my views, on what grounds should I tolerate your views, which I believe to be false? The answer lies partly in my understanding of my limitations as a man. Such understanding is not only the expression of an intellectual humility but is a valid inference from the fact that wise men have made endless mistakes in the past. Furthermore, a belief which does not meet the challenge of criticism and dissent soon becomes inert, habitual, dead. Had there been no heterodoxies, the orthodox should have invented them. A belief which is not envisaged as an answer to a problem is not a belief but a barren formula.

How far should we go in the direction of the open mind? Especially after the first World War, liberals were sometimes too distrustful of enthusiasm and were inclined to abstain from committing themselves as though there were something foolish, even shameful, in belief. Yet especially with youth, which is ardent and enthusiastic, open-mindedness without belief is apt to lead to the opposite extreme of fanaticism. We can all perhaps recall young people of our acquaintance who from a position of extreme skepticism, and indeed because of that position, fell an easy prey to fanatical gospels. It seems that nature abhors an intellectual vacuum. A measure of belief is necessary in order to preserve the quality of the open mind. If toleration is not to become nihilism, if conviction is not to become dogmatism, if criticism is not to become cynicism, each must have something of the other.

CHAPTER 10

DEWEY VERSUS HUTCHINS: THE NEXT ROUND

THOMAS EHRLICH

Several years ago I participated in a public forum at the American Academy of Arts and Sciences. The issue was whether community-service learning is a sound pedagogy for undergraduates. By community-service learning I mean linking academic study and community service through structured reflection so that each reinforces the other. Professor Charles Fried, former Solicitor General of the United States, was among the participants, and he objected to the concept. During the undergraduate years, he said, there should be a "moratorium" on student interactions with society. Young people in those years, he urged, should "be confronted with ideas, with truths, with reflection somewhat detached, perhaps even entirely detached, from the practical consequences of what they are learning." Undergraduates will be "submerged in practical consequences for the whole rest of their lives." College years are a time to learn "things that are to be understood for their own sake, understood for the truths they contain."[1]

I thought of these comments in reflecting on a sharp debate that took place in 1936 between John Dewey and Robert Maynard Hutchins, the young president of the University of Chicago, where Dewey had formerly taught. The key issue was the nature and purpose of a liberal education, including how undergraduates should acquire that education. Hutchins proposed answers that paralleled Fried's "moratorium" approach. The debate was joined when Dewey, in direct response, presented a contrary position.

In Dewey's view, education in our society should be about more than preparation for lives of personal fulfillment and professional accomplishment In *Democracy and Education,* he argued that all aspects of the education systems in the United States ought to be designed to make democracy work. "A democracy," he wrote, "is more than a form of government; it is primarily a mode of associated living, of conjoint communicated experience." This mode of experience requires that "each has to refer his own action to that of others, and to consider the action of others to give point and direction to his own."[2] Educational institutions should be shaped to nurture communal values, abilities, and understandings. This can happen only if students are constantly collaborating and interacting with others both within and outside the institutions. Their teachers should establish, within the controlled environment of a school—but closely linked to the broader societal setting—the cooperative arrangements that enable students to learn from each other and to learn cooperatively. In the process, a democratic community of learning is created that provides education for a lifetime of civic engagement.

Hutchins had a much different view. He certainly believed that an educated citizenry was necessary to a democracy, but he rooted that requirement in what Dewey called "the superficial expla-

---

Source: "Dewey versus Hutchins: The Next Round," by Thomas Ehrlich, reprinted from *Education and Democracy: Re-Imaging Liberal Learning in America,* edited by R. Orrill, 1997, by College Entrance Examination Board. Reprinted with permission.

nation that . . . a government resting upon popular suffrage cannot be successful unless those who elect and who obey their governors are educated."[3] To Hutchins, an education for citizenship meant a liberal education, and a liberal education meant reading and discussing the great books of the Western world, with particular emphasis on metaphysics.

To the contrary, Dewey wrote, students learn best not by sitting in a closed room and reading the works of Aristotle and other great Western minds in search of first principles, as Hutchins proposed, but by opening the doors and windows of experience to the problems that surround us. Learning starts with problems rooted in experiences, Dewey urged, and continues with the application of increasingly complex ideas and increasingly sophisticated skills to increasingly complicated problems. There must be both experiences that interest students and problems that emerge out of those experiences. To resolve the problems, students naturally need information and techniques. Aristotle can be a superb teacher in that process. But learning starts with experience and problems. The goal of education is not intellectual inquiry for its own sake, as Hutchins proclaimed, but the betterment of democratic practice across the whole of American society.

Although the exchange between Dewey and Hutchins has been characterized as a "brisk little spat" in Alan Ryan's splendid biography,[4] it continued in full force up to and through World War II, with each side attracting its own measure of adherence and criticism. In 1945, for example, Harvard's famous Red Book, *General Education in a Free Society,* presented its approach to liberal education in part as a commentary on the opposing positions taken by Dewey and Hutchins. More significant, the debate set the terms of engagement on the substance, the pedagogy, and the recipients of that education in colleges and universities throughout the country. These issues persist today and continue to underly our disagreements about the nature and purpose of undergraduate education, even though we may not readily associate them with the names of Dewey and Hutchins. It is worthwhile, then, to revisit this debate for the purpose of asking where matters now stand and where they are going.

The Purpose of Education

The catalyst for the debate was a little book by Hutchins, *The Higher Learning in America.* He began by deploring "the plight of higher learning" and by attributing most of the mess to a lust for money, a lust that had created "the service-station conception of a university,"[5] a conception that a university must hold itself out to perform all tasks that society asks of it. That debasement of John Henry Cardinal Newman's vision of a university, he argued, had turned that institution away from the cultivation of the intellect for its own sake and toward an anti-intellectual practicality. Hutchins complained that "empiricism, having taken the place of thought as the basis of research, took its place, too, as the basis of education. It led by easy stages to vocationalism."[6] In his view, the university had become a vast center of vocational training. It was past time, he pressed, "to stand firm and show our people what the higher learning is. As education it is the single-minded pursuit of the intellectual virtues. As scholarship it is the single-minded devotion to the advancement of knowledge."[7]

To meet the scourge of vocationalism, which leads to "triviality and isolation" and debases the course of study and the staff, Hutchins proposed "a course of study consisting of the greatest books of the western world and the arts of reading, writing, thinking, and speaking, together with mathematics, the best exemplar of the processes of human reason."[8] In an often-quoted paragraph he proposed this challenge: "Education implies teaching. Teaching implies knowledge. Knowledge is truth. The truth is everywhere the same. Hence education should be everywhere the same."[9]

It could hardly have surprised Hutchins, his protests notwithstanding, that Dewey picked up the challenge. Dewey wrote a series of review articles about the book in a monthly journal called *The Social Frontier,* for which he was an editor and regular contributor. He began by applauding the attack by Hutchins on "the aimlessness of our present educational scheme."[10] But readers should be aware of the Hutchins remedies, he urged, for they are as dangerous as the disease, perhaps worse. Hutchins really wanted to insulate higher learning from contemporary social life, Dewey argued. "This conception is explicitly seen in the constant divorce set up between intellect and practice, and between intellect and experience."[11] The concern of Hutchins for excessive "practicality" masked an effort to separate general education at the university level from the practical problems of the world around us. In the terms that Fried used, Hutchins wanted a "moratorium" on experiences in society at just the time when, Dewey urged, such experiences were the necessary catalysts to learning. Most important, education for democracy could not occur within an institution sealed off from society.

To Hutchins, wrote Dewey, general education began with a set of "ultimate first principles," found in writings by great Western thinkers, particularly Plato, Aristotle, and St. Thomas Aquinas. Perhaps Hutchins wouldn't like the label "authoritarian" applied to his scheme, wrote Dewey. But that is exactly what it was. And while "I would not intimate that the author has any sympathy with fascism, . . . his idea as to the proper course to be taken is akin to the distrust of freedom and the consequent appeal to some fixed authority that is now overrunning the world. There is implicit in every assertion of fixed and eternal first truths the necessity for some human authority to decide, in this world of conflicts, just what these truths are, and how they shall be taught."[12] Some may prefer Aristotle or St. Thomas Aquinas. Others may look to Hegel or Karl Marx or even Mussolini "as the seers of first truths; and there are those who prefer Nazism." Unfortunately, "Hutchins has completely evaded the problem of who is to determine the definite truths that constitute the hierarchy."[13]

Hutchins was not pleased. He rejected the charge that he wanted to divorce thinking from facts and experience. He said he would not apply the terms "fixed" or "eternal" to the principles or truths that he espoused. And he naturally did not take kindly to the "dexterous intimation that I am a fascist in result if not in intention (made the more dexterous by his [Dewey's] remark that he is making no such intimation)."[14]

Dewey responded that *The Higher Learning in America* is "a work of great significance" because it exposed the confused state of higher education, and particularly because it raised a basic issue about the nature of knowledge and learning. In essence, Dewey argued, the classic traditional view was the one Hutchins expounded: "there is a power or faculty of Reason or Intellect . . . which is capable of grasping first and ultimate truths that are the measure and criterion of all inferior forms of knowledge, namely, those which have to do with empirical matters, in which knowledge of both the physical world and practical affairs is included."[15] To the contrary, Dewey urged "the primary place of experience, experimental method, and integral connection with practice in determination of knowledge and the auxiliary role of what is termed Reason and Intellect in the classic tradition."[16] Above all, he saw democracy as a great experiment, one with no "first and ultimate truths." Rather, the policies of a vibrant democracy are constantly changing in response to new evidence, while it maintains a collaborative mode of inquiry and an openness of mind to new ideas and approaches.

Education and Democracy

Dewey's rejoinders to Hutchins are permeated with implicit links between education and the goal of democracy, though he neither makes those links explicit nor provides concrete examples. Indeed, when I perused *Democracy and Education* for the first time, I asked Bob Orrill where in the book Dewey focuses directly on the links. Bob's right answer was that Dewey doesn't do that, because in his vision all dimensions of a good educational institution—the substance and pedagogy of the curriculum, the extracurricular activities, and the social interactions—contribute to training in the practice of democracy. In this sense, the whole book is about the links.

Though Hutchins refused to accept the battleground as defined by Dewey, much of his work in subsequent years was devoted to securing and defending intellectual turf that reads remarkably like what Dewey was so sharply criticizing. As Harry Ashmore describes in his wonderful biography, Hutchins focused enormous energy on the Great Books Project, which included just those works that Hutchins urged were the core of a liberal education.[17] That education, he said in effect, involves going into a library lined with the Great Books, closing the door, and studying those books. When you have gained the learning they contain, you are an educated person. In the introductory volume to the project, Hutchins wrote an extended essay supporting his views and devoted an entire chapter to a critique of Dewey and his views.[18]

Dewey argued that this approach was dangerous nonsense. Dangerous because the notion of fixed truths requires a seal of authenticity from some human authority, which leads away from democracy and toward Fascism. Nonsense because purely intellectual study should not be separated from practical study or from the great social problems confronting society. Separation can only weaken the intellect and undercut the resolution of those problems. Study Aristotle, Plato, Aquinas, and the others, Dewey urged, but recognize that contemporary learning from their writings requires the application of their insights to contemporary issues. The interaction of knowledge and skills with experience, focused on a problem, is key to learning.

The debate continued long after 1936. For example, in 1944 Dewey had a sharp exchange on the substance of a liberal education with Alexander Meiklejohn, a friend of Hutchins and a strong defender of his approach. (Meiklejohn was head of the experimental college at the University of Wisconsin and a member of the editorial board for the Great Books Project.)

Dewey wrote an essay in the pages of *Fortune* magazine, in which he once more blasted the notion that the realm of morals involved a separate and higher level of inquiry than the sciences, that distinct approaches were appropriate to each, and that first principles could be gleaned from a few shelves of great works. "The idea that an adequate education of any kind can be obtained by means of a miscellaneous assortment of a hundred books, more or less, is laughable when viewed practically."[19] He particularly deplored primary reliance on the works of ancient Greek and medieval scholars. That "reactionary movement," as he called it, "ignores and in effect denies the principle of experimental inquiry and firsthand observation that is the lifeblood of the entire advances made in the sciences."[2] The method of inquiry for both morals and sciences should be that same experimental mode. The argument that morals were rooted in first and immutable principles was exactly the one made centuries before about the sciences—and proven false. In both realms, the approach must be the same: "working hypotheses that on the one hand condense the results of continued prior experience and inquiry, and on the other hand direct further fruitful inquiry whose conclusions in turn test and develop for further use the working principles used."[21]

Meiklejohn responded as one of Dewey's opponents.[22] He gave a spirited defense of St. John's College and its curriculum based on the Great Books. Dewey dismissed the response as missing his point, for he was attacking a philosophy much more important than a single institution.[23] Meiklejohn came back once again with the comment that just as he may have misunderstood Dewey, so Dewey misunderstood him.[24] But Dewey would have none of that. In a four-line rejoinder Dewey, the gentle philosopher, wrote that while Meiklejohn was "entitled to admit that he misconstrued" Dewey's views, "when he speaks of a 'joint failure' I find him over inclusive."[25] So much for collegiality when it came to the philosophy of education.

Implications for Today and the Future

Three great issues were at stake in the debate between Dewey and Hutchins on undergraduate education. What is the purpose of that education and who should be the students? What should be learned? What should be the learning process?

On the purpose of an undergraduate education, Hutchins urged that liberal learning should be learning for its own sake and for living the "good life" in the Aristotelian sense. Properly designed, a general education should inculcate students with "the intellectual virtues," which are "good in themselves and good as means to happiness. By the intellectual virtues I mean good intellectual habits."[26] Hutchins cited Aquinas as the primary definer of those habits. Even the professional education that might follow a general education should have little to do with practical issues of society, and even less with baser matters of what he termed "vocationalism."

Dewey took a much different view. Democracy should be the goal of education, and education for democracy requires a community of learning in which members learn together and from each other. Education is obviously necessary for personal fulfillment, he argued. And education for personal goals should not be separated from education for career objectives, for the same skills and substantive knowledge are often relevant to both. But an education system that aims solely at the personal and the professional is still inadequate; democracy should be the ultimate aim.

Dewey rejected the Hutchins attack on "vocationalism" in blunt terms. In a lecture at Harvard a few years before the Hutchins debate, Dewey had quoted with approval the president of Antioch College, Arthur E. Morgan,

> In so far as the liberal arts college stands for a perpetuation of the traditional conflict between vocation and culture, it seems doomed to play a constantly decreasing role in education. . . . It is rapidly becoming a fact that study within one's vocational preparation is an important means of freeing and liberating the mind. This being true, the inevitable trend in education is toward the rapid thinning of the traditional educational wall between vocational and cultural. The liberal arts college will survive and render service in proportion as it recognizes this fact and brings its course of study and administrative setup into effective conformity with it.[27]

Who Should Be the Students?

In contrast, Hutchins believed that his approach to liberal learning provided the best education for leadership. He was an elitist in his views about society and its functioning, and how education should support that functioning. He did hope to expose wide audiences to the Great Books, and his project included a number of guides to help average citizens through the Western wisdom of the ages. He wrote a chapter called "Education for All" for the introductory volume in the Great Books series. In this chapter, Hutchins argued that the democratic ideal requires that everyone should have an education in the Great Books—i.e., a liberal education. His elitism was expressed in terms of who should be the teachers and should control the teachings.

Hutchins also believed that higher education should be restricted to a relatively small segment of the population who could, by his standards, truly benefit from that education. Ideally, they should be chosen on the basis of intellectual potential, not wealth—an aristocracy of intellect, limited in number. He shared that view with most of the presidents of major private universities at the end of World War II, who resisted the GI Bill because it was designed to open higher education to masses of returning servicemen.

Lawrence Cremin put their differences this way: "For Dewey, education was a process of growth that had no end beyond itself, a process in which individuals were constantly extending their knowledge, informing their judgments, refining their sensibilities and illuminating their moral choices. For Hutchins, education was nothing more or less than the cultivation of the intellect, the training of the mind."[28] In Dewey's view, a democratic society is a collaborative, interactive one in which individuals continuously learn from each other in making the whole more than the sum of the parts. It is hardly surprising that, for Dewey, higher education should be open to expanding numbers, while to Hutchins it should be reserved for an elite. Viewed from today's perspective, on this issue, Dewey has won in the court of public opinion. When he crossed swords with Hutchins, fewer than one in five high school graduates went on to college. Today the figure is almost two-thirds.

The Purpose of Education

It is hard to know for certain what the undergraduates of the 1930s, or their parents, wanted from an undergraduate education, but it is clear that the primary concern today is employment. Over the past several years, Richard Hersh, president of Hobart and William Smith Colleges, and Daniel Yankelovich of DYG, Inc. surveyed prospective and current college students and their parents as part of a long-term effort to analyze the challenges facing liberal arts education in America. The results of their surveys are clear: College-bound youth and their parents believe "that the overarching purpose of higher education is help with getting a job and guiding a career and that acquiring 'career skills,' therefore, is the paramount goal."[29] One can bemoan the loss of learning for its own sake, as Hutchins did. Certainly the founding of Rollins College in 1926, rooted in liberal studies and the education of the whole person, would have cheered him. On the basis of anecdotal evidence, however, I am skeptical that most students in most colleges and universities during the years before World War II sought learning for its own sake with anything like the fervor that academics with nostalgia for that era would have us believe.

Can an undergraduate education be liberal if the primary purpose of most students in seeking that education is to find a job? Elsewhere in this volume, Bruce Kimball says "no." He writes that "much liberal learning . . . could be gathered from working and vice versa. But if liberal education . . . becomes vocational, then it loses its principled basis and intellectual warrant. The difference lies in the purpose, and the purpose transforms the experience." Kimball says that Dewey agreed with his position, but I can't square this with Dewey's stress on the necessary joinder of liberal and vocational education. I see no reason to define liberal education in terms of purpose rather than content and skills.

On today's campuses, Hutchins also lost the argument in terms of the substance of undergraduate education, though Dewey can hardly be said to have won it. Almost no one outside the walls of St. John's College urges a primary focus on the Great Books as the source of first principles to guide undergraduates. The issue is not whether those works should be read by undergraduates; they should be read. And it is not whether courses that focus on the texts of those works should be supplemented with works particularly by women and nonwhites; almost all agree that this is also needed. But no undergraduate curriculum that I've read or heard about in recent years takes the Hutchins approach. The problem, of course, is that most of those curricula do not seem to adopt any other coherent approach, either. They certainly are not focused on democracy as a goal in the sense that Dewey proposed.

What should be the essential elements or goals of a baccalaureate degree? During my first year as president of Indiana University, I led an ambitious planning process designed to enhance that university's academic quality. We sought at the outset to answer the question, and concluded that there was broad agreement across all campuses on nine elements. Many would have added a tenth, though there was no consensus on which one should be included. Those nine were:

- writing and speaking English clearly, correctly, persuasively, and interestingly;
- reading carefully and critically, both for personal growth and enjoyment, and to acquire information and knowledge;
- computing and reasoning both quantitatively and analytically;
- understanding the physical world and its relationship to human activities;
- reading, writing, and understanding at least one foreign language;
- using concepts from the behavioral and biological sciences to comprehend human relationships and human communities;
- devising insights and pleasure from intellectual and artistic achievement in both contemporary and historical contexts;
- recognizing and appreciating the contributions of both Western and non-Western cultures in the modern world and throughout human history; and
- developing a consciousness of the ethical implications of human actions and the ability to define and articulate personal and cultural values.

We also found broad agreement that breadth of experience, "which marks the most exciting undergraduate adventure, should be complemented by a rigorous, in-depth exposure to a major discipline, field, or profession. The ideal undergraduate program thus registers the creative tension between the general and speculative curriculum, on the one hand, and the professional, practical, and specialized curriculum on the other."[30]

Similar statements are made in the catalogs of most of the country's 3,000-plus colleges and universities. But I readily acknowledge that they fail to tell much about the learning outcomes that students and others (including those who pay tuition bills) can or should expect from a baccalaureate, and even less about either how colleges and universities should achieve those outcomes or how the public can know whether the institutions succeed in doing so.

What Should Be the Learning Process?

In the realm of pedagogy, Hutchins clearly won. The dominant mode in liberal education is still a pile of books and a closed classroom. Modes of active learning—reaching outside the classroom to engage students in the problems of the world around them—are the exception. Dewey put primary emphasis on the need to link theory and practice, part of his broader view that experience is the catalyst for learning, and that experiential learning is essential for a democratic society.

Although his views have helped shape professional education on the undergraduate as well as graduate level, liberal education has remained relatively immune. The Red Book approach of Harvard in 1945 has been generally followed throughout the country. It emphasizes a spectrum of learning in the humanities, social sciences, and sciences, and a range of techniques of inquiry to reflect those disciplines, but the approach was essentially a victory for Hutchins. It was also a rejection of Dewey's concept of students learning together, as a community, in interaction with the society around them.

The most obvious reason for Hutchins's victory is that the "moratorium" approach is easier for faculty members, for they need not be concerned that they may not know something that their students are learning. But my exchange with Charles Fried illustrates a deeper rationale of many faculty in the arts and sciences. They believe that the "moratorium" approach is sound, that the undergraduate academic experience should occur in an ivory tower surrounded by an invisible moat separating the college or university from the society it serves.

New Learning Strategies—Dewey May Yet Win

Fortunately, from my perspective, a number of "anti-moratorium" strategies, consistent with Dewey's approach and Kimball's analysis, are gaining momentum on many college and university campuses. They may even be reshaping undergraduate education, though I am skeptical of a transformation. They are certainly far removed from issues of political correctness that have so troubled Allan Bloom and other current heirs of Hutchins. These strategies are not focused on the substance of undergraduate learning as much as on the ways in which that learning can be enhanced.

Four strategies seem to me particularly interesting. They are community-service learning, as opposed to closed classroom learning; problem based learning, as opposed to discipline-based learning; collaborative learning, as opposed to individual learning; and the use of interactive technology, as opposed to chalkboards. These are not the only emerging pedagogic strategies in undergraduate education. Increased attention to undergraduate research and expanded use of narratives generally (case studies particularly) could also be cited. But these four seem to me the most promising for realizing Dewey's ideas and ideals, and wholly consistent with the trends that Kimball cites. The strategies also underscore that how a subject is taught is as important as what is taught. Substance and pedagogy are closely intertwined.

Common to these strategies are two threads that spiral through them like a double helix. Education as a social and socializing function is the first—what Professor Jack Lane of Rollins terms the "communalization of education." This is the thread that most directly reflects Dewey's focus on democracy as the overarching goal of education. As Lane stresses,

> For Dewey, the two principles of individualization and communalization of education were interdependent. The one motivated students to learn, the other made that learning worthwhile. Individualization without community led to self-indulgence and to the privatization and atomization of learning; community without individualization tended toward conformity, coercion, and even stagnation.[31]

But, as Lane also notes, the concept of community never infused learning in American higher education, even in progressive colleges such as Sarah Lawrence and Antioch, but was left to extracurricular activities and living arrangements.

The second common thread is a shift from teaching to learning and a shift in the role of faculty member from teacher to coach. In this sense, the thread marks a return to Dewey's concept that student interest should be the starting point in education, as urged in the 1931 Rollins Conference Report. Of all elements comprising Dewey's views on education, this can be the most easily misunderstood, for it sounds suspiciously like a call to let students play in sandboxes or do whatever else they want to do. Instead, it was a call to shape learning experiences around the individual interests and needs of students.

It maybe helpful to use Portland State University and its new programs in general education as an example of the four pedagogic shifts that are occurring nationally. The university is well along in revising its entire undergraduate curriculum, with a particular emphasis on general education. In the words of former President

Judith Ramaley, the new general education curriculum "responds to our students' need to learn how to learn for a lifetime so that they can respond to continuous societal change. We will use real situations and problems as a means to achieve our educational goals, so that our students will learn, and at the same time, serve the community."[32] Dewey would have been delighted.

There is an extensive and growing literature that describes and discusses each of the four strategies, so I will do no more than touch on a few key points. Community-service learning has been my particular interest for some years, in my own courses and in helping to reshape undergraduate education at several institutions, so I begin with that strategy and comment on it at greater length than the others.

Community-Service Learning The substance of community-service-learning courses varies widely, but all include academic study, community service, and structured reflection to integrate that study and service. The community service may assume a variety of forms: direct aid to individuals in need, education and outreach activities, and policy analysis and research. Community-service learning—a subset of experiential learning, which, in turn, is a subset of active learning—has been around a long time, but as with the other movements described here, it has received strong support in recent years.

In the new Portland State undergraduate curriculum, all first-year students must enroll in a program called "Freshman Inquiry" in which they choose from a series of problem based courses. While the problems in each course differ, common learning goals are specified. Teams of five faculty members plan and teach each course. One example is "Embracing Einstein's Universe: Language, Culture, and Relativity," led by faculty from the anthropology, computer science, English, physics, and sociology departments. The course examines both the life and thought of Einstein and "the shift from pre-Einstein to Einsteinian physics as a special case of a profound shift in twentieth-century thought about absolutes . . . (and its expression) in the arts, social theory, literature and the use of language, and other forms of communication."[33]

Students in the course not only learn about these subjects, but are also engaged in community service by teaching about them to high school students who, in turn, teach about them to elementary school students. In an essay in this volume, Lee Shulman recalls that Aristotle judged teaching to be the highest form of understanding, that "no test of human understanding was more demanding than the test of whether you could take something you thought you knew and teach it to someone else." Students in this course were doubly put to that test.

The most important rationale for community-service learning, and the other learning strategies I am discussing, is that it strengthens academic learning. I do not urge that academic learning can be enhanced by community-service learning in every course, any more than I suggest that all intellectual abilities can be developed only through application to community problems. But I am convinced that the academic learning of students in many courses covering most academic fields can be increased by integrating community service with readings, papers, lectures, class discussions, and other course work.

The conclusions of one study may help to illustrate the point. Three political science professors recently reported on a course they taught, "Contemporary Political Problems," at the University of Michigan.[34] From a large class, they randomly selected one group to be involved with community service, along with readings and written assignments, while the other sections did some added traditional assignments. On three scales, they found that the students in the community-service-learning sections succeeded more than did their classmates. Their grades were better (by blind grading), they reported higher satisfaction in course evaluations, and their awareness of societal problems was greater as measured by a questionnaire. The effort was repeated and the results were equally positive. The faculty members emphasized that a key factor in these results was time spent integrating community service into the curriculum through regular discussion sections.

In a broader study, two Vanderbilt professors have coordinated an analysis of data from more than 1,500 students in community-service-learning courses at 20 colleges and universities across the country.[35] Preliminary results indicate that students reported they learn more, are more intellectually stimulated, and work harder in community-service-learning courses than in their other classes. A RAND study of the Learn and Serve Program, sponsored by the Corporation on

National Service, reached similar conclusions.[36] The preliminary results of the Vanderbilt and RAND studies also indicate that community-service learning has a significant impact on citizenship skills and attitudes of social responsibility.

Although different community-service-learning courses emphasize different outcomes, they share a stress on academic learning. Three other learning dimensions are also important. Recognizing that each instructor may have a somewhat different perspective and may use different terminology, I term these dimensions civic learning, moral learning, and social development/career learning. The first two are unique to community-service learning. The third is common to many forms of experiential learning, of which community-service learning is a subset.

Civic learning means coming to understand how a community functions, what problems it faces, the richness of its diversity, the need for individual commitments of time and energy to enhance community life, and, most of all, the importance of working as a community to resolve community concerns. Benjamin Barber of Rutgers, in *An Aristocracy of Everyone,* writes about the importance of education in increasing community involvement.[37] That this is important is attested to by Robert Putnam of Harvard, in a now-famous article titled "Bowling Alone." Putnam has chronicled the sharp decline in participation in community activities throughout the country, with a resulting decline in what he calls "social capital."[38]

Both of these writers, and many others, have stressed that community service is one of the most important ways, often the most important, to counter these trends among students. Civic learning—in the sense of how a community works and how to help it work better—and academic learning are mutually reinforcing, as Dewey stressed. This is also true of the moral learning that students gain through community-service learning. By moral learning I mean reinforcing the elements of character that lead to ethical actions. These elements include respect for the autonomy and dignity of others; compassion and kindness; honesty and integrity; and a commitment to equity and fairness.

The undergraduate years, particularly for those transiting from adolescence to adulthood, have a profound impact on moral character.[39] Robert Coles of Harvard has argued eloquently in *The Call of Service* for the proposition that moral character is enhanced by community-service learning.[40] He has shown that community-service learning helps students think about themselves in relation to others—who are their neighbors and what are their obligations to their neighbors? Service connects thought and feeling in a deliberate way, creating a context in which students can explore how they feel about what they are thinking and what they think about how they feel. The interaction of academic study and community service, linked by guided reflection, offers students opportunities to consider what is important to them—and why—in ways they too rarely experience otherwise.

I link social development and career learning because interpersonal skills such as careful listening, sympathy for others, and abilities to lead, to compromise, to change one's mind, and so forth, as well as personal traits such as self-esteem, are all important to personal interaction in any setting and also vital to success in most careers. Time and again, employers complain that new workers do not "get along" in the workplace, particularly with those from backgrounds different from their own. No community-service-learning course can transform a student, but faculty members frequently report on the significant difference such a course can make in the understanding and insight students have about themselves and their relations with others.

The potential for community-service learning is particularly significant at the great majority of colleges and universities where most of the students commute. These students are usually familiar with their community and its problems, and expect to continue to live and work there. They become undergraduates to gain the knowledge and skills they think they need to lead productive lives in that community. All too often, however, they see little link between their intellectual learning and the issues they want to address personally or professionally. In the experience of faculty members across the country, community-service learning is an important means of providing that link.

Although I have suggested that Dewey would have been delighted by the increased interest in community-service learning, I do not claim that democracy is its goal in the sense that Dewey envisioned for education generally. Civic learning is an important impetus, but it is not the primary rationale in the minds of many—probably most—faculty members who are teaching community-service-learning courses. And civic learning in the sense that Barber and others use such terms is narrower than the learning that Dewey envisaged as preparation for democracy. But the purpose of civic engagement is similar, and the process of community-service learning is itself a democratic process in the sense that Dewey conceived.

Problem Based Learning The second emerging strategy is increased attention to problem areas, as opposed to disciplines. Problem-based learning has been emphasized by some higher-education faculty for a long time, but has received increased attention in recent years. The essential element is not simply that problem based courses are interdisciplinary, but rather that a problem is the starting point in designing a course. As students advance, they tackle increasingly difficult problems, using increasingly sophisticated techniques and increasingly complex knowledge bases.

Among the Freshman Inquiry courses at Portland State, for example, are The Making of a Pluralistic Society: Who We Are and How We Came To Be; The City: Vision and Realities; The Ways of Knowing Home; and Values in Conflict: Knowledge, Power, and Politics. More important than the titles, the subject matter in each course is explored as problems to be solved. Each involves bringing experiences to bear on those problems. Dewey would have been pleased.

General education courses designed around problems use the multiple prisms through which different academic disciplines view a problem to be analyzed. Taken together, those courses can aid students in examining problems, breaking them into component issues, resolving each issue, then putting the pieces back together again.

Case studies have come to be seen, in a number of fields, as a particularly useful means to address problems. Professional schools in business, education, and law have been using various forms of case studies for some time, but they are now becoming increasingly common in liberal arts and science courses as well. The form, organization, and use of case studies varies widely among different disciplines in business, law, and education, for example. A comparative analysis of case studies and their uses across disciplines would be particularly helpful.

Dewey put particular emphasis on the problem or "project" approach as "the way out of educational confusion" that permeated colleges and universities.[41] A central error of higher education, he charged, was the arbitrary categorization of academic study into disciplines divorced from the complex concerns of society and its citizenry. The failure to integrate disciplines, and to focus student inquiry on problems, made learning arid and abstract. Linking liberal and vocational education, which was so important to Dewey, was also tied to the problem approach, for it enabled students to develop skills and insights by training their attention on matters that seemed to them real and important, not remote and bloodless. "A reorganization of subject matter which takes account of out-leanings into the wide world of nature and man, of knowledge and of social interests and uses, cannot fail save in the most callous and intellectually obdurate to awaken some permanent interest and curiosity. Theoretical subjects will become more practical, because more related to the scope of life; practical subjects will become charged with theory and intelligent insight. Both will be vitally and not just formally unified."[42] Shaped in this way, higher education could enhance a lifelong process of growth in all dimensions of intellectual and emotional development.

The problem approach is also key in preparing students for active participation in the ongoing renewal of democracy. That renewal involves much more than attention to the minimum responsibilities of a citizen—to vote, to participate in various civic organizations, and the like—though these responsibilities are certainly both important and ignored by most citizens today. But democracy also calls for citizens to identify community problems and to work communally to resolve those problems. Again, I do not suggest that this benefit of the problem approach is a factor in the minds of most faculty members who use it in their classrooms, but it is another piece in a larger picture that may be moving higher education closer to Dewey's vision.

Collaborative Learning Cooperative or collaborative learning (I use the two terms interchangeably, though some commentators define them differently) is a third strategy that both has a long history and is increasingly part of undergraduate education. A recent volume states that "collaborative learning may well be the most significant pedagogical shift of the century for teaching and learning in higher education."[43] As with the problem-centered approach, collaborative learning is integral to Dewey's view of democracy as the goal of education, though not explicit in the minds of most faculty members who use it.

As president of Indiana University, the most common criticism of graduates I heard from employers was that they were ill-trained to work as members of a team. Although most of the tasks these graduates would be called upon to perform in the workplace would be done as team members, most of their undergraduate work was done alone. Collaborative learning is a pedagogy particularly targeted toward enhancing the skills and abilities required to be a productive team member.

The movement toward collaboration at every stage of undergraduate learning is accelerating in undergraduate education generally, particularly in preprofessional and professional fields such as business, but also in the liberal arts. Students in the Freshman Inquiry courses at Portland State, for example, work in teams on projects, whether papers, research, or field work. A relatively rich literature exists on collaborative learning, so I will not review it here.

Interactive Technology The use of interactive technology is a fourth strategy with potentially significant pedagogical impact on undergraduate learning.[44] Although no one has yet improved on the one-to-one, face-to-face tutorial approach to undergraduate learning in terms of outcomes, it is rarely possible because of cost. However, technology may provide some of the same interactive benefits. I doubt that a "virtual university," along the lines that the western governors are planning, can support student learning in most undergraduate fields without significant face-to-face contact.[45] But many courses can be taught primarily with interactive computer software, as long as opportunities exist for counseling and advising on an individual basis.

Computer conferencing is the best means to break the requirement that the time schedules of teacher and student be the same. As is not true with audio and video conferencing, students can learn from computer conferencing 24 hours a day. E-mail enables students and teachers to communicate with each other at any time. Separate bulletin boards for each course enable teachers to have continuing dialogues with students taking a specific class. Teachers can post a draft document and students can comment on and revise it together. Teachers can also, for example, check on student comprehension by asking each member of even a large class to send an e-mail explanation. Collaborative learning becomes much easier when the collaborating students need not be in the same place at the same time, but can cooperate through computer technology. Community-service-learning sites can also be linked to faculty offices through that technology. In this sense, use of interactive technology is less a separate pedagogy than a means to enhance the others.

Many colleges and universities are engaged in one, or even two, of the four strategies as the result of conscious, campus-wide policies. (At every institution of higher education, individual faculty members are using particular strategies in their individual teaching.) A few campuses are leaders in all of them, though none of those campuses is on the list of major research universities or most prestigious liberal arts colleges. Further, they are not among the "wannabes" for inclusion on that list. Rather, they are campuses where wise leadership and faculty cohesion have supported rigorous rethinking and restructuring across the entire curriculum. Alverno College—a small, private institution—is a prime example. Led by President Joel Reed, its faculty members have done extraordinary work in analyzing the interactions of pedagogy and learning for several decades. Their findings, which have been well publicized, have profoundly important implications for all of higher education. Portland State University—a large, public university formerly under the leadership of President Ramaley—is another example of pedagogic change on an institution-wide basis, though its efforts have been less well publicized.

Education for Undergraduate Teaching

The four learning strategies can make a difference, of course, only to the extent that they are actually being incorporated into the undergraduate classroom. What is going on in terms of training teachers for that classroom? Until recently, unfortunately, the answer was "not much." But another cluster of steps that Dewey would applaud today concern the training of undergraduate teachers. From my perspective as a former administrator at three research universities, the single worst failing of those institutions is the lack of serious training in teaching for graduate students. At Stanford, at Pennsylvania, and at Indiana University, Bloomington, I watched our graduate students leave for teaching positions with little or no education in how to teach. Their faculty supervisors gave close review to scholarly abilities, through supervision of dissertations, but almost no attention to teaching abilities. Perhaps most troublesome, most of our faculty had little firsthand sense of what the professional life of those graduate students would be like when they began at one of the more than 3,000 colleges and universities in the country—usually not at one of the 75 or so research universities. On the regional campuses of Indiana University, teaching loads were at least double what they were at Bloomington. This is equally true at campuses of the California State University, where I now teach.

Disciplines in the arts and sciences are certainly not alone in their lack of attention to education for teaching. Professional schools are at least as guilty. I can use law schools as an example, both because I have taught in them for most of my professional life and because, of all professional school faculty, law professors traditionally pride themselves on being teachers who are also scholars, rather than the reverse. But new law teachers today, as when I began teaching at Stanford, have no formal or informal instruction in pedagogy. They are told to teach, and if lucky, they have a mentor or two who might offer advice from time to time. I recall asking a friend to videotape some of my classes in my first year of teaching and learning a great deal from the terrifying experience of watching. But that was my own idea, done because I had a friend with a video camera. Teaching is certainly considered along with scholarship in terms of promotion and tenure, and most law teachers I know spend considerable time preparing for class. But there are few opportunities for new law teachers to examine carefully what law students are expected to learn, how different students best learn, and what a caring teacher can do to promote the learning process.

Unfortunately, I see only faint signs of change in terms of the education of teachers in law and other professional disciplines. A few schools assign senior faculty members to mentor their new colleagues. Others encourage new faculty to attend workshops organized by one of the professional organizations. The teaching resource centers at some universities have special training sessions for those faculty. But these are modest steps to ameliorate a sad situation.

In the realm of the arts and sciences, I sense more attention to the problem. One important step has been a national initiative on "Preparing Future Faculty," jointly sponsored by the Association of American Colleges and Universities and the Council of Graduate Schools and funded by the Pew Charitable Trusts. This effort was designed to develop model programs for the preparation of college faculty, with a particular emphasis on teaching and service, in addition to scholarship. About one million dollars was awarded in 1994 to 17 doctoral universities. Each of these institutions was expected to create partnerships with a small group of diverse, primarily undergraduate institutions. This joinder was intended to enable graduate students to gain firsthand experience with different types of institutions and student bodies. In a report on the first year of the program, the initiative directors stated that "A total of 85 institutions are part of the project—18 community colleges, 7 historically black colleges and universities, 6 women's colleges, and schools of liberal arts and comprehensive institutions, along with 11 land-grant universities and 9 members of the Association of American Colleges and Universities."[46]

In a survey of students, faculty, and administrators involved in the program, responses from all three groups were overwhelmingly positive at the end of the first year. As might have been expected, training future teachers takes time, energy, and effort, and an insufficient amount of each was sometimes allocated. But the overall picture gives reason for optimism that significant steps are possible with relatively modest funding.

Other universities have started their own teacher-preparation programs. At Indiana University, for example, graduate students at Bloomington now have opportunities to teach at the seven other university campuses in the system. Outstanding faculty from those campuses serve as mentors for the graduate students, who must also participate in a pedagogy program. Ten of the largest departments at Bloomington have developed their own programs, which include pedagogy courses within their disciplines, and the university has a general program, as well.

I do not know how quickly teacher-training efforts for graduate students will replicate along the lines of the Pew-sponsored program and the ones at Indiana and elsewhere. In an essay in this volume, Louis Menand expresses confidence that the move is underway. As he wrote in the *New York Times Magazine,* "Sooner or later, universities engaged in the production of new professors are likely to decide that if they want their graduates to get these jobs, they will have to train them appropriately. And when the way professors are trained changes, the whole picture will start to change. The dog will finally be big enough to wag the tail."[47] I hope he is right, though the tail has proved powerfully independent for a long time.

If colleges and universities hiring new faculty give increasing preference to those with serious and sustained training in teaching, the market will force this move. Because those responsible for hiring were themselves rarely trained as teachers, however, the move will be resisted. But the public pressures for increased attention to teaching may break down the resistance. Particularly within large public systems such as California State University, there is great potential to pressure research universities. In the next 10 years, half of the current CSU faculty will reach retirement age. Not all of those will retire, but many will leave before that age. The 22 campuses of the university plan to hire mainly new Ph.D.'s. A significant share will, in all likelihood, come from the University of California. CSU has great leverage, therefore, to press UC for an enhanced program of teacher training for its graduate students, and a major CSU planning effort now underway includes this step in its proposals.

Learning Assessment

I have described two clusters of change for college and university teachers that would have pleased Dewey. Both show significant promise for enhancing higher education generally and undergraduate education particularly. Although their primary purpose, in the minds of their practitioners, may not be Dewey's vision of democracy, the results can have important benefits in furthering that vision. But the full promise of each cluster will be realized only if they are linked together, only if teacher training for graduate students includes the four pedagogic strategies.

Both clusters of change are directed at enhancing student learning. Underlying the strategies is an assumption that student learning can be improved when students engage in community-service learning, in problem-based learning, in collaborative learning, and in technology- assisted interactive learning. That assumption underscores the need to assess what students learn, and assessment is one of the seven trends that Kimball highlights. When the primary focus is on learning inputs, as it has been in U.S. higher education, assessing learning outputs is not a priority. If the focus shifts to learning outputs, as these four strategies are designed to do, then assessing those outputs becomes critical. A sad reality of the higher education scene, however, is that until recently, relatively little attention has been focused on learning assessment.

Higher education is generally judged by what goes in, not what comes out. The advantages to weaker faculty members of the input approach are obvious: What comes out is not their responsibility. Perhaps most striking, degrees are awarded on the basis of how long students sit in class. The currency of the realm is course credits, or "credit hours," of instruction. A student who completes a course that meets for three 50-minute hours per week generally earns three credit hours, without regard to what she or he has learned. Students are usually entitled to a baccalaureate degree on accumulating 120 semester credit hours (up to 150, depending on the institution and program). The amount of learning varies substantially among three-unit courses, but they are treated the same for degree purposes.

Similarly, faculty workloads are measured in terms of courses and credit hours. A faculty member at Berkeley, for example, will be expected to teach two three-credit courses, or perhaps only one, per semester: At California State, the expected load is generally four such courses. But at both institutions, seat time is the currency of the realm. The advantages of this input approach to the least able faculty members are obvious, and a primary reason for its great attraction. Work and workload are judged without regard to the amount of learning that occurs.

Accountability

Fortunately, not only are internal reforms of undergraduate education imposing pressures to assess learning, and to shift away from the input approach, but external forces are pressing in the same direction, as well. Legislators and their constituents are asking what is the "value added" from a college education and what are the outcomes that they can expect from a baccalaureate? The most obvious pressures are tightening public budgets. "What are we getting for our money?" is always a question that taxpayers and their representatives ask, but they ask it with a special edge when budgets are being cut. Substantial fiscal shortfalls are forcing all institutions and their funders to respond to issues of accountability far more directly and clearly in the 1990s than in preceding decades, and institutions of higher education are not exempt.

The demand for accountability leads directly to calls for measures of success in education—what are the desired learning outcomes and how does the public know whether they are achieved? Public colleges and universities are the primary targets, but public funding of private institutions is substantial, and those institutions are subject to essentially the same lines of inquiry, though not always from the same questioners or with the same intensity.

An even more powerful set of external pressures results from changing public perceptions of education generally and higher education particularly. Throughout our history, Americans have believed that opportunities for their children would be better than their own opportunities, that their children's standards of living would be higher, and that education would be the engine of this progress. In recent decades, increasing numbers of Americans have come to doubt this version of the American dream, to believe that children will not be as well off as their parents have been. Whether this perception will become reality makes less difference than does the fact that it now exists, and that its logical corollary is to blame the engine of progress for having stalled, if not slid back downhill. With that blame come demands for clear evidence that institutions of higher education are producing results. Results can be measured in various ways. "Are graduates getting jobs?" "Are they satisfied with their education?" "Are they good citizens of their communities?" But the most fundamental issue is, "Are they educated?" Answers to those questions require assessment.

In response to these twin pressures—internal pressures for reform of undergraduate education and external pressures for accountability—the assessment movement has gained substantial momentum over the past decade and a half. Some of this progress simply marks a return to techniques that were generally abandoned in the 1970s, such as capstone experiences for seniors and comprehensive examinations in fields of concentration. Other assessment efforts are more substantial.

Assessments of assessment in higher education have been published by numerous commentators.[48] It may be helpful in the context of liberal education, however, to provide a particular example. The Center for Reading and Language Studies at Indiana University, under the leadership of Professor Roger Farr, developed a set of performance-based assessments to determine whether undergraduates at the university were becoming critical readers and writers and in-depth problem solvers. This assessment effort was made because of concerns that there was too much reliance on multiple-choice and short answer questions that gave too little attention to critical skills. Although performance assessment was widely used in the School of Music and in other arts programs, it was not part of general education assessment. The assessments devised by Farr and his colleagues provide students with realistic problems that call on them to read a variety of texts, develop and write thoughtful responses to problems, and direct those responses to particular audiences. Students are urged to take notes while reading the texts, to organize their notes, to prepare a first draft, and then to revise and edit their response as a final draft. Six assessments were prepared that covered the integration of reading and writing, while including science, social science, and literature, and covering an integration of mathematics knowledge and communications skills.

One of the analytic reasoning (mathematics) problems, for example, asked the students to write a memorandum on whether it was practical to tow icebergs from Antarctica into the waters off the coast of Los Angeles as a means of meeting the critical water shortage in southern California. A substantial amount of information is provided about icebergs, how quickly they melt, and so forth. The results are evaluated in terms of reasoning, understanding of mathematical concepts, use of procedures, and communications skills.

The program was tested with about 2,000 undergraduates in 1994. The aim is not to evaluate each student but to assess the institution.

How well is it providing general education to its students? Where the assessments reveal gaps, how can the curriculum be revised to correct them? In considering many more traditional assessments, faculty members voice concerns that they will be forced to "teach to the test." This is a frequent fear in professional fields such as law and nursing, where standardized (often multiple-choice) tests are given on a statewide basis.

By contrast, the Indiana assessments are designed to help in curriculum revision. Faculty are encouraged to shape their courses to these assessments. The Indiana program provides solid evidence that performance-based testing can determine the extent to which undergraduates are able to demonstrate key abilities they need to complete in-depth academic work in a major and to function in the adult world after graduation. It also underscores that assessment and curriculum development should be closely linked.

Any revolution in undergraduate education, as opposed to tinkering, will require a shift away from seat time as the common academic currency. Credit for students and support for faculty must be linked to learning. This does not mean that time spent in performing a task is unimportant, but only that it is an element in the learning process rather than an end in itself. For students, this shift will certainly mean increased attention to self-paced learning, as well as to the four strategies that I discussed. For faculty members, it will mean more effective uses of time to promote learning. It will not be enough to announce that seat time is no longer the measure of academic credit; outcome measures will need to be devised in its place.

A number of innovative efforts to do just that are underway. Some, such as those at Alverno College, have been in operation for some years. Many more are recent developments. Two at California State University campuses may serve as examples. The faculty and administration of the new Monterey campus are committed to outcomes-based learning and to awarding degrees on the basis of demonstrated competencies. Under the leadership of President Peter Smith, they have developed seven broad learning goals. A set of 15 university learning requirements are used to measure achievement of those goals. A student's mastery of learning in each of the 15 can be assessed by an instructor in a course approved as providing the necessary experiences. If the instructor determines that a student has demonstrated proficiency, without regard to hours in class or other traditional standards, the student has met the requirement. In addition, students may design other means for completing each requirement, and then register for assessment in that requirement. It is too early to tell how successful this effort will be, but it holds great promise, not only for the Monterey campus, but for the whole California State University system.

Major efforts are also underway at Sonoma State University to reconceptualize teaching and learning. Over a three-year period, two faculty members are working in each of four disciplines to reformulate the introductory material in those disciplines, with the assistance of a full-time assessment expert, into one-unit modules, each of which has specific learning objectives, anticipated outcomes, and assessment tools. Each faculty member works to take each student as far along in the sequence of modules as the student can progress in a single semester. With the help of the assessment expert, each faculty member assesses the satisfactory completion of each unit of the module by students in the section taught by the other faculty member in the discipline. Students in the program all have computers, and extensive use is made of interactive technology, as well as collaborative learning.

The faculty and administration expect that most students will demonstrate the mastery of more than a single course's worth of concepts and content by the end of a semester and will be given credit accordingly. As a result, a section of 25 students might generate the equivalent of 40 enrollments. When this fact is joined with the reality that the failure-to-completion ratio in these courses usually ranges from 10 to 40 percent, it is entirely possible that faculty productivity may double.

What's Next—A Speculation

What the future will look like depends in great measure on resolution of a fundamental issue that divided Dewey and Hutchins, and still divides U.S. higher education a half century later. Will that education continue to be shaped primarily by a small group of universities dedicated to training an elite cadre of intellectual leaders, using the model if not the substance urged by Hutchins? Or will undergraduate education be increasingly formed by the needs of its consumers and by institutions that view their primary mission as responding to those needs?

Formidable forces favor the status quo. Almost all faculty members in higher education receive their credentials at one of about a hundred so-called research universities. Those credentials are almost exclusively related to research rather than teaching. The credentials are awarded by faculty who themselves were educated in the same system and know no other. The faculty at these institutions are an extraordinarily dedicated group of teachers, but what they learned about teaching and learning did not come from their doctoral programs or the universities that granted their doctoral degrees. Further, my experiences at four research universities—Harvard, Stanford, the University of Pennsylvania, and Indiana University at Bloomington—all suggest that most faculty members at those institutions see and feel no serious impetus to change. Particularly at the most prestigious research universities, demand among potential students is still virtually impervious to extraordinary price increases. The currency of the realm among faculty members at these institutions is not teaching, but rather released time from teaching. These are all elements that do not encourage a rosy view for those of us who think change is essential.

If this analysis is right—that the country's major research universities are not and will not be in the lead in promoting systemic change in undergraduate education—how will change occur and what will be the catalyst? These questions buttress my hesitation to agree with Kimball that the consensus he identifies is actually happening, much as I hope he is right. Arguing against this, though, is the fact that the elite universities that organized the Association of American Colleges and Universities have long been the engines of change in higher education. And these are the institutions most firmly embracing the status quo.

The desire on the part of other colleges and universities to follow the leadership—or lack of leadership—of research institutions is also a dominant force in higher education. Kimball finds evidence of a consensus in the fact that "most of . . . [those] respondents . . . doubtful of the consensus thesis work at institutions in the 'top' 10 percent. . . . Those tending to be persuaded by the consensus thesis come from the other 90 percent" I want to concur, but find no clear evidence now that the latter group really embraces the trends he identifies, or are prepared to do much to pressure change if they do. If systemic change will not be led by the research universities, how might it happen?

One catalyst for change could be money or the lack of it. If higher education continues to face sharp cuts in funding, pressures to change may accelerate, and some of the trends that I have described may be supported as sound means to enhance the value of limited resources. But every academic leader knows how much harder it is to make real change when resources are limited, and it is a tribute to those, such as President Ramaley at Portland State, who manage significant shifts while budgets are slashed.

The other role for money in this realm, of course, is as a positive incentive. I am continually amazed by how relatively small amounts of money lead to substantial changes in higher education. The funding of behavioralism in the social sciences by the Ford Foundation in the 1950s is an example. The entire discipline of political science was altered in a relatively brief period, as Peter J. Seybold has chronicled.[49] But major research universities were chosen by the Ford Foundation to lead the change. The only instance I know of when that was not true was in clinical legal education, also promoted by funding from an offshoot of the Ford Foundation. In that case, faculties at the law schools of most major research universities at least acquiesced in the movement, and Harvard Law School was the home of the major conceptual thinker, Professor Gary Bellow. Whether funds from Kellogg and other interested foundations can have a similar impact in this realm is not clear to me, even assuming that such funds are available. I hope an effort is made to find out. And if money is not the driving force for change, I no less hope that other forces will serve the same end. But I am uncertain what those forces might be.

In spite of the hurdles, I am cautiously optimistic that Dewey's answers will ultimately prevail in the struggle to shape the substance and pedagogy of undergraduate education. This optimism is rooted in a number of forces that should ultimately be unstoppable, though I do not predict how fast they will move.

First, and most obvious, Dewey has clearly won against those who wished, with Hutchins, to reserve higher education for an elite. The percentage of young people seeking a college education is growing at an accelerating rate, and there is ample reason to believe this trend will continue. These students are coming in increasing numbers because they accurately conclude that they cannot utilize their talents and energies in the workplace without a college education. One reason is that a college degree serves as a surrogate for qualities such as maturity and discipline that employers seek. But the more important rationale is the training college students receive in career-related abilities, particularly critical thinking and communications skills.

Second, the numbers of undergraduate students in elite research universities and liberal arts colleges are static, while those in other institutions of higher education are growing. When Dewey wrote, the majority of all undergraduates were attending private institutions. This is one reason he focused more attention on primary and secondary education, which was—and still is—overwhelmingly public. Today only about 20 percent of undergraduates are in private institutions and that share is continuing to decline. Community colleges have exploded; they are a major force in higher education, not holding pens for students waiting to learn in prime time at four-year institutions. The leverage of the elite institutions should erode as their market share shrinks, though the point at which they may lose critical mass is unclear.

Third, and more speculative, voices are increasingly being heard that colleges are doing an inadequate job of providing the career-related skills that are the primary rationale for attending college among undergraduates and their parents. This is hardly surprising because the curriculum that emerges from faculty trained to be research scholars is largely irrelevant to the working futures of most students. When undergraduate education was limited to those transiting from adolescence to adulthood, this disconnect was not as obvious to the consumers of higher education as it is today when many undergraduates are older, part-time, working students with families. These students are demanding that their education be geared to their needs. This does not mean to their next job, but rather to a lifetime of work that will likely involve numerous career shifts. Employers are urging the same changes. These are the forces that want undergraduate education to focus on solving problems in various modes of active learning, to have undergraduate teachers trained in these modes, and to have assessment techniques employed that will define and demonstrate learning outcomes.

Purpose Remains an Issue

There is a deeper level at which the debate between Dewey and Hutchins is again at center stage in U.S. higher education. It has become a commonplace to bemoan a loss of civic responsibility, particularly among young people, and to urge increased attention to civic education among students at every level. If the issue is viewed solely as one of information transfer—fifth-grade civics in a more advanced form—the role of higher education is inevitably a modest one. This is no less true if the issue is seen solely as proselytizing students to vote and pay attention to politics. But Dewey had much more in mind. He viewed U.S. democracy and education as inexorably intertwined. This is not simply because our citizenry must be educated to responsibly choose political leaders and hold them accountable. Much more important, a democratic society is one in which citizens interact with each other, learn from each other, grow with each other, and together make their communities more than the sum of their parts. Dewey urged that a community of learners is the primary mechanism through which this democratizing process can best occur. To be successful, the community needs both vision and skepticism. The vision is of an interactive, collaborative society in which the processes of decision are more important than the decisions themselves. It is balanced by skepticism, which serves as a constant reminder that uncertainty surrounds every decision and every fact on which a decision is based. There are no ultimate answers, as Hutchins had claimed, and tentative answers emerge only through empirical inquiry. What seems certain today, even in science and certainly in society, may prove false tomorrow.

Dewey had two radical insights about U.S. society. One was that most citizens, not just an elite, can have a life of the mind. The other was that a life that is only of the mind is inadequate to the challenges of U.S. democracy. Our society requires civic engagement to realize the potential of its citizens and its communities. These were important lessons that Hutchins failed to grasp.

One of the reasons more has not been done in higher education to promote civic responsibility is that we do not have much empirical knowledge on a range of important issues, and Dewey did not give us many concrete leads. He was never one to practice what he preached—a failing of most of us in the academy. These issues include: What are the essential elements of effective citizenship for an American in the next century? What specific knowledge, skills, and values contribute to those elements of good citizenship, recognizing that there may be a range of different ways to be a good citizen? What evidence is there about the contribution that higher education can make to developing these qualities in sustained and effective ways? What evidence is there about the types of civic education efforts that are most effective in preparing for responsible citizenship? What problems confront colleges and universities that attempt to engage in sustained civic education, and what are the best strategies to overcome these problems?

These are the kinds of issues that must be addressed if Dewey's vision of democracy and education is to be realized. The efforts that I have described are steps in that direction, but they are not yet part of a larger whole that has the sound functioning of a democratic society as its objective. The issues that I just raised are the subject of a multiyear project on civic responsibility and higher education that is being sponsored by the American Council on Education. Other projects in related arenas are underway as well. Together they hold some promise of providing operational insights into how to achieve the linkages between democracy and education that were so clear to Dewey in theory, though continue to be clouded in practice.

If U.S. higher education is to help realize Dewey's vision of democracy, new forms of learning and new forms of defining what we mean by knowledge must emerge. We must recognize that a learning community means one in which no one single member of the community knows everything, in which every member can contribute something, in which there is a clear vision of a better fixture combined with a healthy skepticism about the abilities of anyone to know all the answers—whatever the questions. This was the democratic society that Dewey wanted and for which he posited a powerful role for higher education. It is past time for us in colleges and universities to meet his challenge.

Notes

1. Roundtable on Service Learning in the Academic Curriculum, American Academy of Arts and Sciences, New York, March 13, 1995, 9–10.
2. John Dewey, *Democracy and Education* (New York: Macmillan, 1923), 101.
3. Ibid.
4. Alan Ryan, *John Dewey* (New York: W.W. Norton, 1995), 278.
5. Robert Maynard Hutchins, *The Higher Learning in America* (New Haven, CT: Yale University Press, 1936), 3, 4, 6.
6. Op. cit., 26.
7. Op. cit., 32.
8. Op. cit., 43, 85.
9. Op. cit., 66.
10. John Dewey, "President Hutchins' Proposals to Remake Higher Education," *The Social Frontier* (January 1937), 103. This is the second of two articles. The first was Dewey, "Rationality in Education," *The Social Frontier* (December 1936), 71.
11. Dewey, "President Hutchins' Proposals," 104.
12. Ibid.
13. Ibid.
14. Robert Maynard Hutchins, "Grammar, Rhetoric, and Mr. Dewey," *The Social Frontier* (February 1937), 137–38.
15. John Dewey, "The Higher Learning in America," *The Social Frontier* (March 1937), 167.
16. Ibid.
17. Harry S. Ashmore, *Unreasonable Truths* (Boston: Little, Brown, 1989), 98–103.
18. Robert Maynard Hutchins, "The Great Conversation," in *Great Books of the Western World: Volume 1* (Chicago: Encyclopedia Britannica, 1952).
19. John Dewey "Challenge to Liberal Thought," in Jo Ann Boydston, editor, *John Dewey: The Later Works,* Volume 15 (Carbondale: Southern Illinois University Press, 1989), 261, 266.
20. Op. cit., 267.
21. Op. cit., 272.
22. Alexander Meiklejohn, "A Reply to John Dewey," *Later Works,* 475.
23. "Dewey vs. Meiklejohn," *Later Works,* 333.
24. "Meiklejohn Replies to Dewey," *Later Works,* 486.
25. "Rejoinder to Meiklejohn," *Later Works,* 337.
26. Hutchins, *The Higher Learning in America,* 62.
27. John Dewey, "The Way Out of Educational Confusion," in *Later Works,* Volume 6, 84–85.
28. Lawrence A. Cremin, *Popular Education and Its Discontents* (New York: Harper & Row, 1990), 7.
29. Richard H. Hersh and Daniel Yankelovich, "Intentions and Perceptions: A National Sur-

vey of Public Attitudes Toward Liberal Arts Education," *Change* (March/April 1997), 16.
30. Indiana University, *Academic Planning Paper—Indiana at Its Best* (Fall 1988), 8–9.
31. Jack C. Lane, "The Rollins Conference, 1931, and the Search for a Progressive Liberal Education: Mirror or Prism," *Liberal Education* (70: 1984), 297, 303.
32. Portland State University, "you@psu.pdx.edu: Freshman Inquiry," (Fall 1994), 3.
33. Op. cit., 5.
34. Marcus, Howard, and King, "Integrating Service into a Course in Contemporary Political Issues," *Educational and Policy Analysis* (15: 1993), 410.
35. Janet Eyler and Dwight E. Giles, "The Impact of Service-Learning Program Characteristics on Student Outcomes: Summary of Selected Results for the FIPSE Comparing Models of Service-Learning Research Project," Presented at National Council for Experiential Education Conference, October 1996.
36. Alexander W. Astin, et al., *Evaluation of Learn and Serve America, Higher Education: First Year Report* (Los Angeles: RAND, 1996); see also Alexander W. Astin, Linda J. Sax, and Juan Avalos, *Long-Term Effects of Volunteerism During the Undergraduate* Years (Los Angeles: UCLA, 1997).
37. Benjamin R. Barber, *An Aristocracy of Everyone* (Dubuque, IA: Kendall/Hunt, 1993).
38. Robert D. Putnam, "Bowling Alone: America's Declining Social Capital," *Journal of Democracy* (1:1995), 65.
39. See Ernest T. Pascarella and Patrick T. Tezenzini, *How College Affects Students* (San Francisco: Jossey-Bass, 1991).
40. Robert Coles, *The Call of Service* (Boston: Houghton-Mifflin, 1993).
41. "The Way Out of Educational Confusion," in *The Later Works,* Volume 6, 74, 87.
42. Op. cit., 88.
43. Kris Bosworth and Sharon J. Hamilton, editors, *Collaborative Learning. Underlying Processes and Effective Techniques* (San Francisco: Jossey-Bass, 1994), 2.
44. See Diana Laurillard, *Rethinking University Teaching* (London: Routledge, 1993).
45. See "Western Governors' University: A Proposed Implementation Plan" (Denver: Western Governors' Association, June 24, 1996).
46. Jerry G. Gaff and Anne S. Pruitt, *Preparing Future Faculty: Experiences of Graduate Students, Faculty Members, and Administrators in Programs for Preparing Future Faculty—Year One* (Washington, DC: Association of American Colleges and Universities, November 1995), 1.
47. Louis Menand, "Everybody Else's College Education," *New York Times Magazine* (April 27, 1997), 49.
48. See Peter T. Ewell, "To Capture the Ineffable: New Forms of Assessment in Higher Education," *Review of Research in Education* (17: 1991), 75.
49. Peter J. Seybold, "The Ford Foundation and the Triumph of Behavioralism in American Political Science," in Robert I. Arnove, editor, *Philanthropy and Cultural Imperialism* (New York: Macmillan, 1980), 269.

CHAPTER 11

CONTEMPORARY UNDERSTANDINGS OF LIBERAL EDUCATION

CAROL GEARY SCHNEIDER AND ROBERT SHOENBERG

For more than a decade, a growing number of colleges and universities have been engaged in an important, but largely unremarked, re-examination of their educational purposes and practices. Much of this rethinking has taken the form of extensive changes in general education programs and graduation requirements. Some of it emerges from campus-wide restructuring of major programs and the development of new fields and related programs of study. A further spur to educational change has been the widespread focus on student diversity and a deepening campus engagement with effective ways of supporting student persistence and achievement. Assessment mandates also have contributed to reconsideration of the goals and efficacy of baccalaureate learning.

Taken together, the themes emerging across hundreds of campuses and thousands of separate educational reforms express a renewed and contemporary understanding of the kinds of learning students need to negotiate a rapidly transforming world. Our purpose in this article is to illuminate this emerging understanding and explore its educational potential for the academy in transition.

Teaching and Learning in Transition

Curriculum and instruction have been for more than a decade the major locus of contention about the educational purpose and practice of colleges and universities, both intramurally and extramurally. The issues range from the "culture wars" to the purposes and values of the liberal arts, from the degree of concern for the quality of student learning to the assessment of learning outcomes, from the role of electronic technology in instruction to the value of bringing students into direct engagement with neighboring and global communities.

In both anticipating and responding to these challenges, college and university faculty members have tried much that is genuinely new, or newly emphasized and freshly conceived. The computer has wrought enormous changes in the way faculty teach (not to mention how they carry on their research), in how they interact with students, and even in the constituencies they now reach. If nothing else new were happening, information technology would by itself revolutionize the academy. In particular, it has fueled a profound change in thinking about instruction from teacher-centered to learner-centered education.[1]

But much else has been introduced and become significant in shaping new directions: curricular, particularly general education models that are conceived in terms of development of intellectual skills

Source: "Contemporary Understandings of Liberal Education," by Carol Schneider and Robert Shoenberg, reprinted from *Liberal Education*, Vol. 84, No. 2, Spring 1998, Association of American Colleges and Universities.

as opposed to encountering particular subject matter; new emphases on engaging the diversity of human communities and global cultures; the radiation of experiential teaming and its close congener, service learning; cooperative and collaborative learning; interdisciplinarity; topically linked courses or "learning communities"; undergraduate research; discovery approaches to science, just to name a few.[2] New and insistent demands from the public and from accrediting agencies that institutions clarify and specify their goals and demonstrate their achievement of them are in turn having an increasingly visible, if still uneven, effect on educational practice.

An Emerging Conceptualization of Liberal Learning

From this wealth of new programs and practices, a pattern is emerging that shows promise of providing a conceptual framework for undergraduate learning which is both contemporary and within the traditions of the academy. This conceptualization responds to the reality of a changing and knowledge-intensive society. But it also draws directly on those traditions of excellence the academy has long described as "liberal learning," ways of approaching knowledge that expand imaginative horizons, develop intellectual powers and judgment, and instill in students the capacity and resolve to exercise leadership and responsibility in multiple spheres of life, both societal and vocational.[3] This conceptualization further includes new ways of talking about the content of a liberal education and new approaches to teaching and learning. Indeed, the language many campuses are using to describe the content of a contemporary liberal education implies the necessity for *emphasizing* some learning strategies and reducing the prevalence of others.

Although each institution organizes its educational program in its own way, the following seems a fair description of the *learning goals* implicit in contemporary campus efforts to reconceive both their degree requirements and their undergraduate curricula:

1. *Acquiring intellectual skills or capacities.* Almost universally, institutions include writing and quantitative reasoning in their requirements. Achievement of a certain level of proficiency in oral expression, computer use, and a second language are often expected. In more and more colleges and universities, students are also expected to develop skill in moral reasoning and negotiating difference.
2. *Understanding multiple modes of inquiry and approaches to knowledge.* This is the emergent way of talking about the "distribution requirements" that for much of the twentieth century dominated—and in many institutions still do dominate—general education programs. The commonly encountered requirement that students have some exposure to the knowledge content of the sciences, social sciences, humanities and (less frequently) the arts is being rejustified in epistemological terms. Imparting a sense of the analytic modes of these broad areas of intellectual endeavor forms the rationale for "distribution," and the way in which courses that meet these requirements are taught is being adjusted accordingly. This impetus informs contemporary curricular innovations in science, where "workshop," "studio," and other hands-on approaches are being widely introduced. Many new first year courses and seminars immerse students immediately in the complexities of discovering and validating "knowledge."
3. *Developing societal, civic, and global knowledge.* Traditionally, history and "Western Civilization" requirements have been based on the premise that educated people should know something about societies and events remote in time, but which help to explain contemporary society. The academy is now adding the further expectation that students will learn about cultures separated from the dominant culture by distance and/or by assumptions, experiences, or differential social power. With rapidly increasing frequency, general education requirements include study of a non-European culture and of contemporary cultural diversity (i.e., gender, race, ethnicity, sexual orientation, etc.) and justice issues, both in the United States and abroad. Many campuses promote service learning programs explicitly designed to involve students with challenging societal issues in their own communities. Through

projects to increase student study abroad, colleges and universities are developing more accessible and more diverse ways to support global knowledge and cross-cultural competence.

4. *Gaining self-knowledge and grounded values.* This learning goal is seldom manifested in specific degree requirements but underlies, as implicitly it always has, undergraduate education in general and the general education curriculum in particular. Good teaching, now as ever, tries to help students place and define themselves within their particular cultures and the broader society and to do so within expanding frameworks of knowledge, self-awareness, and increased capacity for reflective judgment. New courses and programs frequently invite students to reflect on their own sources of identity and values and to engage with challenging ethical, moral, and human dilemmas. Fostering social and civic responsibility is an avowed goal of many new curricula. The new self-consciousness about heterogeneity on campus and in society is accelerating many of these trends toward clarifying and exploring value choices and positions.
5. *Concentration and integration of learning.* With rare exception, students are expected to spend anywhere from a quarter to three-quarters of their academic time developing working knowledge and demonstrable skills in a particular field of inquiry and/or practice. The academic major remains the focus of undergraduate education, the curricular element by which students most often and readily define themselves within the institution and through which they explore life and vocational choices and possibilities. Increasingly, however, the boundaries between general education and the major are becoming blurred. Some institutions are acting on their realization that the broad and ambitious goals of general education cannot be met within a small set of discrete courses and are asking both the majors and the co-curriculum to take on some of those responsibilities. At many other institutions, upper level integrative general education courses are taught in ways that intersect and enrich the advanced learning in the major. The rapid growth of interdisciplinary majors and minors accelerates this trend toward intentionally integrative learning.

Learner-Centered Pedagogies

The dominant mode for achieving these learning goals remains lecture and small(er) group discussion, as it has for the last century. Belief in instructor personality, in the professor's ability to induce student commitment to the intellectual content of the course and in his or her skill as an explicator and motivator still governs our practice. But presentational teaching as the quintessential activity of the college professor is retreating before a growing emphasis on the centrality of the student as learner.[4] In this newer conception, the instructor's role as motivator remains fundamental, but now as a mentor in acquiring strategies for learning. As the familiar formulation puts it, the professor is no longer primarily "the sage on the stage," but assumes a new and crucial role as "the guide on the side."

This emerging understanding of the multiple purposes of collegiate instruction is both accompanied and advanced by a raft of increasingly emphasized or newly developed ways of learning. Computer technology, with its capacities for calculation, simulation, and facilitating communication both in real time and at the convenience of the correspondents, has changed teaching forever. Providing new forms of learning and new access to information, information technology is forcefully challenging the model of a single knowledgeable person talking to, or controlling interaction among, a group of people assembled in one place at the same time. New instructional technologies facilitate one-on-one interaction and allow students to do much more on their own, individually, or in groups, with professor-created, problem-focused, often computer-mediated materials to provide guidance and correction.

None of these developments invalidates the importance of the instructor's greater knowledge and wisdom as a powerful resource for students' learning. Nor do they eliminate the significance of the group setting as a stimulus to intellectual development and understanding. Rather, these key elements in the learning process are being reconfigured through an increasing emphasis on course designs that involve students earlier and more frequently in hands-on, inquiry-oriented strategies for learning:

1. *Collaborative inquiry:* learning and problem solving in group settings, both direct and on-line. Students work as a team, both in the classroom and outside it, with the instructor as coach.
2. *Experiential learning:* direct experience in field settings, with open-ended problems, projects, and challenges. The instructor helps the students, either individually or as a group, learn to process their experience, put it in a context of general principle—practical, intellectual, and ethical—and rethink theories in light of the field experience.
3. *Service learning:* direct experiences with societal issues and with groups seeking to solve problems and improve the quality of life for themselves and others. Again, the instructor's role is to provide social, moral, and technical context and to help students generalize from the particular, connect scholarship with practice, and discover grounds for commitment and action.
4. *Research or inquiry-based learning:* helping students develop competence in achieving the ultimate purpose of collegiate education; organizing and dealing with unstructured problems. Often making use of educational technologies, students experience the excitement and the usefulness of creating new knowledge. The instructor serves as guide and mentor, but in many cases is not the expert. This role is shifted to the student.
5. *Integrative learning:* generating links among previously unconnected issues, approaches, sources of knowledge, and/or contexts for practice. Such learning is often multidisciplinary. Increasingly, it occurs in the context of learning communities or thematically linked courses. The instructor serves as exemplar of the person whose role is to find fresh and instructive connections, helping students learn how to test the intellectual and practical usefulness—the explanatory power—of the connections they find. Faculty members teaching linked courses work together to design curricular frameworks and materials that facilitate integrative inquiry and learning.

If we bracket for a moment the transformative power of the new technologies, none of these pedagogies is absolutely new. Some of them draw from the well-established model of the laboratory scientist working in close partnership with apprentice learners. Others have for decades been pedagogies of choice at campuses with high intellectual standards and low student-faculty ratios. What is arresting, rather, is the new emphasis, visible at every kind of institution, on extending to a broad array of students the modes of mentored, engaged, and problem-focused learning that were once reserved for an elite. Equally arresting is the increasing use of educational technologies to frame and reinforce inquiry-based and often collaborative strategies for learning.

The new pedagogical emphases provide a particularly strong match for the emerging curriculum's thrust toward interconnection and relationship. Faculty members are actively encouraging students to develop operational knowledge of their own learning, experiences, and aspirations as they stand in juxtaposition with other knowers. The capacity to engage other knowers is implicitly defined in such curricular themes as communication, epistemologies, cultures, historical time, place, values, and the development of collaborative expertise. Taken together, both the contemporary goals for student learning described above and these pedagogies of engagement express faculty members' expectation that students will emerge from their educational experience with what Elizabeth Minnich has termed "liberal arts of translation," the abilities, commitments, and knowledge required to move productively among diverse subjects, contexts, communities, cultures, and nations.[5]

The newly emphasized learning modes encourage students to develop capacities to deal with the challenging differences that are intrinsic to our pluralist world. The ability to understand, respect, and negotiate multiple forms of diversity is fostered through:

- collaborative work in which students gain an appreciation for the differing and complementary strengths that diverse individuals bring to a group;

- multidisciplinary and integrative learning designed to create an awareness of relationships, tensions, and complementarities among ideas and epistemologies;
- experiential learning and service learning that create a lively sense of students' own life experiences and those of others;
- international study and foreign language learning whose resurgence in new forms and with new methods responds to increasingly urgent needs to communicate across cultures;
- collaborative projects in which students work in diverse teams to frame, address, and propose solutions to significant problems. We might characterize this emerging reconceptualization of curriculum and pedagogy as a movement toward "relational learning."[6] Faculties, like the society as a whole, have been called to new awareness of societal diversities by insistent voices both within and outside the academy. They are struggling to deal responsibly with the intellectual, social, and political implications of this newly acknowledged societal pluralism, both at home and abroad. Colleges and universities are bringing these concerns into the curriculum not simply in terms of individual course content, but in the ways they conceptualize the purposes of education and the pedagogical strategies they employ.[7]

Fifty years ago the Harvard "Red Book," *General Education in a Free Society,* posited a curriculum focused on a unified national culture based in Western thought. By contrast, the emerging curriculum assumes a world society characterized by a multitude of life experiences and informed by complex intersections among historical experiences, gender, race, ethnicity, socioeconomic status, sexual orientation, religious values, political assumptions, cultural styles, and so on. The liberally educated person, many now argue, needs not only substantial knowledge but also the skills and awareness to negotiate a world of plurality.

Thus colleges and universities must educate not in terms of mind alone but also in terms of a life lived in relationships with others whose experiences and assumptions may be very different. Faculties are therefore beginning to pay increased attention to the "civic arts" that lead to an understanding of diversity and to skill in negotiating difficult differences and building communities that respect and acknowledge difference. They are more insistently involving students in an engagement with diversity and equity issues both at home and abroad and in learning experiences that help students develop these capacities and understandings in morally honest and dialogical ways.

When we look at the totality of these curricular and pedagogical themes, a clear and important pattern begins to emerge. What is this pattern? In a sentence, it is a conception of education that holds at its core a vision of, and conscious preparation for, a world lived in common with others.[8] Campuses are asking students not just to deepen their knowledge, but to become self-conscious about the ways in which they can work with others to make knowledge powerful in a changing world.

All in all, we believe these directions constitute an important renewal of liberal learning as we look toward a new era in the history of a long and valuable tradition. The challenge, to all of us, is to help our students and our publics understand these emerging approaches to a liberal education as an indispensable public resource, for our students and through them, for our society.

Notes

1. The *locus classicus* of this reconceptualization is Robert B. Barr and John Tagg. 1995. From teaching to learning: A new paradigm for undergraduate education, *Change* (November-December).
2. A comprehensive overview of contemporary curricular themes and innovations is provided in, *Handbook of the undergraduate curriculum: A comprehensive guide to purposes, structure, practices, and change,* ed. Jerry G. Gaff, James L. Ratcliff, and Associates. 1997. San Francisco: Jossey-Bass Publishers. Additional information on general education reform can be found in *Strong foundations: Twelve principles for effective general education programs.* 1994. Washington, DC: The Association of American Colleges.
3. A window into shifting understandings of liberal education is provided in *Education and democracy: Reimagining liberal learning in Amer-*

ica, ed. Robert Orrill. 1997. New York: The College Examination Board. See also: Frank Wong. 1996. The search for American liberal education, in *Rethinking liberal education.* New York: Oxford University Press, and Bruce Kimball. 1986. *A history of the idea of liberal education.* New York: Teachers College Press.

4. Research on higher education curriculum and pedagogy almost uniformly suggests that colleges and universities generally fail to achieve their broadly stated goals and that our most common lecture-discussion teaching methods produce disappointing results in student learning. An excellent summary of this research and the conclusions to be drawn from it may be found in Lion F. Gardiner. 1994. *Redesigning higher education: Producing dramatic gains in student learning.* Washington, DC: ASHE-ERIC Higher Education Report.
5. Elizabeth Minnich. 1995. *Liberal learning and the arts of connection for the new academy.* Washington, DC: The Association of American Colleges and Universities. This report was written for AAC&Us national initiative American Commitments: Diversity, Democracy and Liberal Learning.
6. The concept of "relational learning" emerged through dialogue among members of the National Panel advising AAC&Us American Commitments initiative. It is explored at greater length by Lee Knefelkamp and Carol Schneider in Orrill, *op. cit.*, Education for a world lived in common with others.
7. Numerous examples of new core curricula and general education courses emphasizing cultural pluralism at home and abroad are provided in Betty Schmitz. 1992. *Core curriculum and cultural pluralism: A guide for campus planners.* Washington, DC: The Association of American Colleges, and in Debra Humphreys. 1997. *General education and American commitments: A national report on diversity courses and requirements* Washington, DC: The Association of American Colleges and Universities.
8. "Education for a world lived in common" is a phrase we borrowed from Maxine Greene. 1988. *The dialectic of freedom.* New York: Teachers College Press.

CHAPTER 12

MULTI-CULTURALISM: THE CRUCIAL PHILOSOPHICAL AND ORGANIZATIONAL ISSUES

PATRICK J. HILL

In higher education today and in American society at large, we are wrestling with an incredible explosion of diversity. There are those who deem higher education complicitous with society's leadership in depreciating or ignoring the diversity of human experience; their attempt is to provide institutional and curricular status of a non-marginal sort for enterprises like women's studies, ethnic studies, and Latin American studies. Then there are those who judge the early responses to diversity to have been more or less appropriate under the circumstances, who worry about incoherence, fragmentation, and "particularism" in the curriculum, and who want to clarify what students should be led to regard as central and what as marginal. In one way or another, all these parties are concerned with the comparative value of the diverse visions, and with how we are to conceive their relationship.

This article attempts to clarify the crucial philosophical and organizational issues that underlie the current struggles in higher education about multi-culturalism. The article is in two parts. The first examines the explosion of diversity and evaluates four major frameworks that have been employed in the West to comprehend or order diversity. The second part reflects on the ramifications of these frameworks for current and possible approaches to the conduct of higher education.

I. Four Frameworks

"The hallmark of modern consciousness," Clifford Geertz observes insightfully, "is its enormous multiplicity." Diversity of opinion, of course, is hardly new; it was, for example, radical diversity of opinion more than 300 years ago that shaped the philosophical projects of Montaigne and Descartes. The novelty in the contemporary engagement with diversity is a function of four other novelties:

1) Awareness on the part of most Western philosophers of the collapse of the Enlightenment goal of objective reason, in the light of which it was hoped to sort and hierarchize the great diversity of opinion. Gadamer's rehabilitation of the concept of prejudice as an inevitable feature of all human thinking may by itself symbolize how far we have moved from the ideal of a disembodied, objective mind.
2) The related awareness, partly philosophical and partly political, of the socioeconomic and political dimensions to the development and sustaining of knowledge-claims. While the claims

Source: "Multi-Culturalism, The Crucial Philosophical and Organizational Issues," by Patrick J. Hill, reprinted from *Change*, Vol. 23, No. 4, July/August 1991, Helen Dwight Reid Educational Foundation.

of scientists were falsely cloaked in the mantle of pure objectivity, the knowledge-claims of other groups (e.g., women, minorities, persons of color, and third-world persons) were and are suppressed, invalidated, and marginalized.

3) The growing incapacity of groups hitherto exercising monopolizing control over judgments of truth and worth to sustain such power. The wealth of Japan and the Arab peoples, for example, and the voting power of women and the elderly in the United States have forced accommodations by the established order to a newly emerging one.

4) The realization on the part of many of the intrinsic beauty and worth of the diverse voices—a realization that came to many people in the United States through the black revolution of the '60s. This shift in consciousness was crisply expressed by Octavio Paz:

> The ideal of a single civilization for everyone, implicit in the cult of progress and technique, impoverishes and mutilates us. Every view of the world that becomes extinct, every culture that disappears, diminishes a possibility of life.

Diversity, again, is not new, and intellectuals have not needed the stimulations of today to construct its analysis. In Western thought, four major frameworks have been employed in the analysis of diversity

1) *Relativism,* which in one way or another regards all knowledge-claims as self-contained within particular cultures or language communities, and which recognizes no higher or commensurable ground upon which objective adjudication might take place.
2) *Perennialism* or *universalism,* which see commonalities or constancies in the great variety of human thought, and which frequently (as in the influential work of Frithjof Schuon) regard those constancies as the essential and more important aspect of diverse historical phenomena.
3) *Hierarchism,* which attempts to sort or rank the multiplicity by a variety of means, among them establishing criteria or methods of inquiry that divide knowledge from opinion, or interpreting world history and human development in such a way that certain opinions and behavior are progressive, developed, and/or mature while others more or less approximate those ideals.
4) *Pluralism,* which in its democratic version is central to the analysis of this article and which I will therefore spend a longer moment here to expand upon.

In the philosophical and political traditions of American pluralism, diversity has played a prominent role. Nowhere was diversity more prominent than in the epistemology and social philosophy of John Dewey. Though aware of the idealized dimension of his thinking, Dewey grounded both science (as a way of knowing) and democracy (as a way of life) in a respect for diverse opinion.

> It is of the nature of science not so much to *tolerate* as to *welcome* diversity of opinion, while it insists that inquiry brings the evidence of observed facts to bear to effect a consensus of conclusions—and even then to hold the conclusions subject to what is ascertained and made public in further new inquiries. I would not claim that any existing democracy has ever made complete and adequate use of scientific method in deciding upon its policies. But freedom of inquiry, toleration of diverse views, freedom of communication, the distribution of what is found out to every individual as the ultimate intellectual consumers, are involved in the democratic as in the scientific method.

In linking science and democracy, Dewey welcomed not just the diversity of opinion of highly trained scientists; he welcomed as an intellectual and political resource the diversity of every human being:

> Every autocratic and authoritarian scheme of social action rests upon a belief that the needed intelligence is confined to a superior few, who because of inherent natural gifts are endowed with the ability and the right to control the conduct of others. . . . While what we call intelligence may be distributed in unequal amounts, it is the democratic faith that it is sufficiently general so that each individual has something to contribute.

For Dewey, the inclusion of diverse perspectives becomes an ethical imperative:

> The keynote of democracy as a way of life may be expressed, it seems to me, as the necessity for the participation of every mature being in the formation of the values that regulate the living of men [sic] together. . . . All those who are affected by social institutions must have a share in producing and managing them.

Finally, appreciation of diversity is linked by Dewey to visions of human nature and community. The resources of diversity will flourish in those social and political forms that allow the pooling of the experience and insights of diversely constituted individuals. Not that the pooled insight is inherently preferable to the workings of intelligence in an individual or within a single-language community—Dewey is forever appreciative of the value of small communities—but that the pooling is an escalation of the power of human intelligence:

> The foundation of democracy is faith in the capacities of human nature; faith in human intelligence and in the power of pooled and co-operative experience. . . . What is the faith of democracy in the role of consultation, of conference, of persuasion, of discussion, in formation of public opinion, which in the long run is self-corrective, except faith in the capacity of the intelligence of the common man [sic] to respond with common sense to the free play of acts and ideas which are secured by effective guarantees of free inquiry, free assembly, and free communication.

In pooled, cooperative experience, Dewey is saying, the powers of human intelligence are increased and human nature or capacity is completed.

This view, or at least the narrowly epistemological dimension of it, is affirmed in other traditions. In Gadamer, the essential and unavoidable partiality of the human knower must be corrected or supplemented in dialogue. In *The Genealogy of Morals,* Nietzsche states the epistemological value of cooperative inquiry quite succinctly:

> The more affects we allow to speak about one thing, the more eyes, different eyes we can use to observe one thing, the more complete will our concept of this thing, our objectivity, be.

Interpreting Diversity

What is at issue among these four competing philosophic frameworks? How night we go about choosing among them?

The philosophical issue in most general terms is the appropriate interpretation of diversity: how to give it its proper due. In an older style of doing philosophy—what Rorty terms the metaphysical as opposed to the "ironist" view—we would now seek to determine which one of these frameworks is true to the nature of things, in this case to the phenomenon of diversity. In a post-metaphysical mode of doing philosophy, we recognize that each of these frameworks is an interpretation, a value-laden interpretation of the variety of human experience. No neutral ground exists upon which we might stand to evaluate either the values or the frameworks objectively.

The choice among the frameworks is to be made (assuming, as I judge to be the case here, that each has dealt honestly and intelligently with the full range of available data) not in terms of conformity to the nature of things, but in terms of each framework's appropriateness for sustaining the values of the culture or language community. The question of the adequacy of each of the interpretations of diversity, then, will be answered differently in different cultures. All answers will be value-laden answers that cannot be justified without reference to these values.

In the United States and much of the Western world, we are at least nominally committed to a democratic social order. The evaluation that follows of the four frameworks is thus done within the context of that cultural commitment. The judgments reached are not abstract ones about the correspondence of particular frameworks to the nature of things, but judgments about their appropriateness to sustaining the vision of "pooled and cooperative experience" articulated above. Crucial to each of those judgments will be the extent to which diversity is "welcomed" and incorporated democratically into pooled experience as well as the extent to which each framework can suggest a relationship of self and diverse other that might motivate the kind of conversation capable of sustaining a public sphere.

With these considerations and a frank commitment to democratic values in mind, I make the following observations about the frameworks for explaining diversity.

1) ***Relativism.*** This is the framework that accords enduring centrality to diversity, both to the fact of diversity and to its defense if not its nurturance. The endless attempts of philosophers to discredit the logical foundations of relativism are convincing to themselves but ineffective in undermining the attractiveness and strength of its straightforward recognition of diverse, frequently non-intersecting (or impermeable) modes of thinking. While those who describe themselves as relativists will endlessly be dogged with logical objections, the opposite position—what Geertz calls "anti-relativism"—can mask a great lack of appreciation for the profound, intractable diversity of our time.

   From the standpoint of democratic values, the problem with relativism is less its logical incoherence than its comparative incapacity to motivate interest or conversation—an incapacity which may stem more from the individualism of our culture than from the framework itself. If we all live in separate and/or incommensurate reality-worlds, the motivation to inquire into the world of the diverse other can be readily relegated to the anthropologist or world traveler. For democracy to work, its citizens must sense if not a commitment to a shared future, then at least an occasional need for each other.

2) ***Perennialism or universalism.*** These philosophies do not ignore diversity, as is frequently charged. They could not uncover perennial themes in diverse cultures or epochs without first immersing themselves in the diversity. Perennialists would claim that they do accord diversity its proper due; indeed, their system is not incapable of explaining anything.

   The problem with perennialism from the standpoint of democratic values is less its capacity to explain diversity than it is the comparative non-centrality it accords it. If the dialogical other is inevitably going to be viewed as an instantiation of a previously known pattern—or, more generously, if the dialogue is at best going to force a modification of a previously known pattern in the light of which I and the other will then be seen as instantiations—it is understandable that the other may feel his/her uniqueness depreciated and forced to fit a mold. Genuine appreciation of diversity must be found to some extent upon an expectation of novelty.

3) ***Hierarchism.*** Philosophies or theologies or social systems that hierarchize or sort differences according to some historical or developmental scheme are obviously taking diversity—especially inequality—seriously. It is not ignored. It is ranked and explained (or explained away, critics would say).

   While inequality is a fact of life and some sort of ranking may for the near term be unavoidable, what is disturbing to a theorist of democracy is the way in which whole epochs and entire peoples—e.g., Native Americans, women, the physically challenged, and the so-called underdeveloped nations—have been and continue to be marginalized and their experience depreciated in such rankings. Democratic social theory cannot in the end be satisfied with an egalitarian epistemology—because some insights and truths are more appropriate than others to particular situations and because we wish to encourage the development of continually diverse perspectives. Still more opprobrious to democratic social theory as an interpretation of human diversity and inequality is a system of ranking joined to a hierarchical structure of association; in any such system, the epistemologically marginalized remain politically vulnerable and effectively voiceless. Whatever inequality currently exists is worsened and perpetuated by structures that de facto operate (in Dewey's words) "as if the needed intelligence" to participate meaningfully "were confined to a superior few."

4) ***Democratic pluralism.*** Within the context of a commitment to democratic values, the diversity of the world's peoples is to be welcomed, respected, celebrated, and fostered. Within that context, diversity is not a problem or a defect, it is a resource. The major problem within all pluralistic contexts (including relativism) is less that

of taking diversity seriously than that of grounding any sort of commonality. It is the problem of encouraging citizens to sustain conversations of respect with diverse others for the sake of their making public policy together, of forging over and over again a sense of a shared future.

Conversations of respect and the making of public policy in a democracy cannot be based on mere tolerance—on the "live and let live" or "to each his own" attitudes of individualistic relativism—at least, not in the Jeffersonian and Deweyan, as opposed to the Federalist, vision of democracy. Democracy needs something at once more binding or relating of diverse viewpoints, and something that grounds the respect in a public sphere, in a world or situation that is at least temporarily shared. It is impossible to respect the diverse other if one does not believe that the views of the diverse other are grounded in a reality—the democratic version of reality—that binds or implicates everyone as much as do our own views.

Conversations of respect between diverse communities are characterized by intellectual reciprocity. They are ones in which the participants expect to learn from each other, expect to learn non-incidental things, expect to change at least intellectually as a result of the encounter. Such conversations are not animated by nor do they result in mere tolerance of the pre-existing diversity, for political or ethical reasons. In such conversations, one participant does not treat the other as an illustration of, or variation of, or a dollop upon a truth or insight already fully possessed. There is no will to incorporate the other in any sense into one's belief system. In such conversations, one participant does not presume that the relationship is one of teacher to student (in any traditional sense of that relationship), of parent to child, of developed to underdeveloped. The participants are co-learners.

My paradigms of such conversations of respect are drawn from my experience in interdisciplinary academic communities. Not all interdisciplinary conversations, to be sure, are respectful: Social scientists often view English professors as providing a service, the service of illustrative examples of their truths, or as high-class entertainment. Humanists often assume that scientists are value-blind dupes of the military-industrial complex. Other interdisciplinary conversations, somewhat less disrespectful, are so complementary as to involve little or no diversity of substance.

In genuinely respectful conversations, each disciplinary participant is aware at the outset of the incapacity of his/her own discipline (and, ideally, of him/herself) to answer the question that is being asked. Each participant is aware of his/her partiality and of the need for the other. One criterion of the genuineness of the subsequent conversations is the transformation of each participant's understanding or definition of the question—perhaps even a transformation of self-understanding.

This definition of a conversation of respect may strike many as too demanding, uncritical, or relativistic. It seems to suggest that the respect easily acknowledged as appropriate to conversations between Christians and Buddhists or between Palestinians and Jews is also appropriate to conversations between biologists and philosophers, between those in higher education and those currently excluded. Or, worse yet, between systems of beliefs on the one hand modernized to accommodate contemporary science and philosophy and, on the other, fundamentalists, traditionalist, pantheists, and all sorts of local and tribal and idiosyncratic cognitive systems.

I have three responses to these concerns. First, we foreclose the ethnographic task that Geertz and others have urged upon us as appropriate to the contemporary explosion of diversity if we presume that we will not discover something about the life of the mind and something valuable for all of us in a dialogue with the radically diverse other. Second, I do not regard these boundary-crossing conversations as the only conversations worth having or the only activity worth engaging in; they just deserve far more of our energy at this time than we have been allotting to them. Third, in view of the collapse of Enlightenment values, of the crisis of the planetary environment, and in view of the many critiques of universalism, the reluctance of modern thought to engage in conversations with communities that retain pre-industrial values ought to be considerably less than it was a quarter of a century ago. The deep distrust of modernity for everything that originated prior to the 16th century has less and less to recommend it.

One last observation about the four frameworks of interpretation: Although particular versions of the four have done so, none of them (as presented in general terms here) attends adequately to the politics of knowledge, to the postmodern awareness of the interplay between power and truth. Democracy's celebration of the diversity of knowers is a healthy corrective to the alternatives of hierarchism; but democracy's framework attends no more sufficiently than the others to the de facto inequality among these alternatives and to the impact of that inequality upon the pursuit of truth. A fuller analysis of the nature of thinking in democratic contexts, which I have attempted elsewhere, would attend to: a) the habits of mind appropriate to participation in a democracy, and b) the creation of conditions under which the power of pooled intelligence might be fully realized.

II.

Having looked at the fact of diversity—at the principal interpretations of it—and attempted to evaluate those interpretations in the context of a democratic pluralism, I turn now to three more topics: 1) the philosophical underpinnings of the current organization of higher education, including the implications of that organization for liberal education; 2) how higher education would be differently organized with the philosophical underpinnings of democratic pluralism; and 3) possible objections to my analysis.

Let me begin with this introductory observation. Higher education, judged by the standards of democratic pluralism, does not take seriously even the diversity within its walls, much less the diversity outside its walls. The diversity of disciplinary or ideological perspectives is muted by what the recent national study of the major conducted by the Association of American Colleges called "the ethos of self-containment." Even in institutions that take interdisciplinarity seriously, the diversity most frequently worked with is not the challenging diversity of unshared assumptions or excluded peoples but the congenial diversity of presumed complementarity. Wedded as most of higher education is to the notion that the point of teaching is to transmit what we already know, few agree with Gerald Graff in seeing a positive pedagogical function for exposing our students to unresolved conflict.

Organizational Philosophy

At first blush, and from the point of view of the student, the organization of the university appears relativistic. It appears that each major, surely each division, constitutes a separate reality-world or, to borrow a recent phrase of Isaiah Berlin's, a "windowless box." The organization of the university seems intended to facilitate each student's discovering a reality-world in which (s)he will feel comfortable. The departments, especially across divisional lines, are at best tolerant of each other, displaying in practice and in their requirements for their majors no great need of each other. Given these assumptions, they pay appropriately little attention to other departments or to general education, both because the major is believed to be self-contained and because there is little-to-no agreement on what might be significantly common across fields of inquiry. Indeed, the disciplines are often viewed, consistent with their historical origins, as correctives to each other.

From the point of view of the self-contained major, the liberally educated person is defined by the habits of mind appropriate to the particular department. From the point of view of the undeclared student, liberal education is de facto defined in a myriad of ways, and the message of the university as a whole seems to be: Define it whichever way you like.

The university, of course, is only speciously relativistic. Hierarchy pervades the institution. Although messages of what is or is not important frequently escape a student's perusal of the catalogue or passage through the pork-barreled distribution requirements, the truth is that the university oozes with uncoded messages about centrality and marginality. While these messages vary from institution to institution, we are all familiar with the value judgments inherent in distinctions like the hard and soft sciences, graduate and undergraduate, required and optional. Discerning observers see the value judgments in the size of departments and buildings, in grading patterns, in the willingness or unwillingness to waive prerequisites, in the frequency of tenure-track appointments, and in the denial of departmental status and budgets to areas like women's studies.

Liberal education in the hierarchical university is spoken of in much the same individualistic terms that an outright relativist might employ: "Do what you're good at." But there is no mistaking the fact that, in the hierarchical university, all the disciplines are not equally valuable. By and large, it is believed by students and professors alike that the better and more serious students will be found in the prestigious departments. It is not a value-free observation to report that so-and-so majored in biochemistry at Johns Hopkins.

What about universalist or perennialist assumptions in the current organization of the university? These assumptions, of course, pervade the separate disciplines themselves (otherwise there would be no point to Geertz's critique). But the assumptions are not apparent in the organization of the university. General education, wherein one would expect the commonality of human experience or disciplinary paradigms to be addressed, is a poor stepchild in most colleges and universities. The university is organized to encourage research and teaching within unshared paradigms. If there are constancies in human cultures and disciplines, the traditional university is certainly not set up to encourage the boundary-crossings that might uncover them.

Democratic Pluralism?

What about democratic pluralism and the conversations of respect upon which it thrives? To what extent is the traditional university grounded on those assumptions?

In my judgment, most universities are not grounded at all on these assumptions. I will make this point by sketching a few features of what a college/university so grounded might look like.

A college that looked upon diversity as a vital resource for learning and wished therefore to encourage conversations of respect under conditions in which unshared or disparate power would not inhibit those conversations would devote itself to three tasks. Two of the tasks are now being done in a token fashion; the third is not being done at all.

Such a college would make it the *highest priority* to recruit women, minorities, persons of color, and persons from other cultures to their faculties and student bodies as soon as possible. As a temporary measure, a measure of significant inadequacy, such colleges would undertake a massive retraining of their faculties (mis)educated in one discipline and one culture.

The second step is a prerequisite of significant multi-cultural education. Having hired some women and persons of color from North America and around the world, it would thus be easy to claim, as many colleges now do, that they are giving diversity its due because they have a study-abroad program, because 10 percent of the faculty are tenured women, because they have a Nigerian in the history department, or because they require one course in non-Western culture. These colleges are still in the grips of the windowless boxes of relativism. In such colleges, it is still quite possible for the vast majority of students and faculty to happily go their independent ways with no experience of a conversation of respect—a transforming conversation of respect—with another culture.

Were a college or university truly committed to democratic pluralism, it would proceed to create conditions under which the representatives of different cultures *need* to have conversations of respect with each other in order to do their everyday teaching and research. As colleges are set up now, there is, except in the highly sequenced departments, virtually no interdependence of the various departments and frequently little of the members of the same department. A democratically pluralistic college would make war upon the ethos of self-containment, upon all boundaries that inhibit or make unnecessary conversations of respect between diverse peoples. General education would be radically reconceived to immerse students in such conversations, in full interaction with their majors. Team-taught programs and interdisciplinary/intercultural majors would become the central (though not the exclusive) mode of study.

The point requires even further elaboration. We would not have changed much if all we achieve is a sprinkling of multi-cultural courses in the departments: "Multi-cultural Cities" in the sociology department, five courses on the Far East in a 120-course history department, or a cross-listed elective for biology majors on the "History of Chinese Medicine." We need to reconceive and restructure the curriculum so that the inquiry cannot fairly be conducted without the contributions or even the presence of the currently marginalized. We would no longer find separate courses on health taught mostly by white males in separate departments of biology, sociology, and philosophy, but instead a team-taught program of 32 credits on "The Human Body in Interdisciplinary and Intercultural Perspective," or "Health and Sickness in Interdisciplinary and Intercultural Perspective," or "Self, Nature and World in Interdisciplinary and Intercultural Perspective."

Marginalization will be perpetuated, in other words, if new voices and perspectives are added while the priorities and core of the organization remain unchanged. Marginalization ends and conversations of respect begin when the curriculum is reconceived to be unimplementable without the central participation of the currently excluded and marginalized.

This point was made in a different language by a team that visited Brown last year. It contrasted the idea of diversity—of mere diversity—with what I have been calling conversations of respect in democratic pluralism:

> By contrast to the idea of [mere] diversity, which gives primary regard to the mere presence of multiple ethnic and racial groups within the community, pluralism asks of the members of all groups to explore, understand and try to appreciate one another's cultural experiences and heritage. It asks a leap of imagination as well as a growth of knowledge. It asks for a most difficult outcome: cultural self-transcendence.

Meaningful multi-culturalism, in other words, transforms the curriculum. While the presence of persons of other cultures and subcultures is a virtual prerequisite to that transformation, their "mere presence" is primarily a political achievement (which different groups will assess differently), not an intellectual or educational achievement. Real educational progress will be made when multi-culturalism becomes interculturalism.

What might such an exploration in intercultural education look and feel like to the student in a democratically pluralistic university? I have framed an answer in terms of the habits of mind I have seen developed by the most responsive students in experiments approximating what I am advocating.

Such persons have immersed themselves in a sustained learning community, a community that is intercultural and interdisciplinary. They have studied something of great human significance and have experienced how their understanding deepens with the additions of each relevant perspective of another discipline, culture, or subculture. They have mastered or at least internalized a feeling for more than one discipline, more than one culture. They know the value and indeed the necessity of seeking many and diverse perspectives, most particularly the inevitable *partiality* of those perspectives. They have mastered the skills of access to those perspectives. They have mastered the skills in understanding and integrating these diverse perspectives. They are comfortable with ambiguity and conflict. Tolerance, empathic understanding, awareness of one's own partiality, openness to growth through dialogue in pluralistic communities—all of these things have become part of their instinctive responses to each novel situation they encounter. (They might even characterize those who proceed otherwise as uncritical thinkers.)

There is one last point I wish to make about the organization of democratically pluralistic colleges. I return to the aforementioned report at Brown to preface the point:

> The ideal of pluralism toward which we would have the University strive is one that can only be realized when a spirit of civility and mutual respect abounds, when all groups feel equally well-placed and secure within the community because all participate in that spirit.

I am less concerned at the moment with the "spirit of civility and mutual respect" than I am with its consequence: "When all groups feel *equally well-placed and secure within the community.*" How would an institution make this happen for currently excluded or marginalized peoples?

In a previous age, we might have been content to say that such security would be provided by allowing all voices to have access to or be represented at the decision-making table. We are now too aware of the interplay of power and knowledge and of the partiality of our own listening to be satisfied with such an answer. Colleges serious about "equal placement and security" would have to be concerned with neutralizing the impact of unshared power in teaching and research as well as in personnel decisions.

I see no holding back from concluding that this suggests an end to the currently inhibiting system of rank, tenure, and promotion. I am not saying flatly that the whole system must be abandoned (though I have heard worse ideas), but if it is not, then ways must be found (as they were found in the Federated Learning Communities and its spin-offs) to conduct the conversations of respect fully within the curriculum but entirely without consequences one way or another for promotion and tenure decisions.

Six Objections

Many reasonable objections might be raised to restructuring the university along the lines I have suggested. Less in the hope of responding definitively to them than in the hope of enhancing the plausibility of a democratically pluralistic vision of the university, I will respond briefly to the objections I have most frequently encountered.

1) Granted, we are living in a radically diverse world, runs the first objection. It is impossible, however, without undermining the coherence of the academic enterprise, to take all of that diversity seriously.

   In reply: I am not suggesting that every institution has to mirror all the diversity in the world. The full diversity should be mirrored by the entire system of higher education, or (less so) by institutions in a region or state. What is important for a single institution is that a challenging, relevant diversity pervade the curriculum, and that its students are thereby exposed to the liberal-education experiences described above.

2) A second objection, inspired by the developmental view of human diversity: It is all well and good to acknowledge the explosion of diversity in our awareness. But all these diverse viewpoints are not equally worthwhile. It is romantic and unreasonable to believe that Native American society, pre-industrial Latin America, or the Gaelic-speaking people of the west of Ireland have as much to contribute to the understanding and shaping of the modern world as do Americans and Europeans and the Japanese.

   In reply: I do not expect Native Americans to leap-frog in the near future over the Japanese and Americans in the production of smart bombs or compact discs. But by and large I will expect, until proven otherwise in sustained conversations of respect, that the marginalized cultures of the world have much to contribute to medicine, to agricultural science, to our understanding of the relationship of humanity and the environment, to child-rearing, to therapy, and to dozens of other important things. The advanced industrial nations of the world have cornered the market on neither wisdom nor science.

3) A related hierarchical objection: Can any education be serious that does not focus centrally on Western civilization? Even ignoring the fact that it is our heritage (and ought therefore to be the focus of our education), it is the most powerful and influential force on the planet.

   In reply: I am not suggesting that we not study Western civilization, nor that it be marginalized or caricatured as the sole root of the world's many problems. I am suggesting, rather: a) that both in its origins (as Martin Bernal has urged) and in its current form it be studied in interaction with other cultures and with its own subcultures (which are also our heritage); and b) that this study take the form of a dialogue with members of those other (sub)cultures in situations of "equal placement and security." Political science majors, for example, ought regularly to encounter professors from Latin America and Africa in dialogue with North American professors on issues of democracy and socio-political organization. Biology majors likewise should participate in curricular-based dialogues with Chinese professors who question the assumptions of Western medicine. While students could scarcely come away from such experiences without some awareness of the partiality of Western approaches, they would also likely leave with as much or more appreciation of the strengths of our approaches than is fostered by the current non-comparative, sprawling, unfocused, and unconnected curriculum.

4) A universalist might object: There is no great need to study Buddhist psychology because the essence of it is available in Jung; and no great need to read Vine Deloria because his tribalism is not significantly

different from the decentralist tradition in America or Russia.

In reply: If these intellectual phenomena are as similar as the objection supposes, that conclusion should emerge in a sustained conversation of respect with Buddhists and Native Americans. We are all too familiar with the distortions and depreciations that occur when a dominant culture or an isolated individual attempts to interpret another by incorporating it into what is already familiar. Additionally the objection presupposes, contrary to the assumptions of democratic pluralism, that the alleged similarities of these intellectual phenomena are more significant than their diversity.

5) A more general (and politically more difficult) version of the previous objection: One or another invasion of diversity has characterized the whole of at least Western history. Geertz and the multi-culturalists are exaggerating the significance of contemporary diversity. Diversity is already receiving its appropriate due.

In reply: In a democratic society, the issue under discussion is not only the philosophical issue of according diversity its proper due, but the politico-philosophical issue of how that judgment is made. Were the predominantly white and male establishment of higher education to decide what changes need to be made to accord contemporary diversity its due, the response would reflect the partiality of their experience and aspirations. Were that decision to emerge from a democratic process in which the currently marginalized and excluded had participated from positions of "equal placement and security," the judgment would understandably be of a different sort. Ultimately we come face-to-face with the depth or shallowness of what Dewey (in a text cited earlier) called "the democratic faith."

6) The last, and most frequently heard, objection: Changes of the sort being discussed would inevitably lead to a watering-down if not a complete collapse of standards.

In reply: There is little doubt that standards would change, just as the standards of the individual disciplines evolve in many interdisciplinary inquiries, or as the skills one values in tennis change from singles to doubles. Whether the new standards are as challenging as the old depends less on the intrinsic nature of these different intellectual enterprises than it does upon the integrity and respectfulness of the conversations.

Conclusion

It is easy to read contemporary experience in the light of simpler times, of a more familiar order, and to regard the explosion of diversity as productive of fragmentation, incoherence, and conflict. From the standpoint of democratic pluralism, wherein diversity is a resource, the explosion is challenging and unsettling but highly welcome. I thus prefer the metaphor of inchoateness to the backward-looking metaphor of fragmentation. We are not staring wistfully at the fragmented ruins of a temple once whole, but poring over the recently discovered jottings for a novel whose form or plot has yet to emerge.

If higher education were to take as its role the creation of new structures of dialogue and invention and cooperative discovery (i.e., structures appropriate to an inchoate world), there may indeed emerge a new world order. I speak not of an order in which technologically powerful Americans try to bring the diversity of the world to heel, but of a new world order that empowers hitherto excluded peoples of our and other nations to contribute their experience on an equal footing to our collective understanding of ourselves, society, and the world.

CASE STUDY

CHAPTER 13

CIVIC EDUCATION AND ACADEMIC CULTURE: LEARNING TO PRACTICE WHAT WE TEACH

CRAIG PLATT

Throughout the wave of liberal education critiques and reform efforts of the 1980s and 1990s, a great deal has been said and written about the need for a revival of "civic education"—that is, education for citizenship—as a central purpose of liberal education. Generally this means not just that students need to be knowledgeable about current public issues or about how government functions (although these outcomes are certainly important), but also that we need to foster the development of the skills, attitudes, and dispositions essential for responsible participation in the democratic process. Kettering Foundation president David Mathews (1991) has aptly summarized this distinction, saying that a democratic education needs to focus not just on educating *about* politics, but on educating *for* politics.

Writing about the civic purpose of liberal education, some have made the point that when faculty members work collaboratively to redesign or reform liberal education curricula, the process can represent an opportunity to model the very same virtues we hope to encourage in students. As David Hiley writes in *Liberal Education* (Winter 1996): "Debate over the curriculum, debate over what we believe is important for all students to know, can become an object lesson in democratic education if we will let it be."

So why is it so notoriously difficult for a faculty to accomplish the kind of collaborative, integrative curriculum planning that would achieve these ends? There are, of course, a multitude of complex factors that impinge on any process of change in American higher education, including internal institutional realities of colleges and universities as well as social and economic dimensions external to the institutions themselves. (A comprehensive treatment of these complexities is given by Jerry Gaff and James Ratcliff, eds. 1997, in *Handbook of the Undergraduate Curriculum.*) Here, I would like to focus on a particular proposition that helps to make sense of the difficulties—and that might have the added virtue of enhancing our empathy for our students.

As I have followed the national conversation about liberal education and citizenship over the past several years, and as we have worked to develop a new liberal education core program at Franklin Pierce College, what has struck me is the extent to which the skills and practices we seek to encourage in our students regarding civic education are precisely those that we ourselves have great difficulty achieving in the academic profession—especially when we deal with issues of curriculum and teaching.

A familiar part of the discourse about interdisciplinary teaching, the concept of "faculty as co-learners," has come to mean a matter of content—that is, that faculty working on interdisciplinary

Source: "Civic Education and Academic Culture: Learning to Practice What We Teach," by Craig Platt, reprinted from *Liberal Education*, Vol. 84, No. 1, 1998, Association of American Colleges and Universities.

projects are often placed in the unaccustomed (and potentially rewarding) role of grappling with unfamiliar subject matter alongside their students. Perhaps a parallel sort of co-learning is required of us when we set out to work together on liberal education reform. To develop purposeful, integrated curricula that prepare students for effective participation in the democratic process, we should be mindful of the often unfamiliar and uncomfortable challenges we are likely to encounter in our own process of collaborating over the curriculum. It may be useful to view ourselves, faculty and administrators, as co-learners of the civic arts.

Liberal Education and the Civic Arts

In *Racing With Catastrophe* (1990), educational philosopher Richard Gambino charged American higher education with "ignoring the needs of the nation, the most essential of these being the needs of a democratic society." Gambino's critique is representative of a continuous wave of calls, from the early 1980s to the present, for a revitalization of the civic purpose of college and university curricula. Concerns about the preparation of young adults for citizenship are not unique to contemporary America, of course, but there clearly has been a groundswell of criticism and calls for reform during the period since the publication in 1981 of the Carnegie Foundation report *Higher Learning in the Nation's Service.* There, Ernest Boyer and Fred Hechinger decried the trend toward "civic illiteracy" in the United States and recommended that an updated version of civics studies be included in college curricula. In the ensuing years, extensive dialogue has taken place in the higher education community about the need to prepare students for citizenship, including lively debate about just what that preparation should entail.

Civic Education

So what is a civic education? What can a liberal education provide to prepare students for effective and responsible citizenship? Part of our answer would certainly be the breadth and depth of knowledge that liberally educated people bring to their participation as citizens—including knowledge of their own and other cultures and their histories, as well as levels of language and science literacy that will allow them to understand and interpret the mass of information they will encounter as they make judgments about public issues. But another thread has woven throughout the recent discussion of civic education, a thread that we might refer to as the *civic arts approach.* Proponents of this approach, including such commentators as Elizabeth Minnich (1991) and David Mathews (1991), have emphasized higher education's potential to provide those skills, dispositions, and habits of mind that are essential for constructive participation in the democratic process.

In "Civic Intelligence," Mathews (1991) writes that "an education for politics is necessarily an education in the practice of making choices with others who are different from us." However simple on its surface, this statement nicely sums up an emerging consensus about the purpose of a civic arts education. According to Mathews, this purpose can best be served by helping students to develop four skills: first, what Kant called the "enlarged mentality," the ability to "understand facts as others would understand them for themselves"; second, the ability to think comprehensively, seeing the whole of a problem rather than compartmentalized aspects; third, an understanding of personal connectedness to the larger world; and fourth, the ability to make public judgments, to make choices together with others in the face of uncertainty.

Academic Culture and the Civic Arts

It may be instructive to consider these same goals in relation to the difficulties that arise when college and university faculties attempt to develop more coherent, meaningful liberal education programs. The issues and problems that tend to impede such curricular reform processes reveal some remarkable parallels to these same dimensions of the civic arts that we want to develop in our students. With regard to our teaching, we are not accustomed to exercising the Kantian enlarged mentality—that is, to considering the differing perspectives of colleagues and integrating them with our own. Few of us have much experience thinking comprehensively about curricular issues beyond our own disciplinary compartments, nor do we often think seriously about connecting our teaching to the larger world of what students are learning in their other coursework. In short, when it comes to liberal education planning, we tend to enter the process poorly equipped to "make choices together in the face of uncertainty."

Given the training we receive and the norms of the professional culture in which we as academics are socialized, it should come as no surprise that collaborative work on the liberal arts curriculum is so difficult for us. First and foremost, we are trained to be specialists—and perhaps more importantly, to *value* specialization. This emphasis is well suited to the kind of disciplinary work that has been the focus of academic life but does little to prepare us to communicate effectively with colleagues who bring their own specialized expertise and disciplinary modes of thinking to the table. Secondly, another fundamental characteristic of the academic profession has been the supreme value we place on autonomy. Clearly, this tradition of freedom from external control serves essential purposes in a healthy higher education community, but the problem for liberal education reform is that any approach designed to enhance coherence—whether it involves a common syllabus, or team teaching, or just a shared thematic structure—is likely to entail some sacrifice of our customary autonomy in the classroom.

The diagnosis I am offering may appear pessimistic, but in fact I would propose that an institution can enhance its prospects for successfully implementing a coherent liberal education program by entering the process with a clear sense of what makes it difficult. With these tensions in mind, we can begin a discussion of how best to bring our own civic skills to bear in our deliberations about the curriculum.

A Laboratory Experience in 'Individual and Community'

The Franklin Pierce faculty began a process of liberal education reform in the fall of 1990, ultimately approving a new core curriculum organized around the theme of "The Individual and Community" that takes the preparation of students for citizenship as one of its central goals. The forty-two semester-hour program, which took effect with the entering class of Fall 1992, consists almost entirely of a sequence of required courses taken in common by all students. Most of the courses in the core are interdisciplinary, designed and taught by teams of faculty from multiple departments. Not surprisingly, the ongoing process of developing and implementing this program has been difficult and sometimes painful, but the opportunity to explore new territory and work in collaboration with colleagues has also been a rewarding experience for faculty—more than 90 percent of whom have been involved in the new core courses.

What stands out in reviewing the history of this project is how clearly it illustrates the analysis I have been offering. Repeatedly, in developing and implementing these new courses, dilemmas have arisen that have challenged our own civic arts. Some issues have involved the design of courses, while others involve administrative aspects of the program. Some have been quite predictable, and others more unexpected. What is striking is how often these various stumbling blocks have returned us to the same kinds of tensions and compromises. A few of the more contentious issues are illuminating.

The question of commonality. Take, for example, one of the more obvious and predictable issues—namely, the question of how much commonality needs to be maintained among different instructors and sections of the same course. The overall curriculum plan approved by the faculty called for "common content," but as faculty teams began work on developing courses, a good deal of debate and anxiety arose about the question of "how common is common?" Clearly, there were legitimate principles underlying the call for commonality: We wanted students to have some shared experience in core courses, and we wanted to be able to build increased coherence from course to course. Just as clearly, however, there were legitimate concerns about what might be sacrificed in the interest of commonality. While some faculty were more vociferous than others, it would be safe to say that all of us felt some discomfort over the loss of our usual individual freedom to choose what and how to teach.

Commonality issues have not magically disappeared over the years, but it has been instructive to see how the faculty sought to resolve these conflicts and how the level of anxiety about this question has been reduced. In general, course teams were given latitude to decide how to pursue the common-content mandate. (One criterion issued by the dean, when pressed by some groups early in the process, was that courses should have at least 50 percent common content.) The resolution that emerged as the first courses were developed was that each course would have an agreed-upon set of goals and a universal thematic structure, and that the same set of primary texts would be used by all instructors. Some degree of individual autonomy was preserved in most courses by designating certain elements of instructor choice, and by the agreement that how to teach a particular text was reserved to individual teaching style.

In retrospect, an important factor in resolving the issues of common content has been that course teams had relative autonomy in their approach. In some courses, the course outline, readings, and assignments have been virtually identical across sections. In others, faculty teams have opted for more individual autonomy, with various creative efforts to ensure genuine commonality.

Collective decision-making. A constant undercurrent to the questions of what to teach in the new courses has been the struggle of each course team to develop its own decision-making processes. While all of us had relevant experience with various kinds of committee work and with decision making at the departmental level, it became clear early on that we were venturing into new territory when we set out to design interdisciplinary courses together. Given that each team member faced the prospect of delivering the course to his or her own students, was it appropriate to make choices of course themes and texts by majority vote? On the other hand, if teams attempted to make every important decision by consensus, would groups inevitably be paralyzed by one intransigent member? Which risk should we seek to minimize: tyranny by the majority or by the minority?

As the project progressed and each course group developed its own norms and history, decision-making styles evolved somewhat differently from one team to another, with some groups operating exclusively by consensus and others adopting formal voting and majority rule. The process has not been easy or entirely harmonious in any of the groups. Questionable text choices have been made to placate one member; individuals overruled by the majority have been alienated. In general, however, it seems safe to say that we have become both more adept and more comfortable in collaborative planning. Also, it seems clear that the opportunity for each team to find its own *modus operandi* has eased some of the initial discomfort about surrendering individual control.

Evaluating courses and instructors. As the newly designed courses began, it was clear that faculty teams needed to have evaluative input from students to inform their work on course revision from year to year. Standard student evaluations of teaching, however, had always been viewed as private information, available to the individual faculty member, the division chair, and the administration, but never seen by colleagues. Thus, what might seem at first glance a fairly trivial administrative question became another dilemma: a legitimate instance of the right to privacy coming into conflict with the commitment to working collectively. Our resolution of this issue is at times unwieldy—and certainly imperfect—but it does seem to represent a fruitful compromise. Each course in the program now administers its own course evaluation questionnaire, asking for student input about course goals, structure, readings, assignments, and so on, entirely separate from the college-wide instrument used for student evaluation of teaching effectiveness. These course evaluation results are compiled by course coordinators to be used for planning purposes by their faculty teams, while the evaluations of teaching effectiveness are not seen by course coordinators or other colleagues.

Balancing *Pluribus* and *Unum*

Perhaps the most important implication to be drawn from the Franklin Pierce story is that what we have been grappling with in developing this Individual and Community curriculum is precisely our own difficulty with the dilemma of individual and community. Furthermore, I would suggest that *any* faculty involved in the task of increasing curricular coherence can expect to deal continuously with issues revolving around that central theme: the tension between the legitimate rights and needs of individual faculty members on the one hand, and the faculty's shared responsibility to the institution and the curriculum on the other. How do we balance the traditions of independent-mindedness and autonomy that have marked the academic endeavor with the increasing constraints imposed by any sort of central thematic or methodological structure? Must we sacrifice autonomy in order to achieve coherence? These difficult questions are likely to be encountered in various forms on any campus where true liberal education reform is undertaken.

A Recurring Theme

Interestingly enough, the individual and community theme has a long history in the discourse about civic education. Observers of American higher education over the past several decades, ranging from the influential Harvard Committee on General Education in the 1940s to the communitarians of the 1990s, have proposed that liberal education should engage students in examining the tension or dialectical relationship between the individual and the collective in a democratic society. Clearly, the difficulties we confront in liberal education reform offer a real-life illustration of the very core subject matter of the civic arts. At a time when countless observers have characterized contemporary American culture as having special difficulty reconciling claims of individual rights with those of community, it seems essential for us in higher education to recognize that these issues are especially salient—and troublesome—in the academic profession. Nowhere is this more the case than in deliberations about liberal education.

As a framework for thinking about this connection, consider a model proposed by Freeman Butts in the 1982 special issue of *Liberal Education* devoted to civic education. In his article, Butts presented a "decalogue" of value-oriented claims that typify democratic communities and that might serve as guidelines for the contents of a common civic curriculum. The ten items include a category of individualistic, pluralistic elements that Butts referred to as "values of pluribus": freedom, diversity, privacy, due process, and international human rights. A set of "values of unum" represent the unifying elements of a democratic society: justice, equality, authority, participation, and personal obligation for the public good. While this summary certainly loses the richness of Butts's proposal, the crux of the argument holds that liberal education can prepare students for citizenship by promoting an understanding and appreciation of these values, and by developing the ability to balance and integrate the claims of pluribus and unum when conflicts between values inevitably arise.

To return to our own efforts as curriculum planners, this model provides a useful perspective on the challenges faced by faculty and administrators dealing with liberal education reform efforts. In general, recent reforms have been motivated by a desire for increasing unity in the curriculum, but ideas for achieving that end often run headlong into conflict with the legitimate values of pluribus that dominate on campus. At Franklin Pierce, we have been continuously challenged by tensions between freedom and personal obligation, privacy and participation, and between diversity and the authority of the group. The ensuing debates can threaten to deteriorate into the same sort of absolutist "rights versus responsibilities" standoff encountered so often in the public forum, and the problems can appear intractable. On the other hand, our rhetoric about civic education would suggest that we believe there are certain attitudes, skills, and perspectives that will help students resolve such issues when they confront them in public life. If we enter the curriculum reform process with our eyes open to these parallels, is it possible for us to engage in an effective civic dialogue of our own, one that seeks to honor the legitimate claims of both pluribus and unum? The work engaging us at Franklin Pierce illustrates that this kind of change is difficult—and that it is indeed possible.

Developing Civic Arts

The particulars of the Franklin Pierce experience may not translate directly to specific curricular approaches attempted at other institutions. However, the broader pattern they illustrate is a fundamental one that needs to be recognized and understood. On any campus, efforts to create a more coherent, unified liberal education program are likely to give rise to tensions and conflicts around the dimension of pluribus and unum, and our customary roles and modes of discourse are unlikely to serve us well in resolving them. For reforms to succeed, we need some mechanism for serious dialogue about how to change ourselves and our institutions while preserving the essential elements of both the individual and the collective good.

While appropriate means to achieve this civic dialogue will vary in significant ways from campus to campus, a few general starting points apply to most institutions. First, if some of the pitfalls of our usual modes of deliberation are to be avoided, curriculum reform initiatives ought to involve new forums for discussion—settings in which fresh ground rules can be set, and new forms of discourse are more likely to emerge.

A second recommendation: any effort to build a coherent curriculum should consciously encourage dialogue across departmental boundaries. A planning committee consisting simply of one representative per department, with members viewing their role primarily as departmental spokespersons, would be unlikely to transcend the usual slice-of-the-pie approach to curriculum design.

A final suggestion for institutions seeking to establish a new civic dialogue around liberal education reform is to start with an emphasis on finding common ground early in the process. What is it that participants can agree on? This may be a statement of the characteristics of an effective curriculum, or a liberal education mission statement, or a list of desired educational outcomes. Whatever form this area of agreement may take, the point is that any civic body engaged in deliberation needs a sense of what is shared in order to shape its discussions.

In introducing this analysis, I suggested that it might have the virtue of increasing our empathy for our students. Consider again the things we ask of students when we engage them in civic arts education: We want them to learn to engage in dialogue with people whose points of view may differ from theirs, to integrate other perspectives with their own, and to make choices about important issues in an uncertain world. We expect them to recognize and value their connectedness to the larger world around them and to find ways to integrate and balance legitimate claims of the individual with those of the collective. This may add up to a daunting—and often unwelcome—set of challenges, especially when they are steeped in a contemporary American culture that, according to so many recent critiques, is especially troubled by an inability to reconcile the traditions of individualism and civic obligation.

We in the academy need to recognize that we ourselves, in addition to being influenced by that same societal milieu, are acculturated in a profession that intensifies these conflicts. We are part of a professional culture that is intensely—perhaps uniquely—committed to the values of individualism, autonomy, and privacy. These core principles serve important and legitimate purposes, even as they leave us poorly prepared to work effectively together on liberal education reform.

To construct the kind of coherent, purposeful approaches that prepare our students to function as citizens, we must realize that we are taking on the task of redefining our own academic culture, campus by campus. Success will require new ways of thinking about our roles, new modes of deliberating together, and creative ways of balancing individual and collective interests. If we hope to foster these civic capacities in our students, we must address ourselves to the same challenges.

References

Boyer, Ernest L., and Fred M. Hechinger. 1981. *Higher learning in the nation's service.* Washington, D.C.: Carnegie Foundation for the Advancement of Teaching.

Butts, R. Freeman. 1982. The revival of civic learning requires a prescribed curriculum. *Liberal Education* 68 (4).

Gaff, Jerry, and James L. Ratcliff, eds. 1997. *Handbook of the undergraduate curriculum.* San Francisco: Jossey-Bass.

Gambino, Richard. 1990. *Racing with catastrophe.* New York: Freedom House.

Harvard Committee on General Education. 1945. *General education in a free society.* Cambridge: Harvard University Press.

Hiley, David R. 1996. The democratic purposes of general education. *Liberal Education* 82 (1).

Mathews, David. 1991. Civic intelligence. In *Higher education and the practice of democratic politics,* edited by Bernard Murchland. Dayton: Kettering Foundation.

Minnich, Elizabeth K. 1991. Some reflections on civic education and the curriculum. In *Higher education and the practice of democratic politics,* edited by Bernard Murchland. Dayton: Kettering Foundation.

PART TWO

PROPOSALS AND CRITIQUES OF THE CONTEMPORARY UNDERGRADUATE CURRICULUM

CHAPTER 14

CURRICULAR TRANSFORMATIONS: TRADITIONAL AND EMERGING VOICES IN THE ACADEMY

JENNIFER GRANT HAWORTH AND CLIFTON F. CONRAD

The purpose, content, and meaning of the undergraduate curriculum has been vigorously debated throughout the history of American higher education. From the antebellum debates over the classical curriculum at Yale and William and Mary to the biting critiques recently leveled against "relativism" in higher education (Bloom, 1987), the undergraduate curriculum has served as an historic theater for defining, producing, and legitimating knowledge. In the past decade, the curriculum has been enacted by a wide range of actors who hold a vital stake in higher education—including academics, policy-makers, students, and representatives of the business community (Conrad, 1989). Their perspectives have focused on both a reassertion—and a reexamination—of the centrality of the traditional canon in the undergraduate curriculum. This dynamic interplay between traditional and emerging stakeholder voices has recently contributed to an intriguing transformation of the American undergraduate curriculum.

By curricular transformation, we are referring to those informal and formal procedures through which knowledge within the curriculum is continually produced, created, and expanded by a wide range of stakeholders acting within a broader social and historical context. The recent introduction—and, in numerous cases, incorporation—of emerging modes of inquiry, perspectives, and pedagogical techniques into the undergraduate curriculum suggests that the purpose, content, and meaning of the undergraduate curriculum is in the midst of major reexamination and change. In this essay, we reflect on the various forces transforming the undergraduate curriculum across three lines of inquiry. First, we explore the contemporary context and discuss four informing forces that have catalyzed recent developments in the undergraduate curriculum. Second, given this contextual background, we discuss the knowledge claims recently articulated by two broad groups of stakeholders and examine their consequences for the undergraduate curriculum. In our final section, we investigate how new knowledge claims are being legitimated by stakeholders within the academy and illustrate how this development has led to a transformation of the undergraduate curriculum.

I. The Contemporary Context

In his inaugural presidential address at Harvard in 1869, Charles William Eliot suggested that "the institutions of higher education . . . are always a faithful mirror in which are sharply reflected the

Source: "Curricular Transformations: Traditional & Emerging Voices in the Academy," by Jennifer Grant Haworth and Clifton F. Conrad, reprinted from *Curriculum in Transition: Perspectives on the Undergraduate Experience*, 1990, Ginn Press.

national history and character" (Rudolph, 1977, p. 5). From the colonial colleges and land-grant colleges to the movement for equality of educational opportunity during the last three decades, American institutions of higher learning have actively responded to the prevailing trends and social values of the day. Three broad societal changes and one significant change within academe have acted as powerful informing forces on the recent development of the undergraduate curriculum.

Changing Demographics

The ethnic composition of American society has diversified markedly over the past decade, a trend that is expected to continue well into the twenty-first century. By 1996, for example, it is expected that one out of every three 15–24 year olds will be a member of a minority group. The percentage of non-minority white youth aged 15–24 is expected to decline by 12 percent while the number of Hispanic youth aged 15–24 is expected to increase by 44 percent (Wetzel, 1987).

This increasing diversity is reflected in college and university enrollments. Since 1980, there has been a richer blend of age, race, and ethnic backgrounds among college and university students than ever before in American higher education. Between 1978 and 1989, the number of adult students (aged 25 years and older) attending college increased by approximately 24 percent, whereas the number of traditional age college students (18–24 years) grew by only 7 percent over the same time period (NCES, 1989). Similarly, the number of women enrolling in postsecondary education increased 26 percent between 1978 and 1989 (NCES, 1989).

Minority enrollment in higher education has also increased over the past decade. Based on data from the National Center for Education Statistics, approximately 18 percent of all college and university students represented minority groups in 1988, an increase from 16 percent in 1980. This increase occurred, despite the drop in black student enrollment from 9.2 percent in 1980 to 8.7 percent in 1988, because Hispanic and Asian/Pacific Islander student enrollments increased notably over the past ten years (NCES, 1989). Although the modest gains in minority student enrollment are troublesome, four out of every five institutions report that they are currently involved in activities designed to increase minority enrollment and retention (El-Khawas, 1989).

Traditionalist Educational Policy Agenda

With the publication of *A Nation at Risk* in 1983, the first indication of an impending traditionalist policy agenda was recognized on American college and university campuses. Under the bully-pulpit political leadership of then Secretary of Education William Bennett, calls for a return to the fundamentals of the higher learning were stressed by both the popular press and many academics. These fundamentals included greater attention on basic skills acquisition, a renewed emphasis on studying the humanities and the great books of Western civilization, and stronger calls for assessing student learning and development.

The back-to-basics movement in higher education has experienced a revival of interest over the past decade. A number of educational reform reports have suggested that colleges and universities must pay greater attention to strengthening basic writing, mathematics, communication, and logical reasoning skills among undergraduate students (NIE, 1984; AAC, 1985; Boyer, 1987). This renewed emphasis on basic skills appears to have been precipitated by studies indicating the academic underpreparedness of today's college-aged youth. According to one recent study of 250 four-year institutions, one out of every seven freshman students was in need of remedial coursework in English or mathematics (Roueche, Baker, and Roueche, 1985). In response to this growing concern, a large number of institutions have recently instituted mandatory basic skill assessments for students. A 1989 study of 366 two- and four-year institutions, for example, found that basic skills testing was firmly in place at 65 percent of all postsecondary institutions and that another 19 percent had initiated plans for testing (El-Khawas, 1989).

The reassertion of the intellectual and social value of the humanities and the traditional great books canon has likewise found expression on college and university campuses across the nation. Initially promoted by Bennett (1984), Allan Bloom (1987) and E.D. Hirsch (1987) have recently penned best-selling volumes that have argued for the inherent worth of the humanities as a course of study—and the great books as the preferred curriculum—in undergraduate education. Colleges and universities have responded to this call: in 1986, 42 percent of universities, and 35 percent of four-year colleges required that original texts be used in their humanities courses (El-Khawas, 1986).

The call for accountability has likewise spread across American colleges and universities. In the mid 1980s, several national reform reports—including those by the National Institute of Education (1984) and the Association of American Colleges (1985)—recommended that colleges and universities implement systematic student assessment programs to monitor and track student learning outcomes. According to a 1989 American Council of Education survey of 366 two- and four-year postsecondary institutions, approximately 70 percent of the surveyed colleges and universities had institutionalized some form of assessment activity (El-Khawas, 1989). For the most part, these assessments have targeted basic skills (65 percent), higher order thinking skills (25 percent), general education (25 percent), and major subject content areas (26 percent) in the undergraduate curriculum (El-Khawas, 1989).

Increasingly Pluralistic Environment

Over the past fifteen years, an increasingly pluralistic environment has emerged both within and outside of the academy. Grounded in societal demographic changes, the international trend toward a global economic marketplace, and the growing environmental recognition of the world as a global village, pluralistic perspectives have surfaced in the American undergraduate curricular landscape in the form of global, gender, and ethnic studies courses.

A number of stakeholders have recently given voice to this pluralistic perspective. In their reform reports, the Association of American Colleges (1980 and 1988) became one of the first major groups to call for the inclusion of multicultural and global perspectives into the undergraduate curriculum: "The first curricular priority is to implant a strong international dimension into the core of general education requirements. The curriculum should be expanded to introduce students particularly to non-Western cultures" (AAC, 1980, p. 4). Several government agencies and private foundations—including the Fund for the Improvement of Postsecondary Education (FIPSE), the Lilly Endowment, and the Andrew W. Mellon Foundation—have provided funding for implementing global, gender, and ethnic studies into the undergraduate curriculum. The entrance of greater numbers of women and minorities into the professioriate has likewise advanced both feminist and multicultural world views.

These pluralistically-inspired courses and program innovations are generally characterized by both a high degree of interdisciplinarity and the use of perspectives and texts not traditionally represented in the Western civilization canon. Pluralists and educational traditionalists have recently locked horns over the legitimacy of representing multiple world views in the undergraduate curriculum. This debate has been most recently illustrated by the curriculum revision projects at the University of California-Berkeley and Stanford University, where both universities have recently revised their general education requirements to include pluralistic perspectives (Mooney, 1988).

Competing Perspectives in the Academy

The recent dynamic interplay between traditionalist and pluralistic perspectives has generated a spectrum of colorful debates among scholars in academe. The anthropologist Renato Rosaldo has used a militaristic metaphor to describe the recent debate as a "raging battle" where the epithet was the weapon of choice: "Name calling has pitted 'objectivists' against 'relativists,' 'presentists' against 'historicists,' and 'foundationalists' against 'interpretivists'" (Rosaldo, 1989, p. 219). Not unlike the debates at the turn of the century between scientists and liberal humanists, this recent exchange over the legitimacy of competing epistemologies, modes of inquiry, and perspectives appears to cut both across—and within—disciplines and professional fields.

This "raging battle" has largely centered on the validity of the traditional, postivist approach to scholarly inquiry. A growing number of scholars have recently objected to the epistemological view that truth is objective and exists "out there" to be discovered through value-free, neutral, scientific methods (Lincoln and Guba, 1985). The emergence of diverse new perspectives—including interpretivism, feminism, multiculturalism and critical theory—has offered competing epistemologies where truth is viewed as subjective and existing, at least in part, within the realm of an individual's personal and cultural experiences. Because of the constructed nature of knowledge, these scholars argue that new modes of inquiry—such as oral history, ethnography, hermeneutics, and the greater use of interdisciplinary and comparative studies—must be used to achieve not only a critical understanding of their own disciplines, but of the world as well.

As the formal medium for communicating knowledge within the university, the curriculum is heavily influenced by the prevailing events, values, and beliefs of the society in which it is situated. In the past ten years, three broad societal changes—the increasing cultural diversity of American society, the resurgence of traditionalist values and attitudes, and the fuller recognition of pluralistic perspectives—as well as the internal conflict over epistemologies and modes of inquiry within academe, have acted to transform the undergraduate curriculum. These contemporary developments have been facilitated by a diverse group of stakeholders holding multiple perspectives for the purpose, content, and meaning of the undergraduate curriculum. As our next two sections will suggest, these perspectives have contributed to fundamental changes in the undergraduate curriculum.

II. Stakeholder Knowledge Claims on the Undergraduate Curriculum

There have been few periods in the history of American higher education when the purpose, content, and meaning of the undergraduate curriculum has been debated as vigorously or as publicly as in the decade of the 1980s. One diverse group has provided high-pitched critiques of American education, arguing that dramatic changes are needed to revitalize the collegiate curriculum. Their proposals have included pleas for reclaiming the national legacy (Bennett, 1984), restoring curricular integrity (AAC, 1985), re-opening the American mind (Bloom, 1987), and ensuring the cultural literacy of our youth (Hirsch, 1987). A second, highly diversified stakeholder group has argued that the current curriculum is narrowly defined by a myopic world view that has minimized the knowledge claims of various groups, including women, minorities, and non-Western authors (see, for example, McIntosh, 1981; Schuster and Van Dyne, 1984; Andersen, 1987; Rosaldo, 1989; Tierney, 1989b). The diversity and vitality of perspectives generated by these two stakeholder groups has drawn national attention to the purpose and substance of the undergraduate curriculum in our nation's colleges and universities. In this section, we discuss the knowledge claims recently articulated by these two stakeholder groups and briefly examine their consequences for the undergraduate curriculum.

Stakeholder Knowledge Claims: Traditional Voices

As noted above, several individuals (Bennett, 1984; Bloom, 1987; Hirsch, 1987; Cheney, 1989) have recently published policy reports and national best-selling books calling for the revitalization of the undergraduate curriculum. Presenting what is widely considered a traditionalist agenda for curricular reform, these stakeholders have argued that the curriculum has become watered down by "relativistic" points of view, becoming little more than a "supermarket" of electives where the central role of the "humanities has been siphoned off, diluted, or so adulterated that students graduating know little of their heritage" (Bennett, 1984, p. 5). These stakeholders have called for a reinstatement of the liberal arts course of study and the traditional great books canon as two mandatory steps toward restoring the educational integrity of the undergraduate curriculum.

From an epistemological perspective, these "traditional voices" are firmly rooted within a particular view of knowledge—logical positivism—that has been the predominant mode of inquiry within the academy since the beginning of the American research university in the late nineteenth century. This epistemology assumes that knowledge exists "out there" and can be discovered through objective and empirical means. From this perspective, knowledge is viewed as a series of lawlike, absolute, universal truths that exist independent of, and external to, the knower. The scholar's task is to act as a detached observer in the pursuit of truth and knowledge.

This guiding epistemology is revealed in the traditionalist's knowledge claims concerning the purpose and content of—and, to a lesser degree, the pedagogy within—the undergraduate curriculum. Believing that the kinds of "knowledge most worth knowing" in a Western, democratic society are based in those universal truths of Western civilization that have endured the test of time, traditionalists argue that the purpose of the undergraduate experience is to expose students to the time-honored truths of their society. For many in this group, these truths are best revealed in the humanities:

> I would describe the humanities as the best that has been said, thought, written, and otherwise expressed about the human experience. The humanities tell us how men and women of our own and other civilizations have grappled with life's enduring questions: What is justice? What should be loved? What deserves to be defended? . . . We should want all students to know a common culture rooted in civilization's lasting vision, its highest shared ideals and aspirations, and its heritage (Bennett, 1984, p. 6).

Many traditionalists further argue that if students are to learn the truths of their common culture, the university must provide programs based upon the "judicious use of great texts" (Bloom, 1987, p. 344) which provoke:

> Awareness of the classic—particularly important for our innocents; an acquaintance with what big questions were when there were still big questions; models, at the very least, of how to go about answering them; and, perhaps, most important of all, a fund of shared experiences and thoughts on which to ground their friendships with one another (Bloom, 1987, p. 344).

These "great texts," according to traditionalist reformers, "embody the best in our culture . . . no student citizen should be denied access to the best that tradition has to offer" (Bennett, 1984, p. 29).

Without these fundamental truths, traditionalists maintain that students will lack the requisite knowledge needed to be productive and informed citizens in American society. Diane Ravitch has argued that "students cannot learn to ask critical questions or to think conceptually about the past or about their own lives as political actors unless they have sufficient background knowledge" (1988, p. 129). Through the study of the humanities and the great thinkers of the past, the traditionalist-crafted undergraduate experience is designed to provide students with the requisite "background knowledge" in order to live wisely and well.

The traditionalists' pedagogical approach is likewise deeply rooted within their epistemology. In her discussion of teaching in the undergraduate core curriculum, Lynne Cheney references the pedagogical wisdom of the *Yale Report of 1828:*

> "The two great points to be gained in intellectual culture," an 1828 report from Yale University noted, "are the *discipline* and the *furniture* [her italics] of the mind; expanding its powers, and storing it with knowledge" (1989, p. 14).

When knowledge is viewed as a series of absolute and universal truths that exist independent of, and external to, the knower, the teacher is viewed as a kind of sage whose task is to impart these universal truths to students neutrally. Given that the aim of a college education is to exercise, condition, and strengthen the intellect, the pedagogical element of the traditionalist's epistemology becomes important only insofar as it more fully engages students in the content of their inquiry.

Traditionalist knowledge claims have contributed significantly to the growing conservative policy agenda that has swept over American education during the past ten years. Their influence over the purpose and content of the undergraduate curriculum has been apparent in a number of areas, including recent movements to increase the amount of general education required by undergraduates, the fuller integration of liberal education into professional undergraduate education programs, as well as the new emphases placed on basic skills, humanities, and great books instruction (Conrad and Haworth, forthcoming). Ironically, perhaps the most instrumental goal of the traditionalists—to establish interdisciplinary core curricula—has not experienced much success. According to a recent survey of 284 four-year institutions, only 2 percent had implemented an interdisciplinary core curriculum for their general education program (Locke, 1989).

Although some recent reform reports, such as Bennett's *To Reclaim a Legacy* and Cheney's *50 Hours,* have recommended that universities select their "most distinguished faculty" to teach core courses, traditional stakeholder perspectives have generally made few recommendations to improve pedagogical practices within the undergraduate curriculum. An exception is the recent AAC report, which includes substantive pedagogical suggestions for "reorienting teaching" that go beyond content issues and address the process of teaching (AAC, 1988). Specifically, the report encourages active student learning through an improved understanding of how students "hear, understand, interpret, and integrate ideas" (AAC, 1988, p. 28) and suggests that teachers enlist their students as "coinquirers" in the learning process.

Stakeholder Knowledge Claims: Emerging Voices

A chorus of new voices has recently been heard in the academy. These stakeholders—although expressing diverse points-of-view—have shared a single perspective in common: the belief that knowledge, as it is currently understood in the undergraduate curriculum, is partial, incomplete, and distorted. Calling for an end to the exclusive dominance of the traditional canon in the undergraduate curriculum, these scholars have argued for an expansion of curricular borders in higher education to include various cultural and theoretical perspectives.

While highly diverse in their own scholarly visions, these new voices share the view that knowledge, at least in large part, is a social construct. This perspective is directly antithetical to the traditionalists' epistemology that knowledge is an objective entity that exists "out there," external to, and independent of, the knower. By contrast, in this other, more contingent approach to knowledge, the interaction between the individual and his or her cultural context is critical to the construction of what is—or is not—considered knowledge. As William Tierney has described it, this epistemological view ". . . assumes that reality is defined though a process of social interchange that cannot be readily mapped, graphed, or controlled" (1989b, p. 43). Rather than employ "one single, simple, unilateral rationality," this epistomological perspective maintains that "there are many rationalities" which are contingent upon "the mores of the enterprise, the individuals involved in the organization, and the socio-historical context in which the organization resides" (Tierney, 1989b, p. 43). Given the belief that knowledge is socially constructed, the scholar's task is to articulate these "multiple constructed realities" (Berger and Luckmann, 1973), not through a detached, neutral stance but, instead, through reflexive inquiry that recognizes the dynamic interplay between the researched and the researcher (Rosaldo, 1989).

An array of emerging knowledge claims regarding content and process in the undergraduate curriculum have been expressed recently by these stakeholders. Firmly rooted within the epistomological assumption that there is no one single objective truth, these stakeholders have proposed that the purpose of an undergraduate education should be, in the words of Nannerl Keohane, president of Wellesley College, not to "reclaim a legacy . . . but to build upon it for a fuller understanding of the works of human beings in the present and the future" (1986, p. 88). To achieve this purpose, the traditional canon must be expanded to include a balanced view of multiple—rather than a single—knowledge perspectives. As Renato Rosaldo has explained it, the traditional canon as a "classic norm should become one mode of representation among others . . . allowing forms of writing that have been marginalized or banned altogether to gain legitimacy" within the curriculum (1989, p. 62).

For these stakeholders, newly emerging knowledge claims from interpretivist, feminist, critical theory, post-structuralist, and multicultural scholarship must be integrated into the curriculum to ensure a holistic undergraduate experience for students (see, for example, McIntosh, 1981; Lather, 1984; Andersen, 1987; Conrad, 1989; Rosaldo, 1989; Tierney, 1989b). The study of these diverse perspectives, these stakeholders suggest, enriches students with a broader context in which to place their own personal experiences and root their future inquiries. Likewise, the incorporation of new inquiry and theoretical perspectives into the curriculum provides new vistas from which both students and scholars alike can explore familiar and emerging topics.

With respect to pedagogy, this diverse group of stakeholders has offered a number of suggestions for strengthening the quality of instruction in the undergraduate curriculum. Based on the epistemological assumption that knowledge is largely a social construct rooted within the context of individual experience, these stakeholders view the current traditionalist approach to education as inherently limited. One critical theorist, Paulo Freire, has likened the traditional educational approach to banking, where the role of the teacher is to deposit objective, "universal truths" into student minds (Freire, 1971). The problems with this approach, these stakeholders argue, are twofold: first, teachers assume that there is a universal canon of thought to be taught; and second, because a predefined school of knowledge is available, teaching is often little more than a one-way transaction where teachers neutrally deposit knowledge into student "savings accounts." This banking approach "anesthetizes" and "attempts to maintain the submersion of consciousness" in students (Freire, 1971, p. 68).

Feminists and critical theorists, by contrast, do not view knowledge as static and objective. Consonant with their view of knowledge as a social construct, they argue that teachers may be better viewed as midwives than as bankers:

> Midwife-teachers are the opposite of banker-teachers. While the bankers deposit knowledge in the learner's head, the midwives draw it out. They assist the students in giving birth to their own ideas, in making their own tacit knowledge explicit and elaborating it . . . they assist in the emergence of consciousness (Belenky, Clinchy, Goldberger, and Tarule, 1986, pp. 217–218).

The role of the teacher in this pedagogical model is to help students unearth their own experiences within the context of the studied material and, within this process, to empower students to recognize their own abilities and to discover their individual "voice" (Shrewsbury, 1987). This pedagogical view suggests that knowledge is not the exclusive property of the teacher whose role is to dole it out to his or her students, but rather an interaction between student and teacher where both equally participate in the "pedagogic struggle to expose the underpinnings of that which is learned" (Tierney, 1989a).

The knowledge claims recently articulated by feminist, critical theorist, and multiculturalist stakeholders have contributed significantly to the growing acceptance of pluralistic points-of-view both within and outside of the academy. The influence of these perspectives over the purpose and content of the undergraduate curriculum has become increasingly apparent in the recent trend to integrate feminist, critical theory, and multicultural perspectives into general education programs previously dominated by the traditional canon of thought and in the rapid expansion of women's and ethnic studies departments and courses across the country (Conrad and Haworth, forthcoming). In addition, a significant number of institutions have recently implemented faculty development programs targeted at integrating many of these emerging theoretical and pedagogical perspectives into the undergraduate curriculum (AAC, 1981; Hoffman, 1986; Conrad and Haworth, forthcoming).

In the past decade, two diverse groups of stakeholders—each subscribing to different epistemologies—have advanced separate knowledge claims in the undergraduate curriculum. The lively exchange between these two groups has resurrected the continual question of "what knowledge is most worth knowing." Although the consequences of this debate have been visibly evidenced in changes in the content and structure of the undergraduate curriculum, this fundamental questioning of what counts as knowledge has also yielded an increasingly visible consciousness of alternative knowledge perspectives among scholars in the academy. It is at this juncture, perhaps, where Jose Ortega y Gasset's observation may offer a useful starting point for grappling with competing stakeholder knowledge claims in the undergraduate curriculum: "Reality happens to be, like a landscape possessed of an infinite number of perspectives, all equally veracious and authentic. The sole false perspective is that which claims to be the only one there is" (cited in Conrad, 1989, p. 215).

III. Stakeholder Knowledge Claims and Curricular Transformations

Between 1983 and 1987, 95 percent of American colleges and universities were either currently reviewing their undergraduate curriculum or had completed fundamental revisions of their undergraduate program (El-Khawas, 1987). This latest revisiting of the purpose and content of the undergraduate curriculum lends credibility to the epistemological position that what is defined as (valued) knowledge in the university changes with different cultural and historical contexts. During the 1980s demographic, traditionalist, and pluralistic societal demands have had an influential effect on the contour and texture of the undergraduate curriculum. It appears that what Frederick Rudolph noted about the curriculum almost fifteen years ago remains true today: "Curricular history is American history and therefore carries the burden of revealing the central purpose and driving directions of American society" (1977, p. 20).

The recent clashes between stakeholders voicing traditional and emerging knowledge claims have likewise provoked a fundamental reexamination of how knowledge is defined, approached, and taught within the academy. As faculty have published articles in scholarly journals, presented papers at professional conferences, and restructured their courses around alternate perspectives and modes of inquiry—such as feminism, critical theory, and multiculturalism—the academic community has responded vigorously to their tentative knowledge claims. The recognition, acceptance—and in many disciplines, the legitimation—of these knowledge claims has led to a significant transformation that has expanded the traditionally-defined canon to include a diversity of new theoretical and pedagogical perspectives. In this section, we examine how stakeholders have facilitated this transformation through the integration of these new knowledge claims into both their research and classroom activities.

Integration of Emerging Knowledge Claims in Disciplinary Scholarship

A merging of the old with the new has generated a fascinating mixture of theoretical perspectives within the traditional arts and science disciplines. Catalyzed by a number of faculty and student-driven initiatives—including newly formed interests in exploring traditionally unstudied populations, re-examining old questions from alternate viewpoints, and utilizing interdisciplinary perspectives in scholarly research—feminist, critical theory, and multicultural perspectives have recently entered the mainstream of scholarly activity in the academy. Each of these perspectives and accompanying modes of inquiry is premised on the epistemological view that knowledge is socially constructed within a cultural and historical context.

Feminist thought has generated widespread influence in a number of traditional social science and humanities disciplines, including psychology, sociology, anthropology, economics, history, and English. Although there are many variations of feminist thought (e.g., radical feminism, liberal feminism, neo-Marxist feminism, black feminism), most are firmly grounded in the belief that knowledge is a social construction. As Margaret Andersen explains:

> Including women refers to the complex process of redefining knowledge by making women's experiences a primary subject for knowledge, conceptualizing women as active agents in the creation of knowledge, looking at gender as fundamental to the articulation of knowledge in Western thought, and seeing women's and men's experiences in relation to the sex/gender system (1987, pp. 224–225).

Within disciplines, feminist research has helped scholars to articulate new meanings in familiar topics. For instance, in anthropology, the study of kinship systems has come to include an examination of gender issues (Coughlin, 1987a, p. A12). In history, scholars have not only begun to focus on the influence of women in the historical process, but have also questioned the legitimacy of traditional historical narratives that have been constructed almost exclusively on the historical accounts of heroic white males (Andersen, 1987). The influence of feminist research in psychology has virtually created a subdiscipline in the psychology of women. Among other things, research in this area has identified how women and men often view reality from contrasting epistemological perspectives (Gilligan, 1982; Belenky, Clinchy, Goldberger, and Tarule, 1986). Sociologists have recently begun to explore the gender-structuring of organizations, the economy, and the workplace (Coughlin, 1987a). And feminist research in economics has investigated the economic relationship between public and private markets, suggesting that household work has a significant economic dimension (Andersen, 1987).

The impact of feminist scholarship has also been felt within the literary disciplines. For instance, in addition to studying works by female authors, literature scholars have begun to investigate why thousands of novels by American women have been excluded from the traditional canon of literary classics (McIntosh, 1981). One scholar has suggested that "reentering knowledge within the experience of women unmasks the invisible paradigms that guide the curriculum and raises questions that require scholars to take a comprehensive and critical look at their fields" (Andersen, 1987, p. 237). If this brief sketch is any indication, it appears that the acceptance of feminist perspectives by social science and humanities scholars has led to the revisiting of such traditional cornerstones as historical periodization, political hierarchies, public sphere economics, sex-role behaviors, and literary canonization.

Critical theory has likewise influenced the development of scholarship in the social sciences and humanities. Critical theory, like feminism, has many variations, but all are tied together by a general critique of the functionalist characteristic of positivist thought. As Henry Giroux explains:

> Critical theory [is] tied to a specific interest in the development of a society without injustice. Theory, in this case, becomes a transformative activity that views itself as explicitly political and commits itself to the projection of a future that is as yet unfulfilled. . . . Rather than proclaiming a [functionalist] notion of neutrality, critical theory openly takes sides in the interest of struggling for a better world (cited in Tierney, 1989b, p. 40).

Critical scholarship has become an identifiable feature across the disciplinary landscapes of sociology, economics, political science, history, literature, law, education, women's studies, and ethnic studies. For example, in sociology and economics, scholars have begun to redefine the concept of class in terms of cultural and political variables (Winkler, 1986). In political science, scholars are questioning if political power elites mechanically mirror economic interests or if other cultural explanations may be insightful in explaining power within a given society (Winkler, 1986). In recent years, literary critical theorists have incorporated post-structuralist and psychoanalytic insights into their interpretations in an attempt to understand how "capitalism affects cultural life and human consciousness" (Winkler, 1987). Critical theory has also influenced legal scholars, who have investigated how notions of class influence the development of legal decisions (Winkler, 1986). In education, critical theory has examined how the curriculum is shaped by cultural and political factors (Tierney, 1989a). More recently, many critical theorists have begun to incorporate other non-traditionalist oriented theoretical perspectives into their scholarship, including post-structuralism, feminism, psychoanalysis, and neoclassical economics (Winkler, 1986).

Just as scholars have embraced feminist and critical theories within their disciplines, many have likewise extended their inquiry to include multicultural perspectives. Rooted as well in the epistemological view that knowledge is socially constructed, multiculturalists seek to understand how meaning is constructed within a specific cultural context. This approach stands in stark contrast to traditional structural-functional approaches which have attempted to explain cultural differences through a Eurocentric lens. In the discipline of black studies, for example, one recent multiculturalist perspective—Afrocentricity—has sought to understand the experiences of blacks around the world as an extension of African history and culture (Coughlin, 1987b). Some historians have criticized the "one-shot approach" to studying minorities in American history and have, instead, adopted multicultural approaches in their research of Hispanics, blacks, Asian-Americans, and American Indians (Winkler, 1986). In sociology, scholars have begun to expand their scope of inquiry to include a new emphasis on cross-national research (Winkler, 1989). In anthropology, a reverse trend has occurred where scholars have become increasingly interested in the study of American society and its many diverse subcultures (Coughlin, 1987a). And, within the literary disciplines, the study of minority and non-Western authors has gained increasing interest over the past decade.

These three perspectives and modes of inquiry—feminism, critical theory, and multiculturalism—have had a profound impact on faculty scholarship in the social sciences and humanities. Tierney has noted that "theory acts as a filter through which we define problems and read answers so that we come to terms with the internal logic of different cultures" (1989b, p. 45). These newly-emergent theoretical perspectives have provided faculty with alternate lenses for understanding how people make sense of reality in a complex, problematic, multicultural world. As faculty have incorporated these perspectives and modes of inquiry into their research, their underlying claim that knowledge is socially constructed has taken on greater legitimacy among scholars in the academy.

Integration of Emerging Knowledge Claims into Classroom Activities

As faculty have expanded their scholarly repertoire to include feminist, critical theory, and multicultural perspectives, they have likewise incorporated these new theoretical views into the undergraduate curriculum. With additional support from the public sector (e.g., private foundation and government agency officials) and from institutional-level and student stakeholders, a number of faculty-driven curricular projects designed to include interpretivist, feminist, critical theory, and multicultural perspectives have been recently integrated into the undergraduate experience at numerous colleges and universities across the country.

Although relatively recent in origin, these curriculum revision/expansion projects have found widespread support from a variety of private foundation and government agencies, including the Ford Foundation, the Andrew Mellon Foundation, the Mott Foundation, the Fund for the Improvement of Postsecondary Education (FIPSE) and the U.S. Office of Education Women's Educational Equity Act (WEEA) Program. In the ten year period between 1975 and 1985, approximately 80 curriculum integration projects were funded by these and other private and public sources; recent trends indicate that institutional support for these projects has increased over the past five years (Andersen, 1987). Similarly, the 48 Centers for Research on Women in the United States have received substantial funding from these stakeholder groups (Hoffman, 1986). These curriculum projects and research centers have sought both to expand the undergraduate curriculum to include feminist, critical theory, and multicultural perspectives and to model a pedagogy that encourages teachers and students to draw upon each other's experiences in the knowledge construction learning process (Hoffman, 1986).

A recent project funded through the New Jersey Department of Higher Education provides a telling indication of the growing support for incorporating diverse perspectives into the curriculum. Declaring 1987 the "inaugural year of integrating the scholarship of women" into the undergraduate curriculum, then New Jersey Governor Thomas Kean awarded $362,500 to the state's 56 public and private colleges for the "New Jersey Project: Integrating the Scholarship on Gender" (McMillen, 1987). The project is designed to provide an impetus to the state's colleges to "revise their courses to reflect a more balanced view of women, as well as minority groups" (McMillen, 1987). At Spelman College, a grant from the Mott Foundation provided funding for the first women's center at a traditionally black women's college. Their recent Ford Foundation funded project, "Integrating Black Women's Studies into the Liberal Arts Curriculum," has led to a fuller integration of race and gender issues in the undergraduate curriculum. Scores of other institutions have likewise received funding from private and public sources to integrate the emerging knowledge claims of women, minorities, and non-Western cultures into undergraduate courses (McIntosh, 1981; AAC, 1981; Hoffman, 1986).

Institutional-level stakeholders have also supported a number of recent initiatives to integrate feminist, critical theory, and multicultural perspectives into the undergraduate curriculum. Primarily driven by student and faculty demands, these changes have been felt at both the institutional and departmental levels. For example, at the University of California-Berkeley, where approximately one out of every two students is a member of a minority group, students have pressured faculty and administrators for a more culturally balanced curriculum (Mooney, 1988). Under mounting pressure from its minority student population, Stanford University's Faculty Senate recently replaced the university's year-long Western civilization requirement with a new multicultural general education sequence entitled "Culture, Ideas, and Values" (Mooney, 1988). The new program is designed to give "substantial attention" to race, gender, class, and multicultural perspectives. Similar institutional level efforts are underway at numerous colleges, including Hartwick College, which recently implemented a "gender-balanced" curriculum (Heller, 1988).

At the departmental level, many faculty have made attempts to integrate feminist, critical theory, and multicultural perspectives into their courses. In the area of women's studies alone, more than 500 programs and approximately 39,000 courses have been offered in American colleges and universities since 1970 (AAC, 1988). At Carnegie-Mellon University, English department faculty recently reoriented the focus of the department and created, in the words of the department chair, the "nation's first post-structuralist undergraduate curriculum" (Heller, 1988). At both the University of Illinois-Chicago and Brown University, faculty members have taken the study of socially constructed meanings seriously by introducing courses in hermeneutics and an undergraduate concentration in semiotics (Heller, 1988). And, in a recent development, Cultural Studies departments have begun to appear at institutions all across the country, often drawing upon the theoretical perspectives of feminism, poststructuralism, multiculturalism, and critical theory within their courses.

The anthropologist Clifford Geertz has suggested that the curriculum can be viewed as a cultural artifact of the knowledge valued by a single—or set of—institutions (1983). Patricia Gumport has further suggested that faculty members, as "mediators of intellectual ideas," validate and legitimate new knowledge claims through their activities within the university. As faculty begin to structure their activities around certain knowledge claims, they concurrently redefine what counts as legitimate knowledge within the university. In no small measure, faculty are encouraged to explore, examine, and integrate these knowledge claims into their scholarship and classroom activities vis-a-vis a larger stakeholder network—including public policymakers, institutional level administrators and students (Conrad, 1989).

Gumport (1988) has suggested that curricular change is rooted within "the cultural life of academic organizations in which faculty, administrators, and students construct and revise their understandings and in which they negotiate about what counts as valid knowledge in particular and historical settings" (1988, p. 50). Over the past decade, a variety of demographic, conservative, and pluralistic societal demands have helped to facilitate the debate between traditional and emerging knowledge claims in the undergraduate curriculum. As traditionalists have continued to argue for the legitimacy of objective, universal truths, other scholars have suggested that truth is neither universal or objective; rather, what is defined as truth is often the byproduct of a cultural social construction process. The result of this recent debate has been an intense interest on the part of a broad range of stakeholders—including faculty, policymakers, institutional administrators, the popular press, and students—in the legitimacy of competing knowledge claims within the university.

One higher education curriculum scholar recently argued that "history is an interaction between participants' lived internalized experiences, and the ideological momentum that becomes institutionalized over the passage of time" (Tierney, 1989b, p. 44). Recent events have witnessed a rapidly growing and widespread interest on the part of faculty, policymakers, institutional administrators, and students in the "tentative" knowledge claims of feminism, critical theory, and multiculturalism. Undergirding these alternate knowledge claims has been a new epistemology that views knowledge as a social construct. As more stakeholders have embraced this epistemological stance, the "tentative" knowledge claims of feminism, critical theory, and multiculturalism have been slowly acknowledged, integrated, and legitimated into these stakeholders' research and classroom activities. The consequence for the undergraduate curriculum has been a fascinating transformation where these knowledge claims have become recognized features on the undergraduate curricular landscape.

In a recent volume, Denise Shekerjian relates an interesting story about perspective that may be helpful in understanding the negotiation of knowledge in the curriculum:

> A story about Picasso tells of how when he was a schoolboy he was terrible at math because whenever the teacher had him write the number 4 on the blackboard, it looked like a nose to him and he'd keep doodling to fill in the rest of the face. Everyone else in the class saw a number on the blackboard; Picasso perceived a face (cited in the *Chronicle of Higher Education,* March 28, 1990, p. B3).

To recent scholars, the debate between traditional and emerging knowledge claims within the undergraduate curriculum has been viewed as a struggle for the prize of what knowledge is most worth knowing. Among others, Shekerjian has suggested that "creativity . . . requires something new, a different interpretation, a break from the twin opiates of habit and cliche" (*Chronicle,* 1990, p. 133) From our perspective, the introduction of new knowledge claims into the academy has provided stakeholders with a fresh perspective on how *we come to know what we know.* It is this development, we believe, which has at once energized and signalled a recent transformation in the undergraduate curriculum.

References

Andersen, M.L. (1987). "Changing the Curriculum in Higher Education." Signs: Journal of Women in Culture and Society, *12* (2), 222–252.

Association of American Colleges. (1980). *Toward Education with a Global Perspective: A Report of the National Assembly on Foreign Language and International Studies.* Washington, D.C.: Association of American Colleges.

Association of American Colleges. (1981). "The Study of Women in the Liberal Arts Curriculum." *The Forum for Liberal Education, 4* (1), pp. 1–18.

Association of American Colleges. (1985). *Integrity in the College Curriculum: A Report to the Academic Community.* Washington, D.C.: Association of American Colleges.

Association of American Colleges. (1988). *A New Vitality in General Education: Planning, Teaching, and Supporting Effective Liberal Learning.* Washington, D.C.: Association of American Colleges.

Belenky, M.F., Clinchy, B.M.; Goldberger, N.R., & Tarule, J.M. (1986). *Women's Ways of Knowing: The Development of Self, Voice, and Mind.* New York: Basic Books.

Bennett, W.J. (1984). *To Reclaim A Legacy: A Report on the Humanities in Higher Education.* Washington, D.C.: National Endowment for the Humanities.

Berger, P.L., & Luckmann, T. (1973). *The Social Construction of Reality.* London: Penguin.

Bloom, A. (1987). *The Closing of the American Mind.* New York: Simon and Schuster.

Boyer, E.L. (1987). *College: The Undergraduate Experience in America.* New York: Harper and Row.

Cheney, L.V. (1989). *50 Hours: A Core Curriculum for College Students.* Washington, D.C.: National Endowment for the Humanities.

Conrad, C.F. (1989). "Meditations on the Ideology of Inquiry in Higher Education: Exposition, Critique, and Conjecture." *The Review of Higher Education, 12,* 199–220.

Conrad, C.F. & Haworth, J.G. (forthcoming). "Curriculum in Higher Education." In M.C. Alkin (Ed.), *The Encyclopedia of Educational Research (sixth edition).* New York: Macmillan.

Coughlin, E.K. (1987a, September 2). "Humanities and Social Sciences: The Sound of Barriers Falling." *Chronicle of Higher Education,* pp. A6–A7, A10, A12.

Coughlin, E.K. (1987b, October 28). "Scholars Work to Refine Africa-centered View of the Life and History of Black Americans." *Chronicle of Higher Education,* pp. A6-A7, A12.

El-Khawas, E. (1986). *Campus Trends, 1986* (Higher Education Panel Reports Number 75). Washington, D.C.: American Council on Education.

El-Khawas, E. (1987). *Campus Trends, 1987* (Higher Education Panel Reports Number 76). Washington, D.C.: American Council on Education.

El-Khawas, E. (1989). *Campus Trends, 1989* (Higher Education Panel Reports Number 78). Washington, D.C.: American Council on Education.

Freire, P. (1971). *Pedagogy of the Oppressed.* New York: Seaview.

Geertz, C. (1983). *Local Knowledge: Further Essays in Interpretive Anthropology.* New York: Basic Books.

Gilligan, C. (1982). In *A Different Voice: Psychological Theory and Women's Development.* Cambridge, MA: Harvard University Press.

Gumport, P.J. (1988). "Curricula as Signposts of Cultural Change." *The Review of Higher Education, 12,* 49–61.

Heller, S. (1988, August 3). "Some English Departments are Giving Undergraduates Grounding in New Literary and Critical Theory." *Chronicle of Higher Education,* pp. A15–A17.

Hirsch, E.D., Jr. (1987). *Cultural Literacy.* Boston: Houghton Mifflin.

Hoffman, N. (1986). "Black Studies, Ethnic Studies, and Women's Studies: Some Reflections on Collaborative Projects." *Women's Studies Quarterly, 14,* 49–53.

Keohane, N.O. (1986, April 2). "Our Mission Should Not Be Merely to 'Reclaim' a Legacy of Scholarship We Must Expand on It." *Chronicle of Higher Education,* p. 88.

Lather, P. (1984). "Critical Theory, Curricular Transformation, and Feminist Mainstreaming." *Journal of Education, 166* (1), 49-62.

Lincoln, Y.S., & Cuba, E.G. (1985). *Naturalistic Inquiry.* Beverly Hills: Sage.

Locke, L. (1989). "General Education: In Search of Facts." *Naturalistic Inquiry, 21* (4), pp. 21–23.

McIntosh, P. (1981). ""the Study of Women: Implications for Reconstructing the Liberal Arts Disciplines." *The Forum for Liberal Education, 4* (1), pp. 1–3.

McMillen L. (1987, September 9). "More Colleges and More Disciplines Incorporating Scholarship on Women in the Classroom." *Chronicle of Higher Education,* pp. A16-A17.

Mooney, C.J. (1988, December 14). "Sweeping Curricular Change is Underway at Stanford as University Phases out Its 'Western Culture' Program." *Chronicle of Higher Education,* pp. A1, A11-A13.

National Center for Education Statistics. (1989). *Digest of Education Statistics, 1989.* Washington, D.C.: National Center for Education Statistics, Office of Educational Research and Improvement, U.S. Department of Education.

National Institute of Education. (1984). *Involvement in Learning: Realizing the Potential of American Higher Education.* Washington, D.C.: National Institute of Education.

Ravitch, D. (1988). "A Response to Michael Apple." *Teachers College Record, 90* (1), 128–130.

Roueche, J.E.; Baker, G.A.; & Roueche, S.D. (1985). *College Responses to Low Achieving Students: A National Study.* Orlando, FL: Harcourt, Brace, Jovanovich.

Rosaldo, R. (1989). *Culture and Truth: The Remaking of Social Analysis.* Boston: Beacon.

Rudolph, F. (1977). *Curriculum: A History of the American Undergraduate Course of Study Since 1636.* San Francisco: Jossey-Bass and the Carnegie Foundation for the Advancement of Teaching.

Schuster, M., and Van Dyne, S. (1984). "Placing Women in the Liberal Arts: Stages of Curriculum Transformation." *Harvard Educational Review, 54* (4), 413–428.

Shekerjian, D. (1990). "Uncommon Genius: How Great Ideas Are Born." *Chronicle of Higher Education,* March 28, 1990, p. B3.

Shrewsbury, C.M. (1987). "What is Feminist Pedagogy?" *Women's Studies Quarterly, 15* (3 & 4), 6–13.

Tierney, W.G. (1989a). "Cultural Politics and the Curriculum in Postsecondary Education." *Journal of Education,* forthcoming.

Tierney, W.G. (1989b). *Curricular Landscapes, Democratic Vistas: Transformative Leadership in Higher Education.* New York: Praeger.

Wetzel, J.R. (1987). *American Youth: A Statistical Snapshot.* New York: The William T. Grant Foundation.

Winkler, K. (1986, July 9). "Flourishing Research in Marxist Theory Belies Signs of Its Demise, Scholars Say." *Chronicle of Higher Education,* pp. 4–5, 7.

Winkler, K. (1987, November 25). "Post-structuralism: An Often-abstruse French Import Profoundly Affects Research in the United States." *Chronicle of Higher Education,* pp. A6-A9.

Winkler, K. (1989, January 11). "Dispute over Validity of Historical Approaches Pits Traditionalists against Advocates of New Methods." *Chronicle of Higher Education,* pp. A4-A5, A7.

CHAPTER 15

TO RECLAIM A LEGACY: A REPORT ON THE HUMANITIES IN HIGHER EDUCATION

WILLIAM J. BENNETT

Introduction

Although more than 50 percent of America's high school graduates continue their education at American colleges and universities, few of them can be said to receive there an adequate education in the culture and civilization of which they are members. Most of our college graduates remain shortchanged in the humanities—history, literature, philosophy, and the ideals and practices of the past that have shaped the society they enter. The fault lies principally with those of us whose business it is to educate these students. We have blamed others, but the responsibility is ours. Not by our words but by our actions, by our indifference, and by our intellectual diffidence we have brought about this condition. It is we the educators—not scientists, business people, or the general public—who too often have given up the great task of transmitting a culture to its rightful heirs. Thus, what we have on many of our campuses is an unclaimed legacy, a course of studies in which the humanities have been siphoned off, diluted, or so adulterated that students graduate knowing little of their heritage.

In particular the study group was disturbed by a number of trends and developments in higher education:

- Many of our colleges and universities have lost a clear sense of the importance of the humanities and the purpose of education, allowing the thickness of their catalogues to substitute for vision and a philosophy of education.
- The humanities, and particularly the study of Western civilization, have lost their central place in the undergraduate curriculum. At best, they are but one subject among many that students might be exposed to before graduating. At worst, and too often, the humanities are virtually absent.
- A student can obtain a bachelor's degree from 75 percent of all American colleges and universities without having studied European history, from 72 percent without having studied American literature or history, and from 86 percent without having studied the civilizations of classical Greece and Rome.

Source: *To Reclaim a Legacy: A Report on the Humanities in Higher Education*, by William J. Bennett, November 1984, National Endowment for the Humanities, Washington, D.C.

- Fewer than half of all colleges and universities now require foreign language study for the bachelor's degree, down from nearly 90 percent in 1966.
- The sole acquaintance with the humanities for many undergraduates comes during their first two years of college, often in ways that discourage further study.
- The number of students choosing majors in the humanities has plummeted. Since 1970 the number of majors in English has declined by 57 percent, in philosophy by 41 percent, in history by 62 percent, and in modern languages by 50 percent.
- Too many students are graduating from American colleges and universities lacking even the most rudimentary knowledge about the history, literature, art, and philosophical foundations of their nation and their civilization.
- The decline in learning in the humanities was caused in part by a failure of nerve and faith on the part of many college faculties and administrators, and persists because of a vacuum in educational leadership. A recent study of college presidents found that only 2 percent are active in their institutions' academic affairs.

In order to reverse the decline, the study group recommended:

- The nation's colleges and universities must reshape their undergraduate curricula based on a clear vision of what constitutes an educated person, regardless of major, and on the study of history, philosophy, languages, and literature.
- College and university presidents must take responsibility for the educational needs of all students in their institutions by making plain what the institution stands for and what knowledge it regards as essential to a good education.
- Colleges and universities must reward excellent teaching in hiring, promotion, and tenure decisions.
- Faculties must put aside narrow departmentalism and instead work with administrators to shape a challenging curriculum with a core of common studies.
- Study of the humanities and Western civilization must take its place at the heart of the college curriculum.

Why Study the Humanities?

The federal legislation that established the National Endowment for the Humanities in 1965 defined the humanities as specific disciplines: "language, both modern and classical; linguistics; literature; history; jurisprudence; philosophy; archaeology; comparative religion; ethics; the history, criticism, and theory of the arts"; and "those aspects of the social sciences which have humanistic content and employ humanistic methods." But to define the humanities by itemizing the academic fields they embrace is to overlook the qualities that make them uniquely important and worth studying. Expanding on a phrase from Matthew Arnold, I would describe the humanities as the best that has been said, thought, written, and otherwise expressed about the human experience. The humanities tell us how men and women of our own and other civilizations have grappled with life's enduring, fundamental questions: What is justice? What should be loved? What deserves to be defended? What is courage? What is noble? What is base? Why do civilizations flourish? Why do they decline?

Kant defined the essence of the humanities in four questions: What can I know? What should I do? What may I hope for? What is man? These questions are not simply diversions for intellectuals or playthings for the idle. As a result of the ways in which these questions have been answered, civilizations have emerged, nations have developed, wars have been fought, and people have lived contentedly or miserably.

If ideas are important, it surely follows that learning and life are poorer without the humanities. Montaigne wrote:

> A pupil should be taught what it means to know something, and what it means not to know it; what should be the design and end of study; what valor, temperance, and justice are; the difference between ambition and greed, loyalty and servitude, liberty and license; and the marks of true and solid contentment.

Further, the humanities can contribute to an informed sense of community by enabling us to learn about and become participants in a common culture, shareholders in our civilization. But our goal should be more than just a common culture—even television and the comics can give us that. We should, instead, want all students to know a common culture rooted in civilization's lasting vision, its highest shared ideals and aspirations, and its heritage. Professor E. D. Hirsch of the University of Virginia calls the beginning of this achievement "cultural literacy" and reminds us that "no culture exists that is ignorant of its own traditions." As the late philosopher Charles Frankel once said, it is through the humanities that a civilized society talks to itself about things that matter most.

How Should the Humanities Be Taught and Learned?

Mankind's answers to compelling questions are available to us through the written and spoken word—books, manuscripts, letters, plays, and oral traditions—and also in nonliterary forms, which John Ruskin called the book of art. Within them are expressions of human greatness and of pathos and tragedy. In order to tap the consciousness and memory of civilization, one must confront these texts and works of art.

The members of the study group discussed at length the most effective ways to teach the humanities to undergraduates. Our discussion returned continually to two basic prerequisites for learning in the humanities: good teaching and a good curriculum.

Good Teaching

Good teaching is at least as essential in the humanities as in other fields of learning. In this connection, it is critical to point out that of all undergraduate credit hours taken in the humanities, 87 percent are taken in the freshman and sophomore years. Because nonhumanities majors account for the largest part of these credit hours, courses taken at the introductory level are the first and only collegiate exposure to the humanities for many students. Therefore, we should want to extend to these students the most attractive invitation to the humanities possible. This requires teachers who can make the humanities live and who can guide students through the landscape of human thought.

Just as students can he drawn to the humanities by good teachers, they can be chased off by poor ones. "Students come to learning through their teachers," wrote Oberlin College Dean Robert Longsworth, "and no list of great works nor any set of curricular requirements can do the work of a good teacher." Although it can take many forms, we all know what poor teaching is. It can be lifeless or tendentious, mechanical or ideological. It can be lacking in conviction. Perhaps most commonly, it can fail to have a sense of the significance of the material it purports to study and teach. It can bore and deaden where it means to quicken and elevate. Giving one example, Harvard Professor David Riesman pointed out that poor teaching can masquerade as good teaching when it "invites students to join a club of sophisticated cynics who are witty, abrasive, and sometimes engrossing; many teachers in the humanities parade and glorify their eccentricities, and only on reflection and at some distance does one realize that they are really lifeless."

What characterizes good teaching in the humanities? First, and foremost, a teacher must have achieved mastery of the material. But this is not enough; there must also be engagement. Professor William Arrowsmith of Emory University described good teachers as "committed to teaching what they have learned to love." In one crucial way, good teachers cannot be dispassionate. They cannot be dispassionate about the works they teach—assuming that they are teaching important works. This does not mean they advocate each idea of every author, but rather that they are moved and are seen to be moved by the power of the works and are able to convey that power to their students. Just as good scholarship is inspired, so must good teaching be.

A Good Curriculum

If the teacher is the guide, the curriculum is the path. A good curriculum marks the points of significance so that the student does not wander aimlessly over the terrain dependent solely on chance to discover the landmarks of human achievement.

Colleges and universities have a responsibility to design general education curricula that identify these landmarks. David Savage of the *Los Angeles Times* expressed the consensus of the study group when he said: "Most students enter college expecting that the university and its leaders have a clear vision of what is worth knowing and what is important in our heritage that all educated persons should know. They also have a right to expect that the university sees itself as more than a catalogue of courses."

Although the study group embraced the principle that all institutions should accept responsibility for deciding what their graduates should know, most members believed that no single curriculum could be appropriate in all places. The study group recognized the diverse nature of higher education under whose umbrella are institutions with different histories philosophies, educational purposes, student body characteristics, and religious and cultural traditions. Each institution must decide for itself what it considers an educated person to be and what knowledge that person should possess. While doing so, no institution need act as if it were operating in a vacuum. There are standards of judgment: Some things are more important to know than others.

The choices a college or university makes for its common curriculum should be rooted firmly in its institutional identity and educational purpose. In successful institutions, an awareness of what the college or university is trying to do acts as a unifying principle, a thread that runs through and ties together the faculty, the curriculum, the students, and the administration. If an institution has no clearly conceived and articulated sense of itself, its efforts to design a curriculum will result in little more than an educational garage sale, possibly satisfying most campus factions but serving no real purpose and adding up to nothing of significance. Developing a common curriculum with the humanities at the core is no easy task. In some institutions, it will be difficult to attain. But merely being exposed to a variety of subjects and points of view is not enough. Learning to think critically and skeptically is not enough. Being well-rounded is not enough if, after all the sharp edges have been filed down, discernment is blunted and the graduate is left to believe without judgment, to decide without wisdom, or to act without standards.

The study group identified several features common to any good curriculum, regardless of institutional particulars:

(1) **Balance between breadth and depth.** A good curriculum should embody both wide reading and close reading. Students should study a number of important texts and subjects with thoroughness and care. They should also become acquainted with other texts and subjects capable of giving them a broader view, a context for understanding what they know well. Excessive concentration in one area however, often abetted by narrow departmentalism, can promote provincialism and pedantry. Conversely, as William Arrowsmith warned, going too far toward breadth could make the curriculum a mere "bus trip of the West" characterized by "shallow generalization and stereotypes."

(2) **Original text.** Most members of the study group believed that the curriculum should be based on original literary, historical, and philosophical texts rather than on secondary works or textbooks. By reading such works, reflecting on them, discussing them, and writing about them, students will come to understand the power of ideas.

(3) **Continuity.** The undergraduate's study of the humanities should not be limited to the freshman and sophomore years. Rather, it should extend throughout the undergraduate career so that continuing engagement with the humanities will complement and add perspective to courses in the major field as well as contribute to students' increasing intellectual maturity as juniors and seniors. Professor Linda Spoerl of Highline Community College said: "The idea that general education requirements should be satisfied as quickly as possible before the student goes on to the 'real' part of education does everyone a disservice."

(4) **Faculty strength.** Because a good curriculum must rest on a firm foundation of good teaching, it follows that the nature of that curriculum should respect areas of faculty competence and expertise. As David Riesman pointed out, it does little good to require study of Shakespeare if there are no scholars on the faculty who can teach Shakespeare with insight and

contagious appreciation. On the other hand, any institution that lacks faculty expertise in the basic fields and work of the humanities should take immediate steps to fill those gaps or to develop such competence in existing faculty.

(5) **Conviction about the centrality of the humanities.** Finally, the humanities must not be argued for as something that will make our students refined, nor should the humanities be presented as a nonrigorous interlude where the young can chew over their feelings, emote, or rehash their opinions. The humanities are not an educational luxury, and they are not just for majors. They are a body of knowledge and a means of inquiry that convey serious truths, defensible judgments, and significant ideas. Properly taught, the humanities bring together the perennial questions of human life with the greatest works of history, literature, philosophy, and art. Unless the humanities are taught and studied in this way, there is little reason to offer them.

Based on our discussions, we recommend the following knowledge in the humanities as essential to a college education:

- Because our society is the product and we the inheritors of Western civilization, American students need an understanding of its origins and development, from its roots in antiquity to the present. This understanding should include a grasp of the major trends in society, religion, art, literature, and politics, as well as a knowledge of basic chronology.
- A careful reading of several masterworks of English, American, and European literature.
- An understanding of the most significant ideas and debates in the history of philosophy.
- Demonstrable proficiency in a foreign language (either modern or classical) and the ability to view that language as an avenue into another culture.

In addition to these areas of fundamental knowledge, study group members recommended that undergraduates have some familiarity with the history, literature, religion and philosophy of at least one non-Western culture or civilization. We think it better to have a deeper understanding of a single non-Western culture than a superficial taste of many. Finally, the study group thought that all students should study the history of science and technology.

What Should Be Read?

A curriculum is rarely much stronger than the syllabi of its courses, the arrays of texts singled out for careful reading and discussion. The syllabi should reflect the college's best judgment concerning specific texts with which an educated person should be familiar and should include texts within the competence and interest of its faculty.

Study group members agreed that an institution's syllabi should not be set in stone; indeed, these syllabi should change from time to time to take into account the expertise of available faculty and the result of continuing scrutiny and refinement. The task, however, is not to take faculty beyond their competence and training, nor to displace students' individual interests and career planning, but to reach and inhabit common ground for a while.

We frequently hear that it is no longer possible to reach a consensus on the most significant thinkers, the most compelling ideas, and the books all students should read. Contemporary American culture, the argument goes, has become too fragmented and too pluralistic to justify a belief in common learning. Although it is easier (and more fashionable) to doubt than to believe, it is a grave error to base a college curriculum on such doubt. Also, I have long suspected that there is more consensus on what the important books are than many people have been willing to admit.

In order to test this proposition and to learn what the American public thinks are the most significant works, I recently invited several hundred educational and cultural leaders to recommend ten books that any high school graduate should have read. The general public was also invited in a newspaper column by George F. Will to send me their lists. I received recommendations from more than five hundred individuals. They listed hundreds of different texts and authors, yet four—Shakespeare's plays, American historical documents (the Constitution, Declaration of

Independence, and Federalist Papers), *The Adventures of Huckleberry Finn,* and the Bible—were cited at least 50 percent of the time.

I have not done a comparable survey on what college graduates should read, but the point to be made is clear: Many people do believe that some books are more important than others, and there is broader agreement on what those books are than many have supposed. Each college's list will vary somewhat, reflecting the character of the institution and other factors. But there would be, and should be, significant overlap.

I am often asked what I believe to be the most significant works in the humanities. This is an important question, too important to avoid. Some works and their authors have profoundly influenced my life, and it is plain that the same works have influenced the lives of many others as well. In providing a list of these works and authors, it is not my intention (nor is it my right) to dictate anyone's curriculum. My purpose is not to prescribe a course of studies but to answer, as candidly as I can, an oft-asked question.

The works and authors I mention virtually define the development of the Western mind. There are, at a number of institutions, strong introductory courses already in place whose syllabi include such works. These institutions do not expect undergraduates to read most of the major works of these authors. They have learned, however, that it is not unreasonable to expect students to read works by some of them and to know who the others were and why they are important.

The works and authors I have in mind include, but are not limited to, the following: from classical antiquity—Homer, Sophocles, Thucydides, Plato, Aristotle, and Vergil; from medieval, Renaissance, and seventeenth-century Europe—Dante, Chaucer, Machiavelli, Montaigne, Shakespeare, Hobbes, Milton, and Locke; from eighteenth- through twentieth-century Europe—Swift, Rousseau, Austen, Wordsworth, Tocqueville, Dickens, Marx, George Eliot, Dostoyevsky, Tolstoy, Nietzsche, Mann, and T. S. Eliot; from American literature and historical documents—the Declaration of Independence, the Federalist Papers, the Constitution, the Lincoln-Douglas Debates, Lincoln's Gettysburg Address and Second Inaugural Address, Martin Luther King, Jr.'s "Letter from the Birmingham Jail" and "I have a dream . . ." speech, and such authors as Hawthorne, Melville, Twain, and Faulkner. Finally, I must mention the Bible, which is the basis for so much subsequent history, literature, and philosophy. At a college or university, what weight is given to which authors must of course depend on faculty competence and interest. But, should not every humanities faculty possess some members qualified to teach at least something of these authors?

Why these particular books and these particular authors? Because an important part of education is learning to read, and the highest purpose of reading is to be in the company of great souls. There are, to be sure, many fine books and important authors not included in the list, and they too deserve the student's time and attention. But to pass up the opportunity to spend time with this company is to miss a fundamental experience of higher education.

Great souls do not express themselves by the written word only; they also paint, sculpt, build, and compose. An educated person should be able not only to recognize some of their works, but also to understand why they embody the best in our culture. Should we be satisfied if the graduates of our colleges and universities know nothing of the Parthenon's timeless classical proportions, of the textbook in medieval faith and philosophy that is Chartres cathedral, of Michelangelo's Sistine ceiling, or of the music of Bach and Mozart?

How Well Are the Humanities Being Taught and Learned on the Nation's Campuses?

Our experience in higher education and study of empirical data convince us that the humanities are being taught and learned with uneven success. Some institutions do an outstanding job, some a poor one. At most colleges and universities, the humanities are taught both well and poorly, with inspiration in one classroom, excruciating dullness or pedantry in another. Overall, however, both teaching and learning in the humanities are not what they should be or can be, and they are neither taught as well nor studied as carefully as they deserve to be.

Evidence for this decline is compelling. Preliminary findings from a 1984–85 survey by the American Council on Education indicate that a student can obtain a bachelor's degree from

75 percent of all American colleges and universities without having studied European history, from 72 percent without having studied American literature or history, and from 86 percent without having studied the civilizations of classical Greece and Rome. The Modern Language Association reports that both entrance and graduation requirements in foreign languages have been weakened significantly since 1966. In that year, 33 percent of all colleges and universities required some foreign language study for admission. By 1975, only 18 percent required a foreign language, and by 1983 only 14 percent. The picture is similar for graduation requirements. In 1966, 89 percent of all institutions required foreign language study for the bachelor's degree, dropping to 53 percent in 1975 and 47 percent in 1983.

Conventional wisdom attributes the steep drop in the number of students who major in the humanities to a concern for finding good-paying jobs after college. Although there is some truth in this, we believe that there is another, equally important reason—namely, that we in the academy have failed to bring the humanities to life and to insist on their value. From 1970 to 1982, the number of bachelor's degrees awarded in all fields increased by 11 percent from 846,110 to 952,998. But during the same period, degrees in English dropped not by a few percentage points, but by 57 percent, in philosophy by 41 percent, in history by 62 percent, and in modern languages by 50 percent. Indications are that the decline is continuing. From 1975 to 1983, the number of high school seniors who took the SAT exam and specified an intended college major rose by 14 percent. Over the same eight-year period, the number who planned to major in the humanities fell by 42 percent. Prospective history majors decreased by 60 percent.

If further evidence of students' estrangement from the humanities is required, one need only refer to the American Council on Education's 1983 survey of academic deans at colleges and universities. Two-thirds of those surveyed indicated that the most able entering undergraduates were turning away from the humanities to other fields, mainly professional and technical. This is not merely a rejection of a career in the humanities, but a rejection of the humanities themselves. The former is not a cause for alarm; the latter is.

Impressionistic or anecdotal evidence for the decline of the humanities surfaces every time I talk with college professors, academic officers, and students. Such evidence is familiar: students who graduate from college unable to write lucidly or reason clearly and rigorously; students who are preoccupied (even obsessed) with vocational goals at the expense of broadening the intellect; students who are ignorant of philosophy and literature and know and care little about the history of their nation and their culture. For example, I know of one university philosophy professor who administers a simple test to his students at the beginning of classes each year to determine how much prior knowledge he can presume. The test consists of identifying twenty important names and events from history (such as Shakespeare, St. Augustine, Beethoven, the Protestant Reformation, and Rembrandt). On the most recent test, his students—mainly sophomores and juniors—correctly identified an average of only six of the twenty.

I must emphasize here that our aim is not to argue for more majors in the humanities, but to state as emphatically as we can that the humanities should have a place in the education of all. Our nation is significantly enriched by the breadth and diversity of its professions and occupations and the interests of its citizens. Our universities should continue to encourage instruction in a full variety of fields and careers. But we do argue that, whatever endeavors our students ultimately choose, some substantial quality instruction in the humanities should be an integral part of everyone's collegiate education. To study the humanities in no way detracts from the career interests of students. Properly taught, they will enrich all.

The State of Teaching in the Humanities

If learning in the humanities is in decline, at least some of the blame must be assigned to those who teach the humanities and to academic administrators who determine the allocation of institutional resources. The study group criticized some universities for surrendering the teaching of introductory and lower division courses to graduate assistants or adjunct, part-time faculty. In making these criticisms, the study group recognized that classes taught by adjunct faculty and graduate students allow the institution to serve more students per faculty salary dollar, and that it is necessary to give future professors experience in the classroom. Nevertheless, the study group was concerned that such persons are not, as a group, the best teachers—the most experienced, most accomplished, and most intellectually mature. They are not capable of extending the most attractive invitation to the humanities to those lower division students who account for nearly 90 percent of all humanities credit hours taken. If students do not experience the best the humanities have to offer early in their undergraduate careers, they are unlikely to come back for more. University of Chicago Professor Wayne Booth said in his 1982 presidential address to the Modern Language Association:

> We have chosen—no one required it of is—to say to the world, almost in so many words, that we do not care who teaches the nonmajors or under what conditions, so long as the troublesome hordes move on and out: forced in by requirements, forced out by discouragement, or by disgust, or by literal failure. The great public fears or despises us because we hire a vast army of underpaid flunkies to teach the so-called service courses, so that we can gladly teach, in our advanced courses, those precious souls who survive the gauntlet. Give us lovers and we will love them, but do not expect us to study courtship.
>
> If we had decided to run up a flag on the quad saying that we care not a whit whether our society consists of people who practice critical understanding, so long as we are left free to teach advanced courses, we could not have given a clearer message.

And Frank Vandiver, president of Texas A&M University, recently analyzed the problem this way: "The liberal arts . . . have allowed this to happen to themselves. They have allowed themselves to sit behind ivy-covered walls and say, 'We are the liberal arts and to hell with you.'"

The problem is more than just who does the teaching it is also how the humanities are taught. Too often introductory humanities courses are taught as if they were initial preparation for majors rather than as general education for all students. This often contributes to a fragmented, compartmentalized curriculum instead of an integrated, coherent one. When the humanities are presented as a series of isolated disciplinary packages, students cannot possibly see the interrelatedness of great works, ideas, and minds.

The study group was alarmed by the tendency of some humanities professors to present their subjects in a tendentious, ideological manner. Sometimes the humanities are used as if they were the handmaiden of ideology, subordinated to particular prejudices and valued or rejected on the basis of their relation to a certain social stance.

At the other extreme, the humanities are declared to have no inherent meaning because all meaning is subjective and relative to one's own perspective. There is no longer agreement on the value of historical facts, empirical evidence, or even rationality itself.

Both these tendencies developed in the hope that we will again show students the relevance of our subjects. Instead of demonstrating relevance, however, they condemn the humanities to irrelevance—the first, by subordinating our studies to contemporary prejudices; the second, by implying that the great works no longer have anything to teach us about ourselves or about life. As David Riesman said, some students are captivated by these approaches and think them modern or sophisticated. But the vast majority of students have correctly thought otherwise and have chosen to vote with their feet, stampeding out of the humanities departments. We cannot blame this on an insufficient number of students, or on the quality of students, or even on the career aspirations of students. We must blame ourselves for our failure to protect and transmit a legacy our students deserve to know.

Effects of Graduate Education on Teaching

Instead of aiming at turning out men and women of broad knowledge and lively intellect, our graduate schools produce too many narrow specialists whose teaching is often lifeless, stilted, and pedestrian. In his recent lecture to the American Council of Learned Societies, Yale Professor Maynard Mask took graduate schools to task for failing to educate broadly:

> When one reads thoughtfully in the works by Darwin, Marx, and Freud, what one finds most impressive is not the competence they show in the studies we associate them with, though that is of course impressive, but the range of what they knew, the staggering breadth of the reading which they had made their own and without which, one comes to

> understand, they could never have achieved the insights in their own areas that we honor them for. Today, it seems to me, we are still moving mostly in the opposite directions despite here and there a reassuring revolt. We are narrowing, not enlarging our horizons. We are shirking, not assuming our responsibilities. And we communicate with fewer and fewer because it is easier to jabber in a jargon than to explain a complicated matter in the real language of men. How long can a democratic nation afford to support a narcissistic minority so transfixed by its own image?

University of Oregon Dean Robert Berdahl described the problem as one of acculturation and unrealistic expectations. Dean Berdahl observed that most of today's college faculty were trained during the 1960s and early 1970s, a period of rapid growth in the academic sector and increasing private and government support for research. As a result, they are oriented more toward research, publication, and teaching graduate students than toward educating nonmajors and generalists. "The successful career to which one is taught to aspire," wrote Dean Berdahl, "is to end up at an institution like that at which one received one's doctorate, where the 'real work' of the profession takes place and where, if one must teach undergraduates, one need only deal with majors or very bright students."

When these former graduate students secure jobs in our college classrooms, they find themselves poorly equipped to teach undergraduates. Again, Robert Berdahl:

> English professors insist that they are not able to teach composition, so that must be left to graduate students or a growing group of underpaid itinerant instructors. Historians who used to be responsible for teaching the entire sweep of Western civilization or the Survey of American History now insist on teaching only that portion of it that corresponds to their specialities. Foreign literature specialists consider it a waste of their talent to teach foreign language classes. Lower division, general education courses are thus often conceptually no different from the upper division courses offered for majors and graduate students; they are only broader. Instead of asking: "What should a student learn from this 'Civ' class or 'Intro to Lit' class if this is the only history or literature class he or she will take in four years?", we ask: "What will best prepare the student to take advanced literature or history classes?"

Graduate education's tendencies toward what Mellon Foundation President John Sawyer called "hyper-specialization and self-isolating vocabularies" often result in a faculty that, even after several years of advanced study, are no better educated than the undergraduates. John Silber, president of Boston University, wrote in a letter to me:

> The Ph.D. is no longer a guarantee that its holder is truly educated. Everyone has seen the consequences of this: How frequently we now meet Ph.D.'s who are incapable of writing correctly or speaking effectively; who are so narrow in their interests that the civilizing effect of the humanities appears to have been entirely lost upon them; who are so jejune in their research interests as to call into question the entire scholarly enterprise.

In a recent article, Harvard Professor Walter Jackson Bate warned that "the humanities are not merely entering, they are plunging into their worst state of crisis since the modern university was formed a century ago in the 1880s." Professor Bate went on to exhort graduate humanities departments to examine their priorities:

> The subject matter—the world's great literature—is unrivaled. All we need is the chance and the imagination to help it work upon the minds and characters of the millions of students to whom we are responsible. Ask that the people you are now breeding up in departments, and to whom you now give tenure appointments, be capable of this.

Training good researchers is vital to the humanities and to the mission of every graduate school. But many graduate schools have become so preoccupied with training narrow research specialists that they no longer address adequately the more pressing need of higher education for good teachers, broadly versed in their fields, inspired by the power of their subjects, and committed to making those subjects speak to the undergraduate. Unless our graduate schools reexamine this misplaced emphasis, much of our teaching will remain mediocre and our students indifferent.

The State of the Humanities Curriculum

The past twenty years have seen a steady erosion in the place of the humanities in the undergraduate curriculum and in the coherence of the curriculum generally. So serious has this erosion become that Mark Curtis, president of the Association of American Colleges, wrote: "The chaotic state of the baccalaureate curriculum may be the most urgent and troubling problem of higher education in the final years of the twentieth century." Clark Kerr has called the undergraduate curriculum "a disaster area," and Professor Frederick Rudolph of Williams College has written:

> . . . when the professors abandoned a curriculum that they thought students needed, they substituted for it one that, instead, catered either to what the professors needed or what the students wanted. The results confirmed the authority of professors and students but they robbed the curriculum of any authority at all. The reaction of students to all this activity in the curriculum was brilliant. They concluded that the curriculum really didn't matter.

A collective loss of nerve and faith on the part of both faculty and academic administrators during the late 1960s and early 1970s was undeniably destructive of the curriculum. When students demanded a greater role in setting their own educational agendas, we eagerly responded by abandoning course requirements of any kind and with them the intellectual authority to say to students what the outcome of a college education ought to be. With intellectual authority relinquished, we found that we did not need to worry about what was worth knowing, worth defending, worth believing. The curriculum was no longer a statement about what knowledge mattered; instead, it became the product of a political compromise among competing schools and departments overlaid by marketing considerations. In a recent article, Frederick Rudolph likened the curriculum to "a bazaar and the students [to] tourists looking for cheap bargains."

Once the curriculum was dissolved, colleges and universities found it difficult to reconstruct because of the pressures of the marketplace. All but the most selective institutions must now compete for scarce financial resources— students' tuition and enrollment-driven state subsidies. As a consequence, many are reluctant to reinstate meaningful course requirements for fear of frightening away prospective applicants. (I believe such a fear is misplaced, but more on this later.)

Intellectual authority came to be replaced by intellectual relativism as a guiding principle of the curriculum. Because colleges and universities believed they no longer could or should assert the primacy of one fact or one book over another, all knowledge came to be seen as relative in importance, relative to consumer or faculty interest. This loss was accompanied by a shift in language. The desired ends of education changed from knowledge to "inquiry," from content to "skills." We began to see colleges listing their objectives as teaching such skills as reading, critical thinking, and awareness of other points of view. These are undeniably essential ends to a college education, but they are not sufficient. One study group member said, "What good is knowing how to write if you are ignorant of the finest examples of the language?" Failure to address content allows colleges and universities to beg the question of what an educated man or woman in the 1980s needs to know. The willingness of too many colleges to act as if all learning were relative is a self-inflicted wound that has impaired our ability to defend our subjects as necessary for learning or important for life.

Effects of the Curriculum on Secondary Education

It is not surprising that once colleges and universities decided the curriculum did not have to represent a vision of an educated person, the secondary schools (and their students) took the cue and reached the same conclusion. Vanderbilt University Professor Chester Finn pointed out that college entrance requirements constitute de facto high school exit requirements for high school graduates—now nearly six of every ten—who seek postsecondary education. With exit requirements relaxed, college-bound students no longer perceive a need to take electives in English and history, let alone foreign languages. Instead, they choose courses thought to offer immediate vocational payoff. Clifford Adelman described research for the National Commission on Excellence in Education that dramatically illustrates this trend. From 1969 to 1981, the humanities declined as a percentage of total high school credits taken, a decline parallel to that in the colleges. Credits in Western civilization are down 50 percent, in U.S. history down 20 percent, and in U.S. government down 70 percent. My own experience attests to the woeful state of the high school curriculum. Recently I met with seventy high school student leaders—all excellent students—from all over the country. When I asked them how many had heard of the Federalist Papers, only seven raised their hands.

As enrollments in basic high school humanities courses fell off, it became more difficult for the schools to justify keeping them. Therefore, many schools dropped humanities courses from the curriculum. When high school graduates enter college, they are poorly prepared in basic knowledge of the humanities as well as in such essential skills as reading and writing. The remedial courses needed by these students cut into the college curriculum, effectively reducing the amount of actual college level course work they can take.

Twenty years ago, William Arrowsmith wrote: "Our entire educational enterprise is . . . founded upon the wholly false premise that at some prior stage the essential educational work has been done." Sadly, this is still true today. The humanities must be put back into the high school curriculum, but this is unlikely to happen unless they are first restored in the colleges. If colleges take the lead in reinstating humanities course requirements, the high schools will surely respond. Evidence of this was related by Professor Noel Reynolds of Brigham Young University, who described how college preparatory course enrollments in Utah's high schools rose after an announcement by the state's two largest universities that preference for admission would be given to students who had completed college preparatory, including humanities, courses. Some Utah secondary schools reported an increase in foreign language enrollments of as much as 200 percent, and only slightly less dramatic increases in English and history.

Bright Spots in the Curriculum

The study group examined in depth the graduation requirements of numerous colleges and universities. The group found enormous variety, ranging from no course requirements of any kind to sequences of highly prescriptive core courses. Types of curricula did not seem to be associated with types of institutions. Some of the least coherent curricula were those of nationally prestigious, highly selective institutions, while some of the most carefully defined were found at less selective local or regional institutions. The most common type of curriculum was the "distribution requirements" model, in which students selected courses from a limited list of regular departmental offerings within a few broad interdepartmental clusters. Typically, "the humanities" is one of the clusters. Often the humanities requirement can be satisfied by taking such courses as speech, remedial writing, or performing arts. Even in institutions where the humanities are defined more rigorously, distribution requirements rarely guarantee that a student will master an explicit body of knowledge or confront a series of important original texts.

A few colleges and universities have rejected this model in favor of a course of studies in which all students share a carefully designed learning experience. Some colleges and universities have been doing this for a long time and have remained steadfast in their commitment. Others have moved in recent years to restore a sound common curriculum. Two of the latter captured the attention of the study group: Brooklyn College and St. Joseph's College.

Brooklyn College, part of the City University of New York system, has about 14,000 undergraduates, many of whom are recent immigrants. Most major in professional fields such as pre-law, accounting, and communications. Yet, since 1981 all bachelor's degree candidates, regardless of major, have taken a sequence of ten core courses, seven of which are in the humanities. Many of the courses emphasize original texts. For example, Core Studies 1, "Classical Origins of Western Culture," requires readings in Homer, Sophocles, Herodotus, Aristophanes, Aristotle, Vergil, and other writers of classical antiquity. Brooklyn's success with the core curriculum has surpassed all expectations. The college reports that its faculty (50 percent of whom teach in the core) are enlivened intellectually by teaching the core courses and that students' writing has improved considerably as a result of a "Writing Across the Core" program. Students, too, are excited by the new curriculum. They say they are able to see relationships among fields, and they talk about a renewed sense of a community of learning, a community that includes faculty, students, and administrators. The administration's commitment to the curriculum can be seen in the fact that both the president and provost teach core courses.

Although it is a very different kind of institution, St. Joseph's College in Indiana has developed a similar curriculum with equally good results. St. Joseph's is a Catholic school of about 1,000 students. Business, finance, and computer science are popular majors. Like Brooklyn College, St. Joseph's requires a sequence of ten core courses. St. Joseph's differs from Brooklyn in distributing these courses over all four years, whereas Brooklyn's core courses are concentrated in the first two. The Brooklyn and St. Joseph's cores also share curricular coherence in the way courses are arranged in logical progression, each course building upon the previous one. All core courses at St. Joseph's involve the humanities. There is tremendous enthusiasm for the core approach among faculty, two-thirds of whom teach core courses. Even more telling is the enthusiasm of St. Joseph's alumni, who frequently write faculty to praise the core as an outstanding feature of their college career.

Among two-year colleges, where vocational training is so important to the institutional mission, some schools have recognized the need for a strong common curriculum in the humanities. Kirkwood Community College in Iowa is a noteworthy example. Kirkwood serves about 6,000 students, half of whom are enrolled in liberal arts degree programs. In 1979, several faculty and administrators formed a Humanities Committee to review the humanities curriculum and recommend improvements. The committee developed and obtained approval for a new twenty-four humanities core requirement. Candidates for the Associate of Arts degree now select from a very limited list of challenging academic courses—in literature, history, philosophy, and languages—which concentrate on reading primary texts and require extensive student writing.

The experience of Brooklyn College, St. Joseph's College, and Kirkwood Community College proves that the drift toward curricular disintegration can be reversed, that colleges and universities—and not just the elite ones—can become true communities of learning, and that it is possible even in this age of skepticism to educate students on the principle that certain areas of knowledge are essential for every college graduate. Their experience also belies the oft-heard fear that students will reject or avoid such a structured curriculum. Intellectually challenging, well-taught courses, whether required or not, will attract good students, and any college that offers a curriculum of such courses will not lack applicants.

The Challenge to Academic Leadership

Revitalizing an educational institution is not easy. Usually it requires uncommon courage and discernment on the part of a few and a shared vision of what can and ought to be on the part of many. Higher education may now be more receptive to decisive leadership than it has been for some time. As University of Puget Sound President Philip Phibbs observed, most colleges and universities sense a crisis on the way and are concerned about the future. Administrators and faculty alike are beginning to perceive that what has traditionally been good for this or that department, one school or another, may be harmful to the institution as a whole and to its overall educational mission.

Recently, educational researchers sought to determine those factors that make some elementary and secondary schools more successful than others. Among the most important was strong leadership from the school principal. Although colleges and universities are more complex institutions than secondary schools, with far stronger fragmenting tendencies, leadership plays the same uncial role.

Curricular reform must begin with the president. In their research on presidential leadership, Clark Kerr and David Riesman found that only 2 percent of the more than seven hundred college and university presidents interviewed described themselves as playing a major role in academic affairs. This is an alarming finding. A president should be the chief academic officer of the institution, not just the chief administrative, recruitment, or fund-raising officer. The president and other principal academic officers (provosts, deans, vice presidents for academic affairs) are solely accountable for all its parts and the needs of all its students. They are ultimately responsible for the quality of the education these students receive.

Members of the study group—which included several deans and presidents—believed strongly that presidents can be an effective force for curricular change only if they define their role accordingly. Bucknell University's Frances Fergusson said that a president's role is to "define, articulate, and defend institutional goals and to redirect the energies of the faculty towards these broader concerns." David Riesman characterized a good president as having "a combination of persuasiveness, patience, ingenuity, even stubbornness." Philip Phibbs said that a president must "have the courage to state and insist upon important, and often uncomfortable, if not initially unacceptable, ideas."

There are a number of concrete steps presidents can take to strengthen the humanities within their institutions. Roland Dille, president of Moorhead State College, said that "in the dozens of speeches that a president makes there ought to be some sign of his having been touched by the humanities." Beyond this, he can set standards for excellence in undergraduate teaching and see that they are met by hiring deans, provosts, and faculty who are committed to those standards. President Hanna Gray of the University of Chicago urged her fellow presidents to "insist on certain priorities" and to "raise certain questions and insist that they be answered." Donald Stewart, president of Spelman College, showed that a president who views himself as all an academic leader can make a real difference. From the beginning of his presidency at Spelman, Stewart sought to cut through the prevalent vocational orientation by stating openly and repeatedly that the humanities are basic to Spelman's mission, and, in so doing, set a new intellectual tone for the institution. Such statements by institutional leaders must, of course, be accompanied by actions. Among these, and not the least important, is rewarding good teaching in hiring, promotion, and tenure decisions.

But as Frederick Rudolph has frequently pointed out, the curriculum cannot be reformed without the enthusiastic support of the faculty. Institutions such as Brooklyn college, St. Joseph's College, and Kirkwood Community College were able to implement strong curricula because their administrators and faculty worked together toward a common goal, not in opposition to one another or to protect departmental turf. Philip Phibbs called upon humanities faculty to recognize their common interests:

> Leadership . . . must also come from the humanities faculty itself. This group must assert itself aggressively within the larger faculty and make its case with confidence and clarity. In too many cases, I think, faculty members in the humanities assume that any intelligent human being, and certainly any intelligent faculty colleague, understands the value of the humanities. It should not, therefore, be necessary to articulate the case. This is a dangerous and misguided assumption.

Concluding Thoughts

The humanities are important, not to just a few scholars, gifted students, or armchair dilettantes, but to any person who would be educated. They are important precisely because they embody mankind's age-old effort to ask the questions that are central to human existence. As Robertson Davies told a college graduating class, "A university education is meant to enlarge and illuminate your life." A college education worthy of the name must be constructed upon a foundation of the humanities. Unfortunately, our colleges and universities do not always give the humanities their due. All too often teaching is lifeless, arid, and without commitment. On too many campuses, the curriculum has become a self-service cafeteria through which students pass without being nourished. Many academic leaders lack the confidence to assert that the curriculum should stand for something more than salesmanship, compromise, or special interest politics. Too many colleges and universities have no clear sense of their educational mission and no conception of what a graduate of their institution ought to know or be.

The solution is not a return to an earlier time when the classical curriculum was the only curriculum and college was available to only a privileged few. American higher education today serves far more people and many more purposes than it did a century ago. Its increased accessibility to women, racial and ethnic minorities, recent immigrants, and students of limited means is a positive accomplishment of which our nation is rightly proud. As higher education broadened, the curriculum became more sensitive to the long-overlooked cultural achievements of many groups with what Janice Harris of the University of Wyoming referred to as "a respect for diversity." This, too, is a good thing. But our eagerness to assert the virtues of pluralism should not allow us to sacrifice the principle that formerly lent substance and continuity to the curriculum, namely, that each college and university should recognize and accept its vital role as conveyor of the accumulated wisdom of our civilization.

We are a part and a product of Western civilization. That our society was founded upon such principles as justice, liberty, government with the consent of the governed, and equality under the law is the result of ideas descended directly from great epochs of Western civilization—Enlightenment England and France, Renaissance Florence, and Periclean Athens. These ideas, so revolutionary in their times yet so taken for granted now, are the glue that binds together our pluralistic nation. The fact that we as Americans—whether black or white, Asian or Hispanic, rich or poor—share these beliefs aligns us with other cultures of the Western tradition. It is not ethnocentric or chauvinistic to acknowledge this. No student citizen of our civilization should be denied access to the best that tradition has to offer.

Ours is not, of course, the only great cultural tradition the world has seen. There are others, and we should expect an educated person to be familiar with them because they have produced art, literature, and thought that are compelling monuments to the human spirit and because they have made significant contributions to our history. Those who know nothing of these other traditions can neither appreciate the uniqueness of their own nor understand how their own fits with the larger world. They are less able to understand the world in which they live. The college curriculum must take the non-Western world into account, not out of political expediency or to appease interest groups, but out of respect for its importance in human history. But the core of the American college curriculum—its heart and soul—should be the civilization of the West, source of the most powerful and pervasive influences on America and all of its people. It is simply not possible for students to understand their society without studying its intellectual legacy. If their past is hidden from them, they will become aliens in their own culture, strangers in their own land.

Restoring the humanities to their central place in the curriculum is a task each college and university will have to accomplish for itself, its faculty and administrators working together toward a common goal with all the vision, judgment, and wisdom they can muster. Every institution has its own unique character, problems, sense of purpose, and circumstances; a successful approach at one school may be impractical at another.

Instead of listing formal recommendations this report concludes with some questions. We believe that if colleges and universities ask these questions of themselves and honestly answer them, the process of reform will have begun.

Questions for the academic community of each institution:

- Does the curriculum on your campus ensure that a graduate with a bachelor's degree will be conversant with the best that has been thought and written about the human condition?
- Does your curriculum reflect the best judgment of the president, deans, and faculty about what an educated person ought to know, or is it a mere smorgasbord or an expression of appeasement politics?
- Is your institution genuinely committed to teaching the humanities to undergraduates? Do your best professors teach introductory and lower division courses? Are these classes designed for the nonmajor, and are they part of a coherent curriculum?

Questions for college and university presidents:

- Do you set an intellectual tone for the institution, articulating goals and ideals?
- Do you take a firm stand on what your institution regards as essential knowledge?
- Do you reward excellent teaching as well as good research in hiring, promotions and tenure decisions?

Questions for humanities faculty:

- Does your teaching make the humanities come alive by helping students confront great texts, great minds, and great ideas?
- Are you as concerned with teaching the humanities to nonmajors as you are with signing up departmental majors?

Questions for graduate humanities departments:

- Are your graduates prepared to teach central humanities texts to undergraduates in addition to being trained as researchers and scholars?
- Are your graduates broadly educated in fields of knowledge other than their primary one? As scholars, are they concerned only with pursuing research of narrow scope or are they able, as well, to ask questions of wide significance?

We conclude with these questions because the spirit of higher education in a free society is the spirit of knowledge and inquiry, the framing of important questions in the vigorous search for good and truthful answers. First, however, we must ask the important questions of ourselves, of our institutions, of our faculties, and of our curricula. We must assure ourselves that the answers we live by are true and valuable. Are we teaching what we should? Are we teaching it as well as we can? No college or university, if it is honest with itself, concerned for its students, and mindful of its largest responsibilities, will reject such questions out of hand or dismiss them with easy affirmatives or conventional excuses.

More than four decades ago, Walter Lippmann observed that "what enables men to know more than their ancestors is that they start with a knowledge of what their ancestors have already learned." "A society," he added, "can be progressive only if it conserves its tradition." The challenge to our colleges and universities, I believe, is to conserve and transmit that tradition, understanding that they do this not merely to pay homage to the wisdom of the past but to prepare wisely for the future.

CHAPTER 16

50 HOURS: A CORE CURRICULUM FOR COLLEGE STUDENTS

LYNNE V. CHENEY

Introduction

A 1989 survey funded by the National Endowment for the Humanities and conducted by the Gallup Organization showed 25 percent of the nation's college seniors unable to locate Columbus's voyage within the correct half-century. About the same percentage could not distinguish Churchill's words from Stalin's, or Karl Marx's thoughts from the ideas of the U.S. Constitution. More than 40 percent could not identify when the Civil War occurred. Most could not identify Magna Carta, the Missouri Compromise, or Reconstruction. Most could not link major works by Plato, Dante, Shakespeare, and Milton with their authors. To the majority of college seniors, Jane Austen's *Pride and Prejudice,* Dostoyevsky's *Crime and Punishment,* and Martin Luther King, Jr.'s "Letter from the Birmingham Jail" were clearly unfamiliar.[1]

Education aims at more than acquaintance with dates and places, names and titles. Students should not only know when Columbus sailed but also perceive the world-altering shock of his voyage. They should not only know what Plato wrote but also understand the allegory of the cave. When education is rightly conceived, events and ideas become, in philosopher Michael Oakeshott's words, "invitations to look, to listen and to reflect."[2] But students who approach the end of their college years without knowing basic landmarks of history and thought are unlikely to have reflected on their meaning.

A required course of studies—a core of learning—can ensure that students have opportunities to know the literature, philosophy, institutions, and art of our own and other cultures. A core of learning can also encourage understanding of mathematics and science, and *50 Hours* includes these fields of inquiry. The National Endowment for the Humanities must be concerned with the literature major who has no understanding of physics as well as with the engineer who graduates without studying history. Both are less prepared than they should be to make the subtle and complex choices today's life demands. Both bring limited perspective to enduring human questions: Where have we come from? Who are we? What is our destiny? Kant struggled for answers in his study; Boyle, in his laboratory. Thoreau, Gauguin, and Einstein took up these questions, approaching them in different ways, but sharing a common goal. All the various branches of human knowledge, as physicist Erwin Schrödinger once observed, have the same objective: "It is to obey the command of the Delphic deity," to honor the ancient injunction, "Know thyself. "[3]

To the task of learning about oneself and the world, a required course of studies can bring needed order and coherence. At one midwestern university, where there is no core, students choose from

Source: "50 Hours: A Core Curriculum for College Students," by Lynne V. Cheney, reprinted from *National Endowment for the Humanities,* 1989.

almost 900 courses, with topics ranging from the history of foreign labor movements to the analysis of daytime soap operas. The result is all too often "a meaningless mosaic of fragments," in naturalist Loren Eiseley's words. "From ape skull to Mayan temple," he wrote, "we contemplate the miscellaneous debris of time like sightseers to whom these mighty fragments, fallen gateways, and sunken galleys convey no present instruction."[4] A core of learning shows the patterns of the mosaic. It provides a context for forming the parts of education into a whole.

A core of learning also encourages community, whether we conceive community small or large. Having some learning in common draws students together—and faculty members as well. When that common learning engages students with their democratic heritage, it invites informed participation in our ongoing national conversation: What should a free people value? What should they resist? What are the limits to freedom, and how are they to be decided?

When students are encouraged to explore the history and thought of cultures different from their own, they gain insight into others with whom they share the earth. They come to understand unfamiliar ideals and traditions—and to see more clearly the characteristics that define their own particular journey.

Is There Time in the Curriculum for a Core?

Almost all colleges and universities have requirements in "general education"—a part of the curriculum that is specified for all undergraduates, regardless of major. The hours set aside for general education are the hours from which a core of learning can be constructed.

The larger and more complex the educational institution, the more difficult it is to commit hours to general education. A school that offers an accredited engineering program has to recognize that few engineering students will be able to graduate in four years if they devote much more than a semester to the humanities and social sciences. Schools offering a bachelor's degree in music must face the demands of the National Association of Schools of Music, an accrediting association that expects students to devote 65 percent of their coursework to studying music.[5]

Nevertheless, even doctorate-granting universities, the most complex institutions of higher education, require, on the average, more than thirty-seven semester hours in general education. For all four-year institutions, the average requirement in general education is fifty-two semester hours.[6] There is time at most schools for a significant core of learning.

As it is now, however, these hours that could be devoted to a core are all too often organized instead into loosely stated "distribution requirements"—mandates that students take some courses in certain areas and some in others. Long lists of acceptable choices are set out in catalogs. Specialized offerings for the most part, they often have little to do with the broadly conceived learning that should be at the heart of general education. Indeed, some courses seem to have little to do with the areas of human knowledge they are supposed to elucidate. At a public university in the West, it is possible to fulfill humanities requirements with courses in interior design. In 1988–89 at a private university in the East, one could fulfill part of the social science distribution requirement by taking "Lifetime Fitness."

Some core programs do offer choices: Alternative possibilities for mathematics and science are almost universal. Choice within a core can work well, so long as each of the choices fits within a carefully defined framework and aims at broad and integrated learning. The University of Denver's core, for example, offers five, year-long options in the arts and humanities. In one course, "The Making of the Modern Mind," philosophy, literature, music, and art are studied from the Enlightenment to the present. A second course, "Commercial Civilization," emphasizes history, political thought and institutions, and classical economic theory from the origins of capitalism to contemporary times.

Is a Core Too Hard for Some Students? Too Easy for Others?

The 1983 report, *A Nation at Risk,* recommended that college-bound high school students take four years of English, three of social studies, science, and mathematics, and two years of foreign language.[7] Students who have completed such a course of studies should be ready to undertake the work required by a program like *50 Hours.* Entering students who lack necessary verbal and mathematical skills should prepare for core work by taking remedial courses. Such a plan benefits the core and can be of value to remedial programs as well by providing a well-defined goal for teaching and learning. The faculty of the remedial and developmental programs of Brooklyn College of the City University of New York recently dedicated a conference to Brooklyn's core curriculum to recognize its importance for their work.

In *50 Hours,* students are expected to write papers of varying length in every course, including those in science and mathematics. The practice of organizing ideas and presenting them coherently is a useful tool for learning in all subjects. Students who write in every course also come to understand that clear and graceful expression is universally valuable, not merely an arbitrary preoccupation of English departments. Some students who are prepared for core work may still need extra practice in composition. For them, writing-intensive sections of required courses can be designated—as they are at Brandeis and Vanderbilt universities.

Students who come to college well-prepared may have read some of the works assigned in the core. But so long as those works are profound provocative, and revealing, these students will again be challenged. Indeed, a criterion for choosing works for the core should be that they repay many readings. They should be books that remain fresh, full of power to quicken thought and feeling, no matter how many times we open their pages.

Why Is Establishing a Core So Difficult?

Curricular change has never been easy: Henry Bragdon, writing about Woodrow Wilson's years at Princeton, called it "harder than moving a graveyard.[8] And the way in which higher education has evolved over the last century has complicated the task.

The forces that have come to dominate higher education are centrifugal rather than centripetal, weakening the ties that individual faculty members have to their institutions. As professional advancement has come increasingly to depend on the esteem of other specialists on other campuses, there has been less and less incentive for scholars at any single college or university to identify fully with that institution and the shared efforts necessary for a complicated task like curricular reform.

At the same time, faculty responsibility for the curriculum has grown. If it is to change, the faculty must come together and act for the common purpose of changing it. "We have a paradox," Professor James Q. Wilson observed after curriculum reform at Harvard. "The faculty is supposed to govern collegially, but it is not a collegium."[9]

The increasingly specialized nature of graduate study is also an impediment. Many Ph.D.'s do not receive the broad preparation necessary to teach courses in general education. Even those who do often step uneasily outside their specialties, concerned that it is unprofessional to teach Dante when one's expertise is Donne. They perceive hours spent teaching in general education—and days consumed devising its courses and curricula—as time away from the labor that the academic system most rewards: research and publication. One young professor called curriculum reform "a black hole," and the time and energy it absorbs are seldom professionally recognized.

Crucial to establishing a core of learning is administrative leadership: college presidents who make general education a priority by putting institutional resources behind it; deans who support those faculty members who are willing to invest the time necessary to develop coherent requirements and seek consensus for them. A recent survey by the American Council on Education suggests that students, parents, alumni, and trustees can also play an important role in encouraging curricular reform: Thirty percent of doctorate-granting institutions that were revising general education requirements reported that the initiators of reform were people other than faculty or administration members.[10]

Successfully establishing and sustaining a core may well require efforts aimed at encouraging intellectual community. Seminars in which faculty members read together the works to be taught in core courses can create common understandings, while at the same time providing background for teaching. At Rice University in Houston, where extensive curricular reform is under way, faculty members met in day-long sessions for two weeks last spring to discuss works to be taught in the humanities foundation course. A classicist led discussion of the *Iliad;* a philosopher, of Plato's *Republic;* a professor of music, of Mozart's *Marriage of Figaro.*

How Should Courses in the Core Be Taught?

"The two great points to be gained in intellectual culture," an 1828 report from Yale University noted, "are the *discipline* and the furniture of the mind; expanding its powers, and storing it with knowledge.[11] For a core of learning to encourage intellectual discipline as well as the acquisition of knowledge, some small classes are essential. Students must have opportunities to participate in discussion and to be encouraged by teachers and peers to think critically about concepts and ideas.

Every course in the core should be taught with other core courses in mind. Students reading Descartes's philosophy in a Western civilization course should be reminded of his contributions to mathematics. Students reading Darwin in a science class should be encouraged to explore in their social science and humanities courses the ways in which evolutionary theory affected social thought and literature. Such connections help demonstrate that human knowledge is not a disconnected series of specialized subjects but interrelated domains of thought.

An institution's most distinguished faculty should teach in the core. Philosopher Charles Frankel once reported that Philipp Frank, Einstein's biographer and collaborator, expressed surprise on learning that in the United States he would not be allowed to teach elementary courses. In Vienna, where Frank had previously taught, beginning courses were considered the greatest honor—one to be bestowed on only those who had mastered their fields sufficiently to be able to generalize. "But in America," Frankel noted, "we thought that was for fellows who know less. Frank believed not—you had to know more and in fact you had to have lived your field and felt the passion of it . . . to communicate it."[12]

Graduate assistants and nontenured faculty, to whom much of the responsibility for undergraduate teaching falls today, are often fine instructors. But the stature of general education is diminished when a college or university's most distinguished faculty do not teach in it. The quality of instruction is diminished when they do not bring their learning and experience to it.

Good teaching is crucial to the success of any curriculum, and it can take a multitude of forms. But teachers who inspire their students to intellectual engagement are themselves always engaged. They do not agree with every book or idea they discuss, but they approach them generously, demonstrating that neither agreement nor disagreement is possible until there has been the hard work of understanding. Learning is not a game for them, not simply an intellectual exercise, but an undertaking that compels mind and heart. Recalling his great teachers, Leo Raditsa of St. John's College in Maryland recently described I. A. Richards. "He conceived reading as the cure of souls. . . ," Raditsa wrote. "And he included his own soul."[13]

In the core, as throughout the curriculum, courses should be taught by men and women who, though deeply knowledgeable, remain eager to learn.

Afterword

If liberal education is a journey, as many have conceived it, then the curriculum is a map. It sets out the past so that we understand that here, in this time and place, Greek temples gleamed, whole and serene under Attic sun. Here Galileo looked through his telescope and saw the shining moons of Jupiter. Here Shakespeare's genius flashed upon the Elizabethan stage, illuminating his time and the human spirit.

But charting a map for learning has this difference from charting land and sea: We are always, as we draw the map, living in the Age of Discovery, likely to find ourselves awed by the significance of what had once seemed of only passing importance, amazed by wonders we didn't know existed. Euclid's parallel postulate, a curiosity for centuries, suddenly becomes crucial to a new understanding. Emily Dickinson's poetry, known to only a few, emerges from obscurity to alter the imaginative horizon. Familiar continents remain, but new islands are discovered and new peninsulas that make us rethink the map we have drawn.

A world dynamic in its details is difficult to chart, and so is a world that is rich in possibilities. Choices must be made, and even when they are meant only to be illustrative, as they are in the core curriculum set forth in this report, the omissions are painful. Where is Pascal? Do we want students to graduate without having encountered his "two infinities" or his wager of faith? Just as the task is finished, one is tempted to go back and add, to suggest that more should be included.

Other authors and topics could have been—and surely will be—suggested, and others would accord with the principle of selection informing this core, particularly in the humanities: that students should encounter works and ideas whose influence can be traced through the history of thought and deed. These works and ideas should be studied not as tribute to the past, though part of education lies in coming to understand that wisdom is to be found there. Rather these works and ideas should be studied because they are part of the present. They exist in the matrix of our experience, whether we know it or not; and to become aware of them is to better understand our lives and ourselves.

An argument sometimes advanced against requirements is that they are limiting, but a core curriculum devised so that students encounter classic works and significant ideas is just the opposite. It expands choices and enriches possibilities for the individual. No two students will come through its complex explorations quite the same. One will love the ordered world of the theorem, another the untamed landscapes of the Romantics. But both will know both, if education has done its duty; and they will share this: an enthusiasm for the journey, a sense of the satisfactions a lifetime of learning can bring.

Ancient mapmakers inscribed legends on their maps—warnings, usually, of monsters and wonders. For a map of learning, another kind of instruction is fitting, a legend drawn from a poet: "Now voyager sail thou forth to seek and find."[14]

Notes

1. *A Survey of College Seniors: Knowledge of History and Literature*, conducted for the National Endowment for the Humanities (Princeton, N.J.: The Gallup Organization, 1989), 33–56.
2. Michael Oakeshott, *The Voice of Learning: Michael Oakeshott on Education*, ed. Timothy Fuller (New Haven, Conn.: Yale Univesity Press, 1989), 29.
3. Erwin Schrödinger, *Science and Humanism: Physics in Our Time* (London: Cambridge University Press, 1951), 4.
4. Loren C. Eiseley, *The Unexpected Universe* (New York: Harcourt, Brace & World, 1964), 6.
5. Joseph S. Johnston, Jr., Susan Shaman, and Robert Zemsky, *Unfinished Design: The Humanities and Social Sciences in Undergraduate Engineering Education* (Washington, D.C.: Association of American Colleges, 1988), 10; *National Association of Schools of Music: 1987–1988 Handbook* (Reston, Va.: National Association of Schools of Music, 1987), 51–57.
6. *Undergraduate General Education and Humanities Requierments*, Higher Education Surveys, no. 7 (Rockville, Md.: Westat, inc., 1989), Table A-4.
7. The National Commission on Excellence in Education, *A Nation at Risk: The Imperative for Educational Reform* (Washington, D.C.: U.S. Government Printing Office, 1983), 24. The Educational Testing Service reports that at least 75 percent of high school seniors taking the Scholastic Aptitude Test in 1988 were meeting these standards. *What Americans Study* (Princeton, N.J.: Educational Testing Service, 1989), 8.
8. Henry Wilkinson Bragdon, *Woodrow Wilson: The Academic Years* (Cambridge, Mass.: Harvard University Press, 1967), 293.
9. James Q. Wilson, "A View from the Inside," *The Great Core Curriculum Debate: Education as a Mirror of Culture* (New Rochelle, N.Y.: Change Magazine Press, 1979), 47.
10. *General Education Reguirements in the Humanities*, Higher Education Panel Reports, no. 66 (Washington, D.C.: American Council on Education, 1985), Table 14.1.
11. *Reports on the Course of Instruction in Yale College* (New Haven, Conn.: Hazekiah Howe, 1830), 7.
12. Charles Frankel, "The Philosopher" (Paper presented at the National Meeting of State-Based Committees, Washington, D.C., 2–3 May 1973), 56.
13. Leo Raditsa, "On Sustenance: Teaching and Learning the Great Works," *Academic Questions* (Spring 1989), 34–35.
14. Walt Whitman, *Leaves of Grass.*

CHAPTER 17

INTRODUCTION: OUR VIRTUE

ALLAN BLOOM

There is one thing a professor can be absolutely certain of: almost every student entering the university believes, or says he believes, that truth is relative. If this belief is put to the test, one can count on the students' reaction: they will be uncomprehending. That anyone should regard the proposition as not self-evident astonishes them, as though he were calling into question 2 + 2 = 4. These are things you don't think about. The students' backgrounds are as various as America can provide. Some are religious, some atheists; some are to the Left, some to the Right; some intend to be scientists, some humanists or professionals or businessmen; some are poor, some rich. They are unified only in their relativism and in their allegiance to equality. And the two are related in a moral intention. The relativity of truth is not a theoretical insight but a moral postulate, the condition of a free society; or so they see it. They have all been equipped with this framework early on, and it is the modern replacement for the inalienable natural rights that used to be the traditional American grounds for a free society. That it is a moral issue for students is revealed by the character of their response when challenged—a combination of disbelief and indignation: "Are you an absolutist?," the only alternative they know, uttered in the same tone as "Are you a monarchist?" or "Do you really believe in witches?" This latter leads into the indignation, for someone who believes in witches might well be a witch-hunter or a Salem judge. The danger they have been taught to fear from absolutism is not error but intolerance. Relativism is necessary to openness; and this is the virtue, the only virtue, which all primary education for more than fifty years has dedicated itself to inculcating. Openness—and the relativism that makes it the only plausible stance in the face of various claims to truth and various ways of life and kinds of human beings—is the great insight of our times. The true believer is the real danger. The study of history and of culture teaches that all the world was mad in the past; men always thought they were right, and that led to wars, persecutions, slavery, xenophobia, racism, and chauvinism. The point is not to correct the mistakes and really be right; rather it is not to think you are right at all.

The students, of course, cannot defend their opinion. It is something with which they have been indoctrinated. The best they can do is point out all the opinions and cultures there are and have been. What right, they ask, do I or anyone else have to say one is better than the others? If I pose the routine questions designed to confute them and make them think, such as, "If you had been a British administrator in India, would you have let the natives under your governance burn the widow at the funeral of a man who had died?," they either remain silent or reply that the British should never have been there in the first place. It is not that they know very much about other nations, or about their own. The purpose of their education is not to make them scholars but to provide them with a moral virtue—openness.

Source: "Introduction: Our Virtue," by Allan Bloom, reprinted from *The Closing of the American Mind*, 1987, Simon & Schuster, Inc.

Every educational system has a moral goal that it tries to attain and that informs its curriculum. It wants to produce a certain kind of human being. This intention is more or less explicit, more or less a result of reflection; but even the neutral subjects, like reading and writing and arithmetic, take their place in a vision of the educated person. In some nations the goal was the pious person, in others the warlike, in others the industrious. Always important is the political regime, which needs citizens who are in accord with its fundamental principle. Aristocracies want gentlemen, oligarchies men who respect and pursue money, and democracies lovers of equality. Democratic education, whether it admits it or not, wants and needs to produce men and women who have the tastes, knowledge, and character supportive of a democratic regime. Over the history of our republic, there have obviously been changes of opinion as to what kind of man is best for our regime. We began with the model of the rational and industrious man, who was honest, respected the laws, and was dedicated to the family (his own family—what has in its decay been dubbed the nuclear family). Above all he was to know the rights doctrine; the Constitution, which embodied it; and American history, which presented and celebrated the founding of a nation "conceived in liberty and dedicated to the proposition that all men are created equal." A powerful attachment to the letter and the spirit of the Declaration of Independence gently conveyed, appealing to each man's reason, was the goal of the education of democratic man. This called for something very different from the kinds of attachment required for traditional communities where myth and passion as well as severe discipline, authority, and the extended family produced an instinctive, unqualified, even fanatic patriotism, unlike the reflected, rational, calm, even self-interested loyalty—not so much to the country but to the form of government and its rational principles—required in the United States. This was an entirely new experiment in politics, and with it came a new education. This education has evolved in the last half-century from the education of democratic man to the education of the democratic personality.

The palpable difference between these two can easily be found in the changed understanding of what it means to be an American. The old view was that, by recognizing and accepting man's natural rights, men found a fundamental basis of unity and sameness. Class, race, religion, national origin or culture all disappear or become dim when bathed in the light of natural rights, which give men common interests and make them truly brothers. The immigrant had to put behind him the claims of the Old World in favor of a new and easily acquired education. This did not necessarily mean abandoning old daily habits or religions, but it did mean subordinating them to new principles. There was a tendency, if not a necessity, to homogenize nature itself.

The recent education of openness has rejected all that. It pays no attention to natural rights or the historical origins of our regime, which are now thought to have been essentially flawed and regressive. It is progressive and forward-looking. It does not demand fundamental agreement or the abandonment of old or new beliefs in favor of the natural ones. It is open to all kinds of men, all kinds of life-styles, all ideologies. There is no enemy other than the man who is not open to everything. But when there are no shared goals or vision of the public good, is the social contract any longer possible?

From the earliest beginnings of liberal thought there was a tendency in the direction of indiscriminate freedom. Hobbes and Locke, and the American Founders following them, intended to palliate extreme beliefs, particularly religious beliefs, which lead to civil strife. The members of sects had to obey the laws and be loyal to the Constitution; if they did so, others had to leave them alone, however distasteful their beliefs might be. In order to make this arrangement work, there was a conscious, if covert, effort to weaken religious beliefs, partly by assigning—as a result of a great epistemological effort—religion to the realm of opinion as opposed to knowledge. But the right to freedom of religion belonged to the realm of knowledge. Such rights are not matters of opinion. No weakness of conviction was desired here. All to the contrary, the sphere of rights was to be the arena of moral passion in a democracy.

It was possible to expand the space exempt from legitimate social and political regulation only by contracting the claims to moral and political knowledge. The insatiable appetite for freedom to live as one pleases thrives on this aspect of modern democratic thought. In the end it begins to appear that full freedom can be attained only when there is no such knowledge at all. The effective way to defang the oppressors is to persuade them they are ignorant of the good. The inflamed sensitivity induced by radicalized democratic theory finally experiences any limit as arbitrary and tyrannical. There are no absolutes; freedom is absolute. Of course the result is that, on the one hand, the argument justifying freedom disappears and, on the other, all beliefs begin to have the attenuated character that was initially supposed to be limited to religious belief.

The gradual movement away from rights to openness was apparent, for example, when Oliver Wendell Holmes renounced seeking for a principle to determine which speech or conduct is not tolerable in a democratic society and invoked instead an imprecise and practically meaningless standard—clear and present danger—which to all intents and purposes makes the preservation of public order the only common good. Behind his opinion there was an optimistic view about progress, one in which the complete decay of democratic principle and a collapse into barbarism are impossible and in which the truth unaided always triumphs in the marketplace of ideas. This optimism had not been shared by the Founders, who insisted that the principles of democratic government must be returned to and consulted even though the consequences might be harsh for certain points of view, some merely tolerated and not respected, others forbidden outright To their way of thinking there should be no tolerance for the intolerant. The notion that there should be no limitation on free expression unless it can be shown to be a clear and present danger would have made it impossible for Lincoln to insist that there could be no compromise with the *principle* of equality, that it did not depend on the people's choice or election but is the condition of their having elections in the first place, that popular sovereignty on the question of black slavery was impermissible even if it would enable us to avoid the clear and present danger of a bloody civil war.

But openness, nevertheless, eventually won out over natural rights, partly through a theoretical critique, partly because of a political rebellion against nature's last constraints. Civic education turned away from concentrating on the Founding to concentrating on openness based on history and social science. There was even a general tendency to debunk the Founding, to prove the beginnings were flawed in order to license a greater openness to the new. What began in Charles Beard's Marxism and Carl Becker's historicism became routine. We are used to hearing the Founders charged with being racists, murderers of Indians, representatives of class interests. I asked my first history professor in the university, a very famous scholar, whether the picture he gave us of George Washington did not have the effect of making us despise our regime. "Not at all," he said, "it doesn't depend on individuals but on our having good democratic values." To which I rejoined, "But you just showed us that Washington was only using those values to further the class interests of the Virginia squirearchy." He got angry, and that was the end of it. He was comforted by a gentle assurance that the values of democracy are part of the movement of history and did not require his elucidation or defense. He could carry on his historical studies with the moral certitude that they would lead to greater openness and hence more democracy. The lessons of fascism and the vulnerability of democracy, which we had all just experienced, had no effect on him.

Liberalism without natural rights, the kind that we knew from John Stuart Mill and John Dewey, taught us that the only danger confronting us is being closed to the emergent, the new, the manifestations of progress. No attention had to be paid to the fundamental principles or the moral virtues that inclined men to live according to them. To use language now popular, civic culture was neglected. And this turn in liberalism is what prepared us for cultural relativism and the fact-value distinction, which seemed to carry that viewpoint further and give it greater intellectual weight.

History and social science are used in a variety of ways to overcome prejudice. We should not be ethnocentric, a term drawn from anthropology, which tells us more about the meaning of openness. We should not think our way is better than others. The intention is not so much to teach the students about other times and places as to make them aware of the fact that their preferences are only that—accidents of their time and place. Their beliefs do not entitle them as individuals, or collectively as a nation, to think they are superior to anyone else. John Rawls is almost a parody of this tendency, writing hundreds of pages to persuade men, and proposing a scheme of government that would force them, not to despise anyone. In *A Theory of Justice,* he writes that the physicist or the poet should not look down on the man who spends his life counting blades of grass or performing any other frivolous or corrupt activity. Indeed, he should be esteemed, since esteem from others, as opposed to self-esteem, is a basic need of all men. So indiscriminateness is a moral imperative because its opposite is discrimination. This folly means that men are not permitted to seek for the natural human good and admire it when found, for such discovery is coeval with the discovery of the bad and contempt for it. Instinct and intellect must be suppressed by education. The natural soul is to be replaced with an artificial one.

At the root of this change in morals was the presence in the United States of men and women of a great variety of nations, religions, and races, and the fact that many were badly treated because they belonged to these groups. Franklin Roosevelt declared that we want "a society which leaves no one out." Although the natural rights inherent in our regime are perfectly adequate to the solution of this problem, provided these outsiders adhere to them (i.e., they become insiders by adhering to them), this did not satisfy the thinkers who influenced our educators, for the right to vote and the other political rights did not automatically produce social acceptance. The equal protection of the laws did not protect a man from contempt and hatred as a Jew, an Italian, or a Black.

The reaction to this problem was, in the first place, resistance to the notion that outsides, had to give up their "cultural" individuality and make themselves into that universal, abstract being who participates in natural rights or else be doomed to an existence on the fringe; in the second place, anger at the majority who imposed a "cultural" life on the nation to which the Constitution is indifferent. Openness was designed to provide a respectable place for these "groups" or "minorities"—to wrest respect from those who were not disposed to give it—and to weaken the sense of superiority of the dominant majority (more recently dubbed WASPs, a name the success of which shows something of the success of sociology in reinterpreting the national consciousness). That dominant majority gave the country a dominant culture with its traditions, its literature, its tastes, its special claim to know and supervise the language, and its Protestant religions. Much of the intellectual machinery of twentieth-century American political thought and social science was constructed for the purposes of making an assault on that majority. It treated the founding principles as impediments and tried to overcome the other strand of our political heritage, majoritarianism, in favor of a nation of minorities and groups each following its own beliefs and inclinations. In particular, the intellectual minority expected to enhance its status, presenting itself as the defender and spokesman of all the others.

This reversal of the founding intention with respect to minorities is most striking. For the Founders, minorities are in general bad things, mostly identical to factions, selfish groups who have no concern as such for the common good. Unlike older political thinkers, they entertained no hopes of suppressing factions and educating a united or homogeneous citizenry. Instead they constructed an elaborate machinery to contain factions in such a way that they would cancel one another and allow for the pursuit of the common good. The good is still the guiding consideration in their thought, although it is arrived at, less directly than in classical political thought, by tolerating faction. The Founders wished to achieve a national majority concerning the fundamental rights and then prevent that majority from using its power to overturn those fundamental rights. In twentieth-century social science, however, the common good disappears and along with it the negative view of minorities. The very idea of majority—now understood to be selfish interest—is done away with in order to protect the minorities. This breaks the delicate balance between majority and minority in Constitutional thought. In such a perspective, where there is no common good, minorities are no longer problematic, and the protection of them emerges as the central function of government. Where this leads is apparent in, for example, Robert Dahl's *A Preface to Democratic Theory.* Groups or individuals who really care, as opposed to those who have lukewarm feelings, deserve special attention or special rights for their "intensity" or "commitment," the new political validation, which replaces reason. The Founding Fathers wished to reduce and defang fanaticism, whereas Dahl encourages it.

The appeal of the minority formula was enormous for all kinds of people, reactionary and progressive, all those who in the twenties and thirties still did not accept the political solution imposed by the Constitution. The reactionaries did not like the suppression of class privilege and religious establishment. For a variety of reasons they simply did not accept equality. Southerners knew full well that the Constitution's heart was a moral commitment to equality and hence condemned segregation of blacks. The Constitution was not just a set of rules of government but implied a moral order that was to be enforced throughout the entire Union. Yet the influence, which has not been sufficiently noted, of Southern writers and historians on the American view of their history has been powerful. They were remarkably successful in characterizing their "peculiar institution" as part of a charming diversity and individuality of culture to which the Constitution was worse than indifferent. The ideal of openness, lack of ethnocentricity, is just what they needed for a modern defense of their way of life against all the intrusions of outsiders who claimed equal rights with the folks back home. The Southerners' romantic characterization of the alleged failings of the Constitution, and their hostility to "mass society" with its technology, its money-grubbing way of life, egoistic individuals and concomitant destruction of community, organic and rooted, appealed to malcontents of all political colorations. The New Left in the sixties expressed exactly the same ideology that had been developed to protect the South from the threat to its practices posed by the Constitutional rights and the Federal Government's power to enforce them. It is the old alliance of Right and Left against liberal democracy, parodied as "bourgeois society."

The progressives of the twenties and thirties did not like the Constitutional protection of private property or the restraints on majority will and on living as one pleased. For them, equality had not gone far enough. Stalinists also found the definition of democracy as openness useful. The Constitution clashed too violently with the theory and practice of the Soviet Union. But if democracy means open-endedness, and respect for other cultures prevents doctrinaire, natural-rights-based condemnation of the Soviet reality, then someday their ways may become ours. I remember my grade-school history textbook, newly printed on fine glossy paper, showing intriguing pictures of collective farms where farmers worked and lived together without the profit motive. (Children cannot understand the issues, but they are easy to propagandize.) This was very different from our way of life, but we were not to be closed to it, to react to it merely on the basis of our cultural prejudices.

Sexual adventurers like Margaret Mead and others who found America too narrow told us that not only must we know other cultures and learn to respect them, but we could also profit from them. We could follow their lead and loosen up, liberating ourselves from the opinion that our taboos are anything other than social constraints. We could go to the bazaar of cultures and find reinforcement for inclinations that are repressed by puritanical guilt feelings. All such teachers of openness had either no interest in or were actively hostile to the Declaration of Independence and the Constitution.

The civil rights movement provides a good example of this change in thought. In its early days almost all the significant leaders, in spite of tactical and temperamental differences, relied on the Declaration of Independence and the Constitution. They could charge whites not only with the most monstrous injustices but also with contradicting their own most sacred principles. The blacks were the true Americans in demanding the equality that belongs to them as human beings by natural and political right. This stance implied a firm conviction of the truth of the principles of natural right and of their fundamental efficacy within the Constitutional tradition, which, although tarnished, tends in the long run toward fulfilling those principles. They therefore worked through Congress, the Presidency, and, above all, the Judiciary. By contrast, the Black Power movement that supplanted the older civil rights movement—leaving aside both its excesses and its very understandable emphasis on self-respect and refusal to beg for acceptance—had at its core the view that the Constitutional tradition was always corrupt and was constructed as a defense of slavery. Its demand was for black identity, not universal rights. Not rights but power counted. It insisted on respect for blacks as blacks, not as human beings simply.

Yet the Constitution does not promise respect for blacks, whites, yellows, Catholics, Protestants, or Jews. It guarantees the protection of the rights of individual human beings. This has not proved to be enough, however, to what is perhaps by now a majority of Americans.

The upshot of all this for the education of young Americans is that they know much less about American history and those who were held to be its heroes. This was one of the few things that they used to come to college with that had something to do with their lives. Nothing has taken its place except a smattering of facts learned about other nations or cultures and a few social science formulas. None of this means much, partly because little attention has been paid to what is required in order truly to convey the spirit of other places and other times to young people, or for that matter to anyone, partly because the students see no relevance in any of it to the lives they are going to lead or to their prevailing passions. It is the rarest of occurrences to find a youngster who has been infused by this education with a longing to know all about China or the Romans or the Jews.

All to the contrary. There is an indifference to such things, for relativism has extinguished the real motive of education, the search for a good life. Young Americans have less and less knowledge of and interest in foreign places. In the past there were many students who actually knew something about and loved England, France, Germany, or Italy, for they dreamed of living there or thought their lives would be made more interesting by assimilating their languages and literatures. Such students have almost disappeared, replaced at most by students who are interested in the political problems of Third World countries and in helping them to modernize, with due respect to their old cultures, of course. This is not learning from others but condescension and a disguised form of a new imperialism. It is the Peace Corps mentality, which is not a spur to learning but to a secularized version of doing good works.

Actually openness results in American conformism—out there in the rest of the world is a drab diversity that teaches only that values are relative, whereas here we can create all the lifestyles we want. Our openness means we do not need others. Thus what is advertised as a great opening is a great closing. No longer is there a hope that there are great wise men in other places and times who can reveal the truth about life—except for the few remaining young people who look for a quick fix from a guru. Gone is the real historical sense of a Machiavelli who wrested a few hours from each busy day in which "to don regal and courtly garments, enter the courts of the ancients and speak with them."

None of this concerns those who promote the new curriculum. The point is to propagandize acceptance of different ways, and indifference to their real content is as good a means as any. It was not necessarily the best of times in America when Catholics and Protestants were suspicious of and hated one another; but at least they were taking their beliefs seriously, and the more or less satisfactory accommodations they worked out were not simply the result of apathy about the state of their souls. Practically all that young Americans have today is an insubstantial awareness that there are many cultures, accompanied by a saccharine moral drawn from that awareness: We should all get along. Why fight? In 1980, during the crisis with Iran, the mother of one of the hostages expressed our current educational principles very well. She went to Iran to beg for her son's release, against the express wishes of the government of her country, the very week a rescue of the hostages was attempted. She justified her conduct by explaining that a mother has a right to try to save her son and also to learn a new culture. These are two basic rights, and her trip enabled her to kill two birds with one stone.

Actually the problem of cultural difference could have been faced more easily here in America forty years ago. When I was in college, a young Mississippian was lodged in my dormitory room for a few days during a visit of the University of Virginia debating team, of which he was a member. It was my first meeting with an intelligent, educated Southerner. He explained the inferiority of blacks to me, the reasons for Jim Crow, and how all that was a part of a unique way of life. He was an attractive, lively, amiable, healthy youngster. I, however, was horrified by him because I was still ethnocentric. I took my Northern beliefs to be universal. The "different strokes for different folks" philosophy had not yet taken full hold. Fortunately the homogenization of American culture that has occurred since that enables us to avoid such nasty confrontations. Only obviously pathological lower-class types now hold the racist views of my young visitor. Southerners helped to fashion our theoretical view of culture, but the Southern culture they intended to defend disappeared.

One of the techniques of opening young people up is to require a college course in a non-Western culture. Although many of the persons teaching such courses are real scholars and lovers of the areas they study, in every case I have seen this requirement—when there are so many other things that can and should be learned but are not required, when philosophy and religion are no longer required—has a demagogic intention. The point is to force students to recognize that there are other ways of thinking and that Western ways are not better. It is again not the content that counts but the lesson to be drawn. Such requirements are part of the effort to establish a world community and train its member—the person devoid of prejudice. But if the students were really to learn something of the minds of any of these non-Western cultures—which they do not—they would find that each and every one of these cultures is ethnocentric. All of them think their way is the best way, and all others are inferior. Herodotus tells us that the Persians thought that they were the best, that those nations bordering on them were next best, that those nations bordering on the nations bordering on them were third best, and so on, their worth declining as the concentric circles were farther from the Persian center. This is the very definition of ethnocentrism. Something like this is as ubiquitous as the prohibition against incest between mother and son.

Only in the Western nations, i.e., those influenced by Greek philosophy, is there some willingness to doubt the identification of the good with one's own way. One should conclude from the study of non-Western cultures that not only to prefer one's own way but to believe it best, superior to all others, is primary and even natural—exactly the opposite of what is intended by requiring students to study these cultures. What we are really doing is applying a Western prejudice—which we covertly take to indicate the superiority of our culture—and deforming the evidence of those other cultures to attest to its validity. The scientific study of other cultures is almost exclusively a Western phenomenon, and in its origin was obviously connected with the search for new and better ways, or at least for validation of the hope that our own culture really is the better way, a validation for which there is no felt need in other cultures. If we are to learn from those cultures, we must wonder whether such scientific study is a good idea. Consistency would seem to require professors of openness to respect the ethnocentrism or closedness they find everywhere else. However, in attacking ethnocentrism, what they actually do is to assert unawares the superiority of their scientific understanding and the inferiority of the other cultures which do not recognize it at the same time that they reject all such claims to superiority. They both affirm and deny the goodness of their science. They face a problem akin to that faced by Pascal in the conflict between reason and revelation, without the intellectual intransigence that forced him to abandon science in favor of faith.

The reason for the non-Western closedness, or ethnocentrism, is clear. Men must love and be loyal to their families and their peoples in order to preserve them. Only if they think their own things are good can they rest content with them. A father must prefer his child to other children, a citizen his country to others. That is why there are myths—to justify these attachments. And a man needs a place and opinions by which to orient himself. This is strongly asserted by those who talk about the importance of roots. The problem of getting along with outsiders is secondary to, and sometimes in conflict with, having an inside, a people, a culture, a way of life. A very great narrowness is not incompatible with the health of an individual or a people, whereas with great openness it is hard to avoid decomposition. The firm binding of the good with one's own, the refusal to see a distinction between the two, a vision of the cosmos that has a special place for ones people, seem to be conditions of culture. This is what really follows from the study of non-Western cultures proposed for undergraduates. It points them back to passionate attachment to their own and away from the science which liberates them from it. Science now appears as a threat to culture and a dangerous uprooting charm. In short, they are lost in a no-man's-land between the goodness of knowing and the goodness of culture, where they have been placed by their teachers who no longer have the resources to guide them. Help must be sought elsewhere.

Greek philosophers were the first men we know to address the problem of ethnocentrism. Distinctions between the good and one's own, between nature and convention, between the just and the legal are the signs of this movement of thought. They related the good to the fulfillment of the whole natural human potential and were aware that few, if any, of the nations of men had ways that allowed such fulfillment. They were open to the good. They had to use the good, which was not their own, to judge their own. This was a dangerous business because it tended to weaken wholehearted attachment to their own, hence to weaken their peoples as well as to expose themselves to the anger of family, friends, and countrymen. Loyalty versus quest for the good introduced an unresolvable tension into life. But the awareness of the good as such and the desire to possess it are priceless humanizing acquisitions.

This is the sound motive contained, along with many other less sound ones, in openness as we understand it. Men cannot remain content with what is given them by their culture if they are to be fully human. This is what Plato meant to show by the image of the cave in the *Republic* and by representing us as prisoners in it. A culture is a cave. He did not suggest going around to other cultures as a solution to the limitations of the cave. Nature should be the standard by which we judge our own lives and the lives of peoples. That is why philosophy, not history or anthropology, is the most important human science. Only dogmatic assurance that thought is culture-bound, that there is no nature, is what makes our educators so certain that the only way to escape the limitations of our time and place is to study other cultures. History and anthropology were understood by the Greeks to be useful only in discovering what the past and other peoples had to contribute to the discovery of nature. Historians and anthropologists were to put peoples and their conventions to the test, as Socrates did individuals, and go beyond them. These scientists were superior to their subjects because they saw a problem where others refused to see one, and they were engaged in the quest to solve it. They wanted to be able to evaluate themselves and others.

This point of view, particularly the need to know nature in order to have a standard, is uncomfortably buried beneath our human sciences, whether they like it or not, and accounts for the ambiguities and contradictions I have been pointing out. They want to make us culture-beings with the instruments that were invented to liberate us from culture. Openness used to be the virtue that permitted us to seek the good by using reason. It now means accepting everything and denying reason's power. The unrestrained and thoughtless pursuit of openness, without recognizing the inherent political, social, or cultural problem of openness as the goal of nature, has rendered openness meaningless. Cultural relativism destroys both one's own and the good. What is most characteristic of the West is science, particularly understood as the quest to know nature and the consequent denigration of convention—i.e., culture or the West understood as a culture—in favor of what is accessible to all men as men through their common and distinctive faculty, reason. Science's latest attempts to grasp the human situation—cultural relativism, historicism, the fact-value distinction—are the suicide of science. Culture, hence closedness, reigns supreme. Openness to closedness is what we teach.

Cultural relativism succeeds in destroying the West's universal or intellectually imperialistic claims, leaving it to be just another culture. So there is equality in the republic of cultures. Unfortunately the West is defined by its need for justification of its ways or values, by its need for discovery of nature, by its need for philosophy and science. This is its cultural imperative. Deprived of that, it will collapse. The United States is one of the highest and most extreme achievements of the rational quest for the good life according to nature. What makes its political structure possible is the use of the rational principles of natural right to found a people, thus uniting the good with one's own. Or, to put it otherwise, the regime established here promised untrammeled freedom to reason—not to everything indiscriminately, but to reason, the essential freedom that justifies the other freedoms, and on the basis of which, and for the sake of which, much deviance is also tolerated. An openness that denies the special claim of reason bursts the mainspring keeping the mechanism of this regime in motion. And this regime, contrary to all claims to the contrary, was founded to overcome ethnocentrism, which is in no sense a discovery of social science.

It is important to emphasize that the lesson the students are drawing from their studies is simply untrue. History and the study of cultures do not teach or prove that values or cultures are relative. All to the contrary, that is a philosophical premise that we now bring to our study of them. This premise is unproven and dogmatically asserted for what are largely political reasons. History and culture are interpreted in the light of it, and then are said to prove the premise. Yet the fact that there have been different opinions about good and bad in different times and places in no way proves that none is true or superior to others. To say that it does so prove is as absurd as to say that the diversity of points of view expressed in a college bull session proves there is no truth. On the face of it, the difference of opinion would seem to raise the question as to which is true or right rather than to banish it. The natural reaction is to try to resolve the difference, to examine the claims and reasons for each opinion.

Only the unhistorical and inhuman belief that opinions are held for no reason would prevent the undertaking of such an exciting activity. Men and nations always think they have reasons, and it could be understood to be historians' and social scientists' most important responsibility to make explicit and test those reasons. It was always known that there were many and conflicting opinions about the good, and nations embodying each of them. Herodotus was at least as aware as we are of the rich diversity of cultures. But he took that observation to be an invitation to investigate all of them to see what was good and bad about each and find out what he could learn about good and bad from them. Modern relativists take that same observation as proof that such investigation is impossible and that we must be respectful of them all. Thus students, and the rest of us, are deprived of the primary excitement derived from the discovery of diversity, the impulse of Odysseus, who, according to Dante, traveled the world to see the virtues and vices of men. History and anthropology cannot provide the answers, but they can provide the material on which judgment can work.

I know that men are likely to bring what are only their prejudices to the judgment of alien peoples. Avoiding that is one of the main purposes of education. But trying to prevent it by removing the authority of men's reason is to render ineffective the instrument that can correct their prejudices. True openness is the accompaniment of the desire to know, hence of the awareness of ignorance. To deny the possibility of knowing good and bad is to suppress true openness. A proper historical attitude would lead one to doubt the truth of historicism (the view that all thought is essentially related to and cannot transcend its own time) and treat it as a peculiarity of contemporary history. Historicism and cultural relativism actually are a means to avoid testing our own prejudices and asking, for example, whether men are really equal or whether that opinion is merely a democratic prejudice.

One might well wonder whether our historical and anthropological wisdom is not just a disguised and rather muddled version of the Romantic dilemma that seemed so compelling and tragic at the beginning of the nineteenth century and produced a longing for the distant past or exotic new lands and an art to satisfy that longing. As the heirs of science, so the argument goes, we know more than did the peoples of other times and places with their unscientific prejudices and illusions, but they were, or are, happier. This dilemma is expressed in the distinction between naive and sentimental art. Lévi-Strauss is an unwilling witness to my hypothesis. With a half-digested Rousseauism, he thinks the best culture is to be found at that moment when men have left the state of nature and live together in simple communities, without real private property or the explosion of *amour-propre.* Such a view requires science, which in turn requires developed and corrupted society, in order to emerge. Science is itself one of the modifications of *amour-propre,* the love of inequality. So this view simultaneously produces melancholy about science. But the dilemma seems so compelling only if we are certain that we know so much, which depends on science. Abandon that certainty, and we might be willing to test the beliefs of those happier peoples in order to see if they know something we do not know. Maybe Homer's genius was not so naive as Schiller thought it was. If we abandon this pride in our knowledge, which presents itself as humility, the discussion takes on a new dimension. Then we could go in one of two directions: abandonment of science, or the reestablishment of the theoretical life as both possible and itself productive of self-sufficient happiness. The Romantic posture is a way of not facing these extremes that masquerades as heroic endurance. Our shuttling back and forth between science and culture is a trivialized spin-off from that posture.

Thus there are two kinds of openness, the openness of indifference—promoted with the twin purposes of humbling our intellectual pride and letting us be whatever we want to be, just as long as we don't want to be knowers—and the openness that invites us to the quest for knowledge and certitude, for which history and the various cultures provide a brilliant array of examples for examination. This second kind of openness encourages the desire that animates and makes interesting every serious student—"I want to know what is good for me, what will make me happy"—while the former stunts that desire.

Openness, as currently conceived, is a way of making surrender to whatever is most powerful, or worship of vulgar success, look principled. It is historicism's ruse to remove all resistance to history, which in our day means public opinion, a day when public opinion already rules. How often I have heard the abandonment of requirements to learn languages or philosophy or science lauded as a progress of openness. Here is where the two kinds of openness clash. To be open to knowing, there are certain kinds of things one must know which most people don't want to bother to learn and which appear boring and irrelevant. Even the life of reason is often unappealing; and useless knowledge, i.e., knowledge that is not obviously useful for a career, has no place in the student's vision of the curriculum. So the university that stands intransigently for humane learning must necessarily look closed and rigid. If openness means to "go with the flow," it is necessarily an accommodation to the present. That present is so closed to doubt about so many things impeding the progress of its principles that unqualified openness to it would mean forgetting the despised alternatives to it, knowledge of which makes us aware of what is doubtful in it. True openness means closedness to all the charms that make us comfortable with the present.

When I was a young teacher at Cornell, I once had a debate about education with a professor of psychology. He said that it was his function to get rid of prejudices in his students. He knocked them down like tenpins. I began to wonder what he replaced those prejudices with. He did not seem to have much of an idea of what the opposite of a prejudice might be. He reminded me of the little boy who gravely informed me when I was four that there is no Santa Claus, who wanted me to bathe in the brilliant light of truth. Did this professor know what those prejudices meant for the students and what effect being deprived of them would have? Did he believe that there are truths that could guide their lives as did their prejudices? Had he considered how to give students the love of the truth necessary to seek unprejudiced beliefs, or would he render them passive, disconsolate, indifferent, and subject to authorities like himself, or the best of contemporary thought? My informant about Santa Claus was just showing off, proving his superiority to me. He had not created the Santa Claus that had to be there in order to be refuted. Think of all we learn about the world from men's belief in Santa Clauses, and all that we learn about the soul from those who believe in them. By contrast, merely methodological excision from the soul of the imagination that projects Gods and heroes onto the wall of the cave does not promote knowledge of the soul; it only lobotomizes it, cripples its powers.

I found myself responding to the professor of psychology that I personally tried to teach my students prejudices, since nowadays—with the general success of his method—they had learned to doubt beliefs even before they believed in anything. Without people like me, he would be out of business. Descartes had a whole wonderful world of old beliefs, of prescientific experience and articulations of the order of things, beliefs firmly and even fanatically held, before he even began his systematic and radical doubt. One has to have the experience of really believing before one can have the thrill of liberation. So I proposed a division of labor in which I would help to grow the flowers in the field and he could mow them down.

Prejudices, strong prejudices, are visions about the way things are. They are divinations of the order of the whole of things, and hence the road to a knowledge of that whole is by way of erroneous opinions about it. Error is indeed our enemy, but it alone points to the truth and therefore deserves our respectful treatment. The mind that has no prejudices at the outset is empty. It can only have been constituted by a method that is unaware of how difficult it is to recognize that a prejudice is a prejudice. Only Socrates knew, after a lifetime of unceasing labor, that he was ignorant. Now every high-school student knows that. How did it become so easy? What accounts for our amazing progress? Could it be that our experience has been so impoverished by our various methods, of which openness is only the latest, that there is nothing substantial enough left there to resist criticism, and we therefore have no world left of which to be really ignorant? Have we so simplified the soul that it is no longer difficult to explain? To an eye of dogmatic skepticism, nature herself, in all her lush profusion of expressions, might appear to be a prejudice. In her place we put a gray network of critical concepts, which were invented to interpret nature's phenomena but which strangled them and therewith destroyed their own *raison d'être.* Perhaps it is our first task to resuscitate those phenomena so that we may again have a world to which we can put our questions and be able to philosophize. This seems to me to be our educational challenge.

CHAPTER 18

THROUGH THE LOOKING GLASS

LAWRENCE W. LEVINE

The titles of the best-known books on contemporary higher education published in the past decade are instructive:

The Closing of the American Mind: How Higher Education Has Failed Democracy and Impoverished the Souls of Today's Students
Profscam: Professors and the Demise of Higher Education
The War Against the Intellect: Episodes in the Decline of Discourse
Tenured Radicals: Horn Politics Has Corrupted Our Higher Education

Killing the Spirit: Higher Education in America
The Hollow Men: Politics and Corruption in Higher Education
Illiberal Education: The Politics of Race and Sex on Campus
The De-Valuing of America: The Fight for Our Culture and Our Children

Impostors in the Temple: American Intellectuals Are Destroying Our Universities and Cheating Our Students of Their Future
Dictatorship of Virtue: Multiculturalism and the Battle for America's Future[1]

It's a small growth industry, this jeremiad against the universities and the professoriate, this series of claims that something has suddenly turned sour in the academe, that the Pure Aims and Honest Values and True Worth of the past have been sullied and fouled by politics, by radicals disguised as professors, by academics consulting only their own interests and completely ignoring those of the students and the society. The charges go on and on, and the tone, as these book tides suggest, is relentlessly apocalyptic.

Patrick Buchanan's assertion during the presidential campaign of 1992 that we were engaged in a war "for the soul of America . . . cultural war, as critical to the kind of nation we will one day be as was the Cold War itself," is echoed again and again in the struggle over the university, and these reverberating echoes have created a culture of hyperbole. The choice facing us today, Roger Kimball cautioned in his assault on contemporary higher education, is "between culture and barbarism." Thomas Aquinas College of Santa Paula, California, advertised its "civilized education for the serious student" under a logo featuring a salivating wolf, teeth bared, wearing an academic mortarboard cap. "Many in today's academy," the ad warned, "bare their teeth, not only at our traditions of government, economics, and social order, but also at the very civilization that gave birth to the university." In 1991 the columnist George F. Will charged that disagreements over the curriculum were "related battles in a single war, a war of aggression against the Western political

Source: "Through the Looking Glass," by Lawrence W. Levine, reprinted from *The Opening of the American Mind: Canons, Culture, and History*, 1996, Beacon Press.

tradition and the ideas that animate it." He declared that Lynn Cheney, who as head of the National Endowment for the Humanities was one of the nation's most vocal critics of universities, was our "secretary of domestic defense." The foreign adversaries that her husband, Secretary of Defense Richard Cheney, faced "are less dangerous, in the long run, than the domestic forces with which she must deal." What is at stake in the battles among intellectuals on the American campus, the sociologist Brigitte Berger assured a *Partisan Review* symposium, is nothing less than "the legitimacy of the Western academic tradition and the cultural values upon which it rests."[2]

In his journal the *New Criterion,* Hilton Kramer inveighed against allowing "the trash of popular culture" onto the campus and declared, "It is our civilization that we believe to be at stake in this struggle." While Kramer spied disaster in professors wallowing in the muck of popular culture, former Secretary of Education William Bennett accused them of the opposite crime, hating the "vulgar" culture of everyday Americans: "If the middle class likes it—be it conventional morality, patriotism, Ronald Reagan, or even *Rocky,* light beer, cookouts, or Disney World—that alone is enough for many of the elites to disdain it." According to Bennett, this all-out academic assault against the tastes and values of the American people has taken its toll: "We ceased being clear about the standards which we hold and the principles by which we judge. . . . As a result, we suffered a cultural breakdown."[3]

The same double bind applies to the subject of politics. If contemporary academics pay attention to politics they are being political, and if they ignore politics they are being political. In either case they are censured as political advocates rather than scholars. George F. Will has used the term "Academic Marxists" to describe those who envision culture as reflecting such broad societal forces as politics and thus deny what Will calls "the autonomy of culture." To suggest that Shakespeare's *Tempest* comments on the imperialism of Elizabethan England robs the play of its aesthetic qualities and reduces it to "a mere index of who had power and whom the powerful victimized." This works to "strip literature of its authority" and opens the way to "social disintegration, which is the political goal of the victim revolution that is sweeping campuses." On the other hand, the historian Gertrude Himmelfarb has used the same term—"Marxists"—to label social historians who pay *insufficient* attention to politics and ignore Aristotle's admonition that "man is by nature a political animal." Where the old history "features kings, presidents, politicians, leaders, political theorists," she complained, "the new takes as its subject the `anonymous masses.'" "Marxism," she concluded, "has succeeded . . . in demeaning and denigrating political events, institutions, activities, and ideas."[4]

Whatever the specifics of the charges, contemporary critics of the university agree that higher education in the United States faces a threat more dire than any in its history and they illustrate their charges in a rollicking blizzard of assertions and accusations. In *The Closing of the American Mind,* which spent thirty-one weeks on the *New York Times* best-seller list, sold some 800,000 copies in its original edition, and was the second best-selling hardback book of 1987, Allan Bloom argued that the student, feminist, and Black power movements of the 1960s and 1970s had resulted in the "democratization of the university" which led to "the collapse of the entire American educational structure." His direct historical analogy was with the populism of Nazi Germany. He compared the New Left to Nazi Youth, the Woodstock concert to the Nuremberg Rally, and the professors who "collaborated" with the American student movements to such supporters of Hitler as Martin Heidegger, the Nazi Rector of Freiburg University. In the fall of 1988 at the first national meeting of the conservative National Association of Scholars (NAS), the historian Alan Kors received a standing ovation when he warned that "the barbarians are in our midst" and enjoined his colleagues "to fight them a good long time." At the second national meeting of the NAS in the spring of 1990, Kors received another standing ovation by urging his colleagues to create within their own ranks "the monasteries of a new dark ages, preserving what is worth preserving amid the barbaric ravages in the countrysides and towns of academe."[5]

The journalist Richard Bernstein compared academic multiculturalists to the "Red Guards of China's Great Proletarian Cultural Revolution" and salted his book about the university with words like "terror," "atrocity," "assault," "dictatorship," and "demagogues," while Robert

Hughes peppered his with "PC-mongers," "lefty thought police," and "PC claptrap." The late Page Smith called the university "a classic Frankenstein monster" and compared the process of achieving university tenure "to ancient rites of human sacrifice." Not to be outdone, Charles Sykes equated curricular change with "the burning of books," and called the contemporary university a "ghetto of appalling intellectual squalor and mediocrity," inhabited by "the obscurantists, sorcerers, and witch doctors of profthink." In his best-selling *Illiberal Education,* Dinesh D'Souza asserted that by the time students graduate, universities have taught them that "all rules are unjust," that individual rights "should be subordinated to the claims of group interest," that "convenient myths and benign lies can substitute for truth," that "justice is simply the will of the stronger party," that "the university stands for nothing in particular," and that "the multiracial society cannot be based on fair rules that apply to every person."[6]

The very manner of their presentation confirmed the apocalyptic tone of many of these condemnations. *New York Magazine* illustrated John Taylor's attack on "political correctness" in the United States with pictures of Nazi youth smiling into the camera as they burned books in the 1930s and Red Guards in Communist China parading academic "dunces" in the 1960s. In 1995 the front cover of the *San Francisco Examiner Magazine* announced an article on multiculturalism by its senior editor Gary Kamiya featuring a white plaster bust of the German composer Richard Wagner with a red book bearing the title *The Multicultural Handbook* in German gothic print opened like a dunce cap on his head, and on his breast in dripping red letters (ink? blood?) the words: "NO DEAD WHITE EUROMALES."[7]

There is no deeper orthodoxy in the minds of contemporary critics of the university than the notion that the university has been politicized and is now controlled by what Roger Kimball has called "tenured radicals." The scenario is simple and is reiterated so often that it appears to be one of those evident truths not even open for discussion. The New Left of the 1960s, having lost the battle in the streets, retreated to the university which it now dominates. According to Robert Brustein, a Harvard professor of Drama and English, "Many, if not most, of today's PC leaders were active members of the New Left twenty-five years ago." The very same radical students who "once occupied university buildings over the Vietnam War, are now officially occupying university offices as professors, administrators, deans, and even presidents." New Left veterans, the historian John Diggins agrees, "are tenured professors within the system and now have the means of expounding their ideas to a captive college audience. The New Left is an idea whose time has passed and whose power has come." George Roche, the president of Hillsdale College in Michigan, argues that once they became the "Establishment on campus," the political and intellectual radicals of the 1960s "took their liberal-left agenda on race, class, and gender and camouflaged it under a mantle of 'diversity,' like the nets of fake foliage used to disguise tanks in Operation Desert Storm." Thus concealed, the "diversity troops" waged a successful war against traditional values and academic discipline. "They have fomented . . . a revolution that is certainly one of the most critical events in modern times." Wilcomb E. Washburn of the Smithsonian Institution spread the alarming news that "academic radicals" have been so dominant on campus that a "small minority" has been able to train "the vast majority of those who write, broadcast, or engage in supporting activities in the press, radio, television, cinema and other opinion-shaping non-academic institutions." One certainly cannot argue with Roger Kimball when he writes, "It has often been observed that yesterday's student radical is today's professor or academic dean." It has indeed![8]

The assumption that large parts of the academe are now controlled by radicals has led to the conviction that the objective search for truth, which once characterized the university, has been eclipsed by conscious partisan advocacy. Professors, of course, have always advocated things in the classroom: sound scholarship, the scientific method, an intelligible writing style, hard work, reading and more reading, and often even independent thinking. But we rarely call these things "advocacy." For the most part in the past one *taught* subjects and approaches and techniques and scholarly ideals, one did not advocate them. There have been periodic exceptions. At the turn of the last century, those teaching Darwinian biology were accused by some of advocacy. During World War I, the teaching of the German language, German literature, or German music was sometimes met by cries of advocacy. Following both world wars, teaching about the Soviet Union or employing a Marxist approach, or even stressing economic causation too vigorously could earn one the same accusation. But it has been left to our own time to normalize what had hitherto been an occasional practice so that entire subjects and whole schools of interpretation are now branded with the hot irons of radical advocacy and political correctness.

Following the lead of Allan Bloom who likened feminism to the "Terror" that followed the French Revolution and who asserted that the "latest enemy of the vitality of classic texts is feminism" since "the Muses never sang to the poets about liberated women," many of these charges have been leveled at women's studies. Page Smith announced in 1990 that by his "rough calculations" there were "approximately" eighty courses focusing on women at the University of California, Santa Cruz, "virtually" all taught by women faculty members. This situation, according to Smith, had some positive consequences: "My impression is that women teachers take a far more personal interest in their students/recruits than do their male counterparts. The older ones play a warm, supportive, mothering role for immature and uncertain young women." But once we move away from mothering and nurturing, the fact that "women have, in effect, seized control over a substantial part of the curriculum," has had uniformly negative results. Smith declared that there are now two Universities of California in Santa Cruz: the "Male Division" where "the traditional pieties still prevail . . . science, objectivity, scholarship," and the "Female Division" where "all pretense of objectivity . . . has been cast aside." Smith's sole documentation for the existence of what he calls "this internal armed feminist camp" is the proliferation of courses in women's studies. Similarly, Charles Sykes counted 50 separate centers devoted to women's issues and 530 programs offering over 30,000 courses in women's studies, and concluded on the basis of this quantitative evidence alone that "obviously women need a vanguard revolutionary elite, just as the proletariat did to lead them to revolutionary consciousness. In its Leninist formulation, this idea is discredited in every capital of Eastern Europe, Moscow not excepted. Miraculously, it is reborn in feminist academia and thus in the curriculum of many of America's elite universities."[9]

When Richard Bernstein of the *New York Times* visited the annual meeting of the American Historical Association in 1987, his sense of the appropriate and significant was offended: "Gone were what I thought of as the Grand Themes, the declines and falls of empires, the waxing and waning of civilizations, the struggles of competing armies, the achievements of Great Men and Women." Instead of the subjects he deemed appropriate, he noted panels on "Women's Definitions of Love Throughout Western History," "Sex, Gender and the Constitution," "Black Women in the Work Force," and "Sodomy and Pederasty Among 19th-Century Seafarers," and without discussing the contents of those papers or the significance of their findings, he concluded that group politics had "replaced even the ideal of disinterestedness," and that "for many historians, history had become advocacy." Once again, the mere presence of certain subjects was all the proof necessary. James Atlas of the *New York Times Magazine* inspected the reading list for one of Stanford's new Culture, Ideas, Values freshman courses in 1989 and reported that along with the Bible, Aeschylus, and Shakespeare, "one finds *With a Pistol in His Hand* by Americo Paredes, *He Who Does Evil Should Expect No Good* by Juana Manuela Gorritti, and something called *Documents from the Tupac Amani Rebellion.*" Atlas fails to tell us what the subject or purpose of the course was and how the readings did or did not fit together to accomplish that purpose. Nor does he demonstrate any familiarity with the latter three books—Paredes's *With a Pistol in His Hand,* for instance, is a superb, original, and deeply scholarly study of Mexican and Mexican American folk culture and thought as manifested in a *corrida* (ballad) about a Mexican bandit. Nevertheless, Atlas concluded that "the presence of such a reading list . . . makes it hard to dismiss as paranoia Hilton Kramer's contention that universities are now firmly in the hands of the radical left." Finding evidence of radicalism in the very title of books whose substance is not examined has become standard practice. Again and again, critics trot out the paper "Jane Austen and the Masturbating Girl," presented by Eve Sedgwick at the 1989 annual meeting of the Modern Language Association. This is probably one of the most heavily cited and least read scholarly papers in history. What it actually says is never discussed and seems to be beside the point; its title—its subject—alone suffices as incontrovertible proof of the advocacy that seriously threatens the academe.[10]

On the day before Christmas, 1990, Charles Krauthammer in his nationally syndicated column announced the death of communism and socialism and asked, "What's left of the left?" His answer: The environmental movement, the antiwar movement, and the literary theory known as deconstruction. Of the three, he concluded, deconstruction posed the most serious threat: "America will survive both Saddam and the snail darter. But the . . . fracturing . . . of the American idea, poses a threat that no outside agent in this post-Soviet world can match." Roger Kimball has epitomized this entire mode of thought by charging that such new subjects and approaches as "women's studies, black studies, gay studies, . . . deconstruction, poststructuralism, new historicism" are "politically motivated" and contain "a blueprint for a radical social transformation that would revolutionize every aspect of social and political life, from the independent place we grant high culture within society to the way we relate to one another as men and women."[11]

Fears of an eroding hierarchy and the encroachment of a democratic society into the academe, as reflected in both the curriculum and the student body, are at the heart of many of the critiques of contemporary higher education. After reading Plato's *Symposium*, a student came to Allan Bloom "with deep melancholy and said it was impossible to imagine that magic Athenian atmosphere reproduced." Bloom assured him that such experiences "are always accessible . . . right under our noses, improbable but always present." But only for a small elite. "The real community of man . . . the community of those who seek the truth, of the potential knowers, . . . includes only a few, the true friends, as Plato was to Aristotle." Bloom contrasted this true community with the spirit of democracy, now all too prevalent on our campuses, which tends "to suppress the claims of any kind of superiority." Comparing today's universities with his memories of the halcyon days he spent as a student at Dartmouth College, Martin Anderson has written with disdain of the transformation he claims has taken place over the past few decades: "From the rather small, quiet dignified institutions of rarefied scholarly pursuits and the teaching of a select few," the "hallowed halls of ivy" have "ballooned . . . staffed by hundreds of thousands of men and women who call themselves professors, offering courses to millions of students."[12]

This expanded student body and faculty have brought the outside world within the walls of the university and have radically altered the curriculum according to the critics. "Superman is as worthy of study as Shakespeare," Gertrude Himmelfarb has charged. "Comic books are as properly a part of the curriculum as *Hamlet* or *Macbeth*." The concern goes beyond popular culture to the inclusion in the curriculum of groups previously ignored. Thus James Atlas complained that the college boards in history "now offer questions on child-rearing practices and the place of women in society," and submitted the following as a disturbing example: "How and why did the lives and status of northern middle-class women change between 1776 and 1876?" Atlas admitted, "It's not a bad question, actually; but how many seventeen-year-olds are prepared to answer it?" The real issue, of course, is the nature of the questions we prepare our students to answer: Should their education include the lives and culture of everyday people? A traditional liberal arts education, Roger Kimball has asserted, "is unquestionably elitist in the sense that it focuses on the pinnacle of human cultural and intellectual achievement," but no longer is "everyone . . . either interested in or capable of taking advantage of a liberal arts education conceived in this way." On a visit to his beloved Harvard, James Atlas was so bewildered by the existence of English Department courses dealing with politics and literature, women in Victorian society, Blacks and Whites in American culture, the rise of mass culture, and family relations and sexuality in the eighteenth-century novel, that he could only turn to a line of W. B. Yeats: "The world is changed, changed utterly"[13]

The extremity of the charges against the university is easily converted to nostalgia for a better past and a sense of dread concerning the future unless something is done to reverse the course universities are now pursuing. Allan Bloom affords a good example. He longed for the time when the university was concerned with the student's *entire* being and conceived as its function the transference of youthful sexual energies to urges of a more metaphysical nature. A significant number of students used to arrive at the university "physically and spiritually virginal, expecting to lose their innocence there. Their . . . literal lust for knowledge, was what a teacher could see in the eyes of those who flattered him by giving such evidence of their need for him. His own satisfaction was promised by having something with which to feed their hunger, an overflow to bestow on their emptiness. His joy was in hearing the ecstatic 'Oh, yes!' as he dished up Shakespeare and Hegel to minister to their need. Pimp and midwife really described him well." Today's students "sated with easy, clinical and sterile satisfactions of body and soul, . . . hardly walk on the enchanted ground they once did . . . they do not seek wholeness in the university."[14]

According to Bloom, once there were many students "who actually knew something about and loved England, France, Germany, or Italy, for they dreamed of living there or thought their lives would be made more interesting by assimilating their languages and literatures." These students have "almost disappeared," to be replaced by those "who are interested in the political problems of Third World countries and in helping them to modernize, with due respect to their old cultures, of course." It is, Bloom grumbled, "the Peace Corps mentality, which is not a spur to learning but to a secularized version of doing good works." Sexual liberation, Bloom maintained, made it impossible for students to learn about their sexual beings from old literature "which from the Garden of Eden on made coupling a very dark and complicated business. On reflection, today's students wonder what all the fuss was about." No longer do they imagine that the sexual plots of such writers as Flaubert, Tolstoy, Shakespeare, or the authors of romantic fiction "could teach them anything about the relations they want to have or will be permitted to have. So they are indifferent." Thirty years ago, Bloom insisted, "university students usually had some early emotive association with Beethoven, Chopin and Brahms, which was a permanent part of their makeup and to which they were likely to respond throughout their lives. This was probably the only regularly recognizable class distinction between educated and uneducated in America." Today, students' musical sensibilities are scarred by rock music which, like all popular culture, Bloom characterized as "pseudo-art" containing "nothing noble, sublime, profound, delicate, tasteful or even decent" with "room only for the intense, changing, crude and immediate." As long as young people "have the Walkman on," Bloom warned, "they cannot hear what the great tradition has to say. And, after its prolonged use, when they take it off, they find they are deaf." In area after area, Bloom portrayed contemporary college students as a generation in serious decline who "know so much less, are so much more cut off from the tradition, are so much slacker intellectually, that they make their predecessors look like prodigies of culture. The soil is ever thinner, and I doubt whether it can now sustain the taller growths."[15]

Much of this nostalgia is fueled by a faulty sense of the history of the American university. We are told again and again that until the 1960s university education was ruled by the study of Western Civilization and a canon of the Great Books. In fact, Great Books and Western Civilization courses enjoyed only a brief ascendancy: they emerged largely after World War I and declined in the decades after World War II. The canon and the curriculum that were supposedly governed by Matthew Arnold's dictum of "the best that has been thought and known in the world . . . the study and pursuit of perfection," were in truth never static and were constantly in the process of revision with irate defenders insisting, as they still do, that change would bring with it instant decline. The inclusion of "modern" writers from Shakespeare to Walt Whitman and Herman Melville came only after prolonged battles as intense and divisive as those that rage today. Thus when John Searle maintains that "until recently" there was no controversy over the existence of a widely agreed upon corpus of writers, knowledge of whom was "essential to the liberal education of young men and women in the United States," he is oversimplifying to the point of distortion, as Part II of this book will demonstrate. What is happening in the contemporary university is by no means out of the ordinary; certainly it is not a radical departure from the patterns that have marked the history of the university—constant and often controversial expansion and alteration of curricula and canons and incessant struggle over the nature of that expansion and alteration.[16]

None of these realities stop James Atlas from asserting: "The Great Books. The best that is known and thought in the world. The canon," were "until a few years ago . . . our educational mandate." We would all benefit if those who tell us where to go understood more clearly where we have been. Atlas, who attended Harvard from 1967 to 1971 and is grateful for what he gained from his years there, can't help longing for an earlier, more glorious day: "What my classmates and I managed to learn in those four years couldn't begin to compare with the knowledge absorbed by earlier generations of students, for whom the study of literature included the study of Greek and Latin classics in the original." Fortunately, we can turn directly to the students he envies who, while they did indeed read the "classics" in the original Greek and Latin, read them not as works of literature but as examples of *grammar,* the rules of which they studied endlessly and by rote. James Freeman Clark, who received his Harvard A.B. in 1829, complained, "No attempt was made to interest us in our studies. We were expected to wade through Homer as though the Iliad were a bog. . . . Nothing was said of the glory and grandeur, the tenderness and charm of this immortal epic. The melody of the hexameters was never suggested to us." Henry Adams proclaimed his years at Harvard from 1854 to 1858 "wasted" and exclaimed in his autobiography: "It taught little, and that little ill. . . . Beyond two or three Greek plays, the student got nothing from the ancient languages." Adams wrote of himself. "He could not afterwards remember to have heard the name of Karl Marx mentioned, or the title of 'Capital.' He was equally ignorant of Auguste Comte. These were the two writers of his time who most influenced its thought." "The entire work of the four years," Adams concluded, "could have been easily put into the work of any four months in after life."[17]

Atlas is on equally shaky ground when he locates the Golden Age at my alma mater. The City College of New York "of forty or fifty years ago," he tells us, operated on such a high plane of excellence that it "seems infinitely remote in time" and we, with our debased standards, cannot even imagine its lofty existence. "Things have gone too far," he laments. " . . . We're on the verge of a new barbarism." Atlas's bleak conclusion is based upon the degradation of higher education he and his fellow critics are convinced has taken place in our own time. Here, for example, is a description in *Newsday* of the university in which I have spent most of my teaching career: "Our first major university with a multiracial, white-minority student body, Berkeley has become a tense no-man's-land of mutually exclusive cultural turfs, where Western civilization is being reduced to something called European-American ethnic studies, and where white students anxiously watch their every word to avoid 'politically incorrect' speech."[18]

In the face of statements like these, which by now are quite common, I feel like Alice in Wonderland living in a topsy-turvy universe that has little to do with my experiences and understanding. Convinced by everything I know and have seen that the American academic world is doing a more thorough and cosmopolitan job of educating a greater diversity of students in a broader and sounder array of courses covering the past and present of the worlds they inhabit than ever before in its history, I walk through the Looking Glass and find myself surrounded by those who see our enterprise as unhealthy and unreliable, built not on the solid foundations of serious inquiry and innovative approaches but on the sands of fashion and politics and coercion.

Both the City College of New York (CCNY) and the University of California at Berkeley have been institutions of the greatest importance in my life. I was a history major at CCNY from 1950 to 1955, the very years Atlas points to as a Pinnacle we can hardly see through the fog of our own decline. I subsequently taught at Berkeley for thirty-two years, from 1962 to 1994, the very years of the presumed Great Decline of the American university. The profound debt I owe City College, which changed my life for the better in a myriad of ways and enabled me not only to dream dreams but to fulfill them, cannot alter the fact that the education I received there does not begin to compare in any respect (save the quality of my classmates) to the one I've been part of during the past few decades at Berkeley. The history courses I took at CCNY required that I read very fat and exceedingly dull and predictable textbooks which rarely diverged from a straightforward narrative, political, Mover-and-Shaker, Whiggish historical approach which recounted a story of never-ending progress. I learned almost nothing about workers, slaves, immigrants, children, or women. I learned almost nothing about how people acted in their families, their churches, their homes, their places of work, what they did with their leisure time, how they felt about their lives and the lives of those about them. I learned nothing about Africa or Asia after the ancient period, nothing about South America and the Caribbean after the Age of Discovery, nothing about the indigenous cultures that once inhabited the very territory I was now living in, nothing about Canada or Australia, nothing about Eastern or Southern Europe after the Classical Era. Vast geographical areas encompassing most of the world's surface, entire cultures, whole peoples remained a wasteland to me and most of my peers.

I clutched my bachelor's degree as I left City College to enter a world most of whose peoples and cultures I knew virtually nothing about. Students at Berkeley are both more burdened and more privileged. They have an array of courses to choose from and requirements to meet that had no parallels in my undergraduate career. They have to read far more than we did, and generally write more as well, and they are treated to a spectrum of history encompassing more peoples and subjects and realities than we could have even imagined in my generation. The depth and range and diversity and sophistication of history education today simply exceeds anything I experienced in my student days. I certainly have not seen as much progress as I had hoped in most aspects of American life, and I have seen almost none in far too many, but higher education has been a happy exception.

It is precisely these developments that trouble so many of the critics whose lament is less about politics in the classroom than about the cultural changes that have taken place in the university. The advocacy they complain about most vigorously is cultural rather than political in nature. It is the *openness* of the contemporary university that is so threatening and the complexity of the education available to students today that is so disturbing to the university's most vigorous detractors. The title of Bloom's *The Closing of the American Mind* was paradoxical. His real target was what he called "the recent education of openness." He characterized the contemporary university as "open to all kinds of men, all kinds of lifestyles, all ideologies," and thus "closed" to the absolute truths of the classical writings and great books that alone constitute true education. Bloom identified the real villain as cultural relativism which he defined as the conviction that all societies and values and beliefs are as "good" as all others. Bloom's anxiety was not relieved by the fact that what cultural relativism commonly taught students is not to make a simple-minded equation between everything as equal, but rather to be open to the reality that all peoples and societies have cultures which we have to respect to the extent that we take the trouble to understand how they operate and what they believe. Bloom found this perspective no less dangerous since it opens students to the possibility that their culture is not necessarily superior and potentially weakens the conviction that Western culture and "Civilization" are synonymous. He condemned contemporary education for "destroying the West's universal or intellectually imperialistic claims, leaving it to be just another culture." Bloom insisted that the permanent and natural state between cultures is one of Darwinian competition. Values, he argued, "can only be asserted or posited by overcoming others, not by reasoning with them. Cultures have different *perceptions*, which determine what the world is. They cannot come to terms. There is no communication about the highest things. . . . Culture means a war against chaos and a war against other cultures."[19]

Writing of the demands to include in the curriculum "populations and points of view that have been 'marginalized,'" "popular culture," "the tradition essential to *un*educated Americans," "native American influences," "Africa," Roger Kimball warned that "a swamp yawns open before us, ready to devour everything. The best response to all this—and finally the only serious and effective response—is not to enter these murky waters in the first place. As Nietzsche observed, we do not refute a disease. We resist it." Richard Bernstein characterized the efforts to demystify Christopher Columbus—whom he calls "our William the Conqueror, our Joan of Arc, our Alexander Nevsky"—begun over a hundred years ago during the celebration of the four-hundredth anniversary of Columbus's voyage and revived with much greater force in 1992, as attempts "to replace healthy nation-building myths with dangerous quests for the complicated truth." Commenting on proposed new curricula for New York elementary and secondary schools, James Atlas lamented, "From now on it won't be enough to know the capital of Idaho or who Pocahantas was; seventh-graders will be expected to know why they should know these facts and not others: `The subject matter content should be *treated as socially constructed* and therefore tentative—as is all knowledge.' Deconstructionism comes to P.S. 87." I can't refrain from commenting that if this be "deconstructionism," I wish it had come to Junior High School its when I was a student there in the 1940s. We had no idea why we were learning what we learned, no clue to how and to what end the facts fed to us were chosen. It was this ignorance of *why* that made history such a perennially dreary subject to legions of students and that makes so many adults to this day, when they hear that I'm a historian, mumble with a combination of guilt and aggression, "History was always my least favorite subject," or, "I *hated* history in school."[20]

The "traditional" curriculum that prevailed so widely in the decades between the World Wars, and whose decline is lamented with such fervor by the conservative critics, ignored most of the groups that compose the American population whether they were from Africa, Europe, Asia, Central and South America, or from indigenous North American peoples. The primary and often exclusive focus was upon a narrow stratum of those who came from a few Northern and Western European countries whose cultures and mores supposedly became the archetype for those of all Americans in spite of the fact that in reality American culture was forged out of a much larger and more diverse complex of peoples and societies. In addition, this curriculum did not merely teach Western ideas and culture, it taught the *superiority* of Western ideas and culture; it equated Western ways and thought with "Civilization" itself. This tendency is still being championed by contemporary critics of the university. "Is it Eurocentric to believe the life of liberty is superior to the life of the beehive?" Charles Krauthammer inquired in his justification of the European conquest of the Americas. Without pretending to have studied the cultures of Asia or Africa in any depth, Secretary of Education William Bennett did not hesitate to inform the faculty and students of Stanford University that "the West is a source of *incomparable* intellectual complexity and diversity and depth."[21]

To say that a curriculum that questions these parochial assumptions is somehow anti-Western or anti-intellectual is to misunderstand the aims of education. If in fact the traditions of Western science and humanities mean what they say, modern universities are performing precisely the functions institutions of higher learning should perform: to stretch the boundaries of our understanding; to teach the young to value our intellectual heritage not by rote but through comprehension and examination; to continually and perpetually subject the "wisdom" of our society to thorough and thoughtful scrutiny while making the "wisdom" of other societies and other cultures accessible and subject to comparable scrutiny; to refuse to simplify our culture beyond recognition by limiting our focus to only one segment of American society and instead to open up the *entire* society to thoughtful examination.

To require more careful study and more convincing documentation for the charges against the university is not to be pedantic or picayune; it is to hold the critics of the university to the same scholarly standards and the same humanistic values they claim the university itself has abandoned. The irony is that the critics of the contemporary university too often have become parodies of the very thing they're criticizing: ideologues whose research is shallow and whose findings are widely and deeply flawed by exaggerated claims, vituperative attacks, defective evidence, and inadequate knowledge of the history of the university in the United States and of the process by which canons and curricula have been formed and reformed since the beginning of American higher education.

While performing the high task of protecting knowledge and scholarly standards against "barbarians," it is obviously not always possible to observe the purest scholarly standards oneself. Dinesh D'Souza's "research" technique, for example, is summed up by the following incident. While visiting the Berkeley campus of the University of California, he wanted to speak with "Asian American students" as part of his investigation. Students of Asian ancestry then constituted roughly one-third of the undergraduates at Berkeley, but D'Souza had trouble locating interviewees: "It is not easy to find an Asian student willing to talk at Berkeley. I passed up two or three who would talk only on condition of anonymity. I approached one student waiting for the library to open, but he was too eager not to miss a minute of reading time. Eventually I found Thuy Nguyen, a cheerful woman who turned out to be a student at UC-Davis. She knew all about Berkeley, though; she was visiting her friend Cynthia Dong, an undergraduate there." Thus his entire direct testimony from "Berkeley" students of Asian descent—a designation covering a wide variety of peoples and cultures—comes from a student enrolled not at Berkeley but at the University of California at Davis, a campus sixty miles away. Ironically,

D'Souza's approach is all too typical of those whose concern about the declining standards and ideals of the academic world has led them to level blistering attacks against it.[22]

After a tour of universities Charles Sykes reported back that "tens of thousands of books and hundreds of thousands of journal articles . . . bloat libraries with masses of unread, unreadable, and worthless pablum." Alas, we never learn whether Mr. Sykes knows this because he himself has performed the heroic task of carefully examining the tens of thousands of books and hundreds of thousands of articles, or if he is synthesizing the Herculean labors of other investigators who remain anonymous, or if he is merely *assuming* that so many books and articles that sit so inertly on library shelves simply *must* be "worthless pablum." Robert Hughes too can't resist the trap of pretending to be able to sum up the scholarly world without having done more than dip the edge of a toenail into it. "With certain outstanding exceptions like Edward Said, Simon Schama or Robert Darnton," he declared, "relatively few of the people who are actually writing first-rate history, biography or cultural criticism in America have professorial tenure." Since in his entire volume Hughes cites only six works of history directly in his notes, it is impossible to discern how he arrived at this ludicrous judgment of the discipline of history which is in one of its most exciting and original periods and has in the past several decades produced large numbers of significant works that have advanced our thinking about the past considerably.[23]

Without taking the trouble to conduct an actual investigation, Martin Anderson, a Fellow at the Hoover Institution, decided: "The work of scholars that is relevant to the critical issues facing Americans is almost nonexistent." This self-generated observation led him to the conclusion that "taken as a whole, academic research and writing is the greatest intellectual fraud of the twentieth century." Based upon precisely the same sort of self-referential "analysis," the historian Page Smith concluded that "the vast majority of the so-called research turned out in the modern university is essentially worthless," though obviously he could have had no actual familiarity with "the vast majority" of university research, most of which is in fields he knew nothing about. Similarly, Allan Bloom presented no evidence whatever to document his assertions that students today appreciate classical music less than they did thirty years ago, or that sexual liberation has robbed them of their ability to relate to the novels of the past, or that students no longer think about or want to visit the countries of Western Europe. Bloom's "research," apart from his own limited personal experience, was primarily internal, conducted largely in the archives of his own mind and the precincts of the sensibilities of the ancient writers as he envisioned them.[24]

In his influential polemic *Tenured Radicals,* Roger Kimball spoke about the "decanonization" of dead, White, European men in recent years but presented no evidence that writers like Shakespeare are actually studied less now than they were before the 1960s. In fact, the most exhaustive surveys of college and university literature courses conducted in 1984–85 and again in 1990 provide no documentation for this accusation made so frequently by conservative critics. The earlier survey concluded that "courses are added to expand the curriculum, not to replace traditional offerings, which remain in place as core requirements for the English major." Of the courses that 80 percent of the English departments insisted their majors take, the three most frequently required were survey courses in British literature, American literature, and Shakespearian drama. The 1990 survey of over nine hundred English teachers indicated that courses in nineteenth-century American literature featured such authors as Nathaniel Hawthorne, Henry David Thoreau, Herman Melville, and Ralph Waldo Emerson, while previously neglected writers like Frederick Douglass and Harriet Beecher Stowe made their way into the curriculum very gradually. "The major works and authors remain preeminent in the courses surveyed," the report concluded. The ways in which curricular change and tradition can and do coexist and constitute the substance of the contemporary university are simply ignored in the impassioned culture of hyperbole which pictures Alice Walker and Toni Morrison displacing Shakespeare.[25]

Like Allan Bloom, Kimball and many of his fellow critics jump from rhetoric to assumption, from assumption to assertion, from assertion to fact. Author after author, critic after critic have recited the catechism concerning how the New Left has captured the academic world. One searches in vain for evidence, for citations, for documentation. Some truths, it seems, are too obvious to require the needless paraphernalia of scholarship. But not too obvious to need constant reiteration so that once again the unproven assertion becomes "documented" through the sheer force of repetition. In 1992, the historian John Diggins asserted that "in the field of American history . . . a liberal Ph.D. who subscribed to consensus instead of class conflict, or a white male conservative who admired Madison more than Marx, had about as much chance of getting hired on some faculty as Woody Allen of starting as point guard for the Knicks." Though Diggins's claim was unaccompanied by any evidence whatever, Lynn Cheney in her 1992 report as chairman of the National Endowment for the Humanities cited it as a "fact" to document her own allegation that a political agenda now often dominated universities and their faculties. Similarly, Professor Jerry Z. Muller has written that political correctness "is a consequence of the institutionalization within the academy of a cohort of New Leftists who came of age politically in the 1960s, who lecture on egalitarianism while practicing elitism, and who exert disproportionate influence through their organizational zeal and commitment to academic politics," and cited Diggins's own totally unsupported assertion that the New Left dominates as his sole "proof." This kind of uninformed and underresearched generalizing is done ostensibly *in defense* of the university by those who seem to understand, or at least to care, little about its purposes, standards, and approaches.[26]

Charges of political advocacy against the university are made also through the process of transforming norms into extremes. Hostility to the writings of "Dead White European Males" is attributed to any scholar who would supplement the canon with the work of those who have been traditionally excluded from it. Afrocentrism and multiculturalism are made synonymous by simply ignoring the large and sophisticated body of recent scholarship on ethnicity which has nothing to do with Afrocentrism or Eurocentrism. Practices and processes that have long exemplified the academe are made to appear to be the contemporary fruits of advocacy. Thus vigorously debating the orthodoxies of prior days, or supplementing and replacing canonical texts and subjects, or altering and experimenting with curricula, or using abstruse theories and complex language, or constructing courses to accommodate the changing nature of the student body, or responding to the major social, cultural, and political forces of the day are treated as evidence of the university's current degradation when in fact they have been endemic in the American academic world. Peter Shaw has complained of "resistance to authority of all kinds" in the modern university: "Literary critics rejected traditional interpretations, scholars found the formal limitations of their disciplines stifling, and humanists objected to the established canon of great works."[27] This condition, of course, is hardly peculiar to our own time but has been an evolving characteristic of American universities throughout the nineteenth and twentieth centuries. Universities are about teaching the methods and dispositions necessary to criticize, question, and test authority.

Similarly, when Gertrude Himmelfarb criticizes many of her fellow historians for daring to "impose upon the past their own determinacy," for acting as if "the past has to be deconstructed and constructed anew," she is, in fact, describing the well-established process of historiography.[28] Historians have always reconstructed the past on the basis of new information, new research, new theories, new approaches, new understandings; on the basis of what the historian Jack Hexter once called the "tracking devices" of their own time. The current emphasis on social and cultural history which so troubles contemporary critics is no more permanent than were past emphases on political, intellectual, economic, or diplomatic history. Neither is it any more—or less—politically motivated. It reflects, as earlier historiographies have reflected, the questions, problems, issues that touch our time and help us make sense of the world. It also reflects the fact that history today is written, as it has always been written, by human beings who are part of their own societies and cultures.

Perhaps the most common of the charges that the contemporary university is guilty of behavior that differentiates it qualitatively from its predecessors and makes it an exception in the history of American higher education are those revolving around what has been called "political correctness" (PC) which has allegedly cast a pall on freedom of expression and action on the American campus. Lynn Cheney has argued that today's students "can disagree with professors. But to do so is to take a risk."[29] In fact, when was it not risky for a socialist student to confront her economics professor who was teaching about the wonders of the free market, for an atheist student to confront his professor of religion who was teaching about the wonders of monotheism, or for African American students to confront their professor of history who was teaching about the wonders of the Founding Fathers, many of whom were slaveholders? This has always been the case in the university. Those professors who would welcome vigorous debate and disagreement on fundamentals often fail to get it either because students don't think this is their place, or because of those of their colleagues who don't welcome it and have taught students to repress their dissident urges. Students have always had to learn to accommodate to the whims and prejudices of professors, to the attitudes and sensitivities of fellow students, and to the values and beliefs of the larger society; to, that is, the complex of considerations that today is referred to much too simply as "political correctness."

The trouble with critics like Cheney is that they have made this long-standing condition in the academe a partisan one (unique to the Left) and an exceptional one (unique to our time). From reading Cheney and most of her fellow critics, you would never dream that there existed a conservative Republican professor or a centrist Democratic professor who stifled freedom of thought and inquiry in the classroom, who intimidated students into silence, who felt it was a student's function to listen and a professor's to dominate the discourse, who was confident of having the True Word to impart to a captive student audience. The problem Cheney is describing—of students fearing to risk debate—is neither new nor confined to one part of the political spectrum, nor is it unique to our time, nor is it particularly virulent in our time, nor does it really characterize the contemporary university which is a more varied, more open, more dynamic place to be in and near than ever before. This problem is inherent in the university which is a dual institution: on the one hand a center of free inquiry and discourse, on the other hand a center of intellectual authority—two characteristics that don't mesh easily and often lead to contradictory or inconsistent behavior. Ironically, it is most often Cheney's fellow conservative critics who have invoked authority in their vision of the classroom. Thus Gertrude Himmelfarb has argued that "it is reasonable and proper to ask students, even scholars, . . . to accept, at least provisionally, until disproved by powerful evidence, the judgment of posterity about great writers and great books. This calls for an initial suspension of private judgment in favor of authoritative opinion, the collective opinion of generations."[30]

It surely was much simpler when the university community was a homogeneous one, not because there was more freedom but because homogeneity ensured that there was more unanimity about what constituted acceptable ideas and behavior; because, that is, there was more, not less, of what today is called political correctness. When Allan Bloom blamed the radical students of the 1960s for opening the university to the "vulgarities present in society at large," he conveniently ignored the truth that long before the student movements universities had hardly transcended the larger society's "vulgarities" but had in fact mirrored its often prejudiced, repressive, and "politically correct" attitudes toward gender, race, and ethnicity in their admissions policies, their hiring practices, and their curricula.[31]

But the American university no longer is and never again will be homogeneous, and much of what we have seen recently in terms of speech codes and the like are a stumbling attempt to adapt to this new heterogeneity. The major consequence of the new heterogeneity on campuses, however, has not been repression but the very opposite—a flowering of ideas and scholarly innovation unmatched in our history. Charles Sykes quotes the educator Robert Maynard Hutchins's dictum that the liberal arts should free the student "from the prison-house of his class, race, time, place, background, family, and even his nation," and goes on to argue that universities today have reversed Hutchins's definition by focusing on race, class, gender, and sexual orientation.[32] On the contrary, today's universities with their diverse student bodies, faculties, and curricula have done more to free us from the confines of self-absorption than Hutchins could have imagined. The problem with Hutchins's vision is that like Bloom's, it was coupled to a homogeneous university community of faculty and students largely from the same class and background who were allowed to assume that *they* were the model and everyone else the deviants, that *they* possessed culture which everyone else lacked. What so troubles many conservatives is the modern university's presumption in believing that it can actually educate a wide array of people and help free them from the prison house of stereotypes and assumptions—those they hold of others and those others hold of them.

The British historian Sir Lewis Namier observed that "the crowning attainment of historical study is a historical sense—an intuitive understanding of how things do not happen." It is exactly this understanding of how things do not happen that the leading critics of the contemporary university lack. Thus they freely spin their facile theories of how the survivors of the New Left lost the political wars but won their ultimate triumph by capturing the university and transforming it from an institution of culture and learning to a high-handed and inflexible purveyor of Political Correctness. The problem with such notions—aside from the fact that they are promulgated, to borrow Carl Becker's memorable phrase, without fear and without research—is that they are telling examples of how things do not happen. Universities in the United States are not transformed by small cabals of political and social radicals who somehow (the process is never revealed) capture venerable private and public institutions of higher learning, convert them to their own agendas, overwhelm and silence the vast majority of their colleagues while boards of regents and trustees benignly look on, and mislead generations of gullible and passive college youth who are robbed of their true heritage and thus compelled to stumble forth into the larger world as undereducated and uncultured dupes mouthing the platitudes taught them by the band of radical mesmerists posing as college professors. "I have never fully understood the notion that faculty could brainwash me into believing whatever they wanted me to," a Stanford undergraduate testified. "Reading Hitler did not make me a fascist; reading Sartre did not make me an existentialist. Both simply enabled me to think about those philosophies in ways I hadn't previously." It should not take a great deal of reflection to realize that neither college students nor college faculties nor college administrations operate in the manner posited by the apocalyptic and conspiratorial views of the contemporary university. This is not how things happen in the American university and to comprehend why some people are convinced that they do we might ponder Richard Hofstadter's notions of the "paranoid style" in American politics.[33]

In no sense did Hofstadter equate what he called the paranoid style with psychological pathology. He argued that while clinical paranoia describes an individual who is convinced of the existence of a hostile and conspiratorial world "directed specifically *against him,*" the paranoid style involves belief in a conspiracy "directed against a nation, a culture, a way of life." Hofstadter found this style recurring throughout American history in the anti-Masonic and anti-Catholic crusades, and in such manifestations of anti-Communism as McCarthyism and the John Birch Society. But there is nothing particularly retrograde about the style; one can find it in aspects of abolitionism, of Populism, and of antiwar movements as well. It is less tied to particular political goals than to a way of seeing the world, a way of understanding how things work by invoking the process of conspiracy. "The paranoid spokesman," according to Hofstadter, "sees the fate of this conspiracy in apocalyptic terms. . . . He is always manning the barricades of civilization. He constantly lives at a turning point: it is now or never in organizing resistance to conspiracy. Time is forever just running out. . . . The apocalypticism of the paranoid style runs dangerously near to hopeless pessimism, but usually stops just short of it."

I would argue that this manner of envisioning reality has frequently characterized those who resisted the changes taking place in American higher education, and never more so than during the past several decades. Perhaps the most unfortunate aspect of this mode of analysis is not merely that it's incorrect but that it's so simple and pat and that we learn little, if anything, from it. "We are all sufferers from history," Hofstadter concluded, "but the paranoid is a double sufferer, since he is afflicted not only by the real world, with the rest of us, but by his fantasies as well."[34]

What is wrong with the dominant critiques is not that they are mistaken in every instance, nor that there aren't things to criticize in contemporary universities. Of course there are. We need to integrate learning more fully and to have more sequential courses that build on one another. We need to minimize the use of inaccessible jargon wherever possible, particularly in those fields where jargon has become a way of life. We need to make a greater effort to communicate with colleagues in other disciplines, with students, and with the general public. We need to ensure that teaching ability is considered seriously in all faculty personnel decisions. We need to learn how to respond to the considerable challenge of teaching the most wide-ranging and heterogeneous body of students in the history of American higher education. The problem is that the charges against the university are so hyperbolic, so angry, so conspiracy-minded, and so one-sided they can find almost nothing positive to say. They see little if any good coming out of the new research and teaching on race and gender, the multifaceted study of American culture, the attempts to more completely understand the world and its peoples and cultures, the exciting development of a student body and faculty that are increasingly becoming more representative of the nation's population.

There *is* fragmentation in the United States; there is distrust; there is deep anger—and much of this is reflected in and acted out in universities, but none of it is *caused* by universities or by professors or by young people. Nevertheless, all three are easy scapegoats for the problems of the larger society. The many changes taking place in the nation's universities have created awkward moments pregnant with the possibilities of progress but also containing an abundance of room for egregious mistakes, and universities have had their share of both. But to collect dozens of anecdotes illustrating the stumbling of many universities in the face of new pressures and challenges—while ignoring all of their many successful adjustments and innovations—and to parade these stories forth as indicative of the great problem we face is mistaken. Those who do so disregard the fact that the real fragmentation confronting this society has nothing to do with the university, which is one of the more successfully integrated and heterogeneous institutions in the United States, and everything to do with the reality that forms of fragmentation—social, ethnic, racial, religious, regional, economic—have been endemic in the United States from the outset. In our own time this historic fragmentation has been exacerbated because a significant part of our population has been removed from the economy and turned into a permanent underclass with no ladders leading out of its predicament and consequently little hope.

Americans' complicated and ambivalent attitudes toward the university have created the myth that universities are not part of the "real" world, and many professors, pleased at the notion that they were apart from and therefore more "objective" about the surrounding society, have been willing to go along with this illusion and to varying extents have even come to believe it. In truth, as this study will illustrate again and again, universities are never far removed from the larger society. To have a literature of crisis built upon the university and the young as the enemy, as the creators of fragmentation, discontent, and social turmoil, is so bizarre as to almost, but not quite, defy understanding. Rather than face the complex of reasons for our present state of unease, it is easier and certainly much more comforting to locate the source of our dilemma in an institution—the university—that has always been deeply suspect in the United States, in a group—professors—who have always been something of an anomaly in a theoretically egalitarian land, and in a generation—college youth—who have always made us nervous because they never *seem* to be our exact replicas.

The trouble with the widespread apocalyptic view of the sudden takeover of the university by forces essentially alien to its basic spirit is that this vision removes the American university from the context of its own extended history and transforms long-term processes of change and development into short-term accidents. When the Mock Turtle asked Alice to explain where she came from, the Gryphon exclaimed impatiently, "No, no! The adventures first, explanations take such a dreadful time."[35] Contemporary critics of the university have shown a similar impatience. Explanations *do* take time, but they remain essential. To understand where the university is we have to understand where it has been and how its present state was constructed. There is no quicker or easier way to proceed; to fathom today requires some awareness of yesterday. In the process we will learn not only about higher education, we will discover truths about our culture and, hopefully, about ourselves as well.

Notes

1. Allan Bloom, *The Closing of the American Mind: How Higher Education Has Failed Democracy and Impoverished the Souls of Today's Students* (New York: Simon and Schuster, 1987); Charles J. Sykes, *Profscam: Professors and the Demise of Higher Education* (New York: Kampmann and

Co., 1988); Peter Shaw, *The War Against the Intellect: Episodes in the Decline of Discourse* (Iowa City: University of Iowa Press, 1989); Roger Kimball, *Tenured Radicals: How Politics Has Corrupted Our Higher Education* (New York: Harper and Row, 1990); Page Smith, *Killing the Spirit: Higher Education in America* (New York: Viking, 1990); Charles J. Sykes, *The Hollow Men: Politics and Corruption in Higher Education* (Washington, D.C.: Regnery Gateway, 1990); Dinesh D'Souza, *Illiberal Education: The Politics of Race and Sex on Campus* (New York: Free Press, 1991); William J. Bennett, *The De-Valuing of America: The Fight for Our Culture and Our Children* (New York: Summit Books, 1992); Martin Anderson, *Impostors in the Temple: American Intellectuals Are Destroying Our Universities and Cheating Our Students of Their Future* (New York: Simon and Schuster, 1992); Richard Bernstein, *Dictatorship of Virtue: Multiculturalism and the Battle for America's Future* (New York: Knopf, 1994).

2. Buchanan's statement is in the *San Francisco Chronicle,* August 19, 1992; Kimball, *Tenured Radicals,* 206; the ad for Thomas Aquinas College is in *National Review,* February 20, 1995, 23; George F. Will, "Curdled Politics on Campus," *Newsweek,* May 6, 1991, 72; George F. Will, "Literary Politics," *Newsweek,* April 22, 1991, 72; Berger's remarks are in *Partisan Review* 58 (1991): 317.
3. Kramer is quoted in James Atlas, *Battle of the Books: The Curriculum Debate in America* (New York: Norton, 1990), 70; Bennett, *The De-Valuing of America,* 28, 33.
4. Will, "Literary Politics," 72; Gertrude Himmelfarb, *The New History and the Old* (Cambridge: Harvard University Press, 1987), 26, 14–18.
5. Bloom, *The Closing of the American Mind,* 314–15, 321. For the book's sales, see "Best Sellers From 1987's Book Crop," *New York Times,* January 6, 1988. The meetings of the NAS are reported in *New York Times,* November 15, 1988, A22; and *Chronicle of Higher Education,* November 23, 1988, A1, A11, and June 20, 1990, A15–16.
6. Bernstein, *Dictatorship of Virtue,* 3–5, 8, 48, 346; Robert Hughes, *Culture of Complaint: The Fraying of America* (New York: Oxford University Press, 1993), 24, 56–57; Smith, *Killing the Spirit,* 9, 122; Sykes, *Hollow Men,* 60; Sykes, *Profscam,* 8, 264; D'Souza, *Illiberal Education,* 228.
7. John Taylor, "Are You Politically Correct?" *New York Magazine,* January 21,1991, 32–40; Gary Kamiya, "Civilization & Its Discontents," *San Francisco Examiner Magazine,* January 22,1995, cover and 14–27.
8. Robert Brustein, "Dumbocracy in America," *Partisan Review* 60 (1993): 527; John Patrick Diggins, *The Rise and Fall of the American Left* (New York: Norton, 1992), 298 and chap. 7; George Roche, *The Fall of the Ivory Tower: Government Funding, Corruption, and the Bankrupting of American Higher Education* (Washington, D.C.: Regnery Gateway, 1994), 3–4; Wilcomb E. Washburn, *The "Treason of the Intellectuals, "1989* (Young America's Foundation, n.d.), 2–3; Kimball, *Tenured Radicals,* xiv.
9. Bloom, *The Closing of the American Mind,* 101, 65; Smith, *Killing the Spirit,* 285–92; Sykes, *Hollow Men,* 37–39.
10. Bernstein, *Dictatorship of Virtue,* 48–50; Atlas, *Battle of the Books,* 72–73. For examples of how the Jane Austen paper is treated, see Kimball, *Tenured Radicals,* 192, 201; John Taylor, "Are You Politically Correct?" *New York Magazine,* January 21, 1991, 36.
11. Charles Krauthammer, "An Insidious Rejuvenation of the Old Left," *Los Angeles Times,* December 24, 1990; Kimball, *Tenured Radicals,* xi-xviii.
12. Bloom, *The Closing of the American Mind,* 381, 329; Anderson, *Impostors in the Temple,* 44.
13. Gertrude Himmelfarb, in *Partisan Review* 58 (1991): 362; Atlas, *Battle of the Books,* 87–88, 48–51; Kimball, *Tenured Radicals,* 204.
14. Bloom, *The Closing of the American Mind,* 135–37.
15. Ibid., 34, 65–66, 107–8, 68–81, 51.
16. For Matthew Arnold's influential and much quoted views, see his *Culture and Anarchy* (London: Smith, Elder and Co., 1875), 44, 47; John Searle, "The Storm Over the University," in Paul Berman, ed., *Debating RC: The Controversy Over Political Correctness on College Campuses* (New York: Laurel, 1992), 88.
17. Atlas, *Battle of the Books,* 136, 43; Clark is quoted in Samuel Eliot Morison, *Three Centuries of Harvard, 1636–1936* (Cambridge: Harvard University Press, 1936), 260; Henry Adams, *The Education of Henry Adams* (1918; New York: Modern Library edition, 1931), 55, 59–60.
18. James Atlas, in *Partisan Review* 58 (1991): 262, 264; Lawrence Auster, "America Is in Danger: Our Ability to Preserve Our Common Heritage Depends on the Continued Existence of a Majority Population that Believes in It," *Newsday,* May 12, 1991, 30.
19. Bloom, *The Closing of the American Mind,* 27, 33, 36–39, 29–30, 202.
20. Roger Kimball, "'Tenured Radicals': A Postscript," *New Criterion* 9 (January 1991): 12; Bernstein, *Dictatorship of Virtue,* 42–45; Atlas, *Battle of the Books,* 90.

21. Charles Krauthammer, "Hale Columbus, Dead White Male," *Time,* May 27, 1991; William Bennett, "Why the West?" *National Review,* May 27,1988, 38 (italics added).
22. D'Souza, *Illiberal Education,* 33.
23. Sykes, *Profscam,* 6; Hughes, *Culture of Complaint,* 67.
24. Anderson, *Impostors in the Temple,* 85; Smith, *Killing the Spirit,* 7; Bloom, *The Closing of the American Mind,* 68–81, 65–66, 97–108, 34.
25. Kimball, *Tenured Radicals,* chap. 1; Bettina J. Huber and David Laurence, "Report on the 1984–85 Survey of the English Sample: General Education Requirements in English and the English Major," ADE *Bulletin* 93 (1989): 30–43; Bettina J. Huber, "Today's Literature Classroom: Findings from the MLA's 1990 Survey of Upper-Division Courses," ADE *Bulletin* 101 (1992): 36–60; Phyllis Franklin, Bettina J. Huber, and David Laurence, "Continuity and Change in the Study of Literature," *Change* (January/February 1992): 42–48.
26. Diggins, *The Rise and Fall of the American Left,* 291, 298; Lynn V. Cheney, *Telling the Truth: A Report on the State of the Humanities in Higher Education* (Washington, D.C.: National Endowment for the Humanities, 1992), 28; Jerry Z. Muller, "Challenging Political Correctness: A `Paranoid Hysteric' Replies to Joan Scott," *Perspectives: American Historical Association Newsletter* 31 (May/June 1993): 13–15.
27. Shaw, *The War Against the Intellect,* xiii.
28. Gertrude Himmelfarb, "Some Reflections on the New History," *American Historical Review* 94 (June 1989): 668.
29. Cheney, *Telling the Truth,* 14.
30. Himmelfarb, in *Partisan Review* 58 (1991): 362.
31. *Bloom, The Closing of the American Mind,* 321.
32. Sykes, *Hollow Men,* 17.
33. Sir Lewis Namier, "History," in Fritz Stern, ed., *The Varieties of History From Voltaire to the Present* (New York: World Publishing, 1956), 375; Raoul V. Mowatt, "What Revolution at Stanford?" in Patricia Aufderheide, ed., *Beyond PC: Toward a Politics of Understanding* (Saint Paul: Graywolf Press, 1992), 131–32.
34. Richard Hofstadter, "The Paranoid Style in American Politics," in Hofstadter, *The Paranoid Style in American Politics and Other Essays* (New York: Knopf, 1965), 3–40.
35. Lewis Carroll, *Alice's Adventures in Wonderland* in Martin Gardner, ed., *The Annotated Alice* (New York: Meridian Books, 1973), 138.

CHAPTER 19

DECENTERING THE CANON: REFIGURING DISCIPLINARY AND PEDAGOGICAL BOUNDARIES

HENRY A. GIROUX

I will begin with what has become a controversial but not insignificant assertion: that the most important questions facing both the liberal arts and higher education in general are moral and political.[1] By invoking the category of the political, I wish to separate myself from a species of neoconservativism that claims that the relationship between the liberal arts and politics is one that taints the scholarship and teaching of those who dare even suggest that such a relationship exists. Nor do I believe that the fashionable but derogatory label of "politically correct" used by liberals and neo-conservatives adequately captures the complex set of motives, ideologies, and pedagogies of diverse progressive and radical scholars trying to engage the relationship between knowledge and power as it is expressed through the history and process of disciplinary canon formation. In fact, the charge that radical scholars are to be condemned for exercising a form of theoretical terrorism appears to be nothing more than a rhetorical ploy that barely conceals the highly charged ideological agenda of neoconservative scholars who refuse to address in any substantive way the political and theoretical considerations currently being raised within the academy by feminists, people of color, and other minority groups.[2]

What is being protested as the intrusion of politics into academic life is nothing less than a refusal to recognize that the canon and the struggle over the purpose and meaning of the liberal arts has displayed a political struggle from its inception. There are no disciplines, pedagogies, institutional structures, or forms of scholarship that are untainted by the messy relations of worldly values and interests.[3] For example, the history, configuration, and legitimation of the canon in the liberal arts cannot be removed from the issue of securing authority. As Gayatri Spivak points out, "canons are the condition and function of institutions, which presuppose particular ways of life and are inescapably political."[4]

More specifically, the various questions that have been raised recently about either defending, reconstructing, or eliminating a particular canon in higher education can only be understood within a broader range of political and theoretical considerations that bear directly on the issue of whether a liberal arts education should be considered a privilege for the few or a right for the vast majority of citizens. This is not merely a matter of deciding who is eligible or can financially afford a liberal arts education; it is fundamentally part of a wider discourse that has increasingly challenged the

Source: "Decentering the Canon: Refiguring Disciplinary and Pedagogical Boundaries," by Henry A. Giroux, reprinted from *Border Crossings: Cultural Workers and the Politics of Education*, 1992, Routledge (US).

American public in the last decade to rethink the role of higher education and its relationship to democratic public life.

This debate raises new and important questions regarding the social and political implications of viewing curriculum as a historically specific narrative and pedagogy as a form of cultural politics. What must be asked about these specific narratives is whether they enable or silence the differentiated human capacities that allow students to speak from their own experiences, locate themselves in history, and act so as to create liberatory social forms that expand the possibility of democratic public life.[5] I believe that the current debate on higher education opens up new possibilities for rethinking the role that university educators might play as critically engaged public intellectuals. While neoconservatives generally view the extensive debate about the fundamental place of literature, culture, ethics, and politics in the academy and the wider society as symptomatic of a crisis of authority and an unmitigated assault on Western civilization itself, I would rather view it as part of a great renewal in academic life.[6]

Before I discuss these issues in detail, I want to stress the importance of recognizing that the university is not simply a place to accumulate disciplinary knowledge that can be exchanged for decent employment and upward mobility. Neither is it a place whose purpose is merely to cultivate the life of the mind or reproduce the cultural equivalent of "Masterpiece Theater." I firmly believe that the institutions of higher education, regardless of their academic status, represent places that affirm and legitimate existing views of the world, produce new ones, and authorize and shape particular social relations; put simply, they are places of moral and social regulation "where a sense of identity, place, and worth is informed and contested through practices, which organize knowledge and meaning."[7] The university is a place that produces a particular selection and ordering of narratives and subjectivities. It is, furthermore, a place that is deeply political and unarguably normative.

Unfortunately, questions concerning higher education in general and liberal arts in particular are often discussed as if they have no relation to existing arrangements of social, economic, and political power. Central to this chapter are the arguments that as a social, political, and pedagogical site, the university is a terrain of contestation and that one can neither understand the nature of the struggle itself nor the nature of the liberal arts unless one raises the question of what the purpose of the university actually is or might be. Or, as Jacques Derrida has put it, "To ask whether the university has a reason for being is to wonder why there is a university, but the question 'why' verges on 'with a view to what?'"[8] It is this question of purpose and practice that illuminates what the limits and possibilities are that exist within the university at a given time in history. Putting aside Derrida's own political agenda, this is essentially a question of politics, power, and possibility. As we know, the liberal arts and various other programs and schools within the university presuppose and legitimate particular forms of history, community, and authority. Of course, the question is what and whose history, community, knowledge, and voice prevails? Unless this question is addressed, the issues of what to teach, how to teach, how to engage our students, and how to function as intellectuals becomes removed from the wider principles that inform such issues and practices.

The sphere of higher education represents an important public culture that cultivates and produces particular stories of how to live ethically and politically; its institutions reproduce selected values, and they harbor in their social relations and teaching practices specific notions regarding "what knowledge is of most worth, what it means to know something, and how one might construct representations of [themselves], others, and the social environment." In many respects, the normative and political language taught in the university can be compared to what Ernst Bloch called the utopian impulse of daydreams.

> Dreams come in the day as well as the night. And both kinds of dreaming are motivated by the wishes they seek to fulfill. But daydreams differ from night dreams; for the day dreaming "I" persist throughout, consciously, privately, envisaging the circumstances and images of a desired, better life. The content of the daydream is not, like that of the night dream, a journey back into repressed experiences and their association. It is concerned with, as far as possible, an unrestricted journey forward, so that instead of reconstituting that which is no longer conscious, the images of that which is not yet can be fantasized into life and into the world.[9]

Bloch's analysis points to an important relation between daydreaming and the liberal arts that is often overlooked. As an introduction to, preparation for, and legitimation of social life, a liberal arts education inscribes students in a present informed by a past that presupposes a particular citizen, society, and future. In other words, like the process of daydreaming, the liberal arts is fundamentally involved in the production of narratives of that which is "not yet." As Roger Simon points out, "the utopian impulse of such programs is represented in the notion that without a perspective on the future, conceivable as a desired future, there can be no human venture."[10] In this respect, the language of education that students take with them from their university experience should embody a vision capable of providing them with a sense of history, civic courage, and democratic community. It is important to emphasize that visions are not only defined by the representations they legitimate and the practices they structure, but also by the arguments they embody for justifying why meaning, knowledge, and social action matter as part of the rewriting and remapping of the events that make up daily life as well as the dynamics of the larger world. The question becomes To what version of the future do the visions of our students speak? To whom do such visions matter and why? As a matter of pedagogical practice, students need to take up these questions through a language of obligation and power, a language that cultivates a capacity for reasoned criticism, for undoing the misuses of power and the relations of domination, and for exploring and extending the utopian dimensions of human potentiality. Needless to say, such a language is at odds with the language of cultural despair, conservative restoration, and aristocratic elitism trumpeted by the educational theorists of the New Right.[11]

It serves us well to remember that the visions presupposed in the structure and discourse of the liberal arts are neither ideologically neutral nor politically innocent. Visions always belong to someone, and to the degree that they translate into curricula and pedagogical practices, they not only denote a struggle over forms of political authority and orders of representation, but also weigh heavily in regulating the moral identities, collective voices, and the futures of others.[12] As institutionalized practices, visions draw upon specific values, uphold particular relations of power, class, gender, ethnicity, and race, and often authorize official forms of knowledge. For this reason, visions always have a moral and political dimension. Moreover, they become important not as a signal for a single-minded preoccupation with academic achievement or social status but as a context from which to organize the energies of a moral vision, to believe that one can make a difference both in combating domestic tyranny and assaults on human freedom and in creating a society that exhibits in its institutional and everyday relations moral courage, compassion, and cultural justice. This is, after all, what university life should be all about: the politics and ethics of dreaming, dreaming a better future, and dreaming a new world.

The current debate about education represents more than a commentary on the state of public and higher education in this country, it is basically a debate about the meaning of democracy, social criticism, and the status of utopian thought in constituting both our dreams and the stories that we devise in order to give meaning to our lives. This debate has taken a serious turn in the last decade and now as before its terms are being set principally by extremists and anti-utopians. Critics such as Allan Bloom, Lynne V. Cheney, Roger Kimball, and John Silber have presented an agenda and purpose for shaping higher education that abstracts equity from excellence and cultural criticism from the discourse of social responsibility. Under the guise of attempting to revitalize the language of morality, these critics and politicians have, in reality, launched a serious attack on some of the most basic aspects of democratic public life and the social, moral, and political obligations of responsible, critical citizens. What is being valorized in this language is, in part, a view of higher education based on a celebration of cultural uniformity and a rigid view of authority; in addition, the neoconservative agenda for higher education includes a call to remake higher education an academic beachhead for defending and limiting the curriculum to a narrowly defined patriarchal, Eurocentric version of the Western tradition and a return to the old transmission model of teaching.

Within this new public philosophy, there is a ruthlessly frank expression of doubt about the viability of democracy.[13] What at first sight appears to be a debate about the meaning and purpose of the canon has become a struggle for "the moral definition of tomorrow's elites."[14] Unfortunately, this is not a debate being conducted within the parameters of critical exchange. It is increasingly taking on the shades of McCarthyism rampant in the 1950s in the United States, with those in power using their influence in the press, in well-funded public symposiums, and through highly financed private think tanks to conjure up charges that academics who are questioning the relationship between the liberal arts and the discourse of power and citizenship are to be judged by their motives rather than their arguments. With great burst of melodramatic rhetoric, we are told, for example, by Roger Kimball, the editor of *The New Centurion,* that politically motivated academic radicals, regardless of their particular theoretical orientation, have as their goal nothing less than the destruction of the values, method, and goals of Western civilization. Equating advocates for a multicultural curriculum with the forces of barbarism, Kimball constructs a reductionistic opposition in which conservatives become the defenders of civilization itself. Kimball spares no words on the importance of *his* messianic struggle:

> The multiculturalists notwithstanding, the choice facing us today is not between a "repressive" Western culture and a multicultural paradise, but between culture and barbarism. *Civilization* is not a gift, it is an achievement—a fragile achievement that needs constantly to be shored up and defended from besiegers inside and out.[15]

Critics such as Allan Bloom and John Silber extend the tone and logic of such attacks by arguing that the very nature of Western civilization is under attack by the infusion of critics in the humanities who constitute a monolithic party (surely an embarrassing overstatement given the endless fragmentation and divisions that characterize the American left). There is more at stake here than the rise of a new nativism; there is also the nature of academic freedom as it has developed in the liberal arts in the last few decades. The poison of McCarthyism is once again being used to limit debate and constrain the so-called excesses of democracy. For instance, instead of addressing the complexity of issues being waged over the nature of the liberal arts and the ideological construction of the canon, John Silber, the President of Boston University, has urged fellow conservatives to abandon any civility toward scholars whose work is considered political. Instead of encouraging rigorous debate, Silber has urged his fellow conservatives to name names, to discredit educators who have chosen to engage in forms of social criticism (work the New Right considers political) at odds with the agenda of the New Rights's mythic conception of the university as a warehouse built on the pillars of an unproblematic and revered tradition.[16] In the Bush Era, there are, sadly, few attempts to engage in dialogue about the assumptions that inform the traditional view of the curriculum and canon; on the contrary, the privileged and the powerful in academia and in government positions now openly advocate crude policing functions as a way to regulate university life. So much for the spirit of democracy and academic freedom.

The loss of utopian vision that characterizes this position is no where more evident than in Allan Bloom's *The Closing of the American Mind* and E. D. Hirsch's *Cultural Literacy.*[17] For Bloom, the impulse to egalitarianism and the spirit of social criticism represent the chief culprits in the decay of higher learning. Bloom argues that the university must give up educating intellectuals, whose great crime is that they sometimes become adversaries of the dominant culture or speak to a wider culture about the quality of contemporary politics and public life. He would prefer that the university curriculum be organized around the Great Books and be selectively used to educate students from what he calls the top twenty elite schools to be philosopher-kings. What Bloom appears to suggest by reform is nothing less than an effort to make explicit what women, people of color, and working-class students have always known: The precincts of higher learning are not for them, and the educational system is meant to reproduce a new mandarin class.

Hirsch, like Bloom, presents a frontal attack aimed at providing a programmatic language with which to defend schools as cultural sites; that is, as institutions responsible for reproducing the knowledge and values necessary to advance the historical virtues of Western culture. Hirsch presents his view of cultural restoration through a concept of literacy that focuses on the basic structures of language, and he applies this version of cultural literacy to the broader consideration of the needs of the business community as well as to maintenance of American institutions. For Hirsch, the new service economy requires employees who can write a memo, read within a specific cultural context, and communicate through a national language composed of the key words of Western culture.

Central to Hirsch's concept of literacy is a view of culture removed from the dynamics of struggle and power. Culture is seen as the totality of language practices of a given nation and merely "presents" itself for all to participate in its language and conventions. Not unlike Bloom's position, Hirsch's view of culture expresses a single durable history and vision, one at odds with a critical notion of democracy and difference. Such a position maintains an ideological silence, a political amnesia of sorts, regarding either how domination works in the cultural sphere or how the dialectic of cultural struggle between different groups over competing orders of meaning, experience, and history emerges within unequal relations of power and struggle. By depoliticizing the issue of culture, Hirsch ends up with a view of literacy cleansed of its own complicity in producing social forms that create devalued others. This is more than a matter of cultural forgetting on Hirsch's part; it is also an attack on difference as possibility. Hirsch's discourse also attempts to undermine the development of a curriculum committed to reclaiming higher education as an agency of social justice and critical democracy and to developing forms of pedagogy that affirm and engage the often silenced voices of subordinate groups.

In the most general sense, Bloom, Hirsch, Cheney, Kimball, and Silber represent the latest cultural offensive by the new elitists to rewrite the past and construct the present from the perspective of the privileged and the powerful.[18] They disdain the democratic implications of pluralism and argue for a form of cultural uniformity in which difference is consigned to the margins of history or to the museum of the disadvantaged. From this perspective, culture, along with the authority it sanctions becomes merely an artifact, a warehouse of goods, posited either as a canon of knowledge or a canon of information that simply has to be transmitted as a means for promoting social order and control. In this view, pedagogy becomes an afterthought, a code word for the transmission and imposition of a predefined and unproblematic body of knowledge. For educators like Bloom and Cheney, pedagogy is something one does in order to implement a reconstituted body of knowledge or information. The notion that pedagogy is itself part of the production of knowledge, a deliberate and critical attempt to influence the ways in which knowledge and identities are produced within and among particular sets of social relations, is far removed from the language and ideology of the neoconservatives.

What is at stake here is not simply the issue of bad teaching, but the broader refusal to take seriously the categories of meaning, experience, and voice that students use to make sense of themselves and the world around them. It is this refusal to enable speech for those who have been silenced, to acknowledge the voices of the other, and to legitimate and reclaim student experience as a fundamental category in the production of knowledge that the character of the current dominant discourse on the canon reveals its totalitarian and undemocratic ideology.

Put in Bloch's terms, this new conservative public philosophy represents a form of daydreaming in which tradition is not on the side of democracy and difference, but is a form of the "not yet" expunged of the language of hope and strangled by a discourse in which history and culture are closed. It is a public philosophy in which teaching is reduced to a form of transmission, the canon is posited as a relationship outside of the restless flux of knowledge and power, and intellectuals are cheerfully urged to take up their roles as clerks of the empire.[19]

It is worth noting that Bloom, Cheney, and other neoconservatives have been able to perform a task that humanists and progressives have generally failed to do. They have placed the question of curriculum at the center of the debate about both education and democracy, but they have argued for a view of the liberal arts fashioned as part of an anti-utopian discourse that serves to disconnect the purpose of higher education from the task of reconstructing democratic public life. This is not to suggest that they have not invoked the notions of democracy and citizenship in their arguments. But in doing so they have reduced democracy to gaining access to an unproblematic version of Western civilization and defined learning as the training of good citizens, that is, "willing subjects and agents of hegemonic authority."[20] By refusing to link democracy to forms of self and social empowerment, neoconservatives have been able to suppress the relationship between learning, social justice, and critical citizenship. This new cultural offensive presents a formidable challenge to humanists who have attempted to defend liberal arts education from the perspective of a highly specialized, self-referential discipline that holds up either a plurality of canons or a canon that serves as a model of scientific rigor and sophisticated methodological inquiry. In such cases, the purpose of the liberal arts is defined, though from different ideological perspectives, from within the perspective of creating a free, enterprising, educated, well-rounded individual. Though well meaning, this discourse discounts the most important social relations that are constitutive of what it means to be educated. That is, it ignores the social and political function of particular knowledge/power/pedagogy relations and how they serve to construct students individually and collectively within the boundaries of a political order that they often take for granted.

The liberal arts cannot be defended either as a self-contained discourse legitimating the humanistic goal of broadly improving the so-called life of the mind or as a rigorous science that can lead students to indubitable truths. Similarly, it is insufficient to defend the liberal arts by rejecting technocratic education as a model of learning. All of these positions share the failure of abstracting the liberal arts from the intense problems and issues of public life. Moreover, the defense of the liberal arts as a gateway to indubitable truths, whether through the discourse of Western civilization or science, often collapses into a not too subtle defense of higher education as a training ground for a "dictatorship of enlightened social engineers."[21] This issue at stake is not one of merely creating a more enlightened or scientific canon but of raising more fundamental questions about how canons are used, what interests they legitimate, what relations they have to the dominant society, and how students are constituted within their prevailing discourses and social relations. How we read or define a "canonical" work may not be as important as challenging the overall function and social uses the notion of the canon has served. Within this type of discourse, the canon can be analyzed as part of a wider set of relations that connect the academic disciplines, teaching, and power to more political considerations defined through broader, intersecting political and cultural concerns such as race, class, gender, ethnicity, and nationalism. What is in question here is not merely a defense of a particular canon, but the issue of struggle and empowerment.[22]

The debate over the canon must be refigured in order to address issues of struggle in which power and knowledge intersect to produce and legitimate specific orders of representations, values, and identities. As such, the issue of canon formation must be engaged in terms that address the historical formation of the canon and the pedagogies through which it is taught and how these pedagogies have either provided or excluded the conditions and knowledge necessary for marginal people to recover their own histories and to speak and learn in places occupied by those who have the dominant power to shape policy and act. In other words, the liberal arts should be defended in the interest of creating critical rather than "good" citizens. That is, the notion of the liberal arts has to be reconstituted around a knowledge-power relationship in which the question of curriculum is seen as a form of cultural and political production grounded in a radical conception of citizenship and public wisdom.

By linking the liberal arts to the imperatives of a critical democracy, the debate on the meaning and nature of higher education can be situated within a broader context of issues concerned with critical citizenship, politics, and the dignity of human life. In this view, it becomes possible to provide a rationale and purpose for higher education, which aims at developing critical citizens and reconstructing community life by extending the principles of social justice to all spheres of economic, political, and cultural life. This position is not far from the arguments posed by John Dewey, George S. Counts, C. Wright Mills, and more recently Hannah Arendt and Alvin Gouldner. These theorists fashioned the elements of a public philosophy in which the liberal arts was seen as a major social site for revitalizing public life. Dewey, for example, argued that a liberal education afforded people the opportunity to involve themselves in the deepest problems of society, to acquire the knowledge, skills, and ethical responsibility necessary for "reasoned participation in democratically organized publics."[23] Mills urged intellectuals to define the liberal arts and their own roles through a commitment to the formation of a critical and engaged citizenry. He envisioned the liberal arts as social site from which intellectuals could mobilize a moral and political vision committed to the reclamation and recovery of democratic public life.[24] In the most general sense, this means fashioning the purpose of higher education within a public philosophy committed to a radical conception of citizenship, civic courage, and public wisdom. In more specific terms, this means challenging the image of higher education as an adjunct of the corporation and rejecting those ideologies and human capital theories that reduce the role of university intellectuals to the status of industrial technicians and academic clerks whose political project or, lack of one, is often betrayed by claims to objectivity, certainty, and professionalism. It means challenging the sterile instrumentalism, selfishness, and contempt for democratic community that has become the hallmark of the Reagan-Bush Era.[25] It means recognizing and organizing against the structured injustices in society that prevent us from extending our solidarity to those others who strain under the weight of various forms of oppression and exploitation. It also means enhancing and ennobling the meaning and purpose of a liberal arts education by giving it a truly central place in the social life of a nation where it can become a public forum for addressing preferentially the needs of the poor, the dispossessed, and the disenfranchised.

A public philosophy that offers the promise of reforming liberal arts education as part of a wider revitalization of public life raises important questions regarding what the notion of empowerment would mean for developing classroom pedagogical practices. That is, if liberal arts education is to be developed in relation to principles consistent with a democratic public philosophy, it is equally important to develop forms of critical pedagogy that embody these principles and practices, a critical pedagogy in which such practices are understood in relation to rather than in isolation from those economies of power and privilege at work in wider social and political formations.

Critical Pedagogy as a Form of Cultural Politics

For many educators, pedagogy is often theorized as what is left after curriculum content is determined. In this view, knowledge "speaks" for itself and teaching is often a matter of providing an occasion for the text to reveal itself. Guided by a concern with producing knowledge that is academically correct or ideologically relevant, educational theorists have largely sidestepped the issue of how a teacher can work from sound ethical and theoretical principles and still end up pedagogically silencing students. Put another way, if educators fail to recognize that the legitimating claims they make in defense of the knowledge they teach is not enough to ensure that they do not commit forms of symbolic violence in their pedagogical relations with students, they will not adequately understand the ways in which students are both enabled and disabled in their own classrooms.

Central to the development of a critical pedagogy is the need to explore how pedagogy functions as a cultural practice to produce rather than merely transmit knowledge within the asymmetrical relations of power that structure teacher-student relations. There have been few attempts to analyze how relations of pedagogy and relations of power are inextricably tied not only to what people know but also to how they come to know in a particular way within the constraints of specific cultural and social forms.[26] Rendered insignificant as a form of cultural production, pedagogy is often marginalized and devalued as a means of recognizing that what we teach and how we do it are deeply implicated not only in producing various forms of domination but also in constructing active practices of resistance and struggle. Lost here is an attempt to articulate pedagogy as a form of cultural production that addresses how knowledge is produced, mediated, refused, and represented within relations of power both in and outside of the university.

Critical pedagogy as a form of cultural politics rejects the reduction of teaching to a narrowly defined concern with instrumental techniques, skills, and objectives. The instrumentalization of teaching erases questions of power, history, ethics, and self-identity. Absent from this discourse is any attempt to understand how pedagogical and institutional practices produce, codify, and rewrite disciplinary practices, values, and social identities in relation to, rather than outside of, the discourse of history, power, and privilege. Critical pedagogy also rejects the notion of knowledge as accumulated capital. Instead, it focuses on the production of knowledge and identities within the specificity of educational contexts and the broader institutional locations in which they are located. Critical pedagogy refers to a deliberate attempt to construct specific conditions through which educators and students can think critically about how knowledge is produced and transformed in relation to the construction of social experiences informed by a particular relationship between the self, others, and the larger world. Rather than reducing classroom practice to forms of methodological reification governed by a pragmatic concern for generating topologies or a reductionist fetish for empirical verification, critical pedagogy stresses the realities of what happens in classrooms by raising a number of crucial questions. These include how identities and subjectivities are produced differently in relation to particular forms of knowledge and power; how cultural differences are coded within the center and margins of power; how the discourse of rationality secures, ignores, or dismisses the affective investments that organize the daily experiences of students; how education might become the practice of liberation and what it means to know something as part of the broader discourses of cultural democracy and citizenship.[27]

The notion of pedagogy being argued for here is not organized in relation to a choice between elite or popular culture, but as part of a political project that takes issues of liberation and empowerment as its starting point. It is a pedagogy that rejects the notion of culture as an artifact immobilized in the image of a storehouse. Instead, the pedagogical principles at work here analyze culture as a set of lived experiences and social practices developed within asymmetrical relations of power. Culture in this sense is not an object of unquestioning reverence but a mobile field of ideological and material relations that are unfinished, multilayered and always open to interrogation. Moreover, this view of culture is defined pedagogically as social practices that allow both teachers and students to construe themselves as agents in the production of subjectivity and meaning. Such a pedagogy transcends the dichotomy of elite and popular culture by defining itself through a project of educating students to feel compassion for the suffering of others, to engage in a continual analysis of their own conditions of existence, to construct loyalties that engage the meaning and importance of public life, and to believe that they can make a difference, that they can act from a position of collective strength to alter existing configurations of power. This notion of pedagogy is predicated on a notion of learned hope, forged amidst the realization of risks, and steeped in a commitment to transforming public culture and life. It is a notion of critical pedagogy that stresses the historical and transformative in its practice.

In the debate about the importance of constructing a particular canon, the notion of naming and transmitting from one generation to the next what can be defined as "cultural treasures" specifies what has become the central argument for reforming the liberal arts.[28] For that reason, perhaps, it appears as though the debate is reducible to the question of the contents of course syllabi. The notion of critical pedagogy for which I am arguing provides a fundamental challenge to this position. For in the great challenges that we confront as university educators, what is called for is a more critical and fundamental argument that transcends the limited focus on the canon. What the issue of critical pedagogy raises in this debate is that the crisis in liberal arts education is one of historical purpose and meaning that challenges us to rethink in a critical fashion the relationship between the role of the university and the imperatives of a democracy in a mass society.

Historically, the liberal arts education was conceived of as the essential preparation for governing, for ruling—more specifically, as the preparation and outfitting of the governing elite. The liberal arts curricula, composed of the "best" that had been said or written, was intended, as Elizabeth Fox-Genovese has observed, "to provide selected individuals with a collective history, culture, and epistemology so that they could run the world effectively."[29] The canon, considered a possession of the dominant classes or groups, was fashioned as a safeguard to insure that the cultural property of such groups was passed on from generation to generation along with the family estates. Thus, in these very terms it seems most appropriate that the literary canon should be subject to revision—as it has been before in the course of the expansion of democracy—such that it might also incorporate and reflect the experience and aspirations of the women, minorities, and children of the working class who have been entering the academy.

As conceived above, a radical vision of liberal arts education is to be found within its elite social origins and purpose. But this does not suggest that the most important questions confronting liberal arts reform lie in merely establishing the content of the liberal arts canon on the model of the elite universities. Instead, the most important questions become that of reformulating the meaning and purpose of higher education in ways that contribute to the cultivation and regeneration of an informed critical citizenry capable of actively participating in the shaping and governing of a democratic society. Within this discourse, the pedagogical becomes political and the notion of a liberal arts canon commands a more historically grounded and critical reading. The pedagogical becomes more political in that it proposes that the ways in which students engage and critically examine knowledge is just as important an issue as the choosing of texts to be used in a class or program. That is, a democratic notion of liberal education rejects those views of the humanities that would treat texts as sacred and instruction as merely transmission. This notion of the canon undermines the possibility for dialogue, argument, and critical thinking. Moreover, it treats knowledge as a form of cultural inheritance that is beyond considerations regarding how it might be implicated, as I previously noted, in social practices that exploit, infantilize, and oppress.

The canons we have inherited, in their varied forms, cannot be dismissed as simply part of the ideology of privilege and domination. Instead, the privileged texts of the dominant or official canons should be explored with respect to the important role they have played in shaping, for better or worse, the major events of our time. Moreover, there are forms of knowledge that have been marginalized by the official canons. There are noble traditions, histories, and narratives that speak to important struggles by women, Afro-Americans, minorities, and other silenced groups that need to be heard so that such groups can lay claim to their own voices as part of a process of both affirmation and critical inquiry. At issue here is a notion of pedagogy as a form of cultural politics that rejects a facile restoration of the past and rejects history as a monolog. A critical pedagogy recognizes that history is constituted in dialogue and that some of the voices that make up that dialogue have been eliminated. Such a pedagogy calls for a public debate regarding the dominant memories and repressed stories that constitute the historical narratives of a social order. In effect, a critical pedagogy recognizes that canon formation is a matter of both rewriting and reinterpreting the past, that canon formation embodies the ongoing "process of reconstructing the 'collective reflexivity' of lived cultural experience . . . which recognizes that the 'notions of the past and future are essentially notions of the present.'"[30] Such notions are central to the politics of identity and power and to the memories that structure how experience is individually and collectively authorized and experienced as form of cultural identity.

As a historical construct, critical pedagogy functions in a dual sense to address the issue of what kinds of knowledge can be put in place that enable rather than subvert the formation of a democratic society. On one level, it authorizes forms of counter-memory. It excavates, affirms, and interrogates the histories, memories, and stories of the devalued others who have been marginalized from the official discourse of the canon. It attempts to recover and mediate those knowledge forms and social practices that have been decentered from the discourses of power. Surely, such knowledge might include the historical and contemporary writings of feminists such as Mary Wollstonecraft, Charlotte Perkins Gilman, and Adrienne Rich; Afro-American writers such as W. E. B. DuBois, Martin Luther King, Jr., and Zora Neale Hurston, as well as documents that helped shape the struggles of labor movements in the United States. The pedagogical practice at work here is not meant to romanticize these subjugated knowledges and "dangerous memories" as much as to critically appropriate and renew them as part of the reconstruction of a public philosophy that legitimates a politics and pedagogy of difference.

On another level, critical pedagogy recognizes that all educational work is at root contextual and conditional. This pedagogy refuses the totalizing unity of discourses that expunge the specific, contingent, and particular from their formulations. In this case, a critical pedagogy can only be discussed from within the historical and cultural specificity of space, time, place, and context. A critical pedagogy does not arise against a background of psychological, sociological, or anthropological universals but from within tasks that are strategic and practical, guided by imperatives that are both historical and ethical.

A critical pedagogy also rejects a discourse of value neutrality. Without subscribing to a language that polices behavior and desire, a critical pedagogy aims at developing pedagogical practices informed by an ethical stance that contests racism, sexism, class exploitation, and other dehumanizing and exploitative social relations as ideologies and social practices that disrupt and devalue public life. This is a pedagogy that rejects detachment, though it does not silence in the name of its own ideological fervor or correctness, acknowledges social injustices, and examines with care and in dialogue with itself and others how injustice works through the discourses, experiences, and desires that constitute daily life and the subjectivities of the students who invest in them. That is, it is a pedagogy guided by ethical principles that correspond to a radical practice rooted in historical experience. It is a pedagogy that comprehends the historical consequences of what it means to take a moral and political position with respect to the horror of, for example, the Gulag, the Nazi holocaust, or the Pol Pot regime, events that not only summon images of terror, domination, and resistance, but also provide a priori examples of what principles have to be both defended and fought against in the interest of freedom and life.

Within this perspective, ethics becomes more than the discourse of moral relativism or a static transmission of reified history. Ethics becomes instead a continued engagement in which the social practices of everyday life are interrogated in relation to the principles of individual autonomy and democratic public life—not as a matter of received truth but as a constant engagement. This provides the opportunity for individual capacities to be questioned and examined so that they can serve both to critically analyze and advance the possibilities inherent in all social forms. Community, difference, remembrance, and historical consciousness become central to the language of public life. This particular ethical stance is one that cannot be separated from the issue of how a socialized humanity develops within ideological and material conditions that either enable or disable the enhancement of human possibilities. It moves beyond moral outrage, attempting instead to provide a critical account of how individuals are constituted as human agents within different moral and ethical discourses and experiences. At the heart of such a pedagogy is the recognition that it is important to stare into history in order to remember the suffering of the past and that out of this remembrance a theory of ethics should be developed in which solidarity, compassion, and care become central dimensions of an informed social practice.

Essential to a critical pedagogy is the need to affirm the lived reality of difference as the ground on which to pose questions of theory and practice. Moreover, a critical pedagogy needs to function as a social practice that claims the experience of lived difference as an agenda for discussion and a central resource for a project of possibility. It must be constructed as part of a struggle over assigned meanings, the viability of different voices, and particular forms of authority. It is this struggle that makes possible and hence can redefine the possibilities we see both in the conditions of our daily lives and in those conditions that are "not yet."

A critical pedagogy for the liberal arts is one that affirms for students the importance of leadership as a moral and political enterprise that links the radical responsibility of ethics with the possibility of having those who are not oppressed understand the experience of oppression as an obstacle to democratic public life. Thus, critical pedagogy as a form of cultural politics is a call to celebrate responsible action and strategic risk taking as part of an ongoing struggle to link citizenship with the notion of a democratic public community, civic courage to a shared conception of social justice. Chantal Mouffe argues that a critical conception of citizenship should be "postmodern" in that it recognizes the importance of a politics of difference in which the particular, heterogeneous, and the multiple play a crucial role in the forming of a democratic public sphere:

> The struggle for democratic citizenship is one strategy among others. It is an attempt to challenge the undemocratic practices of neoliberalism by constructing different political identities. It is inspired by a view of politics, which assumes a community of equals who share rights, social responsibility, and a solidarity based on a common belonging to a political community whose political ends—freedom and equality for all—are pursued in participating institutions. This is a long way from . . . a privatized conception of citizenship that intends to whisk away the notion of political community. Democratic citizenship, on the contrary, aims at restoring the centrality of such a notion.[31]

Mouffe's view of citizenship and my view of a critical pedagogy include the idea that the formation of democratic citizens demands forms of political identity that radically extend the principles of justice, liberty, and dignity to public spheres constituted by difference and multiple forms of community. Of course, this is as much a pedagogical issue as it is a political issue. These political identities have to be constructed as part of a pedagogy in which difference becomes a basis for solidarity and unity rather than for competition and discrimination.

If pedagogy is to be linked with the notion of learning for empowerment, it is important that educators understand theoretically how difference is constructed through various representations and practices that name, legitimate, marginalize, and exclude the cultural capital and voices of subordinated groups in American society. Difference in this case does not become an empty marker for registering such differences within the language of harmony and conflict resolution. On the contrary, difference has to be taken up as a historical and social construction situated within hierarchies of domination and resistance. Hence, differences must be understood historically as part of larger political processes and systems tied to specific forms of exclusion, resistance, and transformation. In this case, difference is about how pedagogical and political practices work within and outside of the university to rewrite, codify, and reshape the practices of some groups within the discourse of privilege, while simultaneously erasing the cultural identities and histories of others.

As part of this theoretical project, a pedagogy of difference must address the question of how representations and practices that name, marginalize, and define difference as the devalued Other are actively learned, internalized, challenged, or transformed. In addition, such a pedagogy needs to address how understanding these differences can be used in order to change the prevailing relations of power that sustain them. It is also imperative to acknowledge and critically interrogate how the colonizing of differences by dominant groups is expressed and sustained through representations: in which the Other is seen as a deficit, in which the humanity of the Other is posited either as cynically problematic or ruthlessly denied. At the same time, it is important for a pedagogy of difference not only to critically unravel the ways in which the voices of the Other are colonized and repressed by the principle of identity that runs through the discourse of dominant groups, but also to understand how the experience of marginality at the level of everyday life lends itself to forms of oppositional and transformative consciousness.[32] This understanding must be based on the Others' reclamation and recreation of their own histories, voices, and visions as part of a wider struggle to change those material and social relations that deny radical pluralism as the basis of democratic political community. For it is only through such an understanding that teachers can develop a pedagogy of difference, one characterized by what Teresa de Lauretis calls "an ongoing effort to create new spaces of discourse, to rewrite cultural narratives, and to define the terms of another perspective—a view from 'elsewhere.'"[33]

What is suggested is a pedagogy in which there is a critical questioning of the omissions and tensions that exist between the master narratives and hegemonic discourses that make up the official curriculum of the university, department, or program and the self-representations of subordinated groups as they might appear in "forgotten" histories, texts, memories, experiences, and community narratives. Not only does a pedagogy of difference seek to understand how difference is constructed in the intersection of the official canon of the school and the various voices of students from subordinate groups, it also draws upon student experience as both a narrative for agency and a referent for critique. This requires forms of pedagogy that both confirm and critically engage the knowledge and experience through which students author their own voices and construct social identities. In effect, we must take seriously, as an aspect of learning, the knowledge and experiences that constitute the individual and collective voices by which students identify and give meaning to themselves and others by first using what they know about their own lives as a basis for criticizing the dominant culture. The student experience has to be first understood and recognized as the accumulation of collective memories and stories that provide students with a sense of familiarity, identity, and practical knowledge. Such experience has to be both affirmed and critically interrogated. In addition, the social and historical construction of such experience has to be affirmed and understood as part of a wider struggle for voice, but it also has to be remade, reterritorialized in the interest of a social imaginary that dignifies the best traditions and possibilities of those groups learning to speak from a position of enablement, that is, from the discourse of dignity and governance. In her analysis of the deterritorialization of women as Other, Caren Kaplan articulates this position well.

> Recognizing the minor cannot erase the aspects of the major, but as a mode of understanding it enables us to see the fissures in our identities, to unravel the seams of our totalities. . . . We must leave home, as it were, since our homes are often sites of racism, sexism, and other damaging social practices. Where we come to locate ourselves in terms of our specific histories and differences must be a place with room for what can be salvaged from the past and made anew. What we gain is a reterritorialization; we reinhabit a world of our making (here "our" is expanded to a coalition of identities—neither universal nor particular).[34]

Furthermore, it is important to extend the possibilities of experience by making it both the object of critical inquiry and by appropriating in a similarly critical fashion, when necessary, the codes and knowledges that constitute broader and less familiar historical and cultural traditions. We need not necessarily indiscriminately abandon the traditions of Western civilization; instead, we need to engage the strengths and weaknesses of such a complex and contradictory tradition as part of a wider effort to deepen the discourse of critical democracy and responsible citizenship.

At issue here is the development of a pedagogy that replaces the authoritative language of recitation with an approach that allows students to speak from their own histories, collective memories, and voices while simultaneously challenging the grounds on which knowledge and power are constructed and legitimated. Critical pedagogy contributes to making possible a variety of human capacities that expand the range of social identities that students may become. It points to the importance of understanding in both pedagogical and political terms how subjectivities are produced within those social forms in which people move but of which they are often only partially conscious. Similarly, it raises fundamental questions regarding how students make particular investments of meaning and affect, how students are constituted within a triad of knowledge, power, and pleasure, and what it is we as teachers need to understand regarding why students should be interested in the forms of authority, knowledge, and values that we produce and legitimate within our classrooms and university. It is worth noting that not only does such a pedagogy articulate a respect for a diversity of student voices, it also provides a referent for developing a public language rooted in a commitment to social transformation.

Another serious challenge of reforming the liberal arts necessitates that university teachers rethink the nature of their role with respect to issues of politics, social responsibility, and the construction of a pedagogy of possibility. Instead of weaving dreams fashioned in the cynical interests of industrial psychology and cultural sectarianism, university educators can become part of a collective effort to build and revitalize critical public cultures that provide the basis for transformative democratic communities. This means, among other things, that they can educate students to work collectively to make "despair unconvincing and hope practical" by refusing the role of the disconnected expert, technician, or careerist and adopting the practice of the engaged and transformative intellectual. This is not a call for educators to become wedded to some abstract ideal that turns them into prophets of perfection and certainty; on the contrary, it represents a call for educators to perform a noble public service, that is, to undertake teaching as a form of social criticism, to define themselves as engaged, critical public intellectuals who can play a major role in animating a democratic public culture.[35] It begs intellectuals to construct their relationship to the wider society by making organic connections with the historical traditions that provide themselves and their students with a voice, history, and sense of belonging. This view resonates with Gramsci's call to broaden the notion of education by seeing all of society as a vast school. It also resonates with his call for critical intellectuals to forge alliances around new historical blocks.[36]

Educators need to encourage students by example to find ways to get involved, to make a difference, to think in global terms, and to act from specific contexts. The notion of teachers as transformative intellectuals is marked by a moral courage and criticism that does not require them to step back from society but only to distance themselves from being implicated in those power relations that subjugate, corrupt, exploit, or infantilize. This is what Michael Walzer calls criticism from within, the telling of stories that speak to the historical specificity and voices of those who have been marginalized and silenced.[37] It is a form of criticism wedded to the development of pedagogical practices and experiences in the interest of a utopian vision that in Walter Benjamin's terms rubs history against the grain, one that gives substance to the development of a public culture that is synonymous with the spirit of a critical democracy.

Educators must therefore develop a public language that refuses to reconcile higher education with inequality, that actively abandons those forms of pedagogical practice that prevent our students from becoming aware of and offended by the structures of oppression at work in both institutional and everyday life. We need a language that defends liberal arts education neither as a servant of the state nor as authoritarian cultural ideology but as the site of a counter-public sphere where students can be educated to learn how to question and, in the words of John Dewey, "break existing public forms."[38] This is a language in which knowledge and power are inextricably linked to the presupposition that to choose life, so as to make it possible, is to understand the preconditions necessary to struggle for it. As engaged public intellectuals committed to a project of radical pedagogy and the reconstruction of democratic public life, academics can create forms of collegiality and community forged in social practices that link their work in the university with larger social struggles. This suggests redefining the borders of knowledge-power relationships outside of the limitations of academic specialties so as to broaden the relationship of the university with the culture of public life. Academic interventions can thus provide the basis for new forms of public association, occasions informed by and contributing to moral and political commitments in which the meanings we produce, the ways in which we represent ourselves, and our relation to others contribute to a wider public discussion and dialogue of democratic possibilities not yet realized. This is a call to transform the hegemonic cultural forms of the wider society and the academy into a social movement of intellectuals intent on reclaiming and reconstructing democratic values and public life rather than contributing to their demise. This is a utopian practice that both critiques and transcends the culture of despair and disdain that has characterized education in the Reagan-Bush Era. It also provides a starting point for linking liberal arts education with a public philosophy in which the curriculum is not reduced to a matter of cultural inheritance, but is posed as part of an ongoing struggle informed by a project of possibility that extends the most noble of human capacities while simultaneously developing the potentialities of democratic public life.

References

1. Of course, a caveat has to be noted here. For many liberal and left academics, the university is generally regarded as a site constituted in relations of power and representing various political and ethical interests. On the other hand, some neoconservative educators believe that the true interests of the university transcend political and normative concerns and that the latter represent an agenda being pushed exclusively by left-wing academics who are undermining the most basic principles of university life. For example, former Secretary of Education William J. Bennett has argued that most universities are controlled "by a left-wing political agenda" pushing the concerns of feminists, Marxists, and various ethnic groups. The neoconservative argument is often made in defense of an objective, balanced, and unbiased academic discourse. The claim to objectivity, truth, and principle that transcend history and power may be comforting to neoconservative but in reality the discourse of such groups is nothing more than a rhetorical mask that barely conceals their own highly charged, ideological agenda. The neoconservative ongoing attacks against affirmative action, ethnic studies, radical scholarship, modernity, and any thing else that threatens the traditional curriculum and the power relations it supports represent a particularized, not universalized view of the university and its relationship with the wider society. The most recent example of neoconservative "objectivity" and public conscience was displayed in a recent meeting in Washington, D.C., of 300 conservative scholars whose major agenda was to reclaim the universities and to find ways to challenge those left-wing academics, referred to by one of the participants as "the barbarians in our midst" (p. 14), who are challenging the authority of the traditional canon. Underlying this form of

criticism is the not so invisible ideological appeal to the "white man's burden" to educate those who exist outside of the parameters of civilized culture; the rhetoric betrays the colonizing logic at the heart of the "reactionary" political agenda that characterizes the new cultural offensive of such groups as the National Association of Scholars. The report on the conference appeared in Joseph Berger, "Conservative Scholars Attack 'Radicalization' of Universities," *New York Times*, November 15, 1988, 14. For a discussion of the conservative offensive in establishing a traditional reading of the liberal arts and the notion of the canon, see William V. Spanos, *Repetitions: The Postmodern Occasion in Literature and Culture* (Baton Rouge, 1987); a special issue on "The Politics of Education," *South Atlantic Quarterly* 89:1, (1990); a special issue on "The Politics of Teaching Literature," *College Literature* 17:2/3 (1990); Henry A. Giroux, *Schooling and the Struggle for Public Life* (Minneapolis, 1988).

2. A characteristic form of this type of evasion can be found in John Searle, "The Storm Over the University," *The New York Review of Books* 37:1 (December 6, 1990); Allan Bloom, *Giants and Dwarf: Essays* 1960–1990 (New York: Simon and Schuster, 1990), and Roger Kimball, *Tenured Radicals: How Politics Has Corrupted Our Higher Education* (New York: Harper and Roe, 1990). All of these books share the lament that progressives and radicals have corrupted the university by politicizing the curriculum. Central to this charge is the assumptions that conservatives are politically neutral and that their call for educational reform is objective and value-free. Searle's claim is a bit more sophisticated, though no less confused. He alleges that because social critics link university reform with the broader goal of social transformation that they must by necessity engage in forms of political indoctrination. Searle cannot, unfortunately, distinguish between rooting one's pedagogy in a particular set of expectations that serve as a referent for engaging students and a pedagogical approach designed to beat them into ideological submission. In other words, Searle collapses the particular ideological values that educators individually profess and the pedagogy they exercise. While I believe that students should be educated to not simply adapt to the system but be able to change it when necessary, the nature of my pedagogy does not have to be reduced to the inculcation of a specific ideology in the service of social transformation. My immediate goal is to get students to think critically about their lives; the specific objectives and ideologies they choose to address and take up are not something that can be forced upon them. Any pedagogy that acts in the service of only one outcome generally constitutes a form of terrorism.
3. Henry Louis Gates, Jr., "The Master's Pieces: On Canon Formation and the African American Tradition," *The South Atlantic Quarterly* 89:1 (1990), 89–111.
4. Gayatri C. Spivak, "The Making of Americans, the Teaching of English, and the Future of Cultural Studies," *New Literary History* 21:4 (Autumn 1990), 785.
5. Philip Corrigan, "In/Forming Schooling," in David W. Livingstone, Critical *Pedagogy and Cultural Power* (New York, New York: Bergin and Garvey, 1987), 17–40.
6. I am borrowing this idea from Peter Brooks, "Western Civ at Bay," *New York Time Literary Supplement*, January 25, 1991, 5.
7. Roger I. Simon, "Empowerment as a Pedagogy of Possibility," *Language Arts* 64:3 (April 1987), 372.
8. Jacques Derrida, "The Principle of Reason: The University in the Eyes of Its Pupils," *Diacritics* 13:3 (Fall 1983), 3.
9. Ernst Bloch, *The Philosophy of the Future* (New York, 1970), 86–87.
10. The quotes before and after the passage by Bloch are from Roger Simon, "Empowerment, as a Pedagogy of Possibility," 371, 372. I am indebted to Simon for a number of the ideas in this section on Bloch and the relationship between daydreaming and the process of schooling.
11. Leon Botstein illuminates some of the ideological elements at work in the language of cultural despair characteristic of the educational discourse of the New Right:

    In particular, the new conservativism evident in the most influential educational critiques and Jeremiads utilizes the language and images of decline and unwittingly makes comparisons to an idealized American past during which far fewer Americans finished high school. It challenges implicitly (Hirsch) and explicitly (Bloom) the post-World War II democratic goal of American schooling: to render excellence and equity incompatible in reality. In the 1980s, the call for educational reform is not being framed, as it was in the late 1950s (when America was concerned about Sputnik and Harvard's Conant studied the American high school), in terms of what might be achieved. Rather the discussion begins with a sense of what has been lost.

See Leon Botstein, "Education Reform in the Reagan Era: False Paths, Broken Promises," *Social Policy* (Spring 1988), 7. For a critique of the ideology of cultural decline among universities, see Jerry Herron, *Universities and the Myth of Cultural Decline* (Detroit, 1988).

12. Simon, "Empowerment as a Pedagogy of Possibility."

13. This criticism is more fully developed in Stanley Aronowitz and Henry A. Giroux, *Postmodern Education* (Minneapolis: University of Minnesota Press, 1991); Henry A. Giroux, *Schooling and the Struggle for Public Life*; Stanley Aronowitz and Henry A. Giroux, *Education Under Siege* (Granby, Mass., 1985).

14. Brooks, "Western Civ at Bay," 5.

15. Roger Kimball, *"Tenured Radicals":* As Post-script," *The New Criterion* (January 1991),13.

16. Silber, cited in Carolyn J. Mooney, "Scholars Decry Campus Hostility to Western Culture at a Time When More Nations Embrace Its Values," *The Chronicle of Higher Education*, January 30, 1991, A16.

17. Allan Bloom, *The Closing of the American Mind: How Higher Education Has Failed Democracy and Impoverished the Souls of Today's Students* (New York, 1987). E. D. Hirsch, Jr., *Cultural Literacy: What Every American Needs to Know* (Boston, 1987).

18. Allan Bloom, *The Closing of the American Mind;* E. D. Hirsch, Jr., *Cultural Literacy;* Kimball, *Tenured Radicals;* Lynne V. Cheney, *Humanities in America: A Report to the President, the Congress, and the American People* (Washington, D.C.: National Endowment for the Humanities, 1988).

19. This position is more fully developed in Jim Merod, *The Political Responsibility of the Critic* (Ithaca, 1987); Aronowitz and Giroux, *Education Under Siege*, 1985; Frank Lentricchia, *Criticism and Social Change* (Chicago, 1983).

20. William V. Spanos, *Repetitions*, 302.

21. Christopher Lasch, "A Response to Fischer," *Tikkun* 3:6 (1988), 73.

22. Mas'ud Zavarzadeh and Donald Morton, "War of the Words: The Battle of (and for) English," *In These Times* (October 28–November 3, 1987), 18–19. Hazel Carby, in "The Canon: Civil War and Reconstruction," *Michigan Quarterly Review* (Winter 1989), 36–38, is clear on this point and is worth quoting at length:

. . . I would argue that debates about the canon are misleading debates in many ways. Arguments appear to be about the inclusion or exclusion of particular texts and/or authors or about including or excluding types of books and authors ("women" and "minorities" are usually the operative categories). It also appears as if debates about the canon are disagreements about issues of representation only. . . . Contrary to what the debate appears to be about, talking about the canon means that we avoid the deeper problem. Focusing on books and authors means that we are not directly addressing ways in which our society is structured in dominance. We live in a racialized hierarchy which is also organized through class and gender divisions. Reducing these complex modes of inequality to questions of representation on a syllabus is far too simple a method of appearing to resolve those social contradictions and yet this is how the battle has been waged at Columbia and Stanford, to take two examples of campuses engaged in debating the importance of canonical works of western culture. What is absurd about these hotly contested and highly emotive battles is that proponents for radical change in canonical syllabi are forced to act as if inclusion of the texts they favor would somehow make accessible the experience of women or minorities as generic types. The same people who would argue in very sophisticated critical terms that literary texts do not directly reflect or represent reality but reconstruct and represent particular historical realities find themselves demanding that the identity of a social group be represented by a single novel. Acting as if an excluded or marginalized or dominant group is represented in a particular text, in my view, is a mistake. . . . Our teaching needs to make connections with, as well as provide a critique of, dominant ideologies and meanings of culture which structure the curricula of departments of English and American studies.

See also Toni Morrison, "Unspeakable Things Unspoken: The Afro-American Presence in American Literature," *Michigan Quarterly Review* (Winter 1989), 1–34.

23. This particular quote is cited in Frank Hearn, *Reason and Freedom in Sociological Thought* (Boston, 1985), 175. The classic statements by Dewey on this subject can be found, of course, in John Dewey, *Democracy and Education* (New York, 1916) and John Dewey, *The Public and Its Problems* in *The Later Works of John Dewey,*

Volume 2, 1925–1927, Jo Ann Boydston, ed. (Carbondale, 1984), 253–372.

24. See, for example, C. Wright Mills, *Power, Politics, and People: The Collected Essays of C. Wright Mills*, Irving Louis Horowitz, ed. (New York, 1963), especially the "Social Role of the Intellectual" and "Mass Society and Liberal Education."

25. For a critical treatment of this issue, see Robert N. Bellah, Richard Madsen, William M. Sullivan, Ann Swidler, and Steven M. Tipton, *Habits of the Heart: Individualism and Commitment in American Life* (Berkeley, 1985); for an excellent analysis and criticism of American life and the decline of community as portrayed in *Habits of the Heart*, see Fredric R. Jameson, "On Habits of the Heart," in Charles H. Reynolds and Ralph V. Norman, eds., *Community in America* (Berkeley, 1988), 97–112.

26. A number of representative essays that deal with pedagogy as a form of cultural production can be found in Henry A. Giroux and Peter McLaren, eds., *Critical Pedagogy, The State and Cultural Struggle* (Albany: SUNY Press, 1988); Henry A. Giroux and Roger I. Simon, eds., *Popular Culture and Critical Pedagogy* (New York: Bergin and Garvey, 1989); Patricia Donahue and Ellen Quandahl, eds., *Reclaiming Pedagogy: The Rhetoric of the Classroom* (Carbondale: Southern Illinois University Press, 1989); Aronowitz and Henry A. Giroux, *Postmodern Education;* and Roger I. Simon, *Teaching Against the Grain* (New York: Bergin and Garvey Press, 1991).

27. Democracy, in this case, is linked to citizenship understood as a form of self-management constituted in all major economic, social, and cultural spheres of society. Democracy as it is being used here take up the issue of transferring power from elites and executives authorities, who control the economic and cultural apparatuses of society, to those producers who wield power at the local level.

28. The next two pages draw from Henry A. Giroux and Harvey J. Kaye, "The Liberal Arts Must Be Reformed to Serve Democratic Ends," *The Chronicle of Higher Education*, March 29, 1989, A44.

29. Elizabeth Fox-Genovese, "The Claims of a Common Culture: Gender, Race, Class and the Canon," *Salmagundi* 72 (Fall 1986), 133.

30. Gail Valasrakis, "The Chippewa and the Other: Living the Heritage of Lac Du Flambeau," *Cultural Studies* 2:3 (October 1988), 268.

31. Chantal Mouffe, "The Civics Lesson," *New Statesman and Society* (October 7, 1988), 30.

32. bell hooks, "Choosing the Margin as a Space of Radical Openness," *Yearning* (Boston: South End Press, 1990), 145–52.

33. Teresa de Lauretis, *Technologies of Gender* (Bloomington, 1987), p. 25.

34. Caren Kaplan, "Deterritorialization: The Rewriting of Home and Exile in Western Feminist Discourse," *Cultural Critique* 6 (Spring 1987), 187–98.

35. On this point, see Russell Jacoby, *The Last Intellectuals* (New York, 1987); Terry Eagleton, *The Function of Criticism* (London, 1984).

36. Antonio Gramsci, *Selections from the Prison Notebooks* (New York, 1971).

37. Michael Walzer, *Interpretation and Social Criticism* (Cambridge, 1985).

38. John Dewey, *The Public and Its Problems in The Later Works of John Dewey, Volume 2, 1925–1927*, Jo Ann Boydston, ed., (Carbondale, 1984), 253–372.

CHAPTER 20

CITIZENS OF THE WORLD

MARTHA C. NUSSBAUM

When anyone asked him where he came from, he said, "I am a citizen of the world."
Diogenes Laertius, *Life of Diogenes the Cynic*

Anna was a political science major at a large state university in the Midwest. Upon graduation she went into business, getting a promising job with a large firm. After twelve years she had risen to a middle-management position. One day, her firm assigned her to the newly opened Beijing office.[1] What did she need to know, and how well did her education prepare her for success in her new role? In a middle-management position, Anna is working with both Chinese and American employees, both male and female. She needs to know how Chinese people think about work (and not to assume there is just one way); she needs to know how cooperative networks are formed, and what misunderstandings might arise in interactions between Chinese and American workers. Knowledge of recent Chinese history is important, since the disruptions of the Cultural Revolution still shape workers' attitudes. Anna also needs to consider her response to the recent policy of urging women to return to the home, and to associated practices of laying off women first. This means she should know something about Chinese gender relations, both in the Confucian tradition and more recently. She should probably know something about academic women's studies in the United States, which have influenced the women's studies movement in Chinese universities. She certainly needs a more general view about human rights, and about to what extent it is either legitimate or wise to criticize another nation's ways of life. In the future, Anna may find herself dealing with problems of anti-African racism, and with recent government attempts to exclude immigrants who test positive for the human immunodeficiency virus. Doing this well will require her to know something about the history of Chinese attitudes about race and sexuality. It will also mean being able to keep her moral bearings even when she knows that the society around her will not accept her view.

The real-life Anna had only a small part of this preparation—some courses in world history, but none that dealt with the general issue of cultural variety and how to justify moral judgments in a context of diversity; none that dealt with the variety of understandings of gender roles or family structures; none that dealt with sexual diversity and its relationship to human rights. More important, she had no courses that prepared her for the shock of discovering that other places treated as natural what she found strange, and as strange what she found natural. Her imaginative capacity to enter into the lives of people of other nations had been blunted by lack of practice. The real-life Anna had a rough time getting settled in China, and the firm's dealings with its new context were not always very successful. A persistent and curious person, however, she stayed on and has made herself a good

Source: "Citizens of the World," by Martha C. Nussbaum, reprinted from *Cultivating Humanity: A Classical Defense of Reform in Liberal Education*, 1997, Harvard University Press.

interpreter of cultural difference. She now plans to spend her life in Beijing, and she feels is making a valuable contribution to the firm.

Two years ago, after several years in China, already in her late thirties, Anna decided to adopt a baby. Through her by then extensive knowledge of the Chinese bureaucracy, she bypassed a number of obstacles and quickly found an infant girl in an orphanage in Beijing. She then faced challenges of a very different kind. Even in the most apparently universal activities of daily life, cultural difference colors her day. Her Chinese nurse follows the common Chinese practice of wrapping the baby's limbs in swaddling bands to immobilize it. As is customary, the nurse interacts little with the child, either facially or vocally, and brings the child immediately anything it appears to want, without encouraging its own efforts. Anna's instincts are entirely different: she smiles at the baby, encourages her to wave her hands about, talks to her constantly, wants her to act for herself. The nurse thinks Anna is encouraging nervous tension by this hyperactive American behavior; Anna thinks the nurse is stunting the baby's cognitive development. Anna's mother, visiting, is appalled by the nurse and wants to move in, but Anna, by now a sensitive cross-cultural interpreter, is able to negotiate between mother and nurse and devise some plan for the baby's development that is agreeable to all. To do this she has had to think hard about the nonuniversality and nonnaturalness of such small matters as playing with a baby. But she has also had to think of the common needs and aims that link her with the nurse, and the nurse with her own mother. Her university education gave her no preparation at all for these challenges.

Had Anna been a student at today's St. Lawrence University, or at many other colleges and universities around the United States, she would have had a better basis for her international role, a role U.S. citizens must increasingly play (whether at home or abroad) if our efforts in business are to be successful, if international debates about human rights, medical and agricultural problems, ethnic and gender relations, are to make progress as we enter the new century. As Connie Ellis, a forty-three-year-old waitress at Marion's Restaurant in Sycamore, Illinois, put it on the Fourth of July, 1996, "You can't narrow it down to just our country anymore—it's the whole planet."[2] We must educate people who can operate as world citizens with sensitivity and understanding.

Asked where he came from, the ancient Greek Cynic philosopher Diogenes replied, "I am a citizen of the world." He meant by this that he refused to be defined simply by his local origins and group memberships, associations central to the self-image of a conventional Greek male; he insisted on defining himself in terms of more universal aspirations and concerns.[3] The Stoics who followed his lead developed his image of the *kosmopolitēs,* or world citizen, more fully, arguing that each of us dwells, in effect, in two communities—the local community of our birth, and the community of human argument and aspiration that "is truly great and truly common." It is the latter community that is, most fundamentally, the source of our moral and social obligations. With respect to fundamental moral values such as justice, "we should regard all human beings as our fellow citizens and local residents."[4] This attitude deeply influenced the subsequent philosophical and political tradition, especially as mediated through the writings of Cicero, who reworked it so as to allow a special degree of loyalty to one's own local region or group. Stoic ideas influenced the American republic through the writings of Thomas Paine, and also through Adam Smith and Immanuel Kant, who themselves influenced the Founders.[5] Later on, Stoic thought was a major formative influence on both Emerson and Thoreau.

This form of cosmopolitanism is not peculiar to Western traditions. It is, for example, the view that animates the work of the influential Indian philosopher, poet, and educational leader Rabindranath Tagore. Tagore drew his own cosmopolitan views from older Bengali traditions, although he self-consciously melded them with Western cosmopolitanism.[6] It is also the view recommended by Ghanaian philosopher Kwame Anthony Appiah, when he writes, concerning African identity: "We will only solve our problems if we see them as human problems arising out of a special situation, and we shall not solve them if we see them as African problems generated by our being somehow unlike others."[7] But for people who have grown up in the Western tradition it is useful to understand the roots of this cosmopolitanism in ancient Greek and Roman thought. These ideas are an essential resource for democratic citizenship. Like

Socrates' ideal of critical inquiry, they should be at the core of today's higher education.

The Idea of World Citizenship in Greek and Roman Antiquity

Contemporary debates about the curriculum frequently imply that the idea of a "multicultural" education is a new fad, with no antecedents in long-standing educational traditions. In fact, Socrates grew up in an Athens already influenced by such ideas in the fifth century B.C. Ethnographic writers such as the historian Herodotus examined the customs of distant countries, both in order to understand their ways of life and in order to attain a critical perspective on their own society. Herodotus took seriously the possibility that Egypt and Persia might have something to teach Athens about social values. A cross-cultural inquiry, he realized, may reveal that what we take to be natural and normal is merely parochial and habitual. One cultural group thinks that corpses must be buried; another, that they must be burnt; another, that they must be left in the air to be plucked clean by the birds. Each is shocked by the practices of the other, and each, in the process, starts to realize that its habitual ways may not be the ways designed by nature for all times and persons.

Awareness of cultural difference gave rise to a rich and complex debate about whether our central moral and political values exist in the nature of things (by *phusis*), or merely by convention (*nomos*).[8] That Greek debate illustrates most of the positions now familiar in debates about cultural relativism and the source of moral norms. It also contains a crucial insight: if we should conclude that our norms are human and historical rather than immutable and eternal, it does not follow that the search for a rational justification of moral norms is futile.

In the conventional culture of fifth-century B.C. Athens, recognition that Athenian customs were not universal became a crucial precondition of Socratic searching. So long as young men were educated in the manner of Aristophanes' Old Education, an education stressing uncritical assimilation of traditional values, so long as they marched to school in rows and sang the old songs without discussion of alternatives, ethical questioning could not get going. Ethical inquiry requires a climate in which the young are encouraged to be critical of their habits and conventions; and such critical inquiry, in turn, requires awareness that life contains other possibilities.

Pursuing these comparisons, fifth-century Athenians were especially fascinated by the example of Sparta, Athens' primary rival, a hierarchical and nondemocratic culture that understood the goal of civic education in a very un-Athenian way. As the historian Thucydides depicts them, Spartan educators carried to an extreme the preference for uniformity and rule-following that characterized the Old Education of Athens in Aristophanes' nostalgic portrait. Conceiving the good citizen as an obedient follower of traditions, they preferred uncritical subservience to Athenian public argument and debate. Denying the importance of free speech and thought, they preferred authoritarian to democratic politics.

Athenians, looking at this example, saw new reasons to praise the freedom of inquiry and debate that by this time flourished in their political life. They saw Spartan citizens as people who did not choose to serve their city, and whose loyalty was therefore in a crucial way unreliable, since they had never really thought about what they were doing. They noted that once Spartans were abroad and free from the narrow constraint of law and rule, they often acted badly, since they had never learned to choose for themselves. The best education, they held, was one that equips a citizen for genuine choice of a way of life; this form of education requires active inquiry and the ability to contrast alternatives. Athenians denied the Spartan charge that their own concern with critical inquiry and free expression would give rise to decadence. "We cultivate the arts without extravagance," they proudly proclaimed, "and we devote ourselves to inquiry without becoming soft." Indeed, they insisted that Sparta's high reputation for courage was ill based: for citizens could not be truly courageous if they never chose from among alternatives. True courage, they held, requires freedom, and freedom is best cultivated by an education that awakens critical thinking. Cross-cultural inquiry thus proved not only illuminating but also self-reinforcing to Athenians: by showing them regimes that did not practice such inquiry and what those regimes lacked in consequence, it gave Athenians reasons why they should continue to criticize and to compare cultures.

Plato, writing in the early to mid-fourth century B.C., alludes frequently to the study of other cultures, especially those of Sparta, Crete, and Egypt. In his *Republic,* which alludes often to Spartan practices, the plan for an ideal city is plainly influenced by reflection about customs elsewhere. One particularly fascinating example of the way in which reflection about history and other cultures awakens critical reflection occurs in the fifth book of that work, where Plato's character Socrates produces the first serious argument known to us in the Western tradition for the equal education of women. Here Socrates begins by acknowledging that the idea of women's receiving both physical and intellectual education equal to that of men will strike most Athenians as very weird and laughable. (Athenians who were interested in cultural comparison would know, however, that such ideas were not peculiar in Sparta, where women, less confined than at Athens, did receive extensive athletic training.)[9] But he then reminds Glaucon that many good things once seemed weird in just this way. For example, the unclothed public exercise that Athenians now prize as a norm of manliness once seemed foreign, and the heavy clothing that they think barbaric once seemed natural. However, he continues, when the practice of stripping for athletic contests had been in effect for some time, its advantages were clearly seen—and then "the appearance of absurdity ebbed away under the influence of reason's judgment about the best." So it is with women's education, Socrates argues. Right now it seems absurd, but once we realize that our conventions don't by themselves supply reasons for what we ought to do, we will be forced to ask ourselves whether we really do have good reasons for denying women the chance to develop their intellectual and physical capacities. Socrates argues that we find no such good reasons, and many good reasons why those capacities should be developed. Therefore, a comparative cultural study, by removing the false air of naturalness and inevitability that surrounds our practices, can make our society a more truly reasonable one.

Cross-cultural inquiry up until this time had been relatively unsystematic, using examples that the philosopher or historian in question happened to know through personal travel or local familiarity. Later in the fourth century, however, the practice was rendered systematic and made a staple of the curriculum, as Aristotle apparently instructed his students to gather information about 153 forms of political organization, encompassing the entire known world, and to write up historical and constitutional descriptions of these regimes. The *Athenian Constitution,* which was written either by Aristotle or by one of his students, is our only surviving example of the project; it shows an intention to record everything relevant to critical reflection about that constitution and its suitability When Aristotle himself writes political philosophy, his project is extensively cross-cultural. In his *Politics,* before describing his own views about the best form of government, he works through and criticizes many known historical examples, prominently including Crete and Sparta, and also a number of theoretical proposals, including those of Plato. As a result of this inquiry, Aristotle develops a model of good government that is in many respects critical of Athenian traditions, though he follows no single model.

By the beginning of the so-called Hellenistic era in Greek philosophy, then, cross-cultural inquiry was firmly established, both in Athenian public discourse and in the writings of the philosophers, as a necessary part of good deliberation about citizenship and political order.[10]

But it was neither Plato nor Aristotle who coined the term "citizen of the world." It was Diogenes the Cynic. Diogenes (404–323 B.C.) led a life stripped of the usual protections that habit and status supply. Choosing exile from his own native city, he defiantly refused protection from the rich and powerful for fear of losing his freedom, and lived in poverty, famously choosing a tub set up the marketplace as his "home" in order to indicate his disdain for convention and comfort. He connected poverty with independence of mind and speech, calling freedom of speech "the finest thing in human life."[11] Once, they say, Plato saw him washing some lettuce and said, "If you had paid court to Dionysius, you would not be washing lettuce."[12] Diogenes replied, "If you had washed lettuce, you would not have paid court to Dionysius." This freedom from subservience, he held, was essential to a philosophical life. "When someone reproached him for being an exile, he said that it was on that account that he came to be a philosopher."

Diogenes left no written work behind, and it is difficult to know how to classify him. "A Socrates gone mad" was allegedly Plato's description—and a good one, it seems. For Diogenes clearly followed the lead of Socrates in disdaining external markers of status and focusing on the inner life of virtue and thought. His search for a genuinely honest and virtuous person, and his use of philosophical arguments to promote that search, are recognizably Socratic. What was "mad" about him was the public assault on convention that accompanied his quest. Socrates provoked people only by his questions. He lived a conventional life. But Diogenes provoked people by his behavior as well, spitting in a rich man's face, even masturbating in public. What was the meaning of this shocking behavior?

It appears likely that the point of his unseemly behavior was itself Socratic—to get people to question their prejudices by making them consider how difficult it is to give good reasons for many of our deeply held feelings. Feelings about the respect due to status and rank and feelings of shame associated with sexual practices are assailed by this behavior—as Herodotus' feelings about burial were assailed by his contact with Persian and Egyptian customs. The question is whether one can then go on to find a good argument for one's own conventions and against the behavior of the Cynic.

As readers of the *Life* of Diogenes, we ourselves quickly become aware of the cultural relativity of what is thought shocking. For one of the most shocking things about Diogenes, to his Athenian contemporaries, was his habit of eating in the public marketplace. It was this habit that gave him the name "dog," *kuōn,* from which our English label Cynic derives. Only dogs, in this culture, tore away at their food in the full view of all. Athenians evidently found this just about as outrageous as public masturbation; in fact his biographer joins the two offenses together, saying, "He used to do everything in public, both the deeds of Demeter and those of Aphrodite." Crowds, they say, gathered around to taunt him as he munched on his breakfast of beets, behaving in what the American reader feels to be an unremarkable fashion. On the other hand, there is no mention in the *Life* of shock occasioned by public urination or even defecation. The reason for this, it may be conjectured, is that Athenians, like people in many parts of the world today, did not in fact find public excretion shocking. We are amazed by a culture that condemns public snacking while permitting such practices. Diogenes asks us to look hard at the conventional origins of these judgments and to ask which ones can be connected by a sound argument to important moral goals. (So far as we can tell, Cynics supplied no answers to this question.)

Set in this context, the invitation to consider ourselves citizens of the world is the invitation to become, to a certain extent, philosophical exiles from our own ways of life, seeing them from the vantage point of the outsider and asking the questions an outsider is likely to ask about their meaning and function. Only this critical distance, Diogenes argued, makes one a philosopher. In other words, a stance of detachment from uncritical loyalty to one's own ways promotes the kind of evaluation that is truly reason based. When we see in how many different ways people can organize their lives we will recognize, he seems to think, what is deep and what is shallow in our own ways, and will consider that "the only real community is one that embraces the entire world." In other words, the true basis for human association is not the arbitrary or the merely habitual; it is that which we can defend as good for human beings—and Diogenes believes that these evaluations know no national boundaries.

The confrontational tactics Diogenes chose unsettle and awaken. They do not contain good argument, however, and they can even get in the way of thought. Diogenes' disdain for more low-key and academic methods of scrutinizing customs, for example the study of literature and history, seems most unwise. It is hard to know whether to grant Diogenes the title "philosopher" at all, given his apparent preference for a kind of street theater over Socratic questioning. But his example, flawed as it was, had importance for the Greek philosophical tradition. Behind the theater lay an important idea: that the life of reason must take a hard look at local conventions and assumptions, in the light of more general human needs and aspirations.

The Stoic philosophers, over the next few centuries, made Diogenes' insight respectable and culturally fruitful.[13] They developed the idea of cross-cultural study and world citizenship much further in their own morally and philosophically rigorous way, making the concept of the "world citizen," *kosmou politēs,* a centerpiece of their educational program.[14] As Seneca writes, summarizing older Greek Stoic views, education should make us aware that each of us is a member of "two communities: one that is truly great and truly common . . . in which we look neither to this corner nor to that, but measure the boundaries of our nation by the sun; the other, the one to which we have been assigned by birth." The accident of where one is born is just that, an accident; any human being might have been born in any nation. Recognizing this, we should not allow differences of nationality or class or ethnic membership or even gender to erect barriers between us and our fellow human beings. We should recognize humanity—and its fundamental ingredients, reason and moral capacity—wherever it occurs, and give that community of humanity our first allegiance.

This does not mean that the Stoics proposed the abolition of local and national forms of political organization and the creation of a world state. The Greek Stoics did propose an ideal city, and the Roman Stoics did put ideas of world citizenship into practice in some ways in the governance of the empire. But the Stoics' basic point is more radical still: that we should give our first allegiance to *no* mere form of government, no temporal power, but to the moral community made up by the humanity of all human beings. The idea of the world citizen is in this way the ancestor and source of Kant's idea of the "kingdom of ends," and has a similar function in inspiring and regulating a certain mode of political and personal conduct. One should always behave so as to treat with respect the dignity of reason and moral choice in every human being, no matter where that person was born, no matter what that person's rank or gender or status may be. It is less a political idea than a moral idea that constrains and regulates political life.

The meaning of the idea for political life is made especially clear in Cicero's work *On Duties (De Officiis)*, written in 44 B.C. and based in part on the writings of the slightly earlier Greek Stoic thinker Panaetius. Cicero argues that the duty to treat humanity with respect requires us to treat aliens on our soil with honor and hospitality. It requires us never to engage in wars of aggression, and to view wars based on group hatred and wars of extermination as especially pernicious. It requires us to behave honorably in the conduct of war, shunning treachery even toward the enemy. In general, it requires us to place justice above political expediency, and to understand that we form part of a universal community of humanity whose ends are the moral ends of justice and human well-being. Cicero's book has been among the most influential in the entire Western philosophical tradition. In particular, it influenced the just-war doctrine of Grotius and the political thought of Immanuel Kant; their views about world understanding and the containment of global aggression are crucial for the formation of modern international law.

Stoics hold, then, that the good citizen is a "citizen of the world." They hold that thinking about humanity as it is realized in the whole world is valuable for self-knowledge: we see ourselves and our customs more clearly when we see our own ways in relation to those of other reasonable people. They insist, furthermore, that we really will be better able to solve our problems if we face them in this broader context, our imaginations unconstrained by narrow partisanship. No theme is deeper in Stoicism than the damage done by faction and local allegiances to the political life of a group. Stoic texts show repeatedly how easy it is for local or national identities and their associated hatreds to be manipulated by self-seeking individuals for their own gain—whereas reason is hard to fake, and its language is open to the critical scrutiny of all. Roman political life in Seneca's day was dominated by divisions of many kinds, from those of class and rank and ethnic origin to the division between parties at the public games and gladiatorial shows. Part of the self-education of the Stoic Roman emperor Marcus Aurelius, as he tells the reader of his *Meditations*, was "not to be a Green or Blue partisan at the races, or a supporter of the lightly armed or heavily armed gladiators at the Circus."[15] Politics is sabotaged again and again by these partisan loyalties, and by the search for honor and fame that accompanies them. Stoics argue that a style of citizenship that recognizes the moral/rational community as fundamental promises a more reasonable style of political deliberation and problem-solving.

But Stoics do not recommend world citizenship only for reasons of expediency. They insist that the stance of the *kosmou politēs* is intrinsically valuable: for it recognizes in people what is especially fundamental about them, most worthy of reverence and acknowledgment, namely their aspirations to justice and goodness and their capacities for reasoning in this connection. This essential aspect may be less colorful than local tradition and local identity, but it is, the Stoics argue, both lasting and deep.

To be a citizen of the world, one does not, the Stoics stress, need to give up local affiliations, which can frequently be a source of great richness in life. They suggest instead that we think of ourselves as surrounded by a series of concentric circles.[16] The first one is drawn around the self; the next takes in one's immediate family; then follows the extended family; then, in order, one's neighbors or local group, one's fellow city-dwellers, one's fellow countrymen—and we can easily add to this list groups formed on the basis of ethnic, religious, linguistic, historical, professional, and gender identities. Beyond all these circles is the largest one, that of humanity as a whole. Our task as citizens of the world, and as educators who prepare people to be citizens of the world, will be to "draw the circles somehow toward the center," making all human beings like our fellow city-dwellers. In other words, we need not give up our special affections and identifications, whether national or ethnic or religious; but we should work to make all human beings part of our community of dialogue and concern, showing respect for the human wherever it occurs, and allowing that respect to constrain our national or local politics.

This Stoic attitude, then, does not require that we disregard the importance of local loves and loyalties or their salience in education. Adam Smith made a serious error when he objected to Stoicism on those grounds, and modern critics of related Kantian and Enlightenment conceptions make a similar error when they charge them with neglect of group differences. The Stoic, in fact, must be conversant with local differences, since knowledge of these is inextricably linked to our ability to discern and respect the dignity of humanity in each person. Stoics recognize love for what is near as a fundamental human trait, and a highly rational way to comport oneself as a citizen. If each parent has a special love for his or her own children, society will do better than if all parents try to have an equal love for all children. Much the same is true for citizenship of town or city or nation: each of us should take our stand where life has placed us, and devote to our immediate surroundings a special affection and attention. Stoics, then, do not want us to behave as if differences between male and female, or between African and Roman, are morally insignificant. These differences can and do enjoin special obligations that all of us should execute, since we should all do our duties in the life we happen to have, rather than imagining that we are beings without location or memory.

Stoics vary in the degree of concession they make to these special obligations. Cicero, for example, takes a wise course when he urges the Roman citizen to favor the near and dear on many occasions, though always in ways that manifest respect for human dignity. These special local obligations have educational consequences: the world citizen will legitimately spend a disproportionate amount of time learning about the history and problems of her or his own part of the world. But at the same time we recognize that there is something more fundamental about us than the place where we happen to find ourselves, and that this more fundamental basis of citizenship is shared across all divisions.

This general point emerges clearly if we consider the relationship each of us has to a native language. We each have a language (in some cases more than one) in which we are at home, which we have usually known from infancy. We naturally feel a special affection for this language. It defines our possibilities of communication and expression. The works of literature that move us most deeply are those that exploit well the resources of that language. On the other hand, we should not suppose—and most of us do not suppose—that English is best just because it is our own, that works of literature written in English are superior to those written in other languages, and so forth. We know that it is more or less by chance that we are English speakers rather than speakers of Chinese or German or Bengali. We know that any infant might have learned any language, because there is a fundamental language-learning capacity that is shared by all humans. Nothing in our innate equipment disposes us to speak Hindi rather than Norwegian.

In school, then, it will be proper for us to spend a disproportionate amount of time mastering our native language and its literature. A human being who tried to learn all the world's languages would master none, and it seems reasonable for children to focus on one, or in some cases two, languages when they are small. On the other hand, it is also very important for students to understand what it is like to see the world through the perspective of another language, an experience that quickly shows that human complexity and rationality are not the monopoly of a single linguistic community.

This same point can be made about other aspects of culture that should figure in a higher education. In ethics, in historical knowledge, in knowledge of politics, in literary, artistic, and musical learning, we are all inclined to be parochial, taking our own habits for that which defines humanity. In these areas as in the case of language, it is reasonable to immerse oneself in a single tradition at an early age. But even then it is well to become acquainted with the facts of cultural variety, and this can be done very easily, for example through myths and stories that invite identification with people whose form of life is different from one's own. As education progresses, a more sophisticated grasp of human variety can show students that what is theirs is not better simply because it is familiar.

The education of the *kosmou politēs* is thus closely connected to Socratic inquiry and the goal of an examined life. For attaining membership in the world community entails a willingness to doubt the goodness of one's own way and to enter into the give-and-take of critical argument about ethical and political choices. By an increasingly refined exchange of both experience and argument, participants in such arguments should gradually take on the ability to distinguish, within their own traditions, what is parochial from what may be commended as a norm for others, what is arbitrary and unjustified from that which may be justified by reasoned argument.

Since any living tradition is already a plurality and contains within itself aspects of resistance, criticism, and contestation, the appeal to reason frequently does not require us to take a stand outside the culture from which we begin. The Stoics are correct to find in all human beings the world over a capacity for critical searching and a love of truth. "Any soul is deprived of truth against its will," says Marcus Aurelius, quoting Plato. In this sense, any and every human tradition is a tradition of reason, and the transition from these more ordinary and intracultural exercises to a more global exercise of critical argument need not be an abrupt transition. Indeed, in the world today it is clear that internal critique very frequently takes the form of invoking what is found to be fine and just in other traditions.

People from diverse backgrounds sometimes have difficulty recognizing one another as fellow citizens in the community of reason. This is so, frequently, because actions and motives require, and do not always receive, a patient effort of interpretation. The task of world citizenship requires the would-be world citizen to become a sensitive and empathic interpreter. Education at all ages should cultivate the capacity for such interpreting. This aspect of the Stoic idea is developed most fully by Marcus Aurelius, who dealt with many different cultures in his role as emperor; he presents, in his *Meditations*, a poignantly personal account of his own efforts to be a good world citizen. "Accustom yourself not to be inattentive to what another person says, and as far as possible enter into his mind," he writes (6.53); and again, "When things are being said, one should follow every word, when things are being done, every impulse; in the latter case, to see straightway to what object the impulse is directed, in the former, to watch what meaning is expressed" (7.4). Given that Marcus routinely associated with people from every part of the Roman Empire, this idea imposes a daunting task of learning and understanding, which he confronts by reading a great deal of history and literature, and by studying closely the individual characters of those around him in the manner of a literary narrator. "Generally," he concludes, "one must first learn many things before one can judge another's action with understanding" (11.18).

Above all, Marcus finds that he has to struggle not to allow his privileged station (an obstacle to real thought, as he continually points out) to sever him, in thought, from his fellow human beings. "See to it that you do not become Caesarized," he tells himself, "or dyed with that coloring" (6.30). A favorite exercise toward keeping such accidents of station in their proper place is to imagine that all human beings are limbs of a single body, cooperating for the sake of common purposes. Referring to the fact that it takes only the change of a single letter in Greek to convert the word "limb" *(meros)* into the word "(detached) part" *(meros)*, he concludes: "if, changing the word, you call yourself merely a (detached) part instead of a limb, you do not yet love your fellow men from the heart, nor derive complete joy from doing good; you will do it merely as a duty, not as doing good to yourself" (7.13). The organic imagery underscores the Stoic ideal of cooperation.

Can anyone really think like a world citizen in a life so full of factionalism and political conflict? Marcus gives himself the following syllogism: "Wherever it is possible to live, it is also possible to live a virtuous life; it is possible to live in a palace; therefore it is also possible to live a virtuous life in a palace" (5.16). And, recognizing that he himself has sometimes failed in citizenship because of impatience and the desire for solitude: "Let no one, not even yourself, any longer hear you placing the blame on palace life" (8.9). In fact, his account of his own difficulties being a world citizen in the turmoil of Roman politics yields some important advice for anyone who attempts to reconcile this high ideal with the realities of political involvement:

> Say to yourself in the morning: I shall meet people who are interfering, ungracious, insolent, full of guile, deceitful and antisocial; they have all become like that because they have no understanding of good and evil. But I who have contemplated the essential beauty of good and the essential ugliness of evil, who know that the nature of the wrongdoer is of one kin with mine—not indeed of the same blood or seed but sharing the same kind, the same portion of the divine—I cannot be harmed by any one of them, and no one can involve me in shame. I cannot feel anger against him who is of my kin, nor hate him. We were born to labor together, like the feet, the hands, the eyes, and the rows of upper and lower teeth. To work against one another is therefore contrary to nature, and to be angry against a man or turn one's back on him is to work against him. (2.1)

One who becomes involved in politics in our time might find this paragraph comforting. It shows a way in which the attitude of world citizenship gets to the root of one of the deepest political problems in all times and places, the problem of anger. Marcus is inclined to intense anger at his political adversaries. Sometimes the anger is personal, and sometimes it is directed against a group. His claim, however, is that such anger can be mitigated, or even removed, by the attitude of empathy that the ideal of the *kosmou polit_s* promotes. If one comes to see one's adversaries as not impossibly alien and other, but as sharing certain general human goals and purposes, if one understands that they are not monsters but people who share with us certain general goals and purposes, this understanding will lead toward a diminution of anger and the beginning of rational exchange.

World citizenship does not, and should not, require that we suspend criticism toward other individuals and cultures. Marcus continues to refer to his enemies as "deceitful and antisocial," expressing strong criticism of their conduct. The world citizen may be very critical of unjust actions or policies, and of the character of people who promote them. But at the same time Marcus refuses to think of the opponents as simply alien, as members of a different and inferior species. He refuses to criticize until he respects and understands. He carefully chooses images that reflect his desire to see them as close to him and similarly human. This careful scrutiny of the imagery and speech one uses when speaking about people who are different is one of the Stoic's central recommendations for the undoing of political hatred.

Stoics write extensively on the nature of anger and hatred. It is their well-supported view that these destructive emotions are not innate, but learned by children from their society. In part, they hold, people directly absorb negative evaluations of individuals and groups from their culture, in part they absorb excessively high evaluations of their own honor and status. These high evaluations give rise to hostility when another person or group appears to threaten their honor or status. Anger and hatred are not unreasoning instincts; they have to do with the way we think and imagine, the images we use, the language we find it habitual to employ. They can therefore be opposed by the patient critical scrutiny of the imagery and speech we employ when we confront those our tradition has depicted as unequal.

It is fashionable by now to be very skeptical of "political correctness," by which the critic usually means a careful attention to the speech we use in talking about minorities, or foreigners, or women. Such scrutiny might in some forms pose dangers to free speech, and of course these freedoms should be carefully defended. But the scrutiny of speech and imagery need not be inspired by totalitarian motives, and it need not lead to the creation of an antidemocratic "thought police." The Stoic demand for such scrutiny is based on the plausible view that hatred of individuals and groups is personally and politically pernicious, that it ought to be resisted by educators, and that the inner world of thought and speech is the place where, ultimately, hatred must be resisted. These ideas about the scrutiny of the inner world are familiar to Christians also, and the biblical injunction against sinning in one's heart has close historical links to Stoicism. All parents know that it is possible to shape a child's attitudes toward other races and nationalities by the selection of stories one tells and by the way one speaks about other people in the home. There are few parents who do not seek to influence their children's views in these ways. Stoics propose, however, that the process of coming to recognize the humanity of all people should be a lifelong process, encompassing all levels of education—especially since, in a culture suffused with group hatred, one cannot rely on parents to perform this task. What this means in higher education is that an attitude of mutual respect should be nourished both in the classroom itself and in its reading material. Although in America we should have no sympathy with the outright censoring of reading material, we also make many selections as educators, both in assigning material and in presenting it for our students. Few of us, for example, would present anti-Semitic propaganda in a university classroom in a way that conveyed sympathy with the point of view expressed. The Stoic proposal is that we should seek out curricula that foster respect and mutual solidarity and correct the ignorance that is often an essential prop of hatred. This effort is perfectly compatible with maintaining freedom of speech and the openness of a genuinely critical and deliberative culture.

In our own time, few countries have been more rigidly divided, more corroded by group hatred, than South Africa. In spelling out its goals for society in its draft for the new Constitution, the African National Congress (ANC) recognized the need to address hatred through education, and specified the goal of education as the overcoming of these differences:

> Education shall be directed towards the development of the human personality and a sense of personal dignity, and shall aim at strengthening respect for human rights and fundamental freedoms and promoting understanding, tolerance and friendship amongst South Africans and between nations.[17]

Some of this language would have been new to Marcus Aurelius—and it would have been a good thing for Roman Stoics to have reflected more about the connections between the human dignity they prized and the political rights they frequently neglected. But the language of dignity, humanity, freedom, understanding, tolerance, and friendship would not have been strange to Marcus. (He speaks of his goal as "the idea of a Commonwealth with the same laws for all, governed on the basis of equality and free speech"; this goal is to be pursued with "beneficence, eager generosity, and optimism.") The ANC draft, like the Stoic norm of world citizenship, insists that understanding of various nations and groups is a goal for every citizen, not only for those who wish to affirm a minority identity. It insists that the goal of education should not be separation of one group from another, but respect, tolerance, and friendship—both within a nation and among nations. It insists that this goal should be fostered in a way that respects the dignity of humanity in each person and citizen.

Above all, education for world citizenship requires transcending the inclination of both students and educators to define themselves primarily in terms of local group loyalties and identities. World citizens will therefore not argue for the inclusion of cross-cultural study in a curriculum primarily on the grounds that it is a way in which members of minority groups can affirm such an identity. This approach, common though it is, is divisive and subversive of the aims of world community. This problem vexes many curricular debates. Frequently, groups who press for the recognition of their group think of their struggle as connected with goals of human respect and social justice. And yet their way of focusing their demands, because it neglects commonalities and portrays people as above all members of identity groups, tends to subvert the demand for equal respect and love, and even the demand for attention to diversity itself. As David Glidden, philosopher at the University of California at Riverside, expressed the point, "the ability to admire and love the diversity of human beings gets lost" when one bases the demand for inclusion on notions of local group identity. Why should one love or attend to a Hispanic fellow citizen, on this view, if one is oneself most fundamentally an Irish-American? Why should one care about India, if one defines oneself as above all an American? Only a human identity that transcends these divisions shows us why we should look at one another with respect across them.

World Citizenship in Contemporary Education

What would an education for world citizenship look like in a modern university curriculum? What should Anna, the future businesswoman in Beijing, learn as an undergraduate if she is to be prepared for her role? What should all students learn—since we all interact as citizens with issues and people from a wide variety of traditions?

This education must be a multicultural education, by which I mean one that acquaints students with some fundamentals about the histories and cultures of many different groups. These should include the major religious and cultural groups of each part of the world, and also ethnic and racial, social and sexual minorities within their own nation. Language learning, history, religious studies, and philosophy all play a role in pursuing these ideas. Awareness of cultural difference is essential in order to promote the respect for another that is the essential underpinning for dialogue. There are no surer sources of disdain than ignorance and the sense of the inevitable naturalness of one's own way. No liberal education can offer students adequate understanding of all they should know about the world; but a detailed understanding of one unfamiliar tradition and some rudiments about others will suffice to engender Socratic knowledge of one's own limitations. It would have helped Anna to have learned a great deal about China; but to have studied the culture of India would have been almost as valuable, since it would have showed her how to inquire and the limitations of her experience.

World citizens will legitimately devote more attention and time to their own region and its history, since it is above all in that sphere that they must operate. This need for local knowledge has important educational consequences. We would be absurdly misguided if we aimed at giving our students an equal knowledge of all histories and cultures, just as we would be if we attempted to provide a bit of knowledge of all languages. Besides the fact that this would produce a ridiculously superficial result, it would also fail in the task of giving students a detailed acquaintance with the local sphere in which most of their actions will be undertaken. Education at all levels, including higher education, should therefore strongly emphasize the history of American constitutional traditions and their background in the tradition of Western political philosophy. In a similar way, literary education should focus disproportionately on the literature of Anglo-American traditions—which, however, are themselves highly complex and include the contributions of many different groups.

On the other hand, it is also extremely important that this material be presented in a way that reminds the student of the broader world of which the Western traditions are a part. This may be done with good educational results in the Western tradition courses themselves, where one can emphasize what is distinctive about this tradition through judicious and illuminating contrasts with developments elsewhere. But it must above all be done by the design of the curriculum as a whole, which should offer students the rudiments of knowledge about the major world traditions of thought and art, and the history that surrounds them, and, even more important, make them aware how much important material they do not know.

Education for world citizenship needs to begin early. As soon as children engage in storytelling, they can tell stories about other lands and other peoples. A curriculum for world citizenship would do well to begin with the first grade, where children can learn in an entertaining arid painless way that religions other than Judaism and Christianity exist, that people have many traditions and ways of thinking. (One such curriculum has been developed by E. D. Hirsch Jr. and is being used in a number of elementary-school districts around the country: first-graders tell stories of Buddha under the *boddhi* tree; they think about Hindu myths of the gods, about African folktales, about the life of Confucius.)[18] By the time students reach college or university, they should be well equipped to face demanding courses in areas of human diversity outside the dominant Western traditions.

This exposure to foreign and minority cultures is not only, and not—though of course this will be one important function such exposure can often serve. It is an education for all students, so that as judges, as legislators, as citizens in whatever role, they will learn to deal with one another with respect and understanding. And this understanding and respect entail recognizing not only difference but also, at the same time, commonality, not only a unique history but also common rights and aspirations and problems.

The world citizen must develop sympathetic understanding of distant cultures and of ethnic, racial, and religious minorities within her own. She must also develop an understanding of the history and variety of human ideas of gender and sexuality. As a citizen one is called upon frequently to make judgments in controversial matters relating to sex and gender—whether as a judge, deciding a case that affects the civil rights of millions, or simply as a democratic voter, deciding, for example, whether to support a referendum like Colorado's Amendment 2, declared unconstitutional by the U.S. Supreme Court in 1996, which restricted the abilities of local communities to pass laws protecting the civil rights of gays and lesbians. To function well as a citizen today, one needs to be able to assess the arguments put forward on both sides; and to do so one needs an education that studies these issues. There are complex connections between cross-cultural study and the study of gender and sexuality. Cross-cultural study reveals many ways of organizing concepts of gender and sexuality; and thinking about gender and sex is essential to thinking critically about a culture. A good undergraduate education should prepare students to be informed and sensitive interpreters of these questions.

Building a curriculum for world citizenship has multiple aspects: the construction of basic required courses of a "multicultural" nature; the infusion of diverse perspectives throughout the curriculum; support for the development of more specialized elective courses in areas connected with human diversity; and, finally, attention to the teaching of foreign languages, a part of the multicultural story that has received too little emphasis.

Basic "diversity" requirements come in two varieties. There are elective requirements that allow the student to choose one or two courses from among a wide range of offerings. Such, for example, is the requirement at the University of Nevada at Reno, where students, in addition to completing a "World Civilizations" core course, must elect a course focusing on at least one area of human diversity outside the dominant culture of her own society. Areas included are the history and culture of non-Western peoples, the history and culture of minorities in the United States, women's studies, and the study of the varieties of human sexuality. Reno, like many institutions, cannot afford to hire new faculty to create integrative courses or to free existing faculty from many of their other commitments. Making a menu of what is on hand, and then giving students a choice from that menu, is these institutions' only option if they wish to diversify their curricula.

Such requirements can fulfill basic Socratic functions, showing students the possible narrowness and limitedness of their own perspective and inviting them to engage in critical reflection. And they can frequently impart methodological tools that will prove valuable in approaching another area of diversity. But this is not always the case: a student who has taken a course on American women writers of the nineteenth century is still likely to be in a weak position with respect to the sort of cultural diversity she will encounter if she finds herself in dialogue with people from China and the Middle East. Even a course in non-Western literature may leave the student blankly ignorant of non-Western history and religion. A student who has studied the history and literature of China may remain unaware of the variety and diversity of minorities within her own nation. It is odd and arbitrary to put all these different topics together in an area called "diversity," as if the grasp of any part of any one of them would somehow yield a person the breadth of learning that could be yielded only by some grasp of each area. This problem will be especially grave if, as at Reno, the courses listed as satisfying the "diversity" requirement are unrelated to one another by any common discussion about methodology, beyond the deliberations of the faculty group that put the requirement together in the first place. Such courses may not even produce a student who knows how to inquire about diversity in a new context.

One can make a still stronger criticism of the amorphous elective requirement: that the failure to confront all the areas of diversity undercuts the encounter with each of them. A student of Chinese history who does not have some awareness of the history of women and the family, and of the different ways of understanding gender roles, will be likely to miss a good deal that is of urgent importance to the person who gets involved with China today, whether through politics or through business. If Anna hears the political rhetoric in today's China about the "natural" suitability of a situation in which women leave the workplace to return home, she will need to evaluate these statements and policies. It would be best to evaluate them against the background not only of the Confucian tradition but also of a critical awareness of gender roles and their variety. Successful and fair business dealings with China require such an awareness, which will not be provided by courses on Chinese history alone.

For these many reasons, an amorphous elective diversity requirement does not adequately prepare students for the complex world they will confront. It is better than no diversity program at all, and it may well be the best that many institutions can do. But it does not provide sufficient direction to fulfill completely the goals of world citizenship.

Despite these drawbacks, the particular version of an elective diversity requirement that was designed at Reno has some strong virtues. Particularly admirable is the reasoning that justified the requirement when it was publicly presented to faculty, students, and the community. The argument crafted by the faculty committee focuses on goals of world citizenship rather than on identity politics. Deborah Achtenberg, professor of philosophy, expert on Aristotle's ethics, and chair of the Diversity Committee, reflects that her approach to curricular politics was colored by her own particular history, as "a woman, a Jew, a former sixties activist, a St. John's College alumna, a philosopher." From St. John's, she says, she learned respect for the intrinsic value of great texts; the diversity requirement strongly emphasizes these values. From the civil-rights movement she learned "how exclusion of groups leaves the dominant culture unable to benefit from the perspectives and contributions of those groups"; this experience gave her a strong motivation to work for inclusion of those perspectives in the curriculum. As a woman, she knows how difficult it is to speak when one wonders whether the terms of the debate have been set by someone else; the courses in which she is involved focus on these issues of voice and methodology. As a Jew, she knows how easy it is for excluded groups to internalize demeaning stereotypes of themselves; she therefore urges questioning of all stereotypes, including those fostered by identity politics. Finally, as a philosopher, she is committed to making the continual attempt to "transcend all this particularity towards commonality," communicating what she perceives to others whose perspectives and experiences are different from her own. The curriculum she helped design draws inspiration both from Greek ideas of world citizenship and from biblical demands for equality of attention and love.

For a university that is skeptical of the elective approach and can support a more ambitious undertaking, a more arduous, but potentially more satisfying, approach is to design a single basic "multicultural" course, or a small number of such courses, to acquaint all students with some basic conceptions and methods. A very successful example of such a course, in a nonelite institution with a mixed student body, is "American Pluralism and the Search for Equality," developed at the State University of New York at Buffalo in 1992. This course is required in addition to a two-semester world civilization sequence that provides basic instruction in non-Western religions and cultures. The pluralism course complements the primarily historical world civilization course by enhancing students' awareness of the many groups that make up their own nation, and of the struggle of each for respect and equality. Since these moral issues arise in the international context as well, reflection about them retrospectively enriches the other course.

The outstanding feature of the pluralism course is its careful design. In striking contrast to the catch-as-catch-can approach to diversity that one often finds, the faculty designing this course met for months to work out a coherent set of goals and methodologies. They justified their plan in documents available not only to the university community but also to the general public. The statement of goals and purposes shows the relation of the course to the goals of citizenship:

> A goal of the course is to develop within students a sense of informed, active citizenship as they enter an American society of increasing diversity by focusing on contemporary and historical issues of race, ethnicity, gender, social class, and religious sectarianism in American life. A goal of the course is to provide students with an intellectual awareness of the causes and effects of structured inequalities and prejudicial exclusion in American society. A goal of the course is to provide students with increased self-awareness of what it means in our culture to be a person of their own gender, race, class, ethnicity, and religion as well as an understanding of how these categories affect those who are different from themselves. . . . A goal

> of the course is to expand students' ability to think critically, and with an open mind, about controversial contemporary issues that stem from the gender, race, class, ethnic, and religious differences that pervade American society.

John Meacham, a professor of psychology who is among its architects, enunciates several principles that contributed to the success of the Buffalo course and that should, in his view, guide the development of other such courses.

1. *"Design multicultural courses with broad content."* The Buffalo course is designed to acquaint students with five categories of diversity: race, gender, ethnicity, social class, and religious sectarianism. Each section of the course must cover all five and must focus in depth on three. This approach gives the advantage of breadth and also ensures that students see one category in its relation to the others. Meacham argues persuasively that such a course contributes a deeper understanding of each of its topics than would a narrower course focusing on a single topic.
2. *"Base multicultural courses on faculty disciplinary expertise."* Faculty staffing the course are drawn from ten different disciplines. Meacham comments: "For example, an intelligent discussion of affirmative action should be grounded at least in history, biology, law, economics, political science, psychology, and sociology." Nothing was included in the course that faculty were not equipped to teach expertly; and different faculty groups in different years approached the basic course plan differently, in accordance with their preparation and training. This allowance for flexibility is very important. Interdisciplinary courses frequently falter if they lack a strong disciplinary base, and faculty cannot do a good job if they are asked to stretch far beyond their training.

   The difficulty of finding enough faculty with the relevant expertise is frequently cited as a point against such multicultural courses, as if they were bound to be specially problematic from this point of view. But "great books" courses, for example the countless courses focusing on ancient Greece and Rome, are hardly free of similar problems. The classics department of any university is small, comprising only a few of the faculty who will be teaching such courses. A large proportion of those who routinely teach Euripides and Sophocles and Plato lack disciplinary expertise in classics and never learn either Greek or Latin. They often do a remarkable job within these limits, and sometimes can bring new life to the material in a way that specialists may not. But they do have limits, and need to rely for guidance on secondary literature prepared by specialists. It would therefore be entirely unfair to mention these problems when criticizing new multicultural courses and not to bring the same objections against standard Western civilization courses.

   There are, of course, special problems involved in teaching any area in which the relevant scholarly literature is small and still evolving. The nonspecialist teaching Plato can choose from among a wide range of translations and annotated editions of the dialogues, and can prepare by using the many helpful and rigorous books and articles that are easily available. The nonspecialist who wishes to teach the history of women in antiquity, or the history of slavery, would have had a much more difficult time twenty years ago, since the materials for such a study were available only to specialists who knew Greek and Latin—and not easily to these, since many documents had not been edited. But by now this is far less a problem in all the areas of human diversity. In most areas, outstanding volumes responsibly present the results of specialist research to nonspecialist academics. In the areas covered by Meacham's course there is no problem at all, since there is no language barrier, and the topics of the course have by now generated an enormous, excellent, and easily available literature.
3. *"Design programs for faculty development."* Faculty should not be asked to teach material that lies to some extent outside their prior expertise without being given financial support for the time spent in retraining. Retraining involves time taken away

from their course preparation in their own original areas, and also from the research that is an integral part of an active scholar's life. First-rate faculty will not choose to get involved in such new courses unless they are compensated for these sacrifices. It is standard practice to pay faculty summer salary for undertaking new course development projects. Where, in addition to retraining, the course will require extensive cooperation among faculty in different fields, such compensation is particularly important. SUNY Buffalo was able to provide funds for four-week faculty development seminars during two consecutive summers. These seminars were absolutely crucial to the program's success, since even faculty who bring a disciplinary expertise to the course are ill prepared for a complex interdisciplinary exchange without concerted preparation, reading, and dialogue. In the seminars the faculty learned about one another's approaches and methods, discussed common readings, and designed readings and methods that were appropriate for the students in their institution.

4. *Spend time reflecting about methodological and pedagogical issues.* Faculty drawn from literature, economics, political science, and philosophy will not intuitively approach a problem such as voting rights or affirmative action with the same set of questions in mind or the same standards of argument and inquiry. This heterogeneity is basically a good thing, since they can complement one another. But careful thought needs to be given to the methods and concerns that will be built into the course. How much, for example, will the course focus on general philosophical questions, such as the nature of rights and the contrast between relativism and universalism? How much empirical information about the history of the relevant issues will students be expected to master? How will quantitative analyses deriving from economics be presented, if at all? If these questions are not settled beforehand, the course will be a grab-bag of issues, with no intellectual cohesion.

Faculty need to devote extra consideration to problems that arise when we approach issues on which people in our society have conflicting and strongly held views. Such issues—and these constitute most of the course—raise particular problems for classroom methodology. Here there is a particular need to be aware of the background and character of one's students and to design classroom methods to elicit the best sort of active critical participation. Buffalo students, Meacham argues, tend to be submissive and deferential. Faculty need to discourage them from simply following authority if the benefits of the course for citizenship are to be gained. In this course more than in others, then, instructors carefully withhold their own personal views, designing strategies for evenhanded classroom debate and not seeking to bring debate to a conclusion prematurely. As one instructor in the course said, it is important "to give students permission to be confused."

The Buffalo course is a success because of the careful thought that went into its design and the availability of funding to support faculty development. One should also commend the determination of faculty to criticize themselves and to monitor carefully the development of the course, insisting on high standards of both expertise and teaching. SUNY Buffalo faculty are under substantial public pressure to justify the development of a multicultural course, since their constituency is aware of many criticisms of such courses. Part of their success is explained by the fact that they have devoted a good deal of thought to public relations both in the university and in the community. They publicize the course and discuss it in a variety of public media, focusing in particular on answering the criticism that such courses are "ideological." They articulate the relation of the course to the goals of democratic citizenship in a convincing way, satisfying the public that the effort contributes to public reasoning, not simply to the affirmation of various groups' identity. This is a legitimate area of public concern, and Buffalo has done more to address it than have many comparable institutions.

A different but equally promising basic core course is the newly designed humanities core course at Scripps College, in Pomona, California. The college enrolls around 700 students, all female; although it shares courses with the other Claremont Colleges, the freshman core course is designed for the entire Scripps entering class, and for them alone. It replaces an earlier Western civilization sequence, which was thought to be too amorphous and unfocused. Called "Culture, Knowledge, and Representation," the course studies the central ideas of the European Enlightenment—in political thought, history, and philosophy, in literature, in religion, to some extent in art and music. Sixteen instructors from all departments in the humanities take turns giving lectures, and each leads a small discussion section. The study of the Enlightenment is followed by a study of critical responses to it—by formerly colonized populations, by feminists, by non-Western philosophy, by Western postmodernist thought. The course ends with an examination of Enlightenment responses to these criticisms. (I was invited to lecture to the group on the ways in which feminists could defend liberalism against the criticisms made by other feminists, and on the responses of the international human rights movement to postcolonial critiques of universal categories.)

This course has produced excitement and lively debate among students. Its clear focus, its emphasis on cross-cultural argument rather than simply on a collection of facts, and its introduction of non-Western materials via a structured focus on a central group of issues all make it a good paradigm of the introductory course. Its ambitious interdisciplinary character has been successful in lecture, less so in sections—where students report that some faculty sections deal far more helpfully with the philosophical texts and issues than do others. This unevenness is to be expected in the first year of such a cooperative venture (the course was instituted in 1995–96) and should not be taken to negate the worth of the experiment. Above all, the course has merit because it plunges students right into the most urgent questions they need to ask today as world citizens, questions about the universal validity of the language of rights, the appropriate ways to respond to the just claims of the oppressed. The college community becomes from the very beginning a community of argument focused on these issues of urgent relevance. (It seemed especially commendable that postmodernism was not given the last word, as though it had eclipsed Enlightenment thinking: students were left with a vigorous debate, as instructors sympathetic to postmodernism welcomed my highly critical challenge to those views.)

Infusing world citizenship into the curriculum is a much larger project than the designing of one or two required courses. Its goals can and should pervade the curriculum as a whole, as multinational, minority, and gender perspectives can illuminate the teaching of many standard parts of the curriculum, from American history to economics to art history to ancient Greek literature. There are countless examples of the successful transformation of familiar courses to incorporate those perspectives. Some involve the redesigning of a basic introductory course. At the University of New Hampshire, a grant from the National Endowment for the Humanities produced a new Western civilization course, team-taught in an interdisciplinary manner by four excellent young faculty hired primarily for this course, from philosophy, the history of science, art history, and comparative literature. The four were given time and support to work together designing a course that integrated all these disciplinary perspectives with a focus on ancient Greece and Rome, at the same time incorporating a comparative dimension that correlated Greek achievements in art, literature, science, and politics with those in China at the same period. (The historian of science specialized in Chinese science; the others were supported in doing research into the comparative dimension of their own discipline.) From the beginning, then, students learned to see familiar landmarks of the Western tradition in a broader world context, understanding what was distinctive about Greek science, for example, in part through the Chinese contrast. As a result of the support and stimulation provided by the program, one of the original four teachers, Charlotte Witt, has gone on to produce not only outstanding scholarship on Aristotle's metaphysics but also admirable discussions of the role of rational argument in feminist criticism.[19]

Some transformations involve the redesigning of a standard departmental course offering.

At Brown University, a standard moral problems course has recently taken as its focus the feminist critique of pornography and related issues of free speech. In this way students learn to confront these divisive issues and learn basic facts about them while learning the techniques of philosophical analysis and debate. At Bentley College, Krishna Mallick offers a non-Western philosophy class, focusing on the philosophy of nonviolent resistance. At Harvard University, Amartya Sen offers a course called "Hunger and Famine." Standard topics in development economics are given a new twist, as students learn to think about the relationship of hunger to gender and also to democratic political institutions in areas of the world ranging from Africa to China to India. At the University of Chicago, historian David Cohen has developed a comparative course on war crimes that brings current events in Bosnia and Rwanda together with historical examples from many cultures. Other topics that invite a global perspective, such as environmental studies and climatology, world population, and religious and ethnic violence, are increasingly taking center stage in the social sciences and are an increasing focus of student interest.

Such integrative courses acknowledge that we are citizens of a world that is diverse through and through—whose moral problems do prominently include the problems of women seeking to avoid violence, whose history does include a complex international history of both nonviolence and war, whose thought about hunger and agriculture must take cognizance of the unequal hunger of women and of the special circumstances of developing nations. This way of incorporating diversity has the advantage of relying on the disciplinary expertise of the instructor. Students who study Indian famines with Sen probably learn more that is important about India than will those who take a broad and general introduction to world civilization, although they will profit more from Sen's course if they have already had such an introduction. They will learn about religious and economic diversity in the process of thinking about hunger, but in a way that will be focused and made more vivid by being connected to a specific problem analyzed with rigor and detail. Such focused courses, taught by expert faculty, should be strongly encouraged, whatever else we also encourage.

In many institutions, however, there are few faculty available to teach such international courses, at least beyond the introductory level. If even the introductory level requires combining existing expertise with new interdisciplinary training, as the Buffalo course shows, the generation of more advanced elective courses integrating the perspective of world citizenship requires even more planning and institutional support. One particularly imaginative and successful example of a program for faculty development has recently been designed at St. Lawrence University. Called "Cultural Encounters: An Intercultural General Education," the program exemplifies the values of world citizenship both in its plan and in its execution. Cultural Encounters is a program containing courses at both the introductory and the more advanced levels. But its focus has been on redesigning disciplinary courses toward an emphasis on the student's encounter with a non-Western culture.

St. Lawrence is a small liberal arts college. It is a relatively wealthy institution, able to attract a high-quality young faculty. It is well known for the high quality of its study-abroad programs, and 33 percent of its students do study in a foreign country at some point. Its students are a mixed group. The 70 percent who receive financial aid tend to be stronger academically than the other 30 percent, many of whom are intellectually unaggressive. This circumstance required careful thought by the faculty as they tried to design a program that would awaken critical and independent thinking about cultural diversity, and about the more general question whether values are universal or culturally relative. Since 1987 the college has had a requirement that all students take one course on a non-Western or Third World culture; the Cultural Encounters program is intended to supplement the strong offerings in these areas by promoting rigorous foundational questioning.

The program began when St. Lawrence received faculty and curriculum development grants from the Andrew Mellon Foundation and the Fund for the Improvement of Post-Secondary Education. In its initial phase, grants were given to a group of seventeen humanities faculty from different departments, enabling them to meet in a weekly seminar throughout the year, discussing common readings and eventually generating new courses, each in their separate disciplines. The course was informed from the beginning by three decisions. The first was to put philosophy at the heart of the matter, in the sense that all participants did a lot of serious discussing of issues of cultural relativism, along with whatever cross-cultural readings they also did. Grant Cornwell of Philosophy and Eve Stoddard of English, the two directors of the program, shared an orientation to the material that stressed the universal aspect of human needs and strivings and was critical of cultural relativism. They did not wish, however, to impose this perspective on the program as a whole; they wished to use the issue as a basis for faculty dialogue.

Cornwell and Stoddard's second decision was to focus on just two areas of diversity, by selecting two non-Western cultures, the cultures of India and Kenya. They decided to start from these two concrete areas in raising issues about ethnic and religious diversity, gender, race, and sexuality. They decided that they had a reasonable shot at understanding something of the history and traditions of these two places if they used the grant-supported faculty seminar to spend an entire year doing common research on each, but that they would have no chance at all of achieving responsible coverage if they cast their net more widely. Faculty in the group were drawn from philosophy, art history, anthropology, English, religious studies, biology, government, geology, economics, and Spanish.

The group's third decision was its most surprising. This was that all ten faculty involved should live for a month in the regions they studied, after a year of intensive seminar preparation, so that their teaching would be informed by a firsthand sense of what it was like to live the life of ordinary women and men in these countries. This undertaking was made financially possible because of the grant, and it proved to be the crucial point in the program. During each of the two visits, the group kept a public diary to exchange and refine views. It is clear that this experience permitted a level of insight into controversial issues such as female circumcision and population control that would not easily have been available from reading alone. It also infused the abstract readings with vividness and made the instructors feel that, for a brief time at least, they had been actual participants in the foreign culture.

Returning to St. Lawrence, the group designed courses reflecting their own disciplinary expertise. David Hornung of Biology and Catherine Shrady of Geology teach a seminar called "Cross-Cultural Perspectives of Healing;" comparing the Western medical tradition with Islamic, Hindu, and traditional African approaches. Economics professor Robert Blewett teaches "African Economies," comparing several African economic institutions with their North American counterparts, and focusing on the impact of cultural difference on economic structure. "Students," Blewett writes, "will learn not only of the diversity and complexity of economic relationships in African societies but will increase their understanding of economics in their own society." Codirector Eve Stoddard teaches a comparative course on the discipline and management of the female body, studying practices ranging from female circumcision to veiling to plastic surgery, dieting, and exercise. There is no naive assumption that all these practices are on a par—indeed, one of the aims of the course is to get students to make increasingly refined evaluations. Stoddard's teaching was informed by lengthy, complicated discussions with women in the regions she visited; she is therefore able to give an informed account of the societies' internal debates about these practices. Student writing is encouraged to analyze issues of cultural relativism in a rigorous way.

At the same time, the group required that students who chose the Cultural Encounters "track," taking both introductory and advanced courses within the program, should have a foreign language requirement. If at all possible, they must live and study abroad for their junior year. Two-thirds of the students who go abroad go to Europe, the other third to Costa Rica, Kenya, India, and Japan. Not all the programs, then, directly support the intellectual aims of the Cultural Encounters course material. But even the apparently unrelated exposure to a European culture and its language indirectly serves the program's goals, since mastery of a foreign language and the ability to make oneself at home in a foreign culture are essential abilities of the world citizen, and build an understanding that can be used to approach a further and even more remote culture.

The Cultural Encounters program is a model of responsible teaching in several areas of human diversity. By design, it encompasses not only the encounter with a foreign culture but also related issues of gender, ethnic and religious pluralism, and sexuality, presenting issues of American pluralism in relation to those of global cultural diversity. Its interdisciplinary character ensures that these issues will be faced from many interlocking perspectives, including those of literary study and anthropology, long prominent in multicultural teaching, but also those of economics, biology, philosophy, and foreign language teaching. Where faculty are concerned, the program's focus on intensive training and dialogue and its demand for actual immersion in the culture sets it apart from many programs of this sort, as does its focus on foundational philosophical questions of relativism and universality. On the side of the student, the requirement to learn a foreign language and, where possible, to visit a foreign culture makes the "encounter" serious and prolonged, while critical discussion of basic issues about culture and values in the classroom ensures that the encounter will be conducted in the spirit of Socratic searching rather than of mere tourism, and will prompt dialectical reflection on the beliefs and practices of the student's own culture while the student explores a foreign culture.

Cornwell and Stoddard write that they prefer the term *interculturalism* to the terms *multiculturalism* and *diversity,* since the latter are associated with relativism and identity politics, suggesting a pedagogy "limited to an uncritical recognition or celebration of difference, as if all cultural practices were morally neutral or legitimate."[20] *Interculturalism,* by contrast, connotes the sort of comparative searching that they have in mind, which, they argue, should prominently include the recognition of common human needs across cultures and of dissonance and critical dialogue within cultures. The interculturalist, they argue, has reason to reject the claim of identity politics that only members of a particular group have the ability to understand the perspective of that group. In fact, understanding is achieved in many different ways, and being born a member of a certain group is neither sufficient nor necessary. Knowledge is frequently enhanced by an awareness of difference.

The Cultural Encounters program has had an influence beyond St. Lawrence. Its success has spawned imitations in a wide range of colleges and universities, including Northern Arizona University, the University of Tulsa, Towson State University, Colgate University, Mount St. Mary's College, and Bowling Green State University. In 1995 a national conference brought the many participants in this movement together for an institute to discuss experiences and methodology. Much thought needs to be given to how such a program, designed for a small, prosperous college, can be adapted to colleges with larger student populations and fewer resources.

Meanwhile, at St. Lawrence itself, the program received a major grant from the Christian Johnson Endeavor Foundation in 1995 to support further curricular development of "intercultural studies." Over four years, the faculty group will focus on interdisciplinary study of four themes: transmission of culture across boundaries; gender and culture; questioning development: equity and the environment; and health across cultures. Expanding its focus to include Latin America, the faculty group spent the summer of 1996 doing research in the Caribbean. Cheerfully describing the group's members as "pathological workaholics," Stoddard expresses keen excitement about their new task.

The Cultural Encounters program brings us back to the issues raised by the Stoics. Its designers firmly reject an approach to "multiculturalism" that conceives of it as a type of identity politics, in which the student receives the impression of a marketplace of cultures, each asserting its own claim. They insist on the importance of teaching that the imagination can cross cultural boundaries, and that cross-cultural understanding rests on the acknowledgment of certain common human needs and goals amid the many local differences that divide us. Like much of the ancient Greek tradition, beginning with Herodotus, Stoics suggest that the encounter with other cultures is an essential part of an examined life. Like that tradition, they believe that education must promote the ability to doubt the unqualified goodness of one's own ways, as we search for what is good in human life the world over.

Becoming a citizen of the world is often a lonely business. It is, in effect, a kind of exile—from the comfort of assured truths, from the warm nestling feeling of being surrounded by people who share one's convictions and passions. In the writings of Marcus Aurelius (as in those of his American followers Emerson and Thoreau) one sometimes feels a boundless loneliness, as if the removal of the props of habit and convention, the decision to trust no authority but moral reasoning, had left life bereft of a certain sort of warmth and security. If one begins life as a child who loves and trusts its parents, it is tempting to want to reconstruct citizenship along the same lines, finding in an idealized image of nation or leader a surrogate parent who will do our thinking for us. It is up to us, as educators, to show our students the beauty and interest of a life that is open to the whole world, to show them that there is after all more joy in the kind of citizenship that questions than in the kind that simply applauds, more fascination in the study of human beings in all their real variety and complexity than in the zealous pursuit of superficial stereotypes, more genuine love and friendship in the life of questioning and self-government than in submission to authority. We had better show them this, or the future of democracy in this nation and in the world is bleak.

Notes

1. "Anna" is a woman I interviewed in China. Her name has been changed.
2. *New York Times,* July 4, 1996, p. 1.
3. All judgments about the Cynics are tentative, given the thinness of our information. The central source is Diogenes Laertius' *Lives of the Philosophers.* See B. Branham and M.-O. Goulet-Cazé, eds., *The Cynics* (Berkeley: University of California Press, 1996).
4. Plutarch, *On the Fortunes of Alexander* 329AB = *SVF* 1.262; see also Seneca, *On Leisure* 4.1.
5. For Paine, see *The Rights of Man,* pt. 2; for Smith, see "Of Universal Benevolence," in *The Theory of Moral Sentiments* (Indianapolis: Liberty Classica, 1982), vol. 6, pt. 2, p. 3, with special reference to Marcus Aurelius; for Kant, see *Perpetual Peace,* in *Kant's Political Writings,* ed. H. Reiss, trans. H. Nisbet, 2nd ed. (Cambridge: Cambridge University Press, 1991). For a discussion of Stoic ideas in Kant's political thought, see Martha C. Nussbaum, "Kant and Stoic Cosmopolitanism," *Journal of Political Philosophy* 5 (1997): 1–25.
6. See Tagore, "Swadeshi Samaj," cited in Krishna Dutta and Andrew Robinson, *Rabindranath Tagore: The Myriad-Minded Man* (London: Bloomsbury, 1995).
7. Kwame Anthony Appiah, *In My Father's House: Africa in the Philosophy of Cultures* (New York: Oxford University Press, 1991).
8. See W. K. C. Guthrie, *History of Greek Philosophy,* vol. 3 (Cambridge: Cambridge University Press, 1969).
9. See Stephen Halliwell, *Plato: Republic V* (Warminster: Aris and Phillips, 1993).
10. The Hellenistic era is usually taken to begin at the death of Alexander the Great, 323 B.C.; Aristotle died in 322. Although Diogenes was a contemporary of Aristotle, his influence is felt in the later period. See A. A. Long, *Hellenistic Philosophy* (London: Duckworth, 1974).
11. The translation by R. D. Hicks in the Loeb Classical Library volume 2 of Diogenes Laertius is inadequate but gives the general idea. All citations here are from that *Life,* but the translations are mine.
12. Dionysius was the one-man ruler of Syracuse in Sicily whom Plato attempted, without success, to turn into a "philosopher-king."
13. The Stoic school had an extraordinarily long life and a very broad influence, extending from the late fourth century B.C. to the second century A.D. in both Athens and Rome.
14. Diogenes uses the single word *kosmopolites,* but Marcus Aurelius prefers the separated form.
15. See Marcus Aurelius, *Meditations,* trans, G. M. A. Grube (Indianapolis: Hackett, 1983).
16. The image is suggested in Cicero and is explicit in Hierocles, a Stoic of the first-second centuries A.D. (quoted here); it is probably older.
17. This is material from a draft written by the ANC for the new constitution; it was presented by Albie Sachs to a meeting on human rights at Harvard University in October 1993.
18. See E. D. Hirsh Jr., ed., *What Your Second Grader Needs to Know* (New York: Doubleday, 1991).
19. Charlotte Witt, *Substance and Essence in Aristotle* (Ithaca: Cornell University Press, 1989); Louise B. Antony and Charlotte Witt, eds., *A Mind of One's Own: Feminist Essays on Reason and Objectivity* (Boulder: Westview Press, 1992).
20. Grant H. Cornwell and Eve W. Stoddard, "Things Fall Together: A Critique of Multicultural Curricular Reform," *Liberal Education,* Fall 1994, pp. 40–51.

CHAPTER 21

THE CHALLENGE OF CONNECTING LEARNING

ASSOCIATION OF AMERICAN COLLEGES

Since the now-ubiquitous major was first introduced in American colleges and universities at Johns Hopkins University in 1878, there never has been a national report devoted to it. Arts and sciences majors consume from one-quarter to one-half of a student's collegiate program and a similar fraction of the faculty's teaching and advising efforts. Yet the major has largely been viewed, within and without the academy, as a self-evident component of college curricula requiring neither an examination of its rationale nor an evaluation of its procedures. After all, when students identify themselves, they most frequently name their major; faculty members find their teaching in major courses most congruent with their professional identities and interests.

Unlike general education, which often lacks either a faculty or a student constituency, major programs are the daily business of small, quite particular, and often well-organized subsets of the faculty. These faculty members design, modify, and implement the major with little, if any, external input or oversight. This contributes to a widely shared ethos that holds each major to be immune from scrutiny and questioning by faculty colleagues outside the field.

The self-containment of the major is especially striking in light of the spirited debates and reform momentum so visible in other parts of higher education. Nine out of ten colleges and universities have embarked upon some form of general education reform, and nearly as many now are considering ways to assess students' learning. There is a heightened awareness of diversity and of the educational changes implied by the rapid diversification of the student body. Terms such as "knowledge explosion," "global awareness," and "blurred disciplinary boundaries" signal an era in which both founding assumptions and scholarly practices in many fields have become the subject of extensive scrutiny and lively debate.

This report seeks to include all arts and sciences majors in the national debate about purposes and practices in liberal education. It does so in part to challenge the widespread assumption that the now-extensive national agenda for educational reform can be fulfilled primarily by changing general education courses and requirements. But this report equally challenges the ethos of self-containment that has grown up around departmental expectations and practices for arts and sciences majors. The major, at the very least, requires the same sort of educational self-consciousness and public debate that now attend the "general" parts of the curriculum.

The more than three thousand colleges and universities in America vary widely. Each confronts different opportunities and constraints; each has its own distinctive quality and style, both historically and at any given time. Curricula are embedded in these local cultures and represent responses to quite particular institutional ecologies. Major programs also have their own styles and histories, nationally and within any given institution or department.

Source: "The Challenge of Connecting Learning," by Association of American Colleges, reprinted from *Project on Liberal Learning, Study In-Depth and the Arts and Sciences Major*, 1991, Association of American Colleges and Universities.

Arts and sciences fields are also different. Each has its own history, language, heroes, central questions, and constitutive debates. Each offers its own ways of seeing and its own values about what should be asked and what counts as persuasive evidence.

Nor are students alike. Today's colleges serve a more diverse set of students than ever before, a trend likely to increase in the future. The presence of so many different racial, ethnic, age, income, and experience groups promises much vitality; it also means that very little can be taken for granted. Approaches that once seemed at least adequate need to be rethought and restructured as faculty members are challenged to reach students who differ both from their predecessors and from one another. In the long run, education should be enhanced as faculty members experiment with an increased variety of styles, contents, and pedagogies to support students' full participation in learning communities. But there is nothing simple about these challenges; faculty members are charting new paths without obvious markers as they seek to serve effectively a very wide range of learners.

There also are significant differences, on many campuses and in many programs, between faculty and student views of the purposes of a liberal arts and sciences major. These differences require and deserve faculty attention. Faculty members often think of the major as a study of a subject valuable in itself, or as a preparation for advanced, postbaccalaureate studies (with the desire that the best students themselves should enter the professoriat). Students often speak of attaining usable capacities, of the "real-world" value of collegiate education. The fact is that most students do not go to graduate school and a career in the learned professions, nor do they use the content of their major directly in their careers.

All of these differences need to be recognized in constructing responsible and responsive major programs. Yet the common equation of arts and sciences majors with liberal learning also implies some larger goals to which each such major should contribute. It is surely not the subject matter alone—which varies not only among departments or programs in the same field but also among student majors in the same program—that constitutes a major program as "liberal" learning. Liberal learning describes—or ought to describe—intellectual habits fostered through and inseparable from successful completion of a course of study.

This report explores this dimension of liberal learning. It argues that liberal arts and sciences majors ought to foster distinctive habits of mind and explores ways that the major can be organized to foster these habits.

This report is indebted to, and draws added strength from, the companion studies completed by task forces from twelve different arts and sciences majors that are reported in Volume Two. For all their differences in content and emphasis, these twelve studies together attest that each arts and sciences field serves, at least for a time, as a learning community for its undergraduate majors. As a learning community, each major program assumes common commitments and responsibilities, including a responsibility to take seriously its own limitations as a framework for knowing and learning. This way of viewing the major provides a much-needed common framework for examining the shared responsibilities of arts and sciences majors. That there are such responsibilities—held across boundaries of topic and program—is the central message of this report.

The Major in the Context of Liberal Learning

In 1985, the Association of American Colleges issued the report *Integrity in the College Curriculum: A Report to the Academic Community,* which sets forth "study-in-depth" as one of nine experiences that constitute, in the authors' view, a minimum curriculum in the liberal arts. While *Integrity* takes considerable pains never to identify "depth" with the traditional major, toward which it exhibits considerable suspicion, it nonetheless provides principles and standards that are widely understood to apply to collegiate concentrations.

Integrity argues that focused study in a particular area or discipline should convey to the student a sense of "both the possibilities and limits of such study." Study-in-depth should include "sequential learning, building on blocks of knowledge that lead to more sophisticated understanding and encourage leaps of imagination and synthesis." By fostering awareness of complexity, it should provide an increasing sense of mastery as well as limitation: "some understanding of the discipline's characteristic questions and arguments, as well as the questions it cannot answer and the arguments it cannot make."

These educational goals remain integral to the work of the major as liberal learning. It may be asked, however, whether "depth" as a metaphor goes far enough in conveying the full range of the agenda that any major needs to address. Certainly "depth" conceals, rather than illuminates, the social dimensions of the major that are intrinsic to its special role in undergraduate learning.

It is perhaps more useful to think about the major in terms of the appropriately social metaphor of "home." As philosopher Herbert Fingarette reminds us, "Home is always home for someone. . . . There is no absolute home in general." Neither students nor faculty members can inhabit the totality of the wide world of human knowledge. Recognizing this, the major invites students to enter a quite particular culture. In this way, the major provides a "home" for learning: a community of peers with whom students can undertake collaborative inquiries and a faculty charged to care about students' intellectual and personal explorations as well as their maturation.

For students, learning in the major means learning to take part in a continuing exploration. The role of faculty members is to provide structures and languages that support this participation: structures and languages that enhance and challenge students' capacities to frame issues, to test hypotheses and arguments against evidence, and to address disputed claims.

The properly structured major enables students to develop an increased capacity to understand and employ a range of topics and analytic tools, as well as characteristic questions and arguments specific to a domain of inquiry. It provides opportunities for students to explore significant questions and generate their own syntheses through carefully structured curricular choices across an extended period of time. It also takes seriously its own necessarily partial vision. The very boundedness of the major should provide an occasion for critical reflection on the successes and limitations of any particular approach to knowledge and for asking searching questions about the values, assumptions, perspectives, consequences, entailments, limits, and choices inherent in any intellectual enterprise.

The work of the major is only partly done when students gain facility in its culture, when they learn the nuances of its special language to such a degree that they can take an active part for a time in its conversations. To fulfill its role in liberal learning, the major also must structure conversations with the other cultures represented in the academy, conversations that more nearly reflect the diversities within our world and require patient labors of translation. Ultimately, the goal of the major should be the development of students' capacities for making connections and for generating their own translations and syntheses. Fostering such capacities is an intrinsic, not an elective, responsibility of each major program.

Viewed in this way, a major requires engagement and disengagement and provides opportunities for both joining and leaving. A student enters the "home" offered by the major in order, finally, to be able to leave it and see it from the outside in, by taking the knowledge, experience, and wisdom gained therein and testing them against the perspectives of other fields and the challenges of the world outside.

For this reason, the traditional distinctions between general education and the major no longer can be sustained. The common curricular model of general studies as preparation for and a preliminary counterweight to the specialized work of the major reinforces the exclusive aspects of the major and subverts its equally necessary inclusive character. Rather, the work of the major needs to open into a larger context of learning in order to develop the fullness of perspective that the discrete disciplines and fields of study cannot help but obscure.

The creative dialogue and tension among diverse domains of inquiry—which is the hallmark of liberal learning and of general education—requires that students know something well enough to consider it from several points of view so that they are able to contextualize it in significant and suggestive ways. Such sophistication cannot be expected of students before they have worked for some time in concentrated studies.

The capacity for generalizing emerges out of and alongside the major; it cannot be relegated to courses that are preparatory to subsequent focused study. Generalizing education is part of the teaching responsibility of the major program. It requires the development of a set of courses separate from more traditional general courses that introduce students to college and encourage them to sample different fields before they choose a major.

Such curricular structuring of the relationships between general education (seen as generalizing education) and the major cannot be the separate responsibilities of the several faculties associated with each of the major programs. Such structuring must be an endeavor of the collegiate faculty as a whole, working together to create courses of study that recognize difference, that bring multiple perspectives and crossdisciplinary dialogue to bear on common issues, that allow students opportunities for reflection on both the power and the limitations of their particular communities of inquiry, and that foster the fashioning of connections.

What Students Should Expect

While education cannot occur apart from specific content, students have the right to assume that education will amount to more than "coverage" of unconnected subjects and more than exposure to information that could be acquired through solitary study apart from the communities that colleges create. The problem with the major is not that it has failed to deliver certain kinds of knowledge. The problem is that it often delivers too much knowledge with too little attention to how that knowledge is being created, what methods and modes of inquiry are employed in its creation, what presuppositions inform it, and what entailments flow from its particular ways of knowing. The problem is further compounded when the major ignores questions about relationships between various ways of knowing, and between what students have learned and their lives beyond the academy.

Students have the right to expect their major to provide a set of learning experiences that will teach them how to use their field's approaches in pursuing significant questions. They have the right to expect opportunities to integrate the learning gained in their various courses to construct increasingly sophisticated structures of knowledge. They have the right to expect learning experiences that will encourage them to shape, reflect on, add to, challenge, and use the knowledge they are gaining. They have the right to expect opportunities for translating and negotiating among different approaches and for exploring the strengths and limitations of the lenses through which they have learned to view issues and problems. They have the right to expect opportunities and support for relating their learning to their own lives and to significant questions in the world beyond the classroom. Finally, students have the right to expect that all of the capacities and knowledge they have gained will be assessed, by faculty members, through carefully designed occasions that challenge them to integrate and demonstrate their learning across their specific programs of study.

In sum, students have the right to expect to experience enculturation into a particular learning community to such a degree that they gain a sense of confidence; they have the right to expect to experience occasions which require critical distance from that community; and they have the right to expect structured moments for conversation between communities, both within and without the academy.

Curricular Coherence

Majors are the responsibility of faculties. They require faculty members' willingness to develop a shared understanding of what study in the major is supposed to accomplish and faculty members' collaboration in designing a coherent program of study sufficient to accomplish it. They require faculty members to consult about ways these common goals intersect with the varying needs of different students.

This is not to ask for some grand intellectual scheme, some universal agreement, that will integrate all the various dimensions of a field in a larger synthesis. It is to insist, however, that suspicion and conflict on such matters does not excuse a faculty at a particular institution from attempting to provide a local structure for a course of study in a major that can specify its goals, ensure that these goals are communicated to students and faculty members alike, and assess the degree to which these aims are achieved. It is also to insist that faculty members concern themselves not just with course requirements but with the ways that a major's parts and practices contribute to its larger purposes.

A major course of study ought to have a principle or principles of organization.

A major in a given field may be organized in a variety of ways, none of which is inevitable or universally appropriate. The chosen mode of organization, however, ought to be the result of deliberate and corporate faculty judgment. An educationally coherent course of study should be designed not prospectively but retrospectively. Faculty members ought to begin with a set of goals for student achievement and then design a curricular structure that fosters their attainment.

The subject matter of a given field may provide the principles of organization. Some majors are organized by units of time, by place, by analytic approach, by subfields, or by a combination of some or all of these and other ways of dividing the subject. Other majors have a sense of logic, a progression of knowledge and techniques that move in sequential order. The first type more often exhibits a loosely structured, highly elective, middle range of courses (including topical courses and offerings in theory and method), preceded by an introduction and, at times, concluding with an independent research project. The latter pattern usually employs some system of prerequisites. Some programs may combine both patterns.

These commonly employed arrangements of subject matter are not the only source of structure. A major can be organized around a set of problems or contested issues characteristic of a given field of study. The various subject courses can provide exemplary cases and a sense of historical situations or contested issues; at the same time, the courses develop students' skills and enable them to address these issues responsibly.

Alternatively, a direct focus on students' learning can provide a major with its overall principles of organization. This focus requires attention to the knowledge students bring to a field and to the ways in which students construct knowledge within a discipline. It can be usefully informed by faculty members' attention to the rich and suggestive scholarship on how students learn that is emerging in a number of academic domains. In some major programs, a faculty member's understanding of cognitive goals and strategies can guide the design and sequence of different parts of the curriculum. In other programs, attention to students' different learning styles can suggest ways of structuring the curriculum. These structural approaches depend on a shared faculty understanding of processes of intellectual development and of modes of learning appropriate for particular domains. They offer a way of bringing shared purpose, organizing principles, and intellectual progression to fields in which the subject matter itself can be organized in any number of courses and patterns.

A major ought to have a beginning, a middle, and an end—each contributing in a different but specific way to the overall aim of the major.

In many majors, the first course frequently is a well-organized survey or introduction. In some programs, the last course may be an individualized research project or a senior seminar. What falls in between—the bulk of the work of the major—is all too often haphazard, at times exhibiting only numerical or political principles of organization: five to ten courses within the department, a course with each faculty member, or the like. Such haphazard procedures—more common in some fields than others—exhibit the fallacy of thinking of the individual course, rather than the program, as the basic educational unit. When the organizing principles for a program are unclear to both faculty members and students, it can be no surprise that each group approaches any particular course as a self-contained unit rather than an experience that ought to contribute discernably to larger aims.

Faculty members responsible for a program must take collective responsibility for shaping a core set of courses that establish an intellectual agenda for their majors. Courses in this core may need to differ from traditional introductory courses designed to serve institutionwide general education purposes. This set of core courses should introduce the kinds of questions a field typically asks, explore the ways it undertakes investigations, specify its frames of reference, and expose its disputed issues. Such courses also should provide exemplary occasions for students' analyses of others' work as well as opportunities to put forth their own. At the very least, faculty members should introduce the methodology and modes of inquiry characteristic of the field to all majors at an early point in their studies; subsequent courses should require students to utilize these methods and modes.

In many fields and programs, the middle-range courses are either highly elective or organized by categories that serve as miniature distribution requirements. This thwarts reasonable expectations that learning is cumulative across courses and that later learning builds on or restructures earlier learning. The major, especially in its middle-range courses, is structured to take time. The length of time the major takes is justified by students' need to return to matters studied earlier and revise what they have learned in the light of fuller understanding. This recursiveness in the curriculum is the enemy of naive acceptance. In many programs, ironically, both the overall number of course offerings and the content of individual courses seem governed by the notion that more is better, producing a hurried and harried educational experience. Less material treated with more attention to reflexivity ought to be the norm.

The middle-range courses—beyond their traditional goals of conveying topical knowledge, characteristic issues, and methods indigenous to the area—provide students with opportunities to explore directly issues attendant on expert inquiry and argumentation: questions as to what counts, what may be taken for granted, and what needs articulation within a given community of discourse. Middle-range courses also should provide opportunities for students to begin the processes of gaining critical perspectives and making connections. They provide an appropriate point through which to structure interactions with other parts of the curriculum in the interests of fostering generalizing education. The middle-range courses also may serve to create and enhance community by experimenting with less solitary modes of discovery such as student internships, collaborative learning projects, or peer teaching.

Given the educational potential of the middle-range courses, the present pattern in many fields of highly individualized student programs leading to few courses in common must be questioned. Cafeteria-style course offerings guarantee little common basis for discourse among majors. If the major is to be a learning community, both curricular goals and intellectual engagement are served better when faculty members ensure that students take in common either some reasoned fraction of a program's offerings or one of several carefully constructed alternative concentrations within a larger program.

Even if faculty members take seriously the challenge to create a set of common experiences for students, in most fields and institutions a significant part of each student's program will remain *de facto* individualized. In most colleges, where the option exists for a self-designed major, the student is expected to account formally for the ways in which each course will contribute to her or his overall program. The same expectation, in principle, ought to govern the traditional major. The individualized work in the major should not remain a student's own private enterprise; occasions must be designed to make it public. Students ought to be asked to consider how their elective choices within the major cohere. Their choices should be subject to periodic review, emendation, discussion, and advice from faculty members and peers. Such collegial discussion of students' individual choices appropriately complements periodic faculty-student dialogue about what is supposed to be accomplished through the common parts of the program and what in fact is being accomplished.

The end of the major ought to be a time for integrating knowledge, concepts, and capacities from the different parts of students' learning experiences. Programs can support this work by establishing structures, such as the "capstone course," which allow broad reflective and critical views of the field of concentration or bring together students from adjacent fields to explore their similarities and differences. Alternatively, programs may encourage each student to construct an intellectual autobiography. Students might be asked to put together a representative "portfolio" illustrating their progress and accomplishments in the major and related courses, or they might be asked to write an interpretive essay that critically examines their own work. Students can revise earlier work or do research that draws on earlier work. Minimally, curricular space should be allotted for faculty-student discussion of this integrating activity; students need to bring together their studies, and the process cannot be a solitary or accidental one.

The structure, organization, and intent of the major course of study ought to be made clear to students.

Faculty members in the major should know and make explicit to their students how their courses relate to the organizing principles of the major as a whole and structure their courses accordingly.

At the very least, these two principles call for catalogue copy and program announcements that are informative of the rationale for the overall course of study, in its several parts and as a whole, as an expression of corporate faculty understanding. These principles suggest, as well, the need for the faculty members in a program to be truly knowledgeable about one another's classes and to organize their classes on the bases of mutual discussions and understandings. Courses in the major can reflect and contribute to the overall purposes of a program only if faculty members talk to each other about what they are attempting and how it is succeeding. Careful advising is also necessary, not only to assure that the requisite number of courses are taken but also to support a continuing discussion about the program's purposes and students' experiences. The sense of community that ought to characterize any major derives not so much from particular requirements as from a shared and enunciated sense of purpose and from activities that sustain engagement.

The organizing principles for a major have their most powerful expression in the structure and substance of particular courses. The course syllabus, therefore, ought to be the first text carefully studied in every class. A mere reading list or itemization of assignments is insufficient as a guide to the work of a course. Students need to understand not only a course's content and procedures but also why they are taking a particular course and how it will contribute to their overall educational experience, within the major and within their entire course of study. Classes also should spend time discussing the choices represented by the syllabus, including the reasons materials are chosen or rejected and the basis for relative time allocation. Such discussion will do much to impeach the apparent self-evidence of the syllabus and establish its status as a constructed plan.

Critical Perspectives

Students join the community of the major briefly; ultimately, they must disengage and leave. An essential step in this process of disengagement is the achievement of some measure of critical distance. Part of the articulated purpose of the major, therefore, is to prepare a student to be sufficiently confident in the discourse of a community to subject the major to sophisticated questions and to compare and connect its proposals with the proposals of other communities. Students must encounter the limitations of their temporary home and explore the possibilities beyond.

Any proposal from any community as to "what is the case" is necessarily partial and bounded; any proposal is necessarily simpler than the complexity it attempts to describe and explain. This is simultaneously the source of its cognitive power and the grounds of its critique. This is a central reason why students and faculty members must work within a collegiate setting with an ethos of communication and contestation that ensures that no proposal stands without alternatives or arrogates to itself the claim of possessing the sole truth.

Every student should experience the intellectual excitement that comes from the capacity to extend the known to the unknown and to discern previously unsuspected relationships. Developing these capacities requires acceptance of specific imperatives. Students must be willing to revise what they have held previously as certain by shifting perspectives and they must engage in the kind of collaborative work in which they become open to criticism. This implies an academic community that sees as an important value of liberal learning bringing private precept into public discourse. It implies equally an academic community which insists that difference be negotiated with civility. Public civil discourse depends, among other conditions, on an ethos of corrigibility. Faculty members must take seriously what students believe about a given subject and engage their prior knowledge so that new learning restructures the old, complicating and correcting it rather than merely living side by side with it.

The culture of a major, like culture in general, is not best understood as a stable deposit transmitted from experts to novices. Culture is not passively appropriated; rather, it consists of a set of highly contested constructs and values that continually must be negotiated and renegotiated by active participants. The coherence of a culture well may lie in its refusal to allow differences to remain incoherent and inarticulate. The academy is one of the privileged social loci devoted to this process, a place where a variety of competing proposals may be explored, experimented with, and evaluated apart from urgent needs and ineradicable consequences.

By attending to the knowledge claims of the major over time and by treating increasingly complex matters from multiple points of view, students discover that nothing is self-evident, that nothing is simply "there," that questions and answers are chosen and created—not given—and that they always are framed by context; for that reason, they always are contingent.

Awareness of contingency takes many forms. It is important for students to know that ideas and methods have origins and histories, that they take place in quite particular times and places. It is important for them to know that ideas represent interests; that ideas are framed by gender, ethnic, social, political, economic, and other cultural and ideological perspectives. It is important for them to know that ideas have power but that this power is not always beneficent. It is important for them to know that there are other points of view that require a sympathetic exercise of the imagination to comprehend. We live in a world characterized by multiplicity, plurality, and difference. We are educated in this world to the degree that we are aware of our own boundedness and partiality, and we that we become skilled in seeking out, understanding, and integrating the perspectives of others.

It is equally important, however, that knowing these things not result in paralysis or some easy relativism. Students cannot be allowed to be content with the notion that issues may be addressed by any number of equally valid formulations among which they cannot choose. They must learn to discriminate by arguing, and they must realize that arguments exist for the purpose of clarifying and making choices. Students need to learn, through the kind of extended and direct experience afforded by concentrated studies, to be able to state why a question or argument is significant and for whom; what the difference is between developing and justifying a position and merely asserting one; and how to develop and provide warrants for their own interpretations and judgments.

Accomplishing these goals cannot be taken for granted or left to students' unaided and solitary musings. It is an iron law of education that students will neither criticize nor integrate what the faculty will not. There must be curricular space and academic credit as well as persuasive guides and models to support student practice in developing critical perspective. Faculty commitment to join disparate points of view within and across disciplinary boundaries is an indispensable foundation for the critical judgment that the major needs to develop.

Connected Learning

For most students in most major programs, fostering capacities for reflection on what happens beyond the academy must be the larger goal. The discourse of the academy is but a means to an end, a developmental step along a path that appropriately points students toward a multitude of contexts and circumstances. Students come into the academic "home," not to become permanent residents, but to be nurtured and supported as they develop the capabilities they need to enter, negotiate, and make connections across communities of discourse both within and without the academy.

There are two ways, by no means unrelated, in which the term "connected learning" may be employed. The first refers to the capacity for constructing relationships among various modes of knowledge and curricular experiences, the capacity for applying learning from one context to another. The second refers to the capacity for relating academic learning to the wider world, to public issues and personal experience. In either case, connected learning means generalizing learning: learning that extends beyond the necessary boundaries of any major and takes seriously its potential translation beyond the limits of a course or program.

Although the structures of departments, academic majors, colleges, and universities reflect traditionally linear and divided ways of organizing, presenting, and producing knowledge, the intellectual practices of faculties today are bursting these boundaries. In many colleges and universities, the traditional disciplinary structures are permeated by crosscutting institutes, seminars, workshops, and the like. Aided by professional societies and the technology of facsimile transmissions and electronic mail, research in many fields is becoming more collaborative, and disciplinary boundaries are increasingly blurred.

These developments have created a marked disparity between the ways academics do their research and the institutional structures that organize curricula and teaching. In the arresting image of historian John Higham, the contemporary academy looks like "a house in which the inhabitants are leaning out of the many open windows gaily chatting with the neighbors, while the doors between the rooms stayed closed."

While faculty members are becoming liberated, however, students experience most acutely the closed doors of classrooms cut off from one another. What are needed are incentives and structures to ensure that the intellectual excitement of discovery, interaction, and critical discourse that many faculty members experience also is available to students.

The forging of connections between seemingly discrete topics and disciplines—the sometimes playful synthetic capacity for discerning previously unsuspected relationships—takes place most often at the boundaries of a field, more rarely at its core. The ability to work at the periphery, however, requires a confident knowing and understanding of the core. At its best, the traditional major has offered a curriculum designed to convey what is central to a given discipline or area of study. But the synthesizing enterprise—the bringing of what one has learned in one context to another, from one community to another—has been left almost entirely to students' private initiative. It ought to take place in public, accredited, curricular space.

The second sort of connected learning hitherto has been even more private, even more unacknowledged by the formal, public curriculum. It is the way students use their studies to think about questions that matter to them personally.

Each field is structured around questions it considers central to examining the reality it studies. The reasons these questions are viewed as central, or even meaningful, may not always be clear to students. The centrality given to these scholarly questions also may teach students to suppress their own questions and concerns as naive or inappropriate. The course of a program of concentrated study should allow students to see and explore the connections between primary issues in the field and their own significant interests and concerns.

While it is important for students to develop a detached critical perspective on subject matter, it is equally important for them to care about subject matter and see its implications for the ways they live their lives. At issue is whether students can connect a field's subject matter and approaches with a variety of pursuits important to them, and whether their curiosity and concerns beyond the classroom can be deepened or shaped by the insights the field brings forth. This requires teaching and opportunities for reflection that encourage students to test the assumptions and proposals of the field against questions and evidence drawn from their own experience.

Students should be invited to engage in both forms of connected learning by participating in collaborative work with other students. Through mutual interviewing—careful questioning and active, attentive listening—students can help each other identify, articulate, and elaborate their own driving questions and build on each other's ideas. Questions about meaning and significance should be addressed in a setting that encourages collaboration in the exploration and reformulation of issues in relation to both academic inquiry and personal experience. This kind of dialogue should give students practice in entering into frames of reference of people with differing experiences of, and assumptions about, the world.

This process—in some way a sharing of stories—can help students shape an intellectual autobiography. Fully conceived, the intellectual autobiography becomes a story that relates students' curricular and extracurricular experiences in significant and connected narratives with both retrospective and prospective clarities or uncertainties and with implications for both personal and public life. The accredited public space that ought to be provided for connecting learning should involve both faculty members and student peers in listening, valuing, and creatively engaging such stories.

In the final analysis, the challenge of college, for students and faculty members alike, is empowering individuals to know that the world is far more complex than it first appears, and that they must make interpretive arguments and decisions—judgments that entail real consequences for which they must take responsibility and from which they may not flee by disclaiming expertise. Major programs characterized by a concern for coherence, critical perspectives, and the construction of connections play significant roles in achieving that end.

Inclusiveness: Reducing Barriers for Underrepresented Students

Even as students from diverse ethnic, racial, and economic backgrounds have entered the academy, they remain underrepresented in many arts and sciences majors. Women also are underrepresented in specific fields, especially in some of the sciences. Redressing imbalances cannot be left to the admissions office or to an institution's promising collaboration with the local public schools. Faculty members in each program must explore what obstacles their fields present to the participation of discrete groups of underrepresented students and make a strong commitment to eliminating those obstacles.

The problem of full participation in arts and sciences majors no longer can be framed in terms of access alone; what is needed is a reformation of present practices. This reformation cannot be separated from the central obligations of major programs already described. Faculty commitment to establishing curricular coherence, critical perspectives, and connected learning provides an overarching framework through which programs can examine their practices and reach for full participation of all students in arts and sciences fields.

Curricular coherence. One of the hallmarks of curricular coherence is a corporate clarity about the differing educational roles of introductory courses, middle-range offerings, and culminating experiences. These distinctions have special relevance when applied to underrepresented students. All too often, courses designed to introduce students to a field's community of inquiry communicate to these students that their participation is not welcome; that the major is not their home; that the field does not recognize, reflect, or value their goals, perspectives, and experiences.

A particular problem is the routine use of introductory courses in some fields as screening devices to filter out, at an exceedingly early stage, students who do not readily fit faculty members' expectations. In programs where disparate patterns of participation are a problem, faculty members need to work together to design multiple entry points to the major. This does not mean remedial courses or separate tracks beyond the purview of the particular program. It means more intensive courses that take as a point of departure "where students are" and the particular difficulties that specific contents frequently present. Where students enter departments with markedly different backgrounds and preparations, there may need to be different versions of the same course, some requiring more time and carrying more credit hours. There are exemplary instances of carefully crafted multiple entry points in some institutions and some fields; there should be many more.

Staggered patterns of attendance as well as movement among institutions (often characteristics of adult and minority students) challenge widespread assumptions that coherence is best achieved through strict serial order. What does it mean for a student to have taken one part of a requisite set of courses at one institution and a second part years later at another? Faculty members in institutions serving significant numbers of intermittent and transfer students may need to design multiple entry points into the community of the major. They may need, further, to follow the example of baccalaureate programs designed specifically for adults and offer their own workshops on educational planning in the major for transfer and returning students in each semester or quarter.

In designing major programs, faculties also need to reflect on appropriate points of entry for adult students returning to college with a broader range of practical experiences than the traditional college-age student. As adults become a major constituency on many campuses, they challenge faculty members in each field to draw on adults' experience outside of school as a resource that enriches the work and discussion of the learning community as a whole.

There is no single approach to initiatory courses that will apply to all colleges and all major programs. What is required of each institution and each field is a strong affirmation of the educational benefits of diversity and a continuing faculty dialogue about the ways initiatory experiences in a field can contribute to, and lay the foundations for, the widest range of students to achieve success.

Attention also must be given to programmatic elements that assist and encourage students in developing increasing competence and confidence in the culture of a particular learning community (the function of middle-range courses) thereby helping more students succeed. Some students "fit" easily; others remain on the fringe; others fall away. Corporate attention to the ways in which a major works as a total program, rather than a set of discrete (and often disparate) courses, can establish a series of points at which faculty members both assess and support students' continuing progress in the field.

When faculty members establish clear understanding of the goals of a major program, they can communicate their expectations more effectively to students and advisors. They also can explore alternative ways to enhance successful participation—for example, through peer advising, workshops on educational planning, focused study groups, linking student course choices to their performance on mid-course assessments, and the like.

Critical perspectives. Encouraging critical perspectives on the limits of the field also can open specific majors to broader participation by including all students in substantive dialogue. For the past two decades, there has been a series of intense scholarly exchanges about the emphases, assumptions, and values of particular fields. Research and criticism from women's studies and from racial and ethnic studies have introduced new dimensions into every area of study. Intense and fruitful debates rage about legitimate areas of inquiry, knowledge in different fields, who possesses knowledge, and the relations between power and knowledge. None of these issues is settled; some ultimately may prove short-lived. But the range of the debate—the issues and consequences it has opened—encourages faculty members and students alike to engage in the critical discourse and arguments that underlie all claims to knowledge.

Too often, faculty members view these debates as separate from their work as educators. Even as they address these issues in their scholarly journals and conferences, they withhold them from their students. Highlighting these strongly contested topics as well as the role of previously excluded groups in shaping these debates can help a broader range of students find a home within a given field, discover their own questions and concerns in fields that once seemed indifferent or closed, and develop a sense of their own role in formulating constructive and critical proposals. Above all, highlighting these strongly contested topics will involve students in fields of liberal learning at their best, functioning as communities committed to collaborative processes of dialogue and inquiry.

Connected learning. Connected learning calls for actively making relationships among fields, applying knowledge from one context to another, and taking seriously students' interests in relating academic learning to the wider world of public issues as well as individual experiences and goals. Even as faculties work to help students develop a richer sense of what liberal education can be, they also should take seriously students' concerns with linking what they learn in college to their lives and careers.

Students who are most likely to enter college with practical and vocational interests also are most likely to shy away from arts and sciences majors. Such students may experience the greatest distance from those faculty members who communicate a conviction that learning is valuable solely in itself, apart from (indeed, indifferent or hostile to) any practical applications. Similarly, many fields communicate to students that it is inappropriate to think about connecting their personal questions and concerns with the contents and methods of the major. To the degree that major programs are reformulated to encourage occasions in which practical and personal concerns publicly enter into dialogue with the assumptions and proposals of specific fields, the goal of full participation in communities of learning and inquiry is advanced.

Conclusion

In 1985, *Integrity*'s authors argued that one of the chief causes for the disarray of the curriculum and the demise of good teaching was the increased professionalization of the professoriat and faculty members' development of primary loyalties to their disciplines rather than to the institutions where they taught or to their students. AAC's Project on Liberal Learning, Study-in-depth, and the Arts and Sciences major has explored an alternative possibility: that there are important resources for educational renewal in the commitments both faculty members and students make to college majors.

In this spirit, this report aims to return the challenge of strengthening both the curriculum and teaching to discrete campuses and to major programs. It suggests that we can link central concerns of liberal education to institutional structures where harmony between professional interests and pedagogical commitments is most likely to be found.

There are long traditions of debate in all fields about what should be taught to majors and about the relationship between requirements for majors and the logic and structure of intellectual developments in the sponsoring fields. These same debates have exhibited too little attention, however, to the *educational* coherence of major programs as they are experienced by the students who take them. It is one thing to say that each student major will take courses addressing particular subject matters; it is quite another to develop educational strategies that help students develop competence in using, interrogating, and integrating their learning across the boundaries of course and field.

This report calls disparate fields into a shared dialogue and a sense of common enterprise. It does so by emphasizing the absolute requirement of bringing students back into the picture and making their need for coherence, critical perspectives, and experiences of connected learning central to the work of the major in the context of liberal learning.

This report also asks for collective and collaborative faculty discussions about ways of translating these common commitments into institutional practices and structures. This translation must begin with time and space for faculty dialogue; it must be supported by visible and concrete rewards for participating in such discussions. It needs, as well, provision of the means to experiment in ways appropriate to the particular institutional settings of diverse fields.

It is not enough for deliberations about the major to be exercises at the blackboard diagramming curricula that "look right" but have little effect either on course practices or student experience of the major. Faculty members' deliberations about majors as educational programs need to become part of a continuing collegial dialogue about the relationship between faculty intentions and student progress.

Departments and programs cannot be expected to make these commitments independently. Collegial leadership within and across programs both deserves and requires full institutional support from presidents and academic administrators. What are needed in the long run are institutional environments that build a sense of common enterprise and institutional priorities that recognize the integral connections between work in the major and overarching goals for liberal learning.

This report suggests a common language through which to explore arts and sciences majors. This language will need translation into a host of specific idioms appropriate to different fields and institutions. But the common language also makes possible conversations and explorations that cut across particular fields and boundaries. The terms of discussion are preliminary; the most important goal of this report is to engage students, faculty members, and administrators in long-needed local conversations about the role of majors within the context of liberal learning.

CHAPTER 22

REINVENTING UNDERGRADUATE EDUCATION: A BLUEPRINT FOR AMERICA'S RESEARCH UNIVERSITIES

BOYER COMMISSION ON EDUCATING UNDERGRADUATES IN THE RESEARCH UNIVERSITY

An Overview

In a great many ways the higher education system of the United States is the most remarkable in the world. The speed with which it developed, its record of achievement, the extent of its reach, the range of its offerings are without parallel. And, particularly in the years since World War II, the system has reached a higher proportion of the national population than that of any other country. Half of the high school graduates in the United States now gain some experience in colleges and universities; we are, as a country, attempting to create an educated population on a scale never known before. The goal of President Harry Truman's 1947 Commission on Higher Education, that the system must provide "the means by which every citizen, youth, and adult, is enabled and encouraged to carry his education, formal and informal, as far as his native capacities permit" is accepted as axiomatic.

In the higher education system in the United States, the research universities have played a leading role: the country's 125 research universities make up only 3 per cent of the total number of institutions of higher learning, yet they confer 32 per cent of the baccalaureate degrees, and 56 per cent of the baccalaureates earned by recent recipients of science and engineering doctorates (1991–95). Their graduates fill the legislatures and board rooms of the country, write the books we read, treat our ailments, litigate our issues, develop our new technologies, and provide our entertainment. To an overwhelming degree, they have furnished the cultural, intellectual, economic, and political leadership of the nation.

Undergraduates Too Often Shortchanged in the Past

Nevertheless, the research universities have too often failed, and continue to fail, their undergraduate populations. Tuition income from undergraduates is one of the major sources of university income, helping to support research programs and graduate education, but the students paying the tuition get, in all too many cases, less than their money's worth. An undergraduate at an American research university can receive an education as good or better than anything available anywhere in

Source: "Reinventing Undergraduate Education: A Blueprint for America's Research Universities," by the Boyer Commission on Educating Undergraduates in the Research University, 1996, Shirley Strum Kenny, Chair of the Commission, President, SUNY Stonybrook.

THE FACTS

University-level education rates in the United States and abroad.

This table indicates the percentage of the population of selected nations that enters college or university; it does not have graduation rates.

Net entry to post-secondary university/college education, for people ages 15 and over:

United States	52%
Canada	49%
United Kingdom	43%
New Zealand	40%
Netherlands	34%
France	33%
Denmark	31%
Germany	27%
Ireland	27%
Austria	26%
Norway	25%
Hungary	20%
Turkey	16%
Switzerland	15%
Average	**30%**

Source: Organization for Economic Cooperation and Development (OECD) Database, Table C4.2, Net Entry rates for university-level education (1995).

THE FACTS

Percentage of recent science and engineering doctoral recipients who earned their bachelor's degrees at U.S. research universities, by field of doctorate.

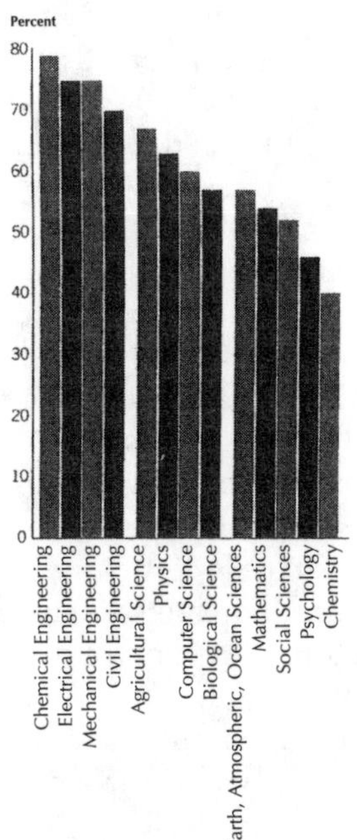

Source: National Science Foundation SRS Survey of Earned Doctorates for the years 1991–95.

the world, but that is not the normative experience. Again and again, universities are guilty of an advertising practice they would condemn in the commercial world. Recruitment materials display proudly the world-famous professors, the splendid facilities and the groundbreaking research that goes on within them, but thousands of students graduate without ever seeing the world-famous professors or tasting genuine research. Some of their instructors are likely to be badly trained or even untrained teaching assistants who are groping their way toward a teaching technique; some others may be tenured drones who deliver set lectures from yellowed notes, making no effort to engage the bored minds of the students in front of them.

Many students graduate having accumulated whatever number of courses is required, but still lacking a coherent body of knowledge or any inkling as to how one sort of information might relate to others. And all too often they graduate without knowing how to think logically, write clearly, or speak coherently. The university has given them too little that will be of real value beyond a credential that will help them get their first jobs. And with larger and larger numbers of their peers holding the same paper in their hands, even that credential has lost much of its potency.

These are not problems that have been totally denied or ignored; there is probably no research university in the country that has not appointed faculty committees and created study groups or hired consultants to address the needs of its undergraduates. There have been results: new courses, new majors, revised curricula. A new study by the Center for Instructional Development at Syracuse University suggests that universities believe they are now giving more attention to teaching. At a sample of eleven research universities, deans, department heads, and other administrators said more emphasis was being given to teaching than five years ago.

Radical Reconstruction

Even so, for the most part fundamental change has been shunned; universities have opted for cosmetic surgery, taking a nip here and a tuck there, when radical reconstruction is called for. Serious responses to complaints about undergraduate teaching have generated original and creative pedagogical and curricular experiments. But too often bold and promising efforts have

THE FACTS

Earned degrees by level and sex, 1969–70 to 2005–06

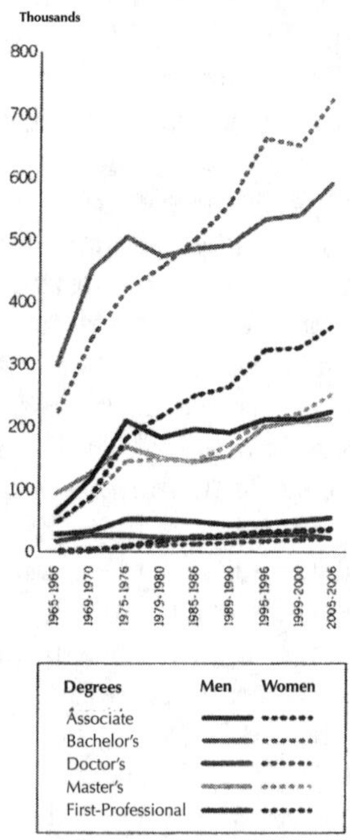

Note: 1995–1996, 1999–2000, and 2005–2006 data is projected.

Source: U.S. Department of Education, National Center for Education Statistics, Earned Degrees Conferred: Projections of Education Statistics to 2006, and Integrated Postsecondary Education Data System (IPEDS), "Completions" surveys. This formation was prepared February 1996.

vanished after external grant support disappeared, have withered on the fringes of the curriculum, or have been so compromised that their originality has been lost. Strikingly, the Syracuse study reported that research productivity was still given "much more" weight in making decisions about promotion and tenure of faculty members than was teaching effectiveness.

The way the research university developed made the present-day situation predictable if not inevitable. The inspiration was the German universities of the nineteenth century, which had redefined themselves as institutions dedicated to advanced research on scientific principles. America's leading colleges adopted parallel goals and began giving advanced degrees, finding honor, excitement, and reward in the exploration of intellectual frontiers made by their faculties. In a country and an era fascinated with discovery and expansion, the research mission has overshadowed the earlier collegiate function of training young men to be ministers, lawyers, and gentlemen. The older function had to be maintained, but the undergraduate experience given the young men, and later the young women as well, was kept isolated from the research activity and still cast in the pre-university mold. Universities on the whole did not see ways to integrate their undergraduates into the research missions that they valued above alt else. As Ernest Boyer said in his *Scholarship Reconsidered* in 1990, "the focus had moved from the student to the professoriate, from general to specialized education, from loyalty to the campus to loyalty to the profession." Advanced research and undergraduate teaching have existed on two quite different planes, the first a source of pleasure, recognition, and reward, and the latter a burden shouldered more or less reluctantly to maintain the viability of the institution.

Defining Worth

The primacy of research within the espoused missions of American universities is attested over and over within the academic world. The standing of a university is measured by the research productivity of its faculty; the place of a department within the university is determined by whether its members garner more or fewer research dollars and publish more or less noteworthy research than other departments; the stature of the individual within the department is judged by the quantity and quality of the scholarship produced. Every research university can point with pride to the able teachers within its ranks, but it is in research grants, books, articles, papers, and citations that every university defines its true worth. When students are considered, it is the graduate students that really matter; they are essential as research assistants on faculty projects, and their placement as postdoctoral fellows and new faculty reinforces the standing of the faculty that trained them. Universities take great pleasure in proclaiming how many of their undergraduates win Rhodes or other prestigious scholarships and how many are accepted at the most selective graduate schools, but while those achievements are lauded, too many students are left alone to pursue them. And the baccalaureate students who are not in the running for any kind of distinction may get little or no attention.

Why, then, should baccalaureate students give their loyalty and their money to research universities? Because the potential remains for acquiring a virtually matchless education. The research universities possess unparalleled wealth in intellectual power and resources; their challenge is to make their baccalaureate students sharers of the wealth. To realize their potential means a complete transformation in the nature of the education offered.

A New Model

What is needed now is a new model of undergraduate education at research universities that makes the baccalaureate experience an inseparable part of an integrated whole. Universities need to take advantage of the immense resources of their graduate and research programs to strengthen the quality of undergraduate education, rather than striving to replicate the special environment of the liberal arts colleges. There needs to be a symbiotic relationship between all the participants in university learning that will provide a new kind of undergraduate experience available *only* at research institutions. Moreover, productive research faculties might find new stimulation and new creativity in contact with bright, imaginative, and eager baccalaureate students, and graduate students would benefit from integrating their research and teaching experiences. Research universities are distinctly different from small colleges, and they need to offer an experience that is a clear alternative to the college experience.

It is obvious that not every student should, or would wish to, attend a research university. Without attempting to characterize students at other kinds of institutions, it might be said that the undergraduate who flourishes at a research university is the individual who enjoys diverse experiences, is not dismayed by complexity or size, has a degree of independence and self-reliance, and seeks stimulation more than security. A research university is in many important ways a city; it offers almost unlimited opportunities and attractions in terms of associations, activities, and enterprises. But as in a city, the requirements of daily living may be taxing, and sorting out the opportunities and finding like-minded individuals may be difficult. The rewards of the ultimate experience, however, can be immeasurable.

THE FACTS

Where students go for higher education
Excluding Two-Year Colleges

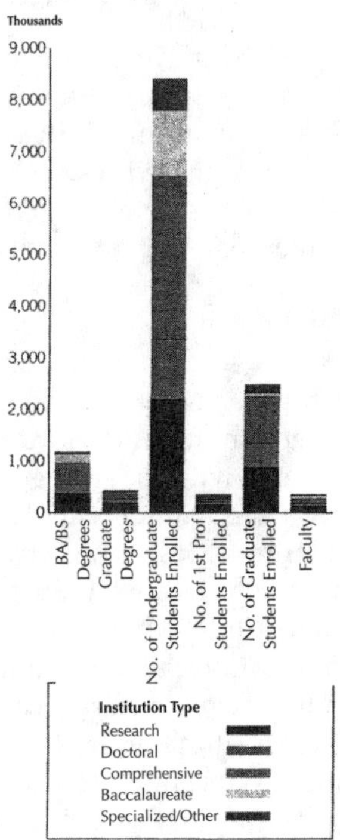

*Includes Masters and Ph.D. Excludes First Professional due to bad data. Excludes certificates
Source: 1994 IPEDS

The University as Ecosystem

Albert Einstein once articulated what many scholars have felt in their own work:

> The history of scientific and technical discovery teaches us the human race is poor in independent thinking and creative imagination. Even when the external and scientific requirements for the birth of an idea have long been there, it generally needs an external stimulus to make it actually happen; man has, so to speak, to stumble right up against the thing before the right idea comes.

Research universities provide the context in which the external stimuli operate with the greatest effectiveness, in which stumbling against the thing should happen with the greatest ease and frequency. The interaction of many kinds of stimuli creates at a university a special kind of intellectual environment, with the health of the whole a manifestation of the health of each part. That environment should become an intellectual ecosystem. Universities are communities of learners, whether those learners are astrophysicists examining matter in the far reaches of space or freshmen new to an expanded universe of learning. The shared goals of investigation and discovery should bind together the disparate elements to create a sense of wholeness.

Searching for a Shared Mission

The ecology of the university depends on a deep and abiding understanding that inquiry, investigation, and discovery are the heart of the enterprise, whether in funded research projects or in undergraduate classrooms or graduate apprenticeships. Everyone at a university should be a discoverer, a learner. That shared mission binds together all that happens on a campus. The teaching responsibility of the university is to make all its students participants in the mission. Those students must undergird their engagement in research with the strong "general" education that creates a unity with their peers, their professors, and the rest of society.

Unfortunately, research universities are often archipelagos of intellectual pursuit rather than connected and integrated communities. Fragmentation has increased drastically during the last fifty years. At many universities, research faculty and undergraduate students do not expect to interact with each other, and both groups distinguish between teachers and researchers as though the two experiences were not inextricably linked. Even those students who encounter an introduction to research technique in one narrow field too often remain ignorant of how diverse fields overlap and intermingle.

The institutional goal of research universities should be a balanced system in which each scholar—faculty member or student—learns in a campus environment that nurtures exploration and creativity on the part of every member.

A Beautiful and Efficient Concept

Ideally, the campus environment is enriched by interaction among faculty members in disparate fields, with graduate students enlivened by their exploration of faculty roles, and with undergraduates, whose questions and fresh approaches may open new paths of inquiry. The faculty member, unlike the full-time non-academic researcher, has interactions with other faculty and with students that broaden his or her intellectual vista and simultaneously provide the opportunity to develop future generations of professors and researchers. The baccalaureate student shares in the environment and develops his or her own research capabilities. The university setting for research is, therefore, much more valuable to our society than the environment in corporate or nonprofit research laboratories and institutes. As Charles M. Vest, President of the Massachusetts Institute of Technology, has pointed out, government funding of research in the universities is also an investment in the education of the next generation, with every dollar doing double duty, "a beautiful and efficient concept." What is more, the university's investment in research faculty also does double duty with teaching ideally enhanced by the research experience of both faculty and students.

Teaching Teachers to Teach

In contrast to this ideal, there is now a distressing and, in the long run, a destructive lack of connection between undergraduate study and the creation of future research faculty. The use of graduate students, particularly in certain fields, has been treated as a necessity for the operation of both research programs and undergraduate instruction. This perceived need has often led to the importation of foreign students new to American education. The international graduate students have been and must be welcomed in our universities; they have added incalculable strengths to research programs and, after graduation, to university faculties and research institutes. But the classroom results of employing teaching assistants who speak English poorly, as a second language, and who are new to the American system of education constitute one of the conspicuous problems of undergraduate education. Unless fully proficient speakers of English are attracted to the professoriate in the United States, these problems will continue to exist. Research universities have, therefore, a strong interest in introducing research-based education to undergraduates who are proficient in English in the hope that many of those research-trained undergraduates will be drawn toward academic careers. Joined by the bright and eager international students, they will furnish unprecedented pools of talent from which future faculties will be drawn.

Needed Now: A Synergistic System

Undergraduates who enter research universities should understand the unique quality of the institutions and the concomitant opportunities to enter a world of discovery in which they are active participants, not passive receivers. Although shared knowledge is an important component of a university education, no simple formula of courses can serve all students in our time. Collaborative learning experiences provide alternative means to share in the learning experiences, as do the multitudinous resources available through the computer. The skills of analysis, evaluation, and synthesis will become the hallmarks of a good education, just as absorption of a body of knowledge once was.

The phrase "student-centered research university" has sprung into the language of several research universities recently. At first glance it seems an oxymoron, and certainly it does not clearly describe the relationship between students and research—can universities be both student-centered and research-centered? The possibility exists that a "research university," properly defined, could embody what the phrase attempts, through a synergistic system in which faculty and students are learners and researchers, whose interactions make for a healthy and flourishing intellectual atmosphere.

An Academic Bill of Rights

When a university accepts an undergraduate student for admission and the student then enrolls, implicit commitments constitute an unwritten contract between them. Each assumes obligations and responsibilities, and each receives benefits. The student commits to a course of study intended to lead to a degree, agrees to follow such rules of civil behavior as the university prescribes, accepts the challenge of making an appropriate contribution to the community of scholars, and pledges to cultivate her or his mind, abilities, and talents with a view to becoming a productive and responsible citizen. The student at a research university, in addition, must come with appropriate preparation for the opportunities that will be provided, must commit to the strenuous burdens of active participation in the educational process, and must be prepared to live in a diverse and heterogeneous environment.

By admitting a student, any college or university commits itself to provide maximal opportunities for intellectual and creative development. These should include:

1. Opportunities to learn through inquiry rather than simple transmission of knowledge.
2. Training in the skills necessary for oral and written communication at a level that will serve the student both within the university and in postgraduate professional and personal life.
3. Appreciation of arts, humanities, sciences, and social sciences, and the opportunity to experience them at any intensity and depth the student can accommodate.
4. Careful and comprehensive preparation for whatever may lie beyond graduation, whether it be graduate school, professional school, or first professional position.

The student in a research university, however, has these additional rights:

1. Expectation of and opportunity for work with talented senior researchers to help and guide the student's efforts.
2. Access to first-class facilities in which to pursue research—laboratories, libraries, studios, computer systems, and concert halls.
3. Many options among fields of study and directions to move within those fields, including areas and choices not found in other kinds of institutions.
4. Opportunities to interact with people of backgrounds, cultures, and experiences different from the student's own and with pursuers of knowledge at every level of accomplishment, from freshmen students to senior research faculty.

The research university must facilitate inquiry in such contexts as the library, the laboratory, the computer, and the studio, with the expectation that senior learners, that is, professors, will be students' companions and guides. The research university owes every student an integrated educational experience in which the totality is deeper and more comprehensive than can be measured by earned credits.

The research university's ability to create such an integrated education will produce a particular kind of individual, one equipped with a spirit of inquiry and a zest for problem solving; one possessed of the skill in communication that is the hallmark of clear thinking as well as

SIGNS OF CHANGE

University Case Study
Undergraduate
Research Opporltunities

University
Massachusetts Institute of Technology

More than half of all undergraduates at the Massachusetts Institute of Technology take part in the Undergraduate Research Opportunities Program, in which students may work with faculty members or on independent projecs. Interested students submit written proposals and are interviewed by the professors leading the projects chosen; the program helps students who propose their own projects find faculty sponsorship. Studens may receive either hourly wages or academic credit. The UROP Research Mentor Program links students just beginning on a project with experienced students. The Undergraduate Research Apprentice Program in science and engineering a the University of California Berkeley, and other universities similarly provides opportunities for undergraduate research.

mastery of language; one informed by a rich and diverse experience. It is that kind of individual that will provide the scientific, technological, academic, political, and creative leadership for the next century.

Ten Ways to Change Undergraduate Education

This concept of integrated education requires restructuring both the pedagogical and the integrative aspects of the research university experience. The Boyer Commission recommends the goals that follow in order to meet the obligations of the university to all students, as expressed in the Academic Bill of Rights.

One caveat: we believe that research universities must be willing and able to break free from the traditions that have thus far governed budget creation and budget approval in order to think creatively about goals and techniques for reaching those goals.

Redirecting Resources

University budgets are now based on the principle of departmental hegemony; as a result, important innovations such as new approaches through interdisciplinarity are often doomed for lack of departmental sponsorship. Departments necessarily think in terms of protecting and advancing their own interests, defined in terms of numbers of faculty, courses, and majors. Initiatives for change coming from sources outside departments are viewed as threats rather than opportunities. New decisions on distributing resources must be carried out at the highest levels in the university, and they can be expected to meet little enthusiasm from those whose interests are protected by existing systems.

Academics have long believed that research universities require large lecture sections combined with study sections run by teaching assistants in order to teach many lower division courses. Yet technology will unquestionably change the nature of pedagogy. We believe that faculty time is best invested in classes in which interaction with students is normal and integral. Used creatively, electronic communication techniques can also be uniquely effective for certain kinds of courses, for example, some of those that have been taught in large lecture sections. Students are able to fit course materials into their own schedules and repeat material as often as desired. Technology provides an alternative context for learning, a context universities need to use. It is also increasingly providing a channel of asynchronous communication between faculty members and students. In the judgment of this Commission, research universities have a special responsibility to develop educational technology that offers students unique opportunities for learning. At the same time, technology cannot be a substitute for direct interactions between human minds.

Definitions of teaching load usually revolve around either how many hours a professor spends in the classroom or the total number of students being taught. However, if guided research becomes an important component of undergraduate education, the professor may well conduct research and class simultaneously but in a very different format. The old definitions of workload will have to be replaced. Time-worn assumptions and practices cannot be allowed to prevent needed change in undergraduate education.

Conventional economic assumptions have governed administrative as well as instructional costs. Universities usually behave as though administrative costs are capable of change in only one direction. It is in the nature of bureaucratic structures to grow, and unrestrained growth again and again absorbs resources that could support academic creativity. Growth in size does not necessarily mean increased usefulness. Universities must be willing to reexamine and re-evaluate every administrative function and pare away everything that cannot demonstrate its value. There must be a willingness to see how functions can be streamlined, combined, or eliminated in order to provide some of the resources that new educational initiatives demand.

We believe universities must recognize the urgency of addressing misdirections and inadequacies in the undergraduate experience, sharpen their own plans and timelines, and move quickly beyond the realm of interesting experiments and innovations to that of the institutionalization of genuine reform. The following recommendations include both general statements on issues of particular importance and specific suggestions for achieving the improvements recommended. Together they envision a major overhaul of baccalaureate education and consequently significant shifts in the balance of relationships of research, graduate, and undergraduate education.

I. Make Research-Based Learning the Standard

Undergraduate education in research universities requires renewed emphasis on a point strongly made by john Dewey almost a century ago: learning is based on discovery guided by mentoring rather than on the transmission of information. Inherent in inquiry-based learning is an element of reciprocity: faculty can learn from students as students are learning from faculty.

Important ideas rarely come fully-developed from the brain of a single individual; all scholars work from the grounding provided by predecessors, and few are not stimulated by the observations and criticisms of their peers. It is one of the functions of a university to provide the context in which ideas can be most productively developed. Bruce Alberts, President of the National Academy of Sciences and a member of the Boyer Commission, has referred to the "accidental collisions of ideas" necessary for the continued productivity of faculty, and has suggested that the presence of students provides a "lubrication" that breaks down intellectual barriers between faculty members. When students at every level—baccalaureate, masters', and doctoral—join with faculty in common inquiry, the opportunities for "accidental collisions of ideas" are optimized.

When asked why, universities expect that teachers both conduct research and teach well, scholar-teachers are fond of replying that their teaching flows from what they have learned through research, and many also say that their research is affected by their teaching. Wayne C. Booth, Dean Emeritus at the University of Chicago and member of the Commission, expressed what many others have felt:

> My books would have been quite different—and to me less valuable—if I had produced them in solitude or after talking only with professional colleagues. It was not just that thinking about how to teach students to read responsibly led me to ideas that I would otherwise have overlooked. Responding to students' rival readings actually changed my opinions about how to appreciate a given novel or work of criticism. For this and other reasons, teaching and publishing have always felt absolutely inseparable.

The non-researcher is too often limited to transmitting knowledge generated by others, but the scholar-teacher moves from a base of original inquiry. In a research university, students should be taught by those who discover, create, and apply, as well as transmit, insights about subjects in which the teacher is expert.

SIGNS OF CHANGE

University Case Study
Studio Format for Introductory Sciences

University
Rensselaer Polytechnic Institute

Rensselaer Polytechnic Institute has redesigned its large introductory science courses for more effective presentation; the traditional format, in which lecture, recitation, and laboratory sections were completely separate, were replaced by a 'studio' format, which integrates the three into one unified program taught in a single facility designed for the purpose. Students are divided into 12–15 "studio workshops," each taught by a single faculty member, with assistance from a graduate student and several undergraduates. Problem-solving, teamwork, and co-operative learning are emphasized.

SIGNS OF CHANGE

University Case Study
Problem-based Learning

University
University of Delaware

Problem-based learning was adopted in all basic science classes at the University of Delaware to promote active learning and connect concepts to applications. Students are not given all the information they need to solve the open-ended "real-world" problems, but are responsible for finding and using appropriate sources. They work in teams with access to an instructor; trained graduate or undergraduate students help lead some groups.

In reality, however, the undergraduate in our time may have little or no direct contact with established scholar-teachers. Instruction very often comes through the scholar's apprentice, the graduate student; the academic luminary featured in admissions bulletins appears rarely if at all in undergraduate classes, and then too often as the lecturer addressing hundreds of students at once. The context is intimidating for many, and they turn away in discouragement. Recognizing that discouragement, some research universities have responded by instituting smaller classes (though usually only for majors) conducted by senior faculty, or undergraduate seminars in which senior students are challenged to produce their own research.

The inquiry-based learning urged in this report requires a profound change in the way undergraduate teaching is structured. The traditional lecturing and note-taking, certified by periodic examinations, was created for a time when books were scarce and costly; lecturing to large audiences of students was an efficient means of creating several compendia of learning where only one existed before. The delivery system persisted into the present largely because it was familiar, easy, and required no imagination. But education by inquiry demands collaborative effort; traditional lecturing should not be the dominant mode of instruction in a research university.

The experience of most undergraduates at most research universities is that of receiving what is served out to them. In one course after another they listen, transcribe, absorb, and repeat, essentially as undergraduates have done for centuries. The ideal embodied in this report would turn the prevailing undergraduate culture of receivers into a culture of inquirers, a culture in which faculty, graduate students, and undergraduates share an adventure of discovery.

Involving Undergraduates in the Research Process

Because of the unique character of a research university, the process of discovery is essentially a public one; the results of research are, through both teaching and publication, offered publicly for critique, correction, and extension. Undergraduates need to become an active part of the audience for research. In a setting in which inquiry is prized, every course in an undergraduate curriculum should provide an opportunity for a student to succeed through discovery-based methods.

The basic idea of learning as inquiry is the same as the idea of research; even though advanced research occurs at advanced levels, undergraduates beginning in the freshman year can learn through research. In the sciences and social sciences, undergraduates can become junior members of the research teams that now engage professors and graduate students. In the humanities, undergraduates should have the opportunity to work in primary materials, perhaps linked to their professors' research projects. As undergraduates advance through a program, their learning experiences should become closer and closer to the activity of the graduate student. By the senior yeas the able undergraduate should be ready for research of the same character and approximately the same complexity as the first-year graduate student; the research university needs to make that zone of transition from senior to graduate student easy to enter and easy to cross. For those who do not enter graduate school, the abilities to identify, analyze, and resolve problems will prove invaluable in professional life and in citizenship.

A Mentor for Every Student

Generations of experienced scholars have known and acted upon the knowledge that the intellectual development of their graduate students is most effectively guided in one-to-one relationships. Essentially the same techniques of tutorship have been practiced at the undergraduate level in areas like art and music, where individual performance is watched, corrected, assisted, and encouraged. In the process, an undergraduate student and instructor can develop a supportive relationship nor unlike that found between doctoral candidate and advisor. This kind of mentoring needs to be emulated throughout universities.

In every discipline, field work and internships should be fostered to provide opportunities for original work. In professional schools, these experiences can occur on campus or externally through linkages with businesses, hospitals, associations, governmental agencies, etc. Professional schools operate primarily at the graduate level. Some, especially law schools, place an emphasis on breadth of background, and some medical schools follow the same kind of practice. But emphasis on breadth is seldom found in graduate schools of business and engineering. Graduate professional schools need to re-cast their admissions procedures to recognize the importance of the kinds of abilities that will be produced by integrated inquiry-based learning. When they do so, they will find their students more adaptive, more resourceful, and better able to accommodate the challenges of specialized training and professional life, as well as the relation of such training to social responsibilities. Those professional schools that train undergraduate students need to accept the same goals that obtain in the arts and sciences. Undergraduate engineers and business majors, as much as their colleagues in literature and political science, will benefit from the educational model being proposed. Particularly in the first years of university life, students in the professional schools should share the common experience.

In the model the Commission proposes, scholar-teachers would treat the sites of their research as seminar rooms in which not only graduate students but undergraduates observe and participate in the process of both discovery and communication of knowledge. Those with knowledge and skills, regardless of their academic level, would practice those skills in the research enterprise and help to develop the proficiency of others. Even though few researchers ever escape the human temptation to compete for rewards, this model is collaborative, not competitive. It assumes that everybody—undergraduate, graduate student, and faculty member alike—is both a teacher and a researcher, that the educational-research process is one of discovery, not transmission, and that communication is an integral part of the shared enterprise.

SIGNS OF CHANGE

University Case Study
Undergraduate Research, URECA

University
State Univesity of New York at Stony Brook

Any interested undergraduate at the State University of New York at Stony Brook may enter the URECA (Undergraduate Research and Creative Activities) Program, in which students work with faculty researchers and artists on selected projects of shared interest, on projects they devise themselves, or on an ongoing research project from one of the academic departments, professional schools, or research centers. Students may also find projects with Brookhaven National Laboratory, Cold Spring Harbor Laboratory, or North Shore University Hospital. Projects require faculty sponsorship and earn academic credit and expense allowances.

University Case Study
Peer Instruction

University
Harvard

A Harvard professor, Eric Mazur, has developed a peer instruction technique, first used in introductory calculus-based physics courses, in which a third of class time is given to asking conceptual questions; student responses are recorded on classroom computers. Students are then asked to discuss their answers with classmates and, if necessary, revise their answers and levels of confidence in them. Finally, clarification of the concept is provided by the instructor, guided by original class responses and later reconsiderations.

Internships

Internships can offer an invaluable adjunct to research-based learning by allowing the student concrete contexts in which to apply research principles. Whether a student has an internship in a physics lab, a news room, a hospital, or a business office, the experience can provide learning that cannot be replicated in the classroom. For undergraduates in the arts and sciences as well as in professional schools, these experiences provide useful, often interdisciplinary, learning

SIGNS OF CHANGE

University Case Study
College Research Opportunities Program (CROP)
University
Univesity of Chicago

Undergraduate students at the University of Chicago may participate in a wide variety of research projects in many disciplines, for which the students receive either academic credit or a salary. Positions are available with the university's on-campus research centers, including the Yerkes Observatory, the Ben May Institute for Cancer Research, the DNA Sequencing Facility, the Center for Medical Genetics, the Film Studies Center, the ARTFL Project (an on-line database of French texts from the 17th to the 20th centuries), the Council for Advanced Studies in Peace and International Cooperation, and the National Opinion Research Center, as well as with affiliated research centers such as the Fermi National Accelerator Lab.

and real-life problem solving. When students need to work to support their education, internships can make that economic requirement a valuable part of university experience.

Specific recommendations to implement this model include:

1. Beginning in the freshman year, students should be able to engage in research in as many courses as possible.
2. Beginning with the freshman year, students must learn how to convey the results of their work effectively both orally and in writing.
3. Undergraduates must explore diverse fields to complement and contrast with their major fields; the freshman and sophomore years need to open intellectual avenues that will stimulate original thought and independent effort, and reveal the relationships among sciences, social sciences, and humanities.
4. Inquiry-based courses should allow for joint projects and collaborative efforts.
5. Professional schools need to provide the same inquiry-based opportunities, particularly in the early years.
6. Provision of carefully constructed internships can turn inquiry-based learning into practical experience; internship opportunities need to be widely available.

II. Construct an Inquiry-based Freshman Year

The first year of a university experience needs to provide new stimulation for intellectual growth and a firm grounding in inquiry-based learning and communication of information and ideas.

The freshman year is crucially important. It marks a transition in the lives of young people both socially and academically. Many of them will spend a long period away from home for the first time and be required to make new friends and organize their lives without the close attention of families. Those who continue to live at home will have different schedules, different expectations, and different relationships. Freshmen who come directly from high school leave a structured academic program for an environment in which they bear far more personal responsibility for the nature of their learning.

The freshman year needs to perform two vital functions: it must be the bridge between high school and home on the one side and the more open and more independent world of the research university on the other, and it must excite the student by the wealth, diversity, scale, and scope of what lies ahead. If it does not perform both those functions successfully, the entire university experience is at risk.

Ironically, the first years of university studies, in many ways the most formative of all years, are usually the least satisfactory in terms of concept, curriculum, and pedagogy. Many universities find, to their great distress, that too many students spend time in the first year in remediation programs. Introductory courses often repeat subject matter that freshmen have studied for years rather than introducing new subjects that broaden their horizons and give them a sense of the adventure of learning. Too often the freshman curriculum is a bore and freshman instruction inadequate. Senior professors, when they teach undergraduates, tend to teach majors in advanced courses, although these students are usually the best equipped of all students for learning on their own in the subject of their chosen major. As a result, freshmen—the students who need the very best teaching—may actually receive the worst, and more of them fall away by the end of the freshman year than at any other time.

The first-year experience at most research universities was in the past governed by the perceived need to give every student a common base of knowledge. The "general education" requirements are now near extinction at many research universities; what has survived is often more influenced by internal university politics than educational philosophies. The freshman experience needs to be an intellectually integrated one, so that the student will not learn to think of the academic program as a set of disparate and unconnected requirements.

Every institution needs to rethink both what every future citizen, regardless of specialty or interests, needs to know in order to receive a degree and at what point that knowledge is best acquired. Radical change is thus essential to make the freshman year successful, a period of perhaps the fastest growth a student experiences during the college years.

Seminar Learning

The freshman year should be reconfigured for maximum benefit, and the sophomore year should evolve as a result of those changes. The focal point of the first year should be a small seminar taught by experienced faculty. The seminar should deal with topics that will stimulate and open intellectual horizons and allow opportunities for learning by inquiry in a collaborative environment. Working in small groups will give students not only direct intellectual contact with faculty and with one another but also give those new to their situations opportunities to find friends and to learn how to be students. Most of all, it should enable a professor to imbue new students with a sense of the excitement of discovery and the opportunities for intellectual growth inherent in the university experience.

Block Scheduling

A supportive atmosphere for adjustment to university life can be created by block scheduling cohorts of freshmen into two or three courses during their first semester or year. Groups can also be joined according to mutual curricular interests in living-learning centers or interest-focused residences.

SIGNS OF CHANGE

University Case Study
Block Scheduling

University
Duke University

First-semester Freshmen at Duke University may enroll in one of about 14 interdisciplinary, thematically-designed programs, in which they take two Focus seminars, a writing course, and a non-Focus elective. Enrollment in each is limited to 30; students in a program live together in a residence hall and meet weekly for dinner.

Remediation Before Admission

The current national attention being given to the idea of fixed graduation standards for public schools recognizes the deficiencies that too many students now bring to college. Entering students should be required to have satisfactory mathematics and oral and written language skills before taking any credit courses. Remediation should not be a function of a research university; for a research university to devote a large portion of its faculty time and its facilities to prepare students for university study represents a dissipation of increasingly scarce resources. Students should acquire the skills they need before entering credit-bearing courses. Intensive summer programs in mathematics and English may in many circumstances provide the necessary skills; students with serious deficits should attend other kinds of institutions prepared to handle their educational needs before enrolling in research universities. International students who need greater experience in spoken or written English should take intensive courses in English as a Second Language, in summers or first semesters, before entering the normal curriculum.

Recommendations

1. A student embarking upon a degree program at a research university should be adequately prepared to meet the intellectual challenges of that program; if remediation is necessary, it should be completed before entering the program.
2. All first-year students should have a freshman seminar, limited in size, taught by experienced faculty, and requiring

SIGNS OF CHANGE

University Case Study
LEAP

University
University of Utah

Entering freshmen at the University of Utah enroll in a year-long seminar led by one instructor and in quarterly Liberal Education Accelerated Program (LEAP) courses linked to the themes of the seminars. Some of these courses meet graduation requirements and some meet core or distribution requirements. LEAP students also enroll in a first-quarter study and computer skills course. Current and past LEAP students are members of the LEAP club, which provides organized social and academic activities such as study groups and guest speakers.

extensive writing, as a normal part of their experience.

3. Every freshman experience needs to include opportunities for learning through collaborative efforts, such as joint projects and mutual critiques of oral and written work.
4. The freshman program should be carefully constructed as an integrated, interdisciplinary, inquiry-based experience by designs such as:
    a. Combining a group of students with a combination of faculty and graduate assistants for a semester or a year of study of a single complicated subject or problem.
    b. Block scheduling students into two or three first-semester courses and integrating those courses so that the professors plan together and offer assignments together.
    c. If possible, integrating those courses with the freshman seminar, so that there is a wholeness as well as a freshness to the first year.
    d. Taking advantage of time freed by advanced placement to explore areas not studied in high school in order to encourage students to range as freely as possible before selecting a major.

III. Build on the Freshman Foundation

The freshman experience must be consolidated by extending its principles into the following years. Inquiry-based learning, collaborative experience, writing and speaking expectations need to characterize the whole of a research university education. Those students who enter the research university later than the freshman year need to be integrated smoothly into this special atmosphere.

After the freshman student is initiated into the life of the research university through a program that is innovative and exciting, the gains will be lost if the rest of the university experience does not match. Moving from a stimulating freshman seminar and an integrated program back into courses that seem unrelated, with requirements that do not evoke the newly-awakened spirit of research, would be dispiriting and disillusioning. So it is incumbent on the university to carry the reforms to every part of the curriculum.

This report does not address the issues of curricular change but rather the questions of how subject matter is presented and how intellectual growth is stimulated. The goal of making baccalaureate students participants in the research process requires faculties to reexamine their methods of delivering education, to ask how, in every course, students can become active rather than passive learners. That task, undertaken seriously, will produce many innovations suited to different disciplinary circumstances; the changes need to include greater expectations of writing and speaking, more active problem-solving, and more collaboration among baccalaureate students, graduate students, and faculty.

Long-term Mentorship

In a successful research experience, a relationship of trust and respect exists among the members of a team; shared goals and community often follow. Universities cannot expect that close personal relationships will or should exist between every student and the faculty members to whom that student has been exposed. But every student at a research university, should be able to feel that some faculty member knows and appreciates that student's situation and progress and is ready to help that progress by setting standards to be met and by offering advice, encouragement, and criticism. To be effective, this kind of mentoring relationship needs to be created early and maintained when possible throughout a student's program. Such a relationship should go beyond the routine suggestions about choice of courses that many departments consider to be "advising"; it requires patience and commitment from the faculty member, but the relationships built can be mutually rewarding.

Integrating Transfer Students

Research universities, particularly the state-supported universities, very often accept into their upper-class majors large numbers of students who have begun their educations elsewhere, at community colleges, at liberal arts colleges, or at other universities. In is not unusual for students to attend more than one institution before settling. Their freshman experience is over, for better or for worse, but they need to be integrated into the atmosphere of the research university and given as much as possible of the kind of inquiry-based experience that they missed. Special seminars or similar courses for transfer students would make up a major part of the deficit.

Recommendations

1. The inquiry-based learning, collaborative efforts, and expectations for writing and speaking that are part of the freshman experience need to be carried throughout the program.
2. Thoughtful and attentive advising and mentoring should integrate major fields with supporting courses so that programs become integrated wholes rather than collections of disparate courses.
3. Mentorships should begin as early as possible and should be maintained, whenever possible, throughout a student's academic career.
4. New transfer students need to be integrated into the research experience with special seminars or similar courses comparable to the freshman seminar.

IV. Remove Barriers to Interdisciplinary Education

Research universities must remove barriers to and create mechanisms for much more interdisciplinary undergraduate education.

SIGNS OF CHANGE

University Case Study
Sophomore Dialogues and Seminars

University
Stanford University

At Stanford University, sophomores who choose to enroll in a Sophomore College program are housed together in student residences and enroll in small-group classes of approximately 10, led by one professor and two upper-class students. Participants earn 1 or 2 academic credits: examples of topics include "Constitutionalism," "Comparative American Urban Cultures," and "The Process of Discovery in Psychology." Workshops in use of university libraries, research opportunities, and academic decision-making are held.

In the earlier decades of the century, research was characteristically confined within traditional boundaries of disciplines that had themselves been defined only a few generations earlier. The anthropologist and the historian rarely ventured into each other's realms; nor did the chemist and the physicist. But in the years since World War II the continuing appearance of new departments and new programs that merge fields has proven repeatedly the permeability of the lines between disciplines. Individual researchers find that pushing the limits of their field takes them into new territories and that the work they are doing may have much more in common with that of colleagues across the campus than with members of their own departments.

The principal barrier to interdisciplinary research and study has been the pattern of university organization that creates vested interests in traditionally defined departments. Administratively, all educational activity needs to "belong" somewhere in order to be accounted for and supported; that which has no home cannot exist. Courses must be offered under some kind of sponsorship; students are asked to place themselves in one discipline or another. The limitations on this kind of structure are recognized in every university by defining new departments, approving new programs, and creating new centers in which to house courses, often experimental, that do not fit into the disciplines. But those centers repeatedly must call on the departments to teach the courses, knowing that the departments may balk at doing so since the interdisciplinary programs deplete staffing for

SIGNS OF CHANGE

University Case Study
Junior Independent Work and Senior Thesis

University
Princeton

All undergraduates at Princeton must conduct independent research or creative work during the junior year and submit a Junior Paper, which then becomes the basis for the required Senior Thesis.

their own departmental courses. Students who find that existing majors do not suit their interests often encounter discouraging barriers; advisors will likely first try to fit those interests into one of the existing patterns.

Breaking the Disciplinary Molds

As research is increasingly interdisciplinary, undergraduate education should also be cast in interdisciplinary formats. Departmental confines and reward structures have discouraged young faculty interested in interdisciplinary teaching from engaging in it. But because all work will require mental flexibility, students need to view their studies through many lenses. Many students come to the university with some introduction to interdisciplinary learning from high school and from use of computers. Once in college, they should find it possible to create individual majors or minors without undue difficulty. Understanding the close relationship between research and classroom learning, universities must seriously focus on ways to create interdisciplinary in undergraduate learning.

Recommendations

1. Lower division courses should introduce students to interdisciplinary study.
2. Academic majors must reflect students' needs rather than departmental interests or convenience.
3. Customizing interdisciplinary majors should be not only possible but readily achievable.

V. Link Communication Skills and Course Work

Undergraduate education must enable students to acquire strong communication skills, and thereby create graduates who are proficient in both written and oral communication.

The failure of research universities seems most serious in conferring degrees upon inarticulate students. Every university graduate should understand that no idea is fully formed until it can be communicated, and that the organization required for writing and speaking is part of the thought process that enables one to understand material fully. Dissemination of results is an essential and integral part of the research process, which means that training in research cannot be considered complete without training in effective communication. Skills of analysis, clear explanation of complicated materials, brevity, and lucidity, should be the hallmarks of communication in every course.

At present, most writing in universities is addressed to professors who know more about the subject matter than the writers, but all students should be taught to write for audiences less informed on the topic than the writer. After college there will be little need to write "up" to a professor; it will be more important to write "down to an audience that needs information and/or opinions, even if that audience happens to be the employer or higher authority. The abilities to explain, to convey new information, and to condense materials for easy absorption will be essential for any profession.

Unfortunately, today's students too often think of composition as a boring English requirement rather than a life skill; moreover, hardly any are exposed to courses or class requirements in oral communication. Faculty too often think of composition as a task the English or composition department does badly, rather than understanding that an essential component of all faculty members' responsibility is making sure that their students have ample practice in both writing and speaking. In evaluating examinations and papers, faculty members are often willing to forgive grammatical and stylistic blunders, thinking such matters the responsibility of composition teachers, as long as they believe they can grasp the essence of the student's text; that behavior reinforces the assumption on the part of students that clear communication is not important.

Communication in Every Course

From the freshman seminar to the senior capstone course, communication skills should be integrated with the subject matter. Freshman composition must be cast in a new form intimately related to a student's other courses. Instructors throughout the curriculum need to build opportunities for written and oral presentations into their course outlines, so that experience and confidence can grow continuously. Faculty members need to assign papers as part of normal course expectations and to create examinations that require demonstration of writing and analytical skills.

Communications must be similarly, emphasized in the education of graduate students (see Section VIII below, Educate Graduate Students as Apprentice Teachers).

Recommendations

1. All student grades should reflect both mastery of content and ability to convey content. Both expectations should be made clear to students.
2. The freshman composition course should relate to other classes taken simultaneously and be given serious intellectual content, or it should be abolished in favor of an integrated writing program in all courses. The course should emphasize explanation, analysis, and persuasion, and should develop the skills of brevity and clarity.
3. Writing courses need to emphasize writing "down" to an audience who needs information, to prepare students directly for professional work.
4. Courses throughout the curriculum should reinforce communication skills by routinely asking for written and oral exercises.
5. An emphasis on writing and speaking in graduate courses will prepare teaching assistants for research, teaching, and professional roles.

VI. Use Information Technology Creatively

Because research universities create technological innovations, their students should have the best opportunities to learn state-of-the-art practices—and learn to ask questions that stretch the uses of the technology.

SIGNS OF CHANGE

Name
World Courses

University
University of Maryland

"World Courses" at the University of Maryland College Park are team-taught lecture courses for core distribution credit; many integrate science with humanities or social science perspectives. Topics include "To Stem the Flow: The Nile, Technology, Politics, and the Environment," taught by faculty from Civil Engineering. Microbiology, and Government and Politics, and "The Creative Drive: Creativity in Music, Architecture, and Science," taught by Mathematics, Music, and Architecture faculty, focusing on the creative process as seen in jazz, modern buildings, and scientific chaos theory.

Continuing technological development, particularly in the areas of information storage, retrieval, and communication, can be expected to alter the manner of teaching at every educational level and in every conceivable setting. We know that emerging technology is ceaselessly changing and will continue to change the ways in which the world functions and the ways in which people live. What we haven't been able to predict is exactly how. In the words of Milton Glaser, designer and Boyer Commission member, "technology is never neutral." It is the role of universities to make technology positive.

No institutions are better suited to make a difference in our technological future than research universities. Much of what we think of as sophisticated technology was created in their halls, and there is every reason to believe that university scholars will lead the way to continuing improvements. Scientific benefits aside, research universities are particularly well suited to take advantage of technology for teaching undergraduates.

The Electronic Classroom

Research universities, because of their size and academic mission, are far more likely than other institutions to possess the technological capabilities for twenty-first century teaching in any area. At many universities, computer networks, wired classrooms, and laser discs are used to bring recent research findings and methods

SIGNS OF CHANGE

University Case Study
Little Red Schoolhouse

University
University of Chicago

The "Little Red Schoolhouse" program at the University of Chicago is a one-quarter writing course taken each year by about 200 undergraduates. It is faculty taught, with assistance from doctoral-student writing interns. The interns are competitively selected and take a quarter-long training program themselves which teaches the "Schoolhouse" analysis of writing and techniques for adapting that analysis to the needs of individual students. In the Schoolhouse the students learn how to adapt their writing to evoke the responses they want and how to work effectively with other writers on revisions.

directly into the classroom. Creative applications of technology abound. A few examples:

- At the University of California, Berkeley, a state-of-the-art center for video conferencing and intercampus instruction allows courses—some of them as esoteric as Armenian History or Medieval Catalan—to be offered in collaboration not only with other University of California campuses but with other universities both in the United States and abroad; they allow any student anywhere to interact with faculty and classmates in real time.
- A freshman non-major science course at the University of Texas uses multimedia software modules with 3-D visuals, animation, and sound in addition to text which has links to remedial and supplementary materials.
- Massachusetts Institute of Technology has developed a large-scale computer service agency, that, among other functions, provides an on-line teaching assistants' program to answer student queries, distributes lectures through a cable-television network, and provides genetics-modeling software for biology courses.

It has become routine in universities for assignments to be sent and received and students' questions answered through electronic mail. If faculty give appropriate attention to reaching innovations, universities can become the technological pacesetters in teaching that they have always been in research; commercial developers await the products now. However, as innovations multiply, so do dangers: in many circumstances, casual over-use of technological aids already increases the real and psychological distance between living faculty members and living students. Technological devices cannot substitute for direct contact.

Enriching Teaching Through Technology

It is incumbent upon the faculties of research universities to think carefully and systematically not only about how to make the most effective use of existing technologies but also how to create new ones that will enhance their own teaching and that of their colleagues. The best teachers and researchers should be thinking about how to design courses in which technology, enriches teaching rather than substitutes for it. And equally important, faculties need to concern themselves with the need to give their students the tools with which they can explore deeply as well as widely, with which they can discriminate, analyze, and create rather than simply accumulate.

If anything is evident, it is that the more information a person can obtain, the greater the need for judgment about how to use it. Obtaining information from the Internet is easy; children in elementary school can do it. But who teaches students how to take advantage of this mass of information? Who teaches them how to tell the difference between valuable information and clutter? How, in short, does a student become a more intelligent consumer in this supermarket of information? The answer, we believe, is by exposure to scholars—experienced, focused guides who have spent their lives gathering and sorting information to advance knowledge.

Recommendations

1. Faculty should be alert to the need to help students discover how to frame meaningful questions thoughtfully rather than merely seeking answers because computers can provide them. The thought processes to identify problems should be emphasized from the first year, along with the readiness to use technology to fullest advantage.

2. Students should be challenged to evaluate the presentation of materials through technology even as they develop an increasing familiarity with technological possibilities.
3. Faculties should be challenged to continue to create new and innovative teaching processes and materials, and they should be rewarded for significant contributions to the technological enrichment of their courses.
4. Planning for academic units, such as block-scheduled courses for freshmen or required courses for individual majors, should include conscientious preparations for exercises that expand computer skills.
5. Active interchange between units on campus and through professional meetings should encourage and inspire faculty, to create new computer capabilities for teaching and to share ideas about effective computer-based learning.

SIGNS OF CHANGE

University Case Study
Rhetoric Department Instructors

University
University of Iowa

Graduate instructors for required basic courses in reading, writing, speaking, and research are recruited not only from the English and Communication departments at the University of Iowa, but also from other humanities and social science departments such as African-American World Studies, Classics, History, and Philosophy. New teachers are provided with background material in the summer before they begin teaching, attend a 3-day intensive workshop before classes begin, and attend a weekly teaching colloquium, required for new faculty as well, during the fall semester. All graduate instructors are paired with faculty teaching advisors, with whom they share drafts of teaching materials and assignments and review students' progress. The department also assists the instructors in preparing a teaching portfolio.

VII. Culminate With a Capstone Experience

The final semester(s) should focus on a major project and utilize to the fullest the research and communication skills learned in the previous semesters.

In order to ensure that the educational experience is drawn together, the student needs a course at the end of the curriculum that corresponds to the capstone of a building or the keystone of an arch. Too many students report a sense of anti-climax in their senior years—just add more to the total of courses, and it is finished! All the skills of research developed in earlier work should be marshaled in a project that demands the framing of a significant question or set of questions, the research or creative exploration to find answers, and the communication skills to convey the results to audiences both expert and uninitiated in the subject matter. When earlier course experience is inquiry-based, the student will be ready for and stimulated by the demands of this course. The nature of the experience will vary widely according to the major discipline of the student, but it should be of value equally to the budding social scientist, bench scientist, artist, humanist, engineer, or business major. The capstone experience needs to allow for collaborative effort whenever appropriate to the discipline, so that undergraduate students can be better prepared for participation in the team projects they will encounter in professional as well as private life.

The Culmination of Academic Effort

The experience should enable the student to bring to a symbolic conclusion the acquisition of knowledge and skills that has preceded this final effort. It should be conducted under the mentorship of a seasoned scholar-teacher who understands the joys and frustrations of a major project. It should allow the student to understand her or his potential for serious work and develop the aspiration to do it well. Ideally, the mentor for the capstone course may be the student's major advisor or a faculty member already, familiar with his or her capabilities and experience.

Although each university will find unique embodiments of the capstone concept, ideally the experience will occur within a small community of learners comprising senior researchers, graduate students, and undergraduate peers. This course should be the bridge to graduate education for the holders of research university baccalaureate degrees who immediately enter

SIGNS OF CHANGE

University Case Study
Capstone Learning Experience
University
University of Wisconsin

A College of Agriculture requirement at the University of Wisconsin is a "problem-solving exercise, in which students under faculty supervision and mentorship, must solve a 'real-world' problem and address societal, economic, ethical, scientific, and professional factors in their solutions." The Capstone Learning Experience must involve more than one department or several areas within a single department. Final work is presented in written, oral, and visual reports.

SIGNS OF CHANGE

University Case Study
Capstone
University
University of Missouri-Columbia

The General Education Program at the University of Missouri, Columbia, mandatory for all students, includes a capstone experience, a senior seminar, thesis, project, performance, internship, or field work, on a topic appropriate to the student's major. The capstone experience is evaluated on both the "quality of the product of the student's investigation and the process of presentation."

graduate school. For graduates entering the work force, the course should provide experience in the analysis, team-building, and problem-solving that most professional situations demand.

We hope that many students will conduct these research or creative projects in interdisciplinary groups, choosing topics and using techniques that break through disciplinary barriers. The flexibility that should mark the graduate of a research university should be fully developed in this final, culminating experience.

Recommendations

1. Senior seminars or other capstone courses appropriate to the discipline need to be part of every undergraduate program. Ideally the capstone course should bring together faculty member, graduate students, and senior undergraduates in shared or mutually reinforcing projects.
2. The capstone course should prepare undergraduates for the expectations and standards of graduate work and the professional workplace.
3. The course should be the culmination of the inquiry-based learning of earlier course work, broadening, deepening, and integrating the total experience of the major.
4. The major project may well develop from a previous research experience or internship.
5. Whenever possible, capstone courses need to allow for collaborative efforts among the baccalaureate students.

VIII. Educate Graduate Students as Apprentice Teachers

Research universities must redesign graduate education to prepare students for teaching undergraduate students as well as for other professional roles.

Although graduate education is not at the center of our concern, clearly the metamorphosis of undergraduate education at research universities can not occur without suitable adjustments in the way that graduate students are prepared for their professional roles. Over the last several decades, universities have prolonged doctoral study, but they have not necessarily improved it by doing so. A graduate degree is a professional degree, intended both to furnish credentials and to prepare students for their life's work. But important aspects of their life's work have been neglected or ignored in their doctoral programs, to their detriment and that of the undergraduates they are expected to teach.

More than half of all doctoral students will seek employment in colleges and universities, 54 per cent according to the National Research Council's 1995 Survey of Earned Doctorates. The percentage of Ph.D.'s who become faculty varies broadly between fields, ranging from 83 per cent of humanities majors to 22 per cent of engineering majors. Most future faculty, however, cannot realistically expect to find positions at the 3 per cent of the nation's colleges and universities that are research universities. Yet graduate education severely neglects the professional goal of the majority of students who will become college professors, that is to say, teaching.

Reshaping Professional Training

Many students go directly from their bachelor's degrees into graduate school. Suddenly they are expected to be experts in their fields; we forget that last year they were mere seniors. They have great needs to acclimate themselves to a very different kind of learning experience. Simultaneously, we burden them with the responsibilities of research or teaching assistantships. Although more affluent institutions may allow them a grace period before beginning their assistantships, too many plunge them directly into their duties. This situation can be most harmful when they begin teaching immediately, sometimes in fields that may well not be their specialty (for example, literature majors teaching composition or foreign language courses). Moreover, they are too often expected to know how to teach with little more than a few days or weeks of casual training and with little or no supervision throughout the year.

When these neophytes enter the classroom, they rarely come armed with serious training in pedagogy. Perhaps they will have a provided syllabus in a multi-sectional course; perhaps they will be placed in charge of sections of freshman mathematics or composition. Too often they will sense that spending time on teaching will hurt them by taking away from their concentration on their own study and research. The situation creates the greatest possibility for poor teaching at the time that the freshman needs the best teaching and mentoring. It also creates great stress at the time the new graduate student is most vulnerable, sometimes leading to early burnout and often to poor teaching.

There is a striking discrepancy now between the nature of graduate work and the nature of the professional careers for which graduate students are being prepared. In particular, people educated to the doctoral level are expected by their employers and by society to be highly proficient in their fields, to be able to evaluate the work of others, to be producers of knowledge that will enrich or improve life, and to be effective communicators to whatever audiences are appropriate. Corporate leaders who recruit new Ph.D.'s seek employees who are accomplished at teamwork, at critical thinking, problem-solving, and oral and written communication. Yet graduate education too often ignores all those expectations. Graduate students are given intensive work in narrowly defined subjects and meticulous training in the technical skills required for research projects; it is the unstated assumption that the other expectations will be met without organized effort—met, presumably, by the general education that preceded gradu-

SIGNS OF CHANGE

University Case Study
Future Professoriate Project

University
Syracuse University

The Future Professoriate Project at Syracuse University, funded by Pew Charitable Trusts, helps develop the teaching abilities of graduate students. Faculty Teaching Mentors lead seminars on effective teaching and serve as advisors; Teaching Associateships provide advanced teaching assistants opportunities to teach classes on their own and to receive a Certificate in University Teaching, awarded by the Graduate School to Teaching Associates who compile a teaching portfolio, which includes observation results as well as examples of syllabi, assignments, and examinations.

THE FACTS

Graduate students who plan to go into teaching.
Percentage of Ph.D. recipients in various fields, with definite employment commitments in the U.S., whose intended employment is in Academe (2 & 4-year colleges and universities and medical schools) or Other (not industry or government; "mainly composed of elementary and secondary schools and nonprofit organizations")

Field	Academe	Other	Total
All Fields	54%	17%	71%
Humanities	83%	10%	93%
Social Sciences	54%	16%	70%
Life Sciences	53%	8.5%	61.5%
Education	50%	38%	88%
Physical Sciences	41.5%	3.5%	45%
Engineering	22%	2.5%	24.5%
Professional/ Other	73%	11%	84%

From the National Research Council, 1995 Survey of Earned Doctorates.

THE FACTS

Where do faculty with Ph.D's work?

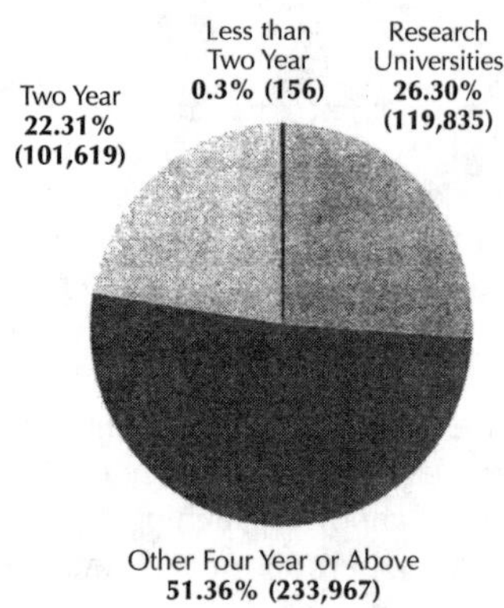

Source: 1994 IPEDS.

THE FACTS

Employment sector of Ph.D. recipients with postgraduation commitments in the United States for selected years, 1975–1995 (U.S. citizens and permanent residents).

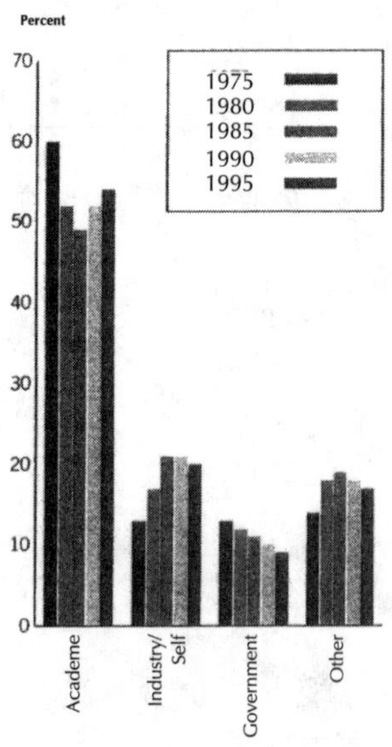

Note: Only Ph.D.s with definite commitments for employment are included. Foreign locations excluded. Percentages are based on the number of Ph.D.s whose employment sector is known. Government includes federal, state and local government agencies in the United State.

Source: National Research Council, Survey of Earned Doctorates.

ate training. For too many people, that assumption is unwarranted.

Restoring Communication

Nowhere are the failures of graduate education more serious than in the skills of communication. Corporate leaders complain that new Ph.D.'s too often fail as communicators and cannot advance their own careers or contribute to the success of their companies. Again and again, effective communication proves to be at least as important as specific knowledge content or technological training.

The importance of communications skills for academic careers is, of course, self-evident, for professors must teach, lecture to colleagues, and publish their research. Yet the skills of writing and speaking are by and large ignored in graduate education, certainly not taught as essential skills required for graduation. Obviously, the lack of emphasis on these skills, even when graduate students become teaching assistants, has a profound effect on undergraduate education.

No student lacking in basic English skills should be expected or required to enter a classroom to teach. The issues here are far bigger than those of accent and grammar; the teacher in any course must also be a teacher of writing and speaking skills. Any graduate student, therefore, who does not possess these skills must acquire them in order both to graduate and to teach.

Solving the Teaching Crisis

Given the fact that so many doctoral students are preparing for academic careers, the reconstitution of doctoral programs will have a profound effect on undergraduate education. If undergraduate programs truly produce good communications skills, then the alumni of those programs will begin their graduate study well prepared, thus reducing the crisis in writing and speaking abilities that exists now in courses taught by some teaching assistants.

Ideally, teaching assistants will also use their classroom opportunities to foster the ability to frame questions, to seek answers independently, and to think in interdisciplinary ways. As those abilities are essential to doctoral study, so they should be initiated and encouraged in undergraduates from their earliest courses, i.e. those often caught by teaching assistants.

Some universities are giving greater emphasis to teaching techniques as part of graduate student education, but few have explored mentoring relationships or the synergy of these interactions (i.e., how do undergraduates teach graduates, and how do graduates stimulate the intellectual growth of faculty members?).

Teaching is a difficult enough task in any setting, and in a research university the difficulties are magnified. The faculties of research universities must demonstrate to their graduate students how to lead undergraduates on their journeys of inquiry and discovery, and graduate students must master those teaching skills if they are to succeed as faculty members. Overdue as those ideas may be, undergraduates can expect to benefit when they are fully put in practice.

Recommendations

1. All graduate students should have time to adapt to graduate school before entering classrooms as teachers.
2. Graduate apprentice teachers should be assisted by one or more of the following means: seminars in teaching, thoughtful supervision from the professor assigned to the course, mentoring by experienced teachers, and regular discussions of classroom problems with other new teachers.
3. Graduate students should be made aware of their classroom roles in promoting learning by inquiry. They should not be limited to knowing the old modes of transmission of knowledge without understanding the role of student and faculty as joint investigators.
4. Graduate courses need particular emphasis on writing and speaking to aid teaching assistants in their preparation for teaching as well as research functions.
5. Graduate students should be encouraged to use technology in creative ways, as they will need to do in their own careers.
6. Compensation for all teaching assistants should reflex more adequately the time and effort expected.
7. Graduate students should be encouraged through special rewards for outstanding teaching. Financial awards should be established for outstanding teaching assistants. The permanent faculty should make it clear through these awards and through all they do that good teaching is a primary goal of graduate education.

SIGNS OF CHANGE

University Case Study
Undergraduate Teaching Initiatives

University
University of Virginia

At the University of Virginia, a Teaching Resource Center way created in 1990, funded primarily by reallocation. It offers evaluation, including videotaped critiques, and teaching improvement workshops, especially for teaching assistants and junior faculty. It also offers graduate courses on effective teaching strategies for special subjects. Outstanding Teaching Awards, five awards of $2,000 each, have been given annually since 1990–91.

IX. Change Faculty Reward Systems

Research universities must commit themselves to the highest standards in teaching as well as research and create faculty reward structures that validate that commitment.

In 1895, the first president of the University of Chicago, William Rainey Harper, asked each new faculty member to agree in writing that advancements in rank and salary would be governed chiefly by research productivity. His stipulation, novel in its time, would raise few eyebrows in most research universities a century later. They might claim otherwise, but research universities consider "success" and "research productivity" to be virtually synonymous terms.

The typical department in a research university will assert that it does place a high value on effective teaching at the baccalaureate level. It will be able to cite faculty members among its ranks who take conspicuous pride in their reputations as successful teachers; it may be able to point to student evaluations that give consistently high ratings to many of its members. At the same time, however, discussions concerning tenure and promotion are likely to focus almost entirely on research or creative productivity. The department head when making salary recommendations may look almost exclusively

SIGNS OF CHANGE

University Case Study
Rhetoric Program

University
University of Iowa

The Rhetoric Department recruits graduate instructors for its basic required courses in reading, writing, speaking and research from about fourteen departments, from African-American World Studies to Political Science to Religion. Before they teach, the instructors receive materials, including a 75-page set of Rhetoric Guidelines, and have a three-day intensive workshop on teaching. A weekly two-hour teaching colloquium is required in the fall. Faculty teaching advisors look over drafts of teaching materials and assignments and discuss student portfolios and exams. These advisors are rotated annually so that graduate instructors experience different points of view. Teaching portfolios are developed before graduate students look for jobs.

at the grants or publication record. The junior faculty member who seems to give disproportionate time and attention to freshman/sophomore courses may well be counseled toward more "productive" redirection; if interest is shown in experimental or interdisciplinary courses at the baccalaureate level, movement toward tenure or promotion may be stalled. The "needs of the department" will be perceived as not being met.

What happens within the department is echoed and reinforced among the established disciplines on a national scale. The professional associations do not as a rule see their responsibilities as embracing the teaching function, even though it is inspired teaching that attracts young minds and pulls new recruits into the disciplines. The national conferences of the disciplines rarely offer sessions dealing with teaching effectiveness, and when they do so, those sessions are likely to be poorly attended.

Synergy of Teaching and Research

The university's essential and irreplaceable function has always been the exploration of knowledge. This report insists that the exploration must go on through what has been considered the "teaching" function as well as the traditional "research" function. The reward structures in the modern research university need to reflect the synergy of teaching and research—and the essential reality of university life: that baccalaureate students are the university's economic life blood and are increasingly self-aware.

The kind of collaborative exploration that is urged here cannot be carried on in lecture sessions with hundreds of students. Budgetary constraints and the nature of survey courses may mean that some such courses continue; still, the teaching schedule of each faculty member needs to provide for small-group situations for baccalaureate students and a context that places them in joint exploration. Faculty course loads must also allow for research mentoring as part of normal operations rather than as poorly-compensated overloads.

Universities rightly assume that whoever appears in front of their classrooms can command the material that should be conveyed. Rare individuals can also captivate and stimulate student audiences, large and small, with their dynamic classroom presentations. Since it is likely that most universities will need to retain some large classes, those individuals capable of striking success in the classroom should be suitably rewarded. Recognition as distinguished teacher-scholars should include added remuneration.

Evaluating Teaching

In calculating academic rewards, it has been painfully difficult to evaluate the quality of research as separated from its mass. Nevertheless, departments and deans find that for passing judgment on peers, research productivity is a much more manageable criterion than teaching effectiveness. Faculty gossip, student evaluations, and alumni testimonials have all been notoriously weak reeds, and reliable self-evaluation is all but impossible. The publication of *Scholarship Assessed,* begun by Dr. Boyer before his death and published by the Carnegie Foundation for the Advancement of Teaching, pursues the issues of evaluating research. Recently the National Research Council has initiated a major study on how to evaluate science and mathematics teaching. But at this point promotion and tenure committees still find teaching effectiveness difficult to measure. Publication is at least a perceptible tool; the relative ease of its use has reinforced the reliance on it for tenure and promotion decisions. Evaluating good teaching will always be difficult, but effective integration of research and teaching should be observable, as should the development of interdisciplinary approaches to learning. Departments and deans must be pressed to give significant rewards for evidence of integrated teaching and research and for the imagination and effort required by interdisciplinary courses and programs. When publication is evaluated, attention should be paid to the pedagogical quality of the work as well as to its contribution to scholarship.

It has been emphasized here that a university is a community of learners. Some of them are more experienced than others; some are far along the way toward academic maturity, and some are not. Still, all are committed to the exploration of defined areas of knowledge, and in the university as envisioned here, they work together. Faculty members, graduate students, baccalaureate students all bring their particular combinations of energy, imagination, experience, and accumulated knowledge to bear. The divisions that have been created between them are artificial and counter-productive and must be bridged for effective collaborations to occur. All members of an academic team can share in the efforts and the rewards.

Recommendations

1. Departmental leaders should be faculty members with a demonstrated commitment to undergraduate teaching and learning as well as to traditionally defined research.
2. The correlation between good undergraduate teaching and good research must be recognized in promotion and tenure decisions.
3. A "culture of teaching" within departments should be cultivated to heighten the prestige of teaching and emphasize the linkages between teaching and research.
4. Prestigious professional research meetings such as national disciplinary conferences and the Gordon Conferences should contain one or more sessions that focus on new ideas and course models for undergraduate education.
5. Sponsors of external research grants can and should promote undergraduate participation, as the National Science Foundation has begun to do, thus facilitating the research experiences of undergraduates.
6. Rewards for teaching excellence, for participation in interdisciplinary programs, and for outstanding mentorship need to be in the form of permanent salary increases rather than onetime awards.
7. Teachers capable of inspiring performance in large classes should be recognized and rewarded appropriately.
8. Committee work at all levels of university life should be greatly reduced to allow more time and effort for productive student-related efforts.

SIGNS OF CHANGE

University Case Study
Eberly Center

University
Carnegie Mellon University

The Eberly Center at Carnegie Mellon University, founded in 1982, conducts programs to provide faculty and teaching assistants with an understanding of the learning process and varied teaching strategies, and offers opportunities for feedback on course design and implementation. Programs emphasize theory, modeling, practice, and feedback and draw on cognitive science research; for example, cross-disciplinary studies of expert-novice differences help faculty understand the difficulties that students new to a subject might have in setting up problems, transferring knowledge to new settings, and interpreting complex patterns.

X. Cultivate a Sense of Community

Research universities should foster a community of learners. Large universities must find ways to create a sense of place and to help students develop small communities within the larger whole.

Diversities of many kinds characterize research universities, which must balance the needs of residential students and commuters, recent high school graduates and returning professionals, native-born and international students. There is more of everything—more students, more professors, more courses, more books in the library, more computers, more laboratories, more student activities. Clearly the complexity of these intellectual cities can give students the opportunity to create their own customized communities within, but that complex-

SIGNS OF CHANGE

University Case Study
Redefining Scholarship

University
Syracuse University

Syracuse University has undertaken a program to redress a perceived overemphasis on research at the expense of teaching. The program has included conferences to enlist administrative support for change and a redefinition of "research and scholarship" by each division to include "the scholarship of teaching." A chancellor's fund was established to support the necessary changes, and a faculty grant program was created to reward teaching excellence and to provide funds for innovations.

ity can also be baffling and overwhelming to students, making them feel lonely, remote, and too anxious for optimal learning.

A sense of community is an essential element in providing students a strong undergraduate education in a research university. Whereas graduate students may readily gravitate to disciplinary colleagues around common research interests, beginning undergraduates rarely arrive with common intellectual connections.

The importance of a sense of personal identity within both large and small communities at the research university entered every discussion of the Boyer Commission. The campus must be a purposeful place of learning in which every student feels special connections. But that personal awareness of connections cannot occur unless there is a responsiveness to place and community. Therefore shared rituals play a powerful role in creating the larger university community in which the smaller, personalized communities of learners can coalesce. Whether the traditions are student convocations, pep rallies or football games, campus-wide celebrations, candlelight ceremonies, or graduation exercises, university-wide traditions feed the need for a connection with place, a unique campus character. These rituals create the aura for a community of learners comprising all members of the university linked by intellectual interests, community values, and interpersonal relations.

Diversity as an Asset

Racial and ethnic diversity is a critical element in building community values, although it is still usually perceived as a problem instead. The presence of international students and nationals of many kinds of backgrounds gives research universities a richness of texture unavailable in most American communities; the challenge facing universities is to make that texture a positive element in the lives of all students. Many extracurricular activities and clubs build on shared interests, sometimes ethnic, religious, or cultural, but sometimes totally race- and ethnicity-blind. Members of an orchestra, for example, care about and rely upon each other's musicianship, not on similarities of background; members of a basketball or mathematics team, actors in a play, or journalists on the student newspaper want the best performers as their colleagues, regardless of ethnicity. Through experiences outside the classroom, students profit from different approaches to the same issues.

The same is true within the classroom. Students enhance the texture of their learning by listening and interacting with faculty and students from different ethnic and cultural backgrounds. Faculty and graduate students become partners and guides for undergraduate study groups and project teams through collaborative learning. When students work in collaborative projects, they can benefit from the range of experiences and perspectives that different backgrounds provide. Diversity of backgrounds and approaches enriches the process of discovery, the ways of thinking about solving problems, the multiple modes of communicating ideas. Therefore a comfort level with difference, as well as flexibility to learn in various ways, must emanate from the institution.

Linking Commuters and Residents

Commuters and residential students alike need to know that they are needed and valued members of the community. Most research universities include large numbers of both commuter students and residents, yet club and community activities tend to be geared for the convenience of the residents and inconvenience of the commuters. Part of the experience of diversity involves the commingling of these two groups, whose experience outside the classroom may be very different. Commuters, who often stay on campus just long enough for their classes, should be drawn into more interaction with residential students, graduate students, and faculty, through collaborative learning situations, co-curricular activities, and shared rituals and celebrations.

Recommendations

1. Research universities need to cultivate a sense of place through appropriate shared rituals that are attractive to the widest possible constituencies within the student population.
2. The enriching experience of association with people of diverse backgrounds, ethnicities, cultures, and beliefs must be a normal part of university life.
3. Residence halls should nurture community spirit.
4. Commuting students must be integrated into university life by making their participation easy and attractive.
5. Collaborative study groups and project teams should be used as a means of creating customized communities for residential and commuting students.
6. Common interests, such as that in maintaining the beauty of the campus setting or supporting charitable or service projects, should be cultivated by creating teams that build community as they work toward a shared goal.
7. Major issues forums, multicultural arts programming, and other extracurricular sharing of ideas, opinions, and arts bring students together, particularly when groups or clubs sponsor or help sponsor the events.
8. Campus programming, such as lectures and performing arts programs, taken as a whole, need to touch the interests of as many audiences as possible.

Conclusion

Research universities are so complex, so multifaceted, and often so fragmented that, short of major crisis, they can rarely focus their attention on a single agenda. We believe that the state of undergraduate education at research universities is such a crisis, an issue of such magnitude and volatility that universities must galvanize themselves to respond. Insofar as they have seen as their primary responsibility the creation and refinement of knowledge, America's research universities have been superbly successful; in ways innumerable and immeasurable they have been the wellsprings of national stature and achievement. But in the education of undergraduates the record has been one of inadequacy, even failure. In a context of increasing stress—declining governmental support, increased costs, mounting outside criticism, and growing consumerism from students and their families—universities too often continue to behave with complacency, indifference, or forgetfulness toward that constituency whose support is vital to the academic enterprise. Baccalaureate students are the second-class citizens who are allowed to pay taxes but are barred from voting, the guests at the banquet who pay their share of the tab but are given leftovers.

Captivated by the excitement and the rewards of the research mission, research universities have not seriously attempted to think through what that mission might mean for undergraduates. They have accepted without meaningful debate a model of undergraduate education that is deemed successful at the liberal arts colleges, but they have found it awkward to emulate. The liberal arts model required a certain intimacy of scale to operate at its best, and the research universities often find themselves swamped by numbers. The model demands a commitment to the intellectual growth of individual students, both in the classroom and out, a commitment that is hard to accommodate to the research productivity that

SIGNS OF CHANGE

University Case Study
Integrated Undergraduate-Faculty Development

University
University of South Carolina

The Integrated Undergraduate-Faculty Development Program at the University of South Carolina includes funding for sending professors to conferences on pedagogy and for supporting curricular innovation; a mentoring program funded by a Lilly Foundation grant assists untenured junior faculty members by pairing them with experienced senior faculty.

brings research universities recognition, professional advancement, and financial security. Almost without realizing it, research universities find themselves in the last half of the century operating large, often hugely extended undergraduate programs as though they are sideshows to the main event. The numbers are there but the attention is elsewhere. It is the purpose of this report to try to bring the undergraduates into the big tent, to explore what kind of education a research university might offer that would fully fit its character and take advantage of its resources.

Commitment to Dramatic Change

For decades we have employed the rhetoric of change; for decades experiments have been undertaken. Now those experiments are becoming more varied, sometimes more successful, and often more serious. Some funding agencies have directed money and attention to undergraduate issues. Still, considering the nation as a whole, efforts have been timid, sporadic, limited, and unavailing. We believe that universities must commit to significant transformation now. Research universities must be willing to approach the issue of undergraduate education free from the blinders of past practice, to ask basic questions and be prepared for answers that require radical reformation of methods of operation. Given the scale of the institutions and the multitude of interests touched, change will be anything but easy. The commitment to dramatic change, not half measures, must be made now, and action must respond to the urgency of the issue.

We believe that the basic direction of change is clear: undergraduates need to benefit from the unique opportunities and resources available in research universities; clumsy adaptations of the practices of liberal arts colleges will no longer serve. The research universities need to be able to give to their students a dimension of experience and capability they cannot get in any other setting, a research experience that is genuine and meaningful. They should turn out graduates who are well on the way to being mature scholars, articulate and adept in the techniques and methods of their chosen fields, ready for the challenges of professional life or advanced graduate study. Research universities have unique capabilities and resources; it is incumbent upon them to equip their graduates to undertake uniquely productive roles.

The recommendations in this report may not attract every institution, but we hope that faculties will be motivated to debate the issues raised here and to accelerate their pace of action. In the hope of speeding that process, we have established a home page [http://www.sunysb.edu/boyerreport] where discussions may continue.

Research universities cannot continue to operate as though the world around them is that of 1930 or 1950 or 1980. As everyone knows, it is changing with dizzying rapidity. These universities must respond to the change; indeed, they ought to lead it. Their students, properly educated for the new millenium, will be required as leaders while that world continues to transform itself.

In the preface to his 1990 study, *Scholarship Reconsidered*, Ernest Boyer wrote, "the most important obligation now confronting the nation's colleges and universities is to break out of the tired old teaching versus research debate and define, in more creative ways, what it means to be a scholar." This report hopes to refine the context of that remark and to affirm that the most important obligation now confronting research universities is to define in more creative ways what it means to be a research university committed to teaching undergraduates. The nation demands and deserves no less.

CHAPTER 23

CREATING MORE LEARNING-CENTERED COMMUNITY COLLEGES

TERRY O'BANION

Introduction

A dip into the literature on American education at any point in this century will reveal a reform movement either flourishing in full bloom or in the early stages of emergence or decline. The impulse to improve, perhaps basic to human nature, flowers again and again in education as we refine past efforts and experiment with new practices in our continuing quest for quality.

Throughout the 1980s, secondary and elementary schools struggled with one of the most massive reform movements in the history of education. Triggered by the 1983 publication of *A Nation at Risk* that lambasted the "rising tide of mediocrity" in the nation's schools, a wave of educational reform swept the country. Over 100 national reports and 300 state reports fueled a number of key changes: increased requirements for high school graduation, increased standards for teacher's certification, increased use of assessment, and increased application of technology. These changes, however, did not bring about the desired results of their champions, and some critics (Daggett 1992, Leonard 1992, and Marchese 1995) observed that after ten years of such reform the nation's schools were no better than at the beginning of the decade.

For the most part, institutions of higher education were largely unaffected by reform efforts in the public schools. Colleges and universities studied these reform efforts, and some assisted public schools in carrying out reforms. The policies, programs, and practices in higher education, however, were left intact until the early 1990s when the impulse to improve surfaced in a number of reform reports directed at higher education.

In 1993, *An American Imperative: Higher Expectations for Higher Education,* published as "An Open Letter to Those Concerned About the American Future," triggered a wave of reform in higher education similar to that of the public schools in the 1980s. In fact, the 1993 report echoed similar alarms sounded in the 1983 report:

> A disturbing and dangerous mismatch exists between what American society needs of higher education and what it is receiving. Nowhere is the mismatch more dangerous than in the duality of undergraduate preparation provided on many campuses. The American imperative for the twenty-first century is that society must hold higher education to much higher expectations or risk national decline (Wingspread Group on Higher Education, p. 1).

Source: "Introduction," by Terry O'Banion, reprinted from *Creating More Learning-Centered Community Colleges*, ERIC Document: 414 980, 1997, League for Innovation in the Community College.

The 1983 and 1993 reports were remarkably similar in their language and in their analysis of the issues. Both reports were issued as "Open Letters" to the public; both reports indicated that the current system of education was inappropriate for the complexity of American society; both reports cited extensive data on the failures of students; both reports sounded the alarm as an "imperative" for a society at "great risk."

But in their recommendations for solutions, the reports were vastly different. For the public schools, the 1983 report recommended shoring-up the current system by increasing standards, revising curricula, adding technology, and increasing spending. For higher education, the 1993 report recommended what many have come to view as a radical departure from past solutions: place learning first and change the historical architecture of education. The 1993 report stated the challenge in succinct terms: "putting learning at the heart of the academic enterprise will mean overhauling the conceptual, procedural, curricular, and other architecture of postsecondary education on most campuses" (Wingspread Group on Higher Education, p. 14).

In the last few years, the reform movement in higher education, triggered by the 1993 report, *An American Imperative,* has spread rapidly and has captured the attention of legislators, national higher education organizations, and a growing number of faculty members and administrators. Some view the reform movement as a learning revolution (*Business Week* 1994, *Time* 1995, Oblinger and Rush 1997), and others view it as a shift in paradigms (Boggs 1993, Gales 1994, Barr and Tagg 1995). Peter Drucker (1992) believes that these changes in education reflect a profound shift in the larger society.

> Every few hundred years throughout Western history, a sharp transformation has occurred. In a matter of decades, society altogether rearranges itself—its world view, its basic values, its social and political structures, its arts, its key institutions. Fifty years later a new world exists . . . our age is such a period of transformation. *Managing for the Future,* p. 95).

Drucker goes on to say that "it is a safe prediction that in the next 50 years schools and universities will change more and more drastically than they have since they assumed their present form 300 years ago when they organized themselves around the printed book" (p. 97).

Regardless of how this reform movement in higher education is described—a revolution in learning, a paradigm shift, a societal transformation—the current impulse to improve what we do in education presents a special challenge and opportunity for community colleges. Community colleges resonate well with the goals of the current reform movement: 1) placing learning first, and 2) overhauling the traditional architecture of education. This monograph addresses the role of the community college in relationship to these two goal, provides basic principles for an idealized institution described as the "learning college," shares practical experiences from a number of community colleges actively engaged in becoming more learning-centered institutions, and reviews briefly some of the key issues and challenges community colleges will face if they decide to take the journey.

Placing Learning First

One of the two key goals of the current reform effort calls for institutions of higher education to place learning as their highest priority. Many educators are offended by this recommendation because they believe they have always placed learning first. Of course educators at all levels place great value on learning, but institutional statements and reward systems often reflect other priorities.

Any student of education can cite the three primary missions most often articulated by universities: teaching, research, and service. However, in many universities, the reward system places higher value on research over teaching and service. "Learning" is seldom, if ever, included as one of the primary missions although its relationship to teaching, research, and service is clearly implied by most educators.

Teaching is probably the most universally acclaimed mission for all levels of higher education. In the most comprehensive survey of its kind (Higher Education Research Institute 1991), involving more than 35,000 faculty members in 392 public institutions of higher education, 99 percent of the community college faculty said they considered "being a good teacher" an essential or very important professional goal; so did 98 percent of the faculty from four-year colleges and 98 percent of the faculty from universities.

In the community college such strong value is placed on teaching that the institution is often referred to as "the teaching college." One of the most significant documents ever written on the community college, *Building Communities* (1988)—the report of the Commission or, the Future of Community Colleges—highlighted over and over the central value placed on teaching in the community college: "Building communities through dedicated teaching is the vision and the inspiration of this report" (p. 8). "Quality instruction should be the hallmark of the movement" (p. 25). "The community college should be the nation's premier teaching institution" (p. 25).

The current reform effort does not ask institutions to place less value on teaching or other missions, but to review their statements and reward systems to ensure that learning is valued as visibly as teaching and other missions. In Barr's 1994 study of California community college mission statements, he noted, "It is revealing that virtually every mission statement contained in the catalogs in California's 107 community colleges fails to use the word 'learning' in a statement of purpose" (p. 2).

For community colleges that want to become more learning-centered institutions, it may make a difference in policies, programs, and practices if learning is embedded in institutional culture as the highest priority. Community colleges that wish to embed this perspective in their culture can ask two basic questions that will keep faculty, staff, trustees, and administrators focused on the major goal: 1) Does this action improve and expand learning? and 2) How do we know this action improves and expands learning? These two questions can be applied to any area of activity in an institution to help its members become more aware of the importance of learning in everyday practice:

Does this budget improve and expand learning? How do we know?

Does this staff development program improve and expand learning? How do we know?

Does the purchase of these six computers improve and expand learning? How do we know?

Does the remodeling of this laboratory improve and expand learning? How do we know?

Does the creation of this new program improve and expand learning? How do we know?

Does this service to the community improve and expand learning? How do we know?

Does this faculty evaluation system improve and expand learning? How do we know?

Does this system of shared governance improve and expand learning? How do we know?

Precise answers to these questions and hundreds of similar questions about every institutional action (department, division, board, etc.) will be hard to come by, but the very voicing of these questions is an expression of commitment and value that will keep the transcendent goal of becoming a more learning-centered institution clearly and constantly visible fear all to see.

Overhauling the Traditional Architecture of Education

The "Carnegie unit" is a metaphor for a vast array of traditional structural elements that have provided the framework for American schooling for generations of students—a framework targeted for major overhaul as the second goal of egie unit" is equivalent to one credit students receive for a yearlong course in high school, an early attempt to measure accumulated learning in order to communicate the amount of learning received. Ideally, students earn five credits in each of four years of high school, and an accumulated 20 credits qualifies them for a high school diploma.

The "Carnegie unit" is but the tip of a very large iceberg that has frozen education into a structure created for an earlier social order. The current architecture of education was created at the end of the last century when 90 percent of the population left school after the eighth grade and when the industrial revolution began to replace an economy built on agriculture. In an agricultural society, students were needed by their families to work on the farms. Schools were designed to end in the middle of the afternoon so that students could be home before dark to milk the cows, gather the eggs, and feed the hogs. Summers were set aside for major farm chores: harvesting crops, tilling new land, building barns, and repairing tools and fences. In Plant City, Florida, a major strawberry-producing center, the schools, as late as the 1946s, were referred to as "strawberry schools" in recognition of their adaptation to an agricultural economy. "Everyone recognizes it (the academic calendar) for what it is: a relic of an agrarian society in which all able-bodied men and women were needed in the fields at certain times of the year" (Lovett 1995, p. 131).

When the nation changed from an agricultural to an industrial economy, the old school structure remained but was updated and streamlined to fit the new industrial model. Scientific management and hierarchical organization, the bedrock principles of bureaucracy, were introduced in the schools, in part to socialize youth in the virtues of order and discipline. More importantly, the modern factory, pioneered by Henry Ford in the production of automobiles, appeared ideally suited to schooling that up to this point had flourished in the cottage industry of one-room schoolhouses. Using the industrial model, schools could be operated like factories with students as products moving through an assembly line. Teachers were the workers who turned out the products, and they were supervised by principals and presidents, the management bureaucracy.

Reformers have been consistent in their criticism of the constraints on learning reflected in the industrial model of schooling. John Dewey said, "Nature has not adapted the young animal to the narrow desk, the crowded curriculum, the silent absorption of complicated facts" (Dewey and Dewey 1962, p. 15). K. Patricia Cross, a leading advocate for educational reform throughout her career, observed over twenty years ago, "After some two decades of trying to find answers to the question of how to provide education for all the people, I have concluded that our commitment to the lock-step, time-defined structures of education stands in the way of lasting progress" (1976, p. 171). More recently, the Tofflers have noted that "America's schools . . . still operate like factories, subjecting the raw material (children) to standardized instruction and routine inspection" (1995, p. 13).

Today this inherited architecture of education places great limits on a system struggling to redefine itself. The school system, from kindergarten through graduate school, is time-bound, place-bound, bureaucracy-bound, and role-bound. (See Figure 1.)

Time-Bound

"Hurry up, the bell's going to ring!" Every teacher who has ever lived knows full well the tyranny of time forced on the system by the creation of the "class hour." "Unyielding and relentless, the time available in a uniform six-hour day and a 180-day year is the unacknowledged design flaw in American education. By relying on time as the metric for school organization and curriculum, we have built the learning enterprise on a foundation of sand" (National Education Commission on Time and Learning 1994, p. 8).

Herding groups of students through one-hour sessions five days a week in high schools and three days a week in college flies in the face of everything known about how learning occurs. No one believes that thirty different students arrive at the appointed hour ready to learn in the same way, on the same schedule, all in rhythm with each other.

Recognizing that schools suffer from a time-bound mentality, the United States Department of Education appointed a national commission in 1992 to study the issue. Members of the commission concluded, "Learning in America is a prisoner of time. For the past 150 years, American public schools have held time constant and let learning vary. . . . Time is learning's warden" (*Ibid.*, p. 7).

The time framework is particularly pernicious when it is extended to credit hours per course. "The vast majority of college courses have three or four hours of credit. Isn't it a coincidence of cosmic proportions that it takes exactly the same billable unit of work to learn the plays of Shakespeare and differential calculus? Or maybe the guest has been amputated to fit the bed" (Peters 1994, p. 23). The National Education Commission on Time and Learning reports that no matter how complex or simple the school subject—literature, shop, physics, gym, or algebra—the schedule assigns each an

Figure 1 Traditional Limits on Education

Time-Bound	**Place-Bound**
• class hours • semester course • school year	• campus • classroom • library
Bureaucracy-Bound	**Role-Bound**
• linear/sequential • ADA/FTE • credit/grade	• expert • lecture • sole judge

impartial national average of 51 minutes per class period, no matter how well or poorly students comprehend the material (1994, p. 7).

The reliance on time as a unit of measure must be changed to reflect mastery instead of time on task, recognizing what is universally understood: human beings learn at different rates. Students should not have to serve time. Time should serve them.

Place-Bound

School is a place. It is a schoolhouse, a schoolroom, a campus, a college. Sometimes school occurs *off-campus* but obviously is defined in relationship to *campus*. Young students go to school. Young adults go *off to college*. Incorrigible students are kicked *out of school*. School/college, and the learning that occurs in that context, is *over there*. It is external to everything else that goes on in the learner and the society. It is cloistered, private, sacrosanct territory. Speed zones control its outer edges and liquor stores cannot be built within its perimeters. School is an ivory tower on the hill; it nestles in the gated groves of academe. Its residents do not mix with "townies." School is a place.

School as a place is deeply embedded in the collective unconscious of a people who made great sacrifices to construct their first college in 1636. This early pattern of school and schoolrooms has been stamped indelibly on each successive generation as the natural order of the world of education. " . . . [T]he design and practices of our childhood schoolrooms tend to be reproduced in most education and training settings, even those that aspire to be nontraditional or 'radically innovative.' Despite decades of experience with models, demonstrations, and experimental programs, the "New American School" persistently gravitates back to our familiar models of school, classrooms, and teaching" (Perelman 1992, p. 125).

Schools are as place-bound as they are time-bound, and together these two traditions constitute a formidable barrier to change. Leonard says, ". . . [T]he conventional classroom . . . is the isolation cell, the lock-up" (1992, p. 28). If the student is to be freed for more powerful learning experiences and the teacher is to be freed to facilitate that learning in a more powerful way, then the walls must crumble, the boundaries made limitless. "The metaphor of a classroom is a powerful one. This most basic and fundamental unit of academic life—the sanctity of the classroom and the authority of the teacher within it—is about to be turned inside out" (Plater 1995, p. 27).

If reform efforts are successful, the campus, the classroom, and the library may no longer serve as the primary sites for learning. There will always be a need for these sites to accommodate some students who learn well in a place-bound context. But in many locations these place-bound constructs will become artifacts abandoned by a great many students and faculty who will embrace the open architecture created by applications of new technology and new knowledge about how human beings learn.

Bureaucracy-Bound

The adoption of business values and practices in education started in about 1900. The great business barons of the time, including Andrew Carnegie, John D. Rockefeller, and J.P. Morgan, powerfully influenced American culture, especially education. President Calvin Coolidge reflected the values of these industrial barons and much of the country when he said, in 1925, "The business of America is business."

Of all the traditional architectural elements of school, critics have been most vocal about the negative influence of the bureaucratic model. Perelman Writes, "Education developed in scale and bureaucratic density to mimic the industrial bureaucracy it was styled to serve. Education in its less than two-century-old modern form is an institution of bureaucracy, by bureaucracy, for bureaucracy" (1992, p. 118–119). Perelman believes that the bureaucratic nature of schools will lead to their ultimate downfall as society in general moves to less bureaucratic models of social interaction. ". . . [T]he disappearance of education is inevitable, not only because education itself has become a huge socialist bureaucracy, but because it is a bureaucracy designed for a bureaucratic society" (*Ibid.*, p. 119).

Leonard makes much the same observation, "from the beginning it was an administrative expediency, an attempt to adapt the tutor-learner system to mass education, a crude way of handling a large number of learners with a much smaller number of teachers. We were able to get away with it in the past chiefly because our society required few academically or technically educated citizens" (1992, p. 26).

Sizer noted a decade ago that the hierarchical bureaucracies of contemporary schools are,

". . . paralyzing American education. The structure is getting in the way of children's learning" (1984, p. 206). And Drucker weighs in with the astute observation that, "Nothing is less productive than to make more efficient what should not be done at all" (1992, p. 29).

The negative effects of the bureaucracy-bound model can be seen in clear relief in the educational code that regulates the California community college system. For 100 years, state and federal laws and structures have been added piece-meal to regulate the delivery of education to California residents; the cumulative effect is mind-boggling. In the California Education Code alone, there are currently over 1,200 statutes that directly regulate and affect the affairs of community colleges. This ponderous code does not even include the 640 regulations adopted by the board of governors and the hundreds and hundreds of federal statutes and regulations that govern the specific activities of colleges. (Nussbaum 1992). Roger Moe, majority leader of the Minnesota State Senate, frustrated in his attempts to bring about educational reform in his state, summed up the basic character of the bureaucratic model: "Higher education is a thousand years of tradition wrapped in a hundred years of bureaucracy" (1994, p. 1).

Role-Bound

By the end of the sixth grade a typical student has experienced at least six different teachers. With high school graduation, assuming six teachers a year for six years, the number climbs to 42. With a bachelor's degree, assuming 124 units divided by 3, the number of teachers for a typical student now totals 83. Ten courses for a master's degree-the minimum level of school achievement for the great majority of instructors working in community colleges today—bring the total number of teachers experienced by a student to 93, not including a vast array of teachers encountered in preschool, scouts, 4-H, Sunday school, summer camp, etc. In short, most educators with a master's degree have spent at least 17 school years under the tutelage of approximately 93 different teachers.

Teaching, however, is the one profession that expects so much of its members and pays so little. Teachers are expected to be knowledge expert, assessors, evaluators, managers, data collectors, artists, group facilitators, counselors, information processors, lecturers, problem analysts, problem solvers, coaches, mentors, behavior controllers, and value clarifiers. Their formal education is ill designed to prepare them for these multiple roles, and postal clerks and cabin personnel on airlines often receive more on-the-job training. Most new teachers are not inducted into the profession, except sometimes in an internship as part of preteaching exercises. Teachers are thrown into the profession, dumped into the classroom to sink or swim on their own. No wonder they fall back on the models they know too well. They teach as they were taught by the 93 teachers who were their models, repeating the catechism that is passed on generation after generation, bound in a role that pretends each is an up-to-date expert in some discipline, that endorses the lecture method as the primary tool of teaching, and that demands each teacher serve as sole judge and jury over the lives of his or her students.

As Kipp has said: "Having observed people teach all our lives, professors-to-be are supposed to know instinctively what to do in the classroom. We're tossed in this rolling sea with no Baywatch lifeguard around, left to sink or swim among the circling students. Small wonder, then, that the worst practices of the profession get passed along from one generation of professors to the next" (1997 p. 11).

Just as schools must be released from the architectural limits of time and place, teachers must be released from their traditional roles to focus their talents and abilities on the learner and learning as their *raison d'être*. "Restructuring the role of faculty members will, at first, prove to be a monumental undertaking. All of the incentives seem against doing so—except, in the end, survival" (Guskin 1994, p. 16).

Perelman describes the basic model of education in vivid terms: "There may be no more common and erroneous stereotype than the image of instruction as injecting knowledge into an empty head. Whether in a typical schoolroom, or a congressional hearing, or a corporate training session, the same one-way process is acted out. In each, the teacher or expert faces the learners, taking on the critical role of "fountain of knowledge." The learner plays the receiver of wisdom," passively accepting the intelligence being dispensed, like an empty bowl into which water is poured" (1992, p. 135). More succinctly, Russell Edgerton (1997), after serving for twenty years as president of the American Association for Higher Education, said, "Professors impart knowledge. Students absorb this knowledge. Examinations test whether students can recall what they have learned. In short, teaching is telling, learning is recalling" (p. 30).

If the dominant role for teachers has been that of conveyor of information, the conveyor belt has been the lecture. "Lecturing is the overwhelming method of choice for teaching undergraduates in most institutions" (Terenzini and Pascarella 1994, p. 29). Despite a large body of evidence gathered over many years regarding the limitations of the lecture method, the current educational architecture supports and encourages its continuing and widespread use. One study (Pollio 1984), for example, found that teachers in the typical classroom spent about 80 percent of their time lecturing to students who were attentive to what was being said about 50 percent of the time.

The historical architecture of education—the time-bound, place-bound, bureaucracy-bound, and role-bound model currently embedded in educational culture—presents a formidable barrier to education reform. Many faculty, administrators, and support staff succeeded as students in this environment, and many work comfortably today within these structures. Furthermore, funding systems, work schedules, and social structures support the continuity of the current architecture. For institutions that want to become more learning-centered, however, the architecture must be changed or there will be significant limits on the extent to which learning can be placed first.

The Learning College

In major reform efforts it is helpful to review both ideal models of proposed alternatives and the experiences of vanguard institutions that are beginning to create their own models. In this section we review the idealized model; in the next section we review the practical experiences of six colleges that are on their way to becoming more learning-centered institutions.

Community colleges will launch the reform efforts to become more learning-centered from a variety of positions. Some will extend their current efforts in Total Quality Management to include more focus on improved and expanded learning for students. Some will use information technology as the catalyst to direct their efforts toward learning. Some community colleges will attempt to apply the experiences they have learned in their "shadow colleges," the divisions that customize education for business and industry, to other programs in the institution. Still others will launch their initiatives from a successful experiment with key innovations such as learning communities or classroom assessment.

Regardless of the point of departure, it will be helpful for those community colleges making visible commitments to becoming more learning-centered to create a frame of reference to serve as a guide for their journey. This frame of reference is more than a vision statement; it is a set of basic principles developed in the context of shared values among the institution's member. What do we really believe? and What can we really become? are questions that focus the institutional conversation.

From hundreds of such conversations over the past four decades, I have constructed a frame of reference that provides a point of departure for creating a more learning-centered college. It is offered here, not as a final answer or even a completely developed guide, but as an example of how the challenge can be approached. I hope this example I call "The Learning College" will serve as a catalyst to assist community colleges in creating their own sets of principles or frameworks to guide their efforts to become more learning-centered institutions.

The learning college places learning first and provides educational experiences for learners anyway, anyplace, anytime (O'Banion 1995–96, p. 22). The model is based on the assumption that educational experiences are designed for the convenience of learners rather than for the convenience of institutions and their staffs. The term "the learning college" is used as a generic reference for all institutions of higher education.

The learning college is based on six key principles:

- The learning college creates substantive change in individual learners.
- The learning college engages learners in the learning process as full partners, assuming primary responsibility for their own choices.
- The learning college creates and offers as many options for learning as possible.

- The learning college assists learners to form and participate in collaborative learning activities.
- The learning college defines the roles of learning facilitators by the needs of the learners.
- The learning college and its learning facilitators succeed only when improved and expanded learning can be documented for its learners.

Principle I

The learning college creates substantive change in individual learners. If the current reform efforts are worth the energy and time they will require, then community colleges should settle for nothing less than substantive change in individual learners. That is a goal highly desired from educational experiences for our own children and all those in our care. No faculty member, administrator, support staff, or trustee will argue with this principle, but it is not often held up visibly as a principle to guide action. Stated upfront and stated often it can become embedded in the institutional culture, undergirding all other principles.

Institutional priorities, however, usually focus on organizing data on the more obvious outcomes of learning and are most often reported for groups: rates of graduation, persistence, or employment for selected cohorts. This is important information and must be collected by all institutions to satisfy external constituencies and to gauge average institutionwide success.

But this general information provides only a rudimentary measure of institutional effectiveness. At some point in their efforts to become more learning-centered institutions, community college staff members will engage in a series of rich conversations about other definitions of learning. There will be discussions regarding the differences among training, education, and learning. Complex constructs regarding basic learning, hardy learning, and more powerful learning will emerge from the discussion of personal values and experience in education.

In my definition, learning kindles new ways of seeing, thinking, and doing that lead to changed behavior. If that definition is even partially correct, then the institutional participants engaged in a conversation about learning may encounter new ways of seeing, thinking, and doing—leading to changes in their behavior. In the learning college, substantive change in individual learners occurs in administrators, faculty, support staff, and trustees, as well as in students. Making learning a central topic of institutional conversation and agreeing that substantive change in individual learners is a basic institutional principle make the current reform effort a great deal more than business as usual.

Principle II

Tire learning college engages learners in the learning process as full partners, assuming primary responsibility for their own choices. At the point a learner chooses to engage the learning college, a series of services will be initiated to prepare the learner for the experiences and opportunities to come. Until there is a seamless system of education for lifelong learning based on principles similar to those of the learning college, these services will be heavily focused on orienting the learner to new experiences and expectations that are not usually found in traditional schools. Two key expectations will be communicated to new learners at the first stage of engagement: 1) learners are full partners in the creation and implementation of their learning experiences, and 2) learners will assume primary responsibility for making their own choices about goals and options.

The services will include assessing the learner's abilities, achievements, values, needs, goals, expectations, resources, and environmental or situational limitations. A personal profile will be constructed by the learner in consultation with an expert assessor to illustrate what this learner knows, wants to know, and needs to know. The learner's self-assessment will be a key activity. A personal learning plan will be constructed from this personal profile, and the learner will negotiate a contract that outlines responsibilities of both the learner and the learning college.

As part of the contract, the learner will be responsible for selecting from among the learning options provided by the learning college. The assessment information, the terms of the contract, historical records from previous learning experiences, external evaluations, work experience, and all other pertinent information will be recorded on the learner's "smart card" which serves as a portfolio of information, a lifelong record of lifelong educational experiences. The "smart card," similar to an Automated Teller

Machine (ATM) card already widely used by banks, will belong to the learner, who will be responsible for keeping it current with assistance from specialists in the learning college. In addition to the "smart card," other educational institutions and employers will develop their own systems to verify what they need to know about the learner.

The learning college will also provide orientation and experimentation for learners who are unfamiliar with the learning environment of the learning college. Some learners will need training in using technology, in developing collaborations, in locating resources, and in navigating learning systems. Specialists will monitor these services carefully and will be responsible for approving a learner's readiness to fully engage the learning opportunities provided.

In the learning college, the orientation and experimentation process will take as much time as necessary to meet the needs of each learner. Some learners seeking minimal learning experiences about which they are very clear can begin their activities immediately following their first point of engagement. Some learners will want to participate in the orientation and experimentation process for a few days or a few weeks. Some learners may be engaged in the process for several months. Since there will be no restrictions on time and place for the engagement, there will be no limitations governing the activities except the needs of the learner. There will be many options for learners to engage the learning college, including self-guided print and video modules, live and Internet-based activities, classes and laboratories "on-campus," and individual consultations with a variety of specialists. Continuing learners will soon learn to navigate the learning college system and use it to their full advantage.

The student will not, however, drive all the choices regarding learning. Colleges are collections of wise educators who know a great deal about the larger values associated with a college education. Faculty may want to require selected liberating experiences for students. A college might, for example, require all students to provide some service to the community, examine their views on diversity, develop special skills such as how to access the Internet, express their creativity in some art form, or understand some special feature of their culture. A college has the right, perhaps even the responsibility, to provide the fullest education possible for its students. Its goal is not always best achieved if the collegiate experience is reduced to a K-Mart in which the customers select only the items with which they are already familiar.

Community colleges attempt to provide experiences that will broaden and deepen the thinking of their students through such programs as critical thinking across the curriculum or a required general education core of courses. And community college faculty and administrators should continue to struggle with what constitutes a common core of learning for all their students. However, in a more learning-centered college the options for how individuals will learn the common core will be greatly increased. The goal is to provide liberating experiences agreed upon by the faculty that are free of the constraints of the historical educational architecture.

Principle III

The learning college creates and offers as many options for learning as possible. In the learning college there are many options for the learner in initial engagement and in continuing educational activities—options regarding time, place, structure, staff support, and methods of delivery. The learner has reviewed these options and experimented with some that are unfamiliar.

Each learning option includes specific goals and competency levels needed for entry, as well as specific outcome measures of competency levels needed for exit. Learning colleges are constantly creating additional learning options for learners, many of them suggested by learners from their own experiences. A major goal of the learning college is to create as many learning options as possible in order to provide successful learning experiences for all learners. If one option does not work, the learner should be able to navigate a new path to an alternative learning option at any point.

If a learning college had to develop a full array of options from scratch, the task would be overwhelming and too costly. Fortunately, there is a tremendous variety of resources available, many of them field tested and free. Thousands of individual faculty members have designed improved or alternative learning materials as part of their sabbaticals, on released time during regular terms, on summer projects, with innovation grants from various institutions, and with support from federal and foundation grants. Individual colleges have initiated programs to design and develop new learning opportunities for students, sometimes with a considerable commitment of college resources. Colleges have initiated consortia to work in collaboration with each other and with agencies and companies to produce new learning programs. State and federal agencies, and most especially the military, have created hundreds of learning options that are free. Business and industry have spent billions on training materials. Educational entrepreneurs such as book publishers, testing agencies, information networks, training organizations, and computer corporations are in the specific business of developing training materials often available to educational institutions for a fee paid by the students.

To "manage" the activities and progress of thousands of learners engaged in hundreds of learning options at many different times, at many different levels, in many different locations, the learning college will rely on expert systems based on early developments such as General Motors' Computer-Aided Maintenance System or Miami-Dade Community College's Synergy Integrator. Without these complex technological systems the learning college cannot function. These learning management systems are the breakthroughs that will free education and educators from the time-bound, place-bound, and role-bound systems that currently "manage" the educational enterprise.

Principle IV

The learning college assists learners to form and participate in collaborative learning activities. In the learning college, the university ideal of a "community of scholars" is transformed into a "community of learners." More than just cute word play, the focus on creating communities among participants in the learning process—including not just students but also the faculty, administrators, and support staff—on creating student cohorts, and on developing social structures that support individual learning is a requirement of a learning college.

Practitioners, as well as researchers, know that group interaction can be very helpful to individual learning. There are examples of effective collaborative learning models at all levels of education. We also know from experience that programs designed to build cohorts of students and then to engage them in a common experience or curriculum greatly increase retention and ultimately program completion. Nursing programs in community colleges have some of the highest success rates in all of education, in part because they are often highly selective, but also because a cohort is guided together through a rigorous competency-based curriculum. Nursing students study together and support each other, and there is no disincentive for all to succeed at high levels because students are not graded relative to each other (as on a Bell curve) but relative to a performance standard.

The most widespread form of collaborative learning in the community college takes place in "learning communities," a specific term that is a curricular intervention to enhance collaboration and expand learning. "Learning communities . . . purposefully restructure the curriculum to link together courses or course work so that students find greater coherence in what they are learning, as well as increased intellectual interaction with faculty and fellow students" (Gablenick *et. al.* 1990, p. 5). These collaborations are also referred to as learning clusters, triads, federated learning communities, coordinated studies, and integrated studies; but "learning communities" has emerged as the favorite descriptor. When the same 30 students enroll for nine credit hours in a sequence of courses under the rubric of "Reading, Writing, and Rats," they have enrolled in a learning community.

In the learning college some learning communities and collaborative learning activities will not look very much like classrooms, and many will have dynamics defined by characteristics of pace, distance, membership, and means of communication. For instance, as the number of adult workers returning to college for education and training continues to grow, a likely venue for establishing learning communities will be in the workplace. Workplaces that value and encourage lifelong learning—whether because of altruism or enlightened self-interest—will make ideal sites for communities of learners, as common interest may be easier to determine and the level of resources available to support the community may be very high. For instance, video-on-demand can distribute information, including interactive training modules, directly to the desktop of employees; information resources can be concentrated at a common work location; and assessment services or learning specialists can be housed at the work site as desired.

Powerful networking technology can also help nurture a learning community by assisting its members to communicate with each other regularly in both synchronous and asynchronous modes. Certainly if courtship can be accomplished in Cyberspace, then learning communities can be formed there. The Electronic Forums established in the Maricopa Community Colleges are pioneering efforts to create communities of learners through technology networks.

The roles that college educators will play in forming and supporting learning communities are yet to be thoroughly defined. However, in a learning college, staff will form and recruit students into cohorts of common interests or circumstances. Process facilitators will orient individuals and help them form groups or communities of learners. Resource specialists will attend to the resource needs of both individuals and groups of learners. Learning facilitators will design experiences that build upon and use group strengths and other dynamics. Assessment specialists will design and implement authentic assessments that can occur both individually and in the context of the learning community. The learning college will be designed not only around the unique needs of individual learners but also around their needs for association. The learning college will foster and nourish communities of learners as an integral part of its design and as a key process for creating substantive change in individual learners.

Principle V

The learning college defines the roles of learning facilitators by the needs of the learners. Everyone employed in the learning college will be a learning facilitator, including categories formerly designated administration or support staff. Trustees will also be considered learning facilitators as they exercise their responsibilities for governance and policy development in creating a more learning-centered institution. Every employee will be directly linked to learners in the exercise of his or her duties, although some activities such as accounting may be more indirectly related. The goal is to have every employee thinking about how his or her work facilitates the learning process.

When the current members of the staff do not have the skills to meet the needs of the learners, the learning college will contract with specialists to provide the needed services. Specialists will be employed on a contract basis to produce specific products or deliver specific services; some will work full time, but many will work part time, often from their homes, linked to the institution and to learners through technology. A number of specialists will be scattered around the world providing unique services and special expertise.

The groundwork is already being prepared for these new roles to emerge. A 1996 report by the Ohio Technology in Education Steering Committee recommended the term "learning consultant" to best describe the educator of the future. "As learning consultants, educators will play many roles:

- Learning consultants will be mentors—guiding each learner to his or her own chosen goals.
- Learning consultants will be facilitators of inquiry—coaching learners and helping them remove barriers as they move toward discovery.
- Learning consultants will be architects of connection—observing the needs of individual learners and joining them to information experiences, resources, experts, and teams.
- Learning consultants will be managers of collaboration and integration—combining the needs and abilities of *their* learning communities with the needs and abilities of *other* learning communities" (1996, p. 13).

Learners will also participate as learning facilitators, and this role could be made part of the options negotiated in the orientation process. Many will not have time, but others will welcome the opportunity to offer their experience and knowledge to assist other learners. Colleges already use students as lab assistants and tutors to facilitate learning. In the learning college, these roles and opportunities will be expanded to capitalize on the resources students bring.

The goal of Principle V is to use the resources of the institution to better meet the needs of students, but it is also designed to free faculty from the restrictions placed on them by the historical role-bound architecture of education. In actual practice, colleges try to implement this principle by employing specialists (counselors, librarians, instructional designers, staff development trainers, etc.) and releasing selected teaching faculty from a class or two to conduct special projects. But the common denominator of the traditional role-bound model—one full-time faculty member teaching four or five courses each term—continues to dominate most of the thinking and most of the action in the institution. An audit of the great variety of skills and expertise residing in the current faculty would be mind-boggling in its richness and complexity. Changing the historical architecture of education to allow the skills and expertise of the faculty to be better matched to the needs of learners would be an overwhelmingly complex task, but a task that could lead to more satisfied and successful faculty and students.

Principle VI

The learning college and its learning facilitators succeed only when improved and expanded learning can be documented for its learners. "What does this learner know?" and "What can this learner do?" are questions that provide the framework for documenting outcomes, both for the learner and the learning facilitators. If the ultimate goal of the learning college is to promote and expand learning, then these questions mark the yardstick by which the learning college and staff are measured. Conventional information may be assembled for students (retention rates and achievement scores) and for faculty (ratings by students, peers, and supervisors, and community service), but the goal will be to document what students know and what they can do and to use this information as the primary measure of success for the learning facilitators and the learning college.

All learning options in the learning college utilize competency requirements for entrance and for exit. These competencies reflect national and state standards when available, or they have been developed by specialists on staff or on special contract. Assessing a learner's readiness for a particular learning option is a key part of the initial engagement process and thereafter a continuing process embedded in the culture of the institution.

Learners negotiate and sign contracts for overall programs (general education core, basic skills, workplace skills, etc.) and may need to negotiate specific contracts for some learning options whether part of a program or not. Moreover, learners will be encouraged to add competencies and goals beyond those established in the standards.

Portfolio assessment will be one of the primary means by which learning is documented. A portfolio is a systematic and organized collection of evidence of what the learner knows and what the learner can do. It builds on prior information, is in constant use through revision and updates, and provides continuity for future learning activities. Specific benchmarks of achievement may be applied to determine credits earned if credits continue to be the hallmarks for moving learners along a seamless path of education.

Guiding the portfolio assessment process will be one of the primary functions of learning facilitators. Since many of the learning options will be stand-alone, student-led collaborations, contracts with specialists, or facilitated by tutors and coaches, learning facilitators will have more time for the portfolio assessment. It may be possible to codify some of the assessment process for easier management, and advances in technology will provide some assistance.

These six principles form the core of the learning college. They refer primarily to process and structure and are built on the basic philosophy that the student is central in all activities of the educational enterprise. There are certainly other principles that must be considered in creating a new paradigm of learning, loosely coupled here into a concept designated "the learning college." Content, funding, and governance are examples of pertinent issues that must be addressed and for which principles must be designed. Still, these six principles provide a starting point for those who wish to create a more learning-centered college, a college that place learning first and provides educational experiences for learners anyway, anyplace, anytime.

References

Barr, Robert B. "A New Paradigm for the Community Colleges," *The News,* Published by the Research and Planning Group for California Community Colleges, San Diego Community College District, February 1994.

Barr, Robert B. and Tagg, John. "A New Paradigm for Undergraduate Education," *Change,* Vol. 27, No. 6, November/December 1995.

Boggs, George R. "Community Colleges and the New Paradigm," *Celebrations*. Austin, Texas: National Institute for Staff and Organizational Development, September 1993.

Commission on the Future of Community Colleges. *Building Communities: A Vision for a New Century*. Washington, D.C.: American Association of Community Colleges, 1988.

Cross, K. Patricia. *Accent on Learning: Improving Instruction and Reshaping the Curriculum*. San Francisco: Jossey-Bass, 1976.

Daggett, Willard R. "Preparing Students for the 1990s and Beyond." Unpublished paper from the International Center for Leadership in Education, January 1992.

Dewey, John and Dewey, Evelyn. *Schools of Tomorrow*. New York: E.P. Dutton and Company, Inc., 1962.

Drucker, Peter T. *Managing for the Future: The 1990s and Beyond*. New York: Penguin, 1992.

Edgerton, Russell. *Higher Education White Paper*. Philadelphia: The Pew Charitable Trusts, September 1997.

Gabelnick, Faith et. al. *Learning Communities: Creating Connections Among Students, Faculty, and Disciplines*. New Directions for Teaching and Learning, Number 41. San Francisco: Jossey-Bass, Inc., Spring 1990.

Gales, R. "Can Colleges Be Reengineered?" *Across the Board: The Conference Board Magazine*, March 1994, pp. 31, 16–22.

Guskin, Alan E. "Restructuring the Role of Faculty;" *Change*, September/October 1994.

Higher Education Research Institute. "The American College Teacher: National Norms for the 1989–90 HERI Faculty Survey." Los Angeles: University of California at Los Angeles. In *The Chronicle of Higher Education*, August 26 1992, p. 30.

Kirp, David L. "Those Who Can't: 27 Ways of Looking at a Classroom." *Change*, Vol. 29, No. 3, May/June 1997.

Leonard, George. "The End of School," *The Atlantic*, Vol. 269, No. 5, May 1992.

Lovett, Clara M. "Small Steps to Achieve Big Changes," *The Chronicle of Higher Education*, November 24, 1995.

"The Learning Revolution," *Business Week*, February 28, 1994, pp. 80–88.

"The Learning Revolution," *Time*, Spring 1995, p. 49–51.

Marchese, Ted. "Getting Smarter about Teaching," *Change*, September/October 1995.

Moe, Roger. Cited in Armajani, Babak, et al. *A Model for the Reinvented Higher Education System: State Policy and College Learning*. Denver: Education Commission of the States; January 1994.

The National Commission on Excellence in Education. *A Nation at Risk: The Imperative for Educational Reform*. Washington, D.C.: U.S. Government Printing Office, April 1983.

National Education Commission on Time and Learning. *Prisoners of Time*. Washington, D.C.: U.S. Government Printing Office, April 1994.

Nussbaum, Thomas J. "Too Much Law . . . Too Much Structure: Together We Can Cut the Gordian Knot." Paper delivered at the 1992 Annual Convention of Community College League of California.

O'Banion, Terry. "A Learning College for the 21st Century," *Community College Journal*, December/January 1995–96.

Oblinger, Diana G. and Rush, Sean C. (Eds.) *The Learning Revolution*. Boston, MA: Anker Publishing Company, Inc., 1997.

Ohio Technology in Education Steering Committee. *Technology in the Learning Communities of Tomorrow: Beginning the Transformation*. Ohio Board of Regents, March 1996.

Perelman, Lewis J. *School's Out: A Radical New Formula for the Revitalization of America's Educational System*. New York: Avon Books, 1992.

Peters, Roger. "Some Snarks Are Boojums: Accountability and the End(s) of Higher Education," *Change*, November/December 1994.

Plater, William M. "Future Work: Faculty Time in the Twenty-First Century," *Change*, May/June 1995.

Pollio, H. *What Students Think about and Do in College Lecture Classes*. Teaching-Learning Issues, No. 53, Knoxville, TN: University of Tennessee, Learning Research Center, 1984.

Sizer, Theodore R. *Horace's Compromise: The Dilemma of the American High School*. Boston: Houghton, 1984.

Terenzini, Patrick T. and Pascarella, Ernest T. "Living With Myths: Undergraduate Education in America," *Change*, January/February 1994.

Toffler, Alvin and Toffler, Heidi. "Getting Set for the Coming Millennium," *The Futurist*, March/April 1995.

Wingspread Group on Higher Education. *An American Imperative: Higher Expectations for Higher Education*. Racine, Wisconsin: The Johnson Foundation, Inc., 1993.

CASE STUDY

CHAPTER 24

DILEMMA: ALPHA UNIVERSITY

AMERICAN COUNCIL ON EDUCATION

University faculty discuss the relative priorities of a multicultural curriculum against one that stresses traditional liberal arts objectives.

Four Professors have arrived an hour early for the first meeting of Alpha University's new Committee on the Goals and Content of the Curriculum. The time of the meeting had been changed, and none of the four had heard of the change. Professor A is at the business school, Professor B is the chair of the mathematics department, Professor C is in the history department, and Professor D is a Professor of engineering.

PROFESSOR A: It's inexcusable the way this place is run. Surely, someone could have telephoned us to let us know the time had been changed.

PROFESSOR B: They could have, if departments had all the secretarial support the administrators have.

PROFESSOR C: Well, we might as well use the time. What were each of you going to say?

PROFESSOR D: Yes. Let's get the bugs out of our speeches.

PROFESSOR A: But first, let me ask why we are here. Why are we going to have this committee? For my part, I want this committee to challenge all the smugness I see around the place. I'm appalled sometimes. But I'm sure all of you have your agendas, too.

PROFESSOR B: Mine is to tighten up on priorities in undergraduate education. Too many trendy, superficial courses have got by the course approval process. But I don't think we are smug, just a fairly happy place, as universities go. We are all pretty comfortable, and I think that includes the students as well as the faculty.

PROFESSOR A: Strike "smug." But aren't we getting just a bit uncomfortable about being so comfortable? I think our students are wondering about the big, strange world out there and worrying that they are not getting much to prepare themselves for it. And that should bother us too.

PROFESSOR C: It does. It's a worry faculty always have.

PROFESSOR D: Well, we engineers have no choice. Our graduates have to know the current state of technology in their fields or they simply won't get jobs.

PROFESSOR A: That may be so, but most of us completely ignore how the world is being reshaped by technology. We produce excellent engineers, of course. But no one thinks much about the implications of technology for everyone else. For example, markets are really different, now that they are

Source: "Dilemma: Alpha University," by the American Council on Education, reprinted from *Dialogues for Diversity: The Project on Campus Community and Diversity*, 1994, Oryx Press.

global. Every securities analyst knows what is happening in Tokyo tomorrow morning.

Professor C: Even the international dateline has become an anachronism. Tomorrow is today.

Professor A: And everything else in the international economy is changing in ways just as confusing. Capital, technology, and management skills are being redistributed, separated, and recombined in ways that give strange twists to our ideas about who does what. An American computer company has Thais assembling parts made in Singapore. Japanese managers teach production techniques to Americans from Kentucky so that they can manufacture Japanese cars in Indiana. TV sets become a commodity like soybeans.

I think our students are generally quite unaware of all this. I hope our MBAs are aware of it, but I don't feel sure even about them. Most of our students think you can still expect to get a job in a firm like the Proctor and Gamble of the 1950s or the federal bureaucracy of the 1960s or the school systems of the 1970s. We have to tell them it isn't so.

Professor B: Fine, you tell them that in the business school. I am too busy teaching them mathematics. And, I hope, the English department is too busy teaching them how to read a book and the psychology department is too busy teaching them about the mind. We have enough on our plates, and our priorities were about right, until multiculturalism and the like came on the scene.

Professor D: Which brings up something that I simply don't understand. What is the conflict over multiculturalism anyway? I guess people who become engineers just want to know how machines work, and from an early age. For us, multiculturalism is really the same: The question is how societies and cultures work.

Professor C: Yes, how they work—but also how they change. Society has changed dramatically for me, as a woman, in my professional lifetime. Students need to understand such changes. Your students need to land jobs. All our students need to land on their feet in a very changeable world, and that is the problem curriculum reform has to deal with.

Professor A: As things are, our students are more likely to land on somebody else's toes. They are often completely unaware of how members of other ethnic groups live. I say our students need a map. Everyone was more or less the same in their suburban high schools, but they won't be the same in the places they end up working. Whether they go into business or become engineers or health professionals, they are going to find themselves among people they will think of as having strange accents, puzzling mannerisms, more muted or more vehement ways of making a point. The chances for missed communication, conflict, inefficiency, and all the little paranoias of the workplace are staggering.

Our graduates are simply not prepared for the kinds of problem solving such workplaces will require of people. This means they are not prepared to be creative and productive in the world as it will exist. And they won't be. Their paychecks will show it.

Do we do anything at all about this? Yes, we do, but it is pretty pathetic. We take in students with a lot of naive goodwill, and by the second semester they are either tongue-tied or mildly hostile in the presence of other ethnic groups. The only students who take international economics are ones who plan to become Professors or MBAs. We have a cooperative education program, but it enrolls a grand total of 50 students. We have an international education program, but it consists mostly of women planning to take a traditional junior year in Florence or Paris.

Professor C: Hold on, I can't let that remark pass about the junior year abroad. Are you aware that more of our women graduates than our men join the Peace Corps? It is we faculty that are isolated from the world around us.

Professor B: Well, maybe this committee is going to be less boring than most. You two are plain wrong. Aren't you assuming that our job is to prepare students for the world as it is right now? But aren't things going to continue to change? If we are out of date, things won't stand still while we catch up.

Professor C: True enough, but don't we have at least to try?

Professor B: Oh, I'm for trying. But exactly what should we try to do? Professor A says our students need a map. I say they need a compass. We can't possibly be all that specific about the world our students will live in. Things change too fast. What we can do is what we do in mathematics:

we concentrate on timeless things. The child that learns to divide an apple into equal shares learns something about fractions that applies equally to the mass of the sun and equally for everybody. It applies in a career on Wall Street or in a career as a pharmacist, and culture, ethnic or otherwise, has nothing to do with it.

And please note, mathematics can be universal because it is abstract. We never hear that children should be spared the learning of fractions because it is too universal and abstract. Teachers of mathematics are spared at least that cross.

PROFESSOR A: Your wonderful uncluttered world of mathematics! But the social sciences and the humanities deal in clutter. These fields are being pressed to deal with the particulars of all kinds of societies, all kinds of ethnic groups. And rightly: if we don't deal with them, that's like saying they don't exist. We just can't talk about justice or the family in the abstract and not imply that kind of denial.

PROFESSOR B: Don't get me wrong! I'm not saying we shouldn't understand particulars, ethnic or otherwise. And we lose much of the richness of life if we do not value them. But when push comes to shove—and you can be sure it is coming for this committee—do we give all these particulars of multiculturalism a license to crowd out what is abstract and universal?

And another thing: You talk as though our students will stop learning once they leave here. Of course they won't stop. They will learn about their varied co-workers when they are actually working with them—and better than they possibly could here at Alpha. They will learn about real particulars, on the spot and on the job, not dubious generalizations about the Black experience or the Chicano experience.

Let's face it, what multiculturalism offers us is new stereotypes for old. There is no reason to think this helps. What good is it to substitute the stereotype of the strong Black family for the stereotype of the weak Black family, if I am to work with a particular Black man? His family may have been strong or weak or—like most families, including mine—strong in some respects and weak in others. What good is it to substitute the stereotype of Asians as dreamy and poetic for the stereotype of Asians as quantitative and entrepreneurial? Both maybe false to the real Asian I am working with.

Aren't we much better off—aren't our students better off—if education concentrates on what is universal? Isn't it most of value to our students to learn about strength and weakness in all families and all people?

PROFESSOR C: But you learn such things through learning from particular people and their histories, including their family histories and—dare I say—from their ethnic histories.

PROFESSOR B: Maybe. But if there must be crowding, I say let the universal crowd out the particular. Students need to learn the abstractions of economics because particular economies change. They need to learn about justice because "cases and controversies" change. They need to learn how scientists think, precisely because the particular problems scientists think about change all the time. To prepare our students for the real world by teaching them about our world of here and now is to give them an education that is instantly obsolete. Bringing education up to date, and only that, is self-defeating. We don't need to bring it up to date so much as to make sure it's good enough.

Yes, our students will live their lives among a diversity of intermingling cultures, but what they need is the equipment to understand the future as well as the present and the past, what are truly the constants and what are the variables. They will then be much better prepared than if they carry around your fading snapshots of the present moment.

PROFESSOR D: Constants and variables I understand. But it seems to me you are not arguing anymore that universals are somehow antagonistic to particulars.

PROFESSOR C: Right. Universals help us understand particulars, and the other way around. You, A and B, seem far apart only because you see the task of preparing students for a multicultural world as first and mainly an issue about subject matter, about what topics should be covered in what courses.

PROFESSOR A: That's right. Courses are what we faculty have some say about.

PROFESSOR B: Yes, not that we don't duck the issues when we can.

PROFESSOR C: But this subject matter perspective leaves out what is much more important: the occasions for multicultural contacts there could be right here on the Alpha campus, and the desire to learn that those contacts can stimulate. You leave out that students learn to care about one another. If a student has a Black roommate or shares a laboratory bench with a Latino student or is in a study group with a student from Vietnam, those contacts are going to stimulate both kinds of inquiry the two of you think important. The student will want to know more about the Black experience in America, the culture of Latin America, and the odysseys of Asian-American students. He will want that kind of particular knowledge, that kind of map.

PROFESSOR A: One would like to think so.

PROFESSOR C: Well, it is my guess that he will also have much more motivation to understand universals of the human condition, to want a compass. He will want to know what he and these fellow students have in common as human beings, as citizens living under a government of laws, as seekers of truth, and as participants in the world economy. That is, he will be motivated in a profoundly personal way to learn particulars and universals.

PROFESSOR B: Maybe, if we have educated him to see the difference.

PROFESSOR C: Sure, we have our work cut out for us. My point is only that the personal contacts that stimulate concern and curiosity about people of other traditions can occur right here, and this is precisely the right place for them. The courses, the books, the scholars are right here to satisfy that concern and curiosity.

Of course, we have to make sure that these great resources really are available to both satisfy and expand these interests. That is, after all, why we really do need a curriculum committee such as this. If we do the job badly we will frustrate all that awakened concern and curiosity about one another—a terrible thing to waste, to paraphrase the slogan of the United Negro College Fund. But we should never lose sight, in debating curriculum proposals, of the kind of intellectual stimulation just being on a diverse campus can provide. Our students' daily lives here are a curriculum outline we would do well to follow.

Questions

1. Do the "map" and "compass" metaphors make sense to you? Are there better metaphors for how education should equip students for life in a changing and diverse society?
2. What kinds of courses do you think each of the Professors might propose to the committee? Could some of their objectives be combined in practice?
3. Do you agree that colleges should seek to impart to their students knowledge that is "universal" and enduring, as contrasted to the particulars of the "here and now"? Can we—do we—make such distinctions in constructing our curricula?
4. How much attention should a college devote to increasing and building upon students' ability to care about one another? What might be the consequences for the curriculum?

PART THREE

CURRICULA UNDER CONSTRUCTION: DESIGN AND ASSESSMENT

CHAPTER 25

DEFINING CURRICULUM: AN ACADEMIC PLAN

JOAN S. STARK AND LISA R. LATTUCA

Defining Curriculum

Common Definitions of Curriculum

Ask any college student or graduate "What is the college curriculum?" and you will get a ready answer. Almost everyone thinks of the curriculum as a set of courses or experiences needed to complete a college degree. Probe more deeply, however, and you will find that these ready answers differ. Some respondents will refer to the total set of courses a college offers, others will mean the set of courses a specific student took, while still others will include informal experiences in college that are not listed in the catalog of courses. Some may include the ways teaching and learning took place as part of their definition, while others will not. At a superficial level, the public assumes it knows what the college curriculum is. Surely the news media commonly discuss the curriculum at this level of generality. But when we get down to specifics, we often focus on quite different phenomena. Even among those closely involved with the curriculum, a consistent definition is lacking. Knowledgeable respondents may point out that the college curriculum cannot be defined unless one knows which college is under discussion since the mission, clients, and programs of colleges vary widely.

Over the years, as we solicited definitions from students, faculty, and others, we noted a certain consistency in the elements included in the definition. Most definitions include at least one and usually more of the following elements:

1. A college's or program's mission, purpose, or collective expression of what is important for students to learn
2. A set of experiences that some authorities believe all students should have
3. The set of courses offered to students
4. The set of courses students actually elect from those available
5. The content of a specific discipline
6. The time and credit frame in which the college provides education (Stark & Lowther, 1986)

Whichever of these elements provides the *primary* basis for an educator's definition of curriculum, an individual often mentions other elements, including the learner, the society, a personal view of the purpose of education, an opinion about how people learn, or some valued techniques for teaching and learning. Faculty members with broad curriculum development responsibilities typically will mention a greater number of elements in their curriculum definitions than persons with-

Source: "Defining Curriculum: An Academic Plan," by Joan Stark and Lisa R. Lattuca, reprinted from *Shaping the College Curriculum: Academic Plans in Action*, 1997, Allyn and Bacon.

out such duties. Yet they may be more definite about which elements should be included or excluded. We can infer that operational definitions of curriculum have evolved locally despite lack of formal agreement.

We have noticed, too, that faculty members seldom link the elements they mention into an integrated definition of the curriculum that suggests how it is developed. Rather, they tend to think of separate educational tasks or processes, such as establishing the credit value of courses, selecting the specific disciplines to be taught or studied, teaching their subject, dealing with student learning problems, and, less frequently, specifying objectives for student achievement or evaluating the curriculum. Probably the most common linkage that faculty do address is the structural connection between the set of courses offered and the related time and credit framework. These "structural" elements, based on the Carnegie credit unit, are relatively recent additions to the curriculum and tend to be emphasized primarily in American colleges (Toombs & Tierney, 1991).

Because college faculty members may feel uncomfortable discussing content in disciplines other than their own, it is not surprising that their efforts at curriculum change focus on curriculum structure, an aspect common to all fields. In fact, some observers have indicated that the most common curriculum change is "tinkering" with the structure (see Bergquist, Gould, & Greenberg, 1981; Toombs & Tierney, 1991). Even among knowledgeable individuals, this common usage of the term *tinkering* leads to an interpretation of "curricular change" as meaning a change in the course listings, college calendar, number of credits required of students, or other dimensions of the framework in which learning typically is arranged and often, by implication, in its cost.

One of the very important consequences of the lack of consensus on a definition of curriculum is that when the American public talks broadly about "improving curriculum," it means not only improving student learning at little or no increased cost, but also demonstrating the improvement. Meanwhile, faculty discussions of curricular change continue to focus on the structural framework rather than on the overall plan for learning envisioned for specific students.

The Need for a Definitional Framework

Since the mid-1980s the extensive literature urging educational reform has focused on the ambiguous term *curriculum*. This use of *curriculum* has been frequently modified by several equally ambiguous adjectives such as *coherent* and *rigorous* or undefined processes such as *integration*. The curriculum is said to "lack integrity" or to be in "disarray," but the meaning of these terms remains subject to the interpretation of the speaker and listener. Is it the mission or purpose of colleges that lacks integrity? the set of courses offered to implement the mission? the choice of courses made by the students? the actual experiences students take away from the courses? the teaching styles and strategies chosen by the professors? or all of the above? Only when there is a working definition of curriculum to guide the discussion and to help us differentiate among the various aspects of education in need of change will we be able to discuss curriculum reform meaningfully.

Nevertheless, faculty members, curriculum committee chairs, deans, instructional development specialists, academic vice presidents, assessment researchers, and teaching assistants regularly make decisions about the curriculum. In doing so, they talk about "curriculum" with the untested assumption that it constitutes a shared language (Conrad & Pratt, 1986). Yet it is no secret that faculty sometimes find it difficult to work together for curriculum improvement. In fact, in many colleges there is little formal discussion of curriculum except under the greatest duress. And when discussions do occur, participants tend to argue from varied definitions and assumptions without spelling them out, particularly in working groups that include many disciplines. Such discussions frequently grow contentious. It is no wonder that curriculum development is not popular work among college faculty.

Yet society and policymakers are calling faculty and administrators to account for perceived failures of the curriculum. Powerful constituencies are urging administrators and faculty to establish clear expectations for students, improve teaching and advising, use new technology, and measure student outcomes. Some forces in society push for a common learning for all college students; other equally vocal groups advocate cultural pluralism in the course of study. To provide a framework for productive discussions and effective decisions, faculty and administrators must come to some agreement on what the curriculum is and what aspects are to be targeted for improvement. Does improving the curriculum mean improving what is offered, what is studied, or what outcomes are measured? A vague definition of curriculum may suffice for the general population, but faculty and administrators have more specialized needs that require more precise definition.

To talk effectively about curriculum change in either an abstract or a technical sense, we must define curricular terms in useful ways. Most current definitions do not provide a framework that helps us understand the assumptions that undergird curriculum development. And because they are general and nonspecific, most are not helpful in strengthening administrative support for the curriculum, in evaluating it, or in communicating its intentions to students. Choosing a definition for curriculum does not mean that everyone must agree about what content should be studied, how it should be studied, or who should study it. It certainly does not mean that everyone must agree on the specific skills or outcomes students must achieve. Our higher education system is characterized—indeed, distinguished—by diversity of students, programs, and institutions. It is unlikely that the college curriculum can, or should be, the same for all Americans.

Yet to see beyond the mechanistic structure of college programs, we need a framework. We must explicitly reject the common but incomplete definition of curriculum as a set of course offerings written down in a bulletin or catalog. Such a definition would require us to confine curricular change to swapping courses, as in a game of checkers, or, at best, deciding that some courses have more power or value than others, as in a game of chess. We must also reject that definition which construes curriculum as the set of courses a student has taken. If, using such a definition, the student has not acquired the desired outcomes, the primary implied adjustment to improve learning is that a different set should have been studied. An appropriate definition of curriculum should allow a wider range of corrective actions.

The Academic Plan as a Useful Definition

To remedy the lack of a comprehensive definition of curriculum, we suggest defining the curriculum as an "academic plan." A plan for any endeavor incorporates a total blueprint for action, including purposes, activities, and ways of measuring success. A plan implies both intentions and rational choices among alternatives to achieve the intentions. We define curriculum as an *academic* plan because its intention is to foster students' academic development. It is devised with a given group of students in mind and within the confines of objectives for those students. An important result of this focus is that it causes planners to put students' education—the primary reason for the existence of the college curriculum—first.

Viewing curriculum as a plan implies a deliberate planning process that focuses attention on important educational considerations which can vary by field, student body, institutional goals, instructor, and others. Despite these variations, the notion of a plan provides a template—a checklist, if you wish—that encourages a careful process of decision making. Every curriculum includes each element of the plan described below, whether conscious attention has been given to it or not, whether a deliberate decision has been made, or whether a default has been accepted. The plan exists whether or not it is (in someone's view) a "correct" plan. Thinking of curriculum as a plan encourages planners to consider major elements, rather than to advocate inclusion of specific content or use of particular instructional strategies.

We are not the first to use *plan* as a synonym for curriculum (see, e.g., Eisner, 1979, and Taba, 1962) or to argue that building a plan involves *decisions* (see Leithwood, 1985). Some have also argued for use of *design* (see Toombs, 1977–1978; Toombs & Tierney, 1991, 1993). We prefer *plan* because it communicates in familiar terms the kind of informal process that a broad range of faculty members shared with us in our extensive research on course and program planning (Stark, Lowther, et al., 1988, 1990). We typically use *plan* to describe the current state of affairs and introduce *design* when we wish to convey a revised and more intentional process that faculty members in any discipline might pursue after considering alternatives we discuss in this book.

Specifically, we propose that the academic plan should include at least the following elements:

1. *Purpose:* The general goals that guide the knowledge, skills and attitudes to be learned
2. *Content:* The subject matter or content within which the learning experiences are embedded
3. *Sequence:* An arrangement of the subject matter intended to lead to specific outcomes for learners
4. *Learners:* Information about the learners for whom the plan is devised
5. *Instructional Processes:* The instructional activities by which learning may be achieved
6. *Instructional Resources:* The materials and settings to be used in the learning process
7. *Evaluation:* The strategies used to determine if skills, knowledge, attitudes, and behavior change as a result of the learning process
8. *Adjustment:* Changes in the plan to increase learning, based on experience and evaluation.

Elements of Academic Plans

In this section we will introduce briefly each of the eight elements of the academic plan mentioned above and displayed in Figure 25-1. We view them as the core of an emerging theory of curriculum, although all the relationships among them have not yet been explored. Thus, in this chapter, we state the theory in its entirety. In later chapters, we will trace its roots, elaborate on it, and discuss its full implications.

One relationship among plan elements is well understood. From our interviews with faculty members, we have learned that purpose and content are nearly always closely related elements of academic plans. Thus, we have shown their reciprocity with a double arrow in Figure 25-1. Frequently, faculty members link content and sequence as they plan but not consistently. Thus, we have shown the relationship between content and sequence with a dotted double arrow. We have arranged the other elements in the approximate order of their mention in many reports of faculty planning. For example, we know that faculty consider learners, resources, and sequence simultaneously, but after purpose and content. Despite our hunches about such relationships among other elements of the plan, we have avoided inserting more arrows because we do not wish to imply that these elements constitute a flow chart or that all curriculum plan-

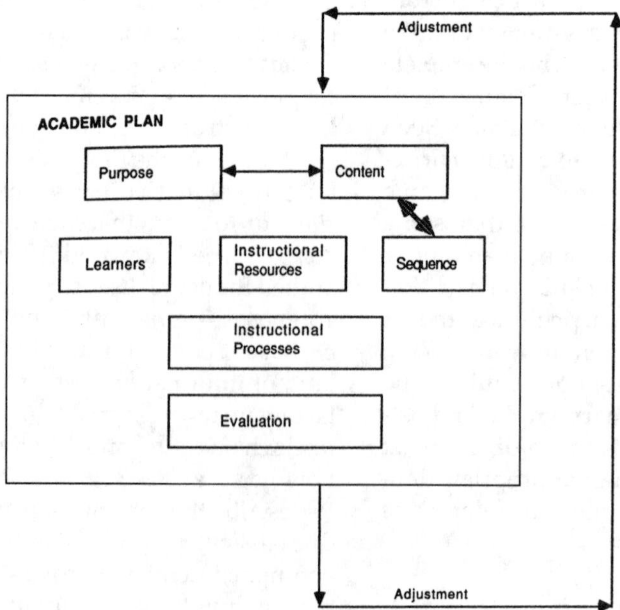

Figure 25-1 Elements of Academic Plans

ners do or must carry out their planning activities in a particular sequence. In fact, faculty reasonably pursue their planning steps in many different orders.

Purpose: Knowledge, Skills, and Attitudes to Be Learned

Discussions about curriculum typically grow out of strong convictions. Thus, we have placed the intended outcomes of education as the first element in the plan. The selection of knowledge, skills, and attitudes to be acquired reflects one's views about the purpose of collegiate education. Thus, in discussions of educational quality, it is not unusual to find that educators, policymakers, and the public express specific views about purposes and cite as support for their own views the opinions of prestigious others with congruent convictions about the curriculum.

In interviews and surveys with college faculty members in different fields, we have found them to hold varying beliefs about educational purpose (Stark, Lowther, Ryan, et al., 1988). Table 25-1 shows several broad statements describing some of these views. Purpose B, which we call "learning to think effectively," is the most commonly espoused purpose, but in any faculty group there are likely to be strong proponents for each of the other statements as well. Some of these statements will be strongly endorsed at one type of college and flatly denied as educational purposes at another type. Considering curriculum as an academic plan can direct attention to these differences in basic purposes of the plan, help to augment this list as necessary for a specific college, and launch discussion of curriculum development with some understanding of the underlying assumptions appropriate to the local setting.

Content: Subject Matter for Learning

Intended educational purposes can be achieved by studying many different topics. Despite the allegiance of most faculty members to their specific disciplines, it would be difficult to argue that any field has a monopoly on encouraging students' intellectual or value development or ability to think effectively. And of course our society demands that students learn concepts and principles in many subjects. Thus, in our definition

TABLE 25-1
Statements of Educational Purpose Common among College Faculty

A. In general, the purpose of education is to make the world a better place for all of us. Students must be taught to understand that they play a key role in attaining this goal. To do this, I organize my course to relate its content to contemporary social issues. By studying content that reflects real life situations, students learn to adapt to a changing society and to intervene where necessary.

B. The main purpose of education is to teach students how to think effectively. As they interact with course content, students must learn general intellectual skills, such as observing, classifying, analyzing, and synthesizing. Such skills, once acquired, can transfer to other situations. In this way, students gain intellectual autonomy.

C. Education should provide students with knowledge and skills that enable them to earn a living and contribute to society's production. I believe a fundamental role for me as an instructor is to help students achieve their vocational goals.

D. Education should involve students in a series of personally enriching experiences. To meet this broad objective, I select content that allows students to discover themselves as unique individuals and thus acquire personal autonomy. I discuss appropriate activities and content with students in an effort to individualize the course.

E. In my judgment, education should emphasize the great products and discoveries of the human mind. Thus, I select content from my field to cover the major ideas and concepts that important thinkers in the discipline have illuminated. I consider my teaching successful if students are able to demonstrate both breadth and depth of knowledge in my field.

F. Whatever the curriculum, it should help students clarify their beliefs and values and thus achieve commitment and dedication to guide their lives. For me, the development of values is an educational outcome as important as acquisition of subject knowledge in the field I teach.

Source: From *Planning Introductory College Courses* by Stark, Lowther, Bentley, et al. (1990). Reprinted by permission of the National Center for Research to Improve Postsecondary Teaching and Learning, The University of Michigan.

of the second element of the academic plan, we indicate that some subject matter typically must be selected to serve as the vehicle for learning. The separation of the first and second elements of the plan emphasizes that the purpose (or desired learning outcomes) and the subject matter are not synonymous.

Although not the same, subject matter goals and educational goals are surely interdependent. Faculty teaching in specific fields are more likely to endorse certain educational beliefs than others and to view their disciplines in ways related to these beliefs. For example, professors in social science fields are more likely than those in physical sciences to endorse Purpose A, "making the world a better place for us all." Furthermore, faculty from different fields may define desirable educational outcomes such as "thinking effectively" in different ways. These disciplinary differences in both intent and meaning complicate discussions of the curriculum. Placing purposes and content in the academic plan as two different interacting elements allows us to emphasize the distinction and helps clarify discussion.

Sequence: A Curricular Arrangement

By curricular *sequence* we mean the ways in which the subject matter is arranged to facilitate the learner's contact with it. We emphasize here not the mechanical and bureaucratic devices by which colleges organize their relationships with students (such as credit hours) but, rather, the assumptions behind how knowledge is conveyed and learned. For example, is the material presented chronologically or thematically? Is there a practice component to accompany theoretical presentations? Is the new material taught meaningful to students because it is connected with their previous experiences? Is it meaningful because it is conveyed in a way that demonstrates its relevance to their future lives? Is the structure arranged so that students will see a broad picture, such as how inquiry is connected in a particular field of study, or how two fields are interrelated? To be sure, the use of resources, such as the existence of internships or laboratories may be related to these rationales for subject matter structure. The point is that the recognized pedagogical reasons should drive the sequencing of content and the choice of resources rather than the reverse.

Learners

The sequence of the academic plan, like other elements, must be related to the ability, previous preparation, and goals of the learner. Although there is little danger that professors will forget the sequencing typical of their discipline, some may overlook the specific students for whom the curriculum is intended. Yet whether the curriculum actually "works" may depend on whether the plan is reasonably congruent with student goals and needs. Stated another way, educators and students each have purpose, objectives, and a plan to reach those objectives. The interaction among all three elements for both—particularly the relation between the two plans—requires advance attention.

Instructional Process: The Learning Activities

Learning processes (and accompanying teaching processes) are often discussed separately from the curriculum, but, realistically, the choice of teaching and learning mode may dictate the learning outcomes. Some learning processes are more often used within certain disciplines than others. But by default, much college teaching is done by the lecture method, while at the same time faculty desire to teach students to think effectively—a process more easily achieved through active learning techniques. Although specific teaching strategies such as self-paced plans, collaborative learning, interdisciplinary seminars, or technological aids should not be viewed as panaceas, we have observed that separating such concepts of teaching from curriculum often results in their easier acceptance. We believe that faculty members will expand their repertoire of teaching strategies if pedagogical choices are consciously recognized as part of curriculum development.

Instructional Resources: Materials and Settings

Curriculum discussions seldom include considerations of learning materials, such as textbooks and media, or availability of settings, including classrooms, laboratories, and practicum sites. Yet the actual educational program is often structured by these items, and sometimes they are the primary source of an academic plan. Many faculty members observe that they arrange their teaching according to the organization of the selected textbook or the configuration of the classroom. This possibility is increasing with the sale of "complete learning packages" by publishers. If for no other reason than to encourage faculty members to examine and weigh varied alternatives to traditional materials, the plan should include these considerations.

Evaluation

Evaluation of the curriculum, through both program review and assessment of student outcomes for specific courses, is strongly emphasized today. Typically, however, curriculum review is viewed as a separate process from curriculum planning. In our view, the best time to devise an evaluation is when the goals and objectives of the program are being clarified and the program designed. We suggest too that the list of elements we have defined in the academic plan helps to draw attention to the students' perspective. Most evaluation plans emphasize educators' goals as measured by student achievement rather than including students' goals.

Adjustment: Improving the Plan

Although some college curriculum development efforts include evaluation plans, we believe that our definition is unique in specifying the use of evaluation results to improve the plan and the planning process. Our scheme calls attention to this important step during the curriculum development process. Careful specification of the steps in the academic planning process can help to identify the particular strategy that needs improvement when the curriculum plan is revised.

Advantages of Defining Curriculum as an Academic Plan

We have pointed out some reasons that we view the idea of a plan as a useful template. Taking a very broad view, several additional advantages of defining curriculum as an academic plan are also apparent. We will discuss them briefly. We will return to them and add other advantages when we have more fully developed each element in our theory of curriculum.

Advantage 1. Promotes clarity about curriculum influences. Although curriculum discussions frequently focus on constraints to change, a variety of factors may influence the development of any plan; only some are constraints. When the curriculum is viewed as a plan, the potential influences on planning can be readily identified, assessed, and even purposefully varied, so that faculty and administrators can recognize both facilitators and constraints. The plan also helps curriculum planners recognize both facilitators and constraints for what they are, rather than confusing them with basic assumptions. This recognition is particularly useful in separating decisions based on constraints due to materials, settings, and structure from the important decisions about desired educational outcomes. We will discuss the importance of recognizing internal, external, and organizational curriculum influences shortly, and often.

Advantage 2. Applicable at lesson, course, program, and college levels. The definition of curriculum as an academic plan is applicable to all levels of curriculum. A plan can be constructed for a single lesson, for a single course, for aggregations of courses (usually called programs or majors), for broader organizational groupings of majors (such as a school or college), and for a college or university as whole (Stark & Lowther, 1988a). Defining curriculum as a plan allows plans at these several organizational levels to be examined for integrity and consistency.

Advantage 3. Encourages explicit attention to student learning. The definition of curriculum as an academic plan can facilitate and make concrete certain concepts that are now widely seen as essential in improving collegiate learning: clarifying expectations for students, encouraging student involvement, and assessing student achievement (National Institute of Education, 1984). The attempt to consider potentially fruitful new curricular approaches such as coherence, active learning processes, and consideration of student goals as part of the plan also builds on recent psychological understandings about how learners reconstruct their knowledge by meshing new information with old.

Advantage 4. Encourages faculty to share views as they plan. By examining their differing beliefs as they construct academic plans, faculty members in diverse fields can better recognize their commonalities, understand how to bridge disciplinary gaps, and gain from each other's pedagogical skills. The recognition of different planning assumptions fosters respect for curricular pluralism and avoids acrimonious debates. Such sharing is especially useful in reducing tension during collegewide curriculum development, in constructing core curricula, or developing interdisciplinary themes.

Advantage 5. Encourages a dynamic view of curriculum development. The assumption of a built-in adjustment mechanism encourages iterative change by making it an expected part of regular practice. Evaluation becomes more closely tied to the curriculum because it is viewed as a normal adjustment in the plan, subject to consideration at every iteration of the planning process. Unlike the static definition of curriculum as a set of courses, a plan implies vigorous strategic adjustment as conditions change because the process of creating the plan can also be examined and influenced.

Constructing Plans: Curriculum Development

To make the most of the opportunity supplied by our definition of curriculum, we distinguish the academic plan itself (curriculum) from the iterative process of planning (curriculum development). Defining curriculum as a plan not only calls attention to the necessity for a planning process but also helps to identify parts of the plan that are subject to specific influences and to identify intervention points for productive curriculum change. Each of the seven elements of the plan implies an associated planning step as follows:

1. *Purpose:* Setting educational goals and objectives
2. *Content:* Selecting subject matter
3. *Sequence:* Organizing content appropriately
4. *Learners:* Considering characteristics, goals, and abilities of learners
5. *Instructional Resources:* Selecting learning materials
6. *Instructional Processes:* Selecting learning and teaching activities
7. *Evaluation:* Assessing student outcomes, and appraising learner and teacher satisfaction with the plan
8. *Adjustment:* Making improvements in both the plan and the planning process

Breaking down the planning process in this way enables us to ask questions about the process itself. We can determine decisions about each element of the plan as well as who influences the decision makers and who bears responsibility for change. For example, we might ask such questions as these:

- Who constructs the plan? Who are the curriculum decision makers operating at each curriculum level?
- How is the plan constructed? What knowledge of curriculum planning do faculty bring to the task? What level of knowledge do they need? What training is needed?
- What premises or purposes undergird the plan? Are these purposes representative of faculty views generally or of those in specific disciplines?
- What stakeholders are included in the plan? Are students included? To what degree are specifications of accreditors, employers, and other external agents congruent with college purposes?
- How is the plan described or represented both formally and informally? How is it articulated to students?
- What educational outcomes do various types of students achieve under the plan?
- How will we know how various types of students experience the plan?
- Who decides when changes in the plan are needed?
- What provisions are made so that changes in the plan can be made promptly?

Some of the questions we pose generate considerable disagreement today. Indeed, some groups may question the legitimacy of the questions themselves or even challenge the notion that any plan should reflect purposes of educational experts or society, rather than those of individual learners. The mere suggestion of such potential questions about the plan and the planning process leads us to a brief consideration of the many influences on curriculum development and thus on the curriculum itself. For us, each question about the planning process suggests an analysis of influences on a step in that process. For example, the plan may be strongly influenced by lack of available information on learner goals or characteristics. Or faculty may need to consider contacts with local employers who could provide important information for planning a vocational program. Or it may become readily apparent that faculty planners are not knowledgeable about changing pedagogical trends. Finally, various interest groups may be trying to change how educational plans are created and implemented. We turn now to a scheme for recognizing and classifying such influences.

Influences on Curriculum Planning

Some years ago the Carnegie Foundation for the Advancement of Teaching (1977) discussed influences on the college curriculum. Elaborating on the scheme they used, we divided the influences into three sets—external influences, organizational influences, and internal influences—to characterize the educational environment for varied professional preparation programs (Stark, Lowther, Hagerty & Orczyk, 1986). In Figure 25-2 we show a simplified version of these three sets of influences acting on the educational environment. External influences stem from society and its agents outside the college or university. Internal and organizational influences both originate within the institution. However, internal influences stem from characteristics, views, and demands of those closest to the decision process, such as faculty and students, whereas organizational influences, for example central administrative officers, are farther removed from the immediate level of planning. We believe that this scheme continues to have broad utility and can be fruitfully applied to influences on curriculum in general. Thus, we suggest here that the interaction of these three sets of influences determines an educational environment for curriculum planning that helps to structure the planning decisions. In turn, curriculum decisions affect educational processes and outcomes.

External Influences

Historically, society's influence on educational planning has resulted in very gradual adaptation of the curriculum to a changing world. In most colleges and universities, curriculum content traditionally has been considered the business of the faculty experts (Toombs & Tierney, 1991) and somewhat insulated from non-student constituencies. Yet other interests do exist and do make themselves heard. Curriculum planning is often subject to strong external influences from disciplinary associations (e.g., the Modern Language Association), publications (like a recent book on cultural literacy by E. D. Hirsch), and accrediting agencies that review both entire colleges and specialized programs. The current era

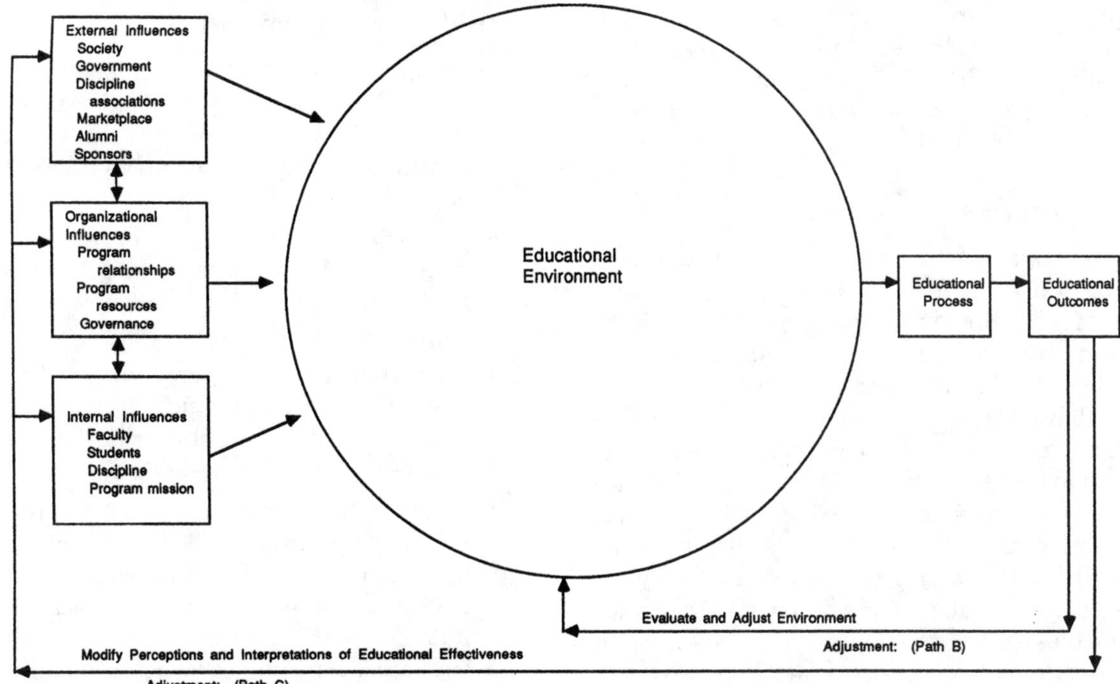

Figure 25-2 Influences on the College Educational Environment

of demand for curriculum reform is an example of a time when the voices of the stakeholders are particularly clear and when change is occurring at a faster pace than usual.

Toombs and Tierney (1991) correctly point out that faculty members often work alone in designing courses without being sufficiently concerned about the various external interest groups. We assert, however, that faculty members in most programs are more attentive to these groups than may be apparent or more than even they may recognize. Influences such as the concerns of employers, the job market, and the society may simply seem muted because they often are filtered through such groups as accreditors, professional associations, and the media. Especially for community colleges, a relatively new type of institution, external groups may exert very strong and direct influence on the curriculum today.

The consideration of curriculum development as a planning process helps us identify the steps that are particularly sensitive to external forces. For example, Purpose, Content, Learners, and Instructional Resources in the planning process outlined earlier are more often subject to pressure from external constituencies. Planning decisions closer to the actual implementation of the plan, such as Instructional Process and Evaluation, are more likely to involve educators as internal forces. Because of their greater susceptibility to external influences, pressures for changes in Purpose, Content, Learners, and Instructional Resources are more politically explosive and, for some types of colleges, result in major curriculum debates.

Organizational Influences

Most academic programs we will discuss exist as part of a larger college context, supported by an organizational infrastructure. Aspects of this infrastructure, particularly college mission, financial stability, and governance arrangements, can have a strong influence on curriculum. The infrastructure provides support for the academic plan to be devised and carried out. But depending on the centrality of the specific course or program to the college or university, resource availability, advising systems, opportunity for faculty renewal, and so on may either be supportive—or not so supportive—influences on curriculum planning. For example, some courses and programs are connected to a wide variety of departments and programs and are influenced strongly by this interdependence; others are more isolated. It is important to distinguish between organizational influences in the college but outside the specific setting where planning occurs, and internal influences closer to the selection of content and teaching process.

Internal Influences

Internal influences are very strong in curriculum planning because faculty are the actual planners. These influences include faculty backgrounds, educational beliefs, and disciplines, as well as student characteristics and goals when they are recognized. These influences vary in salience and intensity at various levels of curriculum development. When the faculty member works alone in planning a course, some influences may be more influential than when a group of colleagues plans an entire program.

Interaction of Influences

In thinking about the curricular planning process, we need to consider simultaneously all three types of influences since they do not operate independently. For simplicity's sake, we say that their interaction produces an environment in which curriculum plans are developed. Here are four of the many potential interactions that might affect the academic plan:

- Society's educational needs interact with faculty members' educational beliefs, views of how people learn, values, and sensitivities to learner needs to produce educational objectives.
- Subject matter, the vehicle for learning, is influenced by society, culture, technological advances, and ways of knowing as well as by institutional mission.
- Instructional processes are influenced by knowledge of pedagogical techniques, technology, and available materials, as well as by discipline preferences.
- Evaluation of academic plans is influenced by the amount of leadership available internally for improvement, by the allocation of organizational resources for data collectors, and by public policies such as state mandates for accountability.

These few selected examples illustrate that the academic plan is not the product of totally rational and context-free deliberations by faculty members. Rather, curriculum development is a complicated process embedded in a larger context that is complex and unpredictable.

Academic Plans in Environmental Context

To provide a total view of curriculum, we must be aware not only of the desired elements of an academic plan and the steps in the planning process but also of the influences on the plan (and on planning) from within and outside the university. Although our analytical approach will be to consider the academic plan elements separately or in related pairs, we must reunite them in recognition of their interdependence. Thus, in Figure 25–3 we link the two frameworks we have just discussed, showing that the interaction of the three sets of influences on curriculum planning produce an environment in which the academic plan is created—an environment that influences the plan's development and eventual shape. The considerable diversity of academic plans in our colleges results from planning processes that cannot escape these three types of influence. Curriculum development can be adequately discussed only when the actual academic plan, its development, and its evaluation are seen as embedded in the environment created by these influences.

We have drawn Figure 25–3 to show that the educational process itself results from the plan but emerges from inside the environment. Just as there is an evaluation and adjustment process for a plan (Path A), there is an evaluation and adjustment process for the educational environment (Path B). Finally, external and internal audiences form perceptions and interpretations of the educational outcomes which cause them to modify the influences they exert (Path C). In proposing this comprehensive framework, which we call "Academic Plans in Environmental Context," we have begun to develop a curriculum theory.

Historically and currently, debate concerning the purposes of college education and the manner in which these purposes should be achieved has engendered much rhetoric but little real understanding. Multiple definitions of *curriculum* are both cause and effect for this rhetorical focus and have hindered the consideration of curriculum planning as a process. Our definition of the curriculum as an academic plan includes the major variables that regularly surface in discussions of the planning, implementation, evaluation, or improvement of teaching and learning.

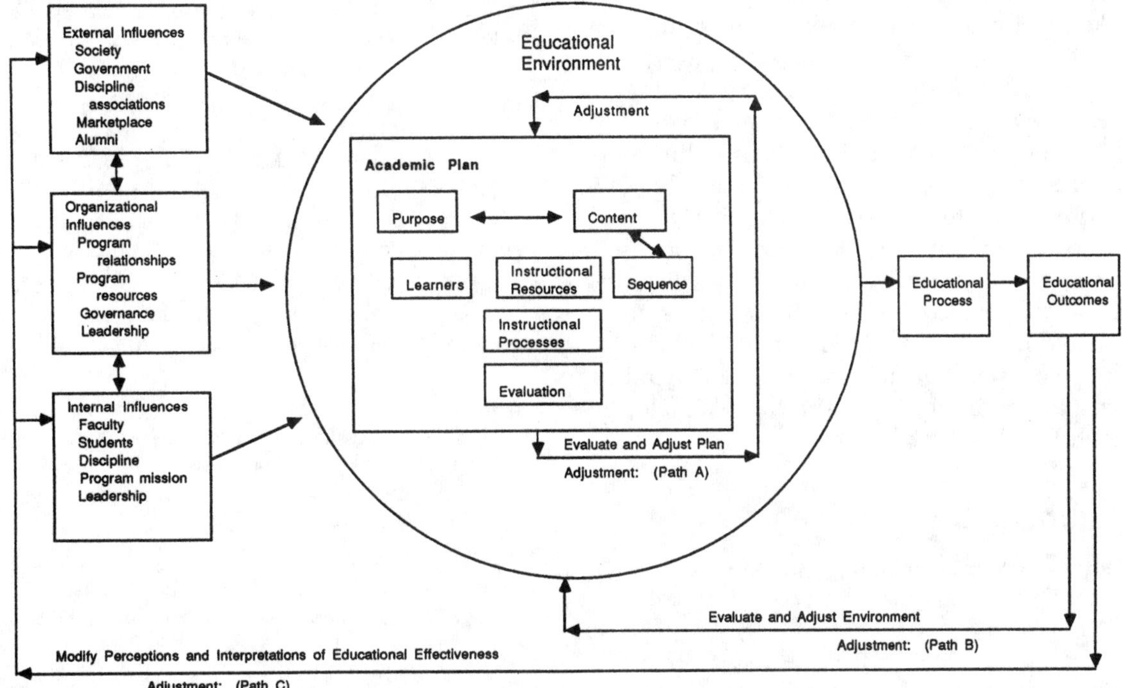

Figure 25-3 Academic Plans in Environmental Context

Without prescribing specific curricula, the idea of the academic plan provides a conceptual umbrella that can incorporate the plans constructed for such diverse fields as liberal arts disciplines, undergraduate professional fields, and vocational programs taught in community colleges. The plan may be constructed for a course, a program of courses, or an entire institution, but in each case the template calls attention to the importance of the context and the learners served.

Is there only one process of constructing an academic plan? Not at all. In keeping with the diversity of collegiate institutions and learners in U.S. higher education, there are many process models. They vary in their underlying purposes, in their implementation, and in how their success might be evaluated. Some of these variations are associated with disciplines, with institutional or program missions, and with prior student preparation. But we have distinguished the plan from the process of planning to focus attention on the important decisions being made.

The diversity within the broad concept of curriculum exists in part because, as the academic plan is developed, the planners are subjected to influences from society and its various agents. Thus, both planning and implementing the plan occur in a specific context of influences from inside and outside the institution. Once this context is recognized, the influences can be acknowledged and their interaction with other influences assessed. As we shall show, awareness of this environment is important if meaningful plans are to be constructed and enhanced.

Although our definition of curriculum synthesizes the research literature and was enhanced by our own interviews and surveys of faculty, it departs from the usual daily terminology used in higher education. The definition is considerably more detailed than any of those in common use and has not yet entered the everyday discourse of faculty members. Thus, we intend to state the definition frequently and develop it carefully in future chapters.

Bibliography

Bergquist, W. H., Gould, R. H., & Greenberg, E. M. (1981). *Designing undergraduate education: A systematic guide.* San Francisco: Jossey-Bass.

Carnegie Foundation for the Advancement of Teaching. (1977). *Missions of the college curriculum: A contemporary review with suggestions.* San Francisco: Jossey-Bass.

Conrad, C. F., & Pratt, A. M. (1986). Research on academic programs: An inquiry into an emerging field. In J. C. Smart (Ed.). *Higher education: Handbook of theory and research* (Vol. 2, pp. 235–273). New York: Agathon Press.

Eisner, E. W. (1979) *The educational imagination: On the design and evaluation of school programs.* New York: Macmillan.

Hirsch, E. D., Jr. (1988). *Cultural literacy: What every American needs to know.* New York: Vintage Books.

Leithwood, K. A. (1985). Curriculum diffusion. In T. Husen & T. N. Postlethwaite (Eds.). *The international encyclopedia of education* (pp. 1181–1183). New York: Pergamon Press.

National Institute of Education. (1984, October). *Involvement in learning: Realizing the potential of American higher education* (Report of the NIE Study Group on the Condition of Excellence in American Higher Education). Washington, DC: U.S. Government Printing Office.

Stark, J. S., & Lowther, M. A. (1986). *Designing the learning plan: A review of research and theory related to college curricula.* Ann Arbor: University of Michigan, National Center for Research to Improve Postsecondary Teaching and Learning.

Stark, J. S. & Lowther, M. A. (1988a). Perspectives on course and program planning. In J. S. Stark & L. Mets (Eds.), *Improving teaching and learning through research* (New Directions for Institutional Research No. 57, pp. 39–52). San Francisco: Jossey-Bass.

Stark, J. S., Lowther, M. A., Bentley, R. J., Ryan, M. P., Martens, G. G., Genthon, M. L., Wren, P. A., & Shaw, K. M. (1990a). *Planning introductory college courses: Influences on faculty.* Ann Arbor: University of Michigan, National Center for Research to Improve Postsecondary Teaching and Learning.

Stark, J. S., Lowther, M. A., Bentley, R. J., & Martens, G. G. (1990b). Disciplinary differences in course planning. *Review of Higher Education,* 13(2), 141–165.

Stark, J. S., Lowther, M. A., Hagerty, B. M. K., & Orczyk, C. (1986). A conceptual framework for the study of preservice professional programs in colleges and universities. *Journal of Higher Education,* 57(3), 231–258.

Stark, J. S., Lowther, M. A., Ryan, M. P., Bomotti, S. Smith, Genthon, M. L., Haven, C. L., & Martens, G. G. (1988). *Reflections on course planning: Faculty and students consider influences and goals.* Ann Arbor: University of Michigan, National Center for Research to Improve Postsecondary Teaching and Learning.

Taba, H. (1962). *Curriculum development: Theory and practice.* New York: Harcourt, Brace and World.

Toombs, W. (1977–1978). The application of design-based curriculum analysis to general education. *Review of Higher Education,* 1, 18–29.

Toombs, W., & Tierney, W. G. (1991). *Meeting the mandate: Renewing the college and departmental curriculum* (ASHE-ERIC Higher Education Report No. 6). Washington, DC: George Washington University, School of Education and Human Development.

Toombs, W., & Tierney, W. G. (1993). Curriculum definitions and reference points. *Journal of Curriculum and Supervision,* 8(3), 175–195.

CHAPTER 26

THINKING THROUGH A CURRICULUM FOR LEARNING THAT LASTS

MARCIA MENTKOWSKI

For curriculum designers—any faculty or staff group who designs learning for students—the essential question is, "What elements of a curriculum could make a difference in our own situation, for our own students?" A broad range of educators need to struggle with such questions in order to advance an effective critique and continuing development of what to teach and how. As faculty and staff take professional responsibility for student learning they also take responsibility for curriculum. In a curriculum that focuses on student learning outcomes, thinking through the curriculum is a continuing, essential activity, where educators question what ought to happen and how to make it happen in practice.

To foster learning that lasts, faculty and staff should conceptualize, design, practice, experience, evaluate, and improve curriculum—all as an ongoing process. Essential considerations are what students bring to it, how students experience it, what students should and do learn across a curriculum, and how graduates should and do learn, develop, and perform beyond college. To explore these complex expectations, we first develop the idea that educators need to be actively taking a curriculum perspective. The value of curriculum for learners depends on it because an effective curriculum functions not only for the time a student participates in it but also throughout the graduate's future as a learner.

Second, we define curriculum as an entire educational program that is a dynamic process with interactive elements; we explore this and other definitions later in this chapter. Because learning is situated, we do not assume that other educators should or would choose to replicate, idealize, or prescribe any one curriculum, given differences in college mission, culture, and dynamics. Nevertheless, learning is transferable and patterned, educators face common issues, and most work within a recognizable approach to organizing learning experiences. Thus, we explore a curriculum as a dynamic process by offering a set of six potentially usable elements of any undergraduate curriculum. Most educators can identify with these elements because we draw them from definitions, debates, and literature on curriculum, framed by an earned sensitivity to practice.

This dynamic understanding of curriculum can serve as a tool for thinking through what is currently in place. Because it is centered on learners and their learning, it points educators toward identifying educational assumptions and learning principles inherent in any curriculum. To illustrate, we analyze a range of current curricular approaches, inferring one assumption and one learning principle from each. A faculty group might use this analysis as another tool to clarify the ideas that ground their own curriculum and to explore the benefits of making conceptual frameworks

Source: "Thinking Through a Curriculum for Learning That Lasts," by Marcia Mentkowski & Associates, reprinted from *Learning that Lasts: Integrating Learning, Development, and Performance in College and Beyond*, 2000, Jossey-Bass Publishers, Inc.

explicit. This activity complements creating the learning-to-teaching connection: Educators benefit by considering educational programs as frameworks for learning and making explicit the educational assumptions and learning principles that ground them.

Third, we recommend analyzing a curriculum in order to foster learning that lasts. We offer an elaborated set of the six elements as essential to such a curriculum. This elaborated set is not that far removed from the initial one, but we extend each element to focus in on what works toward learning that lasts. To determine their essential character, we triangulated the elements that emerged from literature review, Alverno curriculum elements, and the empirical relationships that link this curriculum to learning outcomes. For ease of use by faculty groups, we illustrate the essential elements with cohering evidence from student learning outcomes and faculty curriculum principles. Fourth, we discuss taking up the work of ongoing curriculum development when building on principles for learning that lasts. The chapter encourages ongoing deliberation rather than quick fixes by operating on several levels: as a discussion of critical curriculum processes that can serve a wide variety of groups, as an exploration of essential curriculum elements for learning that lasts, and as a probe of practical strategies.

Educators Taking a Curriculum Perspective

Analysis of the learner Perspectives Interviews emphasized the significance of the faculty and staff taking a curriculum perspective, underlining the connection between the core ideas of a curriculum and each educator's individual work. Students who took a curriculum perspective—who were able to articulate the rationale for and describe the curriculum while they were in college and could still do so five years later—tended to articulate their learning outcomes in a much richer way.

"Having a perspective on curriculum" differs from "taking a curriculum perspective." Each faculty or staff member at any college has a perspective on curriculum. Each could identify his or her own views about what a curriculum is or what it should be—the sequence of the courses, or how disciplinary perspectives shape a program's content—and could contrast this perspective with that of a colleague or with current sources for revisioning curriculum (e.g., Haworth & Conrad, 1995; Diamond, 1998; Gaff, Ratcliff, & Associates, 1997; Stark & Lattuca, 1997). Institutions that have created innovative curricula as they created a college are also enormously instructive (an example is The Evergreen State College, explored in Youtz, 1984). "Taking a curriculum perspective" means that an integrated understanding of curriculum is fused in one's work.

Most faculty and administrators imagine, explore, critique, and pursue various ways of thinking about the purposes and practices of a curriculum. By analyzing transcripts of our institution-level curriculum committee (see Exhibit 26.1), we found that taking a curriculum perspective was a critical first step in framing curriculum discussions that were intellectually stimulating and effective (Alverno College Curriculum Committee, 1998).

On any campus, taking a curriculum perspective might arise while conceptualizing the intent of a major, planning how students experience a range of methods across laboratory courses, or selecting a program of artistic performances on campus. It also arises in designing a student activity or an in-course assessment. Each example involves standing aside to consider one part of a program in relation to the whole, including others' views on curriculum. Faculty, individually or collectively, are called to take a curriculum perspective in a department meeting to resolve student advising issues, when interviewing potential colleagues or participating in resource planning, or during a visit by an accrediting team. This may not always be the reality, but most will recognize these situations as calling for taking a curriculum perspective. Indeed, so does almost every other involvement that a faculty or staff member has. We argue that taking a curriculum perspective frames curriculum inquiry and is also characterized by its consequences, which are themselves integral to liberal education.

Taking a Curriculum Perspective Through Inquiry

The idea of taking a curriculum perspective includes more than sharing responsibility for the curriculum. It also means following through,

Exhibit 26.1
Taking a Curriculum Perspective: A Faculty Conversation

"A department, school, or college that explores its own assumptions may then reflect on what needs to be made explicit and how that informs teaching and learning. How these assumptions connect is an incredibly profound way to point to the need to examine teaching practice. I ask, 'What implications does this assumption have for what I do in the classroom?'"—*professor of philosophy*

"For me, taking a curriculum perspective is taking a perspective on the student's development as a person, not just as a professional. It is a more comprehensive, more global view than your own particular interests and responsibilities at a particular point in the curriculum. In a sense, you're responsible for the whole thing even though there will be a division of labor. You perform with a notion of a hand-off or a handshake from one curriculum element to another so that there is a cumulative and developmental effect. That view of curriculum is more likely to center on the student's learning rather than only on the specific dimension of the discipline that you represent. Each of us is responsible for more than our set of disciplinary constructs. When a student says, 'I have a question for you,' I don't say, 'Well, that's not my specialty; you'd better talk to Professor So-and-So down the hall.'"—*professor of history*

"For me, taking a curriculum perspective also means focusing on the student's interaction with the curriculum and how that works. I might think it's great to read Plato, but if the student doesn't respond, or can't make connections from that experience, then I have to look at how I use the material or even the selection of the material itself.'"—*professor of social sciences*

"What if we started with the definition of taking a curriculum perspective from the student's perspective? How is she aware of connections and relationships, not only for herself, but also for her fellow students, rather than, 'I learned this here, I learned this there.'"—*professor of nursing*

"A beginning student may see a curriculum as a series of courses: Abilities are separate, are extra work. As students experience abilities taught through the disciplines, they develop an integrated perspective on curriculum.'"—*professor of psychology*

"At graduation we say, 'All students with the bachelor of arts degree, stand up.' At that moment they are all sensing that, 'I may have been a management major and a psychology support, but the students next to me had some of the core or common experiences and values, as they have gone through their experience.' They sense that we've all been heading somewhere together, but we've had options in terms of how we focus on different disciplines."—*associate professor of physical sciences*

"Those of us who teach humanities courses to students who aren't our majors get to see the kinds of connections they're making. I don't know if students necessarily have the language to describe themselves that way, but I think they see themselves that way. There's a sense in which they know that they're distinct from many other people in their fields and that what makes them distinct has to do with the kinds of things they're able to do: These are the abilities. Abilities are very much contextualized within the context of their discipline and their major. I think that's how they would first define themselves and then within the context of that say, 'And as a nurse, I am able to do . . .' and then list off very succinctly the abilities that they bring to the career."—*professor of philosophy*

"I think students tend to define themselves in terms of the subject they studied, but I think that students do take a curriculum perspective when they see the commonality among abilities. Then they are able to do that and express it."—*associate professor of business and management*

"Employers take a curriculum perspective when they make judgments: 'You're coming from this school. I have perceptions and knowledge about your curriculum. I don't know all the courses you took, but I'm judging you by the curriculum of the school.'"—*professor of history*

"The question is, how can we describe curriculum perspectives a little more holistically so that students not only have all the right pieces at graduation, but the sense that somehow faculty were consciously making decisions about the whole thing? A faculty member should know what is going to happen to the student in the next course."—*academic dean*

"Taking a curriculum perspective is imagining and empathizing beyond what you do in your classroom and what is happening to your students right then, to what the student experiences cumulatively. It is thinking beyond the momentary experience that you have with your students and that your students have with you, and that's true for students as well."—*associate professor of education*

developing, and refining one's own curriculum based on the implications that flow from (and in turn stimulate) perspective taking. We defined taking a perspective on inquiry as standing in, standing beside, and standing aside simultaneously. Similarly, it means standing in, beside, and aside from one's own and others' roles and standpoints in curriculum—simultaneously—in order to see the curriculum holistically and define and debate the broader educational assumptions and learning principles that ground it.

Taking a curriculum perspective is further characterized by a range of comparisons that faculty make in curriculum meetings, comparing the perspectives and experiences of students, alumnae, and faculty; or comparing previously measured learning outcomes to those observed in current assessments. Faculty members might make explicit connections to external curriculum perspectives that appear to stretch their own. The work of curriculum inquiry requires sustained, extensive, deliberative inquiry by faculty and staff—those who are more directly involved in curriculum design and evaluation, as well as those who share a more general range of curriculum concerns such as determining learning outcomes.

Consequences of Taking a Curriculum Perspective

In the turbulent world of undergraduate curriculum reform, practitioners and curriculum scholars converge on several conceptual directions for improvement in the context of such challenges as degree completion, distributed learning, and satellite campuses. Joan Stark and Lisa Lattuca (1997) identify three challenges that faculty and staff face: incorporating diverse perspectives, increasing coherence, and meeting expectations for quality and access. Jerry Gaff (1997), summarizing the contributions of fifty-seven curriculum experts, argues that the current "renaissance of undergraduate education" should coalesce around the student, "putting students and learning at the center" (p. 691). Consideration of student perspectives can be a powerful catalyst, but it has generally been ignored (Stark & Lattuca, 1997, p. 380). It is our contention that taking a curriculum perspective can address concerns such as respecting learners' purposes for and experiences of their learning, determining student learning outcomes, clarifying the meaning of the baccalaureate, and contributing to faculty and staff vitality.

Respecting Learners' Purposes for and Experiences of Their Learning

Legitimizing students' purposes and experiences is an important factor in making a curriculum meaningful and relevant. Most colleges have used surveys of student attitudes and satisfactions to market education, and most faculty use student course evaluations and students' running commentary in courses to improve teaching and learning (Angelo & Cross, 1993). But students' in-depth perspectives on their learning are less well understood and are thus less often integrated by faculty into collaborative curriculum design.

What has emerged for us, in our inquiries so far, is a much clearer picture of what students consider essential to their learning and how they perceive the outcomes of that learning in relation to faculty curriculum design, the intent of their day-to-day teaching, and faculty experience of it. Fully appreciating student perspectives leads to taking a curriculum perspective. Faculty interpretation becomes paramount in the way faculty seek and use student perspectives—not just student attitudes and course evaluations—in evaluating and improving their teaching. By deeply analyzing student perspectives, faculty and staff also gain a more effective tool for evaluating student work and providing helpful feedback.

Determining Student Learning Outcomes

When curriculum is designed and practiced by faculty who are taking a curriculum perspective in relation to how students experience it, they are more likely to attend to student learning outcomes in their teaching and course designs. Obviously, how students construct learning cannot be the only important source for curriculum development; indeed, student perspectives may be quite limited initially. Other faculty efforts confirm the benefits of digging deeper into student views of learning (Erwin, 1991; Marton, Hounsell, & Entwistle, 1984). Further, taking a curriculum perspective also implies determining student learning outcomes. Joan Stark and Lisa Lattuca (1997) affirm this view. The intent, purpose, content, and development of curricula have been exhaustively debated by educators, they note, but the connection between learning as it is experienced by students and those students' actual learning outcomes continues to be unresearched in curricular studies (pp. 381–382). Distinguishing between student experience of a curriculum and the learning outcomes that accrue from it is difficult. Direct causal connections between particular learning experiences and outcomes often remain a puzzle. Nonetheless, considering student experience in relation to faculty-determined learning outcomes leads to revisiting curriculum intent, purpose, and content.

Clarifying the Meaning of the Baccalaureate

Faculty understanding of students' purposes, experiences, and their learning outcomes stimulates continuous rethinking of the meaning of the college degree. Faculty ask, "What should students know and be able to do upon graduation?" Stark and Lattuca (1997) state that faculty wrested curriculum development responsibilities from administrators in the earlier twentieth century and express a strong desire to retain that role. At a time when the question of what should be taught, learned, and assessed is on the public's agenda, insights about relationships among liberal learning, professional programs, and student learning outcomes are central to educational policymaking. This broader agenda has been punctuated with arguments about what is common learning and what makes up a liberal arts canon. For example, the call for reinstituting a core curriculum that has "integrity" has been part of higher education discussions for some time (Association of American Colleges, 1985). Curricular integrity, which implies that the degree represents what faculty intend and what students experience, requires that a curriculum demonstrate "coherence within diversity." Designing it should, we believe, begin with the question, "Integrated for what and for whom?" The diverse interests and commitments among higher education's multiple stakeholders can yield coherence when educators articulate a key principle: *Curriculum is for the learning of students.* Because centering on learning illuminates the paradox that faculty aim for coherence within diversity, revisiting the meaning of the degree can be a bonding rather than a divisive action for faculty and staff.

Contributing to Faculty and Staff Vitality

Faculty and staff vitality—sustained energy and productivity over time—is essential to collaborative curriculum transformation; it is also a by-product. Students can tell when faculty and staff demonstrate vitality and interdependence. When we studied student and alumna perspectives, we looked for evidence that, in the student's mind, faculty were taking a curriculum perspective. We probed students' beginning and advanced understandings of the rationale they thought faculty had for student involvement and performance across classes. Students' growing understanding of faculty rationale influenced their motivation to stay in school, continue improving, and apply and continue learning outside the classroom and after college. When students became conscious of the design, process, and coherence within the diversity of the curriculum, they reinforced and challenged these practices by expressing their expectations in class, and faculty responded with clarifications or adjustments.

When faculty place student learning at the center of curriculum and build toward student understanding of their curriculum perspective, they also stimulate their own perspective taking in directions that go beyond rethinking the meaning of the degree. These include analyzing the impact of various social forces in shaping curriculum, projecting new majors and the resources needed to develop them, and studying new disciplinary concepts and paradigms that enhance students' grasp of a major. Faculty also create a common bond with each other to support interest in student development. This bond, strengthened by disciplinary connections, fosters what Arthur Applebee (1996) described as *curriculum as conversation.* Faculty and staff, led by their own questions, consider curricular definitions, debates, and conceptual frameworks that stimulate and challenge their own interpretations. Ilene Harris (1991a) has called this *curriculum as deliberative inquiry.* Until recently, as Elizabeth Kamarck Minnich (1990) noted, an invitation to a department discussion on curriculum, mired in academic definitions and debates, would often drive away participants. However, given the fundamental role of interaction in faculty learning, it is all the more important to find the terms and elements that make for effective discourse about curriculum. This leads to a second emphasis: defining and debating curriculum.

Defining and Debating Curriculum

We define curriculum as a dynamic process with a set of six interactive, potentially usable elements of any undergraduate curriculum, drawn from the literature. These elements set the stage for debating the educational assumptions that characterize a faculty's own or other approaches to curriculum. Such a debate can illuminate learning principles, a bridge to the third emphasis of this chapter: a set of essential elements of a curriculum for learning that lasts.

Defining Curriculum as Dynamic Process with Interactive Elements

Educators often comment on how a designed curriculum is changing; this is natural and desirable once they perceive *curriculum as dynamic process with interactive elements.* "I envision curriculum in fluid terms," one social sciences professor says. "We change our curriculum, we evaluate it, we figure out what works, what doesn't work, the world changes, and we change it again." Recognizing curriculum—with its multiple interacting elements—as a dynamic process rather than a static set of structures challenges educators to understand the nature of curriculum change and to ask how and why they are continually shaping and reshaping it. They learn to situate a curriculum in relation to the defining characteristics of their institution, including its history of curriculum development, unique mission, values, and institutional culture. A designed curriculum, however dynamic, is not an entire curriculum. We think of a curriculum as practiced and experienced by faculty and also experienced by students. Observations about a curriculum as it is practiced reflect perspectives from each group. These can test the concepts that seem so important to faculty in the design phase and illuminate ideas that might otherwise be untouched.

Many experts concur that learners and their learning (who they are, what they intend, what they can do and become) should be at the center of how an educator thinks about an undergraduate curriculum (Gaff, 1997), yet this educational assumption may not reflect the ideology or organizational culture of a particular undergraduate institution or program. Organized learning experiences, the "practice" of curriculum, are usually arranged as courses or programs. Whenever faculty start taking a curriculum perspective as a working group, a department, or an institution, reaching a working consensus on content continues to be the most commonly perceived and central task, reflected in consensus on crediting ("consensus," of course, does not mean conformity or absence of conflict, and includes agreeing to disagree). Curriculum is more than learning experiences organized as courses and more than content; it also includes various interactive contexts and cultures (the cocurriculum, the family, and workplace; local and global communities and cultures formed around economic, ethnic, or other dimensions of human identity). Considering such interactive contexts and related subcultures, and examining the idea of hidden or latent curriculum, helps to make clear conceptual frameworks, which may be intended or unintended, explicit or implicit. These frameworks are often reflected in the mission, aims, and philosophy of a curriculum. Program evaluation and assessment are a common element where curriculum inquiry can occur. Figure 26-1 arranges what we found in the literature as key curricular elements into a set of ever widening, concentric circles; the broken lines indicate that each element blends with the others to form a dynamic whole, centered on learners and their learning.

Organized Learning Experiences

With learners and their learning at the center of an undergraduate curriculum in Figure 26-1, the innermost ring addresses how faculty organize learning experiences for students. James Ratcliff (1997) sees an undergraduate curriculum as the formal academic experience of students' pursu-

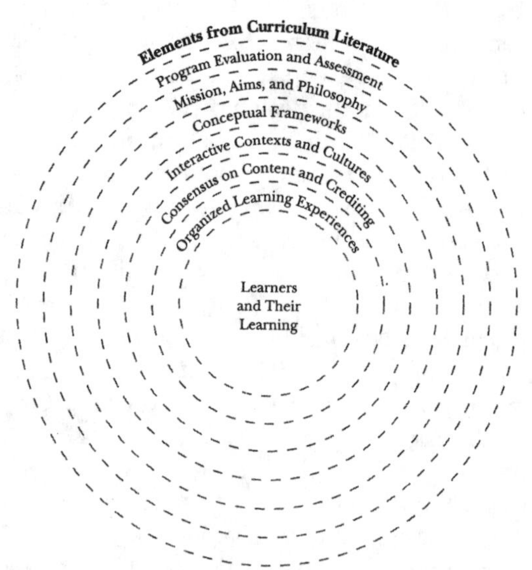

Figure 26-1 Curriculum as Dynamic Process with Interactive Elements

ing the baccalaureate or associate degree: "Such a curriculum is formalized into courses or programs of study including workshops, seminars, colloquia, lecture series, laboratory work, internships, and field experiences. Here, the term *course* is used generically, to designate a formal unit of an undergraduate curriculum. . . . What we call an undergraduate curriculum tends to be a universe of courses, each with its own purpose and environment" (pp. 6–7). Ratcliff notes that 97 percent of curricula, unfortunately, fall in the category of "universe of courses." He usefully extends his definition:

> Curriculum refers to both the *process* and *substance* of an educational program. It comprises the purpose, design, conduct, and evaluation of educational experiences. Curricula exist at different levels, ranging from the single course to the educational program to the department or discipline to the college or university. The organization of curricula is defined by educational philosophy, the structure and content of the knowledge imparted, and the institutional context and climate. Effective curricula have coherence and explicit definitions of aims and standards of attainment. They accomplish their aims through sequence and structure of learning experiences to facilitate student learning and development. They provide sufficient content and coverage to exhibit but not exhaust the limits of the subject of study. They include mastery of basic terms, concepts, models, and theories as well as *some application* [italics added for emphasis] of them to situations appropriate to the student, the learning aims, and the institutional context. Good curricula have the hallmarks of effective instruction and the evidence of the enhancement of student learning. [pp. 12–13]

In our view, "some application" must mean an equal emphasis on what ought to be performed as part of what ought to be learned. A curriculum that specifically fosters learning that lasts, we believe, must also relate structured experiences in the cocurriculum to organized learning experiences in the academic curriculum.

Consensus on Content and Crediting

Consensus on content is a bedrock curricular element, but it is also problematic. "What new content shall we *add*?" often prompts updating curriculum content by introducing newer ideas such as chaos theory (Gleick, 1987) or cultural diversity and gender studies (MacCorquodale & Lensink, 1995; Olguin & Schmitz, 1997); reinvigorating the canon (Bloom, 1987; Hirsch, 1988) or transforming it (Minnich, 1990; Nussbaum, 1997). When updating content means only adding electives or courses to a sequence, a concept of curriculum as bits and pieces may result. Today's challenge is not only, "What content do we include?" but also, "What do we mean by content?"

Content discussions once focused almost entirely on disciplinary knowledge, and faculty debates were more likely about relationships between general education and the major than the broader definitions that appeared in mission statements. More recently, content itself is being articulated as more than knowledge and its transmission. Content has now come to include values and attitudes (respect, tolerance, for example), intellectual capabilities and competencies (for example, critical thinking, problem solving), transition to college or work transition skills (computer literacy, time management, career planning), and interdisciplinary studies, as well as work in the disciplines (Chickering & Reisser, 1993; Doherty, Chenevert, Miller, Roth, & Truchan, 1997; Graham, 1998).

The enlivened debates on curriculum as content include whether and how disciplinary content, attitudes, and values are integrated with intellectual, emotional, and physical abilities and transition skills. These debates are changing the meaning of the degree by introducing a sometimes parallel "content" such as courses in critical thinking, study skills, or diversity workshops; or parallel interdisciplinary majors such as gender studies or cognitive science. Whether these should be or are integrated into a curriculum can lead to discussions about the purposes of undergraduate education and the purposefulness of curriculum design. William Tierny (1995) has observed that each discussion on curriculum can advance or deter a consensus on the meaning of a degree, depending on how content is framed by faculty.

As interactions between content and faculty obligations to student learning become more significant, Stark and Lattuca (1997) propose a view of *curriculum as an academic plan for a student's academic development in action* (pp. 9–10). They call for linking a curriculum's elements to student learning outcomes and report that few, if any, curriculum studies have accomplished this. Exploring these links immediately raises the issue of how learning is credited. When credits are achieved by a combination of time and participation in class and a faculty grade (however well that grade captures expert faculty judgment), it can be difficult to analyze patterns in learning outcomes across a curriculum or to ensure students' academic development. To ensure students' development toward maturity and service is one of the most demanding tasks in curriculum development today, given the changes in the locus of the college and its student body. To accomplish this means considering interactive contexts and cultures.

Interactive Contexts and Cultures

While learners' individual differences are emblematic of cultural, economic, and historical contexts, they also reflect the immediate conditions and events of their lives. Relationships between departmental-institutional mission and local and distant contexts affect a curriculum's potential as a vehicle for student learning. More pointedly, "Do students build on academic and life experiences in their internships?" or "How does the community benefit from service-learning?" Curriculum may also include broader contexts such as experimental colleges (Meiklejohn, 1942), learning environments (Schlossberg, Lynch, & Chickering, 1989), learning communities (Gabelnick, MacGregor, Matthews, & Smith, 1990; Hill, 1982), faculty communities (Kuh & Whitt, 1988), and knowledge communities (Bruffee, 1995).

These and other authors support a view of *curriculum as integrated with the cocurriculum and college experience.* Educators have long been raising questions about what both younger and older students are learning outside the formal academic curriculum. The cocurriculum may include learning experiences organized as courses (for example, transition to college, transition to career); it may include planned or ad hoc student activities, student governance, experiences in the workplace and family, civic commitments, and studies in other countries. Educators question how supportive and challenging the campus culture is for a more diverse population. *Curriculum as social context for learning*—whether on or off campus—becomes as important for the urban, commuter college as it has traditionally been for the residential college, and a goal for the virtual university.

Educators who debate educational intent, beliefs, and values while rethinking or reformulating a curriculum are likely to uncover what some scholars have called the "hidden" or "latent" curriculum. Originally, Benson Snyder (1971) referred to the hidden curriculum as the social or emotional surround of the "what to learn" in the formal curriculum. It included the "how to learn" engendered in faculty values and assumptions, student expectations, and the social contexts where ways of learning developed (p. 4). It involved the ways academic staff ensured sufficient interaction with students or even the nature of the encounters. Faculty and advisors also inferred it from student frustrations that might emerge in peer discussions or advising sessions ("Why doesn't she tell us how long she wants this paper to be?" "Why does he give surprise quizzes?" "Why aren't my views recognized in class?"). For Benjamin Bloom, the "latent" curriculum included student learning of the values implicit in interaction, a kind of learning ethic (as cited in Ratcliff, 1997).

The term *hidden curriculum* has come to imply that an institution's social learning context may be unintended but inherent in a range of student experiences in and outside class. Faculty, students, and others then ask questions about "what is really going on," and whether it is to good effect. A view of *curriculum as social learning process in a learning culture* means that curriculum is much more than learning experiences through which courses are put into practice. It includes the individual aims, philosophy, resources, and planning of the teacher and the "social process in which learning takes place, discoveries are made and [learners] come to terms with culture and [come] to learn independently" (Pring, 1995, p. 81). Learning is reinforced and extended by its culture (Bruner, 1990; Cole, 1996; Shweder, 1990); culture also extends curriculum. Alverno College Education Faculty "understand `curriculum' as much more than a collection of courses. [Curriculum is] the sum total of the courses, the philosophy, and the ways students and faculty interact. It includes what and how students learn, what we do to promote that learning, and what our students are becoming" (1996, p. 4). Faculty and students are likely to perceive *curriculum as social environment—a planned social process for interactive learning.*

At a time when many groups are questioning the purposes and results of educational institutions, curriculum must explicitly include the cocurriculum and other interactive contexts that include patterns of relationships and norms among all members of a campus. Taking a curriculum perspective means discussing what the curriculum includes and thereby building trust, an essential value in relationships between learners and their teachers, as well as faculty and administrators, and between the institution and the public sphere. Conceptualizing curriculum to include all its interactive elements implies an expanded role for faculty, advisors, and student services personnel.

Conceptual Frameworks

A curriculum's conceptual framework is often equated with a particular curricular approach (core curriculum, great books curriculum). Faculty may already have consciously selected or evolved a curricular approach or gradually blended a group of approaches over time. In our view, a curriculum discussion is at its most effective when faculty probe the rationale for their curriculum. It is on *curriculum as conceptual framework*, then, that attempts at curriculum reconceptualization rest. Thus, educators make a habit of standing aside by studying other curricular approaches in the literature or by visiting other campuses to benchmark their own practices.

Any conceptual framework has assumptions, and we have found that a faculty's guided dialogue may make implicit assumptions explicit and specify the connecting principles that guide student learning. Thus, dialogue about assumptions can lead to curriculum change, setting the stage for thinking through educational assumptions that ground a curriculum for learning that lasts. Recent efforts to make assumptions explicit across institutions in problem-based learning (Albanese & Mitchell, 1993; Ravitch, 1997), student-centered and standards-based teacher education (Darling-Hammond, 1997; Diez, 1998), and ability-based learning (Alverno College Faculty, 1976/1992; Consortium for the Improvement of Teaching, Learning and Assessment, 1992; Otter, 1997) illustrate how powerful such discussions of educational assumptions can be in stimulating educational transformation that influences organizational culture.

In these efforts, faculty regularly touched on issues that are seminal in curriculum theory and research, are connected by disciplinary and philosophical foundations of education as a profession, and are reflected in diverse disciplinary or professional paradigms and worldviews. For some, articulating a set of operative educational assumptions and following their implications led to discovering incompatibilities and inconsistencies among the amalgamated approaches to curriculum that had been introduced and adapted over the years. That a shift in assumptions may lead to curricular reconceptualization is a popular topic among many faculty groups who are revising curriculum, as well as curriculum theorists (Pinar, 1999; Wraga, 1999). How educational assumptions affect and are affected by the selection and use of other curricular elements is fundamental to projecting how a curriculum might be experienced by students and which learning outcomes might actually accrue, especially outcomes that ensure learning that endures.

Mission, Aims, and Philosophy

In our experience, faculty are more likely to see an educational program as a curriculum with a conceptual framework that needs to be articulated and discussed when they include *curriculum as mission, aims, and philosophy* as a curricular element. Undergraduate institutions are expected by accrediting boards to have a mission statement; if faculty examine a *curriculum as a funda-*

mental expression of college aims and convictions, the operative meanings of the mission statement come center stage, particularly when discussing curriculum organization or revision.

Often, though, mission statements are so broad that they neither reflect the uniqueness of a college nor illuminate potential gaps between faculty intent, practice, and learner experience at the course or department level that might be helpful in curriculum revision. Aims or purposes and educational philosophy need to be clear as well. Hence, our emphasis on testing curriculum assumptions such as, "teaching leads to learning."

Program Evaluation and Assessment

Program evaluation and assessment functions more as a connecting element than as a large and embracing one. Historically, it has been oriented to the quantitative evidence of program documentation (for example, enrollment, retention, graduation, GPA). However, program assessment directions in the 1980s were grounded in part on the idea that graduation and grades were at best only proxy measures for learning; measurement and judgment would necessarily involve more sophisticated assessment procedures, as well as more integrated and coherent visions of curriculum. Evaluation activities, then, should serve as a means to a dynamic conceptualization of curriculum (Stark & Lattuca, 1997, pp. 266–268). So considered, program evaluation and assessment are part of the lexicon of inquiry and connect the assessment literature to our theme of taking a curriculum perspective (Actin, 1991; Banta & Associates, 1993; Erwin, 1991; Ewell, 1991; Gray, 1989; Loacker, 1988; Mentkowski, 1998; Stark & Thomas, 1994; Taylor & Marienau, 1997).

Exploring Curricular Approaches, Assumptions, and Learning Principles

The dynamic interaction of elements defines a particular curriculum. We have found that exploring how curriculum functions as a conceptual framework of educational assumptions serves as a touchstone for deepening curriculum discussions. As a professor of philosophy suggests, "A department, school, or college that explores its own assumptions may then reflect on what needs to be made explicit and how that informs teaching and learning. How these assumptions connect is an incredibly profound way to point to the need to examine teaching practice. I ask, 'What implications does this assumption have for what I do in the classroom?'" We recommend that a faculty group explore how these elements reveal assumptions that may serve as organizing principles for thinking through their curriculum. Where a group starts makes a difference. For example, *curriculum as course sequence* could start with a debate about timing, scheduling, and faculty course assignments, without ever clarifying concerns about content. *Curriculum as consensus on content* might begin with selecting texts, as in a great books curriculum (Smith, 1983), but then gradually move to rethinking assumptions about how to enhance learning from texts. Further design work might focus on what a particular learned society has set forth as essential for a major in its field.

The power of *curriculum as conceptual framework of educational assumptions* is released when faculty focus on learning-centered education and articulate corresponding learning principles. For example, a primary focus on strengthening learning experiences might lead immediately to redesigning a sequence of courses. Different curricular perspectives can lead to different discussions. Because they see *curriculum as professional problem solving* after college or professional school, a faculty might begin by considering how to construct cases so students must use the essential knowledge base in the field, as in problem-based learning (Barrows, 1994; Barrows & Tamblyn, 1980). *Curriculum as social learning context* might start with identifying principles that foster interactive group learning, as in collaborative learning (Gabelnick et al., 1990). *Curriculum as mission, aims, and philosophy* might involve studying community needs, as in service-learning, so that students can practice contributing effectively in the community (Eyler & Giles, 1999; National Society for Internships and Experiential Education, 1990; Rothman, 1998; Zlotkowski, 1997–1999). *Curriculum as community context* might mean identifying underserved students with limited access to college or gradually increasing diversity in the student body so "all students can learn perspective taking."

Different curricular approaches have contrasting assumptions and principles. Some approaches are conventional; some are emerging, given a developing understanding of the challenges facing postsecondary education in general and undergraduate programs in particular. In reality, most programs integrate at least several approaches to curriculum. However, we have found it helpful to clarify the assumptions already in use because these often influence where a faculty might begin a conversation about curriculum. Here we offer a prompt for moving beyond defining one's own curriculum and its elements, toward external comparisons. We reviewed commonly held curricular definitions and approaches, drawing out educational assumptions and learning principles that underlie them. Table 26-1 lists sixteen approaches to curricula that have identifiable elements; we inferred only one implicit or explicit assumption and one principle from each approach to facilitate faculty discourse that explores the roots of current and potential conceptual frameworks *across* approaches. Each curricular approach actually contains multiple assumptions and learning principles. We selected some that may be embedded and hard to recognize immediately, in part because they rest on different meaning systems. For example, in a core curriculum (Table 26-1, approach 3), consensus on content, that is, common learning, is fundamental to specialized fields. Faculty might ask, "What is the nature of common learning that ensures that students gradually incorporate knowledge, skills, and attitudes over time?" Or, in a profession based curriculum (Table 26-1, approach 5), "What common understandings about the profession are demonstrated via internships, so students learn them?"

Most readers will be familiar with one or another of these curricular approaches and may recognize that each marks a shift in assumptions. For example, faculty might discuss approaches to curriculum and gradually articulate the assumptions and learning principles that underlie these approaches and, by inference, those in their own curriculum. Our premise here is that a conceptual framework for curricular revision should come primarily out of articulated frameworks for good educational practice. Articulating educational assumptions, begun in Table 26-1, can prompt questions about what learning principles a faculty group is committed to and what the priorities and implications are for their own curriculum. For example, specialized content as a framework for learning in a subject-matter curriculum (Table 26-1, approach 4) may work as one learning principle. But if a faculty expands specialized content to include broad abilities or outcomes that define a major field or cross fields, then the principle *learning that lasts is integrative* comes into play (Table 26-1, approach 14). The implication may lead to rethinking the role of subject matter in learning.

In our own case, the faculty began with a shift in focus from what they did as teachers to include what the student and, later, the graduate ought to know and be able to do. Once expected learning outcomes were clearer, the faculty developed student- and program-assessment systems to provide continuing information about progress and substantiate discussions about curriculum with information about actual student learning. This permanently shifted the faculty's focus to study student learning outcomes in relation to curriculum, as well as to alternative curriculum perspectives, structures, and the organizational culture. We now turn to the question of how curricular elements, drawn from the literature, are elaborated when a curriculum embodies a commitment to lasting learning.

Analyzing a Curriculum for Learning That Lasts

Probing the elements of a curriculum in relation to learning outcomes and elaborating them through learner attributions can provide observations about which relationships drive and sustain learning, one basis for inferring the potentially transferable curricular elements for fostering learning that lasts. The perspectives of learners—as students and alumnae—are a critical point of entry to elaborate curriculum elements. In pointing to the powerful and sustaining elements in the curriculum that account for learner outcomes, these perspectives serve a similar role.

Alverno's curriculum is grounded in a particular approach that has gone through extensive changes since its inception in the early 1970s. Further, the interactive relationships among its elements, outcomes, and consequent curricular principles may be quite different from those at any other institution. Recognizing this, we analyzed the Alverno curriculum—its practices, principles, and research—to determine those elements that were stable to a degree; ironically, each element also ensured change in the curriculum.

TABLE 26-1
Inferring One Educational Assumption and One Learning Principle from Selected Curricular Approaches

Curricular Approach[a]	*One Inferred Assumption (Implicit or Explicit)*	*One Learning Principle (Implicit or Explicit)*
1. Cafeteria or shopping mall	1. The content of the curriculum, purposefully selected by faculty, gives structure to the curriculum. Students make informed choices; they enroll prepared to take responsibility for their own learning. A collection of courses has an implicit conceptual framework or lack of one; the student can discern it, supply it, and use it to integrate learning across courses. Individual faculty emphases constitute the content of the curriculum.	1. Choosing is essential for individual motivation for learning. Learning is synonymous with content that changes endlessly.
2. Course of study as a set of sequenced courses (97 percent of curricula, Ratcliff, 1997)	2. Course sequence connects curricula for students; what is taught and learned earlier transfers to later courses in the sequence. Students can infer the philosophy and aims of the department, intended and not, from selection and sequence of courses. They learn coherent aims and learning outcomes informally, or through advising.	2. Learning builds over time; learning is cumulative. Curriculum connections are learned incidentally or individually created.
3. Core curriculum (liberal arts/general education component)	3. Common learning is fundamental to specialized learning in the majors and to a liberal education.	3. What is learned incorporates what has been learned.
4. Subject-matter curriculum	4. All general education requirements are not necessary in all fields (for example, communications, literature, and psychology are not needed in the study of engineering or languages). Coherence among individual theories of teaching and learning depends on the discipline.	4. Specialized content is the framework for learning.
5. Discipline or profession-based curriculum	5. Individual faculty create their own curriculum in courses, but teach out of both their individual and common understanding of what their discipline, as a dynamic field, requires.	5. The discipline and profession is the framework for learning.
6. Selective curriculum	6. Curriculum works when students self-select or are selected at entrance for their prior education, fit with the curriculum, or potential to graduate.	6. Learning potential is predictable.
7. Great books curriculum	7. Selected content or canon centers a curriculum.	7. Learning across selected, diverse texts yields cumulative understanding of liberal arts outcomes.
8. Credit for seat time	8. Credits that are awarded for attendance, prescribed time in class, and achievement represent learning in courses.	8. Rate of learning is constant. Ability to learn varies. Learning potential is predictable.
9. Time constant/learning variable	9. Curriculum units are awarded for mastery of course goals; unsuccessful students may repeat courses.	9. Each student's rate of learning is variable, so time to achieve is variable.

TABLE 26-1 (continued)

Curricular Approach[a]	*One Inferred Assumption (Implicit or Explicit)*	*One Learning Principle (Implicit or Explicit)*
10. Writing across the curriculum	10. Individual faculty who create their own curriculum in courses have consensus on learning outcomes that are taught and assessed across courses.	10. Writing is essential to undergraduate earning.
11. Developmental education	11. Interventions and challenge support what students have learned construct cognitively, so shifts in cognitive development occur.	11. Learning is deep, developmental, and structural.
12. Problem-based learning	12. Faculty hold assumptions and principles in common that ground curriculum and the teaching and learning within it. Predominant learning styles in a profession characterize formal learning.	12. Problem solving integrates learning.
13. Experiential learning	13. Curriculum includes real and simulated experiences that are reflected on, analyzed, and acted on.	13. Learning is experiential.
14. Ability-based learning	14. Curriculum is organized around integrated, explicit learning outcomes that integrate content and ability and are assessed in performance.	14. Learning is integrative and transformative.
15. Collaborative learning community	15. Curriculum is organized so students and faculty learn side by side or interactively in an established learning group.	15. Learning is interactive and interpersonal.
16. Virtual university	16. Curriculum relies on distributed or distance learning to enhance access to education. Learning is not tied to a particular place or time; both may vary.	16. Learning happens all the time, so accessible education provides choice.

[a]Each curricular approach has many assumptions and principles. This analysis provides a starting point for discussion rather than a comprehensive, inclusive analysis.

Essential Curricular Elements for Learning That Lasts

We offer an elaborated set of curricular elements as essential—that is, necessary and sufficient to ensure learning that lasts for a broad range of graduates (see Figure 26-2). They include and extend the findings from the analysis of the literature (introduced in Figure 26-1). These elaborated elements do not guarantee learning that lasts for every student. Rather, the elements, when joined and interactive, create a learning environment that has proved effective for most students in this setting; learners meet the standards set by the faculty and continue to develop and demonstrate them up to at least five years postcollege. If each of these elements is a part of a curriculum dynamic and realized in learner outcomes and attributions, a curriculum may successfully foster learning that lasts.

To obtain the elements we view as essential (Figure 26-2, bottom), we first identified interactive elements of undergraduate curricula from the literature (Figure 26-2, top) and then integrated them with their analysis of elements in the Alverno curriculum. For the latter, we analyzed Alverno faculty construction of practices and principles from their publications (e.g., Alverno College Educators, 1977/1998; Alverno College Faculty, 1976/1992, 1979/1994), including jointly published material from faculty membership in three consortia with other colleges and universities (Cromwell, 1986; Halonen, 1986; Schulte & Loacker, 1994). We used learner outcomes to inform our analysis further. We then submitted seventeen hours of our taped, transcribed deliberations (Alverno College Research and Evaluation Committee, 1998) to a secondary analysis to clarify, synthesize, and confirm the essential elements. In effect, we triangulated our review of the external literature with the literature on this college's curriculum—developed experientially and studied for over twenty years—and the particular studies available in this book that link curricular elements to learning outcomes.

How might a curriculum group use these results to analyze their own curriculum? We are mindful of Stark and Lattuca's (1997) caveat that the use of terms alone to describe aspects of a curriculum is often devoid of meaning. So to make the essential elements more useful, we created Table 26-2. The first column elaborates the essential elements through the context of the Alverno curriculum. Column 2 illustrates each of the essential elements through examples of cohering learner outcomes and causal attributions so a faculty group can see how these elements are reflected in student and alumna perspectives. Column 3 details curriculum principles that cohere to the elements; we inferred them after we had a picture of the essential elements.

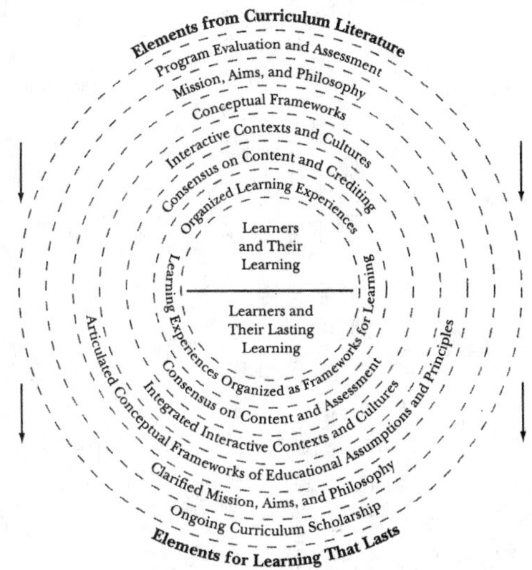

Figure 26-2 Curriculum as Dynamic Process with Interactive Elements: Essential Elements for Learning That Lasts.

Learning Experiences Organized as Frameworks for Learning

Rather than learning experiences organized only as courses, this curriculum's learning experiences are organized primarily as coherent frameworks for learning: (1) abilities integrated with disciplines and interdisciplinary areas of study and professions; (2) student assessment-as-learning; and (3) educating for learning to learn, maturity, and service. These frameworks undergird a level of coherence that balances the deliberately planned diversity within each, recognizing that theories of coherence have an "order bias, a consistency bias" (Quinn & Cameron, 1988b, p. 13) but that the concept resonates well with ineffable educational goals (Buchmann & Floden, 1992). Immediately, one thus confronts what makes liberal learning situated—how learning differs across contexts—and what it means to teach toward transferable abstractions such as

TABLE 26-2
Essential Elements of a Dynamic Curriculum for Learning That Lasts

Essential Elements of a Curriculum for Learning That Lasts[a]	*Curricular Elements as Realized in Learning Outcomes and Learners' Causal Attributions*[b]	*Conceptual framework of Curriculum Principles*
1. *Learning experiences organized as frameworks for learning:* Frameworks are elaborated as expected learning outcomes and experiences that include abilities integrated with disciplines and/or interdisciplinary areas of study, and professions; student assessment-as-learning; educating for learning to learn, maturity, and service.	1. Students and alumnae experience the curriculum as individualized and experiential; interactive and collaborative; coherent and diverse; structured and open-ended; designed for individual and group; and the result of a wide range of teaching, learning, and assessment strategies.	Faculty determine student learning outcomes that inform curriculum. Faculty define learning outcomes as complex and multidimensional abilities integrated with content, that are developmental and integrated in performance and in the person. Faculty designate the learning outcomes that are required for graduation and those that are expected but not required. A curriculum attends to both.
2. *Consensus on content and assessment:* Consensus on content means expected and required learning outcomes that integrate content and ability, abilities in situations, knowing and doing, personal and professional roles, and liberal arts and professions. Consensus on student assessment means student assessment-as-learning, with public, developmental performance criteria, feedback, and self assessment.	2. Public, explicit learning outcomes are developmental, ability based, and performance based. Learners express learning principles in various key components of assessment-as-learning: learning outcomes, criteria, feedback, self assessment.	What and how faculty teach are distinguishable from what students take in and how and when they transform that into knowledge, performance, and personal growth. Teaching, learning, and assessment are variables in the learning process. A curriculum attends to all three. A curriculum that includes distinctive performance outcomes and makes them explicit enables educators to better integrate disciplinary and interdisciplinary frameworks into a student's general education. A curriculum includes diverse opportunities for evaluation of individual performance.
3. *Integrated interactive contexts and cultures:* Contexts include challenging and supportive pedagogy, learning climate, community, and culture with integrated curriculum, cocurriculum, internships, travel abroad, service to community. Consideration of learners' lives and life events. Climate that encourages voice and trust.	3. A curriculum includes diverse opportunities for diverse learners to construct their own ideas, practice, reflect, validate the relevance of learning, and learn to perform. High expectations along with high acceptance, expectations for independent and collaborative achievement. A balance of curricular challenges and supports communicates a climate that encourages voice and trust and provides opportunities for learners to define and realize their own purposes.	A curriculum provides for repeated opportunities for learners to construct, practice, perform, reflect on, and integrate what they are learning in multiple disciplines, interdisciplinary areas of study, and professions. Internships, advising, and instructional and student services are integral to the curriculum.

Essential Elements of a Curriculum for Learning That Lasts[a]	*Curricular Elements as Realized in Learning Outcomes and Learners' Causal Attributions*[b]	*Conceptual framework of Curriculum Principles*
4. *Articulated conceptual frameworks of assumptions and principles:* Frameworks include educational assumptions, learning and assessment principles, curriculum principles, and principles for learning that lasts.	4. A curriculum is learner and learning centered with positive regard toward students. Each learner is respected and can learn.	Curriculum integrity (the degree represents what faculty intend and what students experience) requires that a curriculum be coherent within diversity. A dynamic curriculum requires constantly rethinking and reformulating learning, assessment, and teaching/advising/inquiry/curriculum principles and continually validating educational assumptions.
5. *Clarified mission, aims, and philosophy:* A curriculum is centered on learners and their learning. A curriculum is coherent within its diversity. It is developmental and requires students to meet explicit, common, and evolving expectations that maximize each student's potential.	5. Purposeful, connected curriculum is in the interest of learners. Curriculum is fair in that faculty and staff intent as communicated to students is generally realized in what faculty and staff do and how they interact.	Curriculum diversity yields coherence when curriculum is for the learning of students. A curriculum is designed, practiced, experienced, evaluated, and improved by faculty in relation to what students bring to it, how students experience it, what students learn and ought to learn across a curriculum, and how graduates learn and need to learn beyond college.
6. *Ongoing curriculum scholarship:* Faculty study the relationships between abilities, learning, and their disciplines.	6. Curriculum is continually improving for current and future learners; learners' perspectives on and experiences with the curriculum are considered and changes made. Learners perceive faculty and staff as experts in their fields, and in teaching, advising, and services.	Curriculum scholarship is ongoing, sustained, extensive, deliberative, individual, and collaborative with multiple methods and comparisons across disciplines. Scholarship in the disciplines or an integration of disciplines is shaped by and also shapes student learning

[a]Elements of a dynamic curriculum emerge from a triangulated analysis. Essential elements of curriculum that foster learning that lasts are based on interactive elements of undergraduate curricula derived from the curriculum literature; Alverno faculty perspectives and their current practice; consortia with outside faculty (Cromwell, 1986; Halonen, 1986; Schulte & Loacker, 1994); and by joining empirically derived student and alumna perspectives, performance, and other measurement-based findings. Rather than a uniform and idealized model of curriculum, the emphasis here is on the interaction of elements, and on those that are potentially usable in conversations about design and evaluation of curriculum. The premise is that some of these elements and relationships (for example, regard for the learner, performance assessment, experiential learning) may already be in place or may be implemented in stages in any one department or institution. It is the cohering relationships among these elements that make a difference for learning that lasts.

abilities within disciplines, how students come to evaluate their own work credibly, and how to acknowledge and support the learner as developing person and contributor (Barrowman, 1996; O'Brien, Matlock, Loacker, & Wutzdorff, 1991).

Faculty see abilities integrated with disciplines as one "framework for student learning" (Loacker & Palola, 1981). Disciplines themselves are frameworks for learning, as are abilities. Herein lies the challenge. A barrier to understanding of the concept of abilities integrated with the disciplines is the idea that, prior to integration, abilities and the disciplines can exist separately. Faculty know that this is a false dichotomy. Our way of explaining it away in the past has been to say that we cannot teach for abilities in a void. They must be taught in the context of something, and that "something" is the discipline or interdisciplinary area of study. But that dichotomy is false because disciplines as ways of thinking (particular organizations of procedural knowledge—facts, conventions, concepts, rules of thumb) are already, by this definition, composed of various ability components. The problem is not so much one of integrating abilities and disciplines, but of faculty recognizing and helping students to understand and perform the abilities that compose a discipline. This can be a challenge to faculty because they are generally so proficient at the practice of their disciplines (researching, writing reviews, and so forth) that their ways of thinking are almost second nature to them. Since they seldom articulate the processes underlying their thinking, all students ever notice are the products of faculty practice—the interpretations, the syntheses of current scholarship, the finished writings. What faculty have to do is to reflect upon and break open their professional disciplinary practice to rediscover the specific abilities and habits of mind that constitute them, and thus make them more explicit as they walk students through faculty practice, modeling the discipline for them.

There are various techniques for deconstructing a disciplinary practice; one of the most effective is for faculty to engage in professional dialogue about the meaning of their disciplines *across disciplinary lines.* Unable to rely on the common epistemological assumptions and shared language of a disciplinary community, faculty are forced to explain themselves, identify their assumptions, elaborate the informal rules that guide their thinking and decision making. Once they have done this, it is easier to teach the discipline (not just the disciplinary knowledge base) to students. Faculty must, however, be careful not to model their expectations for students on expectations for themselves. Faculty disciplinary practice is analogous, not identical, to the practice that they want to foster in their students.

Disciplines as a framework for student learning means that faculty make teaching choices based on the suitability of particular dimensions of their own discipline (in itself or integrated with other disciplines) for promoting student learning. They have also come to apply the term *learning framework* to their own thinking in the discipline and to the way they construct meaning through their scholarship. While their own disciplinary thinking differs from that of students in level of sophistication, faculty see their own learning as analogous to their students', and they tend to concentrate in their scholarship on questions about the method and nature of thinking in their disciplines. There is an ongoing interrelationship between the questions they raise about their fields and those that help them to refine student learning. Thinking, for example, about the way they present their discipline's methods for their students refines their own understanding of those methods. As one history professor puts it, "Our practice as teachers in an ability-based learning environment has led us to think differently, or at least more explicitly, about our disciplines. In order for us to help students learn to think in the disciplines, we have to pay serious attention to our own process of learning. Since we explicitly model disciplinary practice and explain this to students, we have to be very conscious of what we are doing."

Learners' outcomes and causal attributions provide additional insight here (see Table 26-2, column 2). Because learners apply what they know, frameworks for learning are *experiential.* An *individualized* curriculum is responsive to individual learners and provides for appropriate challenges from faculty. Extended, multiple interpretations of expectations and achievements express a plural, open-ended standard of excellence revealed in explicit developmental performance criteria; they encourage responsiveness to learning styles and *reinforce diversity* in learner perspectives. *Interactive and collaborative* learning experiences are a source of developing flexibility, as are *coherent and diverse, individual and group* learning experiences. They help to ensure an essential wholeness, continuity of argument, and integrity in the learner—a coherence across the curriculum that supports diversity, making the coherence robust rather than brittle. Learners experience a *wide range of teaching, learning, and assessment strategies.*

Consensus on Content and Assessment

In this curriculum, faculty come to consensus on content as expected learning outcomes and on assessment as an essential process for student learning. "Consensus on content" does not mean uniformity, total agreement, or lack of conflict, just as "ability" does not mean lack of content. Integration of content and ability is essential so that individual academic areas are learned in terms of the range of performances and abilities that represent their learning outcomes, and so that abilities are understood, developed, and demonstrated across multiple disciplinary and interdisciplinary contexts.

Coming to consensus on content as integrated content and abilities has led Alverno's faculty to raise questions about their broader role in student learning. For example, the same history professor asks:

> What is the relationship between faculty teaching and student learning? If we assume a complex epistemology, where subjective processing of experience affects what people know at least to some degree, then what faculty teach is not identical to what students learn. There is no objective transfer of knowledge from the mind of the faculty member to the mind of the student. The data that faculty have reflected upon and transformed into knowledge, through their scholarship, can be experienced by students as a more refined data set—but it will not become knowledge until students transform it into knowledge for themselves.

The language of abilities, integrated with content, has profound implications for learners because how they construct learning influences whether they can transfer it (Doherty et al., 1997; Evers, Rush, & Berdrow, 1998). The younger adult cohorts' experiences reflect what happens when a college is dominated by students directly from high school; the older, work-experienced cohorts reflect the broader adult population, including some young adults. Abilities integrated with disciplines constitutes a roadblock for both kinds of learners at first, but it poses a greater challenge for the eighteen- or nineteen-year-old who comes directly from high school with, in most cases, a less clear sense of career direction. The learner who has been a particularly high performer can stumble just as sharply as the one who has not ("Where's the content? How do I know I'm succeeding or failing?"). The discrepancy between their expectations and the curriculum has definite learning value, but with a major caveat: faculty and advisors must pay careful attention to retention, so their approach does not jeopardize particular kinds of learners. Of course, any college is a new environment, with a new language that the student has not been entirely exposed to before. It is discontinuous from that of the high school, and what appears to be resistance to the new culture may be the persistence of the old one. As Piaget and Perry suggest, when a challenge appears in the new environment, there is a heavy reliance on the prior environment for strategies. Work-experienced, returning, and transfer students are more likely to understand ability-based learning sooner. While similarly challenged at first (they, too, expect more traditional ways of learning), they engage with the complexity of the system sooner.

Performance assessment is inevitably linked conceptually to learning principles, and faculty have come to consensus on how to conceptualize and practice assessment, to the point where student assessment is a framework for learning: assessment-as-learning. With reflective self assessment, it assists learners to shape their future performance based on their understanding of their past and current work and their intellectual processes. A successful active learning process includes engagement, self assessment, and feedback. It must include public, explicit, and developmental criteria for judging performances, as well as feedback and self assessment. At the earliest level, such a framework for learning incorporates student development of self-awareness and self assessment by setting up a visual model (this level is like watching a drama). The next level provides opportunities for students to use the model (like rehearsing the play). At a still higher level, curriculum engages students in the process of self-awareness and self assessment (this would include seeing relevance, showing personal identification, and valuing the process). ("Developmental" does not mean relieving the learner of the obligation to meet standards, since each student must meet criteria in order to graduate.)

As realized in learner outcomes and attributions, an integrated consensus on content and assessment means *public, explicit learning outcomes* that have clarity for learners, faculty, and various groups (Table 26-2, column 2). The analysis of their observations points to the particular elements of the curriculum that they singled out as valuable: the ability framework and the integration of content, the orientation to performance. *Developmental, ability-based, and performance-based learning outcomes* detail the nature and sequence of ability levels, interaction of abilities integrated with content, and how students might build them over time. Interaction of course outcomes with the development of learners is appreciated. Students show development in their *ability to express faculty principles in various aspects of assessment-as-learning, learning outcomes, criteria, feedback, and self assessment.* For example, an advanced learner has developed criteria as a picture of her effectiveness in demonstrating her ability, a picture that is congruent with external standards and highlighting what is unique to her.

Aspects of the curriculum more associated with teaching behaviors and the delivery of the curriculum are student and alumna experiences of the powerful effects of assessment, self assessment, and the procedures for giving feedback on performances. Recent studies with students in transition confirm these conclusions. Faculty find that students who have experienced problems progressing in the curriculum after two or three semesters are often those who have had trouble in working with curriculum frameworks—as in the structure of abilities and disciplinary theories—and in working closely with the feedback they have received. This becomes particularly problematic when, given this learning culture, students are likely to keep receiving greater quantities of feedback than they know how to use. Thus, assisting each student to use feedback to improve becomes the intervention faculty choose (Alverno College Intermediate Student Study Committee, 1994).

Integrated Interactive Contexts and Cultures

The multiple contexts that interact in this curriculum provide important opportunities for an appropriate balance of challenges and supports for learning. In this curriculum, faculty work toward integrating these contexts, so that educating for learning to learn, maturity, and service has become a learning framework. This framework connects the curriculum and cocurriculum in practice to learning that lasts through structured experiences in the cocurriculum (for example, transition-to-college programs, transition to career, learning support groups, residence hall meetings between counselors and residents; negotiating on-campus day care; internships, travel, and community service), as well as an awareness of students' lives and life events and the many subcultures that reflect the intentions and norms of a student population. Integrating interactive contexts has also meant finding ways to create a shared sense of the social process of education for the faculty and staff. The curriculum then provides multiple recurring opportunities for learners to construct what they are learning—and to practice and perform—in different disciplines, contexts, and cultures. Learners themselves come to see the *curriculum as a set of diverse opportunities to construct their own purposes, ideas, and criteria; to practice, to reflect, to validate the relevance of learning; and to learn to perform.* High expectations along with high acceptance, expectations for independent as well as collaborative achievement, challenges and supports—each dynamic is part of their experience, and each communicates a climate for encouraging voice and trust. Considering climate can lead to rethinking the organizational culture.

Articulated Conceptual Frameworks of Assumptions and Principles

In this curriculum, educational assumptions—the ideas that generate frameworks for learning that shape teaching, assessing, advising, and inquiry—are explicit and discussed, and form a basis for generating curricular principles (see Table 26-2, column 3). A conceptual framework of assumptions enables a faculty to discuss what principles for learning that lasts imply for designing and evaluating curriculum. Such articulated conceptual frameworks open up the curriculum rationale for students—one that stays with them as alumnae. Learners projected a strong sense of their own understandings of curricular principles and developed a regard for their own learning. Five-year alumnae who could articulate this rationale also tended to articulate their learning outcomes in more meaningful ways.

Clarified Mission, Aims, and Philosophy

The practice of clarifying mission, aims, and philosophy at this college and its relationship to conceptual frameworks reaffirms a commitment to serving learners and their learning. The focus on abilities integrated with disciplinary and interdisciplinary conceptual frames ties together the students' education, the degree programs, and the cocurriculum. Learners, then, experience the curriculum *as purposeful and connected.* It is purposeful in that faculty have deliberately defined purposes in understandable language rather than just naming them. Thus, learners can connect their learning across the curriculum. The mission, aims, and philosophy require that members of the college community respect each student. There is a democratic dimension to this experience—the sense that each participant is respected and expected to learn. While some curricula may foster learning that lasts but not be purposive, learners understood and experienced the democratic tendencies of this curriculum as a means by which faculty advocated the latent potential for all students to learn and to exceed what is required of them. Learners experienced the curriculum as fair in that faculty generally do what they claim.

Ongoing Curriculum Scholarship

Reflective curriculum practice and inquiry means that faculty and staff, as a community of educators, engage in ongoing studies into the curriculum, student learning, teaching, advising, assessment, and inquiry itself. They also study relationships among abilities, learning, and their disciplines. The professor of history quoted earlier comments, "As great as the challenge has been to unify pedagogical and disciplinary scholarship, it has been an even greater challenge to explain to colleagues who have not experienced it what an integrated and collaborative scholarship discourse sounds like about curriculum because there is, at present, little common language to express the dialogue."

Faculty members' conscious emphasis on disciplines as frameworks for learning may have to do with the environment of a liberal arts college. If they are to have a significant and varied intellectual life with their colleagues, interdisciplinary dialogue is inescapable. Faculty are stepping beyond the comfortable epistemological boundaries of the disciplines. "We can no longer rely on our dialogue partners' automatic understanding of our basic assumptions. We have to be able to explain the structure of our thinking to each other," says the history professor. Accounting for integrated and collaborative scholarship in support of student learning in the disciplines does not, however, explain what it really means to say that disciplinary scholarship is *shaped by* and also *shapes* student learning. To explain this transformation of the disciplines and of student learning, we move to another example.

In a recent faculty fellowship paper, a professor of economics in this college's Business and Management Division explained her dissatisfaction with the assumption of standard economic theory that individual economic agents are autonomous beings who make organized and consistent choices that coherently refer back to a singular self-identity. She wrote that "this account of personal identity has always been problematic for me as a teacher—especially one who teaches adult women. . . . This account in no way explains the choices most of my students have made in their lives, thus making it particularly challenging for them to understand and internalize this theory." Although feminist economists have criticized this assumption of the autonomous individual and have emphasized the way social institutions like the family constrain individual choice, this faculty member went a step further to study the multiple-self literature in philosophy to understand how "individuals constrain themselves in their struggles between multiple selves as they choose between conflicting needs, desires, and values."

This example illustrates many of the characteristics of scholarship in support of student learning:

- Reflection on actual student learning is the stimulus for the examination of the adequacy of fundamental ideas in the discipline.
- The insights derived from this scholarship promise to improve student learning directly.
- The research goes beyond the boundaries of the discipline and presents opportunities for collaboration with colleagues in another field.

- Because the scholarship connects the discipline to the general liberal arts abilities of Analysis and Valuing in Decision-Making, it promises to influence student development of these abilities in courses across this college.
- The formation of method and theory in the discipline is directly addressed through scholarship in the way that term has been traditionally understood.

Curriculum scholarship provides for faculty to continue to develop in their disciplines and to craft cross-college studies as well. For example, learners perceive faculty and staff as competent in their fields—teaching, advising, or service—and experience a curriculum that is evolving in thoughtful response to their expressed learning needs and purposes, leading to the broader study of student outcomes. They also confirmed the power of various challenges and supports to teaching and learning that emerge from the faculty's assumptions and principles, and the opportunities to experience and perform in diverse situations on and off campus, as a dimension of a learning program, as sustaining elements for their continued learning and effectiveness, and for their development as persons.

Confirming the Curriculum in Learner Outcomes

The proof of any curriculum is in learners' performance and their causal attributions. Learner perspectives on their outcomes confirmed essential elements of curriculum for learning that lasts. Most powerful perhaps is the finding that students constructed meaning from their education, with integrity and applicability, to the extent that they experienced a coherent and developing vision of education and learning from the curriculum; multiple, diverse perspectives on their areas of study; and feedback on their performance in a range of modes and contexts. Five-year alumnae linked learning to influential curriculum causes that enabled them to continue to grow. They pointed to the coaching, individualized attention, and positive regard that they experienced from teachers and the cooperative, collaborative work with faculty, external assessors and mentors, and peers as factors that have contributed to sustained learning.

By integrating the statistical analyses on alumna performance, and student and alumna perspectives on their learning outcomes, the character of the curriculum emerges even more sharply:

- The ability framework serves as a metacognitive model as learners deal with work in context.
- Support from the curriculum and faculty teaching toward the learner's growing capacity for self assessment are foundational to becoming an independent and enduring learner.
- The diversity of preparation and the support for in-depth analysis leads to the learner's ability to work with and appreciate multiple viewpoints while effectively constructing and arguing her own position.
- The emphasis on performance and its attendant features (criteria, feedback, practice opportunities, for example) helps the learner integrate the knowledge structures developed across courses with performance opportunities in different contexts.
- Curricular challenges and supports combine to foster independence, and independent and collaborative elements provide for interdependence.

These findings from formal research are reflected not only in the student voice but in the faculty voice drawn from examples of collaborative inquiry.

Taking Up the Work of Ongoing Curriculum Development

Faculty dialogue about interactive and essential curricular elements bears on designing, practicing, reflecting, and deliberating on curriculum. *Designing* means making explicit curricular intent and conceptual frameworks, and planning the underlying structure of curriculum and how it is organized to facilitate particular outcomes. *Practicing* includes instructional interventions and their ongoing adjustments, observing the practices that become critical to their effectiveness. *Reflecting on experience* means using students' experience to learn about curriculum.

Deliberative, collaborative inquiry means participating in constructing, implementing, evaluating, and improving the curriculum's relationship to student learning to ensure its impact and integrity. To do so, educators focus on how their roles intersect and how individual ideas become part of the practice of a community of educators. The ordering of these activities does not mean to imply serial curriculum planning. Rather, they are aspects of academic planning through which faculty gradually move beyond a view of curriculum as a set of learning experiences designed and organized as courses. They thus define content as "more than disciplinary knowledge," cross interactive contexts and cultures of the disciplines, and explore their more intangible assumptions, principles, mission, and philosophy and how they are carried out through curriculum. Dialogue that makes explicit the educational assumptions that underlie curricula, the values that bind a department or school together as a social entity, and the learning principles that undergird curricular principles are particularly helpful. Unarticulated conflicts can stop conversations about what is in the best interest of the learners, and faculty can miss the opportunity to be more accountable for practice.

Particular topics become critical to working on a curriculum: making the learning-to-curriculum connection, realigning faculty and staff roles, and sustaining discourse around activities and challenges. How are these supported by key mechanisms for reflection, deliberation, and inquiry, and how do these contribute to the development, implementation, and evaluation of curriculum?

Making the Learning-to-Curriculum Connection

A range of linking and integrating activities have made up curriculum work over the years:

- Shaping learning-centered curricula in the disciplines, while building opportunities for service-centered performance in the professional areas.
- Identifying, determining, and refining student learning outcomes as an integral feature of learning in the cocurriculum.
- Defining and pursuing problems in determining, revising, and teaching broad abilities or skills integrated with academic content, such as dealing with the "knowledge" problem, including different epistemological paradigms, or deconstructing content for ways of thinking.
- Engendering self-directed student learning through individual and group assignments.
- Modeling the learning gleaned from faculty experience in workshops for new faculty and integrating this learning in criteria for peer review and promotion.
- Using assessment as a tool for student and faculty learning, such as using self-directed learning and self assessment as tools for continuous institutional improvement as well as improvement of individual student performance. (For additional perspectives on such use of portfolio assessments, see O'Brien, 1990.)

Clarifying Roles

The work of curriculum spans a full range of educator roles. It involves the formal groups charged with designing curriculum and making decisions on content, course sequences, and full curricula, but it is just as inclusive of the ad hoc groups and the range of individuals who formulate and carry curricular ideas into program decisions and teaching practice. These activities enable purposive integration of transformative learning processes and learning and action principles into the curriculum. Given this broad involvement, it is all the more important that educators work to understand these roles and their effective interaction. Teachers need to understand their own roles in terms of modeling, building a rationale for, and setting up processes that engage academic work. And, finally, there is the need for processes that enable faculty, as individuals across the dispersion of roles, to take a curriculum perspective as part of their work. There are, as we will see, a number of challenges that emerge directly from this level of integration and collaboration, but it is an important starting point.

Design work that integrates major educational directions seems generally to occur through a committee or task group structure. At the same time, committees with designated curriculum functions may do as much overseeing of course and program policies as with testing the philosophical centers of educational practice. Even with a more or less stable core of educational commitments, much of the work of bringing a curriculum into practice occurs through ad hoc and even less formal group structures that reflect a wide range of college-wide and department meetings.

Creating Opportunities for Sustained Discourse

These meetings, by providing a sustained discourse on educational practice, help maintain the coherence of the curriculum—as a durable core of aims, commitments, and principles—and its flexibility. Revisiting emerging or expanded learning and action principles and educational theories is another part of reflection on curriculum practices. In this kind of context, the broad participation of faculty and academic staff contributes, individually and collectively, to their taking a curriculum perspective. One result is a better understanding of the controversies that can emerge from any structured, purposive endeavor and from curriculum in particular. These include questions of balance between intense collaboration and individual work and initiative; which commitments are shared and which are individual to academic freedom; and strategies for creating pockets of sustained curriculum discourse in a large, diverse faculty. Resource planning, including budgeting, gradually becomes a process that, rather than being delegated solely to a department chair, dean, or provost, is more open and participative, leading to sometimes painful changes in negotiating ways of doing things, including developing more participative strategies for conducting departmental review and self studies for accrediting visits. Thus, conversations about curriculum can lead to targeted, constructive individual and group faculty inquiry that pushes ideas into action.

References

Albanese, M. A., & Mitchell, S. (1993). Problem-based learning: A review of literature on its outcomes and implementation issues. *Academic Medicine, 68*(1), 52–81.

Alverno College Curriculum Committee. (1998). *Taking a curriculum perspective: A faculty conversation.* Milwaukee, WI: Alverno College Institute.

Alverno College Education Faculty. (1996). *Ability-based learning program: Teacher education* [brochure]. Milwaukee, WI: Alverno College Institute.

Alverno College Educators. (1977/1998). *Faculty handbook on learning and assessment.* Milwaukee, WI: Alverno College Institute. (Original work published 1997, revised 1986, 1991, 1992, 1996, 1997, and 1998).

Alverno College Faculty. (1976/1992). *Liberal learning at Alverno College.* Milwaukee, WI: Alverno College Institute. (Original work published 1976, revised 1981, 1985, 1989, and 1992).

Alverno College Faculty. (1979/1994). *Student assessment-as-learning at Alverno College.* Milwaukee, WI: Alverno College Institute. (Original work published 1979, revised 1985 and 1994).

Alverno College Intermediate Student Study Committee. (1994). *Improving the efficiency and effectiveness of teaching and learning of struggling intermediate students at Alverno College: A pilot project.* Milwaukee, WI: Alverno College Institute.

Alverno College Research and Evaluation Committee. (1998). *Transcripts of thirty-eight meetings of the Research and Evaluation Committee: November 1995 to May 1998.* Unpublished manuscript, Alverno College, 3400 South 43rd Street, Milwaukee, WI 53234–3922.

Angelo, T. A., & Cross, K. P. (1993). *Classroom assessment techniques: A handbook for college teachers* (2nd ed.). San Francisco: Jossey-Bass.

Applebee, A. N. (1996). *Curriculum as conversation: Transforming traditions of teaching and learning.* Chicago: University of Chicago Press.

Association of American Colleges (AAC). (1985). *Integrity in the college curriculum: A report to the academic community.* Washington, DC: Author.

Astin, A. W. (1991). *Assessment for excellence: The philosophy and practice of assessment and evaluation in higher education.* New York: Macmillan.

Banta, T. W., & Associates. (1993). *Making a difference: Outcomes of a decade of assessment in higher education.* San Francisco: Jossey-Bass.

Barrowman, C. E. (1996). Improving teaching and learning effectiveness by defining expectations. In E. A. Jones (Ed.), *Preparing competent college graduates: Setting new and higher expectations for student learning.* New Directions for Higher Education, no. 96, 103–114. San Francisco: Jossey-Bass.

Barrows, H. S. (1994). *Practice-based learning: Problem-based learning applied to medical education.* Springfield: Southern Illinois University School of Medicine.

Barrows, H. S., & Tamblyn, R. M. (1980). *Problem-based learning: An approach to medical education.* New York: Springer.

Bloom, A. (1987). *The closing of the American mind.* New York: Simon & Schuster.

Bruffee, K. A. (1995). A nonfoundational curriculum. In J. G. Haworth & C. F. Conrad (Eds.), *Revisioning curriculum in higher education* (pp. 26–34). (ASHE Reader Series). New York: Simon & Schuster.

Bruner, J. S. (1990). *Acts of meaning.* Cambridge, MA: Harvard University Press.

Buchmann, M., & Floden, R. E. (1992). Coherence, the rebel angel. *Educational Researcher, 21*(9), 5–9.

Chickering, A. W., & Reisser, L. (1993). *Education and identity* (2nd ed.). San Francisco: Jossey-Bass.

Cole, M. (1996). *Cultural psychology: A once and future discipline.* Cambridge, MA: Belknap Press.

Consortium for the Improvement of Teaching, Learning and Assessment. (1992). *High school to college to professional school: Achieving educational coherence through outcome-oriented, performance-based curricula.* Final Report to the W. K. Kellogg Foundation. Milwaukee, WI: Alverno Productions.

Cromwell, L. (Ed.). (1986). *Teaching critical thinking in the arts and humanities.* Milwaukee, WI: Alverno Productions.

Darling-Hammond, L. (Chair). (1997, Mar.). *Issues of learner- and learning-centered teacher education: Development and dilemmas.* Interactive symposium conducted at the annual meeting of the American Educational Research Association, Chicago.

Diamond, R. M. (1998). *Designing and assessing courses and curricula: A practical guide* (rev. ed.). San Francisco: Jossey-Bass.

Diez, M. E. (Ed.). (1998). *Changing the practice of teacher education: Standards and assessment as a level for change.* Washington, DC: American Association of Colleges for Teacher Education.

Doherty, A., Chenevert, J., Miller, R. R., Roth, J. L., & Truchan, L. C. (1997). Developing intellectual skills. In J. G. Gaff, J. L. Ratcliff, & Associates, *Handbook of the undergraduate curriculum: A comprehensive guide to purposes, structures, practices, and change* (pp. 170–189). San Francisco: Jossey-Bass.

Erwin, T. D. (1991). *Assessing student learning and development.* San Francisco: Jossey-Bass.

Evers, F. T., Rush, J. C., & Berdrow, I. (1998). *The bases of competence: Skills for lifelong learning and employability.* San Francisco: Jossey-Bass.

Ewell, P. T. (1991). To capture the ineffable: New forms of assessment in higher education. In G. Grant (Ed.), *Review of research in education* (pp. 75–125). Washington, DC: American Educational Research Association.

Eyler, J., & Giles, D. E., Jr. (1999). *Where's the learning in service-learning?* San Francisco: Jossey-Bass.

Gabelnick, F., MacGregor, J., Matthews, R. S., & Smith, B. L. (Eds.). (1990). *Learning communities: Creating connections among students, faculty, and disciplines.* New Directions for Teaching and Learning, no. 41. San Francisco: Jossey-Bass.

Gaff, J. G. (1997). Tensions between tradition and innovation. In J. G. Gaff, J. L. Ratcliff, & Associates, *Handbook of the undergraduate curriculum: A comprehensive guide to purposes, structures, practices, and change* (pp. 684–705). San Francisco: Jossey-Bass.

Gaff, J. G., Ratcliff, J. L., & Associates. (1997). *Handbook of the undergraduate curriculum: A comprehensive guide to purposes, structures, practices, and change.* San Francisco: Jossey-Bass.

Gleick, J. (1987). *Chaos: Making a new science.* New York: Penguin.

Graham, S. E. (1998). Developing student outcomes for the psychology major: An assessment-as-learning framework. *Current Directions in Psychological Science, 7*(6), 165–170.

Gray, P. J. (Ed.). (1989). *Achieving assessment goals using evaluation techniques.* New Directions for Higher Education, no. 67. San Francisco: Jossey-Bass.

Halonen, J. S. (Ed.). (1986). *Teaching critical thinking in psychology.* Milwaukee, WI: Alverno Productions.

Harris, I. B. (1991a). Deliberative inquiry: The arts of planning. In E. C. Short (Ed.), *Forms of curriculum inquiry* (pp. 285–308). Albany: State University of New York Press.

Haworth, J. G., & Conrad, C. F. (Eds.). (1995). *Revisioning curriculum in higher education* (ASHE Reader Series). New York: Simon & Schuster.

Hill, P. J. (1982). Communities of learners: Curriculum as the infrastructure of academic communities. In J. W. Hall (with B. L. Kevles) (Eds.), *In opposition to core curriculum: Alternative models for undergraduate education* (pp. 107–134). Westport, CT: Greenwood Press.

Hirsch, E. D., Jr. (1988). *Cultural literacy: What every American needs to know.* New York: Random House.

Kuh, G. D., & Whitt, E. J. (1988). *The invisible tapestry: Culture in American colleges and universities.* ASHE-ERIC Higher Education Report No. 1. Washington, DC: Association for the Study of Higher Education.

Loacker, G. (1988). Faculty as a force to improve instruction through assessment. In J. H. McMillan (Ed.), *Assessing students' learning.* New Directions for Teaching and Learning, no. 34, 19–32. San Francisco: Jossey-Bass.

Loacker, G., & Palola, E. G. (Eds). (1981). *Clarifying learning outcomes in the liberal arts*. New Directions for Experiential Learning, no. 12. San Francisco: Jossey-Bass.

MacCorquodale, P., & Lensink, J. (1995). Integrating women into the curriculum: Multiple motives and mixed emotions. In J. G. Haworth & C. F. Conrad (Eds.), *Revisioning curriculum in higher education* (pp. 491–503). (ASHE Reader Series). New York: Simon & Schuster.

Marton, F., Hounsell, D., & Entwistle, N. (Eds). (1984). *The experience of learning*. Edinburgh: Scottish Academic Press.

Mentkowski, M. (1998). Higher education assessment and national goals for education: Issues, assumptions, and principles. In N. M. Lambert & B. L. McCombs (Eds.), *How students learn: Reforming schools through learner-centered education* (pp. 269–310). Washington, DC: American Psychological Association.

Minnich, E. K. (1990). *Transforming knowledge*. Philadelphia: Temple University Press.

National Society for Internships and Experiential Education. (1990). *Combining service and learning: A resource book for community and public service*. Raleigh, NC: Author.

Nussbaum, M. C. (1997). *Cultivating humanity: A classical defense of reform in liberal education*. Cambridge, MA: Harvard University Press.

O'Brien, K. (1990). *Portfolio assessment at Alverno College*. Milwaukee, WI: Alverno Productions.

O'Brien, K., Matlock, M. G., Loacker, G., & Wutzdorff, A. (1991). Learning from the assessment of problem solving. In D. Boud & G. Feletti (Eds.), *The challenge of problem based learning* (pp. 274–284). New York: St. Martin's Press.

Olguin, E., & Schmitz, B. (1997). Transforming the curriculum through diversity. In J. G. Gaff, J. L. Ratcliffe, & Associates. *Handbook of the undergraduate curriculum* (pp. 436–456). San Francisco: Jossey-Bass.

Otter, S. (1997, June). *The ability based curriculum: Some snapshots of progress in key skills in higher education*. (Available from Alan Jenkins, ABC Network, Oxford Brookes University, Oxford, United Kingdom).

Pinar, W. F. (1999). Response: Gracious submission. *Educational Researcher, 28*(1), 14–15.

Pring, R. A. (1995). *Closing the gap: Liberal education and vocational preparation*. London: Hodder and Stoughton.

Quinn, R. E., & Cameron, K. S. (Eds.). (1988b). *Paradox and transformation: Toward a theory of change in organization and management*. New York: Ballinger.

Ratcliff, J. L. (1997). What is a curriculum and what should it be? In J. G. Gaff, J. L. Ratcliff, & Associates, *Handbook of the undergraduate curriculum: A comprehensive guide to purposes, structures, practices, and change* (pp. 5–29). San Francisco: Jossey-Bass.

Ravitch, M. (Chair). (1997, Mar.). *What do we mean by problem-based learning? Toward a terminology to better classify and describe some approaches to learning*. Interactive symposium conducted at the annual meeting of the American Educational Research Association, Chicago.

Rothman, M. (Ed.). (1998). *Service matters: Engaging higher education in the renewal of America's communities and American democracy*. Providence, RI: Campus Compact.

Schlossberg, N. K., Lynch, A. Q., & Chickering, A. W. (1989). *Improving higher education environments for adults: Responsive programs and services from entry to departure*. San Francisco: Jossey-Bass.

Schulte, J., & Loacker, G. (1994). *Assessing general education outcomes for the individual student: Performance assessment-as-learning*. Milwaukee, WI: Alverno College Institute.

Shweder, R. A. (1990). Cultural psychology: What is it? In J. W. Stigler, R. A. Shweder, & G. Herdt (Eds.), *Cultural psychology: Essays on comparative human development* (pp. 1–43). New York: Cambridge University Press.

Smith, J. W. (1983). *A search for the liberal college: The beginning of the St. John's Program*. Annapolis, MD: St. John's Press.

Snyder, B. R. (1971). *The hidden curriculum*. New York: Knopf.

Stark, J. S., & Lattuca, L. R. (1997). *Shaping the college curriculum: Academic plans in action*. Needham Heights, MA: Allyn & Bacon.

Stark, J. S., & Thomas, A. (Eds.). (1994). *Assessment and program evaluation*. (ASHE Reader Series). New York: Simon & Schuster.

Taylor, K., & Marienau, C. (1997). Constructive-development theory as a framework for assessment in higher education. *Assessment and Evaluation in Higher Education, 22*(2), 233–243.

Tierney, W. G. (1995). Cultural politics and the curriculum in postsecondary education. In J. G. Haworth & C. F. Conrad (Eds.), *Revisioning curriculum in higher education* (pp. 35–47). (ASHE Reader Series). New York: Simon & Schuster.

Wraga, W. G. (1999). "Extracting sun-beams out of cucumbers": The retreat from practice in reconceptualized curriculum studies. *Educational Researcher, 28*(1), 4–13.

Youtz, B. (1984). The Evergreen State College: An experiment maturing. In R. M. Jones & B. L. Smith (Eds.), *Against the current: Reform and experimen-*

tation in higher education (pp. 93–118). Cambridge, MA: Schenkman.

Zlotkowski, E. (Ed.). (1997–1999). AAHE series on service-learning in the disciplines [monograph series]. Washington, DC: American Association for Higher Education.

CHAPTER 27

WILL DISCIPLINARY PERSPECTIVES IMPEDE CURRICULAR REFORM?

LISA R. LATTUCA AND JOAN S. STARK

Introduction

The recent movement for curricular reform in higher education, sparked by several critical reports in the early 1980s, calls for improvements throughout undergraduate education [8, 11, 22]. Concerned primarily with the general education curriculum, proposed changes have involved both curricular content and educational process. Debate about content has focused on whether colleges and universities should require students to study a common core of courses, and if so, which courses [8, 12]. In the call for commonality some have advocated a core focusing on the Western humanities tradition [8], while others support a curriculum designed to support diversity, economic growth, and global interdependence [1]. When discussing educational processes, most reformers have called for pedagogies that promote students' active involvement and strengthen relationships between faculty and students [22]. For both content and process, many reformers have stressed the need for greater coherence and increased efforts to help students connect what they study with their lives. Nearly all critics have decried "narrow specialization," meaning both early career preparation and professional specialization within the liberal arts and sciences [3].

The Association of American Colleges (AAC) has led discussions about coherence in both general education and advanced studies in liberal arts fields [2, 3, 4]. In the arena of curricular reform, where rhetoric is too seldom followed by useful suggestions for change, the AAC has proposed concrete, positive recommendations for strengthening undergraduate programs. The Association has engaged national task groups of faculty to participate actively in reinvigorating the curriculum, both for general education and the major [3, 4, 5]. First, an AAC task force identified nine experiences that constitute a minimum curriculum in the liberal arts. Second, a faculty group produced a report devoted to improving the eight experiences primarily seen as general education [3]. Finally, the AAC has focused on the ninth experience, "study-in-depth," widely understood to apply to disciplinary concentrations or majors, emphasizing several aspects—the assurance of curricular coherence, the development of critical perspectives, the connection of learning to students' lives, and the reduction of barriers for underrepresented students [2].

Pursuing the emphasis on "connectedness" as important for study-in-depth as well as for general education, in 1988 the AAC National Advisory Committee challenged several arts and sciences fields to address these broad aspects of coherence for the major [4]. Task forces of scholars appointed by their respective learned societies were established, and after three years of study many of the

Source: "Will Disciplinary Perspectives Impede Curricular Reform?" by Lisa R. Lattuca and Joan S. Stark, reprinted from *Journal of Higher Education*, Vol. 65, No. 4 , 1994, Ohio State University Press.

disciplinary societies published reports of the efforts. The AAC compiled the challenge and condensed reports from the task forces in a two-volume set: volume 1, *The Challenge of Connecting Learning,* and volume 2, *Reports from the Fields.*

These reports from teaching scholars in the respective disciplines are potentially powerful influences on the future of liberal education. The AAC effort strikes faculty sensitivities "at home base" by uniquely reflecting the concerns of scholars in each field, rather than those of education generalists. Using the versions of the task force reports assembled in volume 2: *Reports from the Fields,*[1] we explored how ten fields presented the goal of curricular integration or "connectedness." We compared how they expressed their separate disciplinary visions of a coherent curriculum and assessed the extent to which each addressed the challenge set forth by the AAC in volume 1: *Connecting Learning.* We hypothesized that the differences in forms of expression about curriculum are more than semantic; rather, they reveal the disciplines as they are perceived and taught by faculty members [29]. In this article, we discuss some patterns already known to scholars that may reflect enduring epistemological differences among the disciplines but are not always remembered when curricular change is pursued. Examining such differences across disciplines as they attempt to redesign the major may help faculty members and other educational leaders understand that disciplines express themselves differently about their subjects and about how they are taught. This understanding is essential to curriculum leaders who hope to build integrated educational programs fully supported by faculty.

Disciplinary Influences on Curricula

Early theoretical and practical discussions of disciplinary differences have paved the way for recent empirical research. Dressel and Marcus [19] described a discipline as a systematic way of organizing and studying phenomena (p. 86). Building on the earlier work of Phenix [23], they conceptualized disciplinary structures as composed of five components: (1) the substantive component (which includes assumptions, variables, concepts, principles, and relationships); (2) the linguistic component (the symbolism whereby elements can be identified and relationships defined and explored); (3) the syntactical component (the search and organizing process around which the discipline develops); (4) the value component (commitments about what is worth study and how it should be studied); and (5) the conjunctive component (the disciplines' relation to other disciplines). The interaction of these components gives each discipline its distinctive character. Researchers have examined various components of this model and have found important differences in the way disciplines structure knowledge [16, 17], in faculty behaviors and attitudes related to course planning [27, 31], and in cognitive and social patterns that distinguish academicians in different fields [7]. Here we review a few of the more definitive of these studies.

Donald [16] observed that conceptual structures in college courses varied by discipline. Science courses were found to be tightly structured with highly related concepts and principles, whereas social science courses were observed to be more loosely structured, with key concepts acting as organizers, and humanities courses tended to have open structures less dependent upon either organizing strategies or concept interrelatedness. In later studies, Donald [17] discovered that beyond differences in conceptual structures, the disciplines used distinguishable truth and validation strategies to determine the worthiness of new knowledge.

In a series of interview and survey studies of college-level course planning, Stark and a research team [27, 31] found strong correlations among faculty members' background and preparation, the ways they viewed their disciplines, their educational beliefs about the purposes of college, and the influences they believed affected how they planned and sequenced course content. They postulated a model of influences on course planning in which contextual factors in the instructor's specific setting (such as college goals, student characteristics, available services, and student goals) are notably less influential than faculty members' disciplines and educational beliefs.

Through interviews with faculty in both pure and applied fields and reviews of earlier literature, Becher [7] synthesized studies to increase understanding of how the character and structure of knowledge domains influence faculty attitudes and cognitive styles. Noting that some of the more fundamental distinctions are manifested through the medium of language,

Becher adopted (and adapted) the classification system based on organizational strategies and research paradigms developed earlier by Biglan [9, 10] and that based on learning style preferences developed by Kolb [20]. Becher used two of Biglan's classifications—the hard versus soft dimension, which maps disciplines and fields on a continuum according to the degree to which they are paradigmatic,[2] and the pure versus applied dimension, which differentiates fields based on their concern with the application of knowledge. He also utilized the work of Kolb [20], which contrasts preferences for learning in two ways: abstract conceptualization as opposed to experiential learning and active experimentation or detached observation. Becher asserted that the Kolb and Biglan models overlap a great deal, resulting in a model juxtaposing a concrete/applied to hard/pure dimension against a reflective/hard to active/soft dimension.

This appealing synthesis by Becher has caught the attention of academics who have experienced these different ways of thinking in such typical settings as curriculum committees and reform efforts [25]. Combined with earlier studies of disciplinary characteristics, it provides a considerable body of knowledge supporting the thesis of enduring epistemological differences. The research supporting common experience led us to ask if some of these differences would be reflected in the work of disciplinary task forces receiving a common challenge directed at curricular reform.

To examine this question, we attempted to document and describe the approaches the selected disciplines took in answering the AAC challenge. As we will report, we observed disciplinary differences like those suggested by both previous theory and research on faculty views and curricular design.

Methods

We chose content analysis as the method to examine the texts published in *Reports from the Fields*, edited by the AAC in consultation with the individual task forces. Content analysis is a method that utilizes a systematic set of procedures to make valid inferences from text [32]. These inferences may be about the message, its sender(s), or the audience. Although not always scientifically precise, content analysis is useful in establishing relationships and organizing recurring themes or elements, disclosing differences in communication content, auditing content against objectives, identifying intentions and other characteristics of communicators, and revealing the foci of individual, group, institutional, or societal attention [32]. Our purpose in this study was to audit content against objectives.[3]

In this content analysis, we extracted from ten task force reports in *Reports from the Fields* those phrases, sentences, or groups of sentences that reflected the four key components of the AAC challenge as set forth in *Volume 1: Connecting Learning*. These four components—curricular coherence, critical perspective, connected learning, and inclusiveness—were defined in detail by the AAC charge and were intended to guide the discipline task forces in writing their reports. Accordingly, these definitions were the objectives or categories against which the content of the reports were compared. Because we used the condensed reports, we felt it would be overly precise to code each component for intensity based on the amount of space accorded to it, as is often done in content analysis. Instead we coded each new introduction of a component, either its original mention or renewed mention after an intervening discussion of a different category. The frequency count for each component (arranged by field) provided an estimate of the similarities and differences among the reports (see Appendix).

As we will show in the next section, some of the four key components of the AAC charge were composed of subthemes. For example, the concept of connected learning as defined by the AAC refers to five subthemes: (1) constructed relations between various modes of knowledge and experience, (2) relation of academic learning to the larger world, (3) translation of learning beyond the limits of a course or program, (4) synthesis of ideas, principles, and concepts, and (5) testing of the proposals of a field against one's own experience. We coded each subtheme in the content analysis; thus the broader concept of connected learning comprises more than one code. This is true of the other three composite concepts as well.

The coding process involved several steps. First, one coder encoded two reports from *Reports from the Fields* on a trial basis. The trial coding was verified by a second coder specifically concerned with reproducibility (reliability). The few disputed codes were resolved by discussion. The remaining reports were then coded and verified in the same manner. A third coder independently read the reports and differences were again resolved through discussion.

The AAC Challenge: Liberal Learning and Study-in-Depth

The AAC contends that liberal learning fosters distinctive habits of mind or the capacity for "generalizing" and asserts that study-in-depth should also contribute to this broader goal. In this view, the generalizing abilities gained from general education and those gained from the major must be linked. Thus, the major cannot be entirely the "separate responsibilities of several faculties associated with each of the major programs" [4, p. 6]. Rather, structuring the curriculum must be the responsibility of the faculty as a whole "working together to create courses of study that recognize difference, that bring multiple perspectives and cross-disciplinary dialogue to bear on common issues, that allow students opportunities for reflection on both the power and the limitations of their particular communities of inquiry, and that foster the fashioning of connections" [4, p. 6].

While acknowledging that education cannot occur apart from specific content, the AAC argues that it should provide more than coverage of unconnected subjects. The problem, the AAC believes, is not that the major has failed to deliver certain kinds of knowledge, but that it often has delivered knowledge without exposing students to the methods and modes of inquiry that created that knowledge, the presuppositions that inform it, and the consequences of its particular ways of knowing [4]. In dealing with ways to improve this situation, the AAC National Advisory Committee urged the faculty task forces from each major field to address four essential components of curriculum: curricular coherence, critical perspectives, connected learning, and inclusiveness.

Responses from the Fields: Overview of the Content Analysis Results

Twelve fields responded to the challenge set forth by the AAC: biology, economics, history, interdisciplinary studies, mathematics, philosophy, physics, political science, psychology, religion, sociology, and women's studies. We limited our analysis to the ten disciplinary reports,[4] and to facilitate discussion, we grouped them in three fairly traditional categories: (1) natural and physical sciences (biology, mathematics, and physics); (2) social sciences (economics, psychology, political science, and sociology); (3) humanities (history, philosophy, religion). This grouping has two advantages. The first advantage is familiarity: typically in higher education, administrators and curriculum committees work within these groups to accomplish curricular change. The second advantage is that these traditional categories are, for the most part, consistent with the empirically verified typologies developed by Biglan [9, 10] and Kolb [20] and adapted by Becher [7]. The fields in the natural and physical science group would all be classified as hard, pure disciplines according to the Biglan-Kolb-Becher scheme; the social sciences and the humanities would be classed as soft, pure disciplines.

To avoid redundancy, we will describe more fully the AAC rationale for each curriculum component and subtheme prior to presenting the relevant data. In table 27.1, we have provided a synopsis of how the three broad groups responded to each of the four key curriculum components of the AAC challenge, including designated subthemes of the curricular coherence component (coherent design, goals, and sequential learning). Table 27-1 illustrates succinctly and rather dramatically the major finding of our study. We observed substantial variations in the ways the disciplinary groups addressed each component, and these variations were consistent with past research on disciplinary differences. The pattern exhibited by these variations is unequivocal. Fields such as science and mathematics, typically hard and pure fields where a common paradigm is acknowledged, are adept at discussing curricular coherence but find the idea of critical perspectives to be unfamiliar, if not uncomfortable. Fields such as those usually classified as humanities, typically soft, pure fields, show the reverse patterns: helping students develop critical perspectives is their forte, but acceptance of multiple paradigms seems to be associated with reluctance to describe or define coherence, at least as defined by the AAC charge. As expected, the social sciences fall between these

TABLE 27-1
Major Findings of Content Analysis

	Science and Mathematics	*Social Sciences*	*Humanities*
Curricular Coherence Coherent Design	Integration of knowledge and skills readily addressed. Capstone courses and experiences advocated.	Problematic. Content is eclectic, but coherence can be enhanced.	Mixed response from fields. Some objected to or avoided idea. Some attempted to meet challenge.
Goals	Stressed need for local department variation and autonomy.	Need for local department variation and autonomy.	Need for local department variation and autonomy.
Sequential Learning	Possible to sequence. Some fields have natural sequence.	Sequential learning is unfamiliar, but potential.	Objections to prescribed sequences raised.
Critical Perspective	Unfamiliar. Fairly common belief in scientific method as primary perspective.	Addressed in varying ways. Important; diverse approaches acceptable.	Stressed; linked w/ cultural and humanistic sensitivity. Importance of context.
Connecting Learning w/ other fields, life and career	Critical of own efforts to help students connect.	Somewhat more confident that connections are made across disciplines. Few specifics.	Mixed response from fields. Assumed emphasis on connectedness.
Inclusiveness	Should be more open to students w/diverse preparation. Emphasized pedagogy.	Suggested altering content, rather than pedagogy.	Stressed inclusiveness in terms of course content and learning environments.

two extremes, exhibiting some characteristics of sciences and some of humanities.

In the following report we discuss the details that substantiate table 27.1, examining how each field within the broader groups responded to each of the four components of the AAC's challenge. In this discussion, we have emphasized the contrasts and similarities we found in our content analysis rather than provide a detailed description of the data.[5] In some cases, we have used quotations from *Reports from the Fields,* because we believe that the epistemological differences are best displayed and appreciated in the "voices" of those who espouse them.

Results

Curricular Coherence

The charge. The AAC challenged faculty to develop a shared understanding of what study-in-depth in their field should accomplish and to suggest designs for coherent programs of study. The AAC charged the faculty to establish a set of goals for student achievement, design a curriculum that encourages the attainment of these goals, ensure that they are communicated to students and faculty members, and assess the degree to which they are achieved [4, p. 7]. Viewing curricular coherence as the sequential organization of knowledge and techniques, the AAC asserted that the major should have "a beginning, a middle, and an end" each contributing in a different, but specific, way to the overall aim of the major" [4, p. 9]. Faculty must also create a core set of courses that establishes an intellectual agenda for majors: "Courses in this core may need to differ from traditional introductory courses designed to serve general education purposes. This set of core courses should introduce the kinds of questions a field typically asks, explore the ways it undertakes investigations, specify its frames of reference, and expose its disputed issues" [4, p. 9]. The AAC held it to be important that faculty make the structure, organization, and intent of the major clear to students so they understand how a particular course contributes to their total educational experience.

The fields' responses. Each field devoted substantial portions of its report to discussions of curricular coherence. To organize our discussion, we have followed the AAC charge by dividing this element of the challenge into three sections: coherence, goals, and sequential learning.

Coherence. Task forces in the natural and physical sciences had few difficulties determining how to make their study-in-depth programs more coherent. Each field viewed an essential ingredient of coherence to be an emphasis on the repeated integration of knowledge and skills in courses. The biology task force suggested that laboratory methods and processes be used to add curricular cohesion to the major. In mathematics, the task force recommended that topics in major courses include application, problem-solving, and theory components. The physics task force considered a spiral development of teaching increasingly advanced core subjects throughout the program. All the science task forces recommended some form of culminating experience, such as a capstone course, research experience, or thesis.

For the social sciences, coherence was a more problematic idea; the task forces often cited various influences beyond their control as sources of difficulty in achieving it. For example, members of the psychology task force cited increased student heterogeneity, while those on the economics task force criticized textbooks. Focusing on local variations, the political science task force reproved its own colleagues for neglect, noting wide variation in the content of introductory courses in the field. Political scientists characterized the structure of programs beyond the introductory level as "amorphous conceptualizations" [5, p. 135] and questioned whether in-depth study in political science was appropriate given the diversity of the field's conceptualization, organization, and pedagogies.

The other social science fields saw ways to enhance coherence within their respective majors. While the economics task force argued that contextual inquiry (which they defined as courses in economic history, the history of economic thought, comparative economic systems, and area studies) provided sufficient connections, the political science and sociology task forces called for integrating strategies in the form of comprehensive examinations and capstone seminar courses. The psychology task force suggested that thematic clusters of courses be offered to cohorts of students to promote coherence.

The humanities task forces were mixed in their response to the challenge of curricular coherence. The philosophy task force appears to have avoided the issue entirely. The religion task force pointed to the difficulty faculty in this discipline face when trying to integrate the specialities they learned in graduate school. Their solution was to design a major that is progressively more advanced, but they recognized that sequencing could be accomplished in many different ways; capstone courses provided a potential coherence strategy.

The history task force differed from others in the humanities by directly addressing the AAC charge with specific comments.[6] The history task force defined coherence broadly and inclusively. It encouraged faculties to strengthen their programs by engaging students in discussions about the purposes of liberal learning and by leading them to understand how the content and structure of their courses related to these purposes: "History is a discipline in which there is no standard content, no prescribed sequence of courses. The coherence of a history major depends upon the success that student and teachers, working together, achieve in developing clear organizing principles for their work" [5, p. 47]. The history task force recommended using a synthesizing course, integrating subject matter from separate into more comprehensive courses, including a research methods component in all courses, using capstone courses to relate history to other fields, and developing coherent interdisciplinary approaches.

Goals. The task forces from all disciplinary groupings called for autonomy in goal setting. The sciences in particular were reluctant to violate local departmental autonomy by discussing specific goals for a coherent curriculum. The biology task force offered no comments regarding departmental or student goals; the mathematics and physics task forces addressed this issue with varying emphases. Physics enumerated its recommended goals for study-in-depth and suggested that a review process be established to reconsider these regularly. Similarly, the mathematics task force listed curricular goals for the major but softened this by stating that department objectives should match student aspirations, leaving room for debate on how best to achieve objectives.

Like the science task forces, the social science and humanities task forces tended to treat goals as departmental objectives to be articulated locally. The economics task force, however, took a characteristically unique view of goal achievement as it relates to scarce instructional resources, suggesting that rationing of resources must be educationally sound with respect to the major.

Sequential learning. The science task forces treated the charge of sequential learning differently from other disciplinary groups. The mathematics task force provided recommendations regarding possible sequencing but carefully stated that all majors need not take the same sequence of courses. The physics task force saw benefits to sequencing inherent in the field but acknowledged that organizing course work sequentially might work to exclude underrepresented minorities. The biology task force simply noted that course sequences reflect the background, training, and interests of the faculty. In general, the science task forces believed sequencing was a reasonable goal.

Excepting the psychology task force, which viewed its major as generally sequenced, the social sciences task forces perceived sequential learning as an unfamiliar organizing scheme in their fields. They recognized the practical problems encountered by departments that do not sequence their majors and therefore recommended that some sequencing be introduced. In general, however, their discussions seemed to be rhetorical exercises designed to inform faculty of this potential design principle rather than expressions of strong conviction in favor of sequencing.

The humanities task forces, in general, paid little heed to the AAC's challenge to provide sequence for study-in-depth. The history task force simply commented that there is no prescribed sequence in its field. The religion task force merely recommended that advanced courses should evidence increasing student sophistication. And finally, the philosophy task force took an overtly negative view of the concept of sequencing, contending that "it may be inadvisable to shift the burden of creating coherence away from the interaction between philosophy teacher and student in the belief that curricular structure alone suffices for, as opposed to, merely supporting, the desired intellectual ends" [5, p. 105].

Critical Perspective

The charge. As defined by the AAC, the development of critical perspective requires that students become open to criticism, challenge their own views, and become willing to revise what they had assumed was certain. They must actively encounter the limitations of their own learning communities and explore the possibilities beyond them. To achieve these ends, faculty must provide students with sufficient confidence in the discourse of their field so that they may ask sophisticated questions about it. Faculty must take students seriously, engaging their prior knowledge "so that new learning restructures the old, complicating and correcting it rather than merely living side by side with it" [4, p. 13]. As the charge to the task forces elaborates, "It is important for students to know that ideas and methods have origins and histories, that they take place in quite particular times and places. It is important for them to know that ideas represent interests; that ideas are framed by gender, ethnic, social, political, economic, and other cultural and ideological perspectives. It is important for them to know that ideas have power but that power is not always beneficent" [4, p. 13]. To avoid the potential pitfalls of relativism, students must learn how to discriminate between viewpoints and comfortably discern when and for whom an issue or argument is valid; they must learn the difference between simply asserting a position and developing and justifying it. It is the responsibility of the faculty to join disparate crossdisciplinary points of view in order to foster a similar critical perspective in their students. These key points constitute the AAC's guidance to the task forces on critical perspectives.

The fields' responses. Disciplinary differences observed in the case of critical perspective were the inverse of the pattern we described for coherence. Although the science majors had found little difficulty in defining curricular coherence, they had considerable trouble with the challenge of developing critical perspective. The only mention of critical perspective in the biology task force report concerned the desire to instill in students an understanding of science's potential to make contributions to a free society. The mathematics task force spoke of engendering student appreciation for the role of mathematics in ensuring versatility by providing "broad empowerment in the language of our age" [5, p. 94]. Rather than discussing student capabilities, the physics task force examined the capacity of the physics curriculum for fostering critical perspective. It chastized departments for not including information about the history, philosophy, or social implications of physics but included no specific recommendations for amending this oversight.

The social sciences task forces addressed the question of critical perspectives with varying degrees of intensity. The sociology task force defined study-in-depth as a process of intellectual development whereby students become part of the sociological community, a membership that requires the acquisition of a sociological perspective. The political science task force concentrated on the "critical" component of critical perspective, asserting that the goal for study in political science is "to maximize students' capacity to analyze and interpret the dynamics of political events and governmental processes and their significance" ([5] p. 133). Political science students should develop the capacity to understand, evaluate and shape actions and events. The psychology task force offered an expansive conceptualization of critical perspective: "Even at the introductory level, students should be able to inquire about behavioral antecedents and consequences and view with amiable skepticism the explanations and conclusions in popular media reports on psychology and other social sciences. As they advance, psychology students should learn to think critically about themselves, their differences, and their similarities with others; to evaluate their attitudes about people who are different from themselves; and to know how gender, race, ethnicity, culture, and class affect all human perspectives and experiences" [5, p. 158]. The economics task force came closest to the notion of critical perspective as conceived in the AAC charge; its members questioned whether economics students understand the diverse approaches of different economists and the limitations of the prevailing paradigm.

Two themes regarding critical perspectives pervaded the reports of the humanities task forces: the first concerned contextual boundaries, primarily temporal and geographical, of which students must always be aware; the second acknowledged the need for sensitivity, as well as a critical eye, when exploring varying cultural perspectives. Clearly, the idea of critical perspective is a familiar one in the humanities and one that deserved detailed elaboration.

The history task force contended that the study of history incorporates the essential elements of liberal learning, "namely, the acquisition of knowledge and understanding, cultivation of perspective, and development of communication and critical thinking skills; it reflects concern for human values and appreciation of contexts and traditions" [5, p. 44]. Especially important is the knowledge and understanding cultivated through sensitivity to cultural and geographical differences and the awareness of conflicting interpretations of the same events.

Defining the study of religion as the "empathetic study of the other," the religion task force contended that the study of religion in depth is both critical and empathetic: "If criticism is uninformed by an empathetic understanding of the criticized, it chiefly serves to confirm the moral or cultural superiority of the critic. For that, a liberal education is hardly needed. . . . The empathetic understanding grasps the coherence of an alien religious point of view within itself: the student discovers that it makes sense, and the sense it makes enlarges her or his own horizon of human possibility" [5, pp. 175–76]. Through the study of religion, students gain the perspective of knowledge of other times and other places and become aware of the extent to which the world is socially constructed. Like their colleagues in religion, the philosophy task force also stressed the ability to place texts in a wider historical and conceptual context. Philosophy students must be capable of developing their own critiques and must have a knowledge of the history, problems, and methods of the field. Students in advanced classes should be encouraged to reflect on the nature of the discipline itself and on the varied paradigms and methods that challenge one another.

Connecting Learning

The charge. Addressing the concept that gave the challenge to the fields its title, the AAC [4] identified two ways in which the term "connected learning" may be used: "The first refers to the capacity for constructing relationships among various modes of knowledge and curricular experiences, the capacity for applying learning from one context to another. The second refers to the capacity for relating academic learning to the wider world, to public issues and personal experience. In either case, connected learning means generalizing learning: learning that extends beyond the necessary boundaries for any major and takes seriously its potential translation beyond the limits of a course or program" [4, p. 14]. In specifying the first focus, The AAC reasoned that faculty must introduce majors to unsuspected relationships often encountered at the boundaries of a field. In the second focus, the AAC recognized that the major must also allow students to "see and explore the connections between primary issues in the field and their own significant interests and concerns" [4, p. 16]. The curriculum for study-in-depth must encourage students to test assumptions and proposals of their field against their own experiences and help them understand the frames of reference used by those with different experiences.

The field's responses. In their discussions of connected learning, several of the science and social science disciplines were self-critical. Two of the three science reports acknowledged that connected learning is not always evident in their majors. The mathematics task force believed that although connectedness is inherent within mathematics (as "the language of all science"), the design of the mathematics major does not always communicate this connectedness to students. Advanced students who are introduced to a variety of areas will more readily discern the mathematical power of connected ideas and discover unexpected links that offer evidence of a deep, logical unity. This task force recommended that all mathematics students seriously study both the historical context and contemporary impact of mathematics and complete a minor in a discipline that applies mathematics.

The biology task force also criticized the current curriculum for failing to make connections for students: "Many students leave their first and only college course in biology . . . wondering whether there is any connection between the plants and animals of the natural world and what they studied" [5, p. 11]. Arguing that most critical societal problems are interdisciplinary in nature, the task force argued that students must learn to integrate the knowledge, skills, and values of a wide range of intellectual disciplines if they are to help solve these problems.

According to the physics task force, one goal of the physics curriculum should be to help students connect concepts and representations (such as graphs) to objects in the real world and make quantitative models of real-world processes. The task force also opined that the links between physics and mathematics have eroded in recent decades; in their view, dialogue between physics and mathematics faculty should increase.

The social science fields were somewhat more confident that their students were learning to make connections across disciplines, but offered few specifics about how this was accomplished. The sociology task force addressed the concept of connected learning in a circumspect way, by commenting on how the sociological perspective can link students' lives to the external world. In very general recommendations, the task force suggested that departments structure their curricula to recognize and integrate intellectual connections between sociology and other disciplines.

Connected learning, according to the economics task force, involves studying economic arguments that apply to a wide range of problems. The economics group also asserted that good teaching required understanding students' perspectives and orientations, recognizing students' experiences and connecting them with their prior knowledge. The group was uncertain whether students could successfully analyze economic problems encountered in their daily lives after college.

The psychology report expressed similar concerns to those expressed by economics regarding lifelong learning and connectedness. Emphasizing teaching for the transfer of learning, writers contended that psychology majors should be able to recognize and apply concepts and skills in a variety of contexts; looking at relationships, making connections, and struggling with ambiguity: "The critical goal is to help students develop a conceptual framework embracing relevant facts and concepts rather than isolated bits of knowledge, to achieve a base for lifelong learning rather than a static, encyclopedic knowledge of the current state of the field" [5, p. 158]. This task force made few substantive recommendations about relating psychology to other disciplines or relating real world events to student learning.

The political science task force reproved the faculty for offering few incentives for students to integrate disconnected sets of knowledge acquired in their classes. The task force viewed the political science curriculum, particularly at large universities, as capable of presenting students with the opportunity to learn about a wide range of phenomena as well as their own interconnectedness. A capstone course and attention to the role of cognate disciplines were the recommended mechanisms to ensure integration.

To equip student majors for coping with political events and governmental actions, the task force recommended that they experience several kinds of real life political situations off campus (for example, internships, work-study, study abroad, campaign and convention participation). Finally, they recommended that faculty use student evaluations as an integrative tool to help students understand the goals of coherence and interconnectedness.

In the humanities, both the history and the philosophy task forces considered connected learning familiar. Although it did not claim intrinsic connectedness for its field, the philosophy task force stated that "any good philosophy course stresses both "separate" and "connected" knowing, as in drawing distinctions to mark differences and analogies to capture likenesses" [5, p. 102]. The history task force wrote: "History's essence is in the connectedness of historical events and human experiences" [5, p. 43]. Both the history and philosophy task forces considered study in their fields to be additionally enhanced through connections with studies in other disciplines. The philosophy task force specifically stated: "The major should be integrated by patterns of content, by methods of teaching, and by pacing, and externally integrated with the nonphilosophical curriculum by complementary courses in related fields" [5, p. 112]. This integration, the philosophy task force believed, would place philosophy within a coherent vision of the liberal arts.

The history task force recommended that faculties identify and address how to connect research and work in the classroom and how to foster interdisciplinary experiences with the humanities and social sciences. In contrast, the religion task force made few explicit mentions of connected learning. While noting commonalities of religion and other fields in both method and subject matter, the report emphasized instead what distinguishes the religion major from these other fields. For example, the study of foreign language, required by some religion departments, is viewed as a tool for reading original texts rather than as a substantive connection. The religion task force made few references to connecting students' learning to students' experiences, except to note that students' horizons are expanded when they grasp an alien religious point of view.

Inclusiveness

The charge. The AAC asked the faculty to examine obstacles to the participation of underrepresented students within their fields and to work to eliminate those barriers. The AAC contended that faculty commitment to the goals of curricular coherence, critical perspectives, and connected learning provides "an overarching framework through which programs can examine their practices and reach for full participation of all students in arts and sciences fields" [4, p. 17]. By highlighting for students strongly contested topics faculty can open their fields to a broader range of students. By encouraging students to develop critical perspective and to discuss the limits of their fields, faculty may welcome students to their academic home. Specifically, faculty must seriously question the use of introductory courses as gatekeeping devices to exclude students who don't seem to fit traditional expectations and must adjust difficult content to create multiple entry points into the major. The goal of full participation and inquiry is advanced when major programs encourage dialogue that links students' practical and personal concerns with the assumptions and proposals of specific fields.

The fields' responses. All three science task forces agreed that their individual curricula must be more open to students with diverse backgrounds, abilities, and interests. The biology task force, for example, noted that although the abilities and aspirations of today's students had become more varied, biology curricula were highly uniform and had not changed significantly in the past three decades. Similarly, the mathematics task force noted diversity and recommended that the mathematics curriculum be designed for all interested students with appropriate opportunities for average mathematics students and challenges for those who were more advanced. They suggested student tracking as a sensible strategy to respond to the competing interests of students, faculty members, and institutions.

Both the mathematics and physics reports commented on ways pedagogy can address the goal of inclusiveness. The physics task force recognized that a disproportionate number of minority students did not succeed in introductory physics courses that depend upon previously acquired skill in the kind of reasoning needed. Suggesting remedies for the same problem and building on successful existing interventions, the mathematics task force called for a broader spectrum of instructional practice and classroom methods that fit the goals of the major but also provide supportive learning environments. Similarly, biology and physics suggested that role models and mentors play a crucial role for underrepresented students, helping them recognize the sciences as possible careers.

The social sciences task forces recognized barriers to an increasingly diverse student body in their fields and tended to respond with suggestions for altering program content rather than pedagogy, for example, expanding courses dealing with multicultural issues. The sociology task force suggested that instructors recognize and understand the different levels of intellectual development of their students but made no concrete suggestions for dealing with this developmental diversity; the task force did, however, address the issue of diversity in curricular content. Only the economics task force noted that to facilitate learning among a diverse group of students, instructors must explicitly try an array of instructional techniques.

The humanities task forces concentrated their comments on inclusiveness in two areas: course content and learning environments. The history task force argued that the diversity of American society and the growing importance of global interdependence required history faculties to teach the history of other cultures as well as that of the United States and Western civilization. When doing so, the task force urged history departments to provide supportive environments for persons of color and nontraditional students.

The philosophy task force recommended that faculty interact with such students individually to develop a learning community that may attract students from underrepresented groups. The religion task force failed to address the issue of student diversity but noted that multicultural commitments of religion departments have long required studies in more than one tradition.

A recognition of the issues of inclusiveness and self-criticism for not fully addressing them dominates the task force reports with respect to this concept. The paucity of specific suggestions and the lower degree of intensity in the discussions may indicate that this issue is seen as less central to curricular change in the majors than the others.

Summary

The patterns of response to the AAC challenges we describe here are consistent with knowledge about disciplinary differences. They are also consistent with recent research describing different knowledge structures used in college courses [16] and how these structures influence choices faculty members make as they plan and teach courses [31]. The differences we observed in the task force reports were not limited to commonly recognized substantive and linguistic differences among disciplines. Rather, the task force responses highlight the syntactical, value, and conjunctive differences described by theorists but seldom included in curriculum discussions. Here we will summarize how the patterns unearthed in the reports confirm knowledge about disciplinary differences and will extend the application of this knowledge to curriculum development.

Curricular coherence. The syntactical dimension of a discipline is concerned with methods of seeking, acquiring, and organizing new knowledge. Characteristically "hard" fields such as mathematics and sciences grow by accretion [7]. When scholars build a knowledge base systematically, they find curricular coherence easy to describe; the student is helped to place building blocks of the discipline, one upon another, until some prescribed level of understanding is reached. The softer fields acquire knowledge more often by recursive patterns of research than by systematic accretion. These iterative research strategies use multiple perspectives and pursue knowledge in several directions simultaneously, leaving room for curricular diversity. Accordingly, the nature of coherence in the social science and humanities major is quite different than for the hard sciences. The AAC challenge regarding coherence was more attainable for the sciences, which view the major as inherently having "a beginning, a middle and an end," but posed difficulties for faculty in softer fields. Faculty in the humanities and most social science fields did not easily agree on definitions of coherence or that specified sequences of learning content were appropriate for students.

Critical perspective. The value dimension of a discipline, that is, scholars' judgments about what is worth studying and how it should be studied, links with the syntactical dimension to define the validation criteria used to determine the authenticity of knowledge claims. In hard disciplines, validation criteria are clearly established, whereas in soft fields there is less consensus about what constitutes an authentic claim. As Becher noted, causal connections are easier to make in the natural and physical sciences, while judgment and persuasion play a stronger role in complex reasoning about data regarding human and social phenomena [7, p. 14]. Donald substantiated that these differences in validation criteria are observed when content is taught in college classrooms [17].

These studies help explain the cursory attention to critical perspective found in the science task force reports, compared to the explicit and sometimes expansive treatment accorded it by the humanities and social science groups. In the hard disciplines, the quantifiable nature of the phenomena under study, highly developed methods of inquiry, and general agreement on validation criteria render the need for critical perspective less essential. In contrast to its description of coherence, the AAC definition of critical perspective viewed knowledge as contextual and concerned with human experience, rather than absolute. This focus is familiar to faculty members in the humanities and social sciences and is congruent with the strong emphasis they place on fostering the intellectual and personal development of students [28]. In fact, whereas the concept of coherence focuses attention on the structure of the discipline, course, and program, the notion of critical perspective focuses attention on developing student capabilities. The sciences generally seek to enhance students' intellectual growth by developing their capacity to use an accepted scientific perspective; social science and humanities faculty hope to encourage development by inviting students to debate perspectives.

Connecting learning. The component of the AAC challenge to connect learning in the major to other disciplines, to students' lives, and to social problems highlights the "conjunctive" dimension of the disciplines. The humanities task forces responded to this challenge eagerly, stressing the need for cross-fertilization among disciplines and illustrating how their permeable boundaries can promote it. The social science faculty were less explicit about connections among disciplines but mentioned numerous opportunities for connecting students' learning to the external world through the reciprocal relationship with society that characterizes their fields. In contrast, most of the science task force reports left specific links to both other disciplines and social problems underdeveloped.

Because previous research provides less guidance in interpreting patterns of response to this challenge, our commentary is somewhat speculative. Both the humanities and social science task forces were able to interpret comfortably the challenge of connectedness; for the sciences, however, connectedness appeared unimportant or unreasonable. In the sciences, the important connections may be those among the principles and concepts within the fields themselves, classified by the AAC under the challenge of coherence rather than the rubric of connected learning. Such connections, as the mathematics task force indicated, abound within the hard disciplines but are not always apparent to undergraduates. Becher [6, p. 282] suggests that faculty in the pure, hard knowledge areas believe connections with other fields occur much later; only students who have pursued advanced study, mastered a hierarchically structured knowledge base, and understand how scientific phenomena are interrelated are ready to link these phenomena with the social world. In this view, scientific contributions to social problems are made by career scientists, not novices.

Inclusiveness. Despite the AAC's intricate reasoning about how the goal of inclusiveness relates to and enhances the other three goals, this challenge seemed motivated more by a sense of social justice than by pedagogical concerns. Its relations to previous research on disciplinary differences is also less clear; arguably, the challenge would be more readily answered by the humanities and social sciences, which focus on the human condition and are more student-centered [14]. These soft fields readily accepted the challenge, often speaking eloquently about current efforts, but spent little time grappling with new ways to implement it. Rather, it was the hard fields that struggled to address this challenge, perhaps because they are the fields most harshly criticized in this respect.

Traditionally, the doors of hierarchical fields close early to students who have not followed the established sequence of prior preparation, which often begins in high school. Although the science task forces addressed the charge of inclusiveness self-critically, recognizing the barriers that rigid sequencing presents to participation, they nevertheless suggested remedies (like tracking) that might exacerbate the problem. An admission of culpability by the task forces, it appears, is not sufficient motivation to overcome inherent disciplinary characteristics.

Discussion

The differing orientations toward knowledge among the disciplines that we identified in our analysis of *Reports from the Fields* have been previously discussed in the literature. Thus, some may see them as stereotypes rather than as pervasive and enduring characteristics. Typically, these orientations have been explored with regard to their influence on faculty careers and research behaviors as in Becher's analysis [7], or with regard to their organizational implications as in work by Biglan and others [9, 10, 13, 15, 24, 25]. Recently, the curriculum reform movement has stimulated more studies of how disciplinary variations affect course planning [28, 29, 31], course content [16], and development of students' thinking processes [18]. Thus far the results consistently show that disciplinary training and beliefs affect the emphasis faculty give to pedagogy as well as content. Based on these consistent findings, current theoretical models would be enhanced by including a pedagogical dimension to convey the scholar/ teachers in various disciplines differ in the way they translate their discipline's tenets into educational purposes and processes.

Our analysis shows that debate about commonality goes beyond the frequently contested issue of a common core of content; an equally contentious question is whether there should be a common view of teaching and learning. The AAC suggests that curricula can be arranged and sequenced to encourage the development of critical perspective, coherence, and connectedness. This may be an attractive prospect to many in higher education, but our findings prompt us to ask to what extent all three aspects of the AAC charge can be seriously accepted and seriously met by faculty in different fields. The *Reports from the Fields* do not unanimously support the recommended changes, suggesting that the challenge represents too ambitious a goal. The ability of the disciplines to accommodate simultaneously critical perspective, coherence, and connectedness within their vision of study-in-depth appears variable.

Although we did not begin our investigation intending to question the AAC charge, we now wonder if the task posed is feasible. We assume that the task forces, composed of teaching scholars from diverse institutions, responded in good faith to the AAC charge. If some responses appear to those outside a discipline to be self-serving, we believe that it is because epistemological mantles cannot be readily exchanged among disparate disciplines. Lacking any evidence to the contrary, we believe that the task forces grappled with the challenge in distinctive ways based on their disciplinary perspectives.

Because most critics agree that substantial changes are needed to improve undergraduate education, we suggest that curricular reform advocates focus on how each discipline can help students develop those attributes it most readily fosters. For example, curriculum planners might look to mathematics and physics for coherence, to philosophy for critical perspective, and to the social sciences for the connections among disciplinary knowledge and the "real world." To observers this recommendation may either make a strong case for distribution requirements, or alternatively, for interdisciplinarity. Those who argue that the major is, by definition, incompatible with liberal undergraduate education may prefer the latter option. A carefully developed interdisciplinary program may offer an attractive and practical solution for undergraduate study. Appropriate interdisciplinary concentrations could range from uniquely designed thematic fields to combinations of two or more disciplines. The essential requirement would be that a program be deliberately designed to incorporate all of the key dimensions of the AAC charge.

Some might argue that some of the preprofessional and nontraditional undergraduate fields have already achieved this goal. Faculty in women's studies and the interdisciplinary fields assert that successful responses to all these challenges are inherent in their fields.[7] Career-related fields are also inherently interdisciplinary and connected with societal or world problems. Still, few observers believe that the preprofessional fields have achieved their full potential with

APPENDIX
Frequency Counts for Individual Codes by Discipline

	Challenge of Connecting Learning	*Biology*	*Mathe-matics*	*Physics*	*Economics*	*Political Science*	*Psychology*	*Sociology*	*History*	*Philosophy*	*Religion*
Curricular Coherence											
Coherence mechanism	11	6	7	13	5	7	3	16	15		3
Goals/objectives	19	0	15	4	10	13	12	16	4	8	5
Sequential learning	7	2	8	6	7	7	2	17	5	9	5
Connecting Learning											
Connecting Learning	21	8	12	2	8	6	8		7	12	
Relation to external world	15	6	12	4	17	11	4	11	6	14	5
Related fields	10	4	11	11	7	19	2	7	9	17	6
Critical Perspective											
Critical perspectives	14	1	2	1	6	3	2	4	6	7	9
Limitations of field	7	1			5	3	1	1	1	2	
Inclusiveness											
Cultural diversity of students	5	3	4	6		2	4	1	2	3	
Student types/ characteristics	14	5	13	9	7	4	5	12	6	7	1

respect to coherence and critical perspective. Proposals that recommend integrating career and liberal arts perspectives [27] and an enriched major [11] might develop these dimensions more fully. These proposals may represent a more encompassing and potentially more productive, challenge to the faculty.

Notes

1. The condensed reports were used because full reports could not be obtained from all the disciplinary associations.
2. This dimension closely resembles the definition of a paradigm articulated by Thomas Kuhn [21] in *The Structure of Scientific Revolutions.* According to Kuhn, the maturity of a field is based on the existence of one or more paradigms and the nature of these paradigms. Paradigms in mature disciplines and fields provide investigators or practitioners with the tools and techniques to study difficult problems with a greater guarantee of success because methods and clues are supplied as part of the problem.
3. We have also conducted an analysis of the reports by identifying those themes and categories which were not part of the charge given by the AAC but which emerged from the task forces' separate efforts. The results of this analysis, revealing the focus of group attention, is forthcoming.
4. Although two interdisciplinary fields, interdisciplinary studies and women's studies, were included, both are soft, pure disciplines based on their parent disciplines. Other interdisciplinary programs could be descended from the hard, pure disciplines and be classified accordingly. Because the AAC did not include a full balance of soft and hard interdisciplinary programs among its working groups, we decided not to include the interdisciplinary fields in our analysis.
5. Readers interested in the specific codes used in the content analysis and the patterns of response for various disciplines should examine the Appendix.
6. Interestingly, although history is typically considered a soft, pure field, Becher noted that in some ways it resembles hard, pure fields like physics. This is especially true in the field's emphasis on participation in a scholarly community where there is a sense of sharing a definable world and common assumptions of style and thought. See Becher [7], pp. 155-56.
7. Based on content analysis of the task force reports of these fields not included in this article.

References

1. American Association of State Colleges and Universities. *To Secure the Blessings of Liberty.* Washington, D.C.: AASCU, 1986.
2. Association of American Colleges. *Integrity in the College Curriculum: A Report.* Washington, D.C.: Association of American Colleges, 1985.
3. _____. *A New Vitality in General Education.* Washington, D.C.: Association of American Colleges, 1988.
4. _____. *Liberal Learning and the Arts and Sciences Major: The Challenge of Connecting Learning, (Volume 1).* Washington, D.C.: Association of American Colleges, 1991.
5. _____.*Liberal Learning and the Arts and Sciences Major: Reports from the Fields (Volume 2).* Washington, D.C.: Association of American Colleges, 1991.
6. Becher, T. "The Disciplinary Shaping of the Profession." In *The Academic Profession: National, Disciplinary and Institutional Settings,* edited by B. Clark, pp. 271–303. Berkeley: University of California Press, 1987.
7. _____. *Academic Tribes and Territories: Intellectual Enquiry and the Cultures of Disciplines.* Bristol, Pa.: The Society for Research into Higher Education and Open University Press, 1989.
8. Bennett, W. *To Reclaim a Legacy.* Washington, D.C.: National Endowment for the Humanities, 1984.
9. Biglan, A. "The Characteristics of Subject Matter in Different Scientific Areas. *Journal of Applied Psychology,* 57 (1973), 195–203.
10. _____. "Relationships between Subject Matter Characteristics and the Structure and Output of University Departments." *Journal of Applied Psychology,* 57 (1973), 204–13.
11. Boyer, E. *College: The Undergraduate Experience in America.* New York: Harper & Row, 1987.
12. Cheney, L. V. *50 Hours: A Core Curriculum for College Students.* Washington, D.C.: National Endowment for the Humanities, 1989.
13. Creswell, J. W., and J. Bean. "Research Output, Socialization, and the Biglan Model." *Research in Higher Education,* 15 (1981), 69–91.
14. Creswell, J. W., and R. W. Roskens. "The Biglan Studies of Differences among Academic Areas." *Review of Higher Education,* 4 (1981), 1–16.
15. Creswell, J., A. Seagren, and T. Henry. "Professional Development Training Needs of Department Chairpersons: A Test of the Biglan

Model." *Planning and Changing*, 10 (1981), 224–37.

16. Donald, J. G. "Knowledge Structures: Methods for Exploring Course Content." *Journal of Higher Education*, 54 (January/ February 1983), 31–41.
17. _____. "University Professors' Views of Knowledge and Validation Processes." *Journal of Educational Psychology*, 82 (1990), 242–49.
18. _____. "The Development of Thinking Processes in Postsecondary Education: Application of a Working Model." *Higher Education*, 24 (1992), 413–30.
19. Dressel P., and D. Marcus. *Teaching and Learning in College*. San Francisco: Jossey-Bass, 1982.
20. Kolb, D. A. "Learning Styles and Disciplinary Differences." In *The Modern American College*, edited by A. Chickering. San Francisco: Jossey-Bass, 1981.
21. Kuhn, T. S. *The Structure of Scientific Revolutions*. Second Edition, Enlarged. Chicago: The University of Chicago Press, 1970.
22. National Institute of Education. *Involvement in Learning: Realizing the Potential of American Higher Education*. Report of the NIE Study Group on the Condition of Excellence in American Higher Education. U.S. Government Printing Office, 1984.
23. Phenix, P. H. *Realms of Meaning: A Philosophy of the Curriculum for General Education*. New York: McGraw Hill, 1964.
24. Smart, J., and C. Elton. "Goal Orientations of Academic Departments: A Test of Biglan's model." *Journal of Applied Psychology*, 60 (1975), 580–88.
25. ——. "Administrative Roles of Department Chairmen." In *Examining Departmental Management*, edited by J. Smart and J. Montgomery, pp. 39–60. New Directions for Institutional Research. San Francisco: Jossey-Bass, 1976.
26. Stark, J. S. "Seeking Coherence in the Curriculum." In *Improving Undergraduate Education in Large Universities*, edited by C. H. Pazandak, pp. 65–76. New Directions for Higher Education, no. 66. San Francisco: Jossey-Bass, 1989.
27. Stark, J. S., and M. A. Lowther. *Strengthening the Ties That Bind: Integrating Undergraduate Liberal Professional Study*. Ann Arbor: CSHPE, 1988.
28. Stark, J. S., and K. S. Shaw. *Do College Faculty Report Different Influences When Planning Introductory and Advanced Courses?* Ann Arbor, Mich.: NCRIPTAL, circa 1991.
29. Stark, J. S., et al. *Planning Introductory College Courses: Influences of Faculty*. Ann Arbor, Mich.: NCRIPTAL, 1990.
30. Stark, J. S., and B. Morstain. "Educational Orientations of Faculty in Liberal Arts Colleges." *Journal of Higher Education*, 49 (1978), 420–37.
31. Stark, J. S., et al. *Reflections on Course Planning: Faculty and Students Consider Influences and Goals*. Ann Arbor, Mich.: NCRIPTAL, 1988.
32. Weber, R. P. *Basic Content Analysis*. Beverly Hills, Calif.: Sage Publications, 1985.

CHAPTER 28

WHAT DOES IT TAKE TO LEARN?

FERENCE MARTON AND SHIRLEY BOOTH

One thing that people have in common is that they are all different. This disturbing sentence—whether considered conceptually or grammatically—boils down to this: People may be created equal, but they do things differently. There are other ways of putting it—for any one of the things people do, some do it better, others do it worse. To the extent they have learned to do that one thing, they must have learned *to do it differently—some better, some worse.* Rather, they have *learned differently—some better, some worse—to do it.* This is the starting point for our book: If one way of doing something can be judged to be better than another way, then some people must have been better at learning to do it—or have learned to do it better—than others.

Now, if we take that as our starting point, can we reasonably hope that by *finding out* what it takes to learn something we can make people dramatically better at learning it or make them learn it dramatically better? In the rest of this book, argue that it is, and point the way to revealing what it takes to learn the multiplicity of things we are expected to learn.

Inasmuch as we can learn different *sorts of things,* the notion of "what it takes to learn" has to be expressed in different forms. The question "What does it take to learn to do something?" is one form, "How do we gain knowledge about the world?" is another. The latter is the question we are going to address explicitly in this chapter. An answer would empower people to gain knowledge, as well as deeper knowledge, about the world, and it is to develop just such an answer, and just such an empowerment that is our goal in writing this book.

How Do We Gain Knowledge About the World? A Story of Paradoxes

"How do we gain knowledge about the world?" can be seen as the epistemological form of the question "What does it take to learn?" Epistemology has to do with the question of gaining knowledge but also with the question of the truth value of the knowledge gained, as, indeed, does education. We are living in an age of relativism, but a fundamental principle we are assuming in this book is that education has norms—norms of what those undergoing education should be learning, and what the outcomes of their learning should be.

Paradox the First: Meno's Paradox

We find the most famous formulation of the question "How do we gain knowledge about the world?" in one of Plato's early dialogues, written in 403 or 402 BC, when the author was in his mid-20s,

Source: "What Does It Take to Learn?" by Ference Marton and Shirley Booth, reprinted from Learning and Awareness, 1997, Lawrence Erlbaum Associates, Inc.

some 3 or 4 years before Socrates calmly drank the cup of poison administered as punishment for his dangerous ideas (Day, 1994, p. 8). The dialogue was between Socrates and Meno, a young Thessalonian visiting Athens, and started with Meno posing the question: "Can one be taught virtue?" Socrates replied that he did not even know what virtue is, and he argued that neither did Meno. Socrates suggested that they embark upon a search for an answer together, but Meno puts forward an objection that has become known as Meno's paradox: "How can you search for something when you do not know what it is? You do not know what to look for, and if you were to come across it you would not recognize it as what you are looking for." Socrates agreed with this objection, and elaborated:

> It's impossible for a person to search either for what he knows or what he doesn't. . . . He couldn't search for what he knows, for he knows it and no one in that condition needs to search; on the other hand he couldn't search for what he doesn't know, for he won't even know what to search for. (Day, 1994, p. 47)

The surprising answer of Plato—or Socrates—to the question "How do we gain knowledge about the world?" is that we *cannot* gain knowledge about the world. Learning is impossible. The paradox lies in the observation that we certainly do learn!

There is an obvious counterargument to this line of reasoning: Meno's paradox may be valid as far as *searching* for knowledge is concerned, but surely we can learn by being *told?* However, Plato had already ruled out this solution in an earlier dialogue with Protagoras on the grounds that if you do not already know a teacher's assertion when you are told it, then you cannot decide whether it is true or false. Moreover, it is impossible to choose a teacher who knows, on the same grounds as the impossibility of finding knowledge by oneself (Day, 1994, p. 26).

Plato—again using Socrates as mouthpiece—suggested another solution to the apparent paradox, his theory of recollection, which has it that the human soul is immortal even if the human body is not. The soul is reembodied again and again, going repeatedly from one life to the next. All knowledge is laid down in the soul prior to the series of lives. It is then forgotten by its current vessel but is there to be recollected. Learning is such a recollection. Knowledge thus does not originate from the world or, from the outside, but from the immortal soul or, from within. In the course of his dialogue with Meno, Socrates wished to demonstrate that knowledge is innate and called in a young slave boy who was able to count but was ignorant of geometry. Socrates gave him a geometrical problem: to find the length of a side of a square, the area of which is twice the area of a given square. The boy's first answer was wrong, but Socrates managed to act as midwife and draw forth the answer by putting questions that repeatedly showed the inherent contradictions in the boy's way of reasoning. Socrates' method amounts to breaking the problem down into component parts and prompting answers to each part separately, an instance of his famous midwifing, or maieutic, pedagogical method resembling the teaching strategy that in modern educational research has been called *piloting* (Johansson, 1975; Lundgren, 1977). By doing so he claimed to have shown that the knowledge necessary to solve the problem was there in the boy's soul from the beginning, a remnant from some previous embodiment, because the boy did not previously know any geometry.

On hearing what Socrates did we are tempted to rebuff his claim that knowledge comes from within. He did, after all, ask questions, show diagrams, and firmly guide the boy's thinking. But he did not hand over the answers; the boy had to arrive at them using his powers of reason, and in that sense one could argue that knowledge may indeed be gained from within oneself (Day, 1994, p. 23). This does not imply, however, that Socrates presented strong support for the theory of recollection and that he had solved Meno's paradox. As White (1994) convincingly showed, the theory of recollection gives rise to a paradox that is a mirror image of Meno's paradox, which it was supposed to solve. Just as you cannot search for knowledge in the world outside, you cannot recollect knowledge from within. That which is already recollected you do not need to recollect; and that which is not recollected you cannot recollect because you do not know what you are trying to recollect. Indeed, if you were to come upon it, you would not know that it is what you want to recollect.

Thus Plato did not solve the paradox he had formulated. Nor did anyone else (for some fairly recent and less than convincing attempts from the field of education see Bereiter, 1985; Halldén, 1994; Petrie, 1981; Steffe, 1991).

Paradox Avoided: Behavioral Psychology

Some 23 centuries after Plato formulated the paradox of learning—Meno's paradox—learning became an object of research in psychology. Let us take, for example, the pioneering work of Herman Ebbinghaus. His aim was to study memory in a "pure" form—"pure" in the sense of being free from meaningful associations; but in order to study memory it was necessary for someone to learn the stuff that would have to be remembered later. Ebbinghaus prepared lists of pairs of meaningless syllables, and submitting himself to the task of being his own experimental subject, he learned to answer with one of the syllables in a pair when the other was given. His main interest was to find out the extent to which he would be able to recall the missing syllables after different intervals of time. This study was published in 1885 (Ebbinghaus, 1885/1964) and can be viewed in part as a study of learning, or at least of one form of learning—becoming increasingly able to recall something as a function of practice—but nobody would claim that Ebbinghaus had studied how we gain knowledge about the world.

Ivan Pavlov, the Russian Nobel laureate in Medicine in 1904, discovered and studied quite another form of learning (Pavlov, 1927). An organism has a repertoire of innate reflexes: Certain stimuli trigger off certain responses. A toddler starts at a sudden sharp sound; one's pupils dilate when a bright light is shone on them; a hungry mammal salivates more when exposed to the smell or sight of food. Concerning such reactions we talk of unconditioned stimuli resulting in unconditioned responses. What Pavlov found was that if another stimulus is repeatedly presented shortly before the unconditioned stimulus, then eventually a reaction very similar to the unconditioned response will be triggered off by this introduced stimulus. For example, a hungry dog salivates more (unconditioned response) when shown food (unconditioned stimulus). If its keeper repeatedly rings a bell before revealing the food, then increased salivation will eventually be brought about by the sound of the bell alone. The sound of the bell is called a conditioned stimulus, and now the salivation is a conditioned response, being brought about, not by natural reflex, but solely by the sound of the bell.

The father of *behaviorism,* John Watson, applied the same principle in a famous study in which he caused a toddler, Albert, to develop a fear of furry animals (Watson, 1924). When Albert heard a loud noise he reacted naturally with fear: The sound was the unconditioned stimulus that brought about the unconditioned response of fear. Now Watson exposed Albert to a loud noise each time he caught sight of a small furry rabbit: The sight of the rabbit became a conditioned stimulus that triggered off a conditioned response of fear. Albert learned fear of the rabbit, which later become generalized to a fear of any furry animals at all. In our search for illumination, *classical conditioning,* as this form of learning is called, offers no solution at all, because it has nothing at all to do with gaining knowledge about the world; what it does deal with is the transposition of physiological reactions from the stimuli to which they have a built-in response to stimuli that can acquire a conditioned response. Even if the set of stimuli to which reactions can be conditioned is unlimited, what can be learned through classical conditioning is limited to reactions that naturally appear as reflexes.

The American psychologist Burrhus F. Skinner studied learning in the sense of the extent to which a certain behavior appeared as a function of what had followed that behavior in the past (Skinner, 1953). If we think of some sort of organism with a set of behaviors, then Skinner's basic principle can be expressed simply enough: A particular behavior is more likely to appear if its appearance is followed by *reinforcement,* a consequence that is desirable from the organism's point of view. For example, if you have a hungry rat in a box and each time it presses a lever a pellet of food emerges, the likelihood of the rat pressing the lever again will increase because the food is a desirable consequence. If pressing the lever were to be followed by an adverse consequence, a punishment, such as an electric shock from the floor of the box, the rat would be less likely to press the lever again. Such *contingency,* or behavior being related to consequence, can be varied endlessly. If we want to eliminate a certain behavior, we can either punish that behavior or reward another incompatible behavior (and we would probably find that the latter is more efficient). The kind of learning Skinner studied is called *operant conditioning* and deals with how the individual is conditioned by reinforcement and punishment to operate on its environment. Maybe we should not call it a *kind* of learning, but an *aspect* of learning, potentially present in each and every instance of learning. Unlike Pavlov's classical conditioning it is not limited by unconditioned stimulus and response patterns to a finite set of behaviors; it is restricted only by what can be used as reinforcement and punishment.

Operant conditioning can possibly account for the fact *that* someone is doing something. The behavior in question has been directly or indirectly related to reinforcement in the past, whereas alternative behavior has been related to punishment. But even if it can suggest an explanation for the fact *that* someone is doing something, it hardly enables us to make sense of *what* she is doing or *how* she is doing it without reference to the *content* (as opposed to the reinforcing or punishing effect) of her previous experiences. We can try to account for the fact that someone is interested in mathematics in terms of her history of reinforcement, but we can understand her ingenious way of solving, say, differential equations only if we happen to know about her previous experience of mathematics (e.g., that she had studied in the former USSR, for instance, where calculus was taught differently than in Scandinavia). To take another example, what sense can we make of an immigrant to Sweden speaking Swedish with a heavy accent? We might be able to account for his willingness to learn and speak Swedish in terms of his history of reinforcement and even punishment. But to understand the nature of his accent and the grammatical errors he is making we would need to know something of the sound structure of his mother tongue, which interferes with his Swedish, and thus yields a characteristic pattern of deviation from Swedish as it is used by native speakers.

Surprising though it may appear, Skinner was not at all sensitive to the distinction between the reinforcing (or punishing) potential of experiences, on the one hand, and the content and structure of experiences on the other. The former has possible implications for whether or not, or to what extent, people do some particular thing, whereas the latter must betaken into account in order to understand *how* they do what they do. Skinner overgeneralized operant conditioning far beyond the limits of its explanatory power when, for one thing, he sought to account for learning language. He attempted to explain not only that which he possibly could explain but also that which he could not possibly explain.

Paradox the Second: Meno's Mirror

It was largely a result of this overextension that Skinner's entire research program—not only that which was wrong but also that which was right—was in time rejected by a majority of the scientific community. The most devastating criticism of Skinnerian psychology was delivered by the linguist, Noam Chomsky, in his review of Skinner's account of how children learn their mother tongue (Chomsky, 1959). His critique of Skinner's *Verbal Behavior* (Skinner, 1957) has a familiar Platonian ring to it. The main argument is that a grammar cannot be derived from data provided by the environment because the data are simply not always adequate; despite the great variation in richness of the linguistic environment they experience, children nevertheless learn their language. Chomsky concluded that the disposition for a universal grammar, of which the different grammars as realized are a subset, must therefore be innate. But, one ventures to ask, how can a particular grammar be carved out of that preformed, innate, universal grammar when the only tools come from the inadequate data supplied by the environment? Just as Plato's proposed solution to the search for virtue, Chomsky's proposed solution to the problem of learning language runs into a paradox, which this time can be thought of as the mirror image of Meno's paradox: How can that which is innate be formed according to local demands?

The fundamental idea of behaviorism is that it is precisely *behavior* that is the proper subject matter of psychology and related fields. In line with good scientific practice we should stick to that which is observable. This is something that Skinner, Watson, Pavlov, and even Ebbinghaus, whose work predated the behaviorist movement, had in common. With regard to learning it means that change in behavior is studied as a function of practice, contingency of unconditioned and conditioned stimuli, or schedules of reinforcement. Behaviorists studying learning have never encountered Meno's paradox or its mirror image for the very simple reason that they do not ask themselves the question, "How do we gain knowledge about the world?" In fact, they don't even think it is a very good question to ask.

Paradox the Third: Individual Constructivism

Nevertheless, it was just this question that Jean Piaget devoted his long scientific career to exploring. (His first scientific publication appeared when he was 11 years of age in 1907, and the English translation of his last book was printed only in this decade (Piaget & Garcia, 1991). Piaget has never been considered primarily a student of learning, whether by others or himself. Because his main interest was the development of human knowledge, he labeled his field genetic epistemology. For Piaget's sake, then, we perhaps should recast the question "How do we gain knowledge about the world?" as "How do we *develop* knowledge about the world?" But if one is interested in *learning* as gaining knowledge through experience—as we certainly are—and if one is interested in *development* as gaining knowledge through experience as well—as we also are—the distinction between the two is rather slight (Marton & Säljö, 1976c).

Piaget was a *constructivist.* He did not assume that knowledge exists "out there," ready made, and that we somehow "take it in" from the environment, as the empiricists assumed, nor did he assume that knowledge is fundamentally innate as Plato and Chomsky did. According to Piaget, knowledge is constructed by the individual through her acts, through her interaction with the environment, by means of the complementary adaptive mechanisms of accommodation (in which the individual adjusts to the environment) and assimilation (in which the environment is adjusted to suit the individual). In this process progressively more advanced levels of knowledge evolve.

Several questions arise from this view, one of which concerns the locus of development. What gives development its direction? On what grounds can one level of knowledge be replaced by another, more advanced level of knowledge? How can someone select or choose or adopt a more advanced level while still at a less advanced level? This is exactly in line with Meno's paradox: How can we search for (or select) knowledge which we do not yet have? In this case knowledge is supposed to exist within the individual, as in Plato's "solution," but unlike Plato's "solution," it is not present to begin with. Thus the paradox we encounter here is the one we have already identified with Chomsky's solution to language acquisition, which we called the mirror image of Meno's paradox.

A second question has to do with the idea of the individual constructing her world. Because the world as such, the world of Kantian "noumea" (things themselves), is beyond her reach, she is bound in her own subjective, constructed world. Moreover, this world being an individual construction, there is an implication that humans live in their own personal and differing worlds. Where are these worlds and of what do they consist? Or to put our question again: What is the ontological status of the individual's constructed world and the individually constructed worlds? In what sense do they exist at all?

Are these private worlds, isolated solipsistic constructions of individual minds, all that there is? Von Glasersfeld (1990) explained that this is not the case:

> [Constructivism] treats both our knowledge of the environment and of the items to which our linguistic expressions refer as subjective constructs of the cognizing agent. This is frequently but quite erroneously interpreted as a denial of a mind-independent ontological reality, but even the most radical form of constructivism does not deny that kind of independent reality. (p. 37)

Thus, there is an independent reality to weigh in with the individual constructions. Now questions flow: What is it like? Does it exist in a certain way, a way beyond all individual constructions, beyond all descriptions? Is it a material reality of particles? Is the independent world a world of things, plants, animals, humans? Now here is the crux: Is it a world with or without meaning? An independent world with meaning implies someone for whom the meaning is there, "meaners." Then can we individuals, "meaners" all, even think of a world devoid of meaning? The very attempt defies its object, so if this independent world is devoid of meaning, we cannot contemplate it at all, and if it is not devoid of meaning, then it cannot be separate from us, the "meaners."

This brings us to another problem implied by the individual constructivist[1] view. It is held that on the one hand there is an individually constructed world and on the other a real world divorced from this individually constructed world, and that the constructing occurs through interaction between the individual and the environment. Our question is this: How can the individual interact with something she can never reach? Von Glasersfeld suggested that the environment appears in the interaction with the individual in the form of constraints, rather like someone moving around in a dark room: Occasionally she hits a wall and backs away (von Glasersfeld, 1990, p. 33). He likens her movements in the room to the acts of construction; the walls are constraints imposed on her acts by the environment, the world. But, we ask, what is the ontological status of the constraints? Are not even these constructed? The picture changes to one of the individual banging her head against walls she has built herself.

This attempt to pursue the logical consequences of the ontological position underlying the individual constructivist view has led us, somewhat unexpectedly, to the Platonian stand on the epistemological question of learning: We cannot gain knowledge about the world *from* the world, and as individual constructivism does not make the Platonian assumption about the recollection of knowledge, this adds yet a third paradox to Meno's original paradox and to its mirror image from which both the Platonian and the individual constructivist "solutions" suffer. We are left asking, if knowledge is not innate and if it does not come from the world, where does it come from?

Paradoxes Four, Five, and Six: The Cognitive Present

At the risk of oversimplifying things greatly, we can point to two main traditions of answering the question, "How do we gain knowledge about the world?" One set of answers has it that knowledge comes from within, from the powers of mind. This is the rationalist tradition of Plato, Descartes, Kant, Piaget, and Chomsky (whose answers certainly differ in other respects). The other set of answers, also differing in other respects, claim that knowledge comes from the outside, from the world around us. This is the empiricist tradition of Bacon and Locke.

As we pointed out, the epistemological question and the very notion of knowledge was alien to the perspective of behaviorism, which heavily dominated the study of learning in the United States during the first half of this century and a bit beyond. Moreover, throughout the century, it was the United States that dominated the international research community engaged in the study of learning.

In the late 1950s what has been referred to as "the cognitive revolution" occurred, embracing strains of both rationalism and empiricism. Questions about the nature, acquisition, and application of knowledge became central to psychology and related fields, with the emergence of computers contributing strongly. The computer became the new metaphor for the mind, and a new research specialization, cognitive science, evolved, mainly from overlapping interests in psychology, computer science, philosophy, and linguistics (Gardner, 1987). It has been argued that cognitive science has shifted from being a field of study seen with a certain theoretical perspective to being a field of study in the more usual sense of the expression, defined in terms of problems and phenomena, which can be examined from *any* scientifically sound theoretical perspective. We must bear in mind, however, that the very idea that the handling of knowledge by humans and by computers could and should be dealt with within the same framework, the very idea that what is going on in the human mind and in the computer are instances of the same phenomenon, is in itself a very strong theoretical statement that imposes severe constraints on potential descriptions and explanatory models. The computer offers a new, precise, language for describing cognitive phenomena and a way of testing hypothetical models of them. At the same time a description that can be programmed in a computer is, of logical necessity, an algorithmic description.

Although the rationalist Chomskian turn in linguistics contributed to the rise of the cognitive revolution (Gardner, 1987, p. 28), it firmly belongs to the empiricist tradition. The object of research is physical symbol systems, each being "... built from a set of elements, called symbols, which may be formed into symbol structures by means of a set of relations" (Vera & Simon, 1993, p. 8). Such a system receives sensory stimuli from the environment and transforms them into internal symbols allied with perceptual processes. On the other hand it can transform internal symbols into muscular responses allied with motor processes, which in turn connect the symbol system with the environment and interact with the internal processes of information that are akin to thinking. The idea that acts have to be explained in terms of an internal representation of an external reality and in terms of processes by which this internal representation is manipulated is the dogma of cognitivism: "the presumption that all psychological explanation must be framed in terms of internal mental representation, and processes (or rules) by which these representations are manipulated and transformed" (Still & Costall, 1987, p. 2).[2]

This dogma leads to our fourth paradox: The internal representation cannot just lie around in the head; it has to be used somehow by something which is other than the representation itself. This something—or someone—has been called the *homunculus,* "the little human in the head," and is the aspect of the cognitive system that operates on internal representations of the external world. The idea of the homunculus follows logically from the idea of internal representation. But what does it take to operate, act on, or handle this inner world? With what does the operative part of the system's homunculus have to be equipped?

Well, if acting in (or on) the world presupposes a representation of the world, then handling the representation, the inner world, reasonably presupposes a representation of the representation, and handling the representation of the representation presupposes a representation of the representation of the representation of the world. The homunculus must have a homunculus within itself, which must have a homunculus, and so on *ad infinitum.* An intriguing notion? A paradox, we venture to claim, challenging even the computer scientists' sense of logic and reason.

This paradox is structurally identical with what is known as Ryle's regress, named after the philosopher Gilbert Ryle who published his passionate attack on mentalism in the book, *The Concept of Mind* (Ryle, 1949). Because it is the overlapping meanings of cognitivism and mentalism that are relevant for our argument, we will treat the two as synonymous. Ryle argued strongly against what he called "the intellectualist legend," according to which doing a task intelligently means being guided by internally represented declarative knowledge about the task. But then the use of internally represented declarative knowledge must be guided by declarative knowledge about *what* knowledge to use, *how* to use it, and so on. The use of *that* declarative knowledge has to be guided by declarative knowledge on a higher level. Again, there is no end: This is Ryle's regress. His line of reasoning originates from the distinction between two forms of knowledge: knowing *that* and knowing *how.* It is the former that translates into propositional knowledge, knowledge about the world; the latter refers to a capability for doing something in a certain way; it is what we mean by having a skill. The force of his own argument—according to which we have dispositions, whether acquired or developed, for doing things in certain ways, and in which "mind" refers to the ways in which we do things and to the way in which those doings are organized—led Ryle to advocate behaviorism.

For Ryle, mind was not the "ghost in the machine," something *behind* our behavior, but it was an aspect of behavior, and believing otherwise meant making "a category mistake." Ryle's famous example of such a mistake concerns the visitor to Oxford, looking for the University. He sees colleges, libraries, playing fields, museums, scientific laboratories, and administrative offices, but still he feels that in addition to all of these there is the University, another entity of a similar kind but different. Not realizing that the University is exactly the way in which its various parts are organized, he insists he has not yet seen it. Following the same argument, Ryle regards the mind as simply the way in which behavior is organized. There are not two worlds, only one—the observable world, the material world, the world of acts, the world of behavior. Ryle escapes the paradoxes associated with the epistemological question "How do we gain knowledge about the world?" simply by refraining from asking the question. Therefore, and not surprisingly, he does not arrive at an answer.

In addition to the paradox resulting from the idea of making use of an internal representation, the very forming of an internal representation is paradoxical. The notion, as we pointed out earlier, is that we receive sensory data from the outside world through our sense organs. The data as such are meaningless but are synthesized into an inner representation of the outer world. The representation does, of course, carry meaning. The question we have to ask is, "How can something meaningful be built out of that which is devoid of meaning?" Does it not presuppose that we already have knowledge of that which is supposed to be synthesized? But the representation is exactly that knowledge. Thus—and this must by now have a familiar if no less paradoxical ring—in order to obtain the knowledge we must have it already.

Finally, we come to the sixth paradox. Let us assume a representation (ignoring for the moment the fifth and the fourth paradoxes arguing against such an assumption). Assume, furthermore, a person encountering some situation. Let us say she has a problem to solve. What happens? According to the cognitivist explanation, to be able to deal with a particular problem and prior to facing it, she must already have acquired a schema, a paradigm or template, for the class of problems to which this particular problem belongs. By using the appropriate schema the problem can be grasped, dealt with, and eventually solved. But how can the appropriate schema be selected? To make a choice, the problem already must have been identified, hence grasped. Here we are again—the very grasping is supposed to be done by using the schema, and to retrieve that particular schema you must have grasped the problem already—a paradox!

Cognitivism, which has been the dominant paradigm in psychological and educational research for about three decades, is thus seen to suffer from at least three paradoxes.

The Paradox-Free Future of the Situated Cognitivists?

Since the mid-1980s a somewhat heterogeneous movement, referred to as "the situated cognition" or "the situated action" movement, has gained strength. It emanates from studies of learning and thinking in everyday situations outside educational institutions (Chaiklin & Lave, 1993; Lave, 1988), from computer scientists looking for alternative models for human—computer interaction (Clancey, 1992), and from the sociocultural or sociohistorical school of psychology developed originally by Vygotsky and his followers (Wertsch, 1985). We prefer to use "social constructivism" as an umbrella term for a rather diverse set of research orientations that have in common an emphasis on what surrounds the individual, focusing on relations between individuals, groups, communities, situations, practices, language, culture, and society. The main question we ask is, "How do the surrounding social or cultural, forces mould or make certain ways of acting and certain ways of thinking possible for the individual?"

Studies with a situated action orientation are characterized by human acts being explained, not in terms of an individuals' or several individuals' mental states, but in terms of what goes on between individuals, and between individuals and situations. The archetypal study is Hutchins' description of how a ship is navigated on leaving San Diego harbor (Hutchins, 1995). What this takes is not capabilities within one individual, but capabilities distributed over several individuals plus the coordinator of those capabilities. Knowledge is also seen as being embedded in the artifacts used, in this case the navigational instruments.

Human acts also can be seen in terms of their social or cultural situatedness. In a study of police interrogation (Jönsson, Linell, & Säljö, 1991) the point is made that the kind of discourse that evolves cannot be understood other than in terms of the legal system of which the situation is a part. Studies of this kind, of course, do not have the epistemological question "How do we gain knowledge about the world?" as their object, and they do not run into any of the paradoxes we have exposed. They deal instead with a world observed or interpreted by the researchers. There is a similarity with the behaviorist position in that "the inner" is not dealt with, and the situation is described only from the researcher's point of view. As diSessa (1993) pointed out, this implies that the participants are assumed to see the situation in the same way the researcher does.

Vygotskian psychology, however, which at least partially inspired the situated action view, does have an interest in "the inner." Cognitivism puts emphasis on explaining "the outer" (acts, behavior) in terms of "the inner" (mental representation). Vygotskian psychology, in contrast, tries to explain "the inner" (consciousness) in terms of "the outer" (society). Thus the thrusts of the explanations proposed by cognitivists and Vygotskian psychologists are in opposite directions. In the Vygotskian explanation "the outer" and "the inner" are linked by means of "internalization." Bereiter quotes Luria's (1979) firsthand account of Vygotsky and his group who had ". . . recognized this as a problem yet to be solved before there could be an adequate social-cognitive theory" (Bereiter, 1985, p. 204).

Attempts have been made to reconcile the two movements that seem currently to have the most momentum in educational research: social constructivism (Vygotskian psychology, situated cognition, etc.) and what we henceforth refer to as individual constructivism (Cobb, 1994; Driver, Asoko, Leach, Mortimer, & Scott, 1994). The main contribution of individual constructivism is its emphasis on the learner's active role in the acquisition of knowledge. The main contribution made by social constructivism is its emphasis on the importance of cultural practices, language, and other people, in bringing knowledge about.

Our Way Forward

Individual constructivism is a form of cognitivism in the sense that it regards the outer (acts, behavior) as being in need of explanation and the inner (mental acts) as explanatory, whereas, as we have pointed out, the reverse is true for *social constructivism.* The two schools are thus mirror images of each other, their focuses being on different sides of the borderline between "the inner" and "the outer." They share the shortcoming of lacking explanatory power with respect to what they claim to account for because they share the separation between "the inner" and "the outer." In order to combine the insights originating from these two camps that relate to our question "How do we gain knowledge about the world?" one has to transcend the person—world dualism imposed by their respective focus on what is within the person and what surrounds her.[3] One should not, and we do not, consider person and world as being separate. One should not resort to hypothetical mental structures divorced from the world, and we have no intention of doing so. Nor should one resort to the social, cultural world as seen by the researcher only. People live in a world which they—and not only the researchers—experience. They are affected by what affects *them,* and not by what affects the researchers. What this boils down to—as far as learning of the kind to be dealt with in this book is concerned—is taking the experiences of people seriously and exploring the physical, the social, and the cultural world they experience. The world we deal with is the world as experienced by people, by learners—neither individual constructions nor independent realities; the people, the learners, we deal with are people experiencing aspects of that world—neither bearers of mental structures nor behaviorist actors.

Thus in this book the dividing line between "the outer" and "the inner" disappears. There are not two things, and one is not held to explain the other. There is not a real world "out there" and a subjective world "in here." The world is not constructed by the learner, nor is it imposed upon her; it is *constituted* as an internal relation between them. There is only one world, but it is a world that we experience, a world in which we live, a world that is ours.

As we said at the start of this chapter, we are all different, and we do experience the world differently because our experience is always partial. Gaining the most fundamental knowledge about the world is tantamount to coming to experience the world in a different way, and, to rephrase one of our opening statements, if one way of experiencing the world can be judged to be better than another way, then some people must have become better at experiencing the world—or have experienced the world in a better way, or have gained better knowledge—than others, always with the proviso that we are talking in normative educational terms. The rest of this book is devoted to the task of learning about how the world appears to all these different people—how they have come to experience it—following our thesis that by learning about how the world appears to others, we will learn what the world is like, and what the world could be like.

Notes

1. We use the term *individual constructivism* and its derivatives to refer to the view of learning described here, which is usually called simply *constructivism.* Our reason is to draw a contrast with the other currently dominant view of learning that we introduce here and refer to as *social constructivism.*
2. The reader's attention is drawn to the distinction between cognitive science and cognitivism, the former being a field of study, as mentioned earlier, and the latter being grounded in this particular assumption about the relation between mind and world. Not all cognitive scientists subscribe to the dogma of

cognitivism and not all who do subscribe are cognitive scientists.

3. We must point out again that the terms individual *constructivism* and social *constructivism* are umbrella terms that we use to cover quite a heterogeneous range of research perspectives; we have chosen them as representing the most general and outstanding aspects of large fields of work. However, they differ to varying degrees in other respects; for instance, Barbara Rogoff (1990) took an explicitly nondualistic ontological stance within a generally social constructivist framework.

References

Ahlberg, A. (1992). *Att möta matematiska problem. En belysning av barns lärande* [Meeting mathematical problems. An illumination of children's learning]. Göteborg: Acta Universitatis Gothoburgensis.

Ahlberg, A., & Csocsán, E. (1994). Grasping numerosity among blind children. *Report from Department of Education and Educational Research,* Göteborg University, 4.

Alexandersson, M. (1994a). Focusing teacher consciousness: What do teachers direct their consciousness towards during their teaching? In I. Carlgren, G. Handal, & S. Vaage (Eds.), *Teachers' minds and actions: Research on teachers' thinking and practice* (pp. 139–149). London: Falmer Press.

Alexandersson, M. (1994b). *Metod och medvetande* [Method and consciousness]. Göteborg: Acta Universitatis Gothoburgensis.

Anderson, J. R., Pirolli, P., & Farrell, R. (1988). Learning to program recursive functions. In M. T. H. Chi, R. Glaser, & M. J. Farr (Eds.), *The nature of expertise* (pp. 153–183). Hillsdale, NJ: Lawrence Erlbaum Associates.

Andersson, B., & Renström, L. (1979). Temperatur och värme: Kokning [Temperature and heat: Boiling]. *Reports from Department of Teacher Education,* 3, Göteborg University

Andersson, E. (1978). *Bokstav i kunskapens hjärta.* [Letter in the heart of knowledge. Report from the project experiential learning and cognitive development]. *Rapport från projektet Upplevelseinlärning och kognitiv utveckling,* Department of Education, Göteborg University, 19.

Andersson, E., & Lawenius, M. (1983). *Lärares uppfattning av undervisning* [Teachers' conceptions of teaching]. Göteborg: Acta Universitatis Gothoburgensis.

Annerstedt, C. (1991). *Idrottslärarna och idrottsämnet* [Physical education and teachers in physical education]. Göteborg: Acta Universitatis Gothoburgensis.

Ashton-Warner, S. (1963). *Teacher.* New York: Simon & Schuster.

Barnett, S. A. (1973). Homo docens. *Journal of Biosocial Science, 5,* 393–403.

Baxter Magolda, M. B. (1992). *Knowing and reasoning in college: Gender-related patterns in students' intellectual development.* San Francisco: Jossey-Bass.

Beaty, E. (1987). Understanding concepts in social science: Towards an effective strategy. *Instructional Science, 15,* 341–359.

Bereiter, C. (1985). Toward a solution of the learning paradox. *Review of Educational Research, 55,* 201–226.

Bergqvist, K., & Säljö, R. (1994). Conceptually blindfolded in the optics laboratory. Dilemmas of inductive learning. *European Journal of Psychology of Education, 2,* 149–158.

Biggs, J. B. (1979). Individual differences in study process and the quality of learning outcomes. *Higher Education, 8,* 381–394.

Biggs, J. B. (1990). *Approaches to learning in secondary and tertiary students in Hong Kong: Some comparative studies.* Paper presented at the seventh annual conference of the Hong Kong Educational Research Association, University of Hong Kong.

Booth, S. A. (1992a). *Learning to program: A phenomenographic perspective.* Göteborg: Acta Universitatis Gothoburgensis.

Booth, S. A. (1992b). The experience of learning to program. Example: Recursion. In F. Détienne (Ed.), 5 ème workshop sur la psychologie de la programmation, (pp. 122–145) Paris: INRIA.

Bowden, J., Dall'Alba, G., Martin, E., Masters, G., Laurillard, D., Marton, F., Ramsden, P., & Stephanou, A. (1992). Displacement, velocity, and frames of reference: Phenomenographic studies of students' understanding and some implications for teaching and assessment. *American Journal of Physics, 60,* 262–268.

Broady, D. (1981). *Den dolda läroplanen* [The hidden curriculum]. Stockholm: Symposion.

Brown, J. S., Collins, A., & Duguid, P. (1989). Situated cognition and the culture of learning. *Educational Researcher, 18,* 32–42.

Chaiklin, S., & Lave, J. (1993). *Understanding practice. Perspectives on activity and context.* Cambridge: Cambridge University Press.

Chomsky, N. (1957). *Syntactic structures.* The Hague: Mouton & Co.

Chomsky, N. (1959). Review of B. F. Skinner's "Verbal Behavior." *Language, 35,* 26–58.

Clancey, W. J. (1992, June). "Situated" Means coordinating without deliberation. Presented at the McDonell Foundation Conference "The Science of Cognition", Santa Fe, New Mexico.

Cobb, P. (1994). Where is the mind? Constructivist and socio-cultural perspectives on mathematics development. *Educational Researcher, 23,* 13–20.

Colaizzi, P. (1973). *Reflection and research in psychology: A phenomenological study of learning.* Duquesne: Kendall/Hunt.

Coombs, C. H. (1968). *The world educational crisis: A systems analysis.* New York: Oxford University Press.

Coombs, C. H. (1971). *Utbildningens världskris* [The world educational crisis: A systems analysis]. Stockholm: Bonniers.

Csocsán, E. (1988, July). Blind children's model of basic mathematical concepts. Paper presented at the ICME Conference, Budapest.

Dahlgren, G., Gustafsson, K., Mellgren, E., & Olsson, L.-E. (1993). *Barn upptäcker skriftspråket* [Children discover written language]. Stockholm: Liber Utbildning.

Dahlgren, G., & Olsson, L.-E. (1985). *Läsning i barnperspektiv.* Göteborg: Acta Universitatis Gothoburgensis. (The child's conception of reading)

Dahlgren, L. O. (1975). *Qualitative differences in learning as a function of content-oriented guidance.* Göteborg: Acta Universitatis Gothoburgensis.

Dahlgren, L. O. (1985). Higher education: Impact on students. In T. Husén & T. N. Postlethwaite (Eds.), *The International Encyclopedia of Education,* (pp. 2223–2226). Oxford: Pergamon Press.

Dahlgren, L. O. (1989). Fragments of an economic habitus. Conceptions of economic phenomena in freshmen and seniors. *European Journal of Psychology of Education, 4,* 547–558.

Day, J. M., (1994), Introduction. In J. M. Day (Ed.) *Plato's Meno in focus* (pp. 1–34). London: Routledge.

diSessa, A. A. (1993). Between brain and behavior: Response to Marton. *Cognition and Instruction, 10,* 261–280.

Driver, R. Asoko, H., Leach, J, Mortimer, E., & Scott, P. (1994). Constructing scientific knowledge in the classroom. *Educational Researcher, 23,* 5–12.

Ebbinghaus, H. (1964). Memory. A contribution to experimental psychology. New York: Dover. (Original work published, 1885).

Eizenberg, N. (1988). Approaches to learning anatomy: Developing a programme for preclinical medical students. In P Ramsden (Ed.), *Improving learning. New perspectives* (pp. 178–198). London: Kogan Page.

Ekeblad, E. (1993). *Barn som pedagoger Två sätt som sjuåringar använder för art lära en kamrat spelett mattespel* [Children as pedagogues, Two ways that seven year olds teach a friend to play a maths game]. *Rapporter från Institutionen far pedagogik,* Göteborgs Universitet, *15.*

Ekeblad, E. (1994, March). *What's in a case? Conceptions of number in context.* Paper presented at the 22nd congress of the NFPF, Vasa.

Ekeblad, E. (1995, March). *First-grader's conceptions of "How you learn maths".* Paper presented at the 23rd congress of the NFPF, Aarhus.

Ekeblad, E., Lindahl, M., Lindström, B., Marton, F., & Packendorff, M. (1996). *The development of number-sense in a computerized learning environment.* Unpublished manuscript, Institutionen för pedagogik, Göteborgs Universitet.

Ekeblad, E., & Lindström, B. (1995, August). *The role of phenomenographic research in the design of instructional computer applications for number concepts.* Paper presented at the 6th European Conference for Research on Learning and Instruction, Nijmegen, The Netherlands.

Entwistle, N. (1976). The verb "to learn" takes the accusative. Editorial introduction to symposium: Learning processes and strategies—I. *British Journal of Educational Psychology, 46,* 1–3.

Entwistle, N. (1984). Contrasting perspectives on learning. In F. Marton, D. Hounsell, & N. Entwistle (Eds.), *The experience of learning* (pp. 1–18). Edinburgh: Scottish Academic Press.

Entwistle, N., & Marton, F. (1994). Knowledge objects: Understandings constituted through intensive academic study. *British Journal of Educational Psychology, 64,* 161–178.

Eriksson, R., & Neuman, D. (1981). *Räknesvaga elevers matematikundervisning under de sex första skolåren.* [Mathematics teaching for children weak in maths during the first six school years]. Unpublished manuscript, Department of Education, Göteborg University.

Feldman, D. H. (1980). *Beyond universals in cognitive development.* Norwood, NJ: Ablex.

Fensham, P., & Marton, F. (1991). *High-school teachers' and university chemists' differing conceptualizations of the personal activity in constituting knowledge in chemistry.* Department of Education and Educational Research, Göteborg University, 1.

Feynman, R. P., Leighton, R. B., & Sands, M. (1963). *The Feynman lectures on physics. Vol 1.* Reading, MA: Addison-Wesley.

Gardner, H. (1987). *The mind's new science.* New York: Basic Books.

Gibbs, G., Morgan, A., & Taylor, E. (1984). The world of the learner. In F. Marton, D. Hounsell, & N. Entwistle (Eds.), *The experience of learning* (pp. 165–188). Edinburgh: Scottish Academic Press.

Giorgi, A. (1986). *A phenomenological analysis of descriptions of concepts of learning obtained from a phe-*

nomenographic perspective. Publikationer från institutionen för pedagogik, Göteborgs universitet, 18.

Glaser, B., & Strauss, A. (1967). *The discovery of grounded theory*. Chicago, IL: Aldine.

Gurwitsch, A. (1964). *The field of consciousness*. Pittsburgh: Duquesne University Press.

Gustafsson, B., Stigebrant, E., & Ljungvalt, R. (1981). *Den dolda läroplanen* [The hidden curriculum]. Stockholm: Liber.

Halldén, O. (1994). On the paradox of understanding history in an educational setting. In G. Leinhardt, I. L. Beck, & C. Stainton (Eds.), *Teaching and learning in history* (pp. 27–46). Hillsdale, NJ: Lawrence Erlbaum Associates.

Hashisaki, J. (1985). Set theory. In *The New Encyclopedia Britannica* (15th ed., Vol. 27, pp. 238–244). Chicago: Encyclopedia Britannica Inc.

Hasselgren, B. (1981). *Ways of apprehending children at play: A study of pre-school student teachers' development*. Göteborg: Acta Universitatis Gothoburgensis.

Helmstad, G., & Marton, F. (1992, April). *Conceptions of understanding*. Paper presented at the annual meeting of the American Educational Research Association, San Francisco, CA.

Henderson, P. B., & Romero, F. J. (1989). *Teaching recursion as a problem-solving tool using Standard ML*. Paper presented at 20th SIGCSE Technical Symposium on Computer Science Education, Louisville, KY.

Hofstadter, D. R. (1979). *Gödel, Escher, Bach: An eternal golden braid*. London: The Harvester Press

Hounsell, D. (1984). Learning and essay-writing. In F. Marton, D. Hounsell, & N. Entwistle (Eds.), *The experience of learning* (pp. 103–123). Edinburgh: Scottish Academic Press.

Hutchins, E. (1995). *Cognition in the wild*. Cambridge, MA: MIT Press.

Johansson, B. (1975). *Aritmetikundervisning: En rapport om en datainsamling*. [The teaching of arithmetic]. Reports from Pump-project, Department of Education, Göteborg University, 9.

Johansson, B., Marton, F., & Svensson, L. (1985). An approach to describing learning as a change between qualitatively different conceptions. In A. L. Pines & T. H. West (Eds.), *Cognitive structure and conceptual change* (pp. 233–257). New York: Academic Press.

Jönsson, L., Linell, P., & Säljö, R. (1991). Formulating the past: Remembering in the police interrogation. *Activity Theory, 9/10*, 5–11.

Katona, G. (1940). *Organizing and memorizing*. New York: Columbia University Press.

Keller, H. (1908). *The story of my life*. New York: Doubleday.

Kember, D., & Gow, L. (1991). A challenge to the anecdotal stereotype of the Asian learner. *Studies in Higher Education, 16*, 117–128.

Korovessis, P. (1970). *Metoden*. [The method]. Stockholm: Rabén & Sjögren.

Kroksmark, T. (1987). *Fenomenografisk didaktik* [Phenomenographic didactics]. Göteborg: Acta Universitatis Gothoburgensis.

Kullberg, B. (1991). *Learning to learn to read*. Göteborg: Acta Universitatis Gothoburgensis.

Laurillard, D. (1995, May). *Understanding representations*. Paper presented at the symposium Understanding Understanding II, University of Edinburgh.

Lave, J. (1988). *Cognition in practice*. Cambridge, UK: Cambridge University Press.

Lindahl, M. (1996). *Inlärning och Erfarande. Ettåringars möte med förskolans värld* [Learning and Experiencing. One-year-olds' encounters with the world of preschool]. Göteborg: Acta Universitatis Gothoburgensis.

Lundgren, U. P. (1977). Model analysis of pedagogical processes. *Studies in education and psychology*, 2. Stockholm: Institute of Education.

Luria, A. R. (1979). *The making of mind: A personal account of Soviet psychology*. Cambridge, MA: Harvard University Press.

Lybeck, L. (1981). *Arkimedes i klassen. En ämnespedagogiskberättelse* (Archimedes in the class-room]. Göteborg: Acta Universitatis Gothoburgensis.

Lybeck, L., Marton, F., Strömdahl, H., & Tullberg, A. (1988). The phenomenography of "the mole concept" in chemistry. In P. Ramsden (Ed.), *Improving learning: New* perspectives (pp. 81–108). London: Kogan Page.

Martin, E., & Ramsden, P. (1987). *Learning skills, or skill in learning*. In I. T. E. Richardsson, M. W. Eysenck, & D. W. Piper (Eds.), *Student learning* (pp. 155–167). Milton Keynes: Open University Press.

Marton, F. (1970). *Structural dynamics of learning*. Stockholm: Almqvist & Wiksell.

Marton, F. (1974). *Inlärning och studiefärdighet* [Study skills and learning]. *Rapporter från Pedagogiska institutionen*. Göteborgs Universitet, nr 121.

Marton, F. (1976). On non-verbatim learning. IV: Some theoretical and methodological notes. *Scandinavian Journal of Psychology, 17*, 125–128.

Marton, F. (1978). *Describing conceptions of the world around us. Reports from the Institute of Education*. Göteborg University, no 66.

Marton, F. (1981). Phenomenography describing conceptions of the world around us. *Instructional Science, 10*, 177–200.

Marton, F. (1986). Vad är fackdidaktik? [What is pedagogical content knowledge?]. In F. Marton (Ed.), *Fackdidaktik I* (pp. 15–78). Lund: Studentlitteratur.

Marton, F. (1992). Phenomenography and "the art of teaching all things to all men." *International Journal of Qualitative Studies in Education, 5,* 253-267.

Marton, F. (1993). Phenomenograhy. In T. Husén & T. N. Postlethwaite (Eds.) *The International Encyclopedia of Education* (2nd ed. pp. 4424–4429). Oxford: Pergamon Press.

Marton, F. (1994). On the structure of teachers' awareness. In I. Carlgren, G. Handal, & S. Vaage (Eds.), *Teachers' minds and actions: Research on teachers' thinking and practice* (pp. 28–42). London: Falmer Press.

Marton, F., Asplund-Carlsson, M., & Halász, L. (1992). Differences in understanding and the use of reflective variation in reading. *British Journal of Educational Psychology,* 62, 1–16.

Marton, F., Asplund-Carlsson, M., & Halász, L. (1994). The reverse effect of an attempt to shape reader awareness. *Scandinavian Journal of Educational Research, 38,* 291–298.

Marton, F., Beaty, E., & Dall'Alba, G. (1993). Conceptions of learning. *International Journal of Educational Research, 19,* 277–300.

Marton, F., Dahlgren, L. O., Svensson, L., & Säljö, R. (1977). *Inlärning och omvärldsuppfattning* [Learning and conceptions of reality]. Stockholm: Almqvist & Wiksell.

Marton, F., Dall'Alba, G., & Tse, L. K. (1992, January). *Solving the paradox of the Asian learner.* Paper presented at the fourth Asian Regional Congress of Cross-Cultural Psychology, Kathmandu, Nepal.

Marton, F., Fensham, P., & Chaiklin, S. (1994). A Nobel's eye view of scientific intution: Discussions with the Nobel prize-winners in Physics, Chemistry, and Medicine (1970–1986). *International Journal of Science Education, 16,* 457–473.

Marton, F., & Säljö, R. (1976a). On qualitative differences in learning I—Outcome and process. *British Journal of Educational Psychology, 46,* 4–11.

Marton, F., & Säljö, R. (1976b). On qualitative differences in learning II—Outcome as a function of the learner's conception of the task. *British Journal of Educational Psychology, 46,* 115-127.

Marton, F., & Säljö, R. (1976c). Utveckling är inlärning är utveckling [Development is learning is development]. *Forskning om utbildning, 3,* 6–14.

Marton, F., Watkins, D., & Tang, C. (in press). Discontinuities and continuities in the experience of learning: An interview study of high-school students in Hong Kong. *Learning and Instruction.*

Marton, F., Wen, Q., & Nagle A. (in press). Views on learning in different cultures. Comparing patterns in China and Uruguay. *Anales de Psicologia.*

Marton, F., & Wenestam, C.-G. (1988). Qualitative differences in retention when a text is read several times. In M. M. Gruneberg, P. E. Morris, & R. N. Sykes (Eds.), *Practical aspects of memory: Current research and issues* (Vol. 2, pp. 370–376) Chichester: Wiley.

Mathews, M. H. (1992). *Making sense of place: Children's understanding of large-scale environments.* Hemel Hempstead: Harvester Wheatsheaf.

Mugler, F., & Landbeck, R. (1994, November). Student learning at the University of the South Pacific: A pilot study. In R. Ballantyne, & C. Bruce (Eds.), *Proceedings Phenomenography, Philosophy & Practice Conference.* Brisbane.

Nagle, A., & Marton, F. (1993, August-September). *Learning, knowing and understanding. Qualitative changes in student teachers' views of the relationship between some educational phenomena during the first term of pre-school teacher education in Uruguay.* Paper presented at the fifth European Association for Research on Learning and Instruction Conference in Aix en Provence.

Neuman, D. (1987). *The origin of arithmetic skills: A phenomenographic approach.* Göteborg: Acta Universitatis Gothoburgensis.

Neuman, D. (1989). *Räknefärdighetens rötter* [The roots of arithmetic skills]. Stockholm: Utbildningsförlaget.

Neuman, D. (1994, July-August). *Five fingers on one hand and ten on the other: A case study in learning through interaction.* Proceeding of the 18th PME Conference. Lissabon, Portugal.

Newton, I. (1686). *Principia (Philosophiae Naturalis Principia Mathematica).* London, UK: Royal Society.

Patrick, K. (1992, November). *Teachers and curriculum at year 12: Constructing an object of study.* Paper presented at the joint conference of the Australian Association for Research in Education and the New Zealand Association for Research in Education, Deaking University, Geelong, Victoria.

Pavlov, I. P. (1927). *Conditioned reflexes* (G. V. Anrep, Trans.). London: Oxford University Press.

Penrose, R. (1989). *The emperor's new mind: Concerning computers, minds and the laws of physics.* Oxford: Oxford University Press.

Perry, W. G. (1970). *Forms of intellectual and ethical development in the college years: A scheme.* New York: Holt, Rinehart & Winston.

Petrie, H. G. (1981). *The dilemma of enquiry and learning.* Chicago: The University of Chicago Press.

Piaget, J. (1907). Un moineau albinos [An albino sparrow] *Organe du Club Jurassien, 41,* 36.

Piaget, J., & Garcia, R. (1991). *Toward a logic of meanings.* Hillsdale, NJ: Lawrence Erlbaum Associates.

Piaget, J., & Inhelder, B. (1948). *The child's conception of number.* London: Routledge & Kegan Paul.

Pramling, I. (1983). *The child's conception of learning.* Göteborg: Acta Universitatis Gothoburgensis.

Pramling, I. (1986). The origin of the child's idea of learning through practice. *European Journal of Education, 3,* 31–46.

Pramling, I. (1990). *Learning to learn.* New York: Springer Verlag.

Pramling, 1. (1994). *Kunnandets grunder* [The foundations of knowing]. Göteborg: Acta Universitatis Gothoburgensis.

Pramling, I. (1996). Understanding and empowering the child. In D. Olson, & N. Torrance (Eds.), *Handbook of education and human development: New models of learning, teaching and schooling.* Oxford: Blackwell.

Pramling, I., Klerfelt, A., & Williams Graneld, P. (1995). Först var det roligt, sen' blev det tråkigt och sen' vande man sig. . . : Barns möte med skolans värld [It's fun at first, then it gets boring, and then you get used to it. . . : Children meet the world of school]. *Rapporter från Institutionen för metodik i lärarutbildningen, Göteborgs universitet,* 9.

Pramling, I., & Mårdsjö, A-C. (1994). *Att urveckla kunnandets grunder* [Developing the foundations of knowing]. *Rapporter från Institutionen för metodik i lärarutbildningen, Göteborgs universitet, 7.*

Premack, D. (1984). Pedagogy and aesthetics as sources of culture. In M. S. Gazzaniga (Ed.), *Handbook of cognitive neuroscience* (pp. 15–35). New York: Plenum Press.

Prosser, M. (1994). Some experiences of using phenomenographic research methodology in the context of research in teaching and learning. In J. A. Bowden, & E. Walsh (Eds.), *Phenomenographic research: Variations in Method. The Warburton Symposium* (pp. 31–43). Melbourne: RMIT.

Prosser, M., & Millar, R. (1989). The "How" and the "What" of learning physics. *European Journal of Psychology of Education, 4,* 513–528.

Renström, L. (1988). *Conceptions of matter: A phenomenographic approach.* Göteborg: Acta Universitatis Gothoburgensis.

Renström, L., Andersson, B., & Marton, F., (1990). Students' conceptions of matter. *Journal of Educational Psychology, 82,* 555-569.

Roche, J. (1988). Newton's *Principia.* In J. Fauvel, R. Flood, M. Shorthand, & R. Wilson, (Eds.), *Let Newton be! A new perspective on his life and works* (pp. 43–61). Oxford: Oxford University Press.

Rogoff, B. (1990). *Apprenticeship in thinking. Cognitive development in social contexts.* New York: Oxford University Press.

Roth, K. J., & Anderson, C. W. (1988). Promoting conceptual change learning from science textbooks. In P. Ramsden (Ed.), *Improving learning: New perspectives* (pp. 109–141). London: Kogan Page.

Russell, R., & Ginsburg, H. P. (1984). Cognitive analysis of children's mathematical difficulties. *Cognition and Instruction, 1,* 217–244.

Ryle, G. (1949). *The concept of mind.* London: Hutchinson.

Säljö, R. (1975). *Qualitative differences in learning as a function of the learner's conception of the task.* Göteborg: Acta Universitatis Gothoburgensis.

Säljö, R. (1979). Learning in the learner's perspective. 1. Some common-sense conceptions. *Reports from the Department of Education,* Göteborg University, No. 76.

Säljö, R. (1982). *Learning and understanding: A study of differences in constructing meaning from a text.* Göteborg: Acta Universitatis Gothoburgensis.

Säljö, R. (1994). Minding action. Conceiving of the world versus participating in cultural practices. *Nordisk Pedagogik, 74,* 71–80.

Sandberg, J. (1994). *Human competence at work. An interpretative approach.* Göteborg: BAS.

Seuss, Dr. (1966). *Cat in the hat.* New York: Beginner Press.

Skinner, B. F. (1953). *Science and human behavior.* New York: Macmillan.

Skinner, B. F. (1957). *Verbal behavior.* Englewood Cliffs, NJ: Prentice-Hall.

Smedslund, J. (1970). Circular relation between understanding and logic. *Scandinavian Journal of Psychology, 11,* 217-219.

Spiegelberg, H. (1982). *The phenomenological movement: A historical introduction* (3rd ed.). The Hague: Martinus Nijhoff.

Steffe, L. P. (1991). The learning paradox: A plausible counterexample. In L. P. Steffe (Ed.), *Epistemological foundations of mathematical experience* (pp. 26–44). New York: Springer.

Stelmach, M. Z. (1991, July). An application of student learning research in medical education. Paper presented at the annual conference of the Australian and New Zealand Association for Medical Education, The University of Melbourne, Carlton, Victoria.

Still, A., & Costall, A. (1987). Introduction: In place of cognitivism. In A. Costall & A. Still (Eds.), *Cognitive psychology in question* (pp. 1–16). Brighton: Harvester Press.

Strömdahl, H. (1996). *On mole and amount of substance: A study of the dynamics of concept formation and concept attainment.* Göteborg: Acta Universitatis Gothoburgensis.

Sundqvist, R. (1993). *Didaktiskt tänkande: En studie om uppfattningar av undervisning* [Pedagogical thinking. A study of conceptions of teaching]. Unpublished licentiate thesis, .Åbo Akademi, Vasa, Finland.

Svensson, L. (1976). *Study skill and learning.* Göteborg: Acta Universitatis Gothoburgensis.

Svensson, L. (1977). On qualitative differences in learning: III. Study skill and learning. *British Journal of Educational Psychology, 47,* 233–243.

Svensson, L. (1984a). *Människobilden i INOM-gruppens forskning: Den lärande människan* (The image of man in the research of the INOM-group: Man as learner]. *Reports from the Department of Education and Educational Research, Göteborg University, 3.*

Svensson, L. (1984b). Skill in learning. In F. Marton, D. Hounsell, & N. J. Entwistle (Eds.), *The experience of learning* (pp. 56–70). Edinburgh: Scottish Academic Press.

Svensson, L. (1989). The conceptualization of cases of physical motion. *European Journal of Psychology of Education, 4,* 529–545.

Székely, L. (1950). Productive processes in learning and thinking. *Acta Psychologica, 7,* 379–407.

Taylor, E., & Morgan, A. R. (1986, April). *Developing skill in learning.* Paper presented at AERA annual conference, San Francisco.

Theman, J. (1983). *Uppfattningar av politisk makt* [Conceptions of political power]. Göteborg: Acta Universitatis Gothoburgensis.

Torney-Purta, J. (1990). International comparative research in education: Its role in educational improvement in the US. *Educational Researcher, 19,* 32–35.

Trigwell, K., Prosser, M., & Taylor, P. (1994). A phenomenographic study of academics' conceptions of science learning and teaching. *Learning and Instruction, 4,* 217–232.

Tronström, G. (1984). Efter do år började jag forstå . . . [After ten years I started to understand . . .]. *KRUT 2,* 28–30.

Ueno, N., Arimoto, N., & Fujita, G. (1990, April). *Conceptual models and points of view: Learning via making a new stage.* Paper presented at the annual conference AERA, Boston.

van Rossum, E. J., & Schenk, S. M. (1984). The relationship between learning conception, study strategy and learning outcome. *British Journal of Educational Psychology, 54,* 73–83.

Vera, A. H., & Simon, H. A. (1993). Situated action: A symbolic interpretation. *Cognitive Science, 17,* 7–48.

von Glasersfeld, E. (1990). Environment and communication. In L. Steffe & T. Wood (Eds.), *Transforming children's mathematics education: International perspectives* (pp. 30–38). Hillsdale, NJ: Lawrence Erlbaum Associates.

Watson, J. B. (1924). *Behaviorism.* New York: Norton.

Wenestam, C.-G. (1978). *Horisontalisering: Ett sätt att missuppfatta det man läser* [Horizontalization. A way of misunderstanding a text]. Reports from the Department of Education, Göteborg university, 157.

Werner, H. (1948). *Comparative psychology of mental development.* New York: International Universities Press.

Wertheimer, M. (1945). *Productive thinking.* New York: Harper & Row.

Wertsch. J. V. (1985). *Vygotsky and the Social Formation of Mind.* Cambridge, MA: Harvard University Press.

Wertsch, J. V., Minick, N., & Arns, F. J. (1984). The creation of context in joint problem solving. In B. Rogoff & J. Lave (Eds.), *Everyday cognition, Its development in social change contexts* (pp. 151–171). Cambridge, MA: Harvard University Press.

White, N. D. (1994). Inquiry. In J. M. Day (Ed.), *Plato's Meno in focus* (pp. 152–171). London: Routledge.

Wikström, Å. (1987). *Functional programming using Standard ML.* Hemel Hempstead: Prentice-Hall.

Wistedt, I. & Martinsson, M. (1994). *Kvaliteter i elevers tänkande över en oändlig decimalutveckling* [Qualities in how children think about an endlessly repeating decimal]. Rapporter från Stockholms universitet, Pedagogiska institutionen.

CHAPTER 29

THE DEVELOPMENTAL NATURE OF SELF-AUTHORSHIP: THE WORLD OF STUDENTS

MARCIA BAXTER MAGOLDA

Self-authorship is an elusive goal for both students and their instructors. A Doonesbury cartoon about teaching captured this state of affairs. The cartoon depicted a teacher at his lectern, speaking on the topic of Jefferson's defense of basic rights to students in rows below him. In the first frame the teacher asks for students' reactions to his views. Hearing only the sound of scribbling and seeing only blank stares, he muses in the second frame that the students are more interested in getting the information down than responding to his query. He makes his next statement more provocative, calling the Bill of Rights "silly," hoping to spark a response. As the students continue to write faster, the teacher offers increasingly bizarre viewpoints to elicit a discussion. In the last frame he gives up, slumping over the podium in frustration, and pronounces teaching dead. Meanwhile the students comment to one another how interesting the course is becoming given the information just presented. Whereas the teacher invites the students to engage in self-authorship, they appear to miss that point entirely. This scenario repeats itself in real classrooms—where good teachers and bright students come together—because educational practice is rarely organized around students' ways of making meaning.

The students in the cartoon, who in this scenario assume that knowledge is certain and possessed by the authority, see the podium and seating arrangements as an indication that they are to listen to the authority, their educational experience has taught them to listen to authority, and they find the bizarre statements of the professor more interesting than the usual fare. Teachers without an understanding of students' epistemological, intrapersonal, and interpersonal development interpret the students' behavior as indicating that students want nothing more than to fill their notebooks, are too disinterested (perhaps even lazy) to engage in discussion, and cannot distinguish between the professor's view and truth.

A teacher who understands the development of students' meaning-making would be far more hopeful than Doonesbury's teacher would. She would muse that the students seem to believe that knowledge is certain because they write down the teacher's words regardless of their quality. She would further speculate that she would have to adjust her approach to get the students to reconsider their assumptions. She would, as a result, contemplate how to reorganize her practice to take into account where the students are starting as well as where she hopes they will go in thinking about the subject matter. This teacher would also understand the complexity of the task ahead.

Accessing students' ways of making meaning of their experience is a complex task. Students are not accustomed to having their experience valued in the learning process, as is evident in the Doonesbury cartoon. Shor (1992) argues that people are born learners and that their natural curios-

Source: "The Developmental Nature of Self-Authorship: The World of Students," by Marcia Baxter Magdola, reprinted from *Creating Contexts for Learning and Self-Authorship: Constructive- Developmental Pedagogy*, 1999, Vanderbilt University Press.

ity is often stifled by educational environments in which they are expected to memorize rules and existing knowledge. Brown and Gilligan (1992) document the silencing of adolescent girls in educational environments that socialize them in ways that inhibit expression of their true feelings and thoughts. Given these insights, it is not sufficient to simply invite students to practice self-authorship. Somehow instructors must convince students that their perspectives are valued and that education is the process of developing one's own perspectives in the context of existing understandings of the world. Teaching students how to self-author their beliefs is a matter of creating conditions to promote their development. The first step in approaching this task effectively is understanding the developmental nature of self-authorship, the topic to which the rest of this chapter is devoted.

Dimensions of Self-Authorship

Self-authorship has cognitive, intrapersonal, and interpersonal dimensions. Constructive-developmental theorists view these dimensions as parts of a single mental activity rather than separate entities (Kegan 1993). The *cognitive* component of how people make meaning is their assumptions about the nature, limits, and certainty of knowledge, or their epistemic assumptions (Kitchener 1983). These generally move from assuming that knowledge is certain and is possessed by authorities to assuming that knowledge is constructed in a context. The shift of knowledge from certain to uncertain is accompanied by a shift from viewing oneself as a receiver to a constructor of knowledge, a shift central to the development of self-authorship. The *intrapersonal* component of meaning-making involves assumptions about oneself. Intrapersonal growth moves from distinguishing one's impulses from oneself and identifying enduring qualities of the self to experiencing and eventually authoring one's inner psychological life. The latter way of making meaning is a central component of self-authorship. The *interpersonal* component hinges on assumptions about the relation of the self to others. Growth in this arena moves from lack of coordination of one's point of view with that of others, through subsuming one's own view to that of significant others, to developing a system that regulates interpersonal relationships. The latter perspective is necessary for self-authorship.

The pressing issues and tasks that students face and resolve as they mature, what theorists often call psychosocial development, stem from these constructive-developmental frameworks about the self and others. These issues include functioning autonomously, developing healthy relationships with others, dealing with one's identity, and defining one's purpose. This type of development is "concerned with those personal, psychologically oriented aspects of self and the relationships that exist between the self and society" (Miller and Winston 1990, 101). Students' views of themselves as knowers are inextricably intertwined with their views of self and relationships with others. The intrapersonal and interpersonal dimensions, which are often perceived as tangential in the study of pedagogy, are also crucial in understanding the development of self-authorship. Self-authorship means believing one can construct knowledge claims, make one's own inner psychological life, and regulate relationships with others to maintain one's own identity. Genuine self-authorship occurs when one reaches self-authorship in all three dimensions.

Constructive-developmental research describes the nature of each of these dimensions, their interrelationships, and the progression of each from simple to more complex forms. An important characteristic of the constructive-developmental approach is the concept of structure. Structure refers to ways people organize their meaning rather than the content of their meaning-making. Kegan describes this as "the organizing principle we bring to our thinking and our feelings and our relating to others and our relating to parts of ourselves" (1994, 29). For example, the epistemological assumption that knowledge is certain is an organizing principle one can bring to deciding what to believe. Two students can adopt different views from this same structure by believing different authorities; their way of deciding what to believe is the same. Two students could also endorse the same knowledge claim but arrive at it from different underlying structures. These structures are believed to be coherent sets of assumptions people use to make meaning until experiences that are discrepant with the structures cause people to alter them to account for new experience. The notion that these structures evolve through eras according to regular principles of stability and change is referred to as developmentalism (Kegan 1982, 8) and brings the possibility of some order to understanding how students make meaning.

I present constructive-developmental theory here as a *possibility* for understanding students' lived experience in a particular context. No theoretical portrait describes all students; rather, each portrait describes a particular group of students. Marilyn Frye's notion of patterns is useful here. Frye states, "Naming patterns is like charting the prevailing winds over a continent, which does not imply that every individual and item in the landscape is identically affected" (1990, 180). I interpret developmental theories to be the naming of patterns that help make sense of students' development but do not affect all students identically. Thus, they represent possible entrees into students' meaning-making processes, the understanding of which must be achieved through interacting with particular students. Perry argued that the student's organization of experience "can often be deduced by others from the forms of his behavior, including, especially, what he himself has to say on the matter" (1970, 42). Developmental theory is presented here as the basis for dialogue with students to access and understand the meaning they make of their lived experience. This chapter places portraits of epistemological development in the foreground so that the reader can "hear" what the cognitive dimension of self-authorship so central to teaching sounds like first. Then portraits of intrapersonal and interpersonal development are described to illustrate how the three dimensions are integrated in students' meaning-making and development of self-authorship.

Epistemological Development

Jean Piaget (1950) established the cognitive-developmental view of intellectual development, describing intelligence in terms of qualitatively different structures through which persons made meaning of their experience. These structures were characterized by particular assumptions about the nature, limits, and certainty of knowledge, assumptions that Kitchener (1983) later labeled epistemic assumptions. In their synthesis of epistemological theories, Barbara Hofer and Paul Pintrich (1997) identify three intersecting lines of research on epistemological development. Identifying epistemological assumptions and their evolution has been the core focus of one line (e.g., Baxter Magolda 1992; Belenky, Clinchy, Goldberger, and Tarule 1986; Perry 1970). Exploring how epistemological assumptions influence thinking and reasoning processes, such as reflective judgment (King and Kitchener 1994), represents a second line. A third line of research explores epistemological ideas as independent rather than reflective of a developmental structure (e.g., Ryan 1984; Schommer 1994). The perspective I advance here is that epistemic assumptions do evolve via developmental structures; I focus primarily on describing epistemic assumptions and their impact on students' approaches to learning.

Four portraits of students' epistemic assumptions identified through longitudinal studies of college students and adults exist. Perry (1970) offered the first comprehensive account of college students' intellectual development on the basis of a predominantly male sample. He described a progression of epistemic assumptions from knowledge as certain to partially uncertain to completely uncertain to relative in context. Dualistic students viewed knowledge as certain, in right-wrong terms, and acquired from authority. Uncertainty of knowledge appeared in multiplicity, replacing the right-wrong dichotomy with a known-unknown dichotomy. As areas in which knowledge was believed to be uncertain expanded, students began to adopt the stance that all knowledge was uncertain, resulting in less reliance on authority. Relativistic thinking emerged with the realization that some knowledge claims are better than others and can be validated by evidence relevant to the context. Perry also described a segment of the developmental scheme called commitment in relativism to reflect the continual reflection and commitment to perspectives that take place in relativistic thinking.

Due to difficulty interpreting women's experience with Perry's portrait, Belenky, Clinchy, Goldberger, and Tarule (1986) constructed a portrait of intellectual development based on a female sample. They found similar epistemic assumptions, yet learned that women in their study used their own subjectivity in the face of uncertainty more so than Perry's men and also identified an approach to knowing through connection to the object to be known. Belenky et al.'s perspectives of silence, in which participants did not perceive their ability to learn from others, and received knowing, in which the primary mode of learning was listening, demonstrated the belief of knowledge as certain similar to Perry's dualists. When the women discovered uncertainty of knowledge in subjective knowing, however, they moved quickly to rely on their own intuition and personal experiences unlike Perry's multiplicity. Increasing uncertainty led to procedural knowing in which two distinct processes for coming to know were evident. Belenky et al. described these as separate—using a logical, detached approach—and connected—using a subjective, empathic approach. The recognition that knowledge can be judged in a context yielded constructed knowing, a stance similar to Perry's relativist. Although Belenky et al. were careful not to essentialize their ways of knowing to all women, their work raised the question of gender-related patterns within ways of knowing. Continued work by these authors further articulated the relationship of separate and connected knowing (Clinchy 1996) and how gender, race, and class relations mediate negotiations about knowledge (Goldberger 1996).

Another model sparked by Perry's original scheme, the Reflective Judgment model (King and Kitchener 1994), offered a more detailed account of the evolution from certainty to uncertainty. King and Kitchener advance a seven-stage model describing assumptions about knowledge and its justification. The first three stages offer finer distinctions than were previously available in the move from certainty to uncertainty. In stage one, knowledge is certain, and authorities' beliefs are accepted. Knowledge remains certain in stage two, although it is not always available. Temporary uncertainty appears in stage three, with the hope that absolute knowledge will become possible. Recognition that some knowledge is permanently uncertain marks stage four, accompanied by the idiosyncratic evaluation of knowledge claims. In the face of growing uncertainty in stage five, rules of inquiry in particular contexts are used to justify beliefs. Generalized rules of inquiry take over as knowledge is viewed as constructed (stage six), and the value of some knowledge claims over others based on critical evaluation of evidence marks stage seven.

The Reflective Judgment model included both women and men but produced mixed results regarding whether gender made a difference in intellectual development (King and Kitchener 1994). My longitudinal study of college students' epistemological development (Baxter Magolda 1992) resulted in a gender-inclusive model in which women and men share similar epistemic assumptions, yet approach them via gender-related reasoning patterns. King and Kitchener (1994) note that differences in reasoning patterns cannot be discerned from the Reflective Judgment data, saying, "Since the RJI was not designed to elicit such information and since the data reported here have not been scored for this purpose, it cannot be said whether such differences might also exist in the context of the Reflective Judgment Model" (177). Subsequently, I use my Epistemological Reflection model in this chapter because it addresses both reasoning patterns and reflects a portrait of epistemological development consistent with those summarized here.

Epistemological Reflection: Four Ways of Knowing

The Epistemological Reflection model emerged from following eighty students through their four years of college.* It is continually refined through the post-college phase, which currently extends eight years after college. Annual open-ended interviews explored students' thoughts on the role of instructors, learners, and peers in learning; how learning should be evaluated; how to make educational decisions; and the nature of knowledge. Glaser and Strauss's (1967) constant comparative method was used to identify themes in their thinking, resulting in four ways of knowing and gender-related patterns within three of these sets of epistemic assumptions. I use the term *gender-related* to convey that the patterns were used more often by one gender than the other but not used exclusively by one gender. (See the appendices for a brief overview of the method for this study; a complete discussion is found in *Knowing and Reasoning in College: Gender-Related Patterns in Students' Intellectual Development*.)

Absolute Knowing

Discussing his view of learning as a first-year student, Jim offered a perspective that captures the essence of absolute knowing: "The factual information is cut and dried. It is either right or wrong. If you know the information, you can do well. It is easy because you just read or listen to a lecture about the ideas. Then you present it back to the teacher."

The core assumption held by absolute knowers is that knowledge exists in an absolute form, or in Jim's words, it is either right or wrong. They often assume that right and wrong answers exist in all areas of knowledge and that authorities know these answers. Uncertainty does not exist in knowledge per se, although it might exist in the student's lack of knowing the answer. The roles students describe for instructors, peers, and themselves as learners all hinge on knowledge being the purview of the instructor. As learners, absolute knowers focus on obtaining the information—a task Jim describes as reading or listening to lectures. They expect instructors to communicate knowledge clearly to them to aid in their acquiring it. They do not expect peers to have legitimate knowledge, although peers can share what they have learned from authority figures. Notice that Jim does not mention peers in his comment on how to do well. Absolute knowers' views of effective evaluation of students' work reflect the instructor's mastery of knowledge as well as the instructor's ability to determine whether students have acquired knowledge. When Jim presents what he has learned back to the teacher, she will know whether he knows the right answers. Students interpret discrepancies they encounter in the learning process as variations in explanations rather than true differences in knowledge. Finally, they approach educational decisions by looking for the right answers about educational programs, majors, and career directions.

Two reasoning patterns were evident in absolute knowing: receiving and mastery. The *receiving pattern* was used more often by women than men in the study. A central characteristic of the receiving pattern is its internal approach, as shown by Toni's comment: "I like to listen—just sit and take notes from an overhead. The material is right there and if you have a problem you can ask him and he can explain it to you. You hear it, you see it, and then you write it down."

Toni, a sophomore, makes it clear that this approach involves minimal interaction with instructors. Her receiving pattern peers also emphasized the importance of comfort in the learning environment, relationships with peers, and ample opportunities to demonstrate their knowledge. They resolved knowledge discrepancies via personal interpretation.

The *mastery pattern* was used more often by men than by women in the study: Mastery pattern students preferred an active approach to learning, were critical of instructors, and expected interactions with peers and instructors that help them master the material. The active approach to learning permeates most aspects of the learning process. For example, Tim (a first-year student) offered:

> I like getting involved with the class. Just by answering questions, asking questions . . . even if you think you know everything, there's still questions you can ask. When he asks questions you can try to answer them to your best ability. Don't just let the teacher talk, but have him present questions to you.

Tim believes asking and answering questions are necessary to learn; he is not content to listen and take notes as Toni is. Tim and his mastery pattern peers reported engaging one another in debates to further their learning, showing the instructor they were interested, and resolved knowledge discrepancies via research and asking authorities.

Absolute knowers shared the common belief that knowledge is certain and held by authorities. Beyond their shared set of assumptions, receiving and mastery pattern students differed in three areas: voice, identification with authority, and relationships with peers. There was really no student voice per se in absolute knowing. However, mastery pattern students attempted to express themselves while their receiving pattern counterparts remained essentially silent. Mastery pattern students seemed to imitate the voice of authority and worked hard at reproducing it in an effort to join authorities as knowers. Receiving pattern students listened carefully to the voice of authority and repeated it in an effort to show that they had acquired the knowledge.

Although all absolute knowers viewed authorities as holders of truth and knowledge, receiving pattern students exhibited minimal identification with authority figures whereas mastery pattern students exhibited considerable identification with authority. Students in the receiving pattern exhibited a detachment from authority. They described learning as a transaction largely void of interaction with authority unless clarification was needed. Despite their motivation for receiving knowledge, they did not view identification or interaction with authority as a central part of that process. Students in the mastery pattern showed the beginnings of taking their place "next to" authorities in the arena of knowledge. Their learning behaviors resembled those of the active apprentice trying to master the trade.

Relationships with peers were a third point of difference for receiving and mastery pattern students. Receiving pattern students valued peers as providers of comfort in the learning atmosphere. Knowing others in the class made it more intimate, more comfortable, and an easier setting in which to learn and ask questions. For these students peers were a source of assistance in receiving knowledge. Collaboration took the form of support and sharing notes and information. Mastery pattern students valued peers as partners in striving for and testing achievement. They assisted one another in mastering knowledge and took turns testing one another's progress. Collaboration in this form was characterized by individual autonomy.

The path from absolute to transitional knowing involves the realization that not all knowledge is certain, and that authorities are not all-knowing as a result. As the students' stories in transitional knowing reveal, mastery and receiving pattern students encounter this experience differently. Mastery pattern students' identification with authority prompts them to stay with certainty and logic as much as possible in the face of emerging uncertainty. Receiving pattern students' detachment from authority makes it easier to let go of certainty; thus, endorsing uncertainty is preferable. Endorsing uncertainty leads to an increase in activity level over and above listening. Peers are important to students of both patterns, but students endorsing uncertainty more readily assign legitimacy to peers' knowledge.

Transitional Knowing

Uncertainty, upon its discovery, was usually perceived to exist only in particular areas while certainty remained in other knowledge arenas. Fran's statement reflects this perspective:

> Genetics isn't an opinionated kind of subject. Genetics is "These are the experiments; that's what happens. This is what we know now." You wouldn't sit around and have a discussion in calculus . . . or chemistry. In the AIDS class, it's just open discussion, and it makes you really say what you want and think through what you want to think about.

Genetics retained its certainty for Fran, as did calculus and chemistry. On the topic of AIDS, however, uncertainty emerged. This shift in the nature of knowledge sparked changes in the roles students perceived for themselves and others. Students shifted their focus from acquiring knowledge to understanding it. This focus on understanding required that instructors use methods aimed at understanding, many of which included applying knowledge in class and to life in general. Peers took on more active roles, perhaps because understanding was described as requiring more exploration than that required for the acquisition of knowledge. Evaluation was perceived as appropriate to the extent that it measured students' understanding of the material. Uncertainty permeated decision making as well, as students struggled to figure out options for the future. Processes believed to lead to future success replaced direct reliance on authorities for educational decision making. All transitional knowers held these core assumptions.

Within transitional knowing some students, usually women, used an interpersonal approach whereas other students, usually men, used an impersonal approach. *Interpersonal pattern* students were involved in learning through collection of others' ideas, expected interaction with peers to hear their views and provide exposure to new ideas, wanted a rapport with the instructor to enhance self-expression, valued evaluation that takes individual differences into account, and resolved uncertainty by personal judgment. Kris's comments capture the new expectations of peers:

> I get into discussions. Classroom discussions are better for me to learn. You have an opening lecture where you have the professor discuss. Then students can contribute—listening to other students contribute their ideas and putting in my own inputs—that makes learning better for me because it makes me think more and try to come up with more generative ideas as to what I would do in a situation. We react to the material, look at ideas and relate it to ourselves, look at what kinds of action we can take. It's a hands-on type class.

Kris wants to hear the professor but only briefly; then she wants to hear her peers and express her own opinion. Interpersonal pattern knowers tended to focus on areas that were uncertain and viewed this as an opportunity to express their own views for the first time.

Impersonal pattern students wanted to be forced to think, preferred to exchange their views with instructors and peers via debate, expected to be challenged by instructors, valued fair and practical evaluation, and resolved uncertainty by logic and research. Scott described the result of being forced to think:

> The debate and discussion process for me is really interesting; I learn a lot more because I remember questions and I guess I learn the most when I sit and I'm actually forced to raise my hand and then I have to talk. I have to sit there and think on the spot. I learn it better than in a note-taking class that is regurgitation.

Scott has rejected the absolute knowers' approach of presenting information back to the teacher, but he does not endorse Kris's interest in peers' comments. Instead he focuses on his own thinking about the material. Impersonal pattern students also demonstrated a dual focus on certainty and uncertainty, and they wanted to resolve uncertainty when it existed.

Students in both patterns exhibit development of their voice in transitional as compared to absolute knowing. The impersonal pattern voice remains consistent in its closeness to the voice of authority, reflecting now the process of learning rather than the answers. The interpersonal pattern voice diverges more from authority than does the impersonal pattern. The discovery of uncertainty seems to be viewed by interpersonal pattern students as an opportunity to become involved in knowing, resulting in greater activity and exercise of personal judgment. Moreover, a subtle division remains between the interpersonal pattern knower's knowledge and that of authority. Some students remarked that their learning from other students did not necessarily help them learn the material in the book. Yet the interpersonal pattern voice has gained greater distance from authority than has the impersonal pattern voice. Using relationship with authority as a point of departure toward independent knowing, interpersonal pattern students would seem to be more ready to adopt their own voice.

The interpersonal and impersonal difference in the two patterns is clear. Interpersonal pattern students care about their peers' perspectives, want to know their peers, and want instructors to care about them. Relationships are central to the learning process because knowing others promotes sharing perspectives and sharing perspectives promotes adding to one's knowledge. If instructors are uncaring, teaching (and thus learning) is ineffective. For impersonal pattern students these themes did not surface. Although no student wants to be mistreated by instructors, impersonal pattern students prefer challenge to caring. Perhaps this reflects the impersonal pattern students' focus on individual learning whereas the interpersonal pattern students focus on the relationships made possible during learning. Considering peer relationships as a point of departure toward independent knowing, we could expect that interpersonal pattern students would have little difficulty accepting peers' views as valid. For them this will be an extension of knowing in the uncertain arena. For impersonal pattern students a shift will be required to add peers (and themselves) to the ranks of authority.

Independent Knowing

The core assumption of uncertainty in independent knowing changes both the process and the source of knowing substantially. The shift is evident in Laura's description of her discovery of uncertainty:

> Everything's relative; there's no truth in the world, that sort of thing. So I've decided that the only person that you can really depend on is yourself. Each individual has their own truth. No one has the right to decide, "This has to be your truth, too." As long as you feel—it feels right, then it must be right because if everybody is stuck on, "What do the other people think?" then you just waste your whole life. You just do what you feel like you have to do. That's why sometimes I felt that I had to get into business because everybody was going into business. I don't think the world rotates around the business world and money and materialism. Now I'm relaxed and I'm thinking of what I want, what's best for me and not for anybody else.

Given this newfound uncertainty, discrepancies among authorities represent the variety of views possible in an uncertain world. Authorities are no longer the only sources of knowledge but instead become equal with students, who for the first time view their opinions as valid. The emergence of self-authored knowledge rivets the student's attention on thinking for oneself. Learning how to think independently involves expressing one's own views as well as hearing others. Instructors are expected to promote this type of activity in class. They are no longer responsible for providing knowledge; they are responsible for providing the context in which to explore knowledge. Evaluation, likewise, should reward independent thinking and should not penalize the student for holding views different from the instructor or authors of texts. Peers become a legitimate source of knowledge rather than part of the process of knowing. Independent knowers emphasize being open-minded and allowing people to believe what they will, as illustrated by Laura's comment on how she decides what to believe: "I don't know [how I decide on my opinion]. Something works inside my head and it's just there."

Gender-related patterns appeared in independent knowing as well. The *interindividual pattern* was used more often by women than men in the study. Interindividual pattern knowers believed that different perspectives resulted from each person bringing her or his own interpretation, or in some cases bias, to a particular knowledge claim. They simultaneously advocated listening to other interpretations or biases and espousing their own perspectives, describing how the interaction of the two helped them form their perspective. Alexus offered an example of this view during her fifth-year interview. Reflecting on her senior year classes, she commented that the senior year was a time "when you should be most open because you should be able to listen to what other people say and then come up with your own opinion on how you feel about a particular thing." Asked how she did that, she replied,

> I listen to their arguments for it and then I listen to other people's arguments against it. And then basically it's just my own personal view really, whether I can establish the credibility—so I guess it really stems from credibility of the person who's saying it also, as well as just the opinion on it. I listen to both sides. Really I usually throw some of my own views into it as well. So I'm influenced by other people, but in the end I think that each—like each member of the group should be influenced by each other. But then when the final vote comes in, you should go with what you believe.

Alexus valued hearing others' ideas and felt people should be influenced by one another. She simultaneously held her own view and tried to integrate it with the views of others she perceived as credible.

The *individual pattern* knowers, like their interindividual pattern counterparts, espoused thinking independently and exchanging views with others. However, their primary focus was on their thinking, and they sometimes struggled to listen carefully to other voices. Fully acknowledging that everyone had her or his own beliefs, individual pattern knowers described the role theirs played when differences of opinion took place. Lowell shared an experience in which he and other students had different ideas:

> I'd consider myself conservative. And there was one guy in our group who was quite liberal and acknowledged it. I guess it gave me another viewpoint, another aspect to look at this. Like it or not we're all kind of ingrained one way or another, whether it's to the liberal end or the conservative end. He looked at it in this way and I looked at it in another way. And everybody in the group had their own ways on it. It was a spectrum of—and to try to get your point across without sounding too dominating—I'm searching for words and not finding them. To try to listen to theirs, to really listen, not to just hear it and let it go through. And then to try to take that into account and reach a compromise. There was quite a bit of discussion. But I don't think the attempt was to try to change each other's mind. It was just, "Your point is all right, but you've got to look at this part, too, because this is as relevant."

Lowell's genuine attempt to hear his liberal classmate and his insistence that his conservative perspective also be taken into account stopped short of changing either perspective.

The equality of numerous views in the face of prevailing uncertainty made independent thinking possible. Equality of perspectives also changed the relationship of the knower to her or his peers and to authority. In the case of interindividual pattern knowers this prompted connection to peers and to authority. Connection to peers was evident earlier for interpersonal transitional knowers, but interindividual pattern knowers became more open to peers' views. Their exchanges became interindividual by virtue of the knower including her or his own voice. When the potential hazards to connection posed by criticism were removed by equality of views, interindividual pattern knowers connected more intensely with their peers. This connection freed them to express their voices, which appear to have existed internally prior to this point. For them, the adjustment to independent knowing came in the form of including their own voices as equal to those of peers and of authority. Interindividual pattern knowers reconnected to authority once their own voices were legitimized. Thus, the interindividual pattern represents a union of one's own voice and the voices of others.

In the case of individual pattern knowers the equality of perspectives had a different effect on relationships with peers and authority. Peers' role in knowing created a relationship that bordered on becoming a connection. Individual pattern knowers listened to peers but struggled to hear them clearly and also to keep their own voices in the forefront. The adjustment to independent knowing for individual pattern knowers came in the form of including other voices as equal to one's own. Their voices, expressed routinely in previous ways of knowing, were slightly threatened by the genuine consideration of others' voices. Their interest in and attempt to hold both voices in balance appeared to mark the beginning of genuine connection to others. At the same time, equality of views seemed to free individual pattern knowers from authority to pursue their own independent thinking. The individual pattern includes both self-authored knowledge and the views of others, with the balance of the scale tipped toward self-authored knowledge.

The variation in interindividual and individual knowing can also be cast in the language of communion and agency (Bakan 1966). Communion involves connection and relationship with others whereas agency involves separateness from others. Both patterns moved toward communion: interindividual pattern knowers in terms of intense openness to others' views and individual pattern knowers in terms of genuine consideration of others' views. Both patterns also moved toward agency in the emergence of self-authored knowledge and for individual pattern knowers in separation from authority in the learning process. The degree of movement toward communion or agency is best understood in light of the degree to which either was reflected in earlier ways of knowing. Receiving and interpersonal pattern knowers demonstrated communion in previous ways of knowing, but agency represented a shift for them. Mastery and impersonal pattern knowers demonstrated agency in earlier ways of knowing so that communion represented a shift for them. While interindividual pattern knowers still lean toward communion and individual pattern knowers still lean toward agency, both are moving closer together than in previous ways of knowing.

Contextual Knowing: Relational and Impersonal Modes Intertwined

The fourth set of epistemological assumptions noticeable for a few students toward the end of college emerged more completely during the postcollege interviews. Contextual knowers looked at all aspects of a situation or issue, sought out expert advice in that particular context, and integrated their own and others' views in deciding what to think. Gwen, reflecting on her senior year, illustrates this perspective in her comment on whether to believe others' viewpoints: "I don't care if people feel this way or that way about it. But if they can support their stance and have some background and backing for that, to my thinking that is valid." The student voice develops to the point of cognitive self-authorship; both peers and authority have valid knowledge if they can support their stance.

Perhaps the most striking characteristic of contextual knowing is the integration of relational and impersonal modes of knowing. Although relational and impersonal patterns emerged as distinct in previous ways of knowing, contextual knowing necessitated both. Contextual knowers felt that rationality in terms of consulting experts and processing evidence was necessary but simultaneously valued working through their perspectives by accessing their own experience and others' perspectives. Contextual knowing involved constructing one's perspective in the context of one's experience, available information, and the experiences of others. Unlike independent knowers, contextual knowers are unwilling to rely solely on their own perspective or rely solely on the perspectives of others. They attempt to integrate constructing their own perspective with remaining open to considering others' thoughts as part of the process. Contextual knowers make judgments about others' perspectives as well as about information related to the issue under consideration. Contextual knowing incorporates the relational pattern evident in earlier forms of knowing through its focus on accessing one's own and others' perspectives and experiences (Baxter Magolda 1995). Once thinking is connected to, or anchored in, the self, standing outside one's experience is viewed as productive. Contextual knowing incorporates the impersonal pattern evident in earlier forms of knowing through its focus on establishing, or constructing, one's own belief system by abstractly processing experience and information.

Reginald's struggle to establish his perspective and simultaneously remain open to new ideas illustrates how the relational and the impersonal patterns came together in his experience. As Reginald introduced important learning experiences he had encountered in seminary, he brought up his struggle to sort out the meaning of intellect and emotion during his second year there:

> I think what I struggle with . . . is to claim it, to claim the experience. . . . I have to have that identity of what I do believe before I can be—well, not before—but along with the open mind and the openness to other views and respecting that. Because if not I'm just sort of wishy-washy, flimsying around, "Oh, okay, okay." And then if anyone asks, "Well, what do you believe?" "Well, I'm just open to anything." I think that's part of what I was talking about, that self-identity. What is it that makes—that's part of what makes you who you are. That's perhaps the intellect, and then when you live it, that's the emotion or the passion perhaps that you bring to what you do. . . . The belief is sort of a clay that is not hardened, that is always being molded. It can shift; it can take new forms. But it's still the same, still a belief system within your self-identity, within your experience that won't deny your experience. It won't completely just blow away like sand, but it will form and it will be consistent—it has some weight to it.

Reginald chose the word *intellect* to capture the experience he has claimed, the basis of what he believes. Claiming this experience and what he believes forms an identity that helps him balance accessing others' thoughts and acknowledging his experience. He explains this notion further through the idea of boundaries:

> In defining that self, identifying that self, is the creation of boundaries in what we do personally and publicly. . . . If I didn't have that boundary I might not bring out what it is that I need, what it is that I do believe if we're talking about—it can be theological, it can be academic, it can be personal. If I disregard the boundary I can be overwhelmed or just I won't be able to present who I am and what it is that I need. . . . I always considered the word *boundary* as a barrier. And so if I created these things I would be . . . a closed-minded person; I would be a person that when it came to—there wasn't a meeting place because there was this wall in the way. The other person would come to one side of the wall; I'd come to the other side of the wall. And we'd look at brick. And there wouldn't be a place where I could meet them. . . . And if I have those barriers I'm not—well, if I created what I thought would be barriers, I wouldn't have that. But also if I don't have anything, if I don't have boundaries, I lose the sense of who I am and I can't learn. And that's another thing: it restricts my learning and restricts other people's learning because I do bring something to that experience.

Reginald's claiming of intellect connects his belief system to himself, resulting in establishing an identity (the intrapersonal dimension of self-authorship). The boundaries of the identity keep him from being consumed as he meets others in dialogue (the interpersonal dimension of self-authorship). His thoughts suggest that effective connection with others does require some separation—in his case maintaining his self-identity. He argues that one cannot effectively "meet" others without having a self-identity. Reginald's perspective illustrates contextual knowers' integration of knowing via communion and agency. It also illustrates the development of self-authorship with regard to considering evidence—in this case his and others' beliefs and experience—in deciding what to believe.

Summary

Students' epistemic assumptions as well as their reasoning patterns affect the learning process. Expectations of instructors, peers, and learners themselves change as assumptions about the nature of knowledge change and vary according to reasoning patterns. Absolute knowers acquire information from authorities, either by listening (receiving) or by actively questioning and responding to authority (mastery). Transitional knowers focus on understanding knowledge; some do so via accessing others' views regarding uncertainty (interpersonal), and others do so via being forced to think (impersonal). Independent knowers feel free to decide their own opinions. Interindividual pattern students focus primarily on their peers' views in this process whereas individual pattern students focus primarily on their own views. The relational and impersonal dimensions merge in contextual knowing in which students construct knowledge by judging the evidence, others' views, and their own beliefs. Following students longitudinally revealed that their epistemic assumptions evolved from absolute to contextual over the course of the study. Absolute knowing was prevalent during the first two years of college and virtually disappeared by the senior year. Transitional knowing was prevalent during college but dissipated after college. Independent knowing emerged late in college and developed further after college. Contextual knowing was rare in college but developed for most participants in the years following college.

Three threads, or story lines, weave through the four ways of knowing and gender-related patterns—developing the student voice, changing relationships with authority, and changing relationships with peers. As epistemic assumptions evolved, the student voice changed from an echo of authority to an expression of the student's own perspective. Relationships with authority changed as the view of them as omnipotent gave way to viewing them as experts in a given context. Relationships with peers also developed as they evolved from simply helping one understand what authority had said to people whose views counted as valid knowledge if they became experts in a context. All three story lines are mediated by students' cognitive, intrapersonal, and interpersonal development. Because epistemological development is intertwined with these other strands of development, exploring their role is necessary to connect to students' experience in the learning process.

Self-Evolution

The Epistemological Reflection model traces the evolution of student voice in the context of students' assumptions about the nature of knowledge. Students' ability to view themselves as knowers, as persons who can construct valid knowledge, is mediated in part by their self-definition in a broader sense. Kegan's (1982, 1994) constructive-developmental description of the intrapersonal and interpersonal dimensions of self-authorship adds important insights to the epistemological dimension described here. Although numerous theorists describe these dimensions, I use Kegan here because he views these dimensions as an integral part of growth of the mind. Kegan argues that people make meaning from various "orders of the mind," each characterized by a particular organizing principle that affects thinking, feeling, and relating to self and others. These principles are *how* we make meaning of our thinking, feeling, and social relating, not the content of our meaning-making. He describes the core—or structure—of these organizing principles as the subject-object relationship. He defines *object* as "those elements of our knowing or organizing that we can reflect on, handle, look at, be responsible for, relate to each other, take control of, internalize, assimilate, or otherwise operate on" (1994, 32). *Subject*, in contrast, "refers to those elements of our knowing or organizing that we are identified with, tied to, fused with, or embedded in" (1994, 32). The difference, then, is that we cannot operate on what is subject because we cannot stand apart from it. Kegan states, "We *have* object; we *are* subject" (32, italics in original).

Kegan (1994) emphasizes that evolution of the subject-object relationship gives rise to evolution of the organizing principles we use to make meaning. Because what are subject and object for us are not permanent but change as we adjust to account for new experiences, dimensions of our cognitive, intrapersonal, and interpersonal meaning-making that are subject in one organizing principle, or order of the mind, become object in the next. Each new principle subsumes the prior one, resulting in a more complex way of making meaning. Kegan explains,

"Liberating ourselves from that in which we were embedded, making what was subject into object so that we can 'have it' rather than be 'had by it'—this is the most powerful way I know to conceptualize the growth of the mind" (1994, 34). Describing the evolution of what are subject and object, Kegan traces five structures through which people make meaning. Two of Kegan's five orders of the mind are most relevant for understanding the meaning-making activity of college-age students and adults.

The Structure of Self-Development

Kegan describes the third order of mind as

> the mental capacity that enables one to think abstractly, identify a complex internal psychological life, orient to the welfare of a human relationship, construct values and ideals self-consciously known as such, and subordinate one's own interests on behalf of one's greater loyalty to maintaining bonds of friendship, or team or group participation. (1994, 75)

He indicates that this particular balance of what is subject and what is object usually evolves sometime in the teenage years. Its cognitive characteristics—the ability to reason abstractly and to think hypothetically and deductively—are in contrast to the previous order of mind in which these were subject, making the adolescent's thinking concrete. The intrapersonal achievements of the third order are the ability to distinguish between one's needs and oneself (needs were previously subject; now they are object) and to identify enduring qualities of the self. These achievements are made possible by the ability to internalize others' points of view and to coordinate more than one point of view internally, thus the ability to hold values and ideals. This internal coordination also makes possible a change in the interpersonal dimension, that of orienting to shared feelings rather than interacting with others based on getting one's own needs met. This orientation makes subordinating one's own interests on behalf of relationships possible.

The third order of mind is likely to be prevalent among college students, based on Kegan's research (1994). He reports that this order usually evolves sometime between the ages of twelve and twenty, and that half to two-thirds of the adult population have yet to evolve to the fourth order. The third order of mind equips students with some of the cognitive processes to engage in knowledge construction (e.g., ability to think abstractly, hypothetically, deductively). Yet the intrapersonal dimension of the third order embeds the student in making meaning through shared realities with others who are external to the self. Because the system by which meaning is made rests outside the self, the student does not see himself as capable of self-authorship. Being subject to (or "had by" in Kegan's language) shared realities also potentially explains the strong influence of peers in how younger students determine what to believe about themselves, knowledge, values, and their relationships with others. Because their sense of self is coconstructed out of the relation between theirs and others' perspectives, the relationships they participate in heavily influence their sense of self. Kegan notes that "this bringing inside of the other's point of view, this coconstruction of the self, . . . is the triumph and limit of the third order" (1994, 126). The triumph is an ability to become a part of society; the limit is the inability to stand apart from this coconstruction to reflect and act upon it. Common campus issues such as abusive dating relationships, alcohol abuse, and even fraternity hazing might be understood more effectively by understanding how the third order of mind makes meaning.

Kegan notes that values, beliefs, convictions, generalizations, ideals, abstractions, interpersonal loyalty, and intrapersonal states of mind are all subject in the third order. The fourth order is more complex because

> it takes all of these as objects or elements of its system, rather than the system itself; it does not identify with them but views them as parts of a new whole. This new whole is an ideology, an internal identity, a *self-authorship* that can coordinate, integrate, act upon, or invent values, beliefs, convictions, generalizations, ideals, abstractions, interpersonal loyalties, and intrapersonal states. It is no longer *authored by* them, it *authors them* and thereby achieves a personal authority. (1994, 185, italics in original)

This system brings the creation of belief "inside" the self, separate from the shared realities and coconstructions of the third order. The existence of this system that generates beliefs makes self-authorship of knowledge possible. It also makes possible identity formation that is more enduring than the earlier coconstructed versions because the internal self is the source of belief rather than the social surround that was the source of belief in the third order. The ability to relate to one's intrapersonal states, rather than being made up by them, makes it possible to see oneself as the maker (rather than experiencer) of one's inner psychological life. The same ability to relate to one's interpersonal relationships, rather than being made up by them, makes it possible to separate self from relationships with others, to in fact have a relationship to those relationships.

These fourth order capacities form the basis for self-authorship in the cognitive, intrapersonal, and interpersonal dimensions of self-evolution. Complex epistemological development, particularly contextual knowing, necessitates fourth order meaning-making because it necessitates self-authorship. Although self-authorship emerges for the first time in independent knowing, the independent knower is unable to articulate the system through which her beliefs have been established. They no longer come from authority, but it is not clear that they were generated from an internal self-system either. It is likely that early independent knowing is consistent with the third order and that the transition from independent to contextual knowing is consistent with the evolution from third to fourth order.

Multiple Voices Within Self-Evolution

Just as I described gender-related patterns as qualitatively different but equally complex preferences *within* the structure of ways of knowing, theorists have described gender-related patterns in intrapersonal and interpersonal development that Kegan suggests are stylistic preferences existing *within* the structure of orders of the mind. Carol Gilligan (1982) brought the issue of gender-related voices to the attention of developmental theorists and educators in the context of moral orientations. She argued that women often used a care voice in making moral judgments, focusing on responsibility in moral contexts, in contrast to what she called the justice voice, which focused on rights. Research in this arena resulted in identification of a connected, or relational, preference that was often evident in the study of women and a separate preference often evident in the study of men. These preferences seem to reflect Bakan's (1966) communion and agency notions. These preferences have been the source of exploration in most areas of human development; those most closely related to the intrapersonal and interpersonal dimensions are highlighted here.

Chickering (1969) articulated the psychosocial issues of college students as establishing competence, managing emotions, and developing autonomy as precursors to identity after which developing mature interpersonal relationships, purpose, and integrity was possible. His initial theory, based on males, implied that independence was a precursor to a healthy identity and to mature relationships with others. Josselson's (1987) exploration of college women's identity development revealed the integration of connection with others and developing one's sense of self. She concluded that identity development described as agency (e.g., Chickering's theory), or a process toward a separate self, was less important to women than identity development characterized by communion or connection to others. Relationship to others was also central in Straub's (1987) study of women's autonomy development in college. She reported that 36 percent of the critical events students reported as central to autonomy involved connection to others, leading her to conclude that women work on autonomy from a connected standpoint. Lyons (1983) also confirmed two definitions of self—one connected to others and one separate from others. Chickering and Reisser (1993) reframed Chickering's original picture of identity to reflect the voice of connection. Identity development can take place with either separation or connection as the base.

Taub and McEwen (1991) addressed this same issue in comparing white and African-American undergraduate women's development of autonomy and interpersonal relationships. They report that few differences occurred; the data indicate that both groups were concerned with both tasks simultaneously through college. Branch-Simpson (1984) found that both male and female African-American college students stayed connected to others during autonomy development and identity formation as well as in learning. African-American adolescents apparently value connection as well (Ward 1989). Ward also argues that race plays a role in identity development. Parham (1989) describes the additional dynamics African-American students face as they work through the degree to which they endorse Afrocentric or Eurocentric components in identity and encounter others' perceptions of them as African-Americans. In part their identity formation depends on their preference for and encounter of inclusion or exclusion in the campus environment. Kegan (1994) notes that while individuality and separation are promoted by much of North American culture, connection and maintenance of attachment are promoted by many South American, African, and Asian cultures (as, I would add, Native American cultures). He points out that these different expectations may lead to members of those cultures using preferences that stem from their culture. Collectively, the identity development literature conveys that both inclusion (or connection) and independence (or autonomy) are at the core of defining self for white and African-American adolescents and young adults. The voice adopted by the person indicates the preference in the self-evolution process.

Clarifying the distinction between structure and style, or preference, Kegan describes the connected and separate voices as figure and ground rather than as a polarity or dichotomy. He states,

> Some of us may make the experience of connection the base from which we then move toward experiences of agency that may also be greatly important to us. Others may make the experience of independence the base from which we then move to experiences of connection that may also be precious to us or of paramount importance. (1994, 218)

It is possible for a third order mind to be either "connected . . . relationally embedded in the psychological surround . . . or separate . . . separately embedded in the psychological surround" (Kegan 1994, 220). Likewise, the fourth order mind can be either relationally or separately self-authorizing. Kegan uses the contrast between "deciding for oneself" and "deciding by oneself" to explain. Deciding for oneself, or self-authorship, represents the structure of the fourth order. However, within that structure, one could decide by oneself (separate) or decide with others (connected). Regardless of style, the key element here is deciding for oneself. Similarly, independent knowers who are all moving toward self-authorship in knowledge construction may do so in relation to others (the interindividual pattern) or in separation from others (the individual pattern). Understanding both structure and style helps teachers understand how their students make meaning.

Translating Student Development into Educational Practice

Portraits of students' cognitive, intrapersonal, and interpersonal development illustrate the complexity of achieving self-authorship as a young adult. Teaching to promote self-authorship requires understanding the evolution of meaning-making structures that bring it about as well as the stylistic preferences students exhibit within structures. Creating the conditions for students to reorganize their meaning-making structures toward those that reflect self-authorship requires connecting with students' experience in two ways. First, instructors must be able to connect to students' current meaning-making structures in order to determine the kind of experiences that might call those structures into question. Recall Doonesbury's teacher at the outset of this chapter; the conditions he created in his classroom did not connect with his students' assumptions that knowledge was certain, and therefore, they misinterpreted his teaching behavior. Had he instead engaged them in an exploration of how the Constitution was created, by whom and for what purposes, he might have enticed them to call the authority of the writers into question. The traditional objectivist approach to education, in which the learner is separate from knowledge, reinforces early epistemic assumptions that are inconsistent with self-authorship.

Second, connecting to students' stylistic preferences within structures also heightens the probability of their meaningful engagement in reorganizing their ways of making meaning. Kegan argues that the institutionalization of one voice (either separation or connection) gives the persons preferring that voice "home court advantage," leaving those preferring the noninstitutionalized voice feeling like "visitors" (1994, 214). The institutionalization of the separate voice in education could make, and probably has made, connected voice persons feel marginalized. Students who are connection oriented tend to identify less with their teachers as authorities (Baxter Magolda 1992; Belenky et al. 1986; Holland and Eisenhart 1990). If a connection does not exist between student and teacher, yet the student is connection oriented, that connection must be found elsewhere. Some evidence suggests that connection-oriented students find these links with the peer group. Because third order students coconstruct themselves with their peer group, this connection can be detrimental to the evolution of self-authorship if the peer group does not value it. This possibility is most evident in Holland and Eisenhart's (1990) ethnography of African-American and white college women. Studying women on two campuses, they found the women caught up in a culture of romance through which they anticipated, interpreted, and evaluated their experience (probably an example of third order coconstruction of self). Gaining prestige through making themselves attractive to men occupied considerable energy whereas less attention was devoted to academic work. Only five of the twenty-two women balanced peer expectations and academic work to their favor; the remaining seventeen downsized their career and academic aspirations.

Fordham and Ogbu (1986) report similar circumstances with African-American adolescents at Capital High who intentionally scaled back or hid their academic prowess to maintain connection with their peer group—a peer group that viewed academic success as acting white. The adolescent girls Brown and Gilligan (1992) followed also chose to stop expressing their true thoughts in order to be perceived as the "perfect girl" and in doing so exchanged authentic relationships for idealized ones. In the process of maintaining these idealized relationships, they lost their voices and self-authorization. Shared realities with peers in all these cases probably reinforced third order meaning-making. Had these third order students been able to join a shared reality with their teachers, they might have had opportunities to coconstruct themselves differently as it relates to learning, as well as receive encouragement to analyze the source of their values and beliefs.

When connection to the learning environment is possible, the evolution of self-authorship is more likely. The five women in Holland and Eisenhart's study who were able to avoid consumption by their peer group held learning as an important component of their identity. The peer culture can also promote knowing as important, as was the case in my longitudinal study. The receiving, interpersonal, and interindividual pattern students found themselves in a peer culture that supported thinking and exploring ideas. Their relationships with peers helped to develop their voices, and through these relationships, they were able to integrate knowing as a central part of their identities. These shared realities, like ones that could be constructed with teachers, included rather than excluded the notion of self-authorship. It is possible that they also set the conditions for evolution into the fourth order.

Students' development suggests that greater connection in the teaching-learning relationship is useful for creating the conditions that promote self-authorship. Creating these conditions is in effect building a bridge between students' current meaning-making and the structures of meaning-making that reflect self-authorship. Yet it is impossible to build a bridge to something that one does not understand. Most teachers' lived experience is different from that of many of their students, or when similarities do exist, time and growth have a way of diminishing understanding of perspectives previously held. Most teachers have not been exposed to the developmental literature that describes students' meaning-making. It is also impossible to define students as an aggregate in order to provide teachers with a blueprint of students' experience. Connection, given the complexity of student development and learning, can feel like trying to connect to a moving target. Thus, the primary task in connection is the process of accessing and valuing student experience, the dialogue advocated by educational theorists to get into students' worlds..

Note

* Portions of this description are reproduced with permission from Baxter Magolda, M. B. (1992). *Knowing and reasoning in college: Gender-related patterns in students' intellectual development.* San Francisco: Jossey-Bass.

References

Bakan, D. 1966. *The duality of human existence.* Boston: Beacon Press.

Baxter Magolda, Marcia B. 1992. *Knowing and reasoning in college: Gender-related patterns in students' intellectual development.* San Francisco: Jossey-Bass.

_____. 1995. The integration of relational and impersonal knowing in young adults' epistemological development. *Journal of College Student Development* 36, no. 3:205–16.

Belenky, Mary, Blythe Clinchy, Nancy Goldberger, and Jill Tarule. 1986. *Women's ways of knowing: The development of self, voice, and mind.* New York: Basic Books.

Branch-Simpson, G. E. 1984. A study of the patterns in the development of black students at the Ohio State University. Ph.D. diss., Department of Educational Policy and Leadership, Ohio State University.

Brown, Lyn Mikel, and Carol Gilligan. 1992. *Meeting at the crossroads: Women's psychology and girls' development.* Cambridge, Mass.: Harvard University Press.

Chickering, Arthur W. 1969. *Education and identity.* San Francisco: Jossey-Bass.

Chickering, Arthur W., and Linda Reisser. 1993. *Education and identity.* 2d ed. San Francisco: Jossey-Bass.

Clinchy, Blythe McVicker. 1996. Connected and separate knowing: Toward a marriage of two minds. In *Knowledge, difference, and power: Essays inspired by Women's Ways of Knowing,* ed. N. R. Goldberger, J. M. Tarule, B. M. Clinchy, and M. F. Belenky, 205–47. New York: Basic Books.

Fordham, Signithia, and John U. Ogbu. 1986. Black students' school success: Coping with the "burden of acting white." *Urban Review* 18, no. 3:176–206.

Frye, Marilyn. 1990. The possibility of feminist theory. In *Theoretical perspectives on sexual difference,* ed. Deborah L. Rhode, 174–84. New Haven, Conn.: Yale University Press.

Gilligan, Carol. 1982. *In a different voice.* Cambridge, Mass.: Harvard University Press.

Glaser, Barney, and A. Strauss. 1967. *The discovery of grounded theory: Strategies for qualitative research.* Chicago: Aldine.

Hofer, Barbara K., and Paul R. Pintrich. 1997. The development of epistemological theories: Beliefs about knowledge and knowing and their relation to learning. *Review of Educational Research* 67, no. 1:88–140.

Holland, Dorothy C., and Margaret A. Eisenhart. 1990. *Educated in romance: Women, achievement and college culture.* Chicago: University of Chicago Press.

Josselson, Ruthellen. 1987. *Finding herself: Pathways to identity development in women.* San Francisco: Jossey-Bass.

Kegan, Robert. 1982. *The evolving self: Problem and process in human development.* Cambridge, Mass.: Harvard University Press.

_____. 1993. Minding the curriculum: Of student epistemology and faculty conspiracy. In *Approaches to moral development: New research and emerging themes,* ed. Andrew Garrod, 72–88. New York: Teachers College Press.

_____. 1994. *In over our heads: The mental demands of modern life.* Cambridge, Mass.: Harvard University Press.

King, Patricia M., and Karen S. Kitchener. 1994. *Developing reflective judgment: Understanding and promoting intellectual growth and critical thinking in adolescents and adults.* San Francisco: Jossey-Bass.

Kitchener, Karen S. 1983. Cognition, metacognition, and epistemic cognition. *Human Development* 26:222–32.

Lyons, Nona Plessner. 1983. Two perspectives: On self, relationships, and morality. *Harvard Educational Review* 53:125–45.

Miller, Theodore K., and Roger B. Winston Jr. 1990. Assessing development from a psychosocial perspective. In *College student development: Theory and practice for the 1990s,* ed. Don G. Creamer, 99–126. Alexandria, Va.: American College Personnel Association.

Perry, William G. 1970. *Forms of intellectual and ethical development in the college years: A scheme.* Troy, Mo.: Holt, Rinehart, & Winston.

Piaget, Jean. 1950. *The psychology of intelligence.* Translated by M. Piercy and D. Berlyn. London: Routledge & Kegan Paul.

Ryan, M. P. 1984. Conceptions of prose coherence: Individual differences in epistemological standards. *Journal of Educational Psychology,* 76, no. 6:1226–1238.

Schommer, M. 1994. An emerging conceptualization of epistemological beliefs and their role in learning. In *Beliefs about text and instruction with text,* eds. R. Garner and P. A. Alexander, 25–40, Hillsdale, N.J.: Erlbaum.

Shor, Ira. 1992. *Empowering education: Critical teaching for social change.* Chicago: University of Chicago Press.

Straub, Cynthia. 1987. Women's development of autonomy and Chickering's theory. *Journal of College Student Personnel* 28:198–204.

Taub, Deborah J., and Marylou K. McEwen. 1991. Patterns of development of autonomy and mature interpersonal relationships in black and white undergraduate women. *Journal of College Student Development* 32:502–8.

Ward, Jane Victoria. 1989. Racial identity formation and transformation. In *Making connections: The relational worlds of adolescent girls at Emma Willard School,* ed. Carol Gilligan, Nona P. Lyons, and Trudy J. Hanmer. Troy, N.Y.: Emma Willard School.

CHAPTER 30

ON TWO METAPHORS FOR LEARNING AND THE DANGERS OF CHOOSING JUST ONE

ANNA SFARD

This article is a sequel to the conversation on learning initiated by the editors of Educational Researcher *in volume 25, number 4. The author's first aim is to elicit the metaphors for learning that guide our work as learners, teachers, and researchers. Two such metaphors are identified: the acquisition metaphor and the participation metaphor. Subsequently, their entailments are discussed and evaluated. Although some of the implications are deemed desirable and others are regarded as harmful, the article neither speaks against a particular metaphor nor tries to make a case for the other. Rather, these interpretations and applications of the metaphors undergo critical evaluation. In the end, the question of theoretical unification of the research on learning is addressed, wherein the purpose is to show how too great a devotion to one particular metaphor can lead to theoretical distortions and to undesirable practices.*

Educational Researcher, Vol. 27, No. 2, pp. 4–13

O! this learning, what a thing it is.
—W. Shakespeare, *The Taming of the Shrew*

Theories of learning, like all scientific theories, come and go. Some innovations reach deeper than others. Occasionally, theoretical changes amount to a conceptual upheaval. This is what seems to be happening right now in the research on learning. Numerous books and articles in professional journals come up with radically new approaches, and whether one likes the innovative ideas or not, one cannot just brush them aside. The field is in a state of perturbation, with prospects of a new equilibrium not yet in sight. The recent discussion on transfer in *Educational Researcher* (Anderson, Reder, & Simon, 1996; Donmoyer, 1996; Greeno, 1997; Hiebert et al., 1996) brings the controversial nature of current theories of learning into full relief. Strenuous attempts of many authors to come to terms with the change by forging theoretical bridges between competing outlooks (Billett, 1996; Cobb, 1995; Smith, 1995; Vosniadou, 1996) complete this picture. This article will bring a closer look at this controversy, as well as at the issue of theorizing in general. The discussion will be organized around the question of whether the struggle for a conceptual unification of research on learning is a worthwhile endeavor. The first step, however, will be to sketch a bird's-eye view of the competing trends in our present conceptualizations of learning.[1]

To be able to embrace the whole issue at a glance, one has to reach the most fundamental, primary levels of our thinking and bring to the open the tacit assumptions and beliefs that guide us. This means digging out the metaphors that underlie both our spontaneous everyday conceptions and scientific theorizing. Indeed, metaphors are the most primitive, most elusive, and yet amaz-

Source: "On Two Metaphors for Learning and the Dangers of Choosing Just One," by Anna Sfard, reprinted from *Educational Researcher*, Vol. 27, No. 2, 1998, American Educational Research Association.

ingly informative objects of analysis. Their special power stems from the fact that they often cross the borders between the spontaneous and the scientific, between the intuitive and the formal. Conveyed through language from one domain to another, they enable conceptual osmosis between everyday and scientific discourses, letting our primary intuition shape scientific ideas and the formal conceptions feed back into the intuition. Thus, by concentrating on the basic metaphors rather than on particular theories of learning, I hope to get into a position to elicit some of the fundamental assumptions underlying both our theorizing on learning and our practice as students and as teachers. First, however, let me add a few words on the relative status of language, metaphors, and scientific theories.

It was Michael Reddy who, in the seminal paper titled "The Conduit Metaphor," alerted us to the ubiquity of metaphors and to their constitutive role (Reddy, 1978). Using as an example the notion of communication, he showed how the language we use to talk about a given concept may take us in a systematic way to another, seemingly unrelated conceptual domain. (In his example, the figurative projection was from the domain of communication to that of transport.) Since then, the systematic conceptual mappings came to be known as conceptual metaphors and became objects of a vigorous inquiry (Johnson, 1987; Lakoff, 1987, 1993; Lakoff & Johnson, 1980; Sacks, 1978). What traditionally has been regarded as a mere tool for better understanding and for more effective memorizing was now recognized as the primary source of all of our concepts.

The idea that new knowledge germinates in old knowledge has been promoted by all of the theoreticians of intellectual development, from Piaget to Vygotsky to contemporary cognitive scientists. The notion of metaphor as a conceptual transplant clearly complements this view by providing a means for explaining the processes that turn old into new. One may say, therefore, that metaphorical projection is a mechanism through which the given culture perpetuates and reproduces itself in a steadily growing system of concepts.

According to Scheffler (1991), "[t]he line, even in science, between serious theory and metaphor is a thin one—if it can be drawn at all. . . . [T]here is no obvious point at which we may say, 'Here the metaphors stop and the theories begin'" (p. 45). The indispensability of metaphors in science may render them practically transparent, and, as a result, scientists often maintain that figurative representations are not more than explanatory tools. Philosophers of science, however, agreed quite a long time ago that metaphors play a constitutive role, and, in fact, no kind of research would be possible without them (Hesse, 1966; Ortony, 1993). The difficulty with telling the metaphorical from the scientific is aggravated by the fact that scientific vocabulary is usually borrowed from other domains (take as an example such terms as *cognitive strain, closed set, constructing meaning, messenger DNA*) and that the figurative expressions are the only ones in which the theories can be formulated. On the other hand, the fact that concealing the metaphorical origins of ideas in mathematical formalism is a mandatory part of the scientific game can make the figurative roots of scientific theories fairly difficult to restore.[2]

Because metaphors bring with them certain well-defined expectations as to the possible features of target concepts, the choice of a metaphor is a highly consequential decision. Different metaphors may lead to different ways of thinking and to different activities. We may say, therefore, that we live by the metaphors we use. It is also noteworthy that metaphors are a double-edged sword: On one hand, as a basic mechanism behind any conceptualization, they are what makes our abstract (and scientific) thinking possible; on the other hand, they keep human imagination within the confines of our former experience and conceptions. In the process of metaphorical projection, old foundational assumptions and deeply rooted beliefs, being tacit rather than explicit, prove particularly inert. As such, they tend to travel from one domain to another practically unnoticed. Such an uncontrolled migration of metaphorical entailments is not always to the benefit of new theories. It may bar fresh insights, undermine the usefulness of the resulting conceptual system, and—above all—perpetuate beliefs and values that have never been submitted to a critical inspection.

Eliciting the metaphors that guide us in our work as learners, teachers, and researchers is the first aim of the remainder of this article. Given my professional background, I am inclined to use examples taken from mathematics education; this, however, should not diminish the generality of the argument. After identifying two leading metaphors that inform our thinking about learning, I will examine their entailments. While doing so, I will be arguing that implications of a metaphor are a result of contextual determinants not less than of the metaphor itself. Thus, the same figurative idea may engender several greatly varying conceptual frameworks. The principal aim of the analysis that follows is to identify the ways in which one can put the different metaphors for learning to their best uses while barring undesirable entailments. In the end, I will try to show how too great a devotion to one particular metaphor and rejection of all the others can lead to theoretical distortions and to undesirable practical consequences.

Acquisition Metaphor Versus Participation Metaphor

The upshots of the former section can be put as follows: All our concepts and beliefs have their roots in a limited number of fundamental ideas that cross disciplinary boundaries and are carried from one domain to another by the language we use. One glance at the current discourse on learning should be enough to realize that nowadays educational research is caught between two metaphors that, in this article, will be called the *acquisition metaphor* and the *participation metaphor.* Both of these metaphors are simultaneously present in most recent texts, but while the *acquisition metaphor is* likely to be more prominent in older writings, more recent studies are often dominated by the *participation metaphor.*

Acquisition Metaphor

Since the dawn of civilization, human learning is conceived of as an acquisition of something. Indeed, the *Collins English Dictionary* defines learning as "the act of gaining knowledge." Since the time of Piaget and Vygotski, the growth of knowledge in the process of learning has been analyzed in terms of concept development. Concepts are to be understood as basic units of knowledge that can be accumulated, gradually refined, and combined to form ever richer cognitive structures. The picture is not much different when we talk about the learner as a person who constructs meaning. This approach, which today seems natural and self-evident, brings to mind the activity of accumulating material goods. The language of "knowledge acquisition" and "concept development" makes us think about the human mind as a container to be filled with certain materials and about the learner as becoming an owner of these materials.

Once we realize the fact that it is the metaphor of acquisition that underlies our thinking about learning mathematics, we become immediately aware of its presence in almost every common utterance on learning. Let us look at a number of titles of publications that appeared over the last two decades: "The Development of Scientific Knowledge in Elementary School Children," "Acquisition of Mathematical Concepts and Processes," "[C]oncept-Mapping in Science," "Children's Construction of Number," "Stage Theory of the Development of Alternative Conceptions," "Promoting Conceptual Change in Science," "On Having and Using Geometric Knowledge," "Conceptual Difficulties . . . in the Acquisition of the Concept of Function." The idea that learning means acquisition and accumulation of some goods is evident in all of these titles. They may point to a gradual reception or to an acquisition by development or by construction, but all of them seem to imply gaining ownership over some kind of self-sustained entity.

There are many types of entities that may be acquired in the process of learning. One finds a great variety of relevant terms among the key words of the frameworks generated by the *acquisition metaphor:* knowledge, concept, conception, idea, notion, misconception, meaning, sense, schema, fact, representation, material, contents. There are as many terms that denote the action of making such entities one's own: reception, acquisition, construction, internalization, appropriation, transmission, attainment, development, accumulation, grasp. The teacher may help the student to attain his or her goal by delivering, conveying, facilitating, mediating, et cetera. Once acquired, the knowledge, like any other commodity, may now be applied, transferred (to a different context), and shared with others.

This impressively rich terminological assortment was necessary to mark dissimilarities—sometimes easy to see and sometimes quite subtle—between different schools of thought. Over the last decades, numerous suggestions have been made as to the nature of the mechanism through which mathematical concepts may be turned into the learner's private property; however, in spite of the many differences on the issue of "how," there has been no controversy about the essence: The idea of learning as gaining possession over some commodity has persisted in a wide spectrum of frameworks, from moderate to radical constructivism and then to interactionism and sociocultural theories. Researchers have offered a range of greatly differing mechanisms of concept development. First, they simply talked about passive reception of knowledge, then about its being actively constructed by the learner; later, they analyzed the ways in which concepts are transferred from a social to an individual plane and internalized by the student; eventually, they envisioned learning as a never-ending, self-regulating process of emergence in a continuing interaction with peers, teachers, and texts. As long as they investigated learning by focusing on the "development of concepts" and on "acquisition of knowledge," however, they implicitly agreed that this process can be conceptualized in terms of the *acquisition metaphor.*

Participation Metaphor

The *acquisition metaphor* is so strongly entrenched in our minds that we would probably never become aware of its existence if another, alternative metaphor did not start to develop. When we search through recent publications, the emergence of a new metaphor becomes immediately apparent. Among the harbingers of the change are such titles as "Reflection, Communication, and Learning Mathematics," "Democratic Competence and Reflective Knowing," "Development Through Participation in Sociocultural Activities," "Learning in the Community," "Reflective Discourse and Collective Reflection," "Mathematics As Being in the World," "Dialogue and Adult Learning," "Cooperative Learning of Mathematics," and "Fostering Communities of Inquiry." The new researcher talks about learning as a legitimate peripheral participation (Lave & Wenger, 1991) or as an apprenticeship in thinking (Rogoff, 1990).

A far-reaching change is signaled by the fact that although all of these titles and expressions refer to learning, none of them mentions either "concept" or "knowledge." The terms that imply the existence of some permanent entities have been replaced with the noun "knowing," which indicates action. This seemingly minor linguistic modification marks a remarkable foundational shift (cf. Cobb, 1995; Smith, 1995). The talk about states has been replaced with attention to activities. In the image of learning that emerges from this linguistic turn, the permanence of *having* gives way to the constant flux of *doing*. While the concept of acquisition implies that there is a clear end point to the process of learning, the new terminology leaves no room for halting signals. Moreover, the ongoing learning activities are never considered separately from the context within which they take place. The context, in its turn, is rich and multifarious, and its importance is pronounced by talk about situatedness, contextuality, cultural embeddedness, and social mediation. The set of new key words that, along with the noun "practice," prominently features the terms "discourse" and "communication" suggests that the learner should be viewed as a person interested in participation in certain kinds of activities rather than in accumulating private possessions.

To put it differently, learning a subject is now conceived of as a process of becoming a member of a certain community. This entails, above all, the ability to communicate in the language of this community and act according to its particular norms. The norms themselves are to be negotiated in the process of consolidating the community. While the learners are newcomers and potential reformers of the practice, the teachers are the preservers of its continuity. From a lone entrepreneur, the learner turns into an integral part of a team. For obvious reasons, this new view of learning can be called the *participation metaphor.*[3] From now on, to avoid tiresome repetition, I will sometimes use the abbreviations "AM" and "PM" for *acquisition* and *participation metaphor,* respectively.

To clarify the idea of learning-as-participation, a number of explanatory remarks would be in place. First, the question may be asked, "What is metaphorical about the issue of participation?" After all, learning implies participation in instructional activities, and thus its participational nature should perhaps be treated as literal, not as figurative. To answer this, let us take a closer look at the concept of participation as such. A quest after its roots will lead us, once again, to the world of physical objects. "Participation" is almost synonymous with "taking part" and "being a part," and both of these expressions signalize that learning should be viewed as a process of becoming a part of a greater whole. It is now relatively easy to spot those beliefs about learning that may be brought by PM as its immediate entailments. Just as different organs combine to form a living body, so do learners contribute to the existence and functioning of a community of practitioners. While the AM stresses the individual mind and what goes "into it," the PM shifts the focus to the evolving bonds between the individual and others. While AM emphasizes the inward movement of the object known as knowledge, PM gives prominence to the aspect of mutuality characteristic of the part-whole relation. Indeed, PM makes salient the dialectic nature of the learning interaction: The whole and the parts affect and inform each other. On one hand, the very existence of the whole is fully dependent on the parts. On the other hand, whereas the AM stresses the way in which possession determines the identity of the possessor, the PM implies that the identity of an individual, like an identity of a living organ, is a function of his or her being (or becoming) a part of a greater entity. Thus, talk about the "stand-alone learner" and "decontextualized learning" becomes as pointless as the attempts to define lungs or muscles without a reference to the living body within which they both exist and function.

Second, one may oppose the above classification of theories of learning by saying that most conceptual frameworks cannot be regarded as either purely "acquisitional" or purely "participational." The act of acquisition is often tantamount to the act of becoming a participant, and if so, one can find it difficult to consider AM and PM separately, let alone as mutually exclusive.[4] No claim on exclusivity of the metaphors has been made in this article, however. Later, will argue for the inherent impossibility of freeing the discourse on learning from either of the two metaphors. Theories can be classified as acquisition-oriented or participation-oriented only if they disclose a clear preference for one metaphorical ingredient over the other.

Finally, the dichotomy between acquisition and participation should not be mistaken for the well-known distinction between individualist and social perspectives on learning. The examples here have shown that the former division crosses the demarcation lines established by the latter. According to the distinction proposed in this article, theories that speak about reception of knowledge and those that view learning as internalization of socially established concepts belong to the same category (AM), whereas on the individual/social axis, they must be placed at opposite poles. Whereas the social dimension is salient in the PM, it is not necessarily absent from the theories dominated by the AM. It is important to understand that the two distinctions were made according to different criteria: While the acquisition/participation division is ontological in nature and draws on two radically different answers to the fundamental question, "What is this thing called learning?," the individual/social dichotomy does not imply a controversy as to the definition of learning, but rather rests on differing visions of the mechanism of learning. A schematic comparison between the two is presented in Table 30-1.

What Can Go Wrong With AM, and How PM Can Help

It is time to ask for the reasons underlying the metaphorical shift. If we have been living with the AM for millennia, it is not all that obvious why a change should now be necessary. Well, we

TABLE 30-1
The Metaphorical Mappings

Acquisition metaphor		*Participation metaphor*
Individual enrichment	Goal of learning	Community building
Acquisition of something	Learning	Becoming a participant
Recipient (consumer), (re-)constructor	Student	Peripheral participant, apprentice
Provider, facilitator, mediator	Teacher	Expert participant, preserver of practice/discourse
Property, possession, commodity (individual, public)	Knowledge, concept	Aspect of practice/discourse/activity
Having, possessing	Knowing	Belonging, participating, communicating

might have been living with AM, but have we been happy with it? The latest developments make it rather clear that the answer should probably be "no." It does not take much effort to identify at least two areas in which the AM reveals a particular weakness. First, our thinking about learning has always been plagued by foundational quandaries that would not yield to the finest of philosophical minds. Second, the conception of knowledge as property, when not controlled, leads to too literal a translation of beliefs on material properties into beliefs on learning; some of the resulting norms and value judgments are likely to have adverse effects on both the theory and practice of learning and teaching. It may well be that the reason behind the conceptual unrest we are witnessing these days is the hope that the new metaphor will remedy both of these afflictions.

Foundational Dilemmas

Probably the best-known foundational dilemma obviously inherent to the AM was first signaled by Plato in his dialogue *Meno* and came to be known later as "the learning paradox" (Bereiter, 1985; Cobb, Yackel, & Wood, 1992). Although brought up in many different disguises throughout history, the quandary is always the same: How can we want to acquire a knowledge of something that is not yet known to us? Indeed, if this something does not yet belong to the repertoire of the things we know, then, being unaware of its existence, we cannot possibly inquire about it. Or, to put it differently, if we can only become cognizant of something by recognizing it on the basis of the knowledge we already possess, then nothing that does not yet belong to the assortment of the things we know can ever become one of them. Conclusion: Learning new things is inherently impossible.

Philosophers and psychologists have been grappling with the learning paradox for ages, but until recently, no real attempt to transgress the boundaries of the AM was made. The metaphor just did not look like a metaphor at all. How could it be otherwise if the AM has always been engraved in language, from which there is no escape?

Thinking about the epistemological and ontological foundations of our conception of learning intensified a few decades ago, when the doctrine of radical constructivism entangled the psychologists in a new dilemma. Without questioning the thrust of the AM, the constructivists offered a new conception of the mechanism that turns knowledge into one's private possession. It is the central constructivist idea of learners as the builders of their own conceptual structures that, at a closer look, turns problematic. Whatever version of constructivism is concerned—the moderate, the radical, or the social—the same dilemma must eventually pop up: How do we account for the fact that learners are able to build for themselves concepts that seem fully congruent with those of others? Or, to put it differently, how do people bridge individual and public possessions?

One of the reasons some people may be attracted to the PM is that it seems to help us out of these foundational quandaries. It is an escape rather than a direct solution: Instead of solving the problem, the new metaphor simply dissolves vexing questions by its very refusal to objectify knowledge. Here, "objectifying" means treating something as a well-defined entity that can be considered independently of human beings. It should be stressed that the doubt about the soundness of the tendency to objectify knowledge is not new and that the idea of disobjectification has been considered by many thinkers—notably Plato, Hegel, and neo-Kantians (Kozulin, 1990, pp. 22–23; Woodfield, 1993). The PM does the disobjectification job by providing an alternative to talk about learning as making an acquisition. Within its boundaries, there is simply no room for the clearcut distinction between internal and external (concepts, knowledge), which is part and parcel of objectification. By getting rid of the problematic entities and dubious dichotomies and clearing the language of essentialist aftertaste, PMs circumvent the philosophical pitfalls of AMs in an elegant manner.

This account would not be complete without a caveat: It may well be that the PM has in store new foundational dilemmas not yet suspected by its ardent followers. The PM's present appeal stems from the fact that it brings immediate relief from the old headache. There is no guarantee, however, that it is not going to disclose its own maladies one day. The danger of finding ourselves entangled in difficulties as we go on fathoming the intricacies of the participation mechanism is only too real. After all, the physical metaphor of "turning into a part of a greater whole" has its own pitfalls and may eventually lead us to an epistemological dead end just like any other metaphor that crosses ontological boundaries.

The Question of Norms and Values

Whereas the impossibility of "something out of nothing" seems endemic to the property of being an object, so that dismissing the learning paradox would mean rejection of the metaphor itself, there are MA-engendered views and opinions that are optional rather than necessary and only come to the fore if one chooses to endorse them. Metaphorical entailments that have to do with norms and values are usually of the latter kind.

If knowledge is conceived of as a commodity,[5] it is only natural that attitudes toward learning reflect the way the given society thinks about material wealth. When figuratively equated, knowledge and material possessions are likely to play similar roles in establishing people's identities and in defining their social positions. In the class-ridden capitalist society, for example, knowledge understood as property is likely to turn into an additional attribute of position and power. Like material goods, knowledge has the permanent quality that makes the privileged position of its owner equally permanent.

As a result, learning-according-to-AM may draw people apart rather than bring them together. As in a society driven by a pursuit of material goods, so in the AM-based approach to learning, learners and scientists are likely to put forward competition and solitary achievement. The American sociologist of science R. K. Morton notes that a scientist who just arrived at what may count as an important result "will be under pressure to make his *contribution to knowledge* known to other scientists and . . . they, in turn, will be under pressure to acknowledge *his rights to his intellectual property*" (Morton, 1973, p. 294, emphases added). In a footnote to this description, Morton seems to be apologizing for the vocabulary he uses, stating that "[b]orrowing, trespassing, poaching, credit, stealing, a concept which 'belongs' to us—these are only a few of the many terms in the lexicon of property adopted by scientists as matter of course" (p. 295). If this is the language in which this community speaks of intellectual achievement, no wonder that incidents of scientific fraud become more and more frequent in the increasingly crowded academia. While these are certainly extreme cases, there are symptoms much milder than obvious misconduct that can count as consequences of the acquisitionist approach. A not-altogether-infrequent occurrence of self-centered, asocial attitude toward knowing, creating, and learning is certainly a case in point. If people are valued and segregated according to what they have, the metaphor of intellectual property is more likely to feed rivalry than collaboration.

It is noteworthy that within the acquisition paradigm, not only knowledge, but also the means for gaining it, counts as a highly priced possession that, if of a superior quality, can make the possessors themselves superior to others. Such terms as "gift" or "potential," often used to denote a special propensity for learning and creating, suggest that this characteristic is given, not acquired. It is a person's "quality mark." Students' achievements may depend on environmental factors, but the teachers feel they can tell students' real (permanent) potential from their actual performance. The gifts and potentials, like other private possessions, are believed to be measurable and may therefore be used for sorting people into categories. In this climate, the need to prove one's "potential" sometimes overgrows his or her desire to be useful. This is what evidently happened to the Cambridge mathematician G. H. Hardy (1940/1967) who, after confessing that his interest in mathematics was motivated by the wish to show his outstanding abilities (mathematics "gives unrivaled openings for the display of sheer professional skill," p. 80), defiantly admitted to being perfectly happy in the academy without ever doing anything "useful" (the quotes are Hardy's own).

While these distortions are definitely not a necessary outcome of the AM, the metaphor is apparently what made them possible. Attitudes like those presented in the last paragraph are most likely to appear in societies that value—or even just tolerate—uncompromising pursuit of material wealth. As long as a metaphor enjoys full hegemony, its normative implications are usually taken for granted; introduction of a new metaphor is often enough to bring the issue of norms to the fore and turn it into an object of explicit reflection. This is exactly what is likely to happen when the PM enters the scene as a possible alternative to the AM. The new metaphor replaces the talk about private possessions with discourse about shared activities. This linguistic shift epitomizes the democratic nature of the turn toward the PM. The democratization of the language may lead, eventually, to a far-reaching change in awareness and in beliefs about learning.

The promise of the PM seems, indeed, quite substantial. The vocabulary of participation brings the message of togetherness, solidarity, and collaboration. The PM language does not allow for talk about permanence of either human possessions or human traits. The new metaphor promotes an interest in people in action rather than in people "as such." Being "in action" means being in a constant flux. The awareness of the change that never stops means refraining from a permanent labeling. Actions can be clever or unsuccessful, but these adjectives do not apply to the actors. For the learner, all options are always open, even if he or she carries a history of failure. Thus, quite unlike the AM, the PM seems to bring a message of an everlasting hope: Today you act one way; tomorrow you may act differently.

To sum up, the *participation metaphor* has a potential to lead to a new, more democratic practice of learning and teaching. Because, however, social, normative, and ethical morals of metaphors are not inscribed in the metaphors themselves but rather are a matter of interpretation, the intentions and skills of those who harness the metaphor to work are of central significance.[6] In the final account, what shape the practice will take is up to interpreters rather than to legislators. Thus, only time will tell whether the promise of a more democratic process of learning, brought by PM, is going to materialize. When it comes to social issues, PM-based theories are not any less susceptible to abuses and undesirable interpretations than other conceptual frameworks. We can only protect ourselves from falling into such traps by constantly monitoring our basic beliefs. It may well be that the most important merit of the PM is that it serves as an eye-opening device with respect to the *acquisition metaphor.* This relation, by the way, is symmetric: The social implications of the PM, listed above—far from being the only possible—are brought into full relief against the contrasting background of common beliefs induced by the AM and could be much harder to see without it. The mutual dependence of interpretations of the metaphors is something to be remembered when we arrive at the conclusions of the present discussion in the last section of this article.

Why Do We Need AM After All?

After pointing out the weaknesses of the AM and the relative advantages of the PM, I will now argue that giving up the AM is neither desirable nor possible. When it comes to research, some important things that can be done with the old metaphor cannot be achieved with the new one. Besides, the PM, when left alone, may be as dangerous a thing as the AM proved to be in a similar situation.

Research Issues: The Question of Transfer

The refusal to reify knowledge seems to go hand in hand with wondering about the notion of transfer. There are two ways in which the opponents of objectifying and abstracting argue against this notion. Some of them claim that, based on empirical evidence, transfer is a rare event, and the most extreme among them would simply deny its existence. Others reject the very idea of transfer, saying that it is "seriously misconceived" (Lave, 1988, p. 39). Many opponents of the PM argue against the former type of claim (Anderson et al., 1996), but, in fact, only the latter line of reasoning is truly consistent with the PM-based frameworks. As Greeno (1997, p. 5) aptly notices in his contribution to the present discussion, those who overlook this point may, as a result, "talk and write past each other because they address different questions."

A persistent follower of the PM must realize, sooner or later, that from a purely analytical point of view, the metaphorical message of the notion of transfer does not fit into PM-generated conceptual frameworks. Learning transfer means carrying knowledge across contextual boundaries; therefore, when one refuses to view knowledge as a stand-alone entity and rejects the idea of context as a clearly delineated "area," there is simply nothing to be carried over, and there are no definite boundaries to be crossed. It is only natural that when it comes to the centrally important controversy over transfer, many PM adherents, not yet prepared to face the ultimate consequences of the new vision of learning, go only halfway: They bring empirical evidence to refute the claims about the possibility of transfer rather than admit that the notion, at least as it is traditionally understood, is intractable within their framework. By doing so, they unwittingly succumb to the rules of AM-based discourse. Naturally, the discussion between the participationist and acquisitionist is bound to be futile because the former cannot convince the latter of the nonexistence of transfer, just as a physiologist would not be able to convince a psychiatrist about the nonexistence of mental illness: It takes a common language to make one's position acceptable—or even just comprehensible—to another person.

If we agree that there is no room for the traditionally conceived notion of transfer in the PM-based discourse, the long-standing controversy would disappear just as the learning paradox disappeared before. But the benefits of this new disappearance are not so obvious as those of the former one. For one thing, I doubt the very possibility of clearing the discourse on learning from any traces of the AM. Whereas growing numbers of thinkers are ready to agree that the dependence of learning on context is much too great to allow for talk about universal cross-situational invariants, nobody—not even the most zealous followers of the PM-based line of thought—would deny that something does keep repeating itself as we move from situation to situation and from context to context. Our ability to prepare ourselves today to deal with new situations we are going to encounter tomorrow is the very essence of learning. Competence means being able to repeat what can be repeated while changing what needs to be changed. How is all of this accounted for if we are not allowed to talk about carrying anything with us from one situation to another?[7]

Aware of the impossibility of circumventing these questions, some writers are trying to reconcile the idea of transfer with the PM. One such attempt has been presented by Greeno (1997) in his contribution to the present discussion. Greeno's central idea is to provide the old notion with a new interpretation.[8] Defining learning as "improved participation in interactive systems," he proceeds to account "for transfer in terms of transformations of constraints, affordances, and attunements" (p. 12). This description, oriented toward interactions between learners and situations, may indeed be regarded as compatible with the PM framework. In spite of this, one may still wonder whether the proposal has a chance to bring the heated controversy between the two camps to a stop. Even if the new approach is welcome in acquisitionist circles, it may be unacceptable in the eyes of the most devoted adherents of the PM. The latter may claim that the switch to the new framework cannot be regarded as complete until the professional discourse is thoroughly purged of expressions that bring to mind the old metaphor. Indeed, if this is what they said in response to the attempts to preserve the terms "knowledge" and "concept" (see, e.g., Bauersfeld, 1995; Smith, 1995), this is also what they are likely to say about any attempt to save the notion of transfer. Because the notion is fraught with acquisitionist connotations, some people may simply be unable to say "transfer" and "situatedness" in one breath.

Whether fully effective or not, Greeno's attempt shows that even if one agrees with the contention that any human action is a result of a dialectic between the situation and the actor rather than of any predesigned, abstract plan of that action, one may still believe that there is no satisfactory account of learning that does not take into account the actor's previous experience. Thus, if a model of learning is to be convincing, it is probably bound to build on the notion of an acquired, situationally invariant property of the learner, which goes together with him or her from one situation to another.

To sum up, it seems that even if one does not like its objectifying quality, one finds it extremely difficult to avoid the acquisitionist language altogether. Whenever we try to comprehend a change, the perceptual, bodily roots of all our thinking compel us to look for structure-imposing invariants and to talk in terms of objects and abstracted properties. We seem to know no other route to understanding. No wonder, therefore, that those who oppose objectification and try to exorcise abstraction and generalization from the discourse on learning find themselves entangled in conflicting statements. They may be making heroic efforts to free themselves from the idea of learning as acquisition, but the metaphor—engraved in the language—would invariably bounce back. Some of the proponents of the PM framework are aware of the contradictions implicit in the call for disobjectification and wonder about it explicitly: "How can we purport to be working out a theoretical conception of learning without, in fact, engaging in the project of abstraction rejected above?," ask Lave and Wenger (1991, p. 38, emphasis in the original). There is no simple way out of this entrapment. As I argue in the concluding section, even if one cannot solve the dilemma, one can—and probably should—learn to live with it.

Let me finish this section by saying that even if we could create an AM-free discourse, we probably shouldn't. Within the participationist framework, some powerful means for conceptualization of learning are lost, and certain promising paths toward understanding its mechanism are barred. This very article, if it resonates with the readers' thinking, may serve as evidence. This discussion on learning is founded in the theory of conceptual metaphor, according to which any new conceptualization—thus, any learning—is only possible thanks to our ability to transfer existing conceptual schemes into new contexts. The metaphor itself was defined as a "conceptual transplant."[9] The foregoing sections abound in concrete examples of such transplants. All of this testifies to my sustained faith in the power of the AM.

Pedagogical Issues: The Worry About Subject Matter

Whereas the above considerations deal with inevitable implications of the *participation metaphor,* I am now going to focus on metaphorical entailments that are a matter of interpretation and choice rather than of logical necessity.

More often than not, it is not all that obvious how the request to disobjectify knowledge and "put it back into context" should be interpreted. Within the science and mathematics education communities, the claims about inherent contextuality of knowledge are often construed as contentions that scientific and mathematical concepts can be meaningfully learned only within a "real-life" context (see, e.g., Heckman & Weissglass, 1994). As it now becomes clear, however, real-life situations that would be likely to become for mathematics or science students what a craftsman's workshop is for the apprentice are extremely difficult to find. Another translation of PM-engendered theoretical ideas into the language of instructional practice is offered by those who suggest that the student should become a member of a "community of practice" (Lave & Wenger, 1991), within which he or she would have a chance to act as a (beginning) practitioner. According to Ball (1991, p. 35), "the goal [of teaching mathematics] is to help students . . . become active participants in mathematics as a system of human thought," whereas Schoenfeld (1996) promotes the idea of turning mathematics class into a "community of inquiry." At a closer look, this approach also turns quite problematic, as it is far from clear how we should construe the term "community of practice" and whom we should view as "expert practitioners" and the shapers of a given "practice."

Whichever of the two interpretations is chosen, what used to be called "subject matter" may change so dramatically that some people would begin wondering whether the things we would then be teaching could still be called science or mathematics (see, e.g., Hiebert et al., 1996; Sierpinska, 1995; Thomas, 1996). Naturally, the question of naming is not the main reason for concerns expressed by those who hold the PM responsible for current changes in mathematics education. The main problem, it seems, is that of a gradual disappearance of a well-defined subject matter. Without a clearly delineated content,[10] the whole process of learning and teaching is in danger of becoming amorphous and losing direction. No wonder, then, that current talk about "challenges for Reform" (see, e.g., Smith III, 1996)—perhaps even as a backlash to reform—indicate a growing disillusionment with what is going on in many classrooms a few years into the "participation era."

Conclusion: One Metaphor Is Not Enough

The message of the above critical examination of the two basic metaphors for learning is rather confusing: It now seems that we can live neither with nor without either of them. In this concluding section, I wish to make it clear why it is essential that we try to live with both. Later, I make suggestions about the ways in which this seemingly impossible demand might be fulfilled after all.

Why Do We Need More Than One Metaphor?

The relative advantages of each of the two metaphors make it difficult to give up either of them: Each has something to offer that the other cannot provide. Moreover, relinquishing either the AM or the PM may have grave consequences, whereas metaphorical pluralism embraces a promise of a better research and a more satisfactory practice. The basic tension between seemingly conflicting metaphors is our protection against theoretical excesses, and is a source of power.

As was emphasized before, the metaphors we use should not be held responsible for unsatisfactory practices, but rather their interpretations. When a theory is translated into an instructional prescription, exclusivity becomes the worst enemy of success. Educational practices have an overpowering propensity for extreme, one-for-all practical recipes. A trendy mixture of constructivist, social-interactionist, and situationist approaches—which has much to do with the *participation metaphor*—is often translated into a total banishment of "teaching by telling," an imperative to make "cooperative learning" mandatory to all, and a complete delegitimatization of instruction that is not "problem-based" or not situated in a real-life context. But this means putting too much of a good thing into one pot. Because no two students have the same needs and no two teachers arrive at their best performance in the same way, theoretical exclusivity and didactic single-mindedness can be trusted to make even the best of educational ideas fail.

What is true about educational practice also holds for theories of learning. It seems that the most powerful research is the one that stands on more than one metaphorical leg (cf. Sfard, 1997). An adequate combination of the *acquisition* and *participation metaphors* would bring to the fore the advantages of each of them, while keeping their respective drawbacks at bay. Conversely, giving full exclusivity to one conceptual framework would be hazardous. Dictatorship of a single metaphor, like a dictatorship of a single ideology, may lead to theories that serve the interests of certain groups to the disadvantage of others. A metaphor that has been given hegemony serves as an exclusive basis for deciding what should count as "normal" and what is "anomalous," what should be viewed as "below average" rather than "above," and what should be regarded as "healthy" and what as "pathological." The exclusivity is often equated with certainty, whereas the very presence of a competing metaphor may be enough to disclose the arbitrary nature of some of the generally accepted classifications. This disclosure, therefore, has an immediate emancipatory effect. When two metaphors compete for attention and incessantly screen each other for possible weaknesses, there is a much better chance for producing a critical theory[11] of learning (Geuss, 1981; Habermas, 1972). Such a theory would inquire after the true interests of all of the parties involved in the learning process and thus engage the research community in an endeavor likely to have a liberating and consolidating effect on those who learn and those who teach.

Living With Contradictions

After making the case for the plurality of metaphors, I have to show that this proposal is workable. Indeed, considering the fact that the two metaphors seem to be mutually exclusive, one may wonder how the suggested metaphorical crossbreeding could be possible at all. In fact, however, the problem is not new, and it is not restricted to the research on learning. We can turn to contemporary science for many more examples of similar dilemmas, as well as for at least two ways in which the difficulty can be overcome.

First, we can look on the PM- and AM-generated conceptual frameworks as offering differing perspectives rather than competing opinions. Having several theoretical outlooks at the same thing is a normal practice in science, where, for instance, chemistry and physics offer two different—but not incompatible—accounts of matter, while physiology and psychology bring mutually complementing outlooks at human beings. In the spirit of this approach, acquisitionists and participationists might admit that the difference between them is not a matter of differing opinions but rather of participating in different, mutually complementing discourses.

Somebody may argue, however, that the tension between the AM and the PM is too fundamental to be treated with such tolerance. After all, people may say, the AM and the PM make incompatible ontological claims about the nature of learning. To this, Kuhn, Rorty, and many other contemporary philosophers would respond that the metaphors are incommensurable rather than incompatible,[12] and because "[i]ncommensurability entails irreducibility [of vocabularies], but not incompatibility' (Rorty, 1979, p. 388), this means a possibility of their peaceful coexistence. Science and mathematics are a rich source of examples showing that such an option is not purely theoretical. Thus, for instance, today's mathematicians are able to live with Euclidean and non-Euclidean geometries without privileging any of them, whereas contemporary physicists admit a mixture of ostensibly contradictory approaches to subatomic phenomena, sanctioning this decision with Bohr's famous principle of complementarity.

Remembering the metaphorical underpinnings of the claims on the nature of learning, we might find it quite easy to adopt Bohr's principle in our own research. This would mean that, ontological discrepancy notwithstanding, we could view learning as an acquisition or as participation, according to our choice. How this choice is made depends on several factors. First, there are a few necessary conditions a metaphor must fulfill to rank as a candidate. If it is to have any chance at all, the resulting theories must be found convincing and coherent. The seemingly straightforward idea of "convincing" is, in fact, rather complex, and it includes a belief in the usefulness of the theories and an expectation that they will lead to what Rorty (1991) calls an intersubjective agreement. In addition to its role as a potent sense-making tool, a theory has to be an effective producer of new insights about learning.

If the necessary conditions for the acceptance of a metaphor seem relatively easy to pinpoint, the sufficient conditions are rather elusive. Clearly, some metaphors may be more attractive than others because of their accessibility, flexibility, imaginativeness, or aesthetic value. In the final account, however, the choice made by individual researchers would probably depend mainly on what they want to achieve. If, for example, one's purpose is to build a computer program that would simulate human behavior, then the *acquisition metaphor* is likely to be chosen as one that brings forward the issue of representations—something that has to be constructed and quite literally put into a computer. If, on the other hand, one is concerned with educational issues—such as the mechanisms that enable successful learning or make its failure persistent, then the participational approach may be more helpful as one that defies the traditional distinction between cognition and affect, brings social factors to the fore, and thus deals with an incomparably wider range of possibly relevant aspects.[13]

Finally, let me add that being aware of the essentially figurative nature of our sense-making activities, we may sometimes go so far as to merge seemingly conflicting metaphors within one theoretical framework. The merger becomes possible when acquisitionist utterances stop being read as ontological stipulations (as is usually the case within the AM framework) and are interpreted instead as bringing an "as if" message. In this case, their figurative nature is never forgotten and their use is justified pragmatically, with arguments of effectiveness and productivity.

One point cannot be overstated: With all of the flexibility of the proposed multimetaphorical metaframework, plurality of metaphors does not imply that "anything goes;" neither does it result in a complete methodological freedom or in a reduced need for empirical evidence. To count as trustworthy, the resulting theories must still be experimentally testable and congruent with data. The only thing that changes is the relative status of data and theory. While traditionally, data were regarded as previous to, and independent of, theory, now it is assumed that they are already tinted by theory when we first set our eyes on them. As shown by the heated discussion on transfer, the very existence of "facts" may sometimes be a matter of a theoretical lens used by an observer. The relationship between theory and data is dialectic in that they have a tendency for generating each other. It is notable that the persuasive power of data may be confined to the paradigm within which they came into being. Because there is no such thing as "naked facts," the power of empirical findings may sometimes be lost in a transition from one framework to another. For that reason, empirical evidence is unlikely to serve as an effective weapon in paradigm wars.

The basic message of this article can now be put in a few sentences. As researchers, we seem to be doomed to living in a reality constructed from a variety of metaphors. We have to accept the fact that the metaphors we use while theorizing may be good enough to fit small areas, but none of them suffice to cover the entire field. In other words, we must learn to satisfy ourselves with only local sense-making. A realistic thinker knows he or she has to give up the hope that the little patches of coherence will eventually combine into a consistent global theory. It seems that the sooner we accept the thought that our work is bound to produce a patchwork of metaphors rather than a unified, homogeneous theory of learning, the better for us and for those whose lives are likely to be affected by our work.

Notes

This article is an extended version of an invited lecture given at the Eighth International Congress of Mathematics Education in Seville, Spain, in July 1996. I wish to thank Paul Cobb, Robert Thomas, and Devorah Kalekin-Fishman for their patient reading and commenting on different drafts of the article. Special acknowledgments go to anonymous reviewers and to the editor, Dr. Robert Donmoyer, for their helpful questions and suggestions.

1. This article may be read as an interim report on my own face-to-face confrontation with the new approaches to learning and with my conflicting feelings about them. Initially, my mathematical-scientific background made me suspicious—indeed, resentful—of such ideas as abstaining from abstraction and "putting learning back into context" to a total banishment of a "distilled" content that can be carried across situational boundaries (Lave & Wenger, 1991). At the same time, however, I found myself strangely attracted to the new vision of learning that grew out of the innovative approach.
2. Bruner (1986) makes this claim in a particularly clear—and beautifully metaphorical!—way. After stating that metaphors are "crutches to help us get up the abstract mountain," he notes that once we make it to the top, we are eager to get rid of them "in favor of a formal, logically consistent theory that (with luck) can be stated in mathematical or near-mathematical terms" (p. 48).
3. It should be noted that the decision to view learning as an integration with a community in action gave rise to quite a number of conceptual frameworks. The theory of situated learning (Brown, Collins, & Duguid, 1989; Lave, 1988; Lave & Wenger, 1991), the discursive paradigm (Edwards & Potter, 1992; Foucault, 1972; Harre & Gillet, 1995), and the theory of distributed cognition (Salomon, 1993) are probably the best developed among them. All of these are theories of a new kind, differing from the old doctrines not only in their vision of learning but also, and perhaps most importantly, in their epistemological foundations and in the underlying assumption about the mission of research on learning.
4. Harbingers of revolution tend to believe that the old and the new are mutually exclusive. It is only natural that profound change like the one we are witnessing these days is marked by a dose of single-mindedness and zealousness. Often, one feels obliged to declare his or her exclusive devotion to the new metaphor if the other metaphor—the one by which we have been living for centuries—is ever to be made explicit and susceptible to critical scrutiny. As I declared at the outset, however, it is the aim of this article to show the dangers of such total, single-minded devotion to one metaphor.
5. One should not forget that the "knowledge as commodity" metaphor, as any other, can only go so far; for example, while passing a commodity to others deprives its original owner of his or her possession, giving knowledge does not mean the giver loses it.
6. All of this is obviously true, for example, about the NCTM's new *Standards* for teaching and learning mathematics (National Council of Teachers of Mathematics, 1989, 1991), which seem to favor the PM but cannot bring the desired change by their mere existence.
7. The range of possible situations in which we may be able to profit from the given learning sequence differs from person to person; it is interesting that we tend only to talk about transfer when the range is particularly wide. Let us not forget, however, that if so, the difference between the phenomena we recognize as simple cases of successful learning and those we regard as instances of successful transfer is qualitative rather than quantitative, and the line between the two is undefined and probably indefinable.
8. At times of major paradigm shift, endowing old notions with new definitions is a usual practice. In this way, the continuity of the scientific endeavor may be preserved in spite of the apparently unbridgeable breaches. For example, in the transition from the AM to PM framework, Lave and Wenger (1991) proposed to redefine the old terms "learning" and "knowing" as "relations between people in activity in, with, and arising from the socially and culturally structured world" (p. 51). Much earlier, Foucault (1972) redescribed "concept" in discursive terms.
9. The "transplant" is not a simple procedure, and the way a particular conceptual scheme is deemed appropriate for the conceptualization of a given phenomenon is an intricate question to which no satisfactory answer has been found as yet (Johnson-Laird, 1989; Sfard, 1997). A metaphor is built in a complex interaction between the source and the target, and the recognition of similarity between the two, initially regarded as a point of departure for the metaphorical projection, is now considered as something that is only constructed in the course of this projection. All of these intricacies notwithstanding, it is clear that the theory

of the conceptual metaphor belongs to the AM framework.

10. Please note that this notion only makes sense in an AM framework!
11. What came to be known as critical theories can be defined as conceptual frameworks that deal with human beings in asocial context and "aim at emancipation and enlightenment, at making agents aware of hidden coercion, thereby freeing them from that coercion and putting them in a position to determine where their true interests lie" (Geuss, 1981, p. 55). While "theories in natural science are 'objectifying,' critical theories are 'reflective' " (p. 2).
12. "By 'commensurable,' " says Rorty (1979), "I mean able to be brought under a set of rules which will tell us how rational agreement can be reached on what would settle the issue on every point where statements seem to conflict" (p. 316). In other words, incommensurability means that there is no super-theory that would provide tools for proving one framework right while refuting the other. This is certainly the case with the controversy over our two metaphors for learning: There is no possibility of solving this type of conflict with a scientific argument, as it is traditionally understood.
11. Let me remark that when it comes to a choice of a paradigm, a researcher's personal preferences and the question of his or her professional identity, although purportedly irrelevant, may, in fact, be of considerable importance.

References

Anderson, J. R., Reder, L. M., & Simon, H. A. (1996). Situated learning and education. *Educational Researcher, 25*(4), 5–11.

Ball, D. (1991). Research on teaching mathematics: Making subject-matter knowledge part of the equation. In J. Brophy (Ed.), *Advances in research on teaching: Vol. 2. Teacher's subject-matter knowledge* (pp. 1–48.) Greenwich, CT: JAI Press.

Bauersfeld, H. (1995). "Language games" in the mathematics classroom: Their function and their effects. In P. Cobb & H. Bauersfeld (Eds.), *Emergence of mathematical meaning: Interaction in classroom cultures* (pp. 271–291). Hillsdale, NJ: Lawrence Erlbaum Associates.

Bereiter, C. (1985). Towards the solution of the learning paradox. *Review of Educational Research, 55,* 201–226.

Billett, S. (1996). Situated learning: Bridging sociocultural and cognitive theorising. *Learning and Instruction, 6*(3), 263–280.

Brown, J. S., Collins, A., & Duguid, P. (1989). Situated cognition and the culture of learning. *Educational Researcher, 18*(1), 32–42.

Bruner, J. (1986). *Actual minds, possible worlds.* Cambridge, MA: Harvard University Press.

Cobb, P. (1995). Continuing the conversation: A response to Smith. *Educational Researcher, 24*(7), 25–27.

Cobb, P., Yackel, E., & Wood, T. (1992). A constructivist alternative to the representational view of mind in mathematics education. *Journal for Research in Mathematics Education, 23*(1), 2–33.

Donmoyer, R. (1996). This issue: A focus on learning. *Educational Researcher, 25*(4), 4.

Edwards, D., & Potter, J. (1992). *Discursive psychology.* Newbury Park, CA: Sage.

Foucault, M. (1972). *The archaeology of knowledge.* New York: Harper Colophon.

Geuss, R. (1981). *The idea of critical theory: Habermas and the Frankfurt school.* Cambridge, UK: Cambridge University Press.

Greeno, J. G. (1997). On claims that answer the wrong question. *Educational Researcher, 26*(1), 5–17.

Habermas, J. (1972). *Knowledge and human interests.* Boston: Beacon Press.

Hardy, G. H. (1967). *A mathematician's apology.* Cambridge, MA: Cambridge University Press. (Original work published 1940)

Harre, R., & Gillet, G. (1995). *The discursive mind.* Thousand Oaks, CA: Sage.

Heckman, P., & Weissglass, J. (1994). Contextualized mathematics instruction: Moving beyond recent proposals. *For the Learning of Mathematics,* 14(1), 29–33.

Hesse, M. (1966). *Models and analogies in science.* Notre Dame, IN: Notre Dame University Press.

Hiebert, J., Carpenter, T. P., Fennema, E., Fuson, K., Human, P., Murray, H., Olivier, A., & Wearne, D. (1996). Problem solving as a basis for reform in curriculum and instruction: The case of mathematics. *Educational Researcher,* 25(4), 12–21.

Johnson, M. (1987). *The body in the mind: The bodily basis of meaning, imagination, and reason.* Chicago: The University of Chicago Press.

Johnson-Laird, P. N. (1989). Analogy and the exercise of creativity. In S. Vosniadou & A. Ortony (Eds.), *Similarity and analogical reasoning* (pp. 313–365). Cambridge, UK: Cambridge University Press.

Kozulin, A. (1990). *Vygotsky's psychology: A biography of ideas.* New York: Harvester Wheatsheaf.

Lakoff, G. (1987). *Women, fire and dangerous things: What categories reveal about the mind.* Chicago: The University of Chicago Press.

Lakoff, G. (1993). The contemporary theory of metaphor. In A. Ortony (Ed.), *Metaphor and thought* (2nd ed., pp. 202–250). Cambridge, UK: Cambridge University Press.

Lakoff, G., & Johnson, M. (1980). *The metaphors we live by.* Chicago: The University of Chicago Press.

Lave, J. (1988). *Cognition in practice.* Cambridge, UK: Cambridge University Press.

Lave, J., & Wenger, E. (1991). *Situated learning: Legitimate peripheral participation.* Cambridge, UK: Cambridge University Press.

Morton, R. K. (1973). *The sociology of science.* Chicago: The University of Chicago.

National Council of Teachers of Mathematics. (1989). *Curriculum and evaluation standards for school mathematics.* Reston, VA: Author.

National Council of Teachers of Mathematics. (1991). *Professional standards for teaching mathematics.* Reston, VA: Author.

Ortony, A. (Ed.). (1993). *Metaphor and thought* (2nd ed.). Cambridge, UK: Cambridge University Press.

Reddy, M. (1978). The conduit metaphor: A case of frame conflict in our language about language. In A. Ortony (Ed.), *Metaphor and thought* (2nd ed., pp. 164–201). Cambridge, UK: Cambridge University Press.

Rogoff, B. (1990). *Apprenticeship in thinking: Cognitive development in social context.* Oxford, UK: Oxford University Press.

Rorty, R. (1979). *Philosophy and the mirror of nature.* Princeton, NJ: Princeton University Press.

Rorty, R. (1991). *Objectivity, relativism, and truth.* Cambridge, UK: Cambridge University Press.

Sacks, S. (Ed.). (1978). *On metaphor.* Chicago: The University of Chicago Press.

Salomon, G. (Ed.). (1993). *Distributed cognitions: Psychological and educational considerations.* Cambridge, UK: Cambridge University Press.

Scheffler, I. (1991). *In praise of cognitive emotions.* New York: Routledge.

Schoenfeld, A. (1996). In fostering communities of inquiry, must it matter that the teacher knows the "answer"? *For the Learning of Mathematics, 16*(3), 11–16.

Sfard, A. (1994). Reification as the birth of metaphor. *For the Learning of Mathematics, 14*(1), 44–55.

Sfard, A. (1997). Commentary: On metaphorical roots of conceptual growth. In L. English (Ed.), *Mathematical reasoning: Analogies, metaphors, and images* (pp. 339–372). Mahwah, NJ: Erlbaum.

Sierpinska, A. (1995). Mathematics "in context," "pure" or "with applications"? *For the Learning of Mathematics, 15*(1), 2-15.

Smith, E. (1995). Where is the mind? "Knowing" and "knowledge" in Cobb's constructivist and sociocultural perspectives. *Educational Researcher, 24*(7), 23–24.

Smith, J. P., III. (1996). Efficacy and teaching mathematics by telling: A challenge for reform. *Journal for Research in Mathematics Education, 27*(4), 387–402.

Thomas, R. (1996). Proto-mathematics and/or real mathematics. *For the Learning of Mathematics, 16*(2), 11–18.

Vosniadou, S. (1996). Towards a revised cognitive psychology for new advances in learning and instruction. *Learning and Instruction, 6*(2), 95–110.

Woodfield, A. (1993). Do your concepts develop? In C. Hookway & D. Peterson (Eds), *Philosophy and cognitive science* (pp. 41–67). Cambridge, UK: Cambridge University Press.

CHAPTER 31

POWERFUL PARTNERSHIPS: A SHARED RESPONSIBILITY FOR LEARNING

AMERICAN ASSOCIATION FOR HIGHER EDUCATION
AMERICAN COLLEGE PERSONNEL ASSOCIATION
NATIONAL ASSOCIATION OF STUDENT PERSONNEL ADMINISTRATORS

Despite American higher education's success at providing collegiate education for an unprecedented number of people, the vision of equipping all our students with learning deep enough to meet the challenges of the post-industrial age provides us with a powerful incentive to do our work better. People collaborate when the job they face is too big, is too urgent, or requires too much knowledge for one person or group to do alone. Marshalling what we know about learning and applying it to the education of our students is just such a job. This report makes the case that only when everyone on campus—particularly academic affairs and student affairs staff—shares the responsibility for student learning will we be able to make significant progress in improving it.

Collectively, we know a lot about learning. A host of faculty, staff, and institutional initiatives undertaken since the mid-80s and supported by colleges and universities, foundations, government, and other funding sources have resulted in a stream of improvement efforts related to teaching, curriculum, assessment, and learning environments. The best practices from those innovations and reforms mirror what scholars from a variety of disciplines, from neurobiology to psychology, tell us about the nature of learning. Exemplary practices are also shaped by the participants' particular experiences as learners and educators, which is why a program cannot simply be adopted but must be adapted to a new environment.

Despite these examples, most colleges and universities do not use our collective wisdom as well as they should. To do so requires a commitment to and support for action that goes beyond the individual faculty or staff member. Distracted by other responsibilities and isolated from others from whom they could learn about learning and who would support them, most people on campus contribute less effectively to the development of students' understanding than they might. It is only by acting cooperatively in the context of common goals, as the most innovative institutions have done, that our accumulated understanding about learning is put to best use.

There is another reason to work collaboratively to deepen student learning. Learning is a social activity, and modeling is one of the most powerful learning tools. As participants in organizations dedicated to learning, we have a responsibility to model for students how to work together on behalf of our shared mission and to learn from each other.

On behalf of such collaboration, we, the undersigned members of this Joint Task Force on Student Learning, offer the following report. It begins with a statement of the insights gained through the scholarly study of learning and their implications for pedagogy, curricula, learning environments, and assess-

Source: "Powerful Partnerships: A Shared Responsibility for Learning," by the American Association for Higher Education, American College Personnel Association, and the National Association of Student Personnel Administrators, reprinted from *A Joint Report*, 1998, American Association for Higher Education.

ment. Each principle is illustrated by a set of exemplary cooperative practices that bring together academic and student affairs professionals to make a difference in the quality of student learning, a difference that has been assessed and documented. The report ends with a call to all involved in higher education to reflect upon these findings and examples in conjunction with their own and their colleagues' experience and to draw on all these sources of knowledge as the basis for actions to promote higher student achievement.

—Joint Task Force on Student Learning

The following ten principles about learning and how to strengthen it are drawn from research and practice and provide grounds for deliberation and action. All those who participate in the educational mission of institutions of higher education—students, faculty, and staff—share responsibility for pursuing learning improvements. Collaborations between academic and student affairs personnel and organizations have been especially effective in achieving this better learning for students. We advocate these partnerships as the best way to realize fully the benefits of the findings.

Learning Principles and Collaborative Action

1. Learning is fundamentally about *making and maintaining connections:* biologically through neural networks; mentally among concepts, ideas, and meanings; and experientially through interaction between the mind and the environment, self and other, generality and context, deliberation and action.

Rich learning experiences and environments require and enable students to *make connections:*

- through **learning materials** that stimulate comparisons and associations, explore relationships, evaluate alternative perspectives and solutions, and challenge students to draw conclusions from evidence;
- through opportunities to **relate** their **own experience** and knowledge **to materials** being learned;
- through **pedagogies** emphasizing critical analysis of conflicting views and demanding that students make defensible judgments about and demonstrate linkages among bodies of knowledge;
- through **curricula** integrating ideas and themes within and across fields of knowledge and establishing coherence among learning experiences within and beyond the classroom; and
- through **classroom** experiences **integrated with** purposeful activities **outside of class.**

To **make and maintain connections,** faculty and staff collaborators design learning experiences that:

- expose students to alternative world views and culturally diverse perspectives;
- give students responsibility for solving problems and resolving conflicts;
- make explicit the relationships among parts of the curriculum and between the curriculum and other aspects of the collegiate experience; and
- deliberately personalize interventions appropriate to individual students' circumstances and needs.

University of Maryland, College Park offers the College Park Scholars program, a two-year living/learning opportunity for freshmen and sophomores. Students reside and attend most of their classes within residence hall communities. Residence life staff, faculty, and other program staff offices are in the halls. Student scholars live on floors corresponding to thematically linked academic programs. For participating commuting students, access is provided to common areas in host residence halls. The thematic programs **deliberately connect** what the students learn in the classroom to the larger world through weekly colloquia, discussion groups, and field trips dealing with related issues.

The scholars program has improved recruitment and retention of talented undergraduates and has provided an enriched learning experience and a more personalized and human scale to campus life. Faculty offices and classrooms within the residence halls lead to enhanced interaction with faculty.

At *University of Missouri, Kansas City,* Supplemental Instruction and Video-Based Supplemental Instruction help students **make connections.** Supplemental Instruction uses peer-assisted study sessions to increase student academic performance and student retention in historically difficult academic courses. In the sessions, students learn how to integrate course content and develop reasoning and study strategies, facilitated by student leaders who have previously succeeded in these courses and who are trained in study strategies and peer collaborative learning techniques. The video-based program offers an alternative course delivery system. Faculty offer courses on videotape and students enroll in a video section. A facilitator guides review of the video lectures, stopping the tapes in mid-lecture to engage in class discussions, integration, and practice of learning strategies.

More than three hundred studies nationally have documented the impact of supplemental instruction, demonstrating its special impact on students with weak academic preparation. The U.S. Department of Education designated supplemental instruction as an Exemplary Education Program in 1982, noting its ability to increase academic achievement and college graduation rates among students. Program staff at UMKC have further investigated the effects of this instruction through the study of neurological processes. Using a Quantitative Electroencephalography instrument, they have found evidence of improved brain electrical activity in students who participate in the programs.

2. Learning is enhanced by *taking place in* the context of a *compelling situation* that balances challenge and opportunity, stimulating and utilizing the brain's ability to conceptualize quickly and its capacity and need for contemplation and reflection upon experiences.

Presenting students with *compelling situations* amplifies the learning process. Students learn more when they are:

- asked to tackle complex and compelling **problems that invite** them to develop an array of workable and innovative **solutions;**
- asked to produce **work** that will be **shared** with multiple audiences;
- offered opportunities for **active application of skills and abilities** and **time for contemplation;** and
- placed in **settings** where they can **draw upon past knowledge and competencies** while adapting to new circumstances.

To **create compelling situations,** faculty and staff collaborators:

- articulate and enforce high standards of student behavior inside and outside the classroom;
- give students increasing responsibility for leadership;
- create environments and schedules that encourage intensive activity as well as opportunities for quiet deliberation; and
- establish internships, externships, service-learning, study abroad, and workplace-based learning experiences.

The First-Year Experience at the *College of New Jersey* is a collaboration between General Education and Student Life. Students live in residence hall communities with a volunteer nonresident faculty fellow for each floor. Faculty fellows, student life staff, and students plan residence hall activities. Students also take an interdisciplinary core course, *Athens to New York,* taught by full-time faculty and selected student life staff in residence hall classrooms, and incorporating service-learning. Four questions drive the mission of the First-Year Experience: What does it mean to be human? What does it mean to be a member of a community? What does it mean to be moral, ethical, and just? and How do communities respond to differences? Service-learning provides a **compelling situation** in which students can confront complex social issues, apply their talents to marginalized communities, interact and work with diverse populations, and enhance their career preparation.

Student service-learning journals show a clear understanding of the work of the course and its objectives and core questions. Community agency staff provide feedback and guidance to students, and the staffs' evaluations offer evidence that students learn about and contribute to their communities. Students express high levels of satisfaction with the residence hall, the classroom experience, workshops, field trips, and enrichment lectures associated with the core course.

Community College of Rhode Island's 2+4 Service on Common Ground Program is part of the college's extensive service-learning activities. Supported by funds from the Campus Compact National Center for Community Colleges and the Corporation for National Service to develop service-learning partnerships between community colleges and four-year institutions, the college cooperates with Brown University's Center for Public Service. One joint project connects the community college's nursing faculty and students with the university's medical school faculty and students. Students work in many **challenging situations** to meet community needs and discuss and write in journals observations and experiences that relate the activity to their course of study and to social issues.

Student affairs staff began the program with a core team of five faculty. Now the collaborative effort includes some fifty faculty who employ service-learning in more than a dozen academic disciplines.

3. Learning is an *active search for meaning* by the learner—constructing knowledge rather than passively receiving it, shaping as well as being shaped by experiences.

Active participation by the learner is essential for productive learning, dictating that:

- instructional methods **involve students directly** in the discovery of knowledge;
- learning materials challenge students **to transform prior knowledge and experience** into new and deeper understandings;
- students be expected to **take responsibility** for their own learning;
- students be encouraged to **seek meaning** in the context **of ethical values and commitments;** and
- learning be assessed based on students' ability to **demonstrate competencies and use knowledge.**

To stimulate an **active search for meaning,** faculty and staff collaborators:

- expect and demand student participation in activities in and beyond the classroom;
- design projects and endeavors through which students apply their knowledge and skills; and
- build programs that feature extended and increasingly challenging opportunities for growth and development.

Bloomfield College (New Jersey) offers the Student Advancement Initiative, curricular and co-curricular experiences that **develop student competencies** in aesthetic appreciation, communication, citizenship, cultural awareness, problem solving and critical thinking, science and technology, and other professional skills. The program emphasizes computer-aided self-appraisal for students and a student development transcript. The objectives are to **involve students actively** in the assessment process, to provide continuous feedback to students on their progress toward the competencies, and to strengthen programs based on aggregate information about student achievement of the competencies.

Faculty and student affairs joint task forces have defined the competencies and linked them to the general education program. Faculty draw upon student affairs staff expertise in designing course assignments. Student portfolios and assessment information direct students toward self-analysis and synthesis of theoretical and practical knowledge gained through the curriculum and through developmental activities. Faculty and staff participate together in "reflective practice" sessions to improve programming and administration.

DePaul University (Illinois) offers two writing-intensive interdisciplinary and experiential programs for new students to ease the transition to the university. All first-year students enroll in either Focal Point or Discover Chicago. Focal Point highlights an important event, person, place, or issue and is taught using a multidisciplinary format. Students also enroll in a "common hour" course where student affairs professionals **help students evaluate their contributions** to shared learning, develop their study and decision-making skills, create a learning plan, and reflect upon the nature of diversity at the university and in the city. Academic and student affairs personnel are involved in curriculum development, the design of classroom experiences, and student learning outside the classroom. Discover Chicago brings new students together a week before the first term for a course team-taught by a faculty member, a professional staff member, and a student mentor. The course investigates a particular topic using the city as a learning site. The work of the course involves readings and discussions, visits to city locations, and a community service project.

Assessments of the programs are designed to determine their impact on student retention and include qualitative and quantitative pre- and post-test surveys, a standardized test (the College Student Inventory) that is a predictor of student retention, syllabi review, and focus groups. Results provide information about retention and staff-faculty partnering, student expectations about the university and coursework, and the nature of assignments and forms of evaluation in each program.

4. Learning is *developmental,* a cumulative process *involving the whole person,* relating past and present, integrating the new with the old, starting from but transcending personal concerns and interests.

The *developmental* nature of learning implies both a holistic and a temporal perspective on the learning process. This suggests that:

- any **single** learning **experience or** instructional **method** has a **lesser** impact **than** the **overall** educational experience;
- **curricula** should be **additive and cumulative, building upon prior understandings and knowledge** toward greater richness and complexity;
- intellectual **growth** is **gradual,** with periods of rapid **advancement followed by time for consolidation,** an extended and episodic process of mutually reinforcing experiences;
- the goals of undergraduate education should include students' **development of an integrated sense of identity,** characterized by high self-esteem and personal integrity that extends beyond the individual to the larger community and world; and
- **assessment of** learning should encompass **all aspects of** the educational **experience.**

To create a **developmental process** integrating all aspects of students' lives, faculty and staff collaborators:

- design educational programs to build progressively on each experience;
- track student development through portfolios that document levels of competence achieved and intentional activities leading to personal development;
- establish arenas for student-faculty interaction in social and community settings; and
- present opportunities for discussion and reflection on the meaning of all collegiate experiences.

Virginia Polytechnic Institute and State University attends to the overall health of students through its Wellness Environment for Living and Learning. Students who participate make a commitment to a substance-free lifestyle and residence environment. Faculty and student affairs professionals co-teach a wellness forum, a one-credit course in the residence halls in which undergraduate resident advisors also assist. Additional programming emphasizes **social, physical, intellectual, career, emotional, and spiritual purpose and philosophy.** A student-run community board enables students to develop programs and to take responsibility for managing the housing experience. Campus speakers share personal experiences with substance abuse and wellness issues, and faculty and student affairs staff relate their life experiences in class discussions. The residential community, hall programs, and course curriculum encourage students to reflect on past behaviors and to determine how new knowledge can assist them in college and in developing holistic approaches to a healthy life.

Participation in the program has increased dramatically in two years, with a significant rate of returning students and requests for additional residents. The first group of students had a significantly higher grade-point average than a control group in the beginning semester of the program.

University of Richmond (Virginia) provides a four-year experience at its women's residential college, the Women Involved in Living and Learning Program. Participants enroll in an interdisciplinary women's studies minor and in required gender-related educational programs. Goals include increasing self-awareness, self-confidence, independence, and leadership through structured educational experiences; stimulating critical thinking and analysis about gender roles and relationships; nurturing and promoting student potential and talent; fostering awareness and acceptance of difference; and providing students with curricular and co-curricular opportunities to inform and enhance academic, career, and life choices. The professional program coordinator works closely with the women's studies faculty to plan course offerings, serves on its advisory board, and teaches courses. Students complete a supervised internship and attend monthly membership meetings of a student-run organization and sponsored events that complement program goals. Events form the basis for **discussion and reflection in the courses and informally in the residence halls.**

Wellesley College's Center for Research on Women recently completed an assessment of this program using course effectiveness instruments, an annual survey to determine the overall impact, a self-esteem measure, an alumnae survey to evaluate the long-term program impact, and student focus groups. Results confirm the cumulative and developmental effects on participants. The study found the greatest effect on those who completed all four years of the program. Students and alumnae of the program speak of the transformational aspects of their involvement, the ways they learned to think critically that benefit them in diverse situations, their ability to question their own world views, and their tolerance of different viewpoints. Alumnae of the program express greater satisfaction with their undergraduate experience than non-program alumnae.

5. Learning is done by *individuals* who are intrinsically *tied to others as social beings,* interacting as competitors or collaborators, constraining or supporting the learning process, and able to enhance learning through cooperation and sharing.

The *individual and social nature of learning* has the potential for creating powerful learning environments that:

- take into account students' **personal histories and common cultures;**
- feature **opportunities for cooperative learning,** study, and shared research;
- cultivate a climate in which students see themselves as part of an **inclusive community;**
- use the **residential experience** as a resource for collaborative learning and for integrating social and academic life;
- use **school, work, home, and community** as resources for collaborative learning and for integrating social and academic life; and
- give students a chance to fathom and appreciate **human differences.**

To **relate individuals to others as social beings,** faculty and staff collaborators:

- strive to develop a campus culture where students learn to help each other;
- establish peer tutoring and student and faculty mentorship programs;
- sponsor residence hall and commuting student programs that cultivate student and faculty interaction for social and educational purposes; and
- support activities that enable students from different cultural backgrounds to experience each other's traditions.

The Program on Intergroup Relation, Conflict, and Community at the *University of Michigan, Ann Arbor* offers undergraduate coursework and co-curricular programming in several departments, emphasizing intergroup relations and using a variety of pedagogical approaches. Beginning as a faculty initiative, the program is managed and funded by the College of Literature, Science, and the Arts and the Division of Student Affairs. Program features include:

- first-year departmental course seminars, linked through a faculty seminar and taught by faculty seminar and taught by faculty and student affairs teams and incorporating out-of-classroom experiences designed to build communities of students beyond the individual seminars;
- Intergroup Dialogues, two-credit courses **bringing together students from social identity groups** for intensive peer-facilitated dialogues based on integrated readings, discussions, and experiential exercises;
- facilitator training and practicum courses for Intergroup Dialogue leaders;
- advanced courses in intergroup relations in sociology and psychology;
- consultation and workshops by program staff working with university departments and offices, training programs for staff and organizations, and special campus events;
- a resource center on intergroup relations equipped with books, articles, and videos on related topics.

A current study of the program assessed a course that included required Intergroup Dialogues. The study found that the course increased students' structured thinking about racial and ethnic inequality, enabled them to apply this thinking more generally to social phenomena not explicitly covered in the course, and affected the kinds of actions students advocated in intergroup conflicts.

Portland State University (Oregon) faculty developed their general education program using research on student learning and retention and working with student affairs professionals with expertise in student learning, group dynamics, peer facilitation, and the development of community and feelings of inclusion. The program emphasizes **the integration of both affective and cognitive modes of learning** into all aspects of its classes. It strives to overcome the limited opportunity for informal learning and casual interaction characteristic of urban, commuter campuses. Features of the program include:

- CityQuest, an orientation program designed as an activity in a freshman general education course;
- a "leadership cluster" of multidisciplinary upper-division courses on leadership fulfilling general education requirements;
- student affairs fellows who teach in the "freshman inquiry" and "senior capstone" courses;
- Metro Initiative, cooperative agreements with regional community colleges that connect academic support services and general education coursework across all institutions;
- Capstone, a collaboration to facilitate service-learning within the general education curriculum; and
- Student Snapshot, a student affairs newsletter with information about students to help faculty understand students' lives.

Since implementation of the program, student retention between the first and second year has increased, the institution has developed a better sense of who its students are, and it has information on which aspects of students' learning experiences are more or less effective. Faculty are now more likely to request assistance with students from student affairs staff and to involve the staff in teaching program courses.

6. Learning is strongly *affected by the educational climate* in which it takes place: the settings and surroundings, the influences of others, and the values accorded to the life of the mind and to learning achievements.

The *educational climates* in which learning occurs best:

- value **academic and personal success** and **intellectual inquiry;**
- involve **all constituents**—faculty, students, staff, alumni, employers, family, and others—in **contributing** to student learning;
- make student learning and development an integral part of **faculty and staff responsibilities and rewards;**
- incorporate student **academic performance and development goals** into the educational mission, and assessment of progress toward them into unit performance.
- include **subcommunities** in which students feel **connected, cared for, and trusted.**

To construct an effective **educational climate,** faculty and staff collaborators:

- build a strong sense of community among all institutional constituencies;
- organize ceremonies to honor and highlight contributions to community life and educational values;
- publicly celebrate institutional values;
- articulate how each administrative and academic unit serves the institution's mission; and
- share and use information on how units are performing in relation to this mission.

The Youth in Transition Program of *James Madison University* (Virginia) introduces academically underprepared minority students to college life beginning in the summer prior to their freshman year. Students are supported by an intensive, **nurturing educational environment** in which they can overcome prior negative learning experiences and develop new ways to succeed in academics. The program, offered jointly by university faculty and the Office of Multicultural Student Services, continues throughout the school year. Students receive ongoing academic support, educational enrichment opportunities, and mentors. Academic progress is monitored continuously. Faculty and student affairs staff work as an instructional team, with faculty teaching basic mathematics and writing skills and staff teaching study skills and time management and addressing issues of independence and self-confidence. Students live together in residence halls to establish peer relationships and work with their advisors through all four years of college.

A study of program participants tracked their academic progress over a one-year period. Results showed an increase in the proportion of minority students in good standing over the course of the year and a decrease in the number placed on suspension. Further analysis indicated that a significant proportion of those placed on suspension were later able to return to good standing.

New Century College of *George Mason University* (Virginia) coordinates Collaborations: Partnerships for Active Communities, a combination of programs designed to **place students in diverse educational settings.** "Adventure learning" courses, which fulfill the college's requirement for experiential learning, include the Chesapeake Bay Program and the Bahamas Environmental Research Center, where students engage the natural environment firsthand and learn about ecology in the broadest sense, including the people and cultures that shape the environment. Courses contain both a classroom component and a co-curricular final project. Students also can enroll in skill-based short courses, in learning communities that connect classroom study with life experiences, or in an alternative spring break through which they contribute to and learn about communities they serve. Students are encouraged to reflect on their experiences by developing portfolios representative of their work, providing documentation of work in progress, and presenting evidence of self-reflection on how their learning experiences have evolved.

Comparisons show that students who have participated in these programs have higher retention rates, academic performance, and satisfaction with college life than do non-participants.

7. Learning requires *frequent feedback* if it is to be sustained, *practice* if it is to be nourished, and *opportunities* to *use* what has been learned.

The importance to learning of *feedback, practice, and use* of knowledge and skills mandates that students be:

- expected to **meet high but achievable standards** and provided timely information on their progress toward meeting them;
- engaged in a recurring process of **correction and improvement;**
- encouraged to **take risks** and **learn from mistakes;**
- taught how to be **constructive critics** of each other's work;
- required to demonstrate their learning accomplishments through **active problem solving, applying concepts** to practical situations;
- **refining skills** through frequent use; and
- asked to **test theory against practice** and **refine theory based on practice.**

To provide **occasions to use and practice** what has been learned, faculty and staff collaborators:

- recruit students with relevant academic interests as active participants and leaders in related campus life programs and activities;
- organize work opportunities to take advantage of students' developing skills and knowledge;
- collaborate with businesses and community organizations to match students to internship and externship experiences that fit their evolving educational profiles; and
- develop student research and design projects based on actual problems or cases presented by external organizations to be resolved.

Iowa State University's College of Design and Department of Residence have created together the Design Exchange, a living and learning experience to promote academic success. The Exchange houses design students together in a learning community that includes a design studio and computer laboratory. The studio is available twenty-four hours a day and serves as the site of bi-weekly sessions ranging from academic survival skills to portfolio development. Sessions are facilitated by faculty, student affairs, and residence assistance staff; upper-class design students serve as peer mentors and advisors, role models, and programmers. Efforts are made to offer out-of-class activities that extend classroom learning, and to encourage informal interaction among faculty, staff, and students. First-semester survival programs are followed by more intentional faculty involvement in the second semester, during which they discuss with students such issues as design portfolios and career development. The program allows students to **create design projects and receive continual feedback** from peers and teachers. The studio space encourages this sharing on a cooperative rather than a competitive basis.

Preliminary data from a study comparing Exchange students with a control group suggest that students enrolled in the program have higher grade-point averages than design students not involved in the learning community. Students in the program also report higher levels of satisfaction with the university, a greater sense of community, and improved ability to work collaboratively to find solutions to curricular and social issues. Students surveyed cite frequent feedback and living together as major benefits of the program.

The undergraduate division of the Wharton School of the *University of Pennsylvania* has a mission to educate students to become broad-minded, articulate, and effective leaders in the global marketplace. Its course on leadership and communication in groups is a collaboration between student and academic affairs designed to serve this mission. It features community service projects that provide opportunities to **develop and refine leadership skills** both inside and outside the classroom. Other cooperative experiential activities over the course of students' four-year experience include leadership retreats, mentoring programs, skill-building workshops, a leadership lecture series, the management of forty student clubs and organizations, and student-run conferences. The academic and student service partnership is supported by team advisors, trained to offer both academic advice and peer counseling. The collaboration also works to temper the highly competitive business school culture and to foster cooperative community and college leaders.

Student surveys show appreciation for the school's ability to meet their needs for leadership skills. Students evaluate the leadership retreats highly. In addition, students from the school serve an already large and increasing proportion of leadership positions in the university's student organizations.

8. Much learning *takes place informally and incidentally,* beyond explicit teaching or the classroom, in casual contacts with faculty and staff, peers, campus life, active social and community involvements, and unplanned but fertile and complex situations.

Informal and incidental learning is enhanced by:

- activities beyond the classroom that **enrich formal learning** experiences;
- an institutional climate that encourages student **interaction related to educational issues;**
- **mentorship relationships** on and off campus;
- chances for students to meet **faculty and staff in a variety of settings and circumstances;** and
- student participation as **volunteers** and **active citizens in the broader community.**

To facilitate **informal and incidental learning,** faculty and staff collaborators:

- sponsor programs for students, faculty, and staff that serve both social and educational purposes;
- organize community service and service-learning activities performed by faculty, staff, and students together;
- design campus life programs that relate directly to specific courses;
- link students with peers and with faculty, staff, and community mentors; and
- build common gathering places for students, faculty, and staff.

The First-Year Program at the *College of the Holy Cross* (Massachusetts) is a thematically based academic experience for about one-fourth of the first-year class. Each year a new theme is built around the question "How then shall we live?" by connecting that question to a specific issue. The theme gives an explicit ethical focus to the year and is the touchstone for all other components of the program, including a pair of first-year courses extending through both semesters, a two-semester common reading program, a variety of co-curricular events with faculty and students, and a common residency experience. The intellectual community associated with the program encompasses classroom, studio, laboratory, performance space, faculty offices, and residence hall. The program **extends into all aspects of students' lives,** connecting the learning experience with fundamental questions about how to live, to be part of a community, and to make moral choices. The intent is to provide shared experiences that embrace the entire first-year environment and in so doing to provide a framework **that promotes informal learning.**

Student interviews and institutional records show high levels of participation in class discussion and co-curricular events, extensive discussions outside the classroom, and a strong sense of community in the residence halls. Compared with other students, First-Year participants had fewer alcohol-related incidents, received higher grades, and were more likely to assume campus leadership positions, to participate in honors and study abroad programs, and to be active in community programs.

The *University of Missouri, Columbia* creates Freshmen Interest Groups of students enrolled in the same sections of three general education courses, living in the same residence halls (usually on the same floor), and enrolled in a one-semester seminar. The seminar is designed to help students integrate material from the general education courses and to **facilitate informal discussions on issues covered in the courses.** The program's objectives are to make the campus psychologically small by creating peer reference groups of students, to integrate purposefully curricular and co-curricular experiences, to stimulate early registration for related courses, and to encourage faculty to integrate course content and activities across their disciplines. Faculty and staff jointly plan the program, coordinate in- and out-of-classroom activities, and champion desired outcomes and assessment strategies to evaluate the impact of the learning experience. Shared projects and events associated with the courses are especially important for promoting opportunities for discussion. Peer advisors reinforce this learning, serve as study leaders, and use team-building approaches to increase interest group cohesion. Residence halls have been renovated to offer group study space, classrooms, and computer laboratories.

In comparison with other freshmen, students in the Freshmen Interest Groups demonstrate higher levels of interaction and involvement in college life in the first and second years, greater intellectual content in their contacts with faculty and other students, better performance in general education courses, higher grade-point averages, and higher freshmen-to-sophomore retention rates.

9. Learning is *grounded in particular contexts and individual experiences,* requiring effort to transfer specific knowledge and skills to other circumstances or to more general understandings and to unlearn personal views and approaches when confronted by new information.

The *grounded* nature of learning requires that students:

- encounter **alternative perspectives** and **others' realities;**
- grapple with educational materials that **challenge conventional views;**
- confront novel circumstances that extend beyond their own personal experiences and that require the **application of new knowledge or more general principles;** and
- **share** freely with others **experiences** that have shaped their identities.

To transform learning *grounded in particular contexts and individual experiences* into broader understandings, faculty and staff collaborators:

- sponsor events that involve students with new people and situations;
- champion occasions for interdisciplinary discourse on salient issues;
- foster dialogues between people with disparate perspectives and backgrounds; and
- expand study abroad and cultural exchange programs.

St. Lawrence University (New York) strives for a learning environment that integrates multicultural perspectives, influences, and ideas throughout the curriculum and the campus community. In its First-Year Program, students live together in residential colleges and take an intensive, year-long, interdisciplinary, team-taught thematic course in communication. Faculty members work with student affairs staff to ensure that the living and learning nature of the program **encourages students to reflect on course themes, conflicts arising in the residence hall, and connections between the themes and living experiences.** A "residential curriculum" is organized by residential coordinators, college assistants, and faculty to discuss in class and in the colleges both predictable and unique stresses in the residence communities. A residential education committee plans events and designs interventions to address student problems and conflicts. Students are expected to think through and resolve conflicts associated with differences in background, in behavior within the residence halls, and in academic perspectives. In doing so, students explore each other's personal histories, respond to others' views, and examine the relationship between individual perspectives and knowledge-based approaches.

Detailed evaluation forms ask students about the impact of living with people enrolled in a common course, the communication and research skills learned, the effects of the multidisciplinary, team-taught course, and the coverage of residential issues. Data indicate that residential goals and communications skills are being achieved. Students are positive about living with others who share their academic and personal experiences and appreciate having faculty involved in their residential lives.

University of Wisconsin, Whitewater has a mission to serve students with disabilities and has had a formal program to provide services for these students for nearly thirty years. Instructional staff accommodate students with disabilities in classrooms, labs, field work, internships, student teaching, and the workplace. A new work experience project offering academic credit has received exceptional support from faculty and students. The project brings staff into close contact with faculty, and staff work with the State Vocational Rehabilitation Agency to organize the experience. For many severely and multiply disabled students, the work is one of the first successful validations of their capacity to succeed and to establish a strong identity. Efforts are focused on **matching students' needs with a work environment complementing their educational background** and likely to ensure success. The work is an intensive individual experience; however, the individual learning is tied directly to interaction with others in the workplace at several levels. It helps to provide self-definition as a person and to delineate a role and status within the task group. The combination of the workplace routine, supervisory and peer feedback, and the duties of the position offer opportunities for growth and for eliminating non-functional behaviors. The program has proved particularly important for individuals whose learning styles are not conducive to transfer of knowledge from one context to another.

At the university, students with disabilities are retained at a significantly higher rate than the institutional average for all students, and they obtain employment at exceptional rates. These results compare remarkably well with national studies of retention and employment rates for disabled students.

Bowling Green State University (Ohio) created its Chapman Learning Center as a "think tank for learning," to experiment with new pedagogies and program structures to engage students in classroom and outside-the-classroom activities. A freshmen residential program, the Center involves faculty from several disciplines, each with offices in the residence hall, a hall director and junior tutors who work with faculty on required anchor courses, elective courses, and a common learning day. Classes are thematically linked in two anchor courses each semester, and center on difficult social issues during the first term and on aesthetics and imagination during the second. Freshmen composition courses are linked to these disciplinary courses. Community events are planned to relate directly to the course themes. Teaching practices emphasize interactive, experiential activities, learning experiences outside the classroom, **critical thinking about challenging issues,** and support for learning by residential staff. Classes are small, to enable faculty to offer frequent written and verbal feedback on in-class and out-of-class assignments. Students are encouraged to **examine personal beliefs and values** in relation to broader perspectives on social issues, and peer-mediated discussions of social controversies are featured.

Chapman students show disproportionate satisfaction and adjustment to college life when compared with other freshmen. They feel less lonely, are more actively involved in their classes, experience more faculty approval, and are more willing to approach faculty.

10 Learning involves *the ability of individuals to monitor their own learning,* to understand how knowledge is acquired, to develop strategies for learning based on discerning their capacities and limitations, and to be aware of their own ways of knowing in approaching new bodies of knowledge and disciplinary frameworks.

To improve the ability of individuals to *monitor* their *own learning* requires that faculty and staff:

- assist students in **understanding the elements and structures of learning** and the **standards for learning achievements;**
- help students understand their **relative strengths and weaknesses** in learning;
- ask students to observe and record their own **progress in learning;**
- use **multiple pedagogies** suited to the content or skills to be learned and reaching students with different approaches to learning;
- **tailor** education to the **individual learner** rather than exclusively providing mass-delivered presentations;
- use **educational technologies** as a tool for **collaborative learning** and encourage reticent students to participate;
- cultivate students' **desire to know what** they **do not know;** and
- continue to learn what **factors affect student cognition and learning** and to design learning **experiences responsive to learning differences.**

To enable students to **monitor their own learning,** faculty and staff collaborators:

- help them delineate and articulate their learning interests, strengths, and deficiencies;
- reduce the risk to students of acknowledging their own limitations;
- help students select curricular and other educational experiences covering a broad range of learning approaches and performance evaluations; and
- create faculty and staff development activities to learn about advances in learning theory and practice.

The Western College Program of *Miami University. Oxford* (Ohio) is an interdisciplinary residential college featuring a core curriculum in the liberal arts for students' first two years. In their junior year, students are provided opportunities to take greater responsibility for, and to monitor, their learning through individually designed upper-level interdisciplinary programs of study and a year-long senior project based on all four years of study. Completed senior projects are publicly presented using a professional conference format and including faculty respondents from outside the college who have not worked with the students. Faculty and student affairs staff collaborate to fuse the living and study experiences and to challenge and support students as they pursue their core and self-designed studies.

The Student Affairs Assessment Committee, comprising student affairs, academic affairs, and business affairs staff, documents the impact that the university is having on students inside and outside the classroom. Measures include quantitative, nationally normed outcome assessment instruments and qualitative evaluations based on student interviews, free writing, focus groups, portfolios of student work, and ethnographies.

The vice presidents for academic and student affairs at *William Rainey Harper College* (Illinois) established a joint "Statement of Student Success" that endorses two concepts: all students have the right to succeed, and the college has the right to succeed, and the college has the right to uphold high standards for achievement. Based on this statement, the college established a program to support students at this two-year open-door college with academic preparation and counseling services as a way to meet the college's standards and to help them attain success. The college developed five standards of academic performance, established requirements for entry into college-level courses based on level of preparation as determined by entrance tests, and coupled these actions with an "intrusive intervention" program administered by the student development office. The intervention program monitors student course taking and grades. Through computerized tracking and human interaction, students receive information on their progress and work with faculty and staff to create personalized success contracts. These contracts include academic, personal, developmental, and social strategies to assist students making decisions about college and careers. Individual students' strategies are recorded and tracked through a computerized interface with the registration system, allowing possible restrictions to course loads or future registrations, or triggering further interventions when performance falls below standards. Interventions are made by faculty and staff, and students are **asked to assess their own performance** and to learn ways to use the support system to assist them.

Survey results over the years document that at-risk students enrolled in the intervention program have a clear understanding of the academic system, know what factors result in low grades, have reasonable plans to improve their performance, and believe the required interventions will have a positive impact on their future academic success.

What We Have Learned

Collaborative Futures in Support of Learning

The evolving principles of learning, continually informed by future advances in our understanding and knowledge of the learning process, hold great promise for improved student learning. By applying these principles to the practice of teaching, the development of curricula, the design of learning environments, and the assessment of learning, we will achieve more powerful learning. Realizing the full benefit of these applications depends upon collaborative efforts between academic and student affairs professionals—and beyond. It will require attention and action by all those affiliated with our institutions as well as by members of the larger community concerned with higher education to ensure that we achieve our mission of increased higher learning.

We call all those who serve the goals of learning to contribute to these collaborations. We ask that:

Students take charge of their own learning and organize their educational programs to include a broad array of experiences both inside and outside the classroom; become aware of the cumulative nature of their education, and consequently plan and monitor their development; and establish personal relationships with faculty and staff as an essential part of their education.

Faculty become masters of cognitive studies; develop pedagogy and curricula that draw upon and embody learning principles; become involved in all aspects of their institution's community life; and work in partnership with staff and community supporters to create learning activities based on the learning principles.

Scholars of cognition share their findings widely with faculty colleagues and higher education audiences and be attentive in their writings to the application of new findings to the conduct of teaching and learning.

Administrative leaders rethink the conventional organization of colleges and universities to create more inventive structures and processes that integrate academic and student affairs; align institutional planning, hiring, rewards, and resource allocations with the learning mission; offer professional development opportunities for people to cooperate across institutional boundaries; use evidence of student learning to guide program improvement, planning and resource allocation; and communicate information on students' life circumstances and culture to all members of the college or university community.

Student affairs professionals and other staff take the initiative to connect to each other and to academic units; develop programs that purposefully incorporate and identify learning contributions; and help students to view their education holistically and to participate fully in the life of the institution and the community.

Alumni reflect upon how what they learned in college contributed to their life after graduation and share these observations with current students and institutional officials; provide learning opportunities and mentorships outside the classroom for students; and contribute financial support to programs offering students the chance to use their knowledge in a variety of settings.

Governing boards understand the learning enterprise and how the institution conducts it; ask senior managers for information on how the organizational structure supports learning and for evidence of learning outcomes; and reward contributions to learning through promotion and tenure decisions and in evaluation of the president.

Community supporters volunteer workplace and other organizational venues for student learning; team with faculty and staff to design learning experiences in the community or workplace; serve as supervisors and mentors for student learning activities; evaluate student performance and provide models of reflective practice in their own professions; and help colleges and universities to understand the skills and knowledge needed by their graduates.

Accrediting agencies require in their review processes evidence of how institutions integrate learning experiences across administrative units and demand measures of learning effectiveness.

Professional associations disseminate best practices of collaboration on behalf of student learning in their programs, publications, and awards; exemplify the importance of partnerships for learning by establishing cooperative programs with other associations; and emphasize learning as a field of knowledge essential for graduate students planning careers in colleges or universities.

Families help students select a college or university based on its commitments to learning and student development and its learning environment; encourage students to choose and participate in a comprehensive program of educational activities throughout their collegiate experience; and help students to understand the value of reflection and to find time for concentrated study in their complicated lives.

Government agencies sponsor research and development on learning; offer incentives to institutions for new initiatives focused on collaboration for learning; and require evidence of institutional assessment of learning.

All those involved in higher education, as professionals or as community supporters, view themselves as teachers, learners, and collaborators in service to learning.

CHAPTER 32

ASKING THE RIGHT QUESTIONS: WHAT DOES RESEARCH TELL US ABOUT TECHNOLOGY AND HIGHER LEARNING?

STEPHEN C. EHRMANN

"I've got two pieces of bad news about that experimental English comp course where students used computer conferencing.

First, over the course of the semester, the experimental group showed no progress in abilities to compose an essay.

The second piece of bad news is that the control group, taught by traditional methods, showed no progress either."

—From a talk by professor Roxanne Hiltz at the New Jersey Institute of Technology on an early use of computer conferencing

I've been involved with innovation in higher education—its funding, its evaluation, and research about it—for 20 years, especially innovations having to do with computing, video, and telecommunications. During that time I've often been asked: "What do computers teach best?" "Does video encourage passive learning?" "Is it cheaper to teach with telecommunications?" I don't have answers to those questions. I don't think they *can* be answered in any reliable, valid way.

It takes just as much effort to answer a useless question as a useful one. The quest for useful information about technology has to begin, then, with thought about just what are the right questions. This article not only illustrates what I mean by "useless" questions, but discusses a few of the useful ones (and the findings that have resulted from their being asked), as well as one type of question that *ought* to be asked next about how we use technology for learning.

1) *Useless questions and the higher education machine*

The first group of useless questions seeks universal answers to questions about the comparative teaching effectiveness and costs of technology. These kinds of evaluative questions are phrased like, "Do computers do a better job of helping faculty teach English composition than traditional methods?"

Think about it. The question assumes that education operates something like a machine, and that each college is a slightly different version of the same "ideal" machine. In questions like these, the term "traditional methods" is used to represent some widely practiced method that presumably

Source: "Asking the Right Questions: What Does Research Tell Us About Technology and Higher Learning?" by Stephen C. Ehrmann, reprinted from *Change*, Vol.27, No.2, March–April 1995, Helen Dwight Reid Educational Foundation.

has predictable, acceptable results. "If technology performs better than traditional methods," such questions imply, "everyone should use it." A neat picture, but "traditional methods" is a concept that doesn't define the higher education I know and love, nor the higher education revealed by research.

Postsecondary learning is not usually so well structured, uniform, or stable that one can compare an innovation against "traditional" processes without specifying in explicit detail just what those processes are. And specifying in detail what "traditional" means (what materials, what methods, what motives) limits a study to a very small and temporary universe.

Organizationally, our institutions of higher education don't behave like machines, either. Cohen and March did a classic study of presidential decision-making on campuses some years back (see Works Cited), coining the term "organized anarchy" to describe how our institutions function. The term, however, describes any institution, they said, that like the typical college or university, has

1) problematic goals (it "appears to operate on a variety of inconsistent and ill-defined preferences"),
2) unclear technology; or, methods ("Although the organization manages to survive and [where relevant] produce, it does not understand its own processes"), and
3) fluid participation in decision-making ("the boundaries of the organization appear to be uncertain and changing").

Does this sound like a machine being fine-tuned toward a Platonic ideal of efficiency? To me it sounds not only like what colleges are (and ought to be), but also like what college courses are (and ought to be). Unfortunately, this means one can't ask, "How well is this technology-based approach working, relative to the norm?" since there isn't a norm.

It also seems useless to search for global generalizations about the costs of technology relative to "traditional methods." Howard Bowen, a noted economist of higher learning, found that institutions of higher education each raise all the money they can, spend all they get, and spend it in ways that relate closely to the way they spent the money the previous year. His 1980 study found little relationship in patterns of spending even among institutions that appeared on the surface to be quite similar. The institutions spent rather different amounts per student, and they spent each dollar differently. Bowen found no way to state rationally what it ought to cost to educate a student properly. While tougher economic times may have forced some convergence in costs among institutions, we still have no rational way of describing what traditional education *should* cost per student.

Platonic ideals aside, what makes it so difficult to determine what education *does* cost? Prices and accounting methods vary by institution and situation. Services that are inexpensive to some institutions are quite expensive for others. Complicating the cost question still further is the rapid and not always predictable change in technology prices and performance.

None of this suggests that we should ignore issues of cost in looking at new investments in technology. But caution flag should go up whenever you hear someone say, "The nation can teach English composition more cheaply if it uses technology X," be that technology old or new.

2) *If you're headed in the wrong direction, technology won't help you get to the right place*

Questions also are useless if we fail to ask them. Many advocates of technology want to improve current teaching, but too often they fail to ask whether those "traditional methods" are being used to teach the right content. They seek to change education's means but don't ask hard questions first about its objectives.

What makes me uneasy about the "content goals" of undergraduate education is grades—and what research tells us about them. Any undergraduate can tell you that grades are the key to interpreting the mysteries of higher education. Faculty give you high grades when you learn what they value, right? We tell students repeatedly, "Study hard, get good grades, and you will learn what you need in order to do better in life."

But is that true? Let's assume that the curriculum teaches knowledge, skills, and wisdom that are of advantage to graduates. We'll also assume that faculty members are grading rationally, and that although higher education has many goals, not all of them professional or vocational, at least some of them are meant to foster later success in the workplace (in terms of salaries, chances of winning a Nobel Prize, etc.). In that case, research ought to reveal a positive correlation between cumulative grade point average and work outcomes. In other words, "A" graduates should have learned enough to do better in their careers than "C" graduates. (I'll use "graduate" to denote anyone who has completed a course of study, whether or not the person receives a degree.) In contrast, if the curriculum were irrelevant to work outcomes (or if grading were random), then the correlation would be zero. It wouldn't matter how efficiently we taught the wrong stuff, or whether we used technology to teach it three times as well. The correlation between GPA and life outcomes would still be zero.

In 1991, Pascarella and Terenzini synthesized all the research they could find bearing on higher learning and discovered that going to college and graduating indeed pays off in many ways. They also confirmed that the choice of major makes a difference in life outcomes. All of that sounds like good news. But while Pascarella and Terenzini discovered many studies finding a tiny positive correlation between grades and work achievement after graduation, the correlation is so small (about 1 to 2 percent of the total variation) as to be meaningless for the individual student.

Why don't grades predict how well our graduates perform? Is it because we are not even trying to teach them certain knowledge, skills, and wisdom that they need? Or does the problem lie in the way that faculty assess learning?

Are Students Being Taught the Right Stuff?—One possibility is that the curriculum is failing to focus on the knowledge, skills, and wisdom that graduates need. For example, some studies of GPA and work outcomes focus solely on MBA graduates and their success in their first jobs (starting salaries, likelihood of promotion, etc.). Findings about MBA graduates by both Crooks and Livingston are consistent with those of Pascarella and Terenzini: there is little relationship between GPAs for business school grads and their work achievement.

Perhaps the reason for this minimal relationship is that there are important skills the curriculum fails to teach or reward. That's the implicit message of *The Competent Manager* by Richard Boyatzis, a classic work published in 1982 that summarizes many empirical studies of the cognitive skills of effective managers. Each study compares the patterns of thinking of superlative managers to those of average managers.

Boyatzis found that the cognitive skills of highly successful managers didn't seem to bear much relationship to what business schools were teaching. For example, one of the key skills revealed by the studies is the ability to shape and achieve goals by working through coalitions of peers. The habits of thought and action needed to be a good coalition builder must be developed over many courses and extracurricular activities. Do today's business schools do that? Are their highest GPAs usually earned by students who are best at organizing teams?

Boyatzis' findings, however, have broader significance. Skills for working with people, and in organizations, are important for just about every graduate, not just business school types. Most forms of work, citizenship—and even family life—require such knowledge, skills, and wisdom.

If you study your own graduates and find that there is no apparent difference in the fate of those who got A's and those who got C's, perhaps it is because your program is not teaching the right stuff.

Or Is Grading the Problem?—A second way to account for Pascarella and Terenzini's finding is to infer that grading is irrational. Let's assume that most faculty members have no idea what their students think or have learned. By this argument, the students who learn the most may be as likely to get a C as an A. One of the most devastating studies supporting that notion is embodied in the video, "A Private Universe," produced and directed by Matthew H. Schneps, which opens in Harvard Yard during commencement in the late 1980s. Twenty-two graduating seniors, faculty, and alumni were asked one of two questions, "Why is it warmer in the summer than in the winter?" or "Why does the moon seem to have a different shape each night?" Only two of them answered their questions correctly. Yet all should have learned about both these phenomena repeatedly while in school.

The scene then shifts to a good high school nearby. We see ninth graders answering those same two questions incorrectly in the same ways the Harvard seniors did. The ninth graders are interviewed before they're taught the material that year, and then again right afterward. The instruction looks good. But although the teacher repeatedly asks the students canned questions and gets canned answers back, she does not seem to be learning anything about what students believe about these phenomena. The videotaped interviews show that the students' pre-existing theories remain invisible to the teacher, and often go untouched by her instruction.

"A Private Universe" is not the only study that shows that students can get A's without truly understanding the material or being able to apply it. When faculty don't understand what students believe, know, and can do, they are unlikely to teach or to grade appropriately.

So we have two pieces of bad news. We're probably failing to teach the right stuff, but even if we were trying to teach the right stuff, many instructors wouldn't notice whether their students were learning it or not.

I'm not suggesting that we rush out and faddishly transform our curricula, but I do believe that most institutions of higher education are facing a Triple Challenge of outcomes, accessibility, and costs. If not now, then in the next few years they will find it increasingly difficult to offer a modern, effective academic program that reaches and retains the students they should be serving for a price that those students and their benefactors can afford. For many institutions, these three issues of outcomes, accessibility, and costs pose real threats to their reputation and well-being.

I see no evidence that most institutions will be able to meet this Triple Challenge without the substantial use of computers, video, and telecommunication. (In fact, this Triple Challenge is one reason why technology has been rising to the top of budgets and presidential agendas for the last few years. One can no longer afford to ignore technology and still maintain institutional health.) However, if we rush out and buy new technologies without first asking hard questions about appropriate educational goals, the results are likely to be disappointing and wasteful.

3) *The medium isn't the message*

Several decades ago, as educators began to think seriously about using the new technology of the day for teaching, you heard things like "Television will ruin learning" and "Computers will revolutionize instruction." (Twenty-five hundred years earlier in Greece you would have heard the same debate about the written word and its impact on dialogue-based education.) In other words, they were asking whether a technology could be used to teach without specifying anything about the teaching methods involved.

Richard Clark responded to that type of assertion by arguing, in effect, that the medium is not the message. Communications media and other technologies are so flexible that they do not dictate methods of teaching and learning. All the benefits attributed by previous research to "computers" or "video," Clark asserted, could be explained by the teaching methods they supported. Research, Clark said, should focus on specific teaching-learning methods, not on questions of media.

Clark's studies provoked a blaze of responses because he seemed to be saying that technology was irrelevant. A good set of these attacks, with rejoinders by Clark, can be found in two recent issues of *Educational Technology Research and Development*, (listed in the Works Cited box.) Robert Kozma argues, for example, that the particular technology used is not irrelevant, but may be either well or poorly suited to support a specific teaching-learning method. There may indeed be a choice of technologies for carrying out a particular teaching task, he argues, but it isn't necessarily a large choice. There are several tools that can be used to turn a screw, but most tools can't do it, and some that can are better for the job than others. Kozma suggests that we do research on which technologies are best for supporting the best methods of teaching and learning.

I agree with both of them. Clark's message is the more important, however. Too many observers assume that if they know what the "hardware" is (computers, seminar rooms), they know whether student learning will occur. They assume that if faculty get this hardware, they will easily, automatically, and quickly change their teaching tactics and course materials to take advantage of it. Thus, technology budgets usually include almost no money for helping faculty and staff upgrade their instructional programs.

As for useful research, we have both the Clark and the Kozma agendas before us: 1) to study which teaching-learning strategies are best (especially those that would not even be feasible without the newer technologies) and 2) to study which technologies are best for supporting those strategies.

4) *Computer-based tutorials are valuable but . . .*

At this point it may seem like all the research and evaluation are useless. It's time to turn to some questions that have yielded important information.

Since the 1960s the popular image of the computer revolution has rested on individualized computer-assisted instruction. This type of software teaches by offering some text or multimedia instruction, asking the student questions, and providing feedback and new instructional material based on the student's answers. Each student moves through the materials in a different way, and at a different rate.

James Kulik and his colleagues at the University of Michigan have summarized the vast research about such software, re-analyzing data from large numbers of small studies in order to draw more general conclusions. Their basic finding: this method results in a substantial improvement in learning outcomes and speed, perhaps around 20 percent or more on average. Such instruction works best, of course, in content areas where the computer can tell the difference between a student's right answer and wrong answer, for example, in mathematics or grammar exercises. *Few other teaching methods have demonstrated such consistently strong results as this type of self-paced instruction.*

The news is not all good, however.

Studies such as those analyzed by Kulik and his colleagues have focused purely on the educational value of software, not on factors influencing its viability. Unfortunately, even the best computer-assisted instruction of this type often has not found a substantial number of users in higher education. Software intended for educational use often fades away, its revolutionary promise unfulfilled.

A group of us, led by Paul Morris, created a casebook that analyzed 20 pieces of software developed in the 1980s and early 1990s. These software packages had already demonstrated not only *value* (educational power, as evidenced by evaluations and awards) but also *viability* (extensive use over many years). If software is not widely used by many faculty over many years, it is unlikely to foster lasting, national improvement in the way one or more courses are taught. We wanted to understand why a few software packages had proved to be viable, while so many others were not.

Perhaps our most important finding was that it usually takes years for curricular software to be developed and then to become widely accepted. There are many reasons for this. Support services are often under-funded, so faculty can't be certain that the basic hardware and software will consistently be available and in working order. Changing a course involves shifting to unfamiliar materials, creating new types of assignments, and inventing new ways of assessing student learning. It's almost impossible for an isolated faculty member to find the time and resources not only to do all these things, but to take all these risks. Few institutions provide the resources and rewards for faculty to take such risks. For these and other reasons, the pace of curricular change is slow.

We found that the more revolutionary the software, the longer and more arduous was the task of getting a critical mass of users. For large pieces of curricular software, the journey from conception to wide use might take 10 years or more.

Unfortunately, long before most curricular software found such wide use, computer operating systems and interfaces had changed. Instead of looking revolutionary, the software began looking obsolete. Use, instead of growing, began to decline. The lack of obvious returns discouraged funders and publishers from investing in the creation of version 2.0. The original developers had often lost interest, too. Faculty knew that making uninteresting upgrades would win them few rewards. Thus, many valuable curricular software packages died without ever fulfilling their promise.

We did discover a few small families of curricular software had found a niche. However, many of these packages gained use because they were familiar and inexpensive to develop (and thus inexpensive to update regularly). They got into use by being comfortable, not by making instructional waves. Hardly the stuff of revolution.

That doesn't mean that software isn't used for learning. Ironically, while software designed for learning has had a hard time finding a postsecondary market, most of the software that is used for learning was *not* designed for that purpose.

5) *Software that isn't designed for instruction can be good for learning*

"Worldware" is the name we gave software that is developed for purposes other than instruction but also is used for teaching and learning. Word processors are worldware. So are computer-aided design packages. So are electronic mail and the Internet.

Worldware packages are educationally *valuable* because they enable several important facets of instructional improvement. For example, online libraries and molecular modeling software can support experiential learning, while electronic mail, conferencing systems, and voice mail can support collaborative learning by non-residential students.

Worldware packages are *viable* for many reasons: they are in demand for instruction because students know they need to learn to use them and to think with them; faculty already are familiar with them from their own work; vendors have a large enough market to earn the money for continual upgrades and relatively good product support; and new versions of worldware are usually compatible with old files, thus, faculty can gradually update and transform their courses year after year without last year's assignment becoming obsolete.

For reasons like these, worldware often has proved to have great educational potential (value) and wide use for a long period of time (viability). Has that educational potential been realized in improved learning outcomes? There is no substitute for each faculty member asking that question about his or her own students. Here are two such studies.

Karen Smith pioneered what is now an increasingly common application of electronic mail—as an important element in teaching foreign languages. Students of Spanish at the University of Arizona were told to write to one another using a form of electronic mail called computer conferencing. The faculty suggested some topics—for example, the film the class had just seen or reviews for upcoming quizzes. Other topics came from the learners, including an upcoming party and one student's existential angst. Some of these e-mail conversations were private. Conversation in the public conferences was graded, but only for fluency of expression, not for content or grammar.

I met the first cohort of students taking this course. I've never seen a group, before or since, so excited about their course's use of technology. In part they were pleased because computer conferencing was more accessible than a language lab; they could participate from any computer at any time. More importantly, as several put it, "I'm using Spanish for the first time." And they didn't need to feel self-conscious about speaking quickly or with a good accent. All they needed to do was take the time to interpret what had been said to them and then decide how to express their replies.

Surprisingly, Smith's study showed that, relative to a class taught using a traditional language laboratory, the oral performance of these students excelled. In the slower-paced, more anonymous world of the computer conference, they were "speaking" Spanish with a purpose, and learning to express themselves. The evaluation proved that worldware had been used in a way that opened a new dimension of learning for these students.

Another of my favorite evaluations of teaching tactics was never published. The faculty member was simply interested in seeing whether his use of technology was improving his students' learning. Bob Gross, a professor of biology at Dartmouth College, was an early user of personal computers to create animations. In the late 1980s, he became impatient about a bottleneck in his teaching: it was taking him two class hours to teach about a complex series of interactions in biochemistry—"48 blackboards' worth" as he put it. He would draw the molecules, talk, erase some, draw some, and talk some more. Gross wanted to speed up the process and make it more effective. After working several weeks with an undergraduate student, he used worldware to create an animation that enabled him to teach the same material in half an hour. The students could also study the computer-based animation outside class, frame by frame if needed. "I was initially disappointed," he told me the day I visited him at Dartmouth, some months afterward. "There was very little excitement or discussion when I showed it in class. But later, when I gave them my regular exam on the subject, they did better than any previous class."

These two studies show that each faculty member can do his or her own research, asking relevant questions about what students are learning in a particular class. That's what Schneps and others have shown is so important: know thy own students and what they are learning. Without asking hard questions about learning, technology remains an unguided missile.

6) Strategies matter most

Studies by individual faculty of their own students and their own teaching methods and resources are necessary. But such studies are not enough.

I suggest the following hypothesis: Education can affect the lives of its graduates when they have mastered large, coherent bodies of knowledge, skills, and wisdom. Such coherent patterns of learning usually must accumulate over a series of courses and extracurricular experience.

Thus, to make visible improvements in learning outcomes using technology, use that technology to enable large-scale changes in the methods and resources of learning. That usually requires hardware and software that faculty and students use repeatedly, with increasing sophistication and power. Single pieces of software, used for only a few hours, are unlikely to have much effect on graduates' lives or the cost-effectiveness of education (unless that single piece of software is somehow used to foster a much larger pattern of improved teaching).

Thus far, few educators, evaluators, and researchers have paid much attention to educational strategies for using technologies. Too often they've been victims of "rapture of the technologies." Mesmerized, they focus on individual pieces of software and hardware, individual assignments and, occasionally, on individual courses. (Enrolling more adult learners has been a more powerful motive to change strategies and to study those strategies. For a fine strategic evaluation of seven institutional projects to transform whole degree programs, I suggest Markwood and Johnstone's study, *New Pathways to a Degree: Technology Opens the College*.)

Few educators are thinking much about educational strategies for using technology to improve learning outcomes. Does that mean we're not employing such strategies yet? Quite the contrary. Here's an example.

Back in 1987 Raymond J. Lewis and I were looking for faculty members who had had at least two years of teaching in an environment where students had unfettered access to personal computing. One place we visited was Reed College in Portland, Oregon, where the current seniors had had four years of easy access to Macintosh computers. I talked to faculty members from eight departments, asking what they liked about teaching in this environment.

Surprisingly, there was one thing that all of them had noticed. As two of them put it, "I'm no longer embarrassed to ask the student to do it over again." Because computer-based documents and projects are mechanically easier to revise, their students actually pressed to get a second chance to improve their work and their grade. Gradually, the texture of the curriculum in each course was changing toward projects developed in stages—plan, draft, conversation, another draft, final version. Each stage of work was marked by rethinking, and by learning. We called this strategy, "Doing It Again, Thoughtfully," or "DIATing."

I also asked a couple of seniors if they thought their education had been influenced by their use of computers. One of them replied that he'd learned that it's not the first draft or thought that matters, but the final version. In response to my asking in which course he'd learned that, he explained that it had been over a series of courses. Similarly, several faculty members and the director of the writing program independently suggested that the most tangible impact of computer availability would be at the capstone of the curriculum—in the intellectual tightness and coherence of bachelor's theses.

That day at Reed had a surprise ending. When Ray and I sat down with several of the college's educational and technology leaders, they were astonished by what we'd heard that day. The growth of DIATing had been an ecological change, not one directed centrally. They hadn't known that their technology was being used in that way or with those kinds of outcomes. That's because their institutional strategy was the sum of large numbers of independent actions by many faculty members and students across the college.

From this story (and my other experiences with educational uses of information technology), I'd suggest three lessons:

1) Technology can enable important changes in curriculum, even when it has no curricular content itself. Worldware can be used, for example, to provoke active learning through work on complex pro-

jects, rethinking of assumptions, and discussion.

2) What matters most are educational *strategies* for using technology, strategies that can influence the student's total course of study.

3) If such strategies emerge from independent choices made by faculty members and students, the cumulative effect can be significant and yet still remain invisible. (Unfortunately, the converse can also be true. We may be convinced that we have implemented a new strategy of teaching across the curriculum, and yet be kidding ourselves.) As usual, there is no substitute for opening our eyes and looking.

7) *Tools for evaluating strategy: The Flashlight Project*

Ordinarily what matters most is

- not the technology per se but how it is used;
- not so much what happens in the moments when the student is using the technology, but more how those uses promote larger improvements in the fabric of the student's education; and
- not so much what we can discover about the average truth for education at all institutions, but more what we can learn about our own degree programs and our own students.

How can departments and institutions study their educational strategies for using technologies? A faculty member can't do this alone by looking at just one course. As we saw in the DIATing example from Reed, a strategy is a pattern of teaching and learning that extends over many courses. Only a college, university, or department has the range of responsibility and resources to study strategy.

The Annenberg/CPB Project is taking some steps to make it easier for educators to obey the commandment "Know thy students and what they are learning." This January saw the birth of the Flashlight Project, a three-year effort to develop and share evaluation procedures. Colleges and universities will be able to use these procedures to assess their educational strategies for using technology. We're working with the Western Interstate Commission on Higher Education (WICHE), Indiana University Purdue University at Indianapolis (IUPUI) to develop these procedures. IUPUI, the University of Maine at Augusta, the Maricopa Community Colleges, the Rochester Institute of Technology, and Washington State University will test the new procedures.

In a previous planning phase, supported by the Fund for the Improvement of Postsecondary Education, our group identified the educational strategies that the participating institutions most needed to study. Developing good evaluation procedures is expensive. We wanted our procedures to be widely used and important, so we focused them on educational strategies for using technology that are widely used and important.

The chosen educational strategies include:

- project-based learning in an information-rich, tool-rich environment;
- collaborative learning when communication can be synchronous and asynchronous;
- learning at paces and times of students' choosing;
- learning marked by continuous improvement of a piece of work; and
- improved student-faculty and student-student interaction, and enhanced feedback.

Now Flashlight is developing procedures that institutions can use to monitor the evolution, successes, and failures of those strategies locally. Flashlight outcomes measures will focus on graduates' capabilities, changing patterns of enrollment and retention, and the influence of changes in education on total patterns of costs.

As its name indicates, Flashlight's evaluative procedures will not answer all questions that an institution might have, nor will it be easy or inexpensive to ask these evaluative questions. What we do hope is that the answers will prove unusually useful for transforming teaching and setting policy.

Works Cited

Boyatzis, Richard. *The Competent Manager*, NY: Wiley, 1982.

Bowen, Howard R. *The Costs of Higher Education: How Much Do Colleges and Universities Spend per Student and How Much Should They Spend?* San Francisco: Jossey-Bass, 1980.

Cohen, Michael D. and James G. March. *Leadership and Ambiguity: The American College President,* New York: McGraw-Hill, 1974.

Crooks, Lois. "Personal Factors Related to the Careers of MBAs," *Findings,* Vol. 4, No. 1, Princeton, NJ: Educational Testing Service, 1977.

Educational Technology Research and Development, Vol. 42, Nos. 2&3, Washington, DC: Association for Educational Communications and Technology, 1994.

Kulik, Chen-Lin C. and James A. Kulik. "Effectiveness of Computer-Based Instruction: An Updated Analysis," *Computers in Human Behavior,* Vol. 7, Nos. 1–2, 1991, pp. 75–94.

Livingston, J. Sterling. "The Myth of the Well-Educated Manager," *Harvard Business Review,* No. 71108, January 1971.

Markwood, Richard A. and Sally M. Johnstone, eds. *New Pathways to a Degree: Technology Opens the College* and *New Pathways to a Degree: Seven Technology Stories,* Boulder, Colorado: Western Interstate Commission for Higher Education, 1994.

Morris, Paul, Stephen C. Ehrmann, Randi Goldsmith, Kevin Howat, and Vijay Kumar. *Valuable, Viable Software in Education: Cases and Analysis,* New York: Primis Division of McGraw-Hill, 1994.

Pascarella, Ernest T. and Patrick T. Terenzini. *How College Affects Students: Findings and Insights from Twenty Years of Research,* San Francisco: Jossey-Bass, 1991.

Schneps, Matthew H., Producer, Director. "A Private Universe," [Film], Washington, DC: The Annenberg/CPB Project, 1987.

Smith, Karen L. "Collaborative and Interactive Writing for Increasing Communication Skills," *Hispania,* Vol. 73, No. 1, 1990, pp. 77–87.

CHAPTER 33

IMPLEMENTING THE SEVEN PRINCIPLES: TECHNOLOGY AS LEVER

ARTHUR W. CHICKERING AND STEPHEN C. EHRMANN

Since the Seven Principles of Good Practice were created in 1987, new communication and information technologies have become major resources for teaching and learning in higher education. If the power of the new technologies is to be fully realized, they should be employed in ways consistent with the Seven Principles. Such technologies are *tools* with multiple capabilities; it is misleading to make assertions like "Microcomputers will empower students" because that is only one way in which computers might be used.

Any given instructional strategy can be supported by a number of contrasting technologies (old and new), just as any given technology might support different instructional strategies. But for any given instructional strategy, some technologies are better than others: Better to turn a screw with a screwdriver than a hammer—a dime may also do the trick, but a screwdriver is usually better.

This essay, then, describes some of the most cost-effective and appropriate ways to use computers, video, and telecommunications technologies to advance the Seven Principles.

1. Good Practice Encourages Contacts Between Students and Faculty

Frequent student-faculty contact in and out of class is a most important factor in student motivation and involvement. Faculty concern helps students get through rough times and keep on working. Knowing a few faculty members well enhances students' intellectual commitment and encourages them to think about their own values and plans.

Communication technologies that increase access to faculty members, help them share useful resources, and provide for joint problem solving and shared learning can usefully augment face-to-face contact in and outside of class meetings. By putting in place a more "distant" source of information and guidance for students, such technologies can strengthen faculty interactions with all students, but especially with shy students who are reluctant to ask questions or challenge the teacher directly. It is often easier to discuss values and personal concerns in writing than orally, since inadvertent or ambiguous nonverbal signals are not so dominant. As the number of commuting part-time students and adult learners increases, technologies provide opportunities for interaction not possible when students come to class and leave soon afterward to meet work or family responsibilities.

The biggest success story in this realm has been that of time-delayed (asynchronous) communication. Traditionally, time-delayed communication took place in education through the exchange of homework, either in class or by mail (for more distant learners). Such time-delayed exchange

Source: "Implementing the Seven Principles: Technology as Lever," by Arthur W. Chickering and Stephen C. Ehrmann, reprinted from *AAHE Bulletin*, Vol. 49, No. 2, 1996, American Association for Higher Education.

was often a rather impoverished form of conversation, typically limited to three conversational turns:

1. The instructor poses a question (a task).
2. The student responds (with homework).
3. The instructor responds some time later with comments and a grade. The conversation often ends there; by the time the grade or comment is received, the course and student are off on new topics.

Now, however, electronic mail, computer conferencing, and the World Wide Web increase opportunities for students and faculty to converse and exchange work much more speedily than before, and more thoughtfully and "safely" than when confronting each other in a classroom or faculty office. Total communication increases and, for many students, the result seems more intimate, protected, and convenient than the more intimidating demands of face-to-face communication with faculty.

Professor Norman Coombs reports that, after twelve years of teaching black history at the Rochester Institute of Technology, the first time he used email was the first time a student asked what he, a white man, was doing teaching black history. The literature is full of stories of students from different cultures opening up in and out of class when email became available. Communication also is eased when student or instructor (or both) is not a native speaker of English; each party can take a bit more time to interpret what has been said and compose a response. With the new media, participation and contribution from diverse students become more equitable and widespread.

2. Good Practice Develops Reciprocity and Cooperation Among Students

Learning is enhanced when it is more like a team effort than a solo race. Good learning, like good work, is collaborative and social, not competitive and isolated. Working with others often increases involvement in learning: Sharing one's ideas and responding to others' improves thinking and deepens understanding.

The increased opportunities for interaction with faculty noted above apply equally to communication with fellow students. Study groups, collaborative learning, group problem solving, and discussion of assignments can all be dramatically strengthened through communication tools that facilitate such activity.

The extent to which computer-based tools encourage spontaneous student collaboration was one of the earliest surprises about computers. A clear advantage of email for today's busy commuting students is that it opens up communication among classmates even when they are not physically together.

For example: One of us, attempting to learn to navigate the Web, took a course taught entirely by a combination of televised class sessions (seen live or taped) and by work on a course Web page. The hundred students in the course included persons in Germany and the Washington, DC, area.

Learning teams helped themselves "learn the plumbing" and solve problems. These team members never met face-to-face. But they completed and exchanged Myers-Briggs Type Inventories, surveys of their prior experience and level of computer expertise, and brief personal introductions. This material helped teammates size one another up initially; team interactions then built working relationships and encouraged acquaintanceship. This kind of "collaborative learning" would be all but impossible without the presence of the media we were learning about and with.

3. Good Practice Uses Active Learning Techniques

Learning is not a spectator sport. Students do not learn much just sitting in classes listening to teachers, memorizing prepackaged assignments, and spitting out answers. They must talk about what they are learning, write reflectively about it, relate it to past experiences, and apply it to their daily lives. They must make what they learn part of themselves.

The range of technologies that encourage active learning is staggering. Many fall into one of three categories: tools and resources for learning by doing, time-delayed exchange, and real-time conversation. Today, all three usually can be supported with "worldware," i.e., software (such as word processors) originally developed for other purposes but now used for instruction, too.

We've already discussed communication tools, so here we will focus on learning by doing. Apprentice-like learning has been supported by many traditional technologies: research libraries, laboratories, art and architectural studios, athletic fields. Newer technologies now can enrich and expand these opportunities. For example:

- Supporting apprentice-like activities in fields that themselves require the use of technology as a tool, such as statistical research and computer-based music, or use of the Internet to gather information not available in the local library.
- Simulating techniques that do not themselves require computers, such as helping chemistry students develop and practice research skills in "dry" simulated laboratories before they use the riskier, more expensive real equipment.
- Helping students develop insight. For example, students can be asked to design a radio antenna. Simulation software displays not only their design but the ordinarily invisible electromagnetic waves the antenna would emit. Students change their designs and instantly see resulting changes in the waves. The aim of this exercise is not to design antennae but to build deeper understanding of electromagnetism.

4. Good Practice Gives Prompt Feedback

Knowing what you know and don't know focuses your learning. In getting started, students need help in assessing their existing knowledge and competence. Then, in classes, students need frequent opportunities to perform and receive feedback on their performance. At various points during college, and at its end, students need chances to reflect on what they have learned, what they still need to know, and how they might assess themselves.

The ways in which new technologies can provide feedback are many—sometimes obvious, sometimes more subtle. We already have talked about the use of email for supporting person-to-person feedback, for example, and the feedback inherent in simulations. Computers also have a growing role in recording and analyzing personal and professional performances. Teachers can use technology to provide critical observations for an apprentice; for example, video to help a novice teacher, actor, or athlete critique his or her own performance. Faculty (or other students) can react to a writer's draft using the "hidden text" option available in word processors: Turned on, the "hidden" comments spring up; turned off, the comments recede and the writer's prized work is again free of "red ink."

As we move toward portfolio evaluation strategies, computers can provide rich storage and easy access to student products and performances. Computers can keep track of early efforts, so instructors and students can see the extent to which later efforts demonstrate gains in knowledge, competence, or other valued outcomes. Performances that are Time-consuming and expensive to record and evaluate—such as leadership skills, group process management, or multicultural interactions—can be elicited and stored, not only for ongoing critique but also as a record of growing capacity.

5. Good Practice Emphasizes Time on Task

Time plus energy equals learning: Learning to use one's time well is critical for students and professionals alike. Allocating realistic amounts of time means effective learning for students and effective teaching for faculty.

New technologies can dramatically improve time on task for students and faculty members. Some years ago a faculty member told one of us that he used technology to "steal students' beer time," attracting them to work on course projects instead of goofing off: Technology also can increase time on task by making studying more efficient. Teaching strategies that help students learn at home or work can save hours otherwise spent commuting to and from campus, finding parking places, and so on. Time efficiency also increases when interactions between teacher and students, and among students, fit busy work and home schedules. And students and faculty alike make better use of time when they can get access to important resources for learning without trudging to the library, flipping through card files, scanning microfilm and microfiche, and scrounging the reference room.

For faculty members interested in classroom research, computers can record student participation and interaction and help document student time on task, especially as related to student performance.

6. Good Practice Communicates High Expectations

Expect more and you will get it. High expectations are important for everyone—for the poorly prepared, for those unwilling to exert themselves, and for the bright and well motivated. Expecting students to perform well becomes a self-fulfilling prophecy.

New technologies can communicate high expectations explicitly and efficiently. Significant real-life problems, conflicting perspectives, or paradoxical data sets can set powerful learning challenges that drive students to not only acquire information but sharpen their cognitive skills of analysis, synthesis, application, and evaluation.

Many faculty report that students feel stimulated by knowing their finished work will be "published" on the World Wide Web.

With technology, criteria for evaluating products and performances can be more clearly articulated by the teacher, or generated collaboratively with students. General criteria can be illustrated with samples of excellent, average, mediocre, and faulty performance. These samples can be shared and modified easily. They provide a basis for peer evaluation, so learning teams can help everyone succeed.

7. Good Practice Respects Diverse Talents and Ways of Learning

Many roads lead to learning. Different students bring different talents and styles to college. Brilliant students in a seminar might be all thumbs in a lab or studio; students rich in hands-on experience may not do so well with theory. Students need opportunities to show their talents and learn in ways that work for them. Then they can be pushed to learn in new ways that do not come so easily.

Technological resources can ask for different methods of learning through powerful visuals and well-organized print; through direct, vicarious, and virtual experiences; and through tasks requiring analysis, synthesis, and evaluation, with applications to real-life situations. They can encourage self-reflection and self-evaluation. They can drive collaboration and group problem solving. Technologies can help students learn in ways they find most effective and broaden their repertoires for learning. They can supply structure for students who need it and leave assignments more open-ended for students who don't. Fast, bright students can move quickly through materials they master easily and go on to more difficult tasks; slower students can take more time and get more feedback and direct help from teachers and fellow students. Aided by technologies, students with similar motives and talents can work in cohort study groups without constraints of time and place.

Evaluation and the Seven Principles

How are we to know whether given technologies are as useful in promoting the Seven Principles and learning as this article claims? One approach is to look and see, which is the aim of the "Flashlight Project," a three-year effort of the Annenberg/CPB Project to develop and share evaluation procedures. The Flashlight Project is developing a suite of evaluation tools that any campus can use to monitor the usefulness of technology in implementing the Seven Principles and the impacts of such changes on learning outcomes (e.g., the student's ability to apply what was learned in the academic program) and on access (e.g., whether hoped-for gains in time on task and retention are saving money for the institution and its funders).

[For more about the Flashlight Project, see Stephen Ehrmann's "Asking the Right Questions: What Does Research Tell Us About Technology and Higher Learning?" in the March/April 1995 *Change.* Or, check out the Flashlight Project's website at http://www.learner.org/content/ed/strat/eval.html.]

Technology Is Not Enough

The Seven Principles cannot be implemented by technophiles alone, or even by faculty alone. *Students* need to become familiar with the Principles and be more assertive with respect to their own learning. When confronted with teaching strategies and course requirements that use technologies in ways contrary to the Principles, students should, if possible, move to alternatives that serve them better. If teaching focuses simply on memorizing and regurgitating prepackaged information, whether delivered by a faculty lecture or computer, students should reach for a different course, search out additional resources or complementary experiences, establish their own study groups, or go to the professor for more substantial activities and feedback.

Faculty members who already work with students in ways consistent with the Principles need to be tough-minded about the software- and technology-assisted interactions they create and buy into. They need to eschew materials that are simply didactic, and search instead for those that are interactive, problem oriented, relevant to real-world issues, and that evoke student motivation.

Institutional policies concerning learning resources and technology support need to give high priority to user-friendly hardware, software, and communication vehicles that help faculty and students use technologies efficiently and effectively. Investments in professional development for faculty members, plus training and computer lab assistance for students, will be necessary if learning potentials are to be realized.

Finally, it is appropriate for legislators and other benefactors to ask whether institutions are striving to improve educational practice consistent with the Seven Principles. Much depends on the answer.

Note

This article draws on Arthur Chickering's participation in "The Future of Face-to-Face and Distance Learning in Post-Secondary Education," a workgroup chaired by W .L. Renwick as part of a larger effort examining *The Future of Post-Secondary Education and the Role of Information and Communication Technology: A Clarifying Report,* carried out by the Center for Educational Research and Innovation, Organization for Economic Cooperation and Development. Paris: 1993, 1994.

CHAPTER 34

A "TEACHER'S DOZEN": FOURTEEN GENERAL, RESEARCH-BASED PRINCIPLES FOR IMPROVING HIGHER LEARNING IN OUR CLASSROOMS

THOMAS ANTHONY ANGELO

How much trust would you place in an engineer who admitted to having no knowledge of thermodynamics or other basic principles of physics, and who thought, in fact, that those physical laws didn't apply to his work? How much confidence would you have in a physician with no understanding of how bacteria and viruses cause infection, one who believed that biochemistry was irrelevant to her practice? If by some terrible mistake you were arrested and put on trial, would you hire a lawyer who thought that keeping up with the research on jury selection, effective defense strategies, and sentencing patterns was a waste of time?

These questions are obviously rhetorical, because we all expect—or at least hope—that professionals will be knowledgeable and keep current in the research that informs their practice. But, as college teachers, do we expect as much of ourselves?

Unless you're in a field such as cognitive science or educational psychology, chances are slim that your graduate education included any survey of the research on how humans learn. And even within cognitive science and educational psychology doctoral programs, future professors rarely study the research on adolescent and adult learning. As faculty, we tend to assume that knowing a great deal about our specific discipline—say, British literature, biology, business, or Byzantine church history—is sufficient preparation for teaching. Unfortunately, as most department chairs and all faculty who have children in college soon learn, that is a faulty assumption. Mastery of one's discipline may be *necessary* for effective college teaching, but it surely isn't *sufficient*.

Three Assumptions

Before going any further, let me lay out the three main assumptions that undergird this article. The first is that to most effectively and efficiently promote learning, faculty need to know something about how our students—and indeed how we ourselves—learn. The second assumption is that there really are some general, research-based principles that faculty can apply to improve teaching and learning in their classrooms. And the third is that college teaching is so complex and varied that

Source: "'A Teacher's Dozen': Fourteen General, Research-Based Principles for Improving Higher Learning in Our Classrooms," by Thomas Anthony Angelo, reprinted from *AAHE Bulletin*, Vol. 45, No. 8, April 1993, American Association for Higher Education.

faculty members themselves will have to figure out whether and how these general principles apply to their particular disciplines, courses, and students. The discussion that follows rests on these three assumptions like a stool on three legs: If they're sturdy, then what follows will hold up.

While there isn't space here to adequately test these three "legs," a few comments on them might be helpful. First, I assume it's important for faculty to know something about how humans learn because teaching that ignores this knowledge runs the risk of being inefficient, ineffective, and sometimes even counterproductive. The time, energy, and aspirations that we and our students invest in coursework are simply too valuable to spend carelessly.

Second, while few savvy faculty would argue that we know *nothing* useful about learning, many still protest that we don't yet know *enough* to inform teaching practice. It is true that there's still much to discover, but at the same time we do collectively know a great deal about how people learn, far more than we use. Solid research by cognitive scientists, psychologists, ethnographers, and other researchers offers much more direction to college teachers of the 1990s than was available even a decade ago. To argue that we shouldn't use what we know in teaching because our knowledge is incomplete is like arguing that sailors shouldn't use available knowledge about weather and currents in navigation because that knowledge is incomplete. Only by using what we already know can we learn more.

So, what exactly *do* we know about learning that might be useful to college teachers? My response is the "teacher's dozen" referred to in the title. It's my own list of fourteen principles of effective higher learning that are well supported by research. My "teacher's dozen" isn't meant to be definitive or exhaustive. It's simply one college teacher's current list of solid principles to teach by.

Why fourteen? The best known and most discussed list is Chickering and Gamson's "Seven Principles for Good Practice in Undergraduate Education." Their "Seven Principles" remain the standard, and most of those research-based guidelines can be found in my "teacher's dozen." But in making up my list, I found there were also other, more specific principles I couldn't teach without. Though I tried to limit myself to twelve, the teacher in me just couldn't give up that content. So, in the end, I decided that if a "baker's dozen" is thirteen, then surely a "teacher's dozen" could be fourteen.

Three Goals

Of course, whether such a list should include four, fourteen, or forty-four principles is open to discussion and debate. The first goal of this "teacher's dozen" is to encourage just that sort of questioning and dialogue. It's to invite faculty to think, talk, and perhaps even read more about the connections between what we know from research on learning and how we practice teaching. Chickering and Garrison's "Seven Principles," or any other general guidelines based on research, will only stimulate meaningful, long-lasting changes in teaching behavior if faculty make the principles personally meaningful by connecting them to their everyday teaching lives. On your campus, for example, you might begin this connecting process by compiling a list of principles from learning research that guide your own teaching and then comparing it with lists drawn up by your colleagues. At the least, comparing lists could make for stimulating lunchtime discussion or enliven a department meeting.

A second goal is to encourage faculty to use their personal "teacher's dozen" as criteria for assessing their current teaching practices. Once you know what principles you ascribe to, you can better determine how well your teaching embodies them. You can use a simple checklist of learning principles to quickly review your course syllabi, class notes, assignments, tests. Or you might watch a videotape of yourself teaching, checking your actions against your list. The videotape might reveal that, even though you're convinced active engagement is critical to learning, you're still doing most of the work in class, while your students passively observe.

A third, related goal is to encourage faculty to identify the implications of their "favorite" guiding principles and then develop practical classroom applications. If my third assumption is correct, each combination of teacher, course, and students is so unique that general principles have to be either "custom fit" or "custom built" to be useful in a particular class. The operating axiom is: Adapt, don't adopt. Therefore, the classroom implications and applications of these principles must be generated and validated by individual faculty if they are to have any value. Applying your own "teacher's dozen" might involve making changes in your teaching techniques, homework assignments, or tests. To return to the videotape example, once you've observed that your students are not actively engaged in class, you can begin to systematically experiment with new techniques and approaches—and assess how much difference they make.

A Working Definition of Higher Learning

The broader agenda behind these three goals is to help faculty improve the quality of higher learning in their classrooms. But what does that mean? As an exercise in *active* reading and learning, I suggest you take out a pencil and a piece of paper now and write a one- or two-sentence definition of *higher learning* before you read any further. Once you've jotted down your draft definition, we can compare notes to make sure we have similar concepts in mind.

What is higher learning? I define higher learning as an active, interactive process that results in meaningful, long-lasting changes in knowledge, understanding, behavior, dispositions, appreciation, belief, and the like. The key terms in this definition are *meaningful, long-lasting,* and *changes.* Higher learning is *meaningful* if the learner understands and appreciates what is learned; that means that something learned by rote but not understood would not qualify. By *long-lasting,* I mean learning that will endure in accessible memory at least beyond the end of the term. And *changes* here means not simply the addition of knowledge but also the transformation of ways of understanding and organizing the knowledge learned.

This is a demanding definition of higher learning, and I certainly don't always fulfill it, but having an explicit definition does help me make difficult decisions about what and how to teach. Since there is always more worthy course content than time in the semester, I need criteria for making hard choices about what to leave out. Asking myself whether a given class activity, reading, or homework assignment will contribute to meaningful and lasting learning is a helpful decision rule.

A "TEACHER'S DOZEN"

Before I share my current "teacher's dozen," a final caveat is in order: Given the range of human variation, there are bound to be exceptions to nearly every generalization about learning. It's up to individual faculty members to determine which principles apply to whom, when, where, and how.

That said, for each of the fourteen principles listed below, I'll offer a very brief explanation and then suggest one or two implications for or applications to teaching and classroom assessment. These general implications and applications are meant merely as "pump-primers," to stimulate you to come up with more specific, appropriate ones.

1. Active learning is more effective than passive learning.

What I hear, I forget; what I see, I remember, what I do, I understand.

—Chinese proverb

Let the main object of this, our Didactic, be as follows: To seek and find a method by which teachers may teach less, but learners learn more.

—John Amos Comenius

As these quotations suggest, teachers have long known what researchers have only recently confirmed about the value of active learning: Students do learn more and better by becoming actively involved. But activity, in and of itself, doesn't result in higher learning. Active learning occurs when students invest physical and mental energies in activities that help them make what they are learning meaningful, and when they are aware of that meaning-making. As George Stoddard put it, "We learn to do neither by thinking nor by doing; we learn to do by thinking about what we are doing."

Implications/Applications. Having students teach or explain something to others that they have just learned helps them learn it much more effectively, especially if they actively rehearse that "lesson" ahead of time and get feedback. To assess actively, ask students to paraphrase a central concept in a couple of sentences for one specific audience, and then to paraphrase the same explanation for a completely different audience. The two audiences might be parents and children, professionals and laypeople, novices and experts. Assess these directed paraphrases for both accuracy and appropriateness.

2. Learning requires focused attention, and awareness of the importance of what is to be learned.

The true art of memory is the art of attention.
—Samuel Johnson

One of the most difficult tasks for novice learners in a field, whatever their age, is to figure out what to pay attention to and what to ignore. Students in introductory courses often cannot tell what is central from what is peripheral, foreground from background, superordinate from subordinate. Novices find these distinctions elusive, usually not because they lack intelligence but because they lack the experience needed to evaluate the data they encounter. If you've ever found yourself lost and alone in a busy city in a country whose language, culture, and street signs are totally unintelligible (some of you are thinking Boston; others, New York), then you can imagine how many students feel when they encounter a "foreign" discipline for the first time in college.

Implications/Applications. You can help novices by pointing out some of the major landmarks, by writing a list of the five key points in your lecture on the board before class, for example. You also can assess how well they are learning to read the "maps" that lectures or readings provide. Using a "Minute Paper" to find out what students thought were the most important points in a lecture or reading and what questions they still have can provide useful information on where they are getting lost and clues for getting back on track.

3. Learning is more effective and efficient when learners have explicit, reasonable, positive goals, and when their goals fit well with the teacher's goals.

If you don't know where you are going, you will probably end up somewhere else.
—Laurence J. Peter and Raymond Hull

When learners know what their educational goals are and figure out how they can best achieve them, they usually become much more efficient and effective. Adult learners often fit this bill. When learners know how and how well their goals fit the instructor's, they tend to learn more and get better grades.

Implications/Applications. Early in the term, ask students to write down a few specific learning goals they hope to achieve through your course. Then involve them in comparing their learning goals with those of other students, and with your teaching goals. Look for and build on areas of congruence, but don't gloss over potential conflicts or disconnects. Refer back to and assess progress toward shared goals throughout the semester.

4. To be remembered, new information must be meaningfully connected to prior knowledge, and it must first be remembered in order to be learned.

Thinking means connecting things, and stops if they cannot be connected.
—G. K. Chesterton

The more meaningful and appropriate connections students make between what they know and what they are learning, the more permanently they will anchor new information in long-term memory and the easier it will be for them to access that information when it's needed.

Implications/Applications. Provide many and varied examples/illustrations, descriptions/drawings, images, metaphors, and analogies. But ask students to provide them, as well, then give the students feedback on their usefulness and appropriateness. For instance, two simple ways to help students make connections, and to assess the connections they are making, are to ask them to compose a metaphor("Learning is _______") or to complete an analogy ("Teaching is to learning as _______is to _______").

5. Unlearning what is already known is often more difficult than learning new information.

It is what we think we know already that often prevents us from learning.
—Claude Bernard

Habits, preconceptions, and misconceptions can be formidable barriers to new learning, all the more treacherous because, like icebergs, this prior learning is usually 90 percent hidden from view. Before we can help students unlearn or correct prior learning, we need to know something about what is below the surface.

Implications/Applications. Before you present new material, find out what students already believe and know, and what they can do about it. A quick diagnostic "probe," containing a few questions, often can help you locate dangerous "icebergs." By asking a few diagnostic questions you might also find out that the shipping lanes are clear and that your students are more experienced navigators than you had assumed. Whatever you discover, it will help you and the students find more appropriate starting points for your work.

6. Information organized in personally meaningful ways is more likely to be retained, learned, and used.

> *Much goes on in the mind of the learner. Students interpret. They overinterpret. They actively struggle to impose meaning and structure upon new material being presented.*
>
> —Donald A. Norman

Humans are extraordinary pattern seekers. We seek regularity and meaning constantly, and we create them when they are not apparent. Witness our penchant for seeing dragons in clouds, for example. To be most useful, the ways learners organize knowledge in a given domain need to become ever more similar to the ways experts in that field organize knowledge. This requires making what is usually implicit, explicit.

Implications/Applications. Show students a number of different, useful, and acceptable ways to organize the same information. Use prose, outlines, graphs, drawings, and models. Assess students' organizing schemas and skills by getting them to show you their "mental models" in a similar variety of ways.

7. Learners need feedback on their learning, early and often, to learn well; to become independent, they need to learn how to give themselves feedback.

> *Supposing is good, but finding out is better.*
>
> —Mark Twain

Regular feedback helps learners efficiently direct their attention and energies, helps them avoid major errors and dead ends, and keeps them from learning things they later will have to unlearn at great cost. It also can serve as a motivating form of interaction between teacher and learner, and among learners. When students learn to internalize the voice of the "coach," they can begin to give themselves corrective feedback.

Implications/Applications. Don't assume that students understand, ask. Try asking them to jot down what the "muddiest point" was in a particular reading, lab, or lecture, then respond to the most common "muddy points" in your next class. Find out what students are doing with the feedback you're already giving them. Do they read and use the comments you write on papers and exams? If so, how? If not, why not? Explicitly demonstrate how you get feedback on your work and what you do with it.

8. The ways in which learners are assessed and evaluated powerfully affect the ways they study and learn.

> *Let the tutor demand an account not only of the words of his lesson, but of their meaning and substance . . . Let [the learner] show what he has just learned from a hundred points of view, and adapt it to as many different subjects, to see if he has rightly taken in it and made it his own.*
>
> —Michel de Montaigne

Whether faculty "teach to the test" or not, most students are going to try to "study to the test." For generations uncounted, students have annoyed their teachers with the question, "Will this be on the final?" One reason they persist is that most genuinely want to get good grades. But a second reason is that knowing what will be on the final, or on any upcoming test or quiz, helps students figure out where to focus their attention. In other words, they are looking for a roadmap. One way to improve learning, then, is to make sure our test questions require the kind of thinking and learning we wish to promote, and that students know—at least generally—what those questions will be.

Implications/Applications. Once you're sure your questions are testing what you want students to learn, give them a sample exam or a list of study questions from which the exam questions will be selected. Give students regular opportunities to practice answering similar questions and to get feedback on their answers. If students work in study groups, that corrective feedback often can come from their peers.

9. Mastering a skill or body of knowledge takes great amounts of time and effort.

> *There are some things that cannot be learned quickly, and time, which is all we have, must be paid heavily for their acquiring.*
>
> —Ernest Hemingway

In a study of talented young adults who had achieved high levels of mastery in a variety of fields, Benjamin Bloom and his colleagues found that none had achieved mastery in less than a dozen years, and the average time to mastery was sixteen years—at between 25 and 50 hours per week of practice and study. This means that at least 15,000 to 30,000 hours of time and intense practice were required to reach the highest levels of mastery. If we halve those figures to "guesstimate" the time needed to achieve an *acceptable* mastery level, we're still left with about 7,000 to 15,000 hours of preparation—the equivalent of 40-hour weeks, fifty weeks a year, for three-and-a-half to seven years.

Implications/Applications. Unplug all the TVs! Seriously, though, students need to know how long it actually takes to attain mastery in their field. Then they need to find out how much time they actually are devoting to that task. Give students a simple form on which they can log all the times they study/practice for a week and indicate how productively they used each block of time. Discussing their findings with other students in a nonjudgmental way can help them become aware of and gain control over their time use.

10. Learning to transfer, to apply previous knowledge and skills to new contexts, requires a great deal of practice.

Research on learning to transfer generally is depressing. Most learning is highly context-bound, and few students become skilled at applying what they've learned in one context to another similar context. In fact, many students cannot recognize things they've already learned if the context is shifted at all. This is one of the reasons why students will point at questions that are only slightly altered versions of homework questions and protest, "We've never done problems like these before!" Those students who are being honest simply cannot see the similarities. They learned to solve problems involving giraffes, motorcycles, and Cincinnati; they never had to solve problems about wildebeest, cars, or Dayton.

Implications/Applications. If you value transfer, teach transfer. Direct students' attention continually between the general and the specific. Give them many different examples of the same concepts or principles, and make sure they see where the similarities and the differences are. Challenge students to identify and then to create similar but different examples or problems.

11. High expectations encourage high achievement.

For some time now, we've known that younger students tend to achieve more by working with teachers who expect more of them. For the so-called "Pygmalion effect" to work well in college, however, the students must share the teacher's high expectations of themselves and perceive them as reasonable.

Implications/Applications. Begin by finding out what your students expect of themselves in your class, letting them know what you expect, and discussing those expectations. Begin the course with assignments that diligent students can succeed in to build confidence. Have learners interview successful former students, or invite them to class, to illustrate in flesh and blood that high expectations can be realized.

12. To be most effective, teachers need to balance levels of intellectual challenge and instructional support.

In discussing the ways in which mothers help children acquire language by constantly adjusting their speech to stay slightly ahead of the child's, Jerome Bruner writes of "scaffolding." Scaffolding is a useful metaphor for college learning, as well. The weaker or smaller the student's foundation (preparation) in the subject, the stronger and larger the instructional scaffolding (structure and support) that is required. This is one of the many reasons that teaching a first-year course requires a different approach than teaching a third-year course in the same discipline. Students in the third year generally require less structure and direction, and benefit from more autonomy and responsibility. This also helps explain why students of lower ability or much weaker preparation often benefit from and appreciate highly structured courses. They need the scaffolding.

Implications/Applications. Even when learner ability or preparation or both are weak, expectations should remain high. To reach those expectations, less-prepared students will need more and more explicit instructional "scaffolding," such as tutoring, highly structured directions, and more personal contact with the instructor. Students who are better prepared or more able can be encouraged to master their learning by serving as tutors, helping to create scaffolding for others, and to take more responsibility for their own learning through independent studies and special projects.

13. Motivation to learn is alterable; it can be positively or negatively affected by the task, the environment, the teacher, and the learner.

Though we tend to talk about students as being either "motivated" or "not motivated," most of our students are very motivated to learn certain things and not at all motivated to learn others. Research suggests that you stand a good chance of increasing motivation to learn if you can positively influence your students' beliefs and expectations about one or more of the following: Students are likely to be more motivated to learn in your class if they see the value of what you're teaching; believe that learning it will help them achieve other important goals; believe that they are capable of learning it; and expect that they will succeed.

Implications/Applications. Give students lots of specific examples of the value and usefulness of what they're learning and help them make connections between short-term course goals and their own long-term goals. Use simple, anonymous surveys to gauge students' expectations, beliefs, and self-confidence levels, then respond to that information with specific examples, suggestions, and, whenever possible, realistic encouragement.

14. Interaction between teachers and learners is one of the most powerful factors in promoting learning; interaction among learners is another.

As with activity, it isn't interaction in and of itself that promotes academic learning, it's structured interaction focused on achieving meaningful, shared learning tasks. As the professional world never tires of pointing out, our students need to learn to work more effectively in teams.

Implications/Applications. Most students have to believe teachers know and care about them before they can benefit from interactions—or even interact. Learn students' names as a first step, then try to engage them in working with you to learn. Classroom Assessment and Classroom Research projects can engage students and teachers in working together to solve meaningful problems, such as finding ways to ensure that *everyone* in class has a fair chance to master the course content. If you want students to cooperate effectively with other students, first, challenge them with assignments that groups can carry out more effectively than individuals can; second, provide guidelines and guidance for group work, especially for those who haven't had experience; and, third, de-emphasize competition among individuals for grades and approval. Meaningful and positive interactions require mutual trust.

Final Notes

Nothing is so useless as a general maxim.

—Lord Macaulay

Psychology is a science; teaching is an art, and sciences never generate arts directly out of themselves. An intermediary, inventive mind must make the application, by use of its originality.

—William James

I argued at the outset that mastery of an academic discipline is not sufficient for effective college teaching. But even disciplinary mastery complemented by familiarity with research on college learning is not sufficient. Truly effective teachers know their subjects, know something about the research that informs teaching, and also know how to adapt and apply relevant research findings to their own classrooms. Lord Macaulay was partially correct: Nothing is so useless as a general maxim that isn't properly applied to the particular. With James, I'm convinced that we need inventive, original minds to make the applications of these or any other general principles of teaching. I'm also confident we have such "intermediary, inventive" teachers in abundance among our faculty.

Note

This article was adapted from Session 56: "A Teacher's Dozen: Fourteen (General) Findings From Research That Can Inform Classroom Teaching and Assessment and Improve Learning," from AAHE's 1993 National Conference on Higher Education.

Resources

A Few Useful Starting Points

Bloom, B.S. (1986). "The Hands and Feet of Genius: Automaticity." *Educational Leadership*, 43(5):70–77.

Bruner, J.S., and H.W. Haste, eds. (1987). *Making Sense: The Child's Construction of the World.* New York: Routledge.

Gamson, Z., and A. Chickering. (1987). "Seven Principles for Good Practice in Undergraduate Education." *AAHE Bulletin,* 39(7):510.

McKeachie, W.J. (1986). *Teaching Tips: A Guidebook for the Beginning College Teacher,* 8th ed. Lexington, MA: D.C. Heath.

_____, P.R. Pintrich, Y.-G. Lin, and D.A.F. Smith. (1986). *Teaching and Learning in the College Classroom: A Review of the Research Literature.* Ann Arbor. National Center to Improve Postsecondary Teaching and Learning, University of Michigan.

Norman, D.A. (1980). "What Goes On in the Mind of the Learner." In W.J. McKeachie, ed., *Learning, Cognition, and College Teaching.* New Directions for Teaching and Learning, no. 2. San Francisco Jossey-Bass.

Svinicki, M.D. (1991). "Practical Implications of Cognitive Theories." In R.J. Menges and M.D. Svinicki, eds. *College Teaching: From Theory to Practice.* New Directions for Teaching and Learning, no. 45. San Francisco: Jossey-Bass.

Weinstein, C.E., and D.K. Meyer. (1991). "Cognitive Learning Strategies and College Teaching." In R.J. Menges and M.D. Svinicki, eds. *College Teaching: From Theory to Practice.* New Directions for Teaching and Learning, no. 45. San Francisco: Jossey-Bass.

CHAPTER 35

CREATING A CONTEXT WHERE INSTITUTIONAL ASSESSMENT YIELDS EDUCATIONAL IMPROVEMENT

MARCIA MENTKOWSKI

A multitude of settings and a variety of definitions characterize assessment today. Educators and administrators from a wide range of large and small, public and private, institutions are struggling with the process of assessing student performance, program validity, and institutional effectiveness (American Council on Education 1990; El-Khawas 1989; Ewell 1984, 1987, 1988; Heywood 1989; Hutchings and Marchese 1990). Whether we are veterans or novices in this complex, almost chaotic world of discussion about and experience with assessment, we do have much in common.

First, we all want assessment to make a difference. Those of us who are just beginning the discussion in our institutions are wary of jumping onto a bandwagon without a clear view of the pitfalls (Banta 1988; Terenzini 1989). (Some may even feel tempted at times to obstruct or denature assessment for fear it will have a negative impact. Such an attitude is not opposition to assessment; it is a passionate dedication to seeing that assessment makes the right kind of difference.) Indeed, institutions first joining the issue may have the most intense concern with impact and results: they may be the most under the gun to come up with results that people want to use.

Similar issues arise for those of us who are heavily involved in doing assessment (Hutchings 1988). Each of us is trying to figure out how to refine the ways assessment works in our classroom, our department, our institution, or our state. The more we succeed, the more others want in on the action. We become more and more concerned not only with whether and how to do assessment, but with ensuring that our efforts matter (Loacker 1988). And some of us now know the questions, issues, and problems involved in making results matter. We now have something in place and are free to refine assessment, even to create new ways of doing it. But that also puts us in the position, like it or not, of helping to set the tone for the national dialogue about how to make assessment a keystone in educational reform. Assessment will rise or fall as educators like us grapple frankly with the issue of how to improve programs, not just to make institutions accountable.

Second, we share some common educational values that center on expanding human knowledge and educating diverse students for a changing and challenging world. Many of us spend a major part of our lives working to add to or restructure the knowledge in our disciplines and to transform that knowledge into an effective, vital force in individual and public life. Our pilgrims' progress toward assessment represents an unparalleled research opportunity: to discover how adults learn, and in particular how they learn the perspectives and values, the information and skills, the trained habits of mind, that characterize our respective fields.

Source: "Creating a Context Where Institutional Assessment Yields Educational Improvement," by Marcia Mentkowski, reprinted from *Journal of General Education*, Vol. 40, 1991, Pennsylvania State University Press.

Many of us also struggle daily to educate students who will make it in college and in society only if what we do makes a difference. Our dream of effective assessment will not be realized until assessment benefits the learning of each and every student who comes to us. Obviously, the major benefits for students lie in direct assessment of individual student learning (Hutchings 1990; Loacker et al. 1986). But program and institutional assessment will also benefit each and every student—if we build meaning into these broader processes, so that the results matter to educators and administrators who are in a position to use the information to improve teaching and learning.

Qualities of Institutional Assessment

Amid our diverse definitions and practices of assessment nationwide, I have seen a developing consensus about several essential qualities that distinguish assessment as an emerging practice in higher education from measurement practices in other kinds of institutions. Some of these qualities are ones that professionals in measurement (Messick 1988; Tittle 1989), evaluation (Gray 1989; Guba & Lincoln 1989; Patton 1986), educational research (Astin 1985, 1991; Light et al. 1990), and institutional research (Ewell 1985) would recognize as universally desirable; others emerge from the particular goals of the educational enterprise.

1. *Assessment is a means, not an end.* Whether we are conducting an external evaluation of programs at the institutional level or assessing the individual student in the classroom, we are not merely gathering data for its own sake, or measuring just anything because an instrument happens to be available. Our efforts are defined by our values and goals, by what we intend to *do* with the information. Basically, in an educational environment, that intention is always two-fold.

2. *Assessment is a means not only to establish accountability but also to achieve educational benefits.* Educators use assessment both to "prove" and to "improve." The state or the trustees may seek evidence of effectiveness for certification, accreditation, or even funding purposes. Educators also assess in order to increase their knowledge of the learning process and to improve its main outcome—student learning.

We may begin educational assessment in order to demonstrate something, but we will remain committed to it only if it results in tangible, day-to-day benefits—not only examining whether we are doing what we intend to do but also suggesting specific efforts and experiments to do it better.

3. *Assessment purposes, goals, and methods emerge from the setting.* An assessment instrument or process that measures something other than what we are trying to do or why we are doing it is at best pointless, at worst damaging. Educators involved in a program are the best source of definition for their values, rationales, and objectives, for some of the tough questions that need to be asked, and for what kinds of information will make a positive difference.

Even the best external models and materials must be painstakingly adapted to the institution, program, and classroom in which they are being used. This also holds true over time: as courses, programs, and institutions evolve, so will their specific objectives and the challenges they face. Purposes, goals, and methods for assessing their performance must evolve accordingly. Effective assessment considers the immediate context as an essential source of the *what, why,* and *how* of assessing.

4. *Assessment encourages multiplicity.* Successful assessment information, especially in such a complex, rapidly changing environment as higher education, may yield *comparability* of insights and interpretations about diverse programs. Yet each educational institution has a particular mission and serves a unique population; each program and department, each course, and each educator plays a distinct role in meeting that mission and serving that population.

Educators need to shape varied approaches to assessment, responding to their own questions and situations, before they can reach interdepartmental or interinstitutional understandings of what, why, and how to assess. Likewise, different schools and departments will use assessment data to do different things; for a full return on our investment in assessment, we need to encourage and develop such multiple strategies.

5. *Assessment encourages coherence.* Assessment is a means toward connected, purposeful education. It calls for reexamining the explicit and implicit links between educational goals and student outcomes. It focuses a critical eye on relationships among teaching, learning, and any

means that mirror or evaluate the consequences. Assessment encourages coherence when student learning outcomes are mapped in relation to institutional mission, values, and educational assumptions.

Effective assessment ultimately demands that its many forms across the institution be connected—if only to make assessment practical and possible. It joins mechanisms that are already delivering useful information with new strategies and reaches out to reconnect itself with all the elements of an effective curriculum and its administrative functions. This may call for discipline-based as well as interdisciplinary approaches and methods. Thus, assessment draws on multiple modes of inquiry.

Assessment generates even broader connections to all institutions concerned about educational effectiveness. Assessment information stimulates coherence within the institution: students question how to improve; faculty rethink their teaching; departments refine their goals. The results from this process provide a base for communicating with legislators and employers. Ultimately, each of society's institutions in kinship with higher education ask, "How are we linked to higher learning? How do we achieve a connected, supportive interdependence with postsecondary education?"

6. *Feedback is the essence of assessment.* How, and whether, assessment information is communicated critically affects its value. Different audiences—the state, trustees, the registrar, the corporate faculty, the individual instructor, the student, the prospective employer or graduate school—want different kinds of information for their different purposes. But all need timely feedback from the assessment process, data that have been turned into usable information by being made relevant to their concerns. And in educational assessment, two key audiences are educators and students. Unless the data generated by assessment returns to the educational process to improve program and student performance, they will die upon dissemination.

From observing and participating in the nationwide assessment scene for a couple of decades now, this is what I see as an emerging consensus about some essential, distinctive qualities of educational assessment. Against that backdrop, I offer the following guidelines or creating a context where educational assessment program at any level will yield the optimum in educational benefits.

Six Guidelines for Constructing an Assessment Context*

1. *Make a Long-Term Commitment to a Dynamic Plan*

A *long-term commitment* provides stability, allowing us to develop one thing at a time, to stay in the present, and to keep the future in its place. One of the most frustrating aspects of doing assessment is starting up, working to develop one part of a complex plan, and having someone constantly pressuring you to work on another part of the plan, whether you are ready or not.

By 1973, for example, at Alverno, the faculty had created both a new curriculum and a process for assessing each student's abilities sequentially as she moved through it (Alverno College Faculty [1976] 1985, [1979] 1985). But as early as 1974, we began receiving a good deal of outside pressure to do program evaluation. By that time, faculty were ready for validating faculty-designed instruments, testing educational assumptions, researching ability definitions, and evaluating alumnae outcomes. Not until 1976, however, when faculty had their new program well in place and we had our first graduates could we turn our attention to evaluating our program systematically or researching its basic educational assumptions. Having a long-term commitment enabled us to stick to the task at hand, refining our assessment of individual student abilities, before we took up the larger, logically subsequent question of validating the broad outcomes of college.

Once we began program assessment and establishing validity, we used a longitudinal design, working with two complete entering classes. For example, one component assessed student performance on outside measures three times during their college years (Mentkowski & Doherty 1983, [1983] 1984, 1984; Mentkowski & Loacker 1985). We fed each round of data immediately back into the curriculum. But no sooner had we started than we began to get outside pressure to study our alumnae.

Now, any research and evaluation effort should do followup studies of alumni. But at the time, when we had only a few alumnae from

Alverno's new curriculum, it would not have made sense. We held off in fact until 1980, by which time we had researched outstanding professionals (who were not our graduates) for ability models. And by then we had a much clearer view of which overall outcomes of college we wanted to study in our alumnae's lives and careers; we just realized our first full set of longitudinal data in 1988. A long-term commitment helped us keep our eye on what we *could* do and our reasons for doing assessment.

A long-term commitment also creates an atmosphere of purpose and support for using assessment data. Most of us will use information, even though it is at first sketchy and incomplete, if we know there is more coming and that the quality will get better. For example, one group of faculty is currently redesigning one of our in-place, cross-college instruments that we know is not working as well as it might. But because there was a long-term commitment, those who depended on the instrument for individual student feedback as well as those who depended on it for aggregate data were willing to make adjustments until this faculty group had the time—and the insight from other assessment results—to refine it. We were able to deal with what was there, until we had time to make it better (Rogers 1988). An institution, department, or faculty members in the classroom cannot deal with every aspect of assessment at once. But they can resist outside pressures to do something else first, if they have a long-range commitment to what they intend to do.

A *dynamic plan* handles pressure inside the institution as well. It provides an atmosphere of changes, time for redesign, and the constant opportunity to build in elements one might not have thought of at the beginning; the experiences of James Madison University, Kean College of New Jersey, and Kings College bear this out (Farmer 1988; Office of the Vice President for Academic Affairs 1985; Presidential Task Force on Student Learning and Development 1986).

Assessment plans change many times as they are being implemented. A dynamic plan specifically includes the kind of time we need not only to implement but also to revise, rethink, and refine assessment designs. In a dynamic plan, we can at any moment spend time and effort where we really need it, trying out some aspect and making it work on a day-to-day basis, so we can see some results that matter in improved curriculum and student performance.

A dynamic plan is the best response to well-meaning observations from outside about what one should be doing. I learned early on that with a long-range commitment to a dynamic plan, you can satisfy your most stalwart critics. One question we were often asked was, Why not computerize your student information system? We were able to say, "That sounds like a good idea. In fact, we plan to have a completely computerized system including all the relevant information students generate on in-class assessments, so we can see which outcomes of college are realized across the board in classes. That will probably be in 2001. In the meanwhile, we will be working to figure out what kind of information we really want to collect, what we will do with the information once we get it, and how we will use it. In fact, two of our major departments are trying out some ideas like that this semester, to give us a preview of what such a system might look like."

A dynamic plan also influences assessment development. As instructors assess student performance in their courses, discussion and planning for departmental assessment become all but inevitable. Departments planning to collect aggregate data on the outcomes of their major programs are on to a surefire way to inspire better institutional assessment. That puts assessment designers in a better position to create the connections between individual student assessment in the classroom and departmental and curricular evaluation processes. The overlaps in design and multiple uses for assessment data, often from the same instruments, become apparent. Some assessments can be used to give individual feedback to students, enable an instructor to probe the effects of a new teaching strategy, and also form the backbone of a longer-term research and evaluation effort. A dynamic plan encourages such grass-roots development of assessment.

In my early work with assessment, I often made the mistake of being reactive, responding to outside pressure instead of being proactive and communicating the dynamic nature of what we were doing. I have learned that the most convincing argument for what you are doing is actually doing it.

2. Rely on Faculty Questions for Direction

It is a cardinal rule of program evaluation that unless data responds to questions important to those who will *act* as a result of the information it is not good data (Weiss 1983). Students are best helped by information from tests if they can use it to improve. Faculty are best helped by assessment results—to improve instruction or advise students more effectively—when assessment is derived from their questions as educators.

Finding out what educators' questions are has proven to be a remarkably simple process, one that also shows faculty how easily they can become involved in assessment. It presents assessment designers with the issues and realities of their own institution's context. At Alverno, we draw our student-assessment and program-evaluation-research designs from faculty questions. In fact, we have gathered complex arrays of inquiry to guide a year or more of work from a faculty workshop at a year-end institute. Since 1985, the AAHE Research Forum at the AAHE annual conference has engaged nationwide samplings of educators in a similarly compact, productive exercise (Mentkowski & Chickering 1987). In a 1989 preconference session, 42 conference presenters spent three hours generating a host of questions on six conference topics expected to help improve teaching, learning, and assessment. The next day, 129 educators produced additional sets of questions on the six topics, including "assessment of student learning" and "assessment of institutional effectiveness" (AAHE Research Forum 1989; Mentkowski & Banta 1989). The annual AAHE Research Agenda (available from this author) is created from this broad array of educator questions and disseminated to other higher education associations.

Educators know what they need to know to improve education: data gathered in response to educators' questions will more likely be used. Through questions, faculty establish both the meaning of assessment and the uses to which its results will be put. This helps guarantee that assessment's results are linked intimately to its purposes, to create a feedback loop that faculty can rely on. In addition, assessment generated from faculty questions gains credibility among students. Because it is linked to their most important concerns about teaching and learning, faculty reinforce student participation and belief in assessment.

3. Create Interactive Processes

Once an assessment plan is in place, faculty involvement continues to establish its meaning and use. Educators begin to establish which instruments are valid and relevant and which interpretations of results are credible for what purposes. Faculty involvement in deciding which instruments to use, and in designing and developing instruments that measure outcomes they see as essential, is becoming important in assessment practice. Just because an instrument is psychometrically valid does not necessarily mean it will yield results that are credible and useful to a particular educator or group of educators. Credibility emerges only through an interactive process, in which faculty construct assessment and so maintain their involvement.

Such interactive processes create a context where people can respond to each other, connect with each other's interests, work out emerging concerns, and begin to construct a conceptual base for assessment (Mentkowski 1990). They begin to take collaborative responsibility for assessment. For example, the New Jersey Department of Higher Education (College Outcomes Evaluation Program 1987) involved educators across the state in designing assessment. Julia Rogers and her colleagues at the University of Montevallo (Rogers et al. 1988) and Michael McGuire (1988) at the college of Lake County involved faculty at their respective institutions in reviewing a standardized measure of college outcomes against institutional goals to determine whether results would have credibility at their institutions. Would student data from this instrument be meaningful to faculty? Would it help them improve teaching and learning? Faculty at both institutions already had identified goals and detailed views on which information could be used effectively, and how. Soliciting and being guided by those goals and views averted major difficulties and created a system for communicating credible, usable results.

Two task forces—community college and baccalaureate—representing Washington State institutions of higher education engaged in a similar exercise. Along with administering three standardized measures to students in the consortium, more than 100 of their faculty completed some of the same materials and critiqued them for how they reflected institutional goals and whether the information would be useful

(Council of Presidents and State Board for Community College Education 1989). Such critique, in advance as well as after use of standardized measures (Banta et al. 1987), can lead to improved assessment techniques.

A similar kind of faculty involvement occurred in a 24-institution consortium organized on assessment design (Alverno College/FIPSE Assessment Project 1987; Schulte et al. 1989). After designing their own instruments for measuring abilities important at their campus, faculty collaborated in a critique of their work across two Alverno workshops. Among other approaches, they reviewed initial designs against criteria and studied student performance examples to extend the evaluation (Alverno College Office of Research and Evaluation/ Assessment Committee, in press). The result was a set of improved instruments. Similarly, faculty at the University of Wisconsin Medical School at Madison developed ability criteria and refined them over time through progressive tryouts (Stone & Meyer 1989).

At Alverno our interview studies of the abilities of outstanding professionals in nursing and management were designed and conducted by Office of Research and Evaluation staff (DeBack & Mentkowski 1986; Mentkowski et al. 1982). But faculty from both departments were involved in deciding which professionals to interview, choosing and creating instruments, coding the interviews, and interpreting and writing up the results. The next task, comparing the professionals' abilities with those taught in college, proceeded apace, since the study had been crafted to yield results meaningful to educators in both departments. Another interview study extended the method across a range of departments (Schall et al. 1984). Our new computer studies department used a similar interview strategy to test whether their curriculum was advancing or trailing this newly emerging field, and how the abilities of new graduates were actually being played out in a range of postcollege settings (Kennedy 1988). Our faculty and others ("Student Potential Assessed at Rhode Island College" 1989) used modified versions of the interview (Council for Adult and Experiential Learning and McBer & Company 1987) to help determine the abilities of prospective students with weak academic credentials. Taken together, these examples expand the role and benefit of faculty investment in assessment.

Interactivity also enhances student involvement in program assessment. Alverno students whom we asked to volunteer were willing when given extensive rationales for the project and regular reports of individual and group results. By giving them individual feedback on their development in learning styles and then showing how their participation could help lead to greater degree credibility, for example, we were able to sustain participation in a longitudinal study (Mentkowski & Strait 1983).

In our followup study of alumnae five years after college, providing individual and group feedback has been the key to sustaining participation. Preliminary data from a group with 85 percent participation, given to another group to show what graduates were doing five years after graduation, increased the second group's participation (Reisetter & Sandoval 1987).

When faculty, students, and alumnae actively participate in assessment, results are more credible for all of them—and for additional audiences such as trustees, nationwide colleagues, and government agencies.

4. Define Criteria and Comparisons Publicly

To make meaning out of data, people generally try to make some kind of comparison. The notion of "good" student performance, for example, almost inevitably elicits the question, "good compared to what?" Unless we deal with that question, assessment information can lack credibility. Establishing credibility of the criteria—of the comparisons they imply—is one of the most difficult tasks in assessment. If assessment judgments are to be useful for improving performance, the criteria must be *publicly* defined and reflect a *consensus* on the "good" being sought at the level of action and change. This is as true for general education or a major department as for the institution as a whole.

Faculty involvement in defining criteria and making them public is critical. Educators defining general education goals may work across disciplines and from their experience with past student performance to reach consensus on goals, standards, and criteria. They create a community of judgment for deciding what is "good" and work to help each other and their students understand the "why" behind their expert judgment, the "how" of improving.

Faculty in a major department are also the key link between assessment and improvement.

As they make clear what the goals and criteria are and where they come from, they simultaneously point out specific avenues for curricular design. Aided by analyses of student performance on course exams, portfolios, or capstone measures, they continue to illuminate criteria for good performance, relying in part on expertise, on years of deciphering and judging student work. In part, faculty are often relying on fairly clear-cut criteria developed by a discipline for text analysis in literary criticism, for example, or the scientific method in lab experiments. On a psychology department comprehensive exam, students may be meeting criteria established not only by their professors but by all the psychology departments in the state. But in each case—general education or the major—faculty motivation to use information from assessment to improve depends on whether they have implicitly or explicitly defined the criteria explaining what is "good" and why. And these criteria can inform comparisons within and across departments.

Defining standards at the institutional level provides a similar challenge. It is often made more difficult by the temptation to select external measures created outside the department or university, without a faculty review process. Bypassing the faculty may appear justified when curriculum goals and criteria are only implicit and there is outside pressure for immediate results. But insisting that goals and criteria from general education and the major stay up front stimulates faculty investment in this process and can lead to their involvement in clarifying goals.

Some years ago, such external tests often had automatic credibility because they were standardized; now their results often have little credibility with faculty if curriculum goals cannot be clearly linked to what a test measures and its implied comparisons (Council of Presidents and State Board for Community College Education 1989). Standardized tests seldom can publish their assumed criteria or identify enough of the characteristics of norm groups to enable credible comparisons. Many of the most familiar standardized tests were not designed as college-outcomes measures. Nor is it fair to assume that an instrument designer or company creating measures for cross-institutional use could answer for a single institution's faculty what is good, at what level their students should perform, or what the criteria should be.

A faculty, for example, may have decided and set forth in its mission statement that their students should develop "critical thinking." External measures may seem to offer an "objective" or "outside" reading and be readily available. What can such a test really tell this faculty? With a recognition measure, an item-by-item readout may help a faculty analyze patterns for clues to how students perform on items related to department goals.

An objective test, standardized to the current levels of student performance across the country at other colleges, cannot tell the faculty at what level they want their students to perform. Nor can its purveyors offer many clues as to the relationship between scores on the test and the components of critical thinking defined in a department's goals: the latter remains a faculty task—possible only if item-by-item scores are part of the package. Production measures can open up a more in-depth analysis of performance on broad abilities. For example, Perry's patterns of intellectual development in the college years may help a faculty draw relationship between sophistication in intellectual development and students' performance on class or capstone seminar papers and projects (Knefelkamp & Widick 1982; Mentkowski, Moeser & Strait 1983; Perry 1970).

The faculty might find a college in one state that seems similar in size or entrance standards or governance or even programs and compare scores or patterns with that school. But what would they do with the findings then? In fact, such comparison scores may have little educational improvement meaning for either institution, particularly if one cannot easily factor in specific information on students' preparation for college, retention rates, or cultural background.

Faculty are far more likely to be motivated by data from measures they have had a hand in designing, that take into account their own criteria for student performance, drawn from their institutional goals. And they are likely to find far more meaning and use in a range of comparisons. In fact, ACE's 1990 Campus Trends data reports that 66 percent of the respondents design their own instruments (American Council on Education 1990).

Using faculty-designed measures as one basis for comparison, a number of others will likely arise. Many faculty are acutely aware of employers' dissatisfaction with graduates' communication and thinking abilities. Undergraduate professional school students take teacher tests or nursing state boards. Many major departments take readings of student performance on graduate school entrance exams and consequent admissions. Alumni satisfaction, salary, and job surveys are common. While these comparisons may yield success indicators, they are less likely to yield information on the "how" of improving. Extending the range of comparison yields that benefit.

Student's performance data could be compared to criteria drawn from institutional mission statements and department goals. But student performance could also be compared to beginning, developing, and advanced descriptions of student potential; to the judgments of colleagues from other colleges; and to disciplinary or professional standards; and/or the abilities of outstanding alumni and other professionals. In the 1970s, for example, seven colleges agreed to use a number of instruments as part of a study of college outcomes from critical thinking to self-definition and maturity. With the help of a FIPSE grant, students at each college completed McBer & Company's "Cognitive Competence Assessment Battery" at the beginning and end of college. The investigators could have simply compared each college's freshman-senior score gains against the average of the other six, assuming that a high score is the "good" all seven institutions sought. Instead, they analyzed the several mission statements and when they reported their data added whether the college had in fact selected that outcome as one they intended to develop, and then achieved it (Winter et al. 1981). This approach helped set the context for using the data once delivered, because it had been related directly to whether and how closely each institution's goals were being met. Instead of wondering, "Do we look good? Do we look bad?" each faculty could ask some serious questions: "How do we want our students to change?" "Are we satisfied?" and "What could we do better?"

In the Appalachian College Assessment Consortium, assessment questions are likewise drawn from the goals of the general education program at each college (Carey 1987). In one component of their approach, selected faculty members are each directly involved in conducting interviews with three seniors not from the faculty member's discipline. These faculty interviewers pool their information about college outcomes, along with reflections about what worked and did not during the interviews. Such a strategy that involves faculty in the data collection as well as the interpretation provides a unique opportunity for cross-institution comparison within the framework of each college's distinct mission.

Similarly, learning and personal growth outcomes of students can be compared against those descriptions of human growth and potential that emerge from the psychological literature (e.g., cognitive-developmental patterns of growth or arrays of critical thinking skills) (Chickering & Associates 1981; Gardner 1983; Mentkowski 1988; Sternberg 1985). Each of these more external pictures of what students ought to achieve given what is expected in work and personal life can stimulate comparisons that faculty and students consider credible. Trustees, higher education boards, and legislative groups are drawn toward comparisons that ask: Are we educating students toward abilities that project what society will need years from now?

The Association of American Colleges created opportunities for faculty from fifty-one departments in eighteen institutions to collaborate on designing senior-level assessments. Then faculty served as "external examiners" for the culminating work of seniors who were not their own. The comparison led to a new appreciation by departments of an outside view of student achievement. Contrary to their expectations, students greeted with enthusiasm the chance to present their work to a broader range of expert judgments (Fong 1988; Resnick & Schneider, in press).

A dozen learned societies responsible for arts and sciences fields are involved with the Association of American Colleges in rethinking their majors, and are designating content knowledge and intellectual abilities that should be developed by students through the major. As this work develops, these descriptions could form another backdrop against which a department can view its own goals for its undergraduate majors (Carol G. Schneider, personal communication, 22 February 1990).

Another comparison that can be helpful is between abilities selected by faculty and those demonstrated by outstanding members of the discipline's professional groups. For example, the explicit descriptions of the effective professional drawn from performance studies (Boyatzis 1982; Mentkowski et al. 1982) can stimulate a professional school faculty to view the expected abilities of their graduates against the actual performance of partitioners they respect (Evarts 1982); a curriculum can be reviewed with an eye toward how well it prepares students to take on professional roles, abilities, and skills. These professional abilities can be further compared against a department's own effective alumni.

The point is that there is a wide array of meaningful and challenging comparisons that educators and their constituencies can make with their assessment data. And making such comparisons clear and public draws faculty more and more into involvement with assessment while enabling them to learn more and more from it.

5. *Translate Results into Relevant, "Live" Information*

The last two guidelines get down to the nitty-gritty of communicating assessment data so that it results in decisions and action plans for improvement. Assessment information, effectively transmitted, should raise even more questions than it provides answers; our challenge is to turn data into the kinds of "live" information that inspires student or faculty insights and questions that foster change. Whether or not people use information to improve depends on how they get the message. That the medium is the message is as true of assessment data as it is of any other information. Understanding data and interpreting it is a prerequisite for using it.

In the classroom, individual performance data needs to be made understandable and personal to each student; program assessment data often need to be communicated across a wide range of disciplines and even institutions. How do we engage people in the data we are reporting, and how do we provide avenues for them to enter the work of improvement? First, we must speak in plain English. As a developmental psychologist, I tended to throw numbers and charts at faculty, whether they were from the fine arts or the sciences. After one such presentation, a music instructor commented that it was a fine performance but asked, "What did it all mean?" Second, we must address our listeners' common concerns. As one colleague said to me, "You'll need to do more than use beautiful colors and well-executed graphics to draw fine arts faculty into analyzing charts. Maybe you should step back and ask yourself what *all* of our faculty have in common." Of course, what they have in common is students—and that is why assessment data need to evoke understanding of the individual student's performance and perspective. Faculty are eager to learn the educational beliefs, goals, and motivations of students, as well as to see their personal growth, abilities, and learning. After all, understanding students is how educators become better at what they do.

I also learned that most of us have to hear one student voice first. Aggregate data does not relate directly to our experience of students as individuals; we are motivated to help students improve by listening to them one at a time. I finally hit upon the technique of presenting students' testimony and photographs, in a slide-accompanied audiotape. This is something that works; it starts faculty talking, and before you know it, they are asking, "Is this how we want our students to turn out? What in our curriculum might be causing this?" Criteria for good performance get clarified; further inquiries and experiments are born. After an early slidetape, that same music instructor asked whether we also had any *quantitative* patterns that further illustrated students' learning. Once he had heard one student, he began to ask about patterns.

Aggregate data can be valuable if we make the link between it and individual data. Without that connection, and without visible intra- and interindividual patterns, aggregate data seldom makes sense (Collins & Horn, in press; Willett 1988). This flies in the face of the way we are used to seeing data presented—group results, a synthesis of interview topics and patterns, a set of numbers with group averages highlighted.

Experience has also taught me that department or institutionwide assessment programs, no matter how well conceived, are no substitute for the ongoing assessment of individual students in classes and the clues to educational improvement that such data provide. Institutional assessment is a way to step back from a whole curriculum, but it does not do the job that individual educators must do to give ongoing, personal feedback to their students.

6. Create Feedback—Usable Knowledge About Performance—that Stimulates Improvement

Communicating "live" information enables faculty and students to understand assessment data, to make meaning out of it for themselves, and to focus on change. Another element also enables the move from data to decisions: feedback—usable knowledge about performance. Working with both student and program assessment, we have found that the most critical element in using data to improve is feedback that encourages students and faculty to create change. Whether it is presented to a student or to an institution, feedback needs to *focus on strengths as well as weaknesses* (Loacker et al. 1986). In fact, in the beginning of an assessment process, whether individual or institutional, it is essential to begin with strengths, to present confirming information. It is clear that strength-first feedback to a student that clarifies the positive aspects of a performance builds the confidence that allows her to examine more closely what parts missed the mark.

I used a similar strategy in one of the first presentations I made to our faculty on program evaluation data drawn from in-depth interviews of ten students who had just graduated from our new curriculum. I did not attempt to compare one student with another, or to compare this group to earlier graduates. Instead, I prepared a synthesis of some of the constructions these students made about their educational experience, sketching them in broad terms and then illustrating with quotes from the students. This was very confirming for faculty: They had evidence that *some* students were internalizing *some* of the broad educational principles undergirding lifelong learning on which the curriculum was built. Soon afterward they wanted to know, "Do all students make meaning like this?" No, not all; but by that time they were open to hearing about those who did not.

Second, to elicit implications for change, feedback works best when it comes from *more than one data source*, from multiple measures and standards. Data often goes unused when faculty's numerous, urgent questions have been reduced to a single measure, or worse, to one issue. Such data most often elicit dichotomies from listeners. Recall the student who says, "Well, maybe I didn't show I could do it on *that* test, but I did it in class the rest of the semester." Recall the college that says, "Well, maybe our students didn't show change *here*, but after all, this measure is fallible."

One measure we used, an attitude survey, showed that students had upward, positive attitudes toward the curriculum for the first two years of college, followed by a negative drop toward the end of the junior year. At the end of the senior year, attitudes returned to their previous positive levels. The faculty worried about this junior-year decline until we examined data from concurrent student interviews, which suggested students were necessarily experiencing conflicts in the transition to their senior year. Using one measure only, however, faculty had no idea what to do with the data. Feedback should *focus on patterns* to encourage the broadest possible thinking about meaning and implications. When we are interested in complexities, we are less likely to see only problem areas. We look for ways to improve and then think about other data we might need.

In one case, when we were presenting data on several learning outcomes at once, we used learning-style measures, samples from student interviews and samples from interviews with alumnae. This enabled faculty to think about the data broadly, rather than focusing only on negative information. And there did seem to be negatives: Some measures showed up-and-down movement over time (similar to that in the attitude survey), while others showed down-then-up. By no means all showed the steady upward climb we associate with "growth." Another pattern appears to underlie the patterns—a new model of growth. That is, when individuals experience new situations, they recycle through earlier forms of thinking and use less sophisticated methods of coping; development is thus more a spiral than a steady upward curve, or a stepwise series of stages (Mentkowski 1988).

This finding flies in the face of much of the psychological literature, which often seems to describe development as linear progress toward maturity. But it has won immediate acceptance from faculty at Alverno and from faculty visitors from other colleges, who quickly see that it confirms a puzzling part of their own experience. We have all been in the situation of assuming that students would come to a new class with all the learning from previous courses at their fingertips, then blaming other faculty or high school teachers when that did not occur. Once this "spiral" picture of learning was explicit, faculty could stop blaming one another and instead could concentrate on learning how to bring students quickly up to speed in new learning situations, to use the kinds of thinking they are capable of. This cemented new bonds among faculty rather than tearing down morale, although many individual results had looked "negative" at first. By focusing on patterns from many sources of data, we were able to create constructive, significant change.

Feedback should *be developmental;* it should *encourage productive change.* Often, this means that the information generated from assessment should include both the clues and tools that clearly suggest next steps.

Departments at the University of Tennessee at Knoxville have also used assessment data to review and subsequently revise departmental goals. The act of engaging in assessment built faculty confidence to make changes. Most important, faculty began "paying more attention to student experience that will increase their ability to *apply* what they are learning in class—providing opportunities for term projects, field trips, and in-class problem solving" (Banta & Schneider 1988, 79).

In one analysis of longitudinal interviews, Alverno students clearly attributed their ability to gradually take responsibility for their own learning to two components of the assessment-for-learning process: feedback on their performance and the opportunity to self-assess (Mentkowski 1988). A faculty committee quickly moved to review key instruments: Did *each* feedback strategy encourage independence? Did self-assessment opportunities gradually elicit *autonomous* evaluations?

Interview studies of professional competence were designed primarily to hold Alverno faculty's ability definitions to the standards of outstanding professional performance. But these studies also generated many descriptions of complex problem situations and the behaviors that led to their resolution. This library of examples keeps classroom case studies up to date, explicit, and engaging. Here, information from assessment helped refine department goals and assessment criteria while providing concrete examples for creating instruction.

Finally, feedback that can be used to improve performance develops self-confidence—and mutual confidence—in students and faculty. One of the major outcomes of an assessment program that encourages change is that individuals become more independent in their own learning and more able to cooperate effectively. Students and alumnae report that the experience of feedback enables them to undertake active, self-sustained learning during college and afterward. Faculty report that having "live" results and feedback from assessment likewise enables them to take risks. When you know you will be getting feedback on new programs, they say, you are more willing to try things out. No longer is there an all-or-nothing atmosphere or sink-or-swim pressure. Instead, students and faculty are alike buoyed by an attitude of support, encouraged to initiate, and given feedback to reflect on and time to experiment and improve.

Conclusions and Next Questions

Six guidelines help construct a context where program and institutional assessment of student learning outcomes result in improvement. The emphasis is on creating a culture where assessment can become an institutionalized component of a university, college, or department's educational enterprise.

First, *making a long-term commitment to a dynamic plan* with both short- and long-term goals can help an institution respond to expectations for immediate results. This creates space to gradually build processes and systems that meet our more ideal purposes, and time to consider newer approaches to assessment design. Second, *relying on faculty questions for direction* helps identify key issues and specific teaching and learning areas most in need of insight and intervention. Generally, some very simple strategies can tap a wide range of faculty perspectives. Third, *creating interactive processes* sets the stage for gathering the right kinds of information, involving the central players, and holding the kinds of dynamic discussions for interpreting results and debating implications. A culture of assessment is a product of student and faculty investment.

I am persuaded that one of the more challenging tasks in assessment of student learning outcomes is to generate credible assessment information. This leads to the fourth guideline: *Define criteria and comparisons publicly.* What student outcomes are "good"? Are they "good" compared to "what"? The challenge comes in achieving a consensus on the "good" at the level of action and change. Once again, involving faculty and staff directly responsible for using the information to improve student learning is critical.

The kinds of credible comparisons available to answer the "good compared to what" questions are few. That is another part of the challenge. Examples that have some track record include comparison of student learning outcomes to criteria drawn from: (a) institutional mission statements or department goals; (b) developmental pictures of student growth during college; (c) judgments of interdisciplinary colleagues or those from another campus; (d) disciplinary or professional standards as these become available; and/or (e) abilities of outstanding alumni and other professionals. It takes a good deal of effort to identify and then deliver on sets of comparisons that will engage a faculty or staff in interpreting the data and implementing implied changes.

Guidelines 5 and 6 argue for *translating results into relevant, "live" information* and *creating feedback—usable knowledge about performance—that stimulates improvement.* Assisting each audience to build interpretations from information that addresses common concerns, crosses disciplinary boundaries, meets disciplinary criteria, and stimulates improvement is a tall order. But the benefits yield a gradual confidence-building atmosphere where many students, faculty, staff, and administrators are willing to tackle the tough problems a department or institution faces.

Institutional assessment described here reflects an emerging national consensus around several distinctive qualities: these respond to an institution's ideals and purposes as well as the expectations and hopes of its beneficiaries and external audiences. Two of these qualities are: *Assessment is a means, not an end. Assessment is a means not only to establish accountability but also to achieve educational benefits.* Thus assessment-as-improvement is framed and shaped within an institution or department's mission, goals, educational assumptions, and purposes, as well as all the other elements that characterize that particular setting.

As such, assessment-in-context has three other qualities: *Assessment purposes, goals, and methods emerge from the setting. Assessment encourages multiplicity. Assessment encourages coherence.* Thus assessment processes include sets of dynamic methods for examining student learning outcomes that emerge from a particular context. Assessment processes are not relegated to particular office or committee or subsumed under an educational speciality such as measurement, evaluation, or institutional or educational research. Rather, assessment methods emerge from the same, overarching sources as do the teaching and learning processes that shape curriculum and consequent student learning experiences. Does this mean that future assessment methods might be drawn equally from the arts and humanities as from the natural and behavioral sciences? Does this mean that each member of an institution or department will come to see some part of his or her role as assessment?

The complexities of creating assessment-in-context lead to a multiplicity of methods and uses. This diversity creates an apparent paradox with another of its qualities, that assessment encourages coherence. Can assessment processes with many methods and uses simultaneously serve as mechanisms for curricular coherence and connection across departments? Can institution-specific results that benefit students in a single setting also provide effectiveness evidence to higher education's external constituencies?

Solutions to these contradictions may well depend on another of assessment's qualities: *Feedback is the essence of assessment.* Returns may well depend on how results are communicated to each of the many audiences who will directly benefit from the information, and to whom an institution is responsible. Over the long run, will students begin to ask for specific feedback on how to improve after they complete course assessments? Will legislators, state boards, and accrediting agencies begin to ask equally for processes and products, stories and statistics?

Doing assessment often means taking on the paradigms and paradoxes of an emerging field. I believe assessment is new partly because it cannot easily be subsumed under prior categories of inquiry. Assessment seems to require, for example, measurements' long-term validation strategies along with the immediate usefulness of evaluation techniques. It calls for designs to improve a particular setting that can also yield more externally drawn, generalizable insights. Results that meet a faculty's standards and needs may not necessarily speak to all of society's expectations for "improved" undergraduate education. Yet the costs of assessment demand economical data sets that satisfy diverse purposes and users.

Clearly, a consensus around assessment's qualities can benefit from everyone's ongoing experience. Are the difficulties of assessment a reflection of a rough road in a new field? This might mean thinking smarter, but along similar lines. Or are current assessment methods in conflict with our educational values? This might mean reconstructing how we conceptualize assessment, and that task brings us to an examination of our educational assumptions and values.

Summary: Assessment as Values in Action

These six guidelines and the qualities of assessment we come together around say a great deal about our shared educational values. How we design and do assessment reflects—in fact, it embodies and ultimately advances—our educational philosophy. If assessment is to have integrity, the values that underlie it at the classroom, institutional, statewide, and national levels need to be more explicit, so we can question their consistency. If assessment is a means to an end, the values that define that end must be in harmony with the highest values of higher education. Assessment must call us to the best in ourselves, just as we call for the best in each of our students.

Note

*These guidelines have been tested against the insights and experience of college and university faculty, administrators, and assessment specialists from a range of institutions who attended the institutional assessment track of the Alverno College Assessment Workshop in 1987, 1988, 1989, and 1990; and a 24-institution consortium organized on assessment design (Alverno College/FIPSE Assessment Project 1987).

References

Alverno College Faculty. *Liberal Learning at Alverno College.* Milwaukee: Alverno Productions, 1976, revised 1985.

Alverno College Faculty. *Assessment at Alverno College.* Milwaukee: Alverno Productions, 1979, revised 1985.

Alverno College/FIPSE Assessment Project. "Faculty Consortium for Assessment Design." Judeen Schulte, Project Director. 1987.

Alverno College Office of Research and Evaluation/Assessment Committee. *Putting the Validation Process to Work: A Series of Strategies for Establishing the Validity of Faculty-Designed Performance Assessment Instruments.* Milwaukee: Alverno Productions, Forthcoming.

American Association for Higher Education Research Forum. "Improving the Odds for Student Achievement: A Research Agenda." In *Improving the Odds for Student Achievement: A Research Agenda.* Co-chairs Arthur W. Chickering, K. Patricia Cross, Catherine Marienau, and Marcia Mentkowski. Washington, D.C., 1989.

American Council on Education. *Campus Trends, 1990.* Washington, D.C.: Author, 1990.

Astin, Alexander W. *Achieving Educational Excellence: A Critical Assessment of Priorities and Practices in Higher Education.* San Francisco: Jossey-Bass, 1985.

Astin, Alexander W. *Assessment for Excellence: The Philosophy and Practice of Assessment and Evaluation in Higher Education.* New York: Macmillan, 1991.

Banta, Trudy W., ed. "Implementing Outcomes Assessment: Promise and Perils." In *New Directions for Institutional Research,* no. 59, 95–98. San Francisco: Jossey-Bass, 1988.

Banta, Trudy W.; Lambert, E. Warren; Pike, Gary; Schmidhammer, James; and Schneider, Janet. "Estimated Student Score Gain on the ACT COMP Exam: Valid Tool for Institutional Assessment?" *Research in Higher Education: Journal of the Association for Institutional Research* 27, no. 3 (1987): 195–217.

Banta, Trudy W., and Schneider, Janet A. "Using Faculty-Developed Exit Examinations to Evaluate Academic Programs." *Journal of Higher Education* 59, no. 1 (1988): 69–83.

Carey, Karen. *Appalachian College Assessment Program: Assessing General Education; Interview Questions for Seniors.* Lexington: University of Kentucky, College of Education, Educational Policy Studies and Evaluation, 1987.

Chickering, Arthur W., & Associates. *The Modern American College.* San Francisco: Jossey-Bass, 1981.

College Outcomes Evaluation Program, New Jersey Department of Higher Education. *Final Report of the Student Learning Outcomes Subcommittee.* Trenton, N.J.: Author, 1987.

Collins, Linda M., and Horn, John L. *Best Methods for the Analysis of Change?* Washington, D.C.: American Psychological Association Press. Forthcoming.

Council for Adult and Experiential Learning, and McBer and Company. *Student Potential Interview.* Columbia, M.D.: Author, 1987.

Council of Presidents and State Board for Community College Education. *The Validity and Usefulness of Three National Standardized Tests for Measuring the Communication, Computation, and Critical Thinking Skills of Washington State College Sophomores: General Report.* Bellingham: Western Washington University Office of Publications, 1989.

DeBack, Vivien, and Mentkowski, Marcia. "Does the Baccalaureate Make a Difference: Differentiating

Nurse Performance by Education and Experience." *Journal of Nursing Education* 25, no. 7 (1986): 275–85.

El-Khawas, Elaine. "How Are Assessment Results Being Used?" *Assessment Update* 1, no. 4 (Winter 1989): 1–2.

Evarts, H. F. "The Competency Program of the American Management Associations." New York: Institute for Management Competency, American Management Associations, 1982.

Ewell, Peter T. *The Self-Regarding Institution: Information for Excellence.* Boulder, Colo.: National Center for Higher Education Management Systems, 1984.

Ewell, Peter T. "Assessing Educational Outcomes." *New Directions for Institutional Research,* no. 47. San Francisco: Jossey-Bass, 1985.

Ewell, Peter T. "Assessment: Where Are We?" *Change* 19, no. 1 (1987): 23–28.

Ewell, Peter T. "Outcomes, Assessment, and Academic Improvement: In Search of Usable Knowledge." *Higher Education Handbook of Theory and Research* 4, ed. J. C. Smart, 53–108. New York: Agathon, 1988.

Farmer, Donald W. *Enhancing Student Learning: Emphasizing Essential Competencies in Academic Programs.* Wilkes-Barre, P A.: Kings College, 1988.

Fong, Bobby. "Old Wineskins: The ACC External Examiner Project." *Liberal Education* 74, no. 3 (1988): 12–16.

Gardner, Howard. *Frames of Mind: The Theory of Multiple Intelligence.* New York: Basic Books, 1983.

Gray, Peter J., ed. "Achieving Assessment Goals Using Evaluation Techniques." *New Directions for Higher Education,* no. 67. San Francisco: Jossey-Bass, 1989.

Guba, Egon G., and Lincoln, Yvonna S. *Fourth Generation Evaluation.* Newburg Park, Calif.: Sage, 1989.

Heywood, John. *Assessment in Higher Education,* 2d ed. New York: John Wiley & Sons, 1989.

Hutchings, Pat. "Six Stories: Implementing Successful Assessment." Paper presented at the Second National Conference on Assessment in Higher Education, Denver, June 1988.

Hutchings, Pat. "Assessment and the Way We Work." Closing Plenary Address at the Fifth National Conference on Assessment. Washington, D.C.: American Association for Higher Education and the AAHE Assessment Forum, 1990.

Hutchings, Pat, and Marchese, Ted. "Watching Assessment: Questions, Stories, Prospects." *Change* 22, no. 5 (1990): 12–38.

Kennedy, Margaret. "Abilities that Define Computer Studies." Presentation to Alverno Faculty, May 1988 Institute. Milwaukee: Alverno Productions, 1988. Videotape.

Knefelkamp, L. Lee, and Widick, Carole. "The Measure of Intellectual Development." College Park: Center for Applications of Developmental Instruction, University of Maryland, 1982.

Light, Richard; Singer, Judith D.; and Willet, John B. *By Design: Planning Research on Higher Education.* Cambridge, Mass.: Harvard University Press, 1990.

Loacker, Georgine. "Faculty as a Force to Improve Instruction Through Assessment." In *Assessing Students' Learning: New Directions for Teaching and Learning,* no. 34, ed. J. McMillan, 19–32. San Francisco: Jossey-Bass, 1988.

Loacker, Georgine; Cromwell, Lucy, and O'Brien, Kathleen. "Assessment in Higher Education: To Serve the Learner." In *Assessment in Higher Education: Issues and Contexts,* ed. C. Adelman, Washington, D.C.: U.S. Department of Education, 1986, Report No. OR 86–301, 47–62.

McGuire, Michael. "A Content Validity Study of the ACT-COMP for use in the Assessment of Undergraduate Learning." Paper presented at the annual meeting of the American Educational Research Association, New Orleans, April 1988.

Mentkowski, Marcia. "Paths to Integrity: Educating for Personal Growth and Professional Performance." In *Executive Integrity: The Search for High Human Values in Organizational Life,* Suresh Srivasta & Associates, 89–121. San Francisco: Jossey-Bass, 1988.

Mentkowski, Marcia. "Higher Education Assessment: Connecting to Its Conceptual Base." (Cassette Recording No. APA-90-164.) In K. A. Weaver (Chair), *Facing the Challenge of Student, Program, and Institutional Assessment.* Symposium conducted at the Meeting of the American Psychological Association, Boston. Washington, D.C.: American Psychological Association, 1990.

Mentkowski, Marcia, and Banta, Trudy W. "Collaborating in Setting Directions for Assessment Research." *Assessment Update* 1, no. 4 (Winter 1989): 3.

Mentkowski, Marcia, and Chickering, Arthur W. "Linking Educators and Researchers in Setting a Research Agenda for Undergraduate Educators." *The Review of Higher Education* 11, no. 2 (Winter 1987): 137–60.

Mentkowski, Marcia, and Doherty, Austin. *Careering after College: Establishing the Validity of Abilities Learned in College for Later Careering and Professional Performance* (Final Report to the National Institute of Education), Milwaukee: Alverno Productions, 1983. ERIC Document Reproduction Service ED 239 556.

Mentkowski, Marcia, and Doherty, Austin. *Careering after College: Establishing the Validity of Abilities*

Learned in College for Later Careering and Professional Performance (Final Report to the National Institute of Education: Overview and Summary). Milwaukee: Alverno Productions, 1983, revised 1984. ERIC Document Reproduction Service ED 239 556/ED 239 556.

Mentkowski, Marcia, and Doherty, Austin. "Abilities that Last a Lifetime: Outcomes of the Alverno Experience." *AAHE Bulletin* 36, no. 6 (1984): 5–6 and 11–14.

Mentkowski, Marcia, and Loacker, Georgine. "Assessing and Validating the Outcomes of College." In *Assessing Educational Outcomes. New Directions for Institutional Research,* no. 47, ed. P. Ewell, 47–64. San Francisco: Jossey-Bass, 1985.

Mentkowski, Marcia; Moeser, Mary; and Strait, Michael J. *Using the Perry Scheme of Intellectual and Ethical Development as a College Outcomes Measure: A Process and Criteria for Judging Student Performance. Vols. 1 and 2.* Milwaukee: Alverno Productions, 1983.

Mentkowski, Marcia; O'Brien, Kathleen; McEachern, William; and Fowler, Deborah. *Developing a Professional Competence Model for Management Education* (Final Report to the National Institute of Education: Research Report No. 10). Milwaukee: Alverno Productions, 1982. ERIC Document Reproduction Service ED 239 566.

Mentkowski, Marcia, and Strait, Michael J. *A Longitudinal Study of Student Change in Cognitive Development, Learning Styles, and Generic Abilities in an Outcome-centered Liberal Arts Curriculum* (Final Report to the National Institute of Education: Research Report No. 6). Milwaukee: Alverno Productions, 1983. ERIC Document Reproduction Service ED 239 562.

Messick, Samuel. "The Once and Future Issues of Validity: Assessing the Meaning and Consequence of Measurement." In *Test Validity,* ed. Howard Wainer and Henry I. Braun, 33–48. Hillside, N.J.: Erlbaum, 1988.

Office of the Vice President for Academic Affairs. *Initiatives for Excellence and Accountability: A Five Year Plan.* Harrisonburg, V .A.: James Madison University, 1985.

Patton, Michael Quinn. *Utilization-Focused Evaluation,* rev. ed. Newbury Park, Calif.: Sage, 1986.

Perry, William, Jr. *Forms of Intellectual and Ethical Development in the College Years: A Scheme.* New York: Holt, Rinehart and Winston, 1970.

Presidental Task Force on Student Learning and Development. *A Proposal for Program Assessment at Kean College of New Jersey* (Final Report). Union: Kean College of New Jersey, 1986.

Reisetter, Judy, and Sandoval, Pamela. "Flexible Procedures for Efficiently Maximizing Participation in a Longitudinal Study." Paper presented at the annual meeting of the Midwest Educational Research Association, Milwaukee: Alverno Productions, October 1987.

Resnick, Daniel, and Scheider, Carol G. *Assessment and Learning.* Washington, D.C.: Association of American Colleges. Forthcoming.

Rogers, Glen. "Validating College Outcomes with Institutionally Developed Instruments: Issues in Maximizing Contextual Validity." Paper presented at the annual meeting of the American Educational Research Association, New Orleans. Milwaukee: Alverno Productions, 1988.

Rogers, Julia S.; Bullard, Jerri H.; Ernest, Patricia S.; Bolland, Kathleen A.; and McClean, James E. "Evaluating General Education Outcomes Instruments: Relating Test Goals to Institutional Goals." Paper presented at the annual meeting of the American Educational Research Association, New Orleans, April 1988.

Schall, Celestine; Guinn, Katherine; Qualich, Ruth; Kramp, Mary K.; Schmitz, JoAnn; and Stewart, Kyle. *Competence and Careers: A Study Relating Competence; Acquired in College to Career Options for the Liberal Arts Graduate.* Milwaukee: Alverno Productions, 1984.

Schneider, Carol. Telephone conversation with author 22 February 1990.

Schulte, Judeen; Benson, Sterling O.; Scarboro, Allen; and Turcotte, Judith. *Keeping It Local: Report from a Twelve-Campus Faculty Consortium on General Education Assessment.* Presentation at the Fourth National Conference on Assessment in Higher Education sponsored by the American Association for Higher Education, Atlanta, June 1989.

Sternberg, Robert J. *Beyond IQ.* Cambridge: Cambridge University Press, 1985.

Stone, Howard L. and Meyer, Thomas C. *Developing an Ability-Based Assessment Program in the Continuum of Medical Education.* Madison: University of Wisconsin Medical School, 1989.

Student Potential Assessed at Rhode Island College. *Assessment Update* 1, no. 2 (1989): 10.

Terenzini, Patrick T. "Assessment with Open Eyes: Pitfalls in Studying Student Outcomes." *Journal of Higher Education* 60, no. 6 (1989): 643–64.

Tittle, Carol K. "Validity: Whose Construction Is It in the Teaching and Learning Context?" *Educational Measurement: Issues and Practice* 8, no. 1 (1989): 5–13, 34.

Weiss, Carol H. "The Stakeholder Approach to Evaluation: Origins and Promise." In *Stakeholder-Based Evaluation: New Directions for Program Evaluation* 17, ed. A. S. Bryk, 13–14. San Francisco: Jossey-Bass, 1983.

Willett, John B. "Questions and Answers in the Measurement of Change." In *Review of Research in Educations* 15, ed. E. Rothkopf, 345–422. Washington, D.C.: American Educational Research Association, 1988.

Winter, David G.; McClelland, David C.; and Stewart, Abigail J. A *New Case for the Liberal Arts: Assessing Institutional Goals and Student Development*. San Francisco: Jossey-Bass, 1981.

CHAPTER 36

QUALITATIVE PROGRAM ASSESSMENT: FROM TESTS TO PORTFOLIOS

PATRICK L. COURTS AND KATHLEEN H. MCINERNEY

For several years now, [with support from the Fund for the Improvement of Postsecondary Education], Fredonia has been assessing a new general education program, and they've chosen to go the local route in all cases, with faculty-designed exams to cover a variety of cross-cutting general-education outcomes. I think that's a right idea. . . . In [the final] report they set forth what they learned—and equally interesting, what they didn't learn.

They didn't, for instance, ever learn the "Truth" about their students. In fact, much of their work at the outset entailed discussion—and, I dare say, heated debate—about the soundness of this and that instrument, pilot testing, whether the results could be compared with this way or that, what was valid, what not . . . with the result, as I say, that no truth was learned. What the faculty *did* learn was that . . . students were taking and passing individual courses alright, but they weren't seeing connections; they couldn't put the pieces together.

The solution? No doubt there were (and should be) several. . . . [Fredonia faculty] are now working to develop a portfolio approach to assessment that will give them more in-depth information about each student's ability to put the pieces together, but also—and here's the beauty of the thing—help the student *develop* that ability. (Hutchings 1990, 4)

Indeed, the use of portfolios throws light on the very process of measurement or evaluation. For portfolio assessment occupies an interesting in-between area between the clean, artificial world of carefully controlled assessment ("Take out your pencils. Don't turn over your books till I say 'go'.") and the swampy real world of offices and living rooms where people actually write things for a purpose and where we as actual readers look at texts and cannot agree for the life of us (sometimes for the tenure of us) about what they mean and how good they are. Or to put it differently, use of portfolios highlights the tension between *validity* and *reliability*. (Elbow 1991, xii)

Stories from the Front: The Fredonia Experience

As a teacher of English, I became involved with Fredonia's assessment project primarily because I believed then, and continue to believe, that program assessment and outcomes-based educational systems have potential for tremendous damage unless they are created, implemented, and controlled by *teachers* who understand what actually goes on in classrooms and who also understand how genuinely complex it is to quantify human cognition, cognitive growth, or "learning" in any but the most

Source: "Qualitative Program Assessment: From Tests to Portfolios," by Patrick L. Courts and Kathleen H. McInerney, reprinted from *Assessment In Higher Education: Politics, Pedagogy, and Portfolios*, 1993, Greenwood Publishing Group.

primitive terms. Everyone involved must resist the temptation to return to simplistic "competency-based" models of education that emphasize discrete, fragmented, and often irrelevant skills.

But regardless of my opinions about the issue, I feared that the State of New York was moving toward a demand for programmatic assessment at the college level and outcomes-based individual assessment in the public school system. Given that fact, I agreed to be a part of a group composed almost entirely of faculty, who would create a series of instruments designed to assess our General College Program. And lately, as I find the public media filled with calls for a national assessment, I am all the more committed to trying to short-circuit the foolishness that is sometimes associated with assessment. And I reiterate that, from my point of view, assessment of any kind that is not clearly and primarily directed at improving what we do in classrooms is a waste of money and time.

So let me begin at my beginning. I do not believe a detailed description of Fredonia's General College Program (hereafter GCP) is either necessary or particularly interesting for the general reader. Let it suffice for me to say that the program is not "competency-" or "skills-based" in any of the traditional senses of those terms. Students have a broad degree of choice among courses across disciplines that have been specially designed or redesigned to emphasize print literacy, metacognitive or reflexive thinking, problem solving, scientific reasoning, a sense of history, and an understanding of foreign cultures and the degrees to which ethnocentrism can inhibit an understanding of other cultures. The major point here is that we were not trying to find out if our students could write business letters, answer multiple-choice questions about a reading passage, fill in a chart of elements and their atomic weights, find India on a blank map, explain the importance of the year 1492, or itemize the basic tenets of Buddhism. Rather, we wanted to find out how much they had grown or improved as writers and readers, how much their mathematical and scientific thinking had matured, and how their ideas about human history and cultural diversity had been affected between their first and third years of college.

A committee was created of twelve faculty members representing a broad variety of disciplines, and we set about the task of boldly going where none of us had ever gone before; I use this Star Trek allusion purposely because for many of us, myself included, the whole endeavor smacked of science fiction involving uncharted space voyages into an investigation of dimensions we were not at all sure we could investigate.

Like typically good scholars, we began by reading everything we could find that had been written about assessment in the years immediately prior to our project. I would like to say that this reading solved our problems, but for the most part it did not provide us with a test or series of tests we might simply implement. Nor had we really expected it to. Instead, the research confirmed what most of us had expected in the first place: Standardized tests manufactured and sold by Educational Testing Service (ETS) or American College Testing (ACT) were of almost no use for several reasons, not the least of which being that they do not really test much of anything other than how well one does on a standardized test. The best assessment instruments are those created by the individuals intimately involved with students, the institution and the programs that are to be assessed (Aper, Cuver, Hinkle 1990, 476).

Consequently, it became immediately and painfully clear that we would have to create our own instruments, test our tests, so to speak, to find out if they provided the information we were searching for, teach ourselves to evaluate student performance on the tests, find a control group at another college, give the tests, score them, evaluate our findings, and make whatever follow-up recommendations we might wish. It was not so much a problem of realizing that we were "in over our heads" that frightened us, as much as it was the realization that this was going to be a long swim up river against a formidable current.

The Process

The full committee began by considering brief presentations from selected members of the group intended to highlight some of the key issues and potential problems we might encounter as we attempted to create assessment instruments for given areas. Immediately following this series of relatively wide-ranging discussions, we split into temporary subgroups in order to create itemized lists of specific skills, abilities, or processes that should be tested in a given area. The subgroup working with reading, writing, and reflexive thinking, for example, had not decided at this point that reflexive thinking would even be a part of the assessment. The importance of these initial discussions cannot be overemphasized: it was only through these initial discussions, as the group articulated relatively obvious items—things like "the ability to create a central focus in an essay," and "the ability to identify an author's central focus in an article," that we began to articulate more complex items (the ability to infer, or to identify underlying assumptions). And this investigation eventually led the group to items involving metacomprehension and metacognition (meaning the ability to recognize relationships between one's own experience and the experience represented in work produced by another author and consciousness of one's own learning style and ways of approaching learning something or learning how to do something).

The point here is that these subgroups were intensely involved in a discovery process that would lead to an articulation of the kinds of things the assessment would eventually assess. These lists were then reviewed and refined by the entire committee. This review was a particularly important step because it would eventually lead to a fully articulated set of "grids" on which all the skills or abilities to be assessed would be listed and, eventually, matched with the test question or exercise that would allow us to assess student performance. Although this grid would evolve as we more fully articulated the various assessment instruments, this beginning was of central importance as it helped us to engage in the process of creating the tests themselves.

Having established the grid and having agreed that we would create instruments that actively engaged students in "doing" whatever kind of thinking, reasoning, or languaging that we wanted to evaluate, we split into three subgroups: one focusing on reading, writing, and reflexive thinking; one focusing on mathematical and scientific reasoning; and one on historicism and ethnocentrism. Each subgroup then (1) created instruments that might assess growth in these areas (as specified on the grid); (2) identified which specific outcomes listed under the General Education Outcomesm a given instrument might assess; and (3) submitted the "test" to the whole committee for discussion, refinement, and, occasionally, ridicule.

I say *ridicule* with good humor because anyone identified with such a process must become aware that the assessors (a much privileged class) might have tremendous difficulty succeeding on many of the instruments that a given assessment group is using. It was important for all concerned to see me and my sociologist friend laugh in embarrassment when faced with blank maps and told to fill in the names of countries (an instrument later rejected). At another meeting, of course, we had the fun of watching some of our prestigious colleagues fail at some of the problem-solving tasks that had been suggested for use.

As we worked together to examine the tests each subgroup was creating, we also continued to refer to the original grid, making sure that our tests were directly related to our defined purpose. Through this interactive process of examining potential test instruments, referring to the initial grid, trying the tests ourselves, and continual discussion, we eventually arrived at a set of instruments we felt we might use in the assessment. I emphasize these early steps because, without them, without giving them the time and energy they demanded, the project would never have been completed. Throughout the next two years, but especially as we worked together to refine and revise various test instruments, the grid operated as our stable center against which we might consider the value of a given test: (1) matters of efficiency (Does one kind of test allow us to assess more items on the grid than another?); (2) matters of relevance to the task (Does a given instrument assess something that is on the grid?); and (3) matters focusing on the quality of the instrument (Does it address the complexity of the item on the grid, or simply appear to do so?).

An absolutely key point, here is this: anyone engaging in programmatic assessment must be thoroughly familiar with the program that is being assessed and its stated objectives (Aper, Cuver, Hinkle 1990, 476). It was not unusual in our early discussions (and even some later ones) when we were designing the instruments, for one or more individuals to make strong arguments for inclusion of an instrument that would test geographical knowledge, foreign language competency, and so forth. The only problem was that these were not objectives of the program we were assessing. It is all too easy to get caught in the trap of trying to assess everything that some idealized program *should* do or that some group *should* know, regardless of whether or not the program being assessed happens to address all the everythings. It is important to remember that it is rather easy to identify what all educated people *should be able to do,* but we may want to ask whether or not we can do all the things we think that others should do.

At any rate, everyone on the committee tried to do the tests, critiqued them, offered suggestions for change and revision, and sometimes simply decided that a given test was either irrelevant or useless. Once the tests were approved by the larger committee, each group set about articulating the criteria by which degrees of success or failure would be measured for each instrument. Creating clearly articulated criteria and hierarchies of criteria ("outcomes," if you will) that might allow us to clearly differentiate one level of performance from another was much more difficult than creating the tests themselves. And this process, along with training ourselves to score the tests, took the most time and energy, aside from actually scoring the final tests. The first part of the process took place over the period of about one year. When it was over, we had nine tests and we were finally ready to "test the tests" by administering them to small groups of students so that we could find out if the tests gave us the information we wanted and so that we could begin to train ourselves to score the tests.

Once we began to examine the first set of student responses to the tests, we found that things were not going as well as we had hoped. Directions on one test had to be carefully refined so that students could not simply define historical events in terms of the last two years of their lives. Problem-solving tests had to be changed because some of them were so difficult that no one could do them at all: if a test is so difficult that no one can do it, one has no basis for examining change or growth; one simply finds out that no one can do it. On the reading test, some of the follow-up questions showed themselves to be either redundant or unnecessary, and the essay we had chosen for them to read proved to be a little too long for the time period we had allotted. In all cases, as we began to try to score the tests, we found ourselves refining scoring criteria in an attempt to make this subjective process of evaluation reliable and valid.

In a sense we began again. We revised the tests, discussed revisions, gave them again, scored them again, and only then felt that we might finally go ahead with the test itself I will not even go into the problems we had finding another institution with a profile similar to our own that would agree to give the tests, but by the end of two years, we had found an institution to cooperate, we had given the tests, and spent the final year scoring them, evaluating our results, and writing final reports and recommendations.

The following discussion provides a brief description of the tests themselves so that they can be seen in a little better context. But it is important to note that this is simply intended to provide a perspective. If we learned nothing else (and I believe we learned quite a bit) through our involvement with assessment, it is this: qualitative assessment of the kind we are discussing here and the kind that is involved in a portfolio system demands that those doing the assessing create their own instruments, criteria, and scoring system. While a reader may borrow freely from what follows, the first step in assessment is to be sure that you are assessing your program and not someone else's or some fictional program that you have created in your own minds.

All of the following test descriptions are paraphrased and/or quoted from *The GCP and Student Learning: A Report to the Campus,* written by Minda Rae Amiran with The General College Program Assessment Committee, August 1989, and referred to as the GCP Report in the following discussion. (For a complementary discussion of the Fredonia assessment and related assessment projects at Western College at Miami University of Ohio, see Amiran, Schilling, and Schilling).

The Instruments

Writing Test. To test our students' writing ability, we asked entering first-year students, entering transfer students, and upperclass students who had not been transfer students to describe and analyze what they had found to be a major problem with the educational system in their high schools. We chose the subject because we wanted to be sure to present the writers with a topic about which all would have adequate background experience and knowledge to allow them to write concretely and, hopefully, with some engagement. The essays were first scored holistically, and then on the basis of separate criteria like the ability to create a clear central point, offer supporting evidence, analyze reasons, and write Standard English.

Reading Test. Because we desired to avoid the artificiality inherent in most comprehension tests and the multiple-choice questions that characterize such tests, we chose to give the students a twelve-page article from an introductory anthology in sociology. We chose the particular article because it focused on a community's response to two groups of young people, one of which was comprised of "good" kids, and the other of which was composed of rowdier kids. Our primary concern was that the students would have enough background knowledge to bring to the text to allow them to transact with it constructively and with some interest. The students were then asked to provide several sentences of response to a series of questions based on the reading. These questions asked them to identify the author's main point, his supporting evidence, the implications of his essay, his underlying assumptions, and the organizing principle used by the author. Further, in hopes of seeing to what extent students could place the reading in their own context and experience, measuring its sense or nonsense against their own experiences, we also asked them to explain why they agreed or disagreed with the author's main point, illustrating their opinion through a relevant personal experience. Students had ninety minutes in which to complete the test.

Reflexive Thinking. Before describing this particular test, a brief digression may help here. Initially, we had intended to call this test Metacognitive Thinking, but early in the design stages we knew that we could not begin to examine the complexities involved in metacognition through a single test. At the same time, we believe that metacognition is central and essential for the most proficient degrees of learning to occur. Since *metacognition is* a relatively new concept in education, easily oversimplified, some defining should help here. By *metacognition,* we do not simply mean the ability to structure one's own approaches to learning a concept or solving a problem (though this could be a part of the broader definition). Metacognition involves more than the self-knowledge that "I always approach a long writing assignment by making an outline (or by free writing, or whatever)." Metacognition suggests a *meta*-level of consciousness of one's own thought processes. As such, it involves an almost simultaneous, conscious degree of self-awareness. "This is how I approach or think about a situation (problem, issue, concept)"; "this is how I might best approach this particular concept in order to more fully understand it"; "this is how I am thinking about this issue, and it is or is not effective"; "these are the other possible approaches I might take instead."

At its most basic level, a lack of metacognition (or *metacomprehension*) characterizes the learner who has "studied" the chapter for the test, believes that s/he "knows" the material, but is then completely baffled when faced with the test itself. Not only did this learner not know that s/he did not know, she does not understand how to go about knowing (Weaver 1988, 24).

Of course, at its most advanced levels, some kind of full consciousness of self and self's interaction with others, one might reasonably argue that no one is ever genuinely metacognitive. We certainly find it difficult to imagine this degree of metacognition. One is tempted to say that "it takes one to know one," adding that only a self-deceptive egocentric would claim to be fully metacognitive. Anything that involves thinking about one's own thinking presents us with the most serious complexities (and, some might argue, impossibilities). And yet, as difficult as it is to describe, some learners pretty clearly enjoy a higher degree of self-conscious awareness of their own learning processes than others. And it also appears clear to us that the most powerful learners are those who are best able to monitor their own learning processes: These are the learners who "know when they know" and are able to structure their own learning so that they can productively move on from that self-knowledge toward more and fuller knowing. Furthermore, these learners "know when they do not know," which puts them in the position of using a different approach to the problem or seeking help.

While our reflexive thinking test only scratches the surface of assessing students' metacognitive abilities in this more complex sense, it does, at least, approach the issue. But given the obvious importance of developing higher degrees of metacognition, we believe that portfolios most directly suggest ways both to develop and to assess this essential ability.

Likewise, our sense of the importance of metacognition is directly related to the importance we place on actively engaging students in the writing process, across the curriculum, in order that they might consistently attempt to use language to articulate and examine what it is they think: As a linguistic process, writing uniquely allows learners to be surprised by what they know, discover what they do not know, and use what they know to know more (Murray 1985, 7). More directly, writing is first and foremost a self-reflective process that is both regressive and progressive in the same moment. As writers use writing to discover what it is they are trying to say, they also discover more that needs to be said. In the moment of writing, the writer moves between the roles of writer, producing the text, and reader, reading what has been written:

> In the moment of author(iz)ing, the moment of writing, the writer is reading (using language to make sense of) that which is in there (inside the writer) in order to externalize it through the surface structures of language. . . . In the moment of externalizing the meaning, . . . the writer engages in the recursive process of reading what he is writing and writing what he is reading. The two processes are inextricably bound together. (Courts 1991, 110)

In the Fredonia assessment, hoping to find the extent to which our students are conscious of their own learning processes, we asked them to write a brief description of something they learned outside of school and then to answer follow-up questions examining what they had written. These follow-up questions asked them to identify the major factors influencing the learning event they described, to identify any pattern that characterized the learning experience, and to contrast that with any patterns they observed in school learning situations, to draw any conclusions they might about learning in general, and to comment on the ways schools structure the learning experience. They had one hour for the entire task.

Quantitative Problem Solving. We created two similar tests of four questions each

> to assess student problem solving. One question on each test could be solved through very simple algebra, once the equations had been properly set up. Another was an open-ended estimation problem, under realistic conditions of uncertainty. Problems three and four were identical on the two tests, though their order was reversed: the first of the pair was supplied with prompts, the second was not; though the setting of each problem was different, the algebraic solutions were very similar (Amiran 1989, 13–14).

In addition to being asked to solve the problem, students were asked to state their assumptions and explain their reasoning process. For example, one question was as follows: John has a pail with 40 washers in it and finds the total weight to be 175 ounces. Sue weighs the same pail with 20 washers in it and finds the total to be 95 ounces. (a) how much does each washer weigh? (b) how much does the pail weigh? (c) no matter how trivial they may seem, what assumptions did you make in solving the problem? (Throughout the assessment, it was questions like this last one, c, that were particularly important to us because we were trying to assess students' *thinking processes* rather than their knowledge of unrelated bits of information.)

Scientific Reasoning. Students had to do two tasks for this exam: First, they had "to design an experiment to show the relationship between hours of exposure to sunlight and rate of growth in spider plants," and second, they had "to critique the report of a study on the correlation between amount of brown rice consumed and incidence of gout among older men" (Amiran 1989, 17).

Socioethical Understanding. There were three parts to this section of the exam:

1. "'History' asks students to list ten of the most important events in human record, and choosing one of those events, to name three other events that would not have occurred or would have been very different if the chosen even had not taken place."
2. "'Exchange Student' has students answer some uncomplimentary questions about the United States asked by an otherwise friendly Western European exchange student."
3. "'Malbavia' posits a third world kingdom undergoing modernization as a result of newly discovered mineral wealth, and asks the students, as part of a UN team, to infer societal effects and make recommendations, some of which have to do with prevailing practices of hospitality and human sacrifice" (Amiran 1989, 19–20).

What Happened Next: Results

For the sake of brevity, I will only report some of the most interesting generalizations that are supported by the assessment project. Though none of us would agree that what the students wrote in the composition test was particularly well-written, it was in this area that we saw the most obvious and greatest growth. Students clearly had improved as writers. But the results on the reading test were disturbing for several reasons: First, instead of finding improvement in their reading abilities, we found little significant growth in many important areas related to reading. Second, while this might not be reason for alarm if the first-year students had shown strong reading abilities, such was not the case. Third, while most of the students accurately identified the main point of the essay they tread, and many did well in identifying the author's supporting evidence, few did well in identifying the implications of the essay, in articulating the author's assumptions, or in seeing relationships between the article, their own lives, and the society in which they live. In short, after achieving success at a literal level, these readers were unable to do much more.

Unfortunately, this inability to move beyond the literal, to generalize and abstract, characterized our findings on all the other tests. Finally, the results on the reading test caused us to question the results on the writing test: if students had improved significantly as writers, one might reasonably expect similar improvement in their reading abilities. If such results did not occur, then one had to question what it was we had tested on the writing test. This confusion further increased our interest in implementing a portfolio system of some sort.

As for the other tests, let me simply present some findings quoted from the GCP Report: "In absolute terms, few students proved very adept at reflexive thinking" (Amiran 1989, 12). Most of the students "lack the problem-solving or reasoning skills that would help them think the [algebraic] problem through in an orderly way [often complaining] that they don't like math or never have been good at it." (Amiran 1979, 16). Likewise, they were very weak in recognizing the assumptions they had to make in order to solve the problems they had been given.

On the scientific reasoning, students' performance "leaves much to be desired" (Amiran 1989, 18). Their comments suggested a student belief that unless one had a course in which a specific body of information had been studied, one could not conceivably begin to solve the problem. But since the problems were not based on specific knowledge of a given area of science, this indicated to us that the students knew little about scientific reasoning, empirical scientific methodology, complexity of identifying cause-effect relationships without a clearly established control, or researcher bias.

In the area of historical understanding and presentism, students were weak both in terms of establishing a chronology of events and in terms of seeing causal relationships between or among events. And results on socioethical reasoning left us with increasing cause for concern.

The problem is not that there is no growth, but the growth is generally minimal and the level of performance is seldom particularly gratifying.

Obviously, none of us was particularly pleased with what we found. On the other hand, we were not generally too surprised. By trying to measure growth in students' thinking and languaging processes, we knew that we were trying to assess ground that is seldom addressed in schools or colleges. Most testing focuses on assessing students' mastery of discrete bits of information and/or isolated fragmented skills. And we had consciously and purposefully avoided those kinds of tests. We know that our students "know something"; we wanted to find out what they could do with what they know and what kinds of growth they might have experienced as a result of their participation in the General College Program.

If the results are dispiriting, however, they also offer rays of light insofar as they suggest several things: (1) while students did not show a high degree of metacognition, they did indicate a considerable degree of awareness of how schools were failing them and offered plenty of suggestions about what needs to be changed; and (2) the results also indicated that, if we care about our students being something more than repositories of information, if we want them to be thinkers and doers, then we need to emphasize thinking and doing across the curriculum. And we need to empower teachers at the same time.

We at Fredonia know, for example, that our faculty have been participating in highly structured workshops in writing across the curriculum over the past seven years, and this is the only area in which we found significant growth. Of course, it is not particularly revolutionary to suggest that if we want something to change, we need to help faculty make the change instead of simply carping and casting blame. But all too often one finds little support for faculty development workshops of any kind at any level. In our case, however, the dean of General Studies has organized additional workshops for faculty to help them address multiculturalism in their own classrooms and disciplines. And small cadres of mathematicians and science faculty have begun to gather to address some of the more disturbing findings. On its own initiative, the Math Department conducted workshops for the faculty members who teach the introductory mathematics courses that most of our students take to fulfill their general program requirements. These workshops focused on examining ways to help students become more proficient as problem solvers. Likewise, small committees of faculty in the sciences, social sciences, and humanities worked to develop classroom activities that would help students become more aware of their own biases and assumptions. Further, as a result of the findings, many of us involved with the assessment and other interested faculty have worked individually to change the ways in which we teach our courses in order to try to address some of the things the assessment reveals. In terms of curriculum, the English Department is in the process of implementing a three-course core in the major that will emphasize multicultural literatures and engage students in the conscious exploration of ethnocentrism as it affects the critical reader's understanding of a work. Faculty in all disciplines are trying to help students become more conscious of the approaches that characterize the reasoning processes that form the basis of a given discipline.

Have many people simple disregarded the study? Yes, of course. These are real human beings, and they act just as you might expect. In short, there has been no miracle here, but there has been some progress. Have the devastating budget cuts SUNY is presently undergoing severely interfered with the changes that the assessment suggests need to be made? Absolutely. And will the past and continuing budget cuts cause administrators to compromise the quality of the General College Program rather than improve it? Probably. It is, then, fair to say that the Fredonia assessment has not yet had the results many of us hoped it might have. In fairness, however, to all involved, small changes are occurring and a core of interested faculty and administrators remain committed to using assessment to improve programs and classroom instruction.

On the other hand, it is not unusual to find administrators who are more interested in the assessment itself than in the actions that need to be taken as a result of assessment findings. And it is even more common to find that there is more money available for assessment than there is to support the faculty and curricular development that should grow out of assessment projects. Obviously, this presents a seriously pessimistic view of the entire endeavor. Why engage in all this work if it is to come to naught because education in the United States is being devastated by a weak economy? Instead of a trickle-down effect, we seem simply to be trickled on. Why fight for local autonomy in assessment and put forth the time and energy involved in creating qualitative assessment instruments when pressures for a system of standardized national assessment surround us? Why continue to work within a superimposed system that often appears to be characterized by teacher and student bashing orchestrated by secretaries of education? Why bother at all when the destructive rhetoric that has surrounded American education over the past decade is equalled only by the continuing decline of economic support for education in this country?

Our first answer is to return to what we said earlier. If for no other reason, teachers need to be involved in order to defend themselves and their students against inappropriate assessment instruments. Second, we are professionals and must refuse to give in to ignorance or political manipulation. But beyond that, honest, well-planned assessment, carefully evaluated by those directly responsible for instruction and curriculum does offer us the possibility to do a better job. I do not think any of us needs assessment projects to tell us that schools are not teaching students as well as we might like. Thus we do not need assessment to tell us that there is a problem. Rather, we need assessment projects that might help us identify specific elements of teaching and learning that need to be changed.

The Fredonia assessment offers some ideas for the kinds of instruments faculty might create to shape their own assessment projects and suggests some very clear directions we might take to improve the quality of our students learning. Furthermore, as we intend to explain in the next few pages, portfolio assessment, carefully created and implemented, can be one of the most constructive instruments in qualitative assessment. More directly, in the face of the negatives implied above, it is essential that faculties take charge of assessment and create their own instruments *before* something is imposed on them.

Additionally, we know now that faculty development workshops can have an observable effect on instruction. We know that students can and will improve as writers if writing across the curriculum is actually implemented instead of simply being talked about. We know that our system of lecturing and testing appears to reinforce the learning of literal facts but apparently does little to help students become more powerful thinkers and doers. We know that science courses stressing large amounts of discrete facts appear to have little effect on a student's understanding of the nature of science, and that mathematics courses that stress formulaic approaches to solving problems do little to improve students' understanding of mathematics as a discipline or to help them become more adept at solving problems. Also, even with respect to the specific contents of a given course or discipline, it appears clear that students retain very few of those facts that seemed to control the courses while they were taking them. Finally, a good assessment project may also reveal, as it did at Fredonia, that we are not nearly as successful in accomplishing some of our goals as we might wish to pretend. Anyone involved with assessment needs to be prepared to hear some news s/he may not wish to hear.

Our own major interest in the project was and is how it will affect our teaching and our students' learning. And it has. But perhaps the most significant change that has occurred so far has been a direct result of the ironic contradiction that occurs when one considers the difference between students' performance on the writing exam versus the reading exam.

Perhaps because my own major interests lie in the areas of metacognition, reading, and writing, it should be little surprise that I disliked our writing exam from the very beginning, even though I chaired the subcommittee responsible for creating it. Asking our students to engage in a significant act of writing in a fifty-minute period, and then judging that as though it represents real writing borders on a kind of lunacy. We knew from the start that the fifty-minute time limitation, the fact that students did not have time to prewrite, write, receive feedback, and revise all combined to put the students in the middle of an artificial writing activity. But even with all these problems, our results indicated that students improved in this kind of writing, suggesting that our Writing-Across-the-Curriculum efforts had some positive effect. Even so, one cannot create such an assessment tool and not also be haunted by a statement like the following. "'I just don't get it,' said Ruby, a senior at a major state university in the Lower 48. 'In the writing classes, they tell you how important it is to do all this prewriting and revision stuff. Then they give you an exit test where you can't use any of it'" (Wauters 1991, 57).

As has already been mentioned, at the very beginning of the creation of the writing test, we had agreed that portfolios containing student writing over a period of years offered one of the best ways to go about evaluating their writing, but now we became more committed than ever to the idea because we saw that a carefully planned portfolio requirement might not only provide data useful in program assessment (Ewell 1991, 46). More importantly to many of us, such a project might help students become better writers, readers, and thinkers. Consequently, some of us had long ago decided to try to implement a collegewide portfolio requirement consisting of selected pieces of a student's writing over a period of three to four years: these collections of student work might best serve as the instrument for assessing their growth as writers because they would contain writing that students had an opportunity to shape and revise.

Only after the fact, however, did it occur to us that portfolios like this might be shaped in a variety of ways. Students might add critiques of their writing, looking back at what they produced over several years in order to establish a reflective, metacognitive consciousness of their thinking processes and/or the changes in these processes they might constructively undertake. If students had to maintain such portfolios in any given discipline, wherein those portfolios might be shaped in ways most appropriate to the learning demanded in the discipline, the portfolios might serve as instruments for both individual and programmatic assessment. Equally important, the portfolio idea lends itself to helping students examine their own reading, writing, and thinking processes; it gives them an opportunity to examine their own intellectual growth over a period of years; and it gives them an opportunity to see the areas in literacy and thinking in which they need further work. In short, portfolios lend themselves powerfully to outcomes-based assessment.

Having said all that, let me add that designing a portfolio requirement at any level is very complex and needs to be begun with great care. If I have learned nothing else as a teacher and as one interested in assessment and outcomes-based education it is this: never try to do everything at once; keep it simple at first; and make very sure you know what you are trying to achieve before you implement any approach. It is absolutely crucial to be " 'clear on a more-or-less campuswide basis about why assessment is being undertaken, who is to be assessed, and what educational outcomes are to be assessed. An inadequate conceptual foundation for an assessment program will produce confusion, anxiety, and more heat than light' " (Apers, et al. quoting Terenzini 1990, 476).

Portfolios and Program Assessment

From the outset, let us be clear about the following. *First,* this discussion of portfolios is not intended to suggest that we were dissatisfied with the instruments used in the GCP assessment—quite the contrary. We are not suggesting that portfolios are the only useful instruments for assessment of student learning. We will, however, make the case that portfolios might form the center of an any ongoing system of either programmatic or individual assessment. *Second,* we are not in favor of gatekeeping devices; improve teaching and the gates will be unnecessary. *Third,* although many portfolio assessment systems presently focus primarily on assessing student improvement as writers, with the portfolios most often tied directly to first-year, required composition courses and, occasionally, some writing-intensive courses, courses in disciplines other than English—we believe their usefulness extends well beyond assessing a single skill or course. *Fourth,* we are much impressed and encouraged by a considerably different approach to portfolio assessment as exemplified by the work done by faculty at the Evergreen State College, Olympia, Washington: This brave, and apparently successful, group wanted to measure cognitive development in their students over the four-year college experience. Using portfolio collections of student self-evaluations, they used a system of ratings based on Perry's developmental scale to score the writing selections (Thompson 1991; Perry 1970).

Our excitement about projects like the one conducted by the Evergreen group is not intended to minimize the importance of the more focused efforts directed at assessing growth in "Freshman Composition, ENG 101." We simply feel that the potential for portfolios goes well beyond a focus on writing, per se: Perhaps the greatest usefulness of portfolios will occur when their contents are directly related to student performance in academic programs and majors across the curriculum and over several years. Experiments like your own (yet to come) and those of institutions like Fredonia and Evergreen should eventually help us all to understand better what, exactly, it is that we and our students are doing.

What follows, then, is a step-by-step series of suggestions that we encourage you to consider as you begin to articulate your own portfolio requirement. Unfortunately, the step-by-step journey that is outlined next bears more similarity to Dorothy's journey through Oz than it does to a clearly drawn line on a map: Lions and tigers and assessors, oh my!

Following the Yellow Brick Road

Getting Started

Discuss the general concept with sympathetic members in your own discipline or department, and do not try to *convert* your colleagues.

Begin small, using your own classes and those of one or two cooperative colleagues to experiment with portfolios. This step should, necessarily, involve you and some colleagues in a discussion of the kinds of writing required in given courses and additional writing activities that might be appropriate in given courses. This will help significantly when you and others begin to shape the portfolios more specifically for programmatic assessment, because it will give you some sense of the kinds of things students might include in a portfolio and the kinds of student work that might most directly contribute to program assessment.

Try to engage a standing committee in your department, a curriculum committee perhaps, to help articulate the specific goals of the major (or program) you wish to assess. In many cases, this will introduce the first major obstacle in the process. It is not at all unusual to find out that while "everyone knows the objectives of the program, and everyone agrees on the skills or proficiencies that should characterize each successful undergraduate chemistry (or sociology, or philosophy) major," no one has articulated the specifics. In many academic majors, the course contents, directions of the major, and objectives have simply grown, somewhat like Topsy. Members of the discipline at large, some anomalous group or professional association, "agree" that x, y, and z are essential to a given major. Consequently, these courses are required of all undergraduates majoring in the discipline. But then, Professor Smith, a much-published and powerful personality convinces the department that his pet courses are at least as important as x, y, and z, so these become part of the major requirements. And of course, the department rebels know that their courses, intended to deconstruct the major itself and everything the establishment believes is necessary, must also be included. Pretty soon, in desperation, the requirements are discontinued and students are encouraged to take thirty credit hours from among a broad array of wonderful courses offered by the department.

Frankly, we are not terribly dismayed by such a system. Clearly some disciplines demand core requirements and a system of sequencing, but given the arguments that often surround such curricular decisions, we wonder just how clear any of this will ever be. The point, here, is this: until the program or major is defined in terms of observable, albeit qualitative, outcomes that are central to most of the courses in the program, there can be no programmatic assessment. Why? Because in fact, there is no program. An accidental or incidental amalgamation of courses all called *psychology courses* can hardly be called a "program." Nor can it be assessed.

Problems enter rather quickly and obviously at this point. In fact, it looks like a good reason to return to standardized multiple-choice exams and focus on discrete bits of information that are emphasized in isolated courses. Even though this is a fraudulent kind of assessment, at least it's possible to do it. But as most of us know, the discrete facts and unrelated pieces of information are the things we all forgot shortly after we graduated. So assessing this kind of learning is rather silly.

Articulating Objectives

All that we've said above pretty clearly suggests that members of the department or program will necessarily have to reflect on their own courses, looking beyond specific information, to identify the kinds of thinking they are trying to teach their students: what are the thought processes, abilities, and skills that underlie the discipline and most of the courses within it? Fortunately, as problematic as this stage is, it is not impossible and may be one of the most beneficial aspects of being involved in assessment. Students already know that relationships between and among courses are not particularly clear, or at least they do not always see the interrelationships. Instructors need to learn this so that they can begin to help make the interrelationships clearer, when they exist, and create them when it is appropriate.

Of course, you may find some of your colleagues ready to explain, with care and patience, that "you can't assess critical thinking or other complex kinds of reasoning because the students don't know enough yet. First you must teach them the basic facts of the discipline, and only later (in graduate school, we guess) will they know enough to do any complex thinking or reasoning." And it should come as no surprise that this kind of statement is reflected in what students apparently believe when they say that they cannot do something because they never took a course in it. But the fact is that most disciplines genuinely share more in common than is often realized and articulated. Most disciplines and academic programs emphasize (or *believe* they emphasize) some intermixture of the following: (1) critical/analytical thinking; (2) clear reasoning (logical, mathematical, scientific, analogic, metaphoric); (3) creative thinking; and (4) the ability to speak, listen, read, and write with "reasonable" proficiency in the discipline.

More specifically, most disciplines expect students to be able to read, comprehend, and comment articulately on literature in the field. In science and mathematics, students are expected to be able to "do" science and math (but so also are they expected to "do" history, sociology, philosophy . . . if they major in one of those disciplines).

The potential difficulties involved in this step of the process are precisely why each group needs to devise its own assessment program. By identifying the objectives and desired outcomes central to a given major or program, the faculty will necessarily gain a greater sense of their own mission. Likewise, once these have been identified, instructors can begin to examine their own courses to see to what extent they try to help students achieve such objectives or be able to produce specific outcomes.

Consequently, professional self-examination must follow the identification of objectives and outcomes that one wishes to assess. After all, if the instructors teaching the courses are not actively and consciously teaching students to achieve the central objectives of the discipline, why would anyone bother to assess whether or not they are learning them? (Unless, of course, it is to find out that they can already "do" whatever it is we want them to be able to "do," which would attest to the irrelevancy of the discipline, we suppose.) But a reminder of the Fredonia experience is in order—or perhaps just a reminder to use common sense: we already know that we are not doing an adequate job of teaching students to be literate, articulate participants in many of the fields they study. Therefore we first need to more clearly identify what it is we want them to learn as a result of our teaching. And then . . .

Instructors need to identify for themselves and for their colleagues, which activities/requirements in their courses contribute to helping students achieve which objectives, and what exactly will comprise the portfolios. While this step sometimes suggests the trammelling of academic freedom, it need not and should not do so. It is absolutely essential that everyone involved keep in mind the fact that the issue is programmatic assessment; it is not an attempt to point accusatory fingers at particular courses or faculty members. In most cases, faculty will find that key courses already require assignments that will fit naturally and usefully into programmatic assessment. And the portfolio entries need not always be directly tied to course requirements. The following questions might assist in such an examination:

1. How do lab reports (or analytical/critical essays) provide evidence that the fledgling scientist (or philosopher and so on) is doing or is learning to do science (or philosophy and so on): what are the specifics that will indicate a successful report versus a weak one; what activities in the course contribute to teaching the students how to do successful reports; what student work derives from the course that might be included in a portfolio?
2. At the time they declare their desire to major in a given field, should students be asked to write "entry papers" for inclusion in the portfolios? If you wish to find out about the nature of student attitudes toward a discipline, their reasons for choosing it (as opposed to our assumptions about why they have chosen it), what they want to learn—such entry papers are essential. Aside from providing valuable information about the students we are teaching in our courses, these entry papers allow teachers to more fully understand and deal with mismatches between student expectations and program objectives. Of course, it should be obvious that the entry papers must be carefully described in terms of how they are to be used within the portfolio and as part of the program assessment. If entry papers are required, will exit papers also be required? What will they help you find out?
3. Will it be helpful for the fledgling mathematicians or scientists to write descriptions of the processes they go through in solving problems or doing experiments (as opposed to simply including a lab report or mathematical solution)? Likewise, might it be helpful to have the sociology or philosophy students write personal narratives of how they approached understanding a major concept or how they approached a research project? Note, here, that these kinds of written assignments can easily be required *in addition* to the requirements and expectations within a given course. Instructors might simply tell students that during the course of the semester they must complete at least one of these kinds

of narratives for inclusion in their portfolios; a failure to do so will affect the grade in the course. Again, any decision to include such writing in the portfolios must be driven by a prior decision about how the piece will be assessed and how it contributes to assessing the objectives of the program.

4. Should instructors or students decide which work is included in the portfolios (or should they work together to make such decisions)?
5. How much should be included in the portfolio? While one might think that "more is better," it is well to remember that someone is going to have to assess these portfolios, and that almost certainly means more than simply sitting down and reading quickly through the entries to form some generalized judgment (though holistic scoring will often be a significant part of the overall assessment of portfolios). Since most students take courses in a major over a period of about five to six semesters (using the first year or two to complete general college requirements), would it make sense to require that each portfolio contain six entries: an entry paper, papers written in at least four different courses in the major, and an exit paper?
6. Should the portfolio entries be carefully prescribed and described so that each student's portfolio will essentially contain the same amount and kinds of work that another student's portfolio contains? For programmatic assessment, it seems clear to us that this is probably necessary in order for valid, reliable judgements of portfolios to result. For example, though possibilities are endless, students might be expected to include in their portfolios an entry paper, a description of how they approached solving a problem (mastering a complex concept, developing a skill . . .); a research paper (or critical/analytical paper); an out-of-class essay exam (or, perhaps—dare we say it—a creative paper?); a paper explaining the most significant or complex aspect of the discipline they have been studying; and a self-reflective exit paper. Obviously, the contents of the portfolio will be essentially prescribed by the specific objectives/performances/outcomes that the group has decided to assess.
7. Should portfolio entries be limited to written work, or might it be appropriate in some disciplines to include photographs or videotapes of student's productions or of students actually doing something in a lab or teaching situation?

Scoring Portfolios

Now we come to the sticky question of scoring portfolios: that is, having created a system of qualitative, subjective assessment, how does one go about "objectifying" it in any sense of the term *objective?* Needless to say, it is best to start by being at home with relativism and remaining highly conscious of the purpose of the assessment. In programmatic assessment, you begin by (1) clarifying what it is you want to assess; (2) carefully constructing your instruments (in this case the portfolios and their prescribed contents); (3) defining what you consider to accurately represent weak, adequate, and strong performances for each of the pieces required in the portfolio; and (4) articulating highly specified criteria for scoring the quality of performance. Remember the importance of the grid we created for the Fredonia assessment project.

Once the system for scoring has been articulated and agreed upon, it is time to teach yourselves how to score the portfolio entries, a process that will take considerable time, commitment, and the ability to compromise. Quite simply, no matter how well you have planned things up to this point, the entire project will fall apart unless this part of the process is carefully and openly addressed, so it is worth examining what is involved rather carefully.

First, remember that you are not going to score all the portfolios of all the students. Ask your local statistician to tell you what percentage of your majors you must score in order to have a statistically reliable sample. Second, do not underestimate the amount of time and energy the scoring will take. Scorers who are forced to do too much at a given sitting or over an extended period of time will score differently when they are tired (or fed up) than when they began the process. Third, create a system of subgroups. Staying with the example we have already created in which the portfolios contain six entries, it would make sense to create five to six subgroups to score each of the separate entries. Given the description we provided above, one subgroup of scorers might be responsible for comparing the entry and exit papers (unless, of course, it was more appropriate to establish criteria for scoring these two pieces separately). Each of the other subgroups would then be responsible for scoring one specific kind of entry.

Once the groups are created, the training begins. Over and over each scorer will have to be reminded that the scoring system is directly related to the criteria that have been established. It is all too easy to believe that one is scoring a piece of writing to examine the individual's expertise in problem solving when, in fact, the scorer is focusing on punctuation or syntax. Before the scoring is even begun, it is wise for each group to reexamine the criteria and discuss them. Following this discussion, each member of the group begins to score an identical set of selected portfolio entries. Next, the scores are charted, and each individual scorer *explains* his/her score.

This is "sticky wicket" time, indeed, or at least it can be. We italicized the word *explains* because the scorers must avoid defensiveness, argument, sarcasm, personal attacks, and homicide. The key element in this process is coming to a mutual understanding of what is *really* intended by the criteria that were previously established. What seemed perfectly clear before the process began suddenly becomes muddy, and it is essential that the mud be eliminated.

Consider what might occur when a group of scorers used the following criteria to score a portfolio entry focusing on problem solving in which the writer was to solve some specified problem and then produce a brief narrative explaining the steps s/he employed in the process of solving it:

A. The writer clearly articulates each step of the problem-solving process in which s/he engaged.

B. The writer articulates most of the important steps in which s/he engaged, but does not present a full explanation of the solution.

C. The writer is unable to articulately explain the problem-solving process in which s/he engaged.

After scoring an entry, using these criteria, one scorer gives the entry a grade of *A*, another gives it a grade of *B*, and a third gives it a grade of C. Believe us it happens! And at the beginning of the process it occurs more often than you might expect. But why?

The explanation is relatively simple, and very important. One scorer explains the *A* as follows: "This entry is exceptionally well-written; in fact the student writes better than most of the students I teach. The explanation is interesting, clear, and the student clearly arrived at the correct answer to the problem." The scorer who assigned the *B* says, "What you say is true, but the fact is that, even though this is well-written, the writer does not really explain the reasoning process in the step-by-step fashion demanded by the criterion. S/he states many of the steps, but not all of them." And finally the scorer who assigned a *C* says, "In a sense I agree with both of you, but the criteria clearly say that the student is to *explain* the process. But this writer simply *states* a few important steps and leaves the reader to figure it out." And we have not included the fourth scorer who gave the paper a score of *A* because "the solution suggests genuine insight into the problem-solving process, considerably more than I generally see in our students, and there is no way you can give this a low score."

What is important to note here is not which of the individuals is right or wrong—remember we began with a commitment to relativism. In a sense, each of them may be right. But in order to score portfolios, in order to assess anything, the scorers must come to full and conscious agreement on what they *really* mean by those criteria they were applying. The trick is to score the entries in direct relationship to an agreed upon definition of the criteria. And this means, at the beginning of this training process, that most of the criteria that had been originally articulated will undergo laborious reexamination. Indeed, it is not unusual, at this stage, for the individuals to find it necessary to define words that they thought were clearly agreed upon prior to the act of scoring: "What is the difference between 'stating' and 'explaining'? Since it is the writer's prerogative to decide what process s/he engaged in, how can you say that s/he did not include steps in which s/he engaged? Are you not explaining the steps in which *you* engaged?" "To what extent does it matter if the solution is right or wrong if the explanation of the steps is well done?"

In some cases, the group may decide to rewrite criteria to make them clearer or more explicit and eliminate as much confusion as possible. For example, referring to the sample criteria presented above, the group would almost certainly want to rewrite criterion C because the split infinitive "to articulately explain" creates a nonparallel structure (and different meaning) from what is probably intended by the use of the word "explain" in criteria A and B. In other cases, certain criteria may simply have to be eliminated because the scorers cannot mutually agree on their application.

While this may seem like an almost impossible morass, it is not. Even in scoring the reflective thinking exam in the Fredonia assessment, the exam that caused us the most difficulty in scoring, we eventually managed to arrive at a sense of mutual agreement about what we "meant" by the criteria. It is important to keep in mind that this kind of assessment is difficult (and even threatening) precisely because it relies on language and subjective, qualitative decisions about the exact meaning of specific words. One can hardly engage in this kind of assessment without coming to grips with the confusion and sometimes deceit that hides beneath statistical results on standardized, "objective" exams. Quite simply, if it can be this difficult for a small group of highly intelligent people to agree on the meaning of a given term as they apply it to a piece of writing, how much more difficult must it be for the students who must decipher the hidden biases and idiosyncratic meanings of the people who create "objective" reading comprehension tests, or worse yet, tests that rely on analogies? And how much harder to believe that a multiple-choice test that gives you a "critical-thinking" score is addressing relevant criteria or criteria relevant to your college's program.

It should be clear from the above that the Scoring System itself must be clearly articulated and mutually understood. For example, if the group decided to use letter grades (*A, B, C, D* . . .), the letters must eventually be correlated with numbers (*A* = 5 points . . .). Using this system, scorers must remember that the score of *A* is related to the stated criteria and *not* to the *A* that might be given for work in a course in which the criteria might very well be different. Of course, why not simply use numbers instead of letters? And you may find that this works for you. In the Fredonia Assessment, different subgroups used different systems; and by now it should be obvious that the essential element is having all the scorers of a given test understand and be comfortable with whatever system you employ.

Additionally, you must decide how many scoring differentiations you wish to make: one might argue that a scoring system ranging from 1 to 15, clearly related to fifteen carefully differentiated degrees of performance would be better than one ranging from 1 to 6. The finer the differentiations, the more statistically revealing the scores will be. Unfortunately, the finer the distinctions, the more difficult they are for the scorers to make.

And it is important to consider whether or not a *holistic* system of scoring will be helpful, in addition to the itemized scores tied to specific criteria. In the Fredonia assessment, for example, each scorer began by giving each protocol on the writing test a holistic score. In this case, each scorer was directed to read the protocol twice and immediately give it a score ranging from *A* to *E* (including pluses and minuses) based on an overall impression of the general success of the piece of writing. We later found such a system quite useful in judging the relative merit of the itemized criteria and settling disputes between scorers.

While itemized criteria can clearly be important for certain kinds of assessment, we do not mean to imply that they are always necessary. At Miami of Ohio, a university conducting a variety of interesting assessment experiments, scorers examined student writing portfolios in a global manner. As they read through the students' portfolios, the participating faculty were asked

> not to assess *how well* we had met the goals, but rather *where* they saw evidence of an assignment that required skills or abilities that the program faculty viewed as important; for example, assignments that gave evidence of emphasis on "critical thinking," or reflected our "quantitative reasoning across the curriculum" effort. In describing "what" we were doing, rather than "how well" we were doing, we fostered discussion that took

> on a less defensive tone. This permitted a level of sharing that had not occurred in any of our previous discussions of assessment. (Amiran, Schilling, and Schilling forthcoming, 12)

One might clearly apply holistic scoring to find out whether or not the academic program is asking students to write "much" or "enough," whether or not students are encouraged or assisted in any kind of revision process, and whether or not students appear to improve as writer/thinkers over a given period of time. Or scorers might assess portfolios descriptively: What kinds of thinking are evidenced in the portfolio contents? As always, the central problem of *how* any of this is done depends entirely on *what* it is you are trying to find out.

But we must still address some other issues involved in scoring: How many scorers need to score a given protocol (in the Fredonia project we agreed that two scorers would score each protocol)? And what happens when scores for a given protocol seriously conflict: that is, when one scorer scores an item as an *A* but another gives it a *C*-. Obviously, one solution would be to simply average the scores, but such a system is likely to result in most scores ending up in some sort of midrange. Several approaches to the problem suggest themselves: First, the two scorers might discuss their scores trying to determine whether or not each is genuinely committed to a score and can explain its relationship to the stated criteria. Second, in the event that this does not lead to a relatively immediate change by one of the scorers, a third reader can be used to settle the dispute: whichever of the original scores is closest to that of the third reader is averaged with that of the third reader for the official score.

Clearly, it is important to remember that we agreed to accept a relativistic world: qualitative assessment is not "objectively" perfect, but what is, really? In the Fredonia experience, we found the process of training ourselves to score to be the most gruelling part of the entire process. But once it was finished, we were ready to move beyond our self-training and begin the real scoring.

Additional Considerations

So far so good? Maybe, but not quite. Here are some considerations that have yet to be confronted. For example, what about control groups?

It may appear, at first, that program assessment demands the establishment of some sort of control group against which to measure growth and improvement in a given area. Otherwise, all we will have at the end of this long, laborious process is a group of scores unrelated to a group of randomly selected portfolios. To be able to say that a given portfolio is clearly "better" than another hardly provides the information necessary for the evaluation of a program. In the Fredonia assessment, our design included the use of a control group from another college whose student body was similar to our own (based on entrance requirements) but whose general college program was quite different. And while such a design may significantly increase the kinds of information assessments might reveal, it also creates some significant complexities.

At Fredonia we felt the need for a control group because we were not simply trying to find out if students improved in certain areas. Without a control group, we could not have found out if the General College Program, per se, was affecting student learning (as opposed to the growth one might find just because students happen to be in college). Depending on what one is trying to assess, however, control groups may be unnecessary, as Amiran, Schilling, and Schilling point out in their comparative discussion of assessment projects at Fredonia and Western College (at Miami University of Ohio):

> Fredonia began with a focus on locally constructed assessment for an internal audience but found it needed a comparative study with an external institution. Western College began with an external focus on nationally nonmed means of assessment, moved through its collaboration with Fredonia and on to a purely local, internally oriented descriptive approach. It is not a matter of finding what is right for each institution, but of understanding that different foci are right for the same institution at different stages in its assessment process. If Western had not begun with normed instruments it would not have appreciated its need for descriptive measures. If Fredonia had not undertaken its comparative study, it would not have been properly cautious in interpreting its local results. Comparative and local, external and internal foci, outcomes and activities, judgements by others and oneself—these alternate as figure and ground in the assessment "picture," and it may be important to retain one's

> ability to keep reversing them. It is also important to affirm the value of the complexity that baffles us in assessing liberal education: we cannot draw Leviathan with a hook (forthcoming, 18).

Control Groups?

Toward the end of this chapter, we discuss methods of using the portfolios without control groups, but we believe that control groups may, in fact, be necessary to achieve certain ends: that is, especially if the assessment intends to compare one program against another, a demonstrably different one, and probably when the assessment is primarily directed at curriculum revision. To establish such a control group, you must find an institution whose student profile is similar to your own but whose program is significantly different. Second, those who teach in the program must agree to implement portfolio requirements exactly as you have defined them, which is no small task in and of itself. Third, the scorers at your institution must agree to score the portfolios that have been completed by the students at the control institution. To say that the problems of working out all the details involved here are significant is a gross understatement.

A little backtracking will be helpful here. Begin by reconsidering the purpose of the assessment project. As we have stated several times, our purpose for assessment focuses on improving teaching and learning. At present, anyone who has conducted the project as we have thus far described it would be in position of deciding that students are generally performing well, adequately, or inadequately as determined by a variety of measures used for scoring the various kinds of entries within the portfolios. But if your needs demand a control group, must you necessarily go outside your own institution?

Not necessarily. Indeed, a somewhat obvious solution immediately presents itself. For this kind of assessment, you must identify one group of students as the initial group to be assessed and another group of your own students to be the control group. And this system suggests several possible alternatives depending on the make up of your institution. In some larger institutions, for example, a given major or program may offer several distinct "tracks" for students. English Education majors might take a required sequence of courses that significantly differ from those taken by other English majors. In psychology, students heading toward clinical work in the field might take a sequence of courses significantly different from those more interested in research.

More often than not, however, this is unlikely to be the case; students in a given major or program are most likely to take courses that are either distinctly similar or have distinctly similar requirements. In these cases, we suggest that a group of students entering a program or major in a given semester be identified to comprise the control group and that a group of students entering the program or major at least two years later be identified as the experimental group whose progress will be measured against the first group. Still some very significant issues need to be resolved.

At this point, having established a control group and a second group with which to contrast scores, not much has really been accomplished. Consider this hypothetical situation. Group 1 is identified as all those entering the program in September 1994; Group 2 is composed of students entering the program in September 1996. By 1998, the assessors should be in the position of making some powerful judgements about the program, right? Wrong.

By simply establishing two different groups, one must ask what exactly is being compared? In this case, assuming that the program has remained essentially the same over the four-year period, almost no conclusions can be drawn about the program. If the program remains substantially the same, an improvement in student scores would simply indicate that the students had somehow, on their own, done better than their predecessors. If they perform poorly, one might assume that this group of students was simply not as capable as previous groups. In either case, little could be said about the program.

And this returns us to a beginning point. The whole reason for the endeavor, in the first place, is to improve instruction. The idea is to make changes in instruction and to assess whether or not the changes contribute to greater student growth and learning. Consequently, once the portfolio assessment has begun, the faculty should immediately begin the process of redesigning all elements of the program or major or courses that they feel might improve the quality of student learning. By beginning such redesigning immediately, faculty would have a two-year period to prepare to implement changes; thus the second groups of students would be exposed to a program that was significantly different in its attempt to help students improve at the kinds of skills, processes, thinking that the program intends to develop and that the portfolios are designed to measure.

In the short term, what we have described may suggest a kind of madness. The key, here, is to remember the purpose of assessment. First and foremost, it should be aimed at improving instruction rather than simply providing state agencies with "proof" that the program is an effective one through some series of short-term, deceitful assessment instruments. While the system we propose clearly involves long-term involvement and takes a considerable amount of time to complete, these qualities must be recognized as inherent in assessment projects that assess anything of importance. In fact, the system we have just described would be an ongoing one with new groups being identified every two years, or at least as often as the ongoing assessment leads to changes in instruction. We may find out, of course, that nothing changes over time and that all the instructional changes that have been implemented result in no improvements in students' performances. Obviously, this would be disturbing, but important, information. At the very least, it might suggest that the institution needed to look outside itself for help in improving the program or major. More likely, however, the ongoing system of assessment would allow those teaching the program to monitor their continued commitment to good teaching and document needs for changes in what is actually going on in courses or changes resulting from changing student populations.

No Control Groups

While control groups may be essential for certain kinds of assessment, we strongly agree with Minda Rae Amiran who so significantly assisted us in this section of the book. We paraphrase her at length, here, because her comments were so helpful to us. She points out that a portfolio being used to assess a major in a discipline like chemistry would not demand the creation of control groups: it would be clear that "any chemistry the students have learned they have learned through that department (or possibly in related internships or summer jobs). In a department with a defined curriculum, there is no reason why actual portfolios can't be compared to faculty-developed pictures of what a student should know or be able to do as a result of the program." Clearly, she goes on, if students evidence a lack of knowledge or ability deemed essential by the faculty, the department can begin to change its curriculum and/or system of instruction. And while Amiran reiterates that "curricular changes" might be best approached through the use of a control group, she suggests some ways of avoiding the "laborious steps" we itemized in the above section on establishing control groups:

> One could have students collect everything they wrote to answer questions such as [the following]: "How much and what kinds of writing are our students actually doing?" "What kinds of critical thinking are our students engaging in?" "What kinds of problems (texts, theories, authors) can our students address?" One could have students compile selective portfolios with reflections to assess the successes of the program in stimulating the making of connections and metacognition. One could specify the ingredients of portfolios to judge the general level of senior-year seminar papers or projects as compared to sophomore-year research papers. (personal letter, 1992)

Student Commitment

To paraphrase Dorothy, it really does not look much like Kansas, does it? One final qualification must yet be made, however. What good does any of this do if the students do not take it seriously, if the work in the portfolio is viewed by the students as some sort of busy work imposed on them by the institution, as an activity that has nothing to do with their own learning and growth? What if they "borrow" papers from other students in order to fulfill the portfolio requirement? And if they have had the opportunity to work with peer editors to get help from writing tutors, whose work is it that is being evaluated?

Let us take these concerns one at a time. First, we believe that if the portfolios are not directly tied to the students' growth and learning, then there is no reason to expect the students to take them seriously. Portfolio assessment that is divorced from the students' growth invites carelessness and lack of commitment from the students (at best) and plagiarism (at worst). But it has been our experience to find that when students see the contents of a portfolio to be directly tied to their own learning and growth, when the portfolios function as an important part of their discussions with their teachers and advisors, students take them very seriously. And it is for this reason that the next chapter on the role of portfolios in the learning and assessment of the individual student is particularly important to us.

Let us not forget that last question: whose paper is it, really, when the writer has received considerable editorial assistance? The manuscript for this book, for example, has gone through several drafts. We have received feedback from readers and editorial assistance from friends, spouses, and colleagues. Indeed, we quote extensively from Minda Rae Amrian's critical commentary in one of our drafts. Praeger Publishing Company assigned a professional editor to assist in the production of this book. And quite frankly, we appreciated all that help. Nevertheless, we still think that this is our book. Does it not make more sense for us to try to teach our students to be a part of our professional world instead of locking them outside of it with demands that most of us would find ludicrous? What good is assessment of any kind if it does not contribute to students' learning?

Bibliography

Amiran, Minda Rae, Karen Schilling, and Karl Schilling. "Interpreting Liberal Education Assessment Results: Interrelated Stories from Two Schools." In *Are We Making a Difference?* Edited by Trudy Banta. Forthcoming.

Amiran, Minda Rae, with The General College Program Assessment Committee. *The GCP and Student Learning: A Report to the Campus.* Fredonia, N.Y.: State University College of New York at Fredonia, 1989.

Aper, Jeffery P., Steven M. Cuver, and Dennis E. Hinkle. "Coming to Terms with Accountability Versus Improvement Debate in Assessment." *Higher Education* 20 (1990): 471–83.

Courts, Patrick L. *Literacy and Empowerment: The Meaning Makers.* Westport, Conn.: Bergin and Garvey, 1991.

Elbow, Peter, and Pat Belanoff. "State University of New York at Stony Brook Portfolio-Based Evaluation Program." In *Portfolios,* edited by Belanoff and Dickson. 17–36.

Ewell, Peter T. "Assessment and TQM: In Search of Convergence." *New Directions for Institutional Research* 71 (Fall 1991): 39–52.

_____. "Back to the Future." *Change* (November/ December 1991): 12–17.

Hutchings, Pat. "Assessment and the Way We Work." Closing Plenary address, Fifth AAHE Conference on Assessment. June 30, 1990. Reprinted by the American Association for Higher Education and its Assessment Forum.

Murray, Donald M. *A Writer Teaches Writing.* 2nd ed. Boston: Houghton Mifflin, 1985.

Perry, William. *Forms of Intellectual and Ethical Development in the College Years.* New York: Holt, Rinehart and Winston, 1970.

Thompson, Kirk. "Learning at Evergreen: As Assessment of Cognitive Development." Spring 1991. Available in monograph from The Washington Center for Undergraduate Education, The Evergreen State College, Olympia, Washington.

Wauters, Joan K. "Evaluation for Empowerment: A Portfolio Proposal for Alaska." In *Portfolios,* edited by Belanoff and Dickson. 57–68.

Weaver, Constance. *Reading Process and Practice: From Sociolinguistics to Whole Language.* Portsmouth, N.H.: Heinemann, 1988.

CHAPTER 37

PROGRAM REVIEW AND EDUCATIONAL QUALITY IN THE MAJOR

ASSOCIATION OF AMERICAN COLLEGES

Changing the Dynamics of Program Review

Periodic program review is a common practice in most colleges and universities. For some academic programs, particularly preprofessional programs, such review is part of an accreditation process conducted by an external agency. For other programs, including most undergraduate degree programs in the liberal arts and sciences, review is initiated by campus administrators as a means of monitoring program quality and identifying problems that may require administrative action.

Often, program review in reality is a "program audit." The main focus of the review is on data: number of students, number of faculty members, student/faculty ratios, qualifications of faculty members, class size, library holdings, scores of seniors on standardized tests such as the Graduate Record Examination, percentage of students who are admitted to graduate school, percentage of students who are employed within a fixed period after graduation, percentage of classes taught by graduate students or by adjunct faculty members, percentages of women and minorities on the faculty and among the students.

Important though these data may be, they are not sufficient to capture adequately the educational quality of a program. To assess educational quality, one must examine curricular and pedagogical issues—issues that are tied more to intentions, instructional practices, faculty/student interactions, and learning outcomes than to data. From this perspective, *the goal of a program review should be to increase the self-consciousness of faculty members and administrators about their educational practices so they can improve the quality of teaching and learning.*

This handbook is intended for those who wish to initiate a program review focused on educational quality. Although a "program audit" type of review could be combined with the type of review advocated here, supplementary questions eliciting those data either can be constructed easily by anyone who wishes to include them or adapted from one of many available prototypes. Therefore, "audit" questions will not be included here.

The quality of education review, for which guidelines are provided here, is consistent with the national movement toward outcomes assessment. In the end, one cannot truly determine the quality of a program without understanding its effects on students. Thus, a program review that focuses on quality of education depends on a clear specification of desired educational outcomes and carefully gathered evidence that these outcomes are being achieved. A variety of possible approaches to gathering such evidence are included in this handbook.

Source: "Program Review and Educational Quality in the Major: A Faculty Handbook. Liberal Learning and the Arts and Science Major," by Association of American Colleges, reprinted from *ERIC Document 342 295.*

The guidelines for program review provided here address "majors"—programs of concentrated study that in most institutions constitute the intellectual center for students' undergraduate learning. The guidelines reflect the findings of a national review of arts and sciences majors that the Association of American Colleges conducted from 1988 to 1991. The recommendations from that review are contained in the first two volumes of AAC's report on Liberal Learning and the Arts and Sciences Major. The program review guidelines presented here as Volume Three draw especially on Volume One of that report, *The Challenge of Connecting Learning,* which provides organizing principles for liberal learning in any arts and sciences field.

The guidelines presented here also reflect the conclusions of an earlier AAC project, Using External Examiners to Assess Student Learning of the Major. Participants in that project recommended that program reviews begin to incorporate findings from assessment of student learning. They also recommended that program review, which typically invites scrutiny from faculty members external to the program (and often to the institution) ask such external examiners to review direct examples of students' learning across the major as part of their overall review of program quality. Suggestions for linking assessment to periodic program review are presented in this handbook.

The second chapter of this handbook presents a philosophical framework for program review. It is followed in Chapter Three by suggestions for specific procedures that may be utilized in organizing a program review process. Chapter Four presents questions to be asked in a program review process that is concerned primarily with the educational quality of learning in the major.

Key Elements of Strong Programs

AAC's 1991 report, *The Challenge of Connecting Learning,* advocates viewing undergraduate degree programs—programs of concentrated study or academic majors—from a strongly learner-oriented perspective, paying special attention to the needs and expectations of students. This is not to say that students should determine the content of programs—that must be a faculty responsibility—but rather that faculty members, as they design, implement, and review programs, should be sensitive to the students served by the program. This sensitivity cannot be left to one or two faculty members who have a particular interest in undergraduate students; it must be shared by all who teach in the program. The following thirteen characteristics of strong programs, articulated in *The Challenge of Connecting Learning,* provide the underlying philosophy that guides AAC's approach to program review.

1. Clear and Explicit Goals

> *It is not enough for deliberations about the major to be exercises at the blackboard diagramming curricula that "look right" but have little effect either on course practices or on student experience of the major. Faculty members' deliberations about majors as educational programs need to become part of a continuing collegial dialogue about the relationship between faculty intentions and student progress.*
>
> The Challenge of Connecting Learning, page 21

Strong programs articulate clear goals for students' learning, which are made explicit and understandable to the students. These goals should include clear expectations about the purposes and character of introductory, middle-level, and culminating work; the nature of and rationale for program requirements; and the rationale for curricular structures as they relate to these goals.

Faculty members in each program must accept corporate responsibility for the program's goals and curriculum. The faculty as a body periodically should review the program's goals, the extent to which they are realized, and their relation to the goals and structures of general education. Ideally, the faculty will consider thoughtfully, and explain carefully to students, how the articulated goals for learning (and curricular structure) in the program relate to the overarching goals for students' learning in the institution as a whole, including general education.

2. A Focus on Inquiry and Analysis

> *The problem with the major is not that it has failed to deliver certain kinds of knowledge. The problem is that it often delivers too much knowledge with too little attention to how that knowledge is being created, what methods and modes of inquiry are employed in its creations, what pre-*

suppositions inform it, and what entailments flow from its particular ways of knowing. . . .

Students have the right to expect their major to provide a set of learning experiences that will teach them how to use their field's approaches in pursuing significant questions. . . . They have the right to expect learning experiences that will encourage them to shape, reflect on, add to, and use the knowledge they are gaining.

The Challenge of Connecting Learning, 6–7

Strong programs help students develop the capacity to use the methods and perspectives of the discipline(s) in framing questions and in developing increasingly sophisticated analyses of those questions. Recognizing that these capacities develop over time, these programs create curricular structures that provide students with opportunities to revisit issues that they have met in prior courses and to bring to bear on those issues increasingly powerful analytic techniques.

3. Developing Critical Perspective

[Students] have the right to expect opportunities for translating and negotiating among different approaches and for exploring the strengths and limitations of the lenses through which they have learned to view issues and problems.

The Challenge of Connecting Learning, 7

Students join the community of the major briefly; ultimately, they must disengage and leave. An essential step in this process of disengagement is the achievement of some measure of critical distance. Part of the articulated purpose of the major, therefore, is to prepare a student to be sufficiently confident in the discourse of a community to subject the major to sophisticated questions and to compare and connect its proposals with the proposals of other communities.

The Challenge of Connecting Learning, 12

Strong programs help students understand the limitations of a particular field's methods or perspectives by providing opportunities for students to consider the values, biases, and internal conflicts of the field and to examine the ways in which the field may be inadequate (at least on its own) for dealing with some kinds of questions. In some fields, this may require that faculty members engage in more self-conscious analysis of their discipline than they are accustomed to doing.

Strong programs help students learn about the variety of views and perspectives represented within each field. Engaging students in open discussion of questions and conflicts about the presuppositions, methods, and findings of the field represents a powerful teaching technique that fosters intellectual development.

4. Connecting with Students' Needs

Faculty members often think of the major as a study of a subject valuable in itself, or as a preparation for advanced, postbaccalaureate studies (with the desire that the best students themselves should enter the professoriat). Students often speak of attaining usable capacities, of the "real world" value of collegiate education. The fact is that most students do not go to graduate school and a career in the learned professions, nor do they use the content of their major directly in their careers.

The Challenge of Connecting Learning, 3

Programs must acknowledge and respect the perceptions and expectations of students who choose to pursue a particular course of study. This implies that the faculty must be aware of the characteristics of the student body. What are the students' backgrounds, both academic and experiential? What are their aspirations? What do they believe about the value of a college education and about the role of the program in that education? What questions and concerns about the field are of greatest personal interest to them?

Students change; society changes; career opportunities change. Strong programs are dynamic, not static. Faculty members in strong programs actively and regularly seek to learn about their students and respond appropriately to their changing needs. Sometimes the program, or parts of it, must be reformed. Sometimes, extra efforts must be directed to helping students understand more fully the goals of the program as conceived by the faculty. Sometimes, faculty members must articulate the program more carefully to counteract—beforehand—misplaced student assumptions. Always, keen faculty awareness of student perspectives and willingness to rethink their own convictions in the light of new understandings about students are necessary prerequisites to a healthy program.

5. Connecting with Scholarly Inquiry

[There is] a marked disparity between the ways academics do their research and the institutional structures that organize curricula and teaching. . . . What are needed are incentives and structures to ensure that the intellectual excitement of discovery, interaction, and critical discourse that many faculty members experience also is available to students.

The Challenge of Connecting Learning, 15

Strong programs reflect the current state of scholarly understanding. As advances are made in the field, they should impact on the curriculum. As new ideas emerge for organizing and communicating knowledge in the discipline, they should influence the structure and pedagogy of the program. As new issues and controversies arise that relate to the content of the program, they should be brought into the classroom.

Faculty members must be active in the field if they are to design and teach a relevant and vital curriculum. They must be well qualified initially, and they must maintain an active regimen of scholarship. Some will be researchers or creative artists. Others may focus on interpretive, expository, or teaching and learning issues. All, however, must belong to the community of scholars: learning, exploring issues within a collegial community, and sharing new understandings with students. All should have explicitly stated personal goals for professional development and scholarship and for improvement as teachers. Moreover, just as program quality should be reviewed periodically, so should each faculty member's progress toward his or her stated goals be reviewed regularly by peers.

6. Connections within the Major Program

Majors . . . require faculty members' willingness to develop a shared understanding of what study in the major is supposed to accomplish and faculty members' collaboration in designing a coherent program of study sufficient to accomplish it.

The Challenge of Connecting Learning, 7

The program should be organized around a careful plant that views it as a coherent whole rather than as simply a collection of courses. In some programs, coherence is achieved partially through prerequisite structures. In others, it is achieved partially through increasing specialization or methodological sophistication. The need for establishing connections goes beyond either of these, however. A strong program will include opportunities for synthesis and integration across courses—perhaps through junior or senior seminars, a capstone course, or a senior thesis.

Faculty members must be willing to accept responsibility for the entire program—not just for their own courses. They must work collaboratively to ensure that connections among courses are visible to students. This can happen only if faculty members know what their colleagues are teaching and how their own courses fit within the content of the program.

7. Connections with Other Disciplines and Fields

To fulfill its role in liberal learning, the major also must structure conversations that more nearly reflect the diversities within our world and require patient labors of translation. Ultimately, the goal of the major should be development of students' capacities for making connections and for generating their own translations and syntheses.

The Challenge of Connecting Learning, 5

At its best, the traditional major has offered a curriculum designed to convey what is central to a given discipline or area of study. But the synthesizing enterprise—the bringing of what one has learned in one context to another, from one community to another—has been left almost entirely to students' private initiative. It ought to take place in public, accredited, curricular space.

The Challenge of Connecting Learning, 15

Strong programs help students see and appreciate the connections with other disciplines that faculty members may take for granted. Such seeing and appreciating can be accomplished through interdisciplinary courses, seminars, or projects; through course requirements outside the major department; or, perhaps best, through a continual effort by faculty members to examine in their own course insights into, examples, from, and applications to other fields.

8. Connections with Liberal Learning

[T]raditional distinctions between general education and the major no longer can be sustained. . . . [T]he work of the major needs to open into a larger context of learning in order to develop the fullness of perspective that the discrete disciplines and fields of study cannot help but obscure.

The Challenge of Connecting Learning, 5

Strong patterns acknowledge and teach connections between issues of their field and issues of wider academic and "real-world" concern. Every practitioner in every field regularly encounters political, societal, and ethical issues related to the field. Attention to these issues should not be continued to general-education courses. Students must grapple with some of these issues within the context of the major. Students also need opportunities to explore the connections between the various topics and issues in the field and their own interests and concerns.

Each program must accept responsibility for a role in the general education of its students. Strong programs may require, for example, a course on ethics in the discipline, a seminar that examines case studies of major advances in the field and includes attention to the broad issues associated with those advances, or an independent study course that permits the student to explore in depth some topic in the field that is personally meaningful. They may create capstone courses that encourage topical connections across fields.

9. Supportive Community

> *Faculty members must take seriously what students believe about a given subject and engage their prior knowledge so that new learning restructures the old, complicating and correcting it rather than merely living side by side with it.*
>
> The Challenge of Connecting Learning, 13

Strong programs provide practical support and encouragement for students' intellectual growth and development. This includes providing frequent opportunities for interaction and dialogue among students, and between students and faculty members, in addition to that which occurs in the classroom.

The faculty members in a program must take a special interest in the intellectual development of the students in the program. This responsibility can be met only when faculty members recognize that intellectual development is a social as well as an individual process. Program faculty members must provide frequent occasions that enable students to engage with others in a collaborative exploration of knowledge and inquiry in the field of study. Faculty members must be concerned with the many factors that affect students' lives as learners, and they must try to provide an environment in which learning is as natural, stimulating, and fulfilling as possible.

10. Inclusiveness

> *Redressing imbalances [among students due to age, ethnicity, economic background, gender, and race] cannot be left to the admissions office or to an institution's promising collaboration with the local public schools. Faculty members in each program must explore what obstacles their fields present to the participation of discrete groups of underrepresented students and make a strong commitment to eliminating those obstacles.*
>
> *The problem of full participation in arts and sciences majors no longer can be framed in terms of access alone; what is needed is a reformation of present practices.*
>
> The Challenge of Connecting Learning, 17

Those responsible for strong programs are aware of the demographic shifts in representation of minorities and women in the workplace and the benefits to their department of seeking to serve students with diverse characteristics and backgrounds. They work actively to find ways to attract and retain students of all types and backgrounds, including those who have been discouraged from participating in the field due to stereotyping and bias.

Faculty members in strong programs work to improve access to and persistence in the program among groups that are underrepresented in the field. They approach this work with the recognition that focusing on the diverse backgrounds, learning styles, and concerns of new groups of students will result in improved learning experiences and educational quality for all students in the program.

Those responsible for strong programs are alert to the possibility that implicit and unintended messages may be communicated that suggest to students that they are not welcome. They structure introductory courses to acknowledge and respect the goals, perspectives, learning styles, and experiences of all the students in those courses. They take particular are not to use introductory courses as filters that discourage students who in fact have potential for success in the field.

Strong programs provide multiple points of entry. These points of entry may include programs for precollege students that encourage them to enter the field, programs for first-year students whose academic records indicate they are capable of success in the field in spite of stereotypes that may have discouraged them, and courses—or versions of courses—that acknowledge the differing preparations and interests of students.

Strong programs acquaint students and potential students, through orientations or units in first-year courses, with the culture of the field and work actively to make them feel at home. Strong programs actively seek to recruit a diverse faculty that represents the scholarly attainment of traditionally underrepresented groups.

Faculty members and administrators in strong programs seek alliances with ethnic and gender studies programs, such as American ethnic studies and women's studies, to offer joint courses or programs on the history and contributions of these groups to particular fields. They participate in seminars to acquaint themselves with new scholarship. Where appropriate, they incorporate knowledge gathered from these kinds of alliances and inquiries into their own courses and programs. They also acquaint themselves with the nature of racial, ethnic, and sexual harassment and with inadvertent biases that may manifest themselves in teaching.

11. Advising

> *Careful advising is . . . necessary, not only to assure that the requisite number of courses are taken but also to support a continuing discussion about the program's purposes and students' experiences.*
>
> The Challenge of Connecting Learning, 11

Advising students is a faculty responsibility. Advising should begin as soon as a student shows a potential interest in the program, and it should continue through graduation. High-quality advising includes sharing information on the goals and expectations of the program; helping students devise purposeful and coherent plans for study; discussing the culture of, and opportunities in, the field; exploring the aspirations and interests of the student; discussing employment opportunities in the field; and assisting students in the selection of graduate schools.

Throughout the process, advising should help the student successfully "negotiate the system," ensuring that the college experience is as smooth and productive as possible. High-quality advising includes encouraging and supporting student activities outside the formal curriculum, such as academic clubs, student seminars, and interest groups, as well as the traditional one-on-one faculty/student consultations.

12. Evaluation and Assessment

> *[S]tudents have the right to expect that all of the capacities and knowledge they have gained will be assessed, by faculty members, through carefully designed occasions that challenge them to integrate and demonstrate their learning across their specific programs of study.*
>
> The Challenge of Connecting Learning, 7

Strong programs incorporate occasions for assessing student learning that transcend individual courses, for marking educational milestones in the program, and for evaluating cumulative learning. This kind of assessment is essential if faculty members truly are to know how effective their instruction is and how well the goals of the program are being met. Thoughtfully and carefully done, such evaluation also can enhance the process of helping students to make connections: connections between courses in the program, connections with other fields of study, and connections with their own personal experiences and interests.

Although faculty members initially often are suspicious of—and resistant to—assessment, the benefits of assessment usually are recognized quickly by faculty members who engage in assessment activities. Assessment allows the faculty members to identify what they are doing right—what works well and what succeeds in involving students more actively in the field. The results of assessment allow faculty members to streamline their work, abandoning classroom practices and activities that do not significantly enhance learning.

Outcomes assessment is a necessary part of the program review. Analysts of input alone (design of the curriculum, number and qualifications of faculty members, class size, quality of classrooms, and laboratories, library holdings, and so on) cannot yield information on the effectiveness of programs.

13. Administrative Support, Rewards, and Recognition

> *This report . . . asks for collective and collaborative faculty discussions about ways of translating these common commitments into institutional practices and structures. This translation must begin with time and space. . . . [I]t must be supported by visible and concrete rewards. . . .*
>
> The Challenge of Connecting Learning, 21

Any program's faculty members will be committed to a diverse set of activities including teaching, scholarship, course and curriculum development, advising, evaluation, and assessment. The quality of the program depends on strength in all of these areas. This does not mean that every faculty member in the program personally must be committed to excellence in each of these areas. It does mean, however, that all faculty members must acknowledge the importance of each of these areas; that for each area there are faculty members in the program who devote significant time and energy to the area; and that excellence is recognized, appreciated, and rewarded.

Strong programs have clearly articulated policies for supporting and rewarding all of these types of activities. Rewards include salary increases, substantial weight in promotion and tenure decisions, and awards in recognition of excellence. Administrative support includes funds for curriculum development and faculty development (for example, workshops and consultations); for research and scholarly pursuits; for course and teacher evaluation; for assessment; and for travel to meetings and conferences that deal with teaching, learning, and assessment, as well as scholarship in the field.

The Program Review Process

In a very real sense, program review is (or should be) a continuous process. Thoughtful faculty members, as they teach and advise students, constantly reflect on the effectiveness of what they are doing and on the implications for their courses of what they are learning from their students. Ideally, they also reflect on the implications for the program as a whole and share those reflections with other faculty members in faculty meetings or perhaps a faculty retreat. The result is continual fine-tuning of courses and modification of the program whenever the evidence suggests such modification is needed.

Periodically, however, a more structured review is necessary. These structured reviews should occur at regular intervals, not simply occasionally in response to a "crisis" perceived by a chair or dean. Although the stated purpose of the review may vary—to inform external constituencies about the quality of the program, to focus attention on aspects of the program that need attention, or perhaps to justify a request for additional resources—the ultimate goal of a program review should be to examine the extent to which the educational goals of the program are still appropriate and are being achieved satisfactorily. Almost inevitably, a structured program review will result in some (possible minor, sometimes major) changes in the program. The ultimate goal of any program review should be improving the program.

The frequency of structured program review also will vary greatly across institutions and across programs. Typically, structured program reviews occur approximately once every five to seven years, although special circumstances (for example, a program in transition, a program on "probation," or in intervening accreditation review) may indicate the need for a review after fewer than five or more than seven years.

The most useful program reviews are based on evidence that collected on an ongoing basis, not just assembled immediately prior to the review. Continual evidence gathering is important to ensure the availability of the necessary kinds of evidence, the robustness of data, and the ability to analyze trends. It also acts as a reminder of the importance of staying alert to factors that affect program quality.

Program review always invites feedback from reviewers outside the immediate program. Usually, these external reviewers will include colleagues from other institutions. External perspective is an important dimension of program review. It challenges faculty members to reconsider their programs in relation to practices at other institutions and it connects their work with a larger community of dialogue and debate.

Assessment and Program Review

A key ingredient in successful program review is the quality of evidence documenting the educational outcomes of the program. This evidence should assess the quality of student learning. It should be aggregate, focusing on the program and not on individual students or courses. It should be derived from multiple assessment strategies; no one approach can provide adequate information.

Assessment should focus on students' growth from the time they enter the program through their graduation from it. It should provide evidence of the kinds of work students are attempting, their increasing capacity to synthesize and integrate knowledge from different parts of their program, and their ability to use the approaches of their field in framing and analyzing problems and issues. It should provide evidence of the ways they are using their studies and not just evidence of their knowledge of specific information. To serve the purpose of program review, assessment need not include information on every student in the program; information from representative samples is sufficient. If the program has many transfer students, the assessment should provide evidence of how transfer students as a group are adapting to the program's goals and expectations.

Although assessment for program review requires only periodic sampling of students' learning, such assessment is most informative when it is grounded in course and program requirements. Many campuses find that students do not do their best work when assessment is extracurricular and has no consequences for them. Similarly, faculty members may not value evidence developed only for the periodic program review. They may view the evidence as irrelevant because they do not know and trust the measures. When assessment is embedded in the regular curriculum, faculty members are better able to interpret the results and use them for program improvement.

The best assessment strategies provide learning experiences for students as well as evidence for program review. Assessment can be embedded in courses by including common questions on examinations in several courses in the program. Assessment can provide advising experiences for students through "rising junior" exams that assess learning outcomes through the junior year and provide information to guide study during the senior year. Assessment can help students recognize and appreciate their own growth in the program through portfolios or self-assessment essays. Assessment can be structured as a series of assignments in a course—or set of courses—that allow students to try again if their performance is below expectations. Assessment can provide integrative experiences through senior projects.

Program reviews also can incorporate assessment by external examiners. Qualified persons in the external program review group can explore, in oral interviews, the extent to which students have appropriated concepts, approaches, and knowledge in their field. They can evaluate how well students can synthesize or draw upon this learning in addressing new issues or problems. Such external reviews are most effective when the examiners base their questions on students' written work—for example, in a comprehensive examination, a senior project, or in a series of course papers. The results should be summarized in a written report to the program faculty members. When students present their work to external examiners, the review process also should include feedback to the students themselves.

Other assessment strategies may include pre- and post-testing (testing at program entry and retesting at program completion), surveys of graduating seniors and of alumni/ae, exit interviews, analysis of alumni placement, tracking of alumni, standardized tests, and transcript analyses.

Organizing the Program Review

The first step in a structured program review usually is a self-study. This self-study should produce a report that reviews educational goals and rationales for the program, summarizes conclusions of the previous program review, describes changes in the program since the previous review, provides evidence indicating the extent to which program goals are met, identifies critical problems facing the program, and includes short- and long-rage plans and recommendations.

The preparation of the self-study report usually is guided by a set of questions that focus attention on issues considered important by the faculty and administration. A set of possible questions is provided in the next section of this handbook. The self-study report should reflect the corporate judgment of program faculty members, and, ideally, will be the result of a collegial effort that involves the entire program faculty.

A second step in most program reviews is an analysis of the self-study by a group external to the program. This group may include faculty members from other programs in the same institution, faculty members from similar programs at other institutions, alumni, students, members of advisory boards, administrators, or any combination of the above. This group studies the report; reviews course syllabi, final examinations, transcripts of recent graduates, and assessment findings; interviews faculty members, students, and administrators associated with the program; and requests any additional information deemed necessary. Members of the group also may conduct oral interviews with students about their work and experience in the program. Using this information, the group prepares its own report, which comments on the equality of the self-study as well as on the plans and recommendations contained therein. This group also will add its own recommendations.

The final step in the program review process is the institutional and program response, which provides an occasion for constructive dialogue between program faculty members and the responsible dean, as well as an opportunity for program faculty members to revisit the analysis contained in the self-study. The main focus of these discussions should be on educational quality and should return once more to the basic questions: What are the educational goals? How well are they being achieved? What changes should be made in light of the review findings? A follow-up session with the dean should take place after an appropriate interval to discuss any changes that have occurred as a result of the program review.

Program review, done well, is more than simply an activity carried out from time to time in response to a periodic need for information about the health of a program. Program review should be a continual process: of goal identification and review, of faculty conversation about teaching and learning strategies, of assessment and revision. The formal evaluation, which includes the self-study and the report of the external review committee, should be simply a signpost in that process, showing the results of prior assessment activities and pointing the way to a continuation of these activities in the years ahead.

A Framework for Program Review

An efficient and effective program review must be guided by questions that call attention to important issues and suggest standards, and whose answers can provide a basis for evaluation. The set of questions that guides a program review must be tailored to campus goals and priorities. No single set will be appropriate for all campuses or even for all programs on a single campus. Nevertheless, although one can expect considerable variation, most program reviews will need to deal with similar basic issues that reflect areas of common concern. The questions provided here offer a model for campuses to use in constructing their own guidelines for program review. Admittedly and unapologetically, they reflect the views about strong programs of concentrated learning articulated in *The Challenge of Connecting Learning* and summarized in chapter Two of this handbook.

The questions are grouped in categories. We recommend that each campus add one or two additional categories to the list—categories that deal with local concerns—and that the specific questions suggested here be reviewed carefully and modified as necessary to reflect campus priorities.

Goals

> *[Faculty members must attempt] to provide a local structure for a course of study in a major that can specify its goals, ensure that these goals are communicated to students and faculty members alike, and assess the degree to which these aims are achieved.*
>
> The Challenge of Connecting Learning, 7

Prior to any assessment activity there must be an identification of goals and expected outcomes. In a strong program, these will be articulated prior to program implementation. They will be under review continually and, from time to time, under revision.

- What are the educational goals of the program?

  How were these goals determined?

  Are all faculty members in the program aware of the goals, and do they understand how their own courses are intended to contribute to achieving these goals?

How are the goals of the program communicated to students?

Is there clear evidence that the goals of the program are being met?

- Are the goals of the program appropriate for the blend of faculty members and students that are in the program?

  How do the goals of the program compare with the goals of similar programs at other institutions?

  Are program faculty members aware of the characteristics of exemplary programs at other institutions?

- What are the intended outcomes of the program?

  Are these outcomes stated in terms that permit judgments about the extent to which they are realized?

  What procedures are in place for collecting and analyzing evidence that enables such judgments to be made?

  Does this evidence show that the intended outcomes are achieved?

- How does the program monitor its progress toward achieving its goals?

  Are faculty members involved in this process?

  Are occasions provided for sharing the results with all faculty members?

- What are the major changes occurring in similar programs in other institutions?

  How does the faculty learn about these changes?

  How does the faculty assess which of these changes to implement locally?

- What process is used for regularly reviewing goals, courses, and curricular structures in light of the findings of assessment activities?

  Is this a corporate process that involves all faculty members in the program or at least a broadly representative cross-section of the faculty?

  What have been the results of these processes since the previous program review?

- What modifications have been made recently in the goals or in the program?

  How these modifications resulted in documented improvements?

  Are there problems that have not been addressed?

The Structure of the Curriculum

> *[F]aculty members [must] concern themselves not just with course requirements but with the ways that a major's parts and practices contribute to its larger purposes. . . . The chosen mode of organization . . . ought to be the result of deliberate and corporate faculty judgment.*
>
> The Challenge of Connecting Learning, 7–8

In a strong program, required courses and constrained electives fit together in a coherent whole. The organization of the program will vary from field to field and, perhaps, from institution to institution. For all programs, however, the organizing principles and coherence of the curricular plan should be evident to students and faculty members alike. Faculty members should possess a shared understanding of the differences between introductory, intermediate, and culminating work in the program. Their courses and assignments should reflect this shared understanding.

- What is the plan for the curriculum and how was it determined?

  Is it based on a well-defined intellectual agenda?

  Is the plan understood by all faculty members teaching courses in the program?

  Is it understood by students?

  Is it reflected in course rationales, syllabi, and assignments?

- Does the program begin with survey courses or with more specialized introductions to the field?

  What is the rationale for this choice?

  Do the beginning courses serve both majors and nonmajors?

  If so, is there evidence that they serve both constituencies well?

- Is there structure in the middle range of courses?

  What are the organizing principles?

  Do these courses build significantly on the introductory courses?

Do they acknowledge and utilize the learning that is occurring in other middle-range courses?

- Do the middle-range courses include attention to connections with other fields and with the learning that is occurring in the other parts of the curriculum (for example, in general-education courses)?

  Do they allow time and space for reflecting, synthesizing, and generalizing?

- Are students introduced early to the modes of inquiry and methodology of the discipline?

  Are these modes and methods then utilized in assignments for subsequent courses?

  Do students exit the program with a demonstrated ability to apply the approaches of the discipline to formulate and analyze new questions, conjectures, and proposals?

- Do beginning or middle-range courses introduce students to the contested issues of the field and provide students the opportunity to engage actively with these issues?

  Do students understand both the strengths and the limitations of the methodology and perspectives of the field?

  Do they exit the program with some measure of critical distance from the field?

- Is there a common core of courses taken by all students in the program?

  If not, is there an alternate academic structure that stimulates the development of an intellectual community among the students?

- Is there a capstone experience (for example, a senior seminar, a senior project, a thesis, comprehensive examinations) that provides students with an opportunity to integrate the learning that has occurred throughout their college experience?

  Does this capstone experience integrate courses external to the program—including courses in general education—as well as courses within it?

  Does it challenge students to grapple with some of the ethical, political, and societal issues associated with the field?

- What characteristics of the program are evident from an analysis of student transcripts?

  Is the intended structure of the program realized?

  Is it effective in supporting the educational goals of the program?

  Has the structure been reviewed or modified recently?

  Does it need modification?

Connections

> *[F]ostering capacities for reflection on what happens beyond the academy must be the larger goal. The discourse of the academy is but a means to an end, a developmental step along a path that appropriately points students toward a multitude of contexts and circumstances.*
>
> The Challenge of Connecting Learning, 14

> *It is . . . important for [students] to care about subject matter and see its implications for the ways they live their lives. At issue is whether students can connect a field's subject matter and approaches with a variety of pursuits important to them, and whether their curiosity and concerns beyond the classroom can be deepened or shaped by the insights the field brings forth. This requires teaching and opportunities for reflection that encourage students to test the assumptions and proposals of the field against questions and evidence drawn from their own experience.*
>
> The Challenge of Connecting Learning, 16

Strong programs are designed to facilitate connections: with the most recent advances in the field, with the practice of the field in life beyond the academy, with applications to other fields, with liberal learning, and—most important from students' perspectives—with the needs and lives of students. Inattention to these connections will lead to an insularity that is certain to result in a loss of vitality for the program.

- How important are these connections among the stated goals of the program?

  To what extent are connections explicitly addressed in the curricular structure?

Is there evidence that students are making connections as they progress through the program?

As they exit the program?

- What are the modes of scholarship in which the program's faculty members actively are engaged?

  Is there a good representation of differing modes of scholarship among the program faculty members?

  Are all faculty members active?

  Do they bring into the classroom the excitement as well as the results of recent work in the field?

  Do they regularly revise their courses to include the latest results, debates, and open questions?

- Do experiences provided in the program connect with the principal career options available to graduates of the program?

  Are there opportunities for internships or summer employment?

- Do faculty members pay attention in their courses to the links between their courses and the overall goals of the program?

  To the links between their discipline (or approach to the discipline) and others?

  Do they encourage students to take multidisciplinary courses and courses in other fields that extend or use the techniques, ideas, or content of the field?

  Does the program offer opportunities for interdisciplinary courses, seminars, or projects?

- How does the program curriculum interface with the general-education curriculum?

  Do intermediate and advanced courses in the program utilize the knowledge that students bring to these courses from general-education courses?

  Do courses in the program attend to the social, political, and ethical issues associated with the field?

  Are there opportunities for students to connect what they are learning in the program with the wider issues of liberal learning and with issues that are important to them personally?

  Does the program provide opportunities for students to engage in a process of generalizing that reaches beyond the confines of the discipline and into a broader context?

- How does the program connect with the lives of students?

  Does the program actively seek to learn about the characteristics of its students?

  Is there evidence that the program is responsive to changes in those characteristics?

  In particular, is there a regular effort to assess the academic preparation that students bring into the program?

  Is there a regular effort to determine the students' aspirations, beliefs, and expectations with respect to the program?

  Is there evidence that the faculty members are aware of these findings and acknowledge them in their courses?

  Has the program as a whole responded to these findings?

Teaching Quality

For students, learning in the major means learning to take part in a continuing exploration. The role of faculty members is to provide structures and languages that support this participation. . . .

The Challenge of Connecting Learning, 4

Strong programs are taught by faculty members who place a high priority on the quality of their teaching. Teaching quality involves much more than performance in the classroom. It includes attention to the needs of students with a diversity of interests, backgrounds, and learning styles. It includes interacting with students both inside and outside the classroom in relation to the overarching learning goals of the undergraduate academic experience as well as to the goals of a particular course or program. It includes staying current on recent research in teaching and learning, and it includes a willingness to alter teaching styles on the basis of the results of that research. It includes responsibility for addressing the shared goals of the overall program in planning courses and in giving feedback to students on their work and progress.

- How does the program encourage high-quality teaching?

  Are incentives and rewards (such as teaching awards, salary increases, funds to attend conferences on teaching) provided to promote and recognize excellence in teaching?

  Are there mechanisms for mentoring new and temporary faculty members in the art of teaching and in local customs and expectations?

  Are there mechanisms to assist experienced faculty members who wish to improve their teaching?

  If graduate students teach in the program, are they well trained and well supervised?

- How does the program evaluate teaching?

  Are teaching dossiers, peer evaluations, student evaluations, and reviews of syllabi included in the evaluation process?

  Are teaching evaluations taken into account in making teaching assignments?

  In promotion and tenure decisions?

  Are procedures in place to provide counseling for faculty members whose teaching is recognized to be effective for many students?

- Who in the program is cognizant of research in teaching and learning?

  Are these individuals a resource for other faculty members?

  Are there regular occasions (such as faculty meetings, seminars, or brown-bag lunches) for discussing teaching strategies and teaching issues?

- Do faculty members in the program utilize a variety of teaching techniques?

  Are there opportunities for collaborative learning, supervised peer teaching, and independent study?

- How, and how often, do students receive feedback in their courses?

  What form does the feedback take?

  Are there opportunities for students to revise and resubmit their work?

Advising

It is . . . useful to think about the major in terms of the appropriately social metaphor of "home". . . . [T]he major program provides a "home" for learning: a community of peers with whom students can undertake collaborative inquiries and a faculty charged to care about students' intellectual and personal explorations as well as their maturation.

The Challenge of Connecting Learning, 4

Advising must be more than monitoring students to ensure that they are making satisfactory progress toward a degree, and it must be more than suggesting choices among possible options. Quality advising includes discussing goals and expectations: of the program, of the institution, and of the student. It includes discussing opportunities in the field and strategies for achieving students' goals both during and after their program of study. It includes discussing the relationship among courses in the program and between the program and general education.

High-quality advising is built upon knowing each student's background, beliefs, hopes, and expectations. Ideally, advising is an interactive process that makes a definite contribution to the student's education, informs faculty members about students' concerns, and results in a shared understanding of a plan or plans of action that will serve well the needs of the student.

- How are students in the program advised?

  Does each student meet on a regular basis with a faculty member to discuss the student's plans and progress?

  Do these discussions include attention to questions that transcend the requirements of the program (such as the rationale for the program, the culture of the field, the totality of the undergraduate experience, and student goals and expectations)?

- Are there also less formal opportunities for faculty/student interactions?

  Are there student clubs, seminars, or interest groups associated with the program?

  Do program faculty members support these activities?

- Is advising valued in the program?

Are all faculty members expected to participate?

If advising is the responsibility of only a few faculty members, are these few provided with sufficient time for regular one-on-one interactions with students?

Is the knowledge that advisers gain about the characteristics of students shared with all faculty members in the program?

Does it influence the way the program is structured and the way the courses are taught?

Inclusiveness

What is required of each institution and each field is a strong affirmation of the educational benefits of diversity and a continuing faculty dialogue about the ways initiatory [and continuing] experiences in a field can contribute to, and lay the foundations for, the widest range of students to achieve success.

The Challenge of Connecting Learning, 18

It no longer is enough to make simple adjustments to accommodate students who traditionally have been discouraged from study in a field. Institutions and programs must rethink the way they function relative to these students and undertake comprehensive and sustained change efforts. Plans for change, to be effective, must include assessment and accountability measures.

- What are the program's goals for enhancing diversity?

  What do institutional data indicate about the entry and graduation rates of groups of students underrepresented in the field?

  What are the plans to correct any disparities in recruitment and retention of different groups?

  Are the current accountability measures successful in ensuring progress in attaining goals?

  Who is assigned responsibility for monitoring and reporting on progress?

- Does the program assess which courses critically influence students' decisions on whether or not to major in the program?

  Do these courses enroll a reasonable percentage of students from groups underrepresented in the field?

  Do these students stay in the major at the same rate as other students?

  If these students leave the program in large numbers, why do they leave?

- What efforts have been made to identify and remove barriers—such as a climate that communicates to underrepresented groups that their participation is not welcome, that their success in the field is unlikely, or that the field does not value their perspectives and experiences—that may impede entry or success in the program by specific groups of students?

  Have issues of diverse goals, expectations, learning styles, and experiences been considered in planning and implementing courses in the program?

  Does the program sponsor workshops for faculty members on climate issues, including topics such as the dynamics of difference in the classroom, stereotyping and bias, or teaching and learning styles?

- Is the faculty of the program diverse, representing appropriately the availability of faculty members from underrepresented groups?

  If not, has the program evaluated and addressed inequities in recruiting, hiring, promotion, tenure, and salary of faculty members?

  Has the program evaluated policies and procedures for disparate impact?

- If an imbalance persists after extensive efforts have been made to recruit and retain faculty members from underrepresented groups, does the program nonetheless demonstrate to students diversity among professionals in the field, both in perspectives on critical issues in the field and in sex, race, and ethnicity?

- Have faculty members in the program explored the potential benefit of alliance with units on campus that serve diverse groups of students, such as American ethnic studies, women's studies, minority student affairs, or the women's center?

  Does the program sponsor events that highlight the contributions to the field of people of diverse cultures and characteristics?

Does the program sponsor clubs, student focus groups, and advising, mentoring, and mediating services for diverse groups of students?

- Where appropriate, does the program assess its curriculum for the inclusion of relevant new scholarship about women and minorities?

  Do faculty members participate in seminars, workshops, or professional meetings to develop experience in this material?

  Have efforts to incorporate new scholarship in their courses been successful?

Institutional Support

> *Collegial leadership . . . deserves and requires full institutional support from presidents and academic administrators. What are needed in the long run are institutional environments that build a sense of common enterprise and institutional priorities that recognize the integral connections between work in the major and overarching goals for liberal learning.*
>
> The Challenge of Connecting Learning, 21

Strong programs are supported by chairs, deans, provosts, and presidents who value the teaching activities of their faculty members. Administrative support for teaching includes more than access to copy machines, well-equipped classrooms, and laboratory and library facilities. It includes support for course and curriculum development, faculty development, course and teacher evaluation, assessment, and travel to meetings and conferences that focus on curriculum or teaching. It includes promotion and tenure policies that recognize the importance of excellent teaching, advising, research in teaching and learning, and creative activities that enhance quality teaching. In concert with program reviews, administrators at all levels should examine critically their own contributions to creating an institutional environment that is supportive of good teaching.

- What is the track record of the program and the institution in encouraging, rewarding, and promoting excellent teaching?

  What mechanisms are utilized for these purposes?

  Do faculty members describe the atmosphere as one that values teaching and teaching-related activities?

  Is there evidence that teaching excellence is an important factor in promotion and tenure decisions?

- How do the institution and the program orient new faculty members?

  Do the orientations include attention to teaching?

- Are faculty development activities available for faculty members at all levels?

  Are ongoing workshops or seminars on teaching provided for teaching assistants?

- What curriculum development activities have been undertaken recently in the program?

  Were they adequately supported?

  Have they resulted in documentable improvements in the program?

- Are funds available to support assessment and evaluation activities?

  Are these funds well spent?

- Is there evidence that research in teaching and learning, course development, advising, and other teaching-related activities are valued in the program and in the institution?

Outcomes Assessment

> *Corporate attention to the ways in which a major works as a total program, rather than as a set of discrete (and often disparate) courses, can establish a series of points at which faculty members both assess and support students' continuing progress in the field.*
>
> The Challenge of Connecting Learning, 18–19

Every academic program is designed to achieve certain goals. Ultimately, the quality of the program must be judged on how well it achieves those goals. Faculty members' perceptions and anecdotal evidence are not sufficient; evidence on the quality of the teaching process is not sufficient. What is necessary is evidence that the intended outcomes of the program are realized. The key questions are: What are the goals, or intended outcomes, of the program? To what extent are these being achieved?

Strong programs have designed assessment processes to answer these questions. These processes judge the outcomes of the program as a whole rather than the outcomes of a single course or the performance of an individual instructor or the achievements of particular students. Assessment is intended to document the successes of the program: flag areas in which goals are not being met satisfactorily; and, ultimately, lead to improvements in the program. Ideally, many of the assessment processes also will have direct educational value for students.

- What are the intended educational outcomes of the program?

  What processes are in place for measuring the achievements of these outcomes?

  Do the processes provide several kinds of information about student learning and achievement?

  Do these processes reflect faculty discussion and decisions about the kinds of evidence appropriate to their program's goals, strengths, and emphases?
- Are the assessment procedures adopted by the program linked to program goals and curricular priorities?

  Do faculty members periodically discuss the results of assessment in relation to program goals?

  Do they use assessment evidence in making judgments about curriculum development and revisions?
- Does assessment provide opportunities for students to reflect on their progress to the program? To integrate different parts of their learning?

  Do students who take part in assessment activities receive feedback on their performance?

  Is there a culture that invites students to take assessment seriously as a milestone in their learning and intellectual development?
- If assessment examinations and assignments are locally developed, are faculty members given release time or other compensation to design them?

  Who is involved in making judgments about the outcomes of assessment?

  Who uses the results?

  Do faculty members in the program confer with peers in comparable programs in reviewing the outcomes of assessment activities?

  Are there opportunities for students to discuss assessment outcomes in relation to their experience in the program?
- To what extent are intended outcomes achieved?

  To the extent that the intellectual outcomes are not achieved, what changes are being made either in the goals of the program or in the program itself?

Conclusion

This handbook suggests a general framework through which to explore the effectiveness of educational programs in the major. Those consulting it will want to adapt its specific questions to the particular concerns of their institutions and programs.

As they do this adaptation, and as they implement program review focused on educational quality, they should keep at the fore the goal of providing the best possible educational experience for the students served. Connecting the program review—as well as the program—to the needs, abilities, aspirations, experiences, and prior knowledge of students—as well as the goals and expectations of the faculty—will provide the best opportunity for program review and lead to improved programs. This must be the ultimate goal.

As faculty members and academic administrators work together to connect issues addressed here to their own programs and students, they shape the collegial dialogue fundamental to the effectiveness of any educational program.

Selected Bibliography

AAC publications and reports related to arts and sciences majors

The Challenge of Connecting Learning, "Liberal Learning and the Arts and Sciences Major," Volume One. Washington: AAC, 1991.

Volume One of the reports from AAC's three-year review of purposes and practices in arts and sciences majors. *The Challenge of Connecting Learning* proposes organizing principles adaptable to any major and calls for more dialogue among faculty members and between faculty and students, within and across fields.

Reports from the Fields, "Liberal Learning and the Arts and Sciences Major," Volume Two. Washington: AAC, 1991.

Volume Two, *Reports from the Fields,* contains executive summaries of the reports on their majors from twelve learned societies, and discusses important issues and needed changes in each of the following fields: biology, economics, history, mathematics, philosophy, physics, political science, psychology, religion, sociology, and women's studies, as well as interdisciplinary studies. Each review response to an AAC "charge": a set of organizing questions about majors as liberal learning. This volume provides information on how to procure copies of the unabridged reports from the learned societies.

Integrity in the College Curriculum: A Report to the Academic Community. Washington: AAC, 1985.

Integrity proposes a minimum required program of nine essential educational experiences that ensure a liberal education for all students. It severely critiques the formlessness of major programs on many campuses.

Structure and Coherence: Measuring the Undergraduate Curriculum. Washington: AAC, 1989.

Structure and Coherence includes analyses of student transcripts from thirty undergraduate institutions and documents patterns of depth, breadth, and intellectual progression in different subject areas and in different kinds of institutions.

"Frameworks that Enhance Learning," *Liberal Education,* Volume 77, Number 2 (March/April 1991): 1–48.

This issue of AAC's bimonthly journal addresses structural changes in academic programs that enhance student learning.

Resources for good teaching and scholarship

Boyer, Ernest L. *Scholarship Reconsidered: Priorities of the Professoriate.* Princeton: Carnegie Foundation for the Advancement of Teaching, 1990.

Chickering, Arthur W. and Zelda F. Gamson, eds. *Applying the Seven Principles for Good Practice in Undergraduate Education.* New Directions for Teaching and Learning, No. 47, San Francisco: Jossey-Bass, 1991.

CHAPTER 38

AN ENGAGEMENT THEORY OF ACADEMIC PROGRAM QUALITY AND DEVELOPING AND SUSTAINING HIGH-QUALITY PROGRAMS

JENNIFER GRANT HAWORTH AND CLIFTON F. CONRAD

An Engagement Theory of Academic Program Quality

In this chapter, we introduce our theory and, in so doing, advance a new perspective on program quality. This theory is anchored in our definition of high-quality programs—namely, those which provide enriching learning experiences that positively affect students' growth and development—and is based on the weight of the evidence of the 781 people we interviewed. In broad strokes, the theory emphasizes one major idea: that student, faculty, and administrator engagement in teaching and learning is central to a high-quality program.

Engagement Theory

According to our theory, high-quality programs are those in which students, faculty, and administrators engage in mutually supportive teaching and learning: students invest in teaching as well as learning, and faculty and administrators invest in learning as well as teaching. Moreover, faculty and administrators invite alumni and employers of graduates to participate in their programs. In short, the theory accentuates the dual roles that invested participants play in constructing and sustaining programs of high quality.

More specifically, the theory holds that participants in high-quality programs invest significant time and energy in five separate clusters of program attributes, each of which contributes to enriching learning experiences for students that positively affect their growth and development. The five clusters of program attributes are: diverse and engaged participants, participatory cultures, interactive teaching and learning, connected program requirements, and adequate resources. Figure 38-1 provides a visual representation of the theory.

In keeping with the engagement thesis, the most important of these clusters is diverse and engaged participants. In high-quality programs, faculty and administrators continually seek to attract and support faculty and students who infuse diverse perspectives into—and who are engaged in—their own and others' teaching and learning. Faculty, students, and leaders who invest time and effort in their programs strengthen students' learning experiences in ways that significantly enhance students' personal, intellectual, and professional development.

Source: "An Engagement Theory of Academic Program Quality" and "Developing and Sustaining High-Quality Programs," by Jennifer Grant Haworth and Clifton F. Conrad, reprinted from *Emblems of Quality: Developing and Sustaining High-Quality Programs*, 1997, Allyn and Bacon.

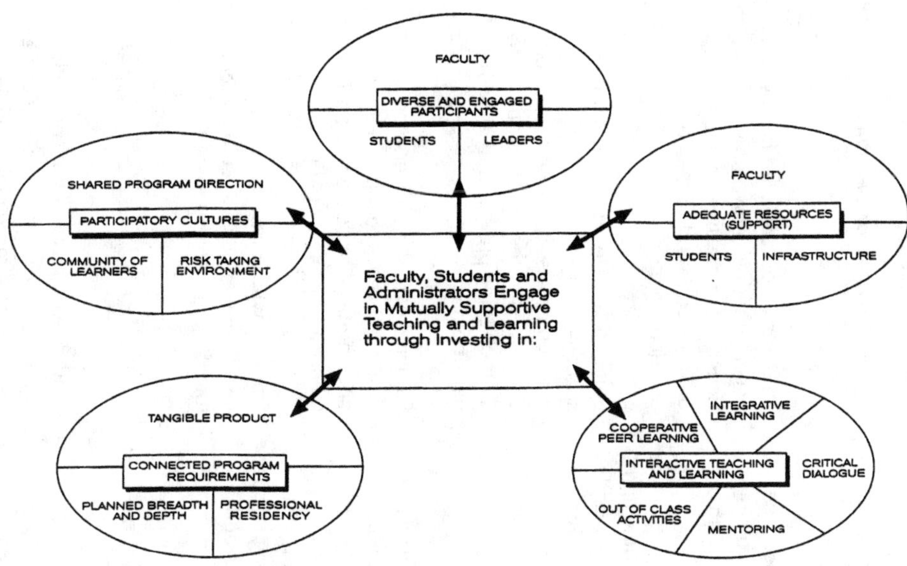

Figure 38-1 Engagement Theory of Program Quality.

Stakeholders in high-quality programs also invest heavily in participatory cultures. Program administrators, faculty, and students—as well as institutional administrators, alumni, and employers—develop and sustain cultures that emphasize a shared program direction, a community of learners, and a risk-taking environment. Program cultures that share these attributes greatly contribute to the quality of students' learning.

Program administrators, faculty, and students in high-quality programs also make strong investments in interactive teaching and learning. Through critical dialogues about knowledge and professional practice, faculty-student mentoring, cooperative peer learning projects, out-of-class activities and integrative, hands on learning activities, stakeholders actively participate in and contribute to one anothers' learning.

Program administrators, faculty, and students in high-quality programs invest in a fourth program cluster: connected program requirements. To wit, faculty and program administrators design program requirements that challenge students to develop more mature and unified understandings of their profession and its practice as they engage in planned breadth and depth course work, apply and test their course-related knowledge and skills in a professional residency, and complete a tangible product (such as a thesis, project report, or performance).

Finally, faculty, program administrators, and institutional administrators in high-quality programs devote substantial time and effort to providing monetary as well as non-monetary support for students, faculty, and basic infrastructure needs. Investing in this program cluster helps to ensure that faculty and students have the resources they need to concentrate fully on teaching and learning.

Table 38-1 summarizes the engagement theory. For each of the theory's seventeen attributes, this figure identifies the actions that stakeholders take to implement the attribute, sketches the major consequences that these actions have for enriching students' learning experiences, and indicates the positive affects that these learning experiences have on students' growth and development.

In presenting the theory, we emphasize that the clusters of attributes that make up our engagement theory represent an "ideal" high-quality program. Further, while each of the attributes discussed in the following chapters was present in at least two-fifths of the programs in our sample, no single program encompassed all seventeen attributes. We encourage readers to use the theory as a "common analytical yardstick" (Turner 1978, 35) for reflecting on similarities and differences between their programs and this "ideal" program.

TABLE 38-1
Overview of Engagement Theory

	Actions	*Consequences for Learning Experiences*	*Effects on Students*
Cluster One: Diverse and Engaged Participants			
Diverse and Engaged Faculty	Faculty and administrators adopt multidimensional hiring policies to attract faculty who will bring diverse theoretical and applied perspectives and a commitment to teaching.	Faculty infuse diverse perspectives into their classroom lectures, discussions, and out-of-class interactions with students.	Students who study with faculty who accent multiple viewpoints develop richer, more creative understandings of knowledge and professional practice.
	Faculty and administrators establish reward structures that support faculty for engaging in diverse scholarly activities and for investing in students.	Faculty dedicate significant time and energy to teaching, including outside-of-class involvement with involvement with students.	Students who learn from committed scholar-teachers become more inspired professionals who are more committed to their profession and to their ongoing professional growth and development.
Diverse and Engaged Students	Faculty and administrators establish admissions policies to attract diverse students who will bring a multiplicity of disciplinary and experientially-based perspectives and who will invest in their experience.	Students contribute fresh perspectives to discussions they have with one another and with faculty.	Students who share diverse perspectives creatively expand and enrich one anothers' understandings of theory and professional practice.
	Faculty and administrators screen and admit students whose professional interests and goals match those of their curriculum and faculty.	Students invest time and energy in their own and others' learning through active participation in formal and informal learning activities.	Students who invest in learning inspire one another to commit more fully to their professions.
Engaged Leaders	Faculty and administrators recruit department or program chairs who will "champion" their program.	Leaders effectively promote their program to internal and external audiences and are adept at securing resources to sustain it.	Leaders who provide students with program leadership opportunities help them become more highly-skilled, self-confident leaders.

	Institutional administrators and faculty engage in activities aimed at supporting program leaders.	Leaders attract and support diverse and engaged faculty and students. Leaders encourage participants to assume informal program leadership roles.	Engaged leaders provide the kinds of support that empowers faculty and students to invest in teaching and learning experiences which, in turn, help students become more competent, committed, and creative leaders.
Cluster Two: Participatory Cultures Shared Program Direction	Faculty and administrative leaders invite stakeholders to join them in developing a shared program direction. Leaders sustain shared understandings of program direction by encouraging faculty, students, alumni, and employers to participate in ongoing evaluation efforts in which they examine the fit between their program's teaching and learning activities and its overall direction. Leaders sustain shared understandings of program direction by communicating it to internal and external audiences.	Stakeholders share an overall program direction that both informs and animates their actions and provides a common thread which knits together students' learning experiences.	Students develop more distinct professional identities in programs in which participants share a common focus. "Connected" learning experiences help students to develop a keener sense of professional direction and a greater awareness of where and how they wish to invest their professional energies upon graduation.
Community of Learners	A leader—or group of leaders—takes responsibility for helping to build a learning community. Faculty develop more collegial and less hierarchical relations with students. Administrators, faculty, and students construct in- and out-of-class teaching and learning experiences to facilitate and sustain co-learning among program participants.	Participants experience their program as a "learning community" in which faculty and students teach and learn from one another more or less as colleagues. Participants experience camaraderie among and between faculty and students that supports and complements the overall sense of community.	The collegial interactions students have with one another and with faculty improve their communication and teamwork skills. Students develop a greater appreciation and respect for the value of collaborative approaches to inquiry, problem-solving, and leadership.

TABLE 38-1 (continued)

	Actions	*Consequences for Learning Experiences*	*Effects on Students*
Cluster Two: Participatory Cultures (continued)			
Risk-Taking Environment	Faculty and administrators develop a supportive learning environment in which students are encouraged to explore new ideas and test developing skills. Faculty and administrators take risks themselves, encourage students to follow their lead and to stretch and grow in new ways.	Supported and challenged to take risks, students regularly question orthodoxies, advance alternative perspectives and approaches, and engage in learning activities that press the boundaries of their potential.	Students who engage in—and learn from—risk-taking activities become more competent, self-assured professionals. Since risk-taking ventures require students to wrestle with their profession in new and creative ways, they become more imaginative and resourceful professionals.
Cluster Three: Interactive Teaching and Learning			
Critical Dialogue	Faculty and administrators emphasize a two-way, interactive approach to teaching and learning that nurtures ongoing dialogue among program participants. Faculty and administrators infuse a critical sensibility into these interactions by encouraging students to take an inquisitive stance on knowledge and professional practice.	Faculty and students engage in disciplined and mutually-enriching dialogue in which they constantly question one another, examine assumptions and differing points-of-view, and generate critically informed understandings of knowledge and professional practice.	Students who engage in critical dialogues with faculty and other students learn to think in a more holistic, questioning, and discriminating manner. The critical and holistic thinking skills students refine through critical dialogue helps them to become more creative and self-confident problem-solvers.
Integrative Learning: Theory with Practice, Self with Subject	Faculty and administrators invest in teaching and learning activities—such as "real-world" lectures and hands-on learning—that invite connections between theory and practice.	Students participate in learning activities in which they connect theoretical and applied knowledge to complex problems, issues, and situations in the real world.	Students who participate in integrative learning activities approach problem-solving from a more holistic standpoint.

	Faculty and administrators model for students how they integrate knowledge and practice as they work with students in class, on-stage, in the laboratory, or in the field.	Students receive individualized advice, guidance, and feedback from faculty in various ways: working together in the lab, field, or studio; in formal meetings; and through informal interactions.	Because they are challenged to connect theoretical and applied knowledge to real-world issues, students become more adept at translating and communicating theoretical and technical knowledge to others.
Mentoring	Faculty take an interest in students' career goals and tailor courses of study to their educational objectives. Faculty periodically instruct students on a one-on-one basis in order to sharpen their understandings of knowledge and professional practice. Faculty regularly provide students with feedback on their professional skills development.		Students become more aware of their strengths and weaknesses, thereby strengthening their professional competence and enhancing their confidence. The mentoring students receive from faculty helps to advance their careers in the university and non-university workplace.
Cooperative Peer Learning	Faculty use in- and out-of-class group activities to promote cooperative learning among students. Faculty themselves engage in collaborative research and team-teaching activities; in so doing, they model peer learning for students and emphasize the importance they place on it in their program and profession.	Students participate in group activities in which they contribute to, and support, one anothers' learning in ways that enrich their understandings of knowledge and professional practice.	Cooperative learning experiences improve students' interpersonal and teamwork skills. As students teach and learn from one another in study groups, research teams, or theater companies, they become more self-confident in their professional abilities.
Out-of-Class Activities	Faculty, administrators, and students develop and sponsor formal and informal out-of-class program activities.	Students—and occasionally faculty—participate in a variety of informal, out-of-class activities in which they explore topics of mutual interest and enrich one anothers' learning.	The interactions students have with one another in out-of-class activities improves their oral communication and interpersonal skills.

TABLE 38-1 (continued)

	Actions	*Consequences for Learning Experiences*	*Effects on Students*
Cluster Three: Interactive Teaching and Learning (continued)	Faculty and administrators support—financially and otherwise—out-of-class activities as an integral part of their program.		As students interact with and learn from one another and from faculty in out-of-class activities, they develop a greater appreciation for collaborative approaches to inquiry, problem-solving, and leadership in their fields.
Cluster Four: Connected Program Requirements			
Planned Breadth and Depth Course Work	Faculty and administrators meet periodically to determine the knowledge, skills, and practices they expect students to learn.	Students complete a combination of core and specialized course work in which they learn both generalized and specialized knowledge.	The advanced knowledge, skills, and practices students learn in core and specialized courses enhances their professional competence.
	Faculty and administrators develop core and specialized course work requirements in line with these expectations.		Since core and specialized course work challenges students to think about their fields in both "broad" and "deep" ways, they develop more holistic understandings of knowledge and practice that improves their workplace effectiveness.
Professional Residency	Faculty and administrators design professional residency experiences with students' career interests and goals in mind.	Residential learning experiences challenge students to build bridges between what they learn in classes and what they encounter in "real-world" settings, thereby helping them to develop more robust and connected understandings of their professions.	The successful application of knowledge and skills in their professional residencies helps students to develop into more confident and competent professionals.
	Faculty and administrators maintain ties with employers, alumni, and community members that, in turn, help them identify and secure residency sites and supervisors for students.		A professional residency strengthens students' professional identities.

	Once students are involved in their residencies, faculty members and site supervisors regularly provide them with regular guidance and feedback.		The confidence, knowledge, and professional networks students develop in their residencies enhances their job prospects upon graduation.
Tangible Product	Faculty and administrators design tangible product requirements in light of their program's overall direction and goals. Faculty and administrators support students throughout this culminating activity, providing them with guidance and feedback as needed.	In developing a tangible product, students are challenged to draw upon and knit together relevant principles, practices, and skills that they have learned in their programs to create a product that is of value to the field as well as to them personally.	The research and writing associated with thesis and project work improves students' analytical and written communication skills. By assuming major responsibility for their projects from start to finish, students develop into more confident and independent professionals. As a culminating—and often an integrative—activity, this learning experience helps students to develop a "big picture" perspective on their professions.
Cluster Five: Adequate Resources Support for Students	Institutional and program administrators, as well as faculty, secure monetary resources for student assistantships, fellowships, and travel to professional conferences. Faculty and administrators design nontraditional course delivery formats to support the educational needs of working professionals. Faculty and administrators provide career planning and placement assistance to help students prepare for and locate employment upon graduation.	Students who receive financial aid for full-time study, or who complete their studies part-time in programs with nontraditional delivery formats, are in a better position to concentrate on their learning. Students who take advantage of career counseling and job placement services learn job-search strategies and develop professional networks that better prepare them for locating employment upon graduation.	Students who utilize career planning and placement services are more likely to secure employment in their field upon graduation. Since financial aid and nontraditional course delivery formats provide students with the support needed to invest more fully in their learning experiences, they indirectly help students to become more committed, lifelong learners. Since support facilitates student investment in many other attributes, it further intensifies many of the effects that these attributes have on students.

TABLE 38-1 (continued)

	Actions	*Consequences for Learning Experiences*	*Effects on Students*
Cluster Five: Adequate Resources (continued)			
Support for Faculty	Campus and departmental administrators allocate monetary resources for faculty salaries, sabbaticals, and travel to professional conferences.	When faculty are adequately supported, they invest significant time and effort in teaching and mentoring students.	Students who study with faculty who take an active interest in them became more self-confident professionals.
	Campus and departmental administrators establish reward structures that support faculty for their involvement in teaching and learning.		Since support facilitates faculty investments in other attributes, it further intensifies many of the effects these attributes have on students.
Support for Basic Infrastructure	Campus and departmental administrators, as well as faculty, secure monetary resources to purchase requisite equipment and supplies; to ensure suitable laboratory, performance, and classroom facilities; and to support institutional library and computer needs.	When basic infrastructure needs are met, students are in a better position to learn advanced knowledge and techniques.	Students who study in programs with up-to-date equipment and facilities become more technically-competent professionals.
			Since this kind of support indirectly complements student investments in other attributes, it further intensifies many of the effects these attributes have on students.

Developing and Sustaining High-Quality Programs

As the previous chapters suggest, developing and sustaining high-quality programs is an organic process, not a mechanical one. The task requires those who have a stake in academic programs to engage in an ongoing process of organizational learning that takes as its focus improved teaching and learning. A high-quality program cannot be reduced to a handful of discrete items or benchmarks that faculty and administrators piece together: Quality demands the collective intelligence and commitment of many people who mutually invest in their own and others' learning. Thus, the metaphor of "assembling" a high-quality program is eclipsed by people "growing" and "cultivating" one.

With this in mind, in this chapter we turn our attention to the practical issue of developing and sustaining high-quality academic programs. In so doing, we propose a framework that is intended to help faculty, administrators, and others learn about, assess, and improve the quality of undergraduate and graduate programs. Anchored in our engagement theory of program quality, the framework also reflects insights from the total quality management, organizational learning, and higher education assessment literatures. Our discussion is divided into three parts: To place our ideas in context, we begin with a critique of how most faculty, administrators, and policymakers assess program quality in higher education and argue for an alternative approach. We then describe our framework and elaborate on its key features. Last, we explain the potential benefits of this framework for cultivating and strengthening the quality of academic programs.

Toward a Learning-Centered Approach to Quality Assessment

In myriad ways, stakeholders both internal and external to academe are involved in examining the quality of academic programs in our nation's colleges and universities. Parents and students, for example, conduct their own quality appraisals during the institutional selection process, often relying on quality rankings published by *U.S. News and World Report* and *The Gourman Report* for assistance. Faculty and administrators frequently take up this task as part of larger institutional program review and accreditation processes. Many others—including alumni, employers, policymakers, state legislators, and members of the media—render quality judgments as they evaluate alumni performances in the workplace, scrutinize faculty productivity on campus, and critique the content and character of undergraduate and graduate curricula in our nation's colleges and universities.

Given that our interest is in improving the ways in which faculty and administrators evaluate academic program quality, we invite readers to reflect critically on the following questions:

- What is the overarching purpose of quality assessment in your program or institution? Is it to determine a program's relative quality in relation to others in the field? To satisfy calls for external accountability? To learn more about the impact of a program on students' learning experiences and outcomes to facilitate ongoing program improvement?
- How are assessment results used? To compare and rank-order programs to determine, in part, resource allocation and program reduction priorities? To meet external mandates (with results having little to no bearing on program improvement)? To inform and guide ongoing efforts to strengthen the learning experiences and outcomes of students?
- What criteria or standards are used to evaluate program quality?
- Who participates in quality assessment efforts? Is there broad participation among diverse stakeholders or does this responsibility rest primarily with a small group of faculty and administrators?
- How frequently is the quality of the program evaluated? Continuously? Every year? Every five years? Every ten years?

We raise these questions both to prompt reflection and to make a broader point. In surveying the higher education literature as well as numerous program review protocols, we have found that there is relatively little variation in how faculty, administrators, and policy-makers evaluate the quality of academic programs.[1] More often than not, such evaluations occur as part of a formal program review process in which a small group of faculty and administrators conduct a program audit, collecting data on a set of pre-established quantifiable "quality indicators" and, in some cases, inviting colleagues from other institutions to review the program. Faculty and administrators then compare their findings to other programs of like size and stature, thus providing a comparative perspective on the program's overall quality. In some cases, these results are used, in part, by institutional administrators and state-level policymakers for resource allocation or program reduction purposes. In the majority of cases, these efforts rarely culminate in reports that have a significant bearing do future program planning or improvement efforts.

While traditional approaches to quality assessment have their merits, they also raise a host of concerns. In particular, we believe they suffer from three major limitations:

First, traditional approaches tend to rely heavily on program comparisons to assess program quality. This practice often leads faculty and administrators to concentrate more on where their program stands in relation to others and less on examining how its inner workings enhance or diminish the quality of students' learning experiences and achievement (Schilling and Schilling, 1993, 171). As faculty busily compare themselves on various proxies of quality—such as faculty research productivity and educational resources—they frequently lose sight of what those proxies were originally intended to represent. The objective no longer becomes to study and understand how various features internal to their program—such as curricular practices and instructional approaches—strengthen student learning and development but, rather, to compete with others to ensure a high "quality ranking." From our perspective, a new approach to quality assessment is needed that redirects faculty and administrators' attention away from their competitors and more on the needs of their own students. Only then will significant improvements be made in academic programs that enrich the quality of students' learning experiences in ways that promote their growth and development.

Second, current quality assessment approaches are informed by a set of widely-shared evaluative criteria and standards—often referred to in the literature as "attributes of quality"—that are presumed to enrich student learning. Yet, as we discussed in Chapter 1, there is very little research that documents causal connections between traditional indicators of quality and their actual effects on students' learning experiences and student outcomes. If student learning and development is the touchstone of a high-quality program, then a new approach to quality assessment is needed—one that advances a new set of evaluative criteria and standards that systematically relate program attributes, learning experiences, and student outcomes.

Third, the infrequency with which faculty and administrators conduct quality assessments tends to undermine efforts aimed at meaningful program improvement. The reasons for this are twofold. To begin with, when quality assessment occurs on a five- or ten-year cycle, it often leads to one-shot data collection efforts that leave faculty and administrators functioning for years at a time with little knowledge of what is and is not working in their programs. Moreover, episodic assessment tends to generate an evaluative climate that is more summative and judgmental than formative and instructive, making faculty less likely to welcome, let alone utilize, assessment results for program improvement. We concur with several scholars in the assessment movement who believe that if quality assessment is to make a difference in academic programs, then it must be formative in character (AAHE 1992; Hutchings 1990; Schilling and Schilling 1993). Formative evaluation promotes the understanding that quality is not a static object to be achieved, but rather a dynamic process requiring constant attention, cultivation, and investment. From our vantage point, such an approach to evaluating program quality is all too rare in higher education today.

The intent of our critique is not to throw traditional approaches to quality assessment out with the proverbial bathwater. For these approaches have their merits, the most important (and, in light of our critique, paradoxical) of which is a fundamental insistence on self-study Nonetheless, we remain fundamentally concerned about the invisibility of the learner and the learning process in most quality assessment efforts today.

Karl Schilling and Karen Maitland Schilling have stated that in order "to change or improve an invisible system, one must first make it visible" (1993, 172). We could not agree more. In our view, a new approach to quality assessment is needed that will shed light on how various learning experiences within programs intersect with and improve the daily lives of students. Faculty, administrators, and other stakeholders need to be challenged to peer inside their own programs to discover how learning environments, instructional practices, and curricular requirements enrich or diminish students' learning and development. In short, we believe that a learning-centered approach to evaluating program quality is necessary—one that will harness the collective intelligence and commitment of faculty, administrators, students, and other participants to invest in a continuous process aimed at improving the quality of students' learning.

A Framework for Assessing and Improving Academic Program Quality

In light of the need for a learning-centered approach to quality assessment, we have developed a framework for assessing and improving the quality of academic programs.[2] Conceptually, this framework places continuous learning among program participants squarely at the center of the program improvement effort and underscores the integral roles that planning and evaluation play in this process. In so doing, it encourages faculty, administrators and other program participants to make their "working space a learning space" (Senge et al. 1994, 35) through an ongoing and dynamic process of study, feedback, modification, and improvement.

In broad strokes, our framework is comprised of a set of guiding principles, questions to inform assessment and improvement, and quality assessment criteria and indicators. We will describe each of these features in detail next, with an eye toward their applicability in program improvement efforts.

But before elaborating on the framework, we introduce three caveats. First, this framework is heavily informed by our engagement theory of program quality. As such, for individuals who disagree with either our definition of a high-quality program or the theory itself, our framework may be of limited value. Second, while our framework promotes a range of strategies for assessing and improving program *quality,* it is not intended to serve as a comprehensive approach to program review. Quality assessment is only one, albeit important, component of program review; our framework does not address its other common components, such as program productivity, student need/demand, or cost. Third, since planning and assessment activities are most effective when they are tailored to the local context in which they occur, we do not view the framework as an authoritative "recipe" for planning and evaluating academic program quality. We believe that readers will be best served if they use the framework as a "thinking device" to promote ongoing dialogues about the quality of undergraduate and graduate programs within their own settings.

Guiding Principles

The framework is grounded in a set of four guiding principles that we believe are fundamental to effective quality assessment. In effect, these principles comprise a statement of "best practices" for evaluating and improving the quality of academic programs. We identified and developed these principles on the basis of what we learned from the nearly 800 interviewees in our study, as well as from a critical reading of the total quality management, organizational learning, and higher education assessment literatures. The four principles are:

- The Linking Pin: A Constant Commitment to Student Learning
- People Make Quality Happen: Inclusivity and Engagement
- Learning Never Ends: Continuous Program Improvement
- Thinking Multidimensionally: Multiple Methods of Assessment

The Linking Pin: A Constant Commitment to Student Learning

At its most fundamental level, improving the quality of academic programs requires faculty and administrators to give thoughtful consideration to their collective core purposes and values and how these, in turn, are reflected in the overall direction and daily practices of their programs. This is not an easy task: it challenges faculty and administrators to examine their beliefs about what their assumptions are, whom they should serve, and what they hope to accomplish in their programs.

Reflecting on the higher education assessment and total quality management literatures as well as findings from our study, we concur with many others that perhaps no "core purpose" is more fundamental to improving the quality of academic programs than a constant commitment to student learning and development (Association of American Colleges 1992; Bergquist and Armstrong 1986; Bowen 1977; Bruffee 1993; Chickering and Gamson 1987; Guskin 1994; Kuh, Schuh, and Whitt 1991; Sanford 1968; Southern Association of Colleges and Schools 1982, Study Group on the Conditions of Excellence in American Higher Education 1984). As a beginning point, such a commitment ensures that students—and their learning experiences, needs, and outcomes—receive appropriate attention, study, and appraisal in ongoing program development.

When faculty and administrators are committed to student learning and development, they take two tasks seriously. First, they know that learning—and attending to and enhancing students' learning, in particular—is fundamental to what they do and who they are as educators. This overriding clarity of purpose provides faculty and administrators with a linking pin that incorporates the learner and the learning process fully into program planning and evaluation efforts. Second, a clear and consistent commitment to students' learning keeps faculty and administrators attuned to the needs and expectations of those whom they directly serve: students and employers. This attention to the "beneficiaries" of higher education (Chaffee, 1992) encourages faculty and administrators not only to ask these stakeholders what they expect students to learn in their programs, but also to assess if the program is effectively meeting these expectations.

From our perspective, a constant commitment to student learning and development is essential to improving the quality of our nation's undergraduate and graduate programs. In contrast to traditional approaches to quality assessment, this guiding principle makes students and their learning the focal point of program evaluation and improvement efforts. In so doing, it ensures that faculty and administrators give full attention to the quality of students' learning in their programs while also recognizing the needs of those whom they serve.

People Make Quality Happen: Inclusivity and Engagement

The total quality management and higher education assessment movements have reminded many of us in higher education that, like it or not, enhancing the quality of a program, good, or service is fundamentally a human activity (AAHE 1992; Chaffee 1992; Mentkowski 1991; Seymour 1992; Sherr and Teeter 1991). It takes human beings to recognize weaknesses in the quality of a learning system, to consider alternatives for its improvement, and to act on proposals for change. In a very real sense, people—not simply curricular requirements or educational resources as many now believe—make quality happen.

With this in mind, and supported by findings from our engagement theory, we understand that meaningful quality assessment demands the collective intelligence and commitment of all parties who have a stake in academic programs. Faculty and administrators need to talk to one another about the salience and impact of various learning experiences in their programs, while also recognizing and including others—especially students, alumni, and employers—in these conversations. The "outsider" perspectives contributed by these latter stakeholders, in particular, often shed considerable light on issues related to program quality (Conrad, Haworth, and Millar 1993; Kuh, Schuh, and Whitt 1991).

Faculty and administrators who take this guiding principle to heart make it a priority to listen to and dialogue with students, alumni, and employers. They establish participatory governance structures (such as alumni councils, employer advisory boards, and open forums with students) and make use of interactive evaluation mechanisms (such as focus group interviews, exit interviews, student advising sessions, and classroom research) to inquire into and listen carefully to stakeholders' appraisals of their programs. More specifically, faculty and administrators use these "feedback loops" to ask students and alumni about their learning experiences—including why they find some more enriching than others, how they promote or hinder their growth and development, and how they would modify or improve these learning experiences in the future. From employers they seek to learn what employers expect of their graduates and if program alumni, in fact, meet these expectations. In both instances, faculty take Ellen Earle Chaffee's advice about listening seriously: "Listen to the people you serve," she writes, for "they are why you care about quality and they will tell you what to do" (1992, 104).

Engaging diverse stakeholders in quality assessment and improvement efforts is important for two primary reasons. First, generating a diversity of perspectives challenges faculty and administrators to question their own assumptions and to delve into the inner workings of their programs in new and creative ways. These forms of creative inquiry almost always provide meaningful fodder for continuous program improvement. Second, when students, alumni, and employers are regularly invited to comment on their program experiences and to suggest improvements, their collective sense of ownership in the program rises dramatically. They begin to understand that they have a voice in the program and that their ideas really matter. They also develop a greater appreciation that faculty and administrators are not the only parties responsible for ensuring program quality, and they assume that mantle more willingly. The idea here is simple: inclusivity fuels stakeholder engagement which, in turn, secures their future investment in the program. For these reasons, the importance of this guiding principle should not be overlooked in program planning and evaluation efforts. Particularly since it is people who, first and foremost, "make quality happen," this principle is especially crucial for ensuring stakeholder investment in the continuing improvement of academic programs.

Learning Never Ends: Continuous Program Improvement

In the Chinese language, "learning" literally means to "study and practice constantly" (Senge 1990, xv). As self-proclaimed "learners" who work in "learning organizations," it is tempting to assume that faculty and administrators devote sustained attention and effort to studying how their programs affect students' learning. To be sure, the literature contains support for this assumption (see, for example, Banta, 1993; Light 1990, 1992; Wright 1990). On balance, however, we concur with Ted Marchese that faculty and administrators in the majority of our nation's colleges and universities lack a "collective sense of obligation toward or avidness about the improvement of student learning" (1993, 12). For too many, self-study has become a relatively meaningless, episodic process targeted primarily at satisfying external mandates rather than a useful, continuous one aimed at understanding and improving the quality of student learning. To be sure, our colleges and universities are chock full of learners. But how many of them are interested, let alone engaged, in studying and learning about themselves?

Like many others, we believe that meaningful quality assessment requires faculty and administrators to make their "working space a learning space" in which they constantly examine and seek to learn about the inner workings of their own programs (AAHE 1992; Chaffee 1992; Ewell 1991; Marchese 1993; Seymour 1992; Sherr and Teeter 1991). More specifically, faculty and administrators need to turn a watchful and discerning eye to how various "processes" within their programs affect the quality of students' learning experiences and learning outcomes. What instructional and curricular practices, for example, do students and alumni find most useful and challenging? Useless and boring? What learning experiences do stakeholders cite (and other forms of evidence confirm) as "adding the most value" in terms of student learning outcomes? How does the learning environment—and, in particular, students' engagement with one another and faculty—enhance or hinder students' learning? Where does the "real learning" take place for students in the program? Ongoing learning of this sort—not least when informed by and interpreted within the context of our engagement theory—is critical if faculty and administrators are to obtain the types of usable information that can lead to meaningful educational change.

Continuous learning and improvement is an important feature of any quality assessment process for two reasons. First, since it requires faculty and administrators to turn a mirror on what they actually do in their programs and to collect data on how these practices affect the quality of students' learning, it provides a crucial evidentiary foundation upon which to base proposals for quality improvement. Again, we invoke the wise counsel of Karl and Karen Maitland Schilling: faculty and administrators cannot improve the quality of a system until they make that system visible. How can quality be improved if we have no idea what needs improving? How can we provide enriching learning experiences for students that positively affect their growth and development if we have little to no knowledge of what we are doing and how it is affecting students? Continuous program improvement—because it is formative in nature and provides useful data on educational practices within the "black box" of academic programs—helps us to see how we look from the inside out, often providing us with strong incentives to improve our appearance. When practiced with the openness and flexibility required of any meaningful learning effort, it promises to reveal program strengths and limitations and to spark informed suggestions targeted at improving the quality of teaching and learning.

Second, continuous program improvement helps to develop in faculty and administrators a new understanding that quality in academic programs—and, in particular, those learning experiences within them that enhance students' growth and development—demands constant attention and investment. Importing more resources or new curricular requirements into a program is no longer a ticket to improving academic quality. Faculty and administrators must now become learners as well as teachers. Without their engagement in studying, understanding, and improving student learning, the overall quality of academic programs—and students' experiences in them—will suffer greatly. Once again, it is people that matter—people make quality happen.

There is wisdom in the old adage, "learning never ends." The principle of continuous program improvement reflects that wisdom. From our perspective, as well as that of many others (AAHE 1992; Chaffee 1992; Ewell 1991; Marchese 1993; Seymour 1992; Sherr and Teeter 1991), it is an important guiding principle that faculty, administrators, and others should heed in assessing and planning academic programs.

Thinking Multidimensionally: Multiple Methods of Assessment

In his novel, *Slaughterhouse Five,* Kurt Vonnegut (1969) paints a vivid image of Billy Pilgrim, the story's main character, lying on a train capturing his only view of the Rocky Mountains through a pipe. He uses the scene in the novel as an analogy to describe how human beings think about time in unidimensional terms; we use it here to caution readers about the hazards of assessing program quality from only one vantage point. As our engagement theory suggests, program quality is a complex phenomenon. To engage and understand that complexity, a broader view is necessary—one that requires faculty and administrators to think about quality in multidimensional terms by surveying the landscape of their programs from multiple points of reference.

Just as many scholars in the higher education assessment movement advocate the use of multiple methods in assessing student learning (Davis 1989; Mentkowski 1991; Prus and Johnson 1992; Sell 1989; Terenzini 1989; Thomas 1991), we strongly believe that faculty and administrators must use multiple methods to assess the quality of academic programs. By drawing upon different data sources through various data collection methods, this guiding principle helps ensure that a more accurate and holistic understanding of program quality will be achieved.

When faculty and administrators take this guiding principle seriously, they dismiss the myth that there is "one true method" for assessing program quality and incorporate a variety of assessment strategies into their programs. These include, among others, course—embedded assessment methods—such as student portfolios (Forrest 1990) and various classroom assessment techniques (Angelo and Cross 1993)—as well as alumni and employer surveys, focus groups with diverse stakeholders, exit interviews with graduating students, and document review.[3]

This guiding principle is important for two reasons. To begin with, when a combination of methods are used, faculty and administrators are far more likely to develop a more holistic understanding of the quality of their programs. For example, qualitative methods—such as portfolios, focus groups, and classroom research—not only help faculty and others to find out what learning experiences really matter to students, but they also allow them to explore how and why those learning experiences make a difference in students' growth and development. Particularly when coupled with larger-scale quantitative surveys of students, alumni, and employers, the resulting mix of information from these methods can create a dynamic and multifaceted empirical foundation for understanding and, in turn, making improvements in a program's overall quality. Multiple methods have another advantage as well. Since they build on the strengths of different approaches, they help to cancel out the weaknesses embedded in a solitary approach to assessment. In short, quality assessments that employ multiple methods tend to produce more accurate and trustworthy (valid) findings.

Billy Pilgrim knew that there was much more to the Rocky Mountains than what he could see through a pipe. Similarly, there is much more to program quality than what any single assessment method can reveal. We urge faculty, administrators, and others to recognize the salience of this guiding principle in their continuing efforts to assess and improve the quality of their own and others' programs.

In summary, we advance four simple principles to guide any quality assessment effort: Stay focused on students and their learning. Involve and engage multiple stakeholders in quality assessment and improvement efforts. Constantly question how program "processes" hinder or promote student learning, and make every effort to improve them. Finally, use multiple methods to learn about and document quality. These principles suggest a process—or a set of "best practices"—for assessing and improving program quality. They are intended to help faculty and administrators understand how to assess and improve the quality of undergraduate and graduate programs. The question of what to assess still looms large. This is the question to which we now turn.

Informing Questions and Quality Standards

Effective program evaluation requires, at a minimum, two key components. First, it must be informed by a set of questions that will call attention to the pertinent issues under study. Second, it must clearly articulate stated standards or criteria against which the answers to those questions can be interpreted and judged. Without either component, the evaluation "will lack focus, and the evaluator will have considerable difficulty explaining what will be examined, how, and why" (Worthen and Sanders 1987, 210).

With this in mind, we propose a range of evaluative questions and quality standards to assist faculty, administrators, and others in assessing and improving the quality of their programs. Grounded in our engagement theory of program quality, these questions and standards provide faculty and administrators with a theoretical basis to guide their quality assessment efforts as well as a theoretical framework through which to interpret their findings. That is, faculty and administrators can use these questions to examine the quality of their program in light of the theory's seventeen attributes and then, on the basis of the evidence collected, they can draw upon these standards to evaluate program strengths and limitations. From our perspective, this is a significant improvement over traditional quality assessment approaches in which faculty and administrators have tended to collect and interpret data on any number of evaluative questions and standards that lacked a firm basis in a theory of quality.

Table 38-1, at the end of this chapter, is a template that consists of guiding questions, quality criteria, and methods of assessment that faculty, administrators, and others may find useful in assessing the quality of their own programs. We are aware that by dividing the template into seventeen components—one for each attribute in the theory—readers could form the impression that program quality can be understood in terms of discrete parts. Such an impression would be a false one, as our engagement theory suggests.

As with any template, we caution readers to use their judgment and to adapt this template to the particularities of their own settings. Not all of the questions we raise can or should be addressed, nor is it feasible to use all of the assessment methods we propose. We believe that the template will be most useful to faculty and administrators if they meet with key stakeholders in their programs to prioritize questions of interest, to develop additional questions as warranted, and to select assessment methods that are most appropriate for collecting data on the questions they seek to answer.

This template specially when combined with the aforementioned four principles of quality assessment—helps to translate our engagement theory into a useful framework for understanding, assessing, and improving program quality. We invite faculty, administrators, and others who have program planning and evaluation responsibilities to consider the framework as they continuously seek to improve and better understand the quality of their own undergraduate and graduate programs.

Benefits of the Framework

What are the potential benefits of using this framework? In our view, the framework promises to benefit faculty and administrators in at least four ways as they seek to develop and sustain high-quality academic programs.

First, the framework—with its clear and consistent focus on student learning and development—provides faculty, administrators, and others with a guide for improving teaching and learning in academic programs. Unlike previous approaches to quality assessment, the framework draws attention to—and offers a template for discovering and understanding—how various instructional, curricular, and cultural practices affect the quality of students' learning. It not only supplies faculty and administrators with a new focal point for understanding program quality, but it also provides them with a guide for making visible those processes within the "black box" of academic programs that promote and enrich student learning. With this information in hand, faculty and administrators can engage in meaningful planning and improvement efforts aimed at enhancing the overall quality of teaching and learning in their programs.

Second, and closely related, the framework proposes a number of principles, guiding questions, criteria, and assessment methods that place continuous quality improvement squarely at the center of the quality assessment process. It challenges faculty, administrators, and others to engage in the kinds of organizational learning that can nurture and promote a culture in which teaching and learning—and its constant improvement—is highly valued (Chaffee 1992). Program participants begin to talk to one another about teaching and learning, to ask questions about student learning in the program, and to voice creative suggestions for change. In a very real sense, ongoing assessment and improvement becomes an important part of organizational life in these programs—a development, no doubt, that can be of obvious value to faculty and administrators in sustaining the quality of academic programs.

Third, the framework has the potential to provide faculty, administrators, and others with useful data on which to base program planning and improvement decisions. In contrast to traditional approaches to quality assessment, this framework makes use of a wider range of data sources and data collection methods by which to compile evidence of program quality. Moreover, it recommends that faculty and others collect evidence in reference to criteria that are directly linked to a theory of quality. On both of these accounts, the framework offers those who have program planning and evaluation responsibilities with a template for collecting relevant and trustworthy evidence that can better inform decisions related to ongoing program improvement.

The framework has potentially salutary consequences for planning and improving the quality of academic programs in one final way: it is likely to enhance stakeholder ownership and investment in ensuring the quality of academic programs. When students, alumni, employers, and other stakeholders are regularly asked to participate in planning, assessment, and improvement efforts, they begin to feel like their ideas and efforts matter in the program. They begin to take more responsibility for sustaining the quality of the program: alumni offer to sponsor interns or to share their perspectives with students in class; students are more likely to initiate out-of-class conversations with their peers and faculty or to put extra effort into their studies; employers take an active interest in mentoring students or working with faculty on collaborative projects. Put simply, an ethic of mutual accountability develops where, in the words of Robert Galvin, Motorola's chairman of the board, quality becomes "very first person" (Seymour 1992, 14). From student to employer and everyone in between, ensuring the future quality of the program becomes a shared responsibility in which everyone has a vital stake.

To be sure, the framework we propose is a demanding one. It requires all stakeholders to devote time and energy to quality assessment and improvement. That said, we believe the benefits that can accrue to students, faculty, and other stakeholders more than justifies these demands. Students (and employers, indirectly) stand to benefit from continuing efforts to develop and sustain high-quality programs. Faculty can gain from this process as well: not only are they likely to develop new and richer insights that will revitalize them as teachers and learners, but they will also experience the satisfaction of engaging in teaching, learning, and assessment activities that make a difference in their own and others' lives.

Notes

1. A notable exception to this general trend is found in a recent document published by the Association of American Colleges entitled, Program Review and Educational Quality in the Major (1992). Its authors argue that program review should take as its primary focus "the quality of learning and achievement in the major" (1992, vi). In turn, they offer a protocol for assessing program quality in the major with this particular focus in mind.
2. Our framework for developing and sustaining high-quality academic programs is informed both by what we learned in our study of program quality and by recent developments in the assessment movement. Yet, while our work emphasizes the underlying value of improving students' learning—as others do in the assessment movement (AAHE 1992; Hutchings 1990; Light 1990, 1992; Schilling and Schilling 1993)—it has a distinctive focus on the evaluation of academic program quality, rather than on the assessment of individual learners.
3. A number of resources are available on various methods of assessment and evaluation. For a general overview, see Banta (1993), Prus and Johnson (1992), Worthen and Sanders (1987). Regarding faculty and student portfolios see, for instance, Centra (1993), Seldin (1993), Courts and McInerney (1993), Forrest (1990), and Knight and Gallaro (1994). For information on individual and focus group interviews, see Guba and Lincoln (1981), Krueger (1994), Morgan (1988), Patton (1987), and Seidman (1991). Also see Angelo and Cross (1993) for information on classroom assessment techniques.

References

American Association for Higher Education, *Principles of Good Practice for Assessing Student Learning.* Washington, D.C.: 1992.

Angelo, Thomas A., and K. Patricia Cross. *Classroom Assessment Techniques: A Handbook for College Teachers* (Second Edition). San Francisco: Jossey-Bass, 1993.

Association of American Colleges. *Program Review and Educational Quality in the Major.* Project on Liberal Learning, Study-in-Depth, and the Arts and Sciences Major, Washington, D.C.: 1992.

Banta, Trudy and Associates. *Making a Difference: Outcomes of a Decade of Assessment in Higher Education.* San Francisco: Jossey-Bass, 1993.

Bergquist, William H., and Jack L. Armstrong. *Planning Effectively for Educational Quality.* San Francisco: Jossey-Bass, 1986.

Bowen, Howard R. *Investment in Learning.* San Francisco: Jossey-Bass, 1977.

Bruffee, Kenneth A. *Collaborative Learning.* Baltimore: Johns Hopkins University Press, 1993.

Centra, John. *Reflective Faculty Evaluation: Enhancing Teaching and Determining Faculty Effectiveness.* San Francisco: Jossey-Bass, 1993.

Chaffee, Ellen Earle, and Lawrence A. Sherr. *Quality: Transforming Postsecondary Education* (ASHE-ERIC Higher Education Report no. 3). Washington, D.C.: The George Washington University, School of Education and Human Development, 1992.

Chickering, Arthur W., and Zelda F. Gamson. "Seven Principles for Good Practice in Undergraduate Education." *AAHE Bulletin* 39 (March, 1987): 3–7.

Conrad, Clifton F., Haworth, Jennifer Grant, and Susan Bolyard Millar. *A Silent Success: Master's Education in the United States.* Baltimore: Johns Hopkins University Press, 1993.

Courts, Patrick L., and Kathleen H. McInerney. *Assessment in Higher Education: Politics, Pedagogy, and Portfolios.* Westport, Conn: Praeger, 1993.

Davis, Barbara Gross. "Demystifying Assessment: Learning from the Field of Evaluation." In *Achieving Assessment Goals Using Evaluation Techniques* (New Directions for Higher Education no. 67), edited by Peter J. Gray. San Francisco: Jossey-Bass, 1989.

Ewell, Peter T. "Assessment and TQM: In Search of Convergence." In *Total Quality Management in Higher Education* (New Directions for Institutional Research no. 71), edited by Lawrence A. Sherr and Deboarah J. Teeter. San Francisco: Jossey-Bass, 1991.

Forrest, Aubrey. *Time Will Tell: Portfolio-Assisted Assessment of General Education.* Washington, D.C.: American Association for Higher Education/The AAHE Assessment Forum, 1990.

Guba, Egon G., and Yvonna S. Lincoln. *Effective Evaluation.* San Francisco: Jossey-Bass, 1981.

Guskin, Alan. "Reducing Student Costs and Enhancing Student Learning: The University Challenge of the 1990s. *Change* 25 (July/August 1994): 23–20.

Hutchings, Pat. "Assessment and the Way We Work." In *Assessment 1990: Understanding the Implications by the American Association for Higher Education Assessment Forum.* Washington, D.C.: American Association for Higher Education, 1990.

Knight, Michael E., and Denise Gallaro, eds. *Portfolio Assessment: Application of Portfolio Analysis.* Lanham, MD: University Press of America, 1994.

Krueger, Richard A. *Focus Groups: A Practical Guide for Applied Research* (Second Edition). Thousand Oaks, Calif.: Sage Publications, 1994.

Kuh, George, Schuh, John H., and Elizabeth J. Whitt. *Involving Colleges: Successful Approaches to Fostering Student Learning and Development Outside the Classroom.* San Francisco: Jossey-Bass, 1991.

Light, Richard J. *The Harvard Assessment Seminars: First Report.* Cambridge, Mass: Harvard University Graduate School of Education and Kennedy School of Government, 1990.

Light, Richard J. *The Harvard Assessment Seminars: Second Report.* Cambridge, Mass: Harvard University Graduate School of Education and Kennedy School of Government, 1992.

Marchese, Ted. "TQM: A Time for Ideas." *Change* 25 (May/June 1993): 10–13.

Mentkowski, Marcia. "Creating a Context Where Institutional Assessment Yields Educational Improvement." *The Journal of General Education* 40 (1991): 255–283.

Morgan, David L. *Focus Groups as Qualitative Research.* Beverly Hills, Calif.: Sage Publications, 1988.

Patton, Michael. *How to Use Qualitative Methods in Evaluation.* Newbury Park, Calif.: Sage Publications, 1987.

Prus, Joseph, and Reid A. Johnson. *A Critical Review of Student Assessment Options.* Rock Hill, S.C.: Winthrop College, 1992.

Sanford, Nevitt. *Where Colleges Fail: A Study of the Student as a Person.* San Francisco: Jossey-Bass, 1968.

Schilling, Karl, and Karen Maitland Schilling. "Descriptive Approaches to Assessment: Moving Beyond Meeting Requirements to Making a Difference." In *A Collection of Papers on Self-Study and Institutional Improvement,* by The Commission on Institutions of Higher Education, North Central Association of Colleges and Schools (98th Annual Meeting). Chicago: 1993.

Seidman, I. E. *Interviewing as Qualitative Research: A Guide for Researchers in Education and the Social Sciences.* New York: Teachers College Press, 1991.

Seldin, Peter. *Successful Use of Teaching Portfolios.* Bolton, Mass.: Anker Publishing, 1993.

Sell, G. Roger. "An Organizational Perspective for the Effective Practice of Assessment." In *Achieving Assessment Goals Using Evaluation Techniques* (New Directions for Higher Education no. 67), edited by Peter J. Gray. San Francisco: Jossey-Bass, 1989.

Senge, Peter M. *The Fifth Discipline: The Art and Practice of the Learning Organization.* New York: Currency/Doubleday, 1990.

Senge, Peter M., Roberts, Charlotte, Ross, Richard B., Smith, Bryan J., and Art Kleiner. *The Fifth Discipline Fieldbook: Strategies and Tools for Building a Learning Organization.* New York: Currency/Doubleday, 1994.

Seymour, Daniel T. *On Q: Causing Quality in Higher Education.* New York: American Council on Education and Macmillan Publishing Company, 1992.

Sherr, Lawrence A., and Deborah J. Teeter. *Total Quality Management in Higher Education* (New Directions for Institutional Research, no. 71). San Francisco: Jossey-Bass, 1991.

Southern Association of Colleges and Schools. *Criteria for Accreditation* (Proposed). Atlanta: Commission on Colleges, Southern Association of Colleges and Schools, 1982.

Study Group on the Conditions of Excellence in American Higher Education. *Involvement in Learning: Realizing the Potential of American Higher Education.* Washington, D.C.: National Institute of Education, 1984.

Terenzini, Patrick T. "Assessment with Open Eyes: Pitfalls in Studying Student Outcomes." *Journal of Higher Education* 60 (November/December, 1989): 644–644.

Thomas, Alice M. "Consideration of the Resources Needed in an Assessment Program." *NCA Quarterly* 66 (1991): 430–443.

Vonnegut, Kurt. *Slaughterhouse Five.* New York: Delacorte Press, 1969.

Worthen, Blaine R., and James R. Sanders. *Educational Evaluation: Alternative Approaches and Practical Guidelines.* New York: Longman, 1987.

Wright, Barbara. "So How Do We Know It Will Work: An Assessment Memoir." *AAHE Bulletin* (April 1990); 14–17.

TABLE 38-2
A Template for Assessing Program Quality

Questions to Guide Assessment	*Criteria and Indicators of Attribute*	*Suggested Methods of Assessment*
Attribute: Diverse and Engaged Faculty 1. How do faculty and administrators define a "good" faculty member? What personal and professional characteristics do they look for in new faculty members? 2. What criteria are reflected in the program's hiring policy for faculty? Which criteria are given the most emphasis in the faculty recruitment and selection process? 3. How diverse are faculty in terms of race, ethnicity, gender, and socioeconomic background? Are faculty diverse in terms of educational and professional workplace experience? 4. Are faculty involved in a range of scholarly activities? Do faculty share their scholarship with students? 5. Is there a good representation of different theoretical, applied, and methodological perspectives among program faculty? Do faculty members infuse these different perspectives into their teaching? If so, how? 6. What effect (if any) does faculty diversity have on students' growth and development? 7. How committed are faculty to students? Where, when, and how do they demonstrate their commitment? 8. How do students describe program faculty? Do they believe that faculty are personally interested in their learning? Disinterested? What effect does faculty engagement (or disengagement) have on students' growth and development?	1. Scholarly Diversity of Faculty • A variety of "ways-of-knowing" are represented among program faculty. • Differing modes of scholarship are represented among program faculty. • Faculty infuse a range of methodological, theoretical, and experiential perspectives into classroom lectures and discussions. 2. Faculty Engagement in Teaching • Faculty share a commitment to student learning and development. • Faculty invest in various teaching related activities. 3. Educational Background and Professional Experience of Faculty • Faculty possess appropriate graduate degrees. • Individuals with professional, nonuniversity workplace experience are represented among the program's faculty. 4. Departmental and Institutional Policies • Faculty hiring policies emphasize criteria such as educational background, research productivity, scholarly diversity, professional experience in the non-university workplace, teaching and advising competence, and dedication to student learning. • Departmental and institutional promotion, tenure, and merit review policies recognize and reward faculty for their participation in a range of scholarly endeavors as well as for their involvement in teaching-related activities.	• Faculty portfolio assessment • Peer evaluations of teaching • Student evaluations of teaching • Focus group interviews with faculty, administrators, students, alumni, and employers • Document review (for evidence of supportive hiring, merit, promotion, and tenure policies)

TABLE 38-2 *(continued)*

Questions to Guide Assessment	*Criteria and Indicators of Attribute*	*Suggested Methods of Assessment*
***Attribute: Diverse and Engaged Faculty* (continued)** 9. What kinds of instructional approaches do faculty members use in their classes? How frequently do faculty members revise the content of their courses to reflect new developments in their field? 10. Do department and institutional merit, promotion, and tenure policies recognize and reward faculty for their involvement in a broad range of scholarly activities? Are each of these activities comparably "weighted" in the departmental and institutional reward structure? 11. How important is teaching—and a demonstrated commitment to student learning and development—in merit, promotion, and tenure policies and practices?		
Attribute: Diverse and Engaged Students 1. How do faculty define a "good student"? What personal and professional characteristics do they look for in student applicants? 2. What criteria are reflected in the program's admissions policy? Which criteria are given the most emphasis by faculty in the student selection process? 3. How much emphasis is placed on matching student goals and interests with those of the program and faculty in the admissions selection process? Do faculty intentionally strive to ensure a "good fit" between students and faculty in this respect, admitting only those who will be well-served by the program?	1. Student Diversity • Students with a variety of educational, life, and professional workplace experiences are represented in the program. • Male and female students from a variety of racial, ethnic, and socioeconomic backgrounds are represented. 2. Engagement in Teaching and Learning • Students actively contribute diverse perspectives on knowledge and practice to class discussions.* • Students demonstrate a visible commitment to their own and others' learning (via their participation in classroom discussions, cooperative learning activities, individual and group projects, independent studies and research).	

4. How diverse are students in terms of race, ethnicity, gender, and socioeconomic background? Are a variety of educational, workplace, and life experiences represented in the student body? 5. How willing are students to share their life and workplace experiences with others in the program? Do faculty members encourage students to share their experiences and views in class? 6. In what ways (if any) do students' perspectives and views on knowledge and practice affect one anothers' learning and development? 7. Are students generally active or passive in their approach to learning? 8. How committed are students to their own and others' learning? Where, when, and how do they express their commitment? 9. How does students' commitment (or lack thereof) to one anothers' learning affect their learning and development?	3. Departmental Policies and Practices • Departmental student admissions policies emphasize a variety of criteria, including educational background, life experience, professional nonuniversity workplace experience, cultural diversity, academic achievement, and motivation for learning. • Admissions decisions are based heavily on the "goodness of fit" between student goals and those of faculty and the program.	• Focus group interviews with students, alumni, and faculty • Student portfolio assessment (for evidence of engagement in learning via individual and collaborative reports, projects, and other products of learning) • Document review (for evidence of supportive admissions policies)
Attribute: Engaged Leaders		
1. How do diverse stakeholders, especially faculty and students, describe the chair of the program? Hierarchical or participatory? Invitational or off-putting? An advocate? Adversary? Disinterested bystander? 2. How committed is the chair to "championing" the program? Where, when, and how does he or she demonstrate his or her commitment? 3. Does the program chair make leadership opportunities available to faculty, students, and others? If so, how does he or she support faculty and students for their involvement in these leadership roles? How are students affected by these leadership experiences?	1. Participatory Leadership • The program director or chair invites a broad range of stakeholders—such as students, alumni, faculty, and employers—to participate in the governance of the program. • The chair provides faculty, students, alumni, and others with opportunities to assume informal leadership roles in the program. • The chair is instrumental in developing a culture that values teaching and learning. 2. Administrative Effectiveness • The chair is effective at promoting the program and building support for it with internal and external audiences.	• Focus group interviews with faculty, institutional administrators, students, alumni, and employers • Faculty survey of administrative effectiveness

TABLE 38-2 *(continued)*

Questions to Guide Assessment	*Criteria and Indicators of Attribute*	*Suggested Methods of Assessment*
***Attribute: Engaged Leaders* (continued)**		
4. Does the program chair invite faculty, students, alumni, and employers to discuss and make decisions regarding program policies and practices? If so, in what ways does he or she do this? 5. What messages does the chair send to faculty and students, in particular, about the importance of teaching and learning in the program? 6. How effective is the chair at promoting the program and its mission to institutional administrators, prospective students, and other external audiences? How does the chair go about this task? 7. How effective is the chair at securing monetary and non-monetary support for the program from institutional administrators? External parties (such as alumni, employers, private foundations)? 8. How effective is the chair in recruiting faculty and students who share a commitment to their own and others' teaching and learning?	• The chair is adept at securing monetary and non-monetary support for the program. • The chair is effective at recruiting new faculty and students whose goals and interests are congruent with those of the program.	
Attribute: Shared Program Direction		
1. What is the overall direction or focus of the program? What do faculty and administrators intentionally hope to accomplish in the program? 2. How do different stakeholders —faculty, program administrators, institutional administrators, students, alumni, and employers— describe the program's overall direction? To what extent do they share similar understandings of the program's direction? 3. How was the program's overall direction determined? Who was involved? Was it a collective process?	1. Stakeholder Involvement in Program • Program leaders involve faculty, students, alumni, and employers in developing and sustaining a shared program direction. • Program leaders involve faculty, students, alumni, and employers in continuous program planning and evaluation efforts in which they examine the congruence between the program's teaching and learning experiences and its overall direction.	• Focus group interviews with faculty, administrators, students, recent program graduates, and employers • Document review of promotional materials, mission statement, student handbooks, course syllabi, and self-studies

4. When, where, how and to whom is the program's overall direction communicated? Is the content of what is communicated consistent with the overall direction of the program and actual practices within it?
5. How frequently are the overall direction and goals of the program reviewed? Who is involved in this process? Is student, alumni, and employer feedback solicited?
6. What kind of graduates are faculty and administrators in the program trying to develop? What kinds of curricular requirements and learning experiences does the program offer to ensure that graduates achieve this goal?
7. How does the program's overall direction inform the content and character of teaching and learning in the program? More specifically, how does it inform what knowledge, skills, and practices are taught to students and in what ways? Are curricular requirements and learning experiences congruent with the program's overall direction?
8. How does a shared program direction (or lack of one) promote or hinder student's learning and development?

2. Shared Support for Program Direction
   - Diverse stakeholders share broadly similar understandings of the program's overall direction and are supportive of it.
3. Fitness-to-Purpose
   - Teaching and learning experiences in the program are congruent with its stated direction.

Attribute: Community of Learners

1. How do faculty define their roles as teachers? Students' roles as learners? What words do they use to describe their relationships with students?
2. How do students define their roles as learners? Faculty members' roles as teachers? What words do they use to describe their relationships with faculty?
3. How do students view one another? As competitive rivals? Disinterested bystanders? Knowledgeable peers? Colleagues? To what extent do students believe that they learn from one another?

1. Collegial Relations among ProgramParticipants
   - Program participants de-emphasize traditional hierarchical relationships (between faculty and students, senior and junior faculty, administrators and staff) and interact with one another more or less as colleagues.
   - Faculty and students regularly collaborate between and among themselves on various research, teaching, and service-related projects.

- Focus groups with students, alumni, faculty, and administrators
- Exit interviews with graduating students
- Student and alumni surveys
- Document review (for evidence of an emphasis on collaborative learning in promotional materials, mission statement, syllabii)

TABLE 38-2 *(continued)*

Questions to Guide Assessment	*Criteria and Indicators of Attribute*	*Suggested Methods of Assessment*
***Attribute: Community of Learners* (continued)**		
4. To what extent do faculty collaborate with one another in their teaching or research? To what extent do they collaborate with students in these areas? 5. To what extent do students feel a camaraderie with one another? To what extent do faculty feel a camaraderie with one another? 6. What words do faculty, students, and administrators use to describe the general "feel" or "ethos" of the program? 7. Which is more pronounced in the program's learning environment: competition or collaboration? What effect does this dominant theme—and the way it is enacted in the program—have on student learning? 8. What is the general tenor of interactions among faculty in the program? Collegial? Indifferent? Antagonistic? Among students? 9. What opportunities exist in the program for students to engage in cooperative or team-based learning? Do faculty encourage cooperative learning? If yes, how? In what ways do these group-centered, interactive learning experiences affect students' growth and development?	2. Sense of Shared Identity and Membership • Program participants share a common identity with the program that generates a positive camaraderie among all. • Program participants feel like—and treat one another as—contributing members in a learning community. 3. Cooperative, Interactive Learning Environment • An ethic of cooperation and interaction, rather than competition and isolation, characterizes the program's learning environment. • The program has structured curricular requirements (such as required field school, laboratory, or core course work requirements) and various teaching and learning activities (such as collaborative research projects, journal clubs, and assorted out-of-class social events) that promote cooperative and interactive learning among program participants.	
Attribute: Risk-Taking Environment		
1. What messages do faculty and administrators send to students about the expectations they hold for their learning? How do students interpret these messages? In what ways, if any, do faculty and administrators develop a learning environment in which students feel "safe to fail"?	1. High Expectations for Student Learning and Development • Faculty and administrators hold high expectations for learning and articulate them clearly to students. 2. Faculty Support for Risk-Taking • Faculty model risk-taking to students and encourage them to follow their lead.	• Focus groups with students, alumni, faculty, and administrators • Exit interviews with graduating students • Student and alumni surveys • Student portfolio assessment (for examples of creative and "risky" projects, papers, and so forth)

2. To what extent do faculty encourage students to take risks in their own learning? How frequently do they provide them with opportunities to do so? 3. Do faculty describe themselves as risk-takers? What kinds of risks do they take? Do they freely and willingly share their failures as well as their successes with students? Are they willing to take risks with new instructional approaches in their classes? 4. What words do students use to describe the learning climate in the program? Do they believe it is an invitational or an intimidating place to learn? Do students feel challenged and supported to do their best? 5. What words do faculty, students, and administrators use to describe the programs learning environment? 6. Do students believe it is "safe" for them to question assumptions, engage in "risky" projects, and take other kinds of risks in the program? Do they fear penalty or reprisal from faculty? 7. To what extent do students take risks in their learning? What effect does risk-taking (or lack thereof) have on students' growth and development? 8. What is more pronounced in the program's learning environment: conformity or creativity? What effect does this dominant theme—and the way it is enacted in the program—have on student learning?	• Faculty provide students with frequent opportunities to take risks in their own learning without penalty. 3. Open and Hospitable Learning Climate • The program has an open, hospitable, and "safe" learning environment in which students feel supported to take risks in their own learning.	
Attribute: Critical Dialogue		
1. How do faculty describe themselves as teachers? What words do they use to describe their overall approach to teaching and learning? Do students offer similar descriptions?	1. Interactive Approach to Teaching and Learning • Faculty utilize a two-way, interactive approach to teaching and learning that emphasizes ongoing dialogue and reflection with students.	• Focus groups with students, alumni, faculty, and administrators • Classroom research • Exit interviews with graduating students • Student, alumni and employer surveys • Peer evaluations of teaching

TABLE 38-2 *(continued)*

Questions to Guide Assessment	*Criteria and Indicators of Attribute*	*Suggested Methods of Assessment*
***Attribute: Critical Dialogue* (continued)**		
2. What kinds of instructional activities (e.g., lectures, discussions, role plays, simulations, student-led seminars, Socratic dialogues) do faculty use most frequently in their classes? Least frequently? 3. What is the character and frequency of faculty-student interaction in class? What metaphors do faculty and students use to describe these interactions? 4. What kinds of opportunities are provided to students to share their ideas, views, and experiences with faculty? How frequently are these opportunities offered? 5. Are faculty respectful of students' views and opinions? How do they evaluate the contributions that students make to class discussions? 6. In what ways do faculty challenge students to examine assumptions, scrutinize theory and practice, and critically evaluate their own and others' ideas? What skills do students hone through discussions such as these? 7. Which is more pronounced in the program: active or passive student learning? 8. How do students describe their involvement in class? Do they believe faculty challenge them to "think aloud" in new and demanding ways?∏ What effect does active engagement in dialogues of this sort have on students' analytical and problem-solving skills? Professional confidence?	• Faculty use a variety of interactive instructional activities, including small and large group discussions, role-playing exercises, and student-led seminars. 2. Critical Inquiry • Faculty and students engage in disciplined and mutually-enriching discussions in which they critically question and scrutinize knowledge and practice in the field. • Students are actively engaged in the learning process, questioning their own and others' assumptions, discussing alternative points of view, and generating critically-informed understandings of knowledge and practice.	• Student evaluations of teaching • Student portfolio assessment (for examples of creative and "risky" projects, papers, and so forth) • Faculty portfolio assessment (examination of syllabi and statement of philosophy of teaching to assess, in part, commitment to and use of critical dialogue in classroom teaching)

Attribute: Integrative Learning

1. How do faculty describe themselves as teachers? What words do they use to describe their overall approach to teaching and learning? Do students offer similar descriptions?
2. What kinds of instructional activities (e.g., lectures, discussions, role plays, simulations, case studies, field research) do faculty use most frequently in the program? Least frequently?
3. How does the program, in terms of curricular content, connect with the lives of students? Important problems in the "real world"?
4. To what extent do faculty model "connected" understandings of theory and practice to students?
5. How frequently do faculty members invite professionals from the non-university workplace to "bridge the gap" between what students are learning in the program with "real world" issues, problems, and concerns of the profession?
6. What kinds of opportunities are provided to students to connect what they are learning in their classes to complex problems, issues, and situations in the real world? How frequently are these opportunities offered? In what ways do learning opportunities of this sort enhance students' growth and development?
7. How do students describe the knowledge and skills they are taught in the program? Theoretical? Applied? A judicious blend of both? Overly-academic? Too practical?
8. In what ways do faculty challenge students to blend theory with practice in the program? What skills do students hone through activities such as these?

1. Integrative Instruction
   - Faculty tie the knowledge and skills they present in their lectures or class discussions to tangible issues and "real world" problems.
   - Faculty use hands-on instructional activities—such as role-plays, case studies, simulations, field trips, artistic performances, field research, and laboratory experiments—that involve students directly in making connections between theory and practice.

- Focus groups with students, alumni, faculty, and administrators
- Classroom research
- Exit interviews with graduating students
- Student, alumni, and employer surveys
- Performance assessment
- Student portfolio assessment (for examples of integrative practice in course papers, projects, and other assignments)
- Peer evaluations of teaching
- Student evaluations of teaching

TABLE 38-2 *(continued)*

Questions to Guide Assessment	*Criteria and Indicators of Attribute*	*Suggested Methods of Assessment*
Attribute: Mentoring		
1. Do faculty actively seek to learn about students as individuals? Do they express an interest in learning about students' career interests and goals? 2. How seriously do faculty take their advising responsibilities? How do they advise students? 3. How frequently do faculty meet with advisees to discuss their academic progress and performance in the program? Who initiates these meetings? 4. Are advising responsibilities equally shared among faculty in the department? 5. Are faculty generally on campus and available to meet with students outside of class? 6. What kinds of opportunities are provided to students for individualized study with faculty? To what extent are faculty willing to offer individualized learning opportunities to students? How frequently do students take advantage of such opportunities? In what ways do learning opportunities of this sort enhance students' growth and development? 7. Do faculty members view mentoring as an important professional responsibility? If so, who do they mentor and how? 8. Do students believe that faculty mentors are available in the program? Do they feel like they have been mentored in any way by faculty? How do they describe these experiences and their effects on their development? 9. How does mentoring positively affect students' knowledge and skills development? Professional confidence? 10. When, where, and how do faculty provide students with individualized feedback on their academic performance and skills development? How often is feedback provided to students? What form does this feedback take?	1. Engaged Advising • Faculty learn about students' career interests and goals and develop individualized program plans consonant with them. • Faculty meet with advisees on a regular basis to discuss their academic progress and performance. • Faculty assist students in locating employment upon graduation. 2. Individualization • Faculty mentor students through various forms of individualized instruction, including informal, one-on-one interactions with students outside-of-class in the lab, field, or studio; individualized tutorials; and independent readings and research courses. • Faculty provide students with regular and timely feedback on their professional development.	• Focus groups with students, alumni, faculty, and administrators • Exit interviews with graduating students • Student and alumni surveys • Student portfolio assessment (for evidence of collaborative work with faculty) • Faculty portfolio assessment (for evidence of collaborative work with students, for listing of advisees)

Attribute: Cooperative Peer Learning

1. What is more pronounced among faculty in the program: individualism or cooperation? Among students? In the instructional approaches of faculty?
2. What kinds of instructional activities (e.g., lectures, discussions, role plays, simulations, case studies, field research) do faculty use most frequently in the program? Least frequently?
3. What opportunities are available to students to learn from one another as members of a team? How frequently do faculty provide students with these opportunities, and how often do students take advantage of them? How do learning opportunities of this sort enhance students' growth and development?
4. Are students required to complete team-based projects, papers, or presentations as part of their courses?
5. What words do students use to describe their interactions with one another?
6. To what extent do students feel like they learn from their peers? Do they actively seek out one anothers' knowledge, ideas, and views?
7. How frequently do students interact with one another in the program? How often do they participate in various out-of-class activities?
8. To what extent do students compete with one another over grades, scholarships, and other "limited goods' in the program? In what ways do faculty members and program policies promote or diminish competition among students?
9. How does cooperative peer learning positively affect students knowledge and skills development? Professional confidence?

1. Team-Oriented Teaching and Learning
   - Faculty engage in collaborative research and team-teaching activities.
   - Faculty use a number of instructional approaches that emphasize team-oriented approaches to learning, including small and large group discussions, role plays, study groups, research teams and group presentations.
   - Faculty require students to complete collaborative assignments and projects, including group presentations, case studies, research projects, and artistic performances.
2. Collaborative and Social Learning
   - Students actively seek to learn from and support one another in the program, both in and out of class.
   - An ethic of cooperation and interaction, rather than competition and isolation, characterizes students' interaction in the program.

- Focus groups with students, alumni, faculty, and administrators
- Classroom research
- Exit interviews with graduating students
- Student, alumni, and employer surveys
- Peer evaluations of teaching
- Student evaluations of teaching
- Student portfolio assessment (for evidence of collaborative work with peers)
- Faculty portfolio assessment (for evidence of the use of cooperative peer learning in courses as documented in syllabi, instructional materials, videotapes of instruction)

TABLE 38-2 *(continued)*

Questions to Guide Assessment	*Criteria and Indicators of Attribute*	*Suggested Methods of Assessment*
Attribute: Out-of-Class Activities		
1. Who initiates planning for out-of-class activities in the program? Who assumes primary responsibility for designing and promoting out-of-class activities? 2. What opportunities are available for faculty, students, and administrators to learn from and socialize with one another outside of class? 3. How frequently do faculty and administrators attend out-of-class activities in the program, such as colloquia, brown bag lunch seminars, departmental parties, and other informal social gatherings? 4. How frequently do students participate in out-of-class activities such as study groups, journal clubs, colloquia, or other informal social gatherings? 5. What words do students use to describe "student life" in the program? 6. To what extent do students feel like they learn from their peers? Do they actively seek out one anothers' knowledge, ideas, and views outside of class? 7. How does student participation in out-of-class activities positively affect their knowledge and skills development? Their attitudes toward collaboration? 8. To what extent do departmental administrators support—financially and otherwise—out-of-class learning activities in the program? What kinds of support do they provide and why?	1. Active Engagement in Out-of-Class Activities • Faculty, administrators, and students design and sponsor an assortment of out-of-class activities, including brown bag seminars, journal clubs, colloquia, and informal social events. • Faculty and administrators frequently attend out-of-class functions. • Students frequently attend out-of-class functions. 2. Departmental Support • Departmental administrators provide adequate financial support to support to sponsor various out-of-class activities.	• Focus groups with students, alumni, faculty, and administrators • Exit interviews with graduating students • Student, alumni, and employer surveys • Document review (for evidence of student clubs, organizations, departmental financial support)

Attribute: Planned Breadth and Depth Course Work

1. What knowledge, skills, and practices do faculty and administrators most want students to learn in the program? To what extent are these expectations reflected in the program's curriculum? In their courses?
2. To what extent do faculty and administrators share common understandings regarding their expectations for student learning in the program? How do they communicate these expectations?
3. Are curricular goals and objectives consistent with the larger goals (or direction) of the program? What processes are in place for monitoring their achievement?
4. How frequently do faculty and administrators meet to review and discuss curricular goals and objectives? What modifications have been made to the curriculum as a result?
5. What is the overall design of the curriculum? How and by whom was it determined?
6. Are foundational, or breadth, courses a part of the curriculum? How many of these courses are required and how are they sequenced? What is the rationale for their inclusion?
7. Are a set of specialized, or depth courses a part of the curriculum? How many of these courses are required and how are they sequenced? What is the rationale for their inclusion?
8. What is the blend of "core" and "specialized" course work in the program? Is it balanced? Does the curriculum emphasize breadth at the expense of depth or vice versa?
9. Are students aware of the connections between "core" and "specialized" courses? How do they describe the kinds of knowledge taught in each?

1. Shared Agreement on Curricular Objectives
   - Faculty and administrators share common understandings of the knowledge, skills, and practices they expect all program graduates to learn.
   - The program's curriculum reflects these expectations.
2. Coherent Sequence of Required Course Work
   - A core of required course work is required in the program that provides students with a broad understanding of foundational knowledge in the field.
   - A set of specialized courses are required in the program that provide in-depth instruction in one or more sub-areas of the field.

- Focus groups with students, alumni, faculty, and administrators
- Exit interviews with graduating students
- Student, alumni, and employer surveys
- Document review (for evidence of clearly stated curricular goals and objectives, descriptions of course work required and its sequencing)
- Transcript analysis
- Comprehensive examinations (for evidence of student learning in required courses)
- Student portfolio assessment (for evidence of student learning in required courses)

TABLE 38-2 *(continued)*

Questions to Guide Assessment	*Criteria and Indicators of Attribute*	*Suggested Methods of Assessment*
***Attribute: Planned Breadth and Depth Course Work* (continued)**		
10. How do students' learning experiences in core courses affect their knowledge and skills development? Specialized courses? The combination of the two?		
Attribute: Professional Residency		
1. Is a professional residency of some sort—an internship, practicum, clinical, or teaching/research assistantship—required of students in the program? What rationale do faculty and administrators provide for requiring, or not requiring, a professional residency? 2. If a residency is required, what is its overall design? How and by whom was it determined? 3. What professional residency opportunities are available to students through the program? How frequently are these opportunities offered? 4. Are professional residency requirements tailored to meet the career goals and objectives of each student? How so? 5. What are students expected to learn and do during their professional residencies? How are these expectations developed and by whom? How are they communicated to students, site supervisors, and faculty? 6. What words do students use to describe their residency experiences? How do they benefit from this learning experience? How does it affect their knowledge and skills development? Professional confidence and identity? 7. To what extent do students make meaningful connections between what they learned in their classes with what they are learning in the residency? How do these connections benefit students?	1. Professional Residency Requirement • Students are required to complete at least one semester-long, hands-on learning experience—such as an internship, practicum, clinical, or teaching/research assistantship—in an applied setting of their choice. 2. Supportive Departmental Practices • Faculty and administrators maintain an up-to-date listing of residency sites and supervisors. • Faculty and administrators assist students in identifying and selecting residency experiences that complement their professional goals and interests. • Faculty members and site supervisors provide students with regular guidance and feedback throughout their residency.	• Focus groups with students, alumni, faculty, and administrators • Exit interviews with graduating students • Student, alumni, and employer surveys • Document review (for evidence of up-to-date listings of residency sites and supervisors; "residency" contracts that clearly describe expectations and responsibilities of students, site supervisors, and faculty; policy statements/handbooks that describe the residency and outline procedures for securing one) Performance assessments (for evidence of student learning during the residency) • Student portfolio assessment (for evidence of student learning in residency via required papers, projects, and journals) • Job placement data

8. To what extent do faculty and administrators assist students in locating residency sites? Does the program maintain a current listing of residency sites and contact persons?
9. Do faculty and administrators maintain close ties with employers, alumni, and community members through advisory councils, alumni associations, and regional professional organizations that help them to identify and secure residency sites for students?
10. Do faculty meet with site supervisors and students prior to placement in order to clarify student and supervisor expectations for the residency, define work responsibilities for the student-resident and determine the frequency and extent of supervisory and faculty feedback to student-residents?
11. When, where, and how frequently do faculty, site supervisors, and student-residents meet to review and discuss the resident's performance? What kinds of feedback are provided to students throughout their residency?

Attribute: Tangible Product

1. Is a tangible product of some sort—either a thesis, project report, or artistic performance—required of students in the program? What rationale do faculty and administrators provide for requiring, or not requiring, a tangible product?
2. If a tangible product is required, what form does it take (e.g., thesis, project report, artistic performance). How does this requirement fit in with the overall direction and goals of the program?
3. What kinds of projects do students produce? How do faculty and other external examiners evaluate their overall quality?

1. Tangible Product Requirement
   - Students are required to complete a tangible product—usually a thesis, project report, or artistic performance—in which they demonstrate their abilities as knowledgeable and skilled professionals in the field.
2. Individualized Guidance and Feedback
   - Faculty members provide students with individualized guidance and feedback as appropriate while completing tangible product requirements.

- Focus groups with students, alumni, faculty, and administrators
- Exit interviews with graduating students
- Student, alumni, and employer surveys
- Document review (for evidence of policy statements/handbooks that describe the requirement and outline procedures for completing it)

TABLE 38-2 *(continued)*

Questions to Guide Assessment	*Criteria and Indicators of Attribute*	*Suggested Methods of Assessment*
***Attribute: Tangible Product* (continued)** 4. What are students expected to demonstrate—in terms of knowledge, skills, and attitudes—to others in completing their tangible product? When and how are these expectations communicated to students? 5. How do students describe their tangible product learning experiences? How do they benefit from this experience? In what ways does the experience enhance their knowledge and skills development? Professional confidence and identity? 6. To what extent do students meaningfully apply and connect knowledge and skills learned in the program to what they are completing for their culminating tangible products? How do these connections benefit students? 7. Are faculty on campus and available to provide students with guidance and feedback on issues or concerns related to their tangible products? How often do faculty meet with students to review and discuss their progress? What kinds of feedback do they provide to students?		• Oral examination on the tangible product (for evidence of students' understandings of what they learned as a result of their experience and how this knowledge connects to previous learning in the program) • Student portfolio assessment (for examples of students' tangible products) • Faculty portfolio assessment (for evidence of faculty involvement in advising students on their theses, project reports, and other culminating projects)
Attribute: Support for Students 1. What forms of financial support are available to students in the program? What percentage of students who request financial support receive it? 2. What efforts do program administrators and faculty make to secure financial support for students? 3. Are courses offered on a flexible schedule and via different formats (such as evening/weekend or satellite-based/videotaped formats? How frequently are courses offered utilizing these formats?	1. Financial Support for Students • The institution and department provides funding to support an adequate number of student scholarships, fellowships, and assistantships. • The institution and department provides funding to support student travel to professional conferences.	• Focus groups with students, alumni, faculty, and administrators • Exit interviews with graduating students • Student, alumni, and employer surveys • Document review (for evidence of financial support to students, flexible course scheduling)

4. In what ways does the university's career planning and placement office assist students in the job search process? How frequently do students take advantage of these services?
5. To what extent do faculty and administrators assist students in preparing for and locating professional employment upon graduation?
6. How do students describe and assess the financial support they receive in the program? Do they believe that the program seeks to accommodate students' needs, particularly in terms of where, when, and how it delivers course-based instruction? How do these forms of support help to facilitate or hinder students' learning?
7. How do students and employers describe the job placement services offered by the university's career counseling and placement center?

2. Flexible Course Delivery Formats
   - The program utilizes flexible course delivery formats—such as evening, weekend, and intensive summer courses and satellite-based or videotaped instruction—that allow students with different schedules and responsibilities to pursue their studies at convenient times.
3. Career Placement Services
   - Faculty and program administrators assist students in preparing for and locating employment upon graduation.
   - Staff in the university's career planning and placement office assist students in preparing for and locating employment upon graduation.

Attribute: Support for Faculty

1. Is financial support available for faculty research, travel to professional conferences, sabbaticals, and professional development opportunities? If so, how much support is available? How is this support distributed among faculty in the program?
2. What efforts do program and institutional administrators make to secure financial support for faculty?
3. How do departmental and institutional reward structures encourage and promote faculty engagement in teaching?
4. Do faculty feel supported for their investments in teaching, mentoring, and advising students? Why or why not? Do they believe that departmental and institutional reward structures value teaching as much as other forms of scholarly activity?

1. Financial Support for Faculty
   - The institution provides competitive salaries to sustain a critical mass of faculty.
   - The program provides adequate funding for faculty travel to professional conferences.
   - The institution and department provide adequate financial support for faculty research, sabbaticals, and professional development opportunities.
2. Supportive Institutional and Departmental Reward Structure
   - Institutional and departmental merit, promotion, and tenure policies recognize and reward faculty for their involvement in a broad range of scholarly activities, including teaching, advising, and mentoring students.

- Focus groups with students, alumni, faculty, and administrators
- Student, alumni, and employer surveys
- Document review (for evidence of financial support to faculty, supportive departmental and institutional merit, promotion, and tenure policies)

TABLE 38-2 *(continued)*

Questions to Guide Assessment	*Criteria and Indicators of Attribute*	*Suggested Methods of Assessment*
***Attribute: Support for Faculty* (continued)**		
5. Do students believe that faculty are supported for their investments in teaching, mentoring, and advising students? Why or why not? Do they believe that departmental and institutional reward structures value teaching as much as other forms of scholarly activity? 6. Is there evidence that faculty investments in teaching, course development, student advising, collaborative research, and program administration and coordination activities are valued in the department? Institution? 7. How does financial support promote or hinder faculty investments in teaching and learning? What impact does a supportive departmental and institutional reward structure have on the time and energy faculty devote to students, their learning, and program improvements?		
Attribute: Support for Basic Infrastructure		
1. What financial support is available to support basic infrastructure needs in the program? Is this support adequate? 2. Is laboratory, classroom, computing and other program equipment up to date and in good repair? 3. Does the program have adequate supplies to support instruction and research? 4. Are classrooms, laboratories, studios, performance areas, and other program facilities suitable to meet the instructional and research needs of students and faculty? Are they in good repair?	1. Financial Support for Basic Infrastructure • The program receives adequate funding from the institution and elsewhere to purchase requisite equipment and supplies. • The program receives adequate funding from the institution to maintain suitable laboratory, classroom, office, and performance facilities. • The institution provides adequate funding to support the college or university's library and computing facilities.	• Focus groups with students, alumni, faculty, and administrators • Student, alumni, and employer surveys • Document review (for evidence of financial support for basic infrastructure needs in the program)

5. What efforts do program and instructional administrators make to secure financial support for the basic infrastructure of the program?
6. Are institutional resources, especially in the library and computing center, adequate to support the instructional and research needs of program faculty and students?
7. How do adequate resources—in terms of equipment, supplies, and facilities—help to facilitate and enrich students' learning? Faculty teaching and research?

CASE STUDIES

CHAPTER 39

BEYOND CHALK AND TALK: STRATEGIES FOR A NEW INTRODUCTORY ECONOMICS CURRICULUM

MEENAKSHI RISHI

Faculty members and administrators are concerned about the decline in the number of economics majors.[1] Students' disenchantment with economics has prompted many to examine critically the content and pedagogy of the introductory economics course. Indeed, the introductory course is the first economics course for many students, and it is here that opinions about the relevance of the discipline are formed. This article offers some strategies for revamping the introductory economics curriculum to make economics more interesting and challenging to a diverse student body. In addition to proposing changes in course content and context, I describe some pedagogical innovations for the introductory economics classroom. In particular, I recommend three learning activities that are likely to capture students' interest by encouraging them to think creatively about standard economic topics.

Economics 100, Principles of Economics, is the introductory course taught at my college over a ten-week quarter. Students who take this course are primarily non-majors who may or may not have had a high school economics course. In redesigning the introductory economics curriculum, I concentrated on two major areas—the course content and the classroom environment.

Course Content and Context

Several studies indicate that a serious drawback of the traditional economics course has been its failure to provide students with an adequate context for thinking critically about real-world issues (Shackleford 1992; Bartlett 1995a; Feiner and Roberts 1995). The literature has also highlighted the presence of subject matter bias in introductory economics textbooks. Feiner and Morgan (1987) document several instances of race and gender bias in introductory economics textbooks. In the same vein, Ferber (1995) concludes that topics that could be of special importance to women and minorities are either completely absent or marginalized as footnotes in several best-selling economics textbooks. For instance, in a majority of the texts surveyed by Ferber (1995), the rise in women's labor force participation rates since World War II is neither discussed nor mentioned. Similarly, the topic of poverty and income distribution is often presented, if at all, as an aggregate phenomenon without adequate reference to its implications for women, minorities, and children.

This is not to suggest that females and students of color may be relatively more interested in topics different from those of white males. Inasmuch as poverty and income distribution are very real

Source: "Beyond Chalk and Talk: Strategies for a New Introductory Economics Curriculum," by Meenakshi Rishi, reprinted from *College Teaching*, Vol. 46, No.3, 1998, Heldref Publications, Helen Dwight Reid Educational Foundation.

economic phenomena, thinking critically about them would benefit all students, regardless of their race or gender.

Such criticisms motivated me to rethink the course content and context of my own introductory economics course.[2] At my college, although course catalogue descriptions are standardized by department, faculty have discretion over course outlines and expectations. Therefore, I attempted to revamp both the course objectives and the course outline to include diversity of content. Prior to that change, the introductory course was structured around coverage of abstract economic concepts—demand, supply, cost curves, types of market structures, and determinants of output, employment, and prices in a decentralized market economy.

The new course supplemented textbook reading with articles, films, and invited speakers in order to enable students to explore, examine, and assess economic theory and practice. Similarly, I revamped course content—where the traditional course had emphasized abstract analytical modeling, the new one used active analysis of categories of race, gender, and class. (I would be happy to send copies of "before and after" syllabi to those who request them.)

Classroom Environment

Within the context of learning environments, Becker and Watts (1996) report that "chalk and talk" is the predominant pedagogical strategy in economics classrooms. Scholars have noted that the mere transmission of knowledge through impersonal lectures may not be an effective learning technique for most college students (see, for example, Meyers and Jones 1993, 3–18). Such an environment may also generate a chilly classroom climate that excludes certain students from the discourse—women and racial-ethnic minorities, in particular.[3] Moreover, the traditional, lecture-like classroom milieu, where "students face forward and rarely have opportunities to interact" can even turn capable students away from the discipline (Bartlett 1995a, 363).

The new course attempted to transform this traditional environment to stimulate a more interactive classroom climate. Seating was arranged in a U-shape that facilitated interchanges and enabled me to maintain eye contact with every student.[4] Additionally, the course evaluation policy was altered to facilitate a cooperative group learning environment that generated frequent feedback.

A cooperative learning environment, as opposed to a traditionally competitive one, is based on the formation of structured groups and requires teamwork on the part of the students. Johnson, Johnson, and Smith (1991) suggest that carefully structured cooperative learning environments can produce higher achievement and enhance positive relationships between students.

Further, many nontraditional students, women, and students of color may actually do better in classrooms that use cooperative learning strategies as opposed to competitive approaches. Treisman (1992) and Bartlett (1995b) note that such environments dispel the otherwise exclusionary classroom atmosphere that women and students of color often encounter. Research by Belenky et al. (1986) notes that women, in particular, are likely to benefit from cooperative learning environments because such environments are more conducive to the "connected" ways in which women have historically acquired knowledge. Preliminary research on ethnicity and learning also proposes a connection between cultural background and learning styles. A literature review of the topic conducted by Banks (1988) led him to conclude that cooperative learning environments may be particularly useful for students whose cultural background emphasizes cooperation rather than competition.

The scholarship on cooperative learning and differences in learning styles, although preliminary, is nevertheless prompting educators to question the usefulness of traditional teaching methods in engaging the interests of a diverse student body (Knowles 1980; Guild and Garger 1985). Several activities such as journals, simulations, case studies, and informal small groups have been suggested as pedagogical techniques designed to enhance learning in today's college classrooms. My own experiments with alternative teaching strategies were, to a large extent, influenced by the classroom innovations discussed in Bartlett (1995b). A brief description follows.

On the first day of classes, I told the students about the potential benefits of working in groups. But the formation of groups was not mandated, and students had the option of not joining a group. To overcome the "hitchhiker" problem often encountered in group work, I changed group testing to a random event. Individual students within a group draw cards from a deck to determine the identity of the test-taker. The test-taking is, therefore, completely random.

Such strategies are often used in cooperative learning to maintain individual accountability within a group (Slavin 1983, 441). A classroom trial run conducted by Bartlett (1995b) documents that adding the element of chance reinforces individual responsibility and motivates both stronger and weaker students to success. The grade earned on tests taken by the randomly selected member was awarded to the group as a whole. Students were, however, given the option of taking the final as individuals if they were dissatisfied with their group grade.

To encourage and reward individual effort, the students were informed that they could earn extra (individual) points above their group grade. The class had access to a *Compendium of Business Statistics,* a World Wide Web site of useful economic links on the Internet. Students could browse these Web links for economic information and e-mail an opinion paragraph to me for extra points. For instance, during a discussion of unemployment, I encouraged them to access the *Compendium* for state and county-level statistics. Students could then write an electronic paragraph on how the data on unemployment related to their perceptions of the economic conditions in their hometowns. These assignments are beneficial because, as we know, research suggests that writing about personal experiences fosters interest, critical thinking, and creativity among students (Kurfiss 1988; Shackleford 1992).

Another classroom innovation was using the "Fast Feedback Questionnaire" that was first developed at the teaching laboratory of the Chicago Business School. Fast feedback entails gathering weekly responses from students about their comprehension of lectures and readings. For genuine communication, the teacher *always* responds with "reverse feedback," that is, she responds orally or in writing. It can take several forms—clarifying concepts, answering specific questions about exams and grades, and stating changes in course coverage of topics.

This two-way process can bring the instructor closer to the class. Because written feedback is anonymous, it also functions well for the otherwise shy person. Students who are weary of the standard faculty evaluation forms greatly appreciate the continuous, two-way communication.

A word of warning is in order—faculty who choose to adopt this feedback approach should be prepared for a bruising of their professional egos! Also, one must invest considerable time and effort. But these shortcomings aside, I found the feedback invigorating, as it enabled me to attend to students' concerns as they arose.

Three Cooperative Learning Activities

These activities present standard economics topics—poverty, inflation, and the budget deficit—from a more inclusive point of view. Students are urged to think from diverse points of view and voice their critiques in a variety of ways.

Poverty

As mentioned above, the introductory economics class is restructured as a cooperative group learning environment. Generally, students take a couple of weeks to grasp the rudiments of demand and supply and to form groups. This is approximately the time that we begin an in-class dialogue on market failure and poverty. We devote one class period to the allocative efficiency implications of a perfectly competitive market economy. My lecture emphasizes that while a free market system is generally able to allocate resources efficiently, it may not be able to distribute income and opportunities equally. In the textbook, the reasons for the unequal distribution of income are ascribed to differences in ability, talent, and opportunity. We discuss this point in class before moving to an analysis of poverty profiles and the disproportionate representation of minorities, women, and children among the poor.

Although the textbook presents a breakdown of poverty statistics by race and gender, it offers no interpretation. To remedy this omission, I assign additional readings that examine poverty and income distribution data from a historical and critical perspective. Over the following week, a speaker from the local Health and Human Services office and an AFDC recipient (a former student and single mother) are invited to participate in an in-class discussion of the myths and realities surrounding poverty and welfare. Students are also guided to a World Wide Web site (http://www.census.gov/hhes/www/poverty.html) maintained by the U.S. Census Bureau to access current income and poverty statistics.

At the end of a lively week of exploration and discussion, the small groups are asked to analyze poverty and welfare from the point of view of an individual welfare recipient. They are allowed to choose the race/gender/class specifics of this person, and they have the option of either submitting a written report or doing a role play exercise for their assignment. After the submission of reports and/or following class presentations, I seek student feedback via the Fast Feedback Questionnaire. Responses indicate that students find the exercise on poverty interesting and thought provoking. Specific comments also document the fact that students enjoy participating in role play activities as they are able creatively to connect classroom learning with a real-world issue.[5]

Inflation

We begin an in-class discussion and disaggregated analysis of the socioeconomic phenomenon of inflation around week five of the ten-week quarter.[6] I provide data (from the Economic Report of the President) on consumer price indices for major expenditure classes, such as food and beverages, housing, apparel, medical care, etc. Students have to choose a particular household from the following three types: (1) a retired couple living on a pension; (2) an affluent professional couple; and (3) a single, working mother of two who is unable to afford medical insurance. Again, students are free to invent the race and gender dynamics of their chosen household.

For their project, individuals/groups are expected to analyze disaggregated data on the Consumer Price Index (CPI) and gauge its effect on their particular household. Results and findings, as in the poverty case, may be submitted in written or role play format. The purpose of this exercise is to enable students to critique aggregate macroeconomic price indices such as the CPI. When students learn to interpret data through many different pairs of eyes, they are able to appreciate that a social phenomenon like inflation does not affect all members of society equally. Consequently, they learn to develop a critical understanding of the race/gender/class implications of policies that are designed to control inflation.

Budget Deficit

An analysis of the budget deficit as a national economic problem sets the stage for another group learning activity. An effective role play opportunity arises during a debate on deficit reduction policies. The class discussion around this issue is highly animated, and cutbacks in entitlement expenditures and defense spending appear as recurring themes.[7] As with the exercise on inflation, students are asked to choose a particular household type in preparation for their class project. I encourage them, as usual, to experiment with their household's race/gender/class composition. The assignment requires students to determine and assess the impact of a specific deficit reduction package, such as cutbacks in public education. I ask groups to submit written reports and encourage them to role play the consequences of deficit reduction policies on their particular household type.

Similar to the exercises on poverty and inflation, the budget deficit activity is intended to stimulate discovery, creativity, and critical thinking among students. The motivation is to enable students to understand that acknowledging the existence of diversity in society implies accepting the differential effects of policy on various groups.

In sum, these are a few of the ways in which we can enliven the classroom to make it intriguing and welcoming to the introductory student. Similar learning activities may be structured around other standard economics topics. Although the design and execution of such activities may require an initial investment of time, the payoff can be substantial as it can kindle students' creativity and an abiding interest in the discipline.

Written comments on evaluations for the 1995–96 academic year indicated that students "enjoyed sitting in a U-shape" as it made the classroom less "lecture-like." Students also liked the way the subject matter "related to real-life situations," and they enjoyed the three cooperative learning activities. On the negative side, some students felt that these activities were "time-consuming." A possible solution to this problem may be to cut down on the number of such exercises planned for the introductory course.

Implications and Conclusions

What are the implications of this curriculum redesign for us as educators? On the one hand, curriculum changes are time-consuming and require constant reassessment. The fact that literature on evaluating alternative pedagogical strategies is still somewhat new may also blunt our enthusiasm for change. But if we are to make economics more appealing and relevant to a wider audience, we must change and diversify the content and context.

Moreover, the creation of an active learning environment enables students to apply what they are learning in the classroom. In this regard, standard economic topics may be enlivened by alternative teaching/learning techniques that go beyond the traditional chalk and talk approach to teaching. Reconstructing the introductory economics course in this fashion will not only foster students' interest in the discipline, it will also enhance our own enjoyment of teaching the subject.

Finally, this article may be seen as a preliminary "cookbook" of strategies for changing the introductory economics classroom. As this perspective becomes part of another academic year, I am aware that real change is not achieved overnight and that we must continue to research ways of making economics more inclusive and its teaching more effective.

Notes

This article was conceived at an NSF-sponsored faculty development conference on Improving Introductory Economics by Integrating the Latest Scholarship on Women and Minorities, Denison University, 1994. Earlier drafts were presented as a paper at the seventh annual Teaching Economics Conference, Robert Morris College, February 1996, and at the ODE-Faculty Advisor session at the ASSA meetings, January 1998. I am grateful to all those who have commented upon various versions of this article.

1. Siegfried and Scott (1994) analyzed data from the National Center for Educational Statistics to report a 2 percent decline in the number of economics degrees awarded in 1990–91 as compared to 1989–90. The underrepresentation of women and ethnic minorities among all economics majors has also been well documented. According to Siegfried and Scott (1994, 285), more than 25 percent of the decline in economics majors between 1999–91 and 1992–93 can be "attributed to the slide in the proportion of majors who are women." Data from the U.S. National Research Council (1995) indicate that out of the 388 economics Ph.D.'s awarded in 1993, minority group members earned only 40.
2. Peggy McIntosh's (1983) model of curriculum development proposes an excellent framework for making course contents more inclusive. Lage and Treglia (1996) provide examples on integrating scholarship on gender in an introductory microeconomics class.
3. A growing body of research (Ferber 1984, 1995; Bartlett and Feiner 1992) has suggested that the recession in female undergraduate majors may be due to the chilly climate in the classroom for women. Hall and Sandier (1982) have studied and documented the existence of such a classroom climate for female students. The classroom interactions between racial-ethnic minority students and instructors are also problematic (Cones et al. 1983).
4. For a discussion of alternative seating configurations, see Meyers and Jones (1993, 43–50).
5. Student comments on the Fast Feedback Questionnaire were illustrative: "The exercise is a good idea, but it is time-consuming." "The exercise on poverty gave us a way to understand real-life economics. I liked the class discussion on the myths and realities of welfare." "It was useful in understanding both sides of an argument and varying opinions." "I got to know how the class thought about the issue."
6. This group activity was initially developed during the NSF-sponsored faculty development conference on Improving Introductory Economics by Integrating the Latest Scholarship on Women and Minorities, Denison University, 1994. I am grateful to Sherry Davis Kasper, Maryville College, for formalizing the same.
7. The class discussion on entitlement programs always comes as a surprise to students unaware of the status of Social Security as an entitlement expenditure.

References

Banks, J. A. 1988. Ethnicity, class, cognitive, and motivational styles: Research and teaching implications. *Journal of Negro Education* 57(4): 452–56.

Bartlett, R. L. 1995a. Attracting "otherwise bright students" to economics 101. *The American Economic Review* 85(2): 362–66.

_____. 1995b. A flip of the coin—A roll of the die: An answer to the free-rider problem in economic instruction. *The Journal of Economic Education* 26 (spring): 131–39.

Bartlett, R. L., and S. Feiner. 1992. Balancing the economics curriculum: Content, method and pedagogy. *American Economic Review* 80(2): 359–64.

Becker, W. E., and M. Watts. 1996. Chalk and talk: A national survey on teaching undergraduate economics. *American Economic Review* 86(2): 448–53.

Belenkey, M., B. Clinchy, N. Goldberger, and J. Tarule. 1986. *Women's ways of knowing: The development of self, voice, and mind.* New York: Basic Books.

Cones, J., III, J. F. Noonan, and D. Janha, eds. 1983. Teaching minority students. *New Directions for Teaching and Learning* 16. San Francisco: Jossey-Bass.

Fassinger, P A. 1995. Understanding classroom interaction: Students' and professors' contributions to students' silence. *Journal of Higher Education* 66(1): January/February: 82–96.

Feiner, S. F, and B. A. Morgan. 1987. Women and minorities in introductory economics textbooks: 1974–1984. *Journal of Economic Education* 18(4): 376–92.

Feiner, S. F., and B. Roberts, 1995. Using alternative paradigms to teach about race and gender: A critical thinking approach to introductory economics. *The American Economic Review* 85(2): 367–71.

Ferber, M. A. 1984. Suggestions for improving the classroom climate for women in the introductory economics course: A review article. *The Journal of Economic Education* 15(spring): 160–68.

_____. M. A. 1995. The study of economics: A feminist critique. *The American Economic Review* 85 (2): 357–61.

Guild, P B., and S. Garger. 1985. *Marching to different drummers.* Alexandria, Va.: Association for Supervision and Curriculum Development.

Hall, R. M., and B. R. Sandier. 1982. The classroom climate: A chilly one for women? *Project on the education and status of women.* Washington, D.C.: Association of American Colleges.

Johnson, D. W., R. T. Johnson, and K. A. Smith. 1991. Cooperative learning: Increased college faculty instructional productivity. In *ASHE-ERIC Higher Education Report 4,* Washington, D.C.: George Washington University.

Knowles, M. 1980. *The modern practice of adult education.* rev. ed. Chicago: Follett.

Kurfiss, J. G. 1988. Critical thinking: Theory, research, practice, and possibilities. In *ASHE-ERIC Higher Education Report* 2, Washington, D.C.: George Washington University.

Lage, M., and M. Treglia. 1996. The impact of integrating scholarship on women into introductory economics: Evidence from one institution. *Journal of Economic Education* 27 (winter): 26–37.

McIntosh, P. 1983. Interactive phases of curricular revision: A feminist perspective. Working paper. Wellesley, Mass.: Wellesley College Center for Research on Women.

Meyers, C., and T. J. Jones. 1993. *Promoting active learning: Strategies for the classroom.* San Francisco: Jossey-Bass.

Rothenberg, P 1996. The politics of discourse and the end of argument. In *Creating an inclusive college curriculum,* ed. E. G. Friedman et al. New York: Teachers College Press.

Shackleford, J. 1992. Feminist pedagogy: A means for bringing critical thinking and creativity to the economics classroom. *American Economic Review* 82(2): 570–76.

Siegfried, J. J., and C. E. Scott. 1994. Recent trends in undergraduate economics majors. *Journal of Economic Education* 25(summer): 281–86.

Slavin, R. E. 1983. Wile" does cooperative learning increase student achievement? *Psychological Bulletin* 94(3): 429–45.

Treisman, U. 1992. Studying students studying calculus: A look at the lives of minority mathematics students in college. *College Mathematics Journal* 23: 362–72.

Walton, G., and F. C. Wykoff. 1993. *Understanding economics today.* 4th ed. Burridge, Ill.: Irwin.

CHAPTER 40

POLICY PERSPECTIVES: EXEMPLARS

MARIA IANNOZZI

The Problem: Reverse shortfalls in student learning and poor attendance in large lecture courses, and reduce a structural budget deficit of $25 million.

The Solution: Reinvent teaching and learning through a comprehensive curriculum renewal to make the educational experience more student-centered and make innovative use of technology in the classroom, replacing the lecture-lab-recitation format with smaller, interactive studio courses.

Rensselaer Polytechnic Institute, an institution renowned for its science and engineering programs, faced a problem common to large research universities: its introductory science and math lectures, some with class enrollments of hundreds of students, simply did not stimulate interest. Faculty realized that the traditional format for instruction in introductory-level science courses—lecture, lab, and recitation sessions—was neither conducive to learning nor cost-effective. "Attention was poor, and attendance was poorer," says Professor Jack Wilson, Rensselaer's dean of undergraduate education. Student test performance demonstrated this point; most simply were not learning the fundamental principles of science or math at a level that would provide adequate tools for subsequent inquiry and analysis.

By 1993, Rensselaer had arrived at a two-stage restructuring process with a dual goal: to realize academic excellence through a new commitment to interactive learning—a movement away from dry lectures in introductory courses to engaging, smaller classes in which students take primary responsibility for learning—while preserving financial equilibrium. As the 1990s began, Rensselaer faced a structural deficit in excess of $25 million. In order to pursue reform in the delivery of undergraduate education without passing the costs onto students, it had to undertake administrative restructuring to create efficiencies throughout the institution and reallocate dollars in key areas: student financial aid, physical plant and infrastructure, endowment, academic renewal, and competitive salaries for senior faculty.

Although one goal was to cut costs and improve efficiency, the primary impetus for reform was an unprecedented opportunity to reinvent the educational experience through technology. In the 1980s, faculty had brought to life the theories of first-year calculus courses by introducing graphical computer software into the classroom, and the mathematics department was quick to introduce computer-enhanced calculus into its standard curriculum. A sense of discontent among a core of faculty in math and science departments—linked with general concerns about retention and Rensselaer's market position as a private institution in competition with lower-cost publics—helped build the case for a different mode of teaching and learning. "Spurred in part by a Pew Campus Roundtable," says Rensselaer's dean of faculty, Gary Judd, "we came to realize that we were in the

---

Source: "Policy Perspectives: Exemplars" Rensselaer Polytechnic Institute, by Maria Iannozzi, reprinted from *ERIC Document 414–811*, 1997.

business of knowledge. As such, we were in competition not just with other higher education institutions but with other information providers who would feel less bound to the traditions of the academy than ourselves."

The initial interactive learning environments soon evolved across the curriculum into studio courses, which Rensselaer has become a pioneer in advancing. Already implemented for introductory physics, chemistry, math, and science and engineering, studio courses replace the large lecture-lab-recitation model with interactive learning classes of up to 60 students. This student-centered and project-based approach to instruction stresses teamwork and problem-solving, with the instructor serving as a resource and catalyst to learning, not as a "talking head" behind a podium. Not only are the courses more lively and better attended, after an initial investment in hardware and software, they are less costly to provide, already realizing savings of $10,000 to $150,000 per course.

Much of the success (and start-up costs) of studio courses is due to a complete redesign of the classroom at Rensselaer—physical changes that give visual witness to this new approach to learning. Rows of desks have disappeared; instead, many classrooms have been transformed into "theaters-in-the-round," where students sit at multimedia-based workstations on specially designed worktables that form concentric ovals. Professors teach and lead discussions from the center of this rough circle, on swivel chairs, students turn to face the professor for brief lectures and return to their workstations when using networked audio, video, graphics, text, and animation capabilities to apply concepts in the lesson.

Professor Wilson describes a typical physics studio, in which instructors move from one mode of teaching to another—uniting functions of the lecture, lab, and recitation in one setting. "During our acceleration-due-to-gravity session," he says, "we videotaped a student throwing a ball. We digitized the video directly into the computer and made it available to every student workstation over the network. Students then analyzed the motion using the on-line scientific tools. Next, they created a spreadsheet illustrating the ball's position-versus-time data, and then plotted their results on computerized graphs. All in one two-hour block." This seamless approach to instruction has a big advantage over the traditional lecture-lab-recitation model, as Davienne Monbleau, a sophomore physics major who also serves as a TA for a physics studio course, explains. "In a lecture course, the elements aren't always connected. What you learned on Monday in a lecture isn't always the topic of discussion in your recitation on Friday. In studios all of the concepts are connected in one session. You're always practicing and reviewing what you've just learned."

From a vantage point at the center of the classroom, professors are able to view all of the students' screens and monitor their progress as they perform virtual experiments, and both professors and TAs can quickly respond to students' questions when problems arise. "In other classes, you don't find out that they don't get it until the test, when it's too late," says Professor Joseph Ecker. "Here, I find out right away." This new format has also improved the relationship between professor and student, contradicting a widely held prejudice against technology instruction. As Professor Gary Adams explains, "Now I actually have more interaction with my students. It's really the difference between knowing the student's name and knowing the student."

And while professor-student interaction has increased, the responsibility for learning has clearly shifted from instructor to student. "There's no step-by-step spoon feeding," says Davienne. "Because you're demonstrating what you've learned, it's more important to come to class prepared. We have more responsibility for what we know, and we're treated more like adults. We learn how to think—how to approach and solve a problem. Studios are also geared toward learning how to work with others, but not in the typical way in large groups, where some students rely on others to get by. We communicate and help each other." In addition to benefiting her scholastically, Davienne believes that her experience will ultimately transfer from the classroom to the workplace. "In today's office, you have to be prepared to work with people in teams, to think critically, and know how to approach problems. Studio courses help to teach those important skills."

Although studio courses reduce the number of contact hours for each re-engineered course, faculty reinvest the saved time by engaging in curriculum reform, research and scholarship, and professional development. In fact, a new culture has evolved among faculty at Rensselaer, one of experimentation and innovation, and they see themselves as agents of change across the institution. Many Rensselaer faculty are actually developing the instructional technology being used in studio classrooms. For example, CUPLE, the software package for physics that students are using to perform virtual experiments, was created by Professor Wilson. To assist faculty in their efforts, Rensselaer offers hands-on technology training on campus at the International Center for Multimedia Education.

Still in the initial years of implementation, acceptance by some of this new approach to learning has been admittedly slow. "Sure, there are cynics," says Professor Wilson. "But once they're shown something new that saves money and works, they come right on board." The results of recent evaluations only fortify the argument. "Our preliminary data show that students in the new classes are doing as well or better than in the traditional classes," explains Professor Wilson. "Students are also learning faster and more effectively; fewer people are failing." And the rates of attendance in studio classes is an astonishing 90 to 100 percent, compared with only 60 to 70 percent for traditional lecture courses. Wilson also describes how Rensselaer's re-engineering process promotes cost efficiency. "There's a myth that it's too expensive to re-engineer courses. But our studios show that by redesigning our process—instead of just trying to fit in technology—we are achieving significant productivity increases. We're serving the same number of students at a lower cost—and serving them more effectively—with more efficient use of our faculty resources. Now that's a breakthrough!"

Institutional Statistics

Private, four-year institution in Troy, New York: **4,400** undergraduate and **2,000** graduate students **380** full-time faculty, **40** part-time faculty.

Milestones on the Path to Reform

- Curriculum renewal began in 1988, when Rensselaer faculty started incorporating technology into introductory science courses, creating the precursor of the institution's "studio course" approach.
- In the late 1980s, a special interdisciplinary program for first-year students was introduced, composed of several courses in the School of Humanities and Social Sciences that were multidisciplinary, team-taught, and committed to interactive learning.
- The Center for Innovation in Undergraduate education was created to oversee curriculum redesign in 1989.
- The calculus initiative prompted faculty to consider new approaches to learning in conjunction with the Anderson Center for Innovation in Undergraduate Education, an incubator for curriculum renewal, founded in 1989.
- As interactive learning gained momentum, the series of stand-alone experiments became a focused, institute-wide initiative. Through a strategic planning process in 1990–91, the Panel on Strategic Initiatives declared that interactive learning should be Rensselaer's top priority.
- By 1993, a two-stage restructuring process was identified the commitment to interactive learning, and the achievement of savings through administrative restructuring to reduce the structural deficit of $25 million.
- The first studio course was implemented in 1993, and Rensselaer began phasing-in these new courses in introductory physics, math, chemistry, and science and engineering over the next three years.
- In 1994, Rensselaer engaged in a Pew Campus Roundtable, which helped to refine its mission and stress the innovative use of technology, as a result of the Roundtable discussions, a goal of $8.4 million in annual savings was targeted through administrative restructuring and the introduction of studio courses.
- "Strategic Initiatives" was established through gifts and endowment to fund faculty proposals to develop renewal projects. From 1992 to 1996, $8 million was allocated for faculty proposals.
- By early 1995, the Curriculum Renewal Implementation team began revising the curriculum, reducing the number of courses students take while increasing the depth of course offerings. The new course menu—called the 4x4 Curriculum—took its name from the introduction of a

standard semester of four, four-credit courses, replacing the former typical semester of five or six three-credit courses.

- In 1995, Rensselaer received a National Science Foundation grant of $4 million to lead Project Links by developing interactive multimedia materials for courses in mathematics, electronics, manufacturing, and management.
- In 1996, the newly renovated Walker Laboratory was reopened, from room layout, to furniture, to computer equipment, Walker classrooms were designed to facilitate student teamwork and faculty mentoring.
- Plans are currently being developed to implement interactive learning across the curriculum, stressing teamwork, leadership, the role of the faculty as mentors, and deploying the studio model as appropriate.
- Two courses, Introduction to Engineering Design and Laboratory Introduction to Embedded Control, have begun to serve as paradigms of interactive learning that takes place in a project-based, team-intensive environment. The nurturing of instructional innovation pays off with courses that augment the studio model.

Part Four

Curriculum in Revision: Curricular Change and Innovation

CHAPTER 41

THE TELIC REFORMS

GERALD GRANT AND DAVID RIESMAN

We might have begun our study of contemporary reform movements in a more philosophical way, inquiring first of all into what education might be, and then dividing it into its formal and informal parts, and higher and lower divisions. Broadly speaking, we know that both the family and the state have a role in education. We are also aware that much "higher education" takes place in settings other than traditional college campuses—in public libraries, over television, in ancillary programs of large corporations, through the military, and through many other channels of civic and cultural life. Reforms in these settings are undoubtedly important, too. But we began with the more restricted view of higher education as formally constituted, degree-granting institutions that play a role in the socialization and education of nearly half of all American youth at the postsecondary level.

Thus we restricted the scope of our inquiry to "merely" 3,000 formally constituted institutions of higher education and focused most of our efforts on what the experimenters themselves claimed to be reforms. Through a variety of methods, we began to investigate these claims and to attempt to understand the intentions of the reformers. Some of the reforms have a large resonance, representing attempts not only to change the university but to set forth new ideals. We call these telic reforms, reforms pointing toward a different conception of the ends of undergraduate education, to distinguish them from the more popular reforms of the last decade which have brought about a general loosening of the curriculum. The telic reforms approach the status of social movements or generic protests against contemporary American life. Of course, to some degree, the telic movements are in conflict with each other as well as in conflict with prevailing societal values. It was John Dewey who said it was the business of an intelligent theory to "ascertain the causes for the conflicts that exist and then, instead of taking one side or the other, to indicate a plan of operations proceeding from a level deeper and more inclusive than as represented by the practices and ideas of the contending parties." Here he has essentially stated our aim, although we have not constructed anything grand enough to be called either a sociological or an educational theory. Rather, in the more usual way of inductively oriented social scientists, we have looked at some cases, compared them, and arranged them in the typology of reform movements to be found in Appendix 1. In this chapter, we explain that typology and attempt to place the telic reform movements in historical perspective.

In Chapter 6, we discuss the popular reforms as partially a response to the meritocratic discontents that came to characterize student life in the most selective colleges and universities. By the early 1960s, the expansion of the American system of higher education had led to fierce competition for the admission to elite colleges and greatly intensified academic pressures for undergraduates who, once admitted, continued to compete for choice graduate-school opportunities. Students sought relief in a wide range of popular reforms that gave them a considerably greater degree of autonomy and

Source: "The Telic Reforms," by Gerald Grant and David Riesman, reprinted from *The Perpetual Dream: Reform and Experiment in the American College,* 1978, University of Chicago Press.

resulted in dramatic changes in their relationships with teachers. Students were freer than before to pick and choose their way through the curriculum and to move at their own pace without penalty. The most popular of these reforms—student-designed majors, free-choice curricula, the abolition of fixed requirements—sought not to establish new institutional aims, but to slow the pace and expand the avenues of approach.[1] While these reforms began in the elite academic institutions, they spread to other colleges and universities. They were adopted in part out of misconceived notions that they would serve to quench campus revolts as well as out of genuinely educational motives on the part of a new generation of faculty who wished to change the processes of education in significant ways. The popular reforms modified the means of education within the constraints of the existing goals of the research-oriented university.

The telic reforms, on the other hand, embody a significantly different conception of the goals of undergraduate education. To some degree, they represent an attack on the hegemony of the giant research-oriented multiversities and their satellite university colleges. In one sense, these telic reforms could be thought of as counterrevolutionary, that is, as counter to the rise of the research-oriented universities that Christopher Jencks and David Riesman described in *The Academic Revolution.*[2] By "revolution," Jencks and Riesman meant the crescent hegemony of the academic professions over previously influential parties: trustees and legislators, students, administrators, religious denominations. That book, like others of its genre, noted that the research universities were producing the faculties for collegiate institutions and took for granted the way in which competition among the colleges led them to imitate the major university model. But because of their resentment and later disaffection with the aims of the academic vanguard, many faculty members trained under its auspices have shown resistance to the model, and their ambivalence as well as lack of resources limited the momentum with which it could be imitated. Until the 1920s, the university college model that was diffused by this imitative process (combined with elements from its English, Scottish and German origins) was neither strong enough at the center nor extensive enough at the periphery of American higher education to incite rebellions that might establish contrasting models of higher education other than those affiliated with denominational groups.[3]

But in the 1930s, two of the telic movements—in our typology the neoclassical and the aesthetic-expressive—arose in opposition to the university college model, and they were followed later by what we have called the communal-expressive and activist-radical. By telic reforms, then, we mean to signify those reforms that emphasize ends and purposes that are different from, if not hostile to, the goals of the regnant research universities.

One could have developed such a typology in abstraction, working out other possible or desirable ideal types. Our scheme does not seek to be exhaustive in this way but grows out of analysis and fieldwork at a wide range of institutions. We proceeded inductively, with the general aim of writing ethnographies or "natural histories" of a range of experiments. We did not write these accounts to fit an a priori scheme; rather the typology emerged as we came to understand the intentions of the founders of these experiments.

Although the institutions illustrating the ideal types are small, the chains of influence represented by these movements may be quite large. For example, from the Committee on the Liberal Arts at Chicago and the neoclassical experiment at St. John's that grew from it, one could trace direct influences to at least a score of colleges. The indirect influences have of course been even greater as vicarious news of these experiments has spread through alumni networks and through articles and books such as our own. (Americans—including many academics—who are tone deaf to philosophical discussions about education—will often attend to an account by someone who has been there, even if only as an occasional visitor.) In the last decade, when any sizable group of faculty has assembled to discuss fundamental curriculum reforms, the debate is likely to become oriented—consciously or unconsciously—toward the directional compass represented by the telic reforms. It even seems probable that a survey instrument could be developed, based upon this typology, that would show that most faculty would be oriented in their purposes, norms, and core values to one of the types of our scheme, despite their frequent confusion and ambivalence.

Essentially, the typology contrasts different models of undergraduate education, which can be translated into ideas about the purposes of such an experience, the values it should embody, and the forms of authority on which it ultimately rests. Each offers a distinctive vision of an educating community. Specific motives are associated with choosing one form or another, and these are accompanied by distinctive processes of education consonant with the ends desired. Students whose primary motivation is to be certified, licensed, and employed, for example, will not stay long at St. John's, where such aims not only have a low priority but are seen as vulgar.

I

St. John's College is the ideal-typical example of what we call the neoclassical college since it has sought to restore the classical curriculum with new intensity and purity. Like the other anti-university experiments, it was basically dominated by a moral imperative: a vision of human unity, of the good life in a Platonic mode. And like Plato's Socratic dialogues, the mode of discourse at St. John's is aporetic: "The argument either leads nowhere or it goes around in circles."[4] Beginning with the Socratic dialogues in the first year, and progressing through the 100-odd Great Books which have come to characterize the program, St. John's teaches that "one dogma and doctrine is not to be compromised: the assertion that learning is first and last for its own sake."[5] The idea of "dogma" in its Greek sense of "a formulated belief" is not foreign at St. John's, a community that believes education should not be instrumental to some other end, but should itself be an end. Thus the college should model the forms of life of liberally educated men, enabling students to join in this process and to experience it as its own reward. The object is to create a great conversation about the great questions. At root, these are connected with intellectual and moral virtue, and with all the Socratic paradoxes about whether and in what ways virtue is "teachable."

Scott Buchanan, the intellectual leader of the new St. John's, had come in 1937 from Robert Hutchins's college at Chicago, where he had taken part in an effort to discover a true curriculum of the liberal arts, which some saw as a return to the ideals of the nineteenth-century liberal-arts college. Buchanan was sympathetic to the disciplinarians' view that the faculties of mind were best sharpened by the classics, mathematics, and philosophy, but he aspired to a vision of the liberal arts that he felt the nineteenth-century colleges failed to realize.[6] He saw himself as a radical not a reactionary, and the transcendent ideals that Buchanan sought led him back to Plato. Buchanan was influenced by the general-education program that had been developed at Columbia College, which moved in this direction in terms of syllabus, but hardly at all in terms of so magisterial a moral intention.[7] For him, the trivium and quadrivium were part of an underlying unity of knowledge: a monism to be attained by the Socratic dialogue. The end of knowledge was virtue: to know the good, and then, in fear and trembling, to live by it. The core values were a faith in the classical texts, the so-called Great Books, and a belief that virtue arose from submitting oneself to their tutelage and from grasping their continuing vitality and import.

If the ideal of the multiversity lies in the scientific method, in which the young teach the old by extending the frontiers of science, the ideal at St. John's is that the wisdom of the elders molds the young in a Socratic process. At St. John's the scale of pay is fixed by one's age; there are no professional ranks, and neither degrees nor teaching experiences elsewhere are taken into account.

The movements of opposition caricature not only each other, but perhaps inevitably the dominant university styles as well. The neoclassicals regarded and still regard the universities and the conventionally departmentalized colleges as vulgar and technocratic. They envisage the universities as sterile, exploiting knowledge for merely technical ends and preparing students not for the "calling" of life, but for superficial though profitable, vocationalism. They underestimated the diversity of what later came to be called the multiversity, and also its incremental inventiveness.[9]

Students were invited to come to St. John's College not for certification or entry into a meritocratic elite, but in order to become more civilized, in order to join an aristocratic great chain of being, stretching back through the medieval university to Plato's Academy. The graduates of St. John's College, an institution which in Scott Buchanan's words was designed to produce cultural misfits, are not rendered unemployable, but have in fact done well in law, teaching, business, and other fields. But though their St. John's virtues are not their undoing, St. John's is hardly the road toward "making it." On the contrary, to think of college as a launching pad for one's career would stamp one as unworthy of St. John's.

It is almost impossible to think of an enterprise like St. John's College existing under public auspices. For one thing, there is the crucial question of scale. A large institution would be wholly antithetical to the ideal of a community of scholars. So far as we know, only in the University of California system has anything like St. John's College been given houseroom without being swamped. A short-lived experiment was started at Berkeley by Professor Joseph Tussman, who, like Scott Buchanan, had come under the influence of Alexander Meiklejohn and his 1920s experiment at the University of Wisconsin.[10] A case could be made that the first college of the University of California at Santa Cruz, Cowell College, which began in 1965, also embodied some aspects of the St. John's model, although it soon abandoned whatever limited requirements it had possessed and lost much of its autonomy vis a vis the Boards of Studies—that is, the academic departments.

The neoclassical concept was obviously more at home in a small setting. Rather than let its community grow beyond four hundred students, St. John's founded a second campus in Santa Fe, New Mexico, in 1964. St. Mary's College of California, which has consciously patterned its curriculum on the St. John's model, is another imitator. Shimer College in Mt. Carroll, Illinois, a 1950s offshoot of Chicago now threatened with extinction, could also be viewed as a kind of analogue of St. John's with its nearly all-required program.

It is striking to realize that all the graduates of St. John's College since it began probably number less than the entering freshman class of one of the great state universities in any given year. Yet, despite its small scale, St. John's began a debate in the 1940s concerning the purposes of higher education that engaged the attention of John Dewey, Alexander Meiklejohn, Sidney Hook, Walter Lippmann, Jacques Maritain, Mark Van Doren, and many others; the cultural resonance continues to this day.

St. John's College resisted the university ideal as being too fractured into specialties, too tainted by careerism. But in one respect. St. John's had a great deal in common with the best Ivy League men's colleges—namely, the premium placed on the written tradition.

II

In the 1920s to learn the performing arts, one's best bet was probably at a conservatory or an art institute. A few liberal-arts colleges had, so to speak, musical appendages, such as Oberlin with its Conservatory. Some of the great state universities, such as Indiana, Illinois, Michigan in music, and Iowa in creative writing, were diverse enough and flexible enough to get away from traditional scholarly canons as to what is appropriate in a university setting.[11] In a way, they followed the land-grant model. Just as they had prepared people who wanted to teach home economics, they prepared people who wanted to teach music or to enter "commercial" callings in the graphic arts as well as those who aspired to the fine arts.

But the creation of colleges whose main emphasis lay in the aesthetic dimension was mirrored by the founding of a kind of second generation of institutions devoted to the education of women. Vassar, Bryn Mawr, Smith, and Mount Holyoke had established that women could equal men in cognitive facility. Now Scripps, and later, to a lesser degree, Mills on the West Coast and Bennington and Sarah Lawrence on the East Coast, took advantage of the somewhat sheltered status of upper-class women to give freer rein to acknowledged creativity in the arts.

When David Riesman was a Harvard College undergraduate, Class of 1931, many of his closest friends were, or considered themselves, aesthetes. When Harvard was not merely muscular, they found it excessively verbal. Bennington College in 1932, the year of its founding, struck him as a dramatic and appealing contrast to all that had seemed donnish and pedestrian at Harvard College. Along with Sarah Lawrence and Black Mountain, it embodied what we have here termed the aesthetic-expressive ideal. That was not all there was to either Bennington or Sarah Lawrence, of course. Both, for example, gave employment to some of the Central European refugee scholars who were not aesthetes: for example, Erich Fromm and Peter Drucker, among others, had joined the Bennington faculty. Still, for many of the Bennington students, creative expression lay at the core of the enterprise.

In more recent decades, Bard College has also shared some of the aims of the colleges we term communal-expressive. Bard has in fact gone through several refoundings, including a ten-year period (1933–44) as an experimental college under the auspices of Teachers College at Columbia. Throughout its history Bard has sought to reject competition and academic pressure, to remove status distinctions between students and faculty, and to seek that elusive goal of "community" which often seems harder to obtain in small isolated antiacademic enclaves than in settings where faculty and students have extramural ties and emotional outlets that soften family quarrels. Black Mountain, particularly in its later days, under the poet-president Charles Olson, was dedicated to the development of creative expression.

To be sure, Black Mountain did not want to be a "one-sided art-music school," as the painter Joseph Albers put it, yet the college saw the academic disciplines as supplementing the arts, not the other way around.[12] The motivation of students was to develop artistic talent; the end of the community was to foster creativity and to experience beauty. The model was that of a bohemian artistic community: and the process of education resembled a studio with its apprenticeship style of mutual creation and criticism, whether it be fiction or sculpture. Black Mountain nurtured a cultural movement that supported and shaped the careers of John Cage, Merce Cunningham, Buckminster Fuller, Paul Goodman, Robert Rauschenberg, Olson, and Albers.

While St. John's College manages to survive only through the dedication of its tutors and the energy and magnanimity of its administrators and supporters, Black Mountain survives in an enormous cultural legacy, even though the college itself, after many rescues from sudden death, perished in 1956. The Bauhaus, undone by Hitler, lives a flourishing life in America; it has influenced the International Style everywhere. Indeed, the native-born Americans among the Black Mountain recruits have helped turn the United States into a mecca for artists from all over the world. They form a major part of what Harold Rosenberg has termed "the tradition of the new."

Correspondingly, although not fully institutionalized in the major university centers,[13] work is now being done in the genres illuminated by these artists; for example, at the Visual Arts Center at Harvard, at the music departments at Princeton or Columbia, and, for a long time now, in the workshops for writers at the University of Iowa. Of course, radicals fear such inclusion as "cooptation," but it is more properly seen as mutual infiltration, or, as Harold Lasswell put it in a marvelous term, "restriction through partial incorporation."

Although the arts did not flourish on American campuses before World War II, major gains were made in the 1960s. More than 80 campuses, three-fourths of them public institutions (UCLA is the largest, awarding 232 fine-arts degrees in a recent year), now award degrees in art. Among the private institutions which have sizable programs are Brigham Young, Wellesley, Boston University, and Northwestern, but no private institutions are among the first twenty in numbers graduated and, with the exception of Stanford, no elite private university awards more than twenty-five art degrees annually.[14] And as more students are trained in the arts, pressure is created for such programs to move downward as graduates seek jobs in the lower schools. In 1976, the U. S. Office of Education initiated a program to assimilate the arts into the regular public-school curriculum. The announcement claimed that it was the "first program supported by Congress for arts education as an integral part of the interdisciplinary teaching of academic subjects rather than an elective course of extra-curricular activity for children with artistic talents or interests."[9] Simultaneously, more money has been flowing into arts programs in public colleges and universities.

Viewed from the perspective of the discipleship that characterized both Black Mountain and the early Bennington, the new palaces of the arts rising in some of the public universities would be seen as corrupting in their giantism. Those early pioneers in education in the arts might also view the Carnegie Commission's recent anointing of the arts as somewhat of a curse.[16] One consequence of the imitation by the broader academic culture is that the colleges founded to give form to the aesthetic impulse have had perhaps an even harder time surviving than the other offbeat enterprises we are discussing here. For one thing, the polarization in terms of sex which relegated creative expression to the female domain has greatly moderated; with men encouraged to develop what would once have been thought "feminine" aspects of themselves, colleges specializing in aesthetic expressivity for women have had to reconsider their mandate. Bennington and Sarah Lawrence, along with most women's colleges, have gone coed; so has Immaculate Heart College, where recently there has been a great emphasis on the arts; Scripps has not had to join the near-panic rush toward coeducation because it is part of the Claremont group. Correspondingly, Bennington[17] and Sarah Lawrence, which have never been exclusively devoted to the arts, have lost their place in the vanguard, while, as we have noted, Black Mountain closed its doors in the mid-1950s. Of the four telic reforms, the aesthetic-expressive has been given short shrift in this volume. We do not devote a chapter to Black Mountain as we have to other illustrations of our typology, but refer the reader to Martin Duberman's brilliant chronicle of the life and death of that incredible experiment.[18]

III

In the nineteenth century, America was seen as the Promised Land by millions of natives and immigrants; but for myriads of small groups, the Covenant had long since been broken and the sense of mission that can be found in John Winthrop's "errand into the wilderness" had long since been betrayed. As higher education spread, and as the specifically religious impulse waned, it is understandable that a few institutions of higher education began to see themselves as the principal expression of the values of community, even though they also operated as peripheral members of a system valuing competition and cognitive rationality. Community was one theme at Black Mountain College, along with the emphasis on the arts; and like other utopian communities, Black Mountain suffered a series of schisms in its search for wholeness. Schisms, in fact, seem to be part of the "natural history" of communal-expressive ventures. Such institutions generally begin with a charismatic leader who is often not good at balancing either books or interests and is subsequently expelled.[19]

The full flowering of the communal-expressive movement in the several colleges that have been dominated by it occurred only with the growing influence of humanistic psychology. Much of the literature of humanistic psychology, including the journal of that name, focuses less on expressing its own particular ethos, than on differentiating itself from such major currents in psychology as behaviorism and traditional Freudian psychoanalysis. Its view of man tends to be Rousseauistic. Carl Rogers, Abraham Maslow, and a more distant and more intellectual mentor, Norman O. Brown, provided the movement with an ideology about the importance of the affective life: "Where ego was, there shall id be." The techniques used in these new ventures are often those of the T-group, the encounter group.[20]

The encounter movement is prominently linked to techniques developed in the National Training Labs in the 1950s and 1960s to help teachers, ministers, businessmen, and civil-rights workers become more sensitive to the feelings of others and more attuned to the factors affecting social interaction. Though Maslow and Rogers have had perhaps the widest influence on the growth of what we have called the communal-expressive movement in higher education, there are less obvious connections to the work of Kurt Lewin, Jacob Moreno, Elton Mayo, Douglas McGregor, and others concerned with creating environments supportive of human growth and change.

Paradoxically, the college that perhaps went furthest in grounding itself in these techniques, Johnston College, was founded in 1969 as an experimental college of the University of Redlands. The college departed from its parent institution with an evangelical fervor that would have been less at odds with the Baptist traditions of the early Redlands. Johnston College opened with a two-week retreat in the woods, in which faculty, students, and staff formed themselves into moderately intrusive encounter groups called Grok Groups in order to share their hopes and aims for the incipient college. The faculty included not only T-group leaders, but also observers of process, whose function it was to report on the affective life of all the constituencies of the college. Many were Rogerians, some of whom brought to their new secular religion the zeal of converts from earlier constraint. The founding chancellor of Johnston College, Pressley McCoy, had been associated with Protestant colleges and is a man of strongly evangelical bent. Indeed, a number of the original faculty of Johnston College had at some previous point either been in a seminary or had entered the priesthood or the ministry. Our impression is that many of the more experimental colleges, public and private, founded in recent years have been influenced by ex-priests and ex-ministers. Most of them, to be sure, are properly equipped with

Ph.D.s, but for them affective education represents something like a return of the repressed or discarded religious impulse. In their own quests for identity, they tend to emphasize the negative identity of the new colleges as being at war with the overwhelming intellectuality and departmentalized rationalism of what they term the academic mainstream.[21]

In the war of negative identities against prevalent patterns at the University of Redlands, Johnston College lost the battle with its parent institution. Chancellor McCoy was ousted, and the struggling enterprise barely escaped termination. Now, five years later, the encounter-group emphasis is still present, but muted; it is no longer the sacred thread that binds the college together. Rather, Johnston College has come to resemble other new private colleges such as New College in Sarasota or Hampshire College in adopting the contract system which allows students and faculty to negotiate what must be done to achieve a terminal degree, and to identify the way stations en route. There is still talk of community, of course, but it is no longer either euphoric or inflamed.

Some of the spirit that animated Johnston College at its founding was also present at the birth of Evergreen State College several years later, but it is considerably attenuated now. However, the communal-expressive impulse was widespread, even though it was often short-lived and seldom established as the dominant metaphor of an entire institution. Seeds of the so-called human potential movement found life at the College Within at Tufts University, the Inner College of the University of Connecticut, at an Esalen-like Center at the University of Oregon, Bensalem College at Fordham University, and a variety of "living-learning" experiments from Old Westbury to Fresno State. Rochdale College, though not actually a degree-granting institution, was set up in an apartment house near Toronto University where resident members were required to contribute labor and hire their own teachers and administrators. The College of the Person in Washington, D. C., advertised itself as a center for encounter, bodily awareness exercises, and Gestalt therapy "that will provide for emotional involvement and support, an opportunity to share feelings, perceptions, insights, love and concern."[22]

As the T-group of encounter style spread to many traditional classrooms in the late 1960s, the seminar table began to resemble the family dinner table.[23] Affective relations came to outweigh intellectual competition, although students as well as their teachers were often ambivalent about awarding academic credit for such explorations. The purest realization of the Communal-Expressive style that we have encountered is the subject of Chapter 4: Kresge College at the University of California at Santa Cruz, which opened in 1970. Kresge appealed to students as "a living learning community which concerns itself with the human as well as the intellectual needs of its members"; the catalogue statement continues: "One favorite Kresge metaphor was the organic image. Last year we thought of ourselves as an infant college, struggling to survive and grow and learn what a college should be. . . . Our eventual objective is to create a diversified system where each species is dependent upon every other for its welfare, and where all of us together make an integrated context which nourishes and sustains life."[24]

In its charter year, Kresge College declared that its aim was to "explore educational innovation through a human relations approach. . . . The excitement and creativity of a learning environment is the result of open, direct and explicit relationships."[25] This aim was to be facilitated by organization into kin groups composed of a faculty member and fifteen or so students who lived near one another, which would meet as a seminar offshoot of a college-wide course, and would often function as an encounter group. Although students attend classes in other boards and colleges at Santa Cruz as well, the kin groups minimize the distinctions of rank and erase any boundary between the curriculum and the life of the residence halls within Kresge.

While the rest of Santa Cruz often views Kresge as a tribal family, it is recognized that there are factions within. Thus, Kresge has faced more slowly the problem of belief that came to an early head at Johnston and the other experiments: the difficulty of eliciting consent from later generations who did not participate in the encounters of the founding cadre and did not share its drama or charisma. By 1976, what had once been a college-wide experiment now retreated as the "Corner of the College." By resisting diffusion, the founders, who had been strengthened by the arrival of Philip Slater and Eliott Aronson, hoped to maintain the intensity of the original experiment on a smaller scale.

At the deepest level, the communal-expressive movement as illustrated by Johnston or by Kresge shows its religious side by a belief in mystical oneness: the desire is to experience unity and to find mutual growth in the support of a group, through openness to others. (And to the Jungians among the founders of Kresge, as with Brother Antoninus, now laicized and writing poetry as William Everson, openness to introspective processes, to one's own subconscious, is a crucial aspect of the Kresge experiment insofar as it enables students to discover their calling by discovering their archetype). Because the aspirations of the covenant are so exalted, the disappointment and disillusion when it breaks down—when the company turns out not to be composed of saints—can run bitter and deep. Mutual openness can lead to exploitation and to what the political scientist, Jo Freeman, writing about women's groups, terms "the tyranny of structurelessness."[26]

While it would be all too easy to parody its saccharine excesses, Kresge strikes us as an experiment of integrity that deserves the careful attention of those who would hope that a better balance can be struck between feeling and intellect,[27] and who believe that we have a great deal to learn about how to be more cooperative without sacrificing essential human diversity.

IV

If the communal-expressive colleges have identified principally with the counterculture, the colleges dominated by political activism in the 1960s have been at odds with the counterculture's softness, its emphasis on consensus. They sought change in the society, less consciously in themselves. In the early days of SDS, the two currents were fused, and often confused; members sought expressive comradeship as well as specific political mobilization and change.[28]

Even now, with the receding wave of protest, departments at many universities, eminent and nonelite alike, are dominated by faculty who were "radicalized" in the 1960s, often, of course, with leadership from the few charismatic elders. As Carnegie Commission surveys of faculty attitudes show, there are dramatic differences among fields, with sociology at one extreme and engineering or veterinary medicine at another. But if one asks not about enclaves within major institutions, but rather about colleges founded by or dominated by activist-radicals, then the list is short indeed.

Before World War I, in the absence of a strong socialist movement, no colleges devoted to working-class or socialist ideals were founded; rather, the YMCA and Catholic and Protestant groups founded a few colleges in the major cities to help give working-class children a start in life according to the traditional American belief in equality of opportunity. The Wobblies started no colleges. Indeed, in the area of the Northwest where the Wobblies have been something of a presence, Reed College began in 1911 as perhaps the purest expression of the university college ideal with no concessions whatever to the gentlemanly collegiate, the evangelical Christian, or the explicitly vocational.

In the period after World War I, several labor schools emerged, such as Brookwood, the Highlander Folk School, Commonwealth, and, as an urban radical institution, the Rand School of Social Science.[29] These schools sought to prepare union leaders rather than those who were likely to get out of the working-class through upward mobility. With the Rand School of Social Science, as in some measure with the New School for Social Research, the aim was more intellectual and less activist; for the faculty, these were scholarly institutions not intended to provide a fortress for direct political activism. In a way, Brookwood and Commonwealth were for the labor movement what Berea was intended to be for Appalachia: places which would help students from a deprived part of the society return to it with more training and a strong sense of mission.

The 1920s saw the founding of the college which was to become in the 1960s the most visible and highly charged base for political activism of any college in America. Antioch College (as it was later reconstituted by Arthur Morgan) represents an ideal-typical instance of the activist-radical college. Its commitment to extramural action began in the 1920s with its focus on the coop program by which Antioch students spent alternate terms on and off campus in work programs. These programs were not, as were those designed for nonaffluent students at Northeastern or Cincinnati, designed to help them finance their education; in fact, their education at parental expense was in effect prolonged in order to help immerse them more fully in the dilemmas and contradictions of American life. Although the work program even to this day has not been fully integrated into the Antioch curriculum, the ideology of the program under the aegis of Arthur Morgan reflected an attempt to get away from bookishness, to provide mentors for students other than scholarly faculty, for whom, in fact, Arthur Morgan had an almost philistine lack of respect.[30]

Antioch was neither founded by radicals originally, nor was it in fact refounded by them during the era of Arthur Morgan. But it has been committed to social, political, and curricular change since that refounding, and in the 1960s it experienced with particular intensity the commitment of a large part of its faculty and student body to using the college for the political ends of the far left. Antioch expanded early, as a few other colleges did, to serve minority groups and had a small cadre committed to expressive-communitarian ideals that were now avowedly political. The college was never wholly "radicalized," but the largest single unit on the campus, although not formally a department, came to be the Marxist-oriented Institute for the Solution of Social Problems. Some departments became collectives in which student voting power outweighed that of the faculty, carrying further the pattern of community self-government that had prevailed at Antioch in an earlier day. The president, James Dixon, a physician who had founded with Marcus Raskin and Dick Gregory the short-lived New Party in the 1960s, encouraged these developments, often, it would appear, using students as leverage against a minority of more traditional faculty. Antioch's elaboration of an extensive network of more than a score of field centers around the country was seen by some as a financial drain on the home campus, further exacerbating confrontation tactics. One student vented his frustration at Antioch's brand of politics: "You can get anything you want on this campus if you place a rock through a pane of glass."[31]

At Goddard College there have been political battles less violent and visible than those at Antioch. The politics there has been more intramural, with fewer links to the national and international agenda of radicalism. And at Staten Island Community College, some faculty saw their mission as that of raising the consciousness of working-class students. But neither of these institutions became quite so polarized and polemical as Antioch; for comparisons, one would have to go to Tokyo or the Free University of West Berlin.

As the more civilized liberal-left consensus at Antioch eroded under radical pressures in the 1960s, everything came to be decided by votes, pressure tactics, strikes, and sit-ins. Violence reached a peak in the 1972–73 academic year. The campus was torn by a series of strikes (by cafeteria workers, minority students, radicals, fired faculty, and others) that went on for months. The grass grew knee-high on campus lawns; buildings were trashed; crime rates rose alarmingly. By June 1975, President James Dixon had been outmaneuvered by the College Council and was dismissed as president. Enrollment fell drastically after years of turmoil; one-fourth of the Yellow Springs faculty were given dismissal notices in one year.

William Birenbaum, who as president of the Staten Island Community College had launched programs for blacks, former drug addicts, veterans, and "community scholars" (chosen by a community group empowered to admit anyone deemed worthy, regardless of previous level of education), succeeded Dixon in 1976. In another of the fascinating connections we keep discovering among the telic reformers, Birenbaum had been influenced by Robert Hutchins during his student days at the University of Chicago (even though as head of the Hyde Park-Kenwood Community Council, Birenbaum later fought Hutchins over the university's seeming lack of concern for the black residents on its border).[32] After Chicago, Birenbaum went to Wayne State and the New School for Social Research, and eventually worked with the late Senator Robert Kennedy to found a new college in the Bedford-Stuyvesant ghetto. These commitments made him a natural choice for the modern Antioch, although even Birenbaum's formidable energies may be exhausted in attempting to coordinate Antioch's disillusioned yet still evolving network.

In fact, Antioch's complex metamorphoses have outrun our own ability to keep pace. Although we had prepared a chapter on Antioch for this volume, we later decided that the College for Human Services would be in some ways a better illustration of the activist-radical model. CHS, as nearly everyone refers to it, was founded on the lower West Side of New York in 1965 by an extraordinary woman, Audrey Cohen. The college grew from earlier efforts to find paraprofessional jobs for black women on welfare.

Known then as the Women's Talent Corps, the college was unaccredited and offered no degrees. Now it seeks to award a master's degree in the human services to students still drawn mainly from the welfare rolls but also including recent Polish immigrants in addition to black and Spanish-speaking minorities. Graduates are urged to take up roles as change agents—not just to enter the helping professions but to transform them. They are to become client advocates skilled at breaking down bureaucratic resistance to "humane and caring" service. Students spend only two days a week at the college, with the other three devoted to internships in a wide variety of service agencies, from schools to mental-health clinics. Faculty act as advocates, too, seeking improved pay and responsibility for students as they make progress in class and on the job. The curriculum has gone far in recent years in the direction of so-called competence-based reforms, requiring students to demonstrate, in a series of "constructive actions," that they can perform as agents of change and improved service.

As at Antioch, students sometimes find it more tempting to try to change the college than the world outside, and the College for Human Services suffered a series of strikes in the early 1970s. But, perhaps because neither student nor faculty rebels had any tenure at CHS, and because Audrey Cohen did not hesitate to show some the door, the experiment not only survived but grew stronger. The curriculum, under development for more than a decade, demands a dedication approaching sainthood from its students. But it is also one of the most ingenious we have seen in terms of engaging students in a carefully articulated series of practical challenges.

Antioch and the College for Human Services illustrate different strains of the activist radical movement. Antioch, in its Marxist Institute for the Solution of Social Problems, was more grandly revolutionary for a brief time, but was not grounded in any stern tradition of radicalism. There has never been any very powerful endemic Socialist movement in America. Going back to Commonwealth and Brookwood, the activist-radical colleges have had only a sporadic life, although Antioch is an exception. The College for Human Services is closer to the impulses of Jane Addams and the early settlement-house leaders than it is to Marxist or more specifically radical political movements. Audrey Cohen is a practical reformer, though she uses the language of a revolutionary. The roots of this movement are manifold and difficult to trace. There are weak connections to European Socialism, although more proximately, the labor-education movement and the civil-rights movements were important influences.

Our typology emphasizes the differences among the telic reforms. But the commonalities are also striking. Each of these experiments has a sense of mission. We suspect that many faculty who are attracted to them are not only dissatisfied with competitive life in the multiversity but yearn for a sense of identity and esprit. They want to join an institution that is capable of evoking the deep loyalties of the whole self and of engendering all-out efforts. They want to believe.[33] A visitor is immediately aware of the basic choices participants have exercised. Bridges have been cut; commitments have been made, and ideals are continually tested, including those of the visitor.

A spirit of vocation and intensity about teaching permeates these communities, partly as a result of the jettisoning of research and publication norms, but also from the growth of a new sense of mission. Of course, new ideals may fade for individuals if not institutions, and faculty who have sacrificed much in their own conversion often hide even from themselves the hurt they feel when their offerings are rejected by the intended acolytes. Yet there is some protection against such wounds since the expertise of the teacher is deemphasized. In all these radical experiments, teachers and students are seen as colearners: at St. John's students and tutors puzzle out the great texts together and at Black Mountain they joined others in creating paintings and poems. The egalitarian spirit[34] does not deny to teachers all authority, although the grounds of that authority do not lie in disciplinary expertise in the way that they do in the university colleges.

Nor is self-governance in itself necessarily egalitarian—certainly not at St. John's, where a small oligarchy on the Instruction Committee rules, nor at Kresge, where in the early years most important decisions were made by a few charismatic figures even while the community sought the ideal of participatory democracy. What does mark these colleges off from most modern universities is the devotion to community. Bonds of community are nourished by reinforcing participation in the full round of life, whether at the Friday night lecture at St. John's or the kin-group meeting at Kresge. At three of these institutions, there are no departments to compete for students. The important judgments have to do with whether students measure up to the ideals of the college, not whether they perform well according to the traditional standards developed by a departmentally organized faculty.[35]

Like the popular reforms, the telic experiments are bound together in their aversions to the multiversity model, but their arena is wider than that of the enemy—their hope is to create some notion of the good life whether in the Platonic or the Rogerian mode.

It is in this deepest sense that these institutions are "transdisciplinary," i.e., there is some notion of an end or a good to which academic disciplines are subordinate. Their sense of mission is reflected in the forms of teaching, too. At St. John's there is the belief that disciplines serve as falsifying lenses through which students preconceive and are likely to misconceive the "natural articulations of the intellectual world. . . . This college chooses to overcome these institutionalized prejudgments by substituting fundamental books for departments and elementary skills for disciplines."[36] The mixed-media event was born at Black Mountain, where poets, musicians, dancers, actors—and on occasion stray dogs—joined together to create productions. At Kresge, the disciplines were viewed as subordinate to the task of building community, and at CHS, subordinate to the aim of discovering the generic competencies of the "humane professional."

These transdisciplinary or interdisciplinary forms are quite distinct from conventional interpretations. If a discipline is the systematic study of a defined field by means of distinctive methods of analysis,[37] then interdisciplinary work has usually meant discussing some topic from a variety of these perspectives. But it would be better to describe that process as multidisciplinary when it means that the conversation is a sandwich with little interpenetration among the layers of sociology, philosophy, or economics. And like a sandwich, multidisciplinary occasions are usually short meals for transitory gatherings.

Interdisciplinary dialogue implies a more sustained conversation subsumed under a fundamental question or problem or set of such questions. It also means that there is an effort to understand the key metaphors and analytical frameworks of the other disciplines. Naturally, participants cannot be expected to master the depth and breadth of many disciplines; to do so clearly requires the power of genius. (More frequently, one finds a new subdiscipline created as the methods of one discipline are applied to another, as in psychohistory.) Interdisciplinary dialogue requires each participant to master at least one discipline and to be capable of understanding the technical apparatus of some others. Participants must become multilingual, acquiring a "reading" knowledge of several languages, more than Berlitz phrase books provide but less than educated citizens of the country would know. This knowledge grows and is tested in discourse with those trained in other disciplines who are equally committed to investigating the common questions.[38]

The telic reform communities provide a setting for such discourse, organizational structures that support and reward it, and transcendent questions that inspire it. The process is most evident at St. John's, where faculty members teach all subjects in a required program. Thus an anthropologist teaches mathematics, mathematicians lead students in biology experiments, and all read Plato. St. John's tutors frequently attend a class along with students a year before they are expected to teach it.

Of course, interdisciplinary dialogue may go stale. Sometimes it becomes fixed in amber because the community, while initially quite diverse in disciplinary make-up, becomes cut off from fresh infusions of disciplinary knowledge. Or later faculty recruits may be only naive generalists with little or inadequate disciplinary training. Without faculty who are grounded in the disciplines there is little hope that the inquiry itself[39] can be disciplined. The difficulty arises if students in such a program never reach any depth themselves in any of the disciplines, particularly if their inadequacy is later projected as mild hostility toward all disciplines.

We speak here of disciplines as guilds of scholars organized in the traditional branches of knowledge: philosophy, history, physics, and the like. But one can speak of discipline in a broad sense: the discipline of a group or a community, the state of order based upon submission to legitimate authority. We have tried to compare the telic reforms in this latter sense—and to contrast them with the multiversity ideal—under the column headed "Authority Grounded in" in Appendix 1. There we point to the grounds of authority that establish what John Dewey called "the moving spirit of the whole group."[40] In the multiversity, discipline in the narrow sense of the scholarly guilds is also the basis of discipline in the broad sense: authority in the research universities ultimately rests with those who possess consensually validated claims to specialized expertise.

In the telic reforms, disciplines in the narrow sense are subordinate to—and usually exist in uneasy tension with—the broad authority that establishes "the moving spirit of the whole group." That authority defines the relation between the student and the community into which he is being inducted. In what we have called the neoclassical model, the authority rests in the wisdom of the Socratic elders as interpreters of the texts of the liberal tradition. The young tutor who questions the selection of any particular reading or its relations to other aspects of the St. John's program is told to be patient: in time he will come to see the wisdom of the choice in the larger scheme of things. For the aesthetic-expressive model, the authority lies in submission to the sensibilities of the master artists. They determine what counts as art and what kind of community discipline will best sustain the tradition of artistic innovation.

In the communal-expressive case, the authority derives from the charisma of the founding prophet or guru, the one who can win the devotion of followers to a particular notion of a nurturing community. As Rosabeth Moss Kanter has written, community of this type is based in part on "the desire for strong relations within a collectivity, for intense emotional feeling among all members, for brotherhood and sharing."[41] The activist-radical model is grounded in an agenda of social or political reform, and the discipline lies in the experience of learning to effect change. The student at the College for Human Services must perform "constructive actions" that result in benefits to clients. The authority attaches to the one who creates a vision of a better society and who acts to bring about change in the desired direction. In the extreme case it is the author of the revolution; in democratic situations it is the one whose program of reform wins the most adherents or votes. Challenges to the authority of the activist-radical inevitably turn on the question of whether one is trying to understand the world or to change it, and at the College for Human Services the curriculum is based on the idea that one will understand it best by trying to change it.

We speak of the transcendent, and even this brief overview hints at the utopian strains that run through these reform movements, which will be more evident in the accounts in the chapters that follow. The utopian impulses are strong, representing a search for a more perfect union that, as we have noted, often leads to disunion and schism. Because the founders have made radical choices, not leaving many options open in the way that the contemporary university does, the alternative to opposition is withdrawal.

In addition to offering more options, the norms of the multiversity are more congruent with dominant societal values: individualistic achievement, pluralism, the production of useful knowledge. In a sense, with the exception of CHS, all the movements we have labeled telic reforms are impractical. They are the luxuries of a society that can afford to educate a leisure class, whether in the neoclassical Greek mode of St. John's or with the more Rousseauistic charms of Kresge. Or they might be justified on the grounds that it is prudent policy to pay for such diversions to keep youth off the streets at a time when a technologically oriented labor market cannot absorb all who seek employment. (St. John's and Black Mountain were in fact founded during the great depression decade, and the reformed Antioch and Kresge blossomed at a time when the labor market was flooded by an unprecedented expansion in the college-age population.) Neo-Marxists would in all likelihood condemn the experiments (excepting Antioch, perhaps) as keeping alive the illusion of change in a decadent capitalist society, as exemplars not of telic reforms but of repressive tolerance.

From a modern functionalist perspective, articulated most notably in the work of Talcott Parsons and Gerald Platt,[42] there is a question of whether these telic reform movements ought to be classified as within the domain of higher education at all. For Parsons and Platt, the primary societal function of the university is to guard cognitive culture and the interests that support it. Thus, scholarly research and graduate faculties, concerned "with the advancement, perpetuation and transmission of knowledge and with the development of cognitively significant competence," constitute the core of the academic system.[43] The primary function of graduate faculties is to maintain the standard of cognitive rationality; this function is blended in varying degrees with three others—undergraduate socialization, training in the professions, and the education of social critics or intellectuals as generalists.

The college experience should develop personalities that "can articulate with a differentiating, rationalizing, and changing society. Intelligence, universalistic standards of evaluation, autonomy, flexibility, and rationally oriented legitimate achievement are features of this extended socialization."[44] The principal aim of undergraduate education ought to be winning students to the values of a pluralistic, cognitively rational culture.

Certainly Parsons and Platt are right that technical skill and cognitive competence are crucially important qualities. And we would agree that internalization of rational standards is difficult, and that care must be exercised so that rationality will not be overwhelmed by emotions or ideology—the former can be seen as a danger in the early Kresge experiment and the latter as a tension at the College for Human Services. But in their concern to counter the excesses of the academic counterculture, Parsons and Platt have taken a position that in some respects limits our vision of what undergraduate education might encompass. They are concerned, for example, that "cultural objects which cannot be described in the pattern-form of a set of propositions should not be called knowledge."[45] Thus art criticism is knowledge but painting itself is not. This is an old distinction, but it comes to have practical importance in a college or university when we must decide whether a student who pots or paints is engaged in as valuable a learning activity as one who writes a critical monograph on pottery or painting. In making a pot, one learns to choose, learns an economy in the use of materials, learns something about the connection between feeling and cognition. Naturally, the position one takes on these matters also determines one's view of who are to be the gatekeepers of knowledge. Should the art historians or the artists themselves be members of teaching faculties? We think both.[46]

In this sense learning and the development of expressive gifts cannot be described in the "pattern-form of a set of propositions," but they have a proper place in the development of aesthetic sensibilities in undergraduate education. We are not served best by identifying the values that justifiably dominate the graduate schools as the core values of all undergraduate education. The pluralism of higher education should not rest on so narrow a base. Higher education in America and life in the multiversity itself, would not be as varied or enriching without the stimulus of the telic reforms, even though these experiments do violate the Parsonian ideals of appropriate university function.

Notes

1. We contrast the telic reforms with the popular as an end-means distinction, and occasionally slip into calling the popular reforms "nontelic." But the latter phrase misleads. Although the popular reformers were concerned with changes in the processes of education more than with changes in institutional goals, their reforms were not without educational purpose. For example, many felt that self-designed programs would result in more relevant or more meaningful educational experiences.
2. Christopher Jencks and David Riesman, *The Academic Revolution* (New York: Doubleday, 1968; paperback, Chicago: University of Chicago Press, 1977).
3. It is arguable whether Catholic colleges ever constituted a contrasting model, and in fact by 1960 they had for the most part moved toward secularism.

   Vatican II served to fragment residual resistance among the lesser Catholic colleges to the processes, already well underway, leading to the creation of a system often only nominally Catholic, increasingly laicized, drawing students from families who still wanted a protective social environment for their offspring but who were no longer likely to insist on a curriculum grounded in Scholastic philosophy and the standard apologetics. Most colleges founded by Protestants have long since given up any strong denominational ties, although there are still a few in the hands of Fundamentalist sects committed to biblical literalism and anti-modernist piety, and, like Protestant Fundamentalism in general, they continue to show vitality at a time when the major more liberal denominations are losing their hold.
4. From Hannah Arendt, "Thinking and Moral Considerations: A Lecture," *Social Research*, 38, no. 3 (Autumn 1971), who makes a point in this essay that would find great favor at St. John's: "Could the activity of thinking as such,

the habit of examining and reflecting upon whatever happens to come to pass, regardless of specific content and quite independent of results, could this activity be of such a nature that it 'conditions' men against evil doing?," p. 148.

5. Eva Brann, "What Are the Beliefs and Teachings of St. John's College," *The Collegian*, St. John's College (May 1975), p. 10.
6. Buchanan was shaped both by his tutelage under Alexander Meiklejohn at Amherst and his graduate days at Oxford, but the Socratic model he created at St. John's differed consciously from the common curricular model of the nineteenth century; his was a grander vision than the "daily textbook assignments and remorseless recitations" that characterized that model as described, for example, in George W. Pierson, *Yale College: An Educational History. 1871–1921* (New Haven, Yale University Press, 1952), p. 69.
7. The best account of the Columbia program and a superbly cogent examination of the larger issues with which our essay deals is Daniel Bell, *The Reforming of General Education: The Columbia College Experience and Its National Setting* (New York: Columbia University Press, 1966).
8. For an evocative discussion of the sorts of innovation that go on in departments without ever being so labeled, and of the pedantry and pretentiousness that are also there, see Martin Trow, "The Public and Private Lives of Higher Education," paper read at the Second National Forum on New Planning and Management Practices in Post-Secondary Education, Education Commission of the States (Chicago, November 16, 1973); revised version in *Daedalus*, 104, no. 1 (Winter 1975), 113–27.
9. For an account of the short, unhappy life of what came to be called Tussman College, see his book, *Experiment at Berkeley* (New York: Oxford University Press, 1969).
10. Syracuse University, which in 1873 established the first degree-granting professional school of art, was an early exception to this pattern.
11. This quotation and our account of Black Mountain are drawn from Martin Duberman's magnificent history, *Black Mountain: An Exploration in Community* (New York: Dutton, 1972).
12. Bernard Beckerman, Dean of the School of Arts at Columbia, describes the checkered career of the arts on Morningside Heights, which have flourished and wilted since the early years of the century but "have never been firmly rooted as part of undergraduate education." See his lecture, "Arts Education for Undergraduates," *Seminar Reports* (New York: Columbia Seminar on General and Continuing Education in the Humanities, May 15, 1974), 1, no. 8: 1–3. Beckerman touches on the problem of the difficulties in the university setting of subordinating creative to scholarly standards, a theme developed by James Ackerman in "The Arts in Higher Education," *Content and Context: Essays on College Education*, ed. Carl Kaysen (New York: McGraw-Hill, 1973), pp. 219–66. Oliver Fulton and Martin Trow also provide survey evidence to show that assessment of creative work causes a strain in the leading universities. See "Research Activity in American Higher Education," *Sociology of Education*, 47, no. 1 (Winter, 1974): 69.
13. For statistics and historical profiles on the growth of the arts on American campuses see the following works: James Cass and Max Birnbaum, eds., *Comparative Guide to American Colleges* (New York: Harper & Row, 1972), pp. 813–15; Laurence Veysey, "The Humanities, 18601920," in Alexandra M. Oleson, ed., *The Organization of Knowledge in American Society, 1860–1920*, forthcoming; Jack Morrison *The Rise of the Arts on the American Campus* (New York: McGraw-Hill, 1973).
14. New York Times, "U.S. Starts Arts Program in the Schools," August 4, 1976, p. 35.
15. Speaking for the commission, Clark Kerr said that in the future the "well-balanced campus" will need to add the creative arts to its endeavors as a fifth stream in addition to the professions, the humanities, the sciences, and the social sciences, "The Carnegie Commission Looks at the Arts," Carnegie Commission, 1973. Kerr also noted that the commission survey showed that students said their campuses did not provide sufficient opportunities for artistic expression.
16. Bennington's long tradition of political and cultural nonconformity and its impact on students is reported in two volumes by Theodore Newcomb: *Personality and Social Change: Attitude Formation in a Student Community* (New York: Dryden, 1943); and Newcomb et al., *Persistence and Change: Bennington College and Its Students after Twenty-Five Years* (New York: John Wiley, 1967); see also David Riesman's review of *Persistence and Change in American Journal of Sociology*, 73, no. 5 (March 1968): 628–30.
17. Duberman, *Black Mountain: An Exploration in Community* (New York: Dutton, 1972; Doubleday Anchor paper edition, 1973).
18. Anyone who, like the authors of this essay, has met a number of these founding fathers is impressed on the one hand by their seemingly innocent plausibility, and on the other hand by

the repeated gullibility of their devotees, including not only supposedly shrewd bankers and other donors but also faculty members and students of higher intellectual caliber than the evangelical leaders they follow.

19. For a discussion of the rubrics of the movement, see Lawrence N. Solomon and Betty Berzon, eds., *New Perspectives on Encounter Groups* (San Francisco: Jossey-Bass, 1972), and Kurt W. Back, *Beyond Words* (Baltimore: Penguin, 1973).
20. In the semi-autobiographical book, *The Quest for Identity,* Allen Wheelis describes the formation of himself as a psychoanalyst, as a refugee from a devout and constraining Fundamentalist Texas family; then he illustrates poignantly the way in which the new vocation has failed to satisfy the impulses which led to its adoption. See "The Vocational Hazards of Psychoanalysis," in *The Quest for Identity* (New York: Norton, 1958). Among some of the leaders of the counterculture one finds such formerly "hard" psychologists as Richard Alpert; in another vein, the former and still practicing classicist Norman O. Brown; and any number of previously rigid academic scholars who found a second career, or a new life, in trying to discard aspects of themselves now regarded as restricting or "unnatural."
21. For brief reports on the College of the Person and similar experiments, see John Coyne and Tom Hebert, *This Way Out: A Guide to Alternatives to Traditional College Education in the United States, Europe and the Third World* (New York: E. P. Dutton, 1972). For an account of experiments at the University of Oregon, see Joseph Fashing and Steven E. Deutsch, *Academics in Retreat: The Politics of Academic Innovation* (Albuquerque: University of New Mexico Press, 1971). The Tufts experiment is treated at length in Richard Millburn, Gerald Grant, Blanche Geer and others, "Report on the College Within," mimeo, Tufts University, 1971.
22 We owe this analogy to Craig Eisendrath's and Thomas J. Cottle's discussion in *Out of Discontent: Visions of the Contemporary University* (Cambridge, Mass.: Schenkman, 1972), pp. 56–58.
23. University of California, Santa Cruz Catalogue (1973/74), pp. 20–21.
24. University of California, Santa Cruz Catalogue (1970/71), p. 41.
25. Jo Freeman, "The Tyranny of Structurelessness," *Berkeley Journal of Sociology,* 17 (1972–73), 151–64; see also the description of the Portland, Oregon, Learning Community, thinly disguised in David French, "After the Fall: What This Country Needs is a Good Counter `Counter-Culture' Culture," *New York Times Magazine,* October 3, 1971, pp. 20–21 ff.
26. We are aware that few things are more complex than the way the affective and cognitive are linked and grounded in human experience. Thought is not without feeling and feeling is entwined with perception and mental processes. Though we speak in uneasy shorthand here, we are not misled into believing that the distinction can be dealt with in brief compass.
27. For accounts by various hands of the impact of student protest on an array of more or less prominent colleges and universities, see David Riesman and Verne Stadtman, eds., *Academic Transformation: Seventeen Institutions under Pressure* (New York: McGraw-Hill 1972); also, Seymour M. Lipset, *Rebellion in the University* (Boston: Little Brown, 1971).
28. A more comprehensive treatment of this period would need to describe the role of the People's Institute at Cooper Union, as well as many others. For a history of Commonwealth, see Raymond and Charlotte Koch, *Educational Commune: The Story of Commonwealth College* (New York: Schocken, 1972). Frank Adams (with Myles Horton) tells the story of Highlander Folk School in *Unearthing Seeds of Fire: The Idea of Highlander* (Winston-Salem, N.C.: John F. Blair, 1975).
29. For the early Antioch (as well as an admirable picture of the early Reed), see Burton Clark, *The Distinctive College: Antioch, Reed, and Swarthmore* (Chicago: Aldine, 1970); for a later portrait see Gerald Grant, "Let a Hundred Antiochs Bloom!" *Change,* 4, no. 7 (September 1972): 47–58.
30. *Antioch Record,* February 13, 1972, p. 2.
31. For his own account of these connections, see Birenbaum's autobiography, *Something for Everybody is Not Enough: An Educator's Search for His Education* (New York: Random House, 1971).
32. In a review of Duberman's *Black Mountain,* in the *Harvard Educational Review,* 43, no. 2 (May 1973), Laurence Veysey beautifully captures that spirit: "Many of us yearn in some part of our minds for a college setting utterly free from bureaucratic harassment, a place where nothing distracts from mutual learning and creation. The dream merges with that of community—an educational environment to be sure, but one where life and the classroom merge into each other, and where status dissolves in genuine human relationships" (p. 258). Veysey himself left the University of Wisconsin to teach at Santa Cruz.

33. For a dramatic contrast with the more usual egalitarianism of American faculty, see Alexander Gerschenkron, "Getting Off the Bullock Cart: Thoughts on Educational Reform," *The American Scholar,* 45 (Spring 1976): 218–33, in which Gerschenkron describes (on p. 223) the shock of a great Swedish economist, Eli F. Heckscher, who gave a guest lecture at Williams College for which an undergraduate walked up to express his admiration. "It was a marvelous lecture, he said . . . Heckscher felt it was bordering on impertinence on the part of the student to presume he was capable of forming any judgment of the quality of a lecture given by a distinguished scholar."
34. Yet ironically, to the extent that such a judgment of the "whole" student reflects an ideology, it can be particularly damaging. To the degree that departmental verdicts are solely cognitive, they can be at least partially discounted, whereas ideological judgments are less easily turned aside, especially if they lead to one's exclusion from the group.
35. Eva Brann, "What Are the Beliefs and Teachings of St. John's College," p. 9.
36. Philip H. Phenix stipulates that "An organized field of inquiry, pursued by a particular group of men of knowledge, may be called a *scholarly discipline." Realms of Meaning: A Philosophy of the Curriculum for General Education* (New York: McGraw-Hill, 1964), p. 312. He leaves out the notion of special methods. And it is true that there is a multiplicity of methods or distinctive angles of vision within traditionally defined disciplines as well as among them: The cognitive, clinical, and humanistic psychologists are worlds apart. One could find analogues *within* most disciplines for what Jurgen Habermas has labeled the empirical-analytic, historical-hermeneutic, and critical ways of knowing in *Knowledge and Human Interests* (Boston: Beacon Press, 1971), see especially the Appendix, "Knowledge and Human Interests: A General Perspective," pp. 301–17.
37. See Hugh G. Petrie's lucid essay, "Do You See What I See, The Epistemology of Interdisciplinary Inquiry," *Educational Researcher,* Journal of the American Educational Research Association, 5, no. 2 (February 1976): 9–15, in which he writes of a test devised for interdisciplinary perception. Martin Trow writes of the dangers of interdisciplinary dialogue in, "Higher Education and Moral Development," *AAUP Bulletin,* Spring 1976, p. 24.
38. Thomas Green makes the point that we only talk about disciplinary or interdisciplinary dialogue "when we focus attention upon what happens *in* the inquiry rather than on the purpose *of* the inquiry . . . But there are settings in which it doesn't make sense to talk about inquiry belonging to any discipline, and therefore it doesn't make sense to say that it *is* inter- or multidisciplinary either . . . one kind would be any situation in which I am called upon to decide what to do rather than to decide what is true." Letter to Gerald Grant, October 6, 1976, emphasis in the original.
39. John Dewey, *Experience and Education* (New York: MacMillan, 1936), p. 56, quoted in Kenneth D. Benne, "Authority in Education," *Harvard Educational Review,* 40, no. 3: 385–410, whose analysis of the authority of rule and authority of the expert helped us to clarify these distinctions. We are also indebted to our colleagues Manfred Stanley, Wendy Kohli, Marian Krizinofski, Thomas Ewens, and Emily Haynes, whose careful attention to an earlier draft of this chapter was invaluable.
40. Kresge College did seek in its early years that commitment to group cohesion that was characteristic of those utopian communities Kanter describes as requiring the "attachment of a person's entire fund of emotion and affectivity to the group." Rosabeth Moss Kanter, *Commitment and Community: Communes and Utopias in Sociological Perspective* (Cambridge, Mass.: Harvard University Press, 1972) p. 72.
41. Talcott Parsons and Gerald M. Platt with Neil J. Smelser, *The American University* (Cambridge; Mass.: Harvard University Press, 1973).
42. *Ibid.,* pp. 109–10.
43. *Ibid.,* p. 215. See also the discussion in Parsons, Platt, and Rita Kirshstein, "Faculty Teaching Goals, 1968–1973," *Social Problems,* December 1976.
44. Parsons and Platt, *American University,* p. 63.
45. Difficulties often arise when traditional departments oriented to the usual scholarly modes of assessment attempt to absorb or to coexist with creative artists. The University of California at San Diego achieved remarkable success by reversing the order, beginning with creators and adding the critics later. In Visual Arts under Paul Brock (who has since gone on to Fordham), they began with a core faculty of painters, sculptors, and film-makers, adding a distinguished faculty in art history and criticism later. The Music and Drama Departments were similarly successful, although we know of other cases when tensions were created when those labeled "critics" and those labeled "creative" were housed in the same department, each group ambivalent not only about the other, but about the parts of themselves represented in the other.

CHAPTER 42

THE PALOMAR COLLEGE EXPERIENCE

GEORGE R. BOGGS AND DIANE G. MICHAEL

Significant discoveries often have their roots in the dynamics of a particular time and place. Caring people, often with a diversity of backgrounds and points of view, come together to solve common problems or to chart a course for the future. Such was the case in the early 1900s when educators began the first junior colleges, starting what would become the largest and most responsive system of higher education the world has ever known—the American community college. Just as the beginning of the twentieth century was a time of invention and the beginning of the community college movement in America, at Palomar College, 1989 was a time for rediscovery. Discussions about the future of the college led to a new focus on student learning and the invention of the "learning paradigm."

Introduction

Palomar College is a public, comprehensive community college in southern California. Founded in 1946, the college grew over the years to serve a geographic area of over 2,500 square miles in northern San Diego County. The college had long prided itself on the comprehensiveness and quality of its programs and its collegial shared governance system. Starting in 1978, however, with the passage of the California property tax limitation initiative (Proposition 13) and subsequent state actions such as the defunding of courses considered frivolous by the state, the enactment of uniform student enrollment fees, and the state-imposed enrollment caps, the college was swept into changes beyond its control.

Challenging Times

In the fall of 1985, the new college district superintendent-president was faced with many challenges. The college, like many other community colleges in California, was going into its fourth consecutive year of enrollment decline, employee salaries had been eroded by inflation, the college was in need of updated instructional equipment and facility improvements, and the district financial reserves had fallen to the point that the new president received a warning letter from the state chancellor's office. The year before, a consultants' report described the college as suffering from a proliferation of committees, which were contributing to distrust, politics, divisiveness, and factionalism.

In his first address to the faculty and staff, the new president asked the college faculty and staff to join him in "gaining control of our own destiny." He talked about the importance of viewing the student as a customer, the need to make students active participants in their learning, and the necessity

Source: "The Palomar College Experience," by George R. Boggs and Diane G. Michael, reprinted from *A Learning College for the 21st Century*, 1997, Oryx Press.

of setting high expectations for students. He explained how everyone at the college must care about students, and why the college must find ways to maximize and document student success.

In the ensuing years, the college instituted many programs intended to raise standards while providing support for students. A new tutorial program was initiated. Serious efforts were made to spread writing and critical thinking across the curriculum. A matriculation program was designed to assess students for their basic skills abilities, to advise them as to proper course placement, and to monitor their progress. Articulation programs with area high schools were strengthened.

Institutional Effectiveness

From 1987 through 1989, the president of Palomar College served as chair of the Commission on Research for the California Association of Community Colleges (CACC). Serving with him as staff was his director of Institutional Research and Planning and a commission member who, in 1990, would become the vice president for Instruction at Palomar College. A major focus of the commission in those years was institutional effectiveness. In 1988, CACC published a report of the research commission, *Indicators and Measures of Successful Community Colleges*, and in 1989, CACC published *Criteria and Measures of Institutional Effectiveness.* Although the reports did not focus solely on learning outcome measures as the most important indicators, it was clear that community college leaders in California were determined to develop methods to document the effectiveness of their colleges.

By 1989, Palomar College had made significant progress. The budget had been stabilized. Student enrollment reached an all-time high of 22,000. The college received a report from the California State University (CSU) system revealing that transfers from Palomar College actually received higher grades after transferring than did CSU native students. The college had just developed a new shared governance system and was beginning to update its policies and procedures. A new flexible academic calendar and a new professional development program for faculty (which would be nationally recognized in 1992) had been implemented.

Pressures to Reform

At the state level, a legislative committee had just concluded an exhaustive review of the California community colleges resulting in the passage of comprehensive community college reform (AB 1725) in 1989. As a result, funding for community colleges in California was now centralized and program-based, and the colleges were being asked to be accountable for the expenditure of scarce resources. At the national level, the American Association of Community and junior Colleges had just issued, in 1988, the report of its Commission on the Future of Community Colleges, *Building Communities: A Vision for a New Century.* This document called on the colleges to expand access, to improve retention of students, to form new partnerships and alliances, to develop a core of common learning, and to build a climate of community.

At the local level, Palomar College found itself in a dynamic environment. The communities it served were among the fastest growing in the country. College leaders and the governing board were challenged to find ways to make classes accessible to the people of the college's large and rapidly growing district without overburdening the San Marcos campus. In addition, the California State University system had chosen to build its twentieth campus just two miles from the San Marcos campus of Palomar College, raising concern about the impact the new university would have on Palomar's mission.

The nature of the college's student body was also changing, becoming, on the average, older, more female, and more diverse. Assessment tests revealed increased weaknesses in basic skills abilities. English as a Second Language classes and developmental courses in mathematics, reading, and English became the fastest growing. Everything around the college, from the local, state, and national environments to its students, seemed to be changing. The questions being asked by Palomar's leaders were whether the college would be prepared for the future and how it could influence what that future might be.

Formation of the Vision Task Force

It was in this environment that the college president convened and chaired the Vision Task Force. The charge for the group was to develop a proposed vision statement for the college, to look into the future, and to envision what the college should be in the year 2003. This 16-member task force was composed of representatives from all segments of the college and one community member. The vice president of the Associated Student Government and a member of the governing board joined faculty members, administrators, and other staff members in an adventure that would last 18 months.

The founders of the college, which had opened its doors in 1946 to 198 students, probably would not have imagined that it would grow by 1989 to enroll 22,000 students in nearly 130 different degree and certificate programs at the San Marcos campus and at seven Education Centers and more than 60 other locations scattered throughout a district larger than Rhode Island or Delaware. Too often, institutions are so busy keeping up with the demands of the present that they are not able to see a future that is any different. The charge of the Vision Task Force, however, was to do just that: to imagine what the college would look like 16 years in the future.

The Initial Reform Process

The Vision Task Force began its work by studying documents about the challenges and roles of community colleges and about the economic and social trends in the country, state, and communities served by the college. The members read *Building Communities,* the reports that led to the California community college reform act, articles on strategic planning, and articles on classroom assessment. They reviewed vision statements from businesses and from other colleges and universities. They surveyed and interviewed faculty, staff, students, and selected community members. They asked business owners in the communities served by the college how many new employees they would need in the next 16 years and what skills future employees would need. They interviewed presidents of local colleges and universities to see what plans neighboring institutions of higher education had for their futures.

Environmental Scan

Data were also gathered from local, county, state, and national governments; public schools; and local planning agencies. The task force was interested in population projections and in the special needs of that population. The members wanted to know whether potential students would need English language or citizenship skills, whether there would be more single-parent households, and what the age and ethnic mix of the population would be. The task force members were also concerned about changes in transportation arteries. Based upon what was found, the task force developed a set of assumptions about the environment in the future.

Next, the task force critically assessed the college's strengths and weaknesses. The members wanted to know both what the college did well and what could be done better. The task force members discussed at length their own values and their own aspirations for the future of the college, how the college did its work, and the nature of its contributions to the community and society. After 18 months of study, discussion, and work, the task force issued its proposed Vision Statement and a revised Mission Statement to the college community. Having concluded its work, the task force was disbanded.

The Vision Statement

In the foreword to the Vision Statement issued in 1991, the college president wrote, "Readers of these statements will note that they reflect a subtle but nonetheless profound shift in how we think of the college and what we do. We have shifted from an identification with process to an identification with results. We are no longer content with merely providing quality instruction. We will judge ourselves henceforth on the quality of student learning we produce. And further, we will judge ourselves by our ability to produce even greater and more sophisticated student learning and meaningful educational success with each passing year, each exiting student, and each graduating class. To do this, we must ourselves continually experiment, discover, grow, and learn. Consequently, we see ourselves as a learning institution in both our object and our method" (Boggs, 1991, p. 1).

The new Mission and Vision statements clearly established Palomar College's goal to become a learning college. The five themes of the statements—empowerment, learning, evaluation, discovery, and growth—all focused on student learning. Under the empowerment theme, the Vision Statement proclaimed, "Palomar College empowers students to learn and empowers our educational team—faculty, staff, and administration—to create powerful learning environments." Under the learning theme, the Vision Statement read in part, "We provide an environment where persons of diverse cultural and ethnic backgrounds become partners in learning, build on the strengths of their own cultural traditions, and respect, embrace, and learn from persons of other traditions." Under the evaluation theme, Palomar College said it "judges its work and its programs and formulates its policies primarily on the basis of learning outcomes. . . ." Under the discovery theme, the Vision Statement committed Palomar College to discovering "new and better ways to enhance learning." And under the growth theme, the college said it will continue "to build on its strengths and shape its growth to promote more efficient and effective learning."

When the proposed Vision Statement was presented to the college constituencies, it was approved without much discussion or even realization of its significance by the Faculty Senate, the Administrative Association, the Associated Student Government, and the Council of Classified Employees. On February 12, 1991, the governing board adopted the Vision Statement and the new Mission Statement as official college policy.

A Paradigm Shift

Members of the Vision Task Force were surprised to find such easy acceptance of such a dramatic change in the college mission and direction. The task force was asking the institution to take responsibility for student learning, not just for delivering instruction, and there was no opposition! Some members speculated that people thought that the Vision Statement would find a comfortable resting place on a shelf, and business would continue as usual. Or perhaps, people felt that this emphasis on learning outcomes was just another passing fad to be endured. What the task force members now think is the real reason for this easy acceptance of the Vision Statement came to them as they viewed Joel Arthur Barker's videotape on paradigms (1989). Task force members realized that people are blinded to the need to change because they are operating from a different paradigm of community colleges, one which college leaders have labeled the "instruction paradigm." The new paradigm envisioned by the Palomar College Vision Statement began, in 1991, to be called the "learning paradigm" by college leaders.

Palomar College leaders knew it would not be easy to change the paradigm that guided the college from one of providing instruction to one of producing student learning. But they began a series of activities to start on the path to change, beginning with the language used. As a result of the work of the Vision Task Force, the college already had a new Mission Statement that defined its purpose as student learning. Next, catalogs, publications, and job descriptions were changed. For example, the job description of the instructional deans was revised to include responsibility for creating effective learning environments for students. Student service deans are now expected to develop and evaluate the performance of assigned personnel in terms of their contributions to student learning and success.

Recruitment brochures were revised to attract a faculty and staff committed to promoting and supporting student learning. Employment procedures were revised to help select faculty and staff who shared the college's values and beliefs. Orientation programs for new full- and part-time faculty and new members of the governing board now emphasize the principles of the learning paradigm.

Student learning forums that brought together faculty, staff, and students were scheduled. These forums were based upon the conviction that if faculty and staff listen carefully to students and respond appropriately to their suggestions, student learning and student success can be improved. For example, in 1993–94, there were three of these forums at Palomar College. The first was facilitated by students who focused on positive and negative classroom and campus experiences and successful techniques that helped them learn.

The second student learning forum was facilitated by faculty and the college president. Its goal was to review the negative experiences identified in the first forum and to develop suggestions to counteract them. The ESL faculty facilitated the third forum, "How to Engage Your Students from Day One," which focused on techniques for assessing student understanding from the first day of class and on skills for improving communications with students.

External Validation

External validation of one's ideas is often helpful. Starting in 1993, Palomar college staff members began to write about the learning paradigm and to present their ideas at conferences. Bob Barr, Palomar's director of Institutional Research and Planning and a member of the Vision Task Force, wrote articles for the Association of California Community College Administrators (1993), the RP Group (1994), and the League for Innovation in the Community College (1995). John Tagg, a member of the English faculty and also a member of the Vision Task Force, joined Barr in an article in *Change Magazine* (1995). Barr's ideas have also influenced the Commission on Educational Policy of the Community College League of California.

The college president, George Boggs, has written articles for the National Institute for Staff and Organizational Development (1993), the California Higher Education Policy Center (1995), and for the American Association of Community Colleges (1993, 1995). Since 1993, Palomar College staff members have made more than 15 presentations about the learning paradigm at individual colleges and at conferences, including three keynote presentations. Palomar College staff participated in two national video conferences on the learning paradigm in 1995.

Feedback from these outside presentations and articles has helped college leaders to clarify their thinking. It has also reinforced the belief in the need to shift to the learning paradigm. An added benefit has been the effect on the reputation of the college. Faculty and staff members who attend conferences are frequently asked by colleagues from other colleges about the innovations at Palomar. When they return, they are not only proud of what is being accomplished at Palomar, but they are even more committed to the paradigm shift.

As a result of a newspaper editorial written by John Tagg on the effective use of technology to improve learning outcomes (1995), Palomar College was asked by Encyclopedia Britannica to be the first community college to pilot-test its Britannica-On-Line service. Faculty members have been experimenting with the potential of the Britannica-On-Line database since the fall semester of 1995. In the spring of 1996, the database was made available to students in selected classes through the Internet.

District Goals

Just prior to the endorsement of the Vision Statement by the governing board, the board identified and distributed district goals for the 1989–90 academic year. The goals were good ones, but there was not any mention of student learning outcomes. The board was concerned about employee salaries, campus appearance, enrollment growth, student parking, policy manuals, and communication. By 1991–92, the district goals were significantly different. At the outset of that goals document, the board stated its commitment "to setting all of its goals in the context of the Palomar College Vision Statement. The college exists to provide and support student learning. The themes of empowerment, learning, evaluation, discovery, and growth, as identified and discussed in the Vision Statement, should guide the college in its decision making and planning." The board's goals included development of the Educational Master Plan, staffing and staff diversity, student diversity, fund raising, and shared governance, all framed within the context of contributions to student learning.

Persistence

Each year since 1991, the governing board has recommitted itself to the Vision Statement by referring to it in the development of the annual district goals. In the 1995–96 district goals, the board calls upon the faculty and staff to identify important learning outcomes and to set goals for improving those outcomes. In that document, the board also states its intent to foster "an attitude which encourages innovation and provides a learning environment that significantly improves student learning and success outcomes."

The college president has made the Vision Statement or the learning paradigm the theme of his annual address to the faculty and staff every year since 1991, recognizing the efforts of innovative faculty and staff members who are contributing to the paradigm shift at Palomar College. Presentations to adjunct faculty members have also emphasized the new direction for the college. Each year, new faculty members are given a three-day intensive orientation to the college and its culture and values. After the college president finished his remarks at the 1995 new faculty orientation, one of the new faculty members was overheard saying, "Now I know why I was hired here."

The 1995 fall Orientation Day for faculty and staff was a unique experience. Returning faculty members were not told that they would become students-for-a-day until they arrived on campus. After a continental breakfast, faculty and staff members were off to their first of three classes patterned after learning communities. The teachers used active-learning methods to involve their "students" in learning. The experience also gave the college president the opportunity to get back into the classroom as a chemistry teacher, allowing him to demonstrate some methods of involving students in learning chemistry. Evaluations of this activity were very positive. Some faculty members commented that it was the best Orientation Day ever at Palomar College.

The president also has an established practice of taking each new faculty member to lunch or breakfast in the first year of employment to see how the faculty member is adjusting to Palomar and to reinforce the college values. New board members experience similar orientations. The values of Palomar College are living and are constantly communicated and reinforced.

The Planning Process

The Vision Statement now guides Palomar's planning processes. But it has not always been easy. Early resistance was encountered in some of the planning committees as exemplified by statements such as, "We should first correct some of the glaring deficiencies in the current system before we conclude that it doesn't work," and "(w)e should simply hire well-educated, high-quality teachers, give them a place to work and a place to be creative, get out of their way and don't work them to death."

After six years of consistent work, however, the learning paradigm seems to be an accepted part of the Palomar College culture. For the first time in 1995, the Goals of the Palomar College Faculty Senate state a commitment to enhancing student learning. College personnel are moving ahead deliberately to make Palomar College a learning institution in both object and method.

Toward a New Learning College at Palomar

Among the things one can expect the learning paradigm to promote are collaborative learning; learning communities; focus on learning outcomes; better use of technology; recognition of the importance of everyone's role in promoting, supporting, and facilitating student learning; and a new unity of purpose among all the college's people.

The College's People

Everyone is familiar with the story of the two bricklayers who, when asked what they were doing, responded very differently. One answered that he was laying bricks. The other responded that he was building a cathedral. The second bricklayer saw himself as an important contributor to the outcome. Likewise, at Palomar College, the goal is for all employees to see their roles as important to the mission of producing student learning. Everyone, from the groundskeeper to the teacher to the librarian to the president to the student, is there for one purpose—student learning.

In the instruction paradigm, the faculty members are the most important people at the college. Their role is to deliver the instruction, primarily by lecturing. The staff is there to support the faculty and the teaching process. Students, all too frequently trained by 12 years of being passive in class and being competitive and individualistic outside class, come to receive the instruction. Administrators and board members set and implement the policies of the college. In the learning paradigm, however, the most important people at the college are the learners. The faculty members are primarily designers of learning environments and methods. The staff is responsible for supporting student learning and success. Students are active participants in their learning. They form study groups and cooperate outside class. College decisions and plans to support student learning are developed through a shared governance system.

Learning Communities

In the fall of 1992, Palomar College offered its first learning community. It was not an idea original to Palomar. The faculty learned of its potential from some colleges in Washington state. To build learning communities, students enroll in a block of classes that are linked by a common theme. The students and the faculty members involved become a community of learners, partners in the examination of important issues from different perspectives.

The first Palomar College learning community, offered in the fall of 1992, had as its theme "Love, Gender, and Sex." The linked courses examined what it means to be a woman or a man; how this society and other societies think and have thought about gender, sex, and sexism; how men and women communicate with each other; and how they learn. Students were awarded credit in speech, English, philosophy, and psychology.

Students and faculty in this first learning community attended all class meetings, read books from a broad interdisciplinary perspective, and engaged in lively discussions in seminar groups. The students wrote extensively to formulate and advance their own thinking and to present their views to others. The discussions proved to be lively as faculty and students alike found their basic beliefs challenged.

Subsequent learning communities at Palomar College have included: "Entrepreneurship—Doing It Right," composed of linked courses in business, speech, and reading; "Persuasion in Popular Film," composed of linked courses in philosophy and speech; "Scholar Athletes," composed of linked courses in English, speech, health, and college success skills; and "Reading, Writing, and Wrenches," composed of linked courses in mathematics, speech, reading, and automotive technology.

"The Reading, Writing, and Wrenches" learning community ran into some unanticipated problems due to the differing math and English backgrounds of the automotive students for whom the learning community was targeted. This problem, however, was somewhat offset by the unanticipated positive outcome of causing the mathematics faculty to redesign Palomar's basic skills mathematics sequence. The result is a one-track, applications-based, technology-supported, seamless mathematics curriculum that takes the students through intermediate algebra and prepares them for transfer courses in mathematics. This new integrated basic skills curriculum now makes it unnecessary to designate specific class sections as emphasizing trade-oriented applications.

Research on the learning communities at Palomar College has shown that they increase student critical thinking skills, and that they improve students' self-assessment of motivation, writing skills, and comfort level in relating to members of different racial/ethnic groups. Student retention has been much higher in the learning communities.

Learning communities are now flourishing at Palomar College. Recent additions include a pairing of the study of Spanish language and culture with natural history studies in Costa Rica; one designed for non-native speakers of English to develop reading and writing skills through exploration and analysis of themes in psychology; and a third combining courses in graphic communications, photography, and English designed to help students learn the principles of mass communications theory and techniques. This last learning community actually produced the college's award-winning literary magazine in 1995.

The college's most ambitious learning community to date began in the spring of 1996. Because of its scheduling, it was called "Afternoon College." This learning community linked English, mathematics, study skills, and supplemental instruction (tutoring). Afternoon College was especially designed for entering first-semester students to ensure that they begin their college experience in a structured and supportive environment and that they enroll early in courses which will help them throughout their college experience.

Afternoon College is similar to a highly successful program called "Starting Blocks," offered through Palomar College's Extended Opportunity Programs and Services (EOPS). Starting Blocks has been offered to 25 students per semester for the past three years. Linked courses for these students include English, college success skills, mathematics, and reading. Students in the Starting Blocks program had a higher retention rate and a slightly higher grade point average than EOPS students in a control group.

Departmental Leadership and Innovations

The mathematics department has perhaps made the most significant changes to its entire curriculum since the inception of the learning paradigm. These changes were facilitated by the acquisition of two computer laboratories through grant funding and by the free time given to several department members to initiate the changes. Even at traditionally off-peak times, visitors to the open-entry math lab find a room full of students working on self-paced assignments. Students check themselves into and out of open labs at Palomar College by swiping the magnetic stripe of their Personal Identification Card (PIC) through an automatic reader.

Across the curriculum, instructors are developing ways to balance lectures with active learning, including group activities. In addition to the changes in basic skills courses, the mathematics faculty has revised its transfer-level curriculum to include a coordinated lecture-laboratory format that takes advantage of technology and allows students to develop higher level cognitive skills.

Math classes frequently begin with a review of the assigned practice sets focusing on the problems that presented difficulties for the students. Having the students "walk through" the solution to the point of confusion or error assures that they have actually attempted the material and reinforces successful approaches to problem-solving. Instructors frequently use class collaboration in working through the steps of the solution. This approach has the dual advantage of acknowledging students for having learned the material, and of reinforcing their learning as they explain the solution to their classmates.

Once a new topic is introduced and one or more examples are worked through by the instructor, work groups are assigned problems to complete together. The instructor moves around the room, listening to the interactions but intervening only when asked and only after the group has made a sincere effort to solve the problem on its own. The group might be asked to choose a spokesperson to put the solution on the board and to explain it to the rest of the class.

In the Life Sciences Department, an anatomy instructor recently developed a series of questions for each unit of the course. Students were randomly assigned to groups to research certain of these questions and to present answers to the entire class. There are rules governing group activities: all members of the group must speak during the presentation, a visual aid must be used, at least four essays related to the material must be presented, and each member of the group must rate the performance of each of the other members and be able to explain the rating.

In the anatomy class, the instructor found this active-learning approach led to higher grades, but attrition was also higher than it would have been in a more traditional course. Students for whom English was a second language had the most difficulty with this approach. The instructor feels that these students were intimidated by the reading assignments and, given the course structure, could not compensate for their difficulties. In future classes, the instructor plans to assess student abilities earlier and to be more assertive in recommending that they receive needed help.

The Palomar College English writing laboratories afford students the opportunity to compose their out-of-class writing assignments on the computer. The access to computers has led to more and better writing because students can easily revise their papers without major retyping. Composition classes are also scheduled to meet in one of the computer labs one hour each week. This hour affords instructors the opportunity to foster small-group collaborative work. For example, one instructor divides students into "conferences" of five or six students to work on writing assignments related to reading material that will be discussed at a subsequent class session.

When composing a group paper, all students in a given conference are networked so that they are working on a common document. Students initial their individual contributions to the composition. The instructor circulates throughout the class, making comments and suggestions as warranted. The students use the resulting paper as a basis for a class presentation. The instructor has found that this group learning experience leads to more insightful analysis, greater participation in class discussions, and greater substance in subsequent individual writing assignments.

In addition to these innovations, instructors at Palomar College are experimenting with new technology to supplement class material, to produce multimedia programs, and to communicate with their students electronically. As this technology becomes more accessible, instructors hope to have students do more collaborative work outside class by assigning electronic mail groups to work on assignments.

Several departments have developed outcome-based criteria for evaluating student work. The art department includes fellow students in the critique and evaluation of projects. The director of the campus art gallery also plays a role in the selection of two projects per class to be displayed in the annual student art show.

The English Department has a holistically graded final examination for one of its courses. Before any grading of exams begins, the entire department reviews a selection of student papers. The criteria by which the papers are to be judged are discussed, and then all members of the group must agree on a grade for each sample paper within one point on a six-point scale. Only then does general grading begin. Each paper is read by two different graders and by a third if the spread between the two grades is greater than one point.

The instructor for the biology majors course is anxious to try new methods in his class. He is concerned, however, that he currently has no way of measuring whether a new technique really improves student learning. As a result, he is developing a comprehensive final examination that he hopes to use in the future as a benchmark against which to evaluate the new methods.

In another example of active learning, a business education teacher has developed a marketing internship class in partnership with General Motors (GM). She provides initial direction and guidance to the class but, before long, changes her role to that of a consultant. The students form a company and develop a complete promotional campaign for a local GM dealership. The students elect a coordinator who actually runs the class, meeting with the instructor as needed for guidance. At the end of the course, the students confidentially rate themselves and their peers in relation to both the role they played and their contribution to the learning experience. These ratings are assessed by the instructor and are considered in the final grade. An important component of the final grade assigned by the instructor is the ability to work effectively as a team member.

Many faculty members at Palomar College are now using the classroom assessment techniques advocated by Angelo and Cross (1993). In addition to providing immediate feedback on student learning, instructors have found these techniques helpful because they are forced to identify clearly what it is they want their students to learn. New techniques can be tested easily to see if they enhance student learning. The use of classroom assessment also demonstrates to the students that instructors are concerned about student learning.

Student Services and the New Technology

Palomar College has also worked to make its student services more user-friendly and more supportive of student learning. Even prior to the development of the Vision Statement, Palomar College Student Services staff adopted the motto, "We support student success." Use of technology has extended college resources and has provided better and faster support to students. For example, in 1990, Palomar College was one of the first community colleges in California to develop a telephone registration system. Then, in 1992, Palomar College developed the Palomar Automated Student Self-Service (PASS) stations. These ATM-type kiosks allow students to access information about the college and their personal academic records through a touch-screen monitor. Students use the magnetic stripe on the back of their Personal Identification Cards (PIC) to access information about grades, class schedules, and course placement recommendations based upon assessment test scores. For security reasons, a personal identification number (PIN) is assigned to each student, without which access to confidential information is denied.

Because students can register for classes over the telephone and can look up their own grades and even print a copy to go, these functions are now rarely performed by staff over the counter. In the fall semester of 1995, more than 14,000 students registered for classes over the telephone. Over 18,000 students each year utilize the three PASS stations in the Student Services Building lobby. These repetitive, staff-intensive transactions are being handled more efficiently for students by using technology, freeing the staff to deal more effectively with less common student needs and concerns.

Palomar technicians are currently working on a system that will allow students to access grades and other information over the telephone by digitizing the database into a voice modality. The paper files are being scanned into an imaging system that stores and retrieves records electronically. With a network CD-ROM, the National College Catalog collection is now online, and the college began transmitting transcripts electronically in 1996. All these efforts are intended to make it easier for staff to provide students with the services and information they need in a quick and efficient manner.

The Counseling Department has made use of new technology in the recent development of a multimedia orientation program. New students are oriented to the college and are informed of its services and requirements through an interesting visual presentation.

The Counseling Department has also employed other innovations to help students. To keep students on track with their learning objectives, the department sends letters to students who have at least 15 units of credit and have not yet declared a major. A Career Center helps students who have not yet decided on a vocational objective, and a Transfer Center helps students who intend to transfer to an upper-division college or university after Palomar.

Other student services intended to support students in accomplishing their learning objectives include student health services, tutorial services, financial aid, job placement, veterans' services, child care, peer advising, services for students with disabilities, and services for students with economic disadvantages. The Student Health Center, for example, provides medical support, physician and nurse care, inoculations, family planning counseling, and low-cost medications to 16,000 students annually. Palomar College has borrowed from an African expression, "it takes an entire village to raise a child." At Palomar, it takes an entire college to retain and support the success of a student. The Student Referral Assistance Guide, which outlines and describes all of Palomar's student support programs and lists local referral agencies, is now distributed to all faculty and is discussed in orientation sessions for new employees.

The Creation of a Learning College Culture

Providing leadership in refocusing a college on learning is not an easy task. Most community colleges have been in existence for a while and have strong, established cultures. All too often, universities are viewed as models for what community colleges should become. In a university, the responsibility for learning is usually considered to be the student's and not the university's. The criteria for judging the quality of universities are almost always based upon inputs and process measures rather than outcomes. Factors such as selectivity of student admissions, number of library holdings, size of the endowments, and number of doctorates on the faculty are commonly used to rate colleges and universities. Perhaps it is time for us to seek a paradigm in which community colleges will be the models, in which colleges will be evaluated based upon their contributions to student learning and success.

The Starting Point

Unless a leader is starting a community college from scratch, it will be necessary to gain support for any new direction. The best way to start is to bring together a group of visionaries and campus leaders from all segments to review and update the college's mission and vision statements. At Palomar College this group was called the Vision Task Force, and it met for 18 months. It studied and argued until consensus was reached about the future of the college. This process cannot be rushed. It is easy to pick up a nice, attractive vision statement from another college and modify it slightly, but it will never be owned by the college unless it is developed from scratch by the people of the college. Educators can learn from what colleagues at other institutions do, but they must shape everything to fit the unique environment of their own college.

Some college leaders may wish to bring in a consultant to work with the group, especially in the beginning. It may be helpful to have someone outside the college set the ground rules of group operations. Other colleges may wish to have an expert on strategic planning help the group discover the steps to take in developing a long-range plan or vision for the college. Colleges that are further along in the learning paradigm may also be able to provide help in the early stages of development of a new vision. Staff members from Palomar College have worked with other colleges to get them started on the path toward developing their own vision statements.

The task force must come to understand the needs of the communities that the college serves and to anticipate what those needs will be in the future. Census data, information from planning agencies, and survey information from area businesses and other educational institutions will be important for the group as it develops environmental assumptions about the future and compares them with the future abilities of the college.

Once the new vision and mission statements that focus the college on the future needs of the communities it serves and that define it as a learning college are prepared, it is important to get official endorsement from all college constituencies before taking them to the governing board for approval. If this new work is to be a truly shared vision and mission, every segment of the college must approve. The effort to iron out problems at this early stage will pay off later.

The Importance of Language

In Bob Barr's 1994 study of California community college mission statements, he found virtually no focus on learning. "When it was used, it was almost always bundled in the phrase 'teaching and learning' as if to say that, while learning may indeed have something to do with community colleges, it is only present as an aspect of teaching" (p. 1). Language is important in American society. College leaders need to be sure they are saying what they intend to say.

College catalogs, schedules, and other publications should all mention student learning as the college's primary purpose. Job descriptions should be revised to make it clear that student learning is everyone's job. Employee recruitment brochures should be unambiguous in stating that the college is interested in receiving applications from individuals committed to student learning. College or district goals should refer to improving student learning outcomes, and they should reinforce the vision and mission statements.

Promotion of the Vision

If the new vision and mission statements are to be taken seriously, they must be actively supported by the CEO and the governing board. If the faculty and staff come to believe that the vision and mission statements are just rhetoric and that there is no real commitment from the top, there will be no progress. The CEO and the chief academic officer must be especially visible and persistent supporters of the new learning mission of the college.

College leaders may experience strong resistance on some fronts, and their message may seem to be ignored at times, but they must never give up. The leaders should use every opportunity to communicate and reinforce the student learning mission of the college. Annual speeches to the faculty and staff, annual "State of the College" messages, "Year in Review" reports, and orientation sessions for new employees and new governing board members are ideal times to discuss the college's commitment to student learning and success and to assess the progress toward realizing the college's vision.

There will, of course, be some people who will never accept the change. These are generally people who are comfortable with doing things the way they always have been done, and perhaps, they are the people who distrust administrators to start with, especially if they try to change things. Not much can be gained by focusing too much energy on this group of people. Instead, the CEO should support the leaders and the innovators and should celebrate their successes at every opportunity.

Although a leader may not have a chance to start a college from scratch, every new employment decision is, in its own way, a new start. The leader should be sure that every new faculty and staff member understands and agrees with the values of the college. For student learning to be the college's mission, it must be every employee's mission. Hiring people who do not want to accept responsibility for contributing to student learning will result in a significant setback.

The CEO can continue to communicate the importance of student learning to new faculty and staff members by personally taking part in new employee orientation sessions. Other members of the staff can explain some of the details about how the college operationalizes its values, but the CEO needs to spend some time with this group and needs to communicate that new employees are expected to take risks and to try new ideas, which might produce better and more student learning. A college is only as good as its people. They must be selected carefully, and they must come to understand the values of the institution and the expectations they must meet.

One of the best ways to bring new people into leadership positions on the learning mission of the college is to invite them to join the leaders in making a presentation at a conference or at another college. The experience at Palomar College is that the faculty and staff members who have been involved in these presentations have become the greatest supporters of the paradigm shift. This should not be surprising to those of us who have been teachers. When one teaches something, one really has to know it.

The College of the Future

The college of the future will have a mission statement which clearly communicates that the college exists to promote and support learning. Indeed, it will take responsibility for the success of its students. Courses, programs, and departments will give way to cross-discipline learning communities. The college staff will be as concerned about the success of a diverse group of students as they are about access.

The criteria for a successful college will also change. Instead of input measures like enrollment growth and participation rates, the college of the future will base its success on the success of its students. The focus will be on constant improvement of student learning outcomes. Both the students and the college will be held to high standards.

The college of the future will not necessarily have the traditional one teacher per classroom. Faculty, instead of being primarily lecturers, will become facilitators of learning and designers of learning environments. Staff, instead of being seen as supporters of the faculty and of the instruction process, will be perceived as important contributors to an environment which promotes and supports learning. Instead of acting independently, faculty members will be part of a learning team that includes all of the college's staff and the students.

The use of new technology and flexible learning systems means that classes will not all necessarily start and end at the same time as most do now. Neither will learning be location bound. Students will be able to make use of new technology to communicate with teachers and fellow students from education centers, work sites, and their homes.

Students, in the college of the future, will not be seen as passive vessels receiving knowledge that the teacher dispenses in lectures. Instead, students will be active constructors of knowledge. Rather than being individualistic and competitive, students will be cooperative and collaborative. They will be partners in a community of learners.

College leaders will move away from the idea that any expert can teach and will acknowledge that empowering learning is a complex activity that requires its own share of research and development. The college of the future will itself be continually learning how it can improve its systems to produce more and better student learning.

A degree from the college of the future will represent more than just time spent in class and accumulated credits. It will mean that the graduate has demonstrated specified skills and knowledge.

Obstacles

Despite the increasing calls for accountability, there are many obstacles to overcome before America's colleges can become responsible for student learning outcomes. As discussed earlier in this chapter, there will be resistance to change on the part of faculty, staff, and students. Faculty will have to make a significant adjustment as they move from being dispensers of knowledge to being facilitators of learning. Staff will have different and increased responsibilities. The Learning Paradigm also requires changes in student behavior. Although public school reform is leading to a more active learning environment, higher education institutions may still receive students who have had 12 years of training to be passive in class and individualistic and competitive outside class. These students may have difficulty adjusting to an environment which requires them to be active participants in a community of learners.

A major obstacle in some states like California is the detailed and prescriptive nature of the Education and Administrative Codes. These laws and regulations seem to be designed to protect and perpetuate the Instruction Paradigm. Most state funding formulas for institutions of higher education are enrollment driven. What really counts under this system is how many students are sitting in class at census week. It does not matter whether the students complete the class or whether they even learn anything. They may even drop out of college completely, but as long as they are replaced by new students so that the seats are occupied when the next census is taken, the college is seen as successful. Funding formulas must change, as they have in some states, to reward learning outcomes.

Another obstacle is the fact that there are not yet very good methods to measure learning outcomes. In fact, most colleges have not addressed which learning outcomes should be measured. This should not be a surprise; learning outcomes are not important in the Instruction Paradigm.

When learning outcomes become important, colleges will find ways to identify and measure them.

Leading the Way

These are challenging times when good leadership can make significant differences for colleges and universities. Colleges can choose to proceed along the same path as always, honoring the sacred traditions of academia and fighting a continual battle for a larger share of diminishing public resources. The alternative is to realize that the present mission of America's colleges no longer fits the needs of today's society and to transform them into the learning colleges of tomorrow.

References

Angelo, Thomas A. and Cross, K. Patricia. *Classroom Assessment Techniques: A Handbook for College Teachers, Second Edition.* San Francisco: Jossey-Bass, 1993.

American Association of Community and Junior Colleges. *Building Communities: A Vision for a New Century.* Washington, D.C.: AACC, 1988.

Barker, J. A. *Discovering the Future: The Business of Paradigms* (2nd Ed.) Videotape. Burnsville, MN: Charterhouse International Learning, 1989.

Barr, R. "From Teaching to Learning: A New Reality for Community Colleges," *Leadership Abstracts,* Mission Viejo, CA: The League for Innovation in the Community College. March 1995, Volume 8, Number 3.

_____. "A New Paradigm for Community Colleges," *News. The RP Group.* The Research and Planning Group for the California Community Colleges. February, 1994.

_____. "New Paradigms for Community Colleges: Focus on Learning Instead of Teaching," *Ad Com* (Newsletter of the Association of California Community College Administrators). Sacramento, CA: ACCCA, October 1993.

Barr, R. and Tagg, J. "From Teaching to Learning—A New Paradigm for Undergraduate Education." *Change,* Washington, D.C.: American Association for Higher Education. November/December 1995.

Boggs, G. R. "Community Colleges and the New Paradigm." *Celebrations,* An occasional publication of the National Institute for Staff and Organizational Development (NISOD), Austin, TX: NISOD, September 1993.

_____. "Focus on Student Learning." *Crosstalk,* San Jose, CA: California Higher Education Policy Center, April 1995, Volume 3, Number 2.

_____. "The Learning Paradigm." *Community College Journal,* Washington, D.C.: American Association of Community Colleges, December/January 1995/96.

_____. "Letter to Colleagues and Friends." *Palomar College 2005: A Shared Vision.* San Marcos, CA: Palomar College, Spring 1991.

_____. "The New Paradigm for Community Colleges—Who's Leading the Way?" *The Catalyst,* Westminster, CO: National Council on Community Services and Continuing Education, Fall 1995, Volume XXV, Number 1.

_____. "Reinventing Community Colleges." *Community College Journal,* Washington, D.C.: American Association of Community Colleges, December/January 1993/94.

California Association of Community Colleges. *Criteria and Measures of Institutional Effectiveness.* Sacramento, CA: CACC, 1989.

_____. *Indicators and Measures of Successful Community Colleges.* Sacramento, CA: CACC, 1988.

Tagg, J. "It's Time to Put Education On-line." *The San Diego Union-Tribune,* March 9, 1995.

Wingspread Group on Higher Education. *An American Imperative: Higher Expectations for Higher Education,* Racine, WI: The Johnson Foundation, Inc., 1993.

CHAPTER 43

CHANGING THE CURRICULUM IN HIGHER EDUCATION

MARGARET L. ANDERSEN

In Susan Glaspell's short story, "A Jury of Her Peers," a man is murdered, strangled in his bed with a rope. The victim's wife, Mrs. Wright, formerly Minnie Foster, has been arrested for the crime. The men investigating—the sheriff, the county attorney, and a friend—think she is guilty but cannot imagine her motive. "It's all perfectly clear, except the reason for doing it. But you know juries when it comes to women. If there was some definite thing—something to make a story about. A thing that would connect up with this clumsy way of doing it," the county attorney says.[1]

This essay has been developed through the many discussions I have had with people working in women's studies curriculum projects around the country. I am particularly grateful for having been able to participate in the Mellon seminars at the Wellesley College Center for Research on Women. Although I cannot name all of the participants in these seminars, their collective work and thought continuously enriches my thinking and teaching; I thank them all. I especially thank Peggy McIntosh, director of these seminars, for her inspiration and ongoing support for this work. She, Valerie Hans, Sandra Harding, and the anonymous *Signs* reviewers provided very helpful reviews of the earlier drafts of this essay. And I appreciate the support of the Provosts Office of the University of Delaware for providing the funds for a curriculum revision project in women's studies at the University of Delaware; working with the participants in this project contributed much to the development of this essay.

When the three men go to the Foster house to search for evidence, two of their wives go along to collect some things for the jailed Minnie Foster. In the house the men laugh at the women's attention to Minnie's kitchen and tease them for wondering about the quilt she was making. While the women speculate about whether she was going to quilt it or knot it, the men, considering this subject trivial, belittle the women for their interest in Minnie's handwork. "Nothing here but kitchen things," the sheriff says. "But would the women know a clue if they did come upon it?" the other man scoffs.[2] The three men leave the women in the kitchen while they search the rest of the house for important evidence.

While in the kitchen, the women discover several things amiss. The kitchen table is wiped half-clean, left half messy. The cover is left off a bucket of sugar, while beside it sits a paper bag only half filled with sugar. Mrs. Hale and Mrs. Peters see that one block of the quilt Minnie Foster was making is sewn very badly, while the other blocks have fine and even stitches. They wonder, "What was she so nervous about?" When they find an empty bird cage, its door hinge torn apart, they try to imagine how such anger could have erupted in an otherwise bleak and passionless house. Remembering Minnie Foster, Mrs. Hale recalls, "She—come to think of it, she was kind of like a bird herself. Real

Source: "Changing the Curriculum in Higher Education," by Margaret L. Andersen, reprinted from *Signs: A Journal of Women in Culture in Society*, Vol. 12, No. 2, 1987, University of Chicago Press.

sweet and pretty, but kind of timid and—fluttery. How—she—did—change."[3] When the women pick up her sewing basket, they find in it Minnie's dead canary wrapped in a piece of silk, its neck snapped and broken. They realize they have discovered the reason Minnie Foster murdered her husband. Imagining the pain in Minnie Foster's marriage to Mr. Wright, Mrs. Hale says, "No, Wright wouldn't like the bird, a thing that sang. She used to sing. He killed that too."[4]

Soon the men return to the kitchen, but the women have tacitly agreed to say nothing of what they have found. Still mocking the women's attentiveness to kitchen details, the men tease them. The county attorney asks, "She was going to—what is it you call it, Ladies?" "We call it, knot it, Mr. Henderson."[5]

"Knot it," also alluding to the method of murder, is a punning commentary on the relative weights of men's and women's knowledge in the search for facts and evidence. Women's culture—"not it" to the men—is invisible, silenced, trivialized, and wholly ignored in men's construction of reality. At the same time, men's culture is assumed to present the entire and only truth.[6]

Glaspell's story suggests the social construction of knowledge in a gender-segregated world. In her story, women's understandings and observations are devalued and women are excluded from the search for truth. How might the truth look different, we are asked, were women's perspectives included in the making of facts and evidence? What worlds do women inhabit and how do their worlds affect what they know and what is known about them?

The themes of Glaspell's story are at the heart of women's studies, since women's studies rests on the premise that knowledge in the traditional academic disciplines is partial, incomplete, and distorted because it has excluded women. In the words of Adrienne Rich, "As the hitherto 'invisible' and marginal agent in culture, whose native culture has been effectively denied, women need a reorganization of knowledge, of perspectives and analytical tools that can help us know our foremothers, evaluate our present historical, political, and personal situation, and take ourselves seriously as agents in the creation of a more balanced culture."[7] Women's studies was born from this understanding and over the past two decades has evolved with two goals: to build knowledge and a curriculum in which women are agents of knowledge and in which knowledge of women transforms the male-centered curriculum of traditional institutions.[8] Curriculum change through women's studies is, as Florence Howe has said, both developmental and transformative: it is developmental in generating new scholarship about women and transformative in its potential to make the traditional curriculum truly coeducational.[9]

Since women have been excluded from the creation of formalized knowledge, to include women means more than just adding women into existing knowledge or making them new objects of knowledge. Throughout this essay, including women refers to the complex process of redefining knowledge by making women's experiences a primary subject for knowledge, conceptualizing women as active agents in the creation of knowledge, including women's perspectives on knowledge, looking at gender as fundamental to the articulation of knowledge in Western thought, and seeing women's and men's experiences in relation to the sex/gender system. Because this multifaceted understanding of "including women in the curriculum" is an integral part of the new scholarship on women and because we have not developed language sufficient to reflect these assumptions, readers should be alert to the fact that phrases like "scholarship on women," "including women," and "learning about women" are incomplete but are meant to refer to the multidimensional reconstruction of knowledge.

Women's studies has developed from feminists' radical critique of the content and form of the academic disciplines, the patriarchal structure of education, the consciousness education reproduces, and the relation of education to dominant cultural, economic, political, and social institutions. Women's studies seeks to make radical transformations in the systems and processes of knowledge creation and rests on the belief that changing what we study and know about women will change women's and men's lives.[10] Hence, curriculum change is understood as part of the political transformation of women's role in society because all teaching includes political values. As Florence Howe has written,

> In the broadest context of that word, teaching is a political act: some person is choosing, for whatever reasons, to teach a set of values, ideas, assumptions, and pieces of information, and in so doing, to omit other values, ideas, assumptions, and pieces of

> information. If all those choices form a pattern excluding half the human race, that is a political act one can hardly help noticing. To omit women entirely makes one kind of political statement; to include women as a target for humor makes another. To include women with seriousness and vision, and with some attention to the perspective of women as a hitherto subordinate group is simply another kind of political act. Education is the kind of political act that controls destinies, gives some persons hope for a particular kind of future, and deprives others even of ordinary expectations for work and achievement.[11]

This discussion raises important questions about how we define women's studies in the future and how, especially in this conservative political period,[12] the radicalism of women's studies can be realized within institutions that remain racist and sexist and integrally tied to the values and structures of a patriarchal society. But, as Susan Kirschner and Elizabeth Arch put it, women's studies and inclusive curriculum projects are "two important pieces of one work."[13] Feminists in educational institutions will likely continue working for both women's studies and curriculum change, since both projects seek to change the content and form of the traditional curriculum[14] and to contribute to social change through curriculum transformation. It is simply impossible, as Howe has put it, "to move directly from the male-centered curriculum to what I have described as `transformation' of that curriculum into a changed and co-educational one—without passing through some form of women's studies."[15]

Building an Inclusive Curriculum

Peggy McIntosh estimates that since 1975 there have been at least eighty projects that, in various ways, examine how the disciplines can be redefined and reconstructed to include us all.[16] This estimate gives some idea of the magnitude of the movement to create new curricula that include women. Moreover, according to McIntosh, although fewer projects are now being funded through sources external to the institutions that house them, internal funding for such projects seems to be increasing.

Curriculum-change projects in women's studies have varied widely in their purposes, scope, institutional contexts, and sources of funding. For example, projects at Wheaton College and Towson State University (both funded through the Fund for the Improvement of Post Secondary Education [FIPSE]) are university-wide projects engaging faculty in the revision of courses across the curriculum. Other projects involve consortia of several campuses, such as those at Montana State University, the Southwest Institute for Research on Women (SIROW) at the University of Arizona, and the University of Massachusetts-Amherst.

The SIROW project has several dimensions, including course development and revision at the University of Arizona and a three-year project for integrating women into international studies and foreign language courses at several universities in Arizona and Colorado. Funded by the Women's Educational Equity Act program (WEEA), the Montana State project began as a two-year faculty development project intended to reduce bias in the curriculum; it was later renamed the Northern Rockies Program on Women and was expanded to develop curriculum resources in a twenty-five school consortium in Montana, Utah, Wyoming, and Idaho. The project "Black Studies/Women's Studies: An Overdue Partnership," funded by FIPSE, includes faculty from the University of Massachusetts, Smith College, Hampshire College, Mount Holyoke College, and Amherst College; twenty-nine faculty from this project met to create new courses and build theoretical and curricular connections between black studies and women's studies. The Mellon seminars at the Wellesley College Center for Research on Women, funded through the Andrew W. Mellon Foundation, have drawn together faculty from the New England area to apply feminist scholarship to curriculum transformation.

At the University of Delaware, the university provided funds for a development project for faculty in the social sciences who were revising introductory and core courses to make them inclusive of gender and race; faculty in the project met in an interdisciplinary faculty seminar on feminist scholarship, followed by a day-long conference on curriculum change and a one-year program for visiting consultants who gave public lectures and advised faculty on the reconstruction of their courses. The Women's Research and Resource Center at Spelman College, funded by the Ford Foundation, has emphasized curriculum revision in freshmen courses in English, world literature, and world civilization with the purpose of building a cross-cultural perspective that would illuminate both the contributions and experiences of Afro-American women and women in the Third World. Still other projects are designed primarily for resource development, such as the project of the Organization of American Historians that produced curriculum packets designed to integrate material on women in the United States and Europe into survey courses at both the college and secondary school level. The Geraldine R. Dodge seminars also focus on the secondary school level. Involving teachers from public and private secondary schools in three regions of the country, these seminars are intended to help teachers become better acquainted with feminist scholarship and to develop high-school curricula that reflect women's history, experiences, and perceptions.

There are so many of these projects that it is impossible to describe all of them here. These few examples do, however, give an idea of the range of activities and the different institutional contexts of inclusive curriculum projects. All of them rest on the concept of faculty development since building faculty knowledge of new interdisciplinary scholarship from feminist studies is an integral and critical part of curriculum transformation.

Directors of these projects typically begin with the recognition that women's studies scholarship has not fully made its way into the "main" curriculum of colleges and universities and that, without programs designed to bring the new scholarship into the whole curriculum, most students—male and female—will remain untouched by scholarship on women and therefore unprepared to understand the world. Elizabeth Minnich suggests that, though liberal arts advocates claim that a liberal arts education instills in students the perspectives and faculties to understand a complex world, instead, students learn about a detached and alienating world outside their own experiences. Were we honest about traditional education, she says, we would teach them the irony of the gap between stated educational missions and actual educational practices. Schools do not typically teach a critical view of the liberal arts we have inherited; we seem to have forgotten that, historically, liberal arts education was an entree into ruling positions for privileged males. Liberal arts education taught privileged men the language of their culture, its skills, graces, principles, and intellectual challenges, modeled on one normative character. It thus emphasized sameness over difference, even in a world marked by vast differences of culture, race, class, ethnicity, religion, and gender.[17] Consequently, there is now entrenched in the liberal arts a curriculum claiming general validity that is, however, based on the experience, values, and activities of a few.

Curriculum-change projects designed to bring the scholarship on women into the whole curriculum have been variously labeled "mainstreaming," "integrating women's studies into the curriculum," and "gender-balancing the curriculum." There are problems with each of these labels, since they may imply that curriculum change through women's studies follows some simple programmatic scheme when women's studies cannot be merely assimilated into the dominant curriculum; McIntosh says the label "mainstreaming" trivializes women by implying that we have been out of, and are only now entering, the mainstream. The term implies that there is only one mainstream and that, by entering it, women will be indistinguishable from men. It makes the reconstructive work of curriculum change seem like a quick and simple process, whereas women's studies builds its understanding on the assumption that there are diverse and plural streams of women's and men's experience.[18]

The use of the terms "integration" and "balance" to describe these projects is also problematic. Feminist scholarship has rested on the assumption that the exclusion of women leads to distorted, partial, and false claims to truth, yet "balancing" may imply that all perspectives are equally accurate or significant. Certainly, women's studies instructors do not want room in the curriculum for all perspectives, thereby including those that are racist, anti-Semitic, ethnocentric, class-biased, and sexist. Furthermore, liberal calls for balance often cloak an underlying appeal for analyses that are detached and dispassionate, as if those who are passionately committed to what they study cannot be objective. Gloria Bowles and Renate Duelli-Klein, among others, argue that it is unrealistic to seek a balanced curriculum in a world that is unbalanced.[19] Their concern reflects the understanding that most educational curricula mirror the values and structure of the dominant culture, yet they may underestimate the power of education to generate change.

Similarly, "integration" implies that women's studies can be assimilated into the dominant curriculum, when women's studies scholarship demonstrates that women cannot be simply included in a curriculum already structured, organized, and conceived through the experience of men. Critics of curriculum-integration projects, including Bowles and Duelli-Klein, caution that these projects might dilute the more radical goals of the women's studies movement by trying to make women's studies more palatable to those who control higher education. Integration is inadequate if it means only including traditionally excluded groups in a dominant system of thinking. So, if integration is interpreted as assimilation, these critics are right, but the history of the black protest movement in America indicates that the concept of integration cannot be dismissed merely as assimilation. Advocates of integration in the black protest movement understood that integration required a major transformation of American culture and values, as well as radical transformation of political and economic institutions. In the development of black studies, integration and separatism have not been either/or strategies, though they do reflect different emphases in black political philosophy and have been used strategically for different, yet complementary, purposes. If we take its meaning from black culture and politics, integration is a more complex idea and goal than assimilation; movements for integration in black history reflect a broad tolerance for diverse efforts to make radical transformations of educational institutions and the society at large.[20]

This controversy is more than a semantic one because the debate about terminology reflects political discussion among feminists who sometimes disagree about the possibilities and desirability of including women's studies in the curriculum. Because women's studies rejects the assumptions of the dominant culture and finds the traditional compartmentalization of knowledge inadequate for the questions women s studies asks, both the language and the work of curriculum change by necessity must maintain that what is wrong with the dominant curriculum cannot be fixed by simple addition, inclusion, and minor revision[21] Feminist critics of curriculum-integration projects fear that these projects change the primary audience of women's studies to "academics who wish to reform the disciplines but see no need to challenge the existing structure of knowledge based on the dominant androcentric culture."[22] Other feminist criticisms reflect a concern that the political radicalism of feminism will be sacrificed in order to make women's studies scholarship more acceptable to nonfeminists.[23] As Mary Childers, former associate director at the University of Maine at Orono project, states it, curriculum-integration projects may transform feminist work more than they transform the people at whom the projects are directed.[24]

The debate about women's studies and curriculum-change projects has been described as a debate between autonomy and integration,[25] and it reflects the origins of women's studies as both an educational project and as a part of broader societal efforts for emancipatory change. Those who argue for autonomy worry that integration projects compromise women's studies by molding it to fit into patriarchal systems of knowledge. Developing women's studies as an autonomous field is more likely, they argue, to generate the new knowledge we need because it creates a sustained dialogue among feminists working on common questions and themes.[26] Integrationists see a dialectical relationship between women's studies and inclusive curriculum projects and recognize that curriculum-revision projects are not a substitute for women's studies.[27] They see curriculum projects as both growing out of women's studies and fostering its continued development (pointing out that on many campuses where inclusive curriculum projects preceded women's studies, the projects resulted in the creation of women's studies programs). Developers of inclusive curriculum projects know that the projects cannot replace women's studies programs and, in fact, rest on the continued development of women's studies programs and research. Moreover, the presence of inclusive curriculum projects in institutions has typically strengthened women's studies programs.[28]

Projects to balance the curriculum also raise the question of what it means to have men doing feminist studies, since curriculum-revision projects are typically designed to retrain male faculty. Elaine Showalter discusses this in the context of feminist literary criticism where a number of prominent men have now claimed feminist criticism as part of their own work. She asks if men's entry into feminist studies legitimates feminism as a form of academic discussion because it makes feminism "accessible and subject to correction to authoritative men."[29] And, does it make feminism only another academic perspective without the commitments to change on which feminist studies have been grounded? The radical shift in perspective found in women's studies stems, in large part, from the breach between women's consciousness and experience and that of the patriarchal world.[30] Merely having men study women as new objects of academic discourse does not necessarily represent a feminist transformation in men's thinking. Showalter concludes that, in literature, only when men become fully aware of the way in which they have been constituted as readers and writers by gender systems can they do feminist criticism; otherwise, she says, they are only engaging in a sophisticated form of girl-watching. By further implication, transforming men through feminist studies must mean more than their just becoming aware of new scholarship on women or understanding how their characters and privileges are structured by gender; it must include their active engagement in political change for the liberation of women.

For women and for men, working to transform the curriculum through women's studies requires political, intellectual, and personal change. Those who have worked in curriculum-revision projects testify that these are mutually reinforcing changes—all of which accompany the process of curriculum revision through women's studies.[31] Understanding the confluence of personal and intellectual change also appears to help women's studies faculty deal with the resistance and denial—both overt and covert—that faculty colleagues in such projects often exhibit.[32] Women's studies scholarship challenges the authority of traditional scholarship and, as a consequence, also challenges the egos of those who have invested their careers in this work. Revising the curriculum is therefore also a process of revising our personalities since our work and our psyches have been strongly intertwined with our educations.[33]

The reconstruction of the curriculum through women's studies is occurring in a context of significant change in the demographic composition of student populations. Women now represent a majority of the college population, and by the year 1990 it is projected that minorities will constitute 30 percent of the national youth cohort.[34] In a report to the Carnegie Foundation, Ernest Boyer and Fred Hechinger conclude that "from now on almost all young people, at some time in their lives, need some form of post-secondary education if they are to remain economically productive and socially functional in a world whose tasks and tools are becoming increasingly complex.[35]

At the same time, current appeals for educational reform threaten to reinstate educational privilege along lines determined by race, class, and sex. Various national reports conclude that there is a crisis in education defined as the erosion of academic standards and the collapse of traditional values in education. In all of these appeals, the decline of academic standards is clearly linked to the proliferation of scholarship and educational programs in women's studies and black studies.[36] And, though seemingly different in tone and intent, conservative academic arguments about the need to "return to the basics" and to reclaim the legacy of "the classics" are actually attempts to reinstate patriarchal authority.[37] The assumption is that, if we do not reclaim the classical legacy of the liberal arts, we will lose the academic rigor on which such forms of education are seen as resting.[38] By implication, women's studies and black studies are seen as intellectually weak and politically biased, while study of the classics is seen as both academically rigorous and politically neutral.

One of the goals of women's studies is to insure that education becomes democratic. Women's studies practitioners know that the skills acquired through education cannot be merely technical and task-oriented but must also address the facts of a multiracial and multicultural world that includes both women and men. Case studies from universities that have had inclusive curriculum projects show that students do learn through women's studies to enlarge their worldviews and to integrate academic learning into their personal experience even though the process by which this occurs is full of conflict, resistance, and anger.[39] Other research shows that, following women's studies courses, students report increased self-esteem, interpret their own experiences within a larger social context, increase their identification with other women, expand their sense of life options and goals, and state more liberal attitudes about women[40] Moreover, faculty in inclusive curriculum projects often report that students are most captivated by the material that focuses specifically on women and gender; students in these projects also report that their classmates and their instructors are more engaged in class material where women are included as agents and subjects of knowledge.[41]

However, given the brief history of inclusive curriculum projects and the fact that balanced courses are still a small percentage of students' total education, evaluating student responses to such projects reveals only part of their significance. Equally important are the opportunities for revitalizing faculty when faculty positions are threatened by budget cuts, retrenchment, and narrowed professional opportunities.[42] Faculty in inclusive curriculum projects report new enthusiasm for their work and see new research questions and directions for their teaching as the result of this work.[43] After her review of inclusive curriculum projects around the country, Lois Banner reported to the Ford Foundation that the projects are also particularly impressive in the degree to which participants discuss and share course syllabi, pedagogical problems and successes, attitudes about themselves, and the changes they are experiencing. She finds this especially noteworthy since college faculty do not ordinarily share course materials with ease and regard their teaching as fundamentally private.[44]

The Phases of Curriculum Change

Several feminist scholars have developed theories to describe the process of curriculum change. These are useful because they provide a conceptual outline of transformations in our thinking about women and because they organize our understanding of curriculum critique and revision as an ongoing process. These phase theories also help unveil hidden assumptions within the curriculum and therefore help move us forward in the reconceptualization of knowledge.[45]

An important origin for phase theories is Gerda Lerner's description of the development of women's history." Lerner describes the theoretical challenges of women's history as having evolved in five phases. The first phase was the recognition that women have a history, which led to the second phase, conceptualizing women as a group. In the third phase, women asked new questions about history and compiled new information about women. In the fourth phase, women's history challenged the periodization schemes of history that had been developed through the historical experiences of men, leading them, in the final phase, to redefine the categories and values of androcentric history through consideration of women's past and present.

Lerner's description of the evolution of feminist thought in history showed feminist scholars in other disciplines that scholarship on women was evolving from simply adding women into existing schemes of knowledge into more fundamental reconstructions of the concepts, methods and theories of the disciplines. She was not the first to see this, but her articulation of these phases of change provided a map for the process through which women were traveling.

McIntosh has developed an analysis of phases in curriculum change that is unique in that it relates patterns of thought in the curriculum to human psyches and their relation to the dominant culture.[47] McIntosh calls phase 1 in the curriculum "womanless" (for example, "womanless history," "womanless sociology," or "womanless literature"). Only a select few are studied in this phase of the curriculum, and highly exclusionary standards of excellence are established. Since the select few in a womanless curriculum are men, we come to think of them as examples of the best of human life and thought. In turn, the curriculum reproduces psyches in students that define an exclusive few as winners and all the rest as losers, second-rate, or nonexistent.

Phase 2 of curriculum change maintains the same worldview as phase 1, since women and a few exceptions from other excluded groups are added in, but only on the same terms in which the famous few have been included. McIntosh defines this phase as "women in history," "women in society," or "women in literature," to use examples from the disciplines. In this phase of curriculum change the originally excluded still exist only as exceptions; their experiences and contributions are still measured through white, male-centered images and ideas. This phase can suggest new questions about old materials, such as, What are the images of women in so-called great literature? Also, this phase raises new questions like, Who were the best-selling women novelists of the nineteenth century? However, while this phase leads to some documentation of women's experience, it tends to see a few women as exceptions to their kind and never imagines women and other underclasses as central or fundamental to social change and continuity.

McIntosh calls the third phase of curriculum change "women as a problem, anomaly, or absence." In this phase, we identify the barriers that have excluded so many people and aspects of life from our studies, and we recognize that, when judged by androcentric standards, women and other excluded groups look deprived. As a result this phase tends to generate anger, but it is also the phase in which feminist scholars begin to challenge the canons of the disciplines and seek to redefine the terms, paradigms, and methods through which all of human experience is understood. Thus, it leads to more inclusive thinking in which class, race, gender, and sexuality are seen as fundamental to the construction of knowledge and human experience. Moreover, we recognize that inclusive studies cannot be done on the same terms as those preceding, thereby moving us to phase 4—"women on their own terms."

Phase 4, exemplified by "women's lives as history" or "women as society," makes central the claim that women's experiences and perspectives create history, society, and culture as much as do those of men. This phase also departs from the misogyny of the first three phases wherein women are either altogether invisible or are seen only as exceptional, victimized, or problematic relative to dominant groups. Phase 4 investigates cultural functions, especially those involving affiliation; understudied aspects of men's lives, such as their emotional lives and nurturant activities, become visible in this phase. In phase 4, according to McIntosh, boundaries between teachers and students break down as the division between the expert and the learner evaporates and teachers and students have a new adjacent relationship to the subjects of study. This phase also leads to a search for new and plural sources of knowledge.

Phase 5, McIntosh says, is harder to conceive because it is so unrealized—both in the curriculum and in our consciousness. She imagines this as a radical transformation of our minds and our work, centered on what she calls "lateral consciousness"—attachment to others and working for the survival of all.

Marilyn Schuster and Susan Van Dyne see curriculum change evolving from recognizing the invisibility of women and identifying sexism in traditional knowledge, to searching for missing women, then to conceptualizing women as a subordinate group, and, finally, to studying women on their own terms.[48] Through these first steps, women's studies poses a challenge to the disciplines by noting their incompleteness and describing the histories that have shaped their developments. Schuster and Van Dyne add women's studies as a challenge to the disciplines to their phase theory and define the last phase as one that is inclusive of human experience and appropriates women's and men's experience and the experiences generated by race and class as relational. The final phase of curriculum transformation, therefore, would be one based on the differences and diversity of human experience, not sameness and generalization. Schuster and Van Dyne identify the implied questions, incentives for change, pedagogical means, and potential outcomes for each of the six phases they identify, and they ask what implications each phase has for changed courses. They also provide a useful index of the characteristics of transformed courses.

In another analysis of curriculum change, Mary Kay Tetreault defines the phases of feminist scholarship as male scholarship, compensatory scholarship, bifocal scholarship, feminist scholarship, and multifocal or relational scholarship.[49] The first phase she identifies, like the first phases described by McIntosh and by Schuster and Van Dyne, accepts male experience as universal. Phase 2 notices that women are missing but still perceives men as the norm. The third phase, bifocal scholarship, defines human experience in dualist categories; curricula in this phase perceive men and women as generalized groups. This phase still emphasizes the oppression of women. Tetreault calls phase 4 "feminist scholarship"; here women's activities, not men's, are the measure of significance, and more attention is given to the contextual and the personal. Sex and gender are seen within historical, cultural, and ideological contexts, and thinking becomes more interdisciplinary. Tetreault's fifth phase, multifocal scholarship, seeks a holistic view in which the ways men and women relate to and complement each other is a continuum of human experience. In this phase, the experiences of race, class, and ethnicity are taken fully into account.

Tetreault suggests that understanding these different phases of curriculum change can be useful for program and course evaluation since they provide a yardstick for measuring the development of feminist thinking in different disciplines. Nevertheless, none of the authors of phase theories intends them to represent rankings or hierarchies of different kinds of feminist scholarship, and it is important to note that these phases have fluid boundaries and that their development does not necessarily follow a linear progression. Still, organizing women's studies scholarship into phases demonstrates how asking certain kinds of questions leads to similar curricular outcomes. As one example, adding black women into the history of science can reveal patterns of the exclusion of black women scientists and can then recast our definition of what it means to practice science and to be a scientist; this shows the necessity of seeing science in terms other than those posed by the dominant histories of science.[50] Furthermore, Showalter points out that different phases of thinking can coexist in our consciousnesses,[51] so for purposes of faculty development, it is important to recognize that certain phases are appropriate as faculty awareness progresses in different institutional, disciplinary, and course contexts.

Finally, identifying the phases of curriculum change is helpful in developing feminist pedagogy. Drawing from work by Blythe Clinchy and Claire Zimmerman[52] on cognitive development among undergraduate students, Francis Maher and Kathleen Dunn[53] discuss the implications of different phases of curriculum change for pedagogy. Clinchy and Zimmerman describe the first level of cognitive functioning for college students as dualist, meaning that students posit right and wrong as absolute and opposite. Maher and Dunn say the pedagogical complement to this phase of student development is the lecture format in which students are encouraged to see faculty members as experts who impart truth by identifying right and wrong.

Multiplism is the second phase in Clinchy and Zimmerman's analysis. This phase of cognitive development describes knowledge as stemming from within; in this phase, students discover the validity of their own experience. According to Maher and Dunn, this produces among students a highly relativistic stance—one in which they accept the legitimacy of different worldviews and experiences, thus opening themselves up to experiences that vary by class, race, and gender but seeing all experiences and perspectives as equally valid. Contextualism is the third phase of cognitive development identified by Clinchy and Zimmerman; according to Maher and Dunn, we can encourage this phase of student development through the creation of a pluralistic curriculum in women's studies.

Like those who have articulated phase theories of curriculum change, Maher and Dunn see the ultimate goal of women's studies as developing a curriculum that is inclusive in the fullest sense taking gender, race, class, and sexuality in their fullest historical and cultural context and developing an understanding of the complexities of these experiences and their relatedness. Such a curriculum would no longer rest on the experiences and judgment of a few. Since phase theories help us move toward this goal, they are an important contribution to faculty and student development through women's studies.

Critique of the Disciplines

The new enthusiasm that participants in women's studies faculty development projects report for their work is a sign that the insights of feminist scholarship are on the theoretical and methodological cutting edge of the disciplines. Working to build a balanced curriculum has renewed faculty and brought them and their students a new level of awareness about women in society, culture, and history. In fact, the revisions in the disciplines that this literature stimulates are so extensive that it is reasonable to conclude that "whether or not you are in women's studies, its scholarship will affect your discipline."[54]

As Schuster and Van Dyne argue,[55] there are invisible paradigms within the educational curriculum that represent tacit assumptions that govern what and how we teach, even when we are unaware of these ruling principles. The feminist movement exposes these unexamined standards by showing their relation to the ideology, power, and values of dominant groups, who in our culture most often are white, European-American men. Thus, although women's studies is often accused of being ideological, it is the traditional curriculum that is nested within the unacknowledged ideology of the dominant culture. The more coherent and tacitly assumed an ideology is, the less visible are the curricular paradigms that stem from it and the more unconsciously we participate in them.

Feminist criticism is generated by the fact that women are both insiders and outsiders to the disciplines; the contradictions imposed by their status create a breach between their consciousnesses and their activity, generating critical dialogue and producing new sources of knowledge.[56] Feminist criticism across the disciplines reveals that what is taken to be timeless, excellent, representative, or objective is embedded within patriarchal assumptions about culture and society. Consequently, recentering knowledge within the experience of women unmasks the invisible paradigms that guide the curriculum and raises questions that require scholars to take a comprehensive and critical look at their fields.

Creating an inclusive curriculum means more than bringing women's studies into the general curriculum because it also means creating women's studies to be inclusive so that women's studies does not have the racist, class, heterosexist, and cultural bias that is found in the traditional curriculum.[57] Feminist curriculum change, then, must not exclude the voices of women of color in posing the research questions, defining the facts, shaping the concepts, and articulating theories of women's studies. How would the work be enriched, both cognitively and emotionally, by listening to the voices and fully including the experiences of women of color? What kind of knowledge is made by ignoring not only class and gender but also race as origins for and subjects of scholarship? If the curriculum—both inside and outside of women's studies—is focused on white cultures, it will continue to define women of color as peripheral and to see white experience as the norm and all others as deviant or exceptional. It will, in effect, reproduce the errors of classical education.[58]

Esther Chow[59] suggests three strategies for incorporating the perspectives of women of color into courses: the comparison method, special treatment, and mainstreaming. The comparison strategy brings materials on women of color into courses for purposes of comparison with the dominant group experience, and it exposes students to a wide range of materials by examining women's experiences from different perspectives. Chow suggests, however, that it can perpetuate the marginality of women of color by leaving white women at the center of the major paradigm for analysis. Alternatively, the special-treatment approach makes women of color the topic of general survey courses, special topic courses, or independent reading, The advantage to such courses is that they allow for in-depth understanding of themes in the lives of women of color, although, since these courses tend to be electives, they do not make an impact on a wide range of students. The mainstreaming strategy incorporates materials on women of color into existing courses so that they appear throughout, not just in segregated areas of courses or the curriculum. Chow is careful to point out that the substance of these courses should not be divided along clear racial and gender lines. Anal she concludes that the effectiveness of these different strategies is dependent on the needs and goals of particular courses, the institutional setting, and interaction between teachers and students of various racial-ethnic backgrounds.

Creating an inclusive curriculum both within women's studies and within traditional disciplines is initiated by asking two questions: What is the present content and scope and methodology of a discipline? and How would the discipline need to change to reflect the fact that women are half the world's population and have had, in one sense, half the world's experience?[60] Those who work in women's studies know that women's studies scholarship cannot be simply added into the existing curriculum, as it challenges the existing assumptions, facts, and theories of the traditional disciplines, as well as challenging the traditional boundaries between the disciplines. The identification of bias in the curriculum is the first step in analyzing the multiple implications of the fact that women have been excluded from creation of formalized knowledge.[61] But as feminist scholarship has developed, more fundamental transformations can be imagined.

Several volumes specifically address the impact of feminist scholarship on the disciplines[62] and, were this essay to review fully the impact of feminist scholarship on the disciplines, the whole of women's studies literature would need to be considered. Of course, this essay cannot possibly do this instead it addresses the major themes that emerge from consideration of curriculum change effected through women's studies.

The Arts and Humanities

Feminist criticism shows that the arts and humanities have in the past created and reinforced definitions of life that exclude the experiences of, deny expression to, and negate the creative works of the nonpowerful, even though the humanities claim to take the concerns of all humanity and the human experience as their subject matter.[63] Women have been excluded from literary and artistic canons on the grounds that their work does not meet standards of excellence,[64] though, as Paul Lauter suggests, "standards of literary merit are not absolute but contingent. They depend, among other considerations, upon the relative value we place on form and feeling in literary expression as well as on culturally different conceptions of form and function."[65]

The exclusion of women from literary and artistic canons suggests that the canons themselves are founded on principles embedded in masculine culture, even though many literature teachers and critics will say that great literature and art speak to universal themes and transcend the particularities of sociocultural conditions like race, class, and gender. In tracing the development of the canon of American literature, Lauter has shown that the exclusion of white women, blacks, and working class writers from the canon of American literature was consolidated in the 1920s when a small group of white elite men professionalized the teaching of literature and consolidated formal critical traditions and conventions of periodization.[66] Since then, the aesthetic standards of the canon have appeared to be universal because without revealing their history, the learned tastes and common experiences of certain academic men are exaggerated as universal. And, as Annette Kolodny argues, once a canon is established, the prior fact of canonization tends to put works beyond questions of merit.[67]

Other feminist critics in the arts and humanities have identified the chronological presentation of materials as deeply problematic. Natalie Kampen and Elizabeth Grossman, for example, say that the idea that time is fundamentally linear and progressive—fundamental in the study and teaching of art history through chronology—produces accounts of the development of human culture that are more linear than the actual historical evolution of the culture has been. Chronological presentation also assumes competition as a part of human creativity and suggests that hierarchical arrangements are inevitable in all organization of cultural reality.[68]

Including women in the curriculum has been especially difficult in fields like the history of philosophy where the canon is fixed and relatively small. Even in ethics, where it is more difficult to ignore variations in human values, the subject tends to be studied from the vantage point of those in power, lending the impression that only elites can understand cultural norms.[69] In the humanities, when women do appear in texts and as artistic objects, their own experiences are seldom primary. In American literature, for example, women, native Americans, and blacks sometimes "inhabit" texts but are rarely given primary voices within them. This reveals a deep sex, class, and race bias in the teaching of the arts and humanities.

Were we to begin study in the arts and humanities through the experience of traditionally excluded groups, new themes would be revealed. Gloria Hull, for example, in her account of reading literature by North American women of color, identifies several themes that arise from immersion in this literature on its own terms.[70] An acute awareness of racial and sexual oppression pervades this literature, but so do themes of bicultural identity (especially expressed through language), alternative understandings of sexuality, and the importance of preserving cultural tradition in forms of expression.

History, like literature and the arts, has tended to focus on the historical experience of a few. Because historians tend to concentrate on heroes, they ignore the lives of ordinary men and women. Thus, much of the impact of feminist scholarship in history has been to expand the "characters" of historical accounts. But, more than adding in new characters, feminist scholarship in history shows how the traditional periodization of historical accounts is organized through the experience of bourgeois men.[71] From a feminist perspective, including women means not only including those who have been left out but rethinking historical paradigms to generate new frameworks in which women are agents of history and that examine the lives of women in their own terms and bring them into accounts of historical change. Feminist revisions of history do more than expand the subjects of history; they introduce gender relations as a primary category of historical experience. So, although the narrative style of history has tended to produce singular tales of historical reality, feminist scholarship in history produces accounts that reflect the multiple layers of historical experience.[72] As one example, in American studies, scholars have focused on a singular myth of the physical and metaphysical frontier of the new world as a place to be conquered and possessed. In contrast, Kolodny's work on women's consciousness and westward expansion shows that women imagined the frontier as a garden to be cultivated.[73]

Feminist scholars suggest that how excellence is produced and defined by literary and cultural institutions should become part of the study of the arts and humanities. This requires methodological self-consciousness, asking, for example, what social conditions are necessary for certain female images to emerge? Whose interests are served by these images? How do they affect women? And what are the varieties of women's tastes, working methods, ideas, and experiences?[74]

These questions help us identify bias in the curriculum and ultimately reveal more deeply embedded habits of thought. In her analysis of foreign language textbooks, Barbara Wright shows that the texts ignore most social classes, except for educated, upper middle-class surgeons, professors, and businessmen.[75] She identifies several phases of critique of the curriculum in foreign language instruction by examining the images of women and girls in textbooks, then studying women's place in the culture being presented, and, finally, developing a critical look at language itself. This last phase of questioning helps us see the value judgments that inform decisions to include or exclude certain semantic and syntactic possibilities in the language and, therefore, reveals ways in which gender, class, and race are embedded in the language of a culture and in our language teaching. Feminist criticism understands that the "circumstances in which culture is produced and encountered, the functions of culture, the specific historical and formal traditions which shape and validate culture these all differ somewhat from social group to social group and among classes. In this respect, the problem of changing curriculum has primarily to do with learning to understand, appreciate and teach about many varied cultural traditions."[76]

Carolyn Heilbrun writes, "The study of literature cannot survive if it cannot . . . illuminate human experience; and human experience cannot today be illuminated without attention to the place of women in literature, in the textuality of all our lives, both in history and in the present."[77] From feminist work in these fields we begin to see past and present cultures as "multi-layered, composites of men's and women's experiences, and rich in complexity and conflict."[78] This vision of cultural multiplicity explored through feminist scholarship would help the humanities to present a full account of human experience.

The Social Sciences

As in the arts and humanities, the exclusion of women from the social sciences leads to distortion and ignorance of their experience in society and culture." Whereas the social sciences claim to give accurate accounts of social reality, the exclusion of women's experiences and perspectives has produced concepts and theories that, while allegedly universal, are, in fact, based on gender-specific experiences, and so these theories often project the assumptions of masculine, Western culture into the social groups under study.[80]

As a result, feminist scholars suggest that core concepts in the social sciences are gender biased. As one example, the assumed split between public and private spheres is reproduced in social science concepts that tend to be grounded in public experience and that ignore private experience and the relation between public and private dimensions of social life. Focus on the public sphere as the primary site for social interaction omits women's experience and much of men's.[81] Economic activity, for example, is defined as taking place only in the public sphere, leading to the total omission of household work as a measurable category of economic activity in economics. Thus, caring for the sick, elderly, or young is productive economic activity when performed for wages but not when performed by persons in the privacy of the household. Moreover, by assuming white Western male experience as the norm, mainstream economists assume that economic activity is based on rational choice and free interaction. A feminist approach, however, would develop economic analyses that identify constraints on choice and the process of choosing.[82]

Likewise, in political science, textbooks describe political activity only as it occurs in formal public political structures. The representation of women and minority groups in elected offices is typically included, as is some recognition of federal legislation on civil rights. But always omitted are such topics as women's and minority groups' participation in community politics, ethnic identity as a dimension of political activity, or sexuality as the basis of organized political movements. Were we to rely on these texts for our understanding of political systems and behavior, as do most faculty and students, the virtual omission of race, sex, gender, class, and ethnicity would lead us to believe that none of these has been significant in the development of political systems and behavior.[83]

The location of social science concepts within the public and masculine realm reflects the dichotomous thinking that prevails in both social science content and method. Dorothy Smith's work in the sociology of knowledge investigates the implications of the fact that men's experience in the public world has been segregated from that of women in the private sphere. She posits that men are able to become absorbed in an abstract conceptual mode because women take care of their everyday emotional, and bodily needs. As a result, concepts in the social sciences, as they have been developed by men, are abstracted from women's experience and do not reflect their realities or worldviews.[84] Others have also argued that social science research methods polarize human experience by forcing respondents into either/or choices to describe their social experiences and attitudes. This is especially the case in experimental and survey research and in research on sex differences.[85] Furthermore, research methods in the social sciences routinely isolate people from the social contexts in which they are studied. And, in empirical research, race and sex, if mentioned at all, are treated as discrete categories and are reported as if they were separate features of social experience. It is an exceptional study that even presents data by race and by sex, and, when this is done, race and sex are most often reported separately. For example, sociologists comparing income by race and by sex typically report blacks' and whites' incomes and, in another table, compare men's and women's incomes. In reporting race and sex separately, the particular experiences of black women, white women, black men, and white men disappear from view. This practice produces false generalizations, perpetuates the invisibility of women of color, and denies that women of color have unique historical and contemporary experiences.

One of the greatest obstacles to curriculum change in the social sciences is the disciplines' search to establish themselves as sciences. The scientific method, as adopted in the social sciences, generates hierarchical methodologies in which the knower is seen as expert in the lives of others and produces research methodologies that deny that social relationships exist between researchers and those they study. Since the relationship between the knower and the known is part of the knowledge produced through research, denial of this relationship distorts the accounts produced by social science. Judith Stacey and Barrie Thorne conclude that, in sociology, positivist epistemology prohibits the infusion of feminist insights because positivism sees knowledge in abstract and universal terms that are unrelated to the stance of the observer. Feminist transformation has been more possible, they argue, in disciplines where interpretive methods are used. Interpretive methods are reflexive about the circumstances in which knowledge is produced and see researchers as situated in the action of their research; thus, they are better able to build knowledge in the social sciences that takes full account of social life.[86]

Feminist methodologies in the social sciences begin from the premise that the relationship between the knower and the known is a socially organized practice. The assumed detachment of scientific observers from that which they observe is, as feminists see it, made possible through organized hierarchies of science where, for example, women work as bottle washers, research assistants, or computer operators.[87] Moreover, feminists argue that the assumption of scientific detachment and rationality is a masculine value, one that is made possible only by ignoring the role of women in the practice of science. Additionally, Shulamit Reinharz suggests that feminist research in the social sciences should see the self-discovery of the researcher as integral to the process of doing research; consequently, it is ludicrous in her view to imagine the act of "data gathering" as separate from the act of "data analysis."[88]

In response to the preoccupation with scientific method in the social science disciplines, feminist scholars suggest that critiques of the scientific method should be a primary concern in feminist revisions of social science courses. In developing, for example, a feminist approach for teaching methods of psychology, Michelle Hoffnung suggests including a variety of approaches and methods and investigating in each case their assumptions about scientists' relations to the worlds being investigated.[89] Similarly, in teaching courses like the history of psychological thought, we need to recognize that women are more active in the history of psychology and social science disciplines than texts lead us to believe. When texts focus only on the internal development of a science, histories of the discipline wrongly ignore the external social and historical conditions that create scientific investigations.[90] As in the arts and humanities, putting women into social scientific courses requires this more reflexive approach—one that puts women and men in the full context of their historical and cultural experiences and that does not assume the universality of concepts, theories, and facts.

Science and Technology

Of all the disciplines, the natural and physical sciences have the closest connections to political and economic structures, yet they make the strongest claims to academic neutrality. For feminist scholars in the sciences, seeing how scientific studies reflect cultural values is a good starting point for understanding the interwoven worlds of science, capitalism, and patriarchy.

To begin with, scientific descriptions project cultural values onto the physical and natural world. Ruth Hubbard explains that kingdoms and orders are not intrinsic to the nature of organisms but have evolved in a world that values hierarchy and patrilineage.[91] Though it is often claimed that scientific explanations run counter to the widely shared beliefs of society, it is also true that scientific explanations are often highly congruent with the social and political ideology of the society in which they are produced.[92] Research on brain lateralization, for example, reflects a seeming intent to find a biological explanation for sexual differences in analytical reasoning, visual-spatial ability, and intuitive thought that cannot itself be clearly and consistently demonstrated in scientific investigations.[93] And perhaps nowhere else are culturally sexist values so embedded in scientific description and analysis as in discussions of sexual selection, human sexuality, and human reproduction.[94]

The feminist critique of science, as in the humanities and social sciences, looks at cultural dualisms associated with masculinity and femininity as they permeate scientific thought and discourse.[95] Some question whether the scientific method is even capable of dealing with collective behavior due to the fact that it parcels out behaviors, cells, categories, and events. In science, like the humanities and social sciences, explanations thought to be true often do not stand up when examined through women's experiences. For example, whereas medical researchers have typically described menopause as associated with a set of disease symptoms, new research by feminist biologists finds that the overwhelming majority of postmenopausal women report no remarkable menopausal symptoms.[96]

The feminist critique of science can be organized into five types of studies: equity studies documenting the resistance to women's participation in science; studies of the uses and abuses of science and their racist, sexist, homophobic, and class-based projects; epistemological studies; studies that, drawing from literary criticism, historical interpretation, and psychoanalysis, see science as a text and, therefore, look to reveal the social meaning embedded in value-neutral claims; and feminist debates about whether feminist science is possible or whether feminists seek simply a better science—undistorted by gender, race, class, and heterosexism.[97]

Building the feminist critique of science can therefore begin from several questions, including, Why are women excluded from science? How is science taught? What are the scientific research questions that, as feminists, we need to ask? How is difference studied in scientific institutions? Or, how is the exclusion of women from science related to the way science is done and thought? Some of these questions are similar to those asked in social studies of science. But feminist discussions of science specifically examine what Evelyn Fox Keller calls the science/gender system—the network of associations and disjunctions between public and private, personal and impersonal, and masculine and feminine as they appear in the basic structure of science and society. Keller argues that asking "how ideologies of gender and science inform each other in their mutual construction, how that construction functions in our social arrangements, and how it affects men and women, science and nature" is to examine the roots, dynamics, and consequences of the science/gender system.[98]

Science bears the imprint of the fact that, historically, scientists have been men. Therefore, asking how and why women have been excluded from the practice of science is one way to reveal deeply embedded gender, race, and class patterns in the structure of scientific professions and, consequently, in the character of scientific thought. As a consequence, while encouraging the participation of women in science is an obvious question of equity, it also reaches deeply into the social construction of science and provides insights about why some concepts gain legitimacy in science while others do not. So, important as it may be, women's experience is excluded from biological theory because it is considered to be subjective and therefore is considered to be outside the realm of scientific inquiry. Moreover, since it cannot be measured in scientific ways, the topic, not the method, is seen as illegitimate.[99]

Collectively, the work of feminist scientists raises new possibilities for the way science is taught[100] and conceived. By making us more conscious of the interrelatedness of gender and science, this work underscores the connection between science and the sex/gender system. Moreover, a feminist view of science would take it as only one of a number of ways to comprehend and know the world around us so that the hegemony of science as a way of knowing would be replaced with a more pluralistic view.

Resource Materials in the Disciplines

New scholarship on women does not automatically get translated into new teaching within the disciplines. Therefore, several of the professional organizations have sponsored projects that have produced guidelines for integrating new material on women into courses in the disciplines. These are especially valuable for assisting faculty teaching core courses in the disciplines and teaching new courses about women. The series published by the American Political Science Association[101] is a five-volume set with review essays, sample syllabi, field exercises, and suggested reading. The authors review explanations for the underrepresentation of women as public officials and examine sex discrimination against women as attorneys, judges, offenders, and victims. Moreover, they examine the traditional assumption that women are apolitical by looking at the political activity of women in community organizations and grassroots movements that are organized around such issues as sexual harassment, women's health, and violence against women.

Other professional groups have developed materials that focus particularly on integrating the study of women into the introductory curriculum; such materials are available in sociology, psychology, American history, and microeconomics.[102] These collections typically include a sample syllabus for introductory courses, with suggestions for new topics, examples, and readings in the different areas usually included in introductory courses. One collection from Feminist Press, *Reconstructing American Literature,* contains sixty-seven syllabi for courses in American literature. The American Sociological Association has recently published an excellent collection that includes syllabi for courses on sex and gender with suggested student assignments and exercises, lists of film resources, and essays on teaching women's studies, dealing with homophobia in the classroom, integrating race, sex, and gender in the classroom, and the experience of black women in higher education.[103]

The appendix of Schuster and Van Dyne's book, *Women's Place in the Academy: Transforming the Liberal Arts Curriculum,* is especially useful because it is organized by disciplines and separates suggested readings into those for classroom use and those more appropriate for teacher preparation. Faculty working to integrate scholarship on women into their courses would be wise to consult the various review essays published in *Signs* that summarize major research and theoretical developments in the academic fields and to consult the papers on curriculum change in the working papers series published by the Wellesley College Center for Research on Women. Newsletters from campuses with inclusive curriculum projects often include essays on revising courses written by faculty who are working to revise their courses.[104] Finally, women's caucuses within the professional associations of the disciplines can typically provide bibliographies and other resources designed to assist in the process of curriculum change.

A wealth of other materials are available to assist faculty specifically in the process of integrating women of color into the curriculum of women's studies and disciplinary courses. Gloria Hull, Patricia Bell Scott, and Barbara Smith's collection, *All the Women Are White, All the Blacks Are Men, But Some of Us Are Brave* is a classic and invaluable source. It includes not only essays on different dimensions of black women's experiences and contributions to knowledge and culture but also a superb selection of syllabi incorporating the study of women of color into courses and bibliographies and bibliographic essays of print and nonprint materials by and about black women.[105]

The Center for Research on Women at Memphis State University publishes a bibliography in the social sciences that is an excellent review of research about women of color;[106] their other projects include summer institutes on women of color and curriculum change, a visiting scholars program, faculty development seminars, and a working papers series. Maxine Baca Zinn's review essay in *Signs* includes an excellent bibliography for including Chicana women in the social sciences,[107] and *Estudios Femeniles de la Chicana* by Marcela Trujillo includes a proposal for Chicana Studies and course proposals and outlines that are useful for curriculum development.[108] Anne Fausto-Sterling and Lydia English have produced a packet of materials on women and minorities in science that is a collaborative project by students enrolled in a course at Brown University on the history of women and minority scientists; their collection includes essays written by the students about their experiences in science. In addition, Fausto-Sterling and English have printed a course materials guide that is an extensive bibliography of books, articles, bibliographies, visual aids, and reference works on the subject of women and minorities in science.[109]

The journal *Sage* is also an invaluable resource for scholars. *Sage* publishes interdisciplinary writing by and about women of color; recent issues have highlighted the topics of education, women writers, and mothers and daughters.[110] Other journals have published special issues devoted to studying women of color.[111] In addition to this growing primary research literature by and about women of color, there are numerous review essays that provide a guide to this important area of research.[112]

Such a wealth of material about women of color invalidates teachers' claims that they would include material on and by women of color if it were available. It also underscores the need to reeducate by recentering toward the lives of those who have been excluded from the curriculum and to do so by changing the materials and experiences we use in constructing classroom contents. Including the study of women of color in all aspects of the curriculum is rooted in a fundamental premise of women's studies: that there is great variation in human experiences and that this diversity should be central to educational studies. Although, as Johnella Butler notes, reductionist habits in the classroom make teaching about multiplicity difficult,[113] if the classrooms are more pluralistic both teachers and students will be better able to understand the pluralistic world.

Materials to assist in the process of curriculum change are abundant—so much so that one of the problems in faculty development projects is that faculty who have not followed the development of feminist scholarship over the past two decades must now learn an entirely new field of scholarship. Obviously, this cannot be accomplished quickly and, although we may sometimes feel discouraged by the magnitude of the needed changes, it is useful to remember that we are trying to reconstruct systems of knowledge that have evolved over centuries. Small changes, while obviously incomplete, do introduce larger changes—both in course content and in the political, intellectual, and personal transformations that this process inspires. Although it is also sometimes difficult to imagine what a revised curriculum would look like, Butler reminds us that working to build an inclusive curriculum requires a willingness to be surprised.

All of the materials reviewed above help us assess the climate for change in particular disciplines and devise appropriate strategies for the different fields in which we work and teach. With this information in mind and with the underlying philosophies of different projects specified, we can better analyze the context for curriculum change in various disciplines and imagine multiple ways of accomplishing educational change within them.

Conclusion

Adrienne Rich pointed the way to curriculum change through women's studies when she distinguished between claiming and receiving an education. Receiving an education is only "to come into possession of; to act as receptacle or container for; to accept as authoritative or true," while claiming an education is "to take as the rightful owner; to assert in the face of possible contradiction."[114] For women, Rich said, this means "refusing to let others do your thinking, talking, and naming for you."[115]

For women's studies to realize Rich's vision means we must develop women's studies itself to be inclusive; building an inclusive curriculum means both working to build women's studies into the curriculum and doing the work and thinking that makes women's studies multicultural and multiracial. These two dimensions will also strengthen women's studies as a field of its own, since they ask us to examine our own assumptions, methods, and relationship to the society in which we live. In this sense, changing the curriculum has three dimensions: changing our selves, changing our work, and changing society.

These are sobering times for women's studies scholars who seek through education an end to the injustices and patterns of exclusion that have characterized our culture. In the current political climate, one in which we are experiencing a serious backlash in educational change, women's studies and the feminist movement will meet new resistance.[116] Current appeals to return to the basics and to stabilize the curriculum threaten once again to exclude women, people of color, and gays and lesbians from the center of our learning, but Howe provides us with hope for change when she writes, "It is essential to revelatory learning to see the opposition clearly. . . . In a period when the opposition will be most visible, we may be able to do our best work."[117]

Notes

1. Susan Glaspell, "A Jury of Her Peers," in *The Best American Short Stories*, ed. Edward J. O'Brien (Boston: Houghton Mifflin Co., 1916), 371–83.
2. Ibid., 376.
3. Ibid., 381.
4. Ibid., 383.
5. Ibid., 385.
6. Building from Simone de Beauvoir's work, Catherine MacKinnon discusses this point. De Beauvoir writes, "Representation of the world, like the world itself, is the work of men; they describe it from their own point of view which they confuse with the absolute truth" (cited in MacKinnon, 537). MacKinnon continues the point by saying that "men create the world from their own point of view which then becomes the truth to be described." As a result, the male epistemological stance is one that is ostensibly objective and uninvolved and does not comprehend its own perspective; it does not take itself as subject but makes an object of all else it looks at. See Catherine MacKinnon, "Feminism, Marxism, Method, and the State: An Agenda for Theory," *Signs: Journal of Women in Culture and Society* 7, no. 3 (Spring 1982): 515–44, esp. 537.
7. Adrienne Rich, "Toward a Woman-centered University," in *On Lies, Secrets, and Silence* (New York: W. W. Norton 8r Co., 1979), 141.
8. Betty Schmitz, *Integrating Women's Studies into the Curriculum* (Old Westbury, N.Y.: Feminist Press, 1985).
9. Florence Howe, *Myths of Coeducation* (Bloomington: Indiana University Press, 1984).
10. Marilyn J. Boxer, "For and About Women: The Theory and Practice of Women's Studies in the United States," *Signs* 7, no. 3 (Spring 1982): 661–95.
11. Howe, 282–83.
12. Deborah Rosenfelt, "What Women's Studies Programs Do That Mainstreaming Can't," in "Special Issue: Strategies for Women's Studies in the 80s," ed. Gloria Bowles, *Women's Studies International Forum* 7, no. 4 (1984): 167–75.
13. Susan Kirschner and Elizabeth C. Arch, "'Transformation' of the Curriculum: Problems of Conception and Deception," in Bowles, ed. 149–51.
14. Florence Howe, "Feminist Scholarship: The Extent of the Revolution," in *Liberal Education and the New Scholarship on Women: Issues and Constraints in Institutional Change: A Report of the Wingspread Conference*, ed. Anne Fuller (Washington, D.C.: Association of American Colleges, 1981), 5–21.
15. Howe, *Myths of Coeducation*, 280.
16. The 1985 directory of such projects from the Wellesley College Center for Research on Women is reprinted in Schmitz. Although such a directory is quickly outdated, it is useful for seeing the diversity of projects that have been undertaken on different campuses across the country, as well as by professional associations. *Women's Studies Quarterly* periodically publishes reports from various projects; see vol. 11 (Summer 1983) and vol. 13 (Summer 1985). See also Peggy McIntosh, "The Study of Women: Processes of Personal and Curriculum Re-vision," *Forum* 6 (April 1984): 2f1; this issue of *Forum* and the vol. 4 (October 1981) issue of *Forum* also contain descriptions of curriculum-change projects on twenty-six campuses. *Forum* is available from the Association of American Colleges, 1818 R Street N. W., Washington D.C. 20009.
17. Elizabeth Kamarck Minnich, "A Feminist Criticism of the Liberal Arts," in Fuller, ed., 22–38.
18. Peggy McIntosh, "A Note on Terminology," *Women's Studies Quarterly* 11 (Summer 1983): 29–30.

19. Gloria Bowles and Renate Duelli-Klein, eds., *Theories of Women's Studies* (Boston: Routledge & Kegan Paul, 1983).
20. Margaret Andersen, "Black Studies/Women's Studies: Learning from Our Common Pasts/ Forging a Common Future," in *Women's Place in the Academy: Transforming the Liberal Arts Curriculum*, ed. Marilyn Schuster and Susan Van Dyne (Totowa, N. J.: Rowman & Allanheld, 1985), 62–72.
21. Johnella Butler, "Minority Studies and Women's Studies: Do We Want to Kill a Dream?" in Bowles, ed., 135–38.
22. Bowles and Duelli0Klein, eds., 9.
23. Marian Lowe and Margaret Lowe Benston, "The Uneasy Alliance of Feminism and Academia," in Bowles, ed. (n. 12 above), 177–84.
24. Mary Childers, "Women's Studies: Sinking and Swimming in the Mainstream," in Bowles, ed., 161–66.
25. This debate can best be reviewed in Bowles, ed. (n. 12 above).
26. Sandra Coyner, "The Ideas of Mainstreaming: Women's Studies and the Disciplines," *Frontiers* 8, no. 3 (1986): 87–95.
27. Peggy McIntosh and Elizabeth Kamarek Minnich, "Varieties of Women's Studies," in Bowles, ed., 139–48.
28. See Myra Dinnerstein, Sheryl O'Donnell, and Patricia MacCorquodale, *How to Integrate Women's Studies into the Traditional Curriculum* (Tucson: University of Arizona, Southwest Institute for Research on Women [SIROW], n.d.); JoAnn M. Fritsche, ed., *Toward Excellence and Equity* (Orono: University of Maine at Orono Press, 1984); and Schmitz (n. 8 above). See also Betty Schmitz, *Sourcebook for Integrating the Study of Women into the Curriculum* (Bozeman: Montana State University, Northwest Women's Studies Association, 1983); and Bonnie Spanier, Alexander Bloom, and Darlene Boroviak, eds., *Toward a Balanced Curriculum: A Sourcebook for Initiating Gender Integration Projects* (Cambridge, Mass.: Schenckman Publishing Co., 1984).
29. Elaine Showalter, "Critical Cross-Dressing: Male Feminists and the Woman of the Year," *Raritan* 3 (Fall 1983): 130–19; quotation is from Gayatri Spivak, "Politics of Interpretations," *Critical Inquiry* 9 (September 1982): 259–78, cited in Showalter, 133.
30. Marcia Westkott, "Feminist Criticism of the Social Sciences," *Harvard Educational Review* 49 (November 1979): 22–30.
31. Peggy McIntosh, "WARNING: The New Scholarship on Women May Be Hazardous to Your Ego," *Women's Studies Quarterly* 10 (Spring 1982): 29–31; and McIntosh, "The Study of Women," (n. 16 above).
32. Dinnerstein et al.
33. Peggy McIntosh, "Interactive Phases of Curricular Re-Vision: A Feminist Perspective," Working Papers Series, no. 124 (Wellesley, Mass.: Wellesley College Center for Research on Women, 1983).
34. Marilyn Schuster and Susan Van Dyne, "Curricular Change for the Twenty-first Century: Why Women?" in Schuster and Van Dyne, eds. (n. 20 above), 3–12.
35. Ernest L. Boyer and Fred M. Hechinger, *Higher Learning in the Nation's Service* (Washington, D.C.: Carnegie Foundation for the Advancement of Teaching, 1981), 28.
36. Michael Levin, "Women's Studies, Ersatz Scholarship," *New Perspectives* 17 (Summer 1985): 7–10. *New Perspectives* is published by the U.S. Commission on Civil Rights.
37. The Family Protection Act, proposed by the New Right, and introduced to Congress on September 24, 1979, would prohibit "any program which produces or promotes courses of instruction or curriculum seeking to inculcate values or modes of behavior which contradict the demonstrated beliefs and values of the community" or any program that supports "educational materials or studies . . . which would tend to denigrate, diminish, or deny role differences between the sexes as it has been historically understood in the United States" (Senate Bill 1808, 96th Congress first session, title 1, sec. 101; cited in Rosalind Petchesky, "Antiabortion, Antifeminism, and the Rise of the New Right," *Feminist Studies* 7 [Summer 1981]: 225). The Family Protection Act would return moral authority to the heterosexual married couple with children and would eliminate women's studies and any other educational programs that suggest homosexuality as an acceptable life-style; it would also severely reduce federal jurisdiction over desegregation in private schools.
38. Nan Keohane, "Our Mission Should Not Be Merely to 'Reclaim' a Legacy of Scholarship—We Must Expand on It," *Chronicle of Higher Education* 32 (April 2, 1986): 88.
39. In Fritsche, ed. (n. 28 above): Christina L. Baker, "Through the Eye of the Storm: Feminism in the Classroom," 224–33; Jerome Nadelhaft, "Feminism in the Classroom: Through the Eye of the Storm," 235–15; and Ruth Nadelhaft, "Predictable Storm in the Feminist Classroom," 247–55.
40. Karen G. Howe, "The Psychological Impact of a Women's Studies Course," *Women's Studies Quarterly* 13 (Spring 1985): 23–24. In addition

to a discussion of her own research, Howe includes an excellent review of literature on this topic.

41. Betty Schmitz, Myra Dinnerstein, and Nancy Mairs, "Initiating a Curriculum Integration Project: Lessons from the Campus and the Region," in Schuster and Van Dyne, eds., 116–29.
42. Marilyn Schuster and Susan Van Dyne, "Placing Women in the Liberal Arts: Stages of Curriculum Transformation," *Harvard Educational Review* 54 (November 1984): 413–28.
43. Dinnerstein et al. (n. 28 above).
44. Lois Banner, "The Women's Studies Curriculum Integration Movement: A Report to the Ford Foundation" (New York: Ford Foundation, March 1985, typescript).
45. For a discussion of phase theories see Mary Kay Thompson Tetreault, "Women in the Curriculum," 1–2; Peggy McIntosh, "Women in the Curriculum," 3; Peggy McIntosh, "Convergences in Feminist Phase Theory," 4; all in the vol. 15 (February 1986) issue of *Comment. Comment* is available from RCI Communications, 680 West 11th Street, Claremont, Calif. 91711.
46. Gerda Lerner, "The Rise of Feminist Consciousness," in *All of Us Are Present*, ed. Eleanor Bender, Bobbie Burk, and Nancy Walker (Columbia, Mo.: James Madison Wood Research Institute, 1984), and "Symposium: Politics and Culture in Women's History," *Feminist Studies* 6 (Spring 1980): 49–54.
47. Peggy McIntosh, "Interactive Phases of Curricular Re-vision" (n. 33 above).
48. Schuster and Van Dyne, eds. (n. 20 above), 27–28.
49. Mary Kay Thompson Tetreault, "Feminist Phase Theory," *Journal of Higher Education* 56 (July/August 1985): 363–84.
50. Evelyn Hammonds, "Never Meant to Survive: A Black Woman's Journey: An Interview with Evelyn Hammonds by Aimee Sands," *Radical Teacher* 30 (January 1986): 8–15. Evelyn Fox Keller, *Reflections on Gender and Science* (New Haven, Conn.: Yale University Press, 1985).
51. Elaine Showalter, *A Literature of Their Own* (Princeton, N. J.: Princeton University Press, 1977).
52. Blythe Clinchy and Claire Zimmerman, "Epistemology and Agency in the Development of Undergraduate Women," in *The Undergraduate Woman: Issues in Educational Equity*, ed. Pamela Perun (Lexington, Mass.: D. C. Heath & Co., 1982), 161–81.
53. Frances Maher and Kathleen Dunn, "The Practice of Feminist Teaching: A Case Study of Interactions among Curriculum, Pedagogy, and Female Cognitive Development," Working Papers Series, no. 144 (Wellesley, Mass.: Wellesley College Center for Research on Women, 1984).
54. F. Howe, *Myths of Coeducation* (n. 9 above), 256.
55. Schuster and Van Dyne, "Placing Women in the Liberal Arts" (n. 42 above).
56. Westkott (n. 30 above).
57. Patricia Bell Scott, "Education for Self-Empowerment: A Priority for Women of Color," in Bender, Burk, and Walker, eds. (n. 46 above), 55–66.
58. Maxine Baca Zinn, Lynn Weber Cannon, Elizabeth Higginbotham, and Bonnie Thornton Dill, "The Costs of Exclusionary Practice in Women's Studies," *Signs* 11, no. 2 (Winter 1986): 290–303.
59. Esther Ngan-Ling Chow, "Teaching Sex and Gender in Sociology: Incorporating the Perspective of Women of Color," *Teaching Sociology* 12 (April 1985): 299–312.
60. McIntosh, "Interactive Phases of Curricular Re-vision (n. 33 above).
61. Mary Childers, "Working Definition of a Balanced Course," *Women's Studies Quarterly* 11 (Summer 1983): 30 ff.
62. See Ellen Carol DuBois, Gail Paradise Kelly, Elizabeth Lapovsky Kennedy, Carolyn W. Korsmeyer and Lillian S. Robinson, eds., *Feminist Scholarship: Kindling in the Groves of Academia* (Urbana: University of Illinois Press, 1985); Diane L. Fowlkes and Charlotte S. McClure, eds., *Feminist Visions: Toward a Transformation of the Liberal Arts Curriculum* (University: University of Alabama Press, 1984); Elizabeth Langland and Walter Gove, eds., *A Feminist Perspective in the Academy: The Difference It Makes* (Chicago: University of Chicago Press, 1981); Julia A. Sherman and Evelyn Torton Beck, eds., *The Prism of Sex: Essays in the Sociology of Knowledge* (Madison: University of Wisconsin Press, 1979); Eloise C. Snyder, ed., *The Study of Women: Enlarging Perspectives of Social Reality* (New York: Harper & Row, 1979); Dale Spender, ed., *Men's Studies Modified: The Impact of Feminism on the Academic Disciplines* (New York: Pergamon Press, 1981); Marianne Triplette, ed., *Women's Studies and the Curriculum* (Winston-Salem, N.C.: Salem College, 1983).
63. Elizabeth Abel, ed., "Writing and Sexual Difference," *Critical Inquiry* 8 (Winter 1981): 173–403.
64. Lillian Robinson, "Treason Our Text: Feminist Challenges to the Literary Canon," Working Papers Series, no. 104 (Wellesley, Mass.: Wellesley College Center for Research on Women, 1983).

65. Paul Lauter, ed., *Reconstructing American Literature* (Old Westbury, N.Y.: Feminist Press, 1983), xx.
66. Paul Lauter, "Race and Gender in the Shaping of the American Literary Canon: A Case Study from the Twenties," *Feminist Studies* 9 (Fall 1983): 435–64.
67. Annette Kolodny, "Dancing through the Minefield: Some Observations on the Theory, Practice, and Politics of a Feminist Literary Criticism," in Spender, ed., 23–42.
68. Natalie Kampen and Elizabeth Grossman, "Feminism and Methodology: Dynamics of Change in the History of Art and Architecture," Working Papers Series, no. 121(Wellesley, Mass.: Wellesley College Center for Research on Women, 1983); and Norma Broude and Mary Garrard, Feminism and Art History: Questioning the Litany (New York: Harper & Row, 1982).
69. Linda Gardiner, "Can This Discipline Be Saved? Feminist Theory Challenges Mainstream Philosophy," Working Papers Series, no. 118 (Wellesley, Mass.: Wellesley College Center for Research on Women, 1983).
70. Gloria Hull, "Reading Literature by U.S. Third World Women," Working Papers Series, no. 141(Wellesley, Mass.: Wellesley College Center for Research on Women, 1984).
71. Joan Kelly-Gadol, "The Social Relations of the Sexes: Methodological Implications of Women's History," *Signs* 1, no. 4 (Summer 1976): 809–24.
72. Susan Armitage, "Women and Western American History," Working Papers Series, no. 134 (Wellesley, Mass.: Wellesley College Center for Research on Women, 1984).
73. Phyllis Cole and Deborah Lambert, "Gender and Race in American Literature: An Exploration of the Discipline and a Proposal for Two New Courses," Working Papers Series, no. 115 (Wellesley, Mass.: Wellesley College Center for Research on Women, 1983); Annette Kolodny, *The Land before Her: Fantasy and Experience of the American Frontiers, 1630–1860* (Chapel Hill: University of North Carolina Press, 1984).
74. Broude and Garrard.
75. Barbara Drygulski Wright, "Feminist Transformation of Foreign Language Instruction: Progress and Challenges," Working Papers Series, no. 117 (Wellesley, Mass.: Wellesley College Center for Research on Women, 1983).
76. Lauter, ed., *Reconstructing American Literature*, xxi.
77. Carolyn G. Heilbrun, "Feminist Criticism in Departments of Literature," *Academe* 69 (September–October 1983): 14.
78. Carroll Smith-Rosenberg, "The Feminist Reconstruction of History," *Academe* 69 (September–October 1983): 26–37.
79. Marcia Millman and Rosabeth Moss Kanter, eds., "Editorial Introduction," *Another Voice* (Garden City, N.Y.: Doubleday & Co., Anchor Press, 1975); Margaret L. Andersen, *Thinking about Women: Sociological and Feminist Perspectives* (New York: Macmillan Publishing Co., 1983); Carolyn Sherif, "Bias in Psychology," in Sherman and Beck, eds. (n. 62 above), 93–134.
80. Rayna Reiter, ed., *Toward an Anthropology of Women* (New York: Monthly Review Press, 1975).
81. Millman and Kanter, vii–xvi.
82. Barbara Bergmann, "Feminism and Economics," *Academe* 69 (September–October 1983): 22–25.
83. James Soles, "Recent Research on Racism" (paper presented at the University of Delaware, 1985 Lecture Series on Racism, Newark, January 1985).
84. Dorothy Smith, "Women's Perspective as a Radical Critique of Sociology," Sociological Inquiry 4 (1974): 7–13, and "Toward a Sociology for Women," in Sherman and Beck, eds., 135–88; Sandra Harding and Merrill B. Hintikka, eds., *Discovering Reality: Feminist Perspectives of Epistemology, Metaphysics, Methodology and Philosophy of* Science (Dordrecht: D. Reidel Publishing Co., 1983).
85. Michelle Hoffnung, "Feminist Transformation: Teaching Experimental Psychology," Working Papers Series, no. 140 (Wellesley, Mass.: Wellesley College Center for Research on Women, 1984); Sherif, 93–134.
86. Judith Stacey and Barrie Thorne, "The Missing Feminist Revolution in Sociology," *Social Problems* 32 (April 1985): 301–16.
87. Marian Lowe and Ruth Hubbard, eds., *Woman's Nature* (New York: Pergamon Press, 1983).
88. Shulamit Reinharz, "Experiential Analysis: A Contribution to Feminist Research," in Bowles and Duelli-Klein, eds. (n. 19 above), 162–91.
89. Michelle Hoffnung.
90. Laurel Furumoto, "Placing Women in the History of Psychology Courses," Working Papers Series, no. 139 (Wellesley, Mass.: Wellesley College Center for Research on Women, 1984).
91. Ruth Hubbard, "Feminist Science: A Meaningful Concept?" (paper presented at the annual meeting of the National Women's Studies Association, Douglass College, New Brunswick, N.J., June 1984).
92. Ruth Hubbard, "Have Only Men Evolved?" in *Biological Woman: The Convenient Myth*, ed. Ruth Hubbard, Mary Sue Henifin, and Barbara Fried (Cambridge, Mass.: Schenckman Publishing Co., 1982), 17–46; Ethel Tobach and Betty Rosof, eds., *Genes and Gender*, vol. 1 (New

York: Gordian Press, 1979); also see the four subsequent volumes of *Genes and Gender.*

93. Ruth Bleier, *Science and Gender* (New York: Pergamon Press, 1984).
94. Mina Davis Caulfield, "Sexuality in Human Evolution: What Is 'Natural' about Sex?" *Feminist Studies* 11 (Summer 1985): 343–63.
95. Helene Longino and Ruth Doell, "Body, Bias, and Behavior: A Comparative Analysis of Reasoning in Two Areas of Biological Science," *Signs* 9, no. 2 (Winter 1983): 206–27; Nancy Hartsock, "The Feminist Standpoint: Developing the Ground for a Specifically Feminist Historical Materialism," in *Money, Sex and Power,* ed. Nancy Hartsock (New York: Longman, Inc., 1983), 231–51; Elizabeth Fee, "Woman's Nature and Scientific Objectivity," in Lowe and Hubbard, eds., 9–28.
96. Anne Fausto-Sterling, *Myths of Gender: Biological Theories about Women and Men* (New York: Basic Books, 1985), 117.
97. Sandra Harding, *The Science Question in Feminism* (Ithaca, N.Y.; Cornell University Press, 1986).
98. Keller (n. 50 above).
99. Patsy Schweickart, lecture presented at Mellon Faculty Development Seminar, Wellesley College Center for Research on Women, Fall 1985.
100. Dorothy Buerk, "An Experience with Some Able Women Who Avoid Mathematics," *For the Learning of Mathematics* 3 (November 1982): 19–24; Anne Fausto-Sterling, "The Myth of Neutrality: Race, Sex, and Class in Science," *Radical Teacher* 19:21–25, and *Myths of Gender;* see also the special issue, "Women in Science," ed. Pamela Annas, Saul Slapikoff, and Kathleen Weiler, *Radical Teacher,* vol. 30 (1986) for several excellent pieces evolving from the feminist critique of science.
101. American Political Science Association, *Citizenship and Change: Women and American Politics,* 9 vols. (Washington, D.C.: American Political Science Association, 1983).
102. Judith M. Gappa and Janice Pearce, "Sex and Gender in the Social Sciences: Reassessing the Introductory Course: Principles of Microeconomics" (San Francisco: San Francisco State University, 1982, mimeographed); Barrie Thorne, ed., *Sex and Gender in the Social Sciences: Reassessing the Introductory Course: Introductory Sociology* (Washington, D.C.: American Sociological Association, 1983); Nancy Felipe Russo and Natalie Malovich, Sex and Gender in the Social Sciences: Reassessing the Introductory Course: Introductory Psychology (Washington, D.C.: American Psychological Association, 1982); Bonnie Lloyd and Arlene Rengert, "Women in Geographic Curricula, "*Journal of Geography* 77 (September-October 1978): 164–91; Organization for American Historians, *Restoring Women to History: Materials for US. I and II,* 2 vols. (Bloomington, Ind.: Organization of American Historians, 1983).
103. Barrie Thorne, Mary McCormack, Virginia Powell, and Delores Wunder, eds., *The Sociology of Sex and Gender: Syllabi and Teaching Materials* (Washington, D.C.: American Sociological Association Teaching Resources Center, 1985).
104. See especially newsletters from the Center for Research on Women, Memphis State University, and "Re-Visions," the newsletter from the Towson State curriculum project funded by the Fund for the Improvement of Post-Secondary Education.
105. Gloria Hull, Barbara Smith, and Patricia Bell Scott, eds., *All the Women Are White, All the Blacks Are Men, But Some of Us Are Brave* (Old Westbury, N.Y.: Feminist Press, 1983).
106. Memphis State University Center for Research on Women, "Selected Bibliography of Social Science Readings on Women of Color in the U.S." (Memphis, Tenn.: Memphis State University Center for Research on Women, n.d.).
107. Maxine Baca Zinn, "Mexican-American Women in the Social Sciences," *Signs* 8, no. 2 (Winter 1982): 259–72.
108. Marcela Trujillo, *Estudios Femeniles de la Chicana* (Los Angeles: University of California Press, 1974).
109. Anne Fausto-Sterling and Lydia L. English, *Women and Minorities in Science: Course Materials Guide.* Pamphlet and other materials are available from Anne Fausto-Sterling, Department of Biology, Brown University, Providence, R.I. 02921.
110. *Sage: A Scholarly Journal on Black Women,* Box 42471, Atlanta, Ga. 30311.
111. See *Journal of Social Issues,* vol. 39 (Fall 1983); *Conditions,* vol. 5 (1979); *Spelman Messenger,* vol. 100 (Spring 1984); *Sinister Wisdom,* vols. 22–23 (1983).
112. Marilyn Jimenez, "Contrasting Portraits: Integrating Materials about the Afro-Hispanic Woman into the Traditional Curriculum," Working Papers Series, no. 120 (Wellesley, Mass.: Wellesley College Center for Research on Women, 1983); Baca Zinn (n. 107 above).
113. Johnella Butler, "Complicating the Question: Black Studies and Women's Studies," in Schuster and Van Dyne, eds. (n. 20 above), 73–86.
114. Rich, "Claiming an Education," in *On Lies, Secrets, and Silence* (n. 7 above), 231.
115. Ibid., 231.
116. Banner (n. 44 above).
117. F. Howe (n. 9 above), 28.

CHAPTER 44

TRANSFORMING THE CURRICULUM: TEACHING ABOUT WOMEN OF COLOR[1]

JOHNNELLA E. BUTLER

Until very recently, teaching about women of color and incorporating material on women of color into the curriculum has been virtually ignored. At best, attention was paid to women of color from a global, culturally different perspective; however, due to various national and state efforts, race, class, gender, and ethnicity within the United States are getting serious attention. Central to this curricular revision are U.S. women of color. I see the resulting methodology and pedagogy of this cross-ethnic, multiethnic endeavor as rooted in the method of critical pedagogy developing in this country and influenced by Brazilian educator and activist Paulo Friere, and evolving from feminist pedagogy as well as the pedagogy implicit in Ethnic Studies. This chapter provides a conceptual framework, an appropriate starting point for teaching about women of color, which, I demonstrate, is at the core of transforming the curriculum.

Why "Women of Color?"

The phrase "women of color" has come into use gradually. Its use immediately brings to mind the differences of race and culture. It also makes clear that Black women are not the only women of color. In an ostensibly democratically structured society, with a great power imbalance signified by race and class privilege, labels representative of reality for those outside the realm of power are difficult to determine. This power imbalance is both cultural and political and consequently further complicates labelling. Selecting the phrase "women of color" by many women of American ethnic groups of color is part of their struggle to be recognized with dignity for their humanity and their racial and cultural heritage as they work within the Women's Movement of the United States. Furthermore, it signals a political coalescence, implying the particular sameness among U.S. women of color while still allowing for their differences. This effort of women of color to name themselves is similar to attempts by Afro-Americans and other ethnic groups to define with dignity their race and ethnicity and to counter the many stereotypical names bestowed on them. Because we tend to use the word "women" to be all-inclusive and general, we usually obscure both the differences and similarities among women.

With the decline of the Civil Rights Movement of the 1960s, the Women's Movement in the second half of the twentieth century got under way. Not long after, Black women began to articulate the differences they experienced as Black women, not only because of the racism within the Women's Movement or the sexism within the Black community, but also because of their vastly differing historical

Source: "Transforming the Curriculum: Teaching About Women of Color," by Johnnella E. Butler, reprinted from *Multicultural Education: Issues & Perspectives*, Third Edition, 1997, Jossey-Bass, Inc.

reality. One major question posed by Toni Cade's pioneering anthology, *The Black Woman*, remains applicable: "How relevant are the truths, the experiences, the findings of White women to Black women? Are women after all simply women?" Cade answers the question then as it might still be answered today: "I don't know that our priorities are the same, that our concerns and methods are the same, or even similar enough so that we can afford to depend on this new field of experts (White, female). It is rather obvious that we do not. It is obvious that we are turning to each other."[2] This anthology served as a turning point in the experience of the Black woman. Previously, White males, for the most part, had interpreted her realities, her activities, and her contributions.[3]

Although we are beyond the point of the complete invisibility of women of color in the academic branch of the Women's Movement—Women's Studies—Black women must still demand to be heard, to insist on being dealt with from the perspective of the experiences of women of color, just as they did in 1970, as the blurb in the paperback *The Black Woman* implies: "Black Women Speak Out. A Brilliant and Challenging Assembly of Voices That Demand to Be Heard." By the latter part of the 1970s, the logic of a dialogue among women of color became a matter of course. We find, as in Cade's *The Black Woman*, women of color speaking to one another in publications such as *Conditions: Five, The Black Women's Issue*, and *This Bridge Called My Back: Writings by Radical Women of Color.*[4] The academic community began to recognize American women of color who identify with the Third World, both for ancestral heritage and for related conditions of colonization; in 1980 we see, for example, the publication of Dexter Fisher's anthology *The Third Woman: Minority Women Writers of the United States.*[5]

The most familiar ethnic groups of color are the Asian Americans, Afro-Americans, Hispanic Americans, and Native Americans. Yet within each group there are cultural, class, and racial distinctions. These ethnic groups can be further delineated: Asian Americans consist of Chinese Americans, Japanese Americans, Filipino Americans, and Korean Americans, in addition to the more recent immigrants from Southeast Asia. Afro-Americans consist of the U.S. Afro-American and the West Indian or Afro-Caribbean immigrants. The number of African immigrants is most likely too small to consider as a group; however, their presence should be accounted for. Hispanic Americans, or Latino Americans as some prefer, are largely Puerto Rican, Chicano, and Cuban. The American Indian is made up of many tribal groups such as Sioux, Apache, Navajo, and Chicahominy.

The phrase "women of color" helps women of all these groups acknowledge both their individual ethnicity and their racial solidarity as members of groups that are racial minorities in the United States, as well as a majority in the world. The concept also acknowledges similarity in historical experiences and political position in relation to the White American. In addition, the use of the phrase and the concept "women of color" implies the existence of the race and ethnicity of White women, for whom the word "women" wrongly indicates a norm for all women or wrongly excludes other women of color.

What We Learn from Studying Women of Color

When we study women of color, we raise our awareness and understanding of the experiences of all women either implicitly or directly. Quite significantly, because of the imbalanced power relationship between White women and women of color, information about one group tends to make more apparent the experiences of the other group. It is well known, for example, that ideals of beauty in the United States are based on the blond, blue-eyed model. Dialogue about reactions to that model ultimately reveals that White women often judge themselves by that model of beauty. White women also serve simultaneously as reminders or representatives of that ideal to women of color and, most frequently, to themselves as failures to meet the ideal.

Another way of stating this is that a way of understanding an oppressor is to study the oppressed. Thus, we come to another level of awareness and understanding when we study women of color. We see clearly that White women function both as women who share certain similar experiences with women of color and as oppressors of women of color. This is one of the most difficult realities to cope with while maintaining viable dialogue among women and conducting scholarship. White women who justifiably see themselves as oppressed by White men find it difficult to separate themselves from the effects of and shared power of White men. White women share with White men an ethnicity, an ancestral heritage, a racial dominance, and certain powers and privileges by virtue of class, race, and ethnicity, by race and ethnicity if not class, and always by virtue of White skin privilege.[6] When we study women of color, we raise our awareness and understanding of the experiences of all women, either explicitly or implicitly.

Once we realize that all women are not White, and once we understand the implications of that realization, we see immediately the importance of race, ethnicity, and class when considering gender. Interestingly, some scholarship that intends to illustrate and analyze class dynamics is blind to racial and ethnic dynamics. In similar fashion, much scholarship that illustrates and analyzes racial dynamics and class dynamics fails to see ethnic dynamics. Other scholarship gives short shrift to, or even ignores, class. We have begun to grapple with the connectedness of the four big "-isms"—racism, sexism, classism, and ethnocentrism. Much scholarship in Women's Studies, however, fails to work within the context of race, class, ethnicity, and gender and their related "-isms," which modulate each other to a greater or lesser extent. Elizabeth V. Spelman illustrates how the racist equating of Blackness with lustfulness in Western culture modulates sexism toward Black women.[7] One resulting stereotype is that the Black woman has a bestial sexuality and, as such, deserves or expects to be raped. This racism is also modulated by an ethnocentrism that further devalues the Black woman, thereby justifying the sexism. Classism may also modulate this sexism if the perpetrator is of a higher class status than are most Black women. However, if this cannot be claimed, racism, ethnocentrism, or both will suffice. Nonetheless, each is operative to some degree. Lower-class Whites or Whites of the same economic class as Blacks can invoke skin privilege to differentiate within the common denominator of class. The categories of race, class, ethnicity, and gender are unified; likewise their related "-isms" and their correctives.

Attention to race makes us aware of the differing perspectives that women have about race and skin color—perceptions of what is beautiful, ugly, attractive, repulsive: what is ordinary or exotic, pure or evil, based on racist stereotypes; the role that color plays in women's lives; and the norms by which women judge themselves physically. Attention to race also brings us to a realization that White women too are members of a race with stereotypes about looks and behavior. These realizations lead us to more sophisticated analyses of institutional racism. Attention to race in women's lives, with the particular understanding that race has a function for White women and within the context of the connectedness among women due to the playing out of the varying gender roles, as well, reveals the oppression of racism, both from the point of view of one oppressed and of one who oppresses or participates in oppression by virtue of privilege.

Attention to class reveals, among other things, that because of different historical experiences, class means different things to different groups. Not necessarily measured by financial status, neighborhood, and level of education, class status frequently is measured by various ways in which one approximates the Anglo-American norm of middle to upper class. Our society encourages such behavior to a great extent, as shown by the popularity of the Dynasty model, the Yuppie, and the Buppie. Simultaneously, our society insists on formally measuring class status by economic means. Yet for the woman of color, as for the man of color, the dynamic of social class becoming a measure for success is particularly insidious, threatening to destroy the affirmation and utilization of ethnic strengths. Chinese Americans who have reached a high education level may move from Chinatown, feel compelled to adhere to Anglo-American norms that dictate certain dress, foods, and lifestyle, and embrace the cultural imperative of the superiority of the Anglo values. This, in turn, may threaten or seriously distort the sense of a sustaining identity that can recognize and negotiate racism and ethnocentrism. Ties to family and friends may be questioned, and the very historical reality and understandings that provided the source of strength for coping in the White world may be devalued and discarded. Poverty, for example, quickly becomes shameful, and the victim is easily blamed for not being a rugged enough individual.

Ethnicity, as a category of analysis, reveals the cultural traditions, perspectives, values, and choices that shape women's lives and their position in society, ranging from hairstyles and jewelry adornment to modes of worship and ways of perceiving a divine force, from moral values to the perception of women's and men's roles. Ethnicity, our cultural and historical heritage, shapes our perception of race and racism, sex, sexism and heterosexism, class and classism.

The element of power or lack of power has a great deal to do with the benefits or deficits of race and ethnicity. Similar to the example regarding classism, ethnic traditions, kinships, and values that are sustaining in the context of an ethnic group that is a minority, and thus, powerless, may become deficits when interacting with the majority or dominant society. On the other hand, when one becomes secure in one's ethnic identity, deficits of powerlessness and the moves to various levels of success (access to limited power) can be negotiated through variations on those strengths. Kinship networks, for example, are of primary importance to people of color for cultural reasons and for survival. Women's friendships have particular significance, specifically friendships of younger women with elder women. The structure of the larger American society does not make allowances for such friendships. Most of us do not live in extended families or in neighborhoods near relatives. Women of color frequently insist that they maintain such relationships over great distances. Time spent with family, especially extended family, must have priority at various times during the year, not just for tradition's sake but for maintaining a sense of rootedness, for a dose of shared wisdom, a balanced perspective of who you are, and often, simply for that affirmation that Momma or Aunt Elizabeth loves you. Ethnicity tells us that women of color celebrate who they are and where they come from, that they are not simply victims of ethnocentrism and other "-isms."

Ethnicity is important in women's lives. Most importantly, ethnicity reveals that besides the usually acknowledged European American ethnic groups, White Anglo-Saxon Protestants are an ethnic group. Even though it is an ethnicity that boasts a defining dominance that makes it unnecessary to name itself, it is an ethnicity. That it is an ethnicity to which many Whites have subscribed, rather than one to which they belong by birth, frequently is cause for confusion. However, it is no less an ethnicity for this reason.

The presence of Anglo-American ethnicity within the ethnicity of ethnic groups of color is often cause for confusion. Nonetheless, American ethnic groups of color manifest ethnicities that constantly balance, integrate, and synthesize the Western European Anglo-American, with what has become, with syncretism over the years, Chinese American, Japanese American, Afro-American, Chicano, American Indian, and Puerto Rican American. In a similar fashion, the English who came here syncretized with the values that emanated from being on this continent and became English Americans. They maintained a position of power so forceful that other Europeans syncretized to their English or Colonial American culture and eventually began to be called Americans. The assumption that people living in the United States are called Americans and that those living in other nations in the hemisphere are Latin Americans, Caribbean Americans, or Canadians attests to this assumed and enforced position of power.

Religion is closely related to ethnicity. Its values are sometimes indistinguishable from ethnic values. Ethnicity as a category of analysis therefore reveals sources of identity, sources of sustenance and celebration, as well as the cultural dynamics that shape women's experience. It makes even more apparent the necessity of viewing women pluralistically.

Gender roles may assume differing degrees of importance. By virtue of the modulation of the other categories, women may see gender or sexism to be of lesser or greater importance. Furthermore, the kind of gender roles or sexism may vary according to the influence of other categories. Attitides towards homosexuality are most frequently shaped by ethnicity (and by religion, which is closely tied to it), as is the depth and form of homophobia.

Gender roles for women of color are more apparently designated, determined, or modulated by ethnocentrism, racism, and sexism. It should not be surprising that women of color argue that racism most frequently assumes primary importance as an oppressive force with which to reckon. The Black woman, harassed in the workplace because she wears her hair in intricate braids and wears clothes associated with her African heritage, receives harsh treatment because of racism, not sexism. Racism also caused Black women to be denied the right to vote after White women gained suffrage rights. The sexism experienced by women of color within their communities is frequently tied to the racist, classist, and ethnocentrist power relationships between men of color and White America. The sexism experienced in the larger society is affected by this relationship as well as by racism, classism, and ethnocentrism directed specifically to the woman of color.

Women of Color: The Agent of Transformation

In dealing with the commonalities and differences among women, a necessity in teaching about women of color, I am reminded that the title of Paula Gidding's work on Afro-American women is taken from Anna J. Cooper's observation: "When and where I enter, then and there the whole . . . race enters with me."[8] Repeated in many forms by women of color, from the nineteenth-century struggle for the vote to the present-day Women's Movement, this truth ultimately contains the goal of transformation of the curriculum: a curriculum that reflects all of us, egalitarian, communal, nonhierarchical, and pluralistic. Women of color are inextricably related to men of color by virtue of ethnicity and traditions as well as by common conditions of oppression. Therefore, at minimum, their struggle against sexism and racism is waged simultaneously. The experiences and destinies of women and men of color are linked. This reality poses a special problem in the relationship between White women and women of color. Moreover, in emphasizing the commonalities of privilege between White men and women, the oppressive relationship between men of color and White men, women of color and White men, and men of color and White women—all implied in Anna J. Cooper's observation—the teaching about women of color provides a natural, pluralistic, multidimensional catalyst for transformation.[9] As such, women of color are agents of transformation.

This section defines transformation and provides the theoretical framework for the pedagogy and methodology of transformation. The final section discusses aspects of the process of teaching about women of color, which, though closely related to the theoretical framework, manifest themselves in very concrete ways.

A review of feminist pedagogy over the past fifteen years or so reveals a call for teaching from multifocal, multidimensional, multicultural, pluralistic, interdisciplinary perspectives. This call, largely consistent with the pedagogy and methodology implied thus far in this chapter, can be accomplished only through transformation. Although many theorists and teachers now see this point, the terminology has still to be corrected to illustrate the process. In fact, we often use the words "mainstreaming," "balancing," "integration," and "transformation" interchangeably. Mainstreaming, balancing, and integration imply adding women to an established, accepted body of knowledge. The experience of White, middle-class women has provided a norm in a way that White Anglo-American ethnicity provides a norm, and all other women's experience is added to and measured by those racial, class, ethnic, and gender roles and experiences.

Transformation, which does away with the dominance of norms, allows us to see the many aspects of women's lives. Understanding the significance of naming the action of treating women's lives through a pluralistic process—transformation—leads naturally to a convergence between Women's Studies and Ethnic Studies. This convergence is necessary to give us the information that illuminates the function and content of race, class, and ethnicity in women's lives and in relation to gender. In similar fashion, treating the lives of people of color through a pluralistic process leads to the same convergence, illuminating the functions and content of race, class, and gender in relation to lives of ethnic Americans and in relation to ethnicity.

We still need to come to grips with exactly what is meant by this pluralistic, multidimensional, interdisciplinary scholarship and pedagogy. Much of the scholarship on, about, and even frequently by women of color renders them systematically invisible, erasing their experience or part of it. White, middle-class, male, and Anglo-American are the insidious norms corresponding to race, class, gender, and ethnicity. In contrasting and comparing experiences of pioneers, White males and females, when dealing with American Indians, for example, often speak of "the male," "the female," and "the Indian." Somehow, those of a different ethnicity and race are assumed to be male. Therefore, both the female and the male Indian experience is observed and distorted. They must be viewed both separately and together to get a more complete view, just as to have a more complete view of the "pioneer" experience, the White male and White female experiences must be studied both separately and together. Thus, even in our attempts to correct misinformation resulting from measurement by one norm, we can reinforce measurement by others if we do not see the interaction of the categories, the interaction of the "-isms," as explained in the previous section. This pluralistic process and "eye" is demanded in order to understand the particulars and the generalities of people's lives.

Why is it so easy to impose norms, effectively erasing the experience of others? I do not think erasing these experiences is always intentional. I do, however, think that it results from the dominance of the Western cultural norms of individuality, singularity, rationality, masculinity, and Whiteness at the expense of the communal, the plural, the intuitive, the feminine, and people of color. A brief look at Elizabeth Spelman's seminal work, "Theories of Race and Gender: The Erasure of Black Women," explains the important aspects of how this erasure comes about.[10] A consideration of the philosophical makeup of transformation both tells us how our thinking makes this erasure happen and how we can think to prevent it from happening.

Spelman gives examples of erasure of the Black woman, similar to the examples I have provided. She analyzes concepts that assume primacy of sexism over racism. Furthermore, she rejects the additive approach to analyzing sexism, an approach that assumes a sameness of women modelled on the White, middle-class, Anglo-oriented woman. Spelman shows that it is premature to argue that sexism and racism are either mutually exclusive, totally dependent on one another, or in a causal relationship with one another. She discusses how women differ by race, class, and culture or ethnicity. Most important, she demonstrates that Black does not simply indicate victim. Black indicates a culture, in the United States the African-American culture. She suggests, then, that we present Women's Studies in a way that makes it a given that women are diverse, that their diversity is apparent in their experiences with oppression and in their participation in United States culture. To teach about women in this manner, our goal must not be additive, that is, to integrate, mainstream, or balance the curriculum. Rather, transformation must be our goal.

Essentially, transformation is the process of revealing unity among human beings and the world, as well as revealing important differences. Transformation implies acknowledging and benefiting from the interaction among sameness and diversity, groups and individuals. The maxim on which transformation rests may be stated as an essential affirmation of the West African proverb, "I am because we are. We are because I am." The communality, the human unity implicit in the proverb, operates in African traditional (philosophical) thought in regard to human beings, other categories of life, categories of knowledge, ways of thinking and being.[11] It is in opposition to the individualistic, difference-is-deficit, European, Western pivotal axiom, on which integration, balancing, and mainstreaming rest (as expressed through the White, middle- class, Anglo norm in the United States): "I think; therefore, I am," as expressed by Descartes.

The former is in tune with a pluralistic, multidimensional process; the latter with a monolithic, one-dimensional process. Stated succinctly as "I am we," the West African proverb provides the rationale for the interaction and modulation of the categories of race, class, gender, and ethnicity, for the interaction and modulation of their respective "-isms," for the interaction and modulation of the objective and subjective, the rational and the intuitive, the feminine and the masculine, all those things that we, as Westerners, see as either opposite or standing rigidly alone. This is the breakdown of what is called variously critical pedagogy, feminist pedagogy, or multifocal teaching, with the end result being the comprehension of and involvement with cultural, ass, racial, and gender diversity; not working simply toward tolerance, but [her toward an egalitarian world based on communal relationships within humanity.

To realize this transformation, we must redefine categories and displace criteria that have served as norms in order to bring about the life context (norms and values) as follows:

1. Non-hierarchical terms and contexts for human institutions, rituals, and actions
2. A respect for the interaction and existence of both diversity and sameness (a removal of measurement by norms perpetuating otherness, silence, and erasure)
3. A balancing and interaction between the individual and the group
4. A concept of humanity emanating from interdependence of human beings on one

another and on the world environment, both natural and human-created

5. A concept of humanity emanating from a sense of self that is not abstract and totally individually defined (I think, therefore, I am), but that is both abstract and concrete, individually and communally defined (I am we; I am because we are; we are because I am).

Such a context can apply to pedagogy and scholarship, the dissemination of ordering of knowledge in all disciplines and fields. Within this context (the context in which the world does operate and against which the Western, individualistic, singular concept of humanity militates) it becomes possible for us to understand the popular music form "rap" as an Americanized, Westernized version of African praise singing, functioning, obviously, for decidedly different cultural and social reasons. It becomes possible to understand the syncretization of cultures that produced Haitian voodoo, Cuban santeria, and Brazilian candomble from Catholicism and the religion of the Yoruba. It becomes possible to understand what is happening when a Japanese American student is finding it difficult to reconcile traditional Buddhist values with her American life. It becomes possible to understand that Maxine Hong Kingston's *Woman Warrior* is essentially about the struggle to syncretize Chinese ways within the United States, whose dominant culture devalues id coerces against syncretization, seeking to impose White, middle-class conformity.

Thinking in this manner is foreign to the mainstream of thought in the United States, although it is alive and well in American Indian traditional philosophy, in Taoist philosophy, in African traditional philosophy, and in Afro-American folklore. It is so foreign, in fact, that I realized that in order to bring about this context, we must commit certain "sins." Philosopher Elizabeth Minnich suggested that these "sins" might be more aptly characterized as "heresies," since they are strongly at variance with established modes of thought and values.[12] The following heresies challenge and ultimately displace the ways in which the Western mind orders the world.[13] They emanate from the experiences of people of color, the nature of their oppression, and the way the world operates. Adopting them is a necessity for teaching about women of color. The conceptualization and the emerging paradigms implied in these heresies surface when we study women of color and lead naturally to the transformation of the curriculum to a pluralistic, egalitarian, multidimensional curriculum.

Heresy 1: The goal of interaction among human beings, action, and ideas must be seen not only as synthesis, but also as the identification of opposites and differences. These opposites and differences may or may not be resolved; they may function together by virtue of the similarities identified.

Heresy 2: We can address a multiplicity of concerns, approaches, and subjects, without a neutral or dominant center. Reality reflects opposites as well as overlaps in what are perceived as opposites. There exist no pure, distinct opposites.

Heresy 3: It is not reductive to look at gender, race, class, and culture as part of a complex whole. The more different voices we have, the closer we are to the whole.

Heresy 4: Transformation demands an understanding of ethnicity that takes into account the differing cultural continua (in the United States, Western European, Anglo-American, African, Asian, Native American) and their similarities.

Heresy 5: Transformation demands a relinquishing of the primary definitiveness of gender, race, class, or culture and ethnicity as they interact with theory, methodology, pedagogy, institutionalization, and action, both in synthesis and in a dynamic that functions as opposite and same simultaneously.

A variation on this heresy is that although all "-isms" are not the same, they are unified and operate as such; likewise their correctives.

Heresy 6: The Anglo-American, and ultimately the Western norm, must be seen as only one of many norms, and also as one that enjoys privilege and power that has colonized, and may continue to colonize, other norms.

Heresy 7: Feelings are direct lines to better thinking. The intuitive as well as the rational is part of the process of moving from the familiar to the unfamiliar in acquiring knowledge.

Heresy 8: Knowledge is identity and identity is knowledge. All knowledge is explicitly and implicitly related to who we are, both as individuals and as groups.

Teaching About Women of Color

The first six heresies essentially address content and methodology for gathering and interpreting content. They inform decisions such as the following:

1. Not teaching Linda Brent's narrative as the single example of the slave experience of Afro-American women in the nineteenth century, but rather presenting it as a representative example of the slave experience of Afro-American women that occurs within a contradictory, paradoxical world that had free Black women such as Charlotte Forten Grimke and abolitionist women such as Sojourner Truth. The picture of Black women that emerges, then, becomes one that illuminates their complexity of experiences and their differing interactions with White people.
2. Not simply teaching about pioneer women in the West, but teaching about American Indian women, perhaps through their stories, which they have "passed on to their children and their children's children . . . using the word to advance those concepts crucial to cultural survival." The picture of settling the West becomes more balanced, suggesting clearly to students the different perspectives and power relationships.
3. Not choosing and teaching separate biographies of a White woman, an Asian American woman, and an Afro-American woman, but rather finding ways through biography, poetry, and storytelling to introduce students to different women's experiences, different according to race, class, ethnicity, and gender roles. The emphases are on the connectedness of experiences and on the differences among experiences, the communality among human beings and the interrelatedness among experiences and ways of learning.

The last two heresies directly address process. After correct content, process is the most important part of teaching. Students who learn in an environment that is sensitive to their feelings and supports and encourages the pursuit of knowledge will consistently meet new knowledge and new situations with the necessary openness and understanding for human development and progress. If this sounds moralistic, we must remember that the stated and implied goal of critical pedagogy and feminist pedagogy, as well as of efforts to transform the curriculum with content about women and ethnicity, is to provide an education that more accurately reflects the history and composition of the world, that demonstrates the relationship of what we learn to how we live, that implicitly and explicitly reveals the relationship between knowledge and social action. Process is most important, then, in helping students develop ways throughout their education to reach the closest approximation of truth toward the end of bettering the human condition.

The key to understanding the teaching process in any classroom in which teaching about women of color from the perspective of transformation is a goal, is recognizing that the content alters all students' perceptions of themselves. First, they begin to realize that we can never say women to mean all women, that we must particularize the term as appropriate to context and understanding (for example, White middle-class women, Chinese American lower-class women, or Mexican-American middle-class women). Next, students begin to understand that using White middle-class women as the norm will seem distortingly reductive. White women's ethnic, regional, class, and gender commonalities and differences soon become apparent, and the role in oppression of the imposed Anglo-American ethnic conformity stands out. Student reactions may range from surprise, to excitement about learning more, to hostility and anger. In the volume *Gendered Subjects*, Margo Culley details much of what happens. Her opening paragraph summarizes her main thesis:

> Teaching about gender and race can create classrooms that are charged arenas. Students

> enter these classrooms inbued with the values of the dominant culture: they believe that success in conventional terms is largely a matter of will and that those who do not have it all have experience a failure of will. Closer and closer ties between corporate American and higher education, as well as the "upscaling" of the student body, make it even harder to hear the voices from the margin within the academy. Bringing those voices to the center of the classroom means disorganizing ideology and disorienting individuals. Sometime, as suddenly as the fragments in a kaleidoscope rearrange to totally change the picture, our work alters the ground of being for our students (and perhaps even for ourselves). When this happens, classrooms can become explosive, but potentially transformative arenas of dialogue.[14]

"Altering the ground of being" happens to some extent on all levels. The White girl kindergarten pupil's sense of the world is frequently challenged when she discovers that heroines do not necessarily look like her. Awareness of the ways in which the world around children is ordered occurs earlier than most of us may imagine. My niece, barely four years old, told my father in a definitive tone as we entered a church farther from her home than the church to which she belongs, "Gramps, this is the Black church." We had not referred to the church as such; yet, clearly, that Catholic congregation was predominantly Black and the girl's home congregation predominantly White. Her younger sister, at age three, told her mother that the kids in the day school she attended were "not like me." She then pointed to the brown, backside of her hand. Young children notice difference. We decide what they do with and think of that difference.

Teaching young children about women of color gives male and female children of all backgrounds a sense of the diversity of people, of the various roles in which women function in American culture, of the various joys and sorrows, triumphs and struggles they encounter. Seeds of awareness of the power relationships between male and female, and among racial, ethnic, and class groups are sown and nurtured.

Teaching about women of color early in students' academic experience, thereby bringing the voices of the margin to the center, disorganizes ideology and ways of being. Furthermore, however, it encourages an openness to understanding, difference and similarity, the foreign and the commonplace, necessary to the mind-set of curiosity and fascination for knowledge that we all want to inspire in our students no matter what the subject.

Culley also observes that "anger is the energy mediating the transformation from damage to wholeness," the damage being the values and perspectives of the dominant culture that have shaped opinions based on a seriously flawed and skewed American history and interpretation of the present.[15] Certain reactions occur and are part of the process of teaching about women of color. Because they can occur at all levels to a greater or lesser extent, it is useful to look for variations on their themes.

It is important to recognize that these reactions occur within the context of student and teacher expectations. Students are concerned about grading, teachers about evaluations by superiors and students. Frequently fear of, disdain for, or hesitancy about feminist perspectives by some students may create a tense, hostile atmosphere. Similarly, fear of, disdain for, or hesitancy about studying people different from you (particularly by the White student) or people similar to you (particularly by the student of color or of a culture related to people of color) also may create a tense, hostile atmosphere. Student expectations of teachers, expectations modulated by the ethnicity, race, class, and gender of the teacher, may encourage students to presume that a teacher will take a certain position. The teacher's need to inspire students to perform with excellence may become a teacher's priority at the expense of presenting material that may at first confuse the students or challenge their opinions. It is important to treat these reactions as though they are as much a part of the process of teaching as the form of presentation, the exams, and the content, for indeed they are. Moreover, they can affect the success of the teaching of the material about women of color.

Specifically, these reactions are part of the overall process of moving from the familiar to the unfamiliar. As heresy #7 guides us, "Feelings are direct lines to better thinking." Affective reactions to content, such as anger, guilt, and feelings of displacement, when recognized for what they are, lead to the desired cognitive reaction, the conceptualization of the facts so that knowledge becomes useful as the closest approximation to the truth. As Japanese American female students first read accounts by Issei women about their picture bride experiences, their reactions might at first be mixed.[16] Raising the issue of Japanese immigration to the United States during the late nineteenth century may challenge the exotic stereotype of the Japanese woman or engender anger toward Japanese males, all results of incomplete access to history. White students may respond with guilt or indifference because of the policy of a government whose composition is essentially White, Anglo-oriented, and with which they identify. Japanese American male students may become defensive, desirous of hearing Japanese American men's stories about picture bride marriages. Afro-American male and female students may draw analogies between the Japanese American experience and the Afro-American experience. Such analogies may be welcomed or resented by other students. Of course, students from varied backgrounds may respond to learning about Issei women with a reinforced or instilled pride in Japanese ancestry or with a newfound interest in immigration history.

Teacher presentation of Issei women's experience as picture brides should include, of course, lectures, readings, audiovisuals about the motivation, the experience, the male-female ratio of Japanese Americans at the turn of the century, and the tradition of arranged marriage in Japan. Presentations should also anticipate, however, student reaction based on their generally ill-informed or limited knowledge about the subject.[17] Discussion and analysis of the students' initial perspectives on Issei women and of how those perspectives have changed, given the historical, cultural, and sociological information, allows for learning about and reading Issei women's accounts to become an occasion for expressing feelings of guilt, shame, anger, pride, interest, and curiosity, and for getting at the reasons for those feelings.

Understanding those feelings and working with them to move the student from damage, misinformation, and even bigotry to wholeness sometimes becomes a major portion of the content, especially when anger or guilt is directed toward a specific group—other students, the teacher, or perhaps even the self. Then it becomes necessary for the teacher to use what I call pressure-release sessions. The need for such sessions may manifest itself in many ways. For example,

> The fear of being regarded by peers or by the professor as racist, sexist or "politically incorrect" can polarize a classroom. If the [teacher] participates unconsciously in this fear and emotional self-protection, the classroom experience will degenerate to hopeless polarization, and even overt hostility. He or she must constantly stand outside the classroom experience and anticipate such dynamics. . . . "Pressure-release" discussions work best when the teacher directly acknowledges and calls attention to the tension in the classroom. The teacher may initiate the discussion or allow it to come about in whatever way he or she feels most comfortable.[18]

The hostility, fear, and hesitancy "can be converted to fertile ground for profound academic experiences. . . . 'Profound' because the students' knowledge is challenged, expanded, or reinforced" by a subject matter that is simultaneously affective and cognitive, resonant with the humanness of life in both form and content.[19] Students learn from these pressure-release sessions, as they must learn in life, to achieve balance and harmony in whatever pursuits; they learn that paradoxes and contradictions are sometimes resolved and sometimes stand separately yet function together (recall heresy #1).

Teaching about women of color can often spark resistance to the teacher or cause students to question subject veracity. Students often learn that the latter part of the nineteenth century and the turn of the century was a time of expansion for the United States. Learning of the experiences of American Indian and Mexican women who were subjected to particular horrors as the United States pushed westward, or reading about Chinese immigrant women whose lives paralleled those of their husbands who provided slave labor for the building of the railroads, students begin to realize that this time was anything but progressive or expansive. Teaching about Ida Wells-Barnett, the Afro-American woman who waged the anti-lynching campaigns at the end of the nineteenth century and well into the twentieth century, also belies the progress of that time. Ida Wells-Barnett brings to the fore the horror of lynchings of Black men, women, and children; the inhuman practice of castration; the stereotyped ideas of Black men and women, ideas that were, as Giddings reminds us, "older than the Republic itself—for they were rooted in the European minds that shaped America."[20] Furthermore, Wells-Barnett's life work reveals the racism of White women in the suffragist movement of the early twentieth century, a reflection of the racism in that movement's nineteenth-century manifestation. The ever-present interaction of racism and sexism, the stereotyping of Black men and women as bestial, the unfounded labelling of Black men as rapists in search of White women, and the horrid participation in all of this by White men and women in all stations of life, make for difficult history for any teacher to teach and for any student to study. The threat to the founding fathers and Miss Liberty versions are apparent.

Such content is often resisted by Black and White students alike, perhaps for different reasons, including rage, anger, or shame that such atrocities were endured by people like them; indifference in the face of reality because "nothing like that will happen again"; and anger, guilt, or shame that people of their race were responsible for such hideous atrocities. Furthermore, all students may resent the upsetting of their neatly packaged understandings of U.S. history and of their world. The teacher must know the content and be willing to facilitate the pressure-release sessions that undoubtedly will be needed. Pressure-release sessions must help students sort out facts from feelings, and, most of all, must clarify the relevance of the material to understanding the world in which we live and preventing such atrocities from recurring. Also, for example in teaching either about the Issei women or about the life of Ida Wells-Barnett, teachers must never let the class lose sight of the vision these women had, how they dealt with joy and sorrow, the triumphs and struggles of their lives, the contributions to both their own people and to U.S. life at large.

In addition to variations on anger, guilt, and challenges to credibility in learning about women of color, students become more aware of the positive aspects of race and ethnicity and frequently begin to take pride in their identities. As heresy #8 states, "Knowledge is identity and identity is knowledge. All knowledge is explicitly and implicitly related to who we are, both as individuals and as groups." The teacher, however, must watch for overzealous pride as well as unadmitted uneasiness with one's ethnic or racial identity. White students, in particular, may react in a generally unexpected manner. Some may predictably claim their Irish ancestry; others may be confused as to their ethnicity, for they may come from German and Scottish ancestry, which early on assumed Anglo-American identity. Students of Anglo-American ancestry, however, may hesitate to embrace that terminology, for it might suggest to them, in the context of the experiences of women and men of color, an abuse of power and "all things horrible in this country," as one upset student once complained to me. Here, teachers must be adept not only at conveying facts, but also at explaining the effects of culture, race, gender, and ethnicity in recording and interpreting historical facts. They also must be able to convey to students both the beautiful and the ugly in all of us. Thus, the Black American teacher may find himself or herself explaining the cultural value of Anglo-American or Yankee humor, of Yankee precision in gardening, of Yankee thriftiness, and how we all share, in some way, that heritage. At whatever age this occurs, students must be helped to understand the dichotomous, hierarchical past of that identity, moving toward expressing their awareness in a pluralistic context.

Now that we have explored the why of the phrase "women of color," identified the essence of what we learn when we study women of color, discussed the theory of transformation, and identified and discussed the most frequent reactions of students to the subject matter, we will now focus more on the teacher.

Teaching about women of color should result in conveying information about a group of people largely invisible in our curricula in a way that encourages students to seek further knowledge and ultimately begin to correct and reorder the flawed perception of the world based on racism, sexism, classism, and ethnocentrism. To do so is no mean feat. Redefining one's world involves not only the inclusion of previously ignored content, but also the revision, deletion, and correction of accepted content in light of missing and ignored content. As such, it might require a redesignation of historical periods, a renaming of literary periods, and a complete reworking of sociological methodology to reflect the ethnic and cultural standards at work. This essay, then, is essentially an introduction to the journey that teachers must embark on to begin providing for students a curriculum that reflects the reality of the past, that prepares students to deal with and understand the present, and that creates the basis for a more humane, productive, caring future.

The implications of teaching about women of color are far-reaching, involving many people in many different capacities. New texts need to be written for college-level students. Teacher education must be restructured to include not only the transformed content but also the pedagogy that reflects how our nation and the world are multicultural, multiethnic, multiracial, multifocal, and multidimensional. College texts, children's books, and other materials need to be devised to help teach this curriculum. School administrators, school boards, parents, and teachers need to participate and contribute to this transformation in all ways that influence what our children learn.

For college professors, high school and elementary teachers, and those studying to teach, the immediate implications of a transformed curriculum can seem overwhelming, for transformation is a process that will take longer than our lifetimes. Presently, we are in the formative stages of understanding what must be done to correct the damage in order to lead to wholeness. I suggest that we begin small. That is, decide to include women of color in your classes this year. Begin adding some aspect of that topic to every unit. Pay close attention to how that addition relates to what you already teach. Does it expand the topic? Does it present material you already cover within that expansion? Can you delete some old material and still meet your objectives? Does the new material conflict with the old? How? Is that conflict a valuable learning resource for your students? Continue to do this each year. Gradually, other central topics will emerge about men of color, White men, White women, class, race, ethnicity, and gender. By beginning with studying women of color, the curriculum then will have evolved to be truly pluralistic.

Once embarked on this journey, teachers must be determined to succeed. Why? Because all the conflicting emotions, the sometimes painful movement from the familiar to the unfamiliar, are experienced by the teacher as well. We have been shaped by the same damaging, ill-informed view of the world as our students. Often, as we try to resolve student conflicts, we are simultaneously working through our own. Above all, we must demand honesty of ourselves before we can succeed.

The difficulty of the process of transformation is one contributing factor to the maintenance of the status quo. Often we look for the easiest way out. It is easier to work with students who are not puzzled, concerned, overly romantic, or angered by what they are studying. Teachers must be willing to admit that while we do not know everything we do know how to go about learning in a way that reaches the closest approximation of the truth. Our reach must always exceed our grasp, and in doing so we will encourage the excellence, the passion, the curiosity, the respect, and the love needed to create superb scholarship and encourage thinking, open-minded, caring, knowledgeable students.

Notes

1. A version of this chapter originally appeared in *Multicultural Education: Issues and Perspectives*, ed. James A. Banks and Cherry M. Banks (Boston: Allyn and Bacon, 1989), 145–65. Reprinted with permission.
2. Toni Cade, *The Black Woman: An Anthology* (New York: New American Library, 1970), 9.
3. The Moynihan Report of 1965, the most notable of this scholarship, received the widest publicity and acceptance by American society at large. Blaming Black social problems on the Black family, Moynihan argues that Black families, dominated by women, are generally pathological and pathogenic. In attempting to explain the poor social and economic condition of the Black lower class, Moynihan largely ignores the history of racism and ethnocentrism and classism in American life and instead blames their victims. His study directly opposes the scholarship of Billingsley and others, which demonstrates the organizational differences between Black and White family units as well as the existence of a vital Afro-American culture on which to base solutions to the social problems Moynihan identifies. See Daniel Moynihan, *The Negro Family* (Washington, D.C.: U.S. Dept. of Labor, 1965); Joyce Ladner, ed., *The Death of White Sociology* (New York: Vintage, 1973); Andrew Billingsley, *Black Families in White America* (Englewood Cliffs, N.J.: Prentice-Hall, 1968); Harriet McAdoo, ed., *Black Families* (Beverly Hills, Calif.: Sage Publications, 1981).
4. *Conditions: Five, The Black Woman's Issue* 2, no. 3 (Autumn 1979); Cherrie Moraga and Gloria Anzaldua, eds., *This Bridge Called My Back: Writings by Radical Women of Color* (Watertown, Mass.: Persephone Press, 1981).
5. Dexter Fisher, ed., *The Third Woman* (Boston: Houghton Mifflin, 1980).

6. See "On Being White: Toward a Feminist Understanding of Race and Race Supremacy," in *The Politics of Reality: Essays in Feminist Theory,* by Marilyn Frye (Trumansburg, N.Y.: The Crossing Press, 1983), 110–27. Also see "Understanding Correspondence Between White Privilege and Male Privilege Through Women's Studies Work," unpublished paper presented by Peggy McIntosh at the 1987 National Women's Studies Association Annual Meeting, Atlanta, GA. Available through Wellesley Center for Research on Women, Washington St., Wellesley, Mass., 02181. These works illuminate race and class power relationships and the difference between race and skin privileges. They emphasize not the rejection of privilege but the awareness of its function in order to work actively against injustice.
7. Elizabeth V. Spelman, "Theories of Gender and Race: The Erasure of Black Women," *Quest: A Feminist Quarterly 5,* no. 4 (1982): 36–62. Also see Renate D. Klein, "The Dynamics of the Women's Studies Classroom: A Review Essay of the Teaching Practice of Women's Studies in Higher Education," *Women's Studies International Forum* 10, no. 2 (1987):187–206.
8. Paula Giddings, *When and Where I Enter: The Impact of Black Women on Race and Sex in America* (New York: William Morrow, 1984).
9. See Lillian Smith, *Killers of the Dream* (New York: Norton, 1949, 1961). Smith provides a useful and clear description of the interaction between racism and sexism and its legacy.
10. Elizabeth V. Spelman, "Theories of Gender and Race," 57–59.
11. See John Mbiti, *Introduction to African Religion* (London: Heineman, 1975); Basil Davidson, *The African Genius* (Boston: Little, Brown, 1969). For a discussion and explication of Western cultural imperatives, see George Kent, *Blackness and the Adventure of Western Culture* (Chicago: Third World Press, 1972).
12. I began to conceptualize this framework while doing consulting work with college faculty to include Black Studies and Women's Studies content in their syllabi at The Conference on Critical Pedagogy at the University of Massachusetts, Amherst, in February 1985. The concept of heresy here implies a reworking of the way that Westerners order the world, essentially by replacing individualism with a sense of communality and interdependence.
13. See also Paulo Friere, *Pedagogy of the Oppressed* (New York: Seabury, 1969); *Education for Critical Consciousness* (New York: Seabury, 1973).
14. Margo Culley, "Anger and Authority in the Introductory Women's Studies Classroom," in *Gendered Subjects: The Dynamics of Feminist Teaching,* ed. Margo Culley and Catherine Portugues (Boston: Routledge and Kegan Paul, 1985), 209.
15. Ibid., 212. See also in same volume, Butler, "Toward a Pedagogy of Everywoman's Studies," 230–39.
16. "Sei" in Japanese means "generation." The concepts of first-, second-, and third-generation Japanese Americans are denoted by adding a numerical prefix. Therefore, Issei is first generation; Nisei, second; and Sansei, third. Most Issei immigrated to the United States during the first quarter of the twentieth century to provide cheap, male, manual labor, intending to return to Japan after a few years. However, their low wages did not provide enough money for them to return. In 1900, out of a total of 24,326 in the United States, 983 were women. Through the immigration of picture brides by 1920, women numbered 38,303 out of a population of 111,010. Because of racist, anti-Japanese agitation, the U.S. government helped bring these brides to the United States. For a complete discussion, see the Introduction and "Issei Women" in Nobuya Tschida, ed., *Asian and Pacific American Experiences: Women's Perspectives* (Minneapolis: University of Minnesota Press, 1982).
17. An important rule in the scholarship of critical pedagogy is that the teacher should build on the ideas and feelings that students bring to a subject, helping them understand how they might be useful, in what ways they are flawed, correct, or incorrect. Sometimes this simply means giving the student credit for having thought about an idea, or helping the student become aware that he or she might have encountered the idea, or aspects of material studied, elsewhere. Generally this process is referred to as moving the student from the familiar to the unfamiliar.
18. Butler, "Toward a Pedagogy," 236.
19. Ibid.
20. Giddings, When and Where I Enter, 31.

CHAPTER 45

INSIDE THE CHANGE PROCESS

SANDRA L. KANTER, ZELDA F. GAMSON, HOWARD B. LONDON, GORDON B. ARNOLD AND JANET T. CIVIAN

Reforming the curriculum is always difficult and fraught with perils.

—Jerry Gaff (1983, p. 164)

A Perilous Journey

As colleges and universities cope with the increasingly turbulent atmosphere of higher education and the internal schisms that seem to intensify in this environment, it is remarkable that so many have undertaken to reform general education. Successful curricular change requires careful maneuvering among the myriad internal and external interests of an institution of higher education. A careful mapping of the change process, then, from consultation to proposal to implementation, is instructive. This chapter looks at the process close up. Drawing on data from the telephone survey of 71 institutions and 15 campus visits, the chapter looks at the underpinnings of organizational change, reviews the survey findings concerning the design and implementation of a new curriculum, and illustrates the design process through a discussion of events on several campuses.

Design of General Education

The Committee

General education reform on college campuses is usually marked by the appointment of a committee responsible for recommending a new program. Table 45-1 summarizes telephone survey data on the characteristics of design committees. Not surprisingly, the committees varied greatly in their size, composition, and duration of work. Slightly more than half (54 percent) of the campuses appointed an ad hoc committee to undertake the redesign of general education, whereas the remainder (46 percent) charged the standing curriculum committee, or one of its subcommittees, with the task. Administrators were solely responsible for making appointments to the design committees on two thirds of the campuses, whereas faculty participated in such appointments on one third of the campuses.

Faculty members generally chaired the design committees, although administrators (a provost, dean, or academic vice-president) did so on about one third of the campuses.

Source: "Inside the Change Process," by Sandra L. Kanter, Zelda F. Gamson, Howard B. London, Gordon B. Arnold and Janet T. Civian reprinted from *Revitalizing General Education in a Time of Scarcity: A Navigational Chart for Administration and Faculty*, 1997, Allyn and Bacon.

TABLE 45-1
Characteristics of General Education Design Committees

Characteristic	%[a]
Committee Type	
Ad hoc committee	54
Standing curriculum committee	46
Appointments to Ad Hoc Committees Made by	
Administrators	67
Faculty	18
Both administrators and faculty	15
Chairperson of Design Committee	
Faculty member	63
Provost, dean, or vice-president of academic affairs	37
Size of Design Committee	
3–6 members	19
7–10 members	40
11–14 members	17
15+ members	23
Design Committee Composition (Position)	
Administrators and at-large faculty	52
At-large faculty only	27
Administrators, department chairs, and at-large faculty	14
Administrators and department chairs	4
Department chairs and at-large faculty	4
Design Committee Composition (Area)	
Only liberal arts faculty	30
Mostly liberal arts faculty	60
Only professional/technical faculty	5
Mostly professional/technical faculty	5

Data are from telephone survey.

[a]Percentages may not add to 100 percent due to rounding.

Committee sizes ranged from 3 to 35 members, with an average of 11 members. The committee composition reflected different configurations of faculty, administrators, and department or division chairpersons. The most popular committee configuration included both administrators and at-large faculty members, followed by committees composed of only at-large faculty. Relatively few department and division chairpersons participated in design committees. The committees tended to have a predominance of liberal arts faculty, with professional and technical faculty in the minority.

Duration

A relatively short but labor-intensive period was typical for designing a new general education curriculum. About half of the campuses reported that their design groups met once a week or more, with the remainder meeting on a biweekly or monthly basis. Among those who were able to make an estimate (and most could not) of the

TABLE 45-2
Duration of Design Process

Duration Measure	*n*	*Median*	*Minimum*	*Maximum*
Total design hours	30	39	12	420
Total number of design months	48	12	1	84
Years from beginning of design discussion until implementation	50	2.5	<1	12

Data are from telephone survey.

TABLE 45-3
Duration of Design Process, Shown by Extent of Curriculum Change

Change	*Median Amount of n*	*Minimum Number of Months*	*Maximum Number of Months*	*Number of Months*
Minimum	18	12	2	48
Moderate	13	13	1	84
Great	8	11	2	24

Data are from telephone survey.

total hours of meeting time, the median was 39 hours, with a range from 12 to 420 hours (see Table 45-2). For the total span of time; most campuses studied general education over a period of 9 months to 2 years; the median duration was 1 year. The median time from the initiation of discussions about design to the actual implementation of a revised general education program was 2.5 years. The range was substantial: A few campuses (4 percent) accomplished the feat in the same year; most campuses (60 percent) took between 1 and 3 years to design and implement a new program; and 36 percent took 4 or more years to do so. One campus implemented its program 12 years after discussions began.

No clear relationship exists between the length of time that the design group met and the amount of change in the new general education curriculum compared with the preexisting curriculum. For 18 campuses that experienced minor changes in their general education curricula the median number of months that the design group met was 12 (see Table 45-3). For 13 campuses with moderate change to their programs the median was 13 months. Eight campuses in the study experienced a great amount of change with a median of only 11 months to design it.

A Closer Look at Actual Campuses

These summary numbers indicate the wide range of committee profiles that produce a new general education curriculum. Committees may be preexisting or ad hoc, small or large; they may meet for a short period or a lengthy one. Understanding the substantive work of the design committees, however, requires a closer look at the context in which they work. Bridgewater State College in Massachusetts and Green Mountain College in Vermont provide two very different contexts for understanding the design process in general education reform. The Bridgewater campus experienced a curriculum development process that was universally viewed as open and inclusive. At Green Mountain the general education program was designed behind closed doors.

On the Bridgewater campus the curriculum committee charged an ad hoc subcommittee with changing the general education program (see Box 1). Members representing a range of disciplines volunteered for this task. No single group dominated the committee, which was chaired by a well-respected senior faculty member.

In its first year the Bridgewater subcommittee on general education was divided into three task forces. The first was charged with gathering information about current students. Members collected data concerning choice of majors, Scholastic Aptitude Test (SAT) scores, and course-taking patterns. The second task force analyzed the results of alumni surveys conducted annually by the college's career planning office. The third reviewed general education requirements at selected colleges in New England. In addition, the subcommittee sent questionnaires to five groups: alumni classes from 1945 to 1975, alumni classes from 1976 to 1982, regional employers, current juniors and seniors, and faculty. Finally, the subcommittee scheduled 27 hearings, often three times a week, with individual departments to solicit opinions about the goals of a new general education program.

In the second year the subcommittee developed a guiding philosophy for general education, identified 12 areas of study to be included in the program, and devised criteria to define the types of courses that would be approved under this program. The proposal was delivered to the curriculum committee, which held hearings. Discussion, debate, and some tinkering ensued, and the proposal was approved pretty much intact. It was then forwarded to the all-college com-

Box 1
Close-up: Bridgewater State College

Bridgewater State College in Bridgewater, Massachusetts is located about an hour's drive from Boston on a picturesque 129-acre campus. The approximately 270 full-time faculty are unionized. Most of its 8,200 students are from the southeastern region of the state, and many are first-generation college students. About half begin their studies directly after being graduated from high school, and most stay in the area after graduation. Because of its large population of nontraditional students and its curriculum, which merges liberal arts and professional education, the college administration sees Bridgewater as an educational service center for the region.

In November 1991 the campus—along with other Massachusetts state colleges and universities—was in the throes of a budget crisis, having suffered legislative funding cuts for several successive years. During this period the college enjoyed an energetic and talented administration which balanced the books with a minimum of sacrifice and a faculty with remarkably high morale. The college boasted a strong liberal arts program and excellent teacher education. The faculty believed that the college was better than any other in the state system.

The impetus for changing the general education curriculum came from the faculty. In the early 1980s the general education program was a loosely structured menu system in which almost any course could fulfill the requirement in its area of study The program was perceived to have no guiding philosophy, coherence, or structure. During the 1983/84 academic year the curriculum committee formed a seven-member ad hoc subcommittee representing a range of disciplines and charged it with reforming the program. After a short term of leadership by one individual the helm was taken by a department head who adopted the strategy of getting people to discuss their differences with one another. Dozens of hearings were scheduled to get feedback on the design of the evolving program.

In fall 1984 the subcommittee proposed the inclusion of 12 areas in the new general education program: writing, speaking, philosophy, locating and processing information, history, literature, artistic modes of expression, physical and biological sciences, behavioral and social sciences, foreign language, mathematics, and non-Western civilization. A key element of the proposal was a set of criteria designed to define the types of courses that would be approved under this program. Although two new elements were introduced into the general education curriculum—a foreign language requirement and a course in non-Western civilization—the new program was not a radical departure from the old. The new criteria for courses in the curriculum, however, made general education "a whole new ball game": All general education courses would have to be approved by the subcommittee.

After much discussion and minor revision of the proposal, the new general education program was approved. The fall of 1985 was spent preparing for its implementation. Extensive meetings with department chairs were held to prepare course proposals and develop a book to describe the new program.

Like the design process, the review of courses for the general education curriculum was open. The agendas of subcommittee meetings were published, and department chairs were informed when their offerings were to be discussed. Votes were made in public, and copies of minutes were sent to department chairs. Subcommittee decisions could be appealed to the curriculum committee.

The implementation of the new program, however, proved somewhat bumpy. Resources had to be reallocated to the foreign languages department to staff introductory courses, and faculty found that no incentives existed to develop courses in non-Western civilization. With no central office or officer charged with directing implementation of the program, students were confused about which rules applied to them, and faculty were seldom prepared to advise them well. Class-size limits were too high, especially in writing-intensive courses. Students complained that the high number of credits consumed by the general education program significantly limited their ability to enroll in electives.

Notwithstanding these difficulties the faculty were largely satisfied with the outcome of the program redesign, due in large part to the integrity of

Box 1 *(continued)*

the subcommittee and the process employed. The design and implementation were almost universally viewed as fair; an unusually large number of faculty took part in an atmosphere of commitment. Although there is discussion on campus about initiating a review of the program, no changes have been made since the redesign.

mittee and to the president for approval. (A unionized campus, Bridgewater does not have a faculty senate or faculty meetings per se.)

Besides having fair-minded leadership and an open process, Bridgewater exemplifies the use of research, an effort advocated by Daniel Seymour (1988), who argued that data should be collected and examined during all stages of an academic change process. Although Bridgewater used data and consulted with the campus at every juncture, the process was not without angst. Philosophical differences and personality problems cropped up, as might be expected in such an intensive and value-laden endeavor. The important point is that all parties perceived not only that they were consulted but also that they were heard.

Green Mountain College offers an example of a process that began as neither open nor inclusive (see Box 2). An administrator selected a group of chairpersons from the liberal arts to design a new general education curriculum. The committee was instructed to work in secret, in the belief that it would be better to avoid the opposition anticipated over such topics as reducing the number of credit hours in professional programs, giving up "pet courses," and developing new courses in all likelihood without release time. Additionally, the administrator believed that a stronger program could be developed if the committee was not second-guessed along the way. As information leaked from the committee and spread throughout campus, it inevitably became distorted. The faculty became both fearful and angry—exactly the situation that the administrator had hoped to avoid.

Other problems befell the design process at Green Mountain. Committee members perceived that they had support from the trustees to develop an ambitious new program. The committee thought that funds would be available to them, within reason, for the new general education program—for faculty to teach in the program and for other types of program support. A sophisticated curriculum was developed that included core courses, multidisciplinary courses, and senior seminars. The trustees, however, rejected the proposal based on the cost and subsequently issued a mandate that any new program must not entail new costs. The faculty, predisposed to dislike any proposal that came from a handpicked and cloistered committee, rejected it as well.

After the failure of the first proposal the committee regrouped and began work on a second program. Although the composition of the committee remained the same, its procedures did not. The committee now actively sought faculty feedback through informal discussions, a survey, presentations at general faculty meetings, and dialogue with the faculty senate.

The final proposal, much less ambitious than the first, offered a modified distribution system with more coherence than the existing system. After minor alterations the committee's proposal was approved by the trustees, faculty senate, and faculty at large.

The Green Mountain process was problematic from two important angles. First was the process itself. The closed, secretive approach engendered anxiety and anger among the very people who must deliver the final product to the students. As Seymour (1988) noted in discussing cultural impediments to innovation, individuals will resist an innovation unless they have been involved in its formulation.

Second, the committee was unrealistic about the resources that would be made available to support the new curriculum. Inattention to implementation issues during the design process undermines the entire effort when a large discrepancy exists between the resources needed for a new program and those available.

The work of design committees can be facilitated when consensus exists not only about available resources but also about the mission of

Box 2
Close-up: Green Mountain College

Lying in a valley in the town of Poultney, Vermont—population 3,220—Green Mountain College is a movie-set New England college. Most of its buildings are brick colonial, some with columns and porticoes, and none more than four stories high. Walkways crisscross the main quadrangle, and stately maples reach into the sky.

Founded in 1834 as the Troy Conference Academy, in 1863 it became Ripley Female College, the first institution of higher learning in Vermont to grant a woman a baccalaureate degree. Eleven years later it reverted to its original name and became coeducational. In 1943, with a wartime shortage of male students, the college became a two-year college for women, renamed Green Mountain College. In 1974, it returned to coeducational, baccalaureate status. The college emphasized career programs until the late 1980s, when it expanded its liberal arts offerings and, through a new general education curriculum, began requiring students to combine liberal and career studies.

With an enrollment of 550, Green Mountain prides itself on providing small undergraduate classes and individual attention to students. Full-time faculty number 35; they are neither tenured nor unionized. Seven academic departments (education, fine arts, language and literature, science, management, recreation and leisure studies, and social sciences) offer a variety of programs. Though small and rural, Green Mountain is not a local college; most students are from out of state, with a handful from other countries. Most students are of traditional age.

The previous general education program was a menu system that required students to choose nine credit hours from each of three areas: science/math, humanities, and social sciences. Several forces contributed to a reform of this loose distribution system. First among these forces was an accreditation visit by the New England Association of Schools and Colleges (NEASC) in 1982. NEASC was critical of the college's general education program and mandated an interim five-year review.

Second, a senior administrator took a keen interest in general education at Green Mountain. Believing that faculty were not opposed to revisions, he appointed a committee to design a new program. Traditionally at Green Mountain the academic dean appoints half of a committee's members and faculty elect the other half. In this case, however, the administrator selected the entire committee and named himself as chair.

Besides the distrust of nonparticipating faculty, the design committee faced an additional hurdle. The committee worked with the understanding that resources would be made available to support a new general education program. Operating under this assumption, it designed a sophisticated, detailed curriculum of core courses, multidisciplinary courses, and senior seminars. The trustees rejected the program because of the high cost of implementing it. The faculty—already predisposed to dislike it—argued that students were academically unprepared for the curriculum and that faculty would need release time to develop it, which the trustees were unwilling to support.

After this proposal was rejected, the general education committee began work on a second, more modest design. Faculty opinions and advice were sought through a survey, informal discussions, and presentations at faculty meetings. The campus was kept informed through the circulation of committee meeting minutes. The committee developed a mission statement and designed a 39-credit modified distribution system: backgrounds of human culture (6 credits), language and expression (6 credits), the scientific endeavor (12 credits), individual and social worlds (12 credits), and health and well-being (3 credits). Trustees and the faculty senate approved the design, with minor modifications, in 1988.

Spurred by a grant from the National Endowment for the Humanities in 1991 and criticisms from NEASC in 1992 concerning the size and lack of coherence of the cafeteria system, faculty discussions continued. In 1993, a broadly representative faculty committee was charged with assessing the general education program. The committee surveyed faculty, obtained information from other institutions, and held its deliberations in an open manner. A task force established in 1994 used the committee's recommendations to propose sweeping changes to the general education curriculum, emphasizing faculty "ownership." These changes were approved by the president and then

Box 2 *(continued)*

discussed in special faculty meetings. In 1995, faculty overwhelmingly endorsed the task force recommendations for fall 1996. The new program, "Perspectives on the Environment," includes three core courses designed and taught by faculty from every discipline. It also includes an interwoven series of distribution courses linked to the core theme of the environment. A faculty governance council is responsible for implementation, assessment, and faculty development.

the program. Gaff (1983) noted that early agreement by the faculty on a rationale and on basic elements makes it easier to design a curriculum: "In the absence of working agreements about the aims, content, or structure of general education, an institution simply cannot build a curriculum" (p. 164). Green Mountain learned this lesson the hard way. Other campuses avoided this error by acquiring early formal approval of general education concepts from their faculties. This method was employed at the University of Hartford and the University of Bridgeport in Connecticut, and Plymouth State in Plymouth, New Hampshire (see Box 3).

Further Resources

In preparing to reform general education, committees at several campuses reviewed current literature, examined general education requirements at other campuses, or did both. For example, Bridgewater investigated requirements at other New England campuses; Plymouth State reviewed literature and contacted other campuses; and Green Mountain, even in its early "closed" attempt, sought information by reviewing the general education literature and visiting three nearby campuses.

Institutions sometimes retained outside consultants to assist in reviewing and redefining the general education curriculum. Some campuses received external grants to assist in the development of general education programs. A few campuses obtained these funds at the beginning of the design process (the University of Hartford and Seattle University), while others obtained funds in the implementation stage to aid in course design and faculty development (the University of Bridgeport, Albertus Magnus, and Kean College).

All campuses made diligent, well-considered efforts to improve general education. The typical design committee, an ad hoc one with 7–10 members appointed by an administrator, was composed of administrators and at-large faculty, predominantly from the liberal arts, with a faculty member as chair. Committees met once a week over a period of 12 months. Implementation occurred a year and a half after design completion. The more successful design committees were composed of a cross section of the various constituencies on campus, and these committees proceeded inclusively—seeking information and feedback from a wide range of sources.

"Closed" and, hence, unsuccessful design efforts were also good-faith attempts. These typically involved a visionary individual or a group of like-minded persons with shared notions about general education. Their desire was to offer a fully developed proposal of an innovative program that would make their campus unique in its bold approach to general education. Given the loosely coupled, decentralized nature of colleges and universities, however, consensus was too remote a possibility without the participation of each element.

Challenges of Implementation

Redesigning general education was an arduous task for the campuses. The debate over what constitutes an educated person was protracted and intense, with all participants having a deeply felt interest in the outcome. Consensus on educational philosophy and resource allocation could not be achieved quickly or easily, even on the most collegial of campuses.

Once the conceptual framework of general education was in place, committee members faced the task of translating plans into a realistic program—more meetings, discussion, disagreement, brokering, compromise. A new general education program was eventually produced and moved through appropriate channels

Box 3
Close-up: Plymouth State College

Located in the small town of Plymouth in rural New Hampshire, Plymouth State College was established during the 19th century as a teachers college. In the early 1960s it expanded its programs, granting baccalaureate degrees in liberal arts and business as well as in teaching. Its student body, drawn from the surrounding region, numbers about 3,500, predominantly traditional-age students 18–22 years old. The college enjoys a healthy enrollment largely because of its popular professional programs in business and physical education. With a full-time faculty of approximately 140, the school is divided into 13 academic departments: art; business; computer science; education; English; foreign languages; health, physical education, and recreation; mathematics; music and theatre; natural science; philosophy; psychology; and social science.

From 1968 to the mid-1980s, general education changed little at Plymouth State. Students were required to take 12 credit hours in the humanities, 12 in social sciences, and 15 in sciences and mathematics and could be graduated without ever having taken a course in history or philosophy. The faculty, dissatisfied with the program, argued that it lacked breadth and depth. Further, they were cognizant of the growing national concern about overspecialization and narrow career-mindedness in undergraduate programs.

In November 1983 the dean named an ad hoc committee to study the general education program and recommend changes. By the summer of 1984 the committee of senior faculty and the associate dean agreed on some minimum requirements: the need for communication and social, scientific, philosophical, historical, and aesthetic understandings as well as the need for some kind of integrative experience among the various disciplines.

From November 1984 through May 1985 the committee surveyed the faculty to ascertain their thinking on needed changes. The ad hoc group schooled itself in the literature on the subject and communicated with colleagues at other institutions concerning successful programs. Throughout its deliberations the committee kept the faculty informed of its work by using liaison members to meet regularly with the academic departments, sponsoring guest speakers and workshops, publishing a newsletter, and anticipating criticism and meeting it openly through handouts explaining its thinking and actions.

Despite some dissension, no opposition arose to reform in the general education program. The final proposal, submitted to the full faculty in May 1985, was accepted with no revisions. The faculty were pleased with the committee's work and felt that the process had been open and aboveboard and that ample opportunities for discussion had been provided.

The new proposal offered a conceptual framework for the general education program with five components: skills, perspectives (areas of knowledge or understanding), integrative or interdisciplinary courses, an emphasis on writing, and a requirement for the study of upper-level courses outside one's major. The proposal sought to balance disciplinary content and methodology and stressed the skills of writing, speaking, and listening.

Since the proposal was implemented, no changes have been made, although minor improvements will likely be made over the next few years, particularly to give students more flexibility in choosing general education courses required by various majors.

for approval and, once passed, was ready to be carried out.

On most campuses, however, design committees failed to anticipate fully the implementation issues—particularly those related to responsibility and resources—that are crucial to the success of a general education program.

Responsibility

"The essential problem with the administration of general education is that, at most institutions, no one has the responsibility and authority to act on behalf of the program as a whole" (Gaff, 1983, p. 135). Data from the telephone survey corroborate Gaff's statement. On two thirds of campuses a committee (a standing curriculum committee or a general education committee) was charged with oversight of general education. Campus visits identified how this type of management tends to be carried out. The committee would retain formal oversight of the program, whereas departments would handle the so-called everyday responsibilities of staffing courses and, sometimes, monitoring course content. Bridgewater State managed its program this way. A subcommittee of the curriculum committee approved courses to be included in the general education program (save for two English courses); day-to-day management was handled at the department level. Only 9 percent of campuses employed a program director for general education, and 11 percent of campuses subsumed the responsibilities for the general education program under the duties of an academic officer (see Table 45-4).

The management of general education was sometimes divided in rather creative ways. For example, at several institutions a director or a coordinator of general education oversaw interdisciplinary aspects of a program, while departments managed the discipline-based requirements. At Albertus Magnus, for example, a director coordinated level I (freshman) courses and level IV (capstone) courses, and departments were responsible for levels II and III.

Discrepancies existed, however, between the responsibility for general education and the authority for it. There was a difference between having responsibility for the day-to-day management of a general education program and having the authority to make decisions about the program. General education directors tended to have great responsibility and little authority, whereas curriculum and general education committees tended to have much authority but little responsibility, which was typically delegated to departments.

"Management by committee" was problematic on several counts. First, when day-to-day responsibilities were relegated to departments, important matters often went unresolved, such as advising students about general education. Second, when departments were responsible for their general education courses, these courses could, over time, come to reflect the interests of those in the department, as opposed to those who governed the general education program; in this way the overall program risked losing its distinctiveness. At Roger Williams College, for example, a new general education program was first created as an entity separate from the disciplinary divisions, with its own director (see Box 4). A campus reorganization elevated the divisions to schools, with a dean heading each. Responsibility for staffing and funding general education then moved to the individual schools and their deans, and courses were renamed to reflect the department instead of being called "General Education XXX." Because general education could no longer be identified as a separate division with its own courses, many on campus feared that the program would lose its flavor and sense of coherence. The worry was that these "general" courses would soon become so heavily identified with the divisions that no distinction would exist between discipline-based courses and general education courses. In effect, it was the first step back to the old, loose distribution system.

At the other end of the spectrum, "management by director" was not without its problems. Some directors of general education were frustrated by their lack of authority; awkward reporting relationships (often to a committee); and lack of status in the community, as they were members neither of the faculty nor of the administration.

TABLE 45-4
Oversight of General Education Program

Source of Oversight	*n*	%
Standing curriculum committee	27	47
General education committee	11	19
Provost, dean, or vice-president of academic affairs	6	11
Program director	5	
Other	5	9
No oversight provided	3	5

Data are from telephone survey.

Box 4
Close-up: Roger Williams College

Roger Williams College in Bristol, Rhode Island is an independent coeducational institution offering liberal arts and selected professional degrees, including business, engineering, and architecture. Students may major in any of 31 fields of study.

The campus, beautifully sited overlooking Mount Hope Bay, is well groomed and relatively new, having been built in 1969. Most of the college's 2,000 full-time students live on campus and come from New England and mid-Atlantic states. Roger Williams employs 300 full- and part-time instructors. Average class size is 20 students.

The institution grew out of a branch campus of Northeastern University's School of Commerce, which was founded in 1919. When the college opened its Bristol campus in 1969, the curriculum reflected the times: The byword was relevance, and students had much freedom of choice. By the mid-1970s the faculty imposed some order by implementing a distribution system in which students were required to take at least one course from each of the divisions at the college. Faculty concern about the curriculum became further evident in 1981/82, when the College Curriculum Committee (CCC) discussed its dissatisfaction with the distribution requirements. Almost all faculty were concerned that students needed better preparation in composition and computation. For some faculty another problem was the lack of breadth in the students' college experience. The liberal distribution requirements meant that students could fulfill requirements without venturing far from their chosen field of study. In addition, some faculty thought that several of the majors required too many courses, thus limiting the students' opportunities for exploring other fields.

In preparing for a visit of the New England Association of Schools and Colleges (NEASC), the college initiated a curriculum review. The report of this self-study, based on the work of the CCC, concluded that the curriculum had "no perceived center or academic focus for either students or faculty" During academic years 1983/84 and 1985/86 the CCC documented the problems of the curriculum and designed a proposal that became the basis of the final version of the general education program. It included foundation or "skills" courses and required students to complete 10 courses (later 9) in seven disciplinary categories. An Ad Hoc Committee on General Education appointed to refine the program disagreed on the program's scope; number of courses; and competing emphases on intellectual processes, such as creative thinking, synthesis, and analysis versus specific course content. Business and technical faculty charged that the emphasis on humanities courses was a thinly veiled attempt of liberal arts faculty to protect their jobs by ensuring enrollment. In November 1985, despite sometimes vociferous opposition from an estimated 20–30 percent of the faculty, the proposal was passed.

Implementation was difficult. The first issue was how to reconcile the new program with the divisional structure of the institution. This was never resolved. A General Education Core Committee was created, and a half-time coordinator of general education was hired. Proposals for courses were solicited from the faculty, and assessment and evaluation mechanisms were devised. No one was sure what the budget should be, but the administration became increasingly concerned about program expenses, particularly those for part-time faculty and for assessment.

In 1990, a reorganization of the college called for divisions to become schools, each headed by a dean. With this reorganization, staffing and funding became the responsibility of school deans and not of a program coordinator. The program no longer existed as a separate entity.

A 1994 internal review of the general education curriculum led to major changes in the program. Since then students must take interdisciplinary core courses in five areas, including the sciences, Western civilization, social sciences, literature and philosophy, and the fine arts. They must also take a five-course core concentration in an academic area other than the major and, at the end of the college experience, an integrative senior seminar.

Despite implementation problems and the sometimes deep divides among faculty in the wake of the design and implementation processes, general education at Roger Williams is considered a success. One faculty member observed: "General education gives students a less myopic view of learning; they see learning as exploration, not memorization." Many faculty felt that the college benefited greatly from looking at the curriculum as a unified whole, rather than division by division, for the first time in the institution's history.

Nevertheless, on campuses where a director was in place, better management of general education prevailed. Directors were able to monitor the quality and staffing of courses; oversee advising; ensure that courses were available to allow students to graduate on time (which requires sensitivity to the size of cohorts moving through the curriculum); offer support to faculty in the development of courses; and, in general, keep the spirit of the program alive. Problems were evident, however, when directors had few resources at their disposal. Without adequate resources, directors were unable, for example, to offer release time and development opportunities for faculty, elements critical to the success of any curricular innovation.

Resources

Resources were crucial to the successful implementation of the new general education program and, not surprisingly, difficult to obtain. About one third of the telephone survey respondents reported that budget constraints had made the implementation of general education difficult. Of the campuses visited, none said that there were adequate resources to support the general education program, particularly for faculty to prepare themselves for designing and teaching interdisciplinary courses.

Among campuses able to find funds for general education, about half patched together funding from a combination of sources (see Table 45-5). About one fourth of the campuses shifted some funds from the operating budget to cover the needs of the new general education program. Only 6 percent located special institutional funds or grant monies. The remaining 13 percent reallocated existing funds. Almost all campuses saw an erosion in the limited funding made available when their general education program was first implemented.

The telephone survey probed for specific areas where resources were expended (see Table 45-6). Two thirds (66 percent) of the campuses reported that they allocated resources to modifying orientation to prepare students for the new general education program, and 57 percent stated that they modified the advising program. Nevertheless, registrars interviewed on campus visits almost universally reported that the advising system regarding general education was poor, with considerable confusion concerning which students were to be "grandfathered" under the old general education guidelines, which were to be bound to the new ones, and what was to be done about transfer students. In addition, staff shortages often resulted in students' being closed out of general education courses. Horror stories were recounted of seniors who were unable to graduate for this reason. The implementation nightmares visited upon campus registrars might have been avoided—or at least mitigated—by ample planning during the design stage of the process.

Slightly more than half of the campuses reported allocating resources for the retraining of faculty members in teaching methods or subject area (see Table 45-6). This retraining was especially important because interdisciplinary courses were part of the new curriculum. Faculty trained in their own disciplines found it extraordinarily difficult to produce coherent courses that wove together several disciplines with a common theme.

On several campuses, the allocation of resources to promote communication with faculty was the hallmark of successful implementation. At the University of Minnesota, Morris the committee developing a freshman core course consulted extensively with the faculty before implementation. The committee made presentations to the faculty, held workshops on

TABLE 45-5
Sources of Funds for Implementing New General Education Programs

Source of Funds	*n*[a]	%
Combination of sources	25	53
Operating budget	13	28
Reallocation of existing funds	6	13
Special institutional funds	2	4
Outside grants	1	2

Data are from telephone survey.

[a]Base number represents campuses (47) that allocated resources for implementing new general education programs.

TABLE 45-6
Types of Expenditures for Implementing New General Education Programs

Type of Expenditure	*n*[a]	%[b]
Modifications to student orientation	31	66
Faculty incentives for creating new courses	31	66
New instructional materials	30	64
Revision of campus publications	29	62
Modifications to the advising program	27	57
Library upgrade	26	55
Retraining of faculty in teaching methods or subject	26	55
Hiring of new faculty	25	53
Revision of campus mission statement	8	17
Revision of admissions policies or procedures	8	17

Data are from telephone survey.

[a]Base number represents campuses (47) that allocated resources for implementing new general education programs.

[b]Percentages add to more than 100 percent due to multiple mentions.

the readings, and developed a course guide. Faculty struggled with the philosophy and essence of the course and gave the committee substantial feedback. The course was refined and, upon implementation, was well understood by the faculty. At Bridgewater State a document called the "Green Book" was created to guide the faculty regarding the new general education program. This comprehensive book clearly presented the goals of the program and provided explicit guidelines for the inclusion criteria for courses. It became an invaluable resource for faculty.

In contrast, at the University of Massachusetts Boston almost no effort was made to educate the faculty about the goals that were to serve as the framework for each core course. Some who understood the goals simply did not know how to incorporate and work toward them. The program floundered for two years until the problems were addressed in a faculty handbook about the core program, and faculty seminars and colloquiums, supported by a Title III grant, were introduced.

Incentives for faculty to create new courses were another important part of resource allocation for general education programs. Two thirds of the campuses surveyed reported that such incentives were available on their campuses. At Seattle University, summer stipends were available for course development, and month-long seminars were held to update and improve course syllabi within the three "phases" of its core program. This support was found to be stimulating for the faculty and revitalizing for the curriculum.

Other campuses, such as the University of Maine at Machias, saw their interdisciplinary courses weaken when funds for course development evaporated. Given the already heavy load of teaching, advising, and community service, faculty had little time (or incentive) to devote to the development of new courses or new themes for existing interdisciplinary courses.

Finally, about half of the campuses reported that they had hired new faculty to help cover the demand for general education courses. Additional faculty were sometimes required to handle newly created courses (especially skills courses and interdisciplinary courses), not all of which could be staffed given the existing commitments of the faculty.

Aside from the sheer volume of courses to be staffed, however, there existed other problems—namely, negative incentives for faculty to teach in the general education program. First, some faculty already had a heavy load of remedial and introductory courses. Teaching in the general education program often meant that they had to give up one or two upper-division courses (typically the most enjoyable ones). At Bridgewater State, for example, this negative incentive existed for the development of courses to satisfy the non-Western heritage requirement. Faculty hesitated to develop courses to fulfill the requirement because such courses were taught at an introductory level. Faculty members would have to give up an upper-division offering to teach yet another lower-level course.

Second, the reward system did not support faculty participation in the general education program. Generally departments made the recommendations for promotion and tenure— recommendations usually supported by upper levels of administration. General education courses taught outside the department (i.e., the interdisciplinary ones) were not valued at department review time because they did not contribute to the department. Similarly, the reward system did not support departmental participation in the general education program. That is, departments themselves typically received no credit for their faculty's teaching of general education courses outside the department.

The use of adjunct faculty in the general education program was commonly practiced for economic reasons but generally viewed as a poor solution. Full-time faculty, feeling overloaded, wanted permanent teaching slots created. The quality of teaching among adjuncts was uneven. Finally, the use of adjunct faculty in general education tended to diffuse the spirit of the program because the adjuncts were not versed in the philosophy and goals of the program.

For those campuses with no resources to hire new faculty, the inevitable shift in resources to cover general education became a bitter pill for some faculty. Existing courses had to be sacrificed so that faculty could be reassigned to interdisciplinary or core courses. For other campuses, such as Colby-Sawyer, this shift may have saved some faculty slots at a time when enrollments were waning. For still other campuses, such as Plymouth State, upper-division courses suffered as faculty were reassigned to teach introductory-level general education courses.

Class size, too, became an issue on many campuses because of the resource and staffing constraints. In an effort to move students through the general education program, class size was frequently increased. This often decreased the effectiveness of the courses (especially writing courses) and resulted in animosity on the part of faculty, some of whom were already feeling aggrieved. Several campuses reported having size limits for general education courses, but according to faculty these limits were often ignored.

Programmatic Outcomes

With few exceptions, general education programs became more structured entities after the attention given to them by the reform process. On two thirds (67 percent) of the campuses, programs became modified distribution systems. In such systems the number of courses that could be taken to fulfill requirements was dramatically reduced, and a few courses were required of all students. Almost half of the institutions (44 percent) required students to take interdisciplinary courses. On about one fifth of the campuses (22 percent) modified core programs were put into place. In these programs the majority of courses that students must take was specified, and students had the freedom to choose courses in only a few areas. Only 12 percent of the campuses retained a loose distribution system in which students had complete freedom of choice.

The change process was indeed perilous for all these institutions in a time of scarcity and insecurity. Poor planning, structural constraints, lack of resources, and passionate individual philosophies of general education all created tremendous barriers to the development of a single, coherent program.

Bibliography

Gaff, Jerry Y. (1983). *General education today: A critical analysis of controversies, practices, and reforms.* San Francisco: Jossey-Bass.

Seymour, D. T. (1988). *Developing academic programs: The climate for innovation.* College Station, TX: Association for the Study of Higher Education (ASHE-ERIC Higher Education report No. 3.)

CHAPTER 46

HABITS HARD TO BREAK: HOW PERSISTENT FEATURES OF CAMPUS LIFE FRUSTRATE CURRICULAR REFORM

CAROL GEARY SCHNEIDER AND ROBERT SHOENBERG

As we write, hundreds of colleges are struggling to update or reform the liberal arts component of their curricula. Often there is excitement about this: during this decade, a sense has emerged that hands-on, inquiry-oriented strategies for learning, built around professor-created, often collaborative materials, may be the approach we need for undergraduate rejuvenation.

Over and over again, however, faculty design teams soon come face-to-face with organizational realities that frustrate their high hopes. Almost whatever plan for integrative, practice-oriented learning they envision, there are structural features of the academic environment that work silently but powerfully to undo it. This article takes up several of the most formidable of these obstacles, and looks at a remedy.

The Discipline as Silo

The 20th-century educational model is ostensibly—indeed was originally—built on a conceptualization of knowledge structured by "'discipline." Each emergent discipline eventually came to be represented by an academic department; then, departments in the arts and sciences fields were organized into "colleges" according to rough principles of common subject matters and epistemologies. If "department" and "discipline" ever were synonymous in the ways the model implies, they certainly are no longer so. The degree to which a discipline represents a paradigmatic structure of knowledge that provides, in and of itself, a viable organizational principle for undergraduate learning is called into question by the increasing "interdisciplinarity" of both student interests and faculty behaviors, not only in their teaching but in their research as well.

The scholarly concerns of individual faculty members within almost any academic department encompass a wide diversity of topics and methods, often including those primarily associated with other disciplines. One anthropologist may be studying evidence derived from analysis of tooth enamel in different cultures; another working in the same department may be producing a history of ideas about race and biology. One economist may study principles of supply and demand across all markets, even as a colleague pursues a cultural analysis of family economic decision-making.

Source: "Habits Hard to Break: How Persistent Features of Campus Life Frustrate Curricular Reform," by Carol Geary Schneider and Robert Shoenberg, reprinted from *Change*, Vol. 31, No. 2, March/April 1999, Helen Dwight Reid Education Foundation.

Above and beyond the migration of scholarly topics and approaches from one discipline to another, new and avowedly interdisciplinary fields of study are springing up everywhere. In the arresting image of the historian John Higham, the contemporary academy is like "a house in which the inhabitants are leaning out of the many open windows gaily chatting with the neighbors, while the doors between the rooms stay closed."

Yet even as scholarship reconfigures knowledge in increasingly intersecting and polycentric designs, students in arts and sciences fields are still socialized not only into the rhetoric of "the discipline" but also into the operational assumption that they have no need or responsibility to integrate their learning across multiple domains of inquiry and practice.

To enter into a discussion of what constitutes a discipline—that is, a distinctive mode of inquiry, as opposed to a subject matter or a community of scholars with overlapping interests—would lead this discussion too far afield. The point to be made here is that the rhetoric and curricular organization associated with inherited concepts of "the discipline" invite students to think of themselves as pursuing a specific, well-defined competence when the entire ethos of the contemporary world calls for the capacity to cross boundaries, explore connections, and move in uncharted directions. Discipline-based conceptions of advanced study become deeply problematic when they allow a student to burrow into only one corner of, say, literature or political science, rather than exploring the field's complex byways and neighboring communities.

Such insularity can be equally problematic for the two-thirds of American undergraduates who choose pre-professional fields. Students in these fields are too seldom invited to connect their vocational studies with larger societal, cultural, historical, or ethical questions. Why ask of the accounting major (a pre-professional field) what is not asked of the biology major (a discipline)? The result, as Ernest Boyer observed a decade ago, is all too often a neglect of the social and ethical responsibilities inherent in the work of any field. As Boyer noted in *College: The Undergraduate Experience in America,*

> [I]n many fields, skills have become ends. Scholars are busy sorting, counting, and decoding. We are turning out technicians. But the crisis of our time relates not to technical competence, but to a loss of social and historical perspective, to the disastrous divorce of competence from conscience. . . . And the values professionals bring to their work are every bit as crucial as the particularities of the work itself.

Lee Shulman, Boyer's successor at the Carnegie Foundation for the Advancement of Teaching, argues that all fields—disciplinary and professional—ought to be guided by an ethic of social obligation and service, and that espousing such an ethic would revitalize the basic conception of a liberal education.

This critique of inherited disciplinary assumptions does not negate the collegial importance of departments. Both faculty and students are sustained by structures that provide small communities of common interest, intellectual "homes" for learning, mentoring, and the give and take of collaborative exploration. As Alexander Astin reports in his 1993 *What Matters in College?* experience and research alike attest to the importance of close relationships between students and faculty in fostering students' intellectual growth and educational attainment. Something like the departmental home seems a necessity in any complex institution.

What we do question is the equating of department with unitary and self-contained courses of study, segregated by catalog design and powerful traditions from all the other parts of student learning. There is no inherent reason why the learning fostered in a departmental community need be narrowly bounded. Many of the newer fields, such as environmental studies, women's studies, or policy studies, not only model but require a problem-centered, multidisciplinary, and integrative approach to learning. The challenge for more traditional departments, disciplinary or pre-professional, is that of rethinking their educational aims and of asserting their own accountability for forms of learning that prepare students to navigate a kaleidoscopically complex world.

In some fields, broadening the recommended course of study to include larger societal perspectives and issues will require challenging and uprooting the encrusted educational assumptions of professional accrediting associations. In other fields, the accrediting associations are already broadening their expectations for student learning in ways that encourage inquiry and interpretive learning.

General Education and the Major

As long as general education was conceived predominantly as study of a range—or "breadth"—of subject matters, with study in a designated major providing "depth," the conventional sharp division between general education and the major made some sense. But with today's educational focus on helping students develop intellectual skills, understand a range of epistemologies, and increase their ability to negotiate intellectual, cultural, civic, and practical topics and relationships, the assumed dividing line between general education and the major is no longer useful.

On the one hand, the usual fraction of the curriculum allocated to general education is simply inadequate for developing, practicing, and integrating—at a reasonable level of proficiency—the complex analytical and inquiry-oriented skills that faculties aim for today. On the other, the development of those abilities requires a full four years of practice and application, which necessarily implicates the major. Developing such abilities, then, is just as much the business of the major as of general education—and it is just as essential to a baccalaureate-level mastery of a field.

Put another way, the logic of today's ambitions for undergraduate education forces us to think about that education as a whole. This whole should include communication skills; analytic, critical, and scientific thinking; and societal perspective and responsibility.

Goals for learning in the major, then, ought to deal at a high level of intentionality with the development of general and integrative as well as field-specific understandings, perspectives, and skills. This blending of general skills with field-specific approaches can already be seen in writing-across-the-curriculum programs and in similar efforts focused on skills such as oral communication, quantitative reasoning, and second-language acquisition. Some departments are introducing diversity content into their curricula in ways appropriate to their field; others are emphasizing issues of social responsibility and global engagement. But such efforts remain for the most part sporadic and elective.

The advantage to major programs of assuming this kind of instructional responsibility for students' integrative learning is a greater share of the attention of their students. What it takes is much clearer formulation of the purposes of the major and a willingness to teach with an intentionality that thoughtfully addresses the goals of the department and of the college, not just those of the individual faculty member.

Courses and Credits

The dysfunctional dichotomy between general and specialized education is discernibly beginning to erode. The challenge, of course, is to replace it with an educationally viable alternative. But standing in the way is another familiar structure, the system of courses and credit hours, which remains in place as strongly as ever.

Use of the word "course"—a shortening of the phrase "course of lectures"—traces its origin to the very beginnings of universities, when students registered and paid for a particular number of lectures by one of the learned men who "professed" at a school. In American higher education, beginning in the early part of this century, the course became standardized in terms of credit hours or an easily translatable equivalent. The modal course, as all know, is three credit hours, which usually implies a set number of class meetings spread over a given term. All sorts of modifications or equivalents are possible, but the three-credit course is the standard coin of the realm.

Equally standard, despite many familiar variants, is the notion of a bachelor's degree as the equivalent of four years of undergraduate study, defined as 40 three-credit courses or 120 credit hours. There is no particular reason why a bachelor's degree should take four years of full-time study, arbitrarily defined as five three-credit courses per semester, to complete. Nor is there any particular reason why all bachelor's degrees should take the same amount of time to complete, or why students in some programs should complete "free electives" to fill out the 120 credits, or why some programs—notably engineering—should try to squeeze themselves into the canonical 120 hours.

This standard for the degree emerged early in the 20th century as a counterweight to diploma mills and other sorts of ventures that awarded degrees on the basis of little or no effort on the part of recipients. The notion of the credit hour was born of the same impulse. Moreover, to a degree probably unforeseen by its inventors, the credit hour, by becoming the standard unit of academic currency, has made possible the American system of student transfer. In fact, transfer has become so pervasive that at many public institutions, both two- and four-year, the transfer process now controls the academic program.

As convenient as this standardization is, it has led—to say the least—to some questionable results . . . some so familiar that their dubiousness seldom occurs to us. For example, instructors have grown used to allowing the size of the package to control the treatment of the subject matter. No matter that some topics might benefit from being taught over a longer period of time, or some a shorter, or that others do not deserve a full course at all: each will appear on the course schedule for the same number of class hours and term time.

This uniform and separate packaging of learning experiences leads both faculty and students to treat courses in isolation from each other. Very seldom—unless courses are explicitly part of a sequence of two or three—do instructors make an effort to relate one course to another, either in terms of the content addressed or the analytical tasks assigned to students.

These problems, however, pale in contrast to the damage done by allowing course titles and credits to stand as surrogates for learning. The establishment of "interchangeable" course units and of declared "equivalencies" has led everywhere to a stunning neglect of what a student is supposed to be able to know and do at the completion of any particular course, and of how capacities fostered in any particular course do or should prepare students for work yet to come.

The result, as many faculty members pioneering with capstone courses and/or portfolios of student work well know, is that significant numbers of students ascend to the final year of study with analytical, problem-solving, and communicative competencies that are at best only shallowly developed.

Credit Transfer Practices

The equating of course titles with learning becomes even more problematic in the context of student transfer, a process increasingly the subject of state mandate in public systems of higher education. Student transfer is built on the presumption that courses with equivalent titles and credits will represent the same learning experience—of content and developed competence—across all institutions.

The flip side of this, of course, is that courses with different titles but equally valid learning experiences will not be accepted in transfer, a practice that enrages transfer students, community colleges, and state legislators alike. All around, the illogic of the practice is patent.

State coordinating boards and, increasingly and notoriously, state legislatures have sometimes responded by establishing a standard set of general education courses for all public institutions, which once completed, must be accepted by the receiving institution in satisfaction of all lower-division general education requirements.

The resulting general education package is frequently a thoroughly retrograde system of distribution requirements in their least intellectually defensible form. This lowest-common-denominator standardization certainly helps reduce barriers to transfer, but it also results in fragmented study and widespread student cynicism about the curriculum while imposing a severe restriction on the curricular and pedagogical imagination of faculties at both two- and four-year institutions.

The Undefined Baccalaureate Degree

The ultimate problem with this entire system of courses and credits is the way it comes to define the baccalaureate degree itself. As course credits become a surrogate for learning, we allow ourselves to shirk responsibility for developing a rigorous definition of what the baccalaureate degree should mean.

This is another way of saying that the academy is insufficiently focused on the kinds of educational outcomes it is trying to achieve. Progress in assessment notwithstanding, colleges and universities have a long way to go in developing functioning frameworks for expected outcomes, let alone in finding adequate ways of judging students' achievement of them.

True, hundreds of campuses have developed statements of their goals for student learning. But these statements are too frequently the stated goals only for that fraction of the curriculum devoted to general education. Seldom are the goals presented as charges to the departments as well.

Thus, having assigned most of the important educational goals to a fraction of the curriculum—often on a principle of a course or two per goal—faculty assessment committees struggle unsuccessfully to figure out some way of assessing these general education outcomes "across the curriculum." One result is that campuses increasingly fall back upon satisfaction surveys as evidence that they are meeting their stated general education goals . . . proof again of how far the academy has to go in developing credible expectations for student performance as an outcome.

Many institutions have noted the powerful example of Alverno College and have sent teams of faculty members and administrators to that college's workshops to learn about assessing entire curricula. In the end, though, few have taken up the challenge of emulating Alverno's system of learning assessments. The example is there; Alverno and a handful of other campuses are pioneers in showing that educational goals can guide the curriculum, that assessment can be done well, and that the combination of faculty-led assessment and student self-assessment can be a powerful spur to demonstrable learning.

Why have so few other institutions shown the will to develop their own performance expectations and assessments? Part of the reason lies in our next topic.

The Faculty Reward Question

Hanging over all this need for rethinking inherited structures is the thorny question of how faculty members will be rewarded for the considerable efforts required to change and assess educational programs. Exhortations abound about the compelling need to change campus reward structures so that curricular and teaching innovations are duly recognized and faculty can devote time to these efforts without fear of jeopardizing their promotion and tenure.

Administrators and sometimes even faculty leaders encourage talented faculty to participate in renewal efforts, but so far, most faculty don't believe them. They've heard too many horror stories about colleagues who spent time on a teaching innovation and curricular reform, only to have it discounted by colleagues or administrators when it came time for promotion or merit increases.

Right now, neither institutions nor faculty members are willing to disarm unilaterally by honoring teaching and service efforts equally with research accomplishments. With the exception of two-year institutions and a fair number of regional liberal arts colleges, the prestige and rewards in higher education continue to lie with published research.

Reforms in teaching and curricula will be absolutely necessary for our colleges to survive and thrive in contexts of technological revolution and multiplying educational providers. But making those reforms will be difficult if not impossible until it becomes the norm for institutions to recognize and honor the intellectual work involved. Faculties will need to know that time spent on creative curricula and teaching will be as well rewarded as equivalent time spent on research. Since much of this work will necessarily be cross-disciplinary and integrative, departments and colleges will have to develop entirely new abilities to assess faculty work.

In short, the disciplinary hold on curriculum, a course-and-credit system of academic bookkeeping, and the atomism of faculty reward systems all stand as formidable impediments to the educational renewal to which campuses aspire. Perfectly reasonable desires to facilitate student transfer and curricular choice serve to keep a number of the more questionable structures in place, indeed to entrench them even more solidly.

Moving from Here to There

Yet these timeworn systems clearly are not total impediments to reform. We could not talk as we have about emerging new practices in baccalaureate education if they were not in fact present and thriving in enough places to attract attention. Whether or not they are involved in such practices, most faculty members are familiar with experiential and service learning, collaborative and cooperative learning, learning communities, capstone courses and projects, and performance assessments. It is not concepts and practices we lack, but a practical consensus about the purposes of baccalaureate education that will encompass them.

We believe an emerging framework for such a consensus exists. It emphasizes a range of intellectual skills; epistemological and research sophistication; global, societal, and self-knowledge; relational learning; and making intellectual connections. It requires seeing undergraduate education as a whole as opposed to splitting it between general and specialized learning. It also argues strongly for aligning the goals and emphases of K-12 education more intentionally with those of collegiate education.

This emerging direction for undergraduate learning is well served by instructional strategies that reflect the resurgent emphasis on the student as learner, with the teacher as mentor rather than sage. The development of problem-solving skills, both as an individual and in collaboration with others, is essential to this pattern, as is experiential learning in its many forms. Institutions' choices of educational technologies ought to reflect this learning-centered, intensively "hands-on" approach.

Connecting Goals with Practice

What we need next for collegiate reform is the parallel embodiment—in a variety of four-year undergraduate programs—of curricula purposely directed toward goals campuses avow. These models should do more than simply reorganize existing individual courses; they should be integrated structures of carefully related learning experiences that pay systematic attention to developmental sequencing and concomitant student assignments. For a variety of practical reasons, the curricula may need to be presented in the standard form of semesters and courses and credits, but the rationale for and instruction within ought to become far less atomistic than in current practice.

To meet fully the challenges of this approach, faculty members will have to give up some old habits of thinking, most significantly the idea that they are sole owners of the courses they teach. Offering their courses within integrated, intentional sequences will require them to acknowledge the stake that their departments and the institution as a whole have in each course and in the student outcomes it is intended to produce. Faculty will have to teach toward some goals about which there has been mutual agreement and around which there is some sense of collective accountability.

This need not mean what faculty most fear—externally imposed constraints on the actual content of a course. But it should mean that designated categories of courses work intentionally and accountably, through the kinds of assignments students undertake, to foster specific capacities and intellectual skills. Models for this combination of flexibility and focus already exist in some fields (the health sciences, for example). The challenge is to build on available examples.

Given the transience of students, particularly within regions or state systems of higher education, some broad agreements within the higher education community about educational goals and what they mean operationally will also be important. If the emphasis is on the mastery of particular intellectual practices rather than on a simple passing of named courses, then faculties within institutions among which students regularly move should be able to negotiate some common understandings about appropriate assignments. Educational goals should not simply be imparted to students; they need to become a continuing framework for students' educational planning, assessments, and self-assessment.

The difficulty of articulating important educational goals across institutions and getting faculty to acknowledge them in what and how they teach, while maintaining a high level of institutional and faculty autonomy, is not to be underestimated. Such coordination requires enormous amounts of educational insight, negotiating skill, and good will. Yet making sense of education for the large numbers of students who increasingly move from institution to institution, and for whom a coherent, purposeful curriculum can never be predesigned at a single campus, would seem to require the effort.

This emphasis on student outcomes rather than on course credits and curricular features implies a wider use of assessment. The assessment will be more appropriate and effective if it is embedded in coursework or grows naturally out of it, rather than taking the form of short-answer instruments created solely for the purpose of external reporting. Ideally, assessment should provide opportunities for students to advance, integrate, and correct their understandings at key junctures in their course of study. Assessments that provide no useful feedback to students themselves defeat what should be an important goal of the assessment effort.

Moving forward with a framework for learning that expects broad, deep, and complex accomplishments for every student is a challenge that invites the participation of the entire array of higher education stakeholders, from the public and its elected representatives to each individual institution, and including accreditors, state higher education agencies, university system offices, learned societies in the disciplines, testing agencies, federal education agencies, and so on. The groundwork for success has already been laid in the form of an emerging consensus about what matters in undergraduate education and some promising pedagogical strategies for getting there. We need to seize the opportunity for building the more purposeful, powerful, and integrative forms of undergraduate education that the consensus now makes possible.

CHAPTER 47

INTEGRATING WOMEN INTO THE CURRICULUM: MULTIPLE MOTIVES AND MIXED EMOTIONS

PATRICIA MACCORQUODALE AND JUDY LENSINK

In the past two decades, women's studies faculty pursued two directions: one promoted the creation, organization and growth of women's studies programs and departments; the other fostered curriculum integration, i.e., efforts to include material on women in already existing courses and disciplines. Some campuses have concentrated on one of these directions while others have followed both. The Women's Studies program at the University of Arizona is a leader on both fronts. This essay will analyze what factors led us to begin our extensive curriculum integration projects, what the outcomes were for students and faculty involved, and what have been the costs and consequences in terms of the Women's Studies program.

Background

In the 1970s, teaching women's studies in the United States was a time of exhilaration; the field was expanding rapidly. The number of women's studies courses rose from 16 in 1969 to over 15,000 by 1980; over half of the 300 programs offered minors, majors or graduate degrees (Stimpson, 1980). The National Women's Studies Association was founded in 1977; *Signs,* a prestigious new interdisciplinary women's studies journal, published its first volume in the fall of 1975.

The atmosphere at University of Arizona was not unlike that on other campuses. Women's Studies began offering courses in 1971 and added a minor in 1979; by 1980 there were thirty courses. Our research component, the Southwest Institute for Research on Women (SIROW), was established in 1979.

In 1979, we were able to enhance our curriculum through a National Endowment for the Humanities (NEH) Pilot Grant. The grant supported an introductory women's studies course, interdisciplinary senior seminars, and faculty workshops. We evaluated the Pilot Grant through teaching evaluations which compared students in women's studies with students in humanities courses. The results of the student questionnaires were both confirmatory and shocking. Women's studies faculty were rated as excellent teachers, who not only expanded students' understanding of humanities, but touched students' lives. Students found women's studies courses rigorous and demanding in the amount of material covered and in their development of writing and analytic skills. We were shocked, however, to realize how few of the students surveyed were exposed to a women's studies perspective. Only seven percent of those in humanities courses had taken women's studies.

Source: "Integrating Women into the Curriculum: Multiple Motives and Mixed Emotions," by Patricia MacCorquodale and Judy Lensink, reprinted from *Women's Higher Education in Comparative Perspecitve*, edited by G.P. Kelly & S. Slaughter, 1991, Kluwer Academic Publishers.

The comparison of women's studies classes to humanities classes revealed clear-cut differences: the humanities courses did not include material on women's roles, status or achievements, or motivate students to get involved in women's issues, or apply the materials to their own lives. The new scholarship on women that had transformed and enriched our own research and teaching had not been incorporated into the traditional humanities curriculum. Thus, most students were not learning about women in the humanities nor were they enrolling in women's studies courses to get this perspective (Auchmuty, Borzello, and Langdell, 1983).

We came to the conclusion that if we wanted to reach those students who would not enroll in women's studies courses, we needed to bring the new scholarship into the traditional curriculum. Hence, our attention turned to curriculum integration, and we entered a debate that continues to this day: should women's studies build its own relatively independent program or should it work to assure that materials on women are included broadly across the curriculum? This is not an either/or choice, but given finite energy and resources, the pursuit of one strategy necessarily sets limits on the other.

Curriculum integration is important for several reasons. The college student body is becoming increasingly female. In the 1960s, women's presence on college and university campuses returned to its prewar level; by 1982, more women than men received bachelor's degrees for the first time in American history (National Center for Education Statistics, 1987). Yet research consistently revealed, for example, that women's self image and self esteem decline during the college years (Astin and Mvint, 1971; Zigili, 1985). The discouragement of women is particularly evident in male dominated fields (Armstrong, 1980; Gornick, 1983; Ware and Steckler, 1983; Reyes and Padilla, 1985). Curriculum integration might make the college experience as well as traditionally male dominated fields more responsive to women's needs.

We wrote and received a multi-year NEH implementation grant to support our efforts in curriculum integration. The primary emphasis was to integrate materials on women into humanities courses by encouraging faculty to revise the curriculum to include materials by and about women. Participating faculty received a stipend. We chose to work with tenured faculty who taught basic courses in humanities and social sciences.[1] Our strategy was to use summer workshops as a forum for discussing interdisciplinary feminist scholarship while participants read intensively in their own fields and prepared annotated bibliographies that dealt with material on women.[2] By the end of the summer, faculty had revised the syllabus for at least one of their courses and agreed to participate in student evaluations of their revised course.

Over the four years of the project, 47 faculty members participated in curriculum integration, although five were involved only marginally for various personal reasons. Because of our decision to work with tenured faculty and because of the structure of the university, the vast majority (91 percent) were male. In terms of disciplines, two-thirds of the participants were from the 'social sciences,' a broad area at our university which included history, psychology, social anthropology, and political theory, while the remaining third were from the humanities, primarily literature and philosophy.[3]

A core group of five women's studies faculty (only one of whom was tenured) designed and led the intensive seminars and served as consultants throughout the year to faculty participants from their own or related disciplines. Although one of us was the 'official' leader of the intensive seminar, we all attended and participated.

Motivations: The Fork in the Road

The women's studies core group felt a sense of mission on behalf of our students because we had seen the impact of women's studies materials in our own classrooms. These materials can motivate and interest students, particularly women, in subjects and materials that they previously dismissed. The materials can help students understand forces in their own lives in ways that provide a new understanding or an impetus to change. Material on women raises aspirations and often provides strategies to overcome barriers. Although students can also be angered or depressed when confronted with the extent of women's oppression, we generally had positive experiences when exposing students to this material. (Recent studies of the impact of women's studies have corroborated our beliefs. Stake and Gerner (1987) found that women's studies students of both genders experienced gains in agentic self esteem, job motivation, and job certainty; that these effects vary by year in college is suggested by Zuckerman (1983). Vedovato and Vaughter (1980) found that women's attitudes became less traditional and their self images more androgynous after taking a women's studies course.) Our initial mood therefore, was optimistic. While there were doubts about how extensively the participants would understand and accept feminist scholarship, we approached the project with the belief that we could convince our colleagues to pursue women's studies.

In order to give us an understanding of the participants' motivations and viewpoints on the project, and to assess changes in their attitudes, we hired an interviewer to talk with each participant. These interviews, based on a series of open-ended questions, were conducted before their participation in the project began and after their year of official involvement ended. What follows is an analysis of participants' motivations before entering the project. It is important to note that while we have categorized the participants' perspectives, the categories are not mutually exclusive. Many people had more than one motive for participating in the project and had multiple reactions to it. What follows is a *post hoc* analysis of data collected as part of the project evaluation. Because we did not set out to study motivations, we did not ask people to rank or prioritize their motives. The categories were created by us after reading and re-reading the interviews. Where patterns appear in the interviews, e.g., motives that often appear together, they will be identified.

Although usually not explicit, one motivation for our colleagues was *financial,* for unlike most curriculum integration projects across the country, ours had external support that enabled us to pay summer stipends.[4] Because resources are very limited and highly competitive in the humanities, most faculty teach summer school; if they spend the summer on their own research, it usually means no salary. To offer faculty the equivalent of what they would have made teaching one summer school course was a powerful incentive. Although external incentives can be powerful motivators, there is a trade-off between external and internal incentives; as one participant explained, 'some of the [participants] look at this as another way to get money and they won't commit to it.' Another said, 'I'm a little embarrassed and guilty. They're paying me money. . . . I plan to sit and think for five weeks. The thing is, I'm not convinced my classes will be substantially changed by this project.'[5] In other cases, internal and external motivations were mutually reinforcing. As one participant commented: 'The idea of getting paid for receiving training that's going to make you a better instructor is marvelous; I think that I would be willing to do it regardless of what the rewards were in terms of monetary [rewards].'

We characterized the most common, explicit motivation of participants as a moral and/or intellectual obligation to include material on women. As one professor said, 'many [female authors] have been excluded. . . . and it is wrong, very wrong, to exclude one-half of all intellectual contribution. Intellectual honesty demands inclusion and redress.' We refer to these professors as the *good liberals;* they wanted to include women because it is the 'right' thing to do. As another professor put it, 'A responsible person would have done it anyway. I feel very open-minded about the whole idea.' Many entered the project with a certain amount of guilt about having previously ignored this material. 'My experience has been that of having good intentions and very little execution.' For some, their liberalism was the latest in a series of causes: 'When I was involved in civil rights, I discovered that I was racist. And I think it was an important discovery because once you get a cognitive handle on what's going on inside of you, you can alter your behavior in ways that you don't otherwise do. I suspect that there are similar feelings in respect to women.'

Ironically, the second most common motivation, also a political rationale, which often coexisted with the good liberal approach, was the desire to incorporate material on women in order to eliminate the need for women's studies. We characterize these participants as *anti-separatists.* As one explained emphatically: 'But I will say the *only* reason I'm in the project is that the mainstreaming idea is precisely what I support. I am vehemently opposed to the idea that Women's Studies should be a separatist, isolated thing.' For many, this position was as much a moral obligation as that of the good liberals: 'I am a non-separatist as a matter of conscience.' They believed that 'self-destruction should be the goal so we could see People's Studies, not Men's or Women's Studies.' Many felt, however, that these changes would not be forthcoming in their lifetimes or that there would still be the need for a permanent, women's studies resource center.'

The anti-separatists were not the only ones concerned with how women's studies should be organized. Opinions as to any need for a separate women's studies program were sharply divided. Some faculty felt they needed more exposure to women's studies material for informed decision making. 'At some point people will probably have to make hard decision about whether (women's studies) constitutes an academic field that you fund in the long term [with] standard positions.' Other participants saw a long-term future for a flourishing women's studies program: 'As a kind of unit, it has a number of uses that probably won't vanish if materials on women are incorporated into the curriculum.'

A third motivation was pedagogical. We call this group the *teachers*:[6] 'I will learn more as a teacher and become better educated,' said one participant before the project began. Another expected new material to 'make the course more interesting and for the students, both more relevant and more timely to what they're going to be doing.' Within this group, different events had triggered their interest. For some, their students had begun the process of curriculum integration by asking questions about gender and bringing materials to the professors. One faculty member had used as class material a play in which the major female character's over-riding ambition is to be a 'faithful shadow' in supporting the male protagonist. This professor was surprised when students questioned the gender dynamics in this example, and made him begin to question his practice with regard to material on women. Another told students they couldn't read material about women because it didn't exist; students began bringing articles on the new scholarship about women and created a bibliography 'that was the biggest launching pad I've had for starting to read in this area intensively myself.' Some were impressed by students' reactions to material on women that they had already used in their courses. 'I don't ever want to hear again my student's comment: "It was so neat to study a woman author; I didn't know there were any."' Several professors saw curriculum integration as an opportunity to change students' orientations: 'Basically, [what interests me the most] is the idea of getting women into my field; I think my students will enjoy and accept the new material,' one commented. Another saw the issue more broadly: 'I'd wish it [an integrated perspective] to be a way of life for all students. . . . We can defeat discrimination with each crop of better-educated students.' The *teachers* saw the transformative potential of women's studies materials. One told the story of a bright, young woman who 'would have dropped out of school had she not found women's studies when she was on campus.' Women's studies gave her 'a focus' and 'confidence' to begin a professional career and later return to law school.

A fourth motivation was the intellectual stimulation that some participants hoped to find in the new scholarship on women.[7] These faculty, who we term *intellectuals*, differed from the other participants in two ways: first, they were more familiar with feminist writings and second, this familiarity usually stemmed from their active involvement in ongoing research. Because they already had some exposure to women's studies, they hoped feminist theory would provide 'new paradigms and new perspectives of how women should be studied.' As one professor said, 'the whole feminist enterprise has given us a new perspective on [the study of literature].' For some, these intellectual motivations extended into the classroom: 'My teaching winds up being an extension of my research.' Or, as another professor said: 'I have been jogged into a new point of view from which I have been teaching. I think it is healthy for anybody who has been teaching for ten years or more every once in a while to be stimulated.'

Finally, cross-cutting all of these motivations were *personal* interests and experiences. Approximately one-third of the participants were married to feminists, most of whom were also in the academy. 'To be honest,' one professor confided, 'my wife is the greatest stimulus for me. It is through her that I have had the most exposure to women's materials.' Another felt 'my wife has also encouraged my interest through her teaching and experiences.' Other family connections also motivated participants; 'I've a daughter coming to the university next year. . . . [By participating] I'd have a better idea of what problems she might face.' Although these personal motivations provided some sensitivity to gender issues, the majority of the participants did not see structural discrimination at the university and claimed it no longer existed.

When we read these interviews before the project began, we primarily focused upon the participants' prior exposure to women's studies material and their initial conceptions of curriculum integration, i.e., did they see it as a major transformation or as a process of merely adding some material. What we failed to focus upon at the time were the ways in which these diverse motives would shape resistances to our efforts.

Resistances: One Step Forward, Two Steps Back

The task of integrating material on women into the curriculum asked the participants to value perspectives and materials that are culturally devalued (Aiken, Anderson, Dinnerstein, Lensink, and MacCorquodale, 1987). This proved to be the most common and greatest difficulty, for the new scholarship on women asks its readers to re-examine assumptions, values, and practices from a new perspective that challenges taken-for-granted viewpoints. For most of the *teachers,* who sought such fresh insights to enliven their classrooms, the resistances were minor. For others, the project asked them to scrutinize their intellectual, emotional and academic beliefs; the majority found this task too threatening and developed strategies of resistance based in part upon their initial motivations. The *good liberals,* for example, were torn between believing they should give feminist scholarship a chance and wanting to avoid association with what they characterized as 'second class' work. Their concern with the quality of the scholarship focused upon the perception that '[women's studies material] doesn't quite fit into the mainstream of the scholarship or the disciplines . . . and it's something that people do 'cause they can't, they're not as competitive in terms of the discipline.' They approached curriculum integration by asking 'are these journals as good as regular journals, is the research as significant as other kinds of research?' Another noted, 'feminist [scholarship] is pretty applied and peripheral so just on straight forward grounds, it would be thought of as less important.'

For the *intellectuals* and some of the *teachers,* this issue of the quality and centrality—the canon—takes the form of questioning what to cut from a course if you want to include new materials on women. 'I don't anticipate, frankly, that we'll put a lot of new things in because that would mean taking the old things out that still *have* to be there.' Another saw this as 'cutting back on the [scholars] that stand out in history . . . who will always be written about as major talents.' For those in the humanities, the canon carries particular weight. As one literature professor remarked, 'when you get to the question of primary materials, it becomes more difficult, because [incorporating new materials] raises the question of the canon, it raises questions of aesthetic value.'

Even the external incentives, time and money, created their own resistances. For those who entered the project reluctantly, the external incentive was accompanied by an uncomfortable sense of obligation: 'I'm given a course off in order to take the seminar, I'm under some kind of an obligation to [incorporate women's material]. That's the hope that [women's studies faculty] have, but I'm not sure that they could actually, physically impose it [integrating women's studies material] upon me to do so.' Others saw the issue in terms of academic freedom. 'My peers,' one believed, 'see it as an encroachment upon academic freedom; women's studies is now telling us what and how we should teach.'

The *good liberals* were extremely troubled by the issue of what is 'objective knowledge.' They described their disciplines as rational and scientific and viewed women's studies as ideological and political. One went so far as to suggest that 'feminist scholarship' was a contradiction in terms. Another professor did not like that fact that 'quite obviously some of the issues that were touched on [in the seminars] were not just objective, intellectual issues, they were emotional issues as well. People responded emotionally.' For another participant, the workshop readings 'had more of a rhetorical purpose than a scholarly one' and feminist scholarship displayed an unnecessary 'tension between advocacy and research.' By dismissing a feminist perspective as 'unobjective,' they minimized their engagement with new materials.

Liberalism itself, with its attention to group rights, afforded another strategy of resistance in that some participants, whether *good liberals* or not, argued that there were many oppressed groups. The uniqueness of women's position and experience was obscured by deflecting the discussion to other groups who experience discrimination (e.g., blacks, the impoverished, the untenured, even 'the ugly'). One participant felt that his status as the only unmarried member of a department 'set[s] me aside in a way and affects people's treatment of me much as they might have reacted if I were the only female or the only black.' Another believed, 'it will probably be difficult for me to incorporate that kind of material because even when women are different from men, the differences are far, far less than similarities . . . men are also outsiders . . . and men face problems that arise from similar kinds of factors.' The curriculum interests of liberals were not enduring; they tended to move on to other 'causes,' i.e., integrating materials on Native American or Black men.

The *good liberals* were particularly bothered by our efforts to keep the focus to women's experience; they reminded us that 'we're the good guys.' Another reflected that 'men [in the project] are sensitive in the first place . . . and what men want coming into something like this is credit for how far they've come so far, before they get pushed down the road any farther.' Liberals did not want to re-think their positions; they used countless personal examples ('I feed the baby' 'I let my wife pay all the bills') to demonstrate that they were 'liberal and on the right side on in all these matters' and simply wanted a quick-fix for their courses.

Anti-separatists' resistances were even more extensive than the liberals. If the *anti-separatists* recognized the quantity and high quality of women's studies scholarship, their antagonistic position vis-a-vis the program would have been called into question. This group resisted curriculum integration in two ways. The first strategy was to search for socio/biological differences to explain sexism. One participant argued that older, white men's power, wealth, and 'sexual prowess' enabled them to have sequential marriages with younger wives. These marital patterns, he believed, ensured that these 'patriarchs' would pass along their genes resulting in a genetic disposition for women to prefer older men as sexual partners. Male dominance, therefore, could be seen as 'natural' and outside of the realm of the humanities and social sciences.

The second strategy was to define their own areas of interest so narrowly that women's studies scholarship was not applicable. One said, 'It's a problem of scarcity [of women's materials in my field].' This stance made the interdisciplinary nature of the project problematic. One participant was disappointed because the workshop 'raised lots of issues in areas that are outside of my area of expertise.' Another felt 'what made [the workshop] frustrating is trying to communicate with people who don't speak the same language.' Many of the participants, but especially the *anti-separatists,* did not acknowledge the differences among women; they treated women, including the women's studies faculty, as a homogeneous, unified group. As one commented, 'it was never made very clear that within the feminists, there is a great divergence of opinion.' For another, 'somehow you feel that you are encountering a monolithic ideology that's pushing you hard . . . and that in starting some of these materials [there] is the appearance that men are all alike.'

These resistances were accompanied by peer pressure. Both male and female participants reported during the interviews that they were subjected to criticism from their colleagues, which ranged from accusations of being 'on a cream-puff project' and 'pokes and giggles' to antagonistic criticism. These comments occur repeatedly through the interviews and are pervasive. As one participant painfully recalled: 'a colleague with whom I've worked in [another department] was very upset and said he wouln't work with me anymore; he said I was selling my soul; that I wasn't professional. In my own department, I received numerous knowing looks, pokes, and giggles.' Another found that 'male colleagues are resistant to the idea. They put on a nice academic front but in day to day conversation you hear all kinds of snide remarks.' Participants took these remarks seriously and saw them as reflections of 'very real resistance," very real bias,' and 'actual viciousness beneath the light matter.' Most professed that 'it doesn't bother me personally,' but one admitted, 'I guess I don't like it much, my colleagues behind my back saying more than they would to my face. It makes me uncomfortable.' A few reacted defensively and redoubled their commitment to the project; for most, the criticism (and 'having to explain and maybe defend what I'm doing') had a more pervasive, enduring effect of dampening their enthusiasm and limiting their involvement in the project.

Outcomes: Baby Steps and Giant Steps

Judging the successes and failures of the project depends, in part, upon the outcomes expected. The core women's studies faculty hoped that exposure to feminist scholarship would be as transformative for the participants as it had been in our own careers. We varied in our assessments of whether anything less than a transformative change could be defined as success, i.e., a significant alteration of the content, structure, and pedagogy of their courses and an almost paradigmatic shift in the questions they raised in and out of the classroom. For many participants, the expectation of extensive change was threatening. After completing the project, one participant, a self-described 'skeptic,' recalled our opening statement "`we hope, and our experience in the past has shown, that this [experience] will change your life,"' and insisted: 'I'm still the same person I was, with the same qualities and flaws. It hasn't changed radically my perception of the world or what academic inquiry should be. . . . It hasn't been a 'religious transformation' for me, as I had the impression some people would expect there would be.'

Outcomes, however, are relative; they must be judged against starting points. As one participant aptly put it, 'a lot of [us] have a much further way to go than others. And there was great variety, at least in our group, where people had only baby steps to take, others had giant steps to take.' As the women's studies faculty looked back over the four-year project, we observed that approximately half of the participants were affected positively. These faculty found materials on women, judged the quality of those materials to be good, and subsequently made changes in their courses, referred to as targeted courses. 'I am very impressed with the development in feminist scholarship from the '60s to the current day. It is much more sophisticated, more solid on an academic basis. . . . [The] program has introduced me to . . . material which I find fascinating and intriguing, well-argued and very convincing.'

Of this half, one-quarter experienced profound changes in their personal or professional orientation which markedly altered their teaching, research, and politics.[8] These participants understood that integration required them to rethink both the structure, content and process of their courses; for them, exposure to feminist scholarship was a transformative experience affecting their theoretical perspectives, research interests, academic politics and personal lives. '[Women's studies scholarship] is a necessary angle of literary interpretation . . . and for literary history. It's a major expansion in all aspects of our discipline and it's got to be there from now on,' concluded one literature professor. Another participant described the challenge of transformation: 'You know values are called into question when you start something like this. This is *not* an intellectual exercise. It is an exercise or reassessment of your commitment on a major part of your life. That can really be unsettling.'

Of the half who were positively affected, the other quarter met the 'official' goals of the project by incorporating new materials on women into their courses; there was great variation in the amount of materials incorporated and the manner in which it was included. These faculty understood that in an integrated course format they 'shouldn't be cuing people by saying "here we have a little lecture on women today."' They believed that 'you can't just add something about women.' Consideration of gender became a regular aspect of their courses.

The remaining half were relatively unchanged in our judgment. Some clearly misunderstood or did not accept the goal of integrating material on women throughout their courses; as one commented, 'I guess I introduce a general topic . . . [and put] women in the examples.' Another wanted to 'spend one whole class period or two surveying just the major aspects of what women do' or fifteen to twenty minutes on male and female sensibilities 'if there's anything remarkable about them.' For some, the extensive change that would be caused by truly integrating women into the curriculum became an excuse. For example, after spending a semester in the project, one participant concluded that 'it will take me a while to think because if I do it properly I would have to re-structure the course far more radically than I was prepared to do on such a short notice.' A few genuinely understood and shared the goal of integration, but were overwhelmed because the task appeared 'beyond [their] capabilities:' 'They are fundamental problems in the basis of [the discipline] that need to be looked at. . . . Going through that experience I realized how much [my field] is not about women. But if [it] is not about women, who is it about? . . . some mythical animal that doesn't exist.'

The *good liberals* and the *anti-separatists* had the greatest number of strategies of resistance and changed the least. Skeptical as to the quantity and quality of feminist scholarship, they used their strategies of resistance to minimize successfully the amount of material 'appropriate' for their courses: 'I feel women's issues are very peripheral to [the focus of my course].' This professor summarized the effect of the project as 'simply affording me the opportunity to shore up my lectures and my professional understanding of the material.' They limited their involvement; several admitted doing 'virtually no reading' or finding materials but 'making no major changes in [course] readings at this time.' Another 'rearranged my lectures and in doing that I went through a lot of my old material and found sexist remarks or sexist material. So I removed some of it.'

The *teachers* took the task of curriculum integration seriously, making changes in both the course that they had agreed to alter, targeted courses, and other non-targeted courses. 'It has caused me to reassess my values in teaching. It's exciting. [But also] I am a bit apprehensive,' one observed. For many of the *teachers* '[the project] has had an almost greater effect on a non-targeted course . . . [where] I was pretty well free to do what I wanted to do.' The *teachers* were also affected by ideas about feminist pedagogy: 'the experience will affect my teaching style in any class I teach regardless of subject matter.'

A natural outgrowth of curriculum integration is feminist pedagogy; changes in what we teach are more effective when we also change how we each. Many participants expressed a desire for more information on feminist pedagogy or wished 'we could have had the pedagogical session first.' One particularly observant participant concluded, 'watching or experiencing the interaction among seminar participants made me aware . . . of just how much resistance there is to feminist thinking in the classroom, and how women bring certain socialized feelings of inadequacy or lack of confidence to a competitive, aggressive, traditionally male-dominated academic setting.' Other participants reported that their interactions with students, especially graduate students, were altered by their new perspective. 'I've become more aware of some of the problems that women in academia have, especially female TA's, who I had always assumed were fairly interchangeable with male TAs. . . . Because they are women, they are facing a very different situation in the classroom' and need 'more training and preparation in giving them confidence in themselves and knowing how to meet these situations.' Many believed that working with graduate students was particularly important because 'they will carry this into their own role as teaching assistants.' Others moved beyond changing their curriculum to advocacy. One participant found a list of fellowships and financial assistance available to women and distributed it to all female graduate students in the department. 'I probably wouldn't have done that the year before. . . . I think that would relate back to heightened awareness and concern,' he concluded. Another found that 'I am very much more an advocate for the women graduate students than I was before. . . . Now I seek them out and I say okay, if you are going to make it through this, this is what you have to do. I feel more radical about making sure that the system works for them.'

The *intellectuals* experienced the most transformation, especially when they saw teaching and research as inseparable. One professor found that 'my participation was greater than expected because what I am teaching links so closely to my research work.' *Intellectuals* were willing to give serious consideration to different, often alien ideas. As one faculty member remarked, 'there are materials that strike me from left field, in the first place, but they do raise issues, important issues, and ones that I hadn't really thought about before.' The professor urged us to concentrate 'more direct attention on [participants'] research . . . because for most college professors, your research leads your teaching rather than the other way around. . . . I'm not going to stop. I'll be writing on this for the next twenty years.' For another, 'the seminar experience was a real eye-opener. It made me realize the extent to which traditional conceptions of males and females, and male-type behavior versus female-type behavior or attributes informs the broad field in which I work. . . . My experience in the seminar has radically changed the way I see my field of study and will affect both the way I talk about it in my classes and the way I actually conduct my research.'

There were also personal and political outcomes.[9] Many found new colleagues across disciplines. As one participant poignantly remarked, 'We have so little contact among faculty members, particularly across disciplines, or even within disciplines, where you sit down and actually talk about ideas; that was very valuable.' Many commented favorably on the women's studies faculty. One participant was struck by 'their enthusiasm and sincerity. . . . It was the first remark I made to my wife—last summer was the first summer that I really enjoyed.' Another found that 'one of the major strengths is the [women's studies faculty] involved in the project. . . . I felt I was working together with them rather than opposed to or against them.' One of the benefits to the program and to female faculty was an increased sensitivity to the problems women face in academia; increased sensitivity and respect for female faculty had political outcomes when some participants moved into administrative posts and began 'pressing these kinds of issues as far as departmental policies and activities.'

Student Reactions

The evaluation design compared students in classes that had been revised to include more material on women (targeted classes) with similar courses that had not been revised (control classes).[10] We asked students to evaluate how often they encountered works by women authors and material on women in their assigned readings, syllabus topics, lectures by the instructor, and class discussions. We also provided a series of statements about students' reactions to the materials. Students could agree or disagree, for example, with the statement 'I do not intend to do reading by or about women in the future.'[11] The next set of statements focused on the effect of the materials on students' lives. For example, 'Since taking this course, my feelings about women have changed in 1) a positive way 2) no change 3) in a negative way.' The last few questions asked about the overall quality of the course and whether the instructor's treatment of materials about women was positive, neutral, negative or hostile.

This evaluation instrument reached over 3500 students during the six semesters. The results revealed marked differences between the courses targeted in our project and those selected as controls.[12] Faculty participants were required to submit a revised syllabus and a narrative description of their course to demonstrate that they had integrated material on women into the course. We were pleased that in all five types of classroom materials—assigned readings, syllabus topics, lectures, class discussion, and works by women authors—students in the targeted classes reported more materials on women than students in the control classes. In targeted classes, a quarter to a third typically said that materials on women were included frequently; in contrast, over half of the students in the control classes observed that material on women was not included at all compared to seventeen percent in the targeted classes. This 'bottom line' measure of the success of curriculum integration—the presence of information about women in a course—proved successful.

We were also interested in assessing effects of curriculum integration on students in subsequent courses. Although students from targeted classes were more likely than students from control classes to report using the materials on women to re-evaluate the content of other courses, when we probed further, the results were disappointing. We expected students from targeted classes to show more 'curricular activism'—the desire by students to have other courses contain materials on women. The data, however, did not support our expectations. Those from the control classes were more likely than those from the targeted classes to say that they would object if other courses omit materials on women or contain biased information. Students from both types of classes were indistinguishable in terms of wanting other courses to contain materials on women or desiring more of these materials in the curriculum. How can we explain these unexpected results? It may be that having attended courses in which there is virtually no information on women throughout their university experience, when students in the targeted group receive some information on women, they believe that it is sufficient. Alternatively, insofar as courses have not included materials on women in the past, all students may believe that these topics belong in specialized courses, such as those offered in the women's studies program. One professor reflected this view in his characterization of student attitudes toward material on women: 'the other [two-thirds] were ambivalent about it. I think they thought, 'What's the point of women's studies in [this course]? I am not paying for women's studies.' Further research is needed to explore students' desire for greater curriculum integration. Although curriculum integration did not increase students' desire for more material on women in the curriculum, the results were encouraging nevertheless; half of both groups would strongly object to classes without materials on women.

Finally, we turn to the issue of how participants' courses were evaluated. Student evaluations are often seen as popularity contests; they measure students' reactions to the professor and the course rather than what students learned or how challenged they were by the course material. Some would argue that the more unsettling and challenging a course is, the more learning occurs (Elbow, 1986). Many faculty participants, however, were quite anxious as to whether their ratings would drop when they included materials and issues on gender. In terms of how the classmates responded to the materials about women, students from control classes rated their classmates as neutral. Students from participants' classes saw fellow students as more positive, more negative, and more hostile. The range of ratings is not surprising, given the controversial issues raised by women's studies material. The controversial nature of the material is reflected in the overall ratings of the quality of the courses. Control courses were more likely to be rated excellent than participants' courses.

Controversy, however, can have a positive effect on students' participation. One faculty member who purposely used controversial issues reported, 'I've noticed that I got more participation . . . not merely from the bright, talkative students, which is easy, but from a wide range of students.'

One question of interest is whether male and female students have different reactions to the inclusion of materials on women. Prior research indicates that male students' attitudes change less than female students' after taking a psychology of women course (Vedovato and Vaughter, 1980). Male students' resistance to materials on women has led some to argue for teaching 'men-free' women's studies courses (Klein, 1983; Mahoney, 1983). Faculty who participated in the project believed that women students responded more favorably to the targeted course.[13] One professor observed, 'Women in the course were very, very positive about it. The men were almost nonverbal on many topics during the whole semester.'

Analyses by gender focused on changes in students' self-image and reactions to the instructors. Three-quarters of students from both targeted and control classes did not change their self-image. Twice as many men in the targeted classes (4%) felt more negative about themselves than those in the control classes. Among women, the same proportion (1.4%) felt more negative in both types of classes. Both male and female students felt more negative about women in the targeted classes (4.6%) than in the control classes (3%). Similarly, among the small proportion who began to feel more negative about relationships, men from the targeted classes were twice as likely as women to have this reaction. These results indicate that the consequences of learning about women influence men more negatively than women.

Women, not surprisingly, find course material on women more attractive. Women from both target and control classes were twice as likely as men to want future classes to contain material on women and to intend to do more reading about women. Female students were more likely than male students to perceive the participants' attitude toward the material as positive and three times as likely as men to rate the course as excellent if the professor's attitudes were positive. Male students in targeted classes were three times more likely than female students to see the instructors as hostile.

In many ways the reaction of the male students parallel the resistances we observed among the participants in the project (who were mostly male). Feminist theory precipitates major reevaluations that are painful for everyone, but especially threatening for men. Given the underlying sexism in contemporary American society, it is not surprising that men are particularly threatened by this material. Men's discomfort in confronting sexism, women's desire for and positive reaction to this material, and increasingly female enrollments on university campuses validate and reaffirm our belief in the necessity of curriculum integration.

Conclusions: The End of the Road?

The curriculum integration project has been over for several years, but it is still difficult to sift and weigh our reactions. At some level we continue to believe in curriculum integration: we have expanded our efforts to community college faculty and women's studies faculty in a four-state area, with an emphasis on international and cross-cultural perspectives. We serve as consultants, speakers, and writers on the topic. Given our experiences with faculty at Arizona, we now work more with younger faculty and with more women, including women's studies faculty. We rely less upon external incentives and more upon internal motivations. Both these factors enable us to find faculty who are more knowledgeable, more motivated, and more interested in learning about women. The greatest benefit to the women faculty and to the women's studies program was the bonds between the core faculty that were strengthened and tested over the years as we worked together. These bonds have enabled us to go on to new projects despite the enormous burn-out and emotional fatigue we experienced during curriculum integration.

However, participation in the curriculum integration program forced us to make trade-offs. Although the number of colleagues sensitive to women's studies was increased by the faculty who underwent extensive intellectual transformations, we might have gained as many sympathetic colleagues if we had focused our efforts upon recruiting specialists in women's studies. The 'success' of the curriculum integration project was used to argue against a campus-wide requirement that all courses include materials on gender and we had to expend energy mobilizing support to have the requirement passed. On the one hand, we gained politically by having more faculty members who had an exposure to women's studies when we came up for promotion and tenure. On the other hand, our careers might have progressed more smoothly and quickly if we had spent the inordinate number of hours devoted to curriculum integration on our own scholarship. Our choice to work with tenured faculty gave us exposure to those in power, but we might have been able to accomplish more change in the academy if we had worked with junior faculty. While focusing upon the undergraduate curriculum, we devoted less time to training and mentoring graduate students.

In many ways, what we experienced was a microcosm of academia: those on the margins, who are most willing to change, often remain marginal, while those within the powerful center—of the canon, the discipline, the androcenteric society—are fairly intransigent. What we learned were insights into the structure and process of the university that will be central to future feminist transformations of the academy.

Notes

1. As part of the granting process, we were required to demonstrate institutional commitment to our project. We chose to work with faculty who taught large, basic, introductory courses in our belief that they were more likely to continue teaching at the University than untenured faculty. The unanticipated result of this decision was the exclusion of many younger faculty members who had some familiarity and interest in women's studies.
2. External funding brought the necessity of evaluation. In our zeal for the project, we designed an ambitious, multi-method approach which included interviews with participants before and after their involvement, formative evaluations of the workshops, seminars and project, consultations and feedback from women's studies faculty about each participant's work, and student evaluations of revised courses. Faculty interviews and student evaluations provide the rich and varied information used in this essay.
3. Because of the small number of participants from particular disciplines, we have decided not to link examples and quotations in this essay to specific fields in order to assure the anonymity of our colleagues. We have examined the information presented in this chapter to search for relationships between discipline and participation, and there do not appear to be significant differences by field. We hesitate to generalize about differences between male and female participants because there were so few female participants in the project.
4. Ironically, we did not design the project to provide equivalent support for the women's studies faculty. The grant provided summer salary for only one women's studies faculty member, and the university provided release time for one person during the fourth year. Since we saw the project as collaborative and interdisciplinary, we all participated fully. Very few of

the participants understood the differences between their economic support and ours, but upon entering the project one explained, 'the women [the women's studies faculty] who participate in it are doing so out of a sense of desire to do so; that is, you don't have to buy their time, you don't have to twist their arms; so those women who are involved are doing a commitment that is really important.' Many of the questions that remain as to whether the project was worth the time and effort that the women's studies faculty devoted are rooted in the enormous personal and professional costs to the core faculty.

5. Our structuring of expectations about the project changed over time in response to our experiences with participants who did not share our goal of actively changing the curriculum. During the first year, several participants entered the project with the belief that they would read materials to see *if* they were appropriate for their courses. Starting in the second year, we structured the project in terms of a contractual situation, expected participants to decide not if, but how, they were going to change their courses, and required a revised course syllabus and an annotated bibliography of the material they read.
6. As discussed above, people are not unidimensional with single motivations driving their behavior. Rather they are motivated by various intentions simultaneously. *Teachers* were divided into two subgroups. One group primarily directed their energy toward teaching. The other combined their enthusiasm for teaching with productive research agendas.
7. As discussed earlier, faculty participants were not unidimensional with single motivations driving their behavior. Rather they often expressed various intentions for their involvement in the project. Thus, some of the researchers were also motivated by their teaching interests, which they saw as going hand-in-hand. Like most large universities, our faculty vary in their involvement in research. Those participants who were not actively involved in scholarly activities were unlike to have intellectual motivations for joining the project. Some participants who did research did not study areas that lend themselves to feminist analyses or *did not see* the connection of their work to women's studies scholarship. Therefore, in spite of their own scholarly activities, these faculty are not motivated by research interest and are not included in this category.
8. Women who participated in the project had various motives; they were *liberals*, *anti-separatists*, and *teachers*. That they were unfamiliar with women's studies scholarship before joining the project reflected a conscious choice on their parts to avoid this kind of research. The material, therefore, was new and revelatory for them, much as it had been for us when we discovered it. In terms of outcomes, the consequences of participation on their personal lives were much greater than for the men. Needless to say, the materials and issues raised in women's studies have profound ramifications for understanding women's lives in and out of academia. Women, therefore, are over-represented among those who underwent a clearly transformative change. For more information on the effects of participants' gender, see Leslie Flemming's essay 'New visions, new methods: The mainstreaming experience in retrospect'. In: Aiken *et al.* (1988).
9. Although we became aware of many profound personal transformations during the project, we were unable to assess adequately the level of personal changes and whether they were actually caused by the project.
10. During the first year, we used the Attitudes toward Women scale (Spence and Helmreich, 1972), which focused upon women's roles and status in society. This scale was given at the beginning and the end of the semester to assess attitudinal change. After the first year, we jettisoned this attitudinal survey because there was not significant change in students' attitudes during the semester. There were three problems in measuring attitude change. First, there was a ceiling effect because the majority of students were strongly liberal at the beginning of the semester, and, therefore, their attitudes would not become more liberal on our scale. Second, attitude changes during one semester are often very small, even in courses that are intended to change attitudes [see Brush, Gold and White (1978)]. Third, gender socialization has long term effects that are difficult to alter in one semester.
11. The directionality of the statements was varied in order to avoid students falling into a response pattern, e.g., agreeing with all statements.
12. Faculty participating in the project identified a faculty member in their departments who taught a course at the same level with similar enrollment. Although faculty could pick an instructor with a bad reputation in order to make themselves look good, few did. Nearly everyone sincerely wanted to know what difference integrating material on women made. They often picked instructors they admired. A few people had us evaluate their courses before their participation in order to serve as their own controls.

13. One faculty member's belief that only certain students would be interested in these materials summarized this sentiment: 'I think the ones who already had an interest in problems of women or problems of gays were confirmed in that interest.' Similar arguments often advance 'self interests' to explain the greater prevalence of female scholars than male scholars researching gender.

References

Aiken, S. H., K. Anderson, M. Dinnerstein, J. Lensink, and P. MacCorquodale. (1987). 'Trying transformations: Curriculum integration and the problem of resistance.' *Signs* 12: 255-275.

Aiken, S. H., K. Anderson, M. Dinnerstein, J. Lensink, P. MacCorquodale (1988). 'Changing our minds: The problematics of curriculum integration.' In: *Changing Our Minds*, pp. 134–163. Albany, NY: State University of New York Press.

Armstrong, J. M. (1980). *Achievement and Participation of Women in Mathematics: An Overview.* (Report 10-MA-00). Denver, CO: Education Commission of the States.

Astin, H. S. and T. Mvint. (1971). 'Career development of young women during the-post-high school years.' *Journal of Counseling Psychology* 18: 369–393.

Auchmuty, R., F. Borzello, and C. D. Langdell (1983). 'The image of women's studies.' *Women's Studies International Forum* 3: 291–298.

Brush, L. R., A. R. Gold, and M. G. White. (1978). 'The paradox of intention and effect: A women's studies course.' *Signs* 3: 870–883.

Elbow, P. (1986). *Embracing Contraries.* New York: Oxford University.

Gornick, V. (1983). *Women in Science.* New York: Simon and Schuster.

Klein, D. D. (1983). 'The men-problem in women's studies: The expert, the ignoramus, and the poor dear.' *Women's Studies International Forum* 6: 413–421.

Mahoney, P. (1983). 'Boys will be boys: Teaching women's studies in mixed-sex groups.' *Women's Studies International Forum* 6: 331–334.

'National Center for Educational Statistics (1987). *Digest of Educational Statistics.* Table 150'Earned degrees conferred by institutions of higher education, by level of degree and sex of student: United States, 1969–70 to 1986–87,' p. 172. Washington, D.C.: Office of Educational Research and Improvement, U.S. Department of Education.

Reyes, L. H. and M. J. Padilla. (1985). 'Science, math and gender.' *The Science Teacher* 52: 46–47.

Spence, J. T. and R. L. Helmreich (1972). 'The attitudes toward women scale: An objective instrument to measure attitudes toward the rights and roles of women in contemporary society.' *Journal Supplement Abstract Service Catalogue of Selected Documents in Psychology* 2: 66.

Stake, J. E. and M. A. Gerner (1987). 'The women's studies experience.' *Psychology of Women Quarterly* 11: 277–284.

Stimpson, C. R. (1980). 'The new scholarship about women: The state of the art.' *Annals of Scholarship* 1, 2: 2–14.

Vedovato, S. and R. M. Vaughter. (1980). 'Psychology of women courses changing sexist and sex-typed attitudes.' *Psychology of Women Quarterly* 4: 587–590.

Ware, N. and N. Steckler (1983). 'Choosing a science major: The experience of men and women.' *Women's Studies Quarterly* 4: 12–15.

Zigli, B. (1985). 'College hurts self-esteem of bright women.' *USA Today*, April 2: 10C.

Zuckerman, A. M. (1983). 'Women's studies, self-esteem and college women's plans for the future.' *Sex Roles* 5: 633–642.

Case Study

CHAPTER 48

WHEN REVISING A CURRICULUM, STRATEGY MAY TRUMP PEDAGOGY: HOW DUKE PULLED OFF AN OVERHAUL WHILE RICE SAW ITS PLANS COLLAPSE

ALISON SCHNEIDER

Curriculum reform often sparks more back-biting than back-patting. Coalitions form. Turf wars erupt. Lofty debate degenerates into low-takes bickering. But there was little of that at Duke University last month.

When it came time to vote on Duke's new general-education requirements—the first major overhaul of the university's curriculum in more than a decade—the challenges were few, the exchanges polite. Everything went like clockwork, even the timing: The vote was called 20 minutes ahead of schedule. And the proposal passed by a two-thirds majority.

It was a particularly sweet victory for a university where the rigor of the curriculum did not seem to equal the rising quality of students who have flocked to Duke in the last 15 years. And it couldn't have happened at a better time, given the bad publicity swirling around Duke's English department, long a minefield of personal feuds and ideological divisions.

By all accounts, political savvy and deft public relations had a lot to do with Duke's curricular coup. Even critics who thought the proposal was more about style than substance acknowledge that it was a smoothly run operation.

It was another picture entirely at Rice University. A new undergraduate curriculum there, which took two and a half years to craft, was hacked to death last November by disgruntled faculty members. Suspicious professors dismissed the proposal as a "postmodern plot."

Rice's president remains philosophical about the defeat. "Changing a curriculum has all the physical and psychological problems of moving a graveyard," Malcolm Gillis says.

He should know. Twelve years ago, he built the curriculum that Duke just dismantled. "These things are political with a little p," says Mr. Gillis, Duke's former dean of arts and sciences. "You can't always get all that you want."

Ironically, Rice and Duke wanted almost exactly the same thing. Each university felt that its curriculum was hit-or-miss in approach, lacking coherence, consistency, and a sense of identity.

Students at both institutions had to take a set number of classes in various subject areas, but at Rice, there are only a couple of specific "foundation" courses that all undergraduates have to fulfill.

Source: "When Revising a Curriculum, Strategy May Trump Pedagogy: How Duke Pulled Off an Overhaul While Rice Saw its Plans Collapse," by Alison Schneider, reprinted from *Chronicle of Higher Education*, February 19, 1999.

At Duke, the curriculum had the consumer-friendly feel of a Burger King commercial: "Have it your way" was the underlying theme. Students had to take courses in at least five out of six subject areas, but there were no specific classes or concepts that undergraduates had to explore, and students were free to opt out of all courses in an entire subject area.

Opt out they did. Some 50 per cent of Duke students regularly avoided all contact with foreign languages, mathematics, or science.

"I was frankly appalled at the number of loopholes that existed in our curricular system that allowed students to escape completely unprepared to live in the world of the 21st century," says William H. Chafe, Duke's dean of the faculty of arts and sciences.

So Duke, like Rice, set out to find a curriculum that would prepare students for a new world—one in which scientific literacy is a necessity, increasing globalization a reality. Both universities wanted to combine seeming opposites: breadth and depth, structure and choice, skills and subject areas, interdisciplinarity and departmental divisions.

It's not rocket science, but it can get complicated.

Dubbed "Curriculum 2000," Duke's new requirements are laid out in a hodgepodge of columns and boxes, known as the "matrix."

Under the plan, students can kiss the opting-out option goodbye. All of them must take three courses in each of the four "areas of knowledge"—arts and literatures, civilizations, natural sciences and mathematics, and social sciences.

Students at Duke must also take two courses in each of two "modes of inquiry"—interpretive and aesthetic approaches; and quantitative, inductive, and deductive reasoning. They have to take two courses in each of three "focused inquiries"—cross-cultural issues; ethics; and science, technology, and society. And there are "competency" requirements, too: three writing classes; two research experiences, one of them in the major; and a foreign-language requirement, ranging from one to three courses, depending on the student's proficiency.

A course can satisfy more than one requirement. So a class in, say, health economics arguably could fulfill not only a social-science requirement, but also the science, technology, and society requirement, and, if it's loaded with math, the quantitative, inductive, and deductive reasoning category as well.

As for the meaning behind the matrix, "it frames what students do," says Angela M. O'Rand, head of the Arts and Sciences Council, a 60-member faculty group. "They're not picking a course just to fulfill a distributional purpose, but to fulfill an intellectual one."

Sound appealing? Rice thought so. Like Duke, it pushed for a curriculum heavy on rigor, one that would call for classes in quantitative reasoning, writing, and oral presentation. Foreign-language requirements were added, as were freshman seminars.

The centerpiece of the Rice plan was five interdisciplinary "ways of knowing": approaches to the past, encounters with texts and the arts, engaging science and technology, interpreting human behavior, and methods, analysis, and inquiry.

There's nothing startling about either the Duke or the Rice curriculum. "Institutions no longer organize curricula around subject matters, but around the ways that people gain knowledge," says Carol Geary Schneider, president of the Association of American Colleges and Universities. "They're emphasizing inquiry itself."

At least, some institutions are. But Rice won't be one of them. "The effort to have the Rice faculty consider major conceptual changes in the general-education curriculum is dead for now," says Gerald McKenny, chairman of the religious-studies department and the man in charge of sifting through the curricular wreckage to see what can be salvaged.

As it turns out, much of it can be saved. The foreign-language requirement was approved. The freshman seminars, cross-divisional courses, and communication-intensive classes will go forth in pilot programs over the next few years. Anything that didn't involve a significant change survived.

But for now, "ways of knowing" is dead and buried, and the name itself might have done it in. "It was a red flag for people," says Carol E. Quillen, an associate professor of history at Rice and a proponent of the new curriculum. "It suggested that we were taking an ideological position about the nature of truth, that we were saying that what you know is determined by the perspective that you take, so there's no objective knowledge. We weren't saying that at all."

But many professors—especially in the sciences, which still reign strong at Rice—didn't believe them. A finger-pointing e-mail message was circulated, criticizing the curriculum committee for harboring postmodern partisans. "Two members of our committee were chosen to be the dean of science and the dean of engineering," responds William Martin, a professor of sociology and the panel's chairman. "We're hardly a bunch of radicals."

But the committee couldn't shake its renegade reputation. Its members held 75 meetings, met with each department before writing the plan, and talked with people after releasing a draft to gauge reactions. They tinkered with language and added a category to "ways of knowing"—methods, analysis, and inquiry—to pacify people in religious studies who felt ignored. Nothing helped.

Perhaps nothing could. Many professors balked at the vagueness of the categories and criticized the "ways of knowing" approach for making false distinctions between the content of a course and the creation of knowledge. "Almost any course at a good university that's content-based has to, of necessity, talk about the way knowledge is found and analyzed," says John Polking, a mathematics professor. His courses certainly do, he adds. "It's a fake issue."

Professors also complained about the speed with which the changes would be made, and questioned the wisdom of requiring courses before they'd been developed. In the end, no one could agree on a single vision of general education. Some wanted to dictate the courses that students would take. Others wanted to leave the choice to the individual.

"I don't want it to sound like a few of us had a golden notion, and a committee of troglodytes spurned it," Mr. Martin says. "But people were very much concerned about, 'What will be the cost to me, my department, and my division? And why should we pay these costs without a demonstration that there would be commensurate gain?'"

Duke, somehow, managed to make the gain seem greater than the cost. To be fair, Rice has some administrative Achilles' heels that Duke does not. For one, Rice is divided into seven schools, while at Duke, there's a faculty of arts and sciences. That doesn't guarantee one big, happy family, but at least everybody's housed under the same roof.

To complicate matters, the entire Rice faculty votes on curricular changes. At Duke, the decision rests in the hands of the 60-member Arts and Sciences Council. What's more, Rice makes its faculty vote twice on a curricular change. The first vote passed by a 3-to-2 margin. But a month later, the plan failed by the same ratio.

"Like all proposals at Rice, this one was hostage to who came to the faculty meeting," Ms. Quillen says.

Apparently, there were a few ringers in the crowd. "Many of the people at the second vote were people we've never seen at a faculty meeting before or since," Mr. Martin says.

But there were no wild cards in the pack at Duke. The Arts and Sciences Council is a known quantity, and the curriculum committee won over key constituencies early in the game. Then, when council members did sit down to vote, they considered the plan as a whole, not piece by piece. That kept the reform from being nickel-and-dimed to death, observers say.

"In the best sense of the word, this succeeded because it was very much a political process," says Mr. Chafe, Duke's dean of arts and sciences. He was an instrumental operator himself. He gave the curriculum committee its initial charge and spoke out strenuously in favor of the proposal. When resistance cropped up, he reassured skeptical professors that Duke would provide the resources needed to turn the plan into reality—nearly $4-million in the first few years to develop new courses and hire more faculty members, among other costs.

"We didn't just come up with a proposal," says Karla F.C. Holloway, a professor of English and a member of the curriculum committee. "We came up with a marketing strategy."

For months, the committee sequestered itself. Members analyzed core curricula at other institutions and picked apart past reform efforts at home, searching for tactical mistakes. And they spent hours anticipating objections and hammering out their answers. They decided where to bend and where to stand firm.

Last spring, they headed out into the field. They met with directors of undergraduate studies, sat down with department heads, consulted with students. In May, they presented an initial draft of their proposal to the Arts and Sciences Council, gathered opinions, and went back to the drawing board. In the fall, the committee made its pitch. It held four open meetings for faculty members and engaged in plenty of behind-the-scenes maneuvering.

Peter Lange, head of the curriculum committee, was a door-to-door salesman, colleagues say. He pounded the pavement, pressed the flesh, met with anyone who would listen. By the end of the process, he had collected more than 1,000 e-mail messages about Curriculum 2000, and had gone through 23 versions of the matrix.

The panel wouldn't budge on the foreign-language requirement, despite complaints from coaches, who worried that it would turn Duke's strong sports programs into an Ivy League version of athletics.

But the committee was anything but rigid. It dropped the number of required courses from 36 to 34 after students complained, and reworded the ethics requirement to sound less preachy. It reduced the number of courses required in each area of knowledge from four to three, because scientists feared that their majors would be overburdened. And it agreed to phase in the research requirement.

The key change, which took two and a half months to broker, speaks volumes about how the curriculum committee did its business. After humanists started complaining that the matrix gave their intellectual enterprise short shrift, Mr. Lange turned the tables. He invited Walter D. Mignolo, chairman of the Romance-studies department, to draft language proposing a new category. The result: A new mode of inquiry, interpretive and aesthetic approaches, was added.

Even people who opposed the reforms admired the committee's tactics. "It was a 'total quality management' approach to curriculum change," says Stuart Rojstaczer, an associate professor of geology, environment, and engineering.

The approach worked. "What kills a curriculum are little oppositions, all of which don't agree with each other, but all of which agree that there's something wrong with the curriculum," Mr. Lange says. "We had big meetings, small meetings, meetings with three people. I don't think anyone felt that this was rammed down their throats."

Just because the plan passed, however, doesn't mean that it hasn't left some professors with a bad taste in their mouths.

Before Duke forces students to take classes in science or Spanish, maybe it should investigate why they're avoiding them, says Peter Muller, an associate professor of statistics. Proponents of the curricular reform argue that most students skip courses because of their difficulty, not their content, "but I'd like some data, not just conjecture," Mr. Muller argues. "It's an irony that we're lamenting that our students avoid quantitative reasoning, yet in our policy document, there's a lack of it."

New requirements aren't the only way to get students to sign up for statistics courses; new teaching styles are another, says Mr. Muller. "If students are avoiding math or languages, maybe there's something that we are doing wrong." Some departmental soul-searching should have preceded wholesale change, he says.

But it's tough to stimulate such debate when most professors don't show up for the discussion. Faculty attendance at the curriculum meetings was dismal at best. "There were more people at the meeting who had worked on the curriculum than in the audience," says Albert F. Eldridge, a political scientist. "It wasn't a defining event of the year for many faculty. It was a distant blip on their intellectual radar."

That's because many professors felt that the new curriculum contained more fat than meat, says Mr. Rojstaczer, the geologist. "Our administration seems to think it's done something substantive in proposing this change, but it's obvious that we've created a curriculum that's merely a rhetorical device. The curriculum is window dressing. It's not that important."

The "inquiry" requirements are "so vague that almost any wine can be poured into those vessels," says Victor Strandberg, an English professor. "I foresee that there will be a lot of fancy footwork with semantics about what constitutes a 'focused inquiry' or a 'mode of inquiry.' We professors will teach courses in the way we always have and will just put different labels on them."

Administrators bristle when asked about the fudge factor. They insist that Duke professors have too much integrity to stoop to gamesmanship and to craftily check off categories that will boost enrollments without retooling content. Besides, they say, there will be oversight.

But Fred Nijhout, a zoologist, says academics have wriggled around curriculum cops before, and will no doubt try again. "It would be the first time if they didn't."